Sociological Realities II

Sociological Realities II

Edited by

Irving Louis Horowitz
Charles Nanry
RUTGERS UNIVERSITY

A Guide to the Study of Society
A Transaction/Society Textbook

Harper & Row, Publishers
New York, Evanston, San Francisco, London

Sponsoring Editor: Ronald K. Taylor
Project Editor: Pamela Landau
Designer: Emily Harste
Production Supervisor: Stefania J. Taflinska

SOCIOLOGICAL REALITIES II:
A Guide to the Study of Society

For information address Harper & Row, Publishers, Inc., 10 East 53rd Street, New York, N.Y. 10022.

Library of Congress Cataloging in Publication Data

Horowitz, Irving Louis, comp.
Sociological realities II.

(A Transaction/Society textbook)
Contains many articles from Society magazine.
Includes index.
1. Sociology—Addresses, essays, lectures.
I. Nanry, Charles, joint comp. II. Society.
III. Title.
HM51.H638 301'.08 75-22055
ISBN 0-06-046639-1

Contents

Photo Essays

Introduction

The first and most important observation to make about *Sociological Realities II* pertains not so much to discontinuities and differences with its predecessor, *Sociological Realities I*, as to a sense of continuity and similarity between the two texts. After all, what makes a book worthwhile, or at least warrants its updating, must in some measure be a response to the success or validity of the first volume. Otherwise, one would surely not bother to publish, much less purchase, a second edition. One gets the impression that, in the rush to announce differences, sociologists, no less than others, lose sight of the things that make revised or new editions valuable to begin with.

Sociological Realities II is a text/reader, but it is not in a conventional sense. It builds on the conception developed in *Sociological Realities I*, an organic orientation toward sociology through the writings of many and diverse people who share common interests and a common sense of what is important and meaningful in the field of sociology today. The goals of this text/reader are the same as those of *Transaction/Society* magazine, from which most of the material presented here has been taken.

The editors have designed this book to accomplish several purposes. One is to gather together the very best sociological writing available that remains true to the mission of sociology and at the same time is understandable to the general reader and beginning student. That kind of sociological writing is hard to do. In many ways it is easier to write in "sociologese" than in plain English. It is also easier to write sensationally than it is to maintain a deep respect for the evidential canons of sociology.

Another important aim of both *Transaction/Society* and *Sociological Realities II* is to present solid, current information about society that is up to date without merely pandering to popular taste. This does not mean that the latest word is necessarily the best word. The "relevance" of a Max Weber, Emile Durkheim, Karl Marx or C. Wright Mills may be timeless. Yet to understand the implications of the work of these men demands a disciplined knowledge of their time as well as ours. The editors believe that students and other readers of this volume will develop a sure sense of what the sociological enterprise is about from its pages, and we fervently hope that it will lead to deeper and broader exploration. The very best contemporary sociologists are represented here, as well as extraordinary sociological writing from nonsociologists. More than 60 percent of the material presented in *Sociological Realities II* has been published since the first edition of *Sociological Realities* appeared in 1971.

At the level of continuities, *Sociological Realities I* and *II* have in common an appreciation of the liberating potentialities of doing scientific sociology. That is to say, like its predecessor, *Sociological Realities II* does not seek by tendentious means to indoctrinate or inculcate a religious, ideological series of values. It does seek to point out, more by example and illustration than by formal theory, the pluralistic nature of the social world and the various forms of human life that not only permit but compel us to recognize that communities, systems and nations differ just as people are different one from another. Indeed, these differences at the interaction level exist precisely *because* people are different.

In the sensitivity that difference is the touchstone of analysis, that the lives we lead are neither necessarily better nor worse than those led by others, inheres the human capability to make scientific comparisons. A capacity to study the validity of differences also allows us to work toward a consensus about what constitutes a good society, no less than what constitutes an operating society. The radical consequences of scientific sociology flow from this recognition of differences between people and societies. This in itself permits new horizons for each of us as individuals. The foundations of sociology disallow any automatic assumption of the superiority of one group over another as if this strength of body or of nation is a preordained, God-given situation. Whether we are better or worse or, more to the point, in what senses we are better and in what senses worse is a function of comparative examination. And such comparison is what *Sociological Realities II* is about.

Yet major changes have taken place between 1969

and 1975 in the social order and in the sociological imagination as well. It is the aim of this text/reader to reflect and record these differences, as well as to maintain a sense of continuity with what occurred before. The first edition of the work assumed the conventional textbook form and attempted to instill, at least in part, a radical content. That is to say, the work was organized, as many textbooks are, in terms of chapters relating to culture, social organization, socialization, social stratification, institutions, interaction and communication, political protest, social movements, and, finally, the style and substance of sociology. In some measure we still hope to provide a useful accompanying reader for any standard text. In addition, however, we are interested in developing a perspective on sociology that will be scientific rather than eclectic, systematic rather than random. To do this means to infuse the volume with a spirit of radical *structure* rather than *content*. By this we seek to convey a sense of the structure of society and not simply a breathless summation of newspaper events.

We have chosen to structure the book in terms of micro, middle and macro levels of sociology. By this tripartite division we mean not simply the range of people covered in any given study, although that may very much be a factor, but, more to the point, an appreciation that work in sociology can cover two people or many, two organizations or many, two nations or many, and yet each of these is a discrete level of analysis. Each has its own fascination, and each is a legitimate area of sociological inquiry. What holds together the ranges of micro, middle and macro is a common-sense conception of methodological purpose and an appreciation that the analysis of two people, like that of two nations, can present us with very much the same dynamics. What we refer to, then, in micro, middle and macro ranges are levels of complexity in social organization, not necessarily new types of analytic tools that have to be adjusted depending on the number of people or organizations to which we refer. Whether we are employing game theory, historical analysis, functionalism or phenomenological analysis, the essential validity and truths of each way of looking at the social system must somehow and in some way incorporate individuals no less than nation-states.

In our view, methodology is the riverbed of social research, infusing all of its branches with a unifying principle that permits diversity rather than choking off innovation. As a result, *Sociological Realities II* makes a much more direct effort to include essays and themes published in *Transaction/Society*, displaying a methodological richness that will enable students to go on to do additional research in the social sciences. *Sociological Realities I* emphasized ethnography, "how" things are done; *Sociological Realities II* lays greater emphasis on methodology, or "why" things are done. In no way is this a critique of ethnography. We simply want to carry the results of observation one step further, so that the student can replicate the same kinds of work in different environments, or different kinds of work using the same kinds of methodological controls. In other words, the methodological emphasis is not simply formalist but, rather, rests on a renewed awareness of content. Many of the essays illustrate how good research can be done, whether at the micro, middle or macro level, and thus provide for independent verification and replication by the student using this text.

This volume emphasizes the inductive nature of sociology, that is, that the discipline moves from particular concrete reality toward generalization. Neither "theory" nor "methods" per se are emphasized but, rather, are allowed to grow organically out of the real sociological work of real sociologists analyzing the real world. The areas of social life discussed by the various writers in this volume range far and wide. Each article provides the kind of data necessary for developing the truly catholic and comparative stance that constitutes the very heart of sociological reasoning. Principles of social behavior arise out of shifting, sorting and abstracting what is common to behavior across different contexts. The generalizability of those principles can only be discovered by exploring what it is that various people do in a myriad of contexts. *Transaction/Society* magazine has for more than a decade contributed an enormous amount of comparative material on social life. This text/reader attempts to organize some of that material into a framework that will allow the student to develop a sociological imagination because it builds on his own experience and the shared experience of others through clear and understandable writing.

The editors also hope that the sociological adventure will be fun. The lively nature of the articles, the aim of the authors represented in these pages to communicate with a general, nonspecialized audience, and the organization of those articles will make the learning process as painless as possible.

Any scheme the editors might have come up with would have been subject to some sort of criticism. The massive amount of material presented in this volume could have been arranged in many different ways. Our organizational system, we believe, permits maximum flexibility for both student and instructor. The book is organized into five parts; each of the parts, in turn, contains from one to seven sections. The sections contain from three to seven articles. Part One, "The Practice of the Sociological Discipline," addresses itself to the overall issues that confront those who would do sociology. While technical discussion is avoided here, the great issues facing the discipline are considered:

the model of social research as a scientific enterprise, the relationship of sociology with other approaches to the study of social life, and the implications of sociological findings for people living in the groups sociologists study—including society as a whole. Part Five, "Social Science and Public Policy," elaborates the last point in greater detail. This last part is relevant in considering the role of social science in shaping public policies, and awareness of the issues joined in Part Five is essential both for an enlightened citizenry and for the development of a more responsive and reflexive sociology.

Between the first and last parts of the book are parts exploring the micro, middle and macro levels of sociology. The editors' intention is to build toward a larger and broader frame of reference as the text/reader unfolds. In Part Two, "The Microlevels of Sociology," the emphasis is on social psychology. Each article in Part Two develops one or another facet of the interaction between individuals and societies, with emphasis on how the individual, in going about his daily round of activities, is affected by the social arrangements around him. The first swells of a long crescendo that will carry the reader to an analytic level within the social structure itself begins in this part dealing with the social psychology of individuals, groups and collectivities.

The middle levels of sociology are the major focus of attention in Part Three. Here a shift occurs away from the individual per se and toward the group process itself. Part Three is concerned with the socialization of individuals by the others who make up the groups he either joins or is placed in by the vagaries of social life. *Socialization*, in this context, simply means the transmission of culture by group representatives who have the power to shape the individual behavior and attitudes of others. The socialization theme, of course, is prominent in the micro section as well, but in that section the angle of vision is more clearly on the socializee. In the third part the linkage function of group life emerges more sharply than in the previous part. Many of these articles dwell on the interaction of socializers with each other, as well as with those who are on the receiving end of the process that binds them into a society of people with shared perspectives and constraints. There is also a blending here of matters that become paramount in the next part, that on macrosociology. Institutions, clusters of patterned roles that contribute regularity to social life, are very much a part of the linkage between people and groups.

Part Four, "The Macro Levels of Sociology," brings the volume to a primary focus on institutions and emphasizes the determinative nature of social structural arrangements. (It should be noted that this does *not* suggest that the editors are convinced that individuals are not "free" to follow plans of action that may lead to very different social arrangements; we believe that the received constraints of group social organization limit the range of alternatives, chiefly, perhaps, by limiting even the alternatives that might be thought of—which is the essential function of culture, the learned way of doing things.) Part Four represents the most traditional concerns of sociology as a distinct discipline, social organization. It leads organically into Part Five, which represents, after all, the "payoff" of having a sociology for the members of society.

Taken as a whole, we believe the editorial material constitutes a coherent statement on the nature of sociology as a discipline. We have avoided the temptation to discuss many of the burning issues involved in the current debate about sociology and its future among practicing sociologists. To do that would unnecessarily burden those who may be coming to sociology for the first time. An alert reading of this volume, however, will make abundantly clear that some of those issues are, as well as some of the alternatives for resolving them. More specialized material in the professional journals and in the sociological literature itself will provide plenty of food for further thought.

A cautionary note must be added for instructors and students who would argue with our organizational scheme. The scheme itself is not a typology in the usual sense. The micro, middle and macro distinctions overlap too much for that to be the case. Instead, we intend them to supply a rough kind of transitivity to the presentation of the material in this volume. One fault we have found with introductory-level texts is that they provide too tight an organizational framework, which belies the fluidity of the sociological enterprise as it functions at present. Other books designed for the beginning student offer little or no organization, only a welter of unrelated material. The advantage of the structure we have used is that it provides a framework that is in harmony with the articles reproduced herein. *Sociological Realities II* comes out of the *Transaction/Society* style and vision of sociology. That very fact lends a kind of organic unity that transcends any editorial scheme.

Instructors and students are urged to rearrange the material in this book to fit their own needs. Taken as a whole, the book provides a sound and consistent collection of articles and editorial content suitable for an introductory course in sociology. It is also useful for social problems courses and as a sourcebook for other, more specialized courses, such as courses in deviance or social organization. Clearly, we have no intention of preempting the instructor's syllabus through the book's organization. Depending on the instructor's teaching style and the needs of his or her students, the material contained herein lends itself to rearrangement. Should the instructor wish, for example, to organize a unit on drug abuse, the articles by Becker (III:6), Christie (III:7), Witter (VII:5), Colburn and Colburn (IX:2) and Graham (XVIII:1) "hang together" for such a unit. For a sequence in women's studies, the articles by Morris (III:2), Stevens (IV:1), Scott (IV:6), Palson and Palson (VI:3), La Rue (X:1), Carter (XI:2), Velarde and Warlick (XI:3), Heyl (XI:5), Salutin (XI:6), Goldman (XI:7) and Nagel and Weitzman (XII:2) might constitute such a unit. A "methods" unit might be constructed from the following articles: all of the articles in Part One; Kiesler (III:1), Gmelch (V:3), Mahigal and Stone (V:4), Sturges (V:5), Silberberg and Silberberg (VII:2), Schafer, Olexa and Polk (VII:3), Bowles (VII:4), Nagel and Weitzman (XII:2), Heussenstamm (XII:3), Whitt (XV:3), Mechanic (XVI:3), Graham (XVIII:1) and Crotty (XVIII:3); and all of Part Five. (It should be obvious that every article included in this volume is about "theory" and "methods." These suggestions represent a concentration on different techniques and on the philosophy of social science.) Other ways of organizing sequences for a substantive approach are limited only by the individual instructor's imagination and proclivities.

A word ought to be added about the potential criticism of this volume to the effect that an article that appears under one heading could have just as easily appeared under another, or that a particular article does not "fit" the organizational scheme very well. Our only response is that we, as editors, have presented one "slant" and that we deliberated about the placing of certain articles that attacked points or presented material in more than one area. We cannot preempt the good judgment of individual instructors here, either. For example, the article by Mahigal and Stone (V:4) *does* distort the concept of collective behavior (although it is clearly a discussion of microlevel interaction); we invite the instructor to place that article elsewhere if his or her syllabus would benefit. To reemphasize a point made previously: Our organizational scheme is tentative and suggestive rather than a reified typology, and it invites reorganization tailored to individual needs.

The first edition of *Sociological Realities* emphasized how people go about doing things in, for and against society. A certain pragmatic series of assumptions were also made concerning the need for social change. This pragmatic emphasis reflected a time of automatic ideological responses: when there was a consensus in American society on the evils of the war in Southeast Asia, the rights of racial minorities to full participation, and the absolute worth of generational, sexual and religious equality. It is not that five years later these issues have been resolved, that American foreign policy is perfect or that racial equity has been achieved. It is, rather, that a sense of the diversity of possible responses has taken hold. Much of what was taken for granted has to do with policy rather than ideology. Even if there remains a wide-scale agreement on the need for equity, how one translates such a need into practice remains a problem of implementation no less than evaluation.

As a result, *Sociological Realities II* displays a stronger emphasis on policy questions, on how it is possible to achieve goals that seem to be universally held. For it is precisely at the level of policy making that the issues are now joined. The consensus that has been reached concerning goals for America now seems less than satisfactory unless techniques at the policy level exist to translate such goals into realistic policies, displaying timetables that are adequate to the task but without causing the fabric of human association itself to collapse simply for the sake of change.

A central difference at the technical level of the organization of this volume is the shift from random photographs accompanying each article to the photographic essay as a form of sociological investigation. The five years between these two texts have brought about a veritable revolution in sociological photography. Indeed, *Transaction/Society* was in some measure responsible for the shift in this photographic vision. The very fact that the visual aspects of the volume have shifted over time along with its literary format is an indication of the cultural revolution of our times, of the use of photography as an instrument of learning rather than simply an instrument of illustration. One would have to say that this, too, is a significant change from the first edition.

Sociological Realities II shares with its predecessor a concern for the human condition, for the varieties of the social experience and for the feeling that social change is part of the fabric of the social system itself. At the same time, the new edition is more sober in its estimates of achieving social change rapidly, a sobriety reinforced by an appreciation of how complex real change is, even when a developing consensus exists on the abstract level of values and ideology or, for that matter, even after revolutionary upheavals take place. For even then the question remains, What next? And this means that sociology, before or after or during times of upheaval, is a valid handmaiden to social change as well as social structure.

Irving Louis Horowitz
Charles Nanry

Rutgers University
New Brunswick, N.J.

PART ONE

The Practice of the Sociological Discipline

There are probably as many definitions of sociology as there are practitioners, but if one yielded to the temptation of saying that the field is nothing more than the sum of individual idiosyncratic definitions of behavior, then there would be no need for a course of study. Despite the admittedly open-ended nature of sociology, certain guidelines do establish what the field is about. In part, these guidelines are matters of convention; that is, decisions are made by the collectivity of sociology to study things in common, such as penal institutions, family groups, social interaction, political agencies and so on. In another sense, sociology is not so much a convention as a response to a felt need to organize the meaning of human behavior in social interaction. Here, what goes on between people rather than in the mind of each person becomes the substance of the discipline.

The boundaries between sociology and other sciences are somewhat artificial. In a sense, all human beings are animals and could be studied zoologically. In another sense, all animals are composites of cellular structures, and therefore chemistry could be the focus of study. In still another sense, all cellular structures are molecular combinations, which are atomic in nature and therefore could be studied by physicists. But, obviously, this *reductio ad absurdum* is just that, a piece of nonsense. In point of fact, the task of sociology, like all sciences, is not merely to know the world or to interpret it, but to live in that world with a sense of knowledge, even anticipation, of what will happen in the future. Thus, sociology starts with the relationship between two people and builds up to that between two nations.

Even posing the situation in such a fashion opens up methodological as well as theoretical dilemmas. What, for example, is the relationship between the behavior of two people and that of two nations? Is the decisive fact the size, the magnitude of each reality? Is it the quality of interrelationships between two parts: two people, two institutions in search of some outcome? Because of such questions, sociology must be at all times both a theoretical and a methodological discipline. It examines not only empirical limits and guidelines but how these guidelines are demonstrable and provable.

No one reader or text can completely satisfy all individuals using such sociological materials, for sociology is not universal, but particular; not collective in its wisdom, but selective in what it extracts from the corpus of information as presentable and/or worthwhile. The inclinations and proclivities of the editors and authors will be clear to those who use this reader. But a discussion of these inclinations and proclivities might well be in order, since this in itself presents openly and unabashedly the limits as well as the scope of the sociological discipline.

1. When the essays deal with micro, middle or macro levels of analysis, each essay is informed by a sense of the humanity intrinsic to the subject matter of sociology, by concern for the people involved and by an interest in equitable treatment for those people.

2. Each essay attempts to show that commonplace wisdom, is, for the most part, either uncommon wisdom or sheer bunk passed along by generations and centuries of mythology. Thus, most of the essays will elicit a response such as "I had no idea this was the case" or "I knew it all along, but this is the first time it has been proved to me." This we hold to be perfectly reasonable procedure within the sociological discipline.

3. The underlying presumption in many, if not all, of the essays is that a major theme throughout American and world history has been the drive for equality. The very emphasis on stratification, that is, structured ordering of society within sociology, does not simply point up inequality but suggests ways of getting beyond such a state into a more equitable arrangement between all people: whites and blacks, men and women, prisoners and custodians, socialists and capitalists. This is not to suggest a sheer, blind denial of differences, or that getting along with all people, whether they be makers of dreams or killers of dreams, is feasible. But the purpose of sociology, and certainly of this book, is to show how reason serves the aims of science and society alike.

Sociology is one of several disciplines that concerns itself with the study of man and his society. Along with the other social sciences, the biological sciences, and literature and the arts, sociology is committed to understanding the human animal living in groups. The special focus of sociology is the human being's relations with other people, the enduring social relations created, and the changing form of these social structures. Sociologists may concentrate their research efforts on groups, associations, communities, institutions or even societies as a whole. In other words, people in interaction, not individuals alone, are the essential focus of sociology; for although each person lives his own life, he or she is also a member in the group that socialized him or her, and he or she lives in collectivities of many sizes and sorts. Society would not exist without individuals, and there would be no human beings if there were no social life.

Sociology has turned its attention to the study of group life in a systematic way with the aim of accumulating a body of knowledge about society that is more reliable than common-sense observations made in the course of ordinary living. There is a great deal of current and accumulated wisdom available about how society works, some of which is mythical, some dependable and true. Sociology attempts to provide a dependable frame of reference for those who want to understand social life in addition to merely living it. Through the eyes of astute sociological observers, we are able to penetrate unknown and often strange social worlds beyond our limited power of observation. Sociology also takes the commonplace "out of play," makes it strange and returns it to us transformed. It grants us a new angle of vision. Sociology makes no claim to eternal truth, but it does lay claim to the status of a discipline; that is, its observations are systematic, open to inspection, natural rather than supernatural and susceptible to test.

Section I

Science, Society and Sociology

In the early days of sociology, the major question on the agenda was: Is sociology a science? Great interest was manifested in this subject, and indeed, most earlier writings on sociology were as dedicated to answering this question as to doing serious sociology as such. This was, perhaps, the inevitable outcome of the philosophical rather than natural scientific origins of many early sociologists. As a result, many techniques of investigation used in the physical sciences were ignored, and sociology remained simple social commentary. This tradition incorporated none of the enormous efforts of some of the early sociologists, whose profound insights overwhelmed any shortcomings in presentation. Indeed, many of the early paradigms are still used in sociology: Superordination and subordination, Gemeinschaft and Gesellschaft, organic society and contract society, and dozens of other antinomies bore enormous fruit and made possible the next stage, namely, which pole of the antinomy is right, and beyond that, how each antinomy is resolved in empirical research and practice.

Several major developments made a science of society realizable. First was the computer revolution, which permitted the study of total information and led to a general societal emphasis on numbers, amounts, ratios, percentages and so on. America, in particular, became the society of sociology par excellence. Worth was defined in terms of election wins and defeats, Gallup Poll voting and general sampling devices to measure individual preferences and tastes in everything from dry cereal to housing. Under such impulses and impetus, sociology quickly shifted from philosophical concerns to consensual concerns, from an earlier critical posture to a constructive one. This, in turn, led to a sociological "counterrevolution" in which critical evaluation has been resurrected, but this is not really the concern of this volume. Clearly, the precondition for a scientific status for sociology was in fact a revolution of considerable proportions, a shift from emphasis on the production of commodity needs to the production of knowledge and information. Sociology, then, is part and parcel of the scientific revolution of the mid-twentieth century, and its character has been largely shaped by this phenomenon.

Sociology has also been shaped by the emergence of institutions dedicated primarily to research rather than teaching. In the past, the only viable means of support for the sociologist was teaching, but of course, teaching is an art engaged in by people interested in everything from Latin classics to astrophysics. Teaching does not define what a sociologist is but, rather, what pedagogy and college life are about.

The development of sociology as a science, therefore, had as its precondition the development of research agencies, bureaus of research and institutes of social science, in which funds were gathered from federal, state and local agencies—private and public, civilian and military—all dedicated to applied research, that is, to the solution of practical problems that had such urgency as to necessitate financial investment in the social research process.

This entire program was made possible by the rise of a military supported technostructure that has given a new, noncivilian direction to American industrial society since the outbreak of World War II. The permanent warfare–welfare economy has bred a new generation of social scientists with a new set of tasks, namely, integrating a new society still employing old labels of capitalism and private sector domination. Sociology became involved in area research centers, international development study groups, crime and delinquency centers, drug rehabilitation programs, social control programs and so on. The sociologist became identified as an entity outside the classroom, having large-scale social tasks ranging from organizational analysis to labor–management studies domestically, to civic action and revolutionary theory internationally.

Later in this volume we shall draw attention to the ethical and moral dilemmas posed by such new tasks of a "postindustrial" society. In the meantime, one must only point out that today, for the first time, more sociologists make a living outside the field of teaching than inside it. Whatever the quality of work performed, the fact is that the new standing of sociology has changed the name of the game and the nature of its problems. One no longer hears "if sociology is a science" but, rather, "given the nature of sociology as a science, how risky is it to the life and limb; what are its advantages and disadvantages; do the former outweigh the latter?" These kinds of issues, as well as the specific techniques of social research, are addressed in the first sections of this volume.

In "Science as a Frame of Reference," Mack suggests the kinship of sociology with other sciences through the unity of method. He makes clear that method does *not* imply specific technique but, rather, a set of underlying assumptions common to the chemist in his laboratory and the social researcher interviewing respondents in a homosexual bar. Mack asserts that reliance on sense data, logic and reliability, that is, the agreement among observers that some observed thing has indeed happened, are the basic assumptions underlying all science.

While all sciences share a logical–philosophical frame of reference, they develop special techniques of study appropriate to the things being studied. In "Intellectual Strategies and Research Tactics," Mack gives an insider's view of how a sociologist goes about tackling a research problem. In the process, we are let in on the sociological reasoning that underlies the selection of particular research tools: the study of past and present documents, participant observation and informal interviews. We see how involved a sociologist becomes, and must become, in the life of the society he is studying in order to arrive at a deeper understanding of it than that of an ordinary observer. Particularly, we see that he enters the society with well-formulated questions in mind and armed with findings from other studies; these questions, based on knowledge from societies previously studied, serve as guidelines for observation, propositions to be tested and the basis for accumulating valid knowledge about society.

Merton and Devereux, in "Practical Problems and the Uses of Social Science," analyze the practical use of social science research by Bell Telephone. They suggest that Bell's use of social research was not random but, rather, depended on three elements: the perceived discrepancy between the goals of the company and the external situation; the need for adjustive activity; and a "puzzle" element, that is, a perceived need for additional facts to explain an ambiguous situation. The real key, however, to understanding "command" research is the *perception* of the need for research by those who control organizational resources. Merton and Devereux point out that those responsible for large-scale organizations learn to "read" trend data and to sensitize themselves to deviations from normal or expected patterns in order to "fine tune" organizational decisions to the outside world.

For financial, ethical and sometimes practical reasons (e.g., unlike that of fruit flies, the length of a human generation may preclude some types of intergenerational research), it is often useful to use computer simulations as models of human behavior. This relatively new field can have a wide variety of applications. Meier and Bradford, in "Creating a World for Research," discuss some of the uses of simulation in planning, political behavior, education, psychology and international relations and in the creation of "artificial intelligence." The computer can generate interesting, albeit nonisomorphic, models of human attitudes and behavior. Having computers available for such uses may even make social scientists less dependent on the whims of governmental agencies and organizational moguls and their "perceptions." As an illustration of one use to which the computer has been put, Skedgell, a former CBS executive, tells us just how those network computers pick winners on election night, often long before the polls are closed.

Aside from obvious inaccuracies, however, computer simulation can involve other dangers. In "The Politics of Information," Webber, a city planner, suggests some of these dangers. Warning that "facts are never neutral," Webber reminds us that simulations can become guides for policy making and may in themselves become instruments of social change. His discussion is a chill reminder that information is power. Webber warns that social scientists may, in fact, become mere pawns in larger political games.

1 *Raymond W. Mack*

Science as a Frame of Reference

"A social scientist is a man who, if he has two little boys, sends one to Sunday School every Sunday and keeps the other one home as an experimental control group." So runs one of our bits of occupational in-group humor. Would that we more often knew such precision!

The scientific *method* in social science is the same scientific method which underlies the work done in the chemist's laboratory, the zoologist's dissecting room, and the astronomer's observatory. But the *techniques* of gathering information vary from discipline to discipline: the chemist has his Bunsen burner and his watch glass, the zoologist his scalpel and his microscope, the astronomer his radio telescope and his charts. The social scientist has his interview schedule and his questionnaire. For each, the controlled experiment is an ideal seldom achieved but often approximated. For all, the canons of the scientific method are identical.

The unity of the sciences lies in their method. The scientific method is a way of trying to make sense out of the booming, buzzing confusion of the universe. It is an intellectual stance toward information. The scientific method is a set of assumptions about when a fact is a fact. The method provides scientists with a set of guideposts for gathering information and for bringing order to congeries of data.

Persons using the scientific method as a frame of reference operate under three assumptions: (1) that the human senses are the most reliable medium for gathering data; (2) that human reason is the most valid tool for organizing data; and (3) that agreement among a number of competent observers is the best check on the efficiency of the data gathering and organizing process called for in the first two assumptions.

Knowledge is scientific, then, when (1) an observer gathers information through one or more of his senses—sight, hearing, touch, taste, or smell—and (2) uses logic to interpret his information, that is, to relate one fact to another, and (3) other scientists sufficiently well-trained in the observer's specialty to understand what he has done use their sense experience and human reason on the information and arrive at the same conclusion.

When one of these criteria is violated in the search for knowledge, the conclusions are not scientific. Science does not provide us with knowledge about God because, by definition, the supernatural cannot be experienced through human senses. A random collection of facts does not constitute a science because facts do not speak for themselves; human reason must be employed to explain the relationships among facts and among sets of facts.

Scientists often use instruments for collecting information: thermometers, stethoscopes, tape recorders, questionnaires. These are the techniques which vary from discipline to discipline. They are simply aids to implementing the scientific method, which is unvarying. These devices are auxiliaries to the human senses. Scientists use them to bring greater precision to their own sense experience.

But the most refined gauge does not measure anything. A human being does the measuring. The instrument extends the range and sharpens the precision of his observations. A yardstick does not measure, and a Geiger counter does not count: a man does. It is the eye and the ear of the scientist using them that translate their sensitive markings and murmurings into scientific facts.

It is hardly correct, then, to speak of facts as being more or less scientific. A set of observations may be more or less precise, but if they are the product of sense experience logically interpreted and independently verified, they are scientific.

While the method of science is unvarying, the bodies of knowledge accumulated via the scientific method are ever-changing. The scientific method does not change, but the content of a scientific discipline does. This does not necessarily mean that a set of facts is disproved, but often that the gaining of additional information leads to a reinterpretation of what is known. Einstein's theory of relativity does not disprove Newton's scientific facts; it explains more by adding to and reinterpreting Newton's observations.

When a man accepts science as a frame of reference, and uses it in his daily work life, it is bound to have some impact upon his frame of mind. The stereotype which nonscientists hold of the scientist offers a clue to that frame of mind. Laymen often see scientists as cold-blooded skeptics, uninvolved in the values of their culture or the issues of their society, and hard to convince of anything. Like most stereotypes, this one is organized around elements of truth. The scientist is neither as bad as some people think in his lack of capacity for emotional conviction, nor as good as others think in his ability to separate his personal preferences from his objective scholarly conclusions.

But his training and practice do lead a scientist to attempt to separate his own wishes and convictions from the process of observing and interpreting data The scientific method, with its commitment to sense experience and independent verification, is an attempt to assure complete objectivity. A social scientist, even more than others, should be aware that his own experience and cultural conditioning will influence his choice of research problems. He has learned in his own society a set of rules and preferences and even a way of thinking. That is why he uses the scientific method: as a guard against confusing what he would like to find with what is actually there.

He may not be able to bring his scientific frame of mind to every problem he addresses as a Republican, as a Baptist, as a father, or as a friend, but when he is working, his commitment to the method helps him to get outside himself and his milieu and to see his physical and social environment objectively. In this sense, too, the stereotype is founded on fact: the scientist *at work* is a man alienated from his society. As a citizen, the bacteriologist may loathe the ravages of tuberculosis and want passionately to find a means of preventing the disease. As a citizen, a sociologist may love democratic concepts of justice and deplore the ways in which poverty and racial discrimination cause his society to fall short of its own ideals. But at work, the bacteriologist must measure, not curse, the virulence of the bacillus; the sociologist must invest his work time in analyzing the effectiveness of special interest groups, not in cheerleading.

Calling something science does not make it scientific, of course. Astrology remains more popular than astronomy. Alchemy preceded chemistry, and there were hosts of economic and political philosophers eager to turn the lead of their opinions into the gold of truth long before there were many economists and political scientists using the scientific method to further their understanding of human behavior. There are still people who call themselves social scientists, but who evidence little inclination to subject their pet theories to the hazards of empirical test.

Nonetheless, this century has seen a larger and larger proportion of scholars using the scientific method as a means to the end of learning more about human social behavior. Every year, more students are exposed to science as a frame of reference. The mass media report and comment upon information gathered by observation, interviews, and questionnaires. Political leaders, educators, businessmen, church administrators make policy decisions based upon data gathered by social scientists. The growing acceptance of science as a frame of reference can encourage belief that decision makers may come to feel more at home with science as a frame of mind.

2 *Raymond W. Mack*

Intellectual Strategies and Research Tactics

Social scientists are perhaps at their most misleading in describing how they do their work. They may be models of objectivity in reporting *what* they find and they will usually work within the canons of scientific method in trying to interpret what their data *mean*. But ask a social scientist *how* he found out, and you are likely to get an outrageous oversimplification.

I know a social scientist who has spent twenty years in learning about factory workers: working in factories himself, observing and interviewing laborers on the job, talking with them casually off the job, studying their personnel records, and reading what other social scientists have written about factory workers. When he was asked how he gathered the data for one of his studies, he replied: "We administered a questionnaire to a random sample of 104 men in one plant." Actually, his conclusions were based upon all the experience I have described. He gathered one set of data with a questionnaire, but he brought to the task of interpreting it all those other sets of data he has acquired as observer, participant observer, interviewer, and reader.

The selection of research techniques is a matter of strategy, not of morals. What is the right way to gather social data? The answer depends on what one is trying to learn about, and on the social setting in which he is trying to find out. Let me use my experience on the Caribbean island of Barbados as an example of what I mean by adopting research techniques to suit the research problem and the research setting.

My involvement with Barbados grew out of my interest in social organization and social classes. As a student of class structure, I have found myself drawn increasingly during the past decade into research on, and analyses of, the role of race in the social structure in the United States.

Having studied and written about race relations in the United States, I thought that I could broaden my perspective and might deepen my insight into the American situation by observing the meaning of race in another society. Reading about Caribbean societies led me to the conclusion that Barbados had experienced enough historical parallels to the American situation to make comparison meaningful and was sufficiently different to make contrast enlightening.

is going on it is therefore particularly important that "face" be mutually respected—and that conflicts do not result in personal antagonisms that can break down the relationship.

To formalize and slightly extend some of Goffman's ideas—to emphasize the role of personal purpose—let us examine further the precise techniques in use (with appropriate jargon to keep it all sounding scientific).

WORDS ABOUT WORDS

To accomplish anything speech must have the favorable impact on the listener that the speaker intends—or hopes for. To try to make sure it does, the speaker can add to the message certain phrases which tell the listener what the message is supposed to mean. Such phrases can be called *communication about communication.*

Suppose an act or statement can have several meanings to a listener, some favorable and others unfavorable. One way to make sure he does not get the wrong meaning is to tell him what meaning he is supposed to get—in other words a *pre-interpretation.* "There's nothing personal about this . . ." is a common pre-interpretation. So are: "objectively speaking . . ." and "Be sure not to take this the wrong way. . . ."

A not uncommon ploy is to start with a *preinterpretation* that asserts that nothing detrimental is intended. This allows the speaker, then, to insult the other at will: "I think you've done a great job and I don't want you to get me wrong, but . . ."

Not all communication about communication need occur before the message; it can also come after. Sometimes it's evident that the listener got the "wrong" meaning; then the speaker may want to rush in and straighten him out. So he uses a *post-interpretation:* "I'm just telling you what's being said—I don't necessarily agree with it." "Now don't misunderstand and think I said. . . ."

The double function of communication about communication—getting your desire while keeping everybody else happy, or at least cooperative—is not always easily accomplished. Sometimes the speaker knows that his message or action may fall flat no matter what he says about it. He may try, then, to separate the listener's personal evaluation of him from the negative effects of the message or action by apologizing ahead of time. He uses a *pre-apology* "I haven't had the chance to read up on this yet . . ." and, "Just speaking off the top of my head, since we have to make a fast decision . . ." are examples that ask others not to downgrade the actor if his act comes below expectations. "I'm really not in practice, but I'll try . . ." asks a little less: that the others not judge the performance too strictly.

The pre-apology is good also for securing a "vote of confidence"—approval even before the action is attempted. This is called "fishing." "I'm really not very good at it," the new lady golfer demurs, and the rest of the foursome (she hopes) immediately choruses, "Oh, of course you are. You're good at everything."

When a pre-interpretation or a post-interpretation reveal causes for one's actions, they are *motive revelations.* If the actor wants to take responsibility and credit for his act, he uses the *personalized* form. If he wants to get off the hook (he was a helpless victim of circumstances) he uses a depersonalized form. A personalized motive revelation identifies the speaker firmly with the good things in the message, or at least with the good intentions implicit in bringing the message: "I'm mentioning this because I think you'd be pleased to know . . ." Depersonalized, it separates him from the bad things: "I didn't want this to happen, but you know what the boss is like when he makes up his mind . . ." The depersonalized motive revelation is, in short, an alibi.

The difference between them becomes most evident in responses to requests. When someone makes a request, he implies that both he and it are worthy of consideration. Denial entails risks on both sides. In consequence, elaborate feelers, and lines of action and reaction, are set up.

One way for a requester to minimize risk is to ask for something without seeming to—to keep the lines of retreat wide open: "It would be very nice if . . ." Assent in such cases tends to take the form of a personalized motive revelation: "Of course, I'd be happy to . . ." The asker can then counter with, "But I don't really want to impose . . . ," a very useful gambit. It serves as a preapology and, at the same time, puts the other in the role of defending the reasonableness of the request—so that before he quite knows what has happened he is urging the requester to accept what was requested. "Oh no, no trouble at all . . . that's perfectly all right . . . don't even mention it . . ."

Depersonalized forms predominate in the opposite tactic —when denying requests. The denier can't be blamed for denial when he demonstrates that he did the best he could. Nor is the requester liable to feel as personally rejected. Usually the matter was simply beyond the denier's control: he was too busy, his wife was sick, the fates were against him. For example; "I only have one vote on that committee. I did the best I could, but I didn't have a chance."

A further refinement is the *altruistic motive revelation.* The request was turned down or the deed was done for the *other's own good.* "No, I didn't put in your name for that apartment, but that was only because I know they don't accept Negroes or children and I just wanted to save you embarrassment." Unless the person using the altruistic form has close personal ties with us or is generally recognized to be in a superior position with superior information (for instance, a physician during illness) he can seem offensively patronizing. Parents however, always know what is best for their children, and often enough it turns out to be exactly opposite what the children want. Children, like adults, learn to be suspicious of such claims, and to discount them.

Altruistic statements are one of a large number of tactics useful in enhancing credibility—a person who has our best interests at heart presumably wouldn't lie to us. We can trust him. Credibility then shifts from the message itself

During the two years between my first look at Barbados and the completion of my study, I was able to spend only about six months actually living in Barbados. If one is going to try to achieve some understanding in such a brief period of how a total society is structured, then he must seize every available tool to help accomplish the mission. My work, therefore, cannot be described as solely library research, nor as participant observation, nor as an interview study. I was shamelessly opportunistic in data gathering.

I read 17th century history, 18th century political science, 20th century travel guides, and both daily newspapers in Barbados, the *News* and the *Advocate.* I studied census bulletins, government economic reports, civil lists, and gossip columns. I was a participant observer at dinner parties, at picnics, on the beach, in bars and restaurants, at dances, at cricket matches, and at horse races. I attended House of Assembly meetings and Town Council welfare hearings. I interviewed cane cutters, planters, taxi drivers, refinery owners, cooks, insurance brokers, maids, automobile salesmen, housewives, newspapermen, storekeepers, waiters, real estate speculators, government ministers, schoolteachers, clergymen, hotel owners, airline employees, leisured expatriates, students, radio announcers, civil servants, one shoeshine boy, and the American Vice-Consul. My interviewees included white Barbadians from the "Big Six" families of the island's power structure; Negro Oxford graduates who have achieved enough political power to make the "Big Six" nervous; mulattoes whom an observer accustomed to the rules in the United States would call "Negro," but who are pass-as-white; old-family members chronically in debt after the fashion of South Carolina "genteel poverty"; working class Negroes; and poor whites viewed with contempt by everyone else regardless of race, color, or creed. My data was gathered from no specifiable sample of the universe of Barbadians, but if total immersion is the way to salvation, I showed good faith.

Since my goal was to learn about race and class and their interrelationship, my strategy led me to start at the bottom of the class structure. The tactic of avoiding early contact with members of the power structure was based on the assumption that I could later produce scholarly credentials which would explain lower class associations to upper class people; but if I became identified early with occupants of the seats of power, it would be extremely difficult later to achieve rapport with workers dependent upon the moguls or with middle class people resentful of their exclusion from the inner circle.

So I talked first with taxi drivers, bus conductors, waiters, the baby sitter, the yard man next door, and gradually became involved in a network of informants: I used to work as a dance band musician before retiring into social science and this provided useful entree into the night world of the island. Many of the musicians working in hotels and night clubs had listened to records and become greatly interested in jazz, and I was able to play with them and talk with them after working hours. My preschool children spent hours on the beach, and were good enough to introduce me to the parents of their friends, who spanned the color spectrum and the power pyramid.

Gradually, my network of middle class acquaintances widened. My landlord introduced me to the extension officer of the University of the West Indies. He in turn introduced me to a school principal, a newspaper columnist, and a government officer. The newsman took me to a welfare hearing; the principal introduced me to a police officer.

I learned to capitalize on the Barbadian's enthusiasm for his island, using it as a probing open-ended question. When new acquaintances asked what I was doing there, I answered truthfully that it was a delightful place for my wife and children to vacation, and that I was writing a book on race relations and social class *in the United States.* Almost invariably, a Barbadian would respond to this information with the observation that "If you're interested in race relations and social class, you ought to study Barbados." Whenever and however a Barbadian phrased this sentiment, I replied with questions. Barbados is pretty similar to the United States, isn't it? Yes, I write about social class and race—why? What's unusual about Barbados? Yes, politics has a good deal to do with race relations in the United States; does it here, too?

Such an informal approach to a design for data-gathering has its obvious disadvantages, as does a multiple strategy in the use of field techniques. But I came to the task of analysis and writing with the idea that shuttling from library to observation to interview and back to library had not only equipped me with reliability checks, but had given me insights I might have missed with a more limited armamentarium.

What did I find in Barbados?

When the division of a population according to race is almost the same as the division according to property or income or some other important criterion of social power, race is highly relevant to the boundaries of groups. In Barbados, class differences created and maintained group boundaries. The recent history of Barbados also suggests that, when class boundaries shift rapidly, the boundaries of races also become fluid. The acquisition of political power by nonwhites allowed them to rock the rest of the system.

But this diminishing importance of racial distinctions in Barbados occurred because there were many non-whites eager and able to fill statuses previously held by whites. The insularity and intimacy of the society also made it difficult to pretend that these ambitious, educated, powerful Negroes were not there. In the United States, on the other hand, it is possible for many white people to have little or no contact with Negroes except as their social inferiors: bellboys, boot-blacks, cleaning women, janitors, parking lot attendants, steel mill laborers, and field hands.

3

Robert K. Merton & Edward C. Devereux, Jr.

Practical Problems and the Uses of Social Science

What determines whether or not a particular problem, or class of problems, is referred to social research? What considerations affect the "demand" for applied research? Which conditions foster and which impede research referral?

The demand for applied social research in a business organization is not simply a result of individual decisions separately made about the usefulness of research for each problem. The demand for research is significantly affected by a variety of factors, by changing business conditions and by broad attitudes and beliefs about the efficacy of social research in general.

Research is not an abstraction carried on in a cultural and organizational vacuum. It is done in various concrete social and cultural settings which may be neutral, friendly, or suspicious. The discussion that follows explores a few of the conditions that affected the demand for social research during the very early stages of its use in the American Telephone and Telegraph Company. The company's interest in the practical possibilities of social research began to develop as early as the end of the 1920's. Documents from that period and the early 1930's indicate some of the questions that were then being raised:

- How do customers feel about the Company and its service?
- Under what circumstances does the telephone change from a luxury to a necessity?
- What attitudes and beliefs act as deterrents to the use of long-distance telephone service?
- What are the special communication needs of different kinds of businesses?

Applied social research at the Bell Telephone Company, as elsewhere, was a response to practical problems. It needs to be asked, therefore, just what constitutes a "practical problem"? In general terms, problems are "puzzles" an individual attempts to "solve," but the solution eludes him, at least at first, because he lacks appropriate knowledge or skills. Practical problems are problems that *require* a solution because the individual has some "interest" in the outcome. Something needs to be done.

At least three essential elements are jointly involved in the emergence of any practical problem:

- a *perceived discrepancy* between some existing (or future) external situation, on the one hand, and the values or goals of an individual or organization, on the other;
- a feeling of a *need for adjustive activity* or for corrective action of some sort;
- a "puzzle element"—an *awareness of ignorance or doubt* about at least some of the facts and relationships believed to be relevant to a decision about what, if anything, should be done.

The existence of such problems is a normal and inescapable circumstance for any individual or for any organization, for there are many discrepancies between external reality and human values or interests. However, discrepancies between external reality and human values or personal interests are not always *perceived* by those who stand to be affected. Unless all three of the above conditions exist, the individual may experience only a vague uneasiness, a diffuse strain, or a mute need; but what he is experiencing is not yet a "practical problem."

A problem may emerge as a concern for decision-makers because something has changed and because this change has acted as a *catalyst*. Various types of change may serve as problem-raising catalysts. Here. however, we propose to discuss only a few of the Bell Telephone materials to explore and expand upon the different ways in which practical problems emerge as a result of only one type of change—a change in the outside objective situation.

Response to Perceived Change

The telephone business like others operates in a situation which is continually changing in some respects and is fairly stable in others. If the objective situation were entirely stable, established policies and routines could be allowed to run on indefinitely once their effectiveness had been demonstrated. Since the situation is in a continuous state of flux, however, policies and routines must be re-examined continually. Existing policies must be modified and new policies must be devised to keep the business aligned with ever-changing circumstances.

If effective action is to be taken, these changes must be seen as soon as possible. The old saying that "what you don't know can't hurt you" is no more true of the business firm than of any other organization. It is true, however, that only *perceived* changes can constitute "problems" in the sense defined above. Yet changes that are not perceived may, and often do, affect the interests of a business.

Continual change virtually forces the business firm, if it does not wish to be caught off guard, to establish and maintain various procedures for *routine* observations and reports about changes in its environment. These give rise to what we may call "instrument-panel" research. In the context of the social science approach this type of research represents a collective "viewing post" of the organization; it takes periodic soundings of trends and notes fluctuations in those aspects of the situation that impinge upon the interests of the business. Instrument-panel researches help an organization to become aware of crucial changes in its outside environment which may affect its public relations or marketing activities.

On this topic, one executive observed:

> "In the advertising field, we are shooting at a fast-moving target. It never stays still. We hope to get from surveys three types of information: (1) some knowledge about where the target is and which way it is moving; (2) what ammunition we should use in trying to hit it; and (3) some indications which would show us how we are doing."

Public opinion is, of course, only one aspect of the changing situation. There are also population movements, fluctuations in the business cycle, constantly shifting markets, changing legal and political arrangements, and varying conditions in the supply and prices of raw materials and labor. These represent but a few of the many social and economic changes about which a firm can use a continuous flow of information.

The Instrument Panel

Instrument-panel studies yield observations that can be plotted as a trend line, and can facilitate the early identification of significant changes. In part, such trend-studies simply provide an assurance that all is well. Just as the airplane pilot occasionally checks his instrument panel to make sure that all is running well, so the business executive checks his routine indicators to satisfy himself that there is no change and no problem. The indicators do not, of course, always stay in their "normal" position, and when one or more of them appears to be getting out of line, the pilot or executive is alerted to a new problem. Instrument-panel studies allow company officials to see at a glance how, for example, public attitudes or other important conditions are fluctuating. Such studies may enable threatening changes to be perceived before they can do any damage.

Problems in the Depression

During the depression of the 1930's the number of telephones in use declined sharply. Revenues fell off, but many items of overhead continued much as before. This dramatic change in the objective situation brought into view a variety of problems that were not present during the prosperous period of the 1920's.

Before the depression, for example, the telephone company had concentrated on the essentially technological problems of extending and improving its equipment. Until then, the demand for its product would be taken more or less for granted. During the depression, however, consumer *demand* became the strategic consideration. As attention shifted to the consumer side of the equation, new awareness was born among company executives that very little was actually known about the nature of the demand for telephone service.

Search for New Information

The heightened awareness of this newly-important problem produced a flood of ideas about new kinds of information that might be useful. In some cases the questions posed were exceedingly broad; should we undertake an extensive program of basic research into all the problems involved in the psychology and sociology of communication? Others were more narrowly limited, for example: should we attempt to measure the effect of changes in telephone rates upon usage? Some questions like these led to the initiation of actual research projects, but the great majority apparently did not.

We may mention briefly a few studies that were

actually carried through. Casting about for new uses of the telephone that might profitably be developed, one of the operating companies decided to explore the use of the telephone for shopping purposes. A survey was made among a sample of customers in a selected community. The pattern of their actual telephone usage was established, and a number of questions were asked about what they perceived to be the advantages and disadvantages of telephone shopping.

The results of this survey were both instructive and useful. It was established, for example, that the inclination among customers to use the telephone for shopping greatly exceeded the facilities of the stores for handling telephone orders. This strategic fact provided leverage for a program. Storekeepers were approached with the idea that it would be good business to provide more clerks and more lines at telephone order desks. Helpful pointers were offered to retailers on the proper training of telephone-order clerks. A series of "shop by telephone" advertisements were based on the information from the survey. The telephone company reported later that these efforts had been very profitable and resulted in a sizeable yearly revenue increase from its small retail accounts in the community.

Another study during this period revealed that 76 percent of the persons interviewed thought that long distance rates were higher than they actually were. This fact, again, provided leverage for a public information program.

Still another study focused upon the nature of the relationships between the people initiating long-distance calls and those whom they called. The knowledge gained in this survey was effectively employed in deciding on advertising approaches to foster the use of long distance facilities for social and family purposes during slack evening hours.

We cannot appreciate why certain of these pioneering studies were carried through during the depression, and why others were not, unless certain general factors are brought into view. Several among these that might be mentioned are:

- Many of the research proposals were too vague or general.
- Policy makers during that earlier period were not yet familiar with the potentialities of research and not yet "sold" on its usefulness.
- Budgets for all items, including research, were sharply curtailed in a time of shrinking revenues.

The War Years

With the outbreak of World War II, new kinds of problems came into focus and those of the depression receded. The demand for telephone service, and for long distance connections, greatly exceeded existing facilities. As the *need* to expand telephone services was increasing, the *ability* to expand was impaired by the acute shortage of many strategic materials and laborpower. Once again, the company's problems became predominantly technological.

But there were also new and special problems of a sociological character, two of which may be mentioned here:

- For the first time in its history, the company found it necessary to undertake activities designed to *restrict* the public's use of telephones that were already installed, to persuade people to limit their long distance calls to three minutes, and to make only essential calls.
- The company also became concerned with the public's reactions to such wartime restrictions. Would they be understood and accepted, or would they undermine the public's good will and its confidence in the company's skills and abilities?

At the beginning of the war, some company executives felt that social research was now less necessary. This was so in part because furthering the war effort was seen as the organization's major objective and, in part, because it was felt that little could then be done to remedy any problems revealed by social research, given the scarcity of materials and manpower. Yet if such considerations restricted social research, others led to the conduct of certain researches.

By 1944, for example, the backlog of unfilled orders for new phones was mounting and it was uncertain when they could be filled. What effect would this wait have upon public attitudes toward the company? How could the public be made to understand and to tolerate these unavoidable delays? Concern with these problems had led certain of the company's executives to propose that the social research group develop and proceed with a survey of the public's feelings.

At the same time, the War Production Board—charged with establishing and administering wartime priorities—also became interested in the backlog problem and considered conducting research on public attitudes toward the existent regulations and priorities for allocating phone services. When the WPB found that the telephone company was planning research in this area, and would be able to include questions of interest to the federal agency, the WPB abandoned the idea of a separate research project.

Evaluation and Support

This episode suggests two other general conditions affecting an organization's readiness to accept and pursue plans for social research:

- whether or not these plans are supported by executives highly placed within the organization;
- whether other, outside, related interests will find the research results acceptable and of value.

It is quite clear, then, that the fate of research proposals does not depend only on the specific problems with which they deal. The decision to accept or table them is influenced also by the general attitudes toward research and by other conditions prevalent within the company.

As the telephone company's experience during the depression and the war suggests, the demand for social research is stimulated when an organization's external situation changes. Change brings with it new kinds of problems, the solution of which requires new kinds of information. Such changes must, however, be visible before they can be identified as *problems* requiring new information and correctives. These changes can be recognized either through the organization's internal records of operations—as they were during the depression—or through special instrument-panel studies. The function of social research, then is not simply to supply information useful in remedying problems already known—it serves also to make the problems known.

SUGGESTED READINGS

The Deadlock of Democracy: Four Party Politics in America, rev. ed., by James MacGregor Burns (Englewood Cliffs, N.J.: Prentice-Hall, 1972).

The American Worker in the Twentieth Century: A History Through Autobiographies by Eli Ginzberg and Hyman Berman (New York: Free Press, 1963).

World Revolution and Family Patterns by William J. Goode (New York: Free Press, 1963).

Revolution in Brazil: Politics and Society in a Developing Nation by Irving Louis Horowitz (New York: E. P. Dutton, 1964).

U.S. Senators and Their World by Donald R. Matthews (New York: Vintage Books, 1960).

4

Dorothy L. Meier & C. H. Bradford

Creating a World for Research

A large metropolitan area wanted to build its first junior college. The ambitious plans called for it to be part trade school and part university, with greatly varied curriculum, faculty, facilities, and student body; large and capable of great expansion, but yet not wasteful; adaptable to future functions which could not be clearly foreseen. The board of directors knew that it would be using public money and be subject to public pressure and it could not afford dramatic mistakes. At the same time, it had to move boldly into new areas, and anticipate and plan for new trends and contingencies, with no reliable precedents. The experiences of somewhat similar colleges around the country emphasized the fact that many major problems only become apparent after buildings are built and classes started—when change is very expensive and difficult.

So the board decided to *simulate* the operation of their proposed school on a large computer—faculty, students, schedules, curriculum, classrooms. The computer feedback brought on modified simulations, using more complete data (an early conclusion of the computer that 8 a.m. might be a nice uncrowded time to schedule lunch was rejected). The plan which was finally adopted cost three million dollars less than the original estimate, required twenty-five fewer classrooms, and provided for more efficient year-round and day-long use of buildings and staff. And before one brick was put on another, the board and administration already had valuable experience in dealing with problems of their school, having, in effect, already coped with them. Total cost of the computer tested plan—about $15,000.

Simulation, as illustrated above, can be loosely characterized as the use of a model or likeness for the real thing. It can range from the little girl playing mother and housekeeper with doll and dollhouse to space engineers "flying" unbuilt rockets and capsules on computers. It can be used for instruction, for experiment, for study. The tremendous advantage is that, except for the intellectual expense involved, it is a marvelously cheap and convenient substitute. If the little girl decided to try to punish her doll by putting it out in the rain, the cost is much less than if she used a real baby. Failure itself is a gain—if the rocket in the computer crashes, or encounters a crisis, the engineer usually knows why with the loss of little money and no lives, and perhaps more precisely than he might have with a real rocket falling into the ocean thousands of miles away. The old cartoon that shows the engineer saying, "Well, back to the drawing board!" while surveying burning wreckage has been largely replaced by the picture of a man putting new instructions into a computer without leaving his chair.

In the social sciences, where experimentation directly with people is so often difficult, expensive, illegal, or immoral, the possibilities of simulation would seem to open new and wide vistas for research.

Simulation, as a social science research technique, has been around a long time. Recently, however, it has undergone a rebirth of usefulness, and is now considered a major new tool for studying social phenomena. Two important developments are primarily responsible.

- Decades—perhaps centuries—of research have begun to reveal systematic results. The sociologist, the psychologist, the educator can now see more clearly the outlines and dimensions of their particular concerns, and can now more precisely conceptualize and compute some of the fundamental variables and relations.
- The fact that computers have such great and unique capacities for handling and analyzing tremendous amounts of complex data has led social scientists to hope that perhaps, finally, the intricate behavior involved in international negotiations or national elections can be dealt with.

COMPUTERS OR PEOPLE

Two main types of simulation techniques are in use in social science research. They depend, roughly, on the extent to which computers or automatic devices are used.

In the first, the programmed computer is king. The ideal is that of an engineer and his rocket flight—it is hoped that the facts and relations of human behavior can be similarly reduced to orderly, easily manipulated equations. The facts are used to determine design of the model, and they are intimately involved in the way it operates. The complexity of forces, and the results of their interactions, are examined. For instance, future elections can be simulated with some accuracy if past voting patterns, changes in the constituency since the last election, the emotional pull of specific issues, and particular (or probable) candidates can be known or closely approximated.

But human behavior, at least at this time, cannot be reduced to precise measurement. Many simulations concentrate on *people* as the precipitating causes of various types of interactions. With our present knowledge and understanding it may be impossible to reduce the actions and reactions of the little girl playing house—or for that matter of her mother keeping house—to computer language. Yet such human reactions are major factors in much experimentation and training, and in attempts to study, through the behavior of small groups of people, phenomena that often involve large masses and whole societies. This does not mean that computers cannot be used in such studies—they may verify or assist—but they cannot rule.

Types of simulation can be said to differ also in the complexity—or completeness—of the model. Relatively few (hopefully the most significant) of the many variables possible in a situation can be included. In this case what is usually sought in a simulation is the end result of continuing interactions over a long period of time. On the other hand, an attempt may be made to make the simulation as complete as possible; here, what is sought is a measure of insight into the complexity of the process itself.

In practice, of course, simulations include all gradations—they are not restricted to being either simple or complex, automated or involving men. But those presently being used in social science research tend to group around the types given above.

UNTIL THE REAL THING

Following are four (among many) of actual simulation procedures being used:

POLITICAL BEHAVIOR. William McPhee, using a few relatively well-established relationships in sociology, political science, and psychology, has built a complex yet beautifully simple simulation model portraying the experiences of many citizens as they reach their final decisions in national political elections. To vote or not vote, and if to vote, then for whom? The simulation includes social background, each individual's past behavior and his interest in elections; the number and nature of political stimuli received through mass media and contacts, and degree of partisanship. With this computer model, the researcher can take advantage of the great masses of data collected through national surveys before each national election.

The conclusions of the simulation model are intended to correspond to the outcomes recorded by actual count of votes cast in national elections. Thus, an almost automatic check for the validity and accuracy of the computer simulation is built in. For both researcher and policy-maker, it permits the transformation of minute bits of data on large aggregates of people into a precise and meaningful picture of an entire voter system.

INTERNATIONAL RELATIONS. Since 1957, many scholars interested in international affairs have followed the lead of Harold Guetzkow and associates in developing a training and research technique to simulate the relations between nations. The Inter-Nation Simulation (INS) includes both men and computers, but puts major emphasis on participants, who act as decision-makers. It has been refined through repeated runs at universities, conference sites, and research institutes, utilizing as participants various adult groups, high school and college students, academic professionals, and diplomatic personnel from a variety of nations.

The Inter-Nation Simulation is a world in miniature, made up of a series of prototypic "nations." Both national and international factors intertwine to determine outcomes. The internal characteristics of each "country" are represented through computations (programmed relations). The decision-makers may enter into trade and aid agreements, form alliances, participate in international organizations, and make policy concerning war and peace. These "heads of state" and their "ministers" must, at the same time, meet demands for both national security and welfare. Internationally, failure to operate effectively may cause the nation to lose its independence and be dominated by another nation. Nationally, failure may bring on the loss of elections, or even revolution.

A particular feature valuable for teaching and training is the immediate feedback of decision consequences, and the necessity for the participant to deal with them, and their effects, throughout a series of events.

Generally, consequences of decisions in the INS follow a predictable course. But this is not always the case. Instability is deliberately programmed into the system, and each decision-maker operates differently; so the simulated world, like the real one, is in constant flux.

PSYCHOLOGY. Psychological simulation can deal with the *results* of a psychological process, or with the *process* itself.

That concerned with results is commonly called research in *artificial intelligence*. Much of this has developed in engineering. It involves building machines capable of performing many of the tasks we used to feel required human intelligence and judgment. Machines are being designed to recognize and act on the basis of human symbolic communication; human speech, writings, drawings. Some are also designed to "learn" from past errors, and adapt accordingly.

The other area of psychological simulation—modeling the process as well as the product—is more directly in the province of the social sciences. Most of it has remained very abstract, using the models to test existing theory, and hoping that they can yield new insights.

Allen Newell, J. C. Shaw, and Herbert Simon have done some of the most influential work on processes. They developed a computer program designed to prove theorems in logic—called the *Logic Theorist.* On the superficial level theorem-proving seems quite straightforward: take a "self-evident" axiom, follow the stated rules of logic, and arrive at a conclusion. This can be done, on the computer, by "brute force" procedures which exhaustively search all possible proofs. However, this is not really the way people think; moreover, Newell, Shaw, and Simon estimate that about 50 million proofs would be required before the correct solution would be found for even elementary problems.

Instead, they built into the *Logic Theorist* a simulation of the way people might attempt such problems. First, the program analyzes the problem to find the types of proofs likely to succeed: it reverses the usual procedure by starting with the theorem to be proved and working *back* to the axioms. The over-all task is broken up into sub-problems which, when solved, lead to the final proof.

Simulations like the *Logic Theorist* are not primarily aimed at solving tasks but at working out techniques to study human problem solving and decision making. Newell, Shaw, and Simon have since developed the *General Problem Solver,* specifically designed to act like a human problem solver—without ulcers. The very construction of such a simulation produces new research insights. Further, the investigator has a perfect subject. The simulated problem-solver will keep at the task for millions of trials if necessary, without fatigue, errors, or grumbling. The investigator can manipulate, distort, and bias his model in a way impossible or unacceptable with human beings.

EDUCATION. Educators (also businessmen) are being trained by working in environments and on problems simulated to include the principle features of their real organizations. Decisions are made; these alter the organization, not always in the way foreseen; the new context requires further decisions, which in turn produce further change in the organization, and on and on.

In *The College and University Planning Game,* developed by John Forbes, the educational and financial planning involved in running a university are simulated. The player must make decisions about projected enrollments, plant expansions, tuition charges, changes in curriculum, faculty recruitment and salaries, admission policies, sources of income, and expenditures for public relations. He must use the limited resources available to manage the simulated school, and he must work toward a planned objective. His decisions are evaluated by the person who has devised the model, and, as in real life, chance elements are involved. The player is faced with a school altered by his previous decisions, and must then make new decisions that, hopefully, will continue toward a successful operation.

Apart from teaching, these models are useful for research. Which interrelationships—and which factors among them—are good representations of real life organizations?

THE FUTURE OF SIMULATION

What do simulation techniques mean for social science?

■ The social scientist can now (and even more effectively in the future) do exploratory experimentation in topics otherwise impossible to study.

■ The construction of simulation models forces the social scientist to *directly face the problem of theory-building.* Formulations must be explicit, definitions must be precise —elements which are unusual in much present social science research. In the long run, these exacting demands of simulation research may be a most significant step toward the development of simulation of adequately verified theory.

■ *Teaching* has been the main non-research use for simulation procedures. Participants feel that they have profited greatly from such teaching, and researchers generally agree. However, objective evidence is difficult to obtain—as it is with any teaching method.

What next? There is an important current problem on which, we believe, non-computer simulation could be used to very good effect—but to which, to our knowledge, it has never yet been systematically applied. We hear much of the bleak and isolated environment of the poor; and of training, therapy, and rehabilitation programs to help them. What kinds of programs? How organized? What specific goals? They must be designed to fit people who need them.

We suggest a series of simulations representing the environments, situations, agencies, and bureaucracies with which the unemployed and "hopelessly depressed" will actually have to cope to get help. The poor themselves could be the "participants," gaining the experience and skills they will need, while researchers and administrators gain clearer insight into the problems and interactions involved.

The design of good simulations takes much time and effort. Often—as with the INS—years of work by several scholars are involved. There are dangers, as with all new techniques—too uncritical acceptance, the drawing of invalid inferences. But there is little doubt that simulation can be a major research tool of the future.

5 *Robert A. Skedgell*

How Computers Pick an Election Winner

When the American electorate goes to the polls in November many winners of statewide races will be announced on radio and television long before any substantial portion of the tabulated or popular vote is available. Also, many important reasons for their victories will be clear at early stages in the vote counting.

This "clairvoyance" will spring from an extensive use of computerized vote projections, based on quickly reported returns from a small number of selected precincts throughout the country. The radio and television networks will put more trust in, and be more dependent upon, their computers than at any time since they sniffed the first 1960 returns—and proclaimed that the odds were 100 to one that Richard M. Nixon would be the next President of the United States.

One system of computer projections—Vote Profile Analysis used by CBS News—has recorded an average deviation of less than 1 percent in estimating the winners' final percentages in 135 elections. It was developed *after* the 1960 general elections by CBS News, Louis Harris & Associates, and the International Business Machines Corporation. VPA was the first effective and accurate system of drawing scientific samples of the electorate so that a small number of key returns would produce close estimations of election outcomes.

Earlier computer systems were excessively rigid because proper weighting was not given to the individual factors involved. So the first scattered returns from just one or two states tended to unduly influence the vote estimates for the entire nation. The resulting projections for major candidates were inflated—more imputed than computed.

The networks did not suffer great embarrassment over the initial performances of their computerized reporting. They had stashed the machines away practically out of sight of the TV cameras and were prepared to drop them entirely at the first suspicious prognostication; in that event, the computers were to be mere comedy gimmicks, more to be belittled than pitied. If, on the other hand, reasonable forecasts seemed to be forthcoming, the broadcasters could claim credit for fathering a rousing advance in the art of election reporting.

Vote Profile Analysis was unveiled in the off-year elections of 1962. The system was applied to 13 key contests in eight states, and it produced accurate results in twelve—up to two hours ahead of the other networks. In the thirteenth race covered that night, the Massachusetts' gubernatorial contest between John Volpe and Endicott Peabody, VPA indicated the outcome as "too close to call." More than a month went by before Volpe was officially designated the winner by a margin of 301 votes out of the total of more than 2,000,000 cast.

VPA Picks Romney

One other VPA projection that same night pointed up the power and value of the new election reporting tool. At 10:05 p.m., Eastern time, CBS News reported—on the basis of VPA—that George Romney was the evident winner over John Swainson. The tabulated vote at that moment read:

SWAINSON 310,000
ROMNEY 236,000

Both Romney and Swainson were as disbelieving as the viewers.

What had happened was that VPA had correctly established that Swainson was running behind his necessary (and expected) strength in Wayne County, and that his showing in the Detroit suburbs was down from two years earlier when he won the governorship. When the computer digested these facts and performed the necessary arithmetic, the projected estimate for Romney came out to 52 percent of the vote. His final, official figure was 51.4 percent.

A modified form of VPA was utilized in the 1964 presidential year in the CBS News coverage of important primary races. From New Hampshire to California, VPA demonstrated its preciseness in pointing to the winners early and accurately. The VPA estimate for Henry Cabot Lodge in the New Hampshire contest was precisely the 35.3 percent of the vote which he officially received; in Oregon, VPA projected that Nelson Rockefeller would win 32.9 percent of the vote, and he won exactly that much.

On November 3, 1964, VPA was put to its first full test—it was applied to a total of 107 contests, including the presidential race in 48 states (excluding Alaska and Hawaii) and the District of Columbia. The average deviation between the final VPA estimates in those 107 races and the final, official returns was less than one percent.

There is no witchcraft about VPA. For all its seeming omniscience, it is simply a formalized effort at systematizing voting data. Its essential function is to measure movement of a particular electorate from their voting history, and to present those findings in an orderly manner. Although it is a sophisticated sampling instrument, it is capable of erring, and proper guidelines must be erected to hold mistakes within acceptable limits.

It is an exercise in simple arithmetic—if there were no rush for the results, it could be done by hand. The computer's contribution to the process—and its only contribution—is to store past voting information for the political units selected; to compare the new results from the special precincts with the old; and to extrapolate an estimate of the final result any time such a projection is requested. Once this point in the process is reached, mortal man takes over to analyze the machine's computations and make judgments based upon political, not arithmetical, knowledge.

Electorate in Miniature

The cornerstone of Vote Profile Analysis is the model of the electorate to be measured in any election. The model is a kind of portrait in miniature of all the voters of a political unit. It has been likened to screening out most of the dots which comprise a newspaper photograph; if a careful selection were made of the dots to remain, the picture would still be recognizable.

As electorates differ from each other, so do models differ. There is no magic formula which will produce a universal model. Each is custom built. For example, the model for the Republican electorate voting in the California primary this year was 90 precincts, selected to represent in their proper proportions the more than 30,000 precincts in the state. In 1964, the model for the Oregon electorate was 42 precincts which served as a microcosm of that state's 3,255 precincts. The number of precincts in a model is set on the basis of having few enough to process quickly on election night, but still enough to represent the state's voters faithfully.

Louis Harris knew from his wide experience in politics and polling that people tend to vote in patterns by groups; the patterns are discernible through the extensive research conducted on voting behavior, and through past polling. The assumption that voters of similar background display similar voting behavior is not to say that all members of a group will vote the same. It simply says that if the rural voters in a state vote 72 percent Democratic, 72 out of every 100 ruralites are performing one way, and 28 out of every 100 are performing another way. Nevertheless, the 72 to 28 ratio is an identifiable pattern which will hold true for all of the rural dwellers in the state.

Every political unit in the nation is made up of groups of voters whose voting patterns can be similarly determined. Harris reasoned that:

—if a small sample could be drawn to represent all of the important groups comprising an electorate by their proportionate voting strengths,

—and if a method could be devised to keep track of their votes on election night,

—and to compare those results with the past voting performance of the same groups,

—then it would be possible to project an accurate result.

To begin with, it would be necessary to determine for each state just what the components of the electorate were, what their history of voting has been, and what proportion of the total vote each group would contribute. In order to accomplish this initial process, teams of researchers pored through Bureau of Census records, demographic reports, and other statistical data. Because there is no central record of precinct results for all states, the researchers had to visit many of the county courthouses around the country and dig out the returns from beneath piles of dust. They studied boundary maps of the precincts to determine if changes had occurred since the last election, for in comparing new returns with the old, it is vital that the perimeters of the current precinct match exactly those of the same precinct as it existed before.

With the initial phase of the research completed, the Louis Harris organization drew up a "recipe" for a model —a specification designed to direct the researchers to the to the kinds of precincts which would ultimately fit the model. If the research indicated that 10 of the model precincts would be metropolitan units, the recipe pointed to the *types* of metropolitan precincts which would qualify as representative of their group.

Each of the precincts in the state models designed for the 1964 elections—nearly 2,000 of them—was classified in four ways:

—by geographic section of the state;

—by the size of community;

—by the ethnic background of a vast majority of the residents;

—and by their religious background.

In Harris' view, each of these four dimensions was a "cutting edge" in the politics of 1964 which would serve to measure political behavior. Economic and social classifications were not used as bases for the VPA controls because of the great difficulty in establishing standards which would apply with equal precision in all sections of the nation. A weekly income of $200 in New York City would produce a standard of living and a political outlook quite different from the same weekly income in a small city elsewhere. The economic status of the model precincts was utilized as an informational guide only and not as a component of the extrapolation formula.

To make certain that the precincts gathered under the terms of the recipe fully qualified for the model, researchers spent many months traveling through and around them. They talked to county and precinct officials and to pastors and rabbis to verify the ethnic and religious background of the residents. They read doorbell names as an additional check.

Blending the Recipe

When the researchers returned from the field, they brought with them data on hundreds of precincts which would meet the technical requirements of the recipe, making them eligible to be among the chosen few to comprise the model. The question then remained: of the hundreds of qualified precincts, which combination of 32 or 40 or 50 would best represent all the voters of the state? For example, of all the precincts classified as predominantly White Anglo-Saxon Protestant, which among them would best portray the political behavior of all of the WASP precincts around the state? Put another way, which combination of precincts meeting all of the weighting criteria of the model would come closest to reproducing or reconstructing the past statewide vote for a particular candidate?

To help find the solution, the computer was put to work running off combination after combination of precincts, averaging their past vote, and comparing them to the statewide average, not for just one past election, but several. The best combinations reproduced past results with only one-tenth or two-tenths of one percent deviation. This process of combining precincts continued section by section until the best grouping for an entire state emerged.

As illustration, VPA for Missouri in the 1964 general elections consisted of 40 precincts assembled to accurately represent more than 4,400 precincts. Missouri was divided into five sections: the St. Louis area and the Kansas City area, the great urban anchor points of the whole state; the rural north, which included St. Joseph; the Ozark country in the southeast; and, the southwest including Springfield. In effect, the geographical map of the state was converted to a political map, with the sectional boundaries marking different kinds of voting behavior.

Since research showed that 33 percent of the electorate resided in the St. Louis area, 33 percent of the model precincts (13 of 40) must be located in that area. Kansas City held 20 percent of the vote (8 of 40 precincts). The remaining three sections of the state produced the other 19 precincts of the model.

This procedure was followed for the other VPA categories: size of place, ethnic composition, and religion. The profile for Missouri showed that 28 percent of the electorate resided in large cities; so 12 of the 40 precincts would come from the large cities. Negro voters would comprise about 8 percent of the vote; so 3 precincts were predominantly Negro.

When the final returns from the Missouri VPA precincts were reported to CBS News election headquarters, and the computer compared those results with the past history of those same precincts, it calculated that Lyndon Johnson would carry the state with a percentage of 63.9. The final, official figure for him was 64.0 percent.

It is seldom necessary to wait for all of the precincts in a particular model to report before the analysts make their decision. More often, those "calls" are made on the basis of partially filled models, when, perhaps, half or fewer of the precincts have reported. It is precisely at this point that the men take over from the machines, bringing their political intelligence to bear on the computer's calculations. In the Missouri election, only 10 of the 40 model precincts had reported at the time that CBS News posted Johnson as the winner.

News reported on the basis of VPA that Goldwater was the winner. What developed through the remainder of that evening, and into the early morning hours of June 3, was enough to try the souls of the CBS News executives who carried the responsibility for the decision.

That decision for Goldwater was based principally on the fact that the first special VPA returns showed him to be making a very strong run in areas where a considerable portion of the Republican electorate resided, especially in Los Angeles County. When the early VPA results were examined by the analysts, it was evident to them that no matter how the vote went in the sections still polling, Rockefeller just could not catch up.

But almost everyone else, on the basis of early returns, thought Rockefeller would win. The trouble was, the tabulated vote as collected and reported by the Associated Press and United Press International did not reflect Goldwater's strong performance in Los Angeles and in Orange and San Diego counties until many hours after the early evening announcement by CBS that Goldwater had won. In fact, the count by the press services at six o'clock the next morning still did not reflect Goldwater's true strength in the southern counties, and Rockefeller seemed to be holding a slim edge. This incomplete wire service tally gave rise to many confusing reports; one San Francisco paper headlined in its afternoon edition the next day, TV PRATFALL—FAST COUNT. ROCKY SWEEPS INTO LEAD. Appearances notwithstanding, the New York governor had not led at any time.

Ethnics and Ethics

VPA's critics, both professional and lay, have held that it is a divisive force on the body politic; that to report elections in terms of how the various ethnic and religious groups perform is an unhealthy, not to say un-American, approach. Irate viewers called the CBS studios following the New York City elections last year to complain about the undue emphasis they thought had been placed upon what Jewish voters had done, or the Italian-Americans, or the Irish-Americans. It was demonstrable, however, that these groups did behave in voting patterns—they were the "cutting edge" in deciding between two major tickets which were neatly balanced with one Jew each, one Irish-American each, one Italian-American, and one white Anglo-Saxon Protestant.

Another widespread charge leveled at computerized voting projections is that they influence voters in those sections of the country where polls remain open longer; that citizens in the Western states either change their vote to join the so-called bandwagon as reported from the East Coast, or simply decide not to vote at all. Three social scientists, Harold Mendelsohn of the University of Denver and Kurt Lang and Gladys Engel Lang of the State University of New York at Stony Brook, studied a sample of California voters following the 1964 elections to assess the validity of such charges. Their independent investigations could find no basis for the assertions that anyone changed his intention to vote for Johnson because the network broadcasts reported that he was the apparent winner, nor that anyone planning to vote for Goldwater refrained from doing so because it was forecast that he would lose badly.

Mendelsohn had interviewed a voter sample on the night before the election to ascertain their preferences. After the polls closed, he interviewed the same persons to see if anyone had changed his mind. The result was that no matter whether the voters had tuned in election broadcasts, 96 to 97 percent voted as they intended. Not more than 2 percent of those interviewed switched their vote, and those last-minute changes that did occur followed no discernible pattern.

VPA and the other vote projection systems were born of the need to fill the information vacuum existing between the time the polls close and the tabulation of sufficient votes to indicate an election trend. Had VPA been operating in the 1960 presidential race, the public would have known that at the time Kennedy seemed to be piling up a commanding lead, the final result would actually be extremely close.

In many states the vote counting process remains excruciatingly slow. Some precinct officials are content to interrupt the tabulation for dinner, a good night's sleep, and a leisurely completion and reporting of the count on the following morning, just as they have done for years. There have been proposals advanced to bring the states' election laws into some orderly scheme. Some have called for a uniform period of voting across the country; others have asked for a common poll closing time; still others have advocated a much more widespread use of electronic and mechanical ballot counters which have been introduced in places with varying degrees of success.

One day the states' antiquated election machinery will be brought into the twentieth century; but it will not occur this year, nor probably for some time to come. In the meantime, reporters will continue to utilize every means available to them to bring the election stories to the public as quickly and accurately as possible.

6 *Melvin M. Webber*

The Politics of Information

Now that three-fourths of Americans are living in urban places—over 50,000,000 in the vast metropolitan centers of the Boston-New York-Washington strip, Chicago, and Los Angeles alone—more and more information is necessary to handle the immense problems of housing, feeding, healing, educating, transporting, and governing them.

A major push is now under way to improve the quality of information about urban life in America. Throughout the country new information centers (or "data banks") are being established, based upon the large storage capacities of electronic computers. These centers are pooling vast stores of facts about a city's people, its real estate, its traffic, its economy, and its governmental activities. In turn, this wealth of new information is being fed into "simulation models" that mimic the behavior of the city's people, its real estate markets, and its over-all economy. These models are used to pre-test the effects of various public actions, as a guide to government officials in deciding among alternative policies.

There are no doubts about the important roles of these new information centers in guiding policy-making, but there is a widespread belief that the facts they contain are neutral, in that data alone favor no decision over another, no group over another. However, because the decisions and actions that people take are shaped by the kinds of information available to them, the centers are likely to become major agents in the processes of social change.

In a field such as astronomy, one's observations and theoretic generalizations are unlikely to make much difference to the phenomena being observed. The remarkable discoveries in astronomy since the war have led to some striking new theories about the histories of stars and the history of the universe. But the stars and the universe remain wholly unaffected by them. In the social sciences, however, as John Seeley has perceptively described it in *Sociology on Trial,* to report one's observations is to change the phenomenon being observed.

To inform a shopping-center investor about consumer travel behavior and about market potentials is to shape his decisions about shopping-center locations and tenant mix. In turn, those decisions will influence the decisions of merchants, shoppers, house-builders, bankers, and others; and they will thus affect the behavioral and market conditions that were initially observed and reported. To supply the facts about national income distribution, as Leon Keyserling and Michael Harrington recently did, was to set loose a chain of responses that may yet change the facts of distribution that were initially reported. The same sort of thing happens with forecasts, of course, as business-cycle theorists and stock-exchange brokers have long known.

Seemingly straightforward facts about a society's things and events are seldom, if ever, neutral. They inevitably intervene into the workings of the systems they describe The information supplier—whatever his motives and methods—is therefore inevitably immersed in politics. The kinds of facts he selects to report, the way he presents them, the groups they are distributed to, and the inferences he invites will each work to shape outcomes and subsequent facts.

ARE FACTS NEUTRAL?

There is a growing belief that better information will make for better actions. But I find a misconception among some urban planners and social scientists who believe that information, *per se,* is nonpolitical—that, as "pure scientists," they can stand outside the system and, with positivistic detachment, record and explain what they observe. This perception of their functions is patently distorted. The scientist, no less than the politician or the merchant or the family is *inside* the system, and his work affects its workings. He cannot escape the fact that his facts are instruments of change. To play the role of scientist in the urban field is also to play the role of intervener, however indirect and modest the interventions.

This pattern is reinforced by the large amount of political and economic capital that information represents. Information, like money, yields power to those who have it. And, like money, the ways in which it is distributed will determine which groups will be favored and which deprived.

An urban intelligence center, quite like the spy or the tipster, cannot be a neutral informant. Even if somehow it succeeded in becoming a nonpartisan supplier of information—making its findings available to all comers—this, too, would represent a powerful intervention into economic, political, and social processes. To redistribute information in such fashion would dramatically change the rules of the political and economic games that are played in the metropolitan areas where vital information is not fully available to all. To reduce secrecy would reduce the advantages that now redound to those favored few who are in on the secrets. To reduce ignorance among those groups that cannot now afford the high costs of good intelligence would strengthen their political and economic positions.

Of course, nothing even approximating equality of access to information is likely, even if an information center were to be established and supported by a diversified group of governments, industries, and foundations. The power that such a center would represent is already clear to many. Indeed, this is one of the reasons that supporting funds have been hard to get. But as such centers are established, we can expect a growing partisan competition to gain control over their activities and to limit outputs; for some sorts of information can be very dangerous weapons.

Thus, the social scientists who staff them will immediately find themselves intimately involved in the internal politics over the centers' programs, mirroring the external politics of the metropolis. Which studies should be conducted? Which hypotheses favored? Which models employed? Which data collected? Which variables accounted? Which analyses made? Which forecasts attempted? Which alternatives explored? Which conclusions reported? And which findings and recommendations reported to which of the competing groups? The staff may wish to believe that their answers are merely scientific conclusions. Simultaneously, however, they would also be political answers of a straightforward sort.

Each group in an urban area seeks its own survival, its own special advantages, its own unique perceptions of self interest and public welfare. Thus, an elected official may promote a costly public-works project as a way of stabilizing his political position. If the analyst should fail to include those so-called "noneconomic variables" in calculating expected returns from the investment, he misses the main point. If he does account for them, he aligns himself with the interests of one partisan group against others. Similarly, a businessmen's group may seek to redevelop a section of the central business district, ostensibly to "revitalize the city's heart" and thereby to "serve the public interest." Unless the analyst is alert to the real business motives driving the project, his information may not give them the indicators of success they really want. If, on the other hand, he *should* serve their purposes, he aligns himself with the project's proponents and against the opponents.

SCIENTIST-POLITICIAN

I use these rather homey examples to say that the man who pursues the urban information sciences also chooses a career in politics, for he cannot avoid becoming a protagonist. He becomes a policy-shaper, if not a policy-maker. For, in addition to being a producer of new facts, an identifier and evaluator of potential action-courses, and a prophet of the future, he also plays the role of planner. By supplying information and reporting scientific findings, he thereby says not only what might happen, but what he thinks ought to happen.

His advice must be even more direct than that, however. The socially responsible student, or planner, or scientist—choose whichever name you happen to like best—has an inherent and an ethical obligation to say what he *thinks* ought to be, just as the physician is obligated to advise his patient to submit to unpleasant therapy or the Federal Reserve System's economist to urge adjustment in the rediscount rate.

The ablest students of human problems have often known their clients' wants better than the clients have, and they often know better what the clients should do. With their superior knowledge of the system's structure, its processes, and the wants of the various publics, the planners who can draw upon an elaborate information center would be well-equipped to design action-programs having high odds of bringing high welfare returns.

In this respect, the scientist-politician-planner may be a peculiar breed in the political scene. He is surely a member of a professional interest group composed of peers who share his particular frames-of-reference and, hence, his social objectives. With them, he sees the world through special filters and holds vested interests in certain concepts, analytic methods, and social programs. With them, he tries to sell his particular brands of rationality and his particular images of the social welfare. In these respects he resembles the members of political parties, trade associations, and civic clubs.

But his special character mirrors the special character of science. To a degree far less common in other interest groups, he has learned to *doubt.* He has been trained to question his beliefs, his data, and his findings; to submit his conclusions to critical evaluation by his peers; to tolerate uncertainty and ambiguity; to bear the frustrations of not knowing, and of knowing he does not know; and, by far the most important, to adopt the empirical test for validity.

Along with improved facts, improved modes of predicting, and the disciplined imagination that the new scientific talent is bringing, it is also injecting the scientific morality into urban policy-making. Partisanship, parochialism, and partial knowledge are inherent to the urban system, as they are to science. The intelligence centers can never eliminate them. The new planners must accept them as facts, no less real and valid than rents, transport costs, interest rates, and topographic conditions. But by more systematically accounting for these variables, and by then exposing alternative action and value hypotheses to critical and systematic examination, those in the information-and-planning sciences may help to eliminate the most negative consequences of partisanship and of ignorance. By offering up their own preferred images of private and public welfare, their own perceptions of good ends and means, and their own proposals for social programs, the new species of scientifically trained urban planners are likely to make significant contributions to relieving the more severe social problems that now mark our cities.

Section II

Theory, Practice and Sociology

Real problems do exist; the study of the poor may give information to the rich for their further oppression, and this is somehow quite different from the study of military officers and their exposure in the minds of society as a whole. In part, however, the difference has to do with sentiment, how we feel about the impoverished vis-à-vis the Department of Defense. In part, it is a matter of risk. Sociology has always taken higher risks in studying the powerful than the powerless. As a result, the real issue is the amount of courage required to perform a sociological task or, to put it more sharply, to recognize that all sociology involves uncovering some truths that might be favorable to one group and unfavorable to another in society. The question is how much to uncover, at whose expense and with what consequences for the society as a whole? Again, we are dealing with serious issues that affect the lives of everyone, not only social scientists. The number of safeguards the system provides for vis-à-vis the kind of information necessary for any given performance itself serves as a task for that society. Thus, the question of the theory and practice of sociology naturally spills over into the study of the theory and practice of the social system itself. One will find in this section of the book both types of examinations.

The important ultimate point is that sociology, like every other discipline and every other interest group, needs its partisans and its loyalists as well as its critics and detractors. It is a field that invites the highest volatile passions because it is closest to the marrow of human needs in a collective world. However, this volatility, while ever-present, itself underlines the fatal truth that sociology is an interest group that is self-serving no less than a profession offering services. It is the path between these two, sociology as a public service and sociology as a professional network, that the field must tread. Its success in this navigation determines the theory and practice of sociology at any given time.

Section II of Part One raises issues about the very core of the sociological enterprise, namely, how practical and theoretical issues arise in the practice of the discipline. Some of the themes suggested in Section I are amplified, and additional sociological leitmotifs are introduced. In "The Sociologist as Naturalist," Rainwater shares with us a very personal account of how his "puzzled curiosity" led him to confront various social problems. Etzioni, in "Social Analysis and Social Action," makes an eloquent plea for the sociologist to apply his partial answers to the large-scale pressing problems in societies. Drawing an analogy from the relation of biochemistry to the practice of medicine, Etzioni suggests that sociologists dare not wait for the "whole truth" before involving themselves in social concerns. For him, the focus of social analysis should be on the major problems of the age and the application of sociology to the understanding of society, its major subcollectivities and society's place in more encompassing communities.

Both the number of professionally trained sociologists and the need for sociologically relevant evaluation in the area of social action programs are growing. In "Evaluating Social Action Programs," Rossi discusses some of the difficulties encountered in such research. Since administrators often have vested interests in the programs for which they are responsible, tension is likely to develop between the evaluator and the administrator whenever the outcome of research is not positive. As more and more social problems are addressed, a period of diminishing returns is likely to set in. That is, the largest gains tend to occur in very early phases of an approach to a problem; as the problem is partially solved, less dramatic results can be expected: It costs more to achieve less. Rossi suggests some alternative solutions to this problem.

Every aspect of social life is grist for the sociological mill. In 1970, *Transaction/Society* magazine published an article by Laud Humphreys about impersonal sex in public restrooms ("tea rooms," in the argot of their users). This research report stirred great controversy.

Journalist von Hoffman wrote a column attacking the article, Horowitz and Rainwater responded to von Hoffman's charges. "Sociological Snoopers and Journalistic Moralizers" joins the issue of what the professional parameters of a responsive sociology ought to be. Horowitz and Rainwater point out how sociology became more relevant in the 1960's and how this new relevance carries certain obligations to society with it. Every statement of "fact" is a political act. Critics on the right and on the left excoriate sociologists for hiding behind the mantle of science. Such charges, Horowitz and Rainwater assert, indicate that the new sociology is a threat to traditional interpreters of society, especially journalists. Sociology has an obligation to demystify society, to describe and interpret it as objectively as possible. The key issue here is the tension between the individual's right to privacy and the citizen's right to know. A discussion of this issue leads to the basic consideration of the moral nature of the discipline.

Moskos, in "Research in the 'Third World'," warns of the danger of "intellectual imperialism" on the part of American social scientists doing work in the Third World. Much of what he has to say is applicable to research among minorities at home as well as abroad. A broadened sociological perspective that includes a focus on change as well as stability is a sine qua non for work of this nature.

The final selection in Section II addresses an issue that is of major concern to both sociologists and psychologists: the use of human subjects in experimental research. Kelman, in "Deception in Social Research," raises issues about the ethics of generating anxiety (and worse) in people who are the subjects of research. His conclusion that subjects must become better, not worse, as a result of their participation is a normative conclusion reached after a thorough discussion of ethical, methodological and future implications of such research. Kelman's alternatives to much "laboratory" sociology resonates well with the feelings of most practicing sociologists.

The problems that emerge from the first section can be placed under the rubric of theory and practice of sociology, and here, too, a series of issues of enormous importance immediately present themselves. First, is sociology primarily a theoretical discipline, or is it a practical one? If theoretical, in what sense: as a philosophy of life or as a defense of the philosophic study of the structure of things? On the other hand, if sociology is a practical discipline, how is it distinguished from social work or the healing arts? In other words, what constitutes its healing essence? These are problems that have plagued sociologists (and others) for years and will not be resolved within the context of this text reader. But we can point to several guiding principles within the theory and practice of sociology. First, sociology attempts to give an overview, i.e., a fair-minded presentation and appraisal of all evidence, not just a selective presentation of information. Second, sociology is not the same as a legal brief: It is not the preparation of information to satisfy only one client or only one part of society. It is a discussion aimed at providing information for the use of society as a whole, especially those whose lives are in a vacuum, who lack power, wealth or the means to produce ideas. The theory and practice of sociology is also concerned with the wealth of the poor and minority groups, not merely as a direct sentimental concern with these groups but, rather, as part of a move toward equity. Those who are locked out of society may make use of that information to change the world.

The theory and practice of sociology must also reserve for itself the right to be critical of and not subordinate to fashionable political ideologies or fads within the field itself. In this sense, such controversial doctrines as Marxism, Functionalism, Existentialism, or any other "ism," must be accounted for. But the mansions of sociology, while large enough to include and incorporate such doctrines, cannot become so flabby as to be overwhelmed by any one of them. This would be self-liquidating in the extreme and would subvert the theory and practice of sociology to an ideology only remotely connected with the pursuit of truth and learning.

For the most part, the area of sociological theory and practice has been shrouded in rhetoric and argued from the point of view of ethics rather than that of performance. The twelve-year history of *Transaction/Society* has been to reverse this ordering of priorities, to show how the work process of sociology creates a culture and climate of opinion and how the barrier placed on research, or limits externally imposed, are automatic first stages to a higher assault on the bastions of ignorance and secrecy.

1 *Lee Rainwater*

The Sociologist as Naturalist

The principal attitude which directs my work is one of puzzled curiosity. I have always felt that I don't understand the people around me very well, and with that feeling has come a strong curiosity to try to figure out exactly what they are doing and why they are doing it. This attitude is perhaps not particularly distinctive to me, but the form by which I have sought to resolve that puzzled curiosity during my professional life is perhaps more distinctive. I have always been drawn to styles of sociological and psychological work that partake of the naturalist's approach—that is, an approach in which there is an effort to observe the forms and behaviors in which one is interested until one feels one understands how they hang together, and then to depict as accurately as possible what one thinks he has observed so that others may apprehend that reality, and perhaps by replicating the observations validate it. This kind of activity has seemed socially worthwhile, as well as personally gratifying, for three reasons.

The first, and I suspect the most enduring for me, is a belief in the intrinsic, almost esthetic value, of an accurate and penetrating depiction of reality. In this I think perhaps I was influenced by my father, who was a historian and who, in his own way, impressed me with the effort to see things as they are, just because they are that way. In addition, I have always felt that if men are to achieve their goals, if they are to avoid troubles and construct a society which meets their needs as fully as it might, they need to understand their world better. The particular part of the country in which I grew up can impress an observer with the extent to which men are their own worst enemies. If one for some reason does not become fully socialized to a particular world view, one can never lose the sense of puzzlement and anger at how men in that society hurt themselves and others to no good purpose.

Finally, I have always hoped that if the social naturalist's task is done well, he provides the best kind of grist for the mill of the social theorist. As a person who has neither interest in, nor talent for, doing other than heavily grounded theoretical work, I nevertheless feel that the other fellow, the theorist, would be more successful in his work if he could draw upon good descriptive work. Unfortunately, few theorists have pursued this strategy systematically, although I would still feel that the best correction for much of the nonsense that passes as sociological theory is the use of work in the ethnographic tradition as raw material for theory.

There are any number of ways one might be led by the puzzled curiosity I have described. A further distinctive characteristic of my work has been the reliance on qualitative data—from participant observation, open-ended interviewing and projective techniques. Such methods have always seemed to me to more closely replicate human life as it is experienced than the more controlling techniques of questionnaires, laboratory experiments and the like. Since these kinds of data have been the ones that have impressed me most—whether in the psychoanalytic case study, the ethnography of the great anthropologists, or the field studies of men like William F. Whyte or Howard Becker—it is ironic that I happen to be a rather poor and indifferent field worker. Were it not for an accident of career development I might never have circumvented this impasse—I might have had perforce to become a survey researcher! The accident was that during graduate studies in the Committee on Human Development at the University of Chicago, I became intrigued with the work being done at Social Research, Inc., in Chicago, a private research firm, then involving such people as Burleigh B. Gardner, W. Lloyd Warner and William E. Henry. This organization was devoted to applying the combined techniques of an anthropologically informed sociology in the style of Warner and a psychodynamically oriented social psychology to studies of "ordinary social life" for such diverse clients as manufacturers, advertising agencies, the movie industry and government agencies. (This kind of research some five years later came to be called "motivation research," but at the time we saw it as simply an extension of more academically oriented community studies.) Because Social Research, Inc., carried out numerous small projects in short periods from beginning to completion (ranging from two months to six months) the organization had adapted survey research techniques to the qualitative approach. I was able, therefore, to make use of a staff of interviewers trained to do focused and nondirective interviewing and to administer specially designed projective techniques, and consequently to work with the kind of data that was meaningful to me without having to collect it myself.

As I have worked as a "secondhand" observer, my respect for the field worker's ability has increased year by year. Apparently my ability to analyze this kind of data has also increased, so that I am often flattered by readers of my work who take it for granted that I myself collected the data about which I write and are surprised and a little unbelieving when I say that I have not. (My most recent experience as a field worker, a study of the

Moynihan Report controversy, again impressed me with how much better other people are at collecting the kind of data I like to work with; fortunately I had a collaborator who is an excellent field worker.) My training in the analysis of projective techniques, particularly the TAT and sentence completions, went a long way toward developing the particular kind of sensitivity to interpreting the lines in between the lines of written material which is the sine qua non of working with qualitative data.

Curiosity and Psychiatry

How did I end up in a place like that? The intellectual and organizational coordinates of my career are hardly typical for a sociologist, except perhaps in that I, no more than other sociologists, aspired to that profession as a child—almost none of us knew it existed! From about 12 years of age I had expected to become first an electrical engineer and then a physicist. But by my first semester in college I had changed my mind. I think I now see that such a choice was a constricting defense against the anxiety that accompanied the puzzled curiosity which I felt about the world. It was a defense that didn't work for me, although, of course, it does work for many others, including quite a few men who have shifted from the physical sciences to productive careers in sociology and psychology. So from physics I shifted to psychiatry; that was about the only model of how one might go about making a career of understanding the what and why of people that penetrated to me in Mississippi. I knew, of course, from having grown up with discussions about history and political science that those, too, were fields that dealt with man, but in the South even an adolescent could get the feeling that such studies were directed more toward justifying the region and its peculiar institutions than to getting at the guts of human behavior. Psychiatry, of course, meant undergraduate work in psychology, but I found that incredibly dull. My interest was sustained only by out-of-class reading of Freud and his followers. Finally, a co-worker at the State Department, where I worked the midnight shift in the code room while studying at George Washington University during the day, told me that given my political and racial views (which put me in a highly argumentative minority against my conservative co-workers who were mostly trainees for the Foreign Service) I should study sociology. George Washington's one sociologist was in the army at the time, so I began reading through the entries that struck my fancy under sociology in the card catalog at the Library of Congress and the public library. This sent me eventually to the University of Southern California (Emory S. Bogardus had more entries in the card catalog than anyone else) and finally to the University of Chicago, where I see-sawed back and forth between sociology and psychology, finally settling down for doctoral work in the Committee for Human Development which regarded both interests as legitimate.

If I had been a somewhat less superficial reader while still in Mississippi, I might not have had to take such a circuitous route to sociology. In my senior year I had read the new book, *An American Dilemma*, and had been fascinated to learn that there seemed to be a great many people who didn't share most white Mississippians' views about white supremacy, segregation and all that. (It must have taken a courageous librarian to buy that book for the Jackson Public Library—fortunately I don't think many people besides myself read it that year.) I knew, of course, from sketchy readings of history, the *Reader's Digest* and *Time* magazine that I was not alone in believing that there was something tragically destructive about how Negroes had been and were being treated in the South, but I had not realized that there was a scientific way of trying to understand all that and perhaps of doing something about it. Myrdal told me that there was, but somehow I did not realize that the pivotal science involved was sociology, and therefore, had to rediscover it some years later. The book that finally persuaded me to a sociological career was *Deep South*, which led me to *Yankee City*, and eventually to the University of Chicago to study with W. Lloyd Warner, Allison Davis and Burleigh Gardner. Like many southerners who became sociologists, the irrationalities of race have been a continuing sociological concern for me. I am pleased, however, that the contingencies of my career took me away from the study of race relations into a broad range of studies of specific aspects of the life-styles of Americans of different social classes. These studies ranged from subjects of substantial social importance such as attitudes toward political candidates to trivia such as attitudes toward breakfast cereal. This research experience provided a kind of perspective which I have found extremely valuable during the past five years, when I have been able to return again to the problem of race that initially sparked by interest in sociology.

As for "influences," they are as varied as the career sketched above might suggest. At the University of Chicago I remember particularly Albert J. Reiss, then a beginning teacher whose courses in urban sociology and "social pathology" were so well organized and presented that one came to feel at home with and impressed by the broad range of traditional Chicago school sociology. I learned more than I knew from Everett C. Hughes, whose work I have come to appreciate increasingly as the years have gone by. The principal influences on me were Allison Davis, William E. Henry, Burleigh B. Gardner and W. Lloyd Warner; the first as a teacher and model, the last three as both teachers and co-workers over a 13-year period. As I look back on it, I regret the influence of the unfortunate Chicago tradition of faculty rivalry and schism. The result was, from the student's point of view, not a dialectic among contending points of view, but rather a series of chasms. As a result, it was not until some time later that I began to appreciate fully the work of men like Louis Wirth, Herbert Blumer and E. A. Shils.

For the first 15 years of my intellectual life by far the strongest influence on my thinking was that of Freud and other psychoanalytic writers. That influence is still strong, but increasingly blended with more traditional sociological perspectives. (This psychoanalytic exposure continues to provide me with delight at the unconscious, or perhaps conscious, cribbing of psychodynamic ideas by the most unlikely sociologists.) Almost as important as the psychoanalytical influence was that of the anthropological writers of the thirties, particularly Ralph Linton and the culture and personality school represented by Ruth Benedict, Kardiner, Kluckhohn, etc. Later the work of Eric Erikson impressed me as a more truly social integration of psychodynamic and anthropological insights. In the past few years I think I have begun to pay increasing attention to people whose work I overlooked because of the feeling that there was some kind of necessary conflict between psychodynamic formulations and the symbolic interactionist social psychology, and therefore, I have been increasingly influence by the works of men such as Anselm Strauss, Erving Goffman, Howard Becker and Edwin Lemert.

Sociology and Social Problems

I like best my first book and my last one, but each for quite different reasons. The first book, ***Workingman's Wife***, represented a combination of researches conducted over a number of years with my colleagues at Social Research, Inc. I enjoyed working with my collaborators, Richard P. Coleman and Gerald Handel, and the book pleases me as an example of what can be produced from comfortable continuing collaboration. I think I like the book most, not for what is unique to it, but for what it shares with the work of a number of other sociologists who were studying the working class at about the same time and without knowing what each other was doing. I continue to be impressed by the similarities, the replication if you will, among the working-class studies of such diverse sociologists as Bennett Berger, Herbert Gans, Mirra Komarovsky, S.M. Miller and Frank Reissman.

The second book, *And The Poor Get Children*, I simply thoroughly enjoyed doing. It represented the application to a particular problem, family planning, of findings developed in previous working-class research and somehow all the pieces fell together right. I think I like the book also because of its shock value, its demonstration that such presumably "sensitive" topics as sexual behavior and contraceptive practice are quite available to qualitative survey methods. Finally, I enjoyed it because I made such a colossal error of prediction—cautioning that large numbers of lower-class women could not be expected to adopt the oral contraceptive because of the demands of the daily pill-taking regimen. That mistake has been a very instructive one for me, and has strongly influenced the way I derive practical implications from social-psychological findings in the research in which I am now engaged.

Finally, I enjoyed the ***Moynihan Report and the Politics of Controversy*** because it gave my coauthor and myself an opportunity to experiment with sociological journalism and because it represented one of the few occasions on which I have strayed outside the area of the sociology of "private" behavior. It has always seemed to me that one of the most profound divisions within sociology is between those who study private behavior (the family, informal social relations, deviant behavior and the like) and those who find such concerns trivial and instead concentrate of the larger questions of formal institutional behavior, political behavior, community power structures, etc. Although I have long had an interest in the operation of government bureaucracies and private cause groups, I had never had an opportunity to shift my focus from the private behavior of individuals and families to this level of social organization. The Moynihan controversy study provided an opportunity to test a number of hypotheses which I had been developing over the previous few years about the operation of the government and civil rights groups in connection with an event which had made the people highly self-conscious about that they were doing.

The question of impact is a difficult one for the person concerned to assess, particularly in the case of one who is not concerned with the development of theory. I believe that my efforts have had an impact in three areas. In family sociology my studies of lower-, working- and middle-class family life have helped to break down the stereotype of one dominant American family life pattern. The particular focus of several of my books on contraception and family planning has, I believe, helped considerably to establish this area as a crucial part of any meaningful effort to understand family behavior.

I believe my work has had some constructive effect as an example of the value of qualitative methodologies. Particularly through the early 1960s, qualitative methodology enjoyed very poor standing in sociology. My work has fit in with that of a number of other sociologists who persisted in the use of these methods and who now seem to have captured the attention of an important segment of the younger men in the field. One hears much less often today than ten years ago the notion that qualitative studies are suitable only for the pilot phase of larger investigations.

Finally, I feel that my recent work has begun to have an impact on policy diagnoses concerning the race and poverty problems. In all of these areas it would be presumptuous to consider that my sociological efforts have had an impact in "reshaping" the field, but such information as I can gather concerning how my work is being used does encourage me to believe that it is playing its part in fostering standards of greater naturalistic accuracy and detail in sociological presentations, and more careful and systematic attention to policy implications.

The relationship of sociology to social problems was at the heart of my initial interest; for many years I functioned as an applier of social science knowledge and research techniques to the concerns of highly varied clients, and more recently I have been concerned to develop knowledge into sociologically informed programs for undoing the damage of racial oppression and economic exploitation of the poor. Even so, I value the wide range of styles of work in the field—from the men who do not want to move out of the ivory tower to those who are willing to work actively for change by getting their hands dirty in political movements and bureaucratic organizations. A sociology that strives so hard for relevance and application that there is no play for pure curiosity must inevitably use up its intellectual capital; a sociology in which application is either rejected or considered "dirty work" better delegated to other professions like social work or planning runs the very real risk of losing touch with the reality its theories are supposed to encompass.

I value the increasing sophistication about application and policy relevance that I think the field has begun to show in the past half-dozen years, with the increasing understanding that policy relevance also involves moral commitment on the part of the sociologist which he needs to acknowledge and address consciously. But I think the central issue has been and will be the one that Irving Louis Horowitz points to in his emphasis on the autonomy of social science. And it is the autonomy of the practicing sociologist, and not just of the field in the abstract, that is important. Sociology is extremely fashionable these days—with undergraduates, with the mass media and with government. But, its popularity comes not so much from an understanding of what sociological knowledge has to offer, as from the belief that other branches of knowledge have failed to "solve" our problems and because sociology talks about some of the most obvious ones (race, poverty, alienation, bureaucracy, etc.) it has the solution. The autonomy of the sociologist to pursue knowledge and develop theory will be seriously threatened by this popularity—not only by the threat of cooptation by the powers that be, but also by the threat of ideological cooptation in the service of the powers against the powers that be. Sociological knowledge is potentially extremely embarrassing to all of these forces since it seldom neatly confirms the preferred world view of any of the contenders in the political process. Sociology is in a position today to make crucial contributions to changing society, but it is in that position only by virtue of several decades of empirical and theoretical work which was relatively insulated from *direct* political interference by the society at large or on the campus. Now the pressures to interfere are strong. And the more accurate sociological depiction becomes, the stronger these forces will be. Sociologists will need a strong sense of solidarity no matter how varied their own individual pursuits of sociological knowledge. If they are to weather these pressures, they will need a deep and sensitive commitment to each other's freedom of responsible inquiry, and an insistent resistance to distortion of their findings by those who perceive themselves to be adversely affected by "sociological truth."

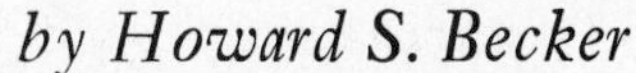

by Howard S. Becker

Blessing the Fishing Fleet in San Francisco

Sometime in the twelfth century, the story goes, a fisherman from the Sicilian village of Porticenno lost his way in a heavy fog. The Madonna appeared and provided light to guide him safely to port. The villagers built a chapel where he landed and placed a picture of the Madonna del Lume, the Madonna of the Lights, in it. Then, feeling the shore not a sufficiently august place for the chapel, they built a grander chapel on the hill overlooking the sea and moved the Madonna to it. But the picture mysteriously disappeared and reappeared in the old chapel.

Inhabitants of Porticenno have celebrated the miracle of the Madonna del Lume ever since. When some of them moved to San Francisco to carry on the fishing trade, they brought the festival with them. Starting in 1923, the parishioners of St. Peter and Paul's Church in the Italian

district of North Beach have yearly held a special mass at the opening of the fishing season in the fall. After the mass, the members of the Society of Saint Dominic, the Knights of Columbus and others join in a parade to nearby Fisherman's Wharf, where they listen to speeches and songs in Italian and English and watch the pastor of the church bless the fishing boats.

Religious and ethnic celebrations rely on the strength of symbols of group solidarity and simultaneously renew that strength. The basic units of the local Italian community express themselves in the parade in religious organization: the men in the Knights of Columbus, the women in the uniforms of the Society of Saint Dominic, the altar boys and young girls in their white Communion dresses. As people celebrate the Madonna and the blessing of the fleet, they feel the power and energy of the entire group of celebrants as an emanation of the symbols they celebrate. Symbol, group and celebration mutually support and strengthen one another.

That, at least, is the classical anthropological interpretation. In contemporary urban America, however, the process works differently. Neighborhood ethnic solidarity

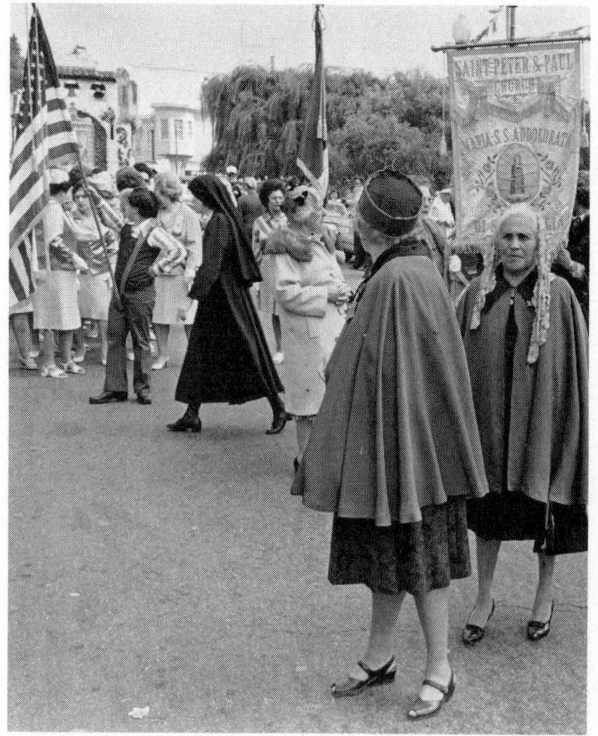

weakens as North Beach Italians move to more "American" parts of the city and to the suburbs. The crabs that made up the bulk of the fishing fleet's catch no longer abound in the ocean beyond the Golden Gate; the fishing industry may fall victim to the same ecological forces that killed off the sardine fleet of Santa Cruz. Even the church is no longer solidly Italian. As group solidarity thus weakens, the celebration no longer grows from and symbolizes the ethnic, religious and occupational solidarity of the Italian fishermen and their families.

Instead, the blessing of the fleet has begun (but only just begun) to move down the road to being another of those civic celebrations that serve the purposes of people beyond the local communities that spawn them as much as those of their originators. North Beach is no longer, has not been for years, solely Italian. The neighborhood now contains large numbers of Chinese and a substantial population of freaks and hippies of all degrees of wealth. For them, the blessing of the fleet is another of the exotic enjoyments of the cosmopolitan city, like Chinese New Year.

Similarly, politicians use the parade as an occasion for electioneering in the time-honored style. It was no surprise that Mayor Joseph Alioto, a son of the neighborhood and a parishioner of St. Peter and Paul's Church, was introduced as "the next governor of the state of California," an office he had not yet announced his candidacy for. It was somewhat more surprising to find George Chinn, the first Chinese member of the San Francisco Board of Supervisors, there (Alioto explained Chinn's presence by asking if people hadn't heard of Marco Polo and the long-standing friendship between Chinese and Italian people). But the city's eccentric politics revealed itself most clearly when Jesus Christ Satan, a transvestite candidate for supervisor (he listed his occupation on the ballot as "Androgynous Human Being"), marched the length of the parade alongside Alioto and the head of the Society of Saint Dominic; Alioto looked a little quizzical but took it in stride. After all, there's no point in alienating the gay vote, and the Italians didn't seem to mind.

2 *Amitai Etzioni*

Social Analysis and Social Action

My interest over the last ten years has moved from the study of smaller social units to that of larger ones, from greater concern with conceptualization to an emphasis on the social relevance of social *science* and from a fair segregation of the role of the sociologist and the active citizen to a greater effort to articulate the two. In so doing, I believe my work reflects trends which affect social sciences in general, sociology in particular. I shall focus first on these trends, then briefly discuss a contribution I might have made to their extension.

Many a sociological article opens with a definition of a new concept (or relationship) and a discussion of methods to be employed to measure it. This is then frequently followed by presentation of some data relevant to the new concept and relating to it familiar sociological variables (e.g., "the distribution of elephantiasis by age and sex in cities with a population of over one hundred thousand"). Most sociologists, the author included, feel that such combination of theory and methods is the very foundation on which sociology as a science ought to be built and is in fact being constructed. But many of us also feel that something is lacking.

What is lacking most is *social analysis,* the systematic exploration of social issues; that is, concern with the methodological questions of sociological analysis of the great issues of our age, which tend to involve the study of macroscopic units. The subject of social analysis, though, is the issues not the sociological building stones; the focus is on the instruments to be utilized to elevate the analysis of societal issues, to improve on amateur, intuitive or journalistic sociology. Traditional training in sociology is no more a preparation for social analysis than training in biophysics or biochemistry is for medical practice. Social analysis requires special training as well as distinct methods, knowledge and a professional tradition. It requires more than a simple application of an existing body of knowledge to the study of a set of problems; it is also a question of studying the problems that application of sociology engenders. When sick, one would hardly exchange treatment by one M.D. for that of two Ph.D.'s in biology. Hence, the call for social analysis as a new element of sociological study and training is a call for the professionalization of sociology—for adding to sociology as a science (as the institutionalized desire to know) the systematic concern with application of knowledge (the institutionalized desire to help).

The *subject matter* of social analysis is all of substantive sociology. However, social analysis as a discipline is not to replace the fields of political sociology, race relations or the study of stratification, but is to deal with the *generic methodological, intellectual and professional problems which the substantive sociologies raise.* Each of the substantive fields combines — in addition to information about the subject matter — three essential elements: to study politics, draw on a general theory and methodology *and* be prepared to handle the generic problems of substantive analysis. The same problems would reappear if one were to study other substantive fields — for example, the sociology or religion of criminology — but would not obtain if one were engaged in sociological theory per se or pure methodology.

Analysis: Substance and Problems

What is the substance of social analysis and what generic problems does its study raise? The focus and raison d'etre of social analysis are the problems of the age, the application of sociology to the understanding of society, its major subcollectivities and a society's place in more encompassing communities. Biochemistry views the blood as having varying chemical compositions; medicine sees it as infested with illnesses. One day — when our knowledge of hematology is much more advanced — the distinction might disappear; meanwhile somebody had better be concerned with how to cure illnesses, using the very partial biochemical information available. The methodological question of medicine is hence how to act under *partial* information. Sociological theory and research slice society into social systems, role sets and reference groups; social analysis is concerned with applying such concepts to the evolution of a world community, the redistribution of social wealth, efforts to advance the growth of human rights, the development of "have-not" countries, etc. In general, we quite correctly train students to achieve higher levels of precision by drawing better samples, using more refined measures, more specified concepts, etc. As a consequence the trained sociologist often shies away from major segments of social data because for one reason or another, he cannot obtain the kind of precision we taught him to look for. The field of analysis of societal problems is thus often left wide open to social commentators who have no methodological training at all. We should develop and teach the methods to be applied when information is fragmentary and vague, as it so often is, because the trained sociologist can still do much better — especially when he is trained to face this problem — than the uninitiated social observer.

A hardly novel historical approach to sociology serves to emphasize our position. We started with grand social theories, formulated in emotion-laden terms (e.g., progress), covering no more and no less than all of history and all of mankind. We began by flying so high on the verbal trapeze that most of our propositions could not be pinned down and those that could often did not withstand empirical tests. Our grandiose designs collapsed.

Then, we foreswore high jumps; we preferred to advance step by step, even if it should take us a hundred years to learn to walk firmly, rather than engage again in breathtaking but also neckbreaking gymnastics. We sharpened our tools on the radio-listening of housewives and focused our concepts by observing small groups of college sophomores. *Such concentration was essential for a transition period;* but behavior which is quite suitable for student days becomes an adolescent fixation when it dominates the behavior of a mature man. While sociological theory ought to be further extended and methods of collecting and analyzing data improved, we should recognize that our wings have sprouted; we are now ready to fly. It would be an overreaction to our earlier misadventures to remain earthbound to a restrictive interpretation of our discipline, to delay a new test flight of social analysis.

Another reason we, as a profession, shy away from social analysis is our fear of value judgments which, we sense, are more rampant in social than in sociological analysis. In the brief period which has elapsed since the publication of my theoretical book *The Active Society,* one question has been raised much more often than any other — how can I maintain that the theory advanced is both critical (i.e., normative) *and* objective. My answer is that we are critical in that we take the human needs and values of those subjects to our study, the members of society, as our basis for evaluation. We compare various social structures in terms of the extent to which they are responsive to their members; asking what factors prevent them from being more responsive than they are, and the conditions under which their responsiveness may be increased. We thus do not evaluate a social structure in terms of *our* preferences but in terms of those of its members.

This position is hardly a novel one — Gunnar Myrdal followed a similar approach in *The American Dilemma:* He did not state that Americans were failing to live up to *his* creed, to his conception of equality, but to theirs. We shall now show in a future publication that Marx's and Mannheim's positions are not too remote from this approach.

The theory is objective in the methodological sense that all empirically minded observers will reach the same conclusions. Whatever their varying personal values, they may observe the same discrepancy between the values the members of society hold and the way of life their society and its component institutions promote or tolerate.

In the past, mainstream sociologists argued that sociology must be neutral to be objective; the critics, on the other hand, have posited that it cannot be neutral and urged that one's normative position ought to be explicitly stated. As long as this course is followed, sociology is either normatively sterile (at least claiming to be), or subjectively based, which undermines its scientific foundation. We suggest that *using the subjects' values rather than our own allows sociology to leave behind this either/or position.*

Another problem arises though. Members of society, the subjects of our study, may be inauthentically committed and unaware of their real needs and preferences. Our proposition is that (a) one can *empirically* test when the declared preferences are the real ones and when they are inauthentic (e.g., when there is a significant gap between the declared and real needs, respondents tend to be defensive about their positions), and that (b) the attributes of the real needs can be empirically determined.

The last point is essential to the whole approach and raises a surprising amount of emotional resistance among many mainstream sociologists while it is considered almost self-evident by many psychologists and psychoanalysts, as well as by anthropologists. One reason for the resistance is that many sociologists subscribe to what Dennis Wrong called the "oversocialized" conception of man, i.e., they assume that human needs are highly pliable by society and culture. Individuals, groups and subcultures may deviate, but the society never does; it sets the norms. As we see it, the social demands (or role expectations) that one society advances may be less responsive to human nature than those another society fosters. In this sense, the first society may be said to be deviant, or more conflicting with human nature, than the other one. Of course, both society and human nature affect each other, but neither has a prior logic nor normative claim for adjustment of the other.

Practice: Needs and Roles

Empirically, the gap between human needs and social roles may be measured by socialization costs, social control costs and the direction of pressure to change. To assess these, take 100 freshmen and put 50 at random into highly bureaucratic roles and the other 50 into a highly particularistic diffuse, affective "organization." If our position is valid, you will see that it will be more difficult to train the freshmen to behave in accordance with bureaucratic norms than with particularistic ones. Sustained conformity will require more agents of social control and more frequent use of sanctions, and when control slackens there will be much more pressure in the bureaucratic organization to shift toward particularistic conduct than in the particularistic organization to shift toward bureaucratic patterns. This would indicate that bureaucratic norms are less fulfilling of human needs that particularistic ones. The same method can be applied to other sociocultural differences and other populations.

There is one catch—if the subjects come from a society which is highly bureaucratic (e.g., Prussia in the late nineteenth century), they *may* initially feel more "comfortable" in highly bureaucratic roles. However, if the study is continued, we expect, they will adapt to nonbureaucratic norms much more easily than subjects from a highly particularistic background will to bureaucratic ones. We frankly do not know how long it will take, but surely longer than the four times 45 minutes many laboratory experiments last, and less than a generation, the extent of many "natural experiments" conducted by society. Finally, we expect those individuals in roles more suitable to human nature, at least after a period of accommodation to their new roles, to be happier and less anxiety ridden than those in less fulfilling roles.

Two more arguments in favor of the present transformation toward a more critical sociology need to be examined. It is said that sociologists, by learning to walk, will find out how to fly. You can learn from the fruit fly, it is correctly suggested, new laws of genetics that apply to all animals and plants. Similarly, we can derive from sophomores' chit-chat universal laws of interaction which enrich our understanding of social behavior in general. But while it is true that in this way we can learn the "universal" elements of our theory — all the universal chemical characteristics of water are represented in any drop — we cannot study the emergent properties of complex units in noncomplex ones. We will not learn much about the anatomy of elephants by studying that of fruit flies. Hence, while we ought to continue to study small groups for their own sake and for the light they cast on social behavior in general, *we ought to invest more of our resources in macroscopic sociology.*

But, as a second line of defense in favor of our present low (though rising) investment in social analysis, it is said you cannot direct scientists and tell them what to study. If sociologists find race relations an unrespectable subject, unless it can be used to perfect survey methods or to redefine the concept of prejudice, what can we do? What we can do is to realize that the distribution of scientific resources is not random, does not follow a laissez-faire pattern, and is "interfered with" regularly anyhow. The distribution of sociological manpower is directly affected by the advantage of required courses, which as a rule include theory and research techniques over optional courses; by Ph.D. committees that approve and encourage some subjects and discourage others; by foundations and federal agencies — which we advise — who support some subjects to the neglect of others; by space awarded in our journals; as well as attention granted at professional meetings, to some subjects over others. All these are occasions where theory and methodology are celebrated while social analysis is given, at best, second-class citizenship.

Finally, sociological scientism is revealed in the aloof attitude toward social action of many members of our profession. This is a severe case of elephantiasis in which the scientist role of the sociologist has made deep inroads into his role as a member of the educated elite of the community. This is not only a question of being a bad citizen but of not living up to a special social obligation we have as persons who know society expertly. To indicate more clearly what I have in mind, let me point out another helpful (for social as well as sociological analysis) term, that of role pairs. ***Role pairs*** are roles which appear frequently together in a society, in the sense that they are carried out by one and the same actor. The importance of such combinations is that they provide the most effective means of communication known between two roles — personal union. They also allow economy of resources, such as that found in the housewife-mother pair, security and elevator boy combination, teacher-researcher, doctor-medical professor, etc.

The role pair of sociologist-intellectual is a particularly effective one. Not that all sociologists were ever intellectuals or vice versa, but there seems to have been a much higher degree of overlap in earlier generations. The growing tendency to dissociate the two roles is particularly regrettable because the virtue of such role combination is greater now than it used to be in the days when it was more common, for now we command a body of theory and methodology as well as a store of validated knowledge about man-in-society which can provide much-needed background for speculation about society. The social analysis of Daniel Bell, Lewis Coser, Nathan Glazer, David Riesman, Dennis Wrong and other contemporary sociologists who fill this role pair is much more hardheaded, soundly based and politically sophisticated than that provided by earlier generations of social analysts or by their former college mates who majored in English literature and still interpret the American scene in the light of moods revealed in ***Moby Dick*** or "understand" the Soviet Union because they suffered with Dostoevsky.

As a discipline we do not encourage, or at least do not train for, the sociologist-social-commentator pairing of roles. In earlier days the clergy and radical movements provided the sparks that fused sociological training with social concern. Today, in the age of specialization, more and more sociologists feel that what is proper behavior in their role as scientists is the proper behavior in their community role as well; the only way they face a social problem is through the lenses of theory and methodology. Civil defense, for example, becomes a subject for study of attitudes ("People who fear war more are also more in favor of fallout shelters.") or an occasion to try out a new computer program in mass dynamics.

The sociologist's role is preempting time, energy and resources that belong to his role as intellectual, as one who is committed to societal issues and expresses his concern about them more effectively than other observers since he knows more than they about the society he is commenting upon. Thus he not only is against nuclear war, but applies his knowledge of society to understand why nations become inflexible in the face of such a danger and freeze rather than act; sharing his analysis with those who seek to reduce the danger through political action, but lack the benefits of the sociologist's training and expertise.

by George Gardner

No Exit?

"Once poverty has locked one into the Crisis Ghetto, the chances of being forced to remain—and the bad consequences of remaining— are greater than if one lived in any other area of the city . . . the ghetto limits and blights the lives of its inhabitants."

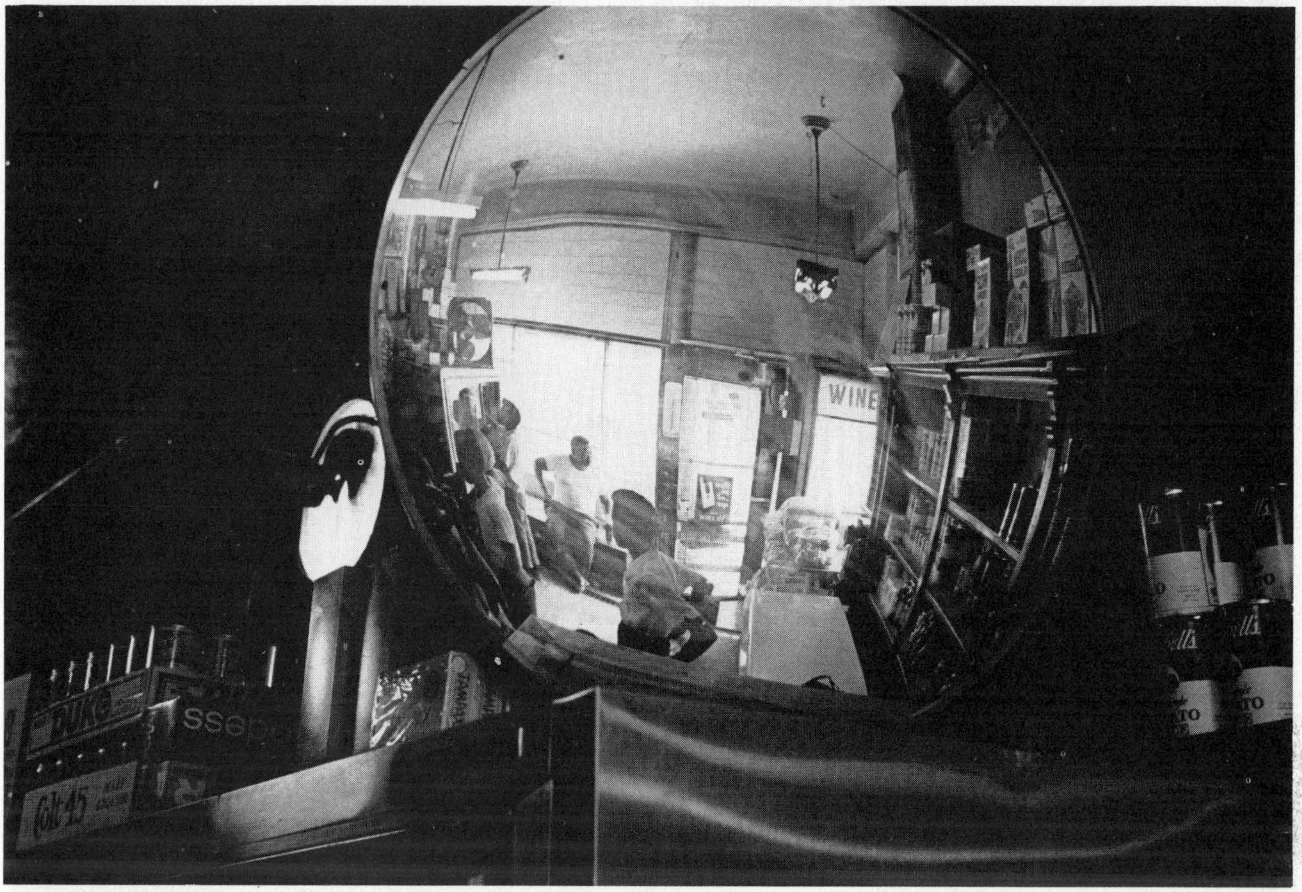

CHILDREN
CROSSING
AHEAD
QA 678

3 *Peter Rossi*

Evaluating Social Action Programs

We are today groping for new and presumably better treatments for a variety of social ills and have enough wealth to correct some of the obvious faults of our society. But, ironically, no matter how heavy our consciences now, we can no longer expect reforms to produce massive results. We have passed the stage of easy solutions. To borrow a parallel from medicine, we can much more easily and decisively reduce death and illness by bringing safe water to a backward land than by trying to get Americans to stop smoking.

Similarly with social ills. Provide schools and teachers to all children and illiteracy goes down dramatically; but to achieve a level of education high enough to assure everyone a good job is a lot more difficult. Diminishing returns set in: The more we have done in the past, the more difficult it becomes to add new benefits. Partly this is because so much has already been achieved; partly because in the past we have not had to deal so much with individual motivation. Almost everyone has enough motivation to learn to read; it takes a lot more to learn a specialized skill.

In short, massive results will not occur, and new social treatments are going to be increasingly expensive in time and money. Practitioners and policy-makers are apprehensive; they want evaluations of program effectiveness, but they are afraid of what might be shown.

Take Project Head Start. Everyone would agree that universal schooling for children has been a huge success—compared to no schooling or schooling only for those who can pay. But poor children are still behind and need help. And a preschool program for them can never make as much change as universal schooling did.

Effective make-up treatment must be expensive. Each trainee at a Job Corps camp costs somewhere between $5,000 and $10,000 a year, as compared to considerably less than $1,000 a year in the usual public high school. Yet Job Corps training is not five to ten times as effective.

Also, the less the effect, the greater is the measurement precision needed to demonstrate its existence—so in evaluation too it will cost more to reveal less.

But if social scientists are pessimistic about results, operators of programs tend to be quite optimistic, at least when facing congressional appropriations committees. Claims made in public are usually much higher than any results we can reasonably expect. So the interests and actions of the program administrators themselves tend to undermine good evaluation.

Finally, controlled experiments—the most desirable model—are not frequently used in evaluation. There is not a single piece of evaluation research being carried out on any of the major programs of the war on poverty that closely follows the controlled experiment model.

The Power of Wishful Thinking

The will to believe that their programs are effective is understandably strong among administrators. As long as the results are positive (or at least not negative), relations between practitioners and researchers are cordial and even effusive. But what if the results are negative?

A few years ago the National Opinion Research Center undertook research on the effects of fellowships and scholarships on graduate study in arts and sciences. The learned societies that sponsored the research sincerely believed that such aids were immensely helpful to graduate students and that heavily supported fields were able to attract better students. The results turned out to be equivocal. First, financial support did not seem to have much to do with selecting a field for study. Second, it did not appear that good students were held back by lack of fellowships or scholarships. The committed ones always found some way to get their PhD's, often relying on their spouses for help.

The first reaction of the sponsors was to attack the study's methodology—leading to the coining of the aphorism that the first defense of an outraged sponsor was methodological criticism. Policy remained unaffected: Sponsors are still asking more and more federal help for graduate students on the grounds that it allows more to go into graduate study, and also spreads talent better among the various fields.

Another example of the power of wishful thinking has to do with the relationship between class size and learning. It is an article of faith among educators that the smaller the class per teacher, the greater the learning experience. Research on this question goes back to the very beginnings of empirical research in educational social science in the early 1920's. There has scarcely been a year since without several dissertations and theses on this topic, as well as larger researches by mature scholars—over 200 of them. The latest was done by James Coleman in his nationwide study for the Office of Education under the Civil Rights Act of 1964. Results? *By and large, class size has no effect on learning by students, with the possible exception of the language arts.*

What effect did all this have on policy? Virtually none. Almost every proposal for better education calls for reduced class size. Even researchers themselves have been apologetic, pointing out how they *might* have erred.

I do not know of any action program that has been put out of business by evaluation research, unless evaluation itself was meant to be the hatchet. Why? Mainly because practitioners (and sometimes researchers) never seriously consider the possibility that results *might* come out negative or insignificant. When a research finding shows that a program is ineffective, and the research director has failed to plan for this eventuality, then the impact can be so devastating that it becomes more comforting to deny the worth of the negative evaluation than to reorganize one's planning.

Getting the Results You Want

Given unlimited resources, it is possible to make some dent in almost any problem. Even the most sodden wretch on skid row can be brought to a semblance of respectability (provided he is not too physically deteriorated) by intensive, and expensive, handling. But there is not sufficient manpower or resources to lead each single skid row inhabitant back to respectability, even briefly.

Many action programs resemble the intensive treatment model. They are bound to produce *some* results, but they cannot be put into large-scale operation.

Note the distinction between "impact" and "coverage." The *impact* of a technique is its ability to produce changes in each situation to which it is applied, while *coverage* of a technique is its ability to be applied to a large number of cases. Thus, face-to-face persuasion has high impact, but its coverage is relatively slight. In contrast, bus and subway posters may have low impact but high coverage.

An extremely effective technique is one that has both high impact and high coverage. Perhaps the best examples can be found in medicine. Immunizing vaccines are inexpensive, easy to administer, and very effective in certain diseases. It does not seem likely, however, that we will find vaccines, or measures resembling them in impact and coverage, for modern social ills. It is a mistake, therefore, to discard out of hand programs which have low impact but the potentiality of high coverage. Programs which show small positive results on evaluation but can be generalized to reach large numbers of people can, in the long run, have an extremely significant cumulative effect.

The Control Group Problem

The scientific integrity of a controlled experiment depends on whether the experimenter can determine which subjects go to the experimental and which to the control groups and whether these allocations are unbiased. But there are many distorting influences.

First, political. Practitioners are extremely reluctant to give the experimenters enough power. For example, to evaluate the worth of a manpower retraining program properly, the potential trainees must be separated into experimental and control groups, and then checked for contrasts after the training. This means that some of them, otherwise qualified, are arbitrarily barred from training. Public agencies are extremely reluctant to authorize such discrimination.

In part, this problem arises because researchers have not sufficiently analyzed what a "control" experience is. A control group need not be deprived of all training—of a chance of any help—merely that type of help.

A placebo treatment for a job retraining program might be designed to help men get jobs that do not involve retraining, and over which the training program should demonstrate some advantage.

Even in the best circumstances, with the best sponsors, controlled experiments can run into a number of booby traps. There was the well-designed evaluation research that could not raise enough volunteers for either experimental or control groups. So the experimenter opted to fill only the experimental groups, abandoning all attempts at proper control.

Or there was the research on the effectiveness of certain means of reaching poor families with birth control information, contaminated by the city health department setting up birth control clinics in areas designated as controls!

Or there is the continuing risk in long-range evaluations that the world will change the control group almost as fast as the experiment changes the experimental group. For instance, David Wilner and his associates undertook to evaluate the effects of public housing in Baltimore when general improvement in housing was on the upswing, and by the end of the period the difference in housing quality between experimental and control groups was minor.

In sum, it is not easy either to get the freedom to undertake properly controlled experiments or to do them when that consent is obtained.

Strategy for Good Evaluation Research

A number of lessons can be drawn to help devise proper evaluation research.

First, most of us are still a long way from full commitment to the outcomes of evaluation research. It is part of the researcher's responsibility to impress on the practitioner that in most cases results are slight and that there is more than an off-chance that they will be unfavorable. What to do about this probability must be worked out in advance; otherwise the research may turn out to be a fatuous exercise.

Second, how can we devise ways of using controlled experiments in evaluation? As noted, political obstacles and our nonsterile world make uncontaminated controls difficult and rare.

Since there is such a high likelihood of small effects, we need very powerful research designs to get clear results. This takes money. But wouldn't it be worthwhile to set up such powerful designs to evaluate *several* items simultaneously, so that the outcome would be more useful for setting policy? For instance, wouldn't it be better to run an evaluation on several types of Job Corps camps simultaneously, comparing them one with the other, rather than comparing one with the Job Corps in general? Such a differential study would give more and better information than a gross evaluation.

If controlled experiments—the desirable model—are used so rarely, what *is* being used? Most frequently quasi-experiments so constructed that some biases do affect the control groups, or correlational designs in which persons getting some sort of treatment are contrasted with others not treated—with relevant characteristics being controlled statistically.

How bad are such "soft" evaluational techniques, particularly correlational designs? When can they be employed with confidence?

First, it seems to me that when massive effects are expected or desired, soft techniques are almost as good as subtle and precise ones. If what is desired, for instance, is complete remission of all symptoms in all persons treated, then a control group is hardly necessary. If a birth control method is judged effective only if all chance of conception is eliminated, then the research design can be very simple. All that needs to be done is administer the technique and then check for any births (or conceptions) thereafter. If effectiveness is defined as fewer births, the design should be more complicated and requires control groups.

The obverse also holds. If a treatment shows no effects with a soft method, then it is highly unlikely that a very precise evaluation will show more than very slight effects. Thus, if children in an ordinary Head Start program show no gain in learning compared to those who do not participate (initial learning held constant), then it is not likely that a controlled experiment, with children randomly assigned to experimental and control groups, is going to show dramatic differences either.

This means that it is worthwhile to consider soft methods as the first stage in evaluation research, discarding treatments that show no effects and retaining more effective ones to be tested with more powerful, controlled designs.

Although checking for possible correlations after the event may introduce biases, such designs are extremely useful in investigating long-term effects. It may be impossible to show a direct laboratory relationship between cigarette smoking and lung cancer, but the long-term correlation between the two, even if not pure enough for the purist, can hardly be ignored. Similarly, though NORC's study of the effect of Catholic education on adults may have selection biases too subtle for us to detect, we still know a great deal about what results might be expected, even if we could manage a controlled experiment for a generation. The net differences between parochial school Catholics and public school Catholics are so slight that we now know that parochial schools are not an effective device for inculcating religious beliefs.

From all these considerations, a useful strategy for evaluational research seems to emerge:

■ A RECONNAISANCE PHASE—a rough screening in which the soft and the correlational designs filter out those programs worthwhile investigating further;

■ AN EXPERIMENTAL PHASE—in which powerful controlled experiments are used to evaluate the relative effectiveness of a variety of those programs already demonstrated to be worth pursuing.

4 *Nicholas von Hoffman*

Sociological Snoopers and . . .

From the Washington Post

WE'RE so preoccupied with defending our privacy against insurance investigators, dope sleuths, counterespionage men, divorce detectives and credit checkers, that we overlook the social scientists behind the hunting blinds who're also peeping into what we thought were our most private and secret lives. But they are there, studying us, taking notes, getting to know us, as indifferent as everybody else to the feeling that to be a complete human involves having an aspect of ourselves that's unknown.

If there was any doubt about there being somebody who wants to know about anything any other human being might be doing it is cancelled out in the latest issue of **Trans**-action, a popular but respected sociological monthly. The lead article, entitled "Impersonal Sex in Public Places," is a resume of a study done about the nature and pattern of homosexual activities in men's rooms. Laud Humphreys, the author, is an Episcopal priest, a duly pee-aich-deed sociologist, holding the rank of assistant professor at Southern Illinois University. The article is taken from a forthcoming book called **Tearoom Trade: Impersonal Sex in Public Places** (Aldine Publishing Company, Chicago, March 1970).

Tearoom is the homosexual slang for men's rooms that are used for purposes other than those for which they were designed. However, if a straight male were to hang around a tearoom he wouldn't see anything out of the ordinary so that if you're going to find out what's happening you must give the impression that you're one of the gang.

"I had to become a participant observer of the furtive felonious acts," Humphreys writes in explaining his methodology, "Fortunately, the very fear or suspicion of tearoom participants produces a mechanism that makes such observation possible; a third man—generally one who obtains voyeuristic pleasure from his duties—serves as a lookout, moving back and forth from door to windows. Such a 'watchqueen,' as he is labeled in the homosexual argot, coughs when a police car stops nearby or when a stranger approaches. He nods affirmatively when he recognizes a man entering as being a 'regular.' Having been taught the watchqueen role by a cooperating respondent, I played that part faithfully while observing hundreds of acts of fellatio."

Most of the people Humphreys observed and took notes on had no idea what he was doing or that they, in disguised form, would be showing up in print at some time in the future. Of all the men he studied only a dozen were ever told what his real purpose was, yet as a sociologist he had to learn about the backgrounds and vital facts of the other tearoom visitors he'd seen. To do this Humphreys noted their license numbers and by tracing their cars learned their identities. He then allowed time to pass, disguised himself and visited these men under the color of doing a different, more innocuous door-to-door survey.

He describes what he did this way: "By passing as a deviant, I had observed their sexual behavior without disturbing it. Now I was faced with interviewing these men—often in the presence of their wives—without destroying them. . . . To overcome the danger of having a subject recognize me as a watchqueen, I changed my hair style, attire and automobile. At the risk of losing the more transient respondents, I waited a year between the sample gathering (in the tearoom) and the interviews, during which time I took notes on their homes and neighborhoods and acquired data on them from the city and county directories."

Humphreys said that he did everything possible to make sure the names of the men whose secrets he knew would never get out: "I kept only one copy of the master list of names and that was in a safe deposit box. I did all the transcribing of taped interviews myself and changed all identifying marks and signs. In one instance, I allowed myself to be arrested rather than let the police know what I was doing and the kind of information I had."

Even so, it remains true that he collected information that could be used for blackmail, extortion, and the worst kind of mischief without the knowledge of the people involved. **Trans**-action defends the ethics of Humphreys' methodology on the basis of purity of motive and the argument that he was doing it for a good cause, that is getting needed, reliable information about a difficult and painful social problem.

Everybody who goes snooping around and spying on people can be said to have good motives. The people whom Sen. Sam Ervin is fighting, the ones who want to give the police the right to smash down your door without announcing who they are if they think you have pot in your house, believe they are well-motivated. They think they are preventing young people from destroying themselves. J. Edgar Hoover unquestionably believes he's protecting the country against subversion when he orders your telephone tapped. Those who may want to overthrow the government are just as well motivated by their lights. Since everybody can be said to be equally well motivated, it's impossible to form a judgment on what people do by assessing their intentions.

To this Laud Humphreys replies that his methods were less objectionable than getting his data by working through the police: "You do walk a really perilous tightrope in regard to ethical matters in studies like this, but, unless someone will walk it, the only source of information will be the police department, and that's dangerous for a society. The methods I used were the least intrusive possible. Oh, I could have hidden in the ceiling as the police do, but then I would have been an accomplice in what they were doing."

Humphreys believes that the police in many cities extort bribes from homosexuals they catch in tearooms. He also thinks that "what's more common is putting an investigation report on file. Often when they catch somebody, they don't arrest him but they get his name, address and employer. There's no defense against this and no way of knowing when the information will be used in the future. I agree there may be a dangerous precedent in studying deviant behavior this way but in some places vice squads use closed circuit TV to look into tearooms and in many cities they use decoys. To my mind **these** are the people who're the dangerous observers."

Some people may answer that by saying a study on such a topic constitutes deviant sociological behavior, a giving-in to the discipline's sometimes peculiar taste for nosing around oddballs. But in the study of man anything men do should be permissible to observe and try to understand. Furthermore, Humphreys has evidence and arguments to show that, far from being a rare and nutty aberration, tearoom activity is quite common.

He cites a UCLA law review study showing that in a four-year period in Los Angeles 274 of a total of 493 men arrested for homosexual activities were picked up in tearooms. He has another study in Mansfield, Ohio, that rural fleshpot, saying that police operating with a camera behind a one-way mirror caught 65 men in the course of only two weeks. FBI national crime figures don't have a special category for tearoom arrests, but Humphreys has enough indicative evidence to allow him to say it's a big problem. Even if it weren't, so many parents are worried about their sons being approached by homosexuals that we believe it's a big problem.

Humphreys' study suggests that tearoom habitues stay clear of teen-agers. "I never saw an instance of a teen-ager being approached. The men in the tearoom are scared to death of teen-agers. When a teen-ager comes in the action breaks off and everybody gets out. You have to give a definite sign before you'll be approached (in his book he goes into detail) so they never approach anyone who hasn't done so. Anyway, there's no problem of recruiting teen-agers because teen-agers are too busy trying to join."

Incontestably such information is useful to parents, teen-agers themselves, to policemen, legislators and many others, but it was done by invading some people's privacy. This newspaper could probably learn a lot of things that the public has a right and need to know if its reporters were to use disguises and the gimmickry of modern, transistorized, domestic espionage, but there is a policy against it. No information is valuable enough to obtain by nipping away at personal liberty, and that is true no matter who's doing the gnawing, John Mitchell and the conservatives over at the Justice Department or Laud Humphreys and the liberals over at the Sociology Department.

Irving Louis Horowitz & Lee Rainwater

... Journalistic Moralizers

COLUMNIST Nicholas Von Hoffman's quarrel with Laud Humphreys' "Impersonal Sex in Public Places" starkly raises an issue that has grown almost imperceptibly over the last few years, and now threatens to create in the next decade a tame sociology to replace the fairly robust one that developed during the sixties. For most of their history, the disciplines of sociology and social psychology were considered a kind of joke, an oddball activity pursued by academic types who cultivated an arcane jargon that either concealed ivory tower views about human reality, or simply said things that everyone knew already.

Somehow, during the 1960s, that image began to shift quite dramatically. People suddenly began to look to sociologists and social psychologists for explanations of what was going on, of why the society was plagued with so many problems. Sociological jargon, perspectives and findings began to enter people's conversation and thinking in a way that no one would have imagined a few years before. All during the sixties enrollment in sociology classes in colleges and universities increased at an accelerating rate. What sociologists had to say about international relations, or race problems, or deviant behavior, or health care or the crisis of the city became standard parts of the ways Americans explained themselves to themselves.

But as the sociological enterprise grew, there also grew up a reaction against it, especially among those who are also in the business of interpreting the society to itself. For, as sociologists know (even if they sometimes forget it), any statement, even of "fact," about a society is also a political assertion in that, whatever the motivation of the speaker, his views can have an impact on the political processes of the society. But there are other kinds of occupations that have traditionally had the right to make these kinds of statements. Foremost among them have been journalists, clergymen, politicians and intellectuals generally. When his perspectives and findings began to gain wider currency, the sociologist became willy-nilly a competitor in the effort to establish an interpretation of what we are all about. And so, these past few years, sociologists have been getting their lumps from those various groups.

With increasing stridency, traditional politicians have railed against university social scientists who exercise undue influence on the way public issues are defined. Right and left militants have sought to dry up their ability to influence public definitions through derision and systematic efforts to deny them access to sources of data. Beginning in the fifties, right wing groups launched successive campaigns against behavioral scientists, as both practitioners and teachers, culminating most recently in the John Birch Society campaign against sex education. All this has had a quiet influence on the research work of social scientists. Slowly but perceptibly over the last couple of years, and with no sign of abatement, sociologists and social psychologists are being told by a varied chorus that they talk too much, or if not too much, at least that too many of the things they say had better be left unsaid, or the saying of them ought to be left to the traditional spokesmen. What has proved particularly galling about the sociologist, as these other spokesmen view him, is his claim to the mantle of science. For all the tentativeness and roughness of sociological science, it makes at least that claim, and so represents a very powerful threat to the more traditional interpreters of reality.

Perhaps the closest competitors of all are journalists. The intertwinings of journalistic and sociological enterprise are complex indeed and have been from the early days of empirical American sociology. After all, Robert Park was a working journalist, and saw sociology simply as a better journalism because it got at the "big picture." Predictably, then, journalists often feel a deep ambivalence about empirical sociology. On the one hand, it represents a resource that can be quite useful in doing journalistic work. On the other hand, for the ambitious practitioner of personal journalism, there is always the threat to his authority, his potential punditry, by a group of fellow interpreters of the world who lay claim to science as the basis of what they say.

It is perhaps for this reason that von Hoffman so readily applies to sociologists a standard of investigative conduct that few journalists could measure up to, and why he is so unwilling to accept the relevance of the socially constructive purpose to which sociological activities are directed.

Sociologists have tended to assume that well-intentioned people fully accept the desirability of demystification of human life and culture. In the age of Aquarius, however, perhaps such a view will be recognized as naive.

"They are there, studying us, taking notes, getting to know us, as indifferent as everybody else to the feeling that to be a complete human involves having an aspect of ourselves that's unknown." Von Hoffman seems to mean this to be a statement about the right to privacy in a legal sense, but it really represents a denial of the ability of people to understand themselves and each other in an existential sense. This denial masks a fear, not that intimate details of our lives will be revealed to *others,* but rather that we may get to know *ourselves* better and have to confront what up to now we did not know about ourselves. Just as psychoanalysis was a scientific revolution as threatening to traditional conceptions as those of Galileo and Kepler had been, it may well be that the sociologist's budding ability to say something about the how's and why's of men's relationships to each other is deeply threatening not only to the established institutions in society, but also in a more personal way to all members of society.

Von Hoffman says he is talking about the invasion of privacy, but his celebration of the "aspect of ourselves that's unknown" shows a deeper worry about making rational and open what he conceives to be properly closed and dark in human reality. Von Hoffman concentrates his outrage on the methods Humphreys used to learn what he did, but we believe that at bottom he is not much different from other critics of behavioral science who make exactly the same points that von Hoffman makes with respect to research, even when it involves people who freely give their opinions, attitudes and autobiographical data to interviewers. This, too, is regarded as a threat because eventually it will remove some of the mystery from human life.

But von Hoffman recognizes that his most appealing charge has to do with privacy, and so he makes much of the fact that Humphreys collected information that could be used for "blackmail, extortion, and the worst kind of mischief without the knowledge of the people involved."

Here his double standard is most glaringly apparent. Journalists routinely, day in, day out, collect information that could be used for "blackmail, extortion, and the worst kind of mischief without the knowledge of the people involved." But von Hoffman knows that the purpose of their work is none of those things, and so long as their information is collected from public sources, I assume he wouldn't attack them. Yet he nowhere compares the things sociologists do with the things his fellow journalists do. Instead, he couples Humphreys' "snooping around," "spying on people" with similarly "well-motivated" invaders of privacy as J. Edgar Hoover and John Mitchell.

To say the least, the comparison is invidious; the two kinds of enterprises are fundamentally different. No police group seeks to acquire information about people with any other goal than that of, in some way, prosecuting them. Policemen collect data, openly or under cover, in order to put someone in jail. Whatever it is, the sociological enterprise is not that. Sociologists are not interested in directly affecting the lives of the particular people they study. They are interested in those individuals only as representatives of some larger aggregate —in Humphreys' case, all participants in the tearoom action. Therefore, in almost all sociological research, the necessity to preserve the anonymity of the respondent is not an onerous one, because no purpose at all would be served by identifying the respondents.

In this respect, journalists are in fact much closer to policemen than sociologists are. Journalists often feel that their function is to point the finger at particular malefactors. Indeed their effort to acquire information about individuals is somewhat like that of the police, in the sense that both seek to affect importantly the lives of the particular individuals who are the object of their attention. Perhaps this kind of misconception of what the sociologist is about, and the total absence of any comment on the role of the journalist, leads von Hoffman to persistently misinterpret Humphreys' research as "invading some people's privacy." Yet everything Humphreys knew about the deviant behavior of the people he studied was acquired in a public context (indeed, on public land).

We believe in the work Humphreys has done, in its principled humaneness, in its courage to learn the truth and in the constructive contribution that it makes toward our understanding of all the issues, including the moral, raised by deviant behavior in our society. *Trans*-action, has always been supportive of and open to the sort of enterprise he has so ably performed; we only wish there were more of it. Furthermore, a vigorous defense of Laud Humphreys' research (and that of others before and after him) is eminently possible and glaringly needed.

Sociologists uphold the right to know in a context of the surest protection for the integrity of the subject matter and the private rights of the people studied. Other groups in society may turn on different pivots: the right of law, the protection of individuals against invasion of privacy and so forth. But whoever is "right" in the abstract, there is a shared obligation for all parties to a controversy to step forth with fullness and fairness to present their cases before the interested public—and to permit that public to enter discussions which affect them so directly. Without this, a right higher than public disclosure or private self will be denied—the right to full public discourse.

Von Hoffman's points are: that in studying the sexual behavior of men in restrooms, Humphreys violated their rights to intimacy and privacy; that the homosexuals were and remain unaware of the true purpose of Humphreys' presence as a lookout; and that in the follow-up questionnaire the researcher further disguised himself and the true nature of his inquiry. For von Hoffman the point of principle is this: that although Humphreys' intent may have been above reproach and that in point of fact his purposes are antithetical to those of the police and other public officials, he nonetheless in his own way chipped away at the essential rights of individuals in conducting his investigations. Therefore, the ends, the goals, however noble and favorable to the plight of sexual deviants, do not justify the use of any means that further undermine personal liberties. Let us respond to these propositions as directly as possible.

Cops and Knowledge

First, the question of the invasion of privacy has several dimensions. We have already noted the public rather than the private nature of park restrooms. It further has to be appreciated that all participants in sexual activities in restrooms run the constant risk that they have among them people who have ulterior purposes. The vocabulary of motives is surely not limited or circumscribed by one man doing research but is as rich and as varied as the number of participants themselves. The fact that in this instance there was a scientific rather than a sexual or criminal "ulterior motive" does not necessarily make it more hideous or more subject to criticism, but perhaps less so.

Second, the question of disguising "the true nature" and purpose of this piece of research has to be put into some perspective. To begin with, let us assume that the research was worth doing in the first place. We know almost nothing about impersonal sex in public places, and the fact that we know so little has in no small way contributed to the fact that the cops feel that *they* know all that needs to be known about the matter. Who, then, is going to gather this countervailing knowledge? Von Hoffman implies that the research enterprise would be ethically pure if Humphreys were himself a full participant, like John Rechey. But to be able to conduct investigations of the type Humphreys performed requires a sociological imagination rare enough among his professional peers, much less homosexuals in public places. Moreover, to assume that the investigator must share all of his knowledge with those being investigated also assumes a common universe of discourse very rarely found in any kind of research, much less the kind involving sexual deviance. Furthermore, the conduct of Humphreys' follow-up inquiries had to be performed with tact and with skill precisely because he discovered that so many of the people in his survey were married men and family men. Indeed, one of the great merits of Humphreys' research is that it reveals clearly etched class, ethnic, political and occupational characteristics of sexual participants never before properly understood. Had he not conducted the follow-up interviews, we would once again be thrown back on simpleminded, psychological explanations that are truly more voyeuristic than analytic, or on the policeman's kind of knowledge. It is the sociological dimensions of sexuality in public places that make this a truly scientific breakthrough.

To take on the ethic of full disclosure at the point of follow-up interviews was impossible given the purposes of the research. If Humphreys had told his respondents that he knew they were tearoom participants, most of them would have cooperated. But in gaining their cooperation in this way he would have had to reveal that he knew of their behavior. This he could not responsibly do, because he could not control the potentially destructive impact of that knowledge. Folding the participants into a larger sample for a different survey allowed for the collection of the data without posing such a threat. And the purpose of the research was not, after all, destruction, as von Hoffman concedes. Therefore, the posture of Humphreys toward those interviewed must be viewed as humane and considerate.

But what von Hoffman is arguing is that this research ought not to have been done, that Humphreys should have laid aside his obligation to society as a sociologist and taken more seriously his obligation to society as a citizen. Von Hoffman maintains that the researcher's intentions—the pursuit of truth, the creation of countervailing knowledge, the demystification of shadowy areas of human experience—are immaterial. "Everybody who goes snooping around and spying on people can be said to have good motives," von Hoffman writes, going on to compare Humphreys' work with policemen armed with a "no-knock" statute.

This is offensive, but it is also stupid. We have called von Hoffman a moralizer, and his moralizing consists precisely in his imputing a moral equivalence to police action, under probably unconstitutional law, and the work of a scholar. Of course the road to hell is paved with good intentions, but good intentions sometimes lead to other places as well. The great achievement of Humphreys' research has been in laying bare the conditions of the tearoom trade, the social classes who engage in such activities and the appalling idiocy and brutality of society's (police) efforts to cope with the situation. Moreover, he has, relative to some of his professional colleagues, answered the question Which side are you on? with uncharacteristic candor, while at the same time he has conducted himself in the best tradition of professional sociology.

The only interesting issue raised by von Hoffman is one that he cannot, being a moralizer, do justice to. It is whether the work one does is good, and whether the good it does outweighs the bad. "No information," he writes, "is valuable enough to obtain by nipping away at personal liberty. . . ." It remains to be proven that Humphreys did in fact nip away at anyone's liberty; so far we have only von Hoffman's assertion that he did and Humphreys' assurance that he did not. But no amount of self-righteous dogmatizing can still the uneasy and troublesome thought that what we have here is not a conflict between nasty snoopers and the right to privacy, but a conflict between two goods: the right to privacy and the right to know.

What is required is a distinction between the responsibilities of social scientists to seek and to obtain greater knowledge and the responsibilities of the legal system to seek and obtain maximum security for the private rights of private citizens. Nothing is more insidious or dangerous than the overprofessionalization of a trade. But for social scientists to play at being lawyers, at settling what the law is only now beginning to give attention to, is clearly not a sound way of solving the problems raised.

Liberal Contradictions

It is certainly not that sociologists should deliberately violate any laws of the land, only that they should leave to the courtrooms and to the legislatures just what interpretation of these laws governing the protection of private citizens is to be made. Would the refusal of a family to disclose information to the Census Bureau on the grounds of the right to privacy take precedence over the United States government's right to knowledge in order to make budgetary allocations and legislation concerning these people? The really tough moral problem is that the idea of an inviolable right of privacy may move counter to the belief that society is obligated to secure the other rights and welfare of its citizenry. Indeed one might say that this is a key contradiction in the contemporary position of the liberal: he wants to protect the rights of private citizens, but at the same time he wants to develop a welfare system that could hardly function without at least some knowledge about these citizens. Von Hoffman's strident defense of the right to privacy is laudable; we are all behind him. What is inexcusable in someone of his intelligence is that he will not see that the issues he raises pose a moral dilemma that cannot be resolved in the abstract, only in the particular case. He may think that Humphreys' research is the moral equivalent of John Mitchell's FBI. We don't, and we have tried to explain why.

Several other minor points in the von Hoffman article require at least brief recollection. First, *Trans*-action has made no statement until this time on the ethics of the kind of research conducted by Laud Humphreys. Indeed, our editorial statements have always emphasized the right to privacy of the researcher over and against the wishes of established authority. To say that *Trans*-action has defended this piece in terms of "priority of motive" is an error of fact. The intent of *Trans*-action is to present the best available social science research, and we believe Humphreys' work admirably fits that description.

Public Rights and Private Agony

Finally, von Hoffman's gratuitous linkage of the "conservatives over at the Justice Department" and the "liberals over at the sociology department" makes for a pleasant balance of syntax, but it makes no sense in real life terms. The political ideology of Laud Humphreys is first of all not an issue. At no point in the article or outside the article is the question of the political preference of the researcher raised.

We would suggest that von Hoffman is the real "liberal" in this argument, for it is he who is assuming the correctness of the classical liberal argument for the supremacy of the private person over and against the public commonweal. This assumption makes it appear that he is willing to suffer the consequences of the abuse of homosexuals by blackmailers, policemen or would-be participants, but that he is not willing to suffer the consequences of a research design or to try to change the situation by a factual understanding of the social sources of these problems.

Laud Humphreys has gone beyond the existing literature in sexual behavior and has proven once again, if indeed proof were ever needed, that ethnographic research is a powerful tool for social understanding and policymaking. And these are the criteria by which the research should finally be evaluated professionally. If the nonprofessional has other measurements of this type of research, let him present these objections in legal brief and do so explicitly. No such attempt to intimidate Humphreys for wrongdoing in any legal sense has been made, and none is forthcoming. The only indictment seems to be among those who are less concerned with the right to know than they are with the sublime desire to remain in ignorance. In other words, the issue is not liberalism vs. conservatism or privacy vs. publicity, but much more simply and to the point, the right of scientists to conduct their work as against the right of journalists to defend social mystery and private agony.

5 *Charles C. Moskos, Jr.*

Research in the "Third World"

Nowadays, American social scientists are making more and more studies of political development, economic growth, and social modernization in foreign countries—especially in those of the "third world" (roughly, Asia, Africa, and Latin America). But as these social scientists range further and further afield, they seem to encounter increasing resistance in the third world from academicians, intellectuals, and political figures. The Americans protest: "We are not spies. We don't have to turn to anyone for permission to publish what we learn here." Those who can, add: "We are not taking any undercover government money." They nonetheless find themselves treated like minions of Project Camelot or the C.I.A., and wonder why.

Their protestations of innocence, however, ignore the larger question. Élites in the third world don't like spies, to be sure, but neither do they feel happy about the prevailing assumptions of American social science.

In light of this hostility from the third world, it is with a sense of *déja vu* that we reread a critique of American social science that sociologist C. Wright Mills made a quarter-century ago. Mills, then in his 20s, identified a number of these assumptions, assumptions that we now see being recapitulated abroad. One of them: conceiving of society as a *cultural* rather than a structural system. And in today's studies of developing nations, we find a strong parallel emphasis on value orientations and related psychological predispositions. A second assumption: that urbanization is linked with undesirable consequences. The third-world students of today write about the allegedly harmful effects that rapid social change has on social integration and personality. Still a third assumption: that problems should be solved through individual action, rather than through collective action for structural change. Now, in the third world "collective action for structural change" really means "revolution." American social scientists of today would much rather study factors fostering stability.

This last point has been made by the German sociologist Ralf Dahrendorf. Indeed, he has noted several "missing traits" in American social-science studies: not just the subject of revolution, but also the subjects of class and history. These subjects are almost central to any serious study of developing countries, but in most of the third-world literature they are ignored. While revolutions break out, Americans inquire into the requisites for social stability; while the social bases of power are changed beyond recognition, Americans talk of "psychological determinants" and "problems of personal identity"; and while the rich nations draw further and further apart from the poor nations, the consequences of international inequality are discussed in a whisper, if at all.

In fact, the American social scientist's lack of concern with social stratification around the world is perhaps his most characteristic blind spot. Americans consistently fail to explore the consequences of the combination of poverty in the third world, and wealth in the other two worlds (capitalist and communist). To them, discussions of neocolonialism, economic exploitation, and military imperialism seem to be in bad taste.

Even the self-consciously "comparative" studies that have been made almost always have been *horizontal*—comparing nations at the same "stage of development." *Vertical* comparisons—explaining how events in industrialized countries and in the third world are intermeshed—would seem to be mandatory, but when such studies do appear they are typically written by foreign social scientists, or by journalists, ideologues, and others on the periphery of social science in the U.S.

A case in point: the increasing autonomy of the socialist countries in Eastern Europe during the 1960s was generally *not* anticipated in the studies that American scholars made in the 1950s. These scholars had gone to great lengths to document the inviolable economic and political ties these countries had to the Soviet Union. Their gigantic error in the 1950s, in overstressing the Kremlin's control over Eastern Europe, has an obverse repetition in the 1960s—because American scholars are playing down the interlocking relationships between the Western countries and the third world.

If we don't have all this information, how can we trust our assertions about the nature of the underdeveloped world? What we must do is to explicitly analyze the role of the industrialized countries, particularly the United States, as one of the determinants of social change in the third world. We must confront the likelihood that the interests of the third world may not be compatible with the present foreign policy of the United States. Moreover, the research we must have—from a genuinely social-scientific viewpoint—need not be the preserve of the Americans. Why should it be so difficult to conceive of a group of Latin American sociologists studying the American military-industrial complex? Or to conceive of African economists looking at patterns of American investments overseas? Or to conceive of Asian political scientists examining the decision-making process in the growth of U.S. military commitments overseas?

In yet another way, American social science is out of balance. I am referring to the very giganticism in the scale of American social science itself. Although only a small fraction of American social-science research is concentrated in the third world, that fraction is still sufficient in many areas to completely overshadow locally generated scholarship. Even in those countries where the indigenous social-science community can counterbalance visiting Americans, these local viewpoints do not have wide currency in academic circles within this country.

At the very least, we must begin to think of changes in the procedure of overseas research that will eliminate some of these errors—such as establishing agencies to sponsor international research; collaborative efforts with local colleagues; domestic dissemination of third-world evaluations of American social science; and the tithing of American scholars going overseas to subsidize third-world social science.

To put it baldly, resistance to American social scientists doing work in the third world will disappear *not* in the never-never when there are no more spies, but when the adjective "American" no longer denotes a social science that ignores what is going on in favor of what it is interested in. Social science is a universal endeavor, and we are part of it. We must acknowledge this universality with an ongoing appraisal of our research strategies and theoretical orientations—and our underlying assumptions. For we must realize that we are also part of another universal: a concern for human dignity, which is the responsibility of all men.

Photos by Joan Dufault

Text by Florence Chanock Cohen

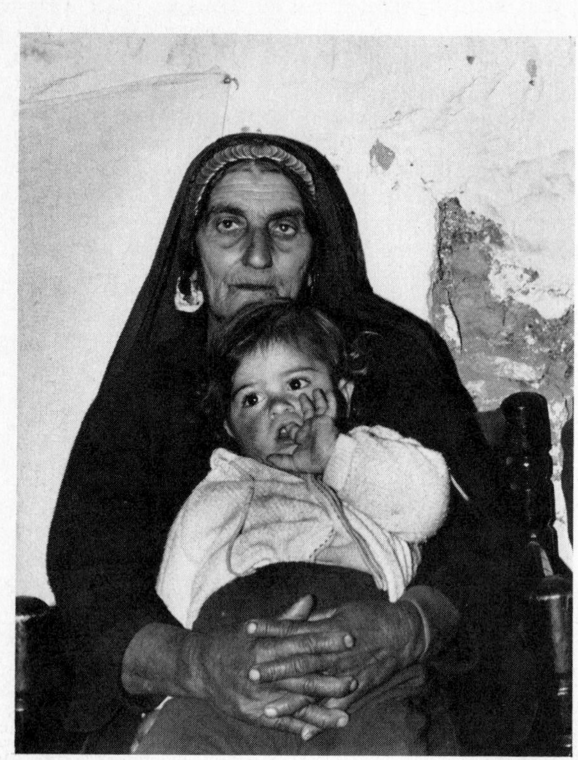

The Many Faces of the Middle East

The one factor common to Israelis and Arabs is that they are victims of history who have been displaced geographically, morally or psychologically at one time or anther. In the Middle East, perhaps for the first time in history, hypocrisy must be replaced with wisdom if the victims are not to become despots. Therefore, one who attempts to mediate wisely between the Arabs and Israelis must empathize with the Palestinian's psychological humiliation and material loss. He must also be acutely conscious of Israel's experience and her justified dread of foul play, treachery and defenselessness.

The mediator in the Middle East has a much more difficult task than that of King Solomon. Today there are no "true mothers" of that ancient land, but there is a lesson, perhaps even a warning, in Solomon's parable. Solomon, the powerful and prestigious mediator, was able to appreciate both legality and human truth; he could differentiate between revenge and "right." He understood that cries for justice had to be heard, but that they should not be confused with the rattles for death.

6 *Herbert C. Kelman*

Deception in Social Research

In order to advance the understanding of human behavior, psychologists regularly use human beings as subjects in a wide variety of experiments. In many of these experiments, the subject is kept in the dark or misinformed about the true purpose of the experiment. Sometimes the deception exposes him to embarrassing, disturbing, or potentially harmful experiences that he had not bargained for.

There is generally a good reason for the use of deception. Many of the phenomena that the psychologist wishes to study would be altered if the subject knew the purpose of the experiment—if he knew, for example, what psychological processes the experimenter is trying to activate and what reactions he is hoping to observe. And yet the use of deception, even when it is done for a scientifically valid reason, poses ethical questions.

These questions are fairly obvious when the deception has potentially harmful consequences for the subject; they are more subtle, but nonetheless important, even in experiments where there is little danger of harmful effects. The issue is: How can we strike a proper balance between the interests of science and the considerate treatment of people who make themselves available as the raw material of research?

The problem of deception has taken on increasingly serious proportions in recent years as its use has become almost a standard feature in psychological experiments. Deception has been turned into a game, often played with great skill and virtuosity. A considerable amount of creativity and ingenuity by social psychologists is given to the development of increasingly elaborate deception situations.

For example, the potentially harmful effects of deception are dramatized in some recent studies of obedience. One volunteer was "smiling and confident" when he entered the laboratory. "Within 20 minutes," the experimenter reported, "he was reduced to a twitching, stuttering wreck, who was rapidly approaching a point of nervous collapse." What caused him to become a "wreck" was an experiment in which subjects were led to believe that they were participating in a learning study. They were instructed to administer increasingly severe shocks to another person, who after a while began to protest vehemently. In fact, of course, the "victim" was an accomplice of the experimenter and did not receive any real shocks. But in some cases, the experimenter instructed the subject to continue to "shock" the "victim" up to the maximum level, which the subject believed to be extremely painful when the victim writhed in pain and pounded his head against the wall.

Not surprisingly, both obedient and defiant (those who refused to administer shocks) subjects exhibited a great deal of stress. And there is surely good reason to believe that at least some of the obedient subjects came away from this experience with lowered self-esteem, realizing that they yielded to authority to the point of inflicting extreme pain on a fellow human being. The fact that, in the experimenter's words, they had "an opportunity to learn something of importance about themselves, and more generally, about the conditions of human action" is beside the point.

If this were a lesson *from life,* it would constitute an instructive confrontation and provide a valuable insight. But do researchers, for purposes of experimentation, have the right to provide such potentially disturbing insights to subjects who do not know that this is what they volunteered for?

And yet, this same research illustrates the complexity of the issues raised by the use of deception. These studies of obedience have produced significant and challenging findings which have posed some basic questions about human behavior and social life. Without deception, this line of investigation could probably not have been pursued.

A GENERATION OF DECEIVERS

It is easy to view the situation with alarm, but it is much more difficult to formulate an unambiguous position on this problem. As a working experimental social psychologist, I know that there are good reasons for using deception in many experiments. There are many significant problems, like the study of obedience, that probably cannot be investigated without the use of deception—at least, given the present level of development of our experimental techniques. Thus, researchers are always confronted with a conflict of values. If they regard the acquisition of scientific knowledge about human behavior as a positive value, and if an experiment using deception constitutes a significant contribution to such knowledge which could not be achieved by other means, then it is difficult to rule out the experiment unequivocally. The question is not simply whether or not to use deception, but whether the amount and type of deception are justified by the significance of the study and the unavailability of alternative procedures.

What concerns me most, then, is not so much that deception is used, but that it is used without question. I sometimes feel that a whole generation of psychologists now in training will not know there is any other way of doing experiments. Too often deception is used, not as a last resort, but as a matter of course. The attitude seems to be: If you can deceive, why tell the truth?

What are some of the major problems posed by the use of this dangerously doubled-edged tool? There are three areas to consider:

- the ethical implications;
- the real effectiveness of deception;
- the implications for the future of psycho-social research in our society.

ETHICAL IMPLICATIONS. Ethical problems of a rather obvious nature arise in those experiments in which deception has potentially harmful consequences for the subject. For example, a brilliant experiment was recently designed to observe the effects of threat on group solidarity and the need for strong leadership. In this study (one of the very rare examples of an experiment conducted in a natural setting) independent food merchants in a number of Dutch towns were brought together for group meetings and informed that a large organization would soon open a chain of supermarkets in the Netherlands. In a "high threat" condition, the subjects were told that their towns would probably be selected as sites for such markets, which would cause a considerable drop in their business. On the advice of the executives of the shopkeepers' organizations who had helped to arrange the group meetings, the investigators never revealed, even after the experiment was over, that the supermarket threat was a fiction.

I have been worried about those Dutch merchants ever since I first heard about this study. Did some of them go out of business in anticipation of the heavy competition? Do some of them have an anxiety reaction every time they see a bulldozer? Chances are that they soon forgot about this threat (unless, of course, supermarkets actually did move into town) and that it became just one of the many little moments of anxiety that occur in every shopkeeper's life. But do investigators have the right to add to life's little anxieties and to risk the possibility of more extensive anxiety purely for the purposes of such experiments?

Two other recent studies provide further example of potentially harmful effects arising from the use of deception. In one set of studies, male college students were led to believe that they had been homosexually aroused by photographs of men. In the other study, subjects of both sexes were given disturbing information about their levels of masculinity or femininity, presumably based on an elaborate series of psychological tests they had taken. In all of these studies, the deception was explained to the subjects at the end of the experiment. One wonders, however, whether this explanation removes the possibility of harmful effects. For many persons in this age group, sexual identity is a live and sensitive issue, and the self-doubts generated by this laboratory experience could linger.

What about the less obvious cases, in which there is little danger of harmful effects? Serious ethical issues are also raised by such deception per se, and the kind of use of human beings that it implies. In other inter-human relationships, most psychologists would never think of doing the things that they do to their subjects—exposing them to lies and tricks, deliberately misleading them, and making promises or giving assurances that they intend to disregard. They would view such behavior as a violation of the respect to which all fellow humans are entitled. Yet they seem to forget that the experimenter-subject relationship—whatever else it is—is a *real* inter-human relationship, in which the experimenter has a responsibility towards the subject as another human being whose dignity he must respect. The difference between the experimenter's behavior in everyday life and his behavior in the laboratory is so marked that one wonders why there has been so little concern with this problem.

The broader ethical problem of the very use of deception becomes even more important when we view it in the present-day historical context. We are living in an age of mass societies, in which the transformation of man into an object, to be manipulated at will, occurs on a mass scale, in a systematic way, and under the aegis of specialized institutions deliberately assigned to this task. In institutionalizing the use of deception in psychological experiments we are contributing to a historical trend that threatens the values most of us cherish.

METHODOLOGICAL IMPLICATIONS. I have increasing doubts about the effectiveness of deception as a method for social research.

A basic assumption in the use of deception is that a subject's awareness of what the experimenter is really trying to find out would affect the subject's behavior in such a way that the experimenter could not draw valid conclusions from it. For example, if the experimenter is interested in studying the effects of failure on conformity, he must create a situation in which subjects actually feel that they have failed, and in which they can be kept unaware of his interest in observing conformity. In short, it is important to keep the subjects naive about the purposes of the experiment so that they can respond spontaneously.

How long, however, will it be possible to find naive subjects? Among college students it is already very difficult. They may not know the exact purposes of the particular experiment in which they are participating, but many of them know that it is *not* what the experimenter says it is. As one subject pithily put it, "Psychologists always lie!"

There are, of course, other sources of human subjects that have not been tapped, but even here it is only a matter of time until word about psychological experiments gets around and sophistication increases. Whether or not a subject knows the true purpose of the experiment, if he does not believe what the experimenter tells him, then he is likely to make an effort to figure out the purpose of the experiment and to act accordingly. This may lead him to do what he thinks the experimenter wants him to do. Conversely, if he resents the experimenter's attempt to deceive him, he may try to throw a monkey wrench into the works. Whichever course the subject uses, however, he is operating in terms of his own conception of the nature of the situation, rather than in terms of the conception that the experimenter is trying to induce. In short, the experimenter can no longer assume that the conditions that he is trying to create are the ones that actually define the situation for the subject. Thus, the use of deception, while it is designed to give the experimenter control over the subject's perceptions and motivations, may actually produce an unspecifiable mixture of intended and unintended stimuli that make it difficult to know just what the subject is responding to. Therefore, is there any future in the use of deception?

IMPLICATIONS FOR THE FUTURE. My third main concern about the use of deception is that, from a long-range point of view, there is obviously something self-defeating about it. As experiments of this kind continue, potential subjects become more and more sophisticated, and scientists become less and less able to meet the conditions that their experimental procedures require. Moreover, potential subjects become increasingly distrustful, and future relations between subjects and experimenters upon which successful research depends are likely to be undermined. Thus, we are confronted with the anomalous circumstance that, the more this research is carried on, the more difficult and questionable it becomes.

The use of deception also involves a contradiction between experimental procedures and the long-range aims of scientists and teachers. In order to be able to carry out experiments, they are concerned with maintaining the naiveté of the population from which they draw subjects. This perfectly understandable desire to keep procedures secret go counter to the traditional desire of the scientist and teacher to inform and enlighten the public. For the long run, it even suggests the possible emergence of a special class, in possession of secret knowledge—a possibility that is clearly antagonistic to the principle of open communication to which scientists and intellectuals are so fervently committed.

ENRICHMENT THROUGH EXPERIMENT

If my concerns about the use of deception are justified—and I think that they are—what are some of the ways they can be dealt with? I would like to suggest two basic remedies:

- exploring ways of counteracting and minimizing the negative efforts of deception;
- giving careful attention to the development of new experimental techniques that can dispense with the use of deception altogether.

In those experiments in which deception could have harmful effects, there is an obvious requirement to build protections into every phase of the process. Subjects must be selected in a way that will exclude individuals who are especially vulnerable; the potentially harmful manipulation (such as the induction of stress) must be kept at a moderate level of intensity; the experimenter must be sensitive to danger signals in the reactions of his subjects and be prepared to deal with crises when they arise; and, at the conclusion of the session, the experimenter must take time, not only to reassure the subject, but also to help him work through his feelings about the experience to whatever degree may be required.

In general, a good principle to follow is that a subject ought not to leave the laboratory with greater anxiety or lower self-esteem than he came with. I would go beyond it to argue that the subject should in some positive way be enriched by the experience—he should come away from it with the feeling that he has learned something, understood something, or grown in some way. And this adds special importance to the kind of feedback—about what was really being done—that is given to the subject at the end of the experimental session.

This post-experimental feedback is also the primary way of counteracting negative effects in those experiments in which the issue is deception as such, rather than possible threats to the subject's well-being. If the subject is deceived, then he must be given a full and detailed explanation of what has been done and of the reasons for doing it. It is not enough to give the subject perfunctory feedback. These explanations should be meaningful and instructive for the subject and helpful in rebuilding his relationship with the experimenter. I feel very strongly that, to accomplish these purposes, the experimenter must keep the feedback itself inviolate and under no circumstance give the subject false feedback, or pretend to be giving him feedback while in fact introducing another experimental manipulation.

THE CASE FOR COOPERATION

My second suggestion is that scientists invest some of the creativity and ingenuity now being devoted to the construction of elaborate deceptions to the search for alternative experimental techniques that do not rely on the use of deception. They would be based on the principle of eliciting the subject's positive motivations to contribute to the experimental enterprise. They would draw on the subject's active participation and involvement in the proceedings and encourage him to cooperate in making the experiment a success by conscientiously taking the roles and carrying out the tasks that the experimenter assigns to him. In short, the kind of techniques I have in mind would be designed to involve the subject as an active participant in a joint effort with the experimenter.

Perhaps the most promising sources of alternative experimental approaches are procedures using some sort of role-playing—that is, procedures in which the experimenter asks the subject to act *as though* he were in a certain situation rather than actually creating that situation experimentally as a "real" one. I have been impressed, for example, with the role-playing that I have observed in the Inter-Nation Simulation, a laboratory procedure in which the subjects take the roles of decision-makers of various nations. This situation seems to create a high level of emotional involvement and to elicit motivations that have a real-life quality to them.

In general, the results of role-playing experiments have been very encouraging. Despite the fact that they know it is all make-believe, subjects usually react realistically to the experimental stimuli, and these reactions follow an orderly pattern.

There are other types of procedure, in addition to role-playing, that are worth exploring. For example, it may be possible to conduct more experiments in a natural non-laboratory setting in which, with the full cooperation of the subjects, specific experimental variations are introduced. The advantages of dealing with motivations at a real-life level of intensity might well outweigh the disadvantages of subjects' knowing the general purpose of the experiment. A much simpler alterative, also worth exploring, would be for experimenters to inform the subjects at the beginning of a laboratory experiment that they will not receive full information about what is going on, but ask them to suspend judgment until the experiment is over.

Whatever alternative approaches are tried, there is no doubt that they will have their own problems and complexities. Procedures effective for some purposes may be quite ineffective for others, and it may well turn out that for certain kinds of problems there is no adequate substitute for the use of deception. But there *are* alternative procedures that, for many purposes, may be as effective or even more effective than procedures built on deception.

These approaches often involve a radically changed set of assumptions about the role of the subject in the experiment: *the subject's motivation to cooperate is utilized rather than by-passed.* These new procedures may even call for increasing the sophistication of potential subjects, rather than maintaining their naiveté.

SUGGESTED READINGS

"The Rights of the Subject in Social Research: An Analysis in Terms of Relative Power and Legitimacy" by H. C. Kelman in *American Psychologist*, 27, 1972, pp. 989–1016.

PART TWO

The Microlevels of Sociology

There has always been a temptation to conceptualize self and society dualistically. A major contribution of sociology to the thoughtways of sophisticated analysts of the social realm has been to mitigate such dualistic consideration of the individual and society. The realization that the individual and the society constitute the warp and the woof of a *single* social fabric permits the central focus of sociology to emerge: interaction. Sociological thinking allows the analytic distinction of individuals and societies (or groups), but it is always informed by the knowledge that such thinking must ultimately lead to the reunification of self and society. Individuals and societies are the products of the process of interaction itself.

The basic construction of reality is atomic, individual; yet we recognize emergence. New units are created out of the combination of preexisting ones. Physical–chemical elements combine to constitute cells, cells combine to constitute organs, organs combine to constitute people. But the process does not stop at this point. People combine to constitute collectivities—groups, institutions, societies. The only thing that is "really real" about us is the basic physical elements our bodies are made of. We know, however, that those elements are constantly being sloughed off; we are literally not the same people we were a short time ago. It is the emergent reality of us, our selves, that is most real. The philosophical paradox thus created can be resolved only one way sociologically: by searching for patterned interaction as the real stuff of social reality. These patterns, some relatively stable, some in the process of formation, some passing out of existence, become the focus of our attention.

The problem with dualistic modes of analysis is the complexity of social reality. Not only is the social realm penetrated by other realms, e.g., the atomic fact that we are physical animals who must one day die, but even the social realm itself is too complex for any kind of monocausal explanation (at least, no such explanation has yet been developed). It is, therefore, necessary to make do with partial truths. This is not the insurmountable obstacle that it might seem. The history of science is littered with the wreckage of grand theories about the physical universe. Salvaged from these wrecks are bits and pieces of verified knowledge recombined in other theories that will also be supplanted by the painstaking confirmation process.

The logic of social inquiry, no less than that of science itself, presses us to search out manifestations of the social, to describe them with the greatest care and accuracy, and to recombine new knowledge with old in a creative manner. This recombination leads to the development of new theory, which, in turn, demands the reanalysis of all that we know. In order to carry out this task, it becomes necessary to cut through the complexity of the "real" world by making analytic distinctions not necessarily found in the real world. These simplifying distinctions become seductive flames, but we must resist the temptation of being drawn into them. When we speak of individuals at some level of our consciousness, we must realize that the individual is penetrated by society and vice versa.

Social psychology represents a focus in sociology where interaction occupies center stage. It should be clear from our previous discussion, however, that this central focus is always informed by the knowledge that individual development is penetrated by the social. This penetration occurs through the process of learning to be human, through socialization. The human infant is very like the young of other species at birth; that is, the infant is a helpless creature possessing only the genetic *potential* for development into a human being. (In fact, anthropologists tell us that the human infant is the most helpless of all animals and yet has the greatest potential—at the cost of a minimum of genetically based "instinct.") This potential becomes actualized through learning to be human from others who have become more or less human. The sheer volume of things to be learned is staggering—what is nourishing, what is dangerous, the meaning of gestures, formal language and the symbol systems of the groups to which the infant belongs (at first the family) and will belong, from peer groups to multinational corporations.

This part of *Sociological Realities II* addresses itself to what we have labeled microsociology. The emphasis is on the socialization process. The emphasis is also on the small social worlds of which we all become part. As this volume unfolds we shall gradually shift our attention toward larger and larger patterns of interaction, and our focus will become more global. For now, let us look at how the socialization process operates to weld the person-group into a single analyzable unit. (It should be noted that the individual–society paradox does not disappear; far from it. The question is: How much energy is directed toward socialization, and how unlikely is it that individuals do not become part of some larger pattern of interaction?)

Section III

Individuals

Social researchers who conduct experiments in laboratories attempt to approach the model of natural science most directly; i.e., they attempt to control as many extraneous variables as possible in order to assess the impact of experimental variables as directly as possible. Although fraught with dangers (see the article by Kelman in Part One, Section II), this approach yields interesting hypotheses about what happens in the walk-around world. In "Conformity and Commitment," Kiesler reports on a project that extends a tradition in small-group research that has given us much insight into the nature of commitment and its pervasive influence in the daily affairs of people. Rejecting the extreme views that people either become committed to a group because of some "personality trait" (that is, some people are "born conformers") or conform to group values and norms solely as a tactic, Kiesler suggests that the true nature of conformity is somewhere between these extremes, but closer to the latter. Conformity as a tactic (compliance) is, in part, a function of commitment. A person committed (that is, stuck in some group) will change his or her opinion to conform as much as those who are attracted, i.e., given to believe that they are well liked in the group.

Inducing commitment in a laboratory under controlled conditions and for a relatively short time is quite different than the longer-lasting levels of commitment required for carrying out prescribed roles in the larger society. Morris, in "Psychological Miscarriage: An End to Mother Love," makes us aware of an important human problem: mothers' rejection of their infants. After demonstrating what a large-scale problem this is, Morris goes on to discuss the dehumanizing aspects of modern delivery room procedures and their possible contribution to the problem of rejection. Her hypotheses about the need for prompt presentation of infants to their mothers and the necessity of "claiming rituals" indicate how social structural arrangements may affect the individual socialization of both mother and child.

In "Why Men Fight," Moskos provides an example of how sociological analysis can shed light on how social organization penetrates the adult socialization process. The system of rotation introduced by the U.S. Armed Services in Vietnam had the effect, according to Moskos, of individualizing and privatizing the war for American soldiers. By actually living wtih combat units during two different periods in Vietnam, Professor Moskos discovered that a series of four patterned stages occurred during the twelve-month rotation. The attitude toward fighting that grew out of this system made the soldier in Vietnam different from his counterpart in either World War II or the Korean War. It was the structure itself, Moskos argues, that made a major difference. He illustrates an important part of the sociological enterprise by his researches in Vietnam, namely, how new conditions modify existing theory. We learn that the military sociologists who did research during other wars did not deal with the same set of conditions. The war in Vietnam created a "natural social science experiment" in which we can see the important impact of changing social organizational variables on individual motivation.

Along with other "human" disciplines, sociology searches for metaphor, for similes, for analogies. Back, in "The Way of Love and Trust: The Sensitivity/Encounter Movement," finds an analogy for the modern sensitivity/encounter movement in the ancient religious pilgrimage. The parallel, Back informs us, is in the conversion experience itself, rejecting the older religious values in favor of a "scientific" justification. Echoing a theme sounded in other readings in this section, Back suggests that the frantic search for meaning in the encounter group reflects individualism, privatization and general societal disturbance. The emphasis of the movement on "the here and now" and on "gut learning" rejects intellectualism, the process of abstraction, as well as history, biography and symbolism. It is the group experience itself that is critical. Under the mantle of science, science itself is rejected in favor of intensive, short-run experience. The movement embraces the cult of the instant and means over ends. Unlike religious and social ritual, the ritual of the encounter movement is concrete and does not represent something else. It uses the procedures and language of science in a mythological sense.

In the delivery room of a big-city hospital, during a fire fight, in a jungle in Southeast Asia and during a weekend encounter session, learning goes on. Larger societal and suprasocietal trends penetrate the experience of everyday life. Individual behavior is shaped and molded by social forces. People, however, are not sheep. People not only react but also act on the larger social networks in which they find themselves. Acting human beings use a "vocabulary of motives," a concept developed by C. Wright Mills, to justify their behavior. People construct rationales, sometimes quite elaborate, which they then employ to explain the "why" of their social activities. In "The Respectable Criminal," Cressey suggests the conditions under which white-collar crime is likely to occur: (1) when someone has the feeling that a personal financial problem is unsharable; (2) when he has the opportunity to solve the problem in secret by violating a position of financial trust; and (3) when he can find a formula that describes the act of embezzling in words that do not conflict with the image of oneself as a trusted person. Cressey suggests that the third condition is most important and is a result of the fact that we usually do not think of cheating on income tax and padding insurance claims in the same way that we think of stealing hubcaps or holding up liquor stores. Although millions of dollars may be "ripped off" by white-collar criminals, the socially arrived at definition of their crime offers a shield of respectability not available to the lower-class criminal.

There is an old Roman proverb that says that "two people who are doing the same thing are not doing the same thing." Two employees may be stealing the same amount from a factory, but as Cressey has demonstrated, if one is an assembly line worker and the other is in the front office, their crimes are likely to be viewed quite differently. One mission of sociology is to point out parallels in behavior where they might be unexpected, for example, likenesses in the socialization process of new recruits into a military academy and into a convent of cloistered nuns. A twin aim of the discipline is to find likenesses *and* to differentiate behaviors that may appear similar at first. In "Consciousness, Power and Drug Effects," Becker admirably demonstrates this twofold nature of the discipline by discussing parallels and differences in the medical and nonmedical uses of drugs. He points out the fact that drugs have different effects on different people. One element that has an important bearing on drug effects is the knowledge users have about drugs. Defining knowledge as ideas that actors believe have been tested against experience, Becker discusses dosage, main and side effects and the process of "testing" that goes on in medical and nonmedical drug cultures. He finds the major factor affecting knowledge about "research and communication" to be that of user control (nonmedical) versus control by the user's agent (medical) in drug taking.

The final reading of Section III provides yet another example of how the larger social structure (in this case national policy) influences individual behavior (in this case drinking patterns). Christie, in "The Scandinavian Hangover," finds that "a strict system of legal and institutional control of accessibility to alcohol seems related to low alcohol consumption—but also to a high degree of public nuisance." Decision makers in a society cause great changes in people's lives. Christie shows how, by changing the definition of alcoholics, for example, from "criminals" to "ill persons," the social control of alcoholics shifts from the criminal justice system to the medical system. In this reading, as in the others in this section, the implicit major theme has to do with the coping behavior of individuals caught up in systems of control and socialization, and how various "definitions of the situation" (to use W. I. Thomas' felicitous phrase) grow out of the self–society dialectic.

1 *Charles A. Kiesler*

Conformity and Commitment

Should I go along with the group?

We have all confronted this question, consciously or not, in one form or another at some time in our multiple relationships with groups at work, in school, in social life, at play, even in the bosom of the family. Will we conform to go along with what others think is right?

People often talk of conformity in the abstract—and like sin in the abstract, they are usually against it. But men face *concrete* situations and decisions every day, often under considerable pressure. What do they do? When will a man change his attitudes and behavior to adjust? To what extent will he change them? What does conformity in this context actually mean? The word conformity implies one of three views of adaptive behavior:

- The first view (the most popular) holds that conformity is an enduring personality characteristic—that organization men are essentially born, not made, so their seduction to conformity comes without strain.
- The second view holds that conformist behavior is a kind of tactic—a superficial "going along with the crowd" because of necessity or temporary advantage—without essential change of private opinion.
- The third is something of a middle ground, although closer to the second. It holds that a conforming individual may actually come to change his private as well as his public opinions and attitudes as a result of continued disagreement with the group; and that this change will last.

In the first view, the natural conformer will try to be like others in most things, finding his satisfactions and support not in personal uniqueness or integrity but in a group identification. There is a germ of truth in this belief. People do wish to be "correct" and in agreement. To some extent we all look to others to validate our opinions. We tend to pick up our cues on proper behavior and personal worth from others. This influence is pervasive and important. After all, the great majority of people conform in rules and customs or our civilization would be impossible.

However, there is little evidence that mankind tends to polarize around two distinct breeds, conformist and nonconformist. People vary in their dependence on, or independence of, the opinions and attitudes of others. They vary in their internal needs and in their perceptions. Thus conformity depends not only on personality and experience, but also on how we analyze our situations.

The second and third views shift emphasis from personality to the situation and how it is perceived.

The second type of conformer goes along with the crowd overtly—while keeping his real disagreement private from the group in question. He is not convinced—he merely pretends he is, whether for convenience or to serve some higher goal. For instance, if a subject in an experiment is told that he and the group would be given $50 if they agreed on some issue, agreement will usually come soon enough.

Does She or Doesn't She?

This second view of conformity is called *compliance.* Its forms and rationalizations are many. People may want to be tactful and considerate, and so pretend to believe things they do not; they may want to get something unpleasant over with as soon as possible; they may be animated by greed or malice; or, as with Galileo disavowing belief in the Copernican theory before church authorities (while, legend has it, muttering to himself, "It's true all the same"), they may simply consider that a certain amount of lip service is a necessary price for peace and the chance to go one's own way in most things. A complier, among friends, may express very different opinions from those he expresses before the group with which he complies.

There has been much research on compliance, most notably that of Solomon Asch and his associates. In Asch's experiments subjects were shown two lines and asked which was longer. When alone, they almost never made a mistake. But in the rigged company of others who insisted that the shorter was longer, one-third went along. Presumably they still believed their eyes, and only their public, but not their private, opinions conformed.

The third view, a logical next step after compliance, has most concerned my students and myself in the last several years. It states that not only the overt opinion, but the private one as well, can be changed as a result of disagreement. Certain consequences follow that would not follow from compliance alone and that do not depend on the presence of the group. If a person changes his opinion, his behavior and attitudes will be changed whether the group is around or not. And this change should last.

Of course, people do not change their opinions easily. They must be motivated to do it. Research has shown that one important motivation is approval—if someone feels that others generally agree with him and find him attractive, he is likely to adjust his opinions to theirs on some issue.

But prior research did not prepare us for a finding in our own work that is more important to us. Our experiments have shown that *commitment*—in this case the expectation by a person that he must continue working and associating with a particular group—is also a major factor in opinion change and conformity to that group's standards. (Elsewhere J. Sakumura and I have defined commitment as "a pledging or binding of the individual to behavorial acts." This is a perfectly reasonable, if somewhat limited, view of commitment, and could include more subjective meanings, such as dedication or resolve. We have evidence that commitment is not, in and of itself, a motivation to change or resistance to change; but the *effect* of commitment is to make particular cognitions, or perceptions, more resistant to change.)

Let us briefly review the complicated experimental procedure that led to this outcome.

The subjects, all volunteers, were told that they would be assigned to discussion groups designed to test how strangers can work together for common goals. Each was told he had to return for four successive one-hour sessions. However, some were told they would continue with the same groups for all sessions (were, in effect, committed to them) while others were told they would be switched later to different groups and had no anticipation of working with the same people all the time.

After a session each privately gave his "first impressions" of the others. He also discussed and ranked various objects by his preferences, including some modern paintings. Each subject was then given bogus information about how others rated him ("Perhaps you would like to see what others thought of you. . . .").

Thus some are told that others find them very attractive, average, or unattractive. All subjects are told that the others disagree with their rankings of the objects. Then each is asked to rerank the objects—" . . . just for the institute; the group will never see them."

Note that every relevant variable is manipulated: the anticipation of continuing with the group; the extent of disagreement; how attractive the group finds each one. The individuals were completely taken in, very serious about cooperating, and unaware that they were being manipulated. (After the experiment the subjects were informed of its purpose, and the manipulation was explained. We found them intrigued, interested, and not offended.)

Under such controlled and cooperative circumstances we could be precise about what factors produced our results and confident that the results could be reliably applied to others. Our studies also demonstrated that:

—the less others like us, the less we like them;

—the less we like them, the less they affect our opinions.

The more we impressed upon a subject that the group didn't like him, the more he indicated that he didn't like them either, and the less he changed his opinion to conform with what we told him theirs was. This much was predictable from other work. However, we found an important exception created by the factor of *commitment.* Results were not the same in those cases when the person was committed to continue associating with the same group.

A committed person—like the noncommitted—generally modified his own opinions when he felt there was a high expression of attraction from the others. They both also modified them, though somewhat less, when the attraction was moderate. *But at the extreme—when least attracted—the committed person (but not the uncommitted) changed his opinions almost as much as the highly attracted did!*

This fascinating finding is not easily accounted for in current psychological theory. The subject does not like the group; they apparently do not like him; yet they have large influence on him. It is passive influence—they do not overtly try to influence him at all, yet they do. Only the individual knows that he disagrees; the group, presumably, does not know he disagrees and would never know unless he brought it up himself. It is a safe position for him to be in, to disagree as much as he pleases privately without external consequence. Yet his opinion changes to meet what he has been told theirs is.

But this is true only if he must continue with the group.

A NOTE ON THE STUDY

This article represents the culmination of a series of studies on consistency, conformity, and commitment. However, it deals primarily with two recent studies.

The first of these, conducted by myself and Lee H. Corbin in 1965, used 180 volunteers, sorted into six-man discussion groups as part of the requirements of an introductory psychology course. Subjects did not know each other personally. They were told of interest by the (fictitious) American Institute for Small Group Research in how strangers worked out certain tasks. They were supposed to rate 10 abstract paintings which, they were told, had previously been rated by experts; theoretically, the individuals and group that came closest to the experts would win cash prizes. Half were made to feel that they would continue with the same group through four sessions; the other half were made to understand that the composition of their groups could and might change and that in time each would have some choice about who would be included in his final group analysis. Half, therefore, felt they would be continuing on with the others, with the problems in adjustment and conformity that this might entail; and the other half should, theoretically, have felt more free of this continuing social pressure.

The second major study, conducted by myself, Mark Zanna, and James De Salvo at Yale and published in 1966, was quite similar in design and procedure. The subjects, however, were 198 high school boys who volunteered to take part in five- and six-man discussion groups. They had been recruited from newspaper advertisements and record shops and did not know one another.

The final study mentioned in this article, by myself, Sara Kiesler, and Michael Pallak, is still in process, and data analyses are not yet complete. Its findings, therefore, while very suggestive, are still tentative.

If he is not so committed the group does not influence him at all, and the relationship between attraction and opinion change proceeds in the predictable straight line.

Further, this opinion change is stable—it lasts. But the obvious suspicion that anyone capable of such change must be a well-oiled weathervane, swinging around to accommodate any new wind, is wrong.

The Deviate Ally

This was well illustrated when we told the committed but low-attracted person that he had an ally (a "deviate ally") who agreed with his original opinion in spite of the rest of the group. Previous studies have demonstrated that if a person who disagrees with a group finds he has even one ally, he will stick by his guns and hold out. But with the committed, low-attracted person it depended on *when* he found out about this ally. If he found out before he had changed his opinion, he stood fast, as expected—opinion change under these circumstances was near zero. But if he found out *after* he had accepted and expressed his new opinion, the ally had little effect. Moreover, he tended to resent this new-found "friend" and even to build up an active dislike for him. Of those who found out about this ally early, before change, 58 percent liked him best in the group. But of those who discovered him late, after change, only 14 percent said they liked him best, and 13 percent said they liked him least.

Let us analyze the implications of this finding a little further. First, they definitely limit the concept that greater attraction must inevitably lead to greater private acceptance; they illustrate at least one significant condition under which it does not. Second, they illustrate how important commitment is for understanding the behavior of groups and of individuals within groups. Commitment obviously can make a difference in attitudes, conclusions, and behavior generally.

It must be reemphasized that commitment makes this difference only when there is very little (or even negative) attraction to the group—the person doesn't like them or the situation, and he doesn't want to keep on, but feels he must. Obviously, therefore, this change of attitude is not what the subject really prefers—it is used only when all other avenues of psychological escape are closed off.

How can we account for this reversal—which seems contrary not only to prior research but to "common sense" as well?

This process can loosely be described in the following way: If a person feels out of harmony with some others or with a group, he has certain alternative methods of response for self-protection or counterattack. He can reject the group—decide to have nothing to do with it, and break off as soon as possible. Or he can devalue it—say that its opinions, importance, and members are of no particular consequence, not worth agreeing with.

There is some evidence that people will act this way if they do not feel bound to continue with the others. But these alternatives are not available to someone who is committed. He must somehow make his peace with them—and with his own concept of himself as someone who acts from conviction.

Appeasement and Aggravation

This is not peace at any price. It is not bland and superficial conformity. As our findings indicate, the important peace is within the subject himself. Also, it takes the long view—it considers consequences for the whole length of the commitment. A person not committed to continue can afford to practice "appeasement"—to bend to immediate pressures in the hope that they will pass. The committed must be much more cautious.

Thus commitment does not only and always tend toward agreement and the easing of tensions. It can lead as well toward sharpened conflict *in the short term,* if this seems necessary for long-term benefits. People who must cooperate cannot forever sweep unpleasant things under the rug.

For instance, how should an individual react to someone else's unpleasant habits or overbearing manners? He can pretend to ignore them once or a very few times. But what if they must keep associating? He may face the same problem at each meeting—aggravated by time and apparent acceptance. This *would* be appeasement in its classical form.

I am now collaborating with Sara Kiesler and Michael Pallak on a series of experiments designed to answer such questions. Specifically, how will people react to a social faux pas made by another? Folklore—in fact, many of the precepts of formal etiquette—suggest we try to save the offender's "face" and "gloss things over" when he is annoying or embarrassing us.

Our data analyses are not yet complete. But so far we have found what we expected. The *un*committed will tend to ignore the faux pas in a private confrontation with the offender; but something very different occurs among people who must continue association. Committed subjects were quite blunt about privately calling the offender's attention to his acts, reproving him, trying to get him to change. They apparently feel compelled to face the problem *now,* rather than keep on suffering from it.

We often notice parallel behavior between husband and wife, people who could hardly be more closely committed. They may reprove each other for acts that each would tolerate without comment from strangers. We usually consider this a sign of breakdown of marriage ties. But could not, as our studies imply, something of the reverse also sometimes be true—a desire to clear away potential sources of friction to make for an easier and more sincere relationship?

It is unfortunate that the effects of commitment have not been given more study, and we can hope that more research will come soon. Any factor that can influence people to change convictions and attitudes is a major force in human behavior and must be reckoned with.

by Sir Benjamin Stone

Manners & Mores of Victorian and Edwardian Englishmen

Sir Benjamin Stone was one of the most prolific amateur photographers of Victorian and Edwardian England. He was born in the Midlands manfacturing town of Birmingham in 1838. He came from a wealthy middle-class family living at Aston Manor. From 1877 until his death in 1914 Sir Benjamin lived at The Grange, Erdington, a fitting country seat for a manufacturer and local politician.

After a traditional grammar-school education he joined the family business of Stone, Fawdry & Stone — Union Glass Works. Benjamin Stone became a pillar of Tory society; he was elected to the Birmingham Town Council, became mayor of Sutton in 1886, was knighted in 1892 and became a member of Parliament for East Birmingham in 1895.

As a boy his interest in antiquities had led him to purchase and collect photographs as we now collect postcards and other souvenirs. In 1868 he decided to learn photography and by the time he died in 1914 he had exposed over 22,000 plates. Sir Benjamin was one of the earliest amateurs when photography was expensive and elaborate. He never seemed to dabble in personal picture-making.

His photographs were taken "always with the same object — to show those who will follow us, not only our buildings, but our everyday life, our manners, and customs. Briefly I have aimed at recording history with the camera, which, I think, is the best way of recording it."

While a member of Parliament he photographed all the noted politicians of his day. He was also an enthusiastic traveler and visited China, Japan, West Indies, South Africa, North and South America as well as most of Europe and he always returned with hundreds of photographs. His interest in antiquities led him to study, from 1889, the survival of ancient customs, pageants, crafts and ceremonies and he traveled thousands of miles, usually by train, with his bulky whole-plate camera equipment, in search of what he called history photography. These photos are reproduced by permission from the Sir Benjamin Stone Collection of Photographs in the Birmingham Public Libraries.

2 *Marian Gennaria Morris*

Psychological Miscarriage: An End to Mother Love

Not long ago a mother in the Midwest, while giving her baby its bath, held its head underwater until it drowned. She said that there was something wrong with the child. Its smell was strange and unpleasant; it drooled; it seemed dull and listless. It reminded her of a retarded relative, and the thought of having to spend the rest of her life caring for such a person terrified her. Her husband was out of work, and she was pregnant again. She said she "felt the walls closing in." When, in her confused and ignorant way, she had asked her husband, a neighbor, and a doctor for help, she got promises, preachments, and evasions. So she drowned the baby.

This mother said she had felt "so all alone." But, unfortunately, she had plenty of company. Many thousands of American women do not love or want their babies. Although few actually kill their infants, the crippling effects of early maternal rejection on children can hardly be exaggerated—or glossed over. The number directly involved is large. The social harm, for everybody, is great. An idea of the size of the problem can be gained from the following figures, taken from federal, state, and local sources:

- 50-70,000 children neglected, battered, exploited annually;
- 150,000 children in foster homes for these reasons;
- over 300,000 children in foster care altogether;
- 8 to 10 percent of all school children in one twenty-county study in need of psychiatric examination and some type of treatment for their problems.

But even these figures can hardly begin to describe the violence, deprivation, and dehumanization involved.

Recently we concluded a study of thirty rejecting mothers and their children, who can serve as examples. Our findings are supported by a number of other studies of parents and their children who have various physical and psychological disorders. Although the poor are hardest hit by family and emotional problems it should be noted that the majority of these families were not poverty-stricken. Psychological miscarriage of motherhood attacks all classes and levels.

Twenty-one of the thirty mothers demonstrated clearly from the time of delivery that they could not properly mother or care for their babies—could not even meet their basic needs. Yet no one who had had contact with them—neither doctors, nurses, nor social workers—had apparently been able to help, effectively, any one of them, nor even seemed aware that severe problems existed.

The entire population of mothers was characterized by old troubles and hopelessness, stretching back to the previous generation—and in one-third of the cases, back to the third generation. Half the children were illegitimate, or conceived before marriage. Sixty percent of the families had been in juvenile, criminal or domestic courts at some earlier time. Two-thirds of the children were either first-borns, or first-borns of their sex—and lack of experience with children increased their mothers' insecurities.

All thirty children needed intensive psychiatric treatment. Only two of the thirty were "well" enough—from homes that were "stable" enough—for out-patient care to even be considered. The remaining twenty-eight were headed for institutions. Their prognoses are grave, their chances doubtful. They will cost us a great deal in the years to come, and their problems will be with us a long time. Some will never walk the streets as free men and women.

Actually, the children were so disturbed that they could not be diagnosed with great accuracy. For instance, it was impossible to tell how intelligent most really were because they were in such emotional turmoil that they could not function properly on tests, and seemed retarded. A fifth of them had been so beaten around the head that it is quite possible their brains were damaged. (One baby had been thrown across the room and allowed to stay where it fell.) Women who feel neglected and less than human in turn neglect their children and treat them as less than human.

Fear and Reality

In our supposedly interdependent society, we are close together in violence, but apathetic to each other's needs. But apathy to their needs constitutes a violence to women facing labor, delivery, and the early and bewildering adjustments of motherhood. And it is in these days and weeks that psychological miscarriage occurs.

During pregnancy, labor, and delivery the basic fears of childhood—mutilation, abandonment, and loss of love—are vividly revived for a woman, and with double force—for herself and the baby. Nor are these fears simply fantasies: mothers *are* frequently cut, torn, and injured, babies *are* born with congenital defects.

The entire pregnancy period, with its lowering of defenses, makes the mother more capable of loving and feeling for her baby. But whether she finds his needs pleasing or threatening depends on what happened to her in the past, and the support she gets in the present.

After delivery, still in physical and emotional stress, under great pressure, she must make the most important, difficult adjustments of all. She must "claim" her baby. That is, she must make it, emotionally, part of herself again; identify it with the qualities and values in herself and her life that she finds good, safe, reassuring, and rewarding. After all the dreams and fears of pregnancy, she now must face and cope with the reality—the baby and his needs. If she miscarries now and rejects the child as something bad that cannot be accepted, then the child cannot grow to be normal. Nor can its society be normal, since the mothers must hand down to each generation the values by which society survives.

In older days, when most women had their babies at home, these adjustments were made in familiar surroundings, with such family support as was available. Now they are made largely in the hospital. What actually happens to mothers in today's hospitals?

Childbirth, once a magnificent shared experience, has increasingly become a technical event. Administrative and physical needs get priority. Emotional needs and personalities tend to get in the way of efficiency. Administrators and medical personnel, like everyone else, respond most readily to those pressures which affect them. Since they are in charge, they pass them down to the patient, whether they help the patient or not.

The mothers of the poor in particular arrive faceless, knowing no one on the ward, with little personal, human contact from before birth until they leave. Increasingly, they arrive already in labor, so that the hospitals cannot turn them away. They also come at this late stage so that they can avoid the constant procession of doctors and the three and four-hour clinic waits, during which they are called "mother" because their names have been lost in the impersonal clinic protocols. In the wards, they may be referred to simply by their bed numbers.

Birth itself may be subordinated to the schedule: some doctors schedule their deliveries, and induce labor to keep them on time. Even "natural" labor may be slowed down or speeded up by drugs for convenience.

A Public Event

Mothers say that they are allowed little dignity or modesty. Doctors strange to them may, and do, examine them intimately, with little attempt at privacy. They say that without their permission they are often used as live lecture material, giving birth before interested audiences of young interns and students while the obstetrician meticulously describes each step and tissue. How apathetic we have become to the routine dehumanization of mothers is well illustrated by the story of an upper-middle-class woman I know. She was in labor, almost hidden by drapes preparatory to vaginal examination, light flooding her perineum (but not her face). Approached by a nurse and gloved physician she suddenly sat up in her short-tailed hospital gown and said, "I don't know who *you* are, doctor, but *I* am Mrs. Mullahy." Good for Mrs. Mullahy! She has a strong sense of personal identity, and is determined to preserve it.

Mothers say they are isolated and humiliated. They say that in addition to their own anxieties they must worry about what their doctors think, and be careful to please and propitiate the staff members, who may have power of life and death over them and their babies.

They say that they are kept in stirrups for hours—shackled in what reduces them to something sub-human—yet afraid to complain.

Is it increasingly true, as mothers say, that babies are not presented to them for from four to twelve hours after birth? Social histories show that prompt presentation is necessary for the mental health of the mothers; studies of other mammals indicate that such delay interrupts mothering impulses and may bring on rejection of the young. Is this happening to human mothers and babies? How necessary, medically, is such a delay? Is it worth the price?

Many women become deeply depressed after childbirth. Is this at least partly a reaction to hospital experiences? Is it an early distress signal of psychological miscarriage? There is very little research that attempts to assess early maternal adaptation, and we need such research badly. Are the violent mothers, so brutal to their children, violent at least in part because of our faceless and impersonal birth practices? Clinical studies show that the less sense of identity and personal worth a mother has, the more easily she displaces her aggressions onto others—*any* others. Are we scapegoating our children?

Staking a Claim

To a mother, the birth of her baby is not a technical event. It starts in intimate contact with the father, and has deep roots in her feelings for and relationship with him, whether positive or negative. It reflects her personality, her state of maturity, the experiences of her most intimate anxieties and special hopes, and her associations with the adults who have had most influence on her. She enters the hospital prey to childhood insecurities, and stripped alike of defenses and clothes. Attitudes and cues from the hospital personnel, and from others, strongly affect her self-respect and her feelings about her own and her baby's worth.

It is difficult to observe most normal claiming behavior in a hospital. But some of it can be observed. Most mothers, for example, do find ways to make contact with their babies' bodies—touching and examining them all over delightedly, even to the tiny spaces between fingers and toes—cooing and listening to them, inhaling their odors, nuzzling and kissing them.

Socially, a major way to claim a child is to name it. Names suggest protective good magic; they establish identity and suggest personality; they emphasize masculinity or femininity; they affirm family continuity and the child's place in it.

Nevertheless, it is usually difficult to follow claiming behavior for two reasons. First, because hospital routines and tasks interfere. To the staff, the process of mothers becoming acquainted with infants is seen as merely cute, amusing, or inconvenient. Babies are presented briefly, pinned and blanketed tightly, making intimate fondling—for women who have carried these infants for months—difficult and sometimes even guilt-producing.

The second reason is related to the nature of normal motherhood. The well-adjusted mother is secure within herself, content to confine her communications mostly to her baby, rather than project them outward. As Tolstoy said of marriage, all happy ones tend to be happy in the same way, and relatively quiet. But the unhappy ones are different and dramatic—and it is by observing unhappy mothers that the pathological breakdown of maternal claiming can be most easily traced.

Let us consider a few examples:

Tim—Breakdown in Early Infancy

When Tim's mother first felt him move in her, and realized then that all evasion and doubt about her pregnancy was past, she blacked out (she said) and fell down a flight of stairs.

Tim was her second child. Her first pregnancy was difficult and lonely and, she had been told, both she and the baby had almost died during delivery. She suffered from migraine headaches, and was terrified of a second delivery.

For the first four months of Tim's life, she complained that he had virulent diarrhea and an ugly odor, and took him from doctor to doctor. Assured by each one that there was nothing wrong with the child (in the hospital the diarrhea cleared up in one day), she took this to mean that there was something wrong with *her*—so she sought another doctor. She took out thirteen different kinds of cancer insurance on Tim.

During an interview, she told a woman social worker that it was too bad that doctors could not look inside a baby and know he was *all* O.K.

The social worker decided to probe deeper: "You would have a hard time convincing me that you *deliberately* threw yourself down those stairs."

"Who, me? Why I told my mother all along that I would never *willingly* hurt a hair of one of my children's heads."

"But suppose you had, unwillingly. Would you blame someone else for doing it, under the circumstances?"

Patterns of Rejection

There are several criteria that can be used to assess the adequacy of a mother's behavior during the early weeks of an infant's life. Mother-infant unity can be said to be *satisfactory* when a mother can:

find pleasure in her infant and in tasks for and with him;
understand his emotional states and comfort him;
read his cues for new experience, sense his fatigue points.

> Examples: she can receive his eye contact with pleasure; can promote his new learnings through use of her face, hands and objects; does not overstimulate him for her own pleasure.

In contrast, there are specific signs that mothers give when they are *not adapting* to their infants:

See their infants as ugly or unattractive.
Perceive the odor of their infants as revolting.
Are disgusted by their drooling and sucking sounds.
Become upset by vomiting, but seem fascinated by it.
Are revolted by any of the infants' body fluids which touch them, or which they touch.
Show annoyance at having to clean up infants' stools.
Become preoccupied with the odor, consistency and numbers of infants' stools.
Let infants' heads dangle, without support or concern.
Hold infants away from their own bodies.
Pick up infants without warning by touch or speech.
Juggle and play with infants, roughly, after feeding, even though they often vomit at this behavior.
Think infants' natural motor activity is unnatural.
Avoid eye contact with infants, or stare fixedly into their eyes.
Do not coo or talk with infants.
Think that their infants do not love them.
Believe their infants expose them as unlovable, unloving parents.
Worry about infants' relaxation following feeding.
Think of their infants as judging them and their efforts as an adult would.
Perceive their infants' natural dependent needs as dangerous.
Fear death at appearance of mild diarrhea or cold.
Are convinced that infants have defects, in spite of repeated physical examinations which prove negative.
Often fear that infants have diseases connected with "eating": leukemia, or one of the other malignancies; diabetes; cystic fibrosis.
Constantly demand reassurance that no defect or disease exists, cannot believe relieving facts when they are given.
Demand that feared defects be found and relieved.
Cannot find in their infants any physical or psychological attribute which they value in themselves.
Cannot discriminate between infant signals of hunger, fatigue, need for soothing or stimulating speech, comforting body contact, or for eye contact.
Develop inappropriate responses to infant needs: over or under-feed; over or under-hold; tickle or bounce the baby when he is fatigued; talk too much, too little, and at the wrong time; force eye contact, or refuse it; leave infant alone in room; leave infant in noisy room and ignore him.
Develop paradoxical attitudes and behaviors.

"No! I was sick and don't even know how it happened."

After that, the demon that had haunted her was in the open, and recovery began. She had felt that she was both criminal and victim, with the child as the instrument of her punishment. (Only a "good" mother deserves a good baby; a "bad" mother deserves a "bad"—damaged or sick—baby.) The implied criticisms of her mother and doctor had aggravated these feelings. She identified Tim not with the good in her but the "evil"—he was something faulty, something to be shunned.

Under treatment she learned to accept herself and regain her role of mother. She was not really the bad little girl her critical mother and doctor had implied; neither, therefore, was Tim bad—she could accept him. It was no longer dangerous to identify with her. She let Tim see her face; she held him comfortably for the first time; she did not mention his "ugly" smell; she stayed by his bed instead of restlessly patrolling the corridors. She referred to our hospital as the place she had "got him *at*," instead of the hospital, ninety miles away, where he had actually been born.

Jack—Effects on an Older Child

Shortly after Jack was born, his mother asked her obstetrician whether Jack's head was all right. Gently touching the forceps marks, he said, "*These* will clear up." Thinking that she had been told delicately that she had a defective child, she did not talk to Jack for five-and-a-half years—did not believe he could understand speech.

At five-and-a-half, approaching school, he had never spoken. A psychologist, thinking that the child was not essentially retarded, referred the mother to a child guidance clinic, where the social worker asked whether she had ever found out if the obstetrician had meant the *inside* of Jack's head. For the first time in all the years it occurred to her that there might have been a misunderstanding. Three months later Jack was talking—though many more months of treatment were still necessary before he could function adequately for his age.

Behind this, of course, was much more than a misunderstanding. Behind it was Jack's mother's feelings of guilt for having caused her own mother's death. Guilt went back many years. During an auto ride long ago, she had an accident in which her mother suffered a mild blow on the head. In the early months of pregnancy with Jack, she had found her mother dead in the tub. The cause was cancer, which had nothing to do with the bump. But deep down she could not believe this, and she developed the fear that Jack's head, too, was damaged—a fitting punishment for a woman who feared she had killed her mother. When her obstetrician seemed to confirm it, she did not question further.

For almost six years Jack was not so much an infant or child as a damaged head. Like her mother he was silent—from "brain injury." It was only under treatment that she accepted the possibility that she might have "misunderstood."

Babs—Hell Revisited

Babs was fourteen months old when she was flown to our hospital from South America, physically ill with diarrhea and dehydration, and emotionally badly withdrawn. In South America, her mother had trouble getting proper drugs and talking effectively with Spanish-speaking doctors—and when she had had to face Babs's pleading eyes with little relief to offer, she had gone into acute panic. She hadn't been able to comfort her child, but had drawn away and could hardly look at her or touch her. From this rejection Babs had in turn withdrawn, and a mutual vicious cycle of rebuff and retreat had come about.

The mother felt that she had lived through all this before in her own childhood. When she was five, she had had a little brother, aged three. Her sick mother often left him in her charge. ("He was *my* baby.") One day both ate sprayed peaches from a tree. Both came down with severe diarrhea. She survived. She remembers vividly seeing him in "his little white coffin."

The pregnancy period with Babs had been stormy, full of family crises; she felt guilty about "not feeding Babs right." She could not accept the reassurances of her obstetrician. After Babs was born she was over-meticulous about cleaning her after bowel movements.

During treatment she shook visibly when asked whether Babs resembled her in any way. But when asked: "Could you have been Jim's *real* mother when you were only five?" she relaxed, and grew radiant. Later she said: "I know *now* that I couldn't have known that the peaches were poisoned."

"Nor that Babs would get sick with diarrhea if you went to South America to live with your husband?"

"No. I know now that the *place* is not good for any of us. I didn't know that before."

In a few days she was admiring in Babs the very qualities she had said she admired in herself—her sense of fun, and her determination. The positive identification between them had been made.

Mothers as Patients

How can we prevent such psychological miscarriages—and how can we limit their ravages once they have already occurred?

The dynamics of maternal rejection are not completely known—we need far more research, far more detailed and orderly observation of early maternal behavior. Nevertheless, enough is known already about the symptoms (detailed in the box on page 11) for us to be able to work up a reliable profile of the kind of woman who is most likely to suffer damage, and to take steps to make sure that help is offered in time. After all, the ultimate cause of maladaptation is lack of human sympathy, contact, and support, even though the roots may go back for more than one generation. We must, therefore, offer that support. We may not be able completely to heal old, festering wounds, but we can palliate their worst effects, and keep them from infecting new babies.

Mothers in our study identified the periods of greatest danger as just before and after delivery. It is then—and swiftly—that intervention by a psychiatric team should occur. What can be done?

■ We must have early recognition of trouble. Early signs of maternal maladaptation are evident in the mutual aversion of mother and child. But these signs have to be watched for—they cannot be ignored because of hospital routine that is "more important."

■ Let the mother have enough time to see and become acquainted with the hospital personnel with whom she will experience birth. Length of hospital stay is geared to technical requirements—five days for middle-class mothers, down (in some places) to twenty-four hours or less for the poor. Therefore, acquaintance should start before birth, at least with the physician, so that when delivery comes the mother will not be faced with a stranger in cap and gown, but a human being she already knows. Nurses and social workers should also be included. (The Hahnemann Medical College and Hospital in Philadelphia already assigns resident physicians to the pre-natal clinics to provide this continuity.)

■ Mothers of young infants suffer from geographical and psychological isolation. Services should work toward reducing both of these isolations. Ideally such services should come from a team, including not only the doctor and nurses, but a sympathetic pediatrician, psychiatric and medical social workers, of both sexes, who could also act as substitute parents. This help should be as available to the middle-class as to the poor (middle-class patients are sometimes denied hospital social services).

■ Help should carry over into home care. *Make sure that each mother has someone to care for her at home.* After their too brief hospital stay, poverty-stricken women, many without husband or family, are often more helpless and lost at home than in the hospital.

■ Mothers should not be left alone for long periods, whether under sedation or not. Schedules should and must be modified to allow them to have normal family support as long as possible. If they have none, substitutes—volunteers—should be found. Isolated mothers, cut off from support or even contact with their physicians, and treated as objects, much too often displace their loneliness, depression, resentment, bitterness, humiliation, rage, and pain onto their babies.

■ Get rid of the stirrups—and the practice of using them to hang mothers' legs in the air for hours! Find some other way to hold women on the delivery table until the last moments. Women often spend months recovering from backaches caused by stirrups.

■ Present the baby as soon as possible. The most frequent comment from mothers who remain conscious in the delivery room is, "The doctor gave him to me." This is psychologically very sound; when the father-image (doctor) presents the baby with the obvious approval of the mother-image (nurse), latent feelings of guilt about having a baby and about the acceptability of the baby—and of motherhood—are lulled and dispelled. Too often, however, the nurse is cast, or casts herself, in the role of unwilling, stingy, critical giver of the baby—in fact the whole institution lends itself to this. Presentation should precede and not depend on feeding; it should be made gladly and willingly; it should allow time and ease of access for the mother to examine her baby's body.

■ Doctors, nurses, and aides should understand and come to know pregnancy, labor, delivery, and early growth as a continuing process, rather than in bits and pieces, a series of techniques. They need to understand and see it from the mothers' viewpoint, as well as in terms of bottles, diapers, rooms, instruments, and procedures.

■ Reassure mothers about their infants. This includes understanding the real meanings of their questions. If a mother continually discounts good reports, rejection may be underway, and psychological miscarriage imminent.

■ First-born children, and the first-borns of each sex, are the ones most commonly rejected; their mothers need special care—as do the mothers of the poor and those without family, husband, or outside human supports.

None of these proposals are radical—even administratively. Most are quite simple, and could be done directly in the wards and the private rooms.

Overall, we need more research. We do not know enough about the earliest signals of psychological miscarriage; we have not trained ourselves, nor taken the trouble, to watch for these early signs. Nor do we know enough about the long-term effects of maladaptation. Are the older children completely lost? Is the process irreversible? Cannot something be done to bring them back to productive life?

There is nothing more important in a maternity pavilion, nor in a home, than the experiences with which life begins. We must stop the dehumanization of mothers. We must give all children a chance for life.

3 *Charles C. Moskos, Jr.*

Why Men Fight

Few stories to come out of the Vietnam War are so poignant as the story of Company A of the 196th Light Infantry Brigade, Third Battalion. As told by Associated Press reporters Horst Fass and Peter Arnett in a cable dated August 26, 1969, Company A had been pushing for five days through enemy-held territory in an effort to recover the bodies of eight Americans killed in a helicopter crash 31 miles south of Da Nang. Now, its strength halved to 60 men, its platoon leaders dead or wounded, Company A was ordered to move down a jungled rocky slope of Nuilon Mountain. They refused. Most of the men were 19 to 20 years old, draftees, and many of them had only a short time to go before being rotated back to the States. They were ordered to move out and they refused.

The rest of the story is unimportant; as far as the military command is concerned the whole story is unimportant. But for many Americans, Company A's refusal to fight that day must have raised terrible questions—perhaps above all questions about one's own personal courage, but questions too about how and why American soldiers continue to expose themselves to death and pain in a war that few civilians any longer believe in.

The most popular notion of how men are brought to kill and be killed in combat has to do with the presumed national character of the soldiers. Different national armies perform better or worse according to the putative martial spirit of their respective citizenries. Italians make "poor" soldiers, Germans "good" ones. Another view has it that combat performance is basically a consequence of the operation of the formal military organization—the strict discipline, military training, unit esprit de corps and so forth. This viewpoint is, naturally enough, found in traditional military thought; but the importance of military socialization is similarly emphasized—albeit from different premises—by antimilitarists concerned with the perversions that military life allegedly inflicts on men's minds. Another interpretation—often the hallmark of political rhetoric—holds that combat performance depends on the soldier's conscious allegiance to the stated purposes of the war. Whether motivated by patriotism or a belief that he is fighting for a just cause, the effective soldier is ultimately an ideologically inspired soldier.

Yet another explanation of combat motivation developed out of the social science studies of World War II. This interpretation deemphasizes cultural, formal socialization and ideological factors and focuses attention instead on the crucial role of face-to-face or "primary" groups. The motivation of the individual combat soldier rests on his solidarity and social intimacy with fellow soldiers at small-group levels. This viewpoint was characteristic of the studies that Samuel Stouffer and his associates reported in *The American Soldier,* as well as of the analysis of the *Wehrmacht* by Edward Shils and Morris Janowitz. The rediscovery of the importance of primary groups by social scientists was paralleled in the accounts given by novelists and other writers about combat behavior such as Norman Mailer, James Jones, J. Glenn Gray and S. L. A. Marshall. In a few of the more extreme elaborations of this theory, primary relations among men in combat were viewed as so intense that they overrode not only preexisting civilian values and formal military goals, but even the individual's own sense of self-preservation.

My own research among American soldiers in Vietnam has led me to question the dominant influence of the primary group in combat motivation on at least two counts. First, the self-serving aspects of primary relations in combat units must be more fully appreciated. War is a Hobbesian world and, in combat, life is truly short, nasty and brutish. But, to carry Hobbes a step farther, primary group processes in combat are a kind of rudimentary social contract, a contract that is entered into because of its advantages to oneself. Second, although the American soldier has a deep aversion to overt political symbols and patriotic appeals, this fact should not obscure his even deeper commitments to other values that serve to maintain the soldier under dangerous conditions. These values—misguided or not—must be taken into account in explaining the generally creditable combat performance American soldiers have given. Put most formally, I would argue that combat motivation arises out of the linkages between individual self-concern and the shared beliefs of soldiers as these are shaped by the immediate combat situation.

The Combat Situation

To convey the immediacy of the combat situation is hard enough for the novelist, not to say the sociologist. But to understand the fighting soldier's attitudes and behavior, it is vital to comprehend the extreme physical conditions under which he must try to live. It is only in the immediate context of battle that one can grasp the nature of the group processes developed in combat squads. For within the network of his relations with fellow squad members, the combat soldier is also fighting a very private war, a war he desperately hopes to leave alive and unscathed.

The concept of relative deprivation—interpreting an individual's evaluation of his situation by knowing the group he compares himself with—has been one of the most fruitful in social inquiry. We should not, however, forget that there are some conditions of life in which deprivation is absolute. In combat, a man's social horizon is narrowly determined by his immediate life chances in the most literal sense. The fighting solider, as an absolutely deprived person, responds pragmatically to maximize any and all short-run opportunities to improve his chances of survival. For the soldier the decisions of state that brought him into combat are irrelevant, meaningless.

Under fire, the soldier not only faces an imminent danger of his own death and wounding; he also witnesses the killing and suffering of his buddies. And always there are the routine physical stresses of combat life—the weight of the pack, tasteless food, diarrhea, lack of water, leeches, mosquitos, rain, torrid heat, mud and loss of sleep. In an actual firefight with the enemy, the scene is generally one of terrible chaos and confusion. Deadening fear intermingles with acts of bravery and, strangely enough, even moments of exhilaration and comedy. If prisoners are taken, they may be subjected to atrocities in the rage of battle or its immediate aftermath. The soldier's distaste for endangering civilians is overcome by his fear that any Vietnamese, of any age or sex, could very well want him dead. Where the opportunity arises, he will often loot. War souvenirs are frequently collected, either to be kept or later sold to rear-echelon servicemen.

As Stendahl and Tolstoy noted long ago, once the fight is over, the soldier still has little idea of what has been accomplished in a strategic sense. His view of the war is limited to his own observations and subsequent talks with others in the same platoon or company. The often-noted reluctance of soldiers to discuss their war experiences when back home doesn't hold true in the field. They talk constantly, repetitiously, of the battles and skirmishes they have been through. They talk about them not just to talk, but more importantly to nail down tactics that may save their lives in future encounters with the enemy.

DEROS and Agape

For the individual soldier, the paramount factor affecting combat motivation is the operation of the rotation system. Under current assignment policies Army personnel serve a 12-month tour of duty in Vietnam. Barring his being killed or severely wounded, then, every soldier knows exactly when he will leave Vietnam. His whole being centers on reaching his personal "DEROS" (Date Expected Return Overseas). It is impossible to overstate the soldier's constant concern with how much more time—down to the day—he must remain in Vietnam.

Within the combat unit, the rotation system has many consequences for social cohesion and individual motivation. The rapid turnover of personnel hinders the development of primary group ties, even as it rotates out of the unit men who have attained fighting experience. It also, however, mitigates those strains (noted in World War II in *The American Soldier*) that occur when new replacements are confronted by seasoned combat veterans. Yet because of the tactical nature of patrols and the somewhat random likelihood of encountering the enemy, a new arrival may soon experience more actual combat than some of the men in the same company who are nearing the end of their tour in Vietnam. Whatever its effects on the long-term combat effectiveness of the American forces as a whole however, the rotation system does largely account for the generally high morale of the combat soldier.

During his one-year stint in Vietnam, the fighting soldier finds his attitude undergoing definite changes. Although attitudes depend a good deal on individual personality and combat exposure, they usually follow a set course. Upon arrival at his unit and for several weeks thereafter, the soldier is excited to be in the war zone and looks forward to engaging the enemy. After the first serious encounter, however, he loses his enthusiasm for combat. He becomes highly respectful of the enemy's fighting abilities and begins to fear and scorn the South Vietnamese. He grows skeptical of victory statements from headquarters and of the official reports of enemy casualties. From about the third to the eighth month of his tour, the soldier operates on a kind of plateau of moderate commitment to his combat role.

Toward the ninth and tenth months, the soldier begins to regard himself as an "old soldier," and it is usually at this point that he is generally most effective in combat. As he approaches the end of his tour in Vietnam, however, he begins noticeably to withdraw his efficiency. He now becomes reluctant to engage in offensive combat operations; and increasingly, he hears and repeats stories of men killed the day they were to rotate back home.

It is significant, though, that "short-timer's fever" is implicitly recognized by the others, and demands on short-timers are informally reduced. The final disengagement period of the combat soldier is considered a kind of earned prerogative which those earlier in the rotation cycle hope eventually to enjoy.

Overall, the rotation system reinforces a perspective which is essentially private and self-concerned. Somewhat remarkably, for example, I found little difference in the attitudes of combat soldiers in Vietnam over a two-year interval. The consistency was largely due, I believe, to the fact that each soldier goes through a similar rotation experience. The end of the war is marked by the date a man leaves Vietnam, and not by its eventual outcome—whether victory, defeat or stalemate. Even discussion of broader military strategy and the progress of the war—except when directly impinging on one's unit—appears irrelevant to the combat soldier: "*My* war is over when I go home."

When the soldier feels concern over the fate of others, it is for those he personally knows in his own outfit. His concern does not extend to those who have preceded him or will eventually replace him. Rather, the attitude is typically, "I've done my time; let the others do theirs." Or, as put in the soldier's vernacular, he is waiting to make the final entry on his "FIGMO" chart—"Fuck it, got my order [to return to the United States]." Whatever incipient identification there might be with abstract comrades-in-arms is flooded out by the private view of the war fostered by the rotation system.

Conventionally, the primary group is described as a network of interpersonal relationships in which the group's maintenance is valued for its own sake rather than as a mechanism that serves one's own interests. And, as has been noted, social science descriptions of combat motivation

Research in the Combat Zone

The information for this article is based on my observations of American soldiers in combat made during two separate stays in South Vietnam. During the first field trip in 1965, I spent two weeks with a weapons squad in a rifle platoon of a paratrooper unit. The second field trip in 1967 included a six-day stay with an infantry rifle squad, and shorter periods with several other combat squads. Although identified as a university professor and sociologist, I had little difficulty gaining access to the troops because of my official status as an accredited correspondent. I entered combat units by simply requesting permission from the local headquarters to move into a squad. Once there, I experienced the same living conditions as the squad members. The novelty of my presence soon dissipated as I became a regular participant in the day-to-day activities of the squad.

The soldiers with whom I was staying were performing combat missions of a patrolling nature, the most typical type of combat operation in Vietnam. Patrols are normally small-unit operations involving squads (9-12 men) or platoons (30-40 men). Such small units made up patrols whose usual mission was to locate enemy forces which could then be subjected to ground, artillery or air attack. Patrols normally last one or several days and are manned by lower-ranking enlisted men, noncommissioned officers leading squads and lieutenants heading platoons.

In the vast majority of instances these patrols turn out to be a "walk in the sun," meeting only sporadic or no enemy resistance. Even when enemy contact is not made, however, patrols suffer casualties from land mines and booby traps. But it is primarily on those occasions when enemy forces are encountered that casualty rates are extremely high. Upon return to the permanent base camp, members of the patrol are able to enjoy a modicum of physical comfort. They live in large tents, eat hot food, get their mail more or less regularly, see movies, and can purchase beer, cigarettes and toilet articles at field Post Exchanges. They spend the bulk of their time in camp on guard duty and maintaining equipment.

In both the 1965 and 1967 field trips, I collected data through informal observations and personal interviewing of combat soldiers. During the second field trip I also conducted 34 standardized interviews with the men of the particular squads with whom I was staying. Some of the information contained in these 34 interviews is amenable to tabular ordering. Yet even when given in tabular form the data are not to be concevied as self-contained, but rather as supportive of more broadly based observations. The attitudes expressed by the formally interviewed soldiers constantly reappeared in conversations I had with numerous other combat soldiers in both 1965 and 1967. Again and again, I was struck by the common reactions of soldiers to the combat experience and their participation in the war. By myself being in the combat situation, I could conduct lengthy interviews on an intimate basis. I assert with some confidence that the findings reflect a set of beliefs widely shared by American combat soldiers throughout Vietnam during the period of the field work.

A prefatory comment is needed on the social origins of the men I interviewed. The 34 soldiers had the following civilian backgrounds prior to entering the service: ten were high-school dropouts, only two of whom were ever regularly employed; 21 were high-school graduates, six directly entering the service after finishing school; and three were college dropouts. None were college graduates. Eighteen of the 34 men had full-time employment before entering the service, 12 in blue-collar jobs and six in white-collar employment. About two-thirds of the soldiers were from working-class backgrounds with the remainder being from the lower-middle class.

As for other social background characteristics: eight were black; one was a Navajo; another was from Guam; the other 20 men were white including three Mexican-Americans and one Puerto Rican. Only seven of the squad members were married (three after entering the service). All the men, except two sergeants, were in their late teens and early twenties, the average age being 20 years. Again excepting the sergeants, all were on their initial enlistments. Twenty of the men were draftees and 14 were Regular Army volunteers. Importantly, except for occasional sardonic comments directed toward the regulars by the draftees, the behavior and attitudes of the soldiers toward the war were very similar regardless of how they entered the service.

in World War II placed particular emphasis on the importance of groupings governed by intimate face-to-face relations. Roger Little's observations of a rifle company during the Korean War differed somewhat by pointing to the two-man or "buddy system" as the basic unit of cohesion rather than the squad or platoon.

My observations in Vietnam, however, indicate that the concept of primary groups has limitations in explaining combat motivation even beyond that suggested by Little. The fact is that if the individual soldier is realistically to improve his survival chances, he must *necessarily* develop and take part in primary relationships. Under the grim conditions of ground warfare, an individual's survival is directly dependent upon the support—moral, physical and technical—he can expect from his fellow soldiers. He gets such support to the degree that he reciprocates to the others in his unit. In other words, primary relations are at their core mutually pragmatic efforts to minimize personal risk.

Interpreting the solidarity of combat squads as an outcome of individual self-interest can be corroborated by two illustrations. The first deals with the behavior of the man on "point" in a patrolling operation. The point man is usually placed well in front of the main body, in the most exposed position. Soldiers naturally dread this dangerous assignment, but a good point man is a safeguard for the entire patrol. What happens, as often as not, is that men on point behave in a noticeably careless manner in order to avoid being regularly assigned to the job. At the same time, of course, the point man tries not to be so incautious as to put himself completely at the mercy of an encountered enemy force. In plain language, soldiers do not typically perform at their best when on point; personal safety overrides group interest.

The paramountcy of individual self-interest in combat units is also indicated by the letters soldiers write. Squad members who have returned to the United States seldom write to those remaining behind. In most cases, nothing more is heard from a soldier after he leaves the unit. Perhaps even more revealing, those still in the combat area seldom write their former buddies. Despite protestations of life-long friendship during the shared combat period, the rupture of communication is entirely mutual, once a soldier is out of danger. The soldier writes almost exclusively to those he expects to see when he leaves the service: his family and relatives, girl friends, and civilian male friends.

Do these contrasting interpretations of the network of social relations in combat units—the primary groups of World War II, the two-man relationships of the Korean War, and the essentially individualistic soldier in Vietnam described here—result from conceptual differences on the part of the commentators, or do they reflect substantive differences in the social cohesion of the American soldiers being described? If substantive differences do obtain, particularly between World War II and the wars in Korea and Vietnam, much of this variation could be accounted for by the disruptive effects on unit solidarity caused by the introduction of the rotation system in the latter two wars.

Latent Ideology

Even if we could decide whether combat primary groups are essentially entities *sui generis* or outcomes of pragmatic self-interest, there remain other difficulties in understanding the part they play in maintaining organizational effectiveness. For it has been amply demonstrated in many contexts that primary groups can hinder as well as serve to attain the formal goals of the larger organization. Thus, to describe effective combat motivation principally in terms of primary group ties leaves unanswered the question of why various armies—independent of training and equipment—perform differently in times of war. Indeed, because of the very ubiquity of primary groups in military organizations, we must look for supplementary factors to explain variations in combat motivation.

I propose that primary groups maintain the soldier in his combat role only when he has an underlying commitment to the worth of the larger social system for which he is fighting. This commitment need not be formally articulated, nor even perhaps consciously recognized. But the soldier must at some level accept, if not the specific purposes of the war, then at least the broader rectitude of the society of which he is a member. Although American combat soldiers do not espouse overtly ideological sentiments and are extremely reluctant to voice patriotic rhetoric, this should not obscure the existence of more latent beliefs in the legitimacy, and even superiority, of the American way of life. I have used the term "latent ideology" to describe the social and cultural sources of those beliefs about the war held by American soldiers. Latent ideology, in this context, refers to those widely shared sentiments of soldiers which, though not overtly political, nor even necessarily substantively political, nevertheless have concrete consequences for combat motivation.

Students of political behavior have too often been uninterested in answers that do not measure up to their own standards of expressiveness. When a person responds in a way that seems either ideologically confused or apathetic, he is considered to have no political ideology. But since any individual's involvement in any polity is usually peripheral, it is quite likely that his political attitudes will be organized quite differently from those of ideologists or political theorists. Yet when one focuses on underlying value orientations, we find a set of attitudes having a definite coherence—especially within the context of that individual's life situation.

Quite consistently, the American combat soldier displays a profound skepticism of political and ideological appeals. Somewhat paradoxically, then, anti-ideology itself is a recurrent and integral part of the soldier's belief system. They dismiss patriotic slogans or exhortations to defend democracy with "What a crock," "Be serious, man," or "Who's kidding who?" In particular, they have little belief that they are protecting an outpost of democracy in South Vietnam. United States Command Information pronouncements stressing defense of South Vietnam as an outpost of the "Free World" are almost as dubiously received as those of Radio Hanoi which accuse Americans of imperialist aggression. As one soldier put it, "Maybe we're supposed to be here and maybe not. But you don't have time to think about things like that. You worry about getting zapped and dry socks tomorrow. The other stuff is a joke."

In this same vein, when the soldier responds to the question of why he is in Vietnam, his answers are couched in a quite individualistic frame of reference. He sees little connection between his presence in Vietnam and the national policies that brought him there. Twenty-seven of the 34 combat soldiers I interviewed defined their presence in the war in terms of personal misfortune. Typical responses were: "My outfit was sent over here and me with it," "My tough luck in getting drafted," "I happened to be at the wrong place at the wrong time," "I was fool enough to join this man's army," and "My own stupidity for listening to the recruiting sergeant." Only five soldiers mentioned broader policy implications—to stop Communist aggression. Two soldiers stated they requested assignment to Vietnam because they wanted to be "where the action is."

Because of the combat soldier's overwhelming propensity to see the war in private and personal terms, I had to ask them specifically what they thought the United States was doing in Vietnam. When the question was phrased in this manner, the soldiers most often said they were in Vietnam "to stop Communism." This was about the only ideological slogan these American combat soldiers could be brought to utter; 19 of the 34 interviewed soldiers saw stopping Communism as the purpose of the war. But when they expressed this view it was almost always in terms of defending the United States, not the "Free World" in general and certainly not South Vietnam. They said: "The only way we'll keep them out of the States is to kill them here," "Let's get it over now, before they're too strong to stop," "They have to be stopped somewhere," "Better to zap this country than let them do the same to us."

Fifteen of the soldiers gave responses other than stopping Communism. Three gave frankly cynical explanations of the war by stating that domestic prosperity in the United States depended on a war economy. Two soldiers held that the American intervention was a serious mistake initially; but that it was now too late to back out because of America's reputation. One man even gave a Malthusian interpretation, arguing that war was needed to limit population growth. Nine of the soldiers could give no reason for the war even after extensive discussion. Within this group, one heard responses such as: "I only wish I knew" "Maybe Johnson knows, but I sure don't" and "I've been wondering about that ever since I got here."

I asked each of the 19 soldiers who mentioned stopping Communism as the purpose of the war what was so bad about Communism that it must be stopped at the risk of his own life. The first reaction to such a question was usually perplexity or rueful shrugging. After thinking about it, and with some prodding, 12 of the men expressed their distaste for communism by stressing its authoritarian aspects in social relations. They saw Communism as a system of excessive social regimentation which allows the individual no autonomy in the pursuit of his own happiness. Typical descriptions of Communism were: "That's when you can't do what you want to do," "Somebody's always telling you what to do," or "You're told where you work, what you eat, and when you shit." As one man wryly put it, "Communism is something like the army."

While the most frequently mentioned features of Communism concerned individual liberty, other descriptions were also given. Three soldiers mentioned the atheistic and antichurch aspects of Communism; two specifically talked of the absence of political parties and democratic political institutions; and one man said Communism was good in theory, but could never work in practice because human beings were "too selfish." Only one soldier mentioned the issues of public versus private property ownership.

I should stress once again that the soldiers managed to offer reasons for the war or descriptions of communism only after extended discussion and questioning. When left to themselves, they rarely discussed the goals of America's military intervention in Vietnam, the nature of Communist systems, or other political issues.

Americanism

To say that the American soldier is not overtly ideological is not to deny the existence of salient values that do contribute to his motivation in combat. Despite the soldier's lack of ideological concern and his pronounced embarrassment in the face of patriotic rhetoric, he nevertheless displays an elemental American nationalism in the belief that the United States is the best country in the world. Even though he hates being in the war, the combat soldier typically believes—with a kind of joyless patriotism—that he is fighting for his American homeland. When the soldier does articulate the purposes of the war, the view is expressed that if Communist aggression is not stopped in Southeast Asia, it will be only a matter of time before the United States itself is in jeopardy. The so-called domino theory is just as persuasive among combat soldiers as it is among the general public back home.

The soldier definitely does *not* see himself fighting for South Vietnam. Quite the contrary, he thinks South Vietnam is a worthless country, and its people contemptible.

The low regard in which the Vietnamese—"slopes" or "gooks"—are held is constantly present in the derogatory comments on the avarice of those who pander to G.I.s, the treachery of all Vietnamese, and the numbers of Vietnamese young men in the cities who are not in the armed forces. Anti-Vietnamese sentiment is most glaringly apparent in the hostility toward the ARVN (Army of the Republic of Vietnam, pronounced "Arvin") who are their supposed military allies. Disparaging remarks about "Arvin's" fighting qualities are endemic.

A variety of factors underlie the soldier's fundamental pro-Americanism, not the least of them being his immediate reliance on fellow Americans for mutual support in a country where virtually all indigenous people are seen as actual or potential threats to his physical safety. He also has deep concern for his family and loved ones back home. These considerations, however, are true of any army fighting in a foreign land. It is on another level, then, that I tried to uncover those aspects of American society that were most relevant and important to the combat soldier.

To obtain such a general picture of the soldier's conception of his homeland, I asked the following question, "Tell me in your own words, what makes America different from other countries?" The overriding feature in the soldier's perception of America is the creature comforts that American life can offer. Twenty-two of the soldiers described the United States by its high-paying jobs, automobiles, consumer goods and leisure activities. No other description of America came close to being mentioned as often as the high—and apparently uniquely American—material standard of living. Thus, only four of the soldiers emphasized America's democratic political institutions; three mentioned religious and spiritual values; two spoke of the general characteristics of the American people; and one said America was where the individual advanced on his own worth; another talked of America's natural and physical beauties; and one black soldier described America as racist. Put in another way, it is the materialistic—and I do not use the word pejoratively—aspects of life in America that are most salient to combat soldiers.

The Big PX

The soldier's belief in the superiority of the American way of life is further reinforced by the contrast with the Vietnamese standard of living. The combat soldier cannot help making invidious comparisons between the life he led in the United States—even if he is working class—and what he sees in Vietnam. Although it is more pronounced in the Orient, it must be remembered that Americans abroad—whether military or civilian—usually find themselves in locales that compare unfavorably with the material affluence of the United States. Indeed, should American soldiers ever be stationed in a country with a markedly higher standard of living than that of the United States, I believe they would be severely shaken in their belief in the merits of American society.

Moreover, the fighting soldier, by the very fact of being in combat, leads an existence that is not only more dangerous than civilian life, but more primitive and physically harsh. The soldier's somewhat romanticized view of life back home is buttressed by his direct observation of the Vietnamese scene, but also by his own immediate lower standard of living. It has often been noted that front-line soldiers bitterly contrast their plight with the physical amenities enjoyed by their fellow countrymen, both rear-echelon soldiers as well as civilians back home. While this is superficially true, the attitudes of American combat soldiers toward their compatriots are actually somewhat more ambivalent. For at the same time the soldier is begrudging the civilian his physical comforts, it is these very comforts for which he fights. Similarly, they envy rather than disapprove of those rear-echelon personnel who engage in sub rosa profiteering.

The materialistic ethic is reflected in another characteristic of American servicemen. Even among front-line combat soldiers, one sees an extraordinary amount of valuable paraphernalia. Transistor radios are practically *de rigueur.* Cameras and other photographic accessories are widely evident and used. Even the traditional letter-writing home is becoming displaced by tape recordings. It seems more than coincidental that American soldiers commonly refer to the United States as "The Land of the Big PX."

Another factor that plays a part in combat motivation is the notion of masculinity and physical toughness that pervades the soldier's outlook toward warfare. Being a combat soldier is a man's job. Front-line soldiers often cast aspersions on the virility of rear-echelon personnel ("titless WAC's"). A soldier who has not experienced combat is called a "cherry" (i.e. virgin). Likewise, paratroopers express disdain for "legs," as nonairborne soldiers are called. This he-man attitude is also found in the countless joking references to the movie roles of John Wayne and Lee Marvin. These definitions of masculinity are, of course, general in America and the military organization seeks to capitalize on them with such perennial recruiting slogans as "The Marine Corps Builds Men" and "Join the Army and Be a Man."

Needless to say, however, the exaggerated masculine ethic is much less evident among soldiers after their units have been bloodied. As the realities of combat are faced, more prosaic definitions of manly honor emerge. (Also, there is more frequent expression of the male role in manifestly sexual rather than combative terms, for example, the repeatedly heard "I'm a lover not a fighter.") That is, notions of masculinity serve to create initial motivation to enter combat, but recede once the life-and-death facts of warfare are confronted. Moreover, once the unit is tempered by combat, definitions of manly honor are not seen to encompass individual heroics. Quite the opposite, the very word "hero" is used to describe negatively any soldier who recklessly jeopardizes the unit's welfare. Men try to avoid going out on patrols with individuals who are overly anxious to make contact with the enemy. Much like the slacker at the other end of the spectrum, the "hero" is also seen as one who endangers the safety of others. As is the case with virtually all combat behavior, the ultimate standard rests on keeping alive.

The Fighting Man's Peace Demonstrator

On both of my trips to Vietnam I repeatedly heard combat soldiers—almost to a man—vehemently denounce peace demonstrators back in the United States. At first glance such an attitude might be surprising. After all, peaceniks and soldiers both fervently want the troops brought home. In fact, however, the troops I interviewed expressed overt political sentiments only when the antiwar demonstrations came up in the talk. Significantly, the soldier perceived the peace demonstrations as being directed against himself personally and not against the war. "Did I vote to come here? Why blame the G.I.?" There was also a widespread feeling that if peace demonstrators were in Vietnam they would change their minds. As one man stated: "How can they know what's happening if they're sitting on their asses in the States. Bring them here and we'd shape them up quick enough." Or as one of the more philosophically inclined put it, "I'd feel the same way if I were back home. But once you're here and your buddies are getting zapped, you have to see things different."

Much of the soldier's dislike of peace demonstrators is an outcome of class hostility. To many combat soldiers—themselves largely working class—peace demonstrators are socially privileged college students. I heard many remarks such as the following: "I'm fighting for those candy-asses just because I don't have an old man to support me." "I'm stuck here and those rich draft dodgers are having a ball raising hell." "You'd think they'd have more sense with all that smart education."

The peace demonstrators, moreover, were seen as undercutting and demeaning the losses and hardships already suffered by American soldiers. Something of this sort undoubtedly contributed to the noticeable hawklike sentiments of combat soldiers. "If we get out now, then every G.I. died for nothing. Is this why I've been putting my ass on the line?" Here we seem to have an illustration of a more general social phenomenon: the tendency in human beings to justify to themselves sacrifices they have already made. Sacrifice itself can create legitimacy for an organization over a short period of time. It is only after some point when sacrifices suddenly seem too much, that the whole enterprise comes under critical reevaluation. But sharp questioning of past and future sacrifices does not generally occur among combat soldiers in Vietnam. I believe this is because the 12-month rotation system removes the soldier from the combat theater while his personal stake remains high and before he might begin to question the whole operation. The rotation system, in other words, not only maintains individual morale but also fosters a collective commitment to justify American sacrifices.

The soldier's hostility toward peace demonstrators is reinforced by his negative reactions to the substance of certain antiwar arguments. For while the combat soldier is constantly concerned with his own and his fellow American's safety, as well as being a fundamental believer in the American way of life and profoundly apolitical to boot, the radical element of the peace movement mourns the suffering of the Vietnamese, is vehement in its anti-Americanism, and is self-consciously ideological. At almost every point, the militant peace movement articulates sentiments in direct opposition to the basic values of the American soldier. Statements bemoaning civilian Vietnamese casualties are interpreted as wishes for greater American losses. Assertions of the United States' immorality for its interventionism run contrary to the soldier's elemental belief in the rectitude of the American nation. Arguments demonstrating that the Viet Cong are legitimate revolutionaries have no credence both because of the soldier's ignorance of Vietnamese history and—more importantly—because the Viet Cong are out to kill him. As one man summed it up: "I don't know who are the good guys or the bad guys, us or the V.C. But anybody who shoots at me ain't my friend. Those college punks are going to answer to a lot of us when we get back."

It must be stressed, however, that the soldier's dislike of peace demonstrators is reactive and does not imply any preexisting support for the war. Paradoxically, then, the more militant peace demonstrations have probably created a level of support for the war among combat soldiers that would otherwise be absent. This is not to say that the soldier is immune to antiwar arguments. But the kind of arguments that would be persuasive among soldiers (e.g. Vietnam is not worth American blood, South Vietnam is manipulating the United States, the corruptness of the Saigon regime and ineptitude of the ARVN make for needless U.S. casualties) are not the ones usually voiced by radical peace groups. *The combat soldier is against peace-demonstrators rather than for the war.* For it should also be known that he has scant affection for "support-the-boys" campaigns in the United States. Again, the attitude that "they don't know what it's all about" applies. As one soldier succinctly put it—and his words spoke for most: "The only support I want is out."

SUGGESTED READINGS

The Warriors by J. Glenn Gray (New York: Harcourt Brace Jovanovich, 1959).

Men Against Fire by S. L. A. Marshall (New York: William Morrow, 1947).

Up Front by Bill Mauldin (New York: Holt, Rinehart and Winston, 1945).

The American Soldier: Combat and Its Aftermath by Samuel A. Stouffer (Princeton, N.J.: Princeton University Press, 1949).

4 *Kurt W. Back*

The Way of Love and Trust

Geoffrey Chaucer in the *Canterbury Tales* describes the tradition of twelfth-century pilgrims going every spring to holy places. Partly they were driven by religious convictions; but in part they were searching for a change of routine, a transformation of themselves, and relief from distress and illness. They were also looking for companionship, and as he describes it, they had a merry time in their groups. They probably were looking, too, for something more: strong emotions which could transport the pilgrim from his mundane existence and create a unique experience he might cherish for a while or even for the rest of his life. And thus, before and after Chaucer, men have longed to go on pilgrimages.

Today we still find them going. For many, the old shrines have lost their magic. The modern pilgrim has often lost his belief in a saint who can help him, but his need for the singular experience a pilgrimage can give is still present, although few would admit it in these times. A great portion of today's pilgrims are looking for strong group experiences. Thus, on weekends and during the summers they journey to places that call themselves by different names: T-group centers, encounter group centers and human potential centers, among others.

The modern pilgrim may not seek rewards in the afterlife, in fact, he frequently rejects belief in it. He does not make a pilgrimage to seek the hereafter, but the here and now. He seeks frankly those experiences sought only indirectly by his ancestors. Today's pilgrim can say that all he is seeking is an encounter with others, help in solving his personal problems and a strong experience, and that no otherworldly power is needed to give it to him. In justifying this argument, the modern pilgrim claims a scientific understanding of the forces he experiences.

The scientific point of view, especially dealing with interpersonal relations and the study of society and the human being, has been widely accepted only within the last century or so. Science has its own rules, justifications and logic in explaining what happens in various social situations. For many people today, the mantle of science can be spread over many activities whose legitimacy might otherwise be questioned. Thus with the rise of science many actions whose basis for justification was formerly religion, the state or other authorities obtain a new sanction, and the scientific mantle covers areas of life and social activity that have little to do with science.

The search for groups in which intense emotional experience can be enjoyed is a sign of disturbance in many societies, occurring at times of deep social unrest, and especially during the rise of new religions. Thus the group experience of the early Christians is clearly a similar phenomenon, as were the underground masses of the Reformation. Paul Goodman, a leading social critic, has called this period in history, our time, the Second Reformation. In more recent times, political movements started the same way—in small political cells or circles. In all these cases, however, the group experience alone has not been the justification, whether to attain religious salvation, some healing process or salvation through secular means. Religious organizations have received attention by issuing eschatological warnings that the end of the world is near, and that therefore attention to the here and now is more vital than to one's future. Secular movements have sought for similar effects by pointing to the imminence of revolution or some upheaval of the present social system.

Here and Now

Sensitivity training is novel in accepting the group experience as having value in itself, without recourse to any ultimate aims. Correspondingly, the group experience has become the center of the movement. In earlier times, intense emotional experiences could always be explained as a working of the agency which gave the movement its own flavor, be it religious or political. In these instances the development of the science of pragmatism de-emphasized the experience itself while emphasizing the ultimate goals.

The catchword for the sensitivity training movement is "here and now." The term was invented by Moreno in his work on psychodrama, one of the techniques which is basic

Excerpted from Kurt W. Back, *Beyond Words: The Story of Sensitivity Training and the Encounter Movement* © 1972 by Russell Sage Foundation.

to much of the work in sensitivity training. In his book *Microcosm*, Philip Slater has contrasted the here-and-now orientation within a group with three other ways in which a group could promote group process: extra-group data, general principles and personal histories. Classroom teaching concentrates on the relation between extra-group data and general principles. Therapy stresses principally the relation between events in the group and personal history. Academic work may also use the general group process, usually as a way to explain general principles. The uniqueness of sensitivity training is that it uses the present experience only, not as a wedge to get into people's past the way therapy does, and not as a wedge to interpretation as teaching methods do. Concentrating on outside events, interpretation and verbal discussion is seen as an escape from the present experience and from the essential work of the group.

This new kind of group activity found in sensitivity training needs a justification to become acceptable for its prospective members. Thus we find a mythology of the here and now which is separate from any social psychological theory developed for the professional audience. This myth of the here and now ties in with the tensions within society. It has taken shape during the period of the growth of a large prosperous mobile middle class left without any central belief or controlled ways to get excitement. It rejects history, even personal history, and any enduring structure. It also rejects symbolization. In effect, one of the main techniques of sensitivity training is to make symbols concrete and active. Thus the statement "I hate you" will be quickly acted out in a fight, the statement "I love you" in an embrace, unhappiness in crying and so on. The implication of this attitude is a complete denial of some recent developments in human history of the importance of abstraction and symbolism.

Gut Learning

The cult of the experience is justified by deprecating symbolic statements, especially higher abstractions, and extolling strong sensual experiences, especially the more direct ones. This value shift is carried out in three ways: from symbols to concrete expression, from intellect to emotions, and from the mind to the body. One part of the here-and-now myth, therefore, is the rejection of a language of symbols in favor of direct experience and action; thus, group exercises, which sometimes look like children's games, are really given a deep meaning. One of the more famous of the exercises, called "trust fall," consists of a person falling backward, confident that his partner is going to catch him. Under the conditions of the group, it is highly unlikely that the partner is not going to catch him. While it is true that to an outsider this may look like a ritual, apparently it assumes deep meaning within the group, so that people really feel that this is the only way to express trust. Similar ways of making abstract concepts concrete are embodied in the myth and ritual of many societies. In all cases, participants realize that the concrete form is known to be a substitute or an explanation of the abstract concept. In the mythology of sensitivity training we learn that concreteness is the high road to understanding. Thus one of the early practitioners of sensitivity training in industry, Douglas McGregor, coined the expression "gut learning" as the only kind of learning that has any meaning and will hold. If we do not have to look beyond the present, any record keeping or symbolization of language would be unnecessary. Language is useful only for recurring situations and to refer to things absent in the present situation.

Rejection of Intellect

Allied with this rejection of symbolism is the rejection of the function that makes symbolism possible—the intellect. Attention is directed toward the exalting of emotion or the direct sensual experience. Group experiences become stronger if their meaning is not mediated by thought but accepted directly. This technique of concentrating on feeling and senses has been for a long time the technique of mysticism and of allied techniques. Here again we must stress the fact that in sensitivity training no ulterior aims can be acknowledged, no ideology gives meaning to the experience, and, therefore, the experience has to be celebrated for itself. Thus we find an emphasis on concentration on sensual experience. Exercises comprise simple concentration on one sense organ, such as one's sight, feeling or hearing. This emphasis extends to whole programs of education based on sensual experience or emotional education or, as it has been called, education for ecstasy.

Using dualistic terminology, we find an emphasis on the body as contrasted to the mind. Bodily exercises have been used, especially by religious groups, for a long time. In fact, some California encounter groups make extensive use of Far Eastern and Indian dance, gymnastics and physical exercises as an aid in their programs. Other physical exercises have been tried which are based on more modern concepts, from gymnastics to psychoanalysis.

Charlotte Selver, Ida Rolfe and Alexander Lowen are the more prominent advocates of this somatic aspect. Selver and Rolfe are physiotherapists who have developed complete methods of practice, movement and exercise intended to lead to a regeneration of the whole person. Lowen is more in the Reichian tradition of psychoanalysis. Like this student and friend of Freud, he poses the liberation of the body, especially the sexual organs, as an equal and even fundamental problem to that of social change. Lowen has developed an integrated psychosomatic "bio-energetic" approach which is intended to release the hidden energy of the body, especially of the lower part. Procedures of sensory awareness or awakening have become the most popular parts of encounter groups and form the subjects of the best-selling publications, notably among them Bernard Gunther's *Sensory Awareness below Your Mind* and *What to Do until the Messiah Comes*. He describes the rationale for this aspect of Esalen as follows:

> I guess largely I feel that most people in our culture tend to carry around a lot of chronic tension, and that they tend to respond largely on the basis of *habit* behavior and often goal-motivated behavior. And what I call sensory awakening is a method to get people to quiet their verbal activity, to let go their tension and focus their awareness on various parts of the body or various activities or feelings in the body. And of experiencing

the *moment*, experiencing what it is they are actually doing as opposed to any kind of concept or conditioned kind of habit behavior.

Sensitivity training represents a reaction to the development of intellectual history. Claude Lévi-Strauss has recently distinguished between the savage mind and the modern mind. The savage mind proposes a completely coherent picture of the world in a concrete manner. What the modern mind would consider a symbol is for the savage mind a real fact. He claims that what is metaphor for the modern mind is metonymy for the savage. The modern mind has developed science by deliberately refusing to assume that different realms of experience, such as animals, stars, trees, human actions and feelings, can be classified in the same way. For the modern mind, these different realms are investigated separately, using purely pragmatic methodology. Mythological thinking, which in a way is what Lévi-Strauss means by the savage mind, tries to put everything into a coherent system. The modern mind, represented by the experimentalists, perceives a fact and uses a symbolization of it for easier manipulation, quite conscious that it is only a symbol.

The last 400 years have gradually seen the increase of the importance of the modern over the savage outlook. While day-by-day activities were always regulated by principles of practicality, they were interpolated into a completely coherent world view. The scientific outlook and its philosophical underpinnings have stressed mainly instrumental value, problem solving, emphasis on the intellect and a free, almost playful use of symbols. Since the rise of science, there has always been a reaction against the values implicit in science. There are several forms which this reaction can take. One is the belief in ultimate nonrational values, the emphasis on ends over means and the rejection of certain scientific facts in order to fit into a preconceived world view. This is a conservative, anti-intellectual way which traditional religion has used in its step-by-step fight against new developments in science from Galileo to Darwin to Freud. As these three examples show, scientific thought has usually prevailed, and much of the approach of science has become ingrained in many people. Science may frustrate some aspects of human life, but this frustration does not lead readily to a return to ideas which have preceded scientific development.

Another way to reject the "modern mind" (in Lévi-Strauss's sense) is to use some of the procedures and language of science in a mythological sense. The central belief of sensitivity training, the use of behavioral science concepts to go from symbol to event, from cognition to emotion, and from mind to body, may be the first comprehensive attempt of this kind.

The progression of behavioral science to a social movement in sensitivity training illuminates one of the paradoxes of the pragmatic outlook. Pragmatism is the philosophy most attuned to the scientific method. It judges a procedure by its outcomes, by whether or not it works. It rejects explicitly the need to integrate each act and idea into an overarching framework. It is satisfied if an idea is useful for a reasonable time. Thus, pragmatics concentrate on choosing means that can be judged in this way and are suspicious of ultimate ends that may only arrive in the distant future and be used as a justification for all kinds of mischief in the meantime. The philosophy of sensitivity training follows this logic in its origins from philosophy based on James and Dewey, as well as in continuous resistance to questions about the ultimate aims of the procedures.

The pragmatic orientation of rejecting ultimate aims can easily slip into a perspective of shorter and shorter time spans. A T-group workshop can be accepted for its short-range objective of leaving the participants with good feelings without worry about ultimate aims. But the same can be said about each session, each interaction, each experience. Thus, denial of ultimate ends may lead beyond a rational short-term time perspective to a cult of the instantaneous and sensual experience. Sigmund Koch described the resulting model of human nature in this way:

> The Group Movement is the most extreme excursion thus far of man's talent for reducing, distorting, evading, and vulgarizing his own reality. It is also the most poignant exercise of that talent, for it seeks and promises to do the very reverse. It is adept at the second remove image-making maneuver of evading human reality within the very process of seeking to reembrace it. It seeks to court spontaneity and authenticity by artifice; to combat instrumentalism instrumentally; to provide access to experience by reducing it to a neuter-pap commodity; to engineer autonomy by group pressure; to liberate individuality by group shaping.

Sensitivity training can be seen as a reaction against the scientific outlook by an emphasis on direct, immediate experience. It can be seen as the logical end point of the transition from the extremely long-range outlook or religion to the middle-range time perspective of science, to the immediacy of the here and now. It has ranged farther and farther away from traditional scientific work. It is treated at best as the outer fringe of group dynamics in discussions of social psychology, and research efforts and theoretical input by people in the movement have decreased almost continually since its inception. By contrast, some adherents of the movement still claim allegiance to social science.

Sensitivity training can be related to the problems of social science and may be seen as a reaction to some of its developments. The central feature of sensitivity training, the strong experience in group interaction, is a very real event, and the conditions that lead to it are central to the concerns of social psychology. During a great part of their history, however, social psychologists have been looking at emotional events, describing them and talking about their importance and then gradually giving up the topic in favor of exact language describing other topics. Thus, group processes have been studied for a long time and discussed by many scholars with interesting ideas. Nevertheless, further work following their pioneering efforts has led them to exact but impersonal laboratory experiments or extremely abstract mathematical models. The Lewinian school, from which at least the Bethel experience started, has gone this course. Although Lewin was extremely concerned with human interaction and social problems and the study of real groups, the basic principles he developed have succumbed more and more to detailed analysis. Lewin's successors in group dynamics have gone from natural groups, then from groups of any kind, to work with individuals. The large laboratories supposed to contain whole groups for observation were gradually subdivided into cubicles where one person could be measured in interaction with a tape recorder or a message that presumably came from another person.

It may be argued, and most practitioners in the field of group dynamics would grant it willingly, that this gradual shift in emphasis has led to increased methodological and theoretical precision, the development of several logical, intricate, but consistent miniature theories, and an amount of cumulative research rare in social science. By the same token, however, many topics that could not be treated in this way, that might depend on the actual functioning of groups or somewhat subtle emotional interchanges, have been lost and neglected. Many practitioners in the field, eager young students, and laymen concerned with problems of everyday living have felt a great loss when they compared what they thought was being done in group dynamics with what was actually being done. Recurrently, in the history of the field, less exact but more encompassing new approaches have arisen, even within academic social psychology, to treat such topics as ethnomethodology and associated techniques. However, sensitivity training has also been ready to receive scientists disappointed in rapid progress by traditional methods. Sensitivity training has been sanctioned by its ancestry in group dynamics as a legitimate field for treating group interaction. It has kept up its reputation by advertising itself as able to treat both practically and experimentally the concerns of many in dealing with their personal problems, with the functioning of groups, and especially with the emotional aspects of man and society. It has been ready to receive them in its centers and workshops and to give them the support and experience they needed.

Anti-intellectual Movement

For many people who have come to the sensitivity training centers in search of a rational understanding of group processes, the experience has been a revelation. Many stay for the experience itself, for the enjoyment of working in the field, and forget the original concern with hard science that brought them there. It has become more and more true with sensitivity training that one is either in it or out of it, and that attraction to it has been in the nature of a conversion experience. Within the field of social science, a person who has followed this school and has become a member of the in-group will neglect any doubts or investigations that may undermine the experience. The social support given to sensitivity training, the proliferation of the centers, the attention given to them in the press and other mass media, the attempts of all kinds of organizations to hire consultants and to institute something like sensitivity training in their fields, has made it easy for people to become full members of the movement and to reject any inside analysis. The field given up by experimental group dynamics has been pre-empted with a vengeance.

This development may explain the paradox of much of sensitivity training, namely, that it is an anti-intellectual movement in the name of science. Its strengths, as well as its weaknesses, derive from this fact. At its best it is an attempt to integrate two aspects of man's existence that are usually kept separate—the analytical, intellectual function and global feelings, emotional attempts to understand man's place in the world. A neat balance between the two may lead to fruitful cross-fertilization. At its worst, however, it may tamper with the procedure of science, introduce questionable emotional practices and disguise easy excitement as experimental research or proved professional practice. Between these extremes, the system frequently becomes exasperating. Believing the language of the movement, one might look for research, proof and the acceptability of disproof. In fact, the followers of the movement are quite immune to rational argument or persuasion. The experience they are seeking exists, and the believers are happy in their closed system which shows them that they alone have true insights and emotional beliefs. Given the cultural context in which they are working, however, the high prestige of science and the necessity of professional control, sensitivity training in general does not want to sell itself as purely a new awakening. Thus it wants not only to become a cult, a new religion of the age of Aquarius, but also to stay on good terms with the scientific establishment. From this dual effort arise certain tensions and new attempts which may show best the place of sensitivity training within social science.

The relation between mind and body, which has been fundamental for the development of modern science, may be the best example of what can be called the post-scientific attitude within the encounter movement. The contrast between mind and body, and the separation of the two, is probably one of the characteristics of Western culture. In part the distinction is implied in Christianity; Descartes used this fact and made the distinction absolute in order to gain freedom for physical science from theological restrictions. One of the effects of this separation has been the development of physical and biological sciences, separate from psychology, psychoanalysis and the social sciences, keeping the mental and physical aspects as separate and closed systems. It was only after both kinds of science developed that attempts were made to show a relationship between the two and to integrate the two systems. In the late nineteenth and early twentieth centuries, the theories of emotion by James, Lange and Cannon, Pavlov's conditioning theories and Freud's theory of symptom formation showed the relationship between the two. The same period saw a frank acknowledgement of the importance of the body and of bodily needs. The original split between mind and body was made with the assumption that the mind was superior and the body was something weak, bad, which one should be ashamed of. Further development in psychosomatic medicine has stressed the profound interaction between mind and body, the importance of bodily well-being for mental adjustment and the influence of psychic disturbances on physical expression.

The sensitivity training movement has been influenced by several strands of this development. It accepts the importance of the body and expends much effort in physical exercises. These exercises are there to develop bodily skills, to get a greater variety of new sensations, and also to use physical conditions to attain certain mental states. On the other hand, partly through the influence of Oriental philosophy and religion, encounter centers also use mental control and techniques such as meditation and, perhaps, trancelike states. The movement seems to have had two influences in its consideration of mind-body relationships: the medical, psychosomatic influence which gives an almost physiological definition for mental changes and uses all kinds of techniques to produce those, and the Oriental one with all its attempts to direct training to achieve new and supposedly superior mental states.

Thus the current problem of the relation of sensitivity training to society and to science has developed. On the one hand, sensitivity training is advertised as the movement that rids man of his overreliance on his overdeveloped brain, especially the cortex, which reverses history, especially the Western history of dominance over nature, and which returns man to his lost garden of innocence. On the other side, sensitivity training is sold to diverse clients as a problem-solving technique and as a new way of working on the traditional problems of behavioral science. The more the movement expands and becomes part of the popular culture, the more both aspects arouse public attention and concern.

The different factions within sensitivity training have looked for ways to maintain, or regain, scientific respectability. In the activities at National Training Laboratory and Bethel and their associated laboratories, a continuous attempt has been made to keep in contact with academic science. Faculty delegates are recruited from university or similar professional settings. The failure of concrete evaluation attempts has been especially crucial here. A reaction has been to proclaim that people trained in these laboratories will become special people, members of an invisible, or perhaps visible, fraternity who have experienced something that may or may not be appropriate in their own work or profession. Connected with this are the attempts to introduce sensitivity training as part of the curriculum in some schools or in professional training.

Attempts to teach some of the concepts of human interaction, especially in courses similar to sensitivity training, combine the sometimes dry textbook psychology with immediate experience. This balance is difficult to maintain, and frequently such teaching leads to excitement for excitement's sake and attracts people who are looking either for therapy or a strong emotional experience. The age of most of the students and the general setting would guarantee in any case the occurrence of some rapid change, and the students who experience this change are greatly impressed by the procedure. It is noticeable, however, that many of the main protagonists of this classroom approach have left sensitivity training and say they are no longer part of the movement, that what they are doing is *not* sensitivity training.

A good example of this trend is Richard Mann, who has taught experientially directed courses in group interaction at Harvard and Michigan.

> I don't have interest in training people how to give feedback or get feedback, or make a good group or be democratic, or be open and honest, or any other damn thing. I mean, that is not my goal. My goal is to go in there and let a group develop. You know, groups aren't all that different, and when I think I understand something, I will say, "Hey, I think I see something happening." Or when I feel something, I will say, "Hey, that is really getting me mad," but it is not, it seems to me, with some underlying purpose of training everybody in the new etiquette of how you say, in this kind of somber tone, "Yes, I have a little feedback to give you, and blah, blah, blah." I don't like it. I think it is Boy Scout moralism, and I think that's the sensitivity training tradition.

Attitudes of this kind exemplify one aspect of the conflict between the emotional experience that is sensitivity training and the demands of hard science. Unwilling to give up the regular procedures in social science, protagonists reject their membership in the clique of sensitivity training and admit only that they use group methods, some more or less orthodox and some of their own devising. In the same way, some of the personnel management people at NTL have left the fold and use group methods in a different context. Among these people, the conflict and ambiguity of the whole field of human relations has led them through different schools of thought, and they may have learned something by having had the experience of having considered sensitivity training.

Perhaps it is the more extreme groups that are looking harder for new ways to adopt scientific respectability. The balance between faith and reason has been precarious wherever one has looked. It is instructive to see how this balance has been worked out in various instances. Recent developments at Esalen are an interesting case in point.

The adoption of the encounter movement by the mass media has in part overwhelmed the encounter centers as well as influenced their development. After all, at a time when restaurants advertise themselves as group encounters with food, going to an encounter session is hardly a novelty and even somewhat conventional. Pure encounter groups have diminished, and the participants at Esalen meetings, as well as at the meetings Esalen holds in San Francisco, are demanding new kinds of programs. The response has been in several directions. One has occurred at Esalen itself, by creating a residential community and acceding in this way to the demand for a complete cultural isolation and riding with the so-called counterculture. This regime includes work time for the paying customer, organic food and similar cultural patterns. The second is the more pronounced drive toward occultism, mysticism and the adoption of cult exercises from the extreme branches of religion around the world. The basic premise of Esalen has always been, at least in the eyes of the founders, an adaptation of Eastern modes of thought into Western science. Encounter groups used this implicitly within the framework of group dynamics and social science. The newer developments have been more explicit about this heritage but lean also on the work of experimental psychology, psychophysiology and biological sciences. These developments include the new interest in all kinds of physical exercise, massage, osteopathy and chiropractic, which have all found a home at Esalen.

Thus, interest in group experience per se has decreased at Esalen, and encounter groups are played down in favor of working with individuals. In this work there is a search for exact scientific instrumentation, the kind of data that can be measured by electronic machines. Science here means neglect of the emotional experience once thought essential for the understanding of groups. However, these experiences still persist with their aura of mystical anti-intellectualism. Thus the attempt is made to obtain the regular data of experimental psychology with the procedures of growth centers and to measure changes within an individual after various forms of treatment. But at the same time, interpretation of these data is made almost intuitively, and the procedure is only used to validate the beliefs of the faithful.

A demonstration of the scientific value of sensitivity training was put on at Esalen for a group of visiting behavioral and biological scientists. A popular Esalen technique was demonstrated, a kind of chiropractic developed by Ida Rolfe but evaluated only by photographs, without any measuring devices or any standardized conditions. The idea that tape measures or other simple devices could be used was rejected emphatically and almost emotionally. One reason given was lack of funds (apparently the cost of tape measures in comparison with that of Polaroid cameras); another was that measurement was impossible because change depended not on simple linear measures but on the ratio of several such measures. Even under these anti-scientific conditions, however, coordinated attempts are being made to attract reputable scientists whose cautious statements can then be easily generalized into wholesale endorsements. Here again, the development has been similar to the one in teaching human relations. Some interesting research areas, such as the physiological and psychological effects of meditation, have been taken out of the setting of the growth centers and into the laboratory by people who are not necessarily part of the movement. Psychologists and physiologists not necessarily connected or identified with the movement may find some of the ideas enriching. Here also, an individual must choose at some point whether he wants to be a scientist or stay within the encounter movement. Some people are able to do both part time, at least for a while.

One of the reasons for this complicated relationship between sensitivity training and organized scientific enterprise is a matter of economics. A great amount of funds is channeled these days from different sources for scientific endeavor. These funds are not obtainable in any other way. Records show that few funds have been used for support of sensitivity training and encounter centers. The main contributions came rather early in the development of the movement. Thus, the Carnegie Corporation supported the National Training Laboratory in its early years; during the same years, NTL was able to obtain government funds, especially through the Office of Naval Research. Since this time little support from government or private foundations has been given. Records of the National Institutes of Health and the National Institute of Mental Health show hardly any support for sensitivity training or research in it as such. Only very recently has NIMH shown interest in the sensitivity training movement, encounter groups and the new cultural phenomena that were analogous to the rise of the drug culture in the 1960s.

Private foundations have been equally cautious. The Carnegie Foundation followed up its initial grant to NTL by an internal small study evaluating the movement which resulted in a privately circulated research report; the researcher has since joined the encounter movement. Other support has come for specific programs of the Western Behavioral Sciences Institute from the Mary Reynolds Babcock Foundation for a study of a school system and from government sources for research on family structure. In addition, some foundations interested in community work have supported sensitivity training as a specific technique in community organization. In general, however, the share of sensitivity training in the general financial support of science has been extremely small in comparison to that of other endeavors.

Client-supported Services

Thus the main support of sensitivity training has come from clients. The National Training Laboratory, through different contracts with industry and government such as the Peace Corps and State Department, has made NTL more a service than a scientific organization. This connection has also served as a conservative check on NTL's activities as they must avoid shocking the potential customer by becoming engaged in some far-out kind of work. The reaction to some financial difficulties in which NTL has recently found itself has been to separate different training functions and to spin off different organizations that can serve specific customers, such as communities or industry. In conformity with its tradition, Esalen has met the challenge of raising money by putting more effort into performances. Benefits in New York and Los Angeles are being mounted; in 1970, the first benefit Esalen held in New York City netted $100,000 for development funds. However, in 1971, the attendance dropped in a catastrophic fashion. In addition, publications, records, tapes and movies bring income to the organizations and to some of the leaders.

The financial picture, therefore, enforces the impression of the whole function of the sensitivity training movement. It is not being supported as a scientific endeavor but is filling a cultural need for people dissatisfied with the efforts of social scientists on their behalf. The basic irony lies in the discrepancy between ends and means. Sensitivity training basically aims at the regeneration of man through a deep, almost spiritual, experience, the kind of effort that has traditionally been part of the field of religion. It uses, however, the methods, the language and some of the ritual of scientific work. One could almost say that, here, science is used to overcome the scientific view of man.

SUGGESTED READINGS

Encounter: Confrontation in Self and Interpersonal Awareness by L. G. Blank, G. Gottsegen, and M. Gottsegen (New York: Macmillan, 1971).

Experimentation with Human Subjects, edited by P. Freund (New York: Praeger, 1970).

The New Reformation by P. Goodman (New York: Random House, 1970).

5 *Donald R. Cressey*

The Respectable Criminal

Spring has returned, and with it two of the major themes of strategy in American life—how to win a baseball pennant and how to beat the income tax collector. Because as a sociologist I'm professionally interested in why people cheat, I'll leave theories about baseball to others.

At this time of year many of us toy with the idea of income tax evasion. Some succumb to the temptation. Those who do are not poor, culturally deprived slum dwellers. They do not like to think of themselves as "criminals." Tax evaders, along with people who pad their insurance claims, embezzle from their employers, or conspire with others to fix the price of goods usually have steady jobs and wear white collars to work. They are, nevertheless, committing what we call "respectable crimes." As recurrent newspaper headlines remind us, these are widespread forms of criminal behavior in our society. To develop a truly comprehensive theory of criminality we must learn more about why such men become violators of the law.

My own interest in "respectable crime" goes back to my days as a graduate student at Indiana University after World War II. My major professor, Edwin H. Sutherland, was conducting a study of the crimes committed by the 70 largest non-financial corporations in the U.S. He invented the concept of white-collar crime and encouraged criminologists, administrators of criminal justice, and laymen to reexamine the generalizations they had traditionally made about crime and criminals.

Sutherland's examination of the laws on certain kinds of business practices—such as restraint of trade, infringement of patents, false and misleading advertising, unfair labor practices—convinced him that these were indeed criminal laws. Violation of these laws is, accordingly, a crime; crimes of this sort must be included in any generalization about crimes and criminals. Sutherland found that the 70 largest corporations had about 980 decisions recorded against them for violation of four laws—an average of about 14 for each corporation. At the time of the study, the most popular criminological theories tended to link criminal behavior to social and personal pathologies of various kinds. Theoreticians emphasized poverty, poor education, broken homes, and psychological characteristics of criminals. The white-collar criminals that Sutherland had discovered, like the high officials of G.E. and Westinghouse who were convicted of conspiracy to fix prices in 1962, were persons of respectability and high social status who had committed crimes in connection with business. They did not fit the theoretical description. It followed that the theory would have to be revised to account for this type of criminality.

Sutherland's position was confused by the fact that he studied corporations, rather than individual white-collar criminals. I tried to correct this defect by making a study of embezzlers. It was my impression that embezzlers are white-collar criminals whose backgrounds are not likely to contain the social and personal pathologies which popular notions and traditional theory ascribe to criminals. Actually I doubt that these characteristics are in fact present in the background of *most* criminals. On the basis of my study, I *know* that they are almost never present in the background of embezzlers.

The Natural History of Embezzling

When I turned, as a first step, to the existing literature for an explanation of embezzling, I found that there was a basic confusion about the nature of this crime. Most books about embezzling are written by accountants—guides to businessmen to help them avoid embezzling in their own firms. Their major thesis is that weak internal controls and poor auditing systems cause defalcations by failing to eliminate the possibility of committing the crime.

While I must agree that a detailed check on all business transactions would prevent defalcations, I doubt whether these crimes can be "explained" by the absence of such checks. In the first place, even the most "foolproof" accounting procedures can never eliminate cheating entirely. The versatility of embezzlers is astounding, and greatly underestimated. In the second place, modern society presupposes business transactions based upon a considerable amount of trust. No matter what accounting system is used, an element of trust remains. A brief review of the history of embezzlement as a crime will make this point clear.

When commerce was beginning to expand in the 16th century, the legal rule regarding financial relations between master, servants, and third persons was simply this: (a) property received from the master remained in his possession, the servant having "mere charge or custody" of it; but (b) property received from a third person for the master *was* in the *servant's* possession, and he was not guilty of a felony if he converted it for his own use. As business expanded and "servants" became in fact clerks and cashiers, the situations in which the master retained possession were expanded. It became the rule that if a clerk placed money in a cash drawer, it thereby came into the possession of the master; if the servant subsequently took the money from the cash drawer to keep, this act was larceny. But until 1799, if a clerk received money from one of his employer's customers and *put it directly into his own pocket,* he had committed no crime; the money had not yet come into his employer's possession. Later that same year the first general embezzlement statute was passed in England. The new law covered "servants" but it did not cover "agents"; when in 1812 a stockbroker took money given to him to invest and converted it for his own uses, the court held that the general embezzlement law did not cover this act. New legislation to cover brokers, agents, etc., was passed almost immediately. Clearly, the common law of fraud and larceny had been sufficient for a relatively simple economy where there was no need to trust servants with business transactions. But with the growth of business firms in the 19th century, embezzlement statutes had to be invented to cover the new offenses which arose with the new economic structure.

Dependence upon trusted employees, agents, brokers, and factors has increased steadily since the passage of these first statutes. To argue that criminal violation of financial trust can be prevented by rigid accounting methods is to overlook the pertinent point: if strict controls were imposed on all trusted persons, embezzlement could be prevented, but very little business could be conducted. To remove "the temptation, the opportunity, and even the suggestion to violate the solemn trust which has been placed in officers and employees," as one accountant-author suggests, would eliminate both "solemn trust" and large numbers of business transactions.

Writers who are not accountants have an alternative explanation of embezzling; they blame it on the weakness, moral depravity, natural dishonesty, weak moral fibre, etc., of the violator. The trouble with explanations of this sort is that they are always after-the-fact. Such hidden variables can be said to cause almost any kind of behavior. They usually become evident only after a person has proved that he is "bad" by stealing from his employer. The notion that an evil result must have something evil as a cause is a fallacy.

In my own attempt to explain this kind of crime, I spent about a year at the Illinois State Penitentiary at Joliet interviewing embezzlers. I then moved to California and talked to some more embezzlers in the California State Institution for Men at Chino. I was also able to gather a considerable number of cases from other studies. But I was disturbed because my sample of embezzlers included very few bankers; this was because bank embezzlement is a federal offense and most of my interviews had been conducted in state prisons. So I spent a summer working in the United States Penitentiary in Terre Haute, Indiana. From these interviews I developed a generalization which I think can be applied to all the embezzlers I talked to. I see no good reason to believe that it does not apply to all embezzlers, although I realize that one should not generalize beyond his data.

The Compleat Cheater

What I came up with was the idea that embezzlement involves three essential kinds of psychological processes:

- the feeling that a personal financial problem is unshareable;
- the knowledge of how to solve the problem in secret, by violating a position of financial trust;
- the ability to find a formula which describes the act of embezzling in words which do not conflict with the image of oneself as a trusted person.

A man has an *unshareable financial problem* if it appears to him that he cannot turn to ordinary, legitimate sources for funds. To an outsider, the situation may not seem so dire; what matters is the psychological perspective of the potential embezzler. Recently I found an example of this state of mind in a newspaper letter to Ann Landers. The writer was a bookkeeper who had taken $75 from petty cash to pay some long-overdue personal bills. "I could have gone to my boss and received a loan for this amount with no trouble, but I had too much pride. My husband makes a small salary, and I was ashamed to admit we were having a difficult time financially." The writer, who signed herself "Ashamed," was paying the money back, but was terrified that she might succumb to the temptation again.

After I first formulated this unshareable problem notion, I tested it by asking a group of fifty embezzlers about an imaginary financial problem. I asked them to suppose that for some reason their fire insurance policy had lapsed and then, through no fault of their own, there was a short circuit in the wiring, or lightning struck, and their home burned down. The family lost everything they owned in the fire. My question was, "Do you think that in a situation like this you would have been tempted to embezzle to get the money you would need?" Sixty percent of the cases indicated clearly that this situation did not seem to them unshareable, and that therefore they would not embezzle. The reasoning is clear in responses like these:

> Case 42. I don't believe I would. I think that in a case like that folks would have sympathized with me and helped me out. There would be outside aid. But in my own case, they didn't know about it and so they couldn't help.
>
> Case 57. Well, I don't doubt that I would if I couldn't borrow the money or something of the sort. There are people or relatives that have money. I've never got along with them, but if it was a necessity like that I would go to them. I'd do anything to give my wife and children what they needed. (He indicated earlier that he had been too proud to go to his relatives for help at the time when he had embezzled.)

The second part of my generalization, the *realization* that the problem could be solved in secret by violating a trust, is a problem in the psychological perception of the opportunity to embezzle. Let me give just one statement, made by an embezzler (and former accountant), about the opportunity and techniques of embezzlement:

> In my case, I would have to say that I learned all of it in school and in my ordinary accounting experience. In school they teach you in your advanced years how to detect embezzlements, and you sort of absorb it. . . . It is

just like a doctor performing abortions . . . I did not use any techniques which any ordinary accountant in my position could not have used; they are known by all accountants, just like the abortion technique is known by all doctors.

The third process in my generalization, *verbalization,* is the crux of the problem. I am convinced that the *words* that the potential embezzler uses in his conversation with himself are actually the most important elements in the process which gets him into trouble, or keeps him out of trouble. If he sees a possibility for embezzlement, it is because he has defined the relationship between the unshareable problem and an illegal solution in language that lets him look on trust violation as something other than trust violation. If he cannot do this, he does not become an embezzler.

To illustrate, let us suppose a man who is a pillar of the community, a respected, honest employee, a man with a background no more criminal than that of most of us. This man finds himself with an unshareable problem, and an objective opportunity to steal money from his company. The chances are very good that if in that situation I walked up to him and said, "Jack, steal the money from your boss," he would look at me in horror, as if I had suggested that he could solve his problem by going down and sticking a pistol into the face of the local cigar store owner. Honest and trusted men "just don't do such things." However, honest and trusted men do "borrow," and if he tells himself that he is borrowing the money he can continue to believe that he is an honest citizen, even as he is stealing the boss blind. Since he wants to remain an honest citizen, the "borrowing" verbalization becomes the key to his dishonest conduct.

I do not wish to overemphasize the idea of "borrowing." There are many verbalizations used, some of them quite complex. The "borrowing" verbalization is simply an example of a vocabulary that can adjust two contradictory roles—the role of an honest man and the role of a crook. I call the use of such a vocabulary a rationalization, which is different from the way psychoanalysts use the term. Let me give an illustration of rationalization that does *not* involve a dishonest role:

Suppose a Dean who is swamped with work in his university is invited to speak at a seminar of businessmen. He might at first feel he should decline the invitation, on the ground that he doesn't have the time, or he has to get the budget in, or he has to finish writing his book. But then suppose he says to himself, "A Dean should get out of the ivory tower now and then," or "Theoretical knowledge is no good unless it is passed on to practical men." *Now* he can accept the invitation, and does.

Vocabularies of motive are not something invented by embezzlers (or anyone else) on the spur of the moment. Before they can be taken over by an individual, these verbalizations exist as group definitions in which the behavior in question, even crime, is in a sense *appropriate.* There are any number of popular ideologies that sanction crime in our culture: "Honesty is the best policy, but business is business"; "It is all right to steal a loaf of bread when you are starving"; "All people steal when they get in a tight spot"; Once these verbalizations have been assimilated and internalized by individuals, they take a form such as: "I'm only going to use the money temporarily, so I am borrowing, not stealing," or "I have tried to live an honest life but I've had nothing but troubles, so to hell with it."

If my generalization about the psychological elements of embezzling is valid, it should have ramifications for crime prevention. Some change in prevention techniques is clearly necessary, for the embezzlement rate in the United States is on the rise. Increasingly complex business organizations need larger proportions of "trusted employees." Business procedures are becoming so involved that the whole fabric of an enterprise depends more and more upon men who have been given independent control over some segment of the enterprise. At the same time, studies of professional and technical workers indicate that many are dissatisfied with their jobs. These disgruntled employees are potential embezzlers.

It follows from my generalization that embezzling can be effectively blocked either at the unshareable problem point or at the verbalization point.

■ Trust violation rates might be reduced by eliminating some of the unshareable problems among employees. This means development of company programs so that employees have fewer financial problems and/or feel that they can share their financial problems with their employer. Wherever a company program solves a financial problem, or makes it shareable, embezzlement will not occur.

■ Companies could introduce educational programs that emphasize how trust violators commonly use verbalizations. These programs would make it increasingly difficult for trusted employees to think of themselves as "borrowers" rather than "thieves" when they take the boss's money. It is highly probable that our current practices in this regard actually encourage embezzlement. We tend to emphasize the notion that embezzlers are people who are the victims of "wine, women, and wagering." Because this lore is so popular, a person with an unshareable problem who is not gambling, drinking, or running around with women can easily think of himself as a nonembezzler who is simply "borrowing." What I am proposing is an educational program in which we say over and over again that a person who "pilfers" or "taps the till" or "borrows" or who is guilty of "defalcation," "peculation," or some other nice term is, in fact, a crook. And if the trusted employee rejects the notion of himself as a crook (and as a "respectable" type, he must), he will also reject the possibility of embezzling.

Crime as Business Policy

The generalization I have developed here was made to fit only one crime—embezzling. But I suspect that the verbalization section of the generalization will fit other types of respectable crime as well. There is a study of crimes among New England shoe manufacturers that supports this notion. In the eight New England communities studied, there were wide variations in the number of shoe firms violating labor relations laws. In Haverhill, Massachusetts, for example, 7 percent of the shoe firms violated these laws, while in Auburn, Maine, 44 percent violated them. The author, Robert E. Lane, concluded that one of the reasons for the differences among the towns was differences in "attitudes toward the law, the government, and the morality of illegality." Those shoe manufacturers who associated with men whose attitudes favored violation were more likely to break the law; those manufacturers who were isolated from these attitudes were less likely to break the law. This influence on attitudes was evident even in the reading habits of these men; those who had violated the law had immersed themselves in a segment of the daily press so hostile to government that violation of the law seemed quite appropriate to them. Here, even the newspapers were providing verbalizations that made crime "all right." Lane predicted, on the basis of such observations, that managers of companies located in bigger cities, with a cosmopolitan press, diversified social life, and greater tolerance for heterodoxy, would accept legal restrictions on how they conducted their businesses more readily than would small town management. This prediction was borne out; firms located in small towns violated the laws much more frequently than did similar firms located in larger cities. The small town atmosphere provided a rationale to justify this particular crime; (government shouldn't tell a man how to run his business; "that man" in Washington is no good anyway; labor unions are corrupt). The bigger cities did not provide this justification. Another study, by Marshall B. Clinard, analyzed O.P.A. violations during World War II and concluded that businessmen violated the regulations simply because they did not "believe in" them.

The G.E. and Westinghouse officials must have had a formula that made their conspiracy to fix the price of electrical equipment something other than a crime. Perhaps it was a generalized dislike of government regulation of business; perhaps they had convinced themselves that no one really abides by the Sherman Anti-trust Act anyway and that, like the prohibition amendment, it could be transgressed without any stigma of criminality. And surely all the income tax evaders do not see themselves as stealing money from the U.S. Treasury—to them the government may seem so rich that "they'll never miss it" or the intricate tax laws may seem a kind of game that allows an advantage to the shrewd player.

But whether the stakes are high or low, whether the financial game is played by an individual or a conspiring group, an aura of personal respectability does not erase (though it may temporarily obscure), the act of a criminal.

SUGGESTED READINGS

The Thief in the White Collar by Norman Jaspan and Hillel Black (New York: Lippincott, 1960). An analysis of the nature and causes of embezzling.

White Collar Criminal: The Offender in Business and the Professions edited by Gilbert Geis (New York: Atherton Press, 1968) is a useful collection of 32 articles. Sutherland and Ross are represented as well as some British social scientists.

White Collar Crime by Edwin H. Sutherland (New York: Holt, Reinhart and Winston, 1949). The seminal work in the field, this book has had an extremely important impact on criminological thought.

"Techniques of Neutralization" by Gresham M. Sykes and David Matza, *American Journal of Sociology* (Vol. 22, Dec. 1957). An interesting and important article that describes different techniques that juvenile delinquents use to rationalize their illegal and immoral behavior.

Other People's Money by Donald R. Cressey (Glencoe, Ill.: Free Press, 1953). A social psychological study of embezzling with interesting sections on the techniques embezzlers use to rationalize their acts.

"Social Structure and Anomie" in *Social Theory and Social Structure,* by Robert K. Merton (New York: The Free Press, 1957). Classic essay on the social structural sources of deviant behavior.

The Sane Society by Erich Fromm (New York: Rinehart, 1955). Details the disorganization in contemporary society and its impact on the individual personality.

Theft of a Nation by Donald R. Cressey (New York: Harper & Row, 1969). Organized crime in America.

Deviance: The Interactionist Perspective edited by Earl Rubington and Martin S. Weinberg (New York: Macmillan, 1968).

The Crime Problem, by Walter C. Reckless (New York: Appleton-Century-Crofts, 1961).

Crime and Society by Gresham M. Sykes (New York: Random House, 1956).

Crime, Correction and Society by Elmer H. Johnson (Homewood, Illinois: Dorsey Press, 1968).

The Sociology of Punishment and Correction edited by Norman Johnson, Leonard Savitz and Martin E. Wolfgang (New York: Wiley, 1962).

Principles of Criminology by Edwin H. Sutherland & Donald R. Cressey (Philadelphia: Lippincott, 1966).

6 *Howard S. Becker*

Consciousness, Power and Drug Effects

Scientists no longer believe that a drug has a single, simple physiological action, essentially the same in all humans. Experimental, anthropological and sociological evidence shows that drug effects differ greatly, depending on variations in the physiology, psychology, knowledge and social situation of the drug taker.

What a person knows about a drug influences the way he uses it, the way he interprets its effects and responds to them, and the way he deals with the sequelae of the experience. What he does not know affects his experience, too, making certain interpretations and actions impossible. "Knowledge" in this sense refers to any ideas or beliefs about the drug that any of the actors in the drug use network (illicit drug sellers, physicians, researchers or lay drug users) believe have been tested against experience.

Dosage. Many drug effects are dose related. A drug has one set of effects if you take *x* amount and quite different effects if you take 5*x*. Similarly, drugs have different effects when taken orally, by inhalation, intramuscularly or intravenously. How much of the drug you take and how you take it depends on what you understand to be the proper amount and route of use. Those understandings depend on what you have learned from sources you consider knowledgeable and trustworthy.

If I have a headache and ask how many aspirins I should take, almost anyone will tell me two; that knowledge is available on the package and in lay medical folklore. It will also be understood that I should swallow the aspirins rather than dissolving them in water and injecting them. Most people, however, have no knowledge about a large variety of drugs, either those medically prescribed (such as cortisone) or those used without benefit of medical advice (like LSD). Would-be users must develop some notions about how much to take and how to take it, either by trial-and-error experimentation or by adopting the ideas suggested by sources they consider reliable (scientists, physicians or more experienced drug users). Those sources can tell the prospective user how much he should take and how he should take it in order to cure his sore throat, control his blood-clotting time, have a mystical experience or get high. They can also tell him how much will be too much, producing unwanted effects or overdose. They may tell him to take four pills of the kind the druggist will sell him, one after each meal and one before retiring; they may give more elaborate instructions, such as those given diabetics about controlling their metabolic balance with food and insulin; they may informally suggest that the novice has probably smoked enough hashish and ought to stop until it takes effect; or tell him that most people find 500 micrograms of "good acid" enough to induce an adequate amount of consciousness expansion.

Using these acquired understandings, the user takes an amount whose effect he can predict fairly accurately. He usually finds that his prediction is confirmed. In this way, his access to knowledge exerts a direct influence on his experience, allowing him to control the physiological input to that experience.

This analysis is based on the assumption that the user has complete control over the amount he takes and the method he uses. Since drug availability is often regulated by law, in reality the user can take only as much as he can get. A user also may lose control over the amount of a drug he takes when someone forces him to take more than he wants or even to take a drug he does not want at all. This occurs commonly when patients in pediatric medicine, in mental hospitals and tuberculosis hospitals are given drugs whose taste or effects they dislike; in chemical and biological warfare; and when chlorine or fluorides are added to city water supplies. In these cases, the relevant knowledge for an understanding of the drug's effects, insofar as they depend on dosage, is the knowledge held by the powerful person or organization which can force the user to ingest the drug.

Main effects. Social scientists have shown how the definitions drug users apply to their experience affect that experience. Persons suffering opiate withdrawal will respond as "typical" addicts if they interpret their distress as opiate withdrawal, but not if they blame the pain on some other cause (such as recovery from surgery). Marijuana users must learn to interpret its subtle effects as being different from ordinary experience and as pleasurable before they can get high. Indians and Caucasians interpret peyote experiences differently, and LSD trips have been experienced as consciousness expansion, transcendental religious experience, mock psychosis or being high.

The user brings to bear, in interpreting his experience, knowledge and definitions derived from participation in particular social groups. Indian culture teaches a different view of the peyote experience than is available to non-Indians. Marijuana users learn to experience the drug's effects from more experienced users. LSD trips are interpreted according to the understandings available in the various settings in which the drug is taken.

The process of interpreting experience has been studied largely in connection with nonmedical drug use, but presumably occurs in medical use also. Here the chief source of authoritative interpretations is the physician who prescribes the drug and, for many people, the pharmacist. Knowledge from authoritative sources lets the user identify the drug's main effect, know when it is occurring, and therefore decide that what is occurring, even when it seems undesirable or frightening, is really acceptable, if only because expected.

Defining Desirable Effects

Side effects. Side effects are not a medically or pharmacologically distinct category of reactions to drugs. Rather, they are effects not desired by either the user or the person administering the drug. Both side effects and main effects are socially defined categories. Mental disorientation might be an unwanted side effect to a physician, but a desired main effect for an illicit drug user.

A drug user's knowledge, if adequate, lets him identify unwanted side effects and deal with them. He interprets his experience most adequately if those who prepare him for the drug's main effects likewise teach him the likely side effects and how to deal with them. Illicit drug users typically teach novices the side effects to look out for, give reassurance about their seriousness, and give instruction in ways to avoid or overcome them; this mechanism probably prevents a great deal of potential pathology, though it can only operate when drug users are connected in information networks. Many LSD users became expert at "talking down" people experiencing bad trips, and marijuana users habitually teach novices what to do if they get extra high. Patients for whom physicans prescribe drugs seldom share a user culture. Since their medication may produce side effects, they can experience profound effects without knowing that their prescribed drug is responsible, should the physician fail to inform them. The physician himself may not know, since the drug may have become available before the effects had been discovered; this seems to have happened when oral contraceptives were introduced and many women experienced edema, depression, vascular difficulties and other undesired effects which no one, at the time, attributed to The Pill.

Research and communication. Knowledge, and the social channels through which it flows, affect the interpretations and responses a drug user makes to the experience the drug produces. This kind of knowledge is produced through "research." Research, so conceived, consists of the accumulation of ideas tested more or less systematically against experience of the empirical world. Researchers may use elaborate techniques and equipment or rely on simple devices and modes of analysis. At one extreme, the research pharmacologist systematically tests the effects of a drug on a wide variety of organ systems; at the other, a casual experimenter takes a "high"-producing drug over a period of weeks, and notes his own reactions, possibly making comparisons with others experimenting with the same drug.

Research, especially concerning subjective experiences produced by drugs, relies heavily on conventionally accepted rules of logic, inference and common sense, and scientific reasoning. Those rules help people decide when they have "experienced" something and what has produced the experience. When a variation from the ordinary occurs, drug users must decide whether it is related to the drug. Marijuana users, for instance, experience considerable hunger and must decide whether it is ordinary appetite or drug-induced.

Are drug effects entirely mental constructs or are they in some way constrained by physiological events? To what degree can people have drug experiences which have no physiological base? Experimental work on placebo effects suggests that there must be some physiological basis for the experience. However, human beings experience a variety of natural physiological events all the time; when one is observing them, even ordinary events can appear to be caused by drugs.

We can distinguish three major social structures in which drug use occurs, according to the degree of control the ultimate users of the drug exercise over their own drug-taking and especially over the production and distribution of drug-relevant knowledge. In one structure users retain control; the major case is illicit drug use for pleasure, though the use of patent medicines provides an interesting comparison. In a second situation the user delegates control to an agent presumed to act on his behalf; modern medical practice is the prime example. Finally, in situations such as chemical warfare, the user has no control over his ingestion of the drug or over the production and distribution of knowledge associated with use of the drug.

User Control

In a situation of user control, such as the illicit use of drugs for pleasure, the user takes as much as he wants on whatever schedule he wants; his dosage is self-initiated and self-regulated. He relies on knowledge generated in user groups to organize his drug-taking activities and interpret his drug experiences. He may feel substantial pressure from drug-using peers with whom he associates, but his use is voluntary and under his control.

Users generate knowledge about drugs largely from their own research, which may include consulting sources such as pharmacology texts or the *Physician's Desk Reference,* and lay techniques, such as self-experimentation and self-observation. While such methods are unreliable in individual cases, they are less likely to be influenced by idiosyncratic errors when a large number of users pool their observations and produce generalizations. The reliability of such generalizations depends on the efficiency of the communication channels through which information moves and the adequacy of the mechanism for collating it.

Pooled information about an illicitly used drug ordinarily accumulates slowly, often over many years. Insofar as users are connected, even tenuously, a large number of experiences eventually circulate through the connected system and produce what can be called a "drug culture" (not the melange of political and cultural attitudes the term is often applied to, but a set of common understandings about the drug, its characteristics and the way it can best be used). The development of knowledge about marijuana probably best approximates this model, many years of extensive marijuana use in the United States having produced a vast body of lore which does not vary much by region or social group.

Other methods of accumulating and collating knowledge occasionally are used. The drug known as STP underwent a hip equivalent of the mass testing of polio vaccines when thousands of pills containing it were thrown from a stage at a be-in. Though no one knew what they were, thousands of participants apparently took them, and within a few days most interested people had heard something about the effects of that drug. Information piled up at the Haight-Ashbury Free Medical Clinic and other places where people suffering adverse reactions were likely to go. In a short time, the major effects, appropriate dosages, likely side effects and effective antidotes were well known.

Knowledge produced this way is unsophisticated. If, as alleged, LSD damages chromosomes and thus produces birth defects in offspring even after drug use ceases, typical styles of user research could not discover the effect, for that kind of knowledge requires more sophisticated equipment and techniques of analysis than users have available. Further, any delayed effects are likely to be missed by user research, which relies on simple and immediate cause-effect relations. If, however, the user population includes well-trained scientists, as was always the case with LSD and is increasingly true with respect to all psychedelic drugs, this problem can be overcome. Finally, the effectiveness of the research is limited by the nature of the user network. Similarity and repetition of experience produce reliability of knowledge, and sparsely connected networks may gather insufficient data to generalize from reliably. The underground news media might be able to link isolated users or user groups.

Knowledge produced by user research has the great virtue of being directed precisely to the questions the user is interested in having answered. If he wants to know whether the drug will make him high, the available research, conducted by people who share his interest, will give him an answer. When knowledge is incomplete, inaccurate or unavailable, users will have predictable troubles. This is particularly obvious when a drug first appears and knowledge has not yet been produced and disseminated.

If we switch to another instance of user control—the case of patent medicines—we see the importance of the character of user networks. I have observed that people produce knowledge about patent medicine effects either on their own or in small family groups. Laxatives are used to relieve constipation, a condition which, presumably, is not widely discussed among people suffering from it. Users cannot easily identify one another as fellow sufferers and thus as potential sources of information. Parents may share the results of their own experiments with their children, as may spouses with one another, but one can imagine that the knowledge would not move much beyond that. Specialized groups (such as fellow inmates of an old people's home) might share such information, but in general knowledge probably would not cumulate. My speculations highlight the importance of communication channels in understanding the experiences of users who control their own drug use.

Control by the User's Agent

When the user delegates control to an agent, interesting variations in the production and distribution of knowledge occur, with equally interesting variations in the kinds of experiences users have. The major empirical case is that of the physician prescribing medication for his patient (though an interesting variation is provided by the religious use of drugs, as in the relation between Don Juan and his pupil, Carlos Castaneda [see *The Teachings of Don Juan,* by Carlos Castaneda]). Here the user takes the drug the doctor prescribes for him, in the amounts and on the schedule the doctor recommends. The doctor's prescription reflects what the doctor wants to accomplish, rather than what the patient wants; their desires may coincide, but need not and in many cases do not.

The doctor uses at least two criteria in evaluating drugs. He wants to alleviate some dangerous or unpleasant condition the patient is suffering from, in a way clearly visible both to him and to his patient. The drug effect which most interests the doctor is one which produces demonstrable (in the best case, visible to the patient's naked eye) improvement. But the doctor also uses a second criterion: he does not want the drug to interfere with his control over the patient. The rationale for that desire is well known: since (the rationale goes) the doctor knows what will help the patient better than the patient himself, the patient must surrender himself to achieve maximum results; if the patient rejects the physician's advice his health may be impaired. Doctors believe they have a legitimate interest in maintaining what Eliot Freidson has usefully labelled "professional dominance."

The patient usually relies on the physician for his

knowledge about dosage, main effects and side effects of the drug prescribed. But the physician may not give the patient all the knowledge that is available to him, because he does not want the patient to use that knowledge as a basis for disobeying medical orders. Henry Lennard has given a telling example. Certain of the tranquilizing drugs sometimes produce an unusual effect on male sexual functioning: while the man experiences orgasm, no ejaculation occurs. This naturally causes some anxiety in those who have the experience. Since these drugs are given to relieve anxiety, Lennard asked psychiatrists why they did not tell patients that this might occur. "If I did that," ran the typical answer, "the patient might not take the drug and, *in my judgment,* he should run the risk of that anxiety in order to protect himself from his basic anxieties." (Physicians also withhold information about side effects because suggestible patients may experience effects they have been told about, even when there is no physiological basis for the experience. Doctors believe that this risk outweighs the risk of morbidity associated with the lack of information.)

Sometimes the physician does not give the patient adequate information about the experience the drug will produce because he does not have the knowledge himself. Research on drugs for medical use is organized quite differently than user's research, and its organization creates substantial barriers to a free flow of information. Drug research is a highly specialized discipline, with its own journals, professional societies and scientific world to which the physician does not belong. He may not follow the latest developments in pharmacology, read its journals or attend meetings of its scientific organizations. So he depends for his knowledge of drug effects on such general medical literature as he keeps up with, on his immediate colleagues, and on the knowledge provided by pharmaceutical companies through their literature and salesmen. Most of his knowledge, especially of new drugs, probably comes from the last source. (Some physicians, especially those specialists who see many cases of the same disease, may, like illicit drug users, try different dosages and treatments on different patients. They may then pool their observations with like-minded specialists and generate knowledge similar to that of drug user cultures, with the same advantages and drawbacks.)

Another serious barrier to the practicing physician's acquisition of knowledge about the drugs he prescribes arises from the organization of pharmaceutical research and manufacture. While pharmaceutical companies, the scientists who work for them and the physicians who participate in their drug testing programs all no doubt want to produce medically valuable drugs that will help physicians combat disease, they are also interested, as Congressional investigations have shown, in profits. They design their research to produce profitably marketable products which can be sold, via physicians' prescriptions, to the public, and which will also pass government tests of purity, efficacy and lack of dangerous side effects. They look primarily for drugs which will produce (or seem to produce) effects on diseased patients, of the kind physicians want, or can be persuaded to want. They appear to investigate possible side effects as Congressional investigations have shown, only so far as required by prudence and law. In general, companies do not seek or force on the practicing physician information which would lessen the profitability of a drug they believe has good commercial possibilities.

The physician, then, may not know that the drug has certain effects or he may not choose to tell the patient what he knows. The uninformed patient runs two risks. He may have experiences which are quite pronounced, extremely unpleasant and even dangerous, but not realize that they result from his medication. As a consequence, he may continue to take the drug that produces the unwanted side effect. For instance, certain commonly prescribed antihistamines occasionally produce urethral stricture; allergic patients who take large quantities may experience this condition but never report it to the allergist because it does not seem to be in his department. If the condition becomes severe they consult a urologist. He may discover they are taking large doses of antihistamine and cure the difficulty by recommending one that does not have this side effect. But not all physicians know of the connection, and failure of the patient to report or the physician to make the connection can lead to serious difficulty.

The patient may also experience symptoms which have an insidious and gradual onset, and never recognize that there is any change in his condition which requires explanation. This was apparently the experience of many women who took birth control pills. They suffered serious and continuing depression, but it appeared gradually, so that they did not realize anything had occurred which might be attributable to the hormone. The mood changes produced by drugs taken for medical purposes will be so gradual that they will be attributed to psychological difficulties, changes in social relationships or other causes unrelated to the medication. Thus, the patient who begins to experience mood changes may be treated as a neurotic. This must have happened frequently among early users of oral contraceptives, especially unmarried women whom physicians often consider especially prone to neurotic symptoms.

Though the medical and scientific professions are organized in a way that ought to promote full communication to practicing physicians of adverse drug reactions, a recent study suggests obstacles which impede that communication. Hospital physicians were asked to report all adverse drug reactions and, simultaneously, clinical pharmacologists made independent checks. From two-thirds to three-quarters of the adverse reactions to prescribed drugs verified by the pharmacologists were *not* reported by the physicians. Physicians tended to report those adverse reactions in which morbidity and danger were high, and in which the connection between the drug and the reaction were already well known. This means that the system works poorly to accumulate new information, although it is relatively efficient in reconfirming what is already known. Add to this the probability that patients are less likely than illicit drug users to compare experiences on a large scale. The result is a substantial risk that adverse information will never be accumulated, and drug users will continue to suffer from this lack of knowledge.

Information Dispersal

Many of the user's difficulties in interpreting his experience will result from the stage of development of knowledge about the drug. Adverse reactions to illicitly used drugs decline as their use increases and a fund of knowledge grows among communicating users, allowing them to regulate dosage and deal with adverse effects. A similar natural history may occur with the use of drugs in medical practice. Doctors seek drugs which will make a decisive and noticeable improvement in a patient's condition. Pharmaceutical companies and researchers attempt to produce such drugs. In the effort to produce a *noticeable* improvement, company recommendations, insufficient research and physician inclinations combine to produce a tendency to prescribe dosages larger than required for the desired medical effect, even large enough to produce serious side effects. Because the research done prior to use on patients has not looked thoroughly into possible side effects, no one connects these occurrences with the new medication. Where the drug is potentially profitable, as in the case of antibiotics, adrenocortical steroids or oral contraceptives, its use will be heavily promoted and widely publicized, so that physicians will feel pressure both from patients and the example of their more innovative peers to begin prescribing the new drug. Massive use, combined with a tendency to overdose, will produce enough adverse reactions that someone will eventually investigate and establish the connection. More such reactions will occur before the information filters through the barriers already discussed, but eventually conventional dosages will be lowered and the incidence of adverse reactions will decline. When they occur, furthermore, they will be recognized and treated more effectively. Eventually, presumably, the number of adverse reactions will reach a minimum based on the number of physicians who are either ignorant of their character or who do not communicate their knowledge to patients so that the reactions can be recognized, reported and treated.

To what degree does the gradual process of information dispersal occur because the investigation and production of medically prescribed drugs is carried on by profit-making corporations in a capitalist economy? Obviously, those elements of the process which reflect marketing strategies designed to maximize profits—focusing research on products likely to produce high sales at low costs and a relative neglect of potential side effects—would not occur in a noncapitalist economy. On the other hand, most of the other elements, reflecting as they do the interests of an organized medical profession as distinct from the interests of patients, would presumably occur in any developed society which contains such a group. The desire of physicians to achieve discernible results and to maintain control over patients would probably continue to influence the dissemination of knowledge from researchers to physicians to patients and, consequently, the kinds of experiences medical patients have as a result of using prescribed drugs.

Carlos Castaneda's account of his instruction in the use of psychedelic substances by Don Juan is the only one I know of the delegation of control to a religious, rather than a medical, agent. The relationship between the two, and its effect on Castaneda's drug experiences, appears similar to the medical model. Don Juan often gave Castaneda insufficient information with which to interpret his experiences and avoid unpleasant panics, because he felt Castaneda's inexperience (or "lack of professional training") would make it impossible for him to understand, because he wished to retain control over his student's progress, and because he wanted his pedagogy to turn out the result he sought, even though the experience might be unpleasant or frightening for Castaneda in the short run and the result might ultimately be failure. The disparity between teacher and student goals parallels the disparity between physician and patient interests and goals, and some of the resulting experiences of the user who has delegated control appear similar.

Control by External Agents

People sometimes find themselves required to ingest drugs involuntarily, under the control of an independent agent. The external agent's purposes sometimes conflict directly with those of the user, as when people find themselves the victims of chemical warfare in the form of a poison gas attack or a contaminated water supply. In other cases, the agent administers the drug because he believes it is in the best interest of the community to do so, as when people with tuberculosis or leprosy are medicated to prevent them from infecting others. In such cases and in such similar instances as the forced medication of mental hospital inmates and the administration of amphetamines to allegedly hyperkinetic schoolchildren, those administering the drug frequently insist, and believe, that the medication serves the ultimate interest of the user as well, however much he may wish to avoid it. In both chemical warfare and forced medication, the crucial feature of the social structure is an imbalance in power between those administering the drug and those to whom it is administered.

Those administering the drug usually have goals totally divorced from anything the user might desire. Although physicians in ordinary medical practice have goals somewhat divergent from those of their patients, they must nevertheless take realistic account of the possibility that patients will cease coming to them unless the treatment proves satisfactory. When the one administering the drug has sufficient control over the user, he can safely ignore the other's interests altogether, and his actions can be designed solely to serve his own interests, personal or (more likely) organizational.

External agents usually look for a maximum dose of a drug—one that will not fail to produce the result they seek. In the case of chemical warfare, they seek to kill or incapacitate those to whom the drug is administered, so they look for the dose at which 50 percent of the subjects will die. In the case of mass administration of tranquilizers in mental hospitals, they look for a dose which will allow patients to continue to take care of themselves but render them incapable of violence and totally suppress psychotic symptoms which interfere with hospital routine. In general, dosages are higher than in medically prescribed or self-regulated use, because they are meant to kill, disable or control the target population, rather than cure their diseases or give them pleasure.

Since goals are set unilaterally, those administering the drug must use coercive measures to insure that the desired dose gets into its target. As the divergence in goals between the two parties increases, the difficulty of administration increases, too. Where the divergence is great and obvious, as in tuberculosis and mental hospitals, hospital personnel usually supervise patients' ingestion of medication very closely; even so, inmates often discover ingenious ways of evading such treatment.

In chemical warfare, where the interests of the parties are diametrically opposed, the problem of an "effective delivery system" becomes extremely important. Chemical warfare agencies concern themselves with foolproof means of dosing entire populations, and so work on such devices as aerosols, which guarantee ingestion by saturating the air everyone must breathe, or methods of contaminating urban water supplies. In their zeal to dose all members of the target population, they create for themselves the problem of inadvertently dosing some of their own personnel, such as the policeman who, attempting to squirt a political demonstrator with Mace, neglects to allow for the wind blowing toward him and gets a faceful of his own medicine.

Those who administer drugs to involuntary users are either indifferent about providing those who get the drug with any knowledge about it or actively attempt to prevent them from acquiring knowledge. Hospital personnel seldom inform inmates receiving forced medication about main or side effects. They may suggest that "this pill will make you feel better" or that "the doctor thinks this will help your condition," but seldom give more detailed information. This lack of knowledge can cause problems, as previously mentioned, but a user's culture may develop among people who are confined in total institutions and subject to the same drug regimen.

Where destruction or incapacitation of the target population is the aim, those who administer the drug may wish to prevent the spread of any knowledge about the administration or effects of the drug. In this way, they hope to prevent countermeasures and, by preventing any understanding of what is happening, create panic in addition to the drug's specific physiological effects. Both Army chemical warriors and those of the psychedelic Left hoped to exploit this phenomenon by putting LSD into urban water supplies. Not only, they hoped, would the drug interfere with people's normal functioning by causing them to misperceive and hallucinate; in addition, people would not even know that they had been given a drug which was causing these difficulties and would be frightened as well. (As it turns out, Mayor Daley need not have worried about the Yippies putting LSD into the Chicago water supply during the 1968 Democratic Convention. As Army CBW investigators had already discovered, LSD breaks down rapidly in the presence of chlorine, and the Chicago water supply usually contains enough chlorine that one can easily taste it. This defect in LSD as a chemical warfare agent has led the Army to attempt to produce a water-soluble version of THC [tetrahydracannabinol, one of the active agents in marijuana], which otherwise is most easily ingested in smoke.)

Drug use in all its varieties—legal, semilegal and illegal—needs far more investigation. If drug experiences somehow reflect or are related to social settings we must note specific settings and determine their exact effects on participants. We must also look further at the role of power and knowledge in each setting: knowledge of whether to take a drug, how to take and what to expect of it; and power over distribution of the drug, knowledge about it, and over the decision to take or not to take it.

SUGGESTED READINGS

The Teachings of Don Juan by Carlos Castenada (Berkeley: University of California Press, 1968).

Medical Innovation by James S. Coleman et al. (Indianapolis: Bobbs-Merrill, 1966).

Professional Dominance by Eliot Freidson (Chicago: Aldine, 1970).

Chemical and Biological Warfare: America's Hidden Arsenal by Seymour Hersh (Indianapolis: Bobbs-Merrill, 1968).

Timetables by Julius Roth (Indianapolis: Bobbs-Merrill, 1963).

7 *Nils Christie*

The Scandinavian Hangover

The Scandinavian countries are sometimes seen as offering useful pre-tests of social welfare arrangements. Some of our arrangements work rather well, but some represent more muddles than models. The field of alcohol control within Scandinavia gives examples of both.

Let me first give some of the Scandinavian experience in regulating the *accessibility* of alcohol, then turn to some of our attempts to cope with the *problem drinker.* Diluted in alcohol, our social arrangements may be perceived as helpful experience for dealing with similar problems in the United States.

Denmark is very lenient about drinking. There is no state monopoly of liquor. Beer, wine, and brandy are widely available through approximately 20,000 stores, restaurants, and pubs.

Finland, Norway, and Sweden are immensely more restrictive. Finland holds a strict state monopoly on beer, wine and whisky. Finland in particular has a strict control of customers. All customers must show special identification cards, complete with photo and signature. They are closely examined to make sure that all drinkers are old enough and that none are known alcoholics. Sweden has a random spot-check system for identification (when an automatic lamp gives a signal, the buyer must produce identification). In Norway a seller will demand identification when, for any reason, he becomes suspicious. Both Norway and Sweden, like Finland, are strict about age limits and deny those with alcohol problems the right to buy.

To find out how to handle alcohol and its problems, we must try to set up a relationship between *accessibility, consumption,* and resulting *public nuisance.* Do countries (like Denmark) that allow easy access to alcohol also have more consumption per capita, more arrests, and more public drunkenness? Or is the opposite true—that making it difficult for the drinker to get the drink creates more alcoholic problems than its solves? It is also possible, of course, that such relationships are not clear—that national peculiarities or differences in cultural drinking patterns (for example, between drinking beer socially at home, or whisky alone in a bar) will have as much impact as the relative availability or consumption of alcohol itself.

What about consumption? As any prohibitionist might have predicted, Danes absorb the most alcohol—about 1.2 American gallons of pure alcohol per year; Finns consume the least, with about half that. Norwegians consume slightly less, per capita, than Swedes.

When we turn from the use of alcohol to its abuse, the picture suddenly reverses. Denmark, the villain in the piece as viewed by a teetotaler, has only 4.6 arrests for drunkenness per 1,000 inhabitants 15 years old and over (1963), while Finland, the villain as viewed by the beverage industry, has nearly 10 times as many (44). Again, Sweden (17.0) and Norway (11.9) have intermediate positions.

Is Something Rotten in Denmark?

How to explain this anomaly? It can be partially explained by differences in the *types* of alcoholic drinks consumed as well as by differences in how they are consumed. For example, the average Dane drinks more beer than his fellows in the other three countries put together, and beer is known to produce a lower blood alcohol level per consumed unit than brandy—especially undiluted brandy. But the Danes also drink brandy—and their consumption is not so far below the Finns as to explain the gap (the average Dane drinks a little more than half as much brandy as the average Finn). Also, after all, Danish beer is not water.

Another possible explanation is that the Danes follow the continental Europeans in their drinking patterns—small, even, frequent imbiding extending throughout the year, while the Finns consume their entire year's quota on a few grand occasions. This explanation might hold true for older people, but it definitely does not hold true for the young. In a study of drinking patterns of 18-year-olds from the four Scandinavian capitals (over a four-month period) it was found that boys from Copenhagen drank most often and those from Helsinki least. But in terms of *quantity* consumed on each occasion, the records were equal. Helsinki youths drink no more on each occasion.

But they do seem to make more noise about it! A comparative study was made on self-reported crime among young males (this time only figures from Oslo and Helsinki were available). We find substantially more self-reporting of drunk and disturbing behavior at public places, and more contacts with police, in Helsinki than in Oslo—and this in spite of the fact that bootleg production of alcohol, and all it entails, is much more common among Oslo youths than among Finns. Self-reported drunken driving is about equal.

Ignoring national peculiarities, let me sum up: A strict system of legal and institutional control of accessibility of alcohol seems related to low alcohol consumption—but also to a high degree of public nuisance.

It probably works something like this: A drinking culture in which there are a lot of noisy drunks on the street, or other highly visible and offensive evidence of the bad effects of drinking, will eventually lead to a crackdown and tightening up, with tighter state control of liquor. This in turn may cut down on part of the visibility of the problem—with liquor harder to get, forbidden to minors and known alcoholics, there may be fewer drunks staggering openly out of state-owned and controlled bars, and somewhat less open revelry.

However, on the other hand as the American experiment with prohibition demonstrated, other forms of alcoholic problems may actually increase.

There is no simple cause and effect relationship. Interactions and interrelationships develop between the system of control, the amount of consumption, and the visible problems resulting from the use of alcohol.

Alcohol problems do not directly bring on a strict system of control. Rather, in political and social life, there are various pressure groups which act both as buffers and catalytic agents. The Scandinavian countries too have their "drys," similar to the WCTU and the Anti-saloon League in the United States. The parliaments in the four countries have the following percentages of teetotalers: Denmark 6.7 percent; Norway 30 percent; Sweden 36 percent; Finland 32.5 percent. The familiar pattern emerges: Denmark at one extreme of permissiveness, the other countries bunched toward the other extreme. Typically, the current prime ministers in Finland, Sweden, and Norway are teetotalers; the Danish prime minister is not.

In my country, Norway, teetotalers make up the largest non-party group in parliament. This, I believe, stems directly from, and represents a reaction against, our not-so-sober background. Most of the Scandinavian countries, from the Vikings on, have long and extreme drinking histories. In 1815 all Norwegian landowners, for instance, were given the right to distill liquor—and most took broad advantage of it. An extremely well-designed questionnaire study made in 1859 showed that more than one-third of the population were hardly, if at all, able to control their use of liquor. Observers described Norway as a thoroughly alcoholized country. Then the reaction set in. This was the time of the birth and very rapid growth of the abstinence movement. Temperance ideas from the United States found fertile ground, made common cause with other abstinence forces, and brought on a change in drinking habits. Even those who continued to drink—both users and abusers—were never the same again. We drink now, but with thorough feelings of guilt and anxiety.

The abstinence movement has, therefore, been successful so far. But the strength of the dry movement seems to be waning in Scandinavia, and this is probably related to the fact that the visibility of problems caused by alcohol is also declining. Norwegians are being arrested for drunkenness less frequently than they used to be. The steam is going out of the drive toward abstinence, and teetotalism is suffering.

Now that the rigidity of controls is declining, authorities feel freer to experiment with details of control. In Finland, beer and wine shops were opened in some rural areas in 1952; results were mixed, but generally good. Consumption went up among adult males, but declined among the young; and (reminiscent of American repeal) consumption of illegal or bootleg alcohol went down from 92 percent of the total to a bare 15 percent. In Sweden, abolition of strict rationing in 1955 (although associated with increases in all prices) led to a severe increase in consumption for heavy drinkers, but at the same time a slight decrease among "normal users." Both in Sweden and Finland the wine monopolies are trying hard, through advertising and price adjustments, to move consumption away from brandy and over to wine and beer.

Drunken Driving

Compared to America, the punishment for drunken driving in Scandinavia is severe. This is true also in Denmark, although the pattern of greatest leniency in Denmark, and greatest stringency in Finland is generally followed. (All four Scandinavian countries work closely together in law-enforcement, and Danish lawmakers are gravitating toward the joint Scandinavian standard.)

Norway has the lowest legal blood alcohol limit, while Denmark has none. Finland has the strictest penalties. If a driver's blood test measures above the legal minimum in Norway he will, typically, draw 21 days in prison and have his license suspended for one year on first offense (more on succeeding offenses). In Finland he would serve six months in prison (and can get up to three years—or, if a death is involved, up to seven) and lose his license for two to three years.

There is little chance that these laws will be changed—they have strong popular support. Poll after poll show that the people approve of them. Only two groups have serious doubts about them—the drunken drivers themselves and the people who administer the laws. The drunk drivers stay prudently quiet; and the administrators are ambivalent, hampered by a feeling that there are many good things about our present practices.

For we feel that our present system curtails drinking in general, and drunk driving in particular. Many people don't drive to parties where they expect to find drink, or they don't drink when they get there. Those who do know that they run the risk of getting caught. More than 2000 persons were imprisoned in Norway in 1963 for drunk driving. That figure may not seem shocking to an American, used to crime on a large scale; but they are very shocking to a Norwegian (America has roughly 200 prisoners per 100,000 population; we have 44.) More people are imprisoned in Norway for drunk driving than for all crimes put together. A sizeable part of the Norwegian people at some time in their lives go through society's most severe ceremony of degradation—imprisonment with criminals.

The skid-row alcoholic is a more universally-defined problem case. He is a reject of society, with few family or social responsibilities, and so probably causes less real hardship to others than other alcoholics. But he is also extremely visible (especially perhaps in my country, which has a strong temperance movement and no slums). But the public demands for some sort of action are strong indeed. He stands out as an offense to the clean streets. He has no place to hide, no run-down building, no privileged areas reserved for chronic sickness and sin. At the same time the skid row person has to stay in the towns to have reliable access to his supply of alcohol.

This whole situation strongly tempts society to use *force*. But application of force means that law is brought into the picture, and law is very sensitive to problems of justice.

Here society is in trouble. Skid row activity is a disturbing one, but not one that can be defined as a very severe crime. And even severe crimes are treated with extreme leniency in Scandinavia as compared to the United States. The "just" punishment for skid row drunkenness should be a few days in prison. But strong forces within society feel the need to get rid of these persons for longer.

Hiding the Problem in Prison

So "compromises" help solve the problem for society. The skid row habitue cannot be *punished* by removal; but, (and here I cite a law professor in the debate that led up to our present law, passed in 1893): ". . . what cannot be inflicted as punishment, cannot be objected to when it is done to take care of a person. . . ." Later the terminology was modernized—incarcerations would not only "take care of" these poor people, but "treat" them as well. Special institutions should be created for them, and they would not be called prisoners, but inmates. So medicine became a justification for the kind of sentence that law itself could not justify. In practice, most skid row alcoholics serve in a very severe prison for a much longer period than the great majority of our ordinary prisoners do for ordinary crimes.

They are, naturally, extremely unhappy and see the whole situation as a great injustice. In a little study I once made, I asked both ordinary thieves and skid row alcoholics waiting for trial what they would do if they could act as judges of their own cases. The thieves came very close to the sentence they actually received some days later; but the skid row people declared themselves not guilty, or only deserving of a fine or a few days in jail. The discrepancy between their evaluation of a just sentence and the sentence they actually received was enormous. However, since their status is so low—and particularly so among puritans who place a high value on working—their plight is seldom of concern to anybody but some researchers who happen to get to know and like them.

What is interesting here is the way words, concepts, and even ideals have been taken out of one context (medicine) and used very efficiently within another one (a legal framework) to curb minorities who have little power to fight back. Skid-row alcoholics are not the only minorities that have been so curbed—nor is this practice confined to Scandinavia.

Another way that three of the four Scandinavian countries (characteristically, Denmark is excluded) have attempted to control alcoholism outside the usual control agencies is by a new device—a committee of *lay specialists* in alcohol problems who, presumably, would be more flexible than the regular agencies, and could help prevent and limit alcoholism by getting to the alcoholic before his public behavior made him a police problem.

In practice it has not worked out that way. These temperance boards seldom get into the act until after the police are already involved—in fact it is usually the police that call them in. In effect they have become, largely, just another arm of law-enforcement when they operate. Usually they are inactive.

A major trend in recent social and criminal policy is toward *combining* the different control disciplines. I doubt the fruitfulness of this approach—certainly when dealing with alcoholics. It may be that the quest for combination is futile—that law and medicine, like oil and water, cannot really mix. Perhaps law, which emphasizes internal control, and must therefore limit the knowledge it can use, and medicine, which must be free to seek unlimited knowledge and must therefore de-emphasize internal control, are basically antagonistic. This does not mean that they should not both be used in alcohol control—but that they should be used separately, each according to its peculiar strengths and insights, at different times in the process of control, rather than mixed together in a form that must eventually subvert both. Medicine—and social work and the other ameliorating disciplines—can study the nature of alcoholism and how to treat it. Law should dispense justice—with due regard for what justice is in each particular circumstance.

I do not believe that law, social work, or medicine should ever be attempting, or at least pretending, to be doing roughly the same things at the same time.

SUGGESTED READINGS

Social Welfare in Denmark by Orla Jensen (Copenhagen: Det Danske Selskab, 1961).

Human Deviance, Social Problems, and Social Control by Edwin M. Lemert (Englewood Cliffs, N.J.: Prentice-Hall, 1967).

Society, Culture, and Drinking Patterns edited by David J. Pittman and Charles R. Snyder (New York: John Wiley, 1962).

Alcoholism in America by Harrison M. Trice (New York: McGraw-Hill, 1966).

Section IV

Groups

While the focus of Section III was on the individual, Section IV changes that focus perceptibly toward the group itself. The theme of socialization, or learning, continues, but now larger issues will be broached about the group process itself. In “Machismo and Marianismo,” Stevens discusses the particular constellation of masculine values called “machismo” found among some Latin men. With the sociologist’s eye Stevens suggests that masculine machismo is joined with feminine marianismo in providing a stable sex role complementarity for those among whom it is found. Machista “behavior” characteristics read like a list of the seven deadly sins, with pride (arrogance) heading the list. Marianismo, on the other hand, pictures the menopausal mother as semidivine, morally superior and spiritually stronger than men. Stevens sees a kind of symbiosis emerging out of this role arrangement.

Whereas the norms of machismo have grown out of a particular cultural setting, Browning’s “Timing of Our Lives” discusses the consequences of abstract demographic changes in the ordinary lives of ordinary people. His synopsis of demography (the study of population—birth, death and migration) from a sociological point of view and his discussion of the consequences of “death control,” the relationship of life expectancy to the life cycles of individuals in developing and developed countries, raise important questions about the need for people living in societies to understand the basic morphology of those societies. His hypothesis that knowledge about longer life expectancy and changing marriage, divorce and child-rearing practices “lags” the demographic processes themselves leads him to make suggestions that ought to be seriously considered.

Henry and Sims, in “Actors’ Search for Self,” shift our attention from the entire life cycle to the part of it that seems so critical for the formation of identity. They introduce us to an important area of social psychological theory, namely, that which has to do with the developmental stages of personality. Focusing on Erik Erikson’s ideas about the importance of identity formation versus identity diffusion, Henry and Sims provide an interesting test of hypotheses about identity formation by studying a sample of actors. Their discussion of the consequences of taking on others’ identities (which is what an actor does in performance) leads to an interesting discussion of the need for all of us to learn to take roles in real life.

While the focus of Section III was on the individual, Section IV changes that focus perceptibly toward the group itself. The theme of socialization, or learning, continues, but now larger issues will be broached about the group process itself. In “Machismo and Marianismo,” Stevens discusses the particular constellation of masculine values called “machismo” found among some Latin men. With the sociologist’s eye Stevens suggests that masculine machismo is joined with feminine marianismo in providing a stable sex role complementarity for those among whom it is found. Machista behavior characteristics read like a list of the seven deadly sins, with pride (arrogance) heading the list. Marianismo, on the other hand, pictures the menopausal mother as semidivine, morally superior and spiritually stronger than men. Stevens sees a kind of symbiosis emerging out of this role arrangement.

Whereas the norms of machismo have grown out of a particular cultural setting, Browning’s “Timing of Our Lives” discusses the consequences of abstract demographic changes in the ordinary lives of ordinary people. His synopsis of demography (the study of population—birth, death and migration) from a sociological point of view and his discussion of the consequences of “death control,” the relationship of life expectancy to the life cycles of individuals in developing and developed countries, raise important questions about the need for people living in societies to understand the basic morphology of those societies. His hypothesis that knowledge about longer life expectancy and changing marriage, divorce and child-rearing practices “lags” the demographic processes themselves leads him to make suggestions that ought to be seriously considered.

Henry and Sims, in “Actors’ Search for Self,” shift our attention from the entire life cycle to the part of it that seems so critical for the formation of identity. They introduce us to an important area of social psychological theory, namely, that which has to do with the developmental stages of personality. Focusing on

Erik Erikson's ideas about the importance of identity formation versus identity diffusion, Henry and Sims provide an interesting test of hypotheses about identity formation by studying a sample of actors. Their discussion of the consequences of taking on others' identities (which is what an actor does in performance) leads to an interesting discussion of the need for all of us to learn to take roles in real life.

In "Rebirth in the Airborne," Weiss gives us a fascinating glimpse into an entire small world, in this case the world of the paratrooper. Important knowledge of how a "new" identity is forged in a total institution has broad application in sociology. Using the conceptual tools of the cultural anthropologist—rites of passage, mana and taboo—Weiss informs us that one becomes a paratrooper through ritual incorporation into the group and that the rite of passage is "quasi-religious" in character.

Howard's "The Making of a Black Muslim" is yet another illustration of the process of group incorporation of individuals. The ascetic nature of the Black Muslims makes them, says Howard, a deviant organization in the Negro community that nonetheless has great appeal. This appeal is based on black nationalism and the emphasis on self-help. These two points of appeal lead to the recruitment of two different types of Black Muslims. The "Muslim militants" are attracted by the former appeal, the "Protestant Ethic Muslims" by the latter. Howard points to a key need for any organization that makes total demands—whether it be Black Muslims or paratroopers—on its members, the need for *insulation* from the larger world. He also points to some of the major problems such groups face in heterogeneous societies.

A persistent problem in many societies has to do with marriage. Status is gained and lost through marriage. In some societies, families solve this problem by arranging marriages. In most societies, institutions of one sort or another develop to facilitate the marriage market. Scott, in "Sororities and the Husband Game," draws parallels between the fattening houses and convents of primitive societies and the college sororities of modern ones. Suggesting that "the right man" is a grave family concern, Scott outlines the historical process whereby the sorority has become an agent of family social control, albeit an indirect one, through alumnae. The sorority exercises "love control," encourages hypergamy and solves the "Brahmin problem" by cornering the marriage market in "dangerously heterogeneous" large public universities. Shifts in the larger society, however, Scott asserts, are creating dark days for the traditional sororities.

1 *Evelyn P. Stevens*

Machismo and Marianismo

"If your wife asks you to jump out the window, pray God that it's from the first floor," is a popular Latin American witticism. Does this sound like the realm of *machismo* and oppressed women? Social scientists and feminists in the North have expressed alarm over the plight of Latin American women. It is time to set the record straight: from the Rio Bravo south to Patagonia it is at least 50 percent a woman's world, even though the men don't know it.

Latin American men and women have unequivocal conceptions of their roles and they play them out, if not in harmony, at least in counterpoint. The interpersonal dynamics of the existing social structure afford each sex a complementary sphere of influence that satisfies basic personal and social needs.

The inference we draw from the available material on Latin American women is that they do not want a change of status. While they almost unanimously complain about their sad lot, their suffering and the unfairness of male domination, they seem to enjoy their martyrdom, and make few concrete proposals for even minimal changes in the status quo. Certainly there has been no movement comparable either to the nineteenth century feminist movement or the twentieth century one in the North Atlantic industrialized nations. Such efforts as have been made were limited almost exclusively to the question of female suffrage; once that was attained, public discussion declined precipitously.

Because much of what has been written about machismo is either moralistic, fragmentary or disguised boasting, it will be helpful to present a more systematic description of its major characteristics before discussing the female attitude and behavior patterns which have developed in a parallel manner.

Mexicans like to think that machismo is an exclusively Mexican phenomenon: the country's principal product. Because Mexico is the nearest culture that exhibits the pattern and because so many Anglo-Americans have visited that country, the misconception persists. A survey of Latin American social science literature reveals that some observers in every country perceive machismo as a widespread, deep-rooted psychosocial problem. Within this general area, however, there are wide variations in the distribution and intensity of its manifestations. Differences can be accounted for in terms of the existing microcultures.

Residents of those areas where indigenous groups have been least affected by contact with "outside" cultural influences show few machista traits. Certain parts of highland Peru, of Bolivia, Colombia, Ecuador and even of Mexico fall into the machismo-free category.

In some Indian communities, matrilineal family structure prevails and women have high prestige, often exercising more authority than the men within the confines of the home. Among the Aymara Indians of Peru, complete premarital sexual freedom prevails for females as well as males. Among the Kuikuru of Brazil, extramarital as well as premarital freedom is the accepted norm for both sexes.

Seven Deadly Sins

In countries populated chiefly by Europeans or their descendants (such as Uruguay, Argentina, Chile and Costa Rica), the machismo behavior pattern exists in somewhat attenuated form. This watering down is particularly interesting because it is generally agreed that the cultural roots of machismo can be traced to the Mediterranean countries, especially to Spain and Italy, from which the Latin American nations have received much of their European immigration.

Machismo seems to flourish in areas where the cultures of two or more great continents have mingled: the urbanized, mestizo sectors of the "Indian" countries as well as the countries of African-European mixture (for example, Brazil, Cuba, Puerto Rico and Venezuela). In all such countries, typical manifestations are reported for all economic classes.

Prevalence of the pattern throughout the class structure seems to contradict the unsupported assertions of recent Afro-American writers in the United States that machismo is found only in the most economically deprived social groups. As a matter of fact, the term *machismo* may be a misnomer for North American black male behavior.

As pictured by some Latin American writers, a description of machista behavior reads like an excerpt from a list of the seven deadly sins.

Pride, better translated as arrogance, heads the list. Resembling the caricature of a sixteenth century Spanish conquistador, today's Latin American male exhibits an overbearing attitude toward anyone in a position inferior to his, demanding menial services and subservience from subordinates.

Burden of Civility

Another manifestation of the trait is his insistence on having his own way, forcing acceptance of his views, winning every argument in which he engages, considering every difference of opinion as a declaration of enmity. For this reason, the macho is reluctant to engage in frank discussion of any important problem, because if he risks expressing an opinion, he must literally be ready to fight for it. Conversely, he must avoid eliciting opinions from other males in order not to appear to be inviting a quarrel which might have physically and psychologically dangerous consequences. Much of the conversation of Latin American male groups consists of "small talk," sparring at arm's length so that all involved can protect themselves from the hazards of conflict. The resultant impoverishment of interpersonal relations makes men lonely and somewhat wistful. Mexicans get drunk, asserts Octavio Paz, when they can no longer bear the burden of civility.

Under the pressures of the machismo ethos, the Iberian concept of *dignidad,* based on the belief that all human beings are equal recipients of grace, becomes deformed into a hypersensitivity, a touchiness, a disposition to interpret almost any remark as an insult. Men bear themselves as though they carried signs reading, "Don't trifle with me," and in smaller print, "Don't josh me, jostle me or cross my will." Almost the only area in which they permit themselves any leeway in disagreeing openly with each other is in discussions of sporting events. Soccer, football and jai alai are immensely popular, in part because betting by spectators affords a ritualized and therefore safe outlet for expressions of hostility. Unfortunately, pride often forces men to bet ruinous sums. Cock fighting and bull fighting are even more popular spectacles, but fall in a separate category, hardly classifiable as sports.

Wrath, the second of the seven deadly sins, manifests itself not only as violence but even more importantly as intransigence. Just as pride leads machos into betting sums they cannot afford, stubbornness traps them into adopting inflexible positions. Once committed to a particular point of view or line of conduct, men refuse to modify or retreat from it. With rare exceptions, Latin American politics leaves little room for accommodation of conflicting policy preferences through negotiation. *He dicho* ("I have spoken") announces that the die is cast and that the speaker is irrevocably bound to his position. For many years Mexico's dominant party, the PRI, kept its conflicts from public view, allowing politicians to contend with each other without risking the dissolution of the entire political system, but there are signs that this arrangement is now failing to contain accumulated hostilities.

Lust and Anxiety

Life is risky for the Latin American male. Even more than in other cultures, the man is forced to act or pretend to act aggressively at all times, yet he must take great care that this aggressiveness does not lead him into a trap, because the penalty for a false move can be death, disgrace or ridicule. For some men, business or professional activities can be nonphysical expressions of aggressiveness, but only a very small band of the social spectrum can enjoy such release. The only safe kind of aggression available to men of all classes is that which they aim at women.

Lust is the theological label for sexual aggressiveness. It is also the behavioral trait that has given machismo its bad press at home and abroad. One suspects, however, that the apparent humility and self-excoriation with which men confess their collective sinfulness to each other and to the outside world contains a thinly concealed boast.

Amorous conquests serve a double purpose. While each seduction gives a man the temporary sensation of having bested an elusive adversary, it also serves to reassure him that the supposed essence of his manhood—his sexual potency—is intact. Trapped by his anxieties, he sees manliness, potency and fertility as an inseparable trio. Because the fear of losing his potency is ever-present, the macho lives in a nightmare world; like a writer between books or an actor between plays, he is desperately unsure about whether he can produce another hit. Miser-like, he reviews his collection of sex partners, hoping to add new ones to the list.

He worries constantly that other men may not believe his boasts. ***Marinerito sobre cubierta*** ("cash on the line"), they may say. Anybody can appear to have slept with a woman, but where is the proof? The only effective proof, the one that will silence even the most skeptical, is to get the woman pregnant. Thus, a man's children, in and out of wedlock, become his insurance against the imputation of impotence.

So that there can be no doubt about the identity of the father, a man does everything possible to restrict his woman's contacts with other men. Some even forbid their women to be seen talking with another member of the opposite sex. "It is a strange kind of civilization," commented a Spanish writer, "where a man's honor depends completely on the fickle behavior of a woman." This jealous watchfulness is an illustration of the way the same behavior pattern can serve different purposes in different cultures. When a Chocó Indian of the Colombian highlands takes his wife to town, she must walk behind him without looking at or speaking with any other man. Women are fewer than men in this Indian group; a Chocó male lucky enough to secure a wife worries constantly that she may be lured away by a more attractive offer. The question for the fearful macho is not whether his wife or mistress may leave him; he worries about giving other men any kind of opening wedge to doubt his claims of potency. Unlike the members of unacculturated Indian communities, *mestizo* males cannot look forward to increasing prestige and dignity as they grow older. As a man leaves his youth behind him, another worry is added to his list: Are his sexual powers diminishing faster than they should? Will he become a *viejo inútil* ("useless old man")? Conscious of this preoccupation, a younger man who wishes to compliment him may make the sly suggestion that some small child in the neighborhood bears a strong resemblance to him.

Callousness towards Women

Among some lower-class males there exists the notion that the sex of the offspring is an indication of the degree of a man's virility; male babies prove that the father is *muy macho,* whereas females reflect a certain "weakness of seed." Particular importance is attached to the sex of the first child, since this can either establish his reputation firmly or leave it hanging in doubt.

The true macho is expected to show callousness toward women except, of course, his mother. This is the cause of women's martyrdom and lamentations, the characteristic women have in mind when they refer to a "repressive and machista society."

When he is behaving according to the stereotype, especially when he is in a group of men, the male feels obliged to express hostility toward women, including his wife and his concubine(s). He is expected to show a regal disdain for their feelings, a lack of concern for the effect his actions may have on their physical or emotional welfare; in fact, ostentatious cruelty toward women can be expected to elicit respectful admiration from male companions and friends. This can take many forms, but probably the most widespread is the practice of seduction, the purpose of which is to persuade an unwilling woman—often by trickery—to engage in sexual intercourse without the man's becoming emotionally involved with her. "To make love without loving" is the basis of the exploits of the prototype Don Juan, whose epithet is *El Burlador* ("The Trickster"), he who makes a laughing-stock of women.

Love and Marriage

Does this mean that a man cannot marry for love? No; he is permitted that temporary lapse into vulnerability, but he is expected to recover his callousness as quickly as possible and to demonstrate it by engaging in extramarital sexual activity and mistreatment of his wife.

Other forms of cruelty may include such petty harassment as deliberately arriving late for meals, prolonged unexplained absences from the home, gratuitous demands for menial services, brusqueness or even verbal abuse of his wife or mistress, unnecessary stinginess and unreasonable restrictions on the woman's freedom of movement (for example, forbidding her to visit with women friends). Wife-beating, although not uncommon, is mostly confined to the lower classes.

The only exception to this behavior pattern is the mother. To her children, but especially to her male children, she is an object of reverence, a royal personage whose wishes must be gratified, and the ever-loving, always forgiving surrogate of the Virgin Mary. Typically, a man may comment that he is going to try to make restitution to his mother for all the suffering his father has caused her. At the same time, he is acting toward his wife in such a way that his children, in turn, will see her as a martyr.

The economics of machismo, as explained by a Puerto Rican professional, are that a middle-class man can easily afford a mistress from the working class. Poverty is so widespread that many individuals live on the border of starvation. Unemployment is widespread, as is underemployment. Peasant women flocking to cities are lucky to find jobs as shockingly underpaid, very badly treated servants. For a few dollars a month, a man can rent a room for a woman, feed her, buy her a few clothes and take her dancing occasionally to a cheap night club (thus making sure that his liaison is noticed by other men). The women who are "bought" in this fashion find at least temporary relief from the pressures of economic necessity. Many of them entertain the hope that they can somehow persuade the men to divorce their present wives and marry them. Such things do happen, though rarely. At any rate, it is more comfortable to be a middle-class man's mistress than a peasant's concubine or an underpaid abused servant. A significant upward trend in economic development would probably reduce the pool of available mistresses.

Rich and middle-income men take advantage of their superior position to recruit women from the more economically deprived strata for their displays of conspicuous sexual consumption. There is a kind of pecking order involved here; rich men usually choose middle-class women, while middle-class men customarily dip into the ranks of poor women for their extramarital partners. Economic deprivation, however, does not bar poor men from acquiring one or more concubines. With his pitifully scant income, the Puerto Rican *jibaro* ("peasant") often maintains a *casa principal* ("main house," a term used to designate the residence of either a legal or a common-law partner) as well as a *casa chica* ("little house," a phrase designating the abode of the principal concubine), and not infrequently a *casa media* ("middle house," the residence of a secondary concubine).

The sexual activity of Latin American males—their proudest claim to high status as machos—bears a curious resemblance to Mark Twain's weather: everybody talks about it, but very little research is done to clarify the point. A decade ago, a investigator commented:

> Just as it is tempting to deduce attitudes from behavior, so it is tempting to deduce a high frequency of sex relations from high fertility, since sex relations are a necessary antecedent to fertility. . . . The available evidence, while unfortunately limited, points in the opposite direction.

Ten years later, there is still no reliable way of determining whether the Latin American male who engages in extramarital sex is more active than one who does not, but researchers agree that the frequency of intercourse for both types of men probably does not vary much from the norm appropriate for their age group. It may very well be that whatever they give to one woman, they deny to another. The *mujeriego* ("philanderer") may simply distribute what he has to offer over a wider field of recipients.

Numbers Game

Latin American wives cooperate in this numbers game in several ways: first by maintaining the attitude that enjoyment of coitus is repugnant to their finer natures, and again by encouraging the notion that men are incurably puerile, unable to restrain their impulses. That these attitudes operate as a self-fulfilling prophecy is confirmed by another Latin American investigator who says that the women in his study do not have orgasm and their frequency of sexual relations does not add up to any more than four times per month in some carefully studied areas.

Lest Anglo-American feminists rush to the conclusion that Latin women have been brainwashed by men, fragmentary data indicate that men are more generous than women in their estimate of the latter's enjoyment of sexual relations.

It appears that in Latin America, each female member of the triangle (or quadrangle or pentagon) derives certain advantages from the male's acknowledged weakness. For the mistress, the compensation is chiefly economic. While the man needs her as visible proof of his proclaimed hypersexuality and aggressiveness, his financial support relieves her of the need to seek more distasteful employment, such as domestic servitude, if she comes from the lower class, or ill-paid drudgery in a store or office. The wife, on the other hand, is able to play on her husband's feelings of guilt at his "moral depravity" by reigning over his "legitimate" household, tyrannizing the servants, basking in the adulation of her children and receiving the approval of society.

But what about our opening epigraph that indicates a man's subservience to his wife's whims? How can that be reconciled with the arrogant, aggressive, lustful figure portrayed above? The quotation reveals men's uneasiness, their fear of being dominated by women and their suspicion that no matter how much they struggle to assert themselves, the battle is irretrievably lost; in fact, has been lost since the beginning of time.

At the core of machista behavior, observes a Mexican male, "there is the obstinate, unshakable, obsessive purpose of proving by all available means that one is free with respect to the woman and that she is absolutely submissive to him. Much of the Latin American literature on the subject reflects a sense of desperation on the part of the men. They seem to feel driven, hounded by the stereotypical prescriptions to conform to the norms of machista behavior. If they want to attain and retain the respect of other human beings, they must go through the ritual of boasting about courage and sexual prowess.

Often they are forced to validate this boasting with some kind of token behavior, which on occasion can lead them into a disastrous cul-de-sac such as the bloody Mexican game of Russian roulette, so ably satirized by the film comic, Mario Moreno ("Cantinflas") in *El Sietemachos*.

Male Hypersexuality

Pressures to conform to the macho stereotype come as strongly from Latin American women as from the men. In women's gossip circles, a favorite topic is the shamelessness with which individual men (designated by name) engage in extramarital promiscuity or in other behavior calculated to humiliate women. A newcomer from another culture is at first shocked and pained by such recitals, until it becomes evident that the only men who are regarded contemptuously for their "pusillanimity" are those who lead blameless lives. Some years ago in Puerto Rico, a dignified justice of the Supreme Court became a candidate for the office of governor, with the support of the local Catholic hierarchy. His campaign slogan, *Vote por Don Martín Travieso; no ha tenido más que una mujer en toda la vida* ("He has had only one woman [wife] in his whole life"), made him the laughing-stock of the island. The slogan was a left-handed reference to the private life of the popular candidate, Luis Muñoz Marín, who won the election by a large majority.

Just as the myth of male hypersexuality glosses over the individual inadequacies of many Latin American men, so the idealization of spiritual love masks the range of temperaments found in women. Because inspiration for this secular cult of femininity is drawn from the adoration of the Virgin Mary, I have called it *marianismo*.

Mary-Worship

Although the church has long counselled women to emulate the virtues of Mary, the excessive veneration of flesh-and-blood women has no support in dogma and in fact remains completely devoid of theological sanction. Interestingly, although Marianism or Mariology, as it is called in liturgical discussions, is a world-wide religious manifestation, only in Latin cultures have its main features been appropriated to forge a powerful lay instrument for the sanctification of all women.

Taking its cue from the worship of Mary, marianismo pictures its subjects as semi-divine, morally superior and spritually stronger than men. This constellation of attributes enables women to bear the indignities inflicted on them by men, and to forgive those who bring them pain. Like Mary, women are seen as mediatrices without whose intercession men would have little chance of obtaining forgiveness for their transgressions. Conversely, a female cannot hope to attain full spiritual stature until her forbearance and abnegation have been tested by male-inflicted suffering. Men's wickedness is therefore the necessary precondition of women's superior status.

Because the *Mater Dolorosa* is the ideal of womanhood, socialization of female children and adolescents is directed toward appreciation of the requisite attitudes toward male members of the family. Within the family, the male ego is the center of attention; mother and sisters cater and defer to him, make excuses and pray for him, and intercede on his behalf with his father during the latter's brief, infrequent but usually harsh exercise of authority. In turn, the male treats his sisters with condescension, more or less tempered by affection, and is expected to watch over their behavior, especially when they venture out of the house. Every male member of the family acts as part of a vigilante network, charged with keeping predatory outside males from making off with the females' "honor" (virginity). A girl who is known as "wild" or "easy" brings disgrace not only on herself, but—more important—on the whole family, in that she reveals the inability of her male relatives—their lack of virile strength and courage—to "protect" her.

Mater Dolorosa

To an outsider it might seem logical to expect that mother and sisters would be scrupulous in their insistence that the males of the family respect the "honor" of other unmarried females, but this is not the case. Sisters will often act as intermediaries for the males' amorous campaigns against their female friends, taking satisfaction in helping their brothers add to their list of conquests. Mothers show a curious lack of concern, amounting at times to spitefulness toward the females involved.

For men, unmarried females are moral and intellectual imbeciles, in need of constant supervision. How is it possible that from such unpromising material each generation produces its own quota of saintly mothers who reign supreme over the extended family or its truncated urbanized version? The apotheosis is neither facile nor swift.

For the woman, the early years of marriage are seen as an apprenticeship, a "trial by fire," in anticipation of a state of blessedness which can be attained only after middle life, when the childbearing period is past and after a woman has supposedly been divested of her specific sexuality. Menopause becomes a sign of divine grace.

Women strive not to avoid suffering but to make known their suffering, for their misfortunes are the stigmata of incipient sainthood which are further validated by the appropriate attitude of abnegation. "The test of womanhood," comments sociologist Lloyd Rogler, "is self-sacrifice." The more closely the husband conforms to stereotyped macho behavior the more rapidly his suffering wife advances toward her anticipated beatification.

It is difficult if not impossible to achieve full sainthood without having born children. The pain of childbirth is the surest proof of martyrdom; loyalty to marianismo would prevent a woman from admitting to an easy delivery. Maternity sections of hospitals resound with the eloquent cries of the parturients, who call upon *their* mothers to help them bear the torture: *"Ay, mamá, no puedo más!"* As there can be no saint unless there are votaries, the multiparous woman provides the setting for her own future cult. Adult daughters will, after socialization, become valuable allies and vestal priestesses, but adult sons will be necessary as worshippers.

Power of Love

Mexican psychiatrist Rogelio Díaz Guerrero agrees that, "far from being victims of this dichotomous portrayal of the sex roles, Latin American women are the deliberate perpetrators of the myth." Guerrero continues:

> For one reason or another, historically, males and females in Mexico realized that whenever there are more than two people together, they will have to accommodate in regards to at least two important dimensions, the dimension of power and the dimension of love. In the Mexican family for one reason or another, it appears that it was decided that the father should have the power and the mother should have the love (and the power of love).

This is an extraordinarily perceptive appreciation of the dynamics involved in the male-female relationship. For women do enjoy great power in Latin America, based on their acknowledged spiritual superiority. In the hierarchy of values of Latin American culture, matters of the spirit stand undisputedly above all others. In comparing themselves with members of other societies, Latin American stress their spirituality, their devotion to "the finer things of life," rather than to the crass materialistic objectives pursued by others. José Enrique Rodó, the revered apostle of Latin American self-affirmation, chose Shakespeare's Ariel to personify the ethereal nature of his people, likening the Anglo Americans to the coarse and brutal Prospero. There is hardly an educated Latin American who cannot quote in their entirety the relevant passages from Rodó's work.

A married woman can be lazy, bad tempered, improvident, but as long as she is not found to be sexually promiscuous, she will be regarded as a good wife and mother. Curiously, as she grows older, her children and even her husband will change the details of her real behavior for a pseudobiography that conforms to the marianismo stereotype.

Secure in the knowledge that her imperfections are immaterial, the Latin American woman wages undeclared war on her husband. Is he stingy? The children are taught to shame him by their tearful begging. Is he abusive? The children are there to comfort their mother. Is he unfaithful? The children's admiration for their mother's abnegation only increases. Does he indulge in petty harassments? The children's silent hostility can be felt. In sum, his efforts to sustain his reputation as a macho in the world outside of the home require that he relinquish his claims to respect and love within the home. He retains his titular authority, but even after he has made a decision he may have the uncomfortable suspicion that he has been manipulated into doing precisely what his wife wanted.

Symbiotic Relationship

If this attempt to set the record straight has given the impression that the role structure for men and women in Latin America is intolerably rigid, this is only due to the oversimplification made necessary by space requirements. In every country, many intelligent individuals, male and female, adopt alternative modes of behavior, sometimes in open defiance of the prescriptions but more often by developing stratagems for quiet noncompliance. It has been my observation—unconfirmed and perhaps unconfirmable by any statistical survey—that Latin American men and women are no more ill at ease with each other than are Europeans or Anglo-Americans.

The marianismo-machismo pattern of attitudes and behavior provides a stable symbiosis in Latin American culture. Within the context of nonindustrialized societies, it has provided clear-cut role definitions for both sexes. As these societies change in the direction of economic growth and development, it will be interesting to observe whether or not new patterns emerge.

SUGGESTED READINGS

Journal of Marriage and the Family (special issue devoted to male-female relationships in Latin America) May 1973.

Mundo Nuevo, April 1970 (special issue devoted to "Machismo y Feminismo en America Latina").

Labyrinth of Solitude by Octavio Paz (New York: Grove Press, 1962).

Female and Male in Latin America, edited by Ann Pescatello (Pittsburgh: University of Pittsburgh Press, 1973).

Profile of Man and Culture in Mexico by Samuel Ramos (Austin: University of Texas Press, 1963).

2 *Harley L. Browning*

Timing of Our Lives

Only quite recently in his history has man been able to exercise any important and lasting influence on the control of his mortality. In Western Europe mortality declines have been documented for periods ranging up to several hundred years, but this accomplishment recently has been overshadowed by the spectacular drops in mortality in many developing countries. They are now accomplishing in a few decades what the European countries took many generations to achieve. In Mexico, to cite one remarkable example, male life expectancy at birth has nearly doubled within the span of a single generation (1930-1965). During this period, the life expectancy of Mexican men rose from 32 to 62 years.

Man's great leap forward in mortality control, which now permits so large a proportion of those born in advanced societies to pass through virtually all important stages in the life cycle, must surely be counted among his most impressive accomplishments. Yet, there has been no systematic effort to follow out all the ramifications of this relatively new condition. If a Mexican boy born in 1965 can expect to live twice as long as his father born in 1930, can he not also expect to pass through a life cycle markedly different in quality and content from that of his father?

One would think that a man who had little chance of living beyond 35 would want to cram all the important stages of his life into a brief period. Conversely, one might expect that if given twice the time in which to live out his life cycle, an individual might plan and space out the major events in his life such as education, marriage, birth of his children and beginning of his work career and so on—to gain the optimal advantage of all this additional time. But, in reality, little intelligent use is being made of the extension of life expectancy in terms of the spacing of key events in the life cycle.

Here, for purposes of exploring the possibilities opened up by recent advances in mortality control, I want first to document the astonishing increase in life expectancy of recent times. From there we can examine some of the implications that can be drawn from it and consider the potential consequences of increased longevity in altering the timing of events in the life cycle. Finally, I shall comment on the feasibility of planning changes in the life cycle to better utilize the advantages of reduced mortality rates. Since my purpose is to set forth a perspective for the linking of life expectancy and life cycle, I have not attempted systematically to provide data for all of my generalizations. Therefore, my conclusions must be taken as exploratory and tentative.

In the investigation of the relationship of changes in life expectancy to changes in the life cycle, it is worthwhile to consider two groupings of countries—the developed countries, where life expectancy has been increasing over a considerable period of time, and the developing countries, with their recent and very rapid increases.

For the developing countries, an important question for which we have little evidence as yet is how much people are aware at all social levels of the dramatic change in life expectancy. Perhaps it is not generally "perceived" because the change has not had time to manifest itself in the lifetime of many persons. The fact that in Mexico there is now so great a generational difference in life expectancy that the son may expect to live almost twice as long as his father surely will have considerable impact upon the family and other institutions. But we can only know these changes for certain as the son passes through his life span, well into the next century, a time when all of us will be dead.

Mexico is a striking case but by no means an isolated one. A number of other developing countries will achieve much the same record within a fifty-year period or less. Thus, for a substantial part of the world's population, the mortality experience of succeeding generations will differ markedly and to an extent unparalleled in any other historical period.

There are striking extremes between conditions in primitive and pre-industrial countries with unusually high death rates and the situation that many countries in Western Europe and Anglo-America either have already reached or are closely approaching. For instance, India between 1901 and 1911 represented the conditions of extremely high mortality under which mankind has lived during most of his time on this earth. A male child born in this period and locale had a life expectancy of slightly less than 23 years. Today such conditions are extremely rare. At the other extreme, a boy born in the United States in 1950, for example, could expect to live almost to age 74.

As is well-known, the greatest improvement in mortality control has come about through the reduction of deaths in infancy and early childhood. In India around 1901, nearly one-half of those born were lost by age five. By contrast, under the conditions prevailing in the United States in 1950, 98.5 per cent of male children were still living five years after birth.

For the purposes of relating life expectancy to life cycle, however, it is not the losses in the early years that are of the most importance. Death at any time, including the first few years of life, is of course a "waste," but the loss on "investment" at these ages for both parents and society is not nearly so great as for those persons who die at just about the time they are ready to assume adult responsibilities. This is when such significant events in the life cycle as higher education, work career, marriage and family take place. For this reason, the focus of this article is upon the fifty-year span from age 15 to 65. By age 15 the boy is in the process of becoming a man and is preparing himself either for college or entry into the labor force. Fifty years later, at age 65, the man is either retired or, if not, his productivity is beginning to decline noticeably in most cases.

But what are the consequences of these changes that have recently permitted a substantial part of the world's population for the first time to live what Jean Fourastie has called "a biologically complete life." What can be the meaning of death in a society where nearly everyone lives out his allotted threescore and ten years? Is death beyond the age of 65 or 70 really a "tragic" occurrence? The specter of early and unexpected death manifested itself symbolically in countless ways in societies with high mortality. Of France in the twelth century, Fourastie writes, "In traditional times, death was at the center of life, just as the cemetery was at the center of the village."

Not everyone believes that the great increase in life expectancy is entirely favorable in its consequences. Some argue that perhaps advanced societies now allow too high a proportion of those born into them to pass through to advanced ages. "Natural selection" no longer works effectively to eliminate the weak and the infirm. In other words, these people maintain that one consequence of improved mortality is that the biological "quality" of the population declines.

While we can grant that a number of individuals now survive to old age who are incapable of making any contribution to their society, the real question is how numerically important a group they are. My impression is that their numbers have generally been exaggerated by some eugenicists. The cost of maintaining these relatively few individuals is far outweighed by the many benefits deriving from high survivorship. In any event, the strong ethical supports for the preservation of life under virtually all conditions are not likely to be dramatically altered within the next generation or so.

Whatever the problems occasioned by the great rise in natural increase, no one would want to give up the very real gains that derive from the control of mortality man now possesses. One of the most interesting features is the biological continuity of the nuclear family (parents and children) during the period when childbearing and childrearing take place. In most societies the crucial period, for men at least, is between ages 25 and 55. But only a little more than a third of the males born under very backward conditions survive from age 15 to age 55. By contrast, almost 94 percent in Europe and Anglo-America reach this age. The fact that until relatively recently it was highly probable that one or both parents would die before their children reached maturity had a profound effect upon family institutions. In "functional" terms, the survival of the society depended upon early marriages and early and frequent conceptions within those marriages. Andrew Collver has shown this very effectively in his comparative study of the family cycle in India and the United States:

> In the United States, the married couple, assured of a long span of life together, can take on long-term responsibilities for starting a new household, rearing children and setting aside some provisions for their old age. In India, by contrast, the existence of the nuclear family is too precarious for it to be entrusted entirely with these important functions. The joint household alone has a good prospect for continuity.

Not all societies with high mortality are also characterized by the importance of joint households. But all societies of the past in one way or another had to provide for children who were orphaned before they reached maturity. One largely uncelebrated consequence of greatly reduced mortality in Western countries, for example, has been the virtual disappearance of orphanages. In the United States, the number of complete orphans declined from 750,000 in 1920 to 66,000 in 1953. In this way a favorite theme of novelists a century or so ago has largely disappeared. Were Dickens writing today he would have to shift his attention from orphans to the children of divorced or separated parents. The psychological and economic consequences of whether homes are broken by divorce or separation rather than by the death of one or both parents obviously may be quite different.

I need not elaborate the obvious advantages of increased life expectancy both for the individual and his society in terms of advanced education and professional career. Under present conditions it is now possible for an individual realistically to plan his entire education and work life with little fear of dying before he can carry out his plans. In this respect, the developed countries have a considerable advantage over developing countries, for the former do not suffer many losses on their investments in the training and education of their youth. But under conditions that are still typical of a large number of countries, a third of those who have reached the age of 15 never reach age 45, the peak productive period of an educated person's life. In such countries, primary education for everyone may be desirable but a part of the investment will be lost for the substantial number who will die during their most productive period.

Another consequence, perhaps overlooked, of the improvement of life expectancy in advanced countries is the fact that while even the rich and powerful were likely to die at early ages in older societies, now everyone, including the poor, can expect to pass through most of the life span. Considerable attention in America is now concentrated on conditions of social inequality, and clearly very large differences exist for characteristics such as education, occupation, and income. But in a society where about eighty-five of every one hundred persons can expect to reach their 65th birthday, extreme differences in longevity among the social strata do not exist. This is not to say that mortality differentials do not exist; they do, but not nearly to the degree found for other major socioeconomic variables. For the poor, unfortunately, increased longevity may be at best a mixed blessing. Too frequently it can only mean a prolongation of ill health, joblessness, and dependency.

What is still not well-appreciated are the consequences of the prolongation of life for the spacing of key events in the life cycle. Obviously, wholesale transformation of the life cycle is impossible because most of the events of importance are to one degree or another associated with age. Retirement cannot precede first job. Nevertheless, the timing of such events or stages as education, beginning of work career, marriage and birth of first and last child is subject to changes that can have marked repercussions on both the individual and the society.

One of the difficulties of dealing with the life cycle is that it is rarely seen in its entirety. Specialists on child development concentrate only on the early years, while the period of adolescence has its own "youth culture" specialists, and so on.

But another important reason why changes in the life cycle itself have not received much attention is the lack of data. Ideally, life histories are required so that the timing of each event can be specified, but until quite recently the technical problems in gathering and especially in processing detailed life histories on a large scale were so great as to make the task unfeasible. Now, however, with the help of computers, many of these problems can be overcome.

Let's examine one particular instance—age at first marriage in the United States—in which one might expect increased life expectancy to have some effect either actual or potential on the life cycle. The data are reasonably good, at least for the last seventy years, and age at first marriage is an event subject to a fair amount of variation in its timing. More interestingly, age at first marriage can greatly affect the subsequent course of a person's life and is indicative of changes in social structure.

In the time period of concern to us, 1890-1960, the generational life expectancy in the United States at age 20 increased 13 years for males and 11 years for females. This is not so great an increase as is now occurring in developing countries but it is still an impressive gain. With an appreciable extension in his life expectancy, a person might reasonably be expected to alter the spacing of key events in his life cycle in order to take advantage of the greater "space" available. In particular, we might expect him to marry at a somewhat later age. But exactly the opposite has happened! Between 1890 and 1960 the median age at first marriage for males declined about four years, a very significant change. For females, the decline was only two years, but their age at first marriage in 1890 (22) already was quite low.

Isn't this strange? During the period of an important extension in life expectancy, a substantial decline in age at first marriage has occurred. Unquestionably, many factors go into an adequate explanation of this phenomenon. One of the reasons why age at first marriage was high around the turn of the century was the numbers of foreign-born, most of them from Europe where marriage at a later age was characteristic, even among the lower strata. Immigrants who arrived as single men had some difficulty finding wives and this delayed their first marriage. In addition, around the turn of the century, middle-class men were not expected to marry until they had completed their education, established themselves in their careers and accumulated sufficient assets to finance the marriage and a proper style of living.

The greatest drop in age at first marriage occurred between 1940 and 1960, especially for females. During this period a great many changes took place in society that worked to facilitate early marriages. "Going steady" throughout a good part of adolescence became accepted practice. Parents adopted more permissive attitudes toward early marriage and often helped young couples to get started. The reduced threat of military conscription after 1946 for married men with children was also a big factor along with a period of general prosperity and easy credit that enabled newlyweds to have a house, furnishings and car, all with a minimal down payment. And not only is marriage easier to get into, it is now easier to get out of; divorce no longer carries the stigma once attached to it.

Of course, many early marriages are not wholly voluntary and in a substantial number of cases the couple either would never have married or they would have married at a later age. David Goldberg has estimated, on the basis of a Detroit survey, that as high as 25 percent of white, first births are conceived outside of marriage, with a fifth of these being illegitimate. As he puts it:

> We have been accustomed to thinking of the sequence marriage, conception and birth. It is apparent that for a very substantial part of the population the current sequence is conception followed by birth, with marriage intervening, following birth or not occurring at all. This may represent a fundamental change in marriage and fertility patterns, but historical patterns are lacking. An increase in illegitimate conceptions may be largely responsible for the decline in marriage age in the postwar period.

Unfortunately, there is no way to determine if the proportion of illegitimate conceptions has risen substantially since 1890.

The causes of early first marriage are not so important for the purposes of this article as their consequences for subsequent events of the life cycle. For one thing, age at first marriage is closely related to the stability of the marriage. The high dissolution of teenage marriages by divorce or other means is notorious. One may or may not consider this as "wastage" but there is no question about the costs of these unsuccessful unions to the couples involved, to their children and often to society in the form of greater welfare expenditures.

Not only has age at first marriage trended downward, especially since World War II, but family formation patterns have also changed. For the woman, the interval between first marriage and birth of her first child has diminished somewhat and the intervals between subsequent births also have been reduced. As a result, most women complete their childbearing period by the time they reach age 30.

Marriage, Work and Babies

The effects of these changes on the family cycle are as yet not very well understood. But the lowering of age at first marriage among men encompasses within the brief span of the early twenties many of the most important events of the life cycle—advanced education, marriage, first stages of work career and family formation. This is particularly true for the college-educated. Since at least four of every ten college-age males will have some college training, this is an important segment of the population. Each important stage of the life cycle requires commitment and involvement of the individual. If he crowds them together, he reduces both the time he can devote to each of them and his chances for success in any or all of them.

From our discussion of increased life expectancy and the timing of one particular aspect of the life cycle, age at first marriage, we might conclude that there is little relationship between the two. Man has been able to push back the threat of death both in developing and developed societies but he has not seen fit to make much use of this increased longevity. Must this be? Would not the "quality" of the populations in both developing and developed countries be improved by a wider spacing of key events in the life cycle? I believe a good argument can be made that it would.

First, take the situation in the developing countries. What would be the consequences of raising the age at marriage several years and of widening the interval between births? The demographic consequences would be very important, for, independent of any reduction of completed family size, these changes would substantially reduce fertility rates. Raising age at marriage would delay births as a short-run effect and in the long run it would lengthen the span of a generation. At a time when there is much concern to slow down the rate of population growth in most developing countries, this would be particularly effective when coupled with a concomitant reduction in completed family size.

A second effect of the raising of age at marriage and widening the spacing of births would be to allow these societies to better gear themselves to the requirements of a modernized and highly-trained population. A later age at marriage for women could permit more of them to enter the labor force. This in itself would probably result in lowered fertility. In most developing societies, the role and position of the woman *outside* of the home must be encouraged and strengthened.

Accommodating the Sex Drive

The case of the developed countries, particularly the United States, is somewhat different. I see very few advantages either for the individual, the couple or the society in the recent practice of squeezing the terminal stages of education, early work career and marriage and family formation into the period of the early twenties. There simply isn't time enough to do justice to all of these events. The negative effects are often felt most by the women. If a woman is married by age 20, completes her childbearing before 30 and sees her children leave home before she reaches 50, she is left with a long thirty years to fill in some manner. We know that many women have difficulty finding meaningful activities to occupy themselves. True, the shortening of generations will permit people the opportunity of watching their great-grandchildren grow up, but does this compensate for the earlier disadvantages of this arrangement? From the standpoint of the society, there are few if any advantages.

If an argument can be made that little intelligent use is being made of the extension of life expectancy in terms of timing key events in the life cycle, what can be done about it? In any direct way, probably very little. "Licensing" people to do certain things at certain ages is, to my mind, appropriate only in totalitarian societies. So far as I am aware, contemporary totalitarian societies have made relatively little effort to actively regulate the timing of events in the life cycle. The Chinese, for example, have only "suggested" that males defer marriage until age 30. But if the state is not to force people to do things at specified ages, at least it might educate them as to the advantages of proper spacing and also make them aware of the handicaps generated by early marriage and, particularly, early family formation. Both in developing and developed countries there probably is very little direct awareness of how spacing will affect one's life chances and how something might be done about it.

Obviously, if marriage is delayed, then something must be done to accommodate the sex drive. Fifty years ago the resolution of this problem was for men to frequent prostitutes while women had fainting spells, but neither alternative is likely to gain favor with today's generation. Perhaps Margaret Mead has once again come to our rescue with her proposal that two kinds of marriages be sanctioned, those with and those without children. Under her "individual" marriage young people could enter into and leave unions relatively freely as long as they did not have children. This, of course, would require effective contraception. Such a union would provide sexual satisfaction, companionship, and assuming the women is employed, two contributors to household expenses. This arrangement would not markedly interfere with the careers of either sex. Marriages with the purpose of having children would be made more difficult to enter into, but presumably many couples would pass from the individual into the family marriage. This suggestion, of course, will affront the conventional morality, but so do most features of social change.

SUGGESTED READINGS

From Generation to Generation by S. N. Eisenstadt (New York: Free Press, 1956).

American Families by Paul Glick (New York: John Wiley, 1957).

Marriage and the Family: A Comprehensive Reader, edited by Jeffrey K. Hadden and Marie L. Borgatta (Itasca, Illinois: F. E. Peacock, 1969).

Photos by Hugo Denisart

Text by Neuma Aguiar

Residents of Brazilian Roads

Translation by Dorit Schneider

A process of rapid urbanization is taking place at the moment in Brazil, but it is not only the cities that are increasing in size. In some areas, such as the south of Ceará in the region of the northeast, we find the phenomenon of small settlements making their appearance next to the rural zone. These populations cannot as yet be classified as urban, nor can they, however, be called rural. They possess an intermediate status for which the classic dichotomies elaborated by the social sciences cannot be used.

Some landowners try to evade the rural legislation, driving the worker to the boundary line between their rural property and the urban zone. This attempt, however, also furthered the growth of the settlements at the cost of maintaining the same rural ties established with the typical resident.

Because of new rural-worker rights, it has become burdensome for the landowner to keep seasonal workers as residents on his land for the whole year. It is just as disagreeable for the resident to work under a system in which he is obliged to do any type of work at a landlord's bidding. The result, then, is the worker's expulsion from the farm and his acquisition of a small plot of land. Although rural legislation forbids the division of the land, the land next to the highways can be considered as part of the urban zone. In other areas the division of the land antedates this legislation. There are also cases in which the land is sold without official recognition, through private contracts, and without legal value. This ownership enables the worker to choose the manner and the place in which he is going to work, usually consisting of subsistence activities in the winter and other types of employment, wherever possible, during the summer.

Contrasted with the resident worker of an estate is the one who lives on the road, that is, the one who has no ties of residence with the landlord and who is, therefore, not subject to him. The estate resident has an obligation to work for his landlord, which does not permit him to arrange a job with another boss. If this should happen, the worker loses his rights of residence. There are men who maintain this tie throughout their whole lives. Entire generations work, at times, for the same landlord. The resident of the road who possesses his own land has no tie of residence and work; he is, to put it in his own words, "loose." He frequently cultivates his plot of land on the basis of sharecropping and rent. He may work for one or for many. He rarely works the whole year for only one person. He rarely has work throughout the whole year.

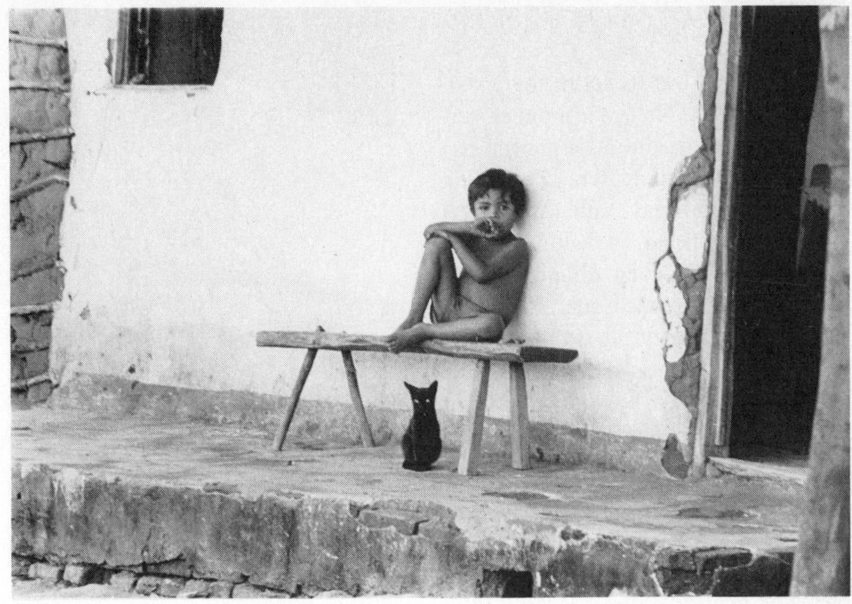

To build a house is an art. First, one needs a small plot of land which, in one of the roads studied, measures 22 palms in front and 14 braces at the back (using the local measurements). A house with three rooms generally measures 4, 5m in width by 5,5m in length. The floor is flattened, then the place where the house is to be built is measured and the place marked where the holes are to be dug to hold up the forked poles or beams of wood acting as cross-beam girders. Then, the smaller vertical and horizontal supports are fixed: ropes and rafters. Following this, the vertical and horizontal spaces are filled in with wooden beams that are even thinner: wattle and daub. The technique consists of elaborating a grid: the wattle is fixed with nails and ***imbira de araticum***, a thin piece of bark which is taken from a type of wood common in the area.

With the minimum resources of subsistence guaranteed, the man puts his house under divine protection and sets up his saints in the place of honor in his residence. He gives thanks for the good year in which the regular rain season permitted cultivation and ensured a good harvest.

The resident of the estate dedicates part of the year to his plot of land, devoting the other part to work that the landlord may require. The resident of the road also dedicates part of the year to his plot of land. The rest of the year he dedicates to complementary activities, such as handicrafts and domestic services, allowing him to earn money to supply the extra needs attached to his production.

3 *William E. Henry & John H. Sims*

Actors' Search for Self

We seem to be of two minds in our thinking about creativity. Almost everyone agrees that creativity is desirable—we all like to think we are creative in our work as architects, social scientists, executives or chemists. And yet, simultaneously, we preserve an older, more exclusive meaning, one that supposes that there is a terrible price to be paid for being creative, a necessary correlation between it and personal disorder and intense unhappiness. This definition tends to be restricted to artists and writers, who in a sense suffer for us as *poètes maudits* and produce their work out of a life informed by the pain of infantile and violent behavior. Writing about Charles Baudelaire, Jean-Paul Sartre sets forth a slightly modified version of the myth:

> He made up his mind that at any rate he would explore himself as the knife explores the wound in the hope of reaching the lonely depths which constitute his real nature . . . the tortures which he inflicted on himself . . . made his flesh grow beneath his fingers so that in the throes of its own sufferings it would recognize that it was his own flesh.

Suffering is conceived as a means of self-exploration. As well as incapacitating the artist, the wounds uncover his essential being, and the process of writing is one of progressively intense self-induced pain. To put the matter slightly differently, in John Berryman's words, "We are using our skins as wallpaper and we cannot win."

There is undeniably something archaic about this notion. The blandly efficient creator is decidedly more the man of our time. The word's reference has become so broad as to be synonymous with such qualities as inventive, even intelligent. According to this formulation, the creative man is the one who performs his job notably, a model of propriety who can find energy for unusually stringent work without backsliding and losing out in the business of ordinary life. The term has become a form of reward offered to the man who most clearly and unequivocally adopts the values of a production economy, someone who yields more of whatever function he performs without breaking the self-imposed restrictions in which his role has involved him.

Private Energy

Yet there remains something meretricious about the second of these definitions. We are not all "truly" creative. Fundamentally, the quality involves using the imagination in order to make new things, books, poems, pictures and so forth. The other creators are necessarily of secondary intensity, since they merely use the imagination as a surrogate in a situation where most of their work is actually routine, a manipulation of objects and persons in sustained collaboration with other people. The "real" creator works alone, sustained by his own resources. He has recourse to history, to tradition, to outside events; but for the most part he is concerned with himself, his private energies. And it is reasonable to assume that his relative independence, his self-concern and freedom of personal conduct will create a character structure that is distinguishable from the one imposed by work in complex interaction with other people in a large or small organization.

The actor's circumstances of work set him somewhat between these two definitions of creativity. His rehearsals bring him into a situation where interaction is possibly more crucial than in any other. It is, after all, what makes the finished play a success or a failure. And yet this interaction is only periodic—actors presumably learn their parts by themselves, and they spend time between roles in an environment where there is no external organization for them whatsoever. Also, although we conceive their function as one where the self is in constant use as a means of self-expression, the actor does not precisely, as creative writers are supposed to, work out of himself.

On the contrary, the actor normally works with other people's material—the script of the play—and his work demands that he make overt behavioral acts characteristic of one or another role model, those presented in the script. He gives to that role from his inner resources of talent, creating the atmosphere of reality that constitutes the play. As a result, he is living someone else's life; he is enacting a role that he did not invent. No matter how much personal style he may give to a particular role, it is not his own. And, furthermore, depending upon a series of events over which he seldom has control, he will shortly be playing the role of still a different person. His life is given over to portraying the identity of others, and his professional success may well depend upon how vividly he enlivens these other identities and, correlatively, how well he suppresses any self-identity that may blur the image of the other currently being played.

But what of the actor himself? What of his personality? We all tend to think of "mature" people as having a personality constellation of some degree of clarity, consistency

This article is based on a study supported by NIMH grant #M-296 (C-1) to Robert Hess, Principal Investigator, William Henry and John Sims, Co-Investigators.

and integrity. In Erik Erikson's terms we anticipate that the individual will resolve the conflicts and polar choices of earlier phases of life and by late adolescence develop a sense of identity—an identity that articulates inner life with outer social events and provides for the person a clear image of a single, if complex, self.

Is Acting Enough?

Yet what happens to the individual whose job consists of being different people and whose identity, if it exists, cannot benefit from a clarity and consistency of job behavior? Is "being an actor" sufficient? Is acting a role enough, when each of those roles requires different behavior and the portrayal of different feelings? To start from a different point, what must be the characteristics of the person who chooses and finds rewarding an occupation and a life style that demand the portrayal of the identities of other people—other people, furthermore, who are invented by still different people, the playwright and the director?

This study of the professional actor is an effort to explore the latter question. We began with the assumption that one prominent characteristic of the professional actor is his failure to develop the identity of which Erikson speaks. We also hypothesized that one of the things that sustains the creative life of the actor is his hope that the repeated portrayal of the lives of others will provide for him that very identity, the absence of which motivates him in this search. At the least, we would propose that long-running plays provide a temporary and fleeting identity sufficiently binding to keep the actor at work but either insufficiently powerful or occurring too late in life to provide the initial basic trust necessary for the sense of confidence that comes with having a firm identity.

Cards of Identity

To test these propositions, we studied a group of professionals from the New York theater and a number of young actors in training. Our sample runs the full range in terms of employment—from actors who have steady work in the theater, who, while performing in one play, are deluged with scripts and offers for the following season, to actors whose economic existence is at best precarious, but who somehow manage to survive on an erratic combination of short-lived bit parts, occasional seasons of summer stock and unemployment compensation. Technically, all our subjects met three basic requirements: they belonged to an actors' union; they derived at least 50 percent of their income from acting; they had been employed as actors within the year previous to being interviewed.

Our actors are similarly varied regarding fame. The names of several would be recognized in most households; others are known widely in the trade; still others are known only by those with whom they have worked. The rough groupings below provide an approximation of the status of our sample of 32 professional actors:

"stars"	3
publicly well known	4
well known in the profession	9
less well known in the profession	7
virtually unknown	9

The term professional actor is used in a wide variety of theatrical enterprises, such as the legitimate theater, movies, television and night clubs, to cover a wide variety of entertainers—actors, comedians, TV panelists, M.C.'s and so forth. Though most of our subjects had experience in several media, all but one, an Academy Award winner, were primarily legitimate stage actors, both in terms of self-definition and in terms of actual professional experience. Sex is split fairly evenly; there is considerable spread regarding both age and success; different schools of acting are quite evenly represented.

Actors, at least highly successful ones, have often been burned by the glare of publicity. As a result, they are realistically cautious about disclosing their private lives. Considering the intimate nature of the data we were requesting, an impersonal method of contacting them was impracticable. Fortunately, we knew several persons prominent in Broadway theater—a playwright, an acting teacher and an actress. Through their influence our first subjects were contacted, and our discretion was guaranteed by them. These first actors, satisfied, even pleased with the testing and interviewing experience, were generous in personally referring us to others. Thus, an ever-widening network of contacts was developed. This method of personal referral did not, as we feared initially, restrict us to a limited number of cliques but led us to actors unknown to any of our other contacts. How representative our sample is, on the basis of this mode of selection, is an open question. However, we can discover no obvious biases.

Even the busiest of actors were generous with their time; the combined testing and interviewing sessions ranged in length from a minimum of four to a maximum of 20 hours. Often this involved tight scheduling and not inconsiderable sacrifice on their part, such as fitting in a couple of hours between their matinee and evening performances, rising early in the morning (rare for an actor) or giving up their day off. With few exceptions, the interviews took place in the actors' homes.

Their enthusiastic cooperation is probably attributable to several factors. First, actors, like many other people like to talk about themselves. Second, actors are fascinated with the process of acting itself, and with the problems involved in using one's self as the artistic medium. Third, we found actors generally to be relatively sophisticated in psychology. They didn't have to be convinced of the relevance of an area of inquiry before answering. Regardless of what we asked, we were never met with the attitude "What has this got to do with anything?" Finally, we found them to be utterly convinced of the value of research; sometimes they expressed envy of what was, for them, the unquestionable worth of the interviewer's profession.

As a framework for the study, we utilized the logic of Erikson's developmental stages. The eight stages of man which compose Erikson's theory of personality development are a formalization of the nature and consequences of a sequence of what he terms "decisive encounters" between the predetermined biological and psychological capacities of the individual and his social environment. These stages are designated by polar terms, such as trust versus mistrust, autonomy versus shame and doubt, intimacy versus isolation, which define the positive and negative extremes of their developmental alternatives. While the issues defining each stage have lifelong relevance, they are normally critical at a particular period in the life cycle because of the human organism's genetic timetable and the impact of social institutions coordinated to it. Each stage exists in some form both before and after its critical moment; all depends on the proper development of each in a correct sequence. Resolution of a stage is defined as a ratio between the positive and negative which remains in dynamic equilibrium throughout life and is either more or less vulnerable to new inner conflict and outer change.

We were primarily interested in Erikson's fifth stage, identity versus identity diffusion. While identity formation is a lifelong process, a constantly evolving configuration of successive ego syntheses and resyntheses, it reaches its normative developmental crisis during adolescence, a time when the physiological changes of puberty, in conjunction with the advent of major social demands, disrupt and challenge the samenesses and continuities of experience upon which the individual had previously based his psychosocial self-definition. The adolescent is threatened by unfamiliar inner experiences and bewildered by the variety of conflicting role possibilities now available to him.

Self-Shopping

Erikson postulates that society meets the individual's needs during this stage of identity crisis and supports his progress through it by granting an institutionalized period of delay between childhood and adulthood. This "psychosocial moratorium" provides the time required for the transition from child to adult, for the operation of the processes of becoming. New models appropriate to the different tasks facing the individual are found for identification, and childhood identifications are reviewed and accepted or repudiated. Most important, the neophyte-adult has the opportunity to establish patterns of consistent and continuous experience in the new roles he has assumed, roles through which his society is able to identify him. In this way, his inner certainty grows, affirmed by outer recognition.

When the individual cannot use the moratorium to find his place in society and fails to establish an identity, he suffers from identity diffusion. Sexually, occupationally, socially, both he and his society are unsure as to who he is or what he wants to become. Acute identity diffusion usually makes its appearance when the individual is faced with urgent and simultaneous demands for physical intimacy, occupational choice and psychosocial self-definition. In such a situation desperate and imprudent decisions and choices contract the range of further alternatives and entrap the individual in a binding, though unwanted, self-definition. At the same time, frightened abstention from making choices leads to isolation and a sense of emptiness. This can lead to psychological paralysis as the individual attempts vainly to reconcile his terror of committing himself with his desire to create and control his future.

Among the many and complex symptoms that characterize identity diffusion, the main features are:

☐ *A lack of intimacy;* an inability for true engagement with others; a tenseness in interpersonal relations that leads to isolation and lonely stereotypic interaction or to frenetic and unsatisfactory attempts at intimacy with inappropriate partners.

☐ *Time diffusion;* the inability to maintain perspective and expectancy; a distrust of waiting, hoping, planning, of one's relationship to the future; a disregard for time as a dimension for organizing one's life.

☐ *Diffusion of industry;* a disruption of the sense of workmanship which manifests itself in an incapacity for concentration and an inability to complete tasks or in an excessive preoccupation with one-sided activities.

☐ *Identity consciousness;* extreme self-consciousness; an ashamed recognition of one's incomplete, inadequate identity; a sense of being exposed and vulnerable and the consequent wish to hide, either within some group uniformity or behind some false self-definition.

☐ *The choice of a negative identity;* a hostile and snobbish rejection of those roles that society offers as proper and desirable and the contrary vengeful choice to become, as Erikson puts it, "nobody or somebody bad." This choice is manifested either in the adoption of a personally defined negative identity based on those roles which in the individual's history have been presented as undesirable and yet real or by membership in groups defying society's values, such as delinquent gangs or homosexual cliques.

The measurement of the continuum identity-identity diffusion presented the difficult problem of translating an imprecisely defined, abstract concept into concrete operational terms. We developed several techniques that approached this task in different ways. A series of Henry Murray's thematic apperception cards was used to explore the fantasies of our actors in order to acquire some insight into their general psychodynamics and, more specifically, to ascertain the appearance of identity problems. We took interviews exploring both contemporary life and past history to investigate current manifestations of identity diffusion and to provide materials relevant to their genesis.

To test the hypothesis—that the actor's creative life was

somehow sustained by his search for an identity in his roles—required an instrument that could be administered twice to the same group of actors over a relatively short period and which, at the same time, would be sensitive enough to register the changes in identity anticipated as resulting from the rehearsal experience. Both of these considerations dictated the need for a short, easily administered instrument which would measure quantitative differences along the continuum of identity-identity diffusion.

To fill this need we devised the Identity Scale, an instrument similar to the seven-point polar choice semantic differential. It is composed of 56 pairs of words or phrases designed to elicit responses relevant to the issue of identity. One item of each pair denotes the negative possibility of a developmental issue, the other, the positive. All eight of Erikson's stages constitute sources of items relevant to the question of identity, for, as he makes clear, the derivatives or precursors of the issues defining each stage "are part and parcel of the struggle for identity." The scale also contains items based upon Erikson's clinical description of the symptoms of identity diffusion already discussed.

Before using the Identity Scale to test the study's hypotheses, we compared subjects' scores on it with another independent measure of identity. By categorizing the symptoms of identity diffusion, we designed an Index of Identity Diffusion on which we rated the current behavior of the actors as reported in the interviews. Scores on the Identity Scale were compared with ratings on the index for 14 male actors and were found significantly related.

For the purpose of exploring the two central hypotheses, we discuss the behavior of actors and criterion groups on the Identity Scale only. Scores referred to as high must be taken as an indication of a well-integrated identity, low scores as a reflection of identity diffusion. For comparison's sake we administered the scale to some 500 men and women in substantially different occupations—nurses, executives, civil servants, schoolteachers, housewives. The instrument was administered to all with the instructions to use the items to describe themselves as honestly as they could.

For the purpose of our first hypothesis, it may be noted that the average scores for groups of professional actors are in all cases lower—more on the identity diffusion side —than any single or all combined comparison groups and are significant in the statistical sense.

The identity instrument produces six fairly distinct factors. The largest is the identity factor mentioned above, and it is here that the major differences between actor and nonactor occur. However, since the symptoms of identity or of identity diffusion inherent in Erikson's theory contain elements of previous polar conflicts, it is not surprising that three of the remaining five factors appear to be echoes of Erikson's basic trust, autonomy and integrity. Elements of intimacy also appear, but these are included in the identity factor as we have defined it. On these three other factors, actors are lower than comparison groups—significantly so on integrity and trust.

One of the remaining factors appears to be a constellation of items relating to highly individualistic expressiveness. It has no social or interpersonal items in it, and hence we are inclined to think of it as a portrayal of ready changeability or adaptability of emotion in spontaneous and nonsocial forms. It has a ready appeal as a correlative to the stereotype of the "emotional" actor. That it may have some basis in reality is suggested by the fact that this is the only factor in which actors and actresses alike are significantly higher than comparison groups.

"Frenetic Search for Intimacy"

In other words, the actors do indeed appear lower, more identity diffuse, than comparison groups. And, further, they also appear lower on several elements which in theory are related to identity diffusion.

Evidence from our interviews can be summarized by saying that the symptoms of aimlessness, of distortion of time perspective, or frenetic search for intimacy are amply displayed. One fact that became apparent during these interviews is relevant and can be simply illustrated. The frenetic search for intimacy is crucial to Erikson's idea of diffused identity, as well as being a commonplace of public portrayals of actors and actresses. To test the truth of this stereotype we constructed an Index of Sexual Modes, with the assumption that sexual behavior was a partial but crucial factor in the intimacy concept. We based this index upon frequency, recentness and mode of sexual experience, taking as its logic the simple moral and psychodynamic view of good and bad sexual acts. Exclusive sexual intercourse with the same partner of the opposite sex scored zero, not as a comment on its worth but in order to emphasize divergences from this supposed norm. To variations in sexual mode, sex of partner, frequent changes of partner, we gave scores of 1, 2 and 3, respectively. This produced some high scores which unfortunately we were unable to compare with other groups for lack of comparable data. However, we made internal comparisons by dividing our actors into two groups, those with more and less identity diffusion. Again, the high group is the less identity-diffused, the one with better-integrated identity; the low group is the one with lower identity scores, more diffused. We gave the sex index additional reference to Erikson's concept of identity diffusion by making different tests for the successive stages of our subjects' lives, thus evaluating their sexual behavior at preschool age, at grammar school, high school, young adult, and adult and present.

The test produced some striking results. The index relates to the evaluation of identity diffusion at a highly significant level. When comparisons were made separately on the basis of age, there were similar relations. The high school period produced least relations to the Identity Scale results, but this too supports our hypothesis, since this stage is precisely the one where, according to Erikson's theories, everyone should be chaotically experiencing the "psychosocial moratorium" of role experimentation.

We have proposed that the life of an actor is in part determined by the effort to create a sense of identity through the portrayal of the varieties of models available in scripts. Our evidence on this point lies partly in what we may generally infer from our long series of interviews. But some is available in readily reportable form. One group of data resides in the administration of the same identity diffusion instrument to actors-in-training with the instructions to describe themselves as they would feel when rehearsal for a role was going particularly well, as compared with scores under the original instructions. On these two administrations actors in training systematically "improve," significantly moving in the direction of identity. This is not unexpected, perhaps, since anyone might do this when things are ideally imagined as going well. And indeed a group of junior executives of similar age does the same. However, actors change more, and the difference between the amount of their change and that of the executives is significant.

We were also able to administer the identity instrument to the cast of a play during rehearsals and under the original instructions to describe themselves as honestly as they could. This was done at two different points in time—two days after the start of a play rehearsal and three weeks later but still during rehearsal periods. The scores move significantly in the direction of firm identity as the actors progressively settle into their roles during the course of their rehearsals. Conclusions to be drawn from these two tests are inescapable; not only do actors believe that they will possess coherent identities under conditions of intense identification with their roles, they also bear out their opinions in practice. The closer they come to total identification with a role utterly alien to their habitual, "real" one, the more identity they seem to possess.

The interviews with experienced actors more than amply documented their own conviction of the vital importance to them personally of acting—an importance far outweighing that which anyone else might be expected to attach to his means of livelihood. The words of two famous actors, in interviews published in the *New Yorker* in 1961, testify to the intensity of the need to act:

Ingrid Bergman: "I hate to make an entrance. It is difficult for me to get up on a dance floor, because I feel everybody is watching. But if I played somebody else walking into a restaurant or getting up on a dance floor, I could do it. I couldn't be blamed. It wouldn't be me."

Henry Fonda: "Acting is putting on a mask. The worst torture that can happen to me is not having a mask to get in back of."

Our professionals are, of course, not our actors in training grown up, but the symptoms of identity diffusion seen in the professionals are, if anything, more marked in the students, and the contrast between those students and comparison groups of the same age are similarly highly significant. If we draw the cross-sectional conclusion, in part from these student data and in part from the retrospective reports of professionals, it is that actors are people whose early lives have been marked by disjunctive experiences, especially experiences calling attention to role differences in intimate family members, to distinctions between inner feelings and overt behavior in such figures, leaving each of our actors with the sense of a quest, a search for the one life style appropriate to them. We think that the role experimentation so begun, and subsequently institutionalized in acting, becomes the modus vivendi that has meaning for them. Especially interesting is the fact that our professionals report that once they had done some acting, commonly in high school, they never subsequently had any doubt as to their future profession. In the unstructured and hectic work world of the actor, the fight necessary to establish oneself is perhaps further evidence of the deeply rooted impulse of that ambition.

This article has suggested that actors are one sort of creative person for whom the inner personality meaning of work is extremely vital to an understanding of their adult lives and to an understanding of their creative work. This is a consequence of their ability to isolate emotional spontaneity from personal interactions, while searching endlessly for an outer form which will have meaning. The real function of their work is indeed internal, residing in the sense of personal identity that it provides. To some extent then, this study moves toward an explanation, to quote Rod Steiger's *New Yorker* interview, of "the way a man can live so beautifully in the fantasy of his art even when he can hardly live at all in the reality of his own life."

SUGGESTED READINGS

The Paradox of Acting by Denis Diderot and *Masks or Faces?* by William Archer (New York: Hill and Wang, 1957).

"On Acting" by Otto Fenichel in *The Psychoanalytic Quarterly*, *15*, 1946, pp. 144–160.

"A Psychological Assessment of Professional Actors and Related Professions" by Ronald Taft in *Genetic Psychology Monographs*, No. 64, 1961, pp. 309–383.

"Studio parties duplicate social occasions on the outside. Guests are an important source of new students."

Front-Stage and Back-Stage

by George Gardner

"Ballroom dance studios have developed a complex and rather standardized set of techniques to convert a potential student into an actual one and to insure continued lesson-taking. In the teachers' room, the inner sanctum in which controls are relaxed, there are no derogatory remarks about ballroom dance teaching. The regular or 'long-course' student who dances well is a source of pride, even in the back regions."

"The studio is designed to give an aura of 'class.' "

"The process of teaching is physically exhausting."

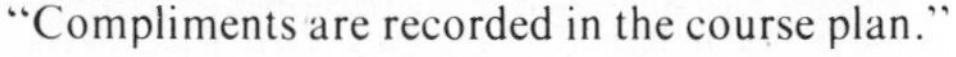

"Compliments are recorded in the course plan."

"The trophy system unites teacher and student and gives them a goal."

"The teacher enters the reception room with 'front-stage' demeanor."

"Teachers in the highly professional studio have high morale and a strong skill orientation."

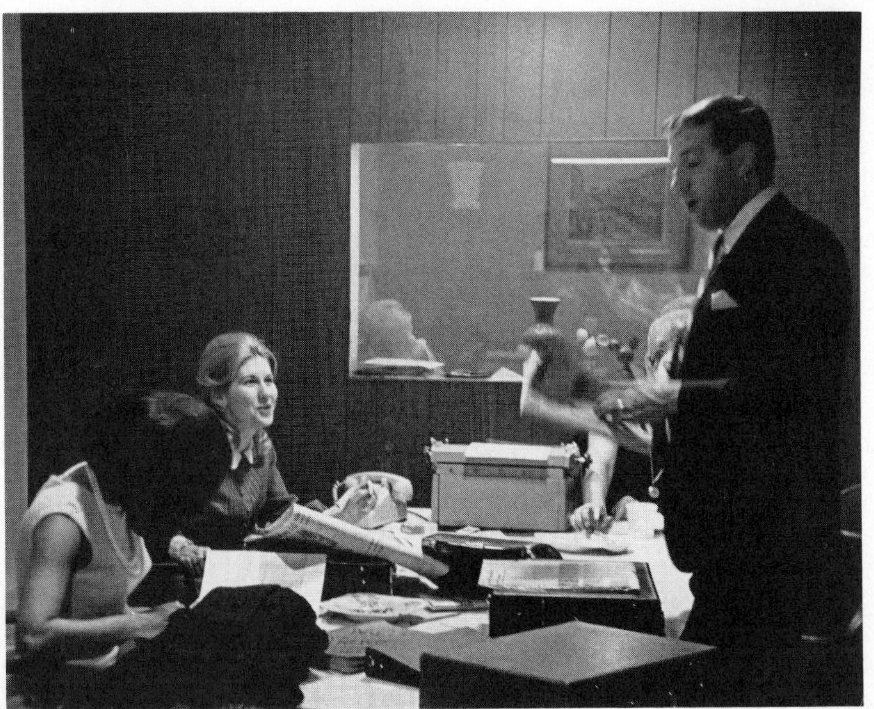

4 *Melford S. Weiss*

Rebirth in the Airborne

When an American paratrooper first learns to jump, he does more than step out of an airplane. He steps into a new way of life. Furthermore, his training even takes note of this major transition in his life in a formal ceremonial manner. This training period—marked by pomp and circumstance, superstition and ritual—is what anthropologists refer to as a *rite of passage.*

Rites of passage are universal features of complex as well as simple societies. They mark critical changes in man's life cycle, such as birth, death, and initiation. The paratrooper training program can best be understood as an initiation, a form of entry into an elite group. The process is interwoven with magical and symbolic ritual practices. In one training unit, for example, each time the trainees enter the airplane, the jumpmaster draws a line on the ground in front of the entrance hatch with the toe of his boot. Each prospective jumper then stomps upon the line before entering the airplane in order to ensure a safe landing. Whether or not they actually believe in the practice (many do not) is of decidedly less importance than the fact that this ritual serves to bind the group together.

A paratooper's training ends in a ceremonial climax. At the close of training it is customary in some military units to reenact the jumping procedure in a fashion symbolic of rebirth. Newly-qualified paratroopers are invited to a "prop blast" at the noncommissioned officers' club. There a wooden model of an airplane has been hastily rigged. The new initiates line up in jump formation inside the plane. They jump and land facing the jumpmaster, their instructor. He hands each a loving cup full of "blast juice." This must be quaffed within the count of "1000, 2000, 3000," the time between an actual jump from a plane and the opening of the chute. Failure to drain it to the dregs within the allotted span is called a "malfunction," the term for chute failure. The process must be repeated, perhaps three or four times, till success is achieved. Then the initiate is ritually one with his fellows.

Initiation Rites

Rites of passage vary in different cultures, but according to Arnold Van Gennep a typical rite has three stages:

—*separation* from the former group or state;

—*transition* to the new;

—and, finally, *incorporation.*

In birth and death rites, for example, separation is emphasized most: "The Lord giveth, the Lord has taken away." In the case of paratrooper training the transitional phase is most important. The paratrooper rite described here is a composite of training programs of many groups from World War II to the present time.

The paratrooper school is inside a compound surrounded by barbed wire and guarded by sentries. In this compound the trainee is fed, trained, and occasionally entertained. He is allowed to go out in the evening but usually does so in the company of other troopers. Fraternization with the non-paratrooper world is not encouraged, but separation from the former civilian environment is only partial.

The transitional phase usually lasts three weeks. During the last week the candidate makes five practice jumps which mark stages in his progress toward final acceptance. Not all the jumps are equally important—the first and fifth are most significant.

Paratrooper training is officially a secular affair. But certain superstitious practices which are interwoven show that, in the broadest sense, it is also a religious rite. From the beginning of the transition period the trainees are subjected to continuous periods of anxiety. Since they are all volunteers with a strong emotional investment in success, these stresses serve to bind them more closely to one another and to the group they seek to enter. So do the "magical" devices they learn to use to relieve anxiety. These include the wearing of charms and fetishes, such as a girl friend's picture above the heart, a pair of sweat socks worn on a previous successful jump, or a replica of the "trooper wings" placed inside a boot.

Use of "sympathetic magic" is fostered by the paratrooper mythology to which the trainee is exposed during this stage. The following examples of paratrooper tales illustrate elements of both *mana* (a spiritual force independent of persons or spirits which explains success, excellence, and potency when these qualities are not otherwise explainable) and *taboo* (a prohibition based upon the assumption that disastrous consequences can be averted if certain acts are not performed):

■ "He was a jinx and was always present at any accident. I would never jump with him in my line. I once touched him before I was about to jump and pretended to be sick in order to avoid jumping that day. Nobody laughed at me when I told them the real reason."

■ A master jumper told this story: "When I was a youngster, I felt that should I ever lose my original set of wings I could never jump again. They had a natural magic about them which protected me. When I went home I put them in the bottom drawer of my mother's dresser. I knew they would be safe there!"

■ Legend maintains that the paratrooper compound is off limits, and one myth relates the unhappy story of the intoxicated soldier from another unit who tried to sneak into the compound and was found next morning with his face severely scratched. The soldier claimed that he was attacked by a small bird and then passed out. But paratroopers claim that the bird was in fact the "screaming eagle," the totemic symbol of the 101st Airborne Division.

During the transition period myth and magic help the trainee to identify with paratroopers in general and share their *esprit de corps*. This becomes a formidable force as airborne units are made up entirely of volunteers. Thus a man becomes a paratrooper by choice and remains one all his military life unless he disobeys a direct order to jump. As in the case of other select military units, paratroopers are bound to one another by pride in a common history and system of training. They consider themselves superior to all other such groups—not only in their military virtues, but in their vices as well. A paratrooper is supposed to be able to outdrink, outbrawl, and outwhore any other member of the armed forces.

The Jumpout Dropout

Systems of initiation depend for their success upon how much the candidate wants to belong to the group. Sometimes, in the case of paratrooper training, he may not want to badly enough. A young man may decide he does not care to spend his active life plunging out of airplanes with nothing but the silkworm's art for support. Since all trainees are volunteers, this is technically no disgrace. All he has to do is request reassignment.

But because of the problem of preserving group morale the dropout is usually eliminated with almost indecent haste. Many instructors feel that to let him hang around will spread the "rot," and other failures or jumping accidents may result. When a would-be dropout says he wants out at the end of a training day, he is more than likely to be called to the orderly room during the next morning's formation. By the time the other trainees return from their midday meal he will have left the training area forever, usually to spend a month's KP duty in some non-elite holding company. For example one dropout said:

> I was scared and I knew it. I dared not let the others know, but I did not think I could hide it very long. We were listening to a master jumper telling us about his first jump and my stomach got queasy and I was sick. I told my sergeant I wanted out. I left the very next day.

If a trainee should quit during the training day, particularly with a public fuss, more brusque tactics may be used. One would-be paratrooper reports:

> I was fed up with this bastard. I made a scene and cursed the Army and shouted that you can shove the paratroopers. I yelled, "I quit." My training NCO rapidly approached me, ripped the patch from my shoulder, and cut the laces of my jump boots.

In some primitive societies those who fail the tests of manhood may be killed outright. The ripping of the patch and the cutting of the laces serves the same function symbolically. It signifies the separation of the dropout from his companions and thus binds the group more closely together, as does the knowledge that the failure is headed for KP or some other nonstatus duty.

As noted before, the transitional phase of paratrooper training has substages. These occur mainly after the first and fifth (last) practice jump. After the first there is no ceremony, but there is a change in the relationship between the trainees and the seasoned paratroopers. As soon as the jumping experience has been shared, the trainee begins to be treated with at least a modicum of respect by his instructors. Conversation in the barracks becomes less guarded. Before any mention of "spilling silk" or "flying a streamer" was avoided. Now jokes about jumping accidents and chute failures are freely bandied about.

The fifth jump is marked by a definite ritual. After the first four the trainee rolls his own chute. After the last he hands it to the platoon sergeant, who rolls it for him and places it in the supply truck. Then the NCO shakes his pupil's hand, congratulates him, and in some cases invites him to use his, the sergeant's, given name. This reversal of roles marks acceptance into the group. The same evening this is confirmed at a party at the enlisted men's club, usually off limits to officers. The paratroopers-to-be, including officer candidates, are invited to join in the drinking and usually do.

The whole transitional period in paratrooper training closely parallels initiation rites in both Western and non-Western societies. During this stage the initiate learns the formulas, gestures, and chants of the brotherhood. These include a paratrooper prayer and a paratrooper song. The latter is a gruesome chant in which the paratrooper verbalizes, jokingly, his fear of sudden and gory death. It is sung to the tune of "The Battle Hymn of the Republic":

> Is everybody ready? cried the Sergeant, looking up.
> Our hero feebly answered yes, as they stood him up.
> He leapt right out into the blast, his static line unhooked.
> O he ain't gonna jump no more!
>
> There was blood upon the risers, there were brains upon the chute,
> His intestines were a dangling from his paratrooper boots;
> They picked him up still in his chute and poured him from his boots;
> O he ain't gonna jump no more!

Chorus: Glory gory what a helluva way to die!
Glory gory what a helluva way to die!
Glory gory what a helluva way to die!
Oh he ain't gonna jump no more!

Wings and a Three-Day Pass

After transition comes incorporation in two stages—an official ceremony and the unofficial "prop blast" described earlier. The official ceremony is a colorful affair in the tradition of most military rituals. It marks the end of the rigorous training and is a welcome climax to weeks of agonizing tension. It takes place the day after the final (fifth) practice jump. The men in the training unit line up in alphabetical order; uniforms are smartly pressed, faces agonizingly clean shaven, and hair close cropped. They stand at attention while the post band plays the national anthem, followed by "Ruffles and Flourishes." The division flag flies just beneath Old Glory.

The men bow their heads as the post chaplain reads from the Bible. After a congratulatory speech the training commandant presents each man with his diploma. The division commandant passes through the ranks, reviews the troops, and pins "wings" to each man's chest. The chaplain delivers the closing benediction. The band continues to play military music as the men now assemble by training platoon and proudly march by the reviewing stand. As the soldiers reach the stand, they are saluted by the senior officers, and the new troopers return the salute. The men are then dismissed and given a three-day pass.

Many features of this ceremony have symbolic significance. The new paratrooper is being initiated into a special brotherhood within the military forces of an American, predominantly Christian, society. The chaplain's benediction gives the ceremony "divine sanction" and links it, however tenuously, with the prevailing Christian religion. The "American heritage" is reflected by the American flag and the national anthem. The polished boots, clean shaves, and close haircuts set up the image of the "clean-cut, all-American boy." The rest of the rite is military, with calculated differences. The marching, the salute, the respect for rank, and the three-day pass remind the paratrooper that he is a member of the armed forces. But the jump-school graduation certificate and the "wings" belong only to paratroopers and serve as permanent marks of that status.

The brotherhood of all troopers is symbolized by the formation itself. While the platoon is the standard military unit, on this one day the men line up in alphabetical order. This wipes out platoon distinctions and incorporates all the men in a pan-paratrooper sodality. Being saluted first by their superiors, against military protocol, shows the "troopers" that they now occupy a coveted status in the military.

Although the training NCO's are not required to attend, they are present throughout the ceremony. At the close they rush to congratulate the new members and welcome them into the brotherhood. The new status of the members has now been recognized and sanctioned by military society. With the evening's "prop blast" and its symbolic reenactment of the jumping process, the rite of passage is complete. The initiate is now wholly separated from his past life and "reborn" into a new, select brotherhood and a new way of life.

SUGGESTED READINGS

The Rites of Passage by Arnold Van Gennep (London, England: Routledge & Kegan Paul, 1960).

Essays in the Ritual of Social Relations, edited by Max Gluckman (Manchester, England: Manchester University Press, 1962).

Reader in Comparative Religion, 2nd ed., by William A. Lessa and Evon Z. Vogt (New York: Harper & Row, 1965).

Religion in Primitive Society by Edward Norbeck (New York: Harper & Row, 1961).

5 *John R. Howard*

The Making of a Black Muslim

You were black enough to get in here. You had the courage to stay. Now be man enough to follow the honorable Elijah Muhammad. You have tried the devil's way. Now try the way of the Messenger.

Minister William X, in a West Coast Black Muslim mosque

The Lost-Found Nation of Islam in the Wilderness of North America, commonly known as the Black Muslim movement, claims a small but fanatically devoted membership among the Negroes of our major cities. The way of the "Messenger" is rigorous for those who follow it. The man or woman who becames a Muslim accepts not only an ideology but an all-encompassing code that amounts to a way of life.

A good Muslim does a full day's work on an empty stomach. When he finally has his one meal of the day in the evening, it can include no pork, nor can he have drink before or a cigarette after; strict dietary rules are standard procedure, and liquor and smoking are forbidden under any circumstances. His recreation is likely to consist of reading the Koran or participating in a demanding round of temple-centered activities, running public meetings or aggressively proselytizing on the streets by selling the Muslim newspaper, *Muhammad Speaks*.

Despite allegations of Muslim violence (adverse publicity from the slaying of Malcolm X supports the erroneous notion that Muslims preach violence), the member's life is basically ascetic. Why then in a non-ascetic, hedonistically-oriented society do people become Muslims? What is the life of a Muslim like? These are questions I asked in research among West Coast members. Specifically, I wanted to know:

- What perspective on life makes membership in such an organization attractive?
- Under what conditions does the potential recruit develop those perspectives?
- How does he happen to come to the door of the temple for his first meeting?
- The Black Muslims are a deviant organization even within the Negro community; the parents or friends of many members strongly objected to their joining. So how does the recruit handle pressures that might erode his allegiance to the organization and its beliefs?

Presenting my questions as an effort to "learn the truth" about the organization, I was able to conduct depth interviews with 19 West Coast recruits, following them through the process of their commitment to the Nation of Islam.

Two main points of appeal emerged—black nationalism and an emphasis on self-help. Some recruits were attracted primarily by the first, and some by the second. The 14 interviewees who joined the organization for its aggressive black nationalism will be called "Muslim militants." The remaining five, who were attracted more by its emphasis on hard work and rigid personal morality, may be aptly termed "Protestant Ethic Muslims."

Muslim Militants: Beating the Devil

Of the 14 Muslim militants, some came from the South, some from border states, and some from the North. All lived in California at the time of the interviews; some migrated to the state as adults, others were brought out by their families as children. They varied in age from 24 to 46, and in education from a few years of grade school to four years of college. Regardless of these substantial differences in background, there were certain broad similarities among them.

At some point, each one had experiences that led away from the institutionally-bound ties and commitments that lend stability to most people's lives. Nine had been engaged in semi-legal or criminal activities. Two had been in the military, not as a career but as a way of postponing the decision of what to do for a living. None had a stable marital history. All of them were acutely aware of being outsiders by the standards of the larger society—and all had come to focus on race bias as the factor which denied them more conventional alternatives.

Leroy X came to California in his late teens, just before World War II:

> I grew up in Kansas City, Missouri, and Missouri was a segregated state. Negroes in Kansas City were always restricted to the menial jobs. I came out here in 1940 and tried to get a job as a waiter. I was a trained waiter, but they weren't hiring any Negroes as waiters in any of the downtown hotels or restaurants. The best I could do was busboy, and they fired me from that when they found out I wasn't Filipino.

Leroy X was drafted, and after a short but stormy career was given a discharge as being psychologically unfit.

> I tried to get a job, but I couldn't so I started stealing. There was nothing else to do—I couldn't live on air. The peckerwoods didn't seem to give a damn whether I lived or died. They wouldn't hire me and didn't seem to worry how I was going to stay alive. I started stealing.

I could get you anything you wanted—a car, drugs, women, jewelry. Crime is a business like any other. I started off stealing myself. I wound up filling orders and getting rid of stuff. I did that for fifteen years. In between I did a little time. I did time for things I never thought of doing and went free for things I really did.

In my business you had no friends, only associates, and not very close ones at that. . . . I had plenty of money. I could get anything I wanted without working for it. It wasn't enough, though.

Bernard X grew up in New York City:

As a kid . . . you always have dreams—fantasies—of yourself doing something later—being a big name singer or something that makes you outstanding. But you never draw the connection between where you are and how you're going to get there. I had to—I can't say exactly when, 13, 14, 15, 16. I saw I was nowhere and had no way of getting anywhere.

Race feeling is always with you. You always know about The Man but I don't think it is real, really real, until you have to deal with it in terms of what you are going to do with your own life. That's when you feel it. If you just disliked him before—you begin to hate him when you see him blocking you in your life. I think then a sense of inevitability hits you and you see you're not going to make it out—up—away—anywhere—and you see The Man's part in the whole thing, that's when you begin to think thoughts about him.

Frederick 2X became involved fairly early in a criminal subculture. His father obtained a "poor man's divorce" by deserting the family. His mother had children by other men. Only a tenuous sense of belonging to a family existed. He was picked up by the police for various offenses several times before reaching his teens. The police patrolling his neighborhood eventually restricted him to a two-block area. There was, of course, no legal basis for this, but he was manhandled if seen outside that area by any policeman who knew him. He graduated in his late teens from "pot" to "shooting shit" and eventually spent time in Lexington.

William 2X, formerly a shoeshine boy, related the development of his perspective this way:

You know how they always talk about us running after white women. There have always been a lot of [white] servicemen in this town—half of them would get around to asking me to get a woman for them. Some of them right out, some of them backing into it, laughing and joking and letting me know how much they were my friend, building up to asking me where they could find some woman. After a while I began to get them for them. I ran women—both black and white. . . . What I hated was they wanted me to do something for them [find women] and hated me for doing it. They figure "any nigger must know where to find it. . . ."

Things Begin to Add Up

Amos X grew up in an all-Negro town in Oklahoma and attended a Negro college. Because of this, he had almost no contact with whites during his formative years.

One of my aunts lived in Tulsa. I went to see her once when I was in college. I walked up to the front door of the house where she worked. She really got excited and told me if I came to see her anymore to come around to the back. But that didn't mean much to me at the time. It is only in looking back on it that all these things begin to add up.

After graduating from college, Amos joined the Marines. There he began to "see how they [the whites] really felt" about him; by the end of his tour, he had concluded that "the white man is the greatest liar, the greatest cheat, the greatest hypocrite on earth." Alienated and disillusioned, he turned to professional gambling. Then, in an attempt at a more conventional way of life, he married and took a job teaching school.

I taught English. Now I'm no expert in the slave masters' language, but I knew the way those kids talked after being in school eight and nine years was ridiculous. They said things like "mens" for "men." I drilled them and pretty soon some of them at least in class began to sound like they had been inside a school. Now the principal taught a senior class in English and his kids talked as bad as mine. When I began to straighten out his kids also he felt I was criticizing him. . . . That little black man was afraid of the [white] superintendent and all those teachers were afraid. They had a little more than other so-called Negroes and didn't give a damn about those black children they were teaching. Those were the wages of honesty. It's one thing to want to do an honest job and another thing to be able to. . . .

With the collapse of his career as a public school teacher and the break-up of his marriage, Amos went to California, where he was introduced to the Muslim movement.

I first heard about them [the Muslims] in 1961. There was a debate here between a Muslim and a Christian minister. The Muslims said all the things about Christianity which I had been thinking but which I had never heard anyone say before. He tore the minister up.

Finding an organization that aggressively rejected the white man and the white man's religion, Amos found his own point of view crystallized. He joined without hesitation.

Norman Maghid first heard of the Muslims while he was in prison.

I ran into one of the Brothers selling the paper about two weeks after I got out and asked him about the meetings. Whether a guy could just go and walk in. He told me about the meetings so I made it around on a Wednesday evening. I wasn't even bugged when they searched me. When they asked me about taking out my letter [joining the organization] I took one out. They seemed to know what they were talking about. I never believed in nonviolence and love my enemies, especially when my enemies don't love me.

Muhammad Soule Kabah, born into a family of debt-ridden Texas sharecroppers, was recruited into the Nation of Islam after moving to California.

I read a series of articles in the Los Angeles *Herald Dispatch,* an exchange between Minister Henry and a Christian minister. It confirmed what my grandfather had told me about my African heritage, that I had nothing to be ashamed of, that there were six thousand books on mathematics in the Library of the University of Timbucktoo while Europeans were still wearing skins. Also my father had taught me never to kow-tow to whites. My own father had fallen away. My parents didn't want me to join the Nation. They said they taught hate. That's funny isn't it? The white man can blow up a church and kill four children and the black man worries that an organization which tells you not to just take it is teaching hate.

Protestant Ethic Muslims: Up by Black Bootstraps

The Protestant Ethic Muslims all came from backgrounds with a strong tradition of Negro self-help. In two cases, the recruit's parents had been followers of Marcus Garvey; another recruit explicitly endorsed the beliefs of Booker T. Washington; and the remaining two, coming from upwardly mobile families, were firm in the belief that Negroes could achieve higher status if they were willing to work for it.

When asked what had appealed to him about the Muslims, Norman X replied:

They thought that black people should do something for themselves. I was running this small place [a photography shop] and trying to get by. I've stuck with this place even when it was paying me barely enough to eat. Things always improve and I don't have to go to the white man for anything.

Ernestine X stressed similar reasons for joining the Muslims.

You learned to stand up straight and do something for yourself. You learn to be a lady at all times—to keep your house clean—to teach your children good manners. There is not a girl in the M-G-T who does not know how to cook and sew. The children are very respectful; they speak only when they are spoken to. There is no such thing as letting your children talk back to you the way some people believe. The one thing they feel is the Negroes' downfall is men and sex for the women, and women and sex for the men, and they frown on sex completely unless you are married.

Despite their middle-class attitudes in many areas, Protestant Ethic Muslims denounced moderate, traditional civil rights organizations such as the NAACP, just as vigorously as the militant Muslims did. Norman X said that he had once belonged to the NAACP but had dropped out.

They spent most of their time planning the annual brotherhood dinner. Besides it was mostly whites—whites and the colored doctors and lawyers who wanted to be white. As far as most Negroes were concerned they might as well not have existed.

Lindsey X, who had owned and run his own upholstery shop for more than 30 years, viewed the conventional black bourgeoisie with equal resentment.

I never belonged to the NAACP. What they wanted never seemed real to me. I think Negroes should create jobs for themselves rather than going begging for them. That's why I never supported CORE.

In this respect Norman and Lindsey were in full accord with the more militant Amos X, who asserted:

They [the NAACP and CORE] help just one class of people. . . . Let something happen to a doctor and they are right there; but if something happens to Old Mose on the corner, you can't find them.

The interviews made it clear that most of the Protestant Ethic Muslims had joined the Nation because, at some point, they began to feel the need of organizational support for their personal systems of value. For Norman and Lindsey, it was an attempt to stop what they considered their own backsliding after coming to California. Both mentioned drinking to excess and indulging in what they regarded as a profligate way of life. Guilt feelings apparently led them to seek Muslim support in returning to more enterprising habits.

Commitment to Deviance

The Nation of Islam is a deviant organization. As such it is subject to public scorn and ridicule. Thus it faces the problem of consolidating the recruit's allegiance in an environment where substantial pressures operate to erode this allegiance. How does it deal with this problem?

The structural characteristics of the Nation tend to insulate the member from the hostility of the larger society and thus contribute to the organization's survival. To begin with, the ritual of joining the organization itself stresses commitment without questions.

At the end of the general address at a temple meeting, the minister asks those nonmembers present who are "interested in learning more about Islam" to step to the back of the temple. There they are given three blank sheets of ordinary stationery and a form letter addressed to Elijah Muhammad in Chicago:

Dear Savior Allah, Our Deliverer:

I have attended the Teachings of Islam, two or three times, as taught by one of your ministers. I believe in it. I bear witness that there is no God but Thee. And, that Muhammad is Thy Servant and Apostle. I desire to reclaim my Own. Please give me my Original name. My slave name is as follows:

The applicant is instructed to copy this letter verbatim on each of the three sheets of paper, giving his own name and address unabbreviated at the bottom. If he fails to copy the letter perfectly, he must repeat the whole task. No explanation is given for any of these requirements.

Formal acceptance of his letter makes the new member a Muslim, but in name only. Real commitment to the Nation of Islam comes gradually—for example, the personal commitment expressed when a chain smoker gives up cigarettes in accordance with the Muslim rules even though he knows that he could smoke unobserved. "It's not that easy to do these things," Stanley X said of the various forms of abstinence practiced by Muslims. "It takes will and discipline and time, . . . but you're a much better person after you do." Calvin X told of periodic backsliding in the beginning, but added, "Once I got into the thing deep, then I stuck with it."

This commitment and the new regimen that goes with it have been credited with effecting dramatic personality changes in many members, freeing alcoholics from the bottle and drug addicts from the needle. It can be argued, however, that the organization does not change the member's fundamental orientation. To put it somewhat differently, given needs and impulses can be expressed in a variety of ways; thus, a man may give vent to his sadism by beating up strangers in an alley or by joining the police force and beating them up in the back room of the station.

"Getting into the thing deep" for a Muslim usually comes in three stages:

■ Participation in organizational activities—selling the Muslim newspaper, dining at the Muslim restaurant, attending and helping run Muslim meetings.

■ Isolation from non-Muslim social contacts—drifting away from former friends and associates because of divergent attitudes or simply because of the time consumed in Muslim activities.

■ Assimilation of the ideology—marking full commitment, when a Muslim has so absorbed the organization's doctrines that he automatically uses them to guide his own behavior and to interpret what happens in the world around him.

The fact that the organization can provide a full social life furthers isolation from non-Muslims. Participation is not wholly a matter of drudgery, of tramping the streets to sell the paper and studying the ideology. The organization presents programs of entertainment for its members and the public. For example, in two West Coast cities a Negro theatrical troupe called the Touring Artists put on two plays, "Jubilee Day" and "Don't You Want to Be Free." Although there was a high element of humor in both plays, the basic themes—white brutality and hypocrisy and the necessity of developing Negro self-respect and courage—were consonant with the organization's perspective. Thus the organization makes it possible for a member to satisfy his need for diversion without going outside to do so. At the same time, it continually reaches him with its message through the didactic element in such entertainment.

Carl X's experiences were typical of the recruit's growing commitment to the Nation. When asked what his friends had thought when he first joined, he replied: "They thought I was crazy. They said, 'Man, how can you believe all that stuff?' " He then commented that he no longer saw much of them, and added:

> When you start going to the temple four or five times a week and selling the newspaper you do not have time for people who are not doing these things. We drifted—the friends I had—we drifted apart. . . . All the friends I have now are in the Nation. Another Brother and I get together regularly and read the Koran and other books, then ask each other questions on them like, "What is Allah's greatest weapon? The truth. What is the devil's greatest weapon? The truth. The devil keeps it hidden from men. Allah reveals it to man." We read and talk about the things we read and try to sharpen our thinking. I couldn't do that with my old friends.

Spelled out, the "stuff" that Carl X had come to believe, the official Muslim ideology, is this:

■ The so-called Negro, the American black man, is lost in ignorance. He is unaware of his own past history and the future role which history has destined him to play.

■ Elijah Muhammad has come as the Messenger of Allah to awaken the American black man.

■ The American black man finds himself now in a lowly state, but that was not always his condition.

■ The Original Man, the first men to populate the earth, were non-white. They enjoyed a high level of culture and reached high peaks of achievement.

■ A little over 6,000 years ago a black scientist named Yakub, after considerable work, produced a mutant, a new race, the white race.

■ This new race was inferior mentally, physically, and morally to the black race. Their very whiteness, the very mark of their difference from the black race, was an indication of their physical degeneracy and moral depravity.

■ Allah, in anger at Yakub's work, ordained that the white race should rule for a fixed amount of time and that the black man should suffer and by his suffering gain a greater appreciation of his own spiritual worth by comparing himself to the whites.

■ The time of white dominance is drawing near its end. It is foreordained that this race shall perish, and with its destruction the havoc, terror, and brutality which it has spread throughout the world shall disappear.

■ The major task facing the Nation of Islam is to awaken the American black man to his destiny, to acquaint him with the course of history.

■ The Nation of Islam in pursuing this task must battle against false prophets, in particular those who call for integration. Integration is a plot of the white race to forestall its own doom. The black bourgeoisie, bought off by a few paltry favors and attempting to ingratiate themselves with the whites, seek to spread this pernicious doctrine among so-called Negroes.

■ The Nation of Islam must encourage the American black man to begin now to assume his proper role by wresting economic control from the whites. The American black man must gain control over his own economic fortunes by going into business for himself and becoming economically strong.

- The Nation of Islam must encourage the so-called Negro to give up those habits which have been spread among them by the whites as part of the effort to keep them weak, diseased, and demoralized. The so-called Negro must give up such white-fostered dissolute habits as drinking, smoking, and eating improper foods. The so-called Negro must prepare himself in mind and body for the task of wresting control from the whites.
- The Nation of Islam must encourage the so-called Negro to seek now his own land within the continental United States. This is due him and frees him from the pernicious influence of the whites.

The Problem of Defection

Commitment to the Nation can diminish as well as grow. Four of the members I interviewed later defected. Why?

These four cases can be explained in terms of a weak point in the structure of the Nation. The organization has no effective mechanisms for handling grievances among the rank and file. Its logic accounts for this. Muslim doctrine assumes that there is a single, ultimate system of truth. Elijah Muhammad and, by delegation, his ministers are in possession of this truth. Thus only Elijah Muhammad himself can say whether a minister is doing an adequate job. The result is the implicit view that there is nothing to be adjudicated between the hierarchy and its rank and file.

Grievances arise, however. The four defectors were, for various reasons, all dissatisfied with Minister Gerard X. Since there were no formal mechanisms within the organization for expressing their dissatisfaction, the only solution was to withdraw.

For most members, however, the pattern is one of steadily growing involvement. And once the ideology is fully absorbed, there is virtually no such thing as dispute or counter-evidence. If a civil rights bill is not passed, this proves the viciousness of whites in refusing to recognize Negro rights. If the same bill *is* passed, it merely proves the duplicity of whites in trying to hide their viciousness.

The ideology also provides a coherent theory of causation, provided one is willing to accept its basic assumptions. Norman X interpreted his victory over his wife in a court case as a sign of Allah's favor. Morris X used it to account for the day-to-day fortunes of his associates.

> Minister X had some trouble. He was sick for a long time. He almost died. I think Allah was punishing him. He didn't run the temple right. Now the Brothers make mistakes. Everyone does—but Minister X used to abuse them at the meetings. It was more a personal thing. He had a little power and it went to his head. Allah struck him down and I think he learned a little humility.

When a man reasons in this fashion, he has become a fully committed member of the Nation of Islam. His life revolves around temple-centered activities, his friends are all fellow Muslims, and he sees his own world—usually the world of an urban slum dweller—through the framework of a very powerful myth. He is still doing penance for the sins of Yakub, but the millennium is at hand. He has only to prepare.

The Nation of Islam does not in any real sense convert members. Rather it attracts Negroes who have already, through their own experiences in white America, developed a perspective congruent with that of the Muslim movement. The recruit comes to the door of the temple with the essence of his ideas already formed. The Black Muslims only give this disaffection a voice.

SUGGESTED READINGS

Outsider: Studies in the Sociology of Deviance by Howard S. Becker (New York: Free Press, 1963).

Black Nationalism: a Search for an Identity in America by E. Essien-Udom (Chicago: University of Chicago Press, 1962).

6 *John Finley Scott*

Sororities and the Husband Game

Marriages, like births, deaths, or initiations at puberty, are rearrangements of structure that are constantly recurring in any society; they are moments of the continuing social process regulated by custom; there are institutionalized ways of dealing with such events.

A. R. Radcliffe-Brown
African Systems of Kinship and Marriage

In many simple societies, the "institutionalized ways" of controlling marriage run to diverse schemes and devices. Often they include special living quarters designed to make it easy for marriageable girls to attract a husband: the Bontok people of the Philippines keep their girls in a special house, called the *olag,* where lovers call, sex play is free, and marriage is supposed to result. The Ekoi of Nigeria, who like their women fat, send them away to be specially fattened for marriage. Other peoples, such as the Yao of central Africa and the aborigines of the Canary Islands, send their daughters away to "convents" where old women teach them the special skills and mysteries that a young wife needs to know.

Accounts of such practices have long been a standard topic of anthropology lectures in universities, for their exotic appeal keeps the students, large numbers of whom are sorority girls, interested and alert. The control of marriage in simple societies strikes these girls as quite different from the freedom that they believe prevails in America. This is ironic, for the American college sorority is a pretty good counterpart in complex societies of the fatting houses and convents of the primitives.

Whatever system they use, parents in all societies have more in mind than just getting their daughters married; they want them married to the *right* man. The criteria for defining the right man vary tremendously, but virtually all parents view some potential mates with approval, some with disapproval, and some with downright horror. Many ethnic groups, including many in America, are *endogamous,* that is, they desire marriage of their young only to those within the group. In *shtetl* society, the Jewish villages of eastern Europe, marriages were arranged by a *shatchen,* a matchmaker, who paired off the girls and boys with due regard to the status, family connections, wealth, and personal attractions of the participants. But this society was strictly endogamous—only marriage within the group was allowed. Another rule of endogamy relates to social rank or class, for most parents are anxious that their children marry at least at the same level as themselves. Often they hope the children, and especially the daughters, will marry at a higher level. Parents of the *shtetl,* for example, valued *hypergamy* —the marriage of daughters to a man of higher status— and a father who could afford it would offer substantial sums to acquire a scholarly husband (the most highly prized kind) for his daughter.

The marriage problem, from the point of view of parents and of various ethnic groups and social classes, is always one of making sure that girls are available for marriage with the right man while at the same time guarding against marriage with the wrong man.

THE UNIVERSITY CONVENT

The American middle class has a particular place where it sends its daughters so they will be easily accessible to the boys—the college campus. Even for the families who worry about the bad habits a nice girl can pick up at college, it has become so much a symbol of middle-class status that the risk must be taken, the girl must be sent. American middle-class society has created an institution on the campus that, like the fatting house, makes the girls more attractive; like the Canary Island convent, teaches skills that middle-class wives need to know; like the *shtetl,* provides matchmakers; and without going so far as to buy husbands of high rank, manages to dissuade the girls from making alliances with lower-class boys. That institution is the college sorority.

A sorority is a private association which provides separate dormitory facilities with a distinctive Greek letter name for selected female college students. Membership is by invitation only, and requires recommendation by former members. Sororities are not simply the feminine counterpart of the college fraternity. They differ from fraternities because marriage is a more important determinant of social position for women than for men in American society, and because standards of conduct associated with marriage correspondingly bear stronger sanctions for women than for men. Sororities have much more "alumnae" involvement than fraternities, and fraternities adapt to local conditions and different living arrangements better than sororities. The college-age sorority "actives" decide only the minor details involved in recruitment, membership, and activities; parent-age alumnae control the important choices. The prototypical sorority is not the servant of youthful interests; on the contrary, it is an organized agency for controlling those interests. Through the sorority, the elders of family, class, ethnic, and religious communities can continue to exert remote control over the marital arrangements of their young girls.

The need for remote control arises from the nature of the educational system in an industrial society. In simple societies, where children are taught the culture at home, the family controls the socialization of children almost completely. In more complex societies, education becomes the province of special agents and competes with the family. The conflict between the family and outside agencies increases as children move through the educational system and is sharpest when the children reach college age. College curricula are even more challenging to family value systems than high school courses, and children frequently go away to college, out of reach of direct family influence. Sometimes a family can find a college that does not challenge family values in any way: devout Catholic parents can send their daughters to Catholic colleges; parents who want to be sure that daughter meets only "Ivy League" men can send her to one of the "Seven Sisters"—the women's equivalent of the Ivy League, made up of Radcliffe, Barnard, Smith, Vassar, Wellesley, Mt. Holyoke, and Bryn Mawr—if she can get in.

The solution of controlled admissions is applicable only to a small proportion of college-age girls, however. There are nowhere near the number of separate, sectarian colleges in the country that would be needed to segregate all the college-age girls safely, each with her own kind. Private colleges catering mostly to a specific class can still preserve a girl from meeting her social or economic inferiors, but the fees at such places are steep. It costs more to maintain a girl in the Vassar dormitories than to pay her sorority bills at a land-grant school. And even if her family is willing to pay the fees, the academic pace at the elite schools is much too fast for most girls. Most college girls attend large, tax-supported universities where the tuition is relatively low and where admissions policies let in students from many strata and diverse ethnic backgrounds. It is on the campuses of the free, open, and competitive state universities of the country that the sorority system flourishes.

When a family lets its daughter loose on a large campus with a heterogenous population, there are opportunities to be met and dangers to guard against. The great opportunity is to meet a good man to marry, at the age when the girls are most attractive and the men most amenable. For the girls, the pressure of time is urgent; though they are often told otherwise, their attractions are in fact primarily physical, and they fade with time. One need only compare the relative handicaps in the marital sweepstakes of a 38-year old single male lawyer and a single, female teacher of the same age to realize the urgency of the quest.

The great danger of the public campus is that young girls, however properly reared, are likely to fall in love, and—in our middle-class society at least—love leads to marriage. Love is a potentially random factor, with no regard for class boundaries. There seems to be no good way of preventing young girls from falling in love. The only practical way to control love is to control the type of men the girl is likely to encounter; she cannot fall dangerously in love with a man she has never met. Since kinship groups are unable to keep "undesirable" boys off the public campus entirely, they have to settle for control of counter-institutions within the university. An effective counter-institution will protect a girl from the corroding influences of the university environment.

There are roughly three basic functions which a sorority can perform in the interest of kinship groups:

- It can ward off the wrong kind of men.
- It can facilitate moving-up for middle-status girls.
- It can solve the "Brahmin problem"—the difficulty of proper marriage that afflicts high-status girls.

Kinship groups define the "wrong kind of man" in a variety of ways. Those who use an ethnic definition support sororities that draw an ethnic membership line; the best examples are the Jewish sororities, because among all the ethnic groups with endogamous standards (in America at any rate), only the Jews so far have sent large numbers of daughters away to college. But endogamy along class lines is even more pervasive. It is the most basic mission of the sorority to prevent a girl from marrying out of her group (exogamy) or beneath her class (hypogamy). As one of the founders of a national sorority artlessly put it in an essay titled "The Mission of the Sorority":

> There is a danger, and a very grave danger, that four years' residence in a dormitory will tend to destroy right ideals of home life and substitute in their stead a belief in the freedom that comes from community living . . . culture, broad, liberalizing, humanizing culture, we cannot get too much of, unless while acquiring it we are weaned from home and friends, from ties of blood and kindred.

A sorority discourages this dangerous weaning process by introducing the sisters only to selected boys; each sorority, for example, has dating relations with one or more fraternities, matched rather nicely to the sorority on the basis of ethnicity and/or class. (A particular sorority, for example, will have dating arrangements not with all the fraternities on campus, but only with those whose brothers are a class-match for their sisters.) The sorority's frantically busy schedule of parties, teas, meetings, skits, and exchanges keeps the sisters so occupied that they have neither time nor opportunity to meet men outside the channels the sorority provides.

MARRYING UP

The second sorority function, that of facilitating hypergamy, is probably even more of an attraction to parents than the simpler preservation of endogamy. American society is not so much oriented to the preservation of the *status quo* as to the pursuit of upward mobility.

In industrial societies, children are taught that if they study hard they can get the kind of job that entitles them to a place in the higher ranks. This incentive actually is appropriate only for boys, but the emphasis on using the most efficient available means to enter the higher levels will not be lost on the girls. And the most efficient means for a girl—marriage—is particularly attractive because it requires so much less effort than the mobility through hard work that is open to boys. To the extent that we do socialize the sexes in different ways, we are more likely to train daughters in the ways of attracting men than to motivate them to do hard, competitive work. The difference in motivation holds even if the girls have the intelligence and talent required for status climbing on their own. For lower-class girls on the make, membership in a sorority can greatly improve the chances of meeting (and subsequently marrying) higher-status boys.

Now we come to the third function of the sorority—solving the Brahmin problem. The fact that hypergamy is encouraged in our society creates difficulties for girls whose parents are already in the upper strata. In a hypergamous system, high status *men* have a strong advantage; they can offer their status to a prospective bride as part of the marriage bargain, and the advantages of high status are often sufficient to offset many personal drawbacks. But a *woman's* high status has very little exchange value because she does not confer it on her husband.

This difficulty of high status women in a hypergamous society we may call the Brahmin problem. Girls of Brahmin caste in India and Southern white women of good family have the problem in common. In order to avoid the horrors of hypogamy, high status women must compete for high status men against women from all classes. Furthermore, high status women are handicapped in their battle by a certain type of vanity engendered by their class. They expect their wooers to court them in the style to which their fathers have accustomed them; this usually involves more formal dating, gift-giving, escorting, taxiing, etc., than many college swains can afford. If upper-stratum men are allowed to find out that the favors of lower class women are available for a much smaller investment of time, money, and emotion, they may well refuse to court upper-status girls.

In theory, there are all kinds of ways for upper-stratum families to deal with surplus daughters. They can strangle them at birth (female infanticide); they can marry several to each available male (polygyny); they can offer money to any suitable male willing to take one off their hands (dowries, groom-service fees). All these solutions have in fact been used in one society or another, but for various reasons none is acceptable in our society. Spinsterhood still works, but marriage is so popular and so well rewarded that everybody hopes to avoid staying single.

The industrial solution to the Brahmin problem is to corner the market, or more specifically to shunt the eligible bachelors into a special marriage market where the upper stratum women are in complete control of the bride-supply. The best place to set up this protected marriage-market is where many suitable men can be found at the age when they are most willing to marry—in short, the college campus. The kind of male collegians who can be shunted more readily into the specialized marriage-market that sororities run, are those who are somewhat uncertain of their own status and who aspire to move into higher strata. These boys are anxious to bolster a shaky self-image by dating obviously high-class sorority girls. The fraternities are full of them.

How does a sorority go about fulfilling its three functions? The first item of business is making sure that the girls join. This is not as simple as it seems, because the values that sororities maintain are more important to the older generation than to college-age girls. Although the sorority image is one of membership denied to the "wrong kind" of girls, it is also true that sororities have quite a problem of recruiting the "right kind." Some are pressured into pledging by their parents. Many are recruited straight out of high school, before they know much about what really goes on at college. High school recruiters present sorority life to potential rushees as one of unending gaiety; life outside the sorority is painted as bleak and dateless.

A membership composed of the "right kind" of girls is produced by the requirement that each pledge must have the recommendation of, in most cases, two or more alumnae of the sorority. Membership is often passed on from mother to daughter—this is the "legacy," whom sorority actives have to invite whether they like her or not. The sort of headstrong, innovative, or "sassy" girl who is likely to organize a campaign inside the sorority against prevailing standards is unlikely to receive alumnae recommendations. This is why sorority girls are so complacent about alumnae dominance, and why professors find them so bland and uninteresting as students. Alumnae dominance extends beyond recruitment, into the daily life of the house. Rules, regulations, and policy explanations come to the house from the national association. National headquarters is given to explaining unpopular policy by any available strategem; a favorite device (not limited to the sorority) is to interpret all non-conformity as sexual, so that the girl who rebels against wearing girdle, high heels, and stockings to dinner two or three times a week stands implicitly accused of promiscuity. This sort of argument, based on the shrewdness of many generations, shames into conformity many a girl who otherwise might rebel against the code imposed by her elders. The actives in positions of control (house manager, pledge trainer or captain) are themselves closely supervised by alumnae. Once the right girls are initiated, the organization has mechanisms that make it very difficult for a girl to withdraw. Withdrawal can mean difficulty in finding alternative living quarters, loss of prepaid room and board fees, and stigmatization.

Sororities keep their members, and particularly their flighty pledges, in line primarily by filling up all their time with house activities. Pledges are required to study at the house, and they build the big papier-mache floats (in collaboration with selected fraternity boys) that are a traditional display of "Greek Row" for the homecoming game. Time is encompassed completely; activities are planned long in advance, and there is almost no energy or time available for meeting inappropriate men.

The girls are taught—if they do not already know—the behavior appropriate to the upper strata. They learn how to dress with expensive restraint, how to make appropriate conversation, how to drink like a lady. There is some variety here among sororities of different rank; members of sororities at the bottom of the social ladder prove their gentility by rigid conformity in dress and manner to the stereotype of the sorority girl, while members of top houses feel socially secure even when casually dressed. If you are born rich you can afford to wear Levi's and sweatshirts.

PRELIMINARY EVENTS

The sorority facilitates dating mainly by exchanging parties, picnics, and other frolics with the fraternities in its set. But to augment this the "fixer-uppers" (the American counterpart of the *shatchen*) arrange dates with selected boys; their efforts raise the sorority dating rate above the independent level by removing most of the inconvenience and anxiety from the contracting of dates.

Dating, in itself, is not sufficient to accomplish the sorority's purposes. Dating must lead to pinning, pinning to engagement, engagement to marriage. In sorority culture, all dating is viewed as a movement toward marriage. Casual, spontaneous dating is frowned upon; formal courtship is still encouraged. Sorority ritual reinforces the progression from dating to marriage. At the vital point in the process, where dating must be turned into engagement, the sorority shores up the structure by the pinning ritual, performed after dinner in the presence of all the sorority sisters (who are required to stay for the ceremony) and attended, in its classic form, by a choir of fraternity boys singing outside. The commitment is so public that it is difficult for either partner to withdraw. Since engagement is already heavily reinforced outside the sorority, pinning ceremonies are more elaborate than engagements.

The social columns of college newspapers faithfully record the successes of the sorority system as it stands today. Sorority girls get engaged faster than "independents," and they appear to be marrying more highly ranked men. But what predictions can we make about the system's future?

All social institutions change from time to time, in response to changing conditions. In the mountain villages of the Philippines, the steady attacks of school and mission on the immorality of the *olag* have almost demolished it. Sororities, too, are affected by changes in the surrounding environment. Originally they were places where the few female college students took refuge from the jeers and catcalls of men who thought that nice girls didn't belong on campus. They assumed their present, endogamy-conserving form with the flourishing of the great land-grant universities in the first half of this century.

ON THE BRINK

The question about the future of the sorority system is whether it can adapt to the most recent changes in the forms of higher education. At present, neither fraternities nor sororities are in the pink of health. On some campuses there are chapter houses which have been reduced to taking in non-affiliated boarders to pay the costs of running the property. New sorority chapters are formed, for the most part, on new or low-prestige campuses (where status-anxiety is rife); at schools of high prestige fewer girls rush each year and the weaker houses are disbanding.

University administrations are no longer as hospitable to the Greeks as they once were. Most are building extensive dormitories that compete effectively with the housing offered by sororities; many have adopted regulations intended to minimize the influence of the Greeks on campus activities. The campus environment is changing rapidly: academic standards are rising, admission is increasingly competitive and both male and female students are more interested in academic achievement; the proportion of graduate students seriously training for a profession is increasing; campus culture is often so obviously pluralist that the Greek claim to monopolize social activity is unconvincing.

The sorority as it currently stands is ill-adapted to cope with the new surroundings. Sorority houses were built to

---

GLOSSARY OF MARRIAGE TERMS

***Endogamy:* A rule or practice of marriage within a particular group.**

***Exogamy:* A practice or rule of marriage only between persons who are *not* members of a well-defined group, such as one based on family or locality.**

***Hypergamy:* The movement of a woman, through marriage, to a status *higher* than that to which she was born.**

***Hypogamy:* The movement of a woman, through marriage, to a status *lower* than that to which she was born.**

***Polygyny:* The marriage of one husband to two or more wives. It is not the same as *polygamy*, which simply means a plurality of mates irrespective of sex.**

---

provide a setting for lawn parties, dances, and dress-up occasions, and not to facilitate study; crowding and noise are severe, and most forms of privacy do not exist. The sorority songs that have to be gone through at rushing and chapter meetings today all seem to have been written in 1915 and are mortifying to sing today. The arcane rituals, so fascinating to high school girls, grow tedious and sophomoric to college seniors.

But the worst blow of all to the sorority system comes from the effect of increased academic pressure on the dating habits of college men. A student competing for grades in a professional school, or even in a difficult undergraduate major, simply has not the time (as he might have had in, say, 1925) to get involved in the sorority forms of courtship. Since these days almost all the "right kind" of men *are* involved in demanding training, the traditions of the sorority are becoming actually inimical to hypergamous marriage. Increasingly, then, sororities do not solve the Brahmin problem but make it worse.

One can imagine a sorority designed to facilitate marriage to men who have no time for elaborate courtship. In such a sorority, the girls—to start with small matters—would improve their telephone arrangements, for the fraternity boy in quest of a date today must call several times to get through the busy signals, interminable paging, and lost messages to the girl he wants. They might arrange a private line with prompt answering and faithfully recorded messages, with an unlisted number given only to busy male students with a promising future. They would even accept dates for the same night as the invitation, rather than, as at present, necessarily five to ten days in advance, for the only thing a first-year law student can schedule that far ahead nowadays is his studies. Emphasis on fraternity boys would have to go, for living in a fraternity and pursuing a promising (and therefore competitive) major field of study are rapidly becoming mutually exclusive. The big formal dances would go (the fraternity boys dislike them now); the football floats would go; the pushcart races would go. The girls would reach the hearts of their men not through helping them wash their sports cars but through typing their term papers.

But it is inconceivable that the proud traditions of the sororities that compose the National Panhellenic Council could ever be bent to fit the new design. Their structure is too fixed to fit the changing college and their function is rapidly being lost. The sorority cannot sustain itself on students alone. When parents learn that membership does not benefit their daughters, the sorority as we know it will pass into history.

Section V

Collectivities

In Section V our attention shifts to collectivities. Here our interest is broadly focused on the process of group formation. In "Communal Life Styles for the Old," Hochschild suggests that the widely noted disengagement of older people may be situational. The key, she tells us, to softening the effects of longer life expectancy is support by a community of appropriate peers. Hochschild's article discusses the formation of group life itself (or "culture"). The very basis of this formation is reciprocity. The implication of her work in this "community" for the elderly has broad application in the sociology of group formation. A quasi-family system emerged in this commune for the elderly based on what Hochschild has called "social siblings" and a status system based on what she has creatively called the "poor dear hierarchy."

In "Carnivals, Road Shows and Freaks," Truzzi and Easto grant us yet another angle on the formation of culture and social structure. Through a careful discussion of the historical development of the carnival, Truzzi and Easto lead us into today's "carnie" society, which is closed to outsiders. A major device used in the formation of this subculture within the larger society is the development of language. The development of a special language sets up a virtually impenetrable barrier to outsiders, and fosters, at the same time, a sense of "oneness" for insiders. This important function of language has long been noted by occupational sociologists and by cultural anthropologists interested in sociolinguistics. The importance of language (in the very broadest sense) can hardly be overestimated in understanding the development of collectivities into groups.

In "Baseball Magic," Gmelch, a professional baseball player turned sociologist, has written a charming article on the use of magic and ritual among professional athletes. Gmelch has applied the hypothesis developed by anthropologist Bronislaw Malinowski about the presence of magic in areas of life where chance and accident are present. In baseball ritual, taboo and fetish are connected only with pitching and hitting, not with fielding (fielding among big leaguers is much more of a sure thing). "Baseball Magic" is a *tour de force* that ably demonstrates the broad range of sociological application to everyday life.

In the article by Truzzi and Easto, we learn about the important social function of verbal language. In "How Card Hustlers Make the Game," Mahigel and Stone instruct us on the importance of nonverbal language as well. They suggest that expert poker players learn to "block" their opponents through the use of body language. They also provide us with a test of that hypothesis by reporting on a "blocking" experiment that they conducted. This article is sheer fun insofar as it is an excellent ethnography of card hustling. One should not underestimate the joy of doing and reading about sociology as a pleasure in and of itself. The articles by Truzzi and Easto, Gmelch, and Mahigel and Stone all underline this last point.

Sturges' "1000 + 1000 = 5000: Estimating Crowd Size" is the final selection in Section V. The article makes an important contribution to the methodology of everyday sociology. Sturges suggests that estimating crowd size is not a random thing but, rather, is patterned. From local editors to advance publicity men for political figures, there is a vested interest in getting an inflated "official" crowd size "guesstimate" accepted.

1 *Arlie Russell Hochschild*

Communal Life-Styles for the Old

The 43 residents of Merrill Court (a small apartment building near the shore of San Francisco Bay), 37 of them women, mainly conservative, fundamentalist widows from the Midwest and Southwest, don't seem likely candidates for "communal living" and "alternatives to the nuclear family." Nonetheless, their community has numerous communal aspects. Without their "old-agers commune" these 60-, 70- and 80-year-olds would more than likely be experiencing the disengagement from life that most students of aging have considered biologically based and therefore inevitable.

The aged individual often has fewer and fewer ties to the outside world, and those which he or she does retain are characterized by less emotional investment than in younger years. This case study, however, presents evidence that disengagement may be situational—that how an individual ages depends largely on his social milieu, and that socially isolated older people may disengage but that older people supported by a community of appropriate peers do not.

Rural Ways in Urban Settings

Merrill Court is a strange mixture of old and new, of a vanishing Oakie culture and a new blue-collar life-style, of rural ways in urban settings, of small-town community in mass society, of people oriented toward the young in an age-separated subculture. These internal immigrants to the working-class neighborhoods of West Coast cities and suburbs perceive their new environment through rural and small-town eyes. One woman who had gone shopping at a department store observed "all those lovely dresses, all stacked like cordwood." A favorite saying when one was about to retire was, "Guess I'll go to bed with the chickens tonight." They would give directions to the new hamburger joint or hobby shop by describing its relationship to a small stream or big tree. What remained of the old custom of a funeral wake took place at a new funeral parlor with neon signs and printed notices.

The communal life which developed in Merrill Court may have had nothing to do with rural ways in an urban setting. Had the widows stayed on the farms and in the small towns they came from, they might have been active in community life there. Those who had been involved in community life before remained active and, with the exception of a few, those who previously had not, became active.

For whatever reason, the widows built themselves an order out of ambiguity, a set of obligations to the outside and to one another where few had existed before. It is possible to relax in old age, to consider one's social debts paid, and to feel that constraints that do not weigh on the far side of the grave should not weigh on the near side either. But in Merrill Court, the watchfulness of social life, the Protestant stress on industry, thrift and activity added up to an ethos of keeping one's "boots on," not simply as individuals but as a community.

Forming the Community

"There wasn't nothin' before we got the coffee machine. I mean we didn't share nothin' before Mrs. Bitford's daughter brought over the machine and we sort of had our first occasion, you might say."

There were about six people at the first gathering around the coffee machine in the recreation room. As people came downstairs from their apartments to fetch their mail, they looked into the recreation room, found a cluster of people sitting down drinking coffee, and some joined in. A few weeks later the recreation director "joined in" for the morning coffee and, as she tells it, the community had its start at this point.

Half a year later Merrill Court was a beehive of activity: meetings of a service club; bowling; morning workshop; Bible study classes twice a week; other classes with frequently changing subjects; monthly birthday parties; holiday parties; and visits to four nearby nursing homes. Members donated cakes, pies and soft drinks to bring to the nursing home, and a five-piece band, including a washtub bass, played for the "old folks" there. The band also entertained at a nearby recreation center for a group of Vietnam veterans. During afternoon band practice, the women sewed and embroidered pillow cases, aprons and yarn dolls. They made wastebaskets out of discarded paper towel rolls, wove rugs from strips of old Wonder Bread wrappers, and Easter hats out of old Clorox bottles, all to be sold at the annual bazaar. They made placemats to be used at the nursing home, totebags to be donated to "our boys in Vietnam," Christmas cards to be cut out for the Hillcrest Junior Women's Club, rag dolls to be sent to the orphanage, place cards to be written out for the bowling league banquet, recipes to be written out for the recipe book that was to go on sale next month, and thank you and condolence cards.

Social Patterns

The social arrangements that took root early in the history of Merrill Court later assumed a life of their own. They were designed, as if on purpose, to assure an "on-going" community. If we were to visually diagram the community, it would look like a social circle on which there are centripedal and centrifugal pressures. The formal role system, centered in the circle, pulled people toward it by giving them work and rewards, and this process went on mainly "downstairs," in the recreation room. At the same time, informal loyalty networks fluctuated toward and away from the circle. They became clear mainly "upstairs," where the apartments were located. Relatives and outsiders pulled the individual away from the circle downstairs and network upstairs although they were occasionally pulled inside both.

Downstairs

Both work and play were somebody's responsibility to organize. The Merrill Court Service Club, to which most of the residents and a half-dozen nonresidents belonged, set up committees and chairmanships that split the jobs many ways. There was a group of permanent elected officials: the president, vice-president, treasurer, secretary and birthday chairman, in addition to the recreation director. Each activity also had a chairman, and each chairman was in charge of a group of volunteers. Some officers were rotated during the year. Only four club members did not chair some activity between 1965 and 1968; and at any time about a third were in charge of something.

Friendship Networks

Shadowing the formal circle was an informal network of friendships that formed over a cup of coffee in the upstairs apartments. The physical appearance of the apartments told something about the network. Inside, each apartment had a living room, kitchen, bedroom and porch. The apartments were unfurnished when the women moved in and as one remarked, "We fixed 'em up just the way we wanted. I got this new lamp over to Sears, and my daughter and I bought these new scatter rugs. Felt just like a new bride."

For the most part, the apartments were furnished in a remarkably similar way. Many had American flag stickers outside their doors. Inside, each had a large couch with a floral design, which sometimes doubled as a hide-a-bed where a grandchild might sleep for a weekend. Often a chair, a clock or picture came from the old home and provided a material link to the past. Most had large stuffed chairs, bowls of homemade artificial flowers, a Bible and porcelain knickknacks neatly arranged on a table. (When the group was invited to my own apartment for tea, one woman suggested sympathetically that we "had not quite moved in yet" because the apartment seemed bare by comparison.) By the window were potted plants, often grown from a neighbor's slip. A plant might be identified as "Abbie's ivy" or "Ernestine's African violet."

Photographs, usually out of date, of pink-cheeked children and grandchildren decorated the walls. Less frequently there was a photo of a deceased husband and less frequently still, a photo of a parent. On the living room table or nearby there was usually a photograph album containing pictures of relatives and pictures of the woman herself on a recent visit "back east." Many of the photographs in the album were arranged in the same way. Pictures of children came first and, of those, children with the most children appeared first, and childless children at the end.

The refrigerator almost always told a social story. One contained homemade butter made by the cousin of a woman on the second floor; berry jam made by the woman three doors down; corn bought downstairs in the recreation room, brought in by someone's son who worked in a corn-canning factory; homemade Swedish rolls to be given to a daughter when she came to visit; two dozen eggs to be used in cooking, most of which would be given away; as well as bread and fruit, more than enough for one person. Most of the women had once cooked for large families, and Emma, who raised eight children back in Oklahoma, habitually baked about eight times as much corn bread as she could eat. She made the rounds of apartments on her floor distributing the extra bread. The others who also cooked in quantities reciprocated, also gratuitously, with other kinds of food. It was an informal division of labor although no one thought of it that way.

Most neighbors were also friends, and friendships, as well as information about them, were mainly confined to each floor. All but four had their *best* friends on the same floor and only a few had a next-best friend on another floor. The more one had friends outside the building, the more one had friends on other floors within the building. The wider one's social radius outside the building, the wider it was inside the building as well.

Neighboring

Apart from the gratification of friendship, neighboring did a number of things for the community. It was a way of relaying information or misinformation about others. Often the information relayed upstairs influenced social arrangements downstairs. For example, according to one widow,

> The Bitfords had a tiff with Irma upstairs here, and a lot of tales went around. They weren't true, not a one, about Irma, but then people didn't come downstairs as much. Mattie used to come down, and Marie and Mr. Ball and they don't so much now, only once and again, because of Irma being there. All on account of that tiff.

Often people seated themselves downstairs as they were situated upstairs, neighbor and friend next to neighbor and friend, and a disagreement upstairs filtered downstairs. For example, when opinion was divided and feelings ran high on the issue of whether to store the club's $900 in a cigar box under the treasurer's bed or in the bank, the gossip, formerly confinced to upstairs, invaded the public arena downstairs.

Relaying information this way meant that without directly asking, people knew a lot about one another. It was safe to assume that what you did was known about by at least one network of neighbors and their friends. Even the one social isolate on the third floor, Velma, was known about, and her comings and goings were talked about and judged. Talk about other people was a means of social control and it operated, as it does elsewhere, through parables; what was told of another was a message to one's self.

Not all social control was verbal. Since all apartment living rooms faced out on a common walkway that led to a central elevator, each tenant could be seen coming and going; and by how he or she was dressed, one could accurately guess his or her activities. Since each resident knew the visiting habits of her neighbors, anything unusual was immediately spotted. One day when I was knocking on the door of a resident, her neighbor came out:

> I don't know where she is, it couldn't be the doctor's, she goes to the doctor's on Tuesdays; it couldn't be shopping, she shopped yesterday with her daughter. I don't think she's downstairs, she says she's worked enough today. Maybe she's visiting Abbie. They neighbor a lot. Try the second floor.

Neighboring is also a way to detect sickness or death. As Ernestine related, "This morning I look to see if Judson's curtains were open. That's how we do on this floor, when we get up we open our curtains just a bit, so others walking by outside know that everything's all right. And if the curtains aren't drawn by mid-morning, we knock to see." Mattie perpetually refused to open her curtains in the morning and kept them close to the wall by placing potted plants against them so that "a man won't get in." This excluded her from the checking-up system and disconcerted the other residents.

The widows in good health took it upon themselves to care for one or two in poor health. Delia saw after Grandma Goodman who was not well enough to go down and get her mail and shop, and Ernestine helped Little Floyd and Mrs. Blackwell who could not see well enough to cook their own meals. Irma took care of Mr. Cooper and she called his son when Mr. Cooper "took sick." Even those who had not adopted someone to help often looked after a neighbor's potted plants while they were visiting kin, lent kitchen utensils and took phone messages. One woman wrote letters for those who "wrote a poor hand."

Some of the caretaking was reciprocal, but most was not. Three people helped take care of Little Floyd, but since he was blind he could do little in return. Delia fixed his meals, Ernestine laundered his clothes, and Irma shopped for his food. When Little Floyd died fairly suddenly, he was missed perhaps more than others who died during those three years, especially by his caretakers. Ernestine remarked sadly, "I liked helping out the poor old fella. He would appreciate the tiniest thing. And never a complaint."

Sometimes people paid one another for favors. For example, Freda took in sewing for a small sum. When she was paid for lining a coat, she normally mentioned the purpose for which the money would be spent (for example, bus fare for a visit to relatives in Montana), perhaps to reduce the commercial aspect of the exchange. Delia was paid by the Housing Authority for cleaning and cooking for Grandma Goodman, a disabled woman on her floor; and as she repeatedly mentioned to Grandma Goodman, she spent the money on high school class rings for her three grandchildren. In one case, the Housing Authority paid a granddaughter for helping her grandmother with housework. In another case, a disabled woman paid for domestic help from her social security checks.

The "Poor Dear" Hierarchy

Within the formal social circle there was a status hierarchy based on the distribution of honor, particularly through holding offices in the service club. Additionally, there was a parallel informal status hierarchy based on the distribution of luck. "Luck" as the residents defined it is not entirely luck. Health and life expectancy, for example, are often considered "luck," but an upper-class person can expect to live ten years longer than a lower-class person. The widows of Merrill Court, however, were drawn from the same social class and they saw the differences among themselves as matters of luck.

She who had good health won honor. She who lost the fewest loved ones through death won honor, and she who was close to her children won honor. Those who fell short of any of these criteria were often referred to as "poor dears."

The "poor dear" system operated like a set of valves through which a sense of superiority ran in only one direction. Someone who was a "poor dear" in the eyes of another seldom called that other person a "poor dear" in return. Rather, the "poor dear" would turn to someone less fortunate, perhaps to buttress a sense of her own achieved or ascribed superiority. Thus, the hierarchy honored residents at the top and pitied "poor dears" at the bottom, creating a number of informally recognized status distinctions among those who, in the eyes of the outside society, were social equals.

The distinctions made by residents of Merrill Court are only part of a larger old age status hierarchy based on things other than luck. At the monthly meetings of the countywide Senior Citizens Forum, to which Merrill Court sent two representatives, the term "poor dear" often arose with reference to old people. It was "we senior citizens who are politically involved versus those 'poor dears' who are active in recreation." Those active in recreation, however, did not accept a subordinate position relative to the politically active. On the other hand, they did not refer to the political activists as "poor dears." Within the politically active group there were those who espoused general causes, such as getting out an anti-pollution bill, and those who espoused causes related only to old age, such as raising social security benefits or improving medical benefits. Those in politics and recreation referred to the passive card players and newspaper readers as "poor dears." Uninvolved old people in good health referred to those in poor health as "poor dears," and those in poor health but living in independent housing referred to those in nursing homes as "poor dears." Within the nursing home there was a distinction between those who were ambulatory and those who were not. Among those who were not ambulatory there was a distinction between those who could enjoy food and those who could not. Almost everyone, it seemed, had a "poor dear."

At Merrill Court, the main distinction was between people like themselves and people in nursing homes. Returning from one of the monthly trips to a nearby nursing home, one resident commented:

> There was an old woman in a wheel chair there with a dolly in her arms. I leaned over to look at the dolly. I didn't touch it, well, maybe I just brushed it. She snatched it away, and said "Don't take my dolly." They're pathetic, some of them, the poor dears.

Even within the building, those who were in poor health, were alienated from their children, or were aging rapidly were considered "poor dears." It was lucky to be young and unlucky to be old. There was more than a 20-year age span between the youngest and oldest in the community. When one of the younger women, Delia, age 69, was drinking coffee with Grandma Goodman, age 79, they compared ages. Grandma Goodman dwelt on the subject and finished the conversation by citing the case of Mrs. Blackwell, who was 89 and still in reasonably good health. Another remarked about her 70th birthday:

> I just couldn't imagine myself being 70. Seventy is old! That's what Daisy said too. She's 80 you know. It was her 70th that got her. No one likes to be put aside, you know. Laid away. Put on the shelf you might say. No sir.

She had an ailment that prevented her from bowling or lifting her flower pots, but she compared her health to that of Daisy, and found her own health a source of luck.

Old people compare themselves not to the young but to other old people. Often the residents referred to the aged back in Oklahoma, Texas and Arkansas with pity in their voices:

> Back in Oklahoma, why they toss the old people away like old shoes. My old friends was all livin' together in one part of town and they hardly budged the whole day. Just sat out on their porch and chewed the fat. Sometimes they didn't even do that. Mostly they didn't have no nice housing, and nothin' social was goin' on. People here don't know what luck they've fallen into.

They also compared their lot to that of other older people in the area. As one resident said:

> Some of my friends live in La Casa [another housing project]. I suppose because they have to, you know. And I tried to get them to come bowling with me, but they wouldn't have a thing to do with it. "Those senior citizens, that's old folks stuff." Wouldn't have a thing to do with it. I tried to tell them we was pretty spry, but they wouldn't listen. They just go their own way. They don't think we have fun.

On the whole, the widows disassociated themselves from the status of "old person," and accepted its "minority" characteristics. The "poor dears" in the nursing home were often referred to as childlike: "They are easily hurt, you know. They get upset at the slightest thing and they like things to be the way they've always been. Just like kids." Occasionally, a widow would talk about Merrill Court itself in this vein, presumably excluding herself: "We're just like a bunch of kids here sometimes. All the sparring that goes on, even with church folk. And people get so hurt, so touchy. You'd think we were babies sometimes."

If the widows accepted the stereotypes of old age, they did not add the "poor dear" when referring to themselves. But younger outsiders did. To the junior employees in the Recreation and Parks Department, the young doctors who treated them at the county hospital, the middle-aged welfare workers and the young bank tellers, the residents of Merrill Court, and old people like them, were "poor dears."

Perhaps in old age there is a premium on finishing life off with the feeling of being a "have." But during old age, one also occupies a low social position. The way the old look for luck differences among themselves reflects the pattern found at the bottom of other social, racial and gender hierarchies. To find oneself lucky within an ill-fated category is to gain the semblance of high status when society withholds it from others in the category. The way old people feel above and condescend to other old people may be linked to the fact that the young feel above and condescend to them. The luck hierarchy does not stop with the old.

The Sibling Bond

There were rivalries and differences in Merrill Court, but neither alienation nor isolation. A club member who stayed up in her apartment during club meetings more often did it out of spite than indifference. More obvious were the many small, quiet favors, keeping an eye out for a friend and sharing a good laugh.

There was something special about this community, not so much because it was an old age subculture, but because the subculture was founded on a particular kind of relationship—the sibling bond. Most residents of Merrill Court are social siblings. The custom of exchanging cups of coffee, lunches, potted plants and curtain checking suggest reciprocity. Upstairs, one widow usually visited as much as she was visited. In deciding who visits whom, they often remarked, "Well, I came over last time. You come over this time." They traded, in even measure, slips from house plants, kitchen utensils and food of all sorts. They watched one another's apartments when someone was away on a visit, and they called and took calls for one another.

There are hints of the parent-child bond in this system, but protectors picked their dependents voluntarily and resented taking care of people they did not volunteer to help. For example, one protector of "Little Floyd" complained about a crippled club member, a nonresident:

> It wasn't considerate of Rose to expect us to take care of her. She can't climb in and out of the bus very well and she walks so slow. The rest of us wanted to see the museum. It's not nice to say, but I didn't want to miss the museum waiting for her to walk with us. Why doesn't her son take her on trips?

The widows were not only equals among themselves, they also were remarkably similar. They all wanted more or less the same things and could give more or less the same things. They all wanted to *receive* Mother's Day cards. No one in the building *sent* Mother's Day cards. And what they did was to compare Mother's Day cards. Although there was some division of labor, there was little difference in labor performed. All knew how to bake bread and can peaches, but no one knew how to fix faucets. They all knew about "the old days" but few among them could explain what was going on with youth these days. They all had ailments but no one there could cure them. They all needed rides to the shopping center, but no one among them needed riders.

Their similar functions meant that when they did exchange services, it was usually the same kinds of services they themselves could perform. For example, two neighbors might exchange corn bread for jam, but both knew how to make both corn bread and jam. If one neighbor made corn bread for five people in one day, one of the recipients would also make corn bread for the same people two weeks later. Each specialized within a specialization, and over the long run the widows made and exchanged the same goods.

Hence the "side by sideness," the "in the same boat" quality of their relations. They noticed the same things about the world and their eyes caught the same items in a department store. They noticed the same features in the urban landscape—the pastor's home, the Baptist church, the nursing homes, the funeral parlors, the places that used to be. They did not notice, as an adolescent might, the gas stations and hamburger joints.

As a result, they were good listeners for each other. It was common for someone to walk into the recreation room and launch into the details of the latest episode of a mid-afternoon television drama ("It seems that the baby is not by artificial insemination but really Frank's child, and the doctor is trying to convince her to tell. . ."). The speaker could safely assume that her listeners also knew the details. Since they shared many experiences, a physical ailment, a death, a description of the past, an "old age joke" could be explained, understood and enjoyed. They talked together about their children much as their children, together, talked about them. Each shared with social siblings one side of the prototypical parent-child bond.

This similarity opened up the possibility of comparison and rivalry, as the "poor dear" hierarchy suggests. Whether the widows cooperated in collecting money for flowers, or competed for prestigious offices in the service club, bowling trophies or front seats in the bus, their functions were similar, their status roughly equal, and their relations in the best and worst sense, "profane."

Not all groups of old people form this sibling bond. Although we might expect subcultures to arise in nursing homes, certain hospital wards or convalescent hospitals, the likes of Merrill Court is rare. It is not enough to put fairly healthy, socially similar old people together. There is clearly something different between institutions and public housing apartments. Perhaps what counts is the kind of relationships that institutions foster. The resident of an institution is "a patient." Like a child, he has his meals served to him, his water glass filled, his bed made, his blinds adjusted by the "mother-nurse." He cannot return the service. Although he often shares a room or a floor with "brother" patients, both siblings have a nonreciprocal relationship to attendants or nurses. Even the research on the institutionalized focuses on the relation between patient and attendant, not between patient and patient. If there is a strong parent-child bond, it may overwhelm any potential sibling solidarity. If the old in institutions meet as equals, it is not as independent equals. The patient's relation to other patients is like the relation between *real,* young siblings, which may exaggerate rather than forestall narcissistic withdrawal.

The widows of Merrill Court took care of themselves, fixed their own meals, paid their own rent, shopped for their own food, and made their own beds; and they did these things for others. Their sisterhood rests on adult autonomy. This is what people at Merrill Court have and people in institutions do not.

The Sibling Bond and Age-Stratification

The sibling bond is delicate and emerges only when conditions are ripe. Rapid currents of social change lead to age-stratification, which, in turn, ripens conditions for the sibling bond. Tied to his fellows by sibling bonds, an individual is cemented side by side into an age stratum with which he shares the same rewards, wants, abilities and failings.

French sociologist Emile Durkheim, in his book *The Division of Labor,* describes two forms of social solidarity. In organic solidarity there is a division of labor, complementary dependence and differences among people. In mechanical solidarity there is no division of labor, self-sufficiency and similarity among people. Modern American society as a whole is based on organic solidarity, not only in the economic but in the social, emotional and intellectual spheres.

Different age strata within the general society however, are more bound by mechanical solidarity. This is important both for the individual and the society. Although division of labor, complementary dependence and differences among people describe society's network of relations as a whole, they do not adequately describe relations among particular individuals. An individual's complementary dependence may be with people he does not know or meet—such as the person who grows and cans the food he eats, or lays the bricks for his house. And in his most intimate relations, an individual may also have complementary relations (either equal or unequal) with his spouse and children. But in between the most and least intimate bonds is a range in which there are many sibling relationships which form the basis of mechanical solidarity.

In fact, many everyday relations are with people similar and equal to oneself. Relations between colleague and colleague, student and student, friend and friend, relations within a wives' group or "the guys at the bar," the teenage gang or army buddies are often forms of the sibling bond. These ties are often back-up relations, social insurance policies for the times when the complementary bonds of parent and child, husband and wife, student and teacher, boy friend and girl friend fail, falter or normally change.

From an individual's viewpoint, some periods of life, such as adolescence and old age, are better for forming sibling bonds than are other periods. Both just before starting a family and after raising one, before entering the economy and after leaving it, an individual is open to, and needs, these back-up relationships. It is these stages that are problematic, and it is these stages that, with longer education and earlier retirement, now last longer.

From society's point of view, the sibling bond allows more flexibility in relations between generations by forging solidarity within generations and divisions between them. This divides society into age layers that are relatively independent of one another, so that changes in one age layer need not be retarded by conditions in another. The institution that has bound the generations together—the family—is in this respect on the decline. As it declines, the sibling bond emerges, filling in and enhancing social flexibility, especially in those social strata where social change is most pronounced. The resulting social flexibility does not guarantee "good" changes and continuity is partly sacrificed to fads and a cult of newness. But whether desirable or not, this flexibility is partly due to and partly causes the growing importance of the sibling bond.

The times are ripe for the sibling bond, and for old-age communities such as Merrill Court. In the social life of old people the problem is not the sibling bond versus the parent-child bond. Rather, the question is how the one bond complements the other. The sisterhood at Merrill Court is no substitute for love of children and contact with them; but it offers a full, meaningful life independent of them.

The Minority Group Almost Everyone Joins

Isolation is not randomly distributed across the class hierarchy; there is more of it at the bottom. It is commonly said that old age is a leveler, that it affects the rich in the same way it affects the poor. It doesn't. The rich fare better in old age even as they fared better in youth. The poorer you are, the shorter your life expectancy, the poorer your health and health care, the lower your morale generally, the more likely you are to "feel" old regardless of your actual age, the less likely you are to join clubs or associations, the less active you are and the more isolated, even from children. Irving Rosow's study of 1,200 people over 62 living in Cleveland found that roughly 40 percent of the working class but only 16 percent of the middle class had fewer than four good friends. Another study of 6,000 white working-class men and women showed that of those over 65 with incomes under $3,000, a full third did not visit with or speak to a friend or neighbor during the preceding week. The rock bottom poor are isolated, but they are not the only ones.

The isolation of old people is linked to other problems. The old are poor and poverty itself is a problem. The old are unemployed and unemployment, in this society, is itself a problem. The old lack community and the lack of community is itself a problem. There is some connection between these three elements. Removed from the economy, the old have been cast out of the social networks that revolve around work. Lacking work, they are pushed down the social ladder. Being poor, they have fewer social ties. Poverty reinforces isolation. To eliminate enforced isolation, we have to eliminate poverty, for the two go together. The social life of Merrill Court residents, who had modest but not desperately low incomes, is an exception to the general link between social class and isolation.

Even if every old person were in a Merrill Court, the problem of old age would not be solved. But, allowing every old person the possibility of such an arrangement could be part of the solution. The basic problem far exceeds the limits of tinkering with housing arrangements. It is not enough to try to foster friendships among the old. Even to do that, it is not enough to set up bingo tables in the lobbies of decrepit hotels or to hand out name cards to the sitters on park benches. This would simply put a better face on poverty, a cheerful face on old age as it now is, at not much social cost.

Merrill Court is not set in any island of ideal social conditions; it is essentially an adjustment to bad social conditions. For the lives of old people to change fundamentally, those *conditions* must change. In the meantime, Merrill Court is a start. It is a good example of what can be done to reduce isolation. I do not know if similar communities would have emerged in larger apartment houses or housing tracts rather than in a small apartment house, with the married rather than the widowed, with rich rather than poor residents, with people having a little in common rather than a lot, with the very old person rather than the younger old person. Only trying will tell.

Merrill Court may be a forecast of what is to come. A survey of 105 University of California students in 1968 suggested that few parents of these students and few of the students themselves expect to be living with their families when they are old. Nearly seven out of ten (69 percent) reported that "under no circumstances" would they want their aged parents to live with them, and only 3 percent expected to be living with their own children when they are old. A full 28 percent expected to be living with *other* old people, and an additional 12 percent expected to be "living alone or with other old people."

Future communities of old people may be more middle class and more oriented toward leisure. Less than 10 percent of the students expected to be working when they passed 65. A great many expected to be "enjoying life," by which they meant studying, meditating, practicing hobbies, playing at sports and traveling.

But some things about future communities may be the same. As I have suggested throughout this book, communal solidarity can renew the social contact the old have with life. For old roles that are gone, new ones are available. If the world watches them less for being old, they watch one another more. Lacking responsibilities to the young, the old take on responsibilities toward one another. Moreover, in a society that raises an eyebrow at those who do not "act their age," the subculture encourages the old to dance, to sing, to flirt and to joke. They talk frankly about death in a way less common between the old and young. They show one another how to be, and trade solutions to problems they have not faced before.

Old age is the minority group almost everyone joins. But it is a forgotten minority group from which many old people dissociate themselves. A community such as Merrill Court counters this disaffiliation. In the wake of the declining family, it fosters a "we" feeling, and a nascent "old age consciousness." In the long run, this may be the most important contribution an old age community makes.

SUGGESTED READINGS

"Minority Group Characteristics of the Aged in American Society" by Milton Barron in *Journal of Gerontology*, *8*, No. 4.

Society, Culture and Depression: The Case of the Middle Aged Woman by Pauline Bart (Cambridge: Schenkman, 1973).

"Changes in Status and Age Identification" by Zena Smith Blau in *American Sociological Review*, *21*, No. 1.

Growing Old: The Process of Disengagement by Elaine Cumming and W. Henry (New York: Basic Books, 1961).

Social Integration of the Aged by Irving Rosow (New York: Free Press, 1967).

by Joan Dufault

Nanterre: An Elderly Confine

Prompted by its description in Simone de Beauvoir's *The Coming of Age*, I decided to visit Nanterre, the huge impersonal hospice for the old outside of Paris. I realized, from her experience, that I would be denied entrance to the buildings and would have to content myself with interviewing those inhabitants who visit the cafés in the environs.

The Maison de Nanterre houses as many as 10,000 old people, I was told, though the figure usually hovers around 5,000; this is lower still when the grape harvest offers temporary employment in the vineyards. It is operated by the Paris municipality and the Prefecture of Police and is the inevitable destination of the police vans that pick up vagrants and homeless alcoholics along the Seine embankment. Those who have no proof of permanent address are summarily brought to Nanterre where they are deloused, bathed and issued uniforms. They must stay for at least three months before they can be released. A great many, like those I interviewed, had been there for years.

Several I spoke to had diagnosed cases of tuberculosis; one woman had cancer; others were walking with crutches or walking sticks, the majority of them toothless. Many seemed to lack sight and memory. The Nanterre inmates live on the small government old-age pension, which is used to pay their keep at the hospice. In addition, they are given a tiny supplement of 25 francs per month, which proves just enough to buy their daily ration of cheap Algerian wine.

At seven o'clock in the morning the imposing iron gates of Nanterre open, disgorging a mass of similarly clad old people. They stream past the doors of the outpatient clinic, past the dapper police guards and on to the indifferent streets of industrial Nanterre. Around the institution cluster the cafés where the inmates of Nanterre sit until lunch, squabbling, making occasional lewd suggestions to each other, complaining about the institutional food. They discuss their ill health and the fact that they must sleep 80 to a ward, the men and women carefully segregated. This holds true even for those who are married. Some get around the lack of privacy by using part of their small allowance to rent a room above a café for an occasional Sunday afternoon. Here they can also keep a few personal clothes locked away. Others, particularly in the summer, resort to deserted alleys in the neighborhood.

Marcel Panel, a kindly faced, moustached man, a roofer, proudly showed me his gold medal received in honor of

35 years employment with the same roofing firm. During the war, for four years, while he was imprisoned by the Germans, he worked in a German brewery until the Russians liberated him. When he returned home he found that his wife had been killed in an air raid. He coughed a great deal, and later he mentioned being under treatment for tuberculosis.

Obviously those old people I was able to interview represented the most well-off of the hospice residents. Although they had been there over a period of years, they had withstood the trauma of being institutionalized and were able to enjoy a part of the outside world: the neighborhood bistro. According to deBeauvoir (quoting figures drawn up by Dr. Pequignot), of healthy old people admitted to an institution for the aged 8 percent die in the first week, 28.7 percent die in the first month, 45 percent die in the first six months, 54.4 percent die in the first year and 64.4 percent die in the first two years.

The general atmosphere of Nanterre is well conveyed by deBeauvoir:

> In summer the Nanterre streets near the institution are filled with old people of both sexes, lying on the ground, sitting, leaning against the wall, clasping bottles of wine to their bosoms and dead drunk already. Their weakened frames cannot stand up to these drinking-bouts, and they go back to the institution staggering, shouting and vomiting: this promiscuity is extremely

painful for those inmates who like cleanliness and peace. Wine stimulates wild notions of grandeur — the momentary compensation for their wretchedness. It also sets free their sexuality . . . .

Most of the inmates find communal life very hard to bear: they are unhappy, anxious, turned in upon themselves, and they are herded together without any social life being arranged for them. Their touchiness, their demanding and often paranoid tendencies lead to frequent antagonistic reactions — to situations of conflict. All of the pathological processes to which old age is subject are accelerated by life in an institution.

In comparison with the typical American old people's home, the physical plant at Nanterre is more rundown and the living conditions of the individuals more degrading. Yet the morale of the people of Nanterre is higher than that of their American counterpart. They are freer and less under the deadening pall of institutional puritanism. There is something to be said for making wine available to these old people. Wine is surely a more humane tranquilizer than pills and mechanical restraints.

Perhaps it is a residue of the gallic wit and sense of proportion that gives these old people a less desperate quality than those in American nursing homes. I became aware of a certain purpose in these people's lives: first to get out of the confines of the hospice, second to make it back with relative sobriety for the noon dinner and again, before the closing of the gates at five. (If they miss this closing they are locked out for the night.) I sensed a bonhommie and comraderie among the men and women even as they accompanied and urged each other back to the depressing drabness of the hospice.

2 *Marcello Truzzi & Patrick Easto*

Carnivals, Road Shows and Freaks

The differences between circus, carnival, fair and bazaar are irrelevant to most people. All evoke the same associations of sights, sounds and smells—memories of balloons and cotton candy, animals and exotica, things to buy and things in cages. Their images blur in a glittering panoply of light and motion, threaded with a pleasing element of mystery. If any thought is given to those who people this world of tinselled splendor, it is probably to characterize them as a loosely bound collection of misfits. Few realize that the world of the "carnie," the carnival worker, is one with an ordered social structure. The carnie society has its own norms, etiquette and hierarchy—even its own language—all of which serve to set its members apart from the rest of the world.

A carnival is best defined by example. Its three major features are riding devices, shows or exhibits and concessions. Riding devices include the familiar merry-go-round (considered by some to be a necessary element in the definition of a carnival), the ferris wheel, the Tilt-a-Whirl and many others which constitute the major rides. In addition, there are the "punk rides" which cater to small children, for example, the boat rides, miniature train and tank rides.

The wide variety of shows and exhibits include presentations of performers (as in girl shows, freak shows), animals (wild life, rare or freak animals) or interesting objects (wax figures, historical objects, even dead people, as in the case of such preserved freak embryos as a two-headed baby). The freak show or "ten-in-one" is almost always the largest show on the midway.

Concessions include a wide variety of both games and refreshment operations. There are two major types of games: "flat-stores" and "hanky-panks." The flat-store or joint is a gambling operation that provides little chance for the patron to win. Examples would include the Swinger, a game in which the customer swings a small bowling ball in such a fashion as to knock over a small bowling pin; the Roll-down, in which the customer spills a number of marbles down a runway filled with numbered depressions; or the Six-cat, in which the object is to toss three baseballs and knock over two large catlike dolls. The hanky-pank differs from the flat-store in that its patron receives a prize each time he plays. Typical hanky-panks are the fish-pond, the ring-toss and dart-throwing games.

Though the worlds of the carnival and the circus occasionally intersect (that is, there are a few people in the carnival world who have worked on circuses and vice versa), they are two distinctly separate and different social and cultural worlds. Circus personnel are generally ranked higher in the outdoor amusement industry's overall stratification system; they often look down upon carnival people.

The circus has been defined as "a traveling and organized display of animals and skilled performances within one or more circular stages, known as rings, before an audience encircling these activities." Its members therefore perceive it as an extension of theater. The origins and connections of the carnival—street fairs and the world of gambling—are very different. Because the circus is primarily a display, its customers are passive; the carnival, which is primarily an entertainment, seeks the active participation of its customers.

Carnivals also differ from circuses in the economic relationship between management and workers. In the circus, virtually all personnel work directly or indirectly (through a chain of authority) for the owner. The carnival, in contrast, is headed by an owner-operator who, though he may own most of the various attractions, enters into contracts with independent ride, show and concession owners in order to enlarge his midway. (An exception is the Royal American Shows, which is reported to be entirely owned by one operator.) Evidence of the often highly informal nature of these economic arrangements is a recent advertisement by the Coleman Brothers Shows in *Amusement Business* stating that "many of our contracts are represented by a handshake only."

Another distinction between the circus and the carnival is that the carnival (unlike most circuses) frequently changes its size and content during the working season. Independent ride, show and concession owners often book with, that is, join, several different carnivals in the span of one season. The weekly advertisements in *Amusement Business* facilitate such moves and contribute to the importance of this periodical in the carnival world.

Unlike circuses, whose numbers have declined since the turn of the century, carnivals have proliferated rapidly over the years. Using data based on route lists, *Billboard* showed an increase from 17 carnivals known to be operating in 1902 to 119 in 1934. Though we have no data for the years from 1934-1970, an examination of the number of carnivals submitting route lists for 1969 showed 163 carnivals, a further increase.

Route list data, however, do not accurately reflect the true number of carnivals for any given year. The inaccuracy is due in part to the fact that carnival owners sometimes fail to submit their route lists for publication; in addition, they may not have the entire season booked. Although estimates vary, the consensus among writers on carnivals is that between 300 and 500 carnivals are currently operating in the United States. But the problem is largely a definitional one, as an editor of *Amusement Business* recently indicated:

> The . . . [number] is elusive. Nobody knows. Estimates range from around 800 to thousands, and the larger number is frequently correct. That is, because whenever the . . . [independent] owner with two or three rides sets up for business he has a carnival. The following week he may tag along as part of a larger show, paying a percentage as an independent operator. But this week, if his name is Pinson, he has every right to call his little display "Pinson's Mighty Grand Spectacular Exposition Show."

The size of carnivals ranges from very small units (called "gillies," "rag-bags" or "forty-milers") with half a dozen trucks to gigantic railroad shows with up to 800 personnel and 45 double-length flat cars. The small carnival can be a forty-miler, so named because it seldom played engagements further than forty miles from its home base; or it can be an ad hoc sort of affair, called a suitcase show, put together by an agent whose sole claim to authority is a set of contracts for a series of engagements. Because the forty-miler usually returns to its home town, it rarely includes concessions that regularly bilk the customers. In marked contrast, the suitcase show, since it is often a one-time-only arrangement, frequently maximizes its profits at the expense of both its public and its sponsors. Within the framework of the small carnival, therefore, both extremes of carnival operation are evident—those in which the public and management know and respect one another, and those in which the carnival sees the townspeople only as sheep ready to be fleeced.

The medium-sized and large carnivals, however, account for the great bulk of the hundreds of thousands of carnival workers, the millions of customers (annual attendance estimates are about 85,000,000), and the hundreds of millions of dollars spent at carnivals. The medium-sized carnival is a truck show with 15 to 20 rides and 50 to 100 concessions, whereas the large show is usually a railroad show with around 100 rides and hundreds of concessions and shows.

While approximately two-thirds of America's carnivals are seasonal (running from around April until October), many are year-round operations. Some of the latter tend to decrease in size during the summer, however, when some of their concessions leave to join the larger carnivals.

Carnival History

The American carnival, like the American circus, can trace its origins back to antiquity. But the American circus as we know it today originated in 1793, whereas the emergence of the American carnival is usually cited as 1893, the date of the World's Columbian Exposition in Chicago. Faced with the exposition's disastrously poor attendance, a number of concessionaires met to grapple with the problem. They agreed that while it was one thing to have a fair, it was quite another to promote it into a paying proposition. Their first overt move in this direction was to induce a prominent Chicago clergyman to denounce the exposition because of a particularly suggestive dance being exhibited on the midway. His diatribe was quickly picked up by the local and national media, and, as a result, attendance figures soared. Everybody, it seemed, wanted to see "that dance."

The second outgrowth of the concessionaires' meeting was the decision to move the assembled attractions to various cities. With the mounting of their attractions on already existing fairgrounds, the idea of the carnival had been born. It was to be fully realized that same year when Frank C. Bostock presented a collection of attractions at Coney Island; his entertainment has been referred to as the first carnival in that his assemblage of a traveling street fair marks the first attempt to make portable a group of attractions.

At first, these early carnivals were moved by horse-drawn wagons, but by 1914 the Smith Greater Shows was moved by truck. A recent advertisement placed by the Royal American Shows in *Amusement Business* provides some notion of the progress since 1914:

> Today Royal American travels on 80 double-length railroad cars, the world's largest train, loaded with 145 massive pieces of equipment. Reflecting the public's change in taste and demands for thrills, the midway features more than 50 rides and attractions and seven under-canvas shows. Royal American has grown in height (tallest ride is 103 feet), length (over a mile-long midway) and capacity (12.5 million annually).

The Carnival Social System

The social structure and stratification system of the average carnival is both complex and highly differentiated. In the simplest terms, carnivals are described in terms of their "front end" and "back end." These do not literally refer to the physical patterning of the carnival although there is some correspondence. Most carnival midways follow a standard horseshoe pattern along which customers are funneled. The geographical front end of the carnival usually contains food and souvenir concessions, games and smaller shows and punk rides. The rear consists of the larger shows and the taller rides (sometimes placed in the rear center of the horseshow rather than on the perimeter) used to draw crowds towards the back. The expression "front end" refers to the games, the refreshment and souvenir concessions, whereas the "back end" refers to the shows. Rides in general are neither clearly seen as being in the front or back end by most carnival members, though they are geographically usually located at the front end.

In a sense, the distinction is between the people who hawk wares and those who are performers. Though this distinction is far from rigid, it does have social meaning in the carnival. Our investigations indicate that the carnival's sociometric patterns tend to cluster along these two poles. Though carnival members usually know about and interact with areas of the carnival outside their own, it is not uncommon to find back-end people with little knowledge of front-end operations; and some back-end carnival workers consider themselves superior to front-end workers, especially so because the more crooked operations usually flourish among the games at the front end. This distinction, constituting a crude but meaningful picture of the carnival system, certainly represents one dimension of the actual complex structure.

Witold Krassowski divided the carnival members into five categories: 1) the boss and his staff, 2) the ride operators, 3) concessionaires, further broken down into owners and operators, 4) the owners, operators and performers of the side shows and 5) the families of the carnival workers. According to Krassowski:

> The kind of work one is doing within the carnival structure is of little or no importance in a status sense to his associates, as long as he is a "true carnie." Once accepted as a carnie—providing he observes the codes, rules, and mores of the carnival world—one will remain a member of the well-knit group, and the kind of work he does will have little or no influence upon his status among the show people of the carnivals.

It is certainly true that his acceptance by his peers as a non-outsider marks the carnival worker as generally superior to non-carnival members. But Krassowski clearly underestimates the carnival's prestige system. His misimpression that there was "no noticeable class differentiation in the carnival society" may be largely due to the following: he worked only at the front end of the carnival; he was recognized as a sociologist and therefore not really allowed "in;" and he investigated a somewhat atypical middle-sized carnival in the Midwest.

Although the carnival's prestige system, like its authority system, is highly informal and flexible, it does exist. Thus, while toleration of differences is great, carnival members who are Negro or who are gypsies are not treated as perfect social equals. Gypsies present a special problem for the carnival in that their identification is primarily with the gypsy world rather than with the carnival subculture. Whereas carnival people feel intense loyalty and a sense of honor towards one another, gypsies see non-gypsy carnival workers as outsiders, too. It is not surprising, then, to see frequent recruitment advertisements specifying "no ragheads" (gypsies).

We would more simply divide the carnival's social hierarchy into four general categories based on personnel: 1) the show owner and other administrative personnel, 2) independent ride, show and concession owners, 3) performers and 4) workers.

The show owner unquestionably occupies the highest prestige position in the carnival. Along with his assistant manager, he arranges the seasonal routes at conventions, decides on new acquisitions like riding devices, and determines booking needs for various spots or locations that may develop during the season. In addition to such long-range decisions, he must tackle the daily problems associated with managing a moderate-size business. Even these everyday operational decisions are complex in the larger carnivals, which are sometimes split into two units and play separately.

The number and type of administrative personnel vary from carnival to carnival but typically include:

☐ A "lot man" who arrives on the grounds ahead of the carnival and decides where to place the various attractions. This role requires solid knowledge about the exact area required by each ride, show and concession when assembled. For example, a ten-in-one may require 110 feet of midway frontage, and the Octopus ride, a circular area of about 80 feet. The staggering complexity of the lot man's task is compounded when he has to deal with mile-long midways.

☐ The "patch" or legal adjuster is a role that involves patching up in a public relations sense (but more often in a financial sense) any carnival-related complaints or misgivings expressed by local officials. In the majority of cases, these officials are simply paid off (bribed). The patch is often called upon to settle other grievances such as those centering around a concessionaire "beating a mark" without giving his customer the coveted panda bear; or even more crucially, those that arise when the local sheriff discovers that one or more of the titillating strippers are in fact female impersonators.

☐ The "ride superintendent" is a kind of grand mechanic who knows how to assemble, disassemble and repair all of the major riding devices. He is also responsible for keeping the tractor-trailer units and other rolling stock in good repair—a formidable task on the larger truck-moved carnivals, such as the Blue Grass Shows, which moves each week in 40 tractor-trailers.

This brief description of the administrative stratum is not only far from complete, but it tends to obfuscate the overlap of jobs. On many carnivals, for example, the assistant manager might double as lot man or the patch might serve as the advance man—a position involving "papering" a town with posters announcing the carnival's arrival. It must also be remembered that the carnival boss may own varying degrees of his midway. The more he owns of the rides, shows and concessions, the greater his authority and thus, to some degree, his status. Carnival owners vary from those who barely earn a living to those whose annual incomes exceed $75,000.

Beneath the administrative stratum in general prestige are the independent ride, show and concession owners. These individuals own their attractions and contract with the show owner, paying him either a flat rate (as is usually the case with concessions) or a percentage of their gross (as is usually the case with rides or shows). Normally, the independent ride or show owner enjoys higher prestige than the concession owner. However, if the concessionaire "books a string of joints," that is, brings a large number of concessions to the midway, he will enjoy comparable status with the independent ride or show owners. Generally, status varies with the number of attractions an independent owner operates.

Only slightly lower in status, and roughly equal to one another socially, are the performers. Here we refer to the girls who perform in the girl shows, the freaks, illusion performers and the like. Krassowski distinguished three categories of shows—freak shows, thrill shows and girl shows.

Although the carnival's unique social climate allows the freak to function in a nearly normal manner, his physical differences remain socially meaningful in the carnival world. Thus, though carnival freaks frequently marry normal persons, such marriages are not viewed with indifference. The freak is seen by his fellows in the carnival world as a person with an unusual physical deformity but not as some sort of "creature" to be stigmatized. In glorifying the position of the freak, some of the carnival literature distinguishes between natural freaks and persons who have intentionally made themselves into freaks, pointing out that natural freaks have higher status within the carnival world than self-made freaks. Our findings indicate otherwise, showing that although freaks are appreciated and often well liked, they are seldom envied.

Second Man is Lowest

Within the ranks of the performers, the generalization made by Krassowski is quite applicable:

> The status position of the individual is determined primarily by the following factors: 1. the length of time spent on the road with the carnival; his skill and success in conducting the business; 2. his financial standing; 3. the ability to adjust to his fellow-carnies; and 4. connections and acquaintances.

The lowest prestige positions in the carnival are held by the workers. Theirs, however, is a highly differentiated stratum. For example, those who operate the riding devices are divided into foremen and second men. The foreman has major responsibility for "upping" and "downing" the ride he is assigned to. The second man is simply his assistant. Usually, the latter is less experienced and is paid less. (The owner of the Blue Grass Shows in Tampa, Florida reported in a recent interview that his ride foremen earn from $85 to $100 per week, and second men earn from about $70 to $80.) After assembling the ride, both the foreman and second man operate it during the week.

Keeping Outsiders Out

The concession agents, who operate the flat-stores and hanky-panks, are paid like salesmen, receiving a small salary plus a commission. The agents who work the flat-stores (the straightforward gambling or con games) might enjoy comparable status with show performers if income were the only criterion for prestige. However, we have often overheard performers suggest that "flatties" are no more than common thieves and that they (the performers) at least give the marks something for their money. The number of flatties is usually limited by the carnival owners, who seek to keep the number of flat-stores on their midways at a minimum; the "gaffed" or rigged character of these joints tends to keep the patch very busy.

The unquestionable presence of social stratification within the carnival community is sometimes obscured to the outsider by the fact that some of its subgroups interact only infrequently and by the strong carnival ideology that "all carnies are in the same boat," that is, all are looked down upon by many if not most of the American people.

The special cultural character of the carnival system is largely reinforced through a series of boundary-maintaining devices which prohibit intrusions from the non-carnival world. These devices are of a variety of types—ecological, demographic, social and cultural.

The carnival system includes rather sharp ecological boundaries. At the rear of the carnival, behind the glittering thoroughfare of rides and shows, there exists a colony of trailers and tents normally never seen by outsiders. Here, off the main midway, is the actual living space of the carnival workers—the areas of the cookhouse (a dining tent for carnival personnel usually found on larger shows), the G-top (a tent set up for socializing activity among carnival employees, often used for gambling on many shows) and the house-trailers. Curious townspeople (especially children) who try to go behind the exhibit or gaming tents are quickly chased away by carnival personnel.

Demographic boundaries are somewhat more subtle and here refer to the entrance and exit aspects of the carnival world. A false impression generated by many writers is that entrance is primarily from the outside. "Carnies are made, not born. I have never known one whose parents were carnival people." People do, of course, enter into carnival occupations from the outside, but it must be remembered that many of them have had previous short experiences traveling with carnivals followed by a departure before becoming fully "with it" (as carnival workers describe the fully-initiated member). Carnival workers even have a name for such a short-timer, a "First-of-May."

Our interviews, however, indicate that possibly a majority come into the carnival world through family connections with the outdoor amusement industry (if not directly from carnivals). Our impressions are corroborated by the findings of Krassowski, who established that 37.7 percent of his carnival sample entered their occupations through either family connections or marriage to a carnival member. In addition, he found that although only 10 percent of the carnival parents in his sample wanted their children to become permanent carnival workers, three-fourths of them wanted their children to have some carnival experience.

It is probably the case that most carnival regulars were born into carnival life. One reason for the misimpression shared by many writers that most carnival workers are fugitives from modern organizational life is due to the general emphasis on freedom as a value among carnival workers. Krassowski noted that the major reason given for joining and staying in carnival life is the greater personal freedom allowed. And he is certainly correct in his general impression that the carnival has tended to attract rugged individuals.

But even if this emphasis on freedom were not a real factor, it would surely have been invented because it represents an important source for superiority feelings over the customers, whose lives are seen as boring and constrained. Carnival workers, therefore, often cite people who have "escaped" from the "normal" world into the glamorous environment of outdoor show business. Recounting examples of one-time successful members of the non-carnival world (like college graduates or the former college professor) who are now "with it" (especially to a journalist who is likely to be surprised and impressed), strengthens and legitimizes the carnival worker's belief in the superiority of his own life style over that of the marks.

Social boundaries are quite rigid. The general rule is simply that carnival workers should not interact with townspeople except along business-relevant lines. The unwritten rule is simply that "you don't talk to the marks." Carnival workers' children are strongly discouraged from interacting with children from the town; they are told to play with other carnival children. The unmarried women of the carnival are expected to have nothing to do with men of the town. Until fairly recently, a carnival girl would not go into town unless she was accompanied by a carnival man.

The protective attitude of carnival workers toward

carnival women takes some odd forms, as in the case of the exhibition of women in the girl shows. Usually included among the attractions of the girl show are exhibitions by the wives of some carnival men. Consequently, it is a general norm that no carnival men are admitted into girl-show performances. The rationale is that it is one thing to allow the women to display their bodies provocatively for the marks—after all, they are suckers—but it is quite another thing to have them ogled by other carnival men. An interesting distinction is made between the boundary-maintaining problems within the carnival system itself and between it and the social system of the community in which it functions.

The distinctive social boundaries of the carnival system are maintained through a host of highly specialized roles—from the highly visible "stick" or carnival worker pretending to be a townsperson as a lure in the gambling activities to the unseen carnival employee who "works the gaff," manipulating the gimmick which makes it impossible for the customer to win the game. Many proscriptive norms control the interaction of carnival people and outsiders and a number of cultural features of carnival life facilitate and reinforce this separation.

The major such cultural factor is the special language of the carnival. There have been few intensive examinations of the importance of language patterns in carnival life, although carnival terms have been sprinkled throughout the many articles written about carnival life and short glossaries of some of the major terms can be found in several sources. In his excellent chapter on the carnival language, Jack Dadswell asserts that:

> Carnival people have a language that belongs exclusively to them . . . [and] there appears no counterpart for it anywhere. Carnie talk can . . . [not] be confused with any other brogue, dialect or jargon on this earth, nor do I believe it can be traced to an ancient foundation as some lexicographers have tried to do. It is purely and simply a convenience language, and its sole purpose is for communication within the clan.

Close examination of the language of the carnival reveals two major components—argot and Z-Latin. Argot consists of the many specialized words of the carnival. In general, these words fall into two categories: 1) words designating unique carnival features for which no simple other words exist; these would include special names for carnival rides, games and technology (e.g., the "caterpillar" ride, the "slum joint"—a concession featuring very inexpensive merchandise; the "fifth wheel"—a section connecting the front wheels of a show wagon) and 2) words used in the carnival which have roughly equivalent terms in everyday language ("mitt-camp" for a fortune-telling concession or "ten-in-one" for a freak show). There are hundreds of such terms used in the carnival world. As David W. Maurer has noted:

> As might be expected, the high birth-rate in show-lingo is equalled by a death-rate sufficient to insure the survival of none but the fittest. Words appear today and sink into oblivion tomorrow. When a word is singularly apt, it may stick for a year or five years or twenty years, accordingly as it fulfills the demands of varying conditions and circumstances.

Most of the 200 terms listed by Maurer in 1931 are still used in the outdoor amusement industry today. Some are seemingly obsolete now, others have persisted with somewhat different meanings, but most have shown a remarkable tenacity.

Regional differences undoubtedly account for the singularity of some carnival terms in much the same way that individual carnivals spawn distinctive words of their own. A study of such variations in carnival language might prove most rewarding, for the diffusion pattern certainly would give a key to the interaction structure between carnivals. For example, the sparsity of terms common to both carnival and circus language (like "ten-in-one" for freak show or "donnicker" for toilet) reflects rather clearly the rare areas of intersection (through personnel mobility) between the two institutions.

The source of carnival argot is very much in question. Many believe it is commonly associated with criminal subcultures (and certainly many of the terms, like "dip," "fuzz" and "fix" probably did migrate into the carnival world). Dadswell argues, however, that carnival language originated in the carnival and was later—largely through newspaper stories—attributed to the criminal underworld. He notes that even such common gangsterisms as the letter "G" meaning one thousand dollars, and a "yard" and "half a yard" meaning one hundred dollars and fifty dollars respectively were used by Coney Island pitchmen as early as 1906.

In many ways far more important than the argot is what Dadswell has called Z-Latin. It is a special language used by carnival people to communicate while blocking out non-carnival listeners. Although its use has even been reported among Chicago school children as early as 1939, it has been universally spoken by carnival people, who claim it originated in the carnival world.

Linguists use the criterion of criminality or non-criminality in distinguishing between argot and cant. They define argot as a non-criminal group's specialized slang, unintelligible to outsiders and used primarily to meet the need for technical terms and secondarily as a way of bolstering group solidarity; cant, however, is defined as a criminal group's specialized slang for excluding outsiders. The special terms of the carnival clearly form an argot by their definition. But we would argue that the Z-Latin constitutes an example of cant, although we are reluctant to use that word because it definitionally implies that the carnival workers who use it would be criminal. Z-Latin, unlike the carnival argot, is most often used as a blocking-out technique to eliminate the comprehension of outsiders. We would suggest, therefore, that the distinction between cant and argot would be far clearer were it to rest solely on whether or not the language were used as a blocking-out technique, bypassing completely the criminality element in the definitions.

We might also add that we have recently learned that Z-Latin is now being used in some California prisons by inmates there outside the carnival world, and the prisoners also call it carnie. Thus, the criminal status of Z-Latin as cant is even more ambiguous.

Dadswell apparently uses the name Z-Latin after the well-known Pig-Latin commonly used by children, but neither he nor any other source provides any rules or guidelines for the language. The name for it within the carnival world is simply carnie. Like Pig-Latin, Z-Latin involves a simple manipulation of normal English words. On the basis of a speaking knowledge of carnie, we offer the following rules for speaking it:

☐ Any word is first separated on the basis of its natural syllables. Each syllable is then divided on the basis of its vowels. The consonant or consonants preceding the vowel are modified by adding a long *e* sound to them. The vowel is replaced by the short *a* sound, and the consonants following the vowel have a *z* sound prefixed to them. The simplest case is a monosyllabic word like "dog" which becomes "dee-a-zog," whereas the polysyllabic word "assumed" becomes "ee-a-zuh-see-a-zumed." The polysyllabic example shows another rule.

☐ If the first syllable is only a vowel or consonant, then the long *e* and short *a* sounds are pronounced first. Then the *z* sound is prefixed to the sound of the single consonant or vowel and pronounced last. Recall the "ah" in assumed being pronounced ee-a-zuh.

☐ Here are several more examples:

The becomes "thee-a-zuh."
Cat becomes "kee-a-zat."
Would becomes "wee-a-zood."
A becomes "ee-a-zay."
Name becomes "nee-a-zame."
Like becomes "lee-a-zike."
People becomes "pee-a-zee, pee-a-zul."
Doorstep becomes "dee-a-zoor, stee-a-zep."
Carnival becomes "kee-a-zar, nee-a-zuh, vee-a-zul."
Publication becomes "pee-a-zub, lee-a-zuh, kee-a-zay, she-a-zun."

The above examples follow the rules to the letter. However, carnie as it is spoken does not always conform exactly to these rules. What commonly occurs is a kind of idiomatic variation where the syllables are not always separated in translating. For example, "separated" should, following our rules, become "see-a-zep, ee-a-zer, ree-a-zay, tee-a-zed," but in common carnie parlance would be "see-a-zep, a, ree-a-zated." In similar fashion, "sucker" or "see-a-zuk, kee-a-zer" would be rendered "see-a-zuker."

Carnival speakers sometimes mix argot with carnie, a combination especially unlikely to be deciphered by the listening mark.

The hundreds of small total institutions that travel across the United States represent a unique opportunity for the ethnographer and analyst. A vast amount of information is needed before further generalizations can be attempted; for as we have indicated, carnivals vary not only in the degree of their integration into the host communities, but in their comparative and individual size and organizational structure.

Despite the public statements about the changing American carnival, the elimination of the grift and the graft, most of the changes have been superficial. The world-view of the carnival is still largely one of hustlers and marks, of carnies and suckers, of insiders and outsiders. Only through a full understanding of the carnival's boundary-maintaining devices can future ethnographers gain entry into this special world.

SUGGESTED READINGS

Hey There, Sucker! by Jack Dadswell (Boston: Bruce Humphries, 1946).

Carnival by Arthur H. Lewis (New York: Trident, 1970).

Step Right Up! by Dan Mannix (New York: Harper & Row, 1951).

"The Decline of the American Circus: The Shrinkage of an Institution," by Marcello Truzzi in *Sociology and Everyday Life*, edited by Marcello Truzzi (Englewood Cliffs, N.J.: Prentice-Hall, 1968).

by Ira Nowinski

Displaced Persons

The San Francisco Examiner *dismissed Yerba Buena residents as "an unsightly burden" with "no stake in the community" . . .*

Plans for San Francisco's Yerba Buena renewal project included the demolition of buildings housing thousands of elderly single men. Though a suit brought by a tenants' group temporarily halted the project, the court's decision seems unlikely to become a landmark—most courts have refused to review renewal plans.

. . . residents don't see it that way. "I'll be here," said an angry Rock Hotel tenant, "when the wrecking ball comes through the wall."

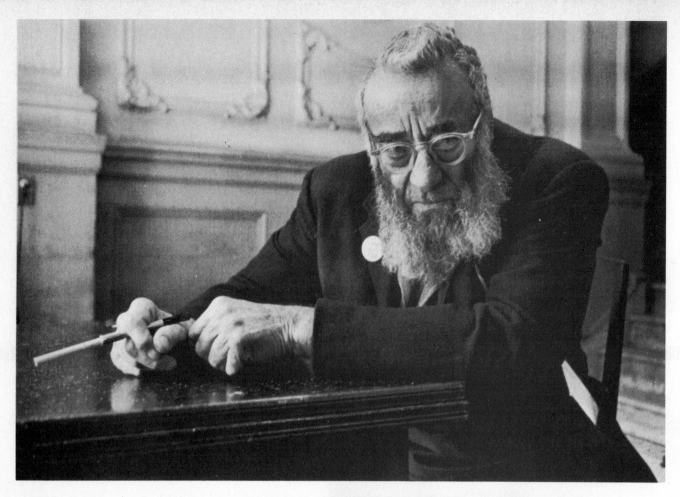

George Wolf, an 84-year-old former union president, is chairman of Tenants and Owners in Opposition to Redevelopment.

The Castle Cafe, a favorite eating place of many of those in the renewal site.

When the Joyce Hotel was torn down, this resident lost his home of 20 years to make way for a gas station.

3 *George Gmelch*

Baseball Magic

We find magic wherever the elements of chance and accident, and the emotional play between hope and fear have a wide and extensive range. We do not find magic wherever the pursuit is certain, reliable, and well under the control of rational methods.

Bronislaw Malinowski

Professional baseball is a nearly perfect arena in which to test Malinowski's hypothesis about magic. The great anthropologist was not, of course, talking about sleight of hand but of rituals, taboos and fetishes that men resort to when they want to ensure that things go their own way. Baseball is rife with this sort of magic, but, as we shall see, the players use it in some aspects of the game far more than in others.

Everyone knows that there are three essentials of baseball—hitting, pitching and fielding. The point is, however, that the first two, hitting and pitching, involve a high degree of chance. The pitcher is the player least able to control the outcome of his own efforts. His best pitch may be hit for a bloop single while his worst pitch may be hit directly to one of his fielders for an out. He may limit the opposition to a single hit and lose, or he may give up a dozen hits and win. It is not uncommon for pitchers to perform well and lose, and vice versa; one has only to look at the frequency with which pitchers end a season with poor won-lost percentages but low earned run averages (number of runs given up per game). The opposite is equally true: some pitchers play poorly, giving up many runs, yet win many games. In brief, the pitcher, regardless of how well he performs, is dependent upon the proficiency of his teammates, the inefficiency of the opposition and the supernatural (luck).

But luck, as we all know, comes in two forms, and many fans assume that the pitcher's tough losses (close games in which he gave up very few runs) are eventually balanced out by his "lucky" wins. This is untrue, as a comparison of pitchers' lifetime earned run averages to their overall won-lost records shows. If the player could apply a law of averages to individual performance, there would be much less concern about chance and uncertainty in baseball. Unfortunately, he cannot and does not.

Hitting, too, is a chancy affair. Obviously, skill is required in hitting the ball hard and on a line. Once the ball is hit, however, chance plays a large role in determining where it will go, into a waiting glove or whistling past a falling stab.

With respect to fielding, the player has almost complete control over the outcome. The average fielding percentage or success rate of .975, compared to a .245 success rate for hitters (the average batting average), reflects the degree of certainty in fielding. Next to the pitcher or hitter, the fielder has little to worry about when he knows that better than 9.7 times in ten he will execute his task flawlessly.

If Malinowski's hypothesis is correct, we should find magic associated with hitting and pitching, but none with fielding. Let us take the evidence by category—ritual, taboo and fetish.

Ritual

After each pitch, ex-major leaguer Lou Skeins used to reach into his back pocket to touch a crucifix, straighten his cap and clutch his genitals. Detroit Tiger infielder Tim Maring wore the same clothes and put them on exactly in the same order each day during a batting streak. Baseball rituals are almost infinitely various. After all, the ballplayer can ritualize any activity he considers necessary for a successful performance, from the type of cereal he eats in the morning to the streets he drives home on.

Usually, rituals grow out of exceptionally good performances. When the player does well he cannot really attribute his success to skill alone. He plays with the same amount of skill one night when he gets four hits as the next night when he goes hitless. Through magic, such as ritual, the player seeks greater control over his performance, actually control over the elements of chance. The player, knowing that his ability is fairly constant, attributes the inconsistencies in his performance to some form of behavior or a particular food that he ate. When a player gets four hits in a game, especially "cheap" hits, he often believes that there must have been something he did, in addition to his ability, that shifted luck to his side. If he can attribute his good fortune to the glass of iced tea he drank before the game or the new shirt he wore to the ballpark, then by repeating the same behavior the following day he can hope to achieve similar results. (One expression of this belief is the myth that eating certain foods will give the ball "eyes," that is, a ball that seeks the gaps between fielders.) In hopes of maintaining a batting streak, I once ate fried chicken every day at 4:00 P.M., kept my eyes closed during the national anthem and changed sweat shirts at the end of the fourth inning each night for seven consecutive nights until the streak ended.

Fred Caviglia, Kansas City minor league pitcher, explained why he eats certain foods before each game: "Everything you do is important to winning. I never forget what I eat the day of a game or what I wear. If I pitch well and win I'll do it all exactly the same the next day I pitch. You'd be crazy not to. You just can't ever tell what's going to make the difference between winning and losing."

Rituals associated with hitting vary considerably in complexity from one player to the next, but they have several components in common. One of the most popular is tagging a particular base when leaving and returning to the dugout each inning. Tagging second base on the way to the outfield is habitual with some players. One informant reported that during a successful month of the season he stepped on third base on his way to the dugout after the third, sixth and ninth innings of each game. Asked if he ever purposely failed to step on the bag he replied, "Never! I wouldn't dare, it would destroy my confidence to hit." It is not uncommon for a hitter who is playing poorly to try different combinations of tagging and not tagging particular bases in an attempt to find a successful combination. Other components of a hitter's ritual may include tapping the plate with his bat a precise number of times or taking a precise number of warm-up swings with the leaded bat.

One informant described a variation of this in which he gambled for a certain hit by tapping the plate a fixed number of times. He touched the plate once with his bat for each base desired: one tap for a single, two for a double and so on. He even built in odds that prevented him from asking for a home run each time. The odds of hitting a single with one tap were one in three, while the chances of hitting a home run with four taps were one in 12.

Clothing is often considered crucial to both hitters and pitchers. They may have several athletic supporters and a number of sweat shirts with ritual significance. Nearly all players wear the same uniform and undergarments each day when playing well, and some even wear the same street clothes. In 1954, the New York Giants, during a 16-game winning streak, wore the same clothes in each game and refused to let them be cleaned for fear that their good fortune might be washed away with the dirt. The route taken to and from the stadium can also have significance; some players drive the same streets to the ballpark during a hitting streak and try different routes during slumps.

Because pitchers only play once every four days, the rituals they practice are often more complex than the hitters', and most of it, such as tugging the cap between pitches, touching the rosin bag after each bad pitch or smoothing the dirt on the mound before each new batter, takes place on the field. Many baseball fans have observed this behavior never realizing that it may be as important to the pitcher as throwing the ball.

Dennis Grossini, former Detroit farmhand, practiced the following ritual on each pitching day for the first three months of a winning season. First, he arose from bed at exactly 10:00 A.M. and not a minute earlier or later. At 1:00 P.M. he went to the nearest restaurant for two glasses of iced tea and a tuna fish sandwich. Although the afternoon was free, he observed a number of taboos such as no movies, no reading and no candy. In the clubhouse he changed into the sweat shirt and jock he wore during his last winning game, and one hour before the game he chewed a wad of Beechnut chewing tobacco. During the game he touched his letters (the team name on his uniform) after each pitch and straightened his cap after each ball. Before the start of each inning he replaced the pitcher's rosin bag next to the spot where it was the inning before. And after every inning in which he gave up a run he went to the clubhouse to wash his hands. I asked him which part of the ritual was most important. He responded: "You can't really tell what's most important so it all becomes important. I'd be afraid to change anything. As long as I'm winning I do everything the same. Even when I can't wash my hands [this would occur when he must bat] it scares me going back to the mound . . . . I don't feel quite right."

One ritual, unlike those already mentioned, is practiced to improve the power of the baseball bat. It involves sanding the bat until all the varnish is removed, a process requiring several hours of labor, then rubbing rosin into the grain of the bat before finally heating it over a flame. This ritual treatment supposedly increases the distance the ball travels after being struck. Although some North Americans prepare their bats in this fashion it is more popular among Latin Americans. One informant admitted that he was not certain of the effectiveness of the treatment. But, he added, "There may not be a God, but I go to church just the same."

Despite the wide assortment of rituals associated with pitching and hitting, I never observed any ritual related to fielding. In all my 20 interviews only one player, a shortstop with acute fielding problems, reported any ritual even remotely connected to fielding.

Taboo

Mentioning that a no-hitter is in progress and crossing baseball bats are the two most widely observed taboos. It is believed that if the pitcher hears the words "no-hitter" his spell will be broken and the no-hitter lost. As for the crossing of bats, that is sure to bring bad luck; batters are therefore extremely careful not to drop their bats on top of another. Some players elaborate this taboo even further. On one occasion a teammate became quite upset when another player tossed a bat from the batting cage and it came to rest on top of his. Later he explained that the top bat would steal hits from the lower one. For him, then, bats contain a finite number of hits, a kind of baseball "image of limited good." Honus Wagner, a member of baseball's Hall of Fame, believed that each bat was good for only 100 hits and no more. Regardless of the quality of the bat he would discard it after its 100th hit.

Besides observing the traditional taboos just mentioned, players also observe certain personal prohibitions. Personal taboos grow out of exceptionally poor performances, which a player often attributes to some particular behavior or food. During my first season of professional baseball I once ate pancakes before a game in which I struck out four times. Several weeks later I had a repeat performance, again after eating pancakes. The result was a pancake taboo in which from that day on I never ate pancakes during the season. Another personal taboo, born out of similar circumstances, was against holding a baseball during the national anthem.

Taboos are also of many kinds. One athlete was careful never to step on the chalk foul lines or the chalk lines of the batter's box. Another would never put on his cap until the game started and would not wear it at all on the days he did not pitch. Another had a movie taboo in which he refused to watch a movie the day of a game. Often certain uniform numbers become taboo. If a player has a poor spring training or a bad year, he may refuse to wear the same uniform number again. I would not wear double numbers, especially 44 and 22. On several occasions, teammates who were playing poorly requested a change of uniform during the middle of the season. Some players consider it so important that they will wear the wrong size uniform just to avoid a certain number or to obtain a good number.

Again, with respect to fielding, I never saw or heard of any taboos being observed, though of course there were some taboos, like the uniform numbers, that were concerned with overall performance and so included fielding.

Fetishes

These are standard equipment for many baseball players. They include a wide assortment of objects: horsehide covers of old baseballs, coins, bobby pins, protective cups, crucifixes and old bats. Ordinary objects are given this power in a fashion similar to the formation of taboos and rituals. The player during an exceptionally hot batting or pitching streak, especially one in which he has "gotten all the breaks," credits some unusual object, often a new possession, for his good fortune. For example, a player in a slump might find a coin or an odd stone just before he begins a hitting streak. Attributing the improvement in his performance to the new object, it becomes a fetish, embodied with supernatural power. While playing for Spokane, Dodger pitcher Alan Foster forgot his baseball shoes on a road trip and borrowed a pair from a teammate to pitch. That night he pitched a no-hitter and later, needless to say, bought the shoes from his teammate. They became his most prized possession.

Fetishes are taken so seriously by some players that their teammates will not touch them out of fear of offending the owner. I once saw a fight caused by the desecration of a fetish. Before the game, one player stole the fetish, a horsehide baseball cover, out of a teammate's back pocket. The prankster did not return the fetish until after the game, in which the owner of the fetish went hitless, breaking a batting streak. The owner, blaming his inability to hit on the loss of the fetish, lashed out at the thief when the latter tried to return it.

Rube Waddel, an old-time Philadelphia Athletic pitching great, had a hairpin fetish. However, the hairpin he possessed was only powerful as long as he won. Once he lost a game he would look for another hairpin, which had to be found on the street, and he would not pitch until he found another.

The use of fetishes follows the same pattern as ritual and taboo in that they are connected only with hitting or pitching. In nearly all cases the player expressed a specific purpose for carrying a fetish, but never did a player perceive his fetish as having any effect on his fielding.

I have said enough, I think, to show that many of the beliefs and practices of professional baseball players are magical. Any empirical connection between the ritual, taboo and fetishes and the desired event is quite absent. Indeed, in several instances the relationship between the cause and effect, such as eating tuna fish sandwiches to win a ball game, is even more remote than is characteristic of primitive magic. Note, however, that unlike many forms of primitive magic, baseball magic is usually performed to achieve one's own end and not to block someone else's. Hitters do not tap their bats on the plate to hex the pitcher, but to improve their own performance.

Finally, it should be plain that nearly all the magical practices that I participated in, observed or elicited, support Malinowski's hypothesis that magic appears in situations of chance and uncertainty. The large amount of uncertainty in pitching and hitting best explains the elaborate magical practices used for these activities. Conversely, the high success rate in fielding, .975, involving much less uncertainty, offers the best explanation for the absence of magic in this realm.

SUGGESTED READINGS

Magic, Science and Religion by Bronislaw Malinowski (New York: Doubleday, 1948).

"Water Witching: An Interpretation of a Ritual Pattern in Rural American Community" by Evon Vogt in *Scientific Monthly*, LXXV, 1952, pp. 175–186.

4

E. Louis Mahigel & Gregory P. Stone

How Card Hustlers Make the Game

Consider the schoolboy football player, the girl on the barstool, the black man on the streetcorner, the white man in the Brooks Brothers suit, or the poker player anywhere. They have something in common, which is that all can be called hustlers with varying degrees of praise or blame, depending on who is doing the labelling and who is being labelled.

We like this moral ambiguity in the word hustler; it is just what is needed for our subjects, gamblers, in that it merely connotes their status as men who happen to derive a substantial amount of their income from playing cards. To say of a gambler that he is a hustler says little about how he plays cards except that he probably plays very well. It certainly doesn't mean that he cheats, either all of the time or only when he can. Cheaters are hustlers who use illegitimate techniques. But not all hustlers are cheaters, even though they are thoroughly familiar with most, if not all, the cheaters' techniques.

There is another useful connotation of the word hustler. It points to a conscious manipulation of people and things in the field of play—football, sex, survival, advertising or gambling—to the end of winning. Social scientists have used various phrases to describe this practice: Ralph Turner has called it role making; Erving Goffman has called it staging or impression management; especially useful is Anselm Strauss' concept of status forcing. These terms place different emphases on different aspects of the situation, but taken together they all remind us that a game is not just played. It can also be made.

Making the game of cards is more than giving them a riffle or a cut, although for most card players, even those who play for serious stakes, that about sums it up. We know that playing cards for money is widespread in this country. Yet there are literally millions of players in every segment of the population who are content to shuffle a deck, cut or decline to cut, and deal or await the deal. They scarcely conceive that making the cards frequently involves for those who financially depend upon gambling a whole range of techniques that have had to be mastered with care and skill.

Of course, the hustler may not use all the techniques we will discuss here. His mere knowledge of the game (hands, pots, bluffs, odds and reading an opponent's style of play) gives him a ten to 25 percent edge in, for example, any poker game. Cheaters, naturally, break the rules in many ways, as we shall see. But in some games cheating may not be possible, and so the cheater may be obliged to hustle legitimately at times. But, for now, let us look at some of the techniques available to him if he does cheat.

Gimmicks, like most equipment used in any industry, are produced in "factories." As used by the gambler, a factory refers to the production and distribution of cheating equipment under the same roof. As far as we know, the largest factory producing and distributing card equipment was once located in Chicago. This particular operation was closed in the early sixties but factories persist today throughout the world, in New York and London, of course, but also in Tulsa, Oklahoma, to name only three cities. Although these factories produce and distribute all kinds of gambling equipment such as dice, "put and take tops," table magnets and radio cue prompters, we will focus on the equipment produced for making the game of cards. Such gimmicks are only used by gamblers who cheat. Categories would include: 1) hold-out equipment, 2) stripped decks, 3) marked decks and 4) equipment to mark or "read" cards. All marking presupposes reading, but not all reading presupposes the use of marking equipment, for some gimmicks are manufactured to permit the reading of conventional cards. With the exception of hold-out equipment, these gimmicks are never mutually exclusive.

Hold-out Equipment are essentially containers. They are designed to facilitate palming or other ways of withdrawing, holding and reintroducing cards during the game. The simplest type is the table card-holder. This is a device that can be attached to the underside of a card table and hold any number of cards for easy retrieval. Only a rank amateur would use such a gimmick, because the skilled card cheat could use his leg, his arm pit or a jacket pocket to accomplish the same results, thereby minimizing the risk of detection. More subtle and complex equipment would include hold-out *machines*, elaborate metallic and vacuumatic devices concealed in the sleeve of the cheater and operated by arm pressure, knee movement or chest expansion. Like table card-holders, these machines enable the cheater to withdraw, hold and reintroduce cards during the course of the game, but they are more subtle because they are on the body of the gambler rather than attached to the props of the game, and bodies are more immune to scrutiny than the props are. Then too if the other players suspect the presence of a hold-out machine, the cheater can flee the scene with it if it's on his person, but the table card-holder, as with all other props, remains on the scene of action. Even so, both these types of devices are used very seldom, as the risks of detection are so great. On those rare occasions when a machine is used, the gambler must be extremely skilled, and the employment of such devices is dependent upon the naivete of the other players as well as the game that is being played. Even then the device is used infrequently. The master of this art is called a "machine man" in the trade.

Paper, Readers and Reading. We have already said that it is impossible to separate writing from reading, so it is with making the game of cards. Marked cards (paper) are useless unless they can be read. Factories supply an incredible range of marked decks, for example, blockout work, brace work, line work, shade work and border work. One of the more popular techniques of marking cards is blocking out. Here a minor portion of the design on the back of the card is inked out, indicating to the cheater the value and sometimes the suit of the card. Brace work is an alteration of the design on the back of the card which conveys the value and/or suit of the card.

On the backs of most cards there are lines. Line work slightly expands these lines to indicate the cards that are in play, and cards so worked are important products of the factory. Shade work is accomplished by darkening a portion of the back of the card. Border work involves very slight alterations of the margin around the design on the back of a card. Sometimes this is called marked edge work and consists of providing minute bumps or bulges in various places around the margin of the design on the back of the card. The location of these bumps or bulges conveys to the skilled reader the value of the card but seldom, if ever, the suit.

At one time cards with a completely white back, devoid of design, were used, possibly as a safeguard against markings. Cheaters quickly got around this barrier by "waxing" or "glazing." Blank white backs of cards could be marked with minute smears of wax detectable only when the cards were held at odd angles. The cheater, of course, was extremely sensitized to the angle that would reveal the markings. We are tempted to say that methods of marking cards during play might well have begun as a reaction against efforts by gambling establishments to eliminate the marked deck, but we are not that naive.

All the above techniques for marking cards permit reading without special equipment. Yet, with the development of technology in the industry, more subtle methods for marking and reading cards have been developed, as, for example, luminous marks. These marks may only be used on red-backed cards, for the marking equipment is green, and, since red and green are primary colors which cancel one another out, the marks cannot be seen with the naked eye and reading them requires special equipment. This equipment once consisted of special spectacles or "shades," called luminous glasses and visors by those who are hip to the trade. Obviously, however, many card players know what rose colored spectacles are, so that they can only be used in making the game for rank fish or true suckers. Only unskilled cheaters would now consider using such reading equipment.

The development of contact lenses opened up new possibilities for reading luminous cards. Contacts can be discerned, of course, but only at a 90 degree angle from the side of the face and the cheater wearing contacts never presents this angle to the other players. Whether or not contact readers will be detected, therefore, is often a function of the skill and competence of the cheater. Cheaters must have poise, keeping the body always firmly in control, to make the game.

Equipment to Mark or "Read" Cards. Marking cards, as opposed to using marked decks, has probably been employed since the beginning of card playing. It has no documented history, like the greatest part of human conduct. Marking white backed cards with wax is a form of daubing, and this gimmick has been considerably elaborated upon and improved over the years. Not too long ago, the daub employed by the cheater had to match the color of the back of the deck but now technology has given the cheater "smoke" or "golden glow." This is a daub that can be applied to the back of almost any card regardless of its color. Daubs may be concealed in various places on the cheater's body—the hair, the moustache—or on clothing, for example, high-rimmed jacket buttons.

Cards can be marked in other ways as well. Sanding, for example, means scratching the edge of cards without borders or margins. The cheater can produce his own devices for sanding, but the factories are in the business. Thus, "sand strips" are available on order from most factories. These are extremely small pieces of sandpaper which can be easily attached to the underside of the index or second finger, or, for that matter, whichever finger the gambler feels he can best use to mark cards.

For those cheaters who have an aversion to sandpaper, the factory provides the "thumb prick." This device is like a thumb tack, except that the tack is reduced to a quarter length. It is concealed by adhesive tape or a band-aid and usually attached to the underside of the thumb. Using such a device, the gambler can make miniscule indentations in salient cards, the position of which he can detect by touch. This ploy is referred to as "pegging."

Yet cheaters are never totally dependent on the factory for marking paper. Two common devices that are employed are "nailing" and "crimping," which unlike pegging, mark the cards for the sight of the reader rather than his touch. When a gambler nails the cards he uses his fingernails to mark the cards along their edges. These indentations are visible, thereby permitting the gambler to read the relevant cards for whatever game he is making. Fingernails nail, and fingers crimp. Fingernails make indentations on cards, while fingers bend them. Crimping, then, requires the dexterous bending of cards in a variety of ways so that, by sight, the gambler can discern the card that best fits his game. Nailing and crimping do not require equipment from the factory. Consequently, the use of these gimmicks depends totally upon the skill of the cheater.

All these marks are "read" by sight or by touch from the backs of the cards. "Shiners" permit the cheater to read from the front. These are small mirrors or reflectors which may be attached to the palm of the dealer's hand, placed in pipe bowls, match boxes, in finger rings or in various places on or under the table. As cards are dealt over the shiner, values and suits are reflected, and the cheater is provided with considerable knowledge of his opponents' hands.

Strippers. Factories carry standardized stripped decks for the trade, but, like tailors, they will provide custom-made equipment for the cheater. Different cheaters may want different cards stripped, and the factory will do this for them. For example, as one factory catalogue, the source of which we shall not reveal, put it:

> We are in a position to furnish special strippers made to cut any card or any combination of cards you desire. Our work is all done by men who are experts in this line of work and the tools we use are the latest and most approved type, resulting in work that is absolutely uniform and cannot be obtained elsewhere.

Most stripped decks used by cheaters are called "side strippers," "belly strippers" or "humps." These terms originate from the fact that the cards to be separated from the rest of the deck, or stripped, protrude slightly—usually one-sixteenth to one-thirty-second of an inch—from the rest of the deck. What this means is that the sucker may shuffle, and the cheater, cutting the deck, can place the stripped cards wherever he wishes in the deck. So the game is made.

Competence, Decks and Pots

The skilled cheater, however, will avoid using these gimmicks because they may be detected, and the detection may mean at least the end of his game, a beating or, in crucial games, his death. Gambling can, indeed, be a matter of life and death for the cheater as well as his mark. For example, one of our acquaintances was playing a game of poker with Filipinos. Throughout the game the Filipinos maintained a running conversation in Filipino-Spanish which the cheater did not understand. He was losing, and he immediately discerned that the Filipino players were conveying information about one another's hands in their patois. To bring an end to this, he laid a thirty-eight calibre revolver on the table and said, "The next sound I want to hear at this table is the bark from this thirty-eight." The game proceeded in silence, and the cheater made his score.

Another example would be the case of Arnold Rothstein, a well known gambler who was taken for $100,000 in a poker game. Suspecting the use of gimmicks, he refused to honor the loss and was later found shot to death. The edge of violence in card games is also demonstrated by the case of "Little Abe," otherwise known as the "Professor." Abe had his heyday in the thirties. He could make any gambling game and would often be called in to make games and take other gamblers who were disliked by insiders. One such character was a small town tough who conspicuously carried a gun at all card games. The Professor was called in to take him at twenty-one. The game had a $100 limit, and the Professor's policy was to get his opponent hooked as soon as possible so he couldn't quit the game with modest winnings. After three hours' play he had the undesirable character "in" for $10,000 (remember this was in the thirties). At that point the local tough put his gun on the table and said "I know you are doing something to me and when I find out I am going to blow your brains out." Since the Professor never used marked cards in a twenty-one game, he knew that his manipulations of the deck could never be detected. Nevertheless, he left town the next day after collecting his commission for the $12,000 he took from the tough.

Quite clearly, competence in manipulating cards is crucial in making games. Without it the cheater may be killed. On occasion even a competent cheater can be beaten or killed when his take becomes too obvious or beyond normal expectations. This depends on the temperament of the sucker coupled with the intensity of his suspicions, what some might call "paranoia." To understand the importance of this observation, imagine the consequences of incompetence displayed by a surgeon, concert pianist or even a sociologist. Surgeons are covered by insurance. There is no insurance for the cheater. Walter Gieseking has recorded the Beethoven Emperor Concerto with an obvious error. The recording is on sale at all music stores. Were he making a card game rather than playing the piano, that might well have been the end of that illustrious pianist. Sociologists, relying as they do on computers rather than competence, may publish errors in the major journals. When such errors are detected, they publicize their apologies in the same journals under a form known as Errata. Cheaters cannot apologize for mistakes. Manipulating the cards requires incredible skill and practice. Concert pianists may practice as often as six hours a day; the surgeon's practice is his surgery; and the sociologist may not practice at all. Yet, the cheater must practice up to eight hours a day before a mirror—preferably a three-way mirror—to master any given technique of manipulating the cards. Only when he cannot perceive his own manipulation can he establish his competence for himself and, consequently, for making future games.

Manipulating the cards takes several forms and is often a co-operative enterprise. These forms include: palming, switches, stacking, peeking and false dealing. Such manipulations of the deck sometimes require shills, for the shill can establish the impression that the cheater has not made the game but rather some apparently naive player who is in fact the cheater's ally. Thus, suspicion is diverted from the one who really makes the game. We shall not discuss the shill except insofar as he facilitates the moves of the cheater.

Palming is the substitution of the hand for the hold-out equipment we discussed earlier. Any valuable card or cards can be removed from the deck, held and reintroduced to the game at propitious stages. We have known of circumstances where as many as five cards have been palmed by cheaters, but the number is usually less, though it may on rare occasion be greater. Extreme competence is required for palming cards, since it is easily detected.

Switching and palming sometimes go together, the difference being that switching a card or cards requires the retrieval of a card from a deck in play and its exchange for some other card in the deck rather than its mere reintroduction. Palming does not require making an exchange but an exchange frequently, but not always, requires palming. Thus, one player may exchange a card in his hand for a card in his partner's hand. Or he may replace a card, cards or an entire deck of cards for a card, cards or the deck employed in the regular game.

Sometimes, then, a different deck may be exchanged for the deck in play. This is often called "cold-decking" and with good reason. Cards in play get warm, and a new deck may well be cool. The skilled gambler can detect such subtle differences in temperature. This risky manipulation may be accomplished by the cheater alone, but sometimes it requires the assistance of a shill, whose function is to distract the attention of the other players from the cheater. He too must be skilled, however. For example, he might turn on a running conversation or "chatter" at the time of the switch; or he might ask for change of a large denomination bill; or he might ask for or offer cigarettes, cigars or a light; or he might focus attention on the pot by conspicuously demanding whether everyone is "in." Such ploys disturb the continuity of the interaction and facilitate the switch.

Looking and Peeking are necessary for many manipulations of cards. Looking simply refers to the observation of cards that are revealed during the course of play or at the end of a hand. The fact that in all card games some of the cards are revealed, except in those cases, bluffing or not, where a hand is not called, is used to the advantage of the cheater or hustler, for the legitimate revelation of cards enables him to make the game. Knowing the cards that have been legitimately revealed permits the hustler to locate or anticipate the location of those same cards during the next deal.

Peeking describes the art of discerning the top or bottom card of the deck without detection by other players, although, on occasion, other cards may be discerned. Gimmicks such as shiners, to which we have referred earlier, may be used in peeking, but the skilled cheater can peek with great effectiveness without the use of any gimmick. This involves an extremely careful control of eye movement. Directly focused peeking must be perfectly timed so that what Edward Hall calls the gaze line is never interrupted. The cultivation of peripheral vision clearly enhances the art of peeking and cheaters know this very well. Above all, looking and sometimes peeking make stacking possible.

Stacking the deck is the craft of placing known cards within the deck at desired locations either prior to or during the shuffling of the deck. This insures that specific cards will be dealt to any player covertly selected by the cheater.

One need not be the dealer to stack a deck of cards. In contract bridge, for example, two decks of cards are ordinarily used in the game so that the labor of shuffling, dealing, and cutting is divided. Thus, the shuffler can stack the deck for his opponent. Cutting the cards may, of course, disturb the stack and render it ineffective. This is particularly true of the "running cut," known in some circles as the "whorehouse cut." Contract bridge, however, is not usually played in whorehouses, so in that game the shuffler may slightly crimp all the cards above the line of cut. In a straight cut the unsuspecting player will quite probably cut the deck at the crimp thus returning the stack to the top of the deck. It should also be observed that, in contract bridge, the shuffler's partner makes the cut, thereby increasing the probability that the stack will be undisturbed.

Clearly, dealers do stack cards and this is often done in those games where shuffling and dealing are performed by the same player, as, for example, in poker, twenty-one and gin rummy, as well as other forms of rummy.

False Dealing. Magicians may deal cards from the center of the deck, but we know of no cheaters who do. To our knowledge, false dealing by cheaters includes dealing "bottoms" and "seconds." Since bottom dealing is by far the most publicized—literally hundreds of American motion pictures, especially westerns, refer to it—the cheater must incur some risk in implementing this deal. Even those who play cards on occasional weekends will be looking for it; they may even have tried clumsily to experiment with it themselves. Bottom dealing is so widely known that it probably accounts for the use of the protective device of sealing the deck in such games as twenty-one and sometimes poker. What the rank amateur does not know, however, is that sealing the deck gives the skilled cheater or hustler an edge. For these gamblers can count and remember.

Second dealing is a different matter. Here the second card from the top of the deck is dealt, retaining the top card which is known to the dealer by reading or peeking. First of all, this gives the dealer an edge simply by making sure the card does not get into the game. Second, the card may be introduced into the game giving the dealer the choice of that card or some unknown card. Third, the card may be introduced into the game to destroy or bust an opponent's hand. Fourth, it may be introduced to build his shill's hand. Since fewer players will be looking for second dealing, the second dealer may enjoy a certain edge over bottom dealers in some games. However, *competent* bottom dealing is objectively as difficult to detect as *competent* second dealing.

Knowing the Odds

Any hustler must know the odds in the game he is making. In draw poker, for example, the odds are four and one-half to one against making a flush by drawing one card to a four flush, or five to one against making a straight by drawing one card to an open ended straight. Of course, it is not our purpose to recount here all the odds for improving one's hand in various games of poker. These have been systematically set down by Oswald Jacoby, one of the foremost poker, bridge and gin players in the world. The point is that *all* of these odds should be known by the full-time gambler. At the very least he must have a contextual, if not a detailed, knowledge of them.

Different techniques of estimating the odds are used in making other games of cards. Probably the currently best known of such techniques are those that have been employed by Edward O. Thorp in making the game of twenty-one, sometimes erroneously referred to as black-jack. To understand the complexity of estimating odds, we would merely observe that Thorp, a mathematician, had to employ the services of an electronic computer to "beat the dealer."

In general, knowing the odds requires not only knowing the odds for any given hand, but also relating those odds to the stakes and the size of the pot.

Stakes. Any player, before he sits in on a game, must know what the stakes are. These range from limit games (one dollar minimum, two dollar maximum, even nickel-dime poker), pot limit, where the player may bet any amount up to the amount in the pot, to table stakes, meaning that players may wager any or all of the money they have before them on the table. One's table stake can never be reduced or supplemented during a single hand. This can only be done between hands. The decision to enter a game of cards depends, to a considerable degree, on knowledge of the stakes in relation to the money that the gambler has available. With table stakes, this is crucial.

If the gambler is "down," that is, has limited funds, he is more likely to join a lower limit game (where he can build up a larger stake) than he is to go where the action really is. Yet, in such games, his own action is limited. Of course he can cheat, but such techniques as "bluffing" and "creating a tell" are not easily employed. Bluffs can be easily called in limit games—the stakes are usually not high. Creating a tell, as we shall see, may hardly be worth the effort, since it requires a considerable investment of time and money.

With higher stakes, the options of the gambler are opened up. In the extreme, given table stakes, the gambler can merely snow the other players by bluffing at bets that they can never see or hope to call. Obviously other forms of bluffing, reverse and double-reverse psychology can be effective in games of high stakes. One such form is creating a tell. Among others, Oswald Jacoby has explained how this is done. He was challenged by an extremely wealthy and arrogant man, described as a "little tin god," to a table stake game of five-card stud poker. The challenger asserted that all bridge experts were poor poker players, since expert poker requires psychological expertise. This annoyed Jacoby. For three hours of the game Jacoby systematically piled chips on his hole card whenever it was an ace or king—losing frequently during that period. Note that it took a lot of time and money to create this tell, but at the end of the time Jacoby was certain that his opponent had taken this "obvious give-away" into account. He then changed his tactics by placing his chips only on aces, not on kings. Ultimately he took his opponent for all he had in one hand with a pair of kings over his opponent's pair of tens. The opponent was convinced that Jacoby's betting was merely a bluff, since he had not piled his chips on the king in the hole.

Pots. Quite clearly, Jacoby's move had to come at an appropriate time—when the pot was very large. Yet, he made it large. The point is that a skilled gambler must relate the stakes, the hand and the pot in making the game.

Pots as well as hands establish odds. The ratio between what is in the pot and the gambler's bet must at least equal or exceed the odds for his making the hand which he estimates will win. Otherwise he must fold. For example, if the gambler in draw poker is drawing to an open ended straight, there must be *at least* five times the amount of money in the pot that he will put up for any particular call. The same principle applies to most games of poker. In other games, for example, twenty-one, there is no pot. One merely plays against the dealer, and the relationship between hands and stakes is the critical one.

Disguises

Often a skilled hustler will be identified by the gambling establishment as precisely that. The house will then take measures to prevent his play. Even the rules of the game may be changed. When Edward Thorp's system for beating twenty-one became widely publicized, the rules of that game were changed in the large gambling houses in April of 1964. The strategem was counterproductive, however. Action at the tables in Las Vegas, as well as the tourist trade, declined so sharply that the original rules were reinstituted by June of 1964. Gambling houses could not afford to lose the suckers, so they were forced to take their chances on the system players. However, recognized system players, like Thorp, were arbitrarily excluded from the action.

Consequently, identified hustlers disguise themselves. Thorp himself adopted a repertoire of disguises including hair sculpture, beards, contact lenses, sweep around sun glasses, clothing and position at the table. On the latter point, one should know that most twenty-one hustlers will sit at "third base"—the first seat on the dealer's right. To disguise his identity, Thorp would sit two seats to the right of the dealer.

These disguises are taken on to con the house, but the

cheater or hustler will use disguises to con other players as well. As only one instance of this, we cite the case of a cheater who makes games of cards in the Negro ghettoes of large mid-western cities. He arrives at the scene of action in soiled bib overalls, a rumpled work shirt, scuffed work shoes, and a typical farmer's hat. He also makes sure there is a visible supply of dirt under his fingernails. He consolidates this rustic appearance with a verbal line, "I just come up from Mississippi with money I've saved so's me and my cousin can open up a chicken farm up here in the north." The players at the game will accept him willingly as a fish. He then proceeds to make the game.

Blocking

As Anselm Strauss has indicated, status-forcing may at least have the consequences of pushing one up or down in some arrangement of status or in or out of participation in some social circle. Strauss' brilliant discussion, however, fails to differentiate systematically verbal from non-verbal techniques. Recently, such observers as Raymond Birdwhistell, Edward T. Hall, Robert Sommer, and Watson and Graves have considerably sharpened up the analysis of non-verbal interaction.

Now all techniques of status-forcing are extremely useful to the gambler. He may wish to build his opponent up for the big take, as in creating a tell, or he may wish to tear him down so that he loses confidence, therefore competence, in his line of play—to destroy his cool. He may wish to force a mark into a game or so control his play that he will throw in his hand or fold prematurely. The latter forcing technique, where accomplished non-verbally, has been termed "blocking" by Albert Scheflen in an outstanding general consideration of the significance of posture in communication.

One of us (Mahigel) has designed and carried out a preliminary experiment on the effects that blocking exerts on the play of poker. His findings show that the use of non-verbal techniques to control interaction in making games of cards holds great promise for establishing a significant advantage to the informed hustler.

Mahigel selected sixteen male poker-players from introductory speech classes at the University of Minnesota. These volunteers were randomly assigned to control and experimental groups, and each was asked to play three hands of draw poker with two other players who had been instructed in the experimental procedure. These latter two players blocked the play of each member of the experimental group, but not the play of members of the control group. The blocking behavior used was mild, to say the least. Each informed player, seated on either side of the experimental subject, merely placed his forearm on the card table between himself and the subject. A dealer, who did not engage in the game, dealt identical cards to all three players in each of three rounds of play, although specific hands were varied from one round to another. In other words, three hands were dealt in the first round. Each of the sixteen volunteers received the same cards, as did the two experimental assistants. In the subsequent two rounds the same procedure was followed, although different hands were dealt in each trial. When no blocking was used in 24 turns of play, there were 17 calls and 7 folds, but when blocking was used in the same number of turns, there were 11 calls and 13 folds. While these figures are not impressive in any statistical sense, they do show that an edge can be established by the gambler through manipulation of posture or body-control.

Making games of cards requires a technology—gimmicks. It also involves skill—cheating and building pots. Such skill moves into knowledge, particularly of the odds. Moreover, one must mask himself if he is very competent. Finally, seemingly insignificant gestures may make a game. In all this, we have omitted the social organization of gambling and gamblers or their universes of discourse and appearance. There are elaborate verbal and nonverbal codes used by cheaters to communicate with one another. When they find themselves together at the same tables where the action is, they can communicate all these things and more. The mark, fish, or sucker will never know. Anyone for poker?

SUGGESTED READINGS

Gamble and Win by "Jack Hart" (Hollywood: Onsco Publications, 1963).

Mirrors and Masks by Anselm L. Strauss (New York: Free Press, 1959).

Beat the Dealer by Edward O. Thorp (New York: Random House, 1966).

The Casino Gambler's Guide by Allan N. Wilson (New York: Harper & Row, 1970).

5 *Gerald D. Sturges*

1000 + 1000 = 5000: Estimating Crowd Size

On October 3, 1970, 20,000 persons (or perhaps 200,000) attended a March for Victory rally in Washington, D.C., led by fundamentalist Christian minister Carl McIntire. The following day, readers of the *Washington Post* were informed that:

> Park police estimated 20,000 at the Monument Grounds. Mr. McIntire refused to give a crowd estimate, although he had predicted a turnout of 500,000 as recently as Friday.
>
> Justice Department observers estimated 15,000 to 20,000 persons attended the afternoon rally at the Monument Grounds.
>
> The *Washington Post* counted 7,150 persons marching at 4th Street and Pennsylvania Avenue. The marchers joined others already assembled at the Monument.

The first word was not to be the last. Undaunted, the religious weekly *Christian Beacon* (edited by Carl McIntire, D.D., Litt.D.) insisted in its October 8 issue "the estimated attendance was between 200 and 250 thousand."

In a bylined sidebar emblazoned "March for Victory—A Glorious Success," McIntire scolded the press for its low estimates:

> The press, however, revealed itself for what it has been doing. The Associated Press sent its story across the world saying that there were only 8000 present. . . . This has angered everyone and all who attended. The evidence of the pictures reveals that there were more than eight or even twenty, which is the highest figure used by the press anywhere.

Perhaps the matter should be dismissed as a simple digit of opinion or as the sort of broadside any promoter might fire in deep disappointment (his handbills had summoned 500,000 to attend). And certainly, if anyone is justified in making inspirational estimates, McIntire is. Even so, basic questions lurk.

How do you count demonstrators when they don't file past a fixed point two by two? How do you count countless heads near the Washington Monument without the help of aerial reconnaissance photos? How do you tabulate a nonstationary crowd that leaves behind no telltale ticker-tape or other paper tribute for a New York sanitation department to weigh?

In general practice the answer is that you guesstimate. And that's what's wrong. Crowd estimating is a mixed bag of art, bravado, padding and a little—very little—counting. As will be seen, it is a symposium of guesses. Consider recent Washington history:

☐ November 1969—With antiwar promoters estimating a gate of one million (high bid) and the Pentagon's analysts coming in at 119,000 (low bid) on the basis of off-hour aerial photography, the count was kicked around for a time. The figure 250,000 won out, though, on a preponderance of evidence—two Washington policemen atop a photographer's scaffold at 15th Street and Pennsylvania Avenue used hand tallies on November 15 to tick off the peace demonstrators as they passed by. They click-clicked a crowd "at least" 250,000 strong.

☐ May 1970—On May 9 there was no convenient file-by, and the military wasn't asked to make a photo flyover. Demonstrators predicted 35,000 would turn out, while the police guesstimator (Inspector Thomas Herlihy, chief of the department's intelligence unit) divulged his formula but not its results. "We use a 2-to-1 formula," he explained. "For every one person we can identify as coming here—by chartered bus, train, by reports from other intelligence sections—we multiply by two. That's a good round guess." One good round guess probably deserves another, so the media settled on a range of 60,000 to 100,000 for the antiwar array that day. It was a pretty solid consensus, more or less.

☐ July 1970—Sometimes it's guesswork from start to finish. Organizers of the Honor America Day rally first hoped for 400,000, but on July 3, just a day ahead, a rally spokesman said he would be happy if it drew 250,000. Meanwhile, the police intelligence unit was reporting it knew of no confirmed special buses or trains arriving, and a survey showed that hotels were booked to only 70 percent of capacity—normal for summer. However they arrived or wherever they stayed, the crowd was estimated by police at 250,000 to 350,000—likely the greatest number ever to go to a Fourth of July celebration in Washington. (The Independence Day crowds of 1951 and 1965 had been estimated at 200,000.)

☐ April-May 1971—It was agreed by most observers that the number of peace marchers who thronged to the Capitol grounds April 24 reached 175,000. McIntire forecast he would top that in a return engagement May 9, but as his marchers reached the Monument Grounds that afternoon he was claiming 25,000 (compared with an official Park police estimate of 14,000 to 15,000 and agreement by newspaper reporters that the crowd looked more like 5,000).

Numbers necessarily matter to us because they matter to editors and news directors. Whether it be a hot summer's day at New York's Far Rockaway beach, a welcoming parade or an animal stampede, these people want a crowd count. This is partly journalistic practice (read unexamined custom), partly the bigger-is-better bias they share with almost everyone. Authoritative estimates are best, but bigger estimates tend to become authoritative. In fact, reporters may be called in to explain only those estimates that are lower than the competition's.

Bigger numbers tend to shore up an editor's confidence that he correctly judged an upcoming event to be newsworthy and perhaps help fend off those citizen letter-writers who belong to the Perspective School (which would hold, for example, that in reporting that several hundred veterans tossed their military decorations onto the United States Capitol grounds on April 23, 1971, a newspaper should point out that there were 28 million living veterans—many of them decorated—who did not attend). While bigger numbers may have these defensive applications, it's doubtful they support the cause of accuracy.

Dead Body Counts

Oddly, the counting of dead bodies is a much more exact enterprise, whether the dead be soldiers or fish. Years of ostensibly precise battlefield counts from Vietnam surely confirm the former, and the impressively unblushing estimate of 15,236,000 fish killed by identifiable pollution sources in 42 states in 1968 verifies the latter. Perhaps combat estimators have been following this advice from the pamphlet, "Investigating Fish Mortalities":

> The number of fish killed should be estimated as accurately as possible. Estimates are often difficult to make because all dead fish are not observable, and in large numbers, counts are impractical. For large rivers and lakes a measured distance of shoreline may be traversed by boat and the number and kinds of dead or dying fish counted. Estimates can be made by projecting representative counts to the total kill area. For smaller streams, the banks may be walked and counts made on the observed numbers of dead fish by species.

To be fair about it, professional crowd estimators labor under handicaps, such as deadline pressure and lack of a convenient vantage point. And they can be victimized by the talented crowd puffer known as the political advance man. Richard M. Cohen of the *Washington Post* recently gleaned some details from Martin E. Underwood, who was President Lyndon Johnson's advance man:

> Getting the crowd there, Underwood would be the first to admit, is only half the task. It is equally important to convince the press that 25,000 persons is really 50,000. One way to do that, Underwood said, is to pick a narrow street for a motorcade and have the crowd bunch up. It looks better. But there is another trick.
>
> "This big sheriff came by in 1966 on one of our state trips," Underwood said. "He came by and kept insisting that he wanted to get into the act. I told him, 'We have a very important job for you but I can't tell you what it is right now.' But every morning he's at my hotel, asking, 'What am I going to do?'
>
> "So the day comes and he comes running over to the platform where the President is and he says, 'Lookit, I'm not doing anything.'
>
> "So I said, 'This is what you're going to do. You're going to get your name in the paper because you're going to give the crowd estimate. Listen, how many people are out here?'
>
> "He said, '25,000.'
>
> " 'You didn't see those over there.'
>
> "He said, '35,000.'
>
> " 'How about those over there by the bridge?'
>
> "He said, '50,000!'
>
> "I said, 'Listen, the president wants you to have this pen.' And Bill Moyers grabbed him and took him over to the press and said, 'This is the sheriff and he wants to give you the crowd estimate.'
>
> "They said, 'How many?' and he said, '50,000.' "

In some other places the police prefer eyeball counting. They would rather not guesstimate. One by one is best, Washington's Herlihy declares, "and there just is no other accurate way to do it." Sometimes police just drop out, as they did in New York City four years ago. They stopped making official estimates in May of 1967 and left it to the newspapers to gauge the number of marchers down Fifth Avenue in the Support Our Boys in Vietnam parade. Using mechanical counters, the papers said roughly 70,000, the organizers claimed three times that, and the police said nothing.

If you don't count heads you can infer their number by weighing sidewalk debris, and the New York sanitation department can tell you the ticker-tape tonnage of major celebrations: Charles A. Lindbergh, 1,750 tons; V-J Day, 5,438; General Douglas MacArthur, 3,249; first orbiter John Glenn, 3,476; Apollo 11,300; and the Miracle Mets, 1,010. Tonnage, though, is no measure of enthusiasm. An ad salesman who'd seen the to-do for Lindbergh, V-J Day and the Apollo astronauts remarked of the Mets' reception, "You could roll all those days together and it wouldn't compare with this." To make an unsure situation more unsure, some demonstrators these days clean up after themselves, leaving litter-ly nothing to weigh.

For well-defined areas you can determine square footage, estimate human density (sometimes almost boundless) and calculate attendance. Herbert Jacobs, a University of California lecturer in journalism, did that a few years ago for Sproul Plaza on the Berkeley campus. And he brought credentials.

Jacobs Crowd Formula

A long-time student of crowd estimating, Jacobs believed the "high tide of estimating" occurred in New York City for the MacArthur parade of 1951, when a police commissioner assessed the crowd at eight million, "despite the fact that it totaled more people than there were in the whole city and suburbs." This was set right in 1960, when a newspaper employed official city maps and measured sidewalk widths to reckon that "the traditional ticker-tape route from Battery Park to City Hall could hold no more than 141,436 spectators." Allowing generously for watchers hanging out of office windows and stationed on side streets, it concluded that the total could not have exceeded 500,000.

Using the same approach, a *Milwaukee Sentinel* reporter substantially deflated the police estimate of 750,000 to

800,000 spectators at this year's Fourth of July parade in Milwaukee and, by implication, the crowd estimate of 600,000 given out for the same event in 1965, 1966, 1967, 1969 and 1970. Dean Jensen calculated square footage for the walks and street crossings along the 33-block route and, after rough adjustment for "especially corpulent parade-goers" and tots who watch while perched on their parents' shoulders, put maximum feasible attendance at 250,000.

At Berkeley in December of 1966, when a plaza parliament voted for a campus strike, Bay Area media estimated the assemblage at 8,000. Jacobs subsequently knocked down the estimate and the estimators by obtaining an 11-by-14 enlargement of a peak-of-the-rally photo, ruling it off into one-inch squares and counting heads.

It took him four hours with a magnifying glass to pinpoint 2,804 persons. Allowing 20 percent for the unphotographed fringes, he asserted the crowd could not have numbered more than 3,400. Then he chastised newsmen for consensus estimating:

> The trouble with all these guesses is that they are themselves based on guesses. Old-time political reporters cover many meetings and observe crowds of various sizes. They soon adopt a scale of values, having seen police officials and their own colleagues give estimates of crowd sizes. But nobody, including the police, stops to actually count the crowd. It is a symposium of guesses, usually erring on the side of optimism.

Hoping for a start toward an estimating formula, Jacobs compared standards for how many persons a given space can hold, noting that one city planner dismissed the classical formula of two square feet per person as applying only to "a thin man in a subway," and that the California Health and Safety Code requirement of seven square feet per person for dance floors and other places of public assembly was made "when dancing was still a body-contact sport."

He chose the University of California campus as his outdoor laboratory because blueprints afforded precise measurements of Sproul Plaza, special stone pavement lines conveniently divided it into squares of 22 feet each, and there was plenty of action. His calculations revealed a density of 6.5 to 8.5 square feet per person for the typical rally, although at times people were tightly packed and used only four square feet and on other occasions spread out to 9.5 square feet per person.

The upshot was the Jacobs Crowd Formula and chastened newsmen quickly embraced it (although the formula was modified when someone discovered it didn't square too well with hypothetically long, thin crowds). The formula applied whether the rally-goers were standing or sitting—in other words, even when it became sprawl plaza.

There's no way of knowing how many newsmen use the Jacobs Crowd Formula, although Julius Fast takes note of it in his book, *Body Language*, in discussing the need for personal space and our resistance to encroachments upon it, and the tenth edition of the *Guinness Book of World Records* enshrines it—sort of—in recording the greatest number of human beings known to have assembled "with a common purpose." This, says the renowned arbiter of tavern arguments, was "more than 5,000,000 at the 21-day Hindu feast of Kumbh-Mela, which is held every 12 years at the confluence of the Yamuna (formerly called the Jumna), the Ganges and the invisible Sarasviti at Allahabad, Uttar Pradesh, India, on January 21, 1966." According to the Jacobs formula, it notes "the allowance of area per person varies from 4 square feet (tight) to 9½ square feet (loose). Thus, such a crowd must have occupied an area of more than 700 acres."

Unfortunately, the Jacobs formula (length times width divided by a correction factor) wasn't devised for application to estimates of unknown origin to derive the area involved, though there's no other choice in this case because the Kumbh-Mela crowd antedates invention of the formula. Maybe at the next feast . . .

Until we know that individual counting or careful use of the Jacobs formula produces our crowd counts, the best credibility insurance might be the use of a mandatory deductible. Just as a property and casualty insurer lists deductibles for certain kinds of hazards, so could we apply them to estimates of certain types of gatherings, for example, X percent for Monument crowds, Y percent for animal stampedes and a standard rake-off (Z percent) for all crowds marshalled by specific advance men. Widespread use of portable turnstiles in open-air settings could work, but would require the crowd's cooperation and, by analogy, might make public authorities feel they have to issue rain checks with parade or rally permits.

It all comes down to one piece of advice: When in doubt—discount.

PART THREE

The Middle Levels of Sociology

Our emphasis in the last part was on the socialized individual. In the part that follows this, we will focus on a strictly sociological area: social organization as it relates to institutional structures. The concern in this part will be with groups that provide linkages between the socialized individual and the larger social system. The idea of a middle level grows out of the notion that learning and the process of becoming human are either facilitated or hindered by linking structures in the middle, mediating between self and society.

Role expectations, reciprocity and norm expectations are transmitted through various agents of socialization. In Part Three the theme of socialization itself will continue. Our focus, however, will shift slightly toward the larger collectivities that shape and mold us into whatever it is that we become.

A major theme of sociology in the past was relativity, pure and simple. Instructors could startle as well as regale their classes with stories about how other folks in other places (and sometimes even friends and neighbors) organized their lives. Until recently, this meant that the boundary between sociology and cultural anthropology tended to become blurred, at least in introductory-level courses. During the 1970's the discipline of sociology has had to shift its focus. No one is startled to learn that different sexual mores, for example, obtain both within and between societies. In one sense, television (the most pervasive of the mass communications media) has "sociologized" the entire population of the United States and begun to do so in the rest of the world. A "hot" war in far-off Asia was brought into our homes in living color; larger numbers of Americans traveled abroad than ever before; the failure of the war on poverty and the scandals of Watergate undermined naïve faith in political institutions. In the words of Alvin Toffler, we have all been "future shocked" into a new level of consciousness. Sociology, too, has had to adjust to the new order (or disorder) by opening up many of its presuppositions to question and by expanding its angle of vision to accommodate to these and other changes.

Section VI

Families

The family is the basic linking unit of every culture. All cultures have beliefs and practices regulating family life, since the survival of the group depends on the procreation and rearing of a new generation to replace the old. Norms for sexual behavior and child rearing always exist, but methods for meeting the needs of the community to regulate sexual behavior and family life are infinitely varied. In other words, some form of the family is found in virtually all societies, although its importance as a separate unit within a larger network of relatives, kin and other significant associates varies greatly all the way from a central and dominating place to a minimal one.

The functions of the modern middle-class family have been so truncated that most of the significant educational, religious, political, health and welfare responsibilities have been taken over by other institutions. The prime function of the family under this contract is to provide emotional and affectual relations. Motz paints a picture of how the middle-class family conforms to society's rules and expectations through the dramaturgical analogy in "The Family as a Company of Players." She emphasizes the cost of the support such arrangements entail.

In "The Family as Cradle of Violence," Steinmetz and Straus raise doubts about the biological linkage of sex and violence. The authors argue that there is widespread evidence of violent family behavior; in order to exercise social control, *most* families from all classes use some physical force. Violence is the result of a violent society—not a biological imperative.

Sociologists have long noted the fact that family functions have shifted. Some of the institutional arrangements of modern families are substantially different from those of their grandparents or even their parents. One such "new" arrangement is "swinging." The Palsons, in "Swinging in Wedlock," explore aspects of a new life-style and suggest a typology of swingers based on their own participant observational research. While it would be foolish to suggest that these arrangements constitute a "wave of the future," it is useful to view such phenomena as natural social science experiments and to consider the consequences of such life-styles for the participants. Swinging provides yet another model for family life.

1 *Annabelle B. Motz*

The Family as a Company of Players

All the world's a stage, and we are all players.

Erving Goffman in his *The Presentation of Self in Everyday Life* views our everyday world as having both front stage and back. Like professionals, we try to give a careful and superior performance out front. Back stage we unzip, take off our masks, complain of the strain, think back over the last act, and prepare anxiously for the next.

Sometimes the "on stage" performances are solos; sometimes we act in teams or groups. The roles may be carefully planned, rehearsed, and executed; or they may be spontaneous or improvised. The presentation can be a hit; or it can flop badly.

Picture a theater starring the family. The "stars" are the husband, wife, and children. But the cast includes a wide range of persons in the community—fellow workers, friends, neighbors, delivery-men, shopkeepers, doctors, and everyone who passes by. Usually husband and wife are the leads; and the appeal, impact, and significance of their performances vary with the amount of time on stage, the times of day and week, the circumstances of each presentation, and the moods of the audience.

Backstage for the family members is generally to be found in their homes, as suggested by the expression, "a man's home is his castle." The front stage is where they act out their dramatic parts in schools, stores, places of employment, on the street, in the homes of other persons; or, as when entertaining guests, back in their own homes.

My aim is to analyze the performances of family members before the community audience—their *front stage* appearances. This behavior conforms to the rules and regulations that society places upon its members; perhaps the analysis of the family life drama will provide insights into the bases of the problems for which an increasing number of middle-class persons are seeking professional help.

Many years ago, Thorstein Veblen noted that although industrialization made it possible for the American worker to live better than at any previous time in history, it made him feel so insignificant that he sought ways to call attention to himself. In *The Theory of the Leisure Class,* Veblen showed that all strata of society practiced "conspicuous consumption"—the ability to use one's income for non-essential goods and services in ways readily visible to others. A man's abilities were equated with his monetary worth and the obvious command he had in the market place to purchase commodities beyond bare necessities. Thus, a family that lives more comfortably than most must be a "success."

While conspicuous consumption was becoming an essential element of front stage performance, the ideal of the American as a completely rational person—governed and governing by reason rather than emotion—was being projected around the world. The writings of the first four decades of this century stress over and over again the importance of the individual and individual opinion. (The growth of unionism, the Social Security program, public opinion polling, and federal aid to education are a few examples of the trend toward positive valuation of each human being—not to mention the impact of Freud and Dewey and their stress on individual worth.) The desirability of rule by majority and democratic debate and voting as the best means of reaching group decisions—all these glorified rationality.

As population, cities, and industry grew, so also did anonymity and complexity; and rationality in organizations (more properly known as bureaucratization) had to keep pace. The individual was exposed to more and more people he knew less and less. The face to face relationships of small towns and workshops declined. Job requirements, duties and loyalties, hiring and firing, had to "go by the book." Max Weber has described the bureaucratic organization: each job is explicitly defined, the rights of entry and exit from the organization can be found in the industry's manual, and the rights and duties of the worker and of the organization toward the worker are rationally defined; above all, the worker acts as a rational being on the job—he is never subject to emotional urges.

With the beams and bricks of "front" and rationality the middle-class theater is built; with matching props the stage is set.

There are two basic scenes. One revolves about family and close personal relationships. It takes place in a well-furnished house—very comfortable, very stylish, but not "vulgar." The actors are calm, controlled, reasonable.

The other scene typically takes place in a bureaucratic anteroom cluttered with physical props and with people treated like physical props. The actors do not want the audience to believe that they *are* props—so they attract attention to themselves and dramatize their individuality and worth by spending and buying far more than they need.

What does this mean in the daily life of the family stars?

Take first the leading lady, wife, and mother. She follows Veblen and dramatizes her husband's success by impressing any chance onlookers with her efficient house management. How does one run a house efficiently? All must be reasoned order. The wife-housekeeper plans what has to be done and does it simply and quickly. Kitchen, closets, and laundry display department store wares as attractively as the stores themselves. The house is always presentable, and so is she. Despite her obviously great labors, she does not seem to get flustered, over-fatigued, or too emotional. (What would her neighbors or even a passing door-to-door salesman think if they heard her screaming at the children?) With minimal household help she must appear the gracious hostess, fresh and serene—behind her a dirty kitchen magically cleaned, a meal effortlessly prepared, and husband and children well behaved and helpful.

Outside the home, too, she is composed and rational. She does not show resentment toward Johnny's teacher, who may irritate her or give Johnny poor marks. She does not yawn during interminable and dull PTA programs (what would they think of her and her family?). At citizen meetings she is the embodiment of civic-minded, responsible, property-ownership (even if the mortgage company actually owns the property). Her supermarket cart reflects her taste, affluence, efficiency, and concern. At church she exhibits no unchurchly feelings. She prays that her actions and facial expression will not give away the fact that her mind has wandered from the sermon; she hopes that as she greets people, whether interested in them or not, she will be able to say the "right" thing. Her clothes and car are extremely important props—the right make, style, finish; and they project her front stage character, giving the kind of impression she thinks she and the other members of the family want her to give.

Enter Father Center Stage

The male lead is husband, father, and man-of-affairs. He acts in ways that, he hopes, will help his status, and that of his family. At all times he must seem to be in relaxed control of difficult situations. This often takes some doing. For instance, he must be both unequal and equal to associates; that is, he is of course a good fellow and very democratic, but the way he greets and handles his superiors at work is distinctly, if subtly, different from the way he speaks to and handles inferiors. A superior who arrives unexpectedly must find him dynamically at work, worth every cent and more of his income; an inferior must also find him busy, demonstrating how worthy he is of superior status and respect. He must always be in control. Even when supposedly relaxing, swapping dirty jokes with his colleagues, he must be careful to avoid any that offend their biases. He has to get along; bigots, too, may be able to do him good or harm.

Sometimes he cannot give his real feelings release until he gets behind the wheel—and the savage jockeying which takes place during evening rush may reflect this simultaneous discharge by many drivers.

The scene shifts back to the home. The other stars greet him—enter loving wife and children. He may not yet be ready or able to re-establish complete emotional control—after all, a man's home is his backstage—and the interplay of the sub-plots begins. If his wife goes on with her role, she will be the dutiful spouse, listening sympathetically, keeping the children and her temper quiet. If she should want to cut loose at the same time, collision will probably still be avoided because both have been trained to restrain themselves and present the right front as parents to their children—if not to each other.

Leisure is not rest. At home father acts out his community role of responsible family head. The back yard is kept up as a "private" garden; the garage as a showroom for tools on display. He must exhibit interest—but not too much enthusiasm—in a number of activities, some ostensibly recreational, retaining a nice balance between appearing a dutiful husband and a henpecked one. Reason must rule emotion.

The children of old vaudevillians literally were born and reared in the theater—were nursed between acts by mothers in spangles, trained as toddlers to respond to footlights as other children might to sunlight. The young in the middle-class family drama also learn to recognize cues and to perform.

Since "front" determines the direction and content of the drama, they are supposed to be little ladies and gentlemen. Proper performances from such tyros require much backstage rehearsal. Unfortunately, the middle-class backstage is progressively disappearing, and so the children too must be prepared to respond appropriately to the unexpected—whether an unwanted salesman at the door who must be discreetly lied to about mother's whereabouts or a wanted friend who must not be offended. They are taught rationality and democracy in family councils—where they are also taught what behavior is expected of them. Reason is rife; even when they get out of hand the parents "reason" with them. As Dorothy Barclay says when discussing household chores and the child, "Appealing to a sense of family loyalty and pride in maturity is the tack most parents take first in trying to overcome youngsters' objections (to household chores). Offering rewards come second, arguing and insisting third."

"Grown-up" and "good" children do family chores. They want the house to look "nice"; they don't tell family secrets when visitors are present, and even rush to close closet and bedroom doors when the doorbell rings unexpectedly.

The child, of course, carries the family play into school, describing it in "show and tell" performances and in his deportment and dress. Part of the role of responsible parenthood includes participation in PTA and teacher conferences, with the child an important player, even if offstage.

To the child, in fact, much of the main dynamic of the play takes place in the dim realm of offstage (not always the same as backstage)—his parents' sex activities, their real income and financial problems, and many other things, some of them strange and frightening, that "children are not old enough to understand."

They early learn the fundamental lessons of front stage: be prepared; know your lines. Who knows whether the neighbors' windows are open? The parents who answers a crying child with, "Calm down now, let's sit down and talk this over," is rehearsing him in stage presence, and in his character as middle-class child and eventually middle-class adult.

Often the family acts as a team. The act may be rehearsed, but it must appear spontaneous. Watch them file in and out of church on Sunday mornings. Even after more than an hour of sitting, the children seem fresh and starched. They do not laugh or shout as on the playground. The parents seem calm, in complete control. Conversations and postures are confined to those appropriate for a place of worship.

Audience reaction is essential to a play. At church others may say, "What nice children you have!" or, "We look forward to seeing you next Sunday." Taken at face value, these are sounds of audience approval and applause; the performers may bask in them. Silence or equivocal remarks may imply disapproval and cause anxiety. What did they really mean? What did we do wrong? Sometimes reaction is delayed, and the family will be uncertain of their impression. In any case, future performances will be affected.

Acting a role, keeping up a front, letting the impressions and expectations of other people influence our behavior, does result in a great deal of good. Organized society is possible only when there is some conformity to roles and rules. Also a person concerned with the impression others have of him feels that he is significant to them and they to him. When he polishes his car because a dirty one would embarrass him, when his wife straightens her make-up before answering the door, both exhibit a sense of their importance and personal dignity in human affairs. Those who must, or want to, serve as models or exemplars must be especially careful of speech and performance—they are always on stage. When people keep up appearances they are identifying themselves with a group and its standards. They need it; presumably it needs them.

Moreover, acting what seems a narrow role may actually broaden experience and open doors. To tend a lawn, or join a PTA, social club, or art group—"to keep up appearances"—may result in real knowledge and understanding about horticulture, education, or civic responsibility.

For the community, front produces the positive assets of social cohesion. Well-kept lawns, homes, cars, clean children and adults have definite aesthetic, financial, and sanitary value. People relate to one another, develop common experiences. People who faithfully play their parts exhibit personal and civic responsibility. The rules make life predictable and safe, confine ad-libs within acceptable limits, control violence and emotional tangents, and allow the show to go on and the day's work to be done. Thus, the challenging game of maintaining front relates unique personalities to one another and unites them in activity and into a nation.

So much for the good which preoccupation with front and staging accomplishes; what of the bad?

First, the inhibition of the free play of emotion must lead to frustration. Human energies need outlets. If onstage acting does not allow for release of tension, then the escape should take place backstage. But what if there is virtually no backstage? Perhaps then the releases will be found in the case histories of psychiatrists and other counselors. Communication between husband and wife may break down because of the contrast between the onstage image each has of the other as a perfect mate and the unmasked actuality backstage. Perhaps when masks crumble and crack, when people can no longer stand the strain of the front, then what we call nervous breakdown occurs.

Growing Up with Bad Reviews

And how does the preoccupation with front affect the growth and development of the child? How can a child absorb and pattern himself after models which are essentially unreal? A mother may "control" her emotions when a child spills milk on her freshly scrubbed floor, and "reason" with him about it; she may still retain control when he leaves the refrigerator open after repeated warnings; but then some minor thing—such as loud laughter over the funnies—may suddenly blow off the lid, and she will "let him have it, but good!" What can he learn from such treatment? To respect his mother's hard work at keeping the house clean? To close the refrigerator door? Not to laugh loudly when reading the comics? That mother is a crab? Or, she's always got it in for him? Whatever he has learned, it is doubtful it was what his mother wanted! Whatever it was it will probably not clarify his understanding of such family values as pride in work, reward for effort, consideration of other people, or how to meet problems. Too, since the family's status is vitally linked with the maintenance of fronts, any deviance by the child, unless promptly rectified, threatens family standing in the community. This places a tremendous burden on a child actor.

Moreover, a concentration on front rather than content must result in a leveling and deadening of values and feelings. If a man buys a particular hat primarily because of what others may think, then its intrinsic value as a hat—in fact, even his own judgment and feelings about it—become secondary. Whether the judgment of those whose approval he covets is good or bad is unimportant—just so they approve. Applause has taken the place of value.

A PTA lecture on "The Future of America" will call for the same attentive front from him as a scientist's speech on the "Effects of Nuclear Warfare on Human Survival." Reading a newspaper on a crowded bus, his expression undergoes little change whether he is reading about nuclear tests, advice to the lovelorn, or Elizabeth Taylor's marital problems. To his employer he presents essentially the same bland, non-argumentative, courteous front whether he has just been refused a much deserved pay raise or told to estimate the cost of light bulbs. He seems impartial, objective, rational—and by so doing he also seems to deny that there is any difference to him between the pay raise and the light bulbs, as well as to deny his feelings.

The Price of Admission

What price does the community pay for its role as audience?

The individual human talents and energies are alienated from assuming responsibility for the well-being and survival of the group. The exaggerated self-consciousness of individuals results in diluted and superficial concern with the community at a time when deep involvement, new visions, and real leadership are needed. Can the world afford to have over-zealous actors who work so hard on their lines that they forget what the play is all about?

It is probable that this picture will become more general in the near future and involve more and more people—assuming that the aging of the population continues, that the Cold War doesn't become hot and continues to need constant checks on loyalty and patriotism, that automation increases man's leisure at the same time as it keeps up or increases the production of consumer goods, and that improved advertising techniques make every home a miniature department store. The resulting conformity, loyalty, and patriotism may foster social solidarity. It may also cause alienation, immaturity, confusion, and much insecurity when new situations, for which old fronts are no longer appropriate, suddenly occur. Unless people start today to separate the important from the tinsel and to assume responsibility for community matters that are vital, individual actors will feel even more isolated; and the society may drift ever further from the philosophy that values every person.

Tomorrow's communities will need to provide new backstages, as the home, work place, and recreation center become more and more visible. Psychiatrists, counselors, confessors, and other professional listeners must provide outlets for actors who are exhausted and want to share their backstage thoughts. With increased leisure, business men will probably find it profitable to provide backstage settings in the form of resorts, rest homes, or retreats.

The state of the world is such today that unless the family and the community work together to evaluate and value the significant and direct their energies accordingly, the theater with its actors, front stage, backstage, and audience may end in farce and tragedy.

SUGGESTED READINGS

People in Places: The Sociology of the Familiar by Arnold Birenbaum and Edward Sagarin (New York: Praeger, 1973).

The Presentation of Self in Everyday Life by Erving Goffman (New York: Overlook Press, 1973, reprint of 1959 edition, Doubleday Anchor Book).

Society and Personality by Tamotsu Shibutani (Englewood Cliffs, N.J.: Prentice-Hall, 1961).

The Pursuit of Loneliness: American Culture at the Breaking Point by Philip Slater (Boston: Beacon Press, 1970).

by Danny Lyon

The Uptowners

"I have found in the most apathetic or lawless people enough unused energy and side-tracked morality to make of them different people, given different circumstances in their everyday lives. . . . The problems these people have is a psychological one only because it continues to be a social and political one."

ROBERT COLES

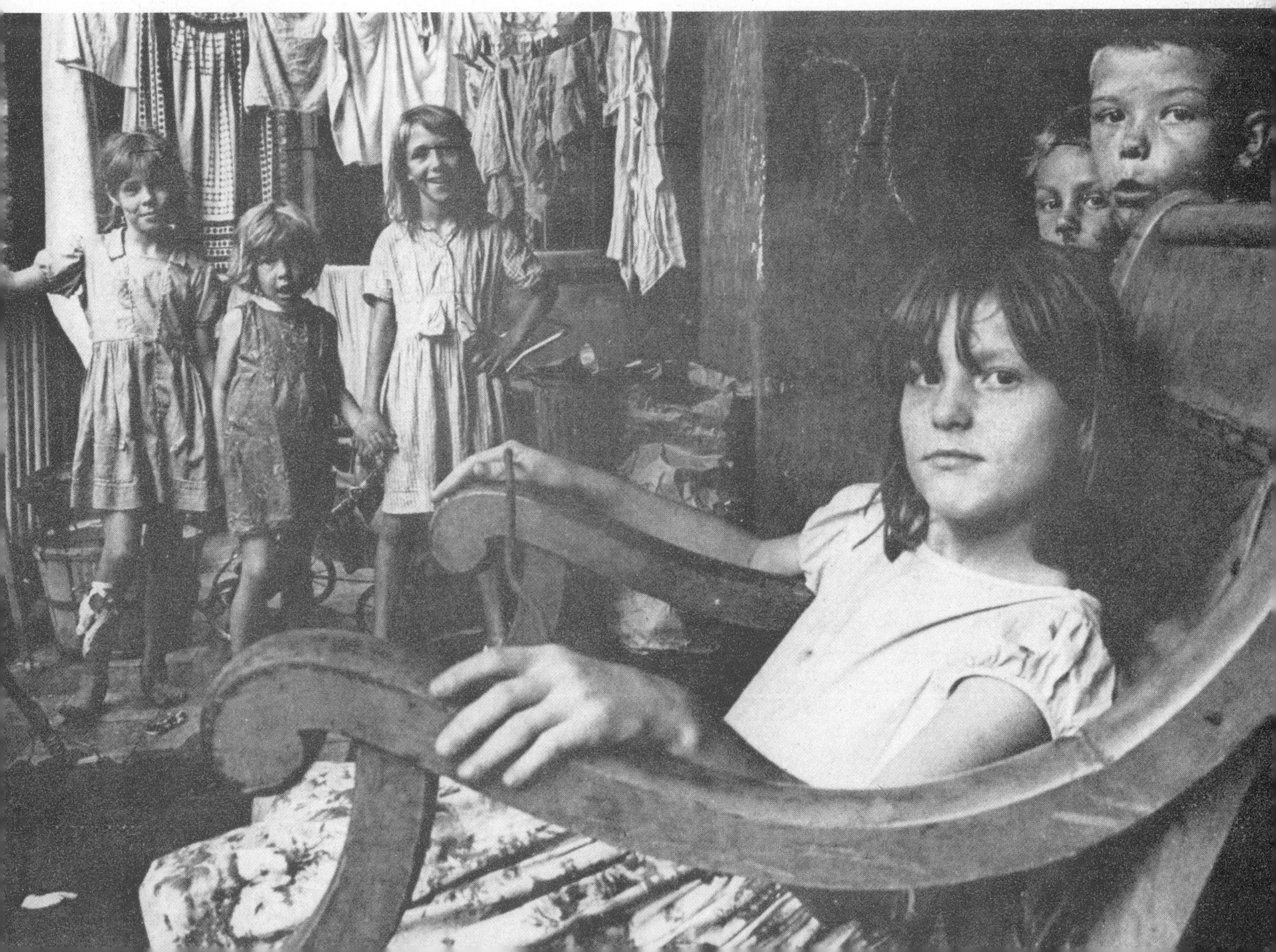

2 *Suzanne K. Steinmetz & Murray A. Straus*

The Family as Cradle of Violence

Lizzie Borden took an ax
And gave her father 40 whacks
When the job was neatly done
She gave her mother 41.

Although intrafamily violence like that attributed to Lizzie Borden is occasionally reported, such behavior is considered totally out of the ordinary—families are supposed to be oases of serenity where love and good feeling flow from each parent and child.

Unfortunately, that lovely picture is not accurate. In fact, the grizzly tale of Lizzie Borden may not be unique. Violence seems as typical of family relationships as love; and it would be hard to find a group or institution in American society in which violence is more of an everyday occurrence than it is within the family. Family members physically abuse each other far more often than do nonrelated individuals. Starting with slaps and going on to torture and murder, the family provides a prime setting for every degree of physical violence. So universal is the phenomenon that it is probable that some form of violence will occur in almost every family.

The most universal type of physical violence is corporal punishment by parents. Studies in England and the United States show that between 84 and 97 percent of all parents use physical punishment at some point in their child's life. Moreover, such use of physical force to maintain parental authority is not confined to early childhood. Data on students in three different regions of the United States show that half of the parents sampled either used or threatened their high school seniors with physical punishment.

Of course, physical punishment differs significantly from other violence. But it is violence, nonetheless. Despite its good intentions, it has some of the same consequences as other forms of violence. Research shows that parents who use physical punishment to control the aggressiveness of their children probably increase rather than decrease their child's aggressive tendencies. Violence begets violence, however peaceful and altruistic the motivation.

The violent tendencies thus reinforced may well be turned against the parents, as in the case of Lizzie Borden. Although most intrafamily violence is less bloody than that attributed to Lizzie, some family abuse does go as far as ax murder. Examination of relationships between murderer and victim proves that the largest single category of victim is that of family member or relative.

Homicide at Home

The magnitude of family violence became particularly obvious during the summer heat wave of 1972. Page 1 of the July 22, 1972 *New York Times* carried an article describing the increase in murders during the previous few days of extreme heat in New York City and summarizing the statistics for murder in New York during the previous six months. Page 2 held an article totalling deaths in Northern Ireland during three and a half years of disturbances. About as many people were murdered by their relatives in one six-month period in New York City as had been killed in three and a half years of political upheaval in Northern Ireland.

Murder, though relatively rare, gets far more attention than less violent abuse. Even though more murders are committed on family members than any other type of person, and even though the United States has a high degree of homicide, the rate is still only four or five per 100,000 population. What about non-lethal physical violence between husband and wife? While accurate statistics are hard to find, one way of estimating the magnitude of the phenomenon is through the eyes of the police.

Just as relatives are the largest single category of murder victim, so family fights are the largest single category of police calls. One legal researcher estimates that more police calls involve family conflict than do calls for all criminal incidents, including murders, rapes, nonfamily assaults, robberies and muggings. "Violence in the home" deserves at least as much public concern as "crime in the streets." The police hate and fear family conflict calls for several reasons. First, a family disturbance call lacks the glamour, prestige and public appreciation of a robbery or an accident summons. More important, such calls are extremely dangerous. Many a policeman coming to the aid of a wife who is being beaten has had a chair or a bottle thrown at him or has been stabbed or shot by a wife who suddenly becomes fearful of what is going to happen to her husband, or who abruptly turns her rage from her husband to the police. Twenty-two percent of all police fatalities come from investigating problems between husband and wife or parent and child.

One cannot tell from these data on police calls just what proportion of all husbands and wives have had physical fights, since it takes an unusual combination of events to have the police summoned. The closest published estimate is found in the research of George Levinger and John O'Brien. In studying applicants for divorce, O'Brien found that 17 percent of his cases spontaneously mentioned overt violent behavior, and Levinger found that 23 percent of the middle-class couples and 40 percent of the working-class couples gave "physical abuse" as a major complaint.

Both of these figures probably underestimate the amount of physical violence between husbands and wives because there may well have been violent incidents which were not mentioned or which were not listed as a main cause of divorce. Even doubling the figure, however, leaves us far from knowing the extent of husband-wife violence. First, there is a discrepancy between the O'Brien and the Levinger figures. Second, these figures apply only to couples who have applied for divorce. It may be that there is a lower incidence of physical violence among a cross-section of couples; or it may be, as we suspect, that the difference is not very great.

A survey conducted for the National Commission of the Causes and Prevention of Violence deals with what violence people would approve. These data show that one out of four men and one out of six women approve of slapping a wife under certain conditions. As for a wife slapping a husband, 26 percent of the men and 19 percent of the women approve. Of course, some people who approve of slapping will never do it and some who disapprove *will* slap—or worse. Probably the latter group is larger. If that is true, we know that husband-wife violence at the minimal level of slapping occurs in at least one quarter of American families.

Our own pilot studies also give some indication of the high rate of violence in the family. Richard Gelles of the University of New Hampshire, who has done a series of in-depth case studies of a sample of 80 families, found that about 56 percent of the couples have used physical force on each other at some time.

In a second study, freshman college students responded to a series of questions about conflicts which occurred in their senior year in high school, and to further questions about how these conflicts were handled. Included in the conflict resolution section were questions on whether or not the parties to the disputes had ever hit, pushed, shoved, thrown things or kicked each other in the course of a quarrel.

The results show that during that one year 62 percent of the high school seniors had used physical force on a brother or sister and 16 percent of their parents had used physical force on each other. Since these figures are for a single year, the percentage who had *ever* used violence is probably much greater. How much greater is difficult to estimate because we cannot simply accumulate the 16 percent for one year over the total number of years married. Some couples will never have used violence and others will have used it repeatedly. Nevertheless, it seems safe to assume that it will not always be the same 16 percent. So, it is probably best to fall back on the 56 percent estimate from the 80 earlier interviews.

Since a vast amount of family violence can be documented, what accounts for the myth of family nonviolence? At least one basis for the rosy, if false, view is that the family is a tremendously important social institution, which must be preserved. In Western countries one supportive device is the ideology of familial love and gentleness, an ideology which helps encourage people to marry and to stay married. It tends to maintain satisfaction with the family system despite the stresses and strains of family life. From the viewpoint of preserving the integrity of a critical social institution, such a mythology is highly useful.

Other simplifications and generalizations also block knowledge and understanding of the nature of violence in the family. The psychopathology myth, the class myth, the sex myth and the catharsis myth must be exposed and examined if the true nature of intrafamily abuse is to emerge.

A growing number of sociologists and psychologists have suggested that a focus on conflict and violence may be a more revealing way of understanding the family than a focus on consensus and solidarity. Most members of this group, however, recognize that family conflict is legitimate, but still consider physical violence only as an abnormality—something which involves sick families. The facts do not support this *psychopathology myth*. According to Richard J. Gelles, only a tiny proportion of those using violence—even child abusers—can be considered mentally ill. Our own studies reveal that physically abusive husbands, wives and children are of overwhelmingly sound mind and body.

The fact that almost all family violence, including everyday beating, slapping, kicking and throwing things, is carried out by normal everyday Americans rather than deranged persons should not lead us to think of violence as being desirable or even acceptable. The important question is, Why is physical violence so common between members of the closest and most intimate of all human groups?

Although social scientists are still far from a full understanding of the causes of violence between family members, evidence is accumulating that family violence is learned—and learned in childhood in the home. This fact does not deny the importance of the human biological heritage. If the capacity for violence were not present in the human organism, learning and social patterning could not produce it.

If a child actually observes and experiences the effects of violence, he will learn to be violent. Husbands, wives and parents play out models of behavior which they learned in childhood from *their* parents and from friends and relatives. Rather than being deviant, they are conforming to patterns learned in childhood. Of course, in most cases they also learned the opposite message—that family violence is wrong. However, a message learned by experience and observation, rather than the message learned Sunday-school-style, has more force, especially when social stresses become great—and family stresses are often very great. The high level of interaction and commitment which is part of the pleasure of family life also produces great tensions.

Another widespread but hard-to-prove belief is the *class myth*, the idea that intrafamily violence occurs mainly in lower- and working-class families. Studying divorce applicants, George Levinger found that 40 percent of the working-class wives and 23 percent of the middle-class wives indicated "physical abuse" as a reason for seeking divorce. If almost one out of four middle-class women can report physical abuse, violence hardly seems absent from middle-class families. The nationwide sample survey conducted for the United States Commission on Violence reveals that over one-fifth of the respondents approve of slapping a spouse under certain conditions. There were no social-class differences in this *approval* of slapping, nor in reports of having ever spanked a child. At the same time, almost twice as many less educated respondents spank *frequently* (42 percent) as more educated respondents (22 percent).

Class Differences

Other research on physical punishment is also contradictory. Most studies report more use of physical punishment by working-class parents, but some find no difference. Howard S. Erlanger undertook a comprehensive review of studies of social-class differences in the use of physical punishment and concluded that, although the weight of the evidence supports the view of less use of this technique among the middle class, the differences are small. Sizeable differences between social classes show up only when the analysis takes into account differences within social classes of such things as race, the sex of the child and of the parent, parental ambition for the child and the specific nature of the father's occupation. Differences *within* social classes are at least as important as differences *between* classes.

Despite the mixed evidence, and despite the fact that there is a great deal of violence in middle-class families, we believe that research will eventually show that intrafamily violence is more common as one goes down the socioeconomic status ladder. Many social scientists attribute this to a lower-class "culture of violence" which encourages violent acts, and to an opposite middle-class culture which condemns violence. Although these cultural elements are well documented, we see them not as a cause, but as a response to fundamental social structural forces which affect families at all social levels but press harder and more frequently on the lower and working classes.

Compensatory Violence

Willingness and ability to use physical violence may compensate for lack of other resources such as money, knowledge and respect. If the social system does not provide an individual with the resources needed to maintain his or her family position, that individual will use violence if he is capable of it. John E. O'Brien asserts that ". . . there is considerable evidence that . . . husbands who . . . displayed violent behavior were severely inadequate in work, earner, or family support roles." While lack of the occupational and economic resources needed to fulfill the position of husband in our society is more characteristic of lower-class families than others, it is by no means confined to that stratum. The 1970-72 recession, with its high rates of unemployment among middle-class occupational groups (such as aerospace engineers) provides an opportunity to test this theory. The *resource theory* of violence would predict that unemployed husbands would engage in more intrafamily violence than comparable middle-class husbands who have not lost their jobs.

Some indication that the predicted results might be found is suggested by statistics for Birmingham, England, which showed a sharp rise in wife-beating during a six-month period when unemployment also rose sharply. A 1971 *Parade* report characterized these men as "frustrated, bored, unable to find a satisfying outlet for their energy, Britishers who are reduced to life on the dole meet adversity like men: they blame it on their wives. Then, pow!!!"

In a society such as ours, in which aggression is defined as a normal response to frustration, we can expect that the more frustrating the familial and occupational roles, the greater the amount of violence. Donald McKinley found that the lower the degree of self-direction a man has in his work, the greater the degree of aggressiveness in his relationship with his son. McKinley's data also show that the lower the job satisfaction, the higher the percentage using harsh punishment of children. The same relationship was found within each social class.

Both husbands and wives suffer from frustration, but since the main avenue of achievement for women has been in the family rather than in occupational roles, we must look within the family for the circumstances that are frustrating to women. Both residential crowding and too many children have been found to be related to the use of physical punishment. As with men, frustrations of this type are more common in the lower class, since lower-class wives are unlikely to have sufficient equipment and money for efficient, convenient housekeeping.

Although intrafamily violence probably is more common among lower-class families, it is incorrect to see it as only a lower-class or working-class phenomenon. What we have called the class myth overlooks the basic structural conditions (such as lack of adequate resources and frustrating life experiences) which are major causes of intrafamily violence and are present at all social levels, though to varying degrees. Some kinds of intrafamily violence are typical of all social classes—such as hitting children—even though the rate may be lower for middle class—while other kinds of intrafamily violence are typical of ***neither*** class—like severe wife-beating—even though the rate is probably greater for the working class and especially the lower class.

The *sex myth* is the idea that sexual drives are linked to violence by basic biological mechanisms developed in the course of human evolution. Violence in sex is directly related to violence in the family because the family is the main way in which sex is made legitimate. To the extent that there is an inherent connection between sex and violence, it would be part of the biological basis for violence within the family.

There is abundant evidence that sex and violence go together, at least in our society and in a number of others. At the extreme, sex and warfare have been associated in many ways, ranging from societies which view sex before a battle as a source of strength (or in some tribes, as a weakness) to the almost universally high frequency of rape by soldiers, often accompanied by subsequent genital mutilation and murder. In the fighting following the independence of the Congo in the early 1960s, rape was so common that the Catholic church is said to have given a special dispensation so that nuns could take contraceptive pills. More recently, in the Pakistan civil war, rape and mutilation were everyday occurrences. In Vietnam, scattered reports suggest that rapes and sexual tortures have been widespread. Closer to home, we have the romantic view of the aggressive he-man who "takes his woman" as portrayed in westerns and James Bond-type novels. In both cases, sex and gunfights are liberally intertwined.

Sexual Repression

Then there are the sadists and masochists—individuals who can obtain sexual pleasure only by inflicting or receiving violent acts. We could dismiss such people as pathological exceptions, but it seems better to consider sadism and masochism as simply extreme forms of widespread behavior. The sex act itself typically is accompanied at least by mild violence and often by biting and scratching.

Nevertheless, despite all of this and much other evidence which could be cited, we feel that there is little biological linkage between sex and violence. It is true that in our society and in many other societies, sex and violence are linked. But there are enough instances of societies in which this is not the case to raise doubts about the biological linkage. What social conditions produce the association between violence and sex?

The most commonly offered explanation attributes the linkage between sex and violence to rules of the culture which limit or prevent sex. Empirical evidence supporting this sexual repression theory is difficult to establish. Societies which are high in restriction of extramarital intercourse are also societies which tend to be violent—particularly in emphasizing military glory, killing, torture and mutilation of an enemy. But just how this carries over to violence in the sex act is not clear. Our interpretation hinges on the fact that sexual restriction tends to be associated with a definition of sex as intrinsically evil. This combination sets in motion two powerful forces making sex violent in societies having such a sexual code. First, since sex is normally prohibited or restricted, engaging in sexual intercourse may imply license to disregard other normally prohibited or restricted aspects of interpersonal relations. Consequently, aggressively inclined persons will tend to express their aggressiveness when they express their sexuality. Second, since sex is defined as evil and base, this cultural definition of sex may create a label or an expectancy which tends to be acted out.

By contrast, in societies such as Mangaia, which impose minimal sex restrictions and in which sex is defined as something to be enjoyed by all from the time they are first capable until death, sex is nonviolent. In Mangaia, exactly the opposite of the two violence-producing mechanisms just listed seem to operate. First, since sex is a normal everyday activity, the normal standards for control of aggression apply. Second, since sex is defined as an act expressing the best in man, it is an occasion for altruistic behavior. Thus, Donald S. Marshall says of the Mangaia: "My several informants generally agreed that the really important thing in sexual intercourse—for the married man or for his unwed fellow—was to give pleasure to his partner; that her pleasure in orgasm was what gave the male partner a special thrill, separate from his own orgasm."

Socially patterned antagonism between men and women is at the heart of a related theory which can also account for the association of sex and violence. The sex antagonism and segregation theory suggests that the higher the level of antagonism between men and women, the greater the tendency to use violence in sexual acts. Since, by itself, this statement is open to a charge of circular reasoning, the theory must be backed up by related propositions which account for the sex role antagonism.

In societies such as ours, part of the explanation for antagonism between the sexes is probably traceable to the sexual restrictions and sexual denigration mentioned above. The curse God placed on all women when Eve sinned is the earliest example in our culture of the sexually restrictive ethic, the placing of the "blame" for sex on women, and the resulting negative definition of women—all of which tend to make women culturally legitimate objects of antagonism and aggression. The New Testament reveals much more antipathy to sex than the Old and contains many derogatory (and implicitly hostile) statements about women.

The present level of antagonism between the sexes is probably at least as great as that in biblical times. In novels, biographies and everyday speech, words indicating femaleness, especially in its sexual aspect (such as "bitch"), are used by men as terms of disparagement, and terms for sexual intercourse, such as "screw" and "fuck," are used to indicate an aggressive or harmful act. On the female side, women tend to see men as exploiters and to teach their daughters that men are out to take advantage of them.

It would be a colossal example of ethnocentrism, however, to attribute antagonism between the sexes to the Western Judeo-Christian tradition. Cultural definitions of women as evil are found in many societies. Obviously, more fundamental processes are at work, of which the Christian tradition is only one manifestation.

Catharsis Myth

A clue to a possibly universal process giving rise to antagonism between the sexes may be found in the cross-cultural studies which trace this hostility back to the division of labor between the sexes and other differences in the roles of men and women. This sex role segregation, gives rise to differences in child-rearing practices for boys and girls and to problems in establishing sexual identity. Beatrice Whiting, for example, concludes: "It would seem as if there were a never-ending circle. The separation of the sexes leads to a conflict of identity in the boy children, to unconscious fear of being feminine, which leads to protest masculinity, exaggeration of the differences between men and women, antagonism against and fear of women, male solidarity, and hence back to isolation of women and very young children." This process can also be observed in the matrifocal family of the urban slum and the Caribbean, the relationships between the sexes have been labeled by Jackson Toby as "compulsive masculinity" and vividly depicted in Eldridge Cleaver's "Allegory of the Black Eunuchs." Slightly more genteel forms of the same sexual antagonism are to be found among middle-class men, as illustrated by the character of Jonathan in the movie *Carnal Knowledge*.

Obviously, the linkages between sex and violence are extremely complex, and many other factors probably operate besides the degree of restrictiveness, the cultural definition of sexuality and antagonism between the sexes. But even these indicate sufficiently that it is incorrect to assume a direct connection between sexual drives and violence, since such an assumption disregards the sociocultural framework within which sexual relations take place. These social and cultural factors, rather than sex drives *per se*, give rise to the violent aspects of sexuality in so many societies.

The *catharsis myth* asserts that the expression of "normal" aggression between family members should not be bottled up: if normal aggression is allowed to be expressed, tension is released, and the likelihood of severe violence is therefore reduced. This view has a long and distinguished intellectual history. Aristotle used the term "catharsis" to refer to the purging of the passions or sufferings of spectators through vicarious participation in the suffering of a tragic hero. Both Freud's idea of "the liberation of affect" to enable reexperiencing blocked or inhibited emotions, and the view of John Dollard and his associates that "the occurrence of any act of aggression is assumed to reduce the instigation of aggression" are modern versions of this tradition.

Applying this approach to the family, Bettelheim urges that children should learn about violence in order to learn how to handle it. Under the present rules (at least for the middle class), we forbid a child to hit, yell or swear at us or his playmates. The child must also refrain from destroying property or even his own toys. In teaching this type of self-control, however, Bruno Bettelheim holds that we have denied the child outlets for the instinct of human violence and have failed to teach him how to deal with his violent feelings.

Proof of the catharsis theory is overwhelmingly negative. Exposure to vicariously experienced violence has been shown to increase rather than decrease both aggressive fantasy and aggressive acts. Similarly, experiments in which children are given the opportunity to express violence and aggression show that they express more aggression after the purported cathartic experience than do controls.

Theoretical arguments against the catharsis view are equally cogent. The instinct theory assumptions which underlie the idea of catharsis have long been discarded in social science. Modern social psychological theories—including social learning theory, symbolic interaction theory and labeling theory—all predict the opposite of the catharsis theory: the more frequently an act is performed, the greater the likelihood that it will become a standard part of the behavior repertory of the individual and of the expectations of others for that individual.

Cultural Beliefs

In light of largely negative evidence and cogent theoretical criticism, the sheer persistence of the catharsis theory becomes an interesting phenomenon. There seem to be several factors underlying the persistence of the catharsis myth:

□ *Prestige and influence of psychoanalytic theory.* Albert Bandura and Richard Walters suggest that the persistence of the catharsis view is partly the result of the extent to which psychoanalytic ideas have become part of both social science and popular culture. Granting this, one must also ask why this particular part of Freud's vast writing is unquestioned. After all, much of what Freud wrote has been ignored, and other parts have been dropped on the basis of contrary evidence.

Whenever an element of cultural belief persists in spite of seemingly sound reasons for discarding it, one should look for ways in which the belief may be woven into a system of social behavior. Certain behavior may be least partially congruent with the "false" belief; various social patterns may be justified by such beliefs.

□ *Justification of existing patterns.* Intrafamily violence is a recurring feature of our society, despite the cultural commitment to nonviolence. It is not far-fetched to assume that, under the circumstances, the catharsis theory which in effect justifies sporadic violence will be attractive to a population engaged in occasional violence.

□ *Congruence with the positive value of violence in non-family spheres of life.* Although *familial* norms deprecate or forbid intrafamily violence, the larger value system of American society is hardly nonviolent. In fact, the overwhelming proportion of American parents consider it part of their role to train sons to be tough. The violence commission survey reveals that 70 percent of the respondents believed it is good for boys to have a few fist-fights. Thus, a social theory which justifies violence as being psychologically beneficial to the aggressor is likely to be well received.

□ *Congruence with the way familial violence often occurs.* Given the antiviolence norms, intrafamily physical abuse typically occurs as a climax to a repressed conflict. As Louis Coser points out:

> Closely knit groups in which there exists a high frequency of interaction and high personality involvement of the members have a tendency to suppress conflict. While they provide frequent occasions for hostility (since both sentiments of love and hatred are intensified through frequency of interaction), the acting out of such feelings is sensed as a danger to such intimate relationships, and hence there is a tendency to suppress rather than to allow expression of hostile feelings. In close-knit groups, feelings of hostility tend, therefore, to accumulate and hence to intensify.

At some point the repressed conflict has to be resolved. Frequently, the mechanism which forces the conflict into the open is a violent outburst. This is one of the social functions of violence listed by Coser. In this sense, intrafamily violence does have a cathartic effect. But the catharsis which takes place comes from getting the conflict into the open and resolving it—not the releasing effects of violent incidents *per se*, but on the ability to recognize these as warning signals and to deal with the underlying conflict honestly and with empathy.

□ *Confusion of immediate with long-term effects.* There can be little doubt that a sequence of violent activity is often followed by a sharp reduction of tension, an emotional release and even a feeling of quiescence. To the extent that tension release *is* produced by violence, this immediate cathartic effect is likely to powerfully reinforce the violence which preceded it. Having reduced tension in one instance, it becomes a mode of behavior likely to be repeated later in similar instances. An analogy with sexual orgasm seems plausible. Following orgasm, there is typically a sharp reduction in sexual drive, most obvious in the male's loss of erection. At the same time, however, the experience of orgasm is powerfully reinforcing and has the long-term effect of increasing the sex drive. We believe that violence and sex are similar in this respect. The short-term effect of violence is, in one sense, cathartic; but the long-term effect is a powerful force toward including violence as a standard mode of social interaction.

While the assumptions outlined in this article in some ways contribute to preserving the institution of family, they also keep us from taking a hard and realistic look at the family and taking steps to change it in ways which might correct the underlying problems. Such stereotypes contain a kernel of truth but are dangerous oversimplifications. Although there are differences between social classes in intrafamily violence, the class myth ignores the high level of family violence present in other social strata. The sex myth, although based on historically accurate observation of the link between sex and violence, tends to assume that this link is biologically determined and fails to take into account the social and cultural factors which associate sex and violence in many societies. The catharsis myth seems to have the smallest kernel of truth at its core, and its persistence, in the face of devastating evidence to the contrary, may be due to the subtle justification it gives to the violent nature of American society and to the fact that violent episodes in a family can have the positive function of forcing a repressed conflict into the open for nonviolent resolution.

SUGGESTED READINGS

The Intimate Enemy by George R. Bach and Peter Wyden (New York: William Morrow, 1969).

Aggression: A Social Learning Analysis by Albert Bandura (Englewood Cliffs, N.J.: Prentice-Hall, 1973).

"Some Social Functions of Violence" by Lewis A. Coser in *Annals of the American Academy of Political and Social Science*, March 1966.

Learning of Aggression in Children by Leonard D. Eron, Leopold O. Walder, and Monroe M. Lefkowitz (Boston: Little, Brown, 1971).

"Force and Violence within the Family" by William J. Goode and "Violence in Divorce-Prone Families: the Relationship between Conflict and Satisfaction" in *Journal of Marriage and the Family*, November 1971.

Violence in the Family, edited by Suzanne K. Steinmetz and Murray A. Straus (New York: Dodd, Mead, 1973).

3 *Charles Palson & Rebecca Palson*

Swinging in Wedlock

Since the later 1960s, an increasing number of middle-class couples have turned to mate swapping or "swinging" as an alternative to strictly monogamous marriage. That is, married couples (or unmarried couples with an apparently stable relationship) willingly and knowingly relinquish sexual rights to their own mates so that others may temporarily enjoy these rights. This phenomenon, which is fairly recent in its openness and proportions, provides an opportunity of testing, on a large scale, the traditional theories about the consequences of extramarital sexual activity. It has often been assumed that sexual infidelity, where all the concerned parties know of it, results to some degree in jealousy. The intensity of jealousy is thought to increase in proportion to the amount of real or imagined emotional involvement on the part of the unfaithful member of the couple. Conversely, the more "purely physical" the infidelity, the less likely that there will be any jealousy. Thus it is often hypothesized that where marital stability coexists with infidelity, the character of the extramarital involvement is relatively depersonalized.

In the film *Bob and Carol and Ted and Alice,* Bob finds Carol, his wife, entertaining another man in their bedroom. Although he had previously told her that he was having an affair, and they had agreed in principle that she too could have affairs, he is obviously shaken by the reality. Nervously trying to reassure himself, he asks, "Well, it's just *sex,* isn't it? I mean, you don't *love* him?" In other words, Bob attempts to avoid feelings of jealousy by believing that Carol's affair involves only depersonalized sex in contrast to their own relationship of love.

In his book, *Group Sex,* Gilbert Bartell offers the same hypothesis about those people he calls "organization swingers:"

> They are terrified of the idea that involvement might take place. They take comfort from the fact that if they swing with a couple only once or at most twice, the chances of running into a marriage-threatening involvement are small.

These swingers, who can be described as organizational only in the sense that they tend to use swinger magazines or special swinging nightclubs to make their contacts, are mostly beginners who *may* act in ways that approximate Bartell's description. Near the end of the book, however, he mentions some couples he interviewed whom he calls dropouts. These people either had never desired depersonalized swinging or had passed through a depersonalized stage but now preferred some degree of emotional involvement and long-term friendship from their swinging relationships. Bartell does not explain how these couples continue to keep stable relationships and can remain free of jealousy, but the fact that such couples exist indicates that depersonalization is not the only way to jealousy-free swinging.

Our involvement with the subject has been partly a personal one, and this requires some introductory explanation. In September 1969, we read an article about swinging and became fascinated by the questions it raised about sex and the American family. Did this practice signal the beginning of the breakup of the family? Or was it a way to inject new life into marriage as the authors of the article suggested? How do people go about swinging and why? We contemplated these and many other questions but, not knowing any swingers, we could arrive at only very limited answers. It seemed to us that the only way to find out what we wanted to know was to participate ourselves. In one way this seemed natural because anthropologists have traditionally lived with the people they have studied. But our curiosity about swinging at that time was more personal than professional, and we knew that ultimately our participation would have personal consequences, although we had no idea what their nature might be. We had to decide whether exploration of this particular unknown was worth the risk of changing the perfectly sound and gratifying relationship which we had built during the previous three-and-a-half years. Finally, our misgivings gave way to curiosity and we wrote off to some couples who advertised in a national swinger's magazine.

Although, like most beginners, we were excited about swinging, we were nervous too. We didn't know what swinging in reality was like or what "rules" there were, if any. In general, however, we found those first experiences not only enjoyable from a personal point of view, but stimulating intellectually. It was then that we decided to study swinging as anthropologists. But, like many anthropologists who use participant observation as a method of study, we could never completely divorce ourselves from the personal aspects of our subject.

The method of participant observation is sometimes criticized as being too subjective. In an area such as sex, where experiences are highly individual and personal, we feel that participant observation can yield results even more thorough and disciplined than the more so-called objective methods. Most of our important insights into the nature of swinging could only have been found by actually experiencing some of the same things that our informants did. Had we not participated, we would not have known how to question them about many central aspects of their experience.

This article presents the results of our 18-month, participant observation study of 136 swingers. We made our contacts in three ways. First, we reached couples through swinger magazines. These are magazines devoted almost exclusively to ads placed by swingers for the purpose of contacting other interested couples and/or singles. Many, although not all, of the couples we contacted in this way seemed to be beginners who had not yet found people with whom they were interested in forming long-term relationships. Second, we were introduced to couples through personal networks. Couples whom we knew would pass our name on to others, sometimes explicitly because they wanted our study to be a success. Third, some couples contacted us as a result of lectures or papers we presented, to volunteer themselves as informants. It should be noted that we did not investigate the swingers' bars, although second-hand reports from couples we met who had used them for making contacts seem to indicate that these couples did not significantly differ from those who do not use the bars. Our informants came from Pennsylvania, New Jersey, New York, Massachusetts, Louisiana, California, Florida and Illinois. They were mostly middle class, although ten could be classified as working class.

Usually we interviewed couples in very informal settings, and these interviews were often indistinguishable from ordinary conversation that swingers might have about themselves and their activities. After each session we would return home, discuss the conversation and write notes on our observations. Later several couples volunteered to tape interviews, enabling us to check the accuracy of the field notes we had taken previously.

In spite of our efforts to find informants from as many different sources as possible, we can in no way guarantee the representativeness of our sample. It should be emphasized that statistics are practically useless in the study of swingers because of insurmountable sampling problems. We therefore avoided the statistical approach and instead focused the investigation on problems of a nonstatistical nature. The information we obtained enabled us to understand and describe the kinds of cultural symbols—a "symbolic calculus," if you will—that swingers must use to effectively navigate social situations with other swingers. This symbolic calculus organizes widely varying experiences into a coherent whole, enabling swingers to understand and evaluate each social situation in which they find themselves. They can thereby define the choices available to them and the desirability of each. Our research goal, then, was to describe the symbols that infuse meaning into the experiences of all the swingers that we contacted.

Unlike Bartell, we had no difficulty finding couples who either wanted to have or had succeeded in having some degree of emotional involvement and long-term friendship within a swinging context. In fact, many of them explained to us that depersonalization simply brought them no satisfaction. In observing such couples with their friends it was evident that they had formed close and enduring relationships. They host each other's children on weekends, celebrate birthdays together, take vacations together and, in general, do what close friends usually do. It should be noted that there is no way of ascertaining the numbers of couples who have actually succeeded in finding close friends through swinging. In fact, they may be underrepresented because they tend to retreat into their own small circle of friends and dislike using swinger magazines to find other couples. Thus they are more difficult to contact.

In order to see how swingers are able to form such relationships it is necessary to understand not how they avoid jealousy, but how they deal with its causes. Insecurity and fear of being replaced are the major ingredients in any experience with jealousy. An effective defense against jealousy, then, would include a way to guarantee one's irreplaceability as a mate. If, for example, a wife knows that she is unlike any other woman her husband has ever met or ever will meet, and if they have a satisfying relationship in which they have invested much time and emotion, she can rest assured that no other relationship her husband has can threaten her. If, on the other hand, a woman feels that the continuance of her marital relationship depends on how well she cooks, cleans and makes love, jealousy is more likely to occur, because she realizes that any number of women could fill the same role, perhaps better than she.

Similarly, a man who feels that the continuance of his wife's loyalty depends on how well he provides financial security will be apt to feel more jealousy because many men could perform the same function. To one degree or another, many swingers naturally develop towards a more secure kind of marital relationship, a tendency we call *individuation.* Among the couples we contacted, individuation was achieved for the most part at a level that precluded jealousy. And we found that, to the extent that couples did not individuate, either jealousy occurred or swinging had to take other, less flexible forms in order to prevent it.

We found evidence of individuation in two areas. First, we found that patterns of behavior at gatherings of swingers who had passed the beginning stages were thoroughly pervaded by individuation. Second, we found that by following changes in a couple's attitudes toward themselves, both as individuals and as a couple and toward other swingers, a trend of increasing individuation could be observed.

Individuating Behavior at Gatherings

When we first entered the swinging scene, we hypothesized that swinging must be characterized by a set of implicit and explicit rules or patterns of behavior. But every time we thought we had discovered a pattern, another encounter quickly invalidated it. We finally had to conclude that any particular swinging gathering is characterized by any one of a number of forms, whatever best suits the individuals involved. The ideal, as in nonswinging situations, is for the initiation of sexual interaction to appear to develop naturally—preferably in a nonverbal way. But with four or more people involved and all the signaling and cross-signaling of intentions that must take place, this ideal can only be approached in most cases. The initiation may begin with little or no socializing, much socializing with sex later on as a natural outgrowth of the good feelings thus created, or some mixture in-between. Socializing is of the variety found at many types of nonswinging gatherings. The sexual interaction itself may be "open" where couples participate in the same room or "closet" where couples pair off in separate rooms. In open swinging, a "pretzel," "flesh pile" or "scene" may take place, all terms which signify groups of more than two people having sex with each other. Like Bartell, we found that females are much more likely to participate in homosexuality—probably near 100 percent—while very few men participate in homosexuality. Younger people tend to be much more accepting about the latter.

All of this flexibility can be summed up by saying that swingers consider an ideal gathering one in which everyone can express themselves as individuals *and* appreciate others for doing the same. If even one person fails to have an enjoyable experience in these terms, the gathering is that much less enjoyable for everyone.

An important consequence of this "do your own thing" ethic is that sexual experiences are talked about as a primarily personal matter. Conversely they are not evaluated according to a general standard. Thus one hears about "bad experiences" rather than "bad swingers." This is not to say that swingers are not aware of general sexual competence, but only that it is largely irrelevant to their appreciation of other people. As one informant said:

> Technique is not that much. If she's all right, I don't care if she's technically terrible—if I think she's a beautiful person, she can't be that bad.

Beginners may make certain mistakes if they do not individuate. They may, for example, take on the "social director" role. This kind of person insists that a party become the materialization of his own fantasies without regard for anyone else's wishes. This can make the situation very uncomfortable for everyone else unless someone can get him to stop. Or, a nervous beginner may feel compelled to look around to find out what to do and, as a result, will imitate someone else. This imitation can be disturbing to others for two reasons. First, the imitator may not be enjoying himself. Second, he may be competing with someone else by comparing the effects of the same activity on their different partners. In either case, he is not involved with perceiving and satisfying the individual needs of his own partner. This would also be true in the case of the person who regularly imitates his or her own previous behavior, making an unchanging formula for interaction, no matter who he is with. Swingers generally consider such behavior insensitive and/or insincere.

Modification of Attitudes

Beginners tend to approximate the popular stereotype of sex-starved deviates. A 50-year-old woman described one of her beginning experiences this way:

> It was one after another, and really, after a point it didn't make any difference *who* it was. It was just one great big prick after another. And I *never* experienced anything like that in my whole life. I have never had an experience like that with quite so many. I think in the course of three hours I must have had 11 or 12 men, and one greater than the next. It just kept on getting better every time. It snowballed.

The manner in which she describes her experience exemplifies the attitudes of both male and female beginners. They are not likely to develop a long lasting friendship with one or a small number of couples, and they focus much more on sex than the personalities involved. Frequently, they will be more interested in larger parties where individual personality differences are blurred by the number of people.

Simple curiosity seems to be the reason for this attitude. As one beginner told us, "Sometimes, we get titillated with them as people, knowing in the long run that it won't work out." It seems that because the beginner has been prevented so often from satisfying his curiosity through sexual liaisons in "straight" life, an important goal of early swinging is to satisfy this curiosity about people in general. This goal is apt to take precedence over any other for quite some time. Thus, even if a couple sincerely hopes to find long-lasting friendships, their desire to "move on" is apt to win out at first.

Bartell has asserted that both personality shallowness and jealousy are always responsible for this focus on sex and the search for new faces. For the most part, neither of these factors is necessarily responsible. First, the very same couples who appear shallow in fact may develop friendships later on. Second, as we shall see below, some couples who focus almost exclusively on sex nevertheless experience jealousy and must take certain precautions. On the other hand, some swingers *do* couple-hop because of jealousy. The Races, for example, dislike swinging with a couple more than once or twice because of the jealousy that arises each time. Very often only one member is jealous of the other's involvement but the jealousy will be hidden. Pride may prevent each from admitting jealousy for quite some time. Each partner may feel that to admit jealousy would be to admit a weakness and instead will feign disinterest in a particular couple to avoid another meeting.

This stage of swinging eventually stops in almost all cases we know of, probably because the superficial curiosity about people in general is satisfied. Women are usually responsible for the change, probably because they have been raised to reject superficial sexual relationships. Sometimes this is precipitated by a bad experience when, for example, a man is particularly rough or inconsiderate in some way. Sometimes a man will be the first to suggest a change because of erection problems which seem to be caused in some cases by a general lack of interest in superficial sexual contacts. In other words, once his general curiosity is satisfied, he can no longer sustain enough interest to be aroused.

The termination of the curiosity stage and the beginning of a stage of relative selectivity is characterized by increasing individuation of self and others. Among men this change manifests itself in the nature of fantasies that give interest to the sexual experience. The statement of one male informant exemplifies the change:

> Now, I don't fantasize much. There's too much reality to fantasize, too much sex and sex realities we've experienced. So there is not too much that I *can* fantasize with. I just remember the good times we've actually had.

Instead of fantasies being what one would wish to happen, they are instead a kind of reliving of pleasant past experiences with particular people. Also, some informants have noticed that where their previous fantasies had been impersonal, they eventually became tied to specific people with whom pleasant sexual experiences had been shared.

FIVE TYPES OF SWINGING COUPLES:
The Eversearches, the Closefriends, the Snares, the Races and the Successes

The following are composite case histories of five swinging couples. Although each case history is closely tied to one couple whom we knew fairly well, the case itself is more generalized to represent at least a few couples we have met. To check the accuracy of our perceptions of these different types of couples, we showed these case histories to five couples. All recognized other swinging couples whom they had also met.

Two problems present themselves here—the representativeness of the individual cases and the comprehensiveness of the five cases taken as a whole. In regard to the former, there is no way to know what proportion of swingers represent each case. In fact, to judge proportions from our sample might very well be misleading. This is because couples such as the Eversearches use swinging media and are therefore more visible and easier to contact, while couples like the Closefriends are very difficult to locate because they stay within their own circle of close friends. Hence, even though the Eversearches probably represent a higher proportion of our sample, this in no way tells us about the actual proportion of Eversearch types. In regard to the question of comprehensiveness, these case histories are only meant to intuitively represent the possible range of types. Many couples may better be seen as a mixture of types, and some types of couples may not be represented at all.

Jack and Jeanine Eversearch

Jack and Jeanine grew up in the same small town. They went to the same schools and the same church. In their sophomore year of high school they began to go steady. Just before she was to graduate, Jeanine, to her dismay, became pregnant, and her parents, experiencing a similar reaction, finally decided on abortion. They wanted her to go to college, enlarge her experiences, and perhaps find some other marriage prospect than the rather placid Jack.

At college, however, the two continued to see each other frequently. Jeanine occasionally went out with other men, but never felt as comfortable with them as she did with Jack. Jack never went out with anyone but Jeanine, mainly because his shyness prevented him from meeting other girls. It was predictable that the two would marry the June they graduated.

Five years and two children later, Jack and Jeanine were living much as they always had, in a new suburban home, close to their families. Life had become a routine of barbecues and bridge parties on weekends and children to get ready for school during the week, marked by occasional special events like a church social or a ride in the country. To all appearances, they seemed to have a model marriage.

But their marriage had actually changed, so gradually that the shift was almost imperceptible. Like most married couples, they had experienced a waning of sexual interest from time to time. But in their case, the troughs had lengthened until sex had become a perfunctory gesture, something they did just because they were married. As Jeanine said, "We didn't fight, because there was nothing to fight about. We just felt the inevitability of being together for the rest of our lives—something like brother and sister without the blood."

They had used the church before in a social way; they turned to it now for inspiration. Their congregation had recently acquired a new pastor, a sincere and intelligent man, whom almost everyone liked.

But the home situation continued to disintegrate. Jeanine, on her own there most of the day, found the situation intolerable and decided to seek help from the pastor:

> I knew something was wrong but it was too vague to talk about very clearly. I just kept stammering about how . . . things weren't what they used to be. But I couldn't say exactly why. In fact, I was so fuzzy that I was afraid he'd misunderstand me and that instead of advice I'd get a lecture about how God is the source of all meaning in life or something like that. So, when he started telling me about the problems that he and his wife had, I was quite surprised but also delighted.

They continued to meet as friends, and it became apparent that the pastor needed Jeanine for personal comfort and support as much as she needed him. This led to an affair, which lasted until Jack came home unexpectedly early from work one day three months later.

After the initial shock faded, Jack was left with a feeling of total inadequacy:

> I guess I thought that if Jeanine wanted to sleep with someone else, that meant I had disappointed her. I felt that my inability to rise in the company reflected on our marriage and on her choice of me as a husband—which didn't do my ego any good.

The episode proved fortunate, because it provided them with a reason to talk about their problems, and with the channels of communication open once more, their marriage began to seem fulfilling again. Their sexual interest in each other returned:

> We started doing things in bed that we'd always been curious about but had never bothered to try or had been too embarrassed to mention. There were many nights when we couldn't wait to get into bed.

About a year after Jeanine's affair ended, they started discussing the possibility of swinging. But when they thought of it seriously, they realized that not one other couple they knew would be willing partners. Jack had heard of swingers' magazines, gave the local smut peddler a try, and brought one home.

They examined the magazine for hours, wondering about the people who had placed the ads and looking at the pictures. Finally, caution gave way to curiosity, and they answered four of the more conservative ads. Within a few weeks they had received encouraging answers from all four.

Jack and Jeanine found their first swinging experience very pleasant. They felt nervous at first when they were greeted at the door by the other couple because they did not know what to expect. Nevertheless, they enjoyed themselves enough to agree to swing when it was suggested by their hosts. Having their fantasies and desires come true in the bedroom was intensely pleasurable to them both, and when they returned home they longed to share their elation with someone else, but could think of no one who would not be shocked. So they called the other couple back and told *them* what a good time they'd had.

Encouraged by this first happy experience, the Eversearches began to swing with practically every couple they could contact. Lately, they have become more selective, but they still devote some time to contacting and meeting new people.

Looking back, both feel that swinging has changed them. Before, Jack had always gone along with the men he knew, accepting, at least verbally, their values, attitudes and behavior:

> It bugs me now that I have to play some kind of he-man role all the time. I never used to notice it. You know how guys are always talking about this girl and how they would like to get her in bed? Well . . . I'm not interested in just sex anymore—I mean, I want to have someone I like, not just a writhing body.

Jeanine feels similarly:

> All of a sudden it seems I have more insight into everybody, into how they interact with each other. Maybe because we've met so many different kinds of people. And I have to be very careful that I don't express some of my liberal views. Sometimes, I really want to tell our nonswinging friends about our new life—but then I'm sure they wouldn't understand.

Mike and Maryann Closefriend

Mike and Maryann are 30 and 25 years old and have been married five years. They originally met when Mike, then an advanced graduate student, gave a lecture about inner-city family structure to a group of volunteer social workers. Maryann was in the audience and asked several penetrating questions. After the talk, she approached him to find out more. They were immediately attracted to each other and started going out frequently. After about six months they rented an apartment together, and when Mike got his Ph.D. in social science a year later, they married and moved to the East Coast, where he had obtained a teaching post.

Their early life together seemed an experience of endless enjoyment. They went camping on weekends, took pottery classes, and were lucky in meeting several people whose outlook on life was similar to theirs, with whom they developed close relationships. These friends have helped not only in practical things, such as moving or house painting, but in emotional crises. When, for example, Mike and Maryann seemed to be on the verge of breaking up about two years ago, their friends helped to smooth things over by acting as amateur psychologists.

The Closefriends don't remember exactly how they started swinging. Mike says it was "just a natural consequence of our friendship—our feeling for our friends." They remember some nudity at their parties before they swung, mostly unplanned. People took off their clothes because of the heat or just because they felt more comfortable that way. Sometimes they engaged in sexual play of various kinds, and this led to intercourse as a natural part of these occasions. Sometimes just two people felt like swinging, and sometimes everyone. If the former was the case, people could just watch, or if the couple wanted privacy, they went to another room. And sometimes no one felt like swinging, and the subject was never brought up.

For the Closefriends, swinging seems to be a natural outgrowth of the way they approached marriage and friendship, and the way they feel about and relate to people in general. As Maryann puts it:

> I guess it has to do with our basic belief in the totality of sharing and the kind of dialogue that we have with each other. Our no-holds-barred, no secrets kind of relationship produces such a lovely kind of glow that we just naturally like to share it with our friends. Our having close relationships with people is actually like having a second marriage. Not that we would all want to live together, although that might be possible some day. Some of the men, for example, couldn't live with me—we would be incompatible—but that doesn't make us any less desirable to each other.

Paul and Georgia Snare

When Paul met Georgia, he had been married about a year and was beginning to find his wife Serita both boring and demanding. A handsome young man, Paul had led an exciting life as a bachelor and found the daily routine of marriage very depressing:

> I felt awfully trapped. . . . It just got worse and worse until I couldn't see going home anymore. I bought a motorcycle and joined up with a bunch of guys pretty much like me. We'd ride around all night so we wouldn't have to go home to our old ladies.

Georgia was a salesgirl in the drugstore next door to the camera shop where Paul worked. He used to drop by daily for cigarettes and a chat, and they became friendly. Paul even made a few passes, but Georgia knew he already had a wife and refused his attentions. Unused to this kind of treatment, Paul took her refusals as a challenge and became quite serious in his efforts to persuade her to go out with him. Finally, when Paul and Serita got a formal separation, Georgia accepted his invitations, and they began to date steadily.

Georgia became pregnant about three months before Paul's divorce was due to come through, so they were married the week after the decree became final. At first things went well. Georgia stayed home and took care of the small house in the suburbs that Paul had bought for her, and the marriage ran smoothly for about six months, until the baby came. Then Paul began to feel trapped again, "going to work every day, coming home to dinner and going to bed. I didn't want it to happen again but it did."

Paul resorted to outside affairs, but found them unsatisfactory because they took too much time and money, and "it just wasn't worth all the lying." He suggested to Georgia the possibility of swinging with some friends of theirs, pointing out that he loved her but that "every man needs a bit of variety." Georgia initially thought the idea was crazy, but Paul persisted and finally persuaded her to try it.

Persuading their friends, however, was another matter. They didn't want to come right out and proposition them, so they decided on seduction as the method of persuasion. They would "date" a couple each weekend, and go dancing to provide an excuse for body contact. Paul would get increasingly intimate with the wife, and if the husband followed his example, Georgia would accept his advances.

They decided their first couple would be their old friends Bill and Jean. Everything went as planned for a while until Bill became suspicious and asked Paul to explain his attentions to Jean. When Paul did so, the couple became upset and left almost immediately.

Somewhat depressed by the loss of their friends, Paul and Georgia tried another couple they knew, but this time they enacted their plan more slowly. It took about six months, but it worked, and they continued to swing with the couple exclusively for about a year, until they discovered swinging magazines and began making new contacts through them.

Neither of the Snares have any problems with jealousy, and agree that this is because "we are so good in bed with each other that no one could really compete." From time to time Paul even brings home girls he has met;

Georgia doesn't get jealous "just so long as he introduces them to me first and they do their thing in my house." For her part, Georgia has discovered that she likes women too and regularly brings home girls from a nearby homosexual bar. "Men," she says, "are good for sex, but it isn't in their nature to be able to give the kind of affection a woman needs." Georgia's activities don't worry Paul a bit:

> A woman couldn't provide the kind of support I do. They just don't know how to get along in the world without a man. A lot of these lesbians she meets are really irresponsible and would never be able to take care of the kid.

Swinging has affected Georgia's self-confidence as well as changing her sex habits. She now feels much more confident in social situations, a change that occurred after she began making her own choices about whom she would swing with. At first, she had let Paul make all the decisions:

> If he liked the woman, then I would swing with the man. But it got so I couldn't stand it anymore. I had to make it with so many creeps! I just got sick of it after a while. Paul kept getting the good deals and I never found anybody I liked. Finally, I just had to insist on my rights!

Paul agrees that this is good and points out that one swinger they know constantly forces his wife to swing with men she has no desire for, and as a result their marriage is slowly disintegrating. He credits swinging with saving his own marriage with Georgia and thinks that, had he known about it before, it could have saved his first marriage too.

Frank and Helen Race

Frank and Helen met at a well-known West Coast university where both were top-ranked graduate students in biochemistry. Both were from Jewish backgrounds, strongly oriented toward academic achievement.

Frank, largely because of his parents' urging, had excelled in high school, both academically and in extracurricular activities. After high school, he enlisted in the marines, was commissioned after OCS training and commanded one of the best units on his base. Ultimately, he became dissatisfied with the life of a marine officer and left to attend college, where he finished his bachelor degree in three years, graduated with honors and went on to graduate school.

As a child, Helen had experienced much the same kind of pressure. Her father, an excellent musician, dominated the family and drove her endlessly. She began piano lessons at age four and remembers that he was always at her shoulder to scold her when she made a mistake. She was able to end music lessons only because she attended a college where no facilities were available, leaving her free to devote all her time to the study of biochemistry, which she much preferred.

Helen and Frank married during their third year of graduate school. It seemed a perfect match—two fine scholars with identical interests, who could work as a team. For the next four years they did work closely together on their respective Ph.D. dissertations, which were published and became well known in the field. Despite this success, however, they could not find jobs with prestige schools and had to take posts at a less well known institution.

They settled into their professional lives, both publishing as much as possible in the hope of eventually gaining positions at a more prestigious university. They worked together closely, constantly seeking each other's help and proffering severe criticisms. If either published more than the other during the year, the "underpublished" one would experience intense jealousy. Realizing this disruptive competition was a serious threat to their marriage, they sought help from a psychotherapist and from group therapy sessions.

The most important thing Frank and Helen learned about themselves in therapy was that by making their relationship competitive they had forfeited their appreciation of each other as individuals. They also discovered another element in their lives, which Frank links directly to their decision to take up swinging:

> I told Helen that I missed terribly the experiences that other men had as kids. I was always too busy with school to ever have a good time dating. I only had a date once in high school, for the senior prom, and I had only had one girl friend in college. I felt that a whole stage of my life was totally absent. I wanted to do those things that I had missed out on—then maybe I'd feel more able to cope with our problems. Much to my surprise, Helen felt she too had missed out.

Like the Eversearches, the Races met their first couple through an ad in a swinger publication. Their first meeting, however, was somewhat unpleasant. Frank felt jealous because he feared the man might be sexually better than he. He did not tell Helen this, however, but simply refused to return, on the grounds that he had not enjoyed the woman. Helen suspected Frank was in fact jealous, and many arguments ensued.

The Races have been swinging for about three years and average one contact every two or three months, a rate of frequency considerably lower than usual. Both agree that they have a lot of difficulty with jealousy. If, for example, they meet a couple and Helen is very attracted to the man, Frank will invariably insist he does not find the woman desirable. They have come to realize that the one who exercises the veto is probably jealous of the good time the other has had or is about to have and thus insists on breaking off the threatening relationship. They also realize that swinging may not be the best way to use their leisure time—but somehow they can't give up the hope that they may find the experiences they missed as young people.

Glen and Andrea Success

Glen and Andrea were married shortly before the end of the war, immediately after Glen graduated with a Ph.D. in biology. Because he felt that teaching at a university would be financially limiting, he found a job with a medical supply manufacturing company, which promised him a high-ranking executive position in the future. He has stayed with the company for nearly 20 years, rising to positions of increased responsibility.

Five years after he had begun work, Andrea and Glen were able to afford a luxurious suburban home. Well settled into their house and community, they started their family. Andrea enjoyed motherhood and raised her two boys and a girl as model children:

> There wasn't a thing we couldn't do. Glen and I traveled all over the States and Europe. We even went to Australia. We had bought ourselves a lovely house, we had a fine marriage and wonderful, healthy children. We had many fine friends too.

Glen claims it was this unusual good luck that eventually turned them to swinging. About seven years ago, they began to feel they had achieved everything that people usually want and anything else would be anticlimactic:

> We knew one couple with whom we

could talk about anything and everything, and we did! One conversation especially, I think, led to our considering swinging. We were talking about success and trying to define exactly what it meant. Andrea and I thought it was something like having all the money you need and a good marriage. They said that if that was true, then we already had everything we would ever want. . . . Later on, when I thought about what he'd said, I got a funny kind of hollow feeling. Forty-five, I said to myself, and at the end of the line.

In this state of mind Glen got the idea that swinging might be a way out. He and Andrea spent about a month discussing the possibility and finally decided to try it out. Their first meeting with another couple was disturbing for them both, but they continued to look for more satisfactory people. If the second meeting had been equally bad, they probably would have given up the whole idea. But it ended pleasantly in a friendship that lasted about three years.

At first they had to rely on contacts from the *National Enquirer,* but about a year after they started swinging their local newspaper began running ads on the lines of "Modern couple interested in meeting the same. Box 1023." About ten of these ads appeared during the brief period before the paper found out what they were for and ceased to accept any more. By then Glen and Andrea had contacted all the couples who had advertised. These people, in turn, knew other swingers whom they had either met through national publications or had initiated themselves. Soon a large network began to form.

Glen applied his organizational talents to the swinging scene and was soon arranging parties for couples he felt would be compatible, spending his own money to rent halls for get-togethers. Many couples started coming to him with their problems, and to help them out, he arranged for a doctor to direct group discussions dealing with typical swinging problems. He even contacted lawyers whom he knew personally to protect "his swingers," as he was beginning to call them, should they have any difficulties with the law. In fact, the Successes knew so many couples that other swingers began to rely on them as a kind of dating service that could arrange for either quiet evenings or major parties.

The Successes feel that in swinging they have finally found an activity which offers lasting interest and stimulation. Says Andrea:

Glen and I have done everything—I don't just mean sex. Just doing things doesn't really appeal to us anymore. But swinging has managed to hold our attention for a long time. If you give me a choice between going to South America, nightclubbing or swinging, I think swinging is the most satisfying and interesting.

Why? Glen says:

I think it's because in swinging you can see people for who they really are—as individuals, without the masks they have to wear most of the time. In a way, I guess I never knew people before, and I'm amazed at the variety. Maybe that's why swinging holds my interest—everybody is different, a challenge to get to know.

---

continued from page 187

Increasing individuation is also noticeable in beginners' changing perceptions of certain problems that arise in swinging situations. Many male swingers have difficulty with erections at one time or another. Initially, this can be quite ego shattering. The reason for this trauma is not difficult to understand. Most Americans believe that the mere sight of a nude, sexually available woman should arouse a man almost instantly. A male who fails to be aroused may interpret this as a sign of his hitherto unknown impotency. But if he is not too discouraged by this first experience he may eventually find the real reasons. He may realize that he does not find some women attractive mentally and/or physically even though they are sexually available. He learns to recognize when he is being deliberately though subtly discouraged by a woman. He may discover that he dislikes certain situational factors. For example, he may find that he likes only open or only closet swinging or that he cannot relax sufficiently to perform after a hard day's work. Once a swinger realizes that his physical responses may very well be due to elements that inhere to the individual relationship rather than to an innate sexual inadequacy, he has arrived at a very different conception of sexual relationships. He is better able to see women as human beings to whom he may be attracted as personalities rather than as objects to be exploited for their sexual potential. In our terms, he can now more successfully individuate his relationships with women.

Women must cope with problems of a slightly different nature when they begin to swing. Their difficulties develop mostly because of their tendency to place decorum above the expression of their own individual desires in social situations. This tendency manifests itself from the time the husband suggests swinging. Many women seem to swing merely because their husbands want to rather than because of their own positive feelings on the matter. This should not be interpreted to mean that wives participate against their will, but only that as in most recreational activity, the male provides the initial impetus that she can then choose to go along with or reject. Her lack of positive initiative may express itself in the quality of her interaction. She is apt to swing with a man not because he manifests particular attributes that she appreciates, but because he lacks any traits that she finds outright objectionable. One woman describes one of her first experiences this way:

As I recall, I did not find him particularly appealing, but he was nice, and that was OK. He actually embarrassed me a bit because he was so shy and such a kind of nonperson.

This is not to say that women do not enjoy their experiences once they begin participating. The same woman remarks about her first experience in this way:

Somehow, it was the situation that made the demand. I got turned on, although I hadn't anticipated a thing up to that point. In fact, I still have a hard time accounting for my excitement that first time and the good time which I did actually have.

In fact, it sometimes happens at this stage that women

become more enthusiastic about swinging than men, much to the latter's embarrassment.

Their enjoyment, however, seems to result from the same kind of psychology that is likely to propel them into swinging in the first place, the desire to please men. Hence, like her nonswinging counterparts, a woman in swinging will judge herself in terms of her desirability and her attractiveness to men much more than thinking about her own individuality in relation to others.

After swinging for awhile, however, her wish to be desired and to satisfy can no longer be as generalized because it becomes apparent that she is indeed desired by many men, and thus she has no need to prove it to herself. In order to make the experience meaningful, she arrives at a point where she feels that she must begin to actually refuse the advances of many men. This means that she must learn to define her own preferences more clearly and to learn to act on these preferences, an experience that many women rarely have because they have learned to rely on their husbands to make these kinds of decisions in social situations. In short, a woman learns to individuate both herself and others in the second stage of swinging.

Another change that swingers mention concerns their feelings towards their mates. They say that since they started swinging they communicate better than they did before. Such couples, who previously had a stable but uninteresting or stale marriage ("like brother and sister without the blood"), say that swinging has recreated the romantic feelings they once had for each other. These feelings seem to find concrete expression in an increasing satisfaction with the sexual aspects of the marital relationship, if not in an actual increase in sexual intercourse. This is almost always experienced by older couples in terms of feeling younger.

An explanation for this change, again, involves the individuation process. Marriage can grow stale if a couple loses a sense of appreciation of each other's individuality. A husband may look too much like an ordinary husband, a wife like an ordinary wife. This can happen easily especially when a couple's circumstances (job, children and so forth) necessitate a great deal of routinization of their life together. Such couples find in swinging the rare opportunity to escape from the routine roles that must be assumed in everyday life. In this setting individual differences receive attention and appreciation and, because of this, married couples can again see and appreciate their own distinct individuality, thus reactivating their romantic feelings for each other.

It is interesting to note that, those couples who do not answer in this way almost always experience jealousy, not romanticization, as a result of swinging. This is the case with one couple we interviewed, each of whom insists that the other is "better than anyone else," although it was clear by their jealousy of each other that neither was entirely confident of this.

Individuation, then, pervades the swinging scene and plays an important role in minimizing jealousy. But it alone cannot guarantee the control of jealousy—because there is always the possibility that a person will appreciate and be equally attracted to two unique individuals. Clearly, individuation must be complemented with something more if the marriage is to be effectively distinguished from other extramarital relationships.

This "something else" is compatibility. Two individuals who perceive and appreciate each other's individuality may nevertheless make poor living mates unless they are compatible. Compatibility is a kind of superindividuation. It requires not only the perception and appreciation of uniqueness, but the inclusion of this in the solutions to any problems that confront the relationship. Each partner must have the willingness and the ability to consider his or her mate's needs, desires and attitudes, when making the basic decisions that affect them both. This is viewed as something that people must work to achieve, as indicated by the phrase, "He failed in his marriage."

Unlike swinging, then, marriage requires a great deal of day-to-day giving and taking, and an emotional investment that increases with the years. Because such an investment is not given up easily, it provides another important safeguard against jealousy.

The dimension of marital compatibility often shows itself in swinging situations. If and when serious problems are encountered by one marriage partner, it is expected that the other partner will take primary responsibility for doing what is necessary. One couple, for example, was at a gathering, each sitting with their swinging partners. It was the first time they had ever tried pot, and the wife suddenly became hysterical. The man she was with quickly relinquished his place to her husband, who was expected to take primary responsibility for comforting his wife, although everyone was concerned about her. Another example can occur when a man has erection problems. If he is obviously miserable, it is considered wrong for his wife to ignore his condition, although we have heard of a few cases where this has happened. His wife may go to his side and they will decide to go home or she may simply act worried and less than completely enthusiastic, thus evincing some minimal concern for her husband. In other words, the married couple is still distinguished as the most compatible partners and remains therefore the primary problem-solving unit.

The importance of compatibility also shows up in certain situations where a couple decides that they must stop swinging. In several cases reported to us, couples who had been married two years or less found that swinging tended to disrupt their marital relationship. We ourselves encountered three couples who had been married for under one year and had not lived together before marriage. All three had difficulties as a result of swinging, and one is now divorced. These couples evidently had not had the time to build up the emotional investment so necessary to a compatible marriage.

It is clear, then, that to the degree that couples individuate and are compatible, jealousy presents no major problems. Conversely, when these conditions are not satisfied, disruptive jealousy can result.

There are, however, some interesting exceptions. For a few couples who seem to place little emphasis on individuation, marital compatibility is an issue which remains chronically unresolved. Compatibility for them is a quality to be constantly demonstrated rather than a fact of life to be more or less taken for granted. Hence, every give-and-take becomes an issue.

These couples focus on the mechanics of sexual competence rather than on personal relationships. These are the people who will talk about "good swingers" and "bad swingers" rather than good and bad experiences. One of these husbands once commented:

> Some people say there's no such thing as a good lay and a bad lay. But in my experience that just isn't true. I remember this one woman I went with for a long time. She was just a bad lay. No matter what I did, she was just lousy!

In other words, his bad lay is everyone's bad lay. One of his friends expressed it differently. He didn't understand why some swingers were so concerned with compatibility; he felt it was the sex that was important—and simply "having a good time."

Because they do not consider individuation important, these couples tend to approximate most closely the popular stereotypes of swingers as desiring only "pure sex." Swinging for these couples is primarily a matter of sexual interaction. Consequently, they are chiefly interested in seeing how sexually competent a couple is before they decide whether or not to develop a friendship. Competence may be defined in any or all of a number of ways. Endurance, size of penis, foreplay competence—all may be used to assess competence during the actual sexual interaction whether it be a large open party or a smaller gathering.

It is clear, then, that such couples perceive sex in a way that individuators find uncongenial or even repugnant. When we first observed and interviewed them, we interpreted their behavior as the beginning stage of promiscuity that new couples may go through. But when we asked, we would find that they had been swinging frequently for a period of two years, much too long to be considered inexperienced. How, we asked ourselves, could such couples avoid jealousy, if they regularly evaluated sexual partners against a common standard? It seemed to us that a husband or wife in such a situation could conceivably be replaced some day by a "better lay," especially if the issue of marital compatibility remained somewhat unresolved. Yet these couples did not appear to experience any disruptive jealousy as a result of swinging. We found that they are able to accomplish this by instituting special, somewhat less flexible arrangements for swinging. First, they are invariably exclusive open swingers. That is, sexual interaction must take place in the same room. This tends to reduce any emotional involvement in one interaction. They think that closet swinging (swinging in separate rooms) is "no better than cheating." They clearly worry about the possibility of emotional infidelity more than individuators. An insistence on open swinging reduces the possibility of emotional involvement, and with it, the reason for jealousy. Second, they try to control the swinging situation as much as possible. So, for example, they are much more likely to insist on being hosts. And they also desire to state their sexual preferences ahead of time, thereby insuring that nothing very spontaneous and unpredictable can happen. Third, the women are more likely to desire female homosexuality and more aggressively so. This often results in the women experiencing more emotional involvement with each other than with the men, which is more acceptable because it does not threaten the marital relationship.

Sexual Revolution?

We are now at the point where we can answer some of the questions with which we began our research. Contrary to many who have assumed that any extramarital activity results in at least some jealousy and possibly even marital breakup, especially when there is emotional involvement, we have found that swinging often succeeds in solidifying a marriage. It does this by reromanticizing marriage, thereby making it tolerable, even enjoyable to be married. In a very important way, then, swinging is a conservative institution.

It is usually assumed that the present "sexual revolution" of which swinging is a part will continue. Bartell, reflecting this view, points out that an increasing number of people are becoming interested in swinging. Basing his prediction on a projection of present trends, he believes that swinging will probably grow in popularity and become in some way a permanent part of American culture. A similar view is expressed by James and Lynne Smith. Although they do not believe that it will become a universal form in marriage, they believe that eventually as many as 15 to 25 percent of married couples will adopt swinging.

But predictions based on projection are inadequate because they do not consider the causal processes involved and therefore cannot account for future deviations. In other words, in order to predict increasing sexual freedom, one must first understand what caused it to appear in the first place.

Although we cannot at this time make rigorous scientific statements amenable to disciplined criticism, a glance at American history in this century reveals trends that suggest some tentative answers. Since the 1920s, greater sexual freedom has always been followed by periods of relatively greater sexual repression. The flappers of the 1920s were followed by the more conservative women of the 1930s, and the freer women of World War II were followed by an era where women flocked back to conservative roles in the home. And finally, of course, we have the counterculture which expresses an unprecedented height of sexual freedom in this century. An important factor present in all of these periods seems to be the economic ebb and flow. Economic depressions and recessions have preceded all years of more conservative sexual norms. And it is probably no accident that the present summit of sexual freedom has taken place in the longest run of prosperity this country has ever experienced. With increased economic independence, women have gained sexual privileges more nearly equal to those of men. Even homosexuality has become more acceptable. Further evidence that economic ebbs and flows may directly affect sexual norms can be seen by comparing class differences in sexual behavior. For example, working-class attitudes towards sex tend to be more conservative than those of the middle and upper classes. In general it would seem that as economic resources become more plentiful so do acceptable alternative norms of sexual behavior.

If this is so, given the present decline of economic prosperity, we should find the numbers of acceptable alternative norms shrinking. One of the more obvious indications of this is the back-to-Jesus trend which is attracting increasing numbers of young people who would have formerly been drawn to the rock-drug counterculture.

It is possible, then, that swinging and sexual freedom in general is a function of factors that are beyond the immediate control of individuals. Such factors as investment flows, limited resources, fluctuations in world markets and so forth, all events that seem isolated from the arena of intimacy which people carve out for themselves are in fact very much a part of their most personal relationships. These superstructural events are critical in that they regulate the resources at the disposal of groups of people, thereby limiting the alternatives available to any one individual in his social relations including his sexual relations.

Given economic prosperity as a necessary condition for increasing sexual freedom, it is quite possible that with the economic difficulties this country is now facing the number of available acceptable sexual alternatives will decline and swinging may all but disappear from the American scene.

Section VII

Schools

Anthropologist Ralph Linton has suggested that each succeeding generation of children is like an invading horde of barbarians who must be civilized. While it is a truism to say that the hope of the future rests with the children in any society, the socialization of children is a most important function in any society. The family is typically the most important agent of socialization. In modern industrial societies, however, the school is also vitally important in transmitting the folkways and mores of a culture to its young. Children spend increasingly large portions of their time in school, and the schools themselves act as social control agents on behalf of the larger society.

In "Children and their Caretakers," Denzin asserts that the schools represent the intersection of the moral, political and social orders in society. The schools become, says Denzin, an arena of competition for ideology and power where control is objectified and removed from the children themselves. The schools are moral, fate-controlling agencies where children are defined as objects to be shaped and molded as extensions of the adults who control the social order. He suggests that schools in the United States have two major functions: (1) to Americanize students and (2) to sort, filter and accredit social selves. In addition to other functions like caretaking and babysitting, the schools provide age–sex socialization and, in America, racial socialization. Denzin goes on to explore the implications of testing procedures and how these teach some children how to become failures.

The Silberbergs, in "Reading Rituals," develop a theme sounded by Denzin by examining the testing procedures used in assessing the impact of reading levels in schools. They point out an interesting statistical problem, namely, that 50 percent of all children tested must read at grade level or below. These children, in the words of the authors, are "up against the curve." Rampant credentialism means that children who are up against the curve need an advocate, someone who will recognize their strengths rather than their weaknesses. They suggest that we need to restructure the schools, not the children.

Schafer, Olexa and Polk develop further the implications of the fetish for testing in American schools in "Programmed for Social Class: Tracking in High School." They suggest that, with education as the key to mobility in America, children's class background has a strong effect on the tracking process, i.e., placing children in specialized curricula. Blue-collar whites and minorities end up most often in noncollege tracks, and this process is almost irreversible. The growth of the formal educational enterprise in the United States has been a result of several trends in the larger society: (1) a decline in the number of jobs relative to the total population, (2) more requirements placed on job applicants, and (3) less need for teen-age input into family income. With intelligence tied to previous academic performance, those who fall into a noncollege track in high school end up stigmatized and victims of a self-fulfilling prophesy—they turn out the way they do because of the predictions made about them through the tracking system.

The conventional wisdom about the school system suggests that it provides an avenue of mobility in American society. Bowles, in "Getting Nowhere: Programmed Class Stagnation," argues that it actually preserves inequality (class). His discussion, informed by a Marxist perspective, insists that programming is a result of the need in a capitalistic system for socialized workers and managers, and that it leads to a preservation of the class structure.

Each of the articles presented in this section so far has argued that such things as tracking, curricular programming and testing are mechanisms of social control. A good sociologist, the implication is, must keep the ancient Latin injunction *cui bono* (literally, "to whose benefit") in mind in looking at institutional arrangements. In "Drugging and Schooling," Witter suggests that even the use of medicine in the schools is part of the same social control enterprise. He argues that the discovery of MBD (minimum brain dysfunctions) in young children serves the system by using drugs to regulate behavior rather than searching for the social causes of that behavior.

Up to this point, the emphasis of discussion has been the American school system. Lipset, in "Education and Equality: Israel and the United States Compared," invites us to take a comparative stance toward the issue of formal education. Lipset suggests that in the United States education has been valued (ideologically) as a means toward open mobility. The emphasis is on equality of opportunity. In Israel, on the other hand, there has been much more emphasis on the equality of result, with a more elitist attitude toward education itself. Professor Lipset sees problems with both orientations, and an analogy between the condition of Arabs in Israel and pre-World War II blacks in the United States.

1 *Norman K. Denzin*

Children and Their Caretakers

Schools are held together by intersecting moral, political and social orders. What occurs inside their walls must be viewed as a product of what the participants in this arena bring to it, be they children, parents, instructors, administrators, psychologists, social workers, counselors or politicians. A tangled web of interactions—based on competing ideologies, rhetorics, intents and purposes—characterizes everyday life in the school. Cliques, factions, pressure groups and circles of enemies daily compete for power and fate in these social worlds.

Children and their caretakers are not passive organisms. Their conduct reflects more than responses to the pressures of social systems, roles, value structures or political ideologies. Nor is their behavior the sole product of internal needs, drives, impulses or wishes. The human actively constructs lines of conduct in the face of these forces and as such stands over and against the external world. The human is self-conscious. Such variables as role prescription, value configurations or hierarchies of needs have relevance only when they are acted on by the human. Observers of human behavior are obliged to enter the subject's world and grasp the shifting definitions that give rise to orderly social behavior. Failing to do so justifies the fallacy of objectivism: the imputing of motive from observer to subject. Too many architects of schools and education programs have stood outside the interactional worlds of children and adults and attempted to legislate their interpretation of right and proper conduct.

Such objectivistic stances have given schools a basic characteristic that constitutes a major theme of this essay. Schools are presently organized so as to effectively remove fate control from those persons whose fate is at issue, that is, students. This loss of fate control, coupled with a conception of the child which is based on the "underestimation fallacy" gives rise to an ideology that judges the child as incompetent and places in the hands of the adult primary responsibility for child-caretaking.

Schools as Moral Agencies

Schools are best seen, not as educational settings, but as places where fate, morality and personal careers are created and shaped. Schools are moral institutions. They have assumed the responsibility of shaping children, of whatever race or income level, into right and proper participants in American society, pursuing with equal vigor the abstract goals of that society.

At one level schools function, as Willard Waller argued in 1937, to Americanize the young. At the everyday level, however, abstract goals disappear, whether they be beliefs in democracy and equal opportunity or myths concerning the value of education for upward mobility. In their place appears a massive normative order that judges the child's development along such dimensions as poise, character, integrity, politeness, deference, demeanor, emotional control, respect for authority and serious commitment to classroom protocol. Good students are those who reaffirm through their daily actions the moral order of home, school and community.

To the extent that schools assume moral responsibility for producing social beings, they can be seen as agencies of fate or career control. In a variety of ways schools remind students who they are and where they stand in the school's hierarchy. The school institutionalizes ritual turning points to fill this function: graduations, promotions, tests, meetings with parents, open-houses, rallies and sessions with counselors. These significant encounters serve to keep students in place. Schools function to sort and filter social selves and to set these selves on the proper moral track, which may include recycling to a lower grade, busing to an integrated school or informing a student that he has no chance to pursue a college preparatory program. In many respects schools give students their major sense of moral worth—they shape vocabularies, images of self, reward certain actions and not others, set the stage for students to be thrown together as friends or enemies.

Any institution that assumes control over the fate of others might be expected to be accountable for its actions toward those who are shaped and manipulated. Within the cultures of fate-controlling institutions, however, there appears a vocabulary, a rhetoric, a set of workable excuses and a division of labor to remove and reassign responsibility. For example, we might expect that the division of labor typically parallels the moral hierarchy of the people within the institution, that is, the people assigned the greatest moral worth are ultimately most blameworthy, or most accountable. Usually, however, moral responsibility is reversed. When a teacher in a Head Start program fails to raise the verbal skills of her class to the appropriate level she and the project director might blame each other. But it is more likely that the children, the families of the children or the culture from which the children come will be held responsible. Such is the typical rhetorical device employed in compensatory education programs where the low performances of black children on white middle-class tests is explained by assigning blame to black family culture and family arrangements. Research on the alleged genetic deficiences of black and brown children is another example of this strategy. Here the scientist acts as a moral entrepreneur, presenting his findings under the guise of objectivity.

What is a Child?

Any analysis of the education and socialization process must begin with the basic question, "what is a child?" My focus is on the contemporary meanings assigned children, especially as these meanings are revealed in preschool and compensatory education programs.

In addressing this question it must be recognized that social objects (such as children) carry no intrinsic meaning. Rather, meaning is conferred by processes of social interaction—by people.

Such is the case with children. Each generation, each social group, every family and each individual develops different interpretations of what a child is. Children find themselves defined in shifting, often contradictory ways. But as a sense of self is acquired, the child learns to transport from situation to situation a relatively stable set of definitions concerning his personal and social identity. Indeed most of the struggles he will encounter in the educational arena fundamentally derive from conflicting definitions of selfhood and childhood.

Child Production as Status Passage

The movement of an infant to the status of child is a socially constructed event that for most middle-class Americans is seen as desirable, inevitable, irreversible, permanent, long term in effect and accomplished in the presence of "experts" and significant others such as teachers, parents, peers and siblings.

For the white middle income American the child is seen as an extension of the adult's self, usually the family's collective self. Parents are continually reminded that the way their child turns out is a direct reflection of their competence as socializing agents. These reminders have been made for some time; consider this exhortation of 1849:

> Yes, mothers, in a certain sense, the destiny of a redeemed world is put into your hands; it is for you to say whether your children shall be respectable and happy here, and prepared for a glorious immortality, or whether they shall dishonor you, and perhaps bring you grey hairs in sorrow to the grave, and sink down themselves at last to eternal despair!

If the child's conduct reflects upon the parent's moral worth, new parents are told by Benjamin Spock that this job of producing a child is hard work, a serious enterprise. He remarks in *Baby and Child Care*:

> There is an enormous amount of hard work in child care—preparing the proper diet, washing diapers and clothes, cleaning up messes that an infant makes with his food . . . stopping fights and drying tears, listening to stories that are hard to understand, joining in games and reading stories that aren't very exciting to an adult, trudging around zoos and museums and carnivals . . . being slowed down in housework . . . . Children keep parents from parties, trips, theaters, meetings, games, friends . . . . Of course, parents don't have children because they want to be martyrs, or at least they shouldn't. They have them because they love children and want some of their very own . . . . Taking care of their children, seeing them grow and develop into fine people, gives most parents—despite the hard work—their greatest satisfaction in life. This is creation. This is our visible immortality. Pride in other worldly accomplishments is usually weak in comparison.

Spock's account of the parent-child relationship reveals several interrelated definitions that together serve to set off the contemporary view of children. The child is a possession of the adult, an extension of self, an incompetent object that must be cared for at great cost and is a necessary obligation one must incur if he or she desires visible immortality.

These several definitions of childhood are obviously at work in current educational programs. More importantly, they are grounded in a theory of development and learning that reinforces the view that children are incompetent selves. Like Spock's theory of growth, which is not unlike the earlier proposals of Gesell, contemporary psychological theories see the child in organic terms. The child grows like a stalk of corn. The strength of the stalk is a function of its environment. If that environment is healthy, if the plant is properly cared for, a suitable product will be produced. This is a "container" theory of development: "What you put in determines what comes out." At the same time, however, conventional wisdom holds that the child is an unreliable product. It cannot be trusted with its own moral development. Nor can parents. This business of producing a child is serious and it must be placed in the hands of experts who are skilled in child production. Mortal mothers and fathers lack these skills. Pressures are quickly set in force to move the child out of the family into a more "professional" setting—the preschool, the Head Start program.

Caretaking for the Middle Classes

Preschools, whether based on "free school" principles, the Montessori theory, or modern findings in child development, display one basic feature. They are moral caretaking agencies that undertake the fine task of shaping social beings.

Recently, after the enormous publicity attendant to the Head Start program for the poor, middle income Americans have been aroused to the importance of preschool education for their children. "Discovery Centers" are appearing in various sections of the country and several competing national franchises have been established. Given names such as We Sit Better, Mary Moppit, Pied Piper Schools, Les Petites Academies, Kinder Care Nursery and American Child Centers, these schools remind parents (as did the Universal Education Corporation in the *New York Times*) that:

> Evaluating children in the 43 basic skills is part of what the Discovery Center can do for your child. The 43 skills embrace all the hundreds of things your child has to learn before he reaches school age. Fortunately preschoolers have a special genius for learning. But it disappears at the age of seven. During this short-lived period of genius, the Discovery Center helps your child develop his skills to the Advanced Level.

Caretaking for the middle classes is a moral test. The parent's self is judged by the quality of the product. If the product is faulty, the producer is judged inadequate, also faulty. This feature of the socialization process best explains why middle-class parents are so concerned about the moral, spiritual, psychological and social development of their children. It also explains (if only partially) why schools have assumed so much fate control over children; educators are the socially defined experts on children.

The children of lower income families are often assumed to be deprived, depressed and emotionally handicapped. To offset these effects, current theory holds that the child must be "educated and treated" before entrance into kindergarten. If middle income groups have the luxury of withholding preschool from their children, low income, third-world parents are quickly learning they have no such right. Whether they like it or not, their children are going to be educated. When formal education begins, the culturally deprived child will be ready to compete with his white peers.

What is Cultural Deprivation?

The term "culturally deprived" is still the catchall phrase which at once explains and describes the inability (failure, refusal) of the child in question to display appropriate conduct on I.Q. tests, street corners, playgrounds and classrooms. There are a number of problems with this formulation. The first is conceptual and involves the meanings one gives to the terms *culture* and *deprived*. Contemporary politicians and educators have ignored the controversy surrounding what the word *culture* means and have apparently assumed that everyone knows what a culture is. Be that as it may, the critical empirical indicator seems to be contained in the term *deprived*. People who are deprived, that is, people who fail to act like white, middle income groups, belong to a culture characterized by such features as divorce, deviance, premarital pregnancies, extended families, drug addiction and alcoholism. Such persons are easily identified: they tend to live in ghettos or public housing units, and they tend to occupy the lower rungs of the occupation ladder. They are there because they are deprived. Their culture keeps them deprived. It is difficult to tell whether these theorists feel that deprivation precedes or follows being in a deprived culture. The causal links are neigher logically or empirically analyzed.

The second problem with this formulation is moral and ideological. The children and adults who are labeled culturally deprived are those people in American society who embarrass and cause trouble for middle income moralists, scientists, teachers, politicians and social workers. They fail to display proper social behavior. The fact that people in low income groups are under continual surveillance by police and social workers seems to go unnoticed. The result is that members of the middle class keep their indelicacies behind closed doors, inside the private worlds of home, office, club and neighborhood. Low income people lack such privileges. Their misconduct is everybody's business.

The notion of cultural deprivation is class based. Its recurrent invocation, and its contemporary institutionalization in compensatory education programs reveals an inability or refusal to look seriously at the problems of the middle and upper classes, and it directs attention away from schools which are at the heart of the problem.

Herbert Gans has noted another flaw in these programs. This is the failure of social scientists to take seriously the fact that many lower income people simply do not share the same aspirations as the middle class. Despite this fact antipoverty programs and experiments in compensatory education proceed as if such were the case.

Schools are morally bounded units of social organization. Within and from them students, parents, teachers and administrators derive their fundamental sense of self. Any career through a school is necessarily moral; one's self-image is continually being evaluated, shaped and molded. These careers are interactionally interdependent. What a teacher does affects what a child does and vice versa. To the extent that schools have become the dominant socializing institution in Western society it can be argued that experiences in them furnish everyday interactants with their basic vocabularies for evaluating self and others. Persons can mask, hide or fabricate their educational biography, but at some point they will be obliged to paint a picture of how well educated they are. They will also be obliged to explain why they are not better educated (or why they are too well educated), and why their present circumstances do not better reflect their capabilities (e.g., unemployed space engineers). One's educational experiences furnish the rhetorical devices necessary to get off the hook and supply the basic clues that will shore up a sad or happy tale.

The School's Functions

I have already noted two broad functions served by the schools: they Americanize students, and they sort, filter and accredit social selves. To these basic functions must be added the following. Ostensibly, instruction or teaching should take precedence over political socialization. And indeed teaching becomes the dominant activity through which the school is presented to the child. But if schools function to instruct, they also function to entertain and divert students into "worthwhile" ends. Trips to zoos, beaches, operas, neighboring towns, ice cream parlors and athletic fields reveal an attempt on the part of the school to teach the child what range of entertaining activities he or she can engage in. Moreover, these trips place the school directly in the public's eye and at least on these excursions teachers are truly held accountable for their class's conduct.

Caretaking and babysitting constitute another basic function of schools. This babysitting function is quite evident in church oriented summer programs where preschools and day-care centers are explicitly oriented so as to sell themselves as competent babysitters. Such schools compete for scarce resources (parents who can afford their services), and the federal government has elaborated this service through grants-in-aid to low income children.

Formal instruction in the classroom is filtered through a series of interconnected acts that involve teacher and student presenting different social selves to one another. Instruction cannot be separated from social interaction, and teachers spend a large amount of time teaching students how to be proper social participants. Coaching in the rules and rituals of polite etiquette thus constitutes another basic function of the school. Students must be taught how to take turns, how to drink out of cups and clean up messes, how to say please and thank you, how to take leave of a teacher's presence, how to handle mood, how to dress for appropriate occasions, how to be rude, polite, attentive, evasive, docile, aggressive, deceitful; in short, they must learn to act like adults. Teachers share this responsibility with parents, often having to take over where parents fail or abdicate, though, again, parents are held accountable for not producing polite children. Because a child's progress through the school's social structure is contingent on how his or her self is formally defined, parents stand to lose much if their children do not conform to the school's version of good conduct. When teachers and parents both fail, an explanation will be sought to relieve each party of responsibility. The child may be diagnosed as hyperactive, or his culture may have been so repressive in its effects that nothing better can be accomplished. Career tracks for these students often lead to the trade school or the reformatory.

Another function of the schools is socialization into age-sex roles. Girls must be taught how to be girls and boys must learn what a boy is. In preschool and daycare centers this is often difficult to accomplish because bathrooms are not sex segregated. But while they are open territories, many preschools make an effort to hire at least one male instructor who can serve as male caretaker and entertainer of boys. He handles their toilet problems among other things. Preschool instructors can often be observed to reinterpret stories to fit their conception of the male or female role, usually attempting to place the female on an equal footing with the male. In these ways the sexual component of self-identity is transmitted and presented to the young child. Problem children become those who switch sex roles or accentuate to an unacceptable degree maleness or femaleness.

Age-grading is accomplished through the organization of classes on a biological age basis. Three-year-olds quickly learn that they cannot do the same things as four-year-olds do, and so on. High schools are deliberately organized so as to convey to freshmen and sophomores how important it is to be a junior or senior. Homecoming queens, student body presidents and athletic leaders come from the two top classes. The message is direct: work hard, be a good student and you too can be a leader and enjoy the fruits of age.

It has been suggested by many that most schools centrally function to socialize children into racial roles, stressing skin color as the dominant variable in social relationships. Depictions of American history and favored symbolic leaders stress the three variables of age, sex and race. The favored role model becomes the 20 to 25-year-old, white, university-educated male who has had an outstanding career in athletics. Implicitly and explicitly students are taught that Western culture is a male oriented, white-based enterprise.

Shifting from the school as a collectivity to the classroom, we find that teachers attempt to construct their own versions of appropriate conduct. Students are likely to find great discrepancies between a school's formal codes of conduct and the specific rules they encounter in each of their courses and classes. They will find some teachers who are openly critical of the school's formal policies, while at the same time they are forced to interact with teachers who take harsh lines toward misconduct. They will encounter some teachers who enforce dress standards and some who do not. Some teachers use first names, others do not, and so on. The variations are endless.

The importance of these variations for the student's career and self-conception should be clear. It is difficult managing self in a social world that continually changes its demands, rewards and rules of conduct. But students are obliged to do just that. Consequently the self-conception of the student emerges as a complex and variegated object. He or she is tied into competing and complementary worlds of influence and experience. Depending on where students stand with respect to the school's dominant moral order, they will find their self-conception complemented or derogated and sometimes both. But for the most part schools are organized so as to complement the self-conception of the child most like the teacher and to derogate those most unlike him or her. And, needless to say, the moral career of the nonwhite, low income student is quite different from the career of his white peer.

I have spelled out the dimensions around which a student comes to evaluate himself in school. Classrooms, however, are the most vivid stage on which students confront the school, and it is here that the teacher at some level must emerge as a negative or positive force on his career. While the underlife of schools reflects attempts to "beat" or "make-out" in the school, in large degree the student learns to submit to the system. The ultimate fact of life is that unless he gets through school with some diploma he is doomed to failure. Not only is he doomed to failure, but he is socially defined as a failure. His career opportunities and self-conceptions are immediately tied to his success in school.

Schools, then, inevitably turn some amount of their attention to the problem of socializing students for failure. Indeed, the school's success as a socializing agent in part depends on its ability to teach students to accept failure. A complex rhetoric and set of beliefs must be instilled in the students. Children must come to see themselves as the school defines them. They are taught that certain classes of selves do better than other classes, but the classes referred to are not sociological but moral. A variation of the Protestant ethic is communicated and the fiction of equality in education and politics is stressed. Students must grasp the fact that all that separates them from a classmate who goes to Harvard (when they are admitted to a junior college) are grades and hard work, not class, race, money or prestige. Schools, then, function as complex, cooling out agencies.

Two problems are created. School officials must communicate their judgments, usually cast as diagnoses, prescriptions, treatments and prognoses, to students and parents. And second, they must establish social arrangements that maximize the likelihood that their judgments will be accepted, that is, submission to fate control is maximized, and scenes between parents and students are minimized.

Fate Control

The most obvious cooling out agents in schools are teachers and counselors. It is they who administer and evaluate tests. It is they who see the student most frequently. In concert these two classes of functionaries fulfill the schools' functions of sorting out and cooling out children. Their basic assignment is to take imperfect selves and fit those selves to the best possible moral career. They are, then, moral entrepreneurs. They design career programs and define the basic contours around which a student's self will be shaped.

A basic strategy of the moral entrepreneur in schools is co-optation. He attempts to win a child's peers and parents over to his side. If this can be accomplished, the job is relatively easy. For now everyone significant in the child's world agrees that he is a failure or a partial success. They agree that a trade school or a junior college is the best career track to be followed.

Another strategy is to select exemplary students who epitomize the various tracks open to a student. Former graduates may be brought back and asked to reflect on their careers. In selecting types of students to follow these various paths, schools conduct talent searches and develop operating perspectives that classify good and bad prospects. Like the academic theorist of social stratification, these officials work with an implicit image of qualified beings. They know that students from middle and upper income groups perform better than those from lesser backgrounds. They know that students who have college educated parents do better than those whose parents dropped out of high school. They learn to mistrust nonwhites. In these respects schools differ only slightly from medical practitioners, especially the psychiatrist who has learned that his trade works best on persons like him in background. Teachers too perpetuate the system of stratification found in the outside world.

Student Types

Schools can cool out the failures in their midst. They have more difficulty with another type of student, the troublemakers or militants. Troublemakers, as would be predicted, typically come from low income white and nonwhite ethnic groups. Forced to process these children, school systems developed their own system of stratification, making low status schools teach troublemakers. This has become the fate of the trade school or the continuation high school. Here those who have high truancy or arrest records, are pregnant, hyperactive or on probation are thrown together. And here they are presented with white middle-class curriculums.

Militants and troublemakers refuse to accept the school's operating perspective. To the extent that they can band together and form a common world view, they challenge the school's legitimacy as a socializing agent. They make trouble. They represent, from the middle-class point of view, failures of the socializing system.

In response to this, schools tend to adopt a strategy of denial. Denial can take several forms, each revealing a separate attempt to avoid accountability. Denial of responsibility takes the form of a claim that "we recognize your problem, but the solution is outside our province." The need for alternative educational arrangements is recognized, but denied because of reasons beyond control. Private and public guilt is neutralized by denying responsibility and placing blame on some external force or variable such as the state of the economy.

When some resource is denied to a social group, explanations will be developed to justify that denial. My earlier discussion has suggested that one explanation places blame on the shoulders of the denied victim. Thus the theory of cultural deprivation removes blame, by blaming the victim. Scientific theory thus operates as one paradigm of responsibility.

Another form of the strategy is to deny the challengers' essential moral worth. Here the victim is shown to be socially unworthy and thereby not deserving of special attention. This has been the classic argument for segregation in the South, but it works only so long as the victim can be kept in place, which has lately in that part of the world involved insuring that the challenger or victim is not presented with alternative self models. Shipping black instructors out of the South into northern urban ghettos represents an attempt to remove alternative self models for the southern black child.

The Victim's Response

Insofar as they can organize themselves socially, victims and challengers may assume one of three interrelated stances. They may condemn the condemner, make appeals to higher authorities or deny the perspective that has brought injury. In so doing they will seek and develop alternative scientific doctrines that support their stance.

Condemning the condemner reverses the condemner's denial of moral worth. Here the school or political and economic system is judged hypocritical, corrupt, stupid, brutal and racist. These evaluations attempt to reveal the underlying moral vulnerability of the institution in question. The victim and his cohort reverse the victimizer's vocabulary and hold him accountable for the failures they were originally charged with (for example, poor grades or attendance records).

These condemnations reveal a basic commitment to the present system. They are claims for a just place. They are a petition to higher authority. Democratic ideology is proclaimed as a worthy pursuit. The school is charged with failure to offer proper and acceptable means to reach those goals. Here the victims' perspective corresponds with dominant cultural ideologies.

Denial of perspective is another stance. Best seen in the Nation of Islam schools, the victim now states that he wants nothing the larger system can offer. He leaves the system and constructs his own educational arrangements. He develops his own standards of evaluation. He paints his own version of right and proper conduct. (Private educational academies in the South, partly a function of the Nixon administration, serve a similar function for whites.)

Denials of perspective thus lead to the substitution of a new point of view. If successfully executed, as in the case of the Nation of Islam, the victims build their own walls of protection and shut off the outside world. In such a setting, one's self-conception is neither daily denied nor derided. It is affirmed and defined in positive terms.

Lower self-conceptions would be predicted in those settings where the black or brown child is taught to normalize his deficiencies and to compensate for them. This is the setting offered by Head Start and Follow-Through. The victim accepts the victimizers' judgments and attempts to compensate for socially defined flaws.

Americans of all income levels and from all racial groups, including white, are troubled over the current educational system. They are demanding a greater say in the social organization of schools; they are challenging the tenure system now given teachers; they feel that schools should accept greater responsibilities for the failures of the system. (A Gallup Poll in late 1970 showed that 67 percent of those surveyed favor holding teachers and administrators more accountable for the progress of students.) Accordingly it is necessary to consider a series of proposals that would bring education more in line with cultural and social expectations.

From this perspective education must be grounded in principles that recognize the role of the self in everyday conduct. The child possesses multiple selves, each grounded in special situations and special circles of significant others. Possessing a self, the child is an active organism, not a passive object into which learning can be poured.

Conventional theories of learning define the child as a passive organism. An alternative view of the social act of learning must be developed. George Herbert Mead's analysis provides a good beginning. Creativity or learning occurred, Mead argued, when the individual was forced to act in a situation where conventional lines of conduct were no longer relevant. Following Dewey's discussion of the blocked act, Mead contended that schools and curricula must be organized in ways that challenge the child's view of the world. Standard curricula are based on an opposite view of the human. Redundancy, constant rewards and punishments, piecemeal presentation of materials, and defining the child as incompetent or unable to provoke his own acts best characterizes these programs. Course work is planned carefully in advance and study programs are assiduously followed. The teacher, not the child, is defined as the ultimate educational resource. Parents and local community groups, because they tend to challenge the school's operating perspective, are treated only ritualistically at P.T.A. meetings, open houses, school plays, athletic contests. Their point of view, like the child's, is seldom taken seriously. They are too incompetent. Taking them seriously would force a shift in existing power arrangements in the school.

Mead's perspective proposes just the opposite view of parents, children and education. Education, he argued, is an unfolding, social process wherein the child comes to see himself in increasingly more complex ways. Education leads to self-understanding and to the acquisition of the basic skills. This principle suggests that schools must be socially relevant. They must incorporate the social world of child and community into curriculum arrangements. Cultural diversity must be stressed. Alternative symbolic leaders must be presented, and these must come from realistic worlds of experience. (Setting an astronaut as a preferred "self model" for seven-year-old males as a present text book does, can hardly be defined as realistic). Problematic situations from the child's everyday world must be brought into the classroom. Mead, for example, proposed as early as 1908 that schools teach sex education to children.

Children and parents, then, must be seen as resources around which education is developed and presented. They must be taken seriously. This presupposes a close working relationship between home and school. Parents must take responsibility for their children's education. They can no longer afford to shift accountability to the schools. This simple principle suggests that ethnic studies programs should have been central features of schools at least 50 years ago. Schools exist to serve their surrounding communities, not bend those communities to their perspective.

Redefining Schools

If this reciprocal service function is stressed, an important implication follows. Schools should educate children in ways that permit them to be contributing members in their chosen worlds. Such basics as reading, writing and counting will never be avoided. But their instruction can be made relevant within the worlds the child most directly experiences. This suggests, initially at least, that black and brown children be taught to respect their separate cultural heritages. Second, it suggests that they will probably learn best with materials drawn from those cultures. Third, it suggests that they must be presented with self models who know, respect and come from those cultures—black teachers must not be removed from southern schools.

To the extent that schools and teachers serve as referent points for the child's self-conception it can be argued that it is not the minority student who must change. But instead it is the white middle-class child who must be exposed to alternative cultural perspectives. Minority teachers must be made integral components of all phases of the educational act.

Mead's perspective suggests, as I have attempted to elaborate, that the classroom is an interactive world. Research by Roger G. Barker and Paul V. Gump on big schools and little schools supports this position and their findings suggest an additional set of proposals. Briefly, they learned that as class and school size increases student satisfaction decreases. Teaching becomes more mechanized, students become more irrelevant and activities not related to learning attain greater importance, social clubs, for example. In short, in big schools students are redundant.

Classroom size and school size must be evaluated from this perspective. If schools exist to serve children and their parents, then large schools are dysfunctional. They are knowledge factories, not places of learning or self-development. Culturally heterogeneous, small-sized classes must be experimented with. Students must have opportunities to know their teachers in personal, not institutional terms. Students must be taught to take one another seriously, not competitively. Small, ecologically intimate surroundings have a greater likelihood of promoting these arrangements than do large-scale, bureaucratically organized classes.

At present, standardized, state and nationally certified tests are given students to assess their psychological, emotional, intellectual and social development. Two problems restrict the effectiveness of these methods, however. With few exceptions they have been standardized on white middle-class populations. Second, they are the only measurement techniques routinely employed.

A number of proposals follow from these problems. First, open-ended tests which permit the child to express his or her perspective must be developed. These tests, such as the "Who Am I?" question, would be given to students to determine the major contours of their self-conceptions. With this information in hand teachers would be in a better position to tailor teaching programs to a child's specific needs, definitions, intentions and goals.

Second, tests such as "Who is Important to You?" could be given students on a regular basis to determine who their significant others are. It is near axiomatic that derogation of the people most important to one leads to alienation from the setting and spokesman doing the derogation. Teachers must learn to respect and present in respectful terms those persons most important to the child.

A third methodological proposal directs observers to link a student's utterances, wishes and self-images to his or her day-to-day conduct. Written test scores often fail to reflect what persons really take into account and value. In many social settings verbal ability, athletic skill, hustling aptitudes, money and even physical attractiveness serve as significant status locators. I.Q. tests often do not. Furthermore, a person's score on a test may not accurately reflect his ability to handle problematic situations, which is surely a goal of education. Observations of conduct (behavior) in concrete settings can provide the needed leads in this direction.

Methodological Implications

A critic of these proposals might remark that such measures are not standardized, that their validity is questionable, that they cannot be administered nationally, and that they have questionable degrees of reliability. In response I would cite the ability of Roger Barker and colleagues to execute such observations over time with high reliability (.80-.98 for many measures). But more to the point I would argue that conventional tests are simply not working and it is time to experiment with alternative techniques, perspectives and theories.

This defense suggests that schools of education must begin to consider teaching their students the methodologies of participant observation, unobtrusive analysis and life history construction. These softer methods have been the traditional province of sociologists and anthropologists. Members of these disciplines must consider offering cross-disciplinary courses in methodology, especially aimed for everyday practitioners in school settings. Graduate requirements for teaching credentials must also be reexamined and greater efforts must be made to recruit and train minority students in these different approaches.

These proposals reflect a basic commitment. Schools should be organized so as to maximize a child's self-development and they should permit maximum child-parent participation. It is evident that my discussion has not been limited to an analysis of compensatory education programs. This has been deliberate. It is my conviction that education, wherever it occurs, involves interactions between social selves. Taking the self as a point of departure I have attempted to show that what happens to a preschool child is not unlike the moral experiences of a black or brown 17-year-old senior. But most importantly, both should find themselves in schools that take them seriously and treat them with respect. Schools exist to serve children and the public. This charge must be also taken seriously.

SUGGESTED READINGS

Centuries of Childhood by Phillipe Aries (New York: Random House, 1962).

Big School and Small School by Roger Barker and Paul V. Gump (Stanford, California: Stanford University Press, 1964).

The Sociology of Teaching by Willard Waller (New York: John Wiley, 1967, originally published in 1937).

2 *Norman E. Silberberg & Margaret C. Silberberg*

Reading Rituals

Back in 1969, when he was United States Commissioner of Education, James E. Allen, Jr., declared that for the quarter of our population who do not do well in reading, "education, in a very important way, has been a failure, and they [the failures] stand as a reproach to all of us who hold in our hands the shaping of the opportunity for education." In the same speech, Allen further pointed out that "one of every four students nationwide has significant reading deficiencies," and "in large city school systems, up to half of the students read below expectation." He went on about the "knowledge and inspiration available through the printed word" despite the fact, or because of it, that a Gallup poll showed that 58 percent of the American people admit that they have *never* read a book. Allen then demanded the public and political recognition of "The Right to Read."

With all the studies done on reading, we still don't know why some children do not read efficiently. It is difficult, when a parent asks why a child can't read well, to suggest (in professional language, of course) that "that's not his bag." Yet, that is what most such appraisals often come down to. There are thousands of diagnoses of what is "wrong" with a child who does not read efficiently, and nearly as many supposed "cures" for these problems, but no one seems to have considered the possibility that we may be barking up the wrong tree in *expecting* all children to read well. These studies have identified many correlates of inefficient reading, but in none has a causal relationship been satisfactorily demonstrated. For example, although there is high correlation between socioeconomic class and reading skills, closer inspection of the terms reveals that the same thing may be lurking under the middle classes' "learning disabilities" and the poor's "cultural deprivation." For the poor, home environment is blamed for inefficiency in reading. For the rich, it is brain damage, which is presumably less reversible. In neither case do we really know why children in all socioeconomic classes read inefficiently—only that they do.

More important is the fact that, by definition, 50 percent of children must read at grade level or below, since grade level only means the median level achieved in a particular grade. Thus, it is not too surprising that Commissioner Allen finds as many as 50 percent of children who are encountering difficulties in reading. As long as grade equivalent is used as a criterion of reading skill, there has to be 50 percent who are below the median in this skill area. One could question the statistical appropriateness of labeling 50 percent of the population as "abnormal," but the real point is that we as a society are attempting to narrow the range of acceptable learning behavior to a specific point, which we have predetermined as appropriate conformity. This seems, at least, a self-defeating task.

Up Against the Curve

We have found seven longitudinal studies of remedial reading. Not one shows any long-term beneficial effect. The current administration is also rather skeptical of these efforts. In a speech given early in 1970, President Richard Nixon described the results after almost $1 billion had been spent yearly on reading programs under Title I of the Elementary and Secondary Education Act of 1965: "Before-and-after tests suggest that only 19 percent of the children in such programs improve their reading significantly; 15 percent appear to fall behind more than expected, and more than two-thirds of the children remain unaffected—that is, they continue to fall behind." There is currently no evidence that one can "remediate" reading as long as reading is measured in relative rather than absolute terms. We can strive to move the whole reading curve up, but we cannot possibly eliminate its bottom half. Research on the cost effectiveness of such efforts, however, indicates, as they would say at the Pentagon, there is not much bang obtained for the remedial buck.

The better we get at measuring school learning skills, the better able we are to describe them. As the social sciences amass more and better measurements of behavior, we can define with good accuracy what percent of children will have difficulty in reading, what percent of children will have behavior problems and so forth. The only thing that we cannot do is to predict into which family such a child will fall. When parents come to us and ask why their child does not achieve or adjust properly in school, we are often tempted to tell the parents it's just their tough luck. What else can we tell them?

The only other response, it seems to us, is the reminder that bearing or adopting children guarantees parents nothing. We—as a society—have not communicated to parents the probabilities of their having children who do not conform to our predetermined narrow range of achievement. Someone should tell parents that they stand at least a 50 percent chance of having a child who will not be successful in school. This is not as difficult for most people to take as one might expect. Parents, for example, are not particularly shocked if it is suggested to them that their children are likely to resemble them in school learning abilities. (In speeches to upwardly mobile suburban parent groups, our suggestion that the parents pull their old report cards out of the attic to hang on the refrigerator as an inspiration to their children is always met with embarrassed laughter.) Unfortunately, however, parents and teachers take personal responsibility for altering a child's behavior so that he conforms to the standards set forth by the media, industry, the whole striving ethos of our culture. We have had parents of children accept the diagnosis of poor school achievement but fall to pieces when told the child should *not* attend college.

Marking Time

American society is moving more and more toward establishment of academic skill as the *sine qua non* of acceptance within that society. Even though we are, for all intents and purposes, attempting to provide some form of academic education to the total society, our demands become less and less realistic. In 1941, the median educational level in this country was ninth grade. Now we keep almost all of our children through tenth grade. Thus, those children who, in our parents' days, were not learning in school and left in sixth grade to work in mines or on farms are now forced *by law* to sit in school for three or four years longer. While they sit in school, they are usually offered either watered-down versions of the same reading-based curriculum the more talented children receive, or woodworking and shop courses which, it is realized by both teachers and students, provide no entry to a meaningful occupation. Even much of the curriculum research for educable retarded children is aimed not at the experience unit, but rather at ways of improving literacy in this group of persons whose tested language skills are in the bottom 5 percent of the population.

Credentialism

Despite the fact that academic potential (IQ) and intelligence (ability to survive in the environment) are very poorly related in many individuals, more and more sectors of the society are being forced into the high school graduate and college craze. We hear reports that companies will not even interview high school dropouts, even though there is no demonstrated relationship between the job task and academic achievement. A local chain of stores insists that their carry-out boys take a *written* test to get this job, even though the only reading required is occasionally setting a price on a stamp which is then used to stamp hundreds of cans. Carole Williams found that

> only 5 percent of the graduates of inner-city high schools are placed in colleges, jobs, or job-training programs by fall, while 50 percent of the dropouts scheduled to be graduated with the same class have found employment . . . . Inner-city schools don't teach these youngsters job skills, so they seek jobs as unskilled workers—jobs that have already been grabbed by the dropouts. In effect, they have been betrayed by the myth that they should stay in school.

Do these young people need an academic education, or do the personnel managers need an education into the types of skills needed for these jobs?

One example of the frustration encountered because of this thinking is a ninth-grade, 15-year-old boy recently evaluated at the Kenny Institute. He had academic potential within the average range, but, despite years of remedial help, he was still reading at about beginning fourth-grade level and was, of course, flunking most of his courses. He did not make friends easily, so it was not too surprising that when his family moved he refused to attend the new school. He could not bear to demonstrate his "dumbness" to the other students who, not atypically for their age, teased him. He was artistically gifted and good at working with things. What could we do for him? There were no vocational schools where he lived, and even if there had been, most such schools insist on passing grades in academic courses before admission. He was too young for the Department of Vocational Rehabilitation, which also usually encourages high school graduation or else sends the client back for additional course work in books. We could not locate a place where he might study art below a college level. Apprenticeship programs were not available for a high school dropout, as this boy was soon to become. Thus, we had a child who logically could contribute to society, but, because of his reading, was barred from education for an occupation—or rather was barred because the agencies that could help him would not because of their insistence on academic competence.

No one is attempting realistically to assess the wide variations in abilities and talents that exist among young children. Elitists claim that IQ differences among children are not only quantitative, they also represent qualitative differences: a child with a higher IQ is "smarter" than a child with a lower IQ. The trouble with this view is that it expects too much of IQ tests, which do only what they are supposed to do: predict success within an academic curriculum. In addition, it does not recognize the fact that academic curricula were developed for a small portion of the society and cannot be expected to be appropriate for everyone. Elitists regard children with low IQs as deadwood; one influential government official was recently quoted as saying, "Let's teach them to turn a lathe and leave it at that."

On the other side, we find equalitarians whose philosophy is diametrically opposed to that of the elitists. They seem to view people as having equal potential. Thus, we can teach anyone anything, if our teaching techniques are appropriate and if the reward system is appropriate.

We feel the truth lies somewhere between these two points of view. Unquestionably, there are innate differences between individuals. It is also true that most people learn to survive quite well in this society, independent of their success in school. The problems come, however, because society places hierarchical values upon these differences. Higher IQ does not mean "better," it only means "different." Children with lower IQs can learn to do many things that are possibly more important and appropriate to a modern society than the tasks performed by college professors.

Most agencies and professionals exist to satisfy the parents or the school. Most also accept the narrow limits of behavior considered appropriate for children, and then try to fit the individual child into these narrow limits. But who is to speak for the child? What is needed is an advocate for the child.

The function of the advocate is not to attempt to satisfy unrealistic demands by parent or school or government. Rather, the advocate should interpret the child realistically to all concerned and attempt to help the child make it through childhood with the least possible stress. He should focus on the strengths of the child, rather than attempting to remake his weaknesses. Children are not clay; they have their own personalities, traits and talents, as do adults. Parents and the school must begin to recognize these individual differences, and appreciate them, rather than attempt to change them. Options must be made available for those children who are unable to conform, whatever the reason. To view those children who read poorly as defective and requiring a "cure" only increases the frustrations and unhappiness of these children, many of whom are already suffering from the pressure of overzealous parents and educators. A child's advocate would try to relieve this pressure and bring reality into planning for the individual.

If one is willing to accept this point of view, one can then reassess the child. Does the child truly have a learning disability, or, alternatively, do we as a society have a teaching disability? Most of the children we see in clinics or private practice are not incapable of learning. Many of them are incapable of reading comfortably, and many of them, often because of this inefficiency in reading, are unable to behave in a conforming manner. The relationship of poor school achievement to antisocial behavior is well documented. The question is, should we be devoting so much effort to changing the children, or should we be channeling some of our efforts into changing how and what we teach them? Does a child have a right to read, or does he have a right to learn?

As we have pointed out earlier, many children can be taught by other means. One can easily imagine a bookless curriculum which teaches through media other than the printed word, while the teaching of reading takes place much as other skills, such as lathe work, are taught. Art is taught as a skill, but nobody thinks of a child's proficiency in this medium as important to his education. Nevertheless, one should keep in mind that reading is only one skill in a vast repertoire of skills possessed by most children. If we could find ways to teach children by presenting them with more curricular options, we might reduce the stress on them and possibly reduce their rejection of the learning situation as well.

Alternative Skills

John Dewey, decrying the fetish of reading, recommended that books be thrown out of the elementary grades while we get on with the business of educating children. We are not advocating the burning of books or the elimination of reading instruction. Rather, reading should be taught as is any other specific skill, while other available resources are used to ensure that children are not excluded from education. The use of experience units, films, field trips, records, tapes, observation, readers (good readers can put books on tape), verbal interaction between children, and verbal interaction with teachers can be learning experiences.

Education need not be an either-or situation, where a child either learns by the narrow methods traditionally used in schools (book learning) or is shunted off to something called "job training." In a democracy, it is exceedingly important that each citizen be afforded the opportunity to be educated in the fullest sense of the word. Different responses to one skill such as reading should not bar children from a serious education in the name of training. The assumption that the inefficient reader and/or verbally less proficient child is unable to learn or cannot be educated is specious and cruel.

To rid ourselves of this assumption requires not only the restructuring of education but the restructuring of society with its artificial literary requirements. Let us look at some examples of how this could be done. The United States Department of Health, Education, and Welfare, in its request for research proposals relating to "The Right to Read" Program (RFP 70-6), describes a "reading task" in the following way:

> Reading task: A real-life incident which creates an internally or externally imposed requirement for an individual to perform a discrete, observable operation which is highly dependent upon his having satisfactorily read a specific passage of written material. Examples of reading tasks are: (a) looking up a telephone number; (b) following written directions which tell how to assemble a toy or appliance; (c) responding to a written social invitation; and (d) completing a written job application.

Now, seldom, if ever, does one encounter a truly word-blind person. Even inefficient readers can look up telephone numbers, and for those who cannot, there is always "Information" (if you can get it) through the telephone itself. Following written instructions is a stickier matter. Many of us who read well are totally unable to comprehend the written instructions that come with appliances. And there are many other people, good at working with things, though not talented in the use of language, who can assemble appliances with minimal instruction in language. If records can be produced cheaply enough to put them on the backs of breakfast cereal boxes, it would seem logical that recorded instructions could be included *with* the written directions as an option. As for written social invitations, we will let Tiffany's worry about that.

The problem of the written job application is most critical. Current practice screens out people who want to work on assembly or other non-language-based tasks—tasks that can be and usually are demonstrated by the foreman without benefit of text, without determining if there is a relationship between filling out an application blank and the skill required for that job. Application blanks could be mailed out on telephone request so that the inefficient reader can get help from friends or family in filling it out, with options provided on the job (records, demonstrations and the like) to eliminate the need to read print. The current unemployment or underemployment of many Ph.D.'s raises the question of whether higher education guarantees financial security. Despite the fact that close to 50 percent of high school graduates attend college, less than 20 percent graduate. Vocational school is now becoming more and more a college level program, which means that persons who want to work in nonacademic vocations must first achieve academically for 12 years before they are even permitted access to training. For the first time, society is demanding that schools instruct today's total population of children as successfully as when less than 10 out of 100 children entered high school. Unfortunately, "The Right to Read" suggests that we educate our masses *in the same way* as we used to educate a small number of children who were talented in reading.

We therefore propose that people who are concerned about the academically underachieving child switch their focus. Rather than functioning as agents of changing the child, we need more people to stand up for these children. We must advocate change so that these children can be included in society as they are, so that they can be valued for persons as they are and so that they can be proud of what they are. If parent groups and professionals become advocates for the child, demanding that schools and industry focus on ways of including these children rather than develop more requirements to exclude them, some change might be achieved.

The "that's not his bag" approach is not a pessimistic one. The focus switches to defining the limits in expected variations of specific behaviors within the population. It then becomes the responsibility of the schools to alter their curricula to fit the characteristics of the entire population, rather than attempt to restructure the population to fit society's descriptions of how children *should* perform. In this technological age, it is difficult to understand why literacy has maintained such importance. With education focusing almost solely on a curriculum based on literacy, we are excluding a sizable number of potentially capable citizens from an opportunity to be educated, informed and employed in meaningful jobs.

Educators must decide what it is they want to teach children. Must education continue to emphasize the value of traditional academic education to the exclusion of all else? Couldn't we reorder our priorities so that the teaching of reading requires less of the educator's time and energies? Can't we teach children about the world around them, their own and other cultures, the similarities and differences of other peoples, the social and ecological needs of people, past, present and future? The child's right to learn these things should outweigh his right to read.

SUGGESTED READINGS

The Psychology and Pedagogy of Reading by E. B. Huey (Cambridge: MIT Press, 1968).

"The Bookless Curriculum" by Norman E. Silberberg and Margaret C. Silberberg in *Journal of Learning Disabilities*, 2, No. 6, 1969, pp. 302–307.

Who Speaks for the Child? by Norman E. Silberberg and Margaret C. Silberberg (Springfield, Ill.: Charles C. Thomas, 1974).

3 *Walter E. Schafer, Carol Olexa & Kenneth Polk*

Programmed for Social Class

If, as folklore would have it, America is the land of opportunity, offering anyone the chance to raise himself purely on the basis of his or her ability, then education is the key to self-betterment. The spectacular increase in those of us who attend school is often cited as proof of the great scope of opportunity that our society offers: 94 percent of the high school age population was attending school in 1967, as compared to 7 percent in 1890.

Similarly, our educational system is frequently called more democratic than European systems, for instance, which rigidly segregate students by ability early in their lives, often on the basis of nationally administered examinations such as England's "11-plus." The United States, of course, has no official national policy of educational segregation. Our students, too, are tested and retested throughout their lives and put into faster or slower classes or programs on the basis of their presumed ability, but this procedure is carried out in a decentralized fashion that varies between each city or state.

However, many critics of the American practice claim that, no matter how it is carried out, it does not meet the needs of the brighter and duller groups, so much as it solidifies and widens the differences between them. One such critic, the eminent educator Kenneth B. Clark, speculates: "It is conceivable that the detrimental effects of segregation based upon intellect are similar to the known detrimental effects of schools segregated on the basis of class, nationality or race."

Patricia Cayo Sexton notes that school grouping based on presumed ability often reinforces already existing social divisions:

> Children from higher social strata usually enter the "higher quality" groups and those from lower strata the "lower" ones. School decisions about a child's ability will greatly influence the kind and quality of education he receives, as well as his future life, including whether he goes to college, the job he will get, and his feelings about himself and others.

And Arthur Pearl puts it bluntly:

> . . . "special ability classes," "basic track," or "slow learner classes" are various names for another means of systematically denying the poor adequate access to education.

In this article we will examine some evidence bearing on this vital question of whether current educational practices tend to reinforce existing social class divisions. We will also offer an alternative aimed at making our public schools more effective institutions for keeping open the opportunities for social mobility.

Education Explosion

Since the turn of the century, a number of trends have converged to increase enormously the pressure on American adolescents to graduate from high school: declining opportunity in jobs, the upgrading of educational requirements for job entry, and the diminishing need for teenagers to contribute to family income. While some school systems, especially in the large cities, have adapted to this vast increase in enrollment by creating separate high schools for students with different interests, abilities or occupational goals, most communities have developed comprehensive high schools serving all the youngsters within a neighborhood or community.

In about half the high schools in the United States today, the method for handling these large and varied student populations is through some form of tracking system. Under this arrangement, the entire student body is divided into two or more relatively distinct career lines, or tracks, with such titles as college preparatory, vocational, technical, industrial, business, general, basic and remedial. While students on different tracks may take some courses together in the same classroom, they are usually separated into entirely different courses or different sections of the same course.

School men offer several different justifications for tracking systems. Common to most, however, is the notion that college-bound students are academically more able, learn more rapidly, should not be deterred in their progress by slower, non-college-bound students, and need courses for college preparation which non-college-bound students do not need. By the same token, it is thought that non-college-bound students are less bright, learn more slowly, should not be expected to progress as fast or learn as much as college-bound students, and need only a general education or work-oriented training to prepare themselves for immediate entry into the world of work or a business or vocational school.

In reply, the numerous critics of tracking usually contend that while the college-bound are often encouraged by the tracking system to improve their performance, non-college-bound students, largely as a result of being placed in a lower-rated track, are discouraged from living up to their potential or from showing an interest in academic values. What makes the system especially pernicious, these critics say, is that non-college-bound students more often come from low-income and minority group families. As a result, high schools, through the tracking system, inadvertently close off opportunities for large numbers of students from lower social strata, and thereby contribute to the low achievement, lack of interest, delinquency and rebellion which school men frequently deplore in their noncollege track students.

If these critics are correct, the American comprehensive high school, which is popularly assumed to be the very model of an open and democratic institution, may not really be open and democratic at all. In fact, rather than facilitating equality of educational opportunity, our schools may be subtly denying it, and in the process widening and hardening existing social divisions.

Tracks and Who Gets Put on Them

During the summer of 1964, we collected data from official school transcripts of the recently graduated senior classes of two midwestern three-year high schools. The larger school, located in a predominantly middle-class, academic community of about 70,000, had a graduating class that year of 753 students. The smaller school, with a graduating class of 404, was located nearby in a predominantly working-class, industrial community of about 20,000.

Both schools placed their students into either a college prep or general track. We determined the positions of every student in our sample by whether he took tenth grade English in the college prep or the general section. If he was enrolled in the college prep section, he almost always took other college prep sections or courses, such as advanced mathematics or foreign languages, in which almost all enrollees were also college prep.

Just how students in the two schools were assigned to—or chose—tracks is somewhat of a mystery. When we interviewed people both in the high schools and in their feeder junior highs, we were told that whether a student went into one track or another depended on various factors, such as his own desires and aspirations, teacher advice, achievement test scores, grades, pressure from parents, and counselor assessment of academic promise. One is hard put to say which of these weighs most heavily, but we must note that one team of researchers, Cicourel and Kitsuse, showed in their study of *The Educational Decision-Makers* that assumptions made by counselors about the character, adjustment and potential of in-coming students are vitally important in track assignment.

Whatever the precise dynamics of this decision, the outcome was clear in the schools we studied: socioeconomic and racial background had an effect on which track a student took, quite apart from either his achievement in junior high or his ability as measured by IQ scores. In the smaller, working-class school, 58 percent of the incoming students were assigned to the college prep track; in the larger, middle-class school, 71 percent were placed in the college prep track. And, taking the two schools together, whereas 83 percent of students from white-collar homes were assigned to the college prep track, this was the case with only 48 percent of students from blue-collar homes. The relationship of race to track assignment was even stronger: 71 percent of the whites and only 30 percent of the blacks were assigned to the college prep track. In the two schools studied, the evidence is plain: Children from low income and minority group families more often found themselves in low ability groups and non-college-bound tracks than in high ability groups or college-bound tracks.

Furthermore, this decision-point early in the students' high school careers was of great significance for their futures, since it was virtually irreversible. Only 7 percent of those who began on the college prep track moved down to the noncollege prep track, while only 7 percent of those assigned to the lower, noncollege track, moved up. Clearly, these small figures indicate a high degree of rigid segregation within each of the two schools. In fact, greater mobility between levels has been reported in English secondary modern schools, where streaming—the British term for tracking—is usually thought to be more rigid and fixed than tracking in this country. (It must be remembered, of course, that in England the more rigid break is between secondary modern and grammar schools.)

Differences Between Tracks

As might be expected from the schoolmen's justification for placing students in separate tracks in the first place, track position is noticeably related to academic performance. Thirty-seven percent of the college prep students graduated in the top quarter of their class (measured by grade point average throughout high school), while a mere 2 percent of the noncollege group achieved the top quarter. By contrast, half the noncollege prep students fell in the lowest quarter, as opposed to only 12 percent of the college prep.

Track position is also strikingly related to whether a student's academic performance improves or deteriorates during high school. The grade point average of all sample students in their ninth year—that is, prior to their being assigned to tracks—was compared with their grade point averages over the next three years. While there was a slight difference in the ninth year between those who would subsequently enter the college and noncollege tracks, this difference had increased by the senior year. This widening gap in academic performance resulted from the fact that a higher percentage of students subsequently placed in the college prep track improved their grade point average by the senior year, while a higher percentage of noncollege prep experienced a decline in grade point average by the time they reached the senior year.

Track position is also related strongly to dropout rate. Four percent of the college prep students dropped out of high school prior to graduation, as opposed to 36 percent of the noncollege group.

Track position is also a good indication of how deeply involved a student will be in school, as measured by participation in extracurricular activities. Out of the 753 seniors in the larger school, a comparatively small number of college prep students—21 percent—did not participate in any activities, while 44 percent took part in three or more such activities. By contrast, 58 percent, or more than half of the noncollege group took part in no extracurricular activities at all, and only 11 percent of this group took part in three or more activities.

Finally, track position is strikingly related to delinquency, both in and out of school. Out of the entire school body of the larger school during the 1963–1964 school year—that is, out of 2,565 boys and girls—just over one-third of the college-bound, as opposed to more than half of the non-college-bound committed one or more violations of school rules. Nineteen percent of the college-bound, compared with 70 percent of the non-college-bound, committed three or more such violations. During this year, just over one-third of all the college-bound students were suspended for infractions of school rules, while more than half of all the non-college-bound group were suspended.

Furthermore, using juvenile court records, we find that out of the 1964 graduating class in the larger school, 6 percent of the college prep, and 16 percent of the non-college-bound groups, were delinquent while in high school. Even though 5 percent of those on the noncollege track had already entered high school with court records, opposed to only 1 percent of the college prep track, still more non-college-bound students became delinquent during high school than did college prep students (11 percent compared with 5 percent). So the relation between track position and delinquency is further supported.

We have seen, then, that when compared with college prep students, noncollege prep students show lower achievement, great deterioration of achievement, less participation in extracurricular activities, a greater tendency to drop out, more misbehavior in school, and more delinquency outside of school. Since students are assigned to different tracks largely on the basis of presumed differences in intellectual ability and inclination for further study, the crucial question is whether assignment to different tracks helped to meet the needs of groups of students who were already different, as many educators would claim, or actually contributed to and reinforced such differences, as critics like Sexton and Pearl contend.

The simplest way to explain the differences we have just seen is to attribute them to characteristics already inherent in the individual students, or—at a more sophisticated level—to students' cultural and educational backgrounds.

It can be argued, for example, that the difference in academic achievement between the college and noncollege groups can be explained by the fact that college prep students are simply brighter; after all, this is one of the reasons they were taken into college prep courses. Others would argue that non-college-bound students do less well in school work because of family background: they more often come from blue-collar homes where less value is placed on grades and college, where books and help in schoolwork are less readily available, and verbal expression limited. Still others would contend that lower track students get lower grades because they performed less well in elementary and junior high, have fallen behind, and probably try less hard.

Fortunately, it was possible with our data to separate out the influence of track position from the other suggested factors of social class background (measured by father's occupation), intelligence (measured by IQ—admittedly not a perfectly acceptable measure), and previous academic performance (measured by grade point average for the last semester of the ninth year). Through use of a weighted percentage technique known as test factor standardization, we found that even when the effects of IQ, social class and previous performance are ruled out, there is still a sizable difference in grade point average between the two tracks. With the influence of the first three factors eliminated we nevertheless find that 30 percent of the college prep, as opposed to a mere 4 percent of the noncollege group attained the top quarter of their class; and that only 12 percent of the college prep, as opposed to 35 percent of the noncollege group, fell into the bottom quarter. These figures, which are similar for boys and girls, further show that track position has an independent effect on academic achievement which is greater than the effect of each of the other three factors—social class, IQ and past performance. In particular, assignment to the noncollege track has a strong negative influence on a student's grades.

Looking at dropout rate, and again controlling for social class background, IQ and past performance, we find that track position in itself has an independent influence which is higher than the effect of any of the other three factors. In other words, even when we rule out the effect of these three factors, non-college-bound students still dropped out in considerably greater proportion than college-bound-students (19 percent vs. 4 percent).

When the Forecasters Make the Weather

So our evidence points to the conclusion that the superior academic performance of the college-bound students, and the inferior performance of the noncollege students is partly caused by the tracking system. Our data do not explain how this happens, but several studies of similar educational arrangements, as well as basic principles of social psychology do provide a number of probable explanations. The first point has to do with the pupil's self-image.

Stigma. Assignment to the lower track in the schools we studied carried with it a strong stigma. As David Mallory was told by an American boy, "Around here you are *nothing* if you're not college prep." A noncollege prep girl in one of the schools we studied told me that she always carried her "general" track books upside down because of the humiliation she felt at being seen with them as she walked through the halls.

The corroding effect of such stigmatizing is well known. As Patricia Sexton has put it, "He [the low track student] is bright enough to catch on very quickly to the fact that he is not considered very bright. He comes to accept this unflattering appraisal because, after all, the school should know."

One ex-delinquent in Washington, D.C. told one of us how the stigma from this low track affected him.

> It really don't have to be the tests, but after the tests, there shouldn't be no separation in the classes. Because, as I say again, I felt good when I was with my class, but when they went and separated us—that changed us. That changed our ideas, our thinking, the way we thought about each other and turned us to enemies toward each other—because they said I was dumb and they were smart.
>
> When you first go to junior high school you do feel something inside—it's like ego. You have been from elementary to junior high, you feel great inside. You say, well daggone, I'm going to deal with the *people* here now, I am in junior high school. You get this shirt that says Brown Junior High or whatever the name is and you are proud of that shirt. But then you go up there and the teacher says—"Well, so and so, you're in the basic section, you can't go with the other kids." The devil with the whole thing—you lose—something in you—like it just goes out of you.
>
> *Did you think the other guys were smarter than you?* Not at first—I used to think I was just as smart as anybody in the school—I knew I was smart. I knew some people were smarter, and I *wanted* to go to school, I wanted to get a diploma and go to college and help people and everything. I stepped into there in junior high—I felt like a fool going to school—I really felt like a fool. *Why?* Because I felt like I wasn't a part of the school. I couldn't get on special patrols, because I wasn't qualified. *What happened between the seventh and ninth grades?* I started losing faith in myself—after the teachers kept downing me. You hear "a guy's in basic section, he's dumb" and all this. Each year—"you're ignorant—you're stupid."

Considerable research shows that such erosion of self-esteem greatly increases the chances of academic failure, as well as dropping out and causing "trouble" both inside and outside of school.

Moreover, this lowered self-image is reinforced by the expectations that others have toward a person in the noncollege group.

The Self-fulfilling Prophecy. A related explanation rich in implications comes from David Hargreaves' *Social Relations in a Secondary School*, a study of the psychological, behavioral and educational consequences of the student's position in the streaming system of an English secondary modern school. In "Lumley School," the students (all boys) were assigned to one of five streams on the basis of ability and achievement, with the score on the "11-plus" examination playing the major role.

Like the schools we studied, students in the different streams were publicly recognized as high or low in status and were fairly rigidly segregated, both formally in different classes and informally in friendship groups. It is quite probable, then, that Hargreaves' explanations for the greater antischool attitudes, animosity toward teachers, academic failure, disruptive behavior and delinquency among the low stream boys apply to the noncollege prep students we studied as well. In fact, the negative effects of the tracking system on non-college-bound students may be even stronger in our two high schools, since the Lumley streaming system was much more open and flexible, with students moving from one stream to another several times during their four-year careers.

Streamed Schools

As we noted, a popular explanation for the greater failure and misbehavior among low stream or non-college-bound students is that they come from homes that fail to provide the same skills, ambition or conforming attitude as higher stream or college-bound students. Hargreaves demonstrates that there is some validity to this position: in his study, low stream boys more often came from homes that provided less encouragement for academic achievement and higher level occupations, and that were less oriented to the other values of the school and teachers. Similar differences may have existed among the students we studied, although their effects have been markedly reduced by our control for father's occupation, IQ and previous achievement.

But Hargreaves provides a convincing case for the position that whatever the differences in skills, ambition, self-esteem or educational commitment that the students brought to school, they were magnified by what happened to them in school, largely because low stream boys were the victims of a self-fulfilling prophecy in their relations with teachers, with respect to both academic performance and classroom behavior. Teachers of higher stream boys expected higher performance and got it. Similarly, boys who wore the label of streams "C" or "D" were more likely to be seen by teachers as limited in ability and troublemakers, and were treated accordingly.

In a streamed school the teacher categorizes the pupils not only in terms of the inferences he makes of the child's class room behavior but also from the child's stream level. It is for this reason that the teacher can rebuke an "A" stream boy for being like a "D" stream boy. The teacher has learned to *expect* certain kinds of behavior from members of different streams. . . . It would be hardly surprising if "good" pupils thus became "better" and the "bad" pupils become "worse." It is, in short, an example of a self-fulfilling prophecy. The negative expectations of the teacher reinforce the negative behavioral tendencies.

A recent study by Rosenthal and Jacobson in an American elementary school lends further evidence to the position that teacher expectations influence student's performance. In this study, the influence is a positive one. Teachers of children randomly assigned to experimental groups were told at the beginning of the year to expect "unusual intellectual" gains, while teachers of the control group children were told nothing. After eight months, and again after two years, the experimental group children, the "intellectual spurters," showed significantly greater gains in IQ and grades. Further, they were rated by the teachers as being significantly more curious, interesting, happy and more likely to succeed in the future. Such findings are consistent with theories of interpersonal influence and with the interactional or labelling view of deviant behavior.

If, as often claimed, American teachers underestimate the learning potential of low track students and expect more negative attitudes and greater trouble from them, it may well be that they partially cause the very failure, alienation, lack of involvement, dropping out and rebellion they are seeking to prevent. As Hargreaves says of Lumley, "It is important to stress that if this effect of categorization is real, it is entirely unintended by the teachers. They do not wish to make low streams more difficult than they are!" Yet the negative self-fulfilling prophecy was probably real, if unintended and unrecognized, in our two schools as well as in Lumley.

Two further consequences of the expectation that students in the noncollege group will learn less well are differences in grading policies and in teacher effectiveness.

Grading Policies. In the two schools we studied, our interviews strongly hint at the existence of grade ceilings for noncollege prep students and grade floors for college-bound students. That is, by virtue of being located in a college preparatory section or course, college prep students could seldom receive any grade lower than "B" or "C," while students in non-college-bound sections or courses found it difficult to gain any grade higher than "C," even though their objective performance may have been equivalent to a college prep "B." Several teachers explicitly called our attention to this practice, the rationale being that noncollege prep students do not deserve the same objective grade rewards as college prep students, since they "clearly" are less bright and perform less well. To the extent that grade ceilings do operate for non-college-bound students, the lower grades that result from this policy, almost by definition, can hardly have a beneficial effect on motivation and commitment.

Teaching Effectiveness. Finally, numerous investigations of ability grouping, as well as the English study by Hargreaves, have reported that teachers of higher ability groups are likely to teach in a more interesting and effective manner than teachers of lower ability groups. Such a difference is predictable from what we know about the effects of reciprocal interaction between teacher and class. Even when the same individual teaches both types of classes in the course of the day, as was the case for most teachers in the two schools in this study, he is likely to be "up" for college prep classes and "down" for noncollege prep classes—and to bring out the same reaction from his students.

A final, and crucial factor that contributes to the poorer performance and lower interest in school of non-college-bound students is the relation between school work and the adult career after school.

Future Payoff. Non-college-bound students often develop progressively more negative attitudes toward school, especially formal academic work, because they see grades—and indeed school itself—as having little future relevance or payoff. This is not the case for college prep students. For them, grades are a means toward the identifiable and meaningful end of qualifying for college, while among the non-college-bound, grades are seen as far less important for entry into an occupation or a vocational school. This difference in the practical importance of grades is magnified by the perception among non-college-bound students that it is pointless to put much effort into school work, since it will be unrelated to the later world of work anyway. In a study of *Rebellion in a High School* in this country, Arthur Stinchcombe describes the alienation of non-college-bound high school students:

> The major practical conclusion of the analysis above is that rebellious behavior is largely a reaction to the school itself and to its promises, not a failure of the family or community. High school students can be motivated to conform by paying them in the realistic coin of future advantage. Except perhaps for pathological cases, any student can be motivated to conform if the school can realistically promise something valuable to him as a reward for working hard. But for a large part of the population, especially the adolescent who will enter the male working class or the female candidates for early marriage, the school has nothing to offer. . . . In order to secure conformity from students, a high school must articulate academic work with careers of students.

Being on the lower track has other negative consequences for the student which go beyond the depressing influence on his academic performance and motivation. We can use the principles just discussed to explain our findings with regard to different rates of participation in school activities and acts of misbehavior.

Tracks Conformity & Deviance

For example, the explanations having to do with self-image and the expectations of others suggest that assignment to the non-college-bound track has a dampening effect on commitment to school in general, since it is the school which originally categorized these students as inferior. Thus, assignment to the lower track may be seen as independently contributing to resentment, frustration and hostility in school, leading to lack of involvement in all school activities, and finally ending in active withdrawal. The self-exclusion of the noncollege group from the mainstream of college student life is probably enhanced by intentional or unintentional exclusion by other students and teachers.

Using the same type of reasons, while we cannot prove a definite causal linkage between track position and misbehavior, it seems highly likely that assignment to the non-college prep track often leads to resentment, declining commitment to school, and rebellion against it, expressed in lack of respect for the school's authority or acts of disobedience against it. As Albert Cohen argued over a decade ago in *Delinquent Boys,* delinquency may well be largely a rebellion against the school and its standards by teenagers who feel they cannot get anywhere by attempting to adhere to such standards. Our analysis suggests that a key factor in such rebellion is noncollege prep status in the school's tracking system, with the vicious cycle of low achievement and inferior self-image that go along with it.

This conclusion is further supported by Hargreaves' findings on the effect of streaming at Lumley:

> There is a real sense in which the school can be regarded as a generator of delinquency. Although the aims and efforts of the teachers are directed towards deleting such tendencies, the organization of the school and its influence on subcultural development unintentionally fosters delinquent values. . . . For low stream boys . . . , school simultaneously exposes them to these values and deprives them of status in these terms. It is at this point they may begin to reject the values because they cannot succeed in them. The school provides a mechanism through the streaming system whereby their failure is effected and institutionalized, and also provides a situation in which they can congregate together in low streams.

Hargreaves' last point suggests a very important explanation for the greater degree of deviant behavior among the non-college-bound.

The Student Subculture. Assignment to a lower stream at Lumley meant a boy was immediately immersed in a student subculture that stressed and rewarded antagonistic attitudes and behavior toward teachers and all they stood for. If a boy was assigned to the "A" stream, he was drawn toward the values of teachers, not only by the higher expectations and more positive rewards from the teachers themselves, but from other students as well. The converse was true of lower stream boys, who accorded each other high status for doing the opposite of what teachers wanted. Because of class scheduling, little opportunity developed for interaction and friendship across streams. The result was a progressive polarization and hardening of the high and low stream subcultures between first and fourth years and a progressively greater negative attitude across stream lines, with quite predictable consequences.

> The informal pressures within the low streams tend to work directly against the assumption of the teachers that boys will regard promotion into a higher stream as a desirable goal. The boys from the low streams were very reluctant to ascent to higher streams because their stereotypes of "A" and "B" stream boys were defined in terms of values alien to their own and because promotion would involve rejection by their low stream friends. The teachers were not fully aware that this unwillingness to be promoted to a higher stream led the high informal status boys to depress their performance in examinations. This fear of promotion adds to our list of factors leading to the formation of anti-academic attitudes among low stream boys.

Observations and interviews in the two American schools we studied confirmed a similar polarization and reluctance by noncollege prep students to pursue the academic goals rewarded by teachers and college prep students. Teachers, however, seldom saw the antischool attitudes of noncollege prep students as arising out of the tracking system—or anything else about the school—but out of adverse home influences, limited intelligence or psychological problems.

Implications. These, then, are some of the ways the schools we studied contributed to the greater rates of failure, academic decline, uninvolvement in school activities, misbehavior and delinquency among non-college-bound students. We can only speculate, of course, about the generalization of these findings to other schools. However, there is little reason to think the two schools we studied were unusual or unrepresentative and, despite differences in size and social class composition, the findings are virtually identical in both. To the extent the findings are valid and general, they strongly suggest that, through their tracking system, the schools are partly causing many of the very problems they are trying to solve and are posing an important barrier to equal educational opportunity to lower income and black students, who are disproportionately assigned to the noncollege prep track.

The notion that schools help cause low achievement, deterioration of educational commitment and involvement, the dropout problem, misbehavior and delinquency is foreign and repulsive to many teachers, administrators and parents. Yet our evidence is entirely consistent with Kai Erikson's observation that " . . . deviant forms of conduct often seem to derive nourishment from the very agencies devised to inhibit them."

What, then, are the implications of this study? Some might argue that, despite the negative side effects we have shown, tracking systems are essential for effective teaching, especially for students with high ability, as well as for adjusting students early in their careers to the status levels they will occupy in the adult occupational system. We contend that however reasonable this may sound, the negative effects demonstrated here offset and call into serious question any presumed gains from tracking.

Others might contend that the negative outcomes we have documented can be eliminated by raising teachers' expectations of noncollege track students, making concerted efforts to reduce the stigma attached to noncollege classes, assigning good teachers to noncollege track classes, rewarding them for doing an effective job at turning on their students, and developing fair and equitable grading practices in both college prep and noncollege prep classes.

Attractive as they may appear, efforts like these will be fruitless, so long as tracking systems, and indeed schools as we now know them, remain unchanged. What is needed are wholly new, experimental environments of teaching-learning-living, even outside today's public schools, if necessary. Such schools of the future must address themselves to two sets of problems highlighted by our findings: ensuring equality of opportunity for students now "locked out" by tracking, and offering—to all students—a far more fulfilling and satisfying learning process.

One approach to building greater equality of opportunity, as well as fulfillment, into existing or new secondary schools is the New Careers model. This model, which provides for fundamentally different ways of linking up educational and occupational careers, is based on the recognition that present options for entering the world of work are narrowly limited: one acquires a high school diploma and goes to work, or he first goes to college and perhaps then to a graduate or professional school. (Along the way, of course, young men must cope with the draft.)

The New Careers model provides for new options. Here the youth who does not want to attend college or would not qualify according to usual criteria, is given the opportunity to attend high school part time while working in a lower level position in an expanded professional career hierarchy (including such new positions as teacher aide and teacher associate in education). Such a person would then have the options of moving up through progressively more demanding educational and work stages; and moving back and forth between the work place, the high school and then the college. As ideally conceived, this model would allow able and aspiring persons ultimately to progress to the level of the fully certified teacher, nurse, librarian, social worker or public administrator. While the New Careers model has been developed and tried primarily in the human service sector of the economy, we have pointed out elsewhere that it is applicable to the industrial and business sector as well.

This alternative means of linking education with work has a number of advantages: students can try different occupations while still in school; they can earn while studying; they can spend more time outside the four walls of the school, learning what can best be learned in the work place; less stigma will accrue to those not immediately college bound, since they too will have a future; studying and learning will be inherently more relevant because it will relate to a career in which they are actively involved; teachers of such students will be less likely to develop lower expectations because these youth too will have an unlimited, open-ended future; and antischool subcultures will be less likely to develop, since education will not be as negative, frustrating or stigmatizing.

Changes of this kind imply changes in the economy as well and, therefore, are highly complicated and far-reaching. Because of this, they will not occur overnight. But they are possible, through persistent, creative and rigorously evaluated educational, economic and social experimentation.

Whatever the future, we hope teachers, administrators and school boards will take one important message from our findings: what they do to students makes a difference. Through the kind of teaching-learning process they create, the schools can screen out and discourage large numbers of youth, or they can develop new means for serving the interests and futures of the full range of their students.

SUGGESTED READINGS

"Delinquency and the Schools" by Walter E. Schafer and Kenneth Polk in *Task Force Report: Juvenile Delinquency and Youth Crime* (President's Commission on Law Enforcement and Administration of Justice, 1967).

4 *Samuel Bowles*

Getting Nowhere: Programmed Class Stagnation

Education has long been the chosen instrument of American social reformers. Whatever the ills that beset our society, education is thought to be the cure. Most Americans share the faith—voiced by Horace Mann over a century ago—that education is the "great equalizer." With access to public schools, the children of every class and condition have an equal chance to develop their talents and make a success of themselves. It is our public system of education—so the conventional wisdom goes—that guarantees an open society where any citizen can rise from the lowliest background to high social position according to his ability and efforts.

The record of educational history in the United States and scrutiny of the present state of our colleges and schools lend little support to this comforting optimism. Rather, the available data suggest an alternative interpretation. Apparently our schools have evolved not as part of a pursuit of equality but rather to meet the needs of capitalist employers for a disciplined and skilled labor force and to provide a mechanism for social control in the interests of political stability. As the economic importance of skilled and well-educated labor has grown, inequalities in the school system have become increasingly important in reproducing the class structure from one generation to the next. In fact, the United States school system is pervaded by class inequalities which have shown little sign of diminishing over the last half-century. The evidently unequal control over school boards and other decision-making bodies in education does not provide a sufficient explanation of the persistence and pervasiveness of these inequalities. Although the unequal distribution of political power serves to maintain inequalities in education, their origins are to be found outside the political sphere in the class structure itself and in the class subcultures typical of capitalist societies. Thus unequal education has its roots in the very class structure which it serves to legitimize and reproduce.

In colonial America, as in most pre-capitalist societies of the past, the basic productive unit was the family. For the vast majority of male adults, work was self-directed and was performed without direct supervision. Though constrained by poverty, ill health, the low level of technological development and occasional interferences by the political authorities, a man had considerable leeway in choosing his working hours, what to produce and how to produce it. While great inequalities in wealth, political power and other aspects of status normally existed, differences in the degree of autonomy in work were relatively minor, particularly when compared with what was to come.

Parents as Teachers

Transmitting the necessary productive skills to the children as they grew up proved to be a simple task, not because the work was devoid of skill, but because the quite substantial skills required were virtually unchanging from generation to generation, and because the transition to the world of work did not require that the child adapt to a wholly new set of social relationships. The child learned the concrete skills and adapted to the social relations of production through learning by doing within the family.

All of this changed with the advent of the capitalist economy in which the vast majority of economically active individuals relinquished control over their labor power in return for wages or salaries and in which the non-labor means of production were privately owned. The extension of capitalist production (particularly the factory system) undermined the role of the family as the major unit of both socialization and production. Small farmers were driven off the land or competed out of business. Cottage industry was destroyed. Ownership of the means of production became heavily concentrated in the hands of the owners of capital and land. Increasingly, production was carried on in large organizations in which a small management group directed the work activities of the entire labor force. The social relations of production—the authority structure, the prescribed types of behavior and response characteristic of the work place—became increasingly distinct from those of the family.

The divorce of the worker from control over production—from control over his own labor—is particularly important in understanding the role of schooling in capitalist societies. The resulting social division of labor between controllers and the controlled is a crucial aspect of the class structure and will be seen as an important barrier to the achievement of social-class equality in schooling.

While undermining both family and church—the main institutions of socialization—the development of the capitalist system created at the same time an environment which would ultimately challenge the political order. Workers were thrown together in oppressive factories, and the isolation which had helped to maintain quiescence in earlier, widely dispersed peasant populations was broken down. With an increasing number of families uprooted from the land, the workers' search for a living resulted in large-scale labor migrations. Transient (and even foreign) elements came to constitute a major segment of the population and began to pose seemingly insurmountable problems of assimilation, integration and control. Inequalities of wealth became more apparent and were less easily justified and less readily accepted. The simple legitimizing ideologies of the earlier period—for example, the divine right of kings and the divine origin of social rank—fell under the capitalist attack on the royalty and the traditional landed interests. The broadening of the electorate, first sought by the capitalist class in the struggle against the entrenched interests of the pre-capitalist period, soon threatened to become an instrument for the growing power of the working class. Having risen to political power, the capitalist class sought a mechanism to insure social control and political stability.

An institutional crisis was at hand. The outcome, in virtually all capitalist countries, was the rise of mass education. In the United States, the many advantages of schooling as a socialization process were quickly perceived. The early proponents of the rapid expansion of schooling argued that education could perform many of the socialization functions which earlier had been centered in the family and to a lesser extent in the church.

An ideal preparation for factory work was found in the social relations of the school, specifically in its emphasis on discipline, punctuality, acceptance of authority outside the family and individual accountability for one's work. A manufacturer writing to the Massachusetts State Board of Education from Lowell in 1841 commented:

> I have never considered mere knowledge. . .as the only advantage derived from a good education. . . . [Workers with more education possess] a higher and better state of morals, are more orderly and respectful in their deportment, and more ready to comply with the wholesome and necessary regulations of an establishment. . . . In times of agitation, on account of some change in regulations or wages, I have always looked to the most intelligent, best educated and the most moral for support. The ignorant and uneducated I have generally found the most turbulent and troublesome, acting under the impulse of excited passion and jealousy.

The social relations of the school would replicate the social relations of the workplace and thus help young people adapt to the social division of labor. Schools would further lead people to accept the authority of the state and its agents—the teachers—at a young age, in part by fostering the illusion of the benevolence of the government in its relations with citizens. Moreover, because schooling would ostensibly be open to all, one's position in the social division of labor could be portrayed as the result not of birth, but of one's own efforts and talents. And if the children's everyday experiences with the structure of schooling were insufficient to inculcate the correct views and attitudes, the curriculum itself would be made to embody the bourgeois ideology. Thomas Cooper, an American economist, wrote in 1828:

> Education universally extended throughout the community will tend to disabuse the working class of people in respect of a notion that has crept into the minds of our mechanics and is gradually prevailing, that manual labor is at present very inadequately rewarded, owing to combinations of the rich against the poor; that mere mental labor is comparatively worthless; that property or wealth ought not to be accumulated or transmitted; that to take interest on money lent or profit on capital employed is unjust. . . . The mistaken and ignorant people who entertain these fallacies as truths will learn, when they have the opportunity of learning, that the institution of political society originated in the protection of property.

The movement for public elementary and secondary education in the United States originated in the nineteenth century in states dominated by the burgeoning industrial capitalist class, most notably in Massachusetts. It spread rapidly to all parts of the country except the South. In Massachusetts the extension of elementary education was in large measure a response to industrialization and to the need for social control of the Irish and other non-Yankee workers recruited to work in the mills. The fact that some working people's movements had demanded free instruction should not obscure the basically coercive nature of the extension of schooling. In many parts of the country, schools were literally imposed upon the workers.

A system of class stratification developed within this rapidly expanding educational system. Children of the social elite normally attended private schools. Because working-class children tended to leave school early, the class composition of the public high schools was distinctly more elite than that of the public primary schools. And as a university education ceased to be merely training for teaching or the divinity and became important in gaining access to the pinnacles of the business world, upper-class families increasingly used their money and influence to get their children into the best universities, often at the expense of the children of less elite families.

Around the turn of the century, large numbers of working-class (and particularly immigrant) children began attending high schools. At the same time, a system of class stratification developed within secondary education.

The older democratic ideology of the common school—that the same curriculum should be offered to all children—gave way to the "progressive" insistence that education should be tailored to the "needs of the child." The superintendent of the Boston schools summed up the change in 1908:

> Until very recently [the schools] have offered equal opportunity for all to receive *one kind* of education, but what will make them democratic is to provide opportunity for all to receive such education as will fit them *equally well* for their particular life work.

In the interests of providing an education relevant to the later life of the students, vocational schools and tracks were developed for the children of working families. The academic curriculum was preserved for those who would later have the opportunity to make use of book learning either in college or in white-collar employment. This and other educational reforms of the progressive education movement reflected an implicit assumption of the immutability of the class structure.

Tracking by Social Class

The frankness with which students were channeled into curriculum tracks on the basis of their social-class background raised serious doubts concerning the openness of the class structure. The apparent unfairness of the selection and tracking procedures was disguised (though not mitigated much) by another "progressive" reform—"objective" educational testing. Particularly after World War I, the capitulation of the schools to business values and the cult of efficiency led to the increased use of intelligence and scholastic achievement testing as an ostensibly unbiased means of measuring school outputs and classifying students. The complementary growth of the guidance counseling profession allowed much of the channeling to proceed from the students' own well-counselled choices, thus adding an apparent element of voluntarism to the mechanisms perpetuating the class structure.

As schooling became the standard for assigning children positions in the class structure, it played a major part in legitimizing the structure itself. But at the same time it undermined the simple processes by which the upper class had preserved its position from one generation to the next—the inheritance of physical capital. When education and skills play an important role in the hierarchy of production, the inheritance of capital from one generation to the next is not enough to reproduce the social division of labor. Rather skills broadly defined and educational credentials must somehow be passed on within the family. It is in furthering this modern form of class structure that the school plays a fundamental role. Children whose parents occupy positions at the top of the occupational hierarchy receive more and better schooling than working-class children. Inequalities in years of schooling are particularly evident. My analysis of United States Census data indicate that if we define social-class standing by the income, occupation and educational level of the parents, a child from the 90th percentile in the class distribution may expect on the average to achieve over four-and-a-half more years of schooling than a child from the tenth percentile. Even among those who had graduated from high school, children of families earning less than $3,000 per year were over six times as likely not to attend college as were the children of families earning over $15,000.

Because schooling is heavily subsidized by the general taxpayer, the longer a child attends school, the more public resources he has access to. Further, public expenditure per student in four-year colleges greatly exceeds that in elementary schools; those who stay in school longer receive an increasingly large *annual* public subsidy. In the school year 1969-70, per-pupil expenditures of federal, state and local funds were $1490 for colleges and universities and $747 for primary and secondary schools. Even at the elementary level, schools in low income neighborhoods tend to be less well endowed with equipment, books, teachers and other inputs into the educational process.

The inequalities in schooling go deeper than these simple measures. Differences in rules, expected modes of behavior and opportunities for choice are most glaring when we compare levels of schooling. Note the wide range of choice over curriculum, life style and allocation of time afforded to college students compared with the obedience and respect for authority expected in high school. Differentiation also occurs within each level of schooling. One needs only to compare the social relations of a junior college with those of an elite four-year college, or those of a working-class high school with those of a wealthy suburban high school, for verification of this point. It is consistent with this pattern that the play-oriented, child-centered pedagogy of the progressive movement found little acceptance outside of private schools and public schools in wealthy communities.

Mirror of the Factory

These differences in socialization patterns do not arise by accident. Rather, they are the product of class differences in educational objectives and expectations held by parents and educators alike and of differences in student responsiveness to various patterns of teaching and control. Further, a teacher in an understaffed, ill-equipped school may be compelled to resort to authoritarian tactics whether she wants to or not. Lack of resources precludes having small intimate classes, a multiplicity of elective courses, specialized teachers (except disciplinary personnel), free time for the teachers and the free space required for a more open, flexible educational environment. Socialization in such a school comes to mirror that of the factory; students are treated as raw materials on a production line. There is a high premium on obedience and punctuality and there are few opportunities for independent, creative work or individualized attention by teachers.

Even where working-class children attend a well-financed school they do not receive the same treatment as the children of the rich. Class stratification within a given school is achieved through tracking and differential participation in extracurricular activities; it is reinforced by attitudes of teachers and particularly guidance personnel who expect working-class children to do poorly, to terminate schooling early and to end up in jobs similar to their parents.

Not surprisingly, the results of schooling differ greatly for children of different social classes. On nationally standardized achievement tests, children whose parents were themselves highly educated outperform by a wide margin the children of parents with less education. A recent study revealed, for example, that among white high school seniors, those whose parents were in the top education decile were on the average well over three grade levels ahead of those whose parents were in the bottom decile.

Given class differences in scholastic achievement, class inequalities in college attendance are to be expected. Thus one might be tempted to argue that the data in Table I are simply a reflection of unequal scholastic achievement in high school and do not reflect any additional social-class inequalities peculiar to the process of college admission. This view, so comforting to the admissions personnel in our elite universities, is unsupported by the available data, some of which is presented in Table 2. Access to a college education is highly unequal, even for students of the same measured academic ability.

And inequalities of educational opportunity show no signs of abatement. In fact, data from a recent United States Census survey reported in Table 3 indicate that graduation from college is at least as dependent on one's class background now as it was 50 years ago. Considering access to all levels of education, the data suggest that the number of years of schooling attained by a child depends upon the social-class standing of the father slightly more in the recent period than it did at the beginning of the century.

The pervasive and persistent inequalities in the United States system of education pose serious problems of interpretation. If the costs of education borne by students and their families were very high, or if nepotism were rampant, or if formal segregation of pupils by social class were practiced, or educational decisions were made by a select few whom we might call the power elite, it would not be difficult to explain the continued inequalities in the system. The problem is to reconcile the above empirical findings with the facts of our society as we perceive them: public and virtually tuition-free education at all levels, few legal instruments for the direct implementation of class segregation, a limited role for contacts or nepotism in the achievement of high status or income, a commitment (at the rhetorical level at least) to equality of educational opportunity and a system of control of education which if not particularly democratic extends far beyond anything resembling a power elite. The attempt to reconcile these apparently discrepant facts leads us back to a consideration of the social division of labor, the associated class cultures and the exercise of class power.

The social division of labor—based on the hierarchical structure of production—gives rise to distinct class subcultures, each of which has its own values, personality traits and expectations. The social relations of production characteristic of advanced capitalist societies (and many socialist societies) are most clearly illustrated in the bureaucracy and hierarchy of the modern corporation. Occupational roles in the capitalist economy may be grouped according to the degree of independence and control exercised by the person holding the job. The personality attributes associated with the adequate performance of jobs in occupational categories defined in this broad way differ considerably, some apparently requiring independence and internal discipline, and others emphasizing such traits as obedience, predictability and willingness to subject oneself to external controls.

These personality attributes are developed primarily at a young age, both in the family and to a lesser extent in secondary socialization institutions such as schools. Daily experience in the work place reinforces these traits in adults. Because people tend to marry within their own class, both parents are likely to have a similar set of these fundamental personality traits. Thus children of parents occupying a given position in the occupational hierarchy grow up in homes where child-rearing methods and perhaps even the physical surroundings tend to develop personality characteristics appropriate to adequate job performance in the occupational roles of the parents. The children of managers and professionals are taught self-reliance within a broad set of constraints; the children of production-line workers are taught conformity and obedience.

Melvin Kohn summarizes his extensive empirical work on class structure and parental values as follows:

> Whether consciously or not, parents tend to impart to their children lessons derived from the condition of life

Table 1 — College Attendance in 1967 among High School Graduates, by Family Income

Family income	Percent who did not attend college
Total	53.1
under $3,000	80.2
$3,000 to $3,999	67.7
$4,000 to $5,999	63.7
$6,000 to $7,499	58.9
$7,500 to $9,999	49.0
$10,000 to $14,999	38.7
$15,000 and over	13.3

Refers to high school seniors in October 1965 who subsequently graduated. Bureau of the Census, *Current Population Report*, 1969. College attendance refers to both two- and four-year institutions.

Table 2 — Probability of College Entry for a Male Who Has Reached Grade 11

		Socioeconomic quartiles			
		Low 1	2	3	High 4
	1 Low	.06	.12	.13	.26
Ability	2	.13	.15	.29	.36
quartiles	3	.25	.34	.45	.65
	4 High	.48	.70	.73	.87

Based on a large sample of U.S. high school students studied by Project Talent at the University of Pittsburgh, 1966.
The socioeconomic index is a composite measure including family income, father's occupation and education, mother's education and so forth. The ability scale is a composite of tests measuring general academic aptitude.

Table 3 — Among Sons Who Had Reached High School, Percentage Who Graduated from College, By Son's Age and Father's Level of Education

		Father's Education						
Son's age in 1962	Likely dates of college graduation	Less than 8 years	Some high school: Percent graduating	Some high school: Ratio to less than 8 years	High school graduate: Percent graduating	High school graduate: Ratio to less than 8 years	Some college or more: Percent graduating	Some college or more: Ratio to less than 8 years
25-34	1950-1959	07.6	17.4	2.29	25.6	3.37	51.9	6.83
35-44	1940-1949	08.6	11.9	1.38	25.3	2.94	53.9	6.27
45-54	1930-1939	07.7	09.8	1.27	15.1	1.96	36.9	4.79
55-64	1920-1929	08.9	09.8	1.10	19.2	2.16	29.8	3.35

Based on U.S. Census data for 1962 as reported in William G. Spady, "Educational Mobility and Access: Growth and Paradoxes," *American Journal of Sociology*, November 1967.
Assumes college graduation at age 22.

of their own class—and thus help to prepare their children for a similar class position. . . . The conformist values and orientation of lower- and working-class parents are inappropriate for training children to deal with the problems of middle-class and professional life. . . . The family, then, functions as a mechanism for perpetuating inequality.

This relation between parents' class position and child's personality attributes is reinforced by schools and other social institutions. Teachers, guidance counselors and school administrators ordinarily encourage students to develop aspirations and expectations typical of their social class, even if the child tends to have deviant aspirations.

It is true that schools introduce some common elements of socialization for all students. Discipline, respect for property, competition and punctuality are part of implicit curricula. Yet the ability of a school to appreciably change a child's future is severely limited. However, the responsiveness of children to different types of schooling seems highly dependent upon the personality traits, values and expectations which have been developed through the family. Furthermore, since children spend a small amount of time in school—less than a quarter of their waking hours over the course of a year—schools are probably more effective where they complement and reinforce rather than oppose the socialization processes of the home and neighborhood. Not surprisingly, this relationship between family socialization and that of the schools reproduces patterns of class culture from generation to generation.

Among adults the differing daily work experiences of people reinforce these patterns of class culture. The reward structure of the workplace favors the continued development of traits such as obedience and acceptance of authority among workers. Conversely, those occupying directing roles in production are rewarded for the capacity to make decisions and exert authority. Thus the operation of the incentive structure of the job stabilizes and reproduces patterns of class culture. The operation of the labor market translates these differences in class culture into income inequalities and occupational hierarchies. Recent work by Herbert Gintis and other economists shows that the relation between schooling and economic success cannot be explained by the effect of schooling on intellectual capacity. Rather, the economic success of individuals with higher educational attainments is explained by their highly rewarded personality characteristics which facilitate entry into the upper echelons of the production hierarchy. These personality characteristics, originating in the work experiences of one's parents, transmitted in turn to children through early socialization practices and reinforced in school and on the job are an important vehicle for the reproduction of the social division of labor.

But the argument thus far is incomplete. The perpetuation of inequality through the schooling system has been represented as an almost automatic, self-enforcing mechanism, operating through the medium of class culture. An important further dimension is added to this interpretation if we note that positions of control in the productive hierarchy tend to be associated with positions of political influence. Given the disproportionate share of political power held by the upper classes and their capacity for determining the accepted patterns of behavior and procedures, to define the national interest and to control the ideological and institutional context in which educational decisions are made, it is not surprising to find that resources are allocated unequally among school tracks, between schools serving different classes and between levels of schooling. The same configuration of power results in curricula, methods of instruction and criteria which, though often seemingly innocuous and ostensibly even egalitarian, serves to maintain the unequal system.

Illusion of Fair Treatment

Take the operation of one of these rules of the game—the principle that excellence in schooling should be rewarded. The upper class defines excellence in terms on which upper-class children tend to excel (for example, scholastic achievement). Adherence to this principle yields inegalitarian outcomes (for example, unequal access to higher education) while maintaining the appearance of fair treatment. Those who would defend the "reward excellence" principle on the grounds of efficient selection to ensure the most efficent use of educational resources might ask themselves this: why should colleges admit those with the highest college entrance examination board scores? Why not the lowest or the middle? According to conventional standards of efficiency, the rational social objective of the college is to render the greatest increment in individual capacities ("value added," to the economist), not to produce the most illustrious graduating class ("gross output"). Thus the principle of rewarding excellence does not appear to be motivated by a concern for the efficient use of educational resources. Rather it serves to legitimize the unequal consequences of schooling.

Though cognitive capacities are relatively unimportant in the determination of income and occupational success, the reward of intellectual ability in school plays an important role. The "objective" testing of scholastic achievement and relatively meritocratic system of grading encourages the illusion that promotion and rewards are distributed fairly. The close relationship between educational attainments and later occupational success further masks the paramount importance of race and social-class background for getting ahead.

At the same time, the institution of objectively administered tests of performance serves to allow a limited amount of upward mobility among exceptional children of the lower class, thus providing further legitimation of the operations of the social system by giving some credence to the myth of widespread mobility.

The operation of the "reward excellence" rule illustrates the symbiosis between the political and economic power of the upper class. Adherence to the rule has the effect of generating unequal consequences via a mechanism which operates largely outside the political system. As long as one adheres to the reward (academic) excellence principle, the responsibility for unequal results in schooling appears to rest outside the upper class, often in some fault of the poor—such as their class culture—which is viewed as lying beyond the reach of political action or criticism.

Thus it appears that the consequences of an unequal distribution of political power among classes complement the results of class culture in maintaining an educational system which has thus far been capable of transmitting status from generation to generation, and capable in addition of political survival in the formally democratic and egalitarian environment of the contemporary United States.

The role of the schools in reproducing and legitimizing the social division of labor has recently been challenged by popular egalitarian movements. At the same time, the educational system is showing signs of internal structural weakness. I have argued elsewhere that overproduction of highly educated workers by universities and graduate schools and a breakdown of authority at all levels of schooling are not passing phenomena, but deeply rooted in the pattern of growth and structural change in the advanced capitalist economy. These two developments suggest that fundamental change in the schooling process may soon be possible.

But it should be clear that educational equality cannot be achieved through changes in the school system alone. Attempts at educational reform may move us closer to that objective (if, in their failure, they lay bare the unequal nature of our school system and destroy the illusion of unimpeded mobility through education). Yet if the record of the last century and a half of educational reforms is any guide, we should not expect radical change in education to result from the efforts of reformers who confine their attention to the schools. My interpretation of the educational consequences of class culture and class power suggests that past educational reform movements failed because they sought to eliminate educational inequalities without challenging the basic institutions of capitalism.

Efforts to equalize education through changes in school finance, compensatory education and similar programs will at best scratch the surface of inequality. As long as jobs are structured so that some have power over many and others have power over nothing—as long as the social division of labor persists—educational inequality will be built into U.S. society.

SUGGESTED READINGS

"Contradictions in U.S. Higher Education" by Samuel Bowles in *Political Economy: Radical vs. Orthodox Approaches*, edited by James Weaver (Boston: Allyn & Bacon, 1972).

The Irony of Early School Reform by Michael B. Katz (Cambridge: Harvard University Press, 1968).

"Unequal Education and the Reproduction of the Social Division of Labor" in the *Review of Radical Political Economy*, Winter 1971.

5 *Charles Witter*

Drugging and Schooling

Minimal brain dysfunction (MBD), one of at least 38 names attached to a subset of learning disabilities, can significantly hinder a grammar school student of average or above-average intelligence from achieving his full potential. Hyperactive, often loud and demanding and little responsive to the feelings of others (or himself), the MBD child can be seen as the very model of the uncontrollable student. Then, 30 years ago, it was discovered that amphetamines, stimulants and/or tranquilizers could calm the hyperactive child who was so often disruptive in class or at home. Amphetamines and stimulants such as Ritalin have a "paradoxical effect" in the prepubescent child: instead of being "speed," they actually slow him down, make him more tractable and teachable and permit calm to be restored for the harassed parent and overburdened teacher.

Such was the conventional wisdom on 29 September 1970 when Congressman Cornelius E. Gallagher (D-New Jersey) convened a hearing of his House Privacy Subcommittee. This article is a critique of the hearing and an urgent appeal for social scientists to assert humanist concern in a world increasingly reliant on biochemical manipulation.

For the child who is very carefully tested by a team of neurologists, pediatricians, psychologists and educators, the symptoms of MBD can be masked by drugs in as high as 80 percent of the cases, according to some authorities. Others say 50 percent, while dissenters state that the good results are either the result of increased personal attention received by the child or the magical properties the child ascribes to the drug. A careful reading of Department of Health, Education, and Welfare (HEW) testimony at the Gallagher hearing suggests that 200,000 children in the United States are now being given amphetamine and stimulant therapy, with probably another 100,000 receiving tranquilizers and antidepressants.

All the experts agree, however, that the use of medication to modify the behavior of grammar school children will radically increase—"zoom" was the word connected with the man most responsible for the promotion of the program at the National Institute of Mental Health (NIMH). Already specialists in this therapeutic method state that at least 30 percent of ghetto children are candidates, and this figure could run as high as four to six million of the general grammar school population. The authoritative *Journal of Learning Disabilities* puts it bluntly: "Disadvantaged children function similarly to advantaged children with learning disabilities."

Not all children with the ill-defined, perhaps indefinable, syndrome are likely to be treated with medication, but it must be recognized that drugs are a cheap alternative to the massive spending so obviously necessary to revitalize the public school system. Lest there be any doubt about whether leadership in America would be reluctant to embrace quick, inexpensive answers to social problems, consider the plan of the president's former internist, Dr. Arnold Hutschnecker, who would give all six-to eight-year-olds in the nation a predictive psychological test for their criminal potential. Those who flunked these tests—which have been shown to provide successful individual prognosis slightly over 50 percent of the time—would be sent to rehabilitation centers "in a romantic setting with trees out West," as Hutschnecker phrased it. This late, unlamented proposal was sent on White House stationery to the secretary of HEW with a request for suggestions on how to implement it. Once again, Mr. Gallagher's was the only congressional voice raised in opposition, and he branded those camps "American Dachaus." After hearings were threatened, HEW reported unfavorably, and the White House dropped the idea. Many other plans have gone forward, but the Hutschnecker proposal is important because of its high-level endorsement and encouragement, and the distressing impact it would have had on virtually every American family.

The National Institute of Mental Health, which studied the Hutschnecker plan for some three months, has granted at least $3 million to study drug therapy. The clearest statement on the reality of minimal brain dysfunction, however, has come from Dr. Francis Crinella, a grantee of the Office of Education. He said that MBD "has become one of our most fashionable forms of consensual ignorance." No simple medical examination or even an electroencephalogram can disclose the presence of the disorder; "soft" neurological signs seem to be the only physical manifestation.

Passing the Buck

Dr. John Peters, director of the Little Rock Child Study Center of the University of Arkansas, testified that the only way to separate the active child from the hyperactive one was to have had his long experience in seeing thousands of normal and "deviant" children and then making a personal judgment. In Omaha, where the drugging was first discovered by the *Washington Post's* Robert Maynard, the doctors are not even that confident. How else does one explain the lines, reported also by Nat Hentoff, from the *Bulletin of the Omaha Medical Society*: "The responsibility of the prescription was not that of the doctor, but rather of the parent. The parent then vests responsibility in the teacher."

Wow! One could say with equal validity that the facts in a book are not the responsibility of the author; rather, he has vested responsibility in the researcher, who in turn has relied solely on secondary sources.

The conclusion must be that it is behavior and behavior alone that creates the diagnosis of MBD, and this behavior can only be found in the classroom or at home. Mark

Stewart, who received NIMH support, wrote in the July 1970 *Scientific American*: "A child who has been described by his mother as a demon may be an angel when he comes to a psychiatrist's office. Most hyperactive children tend to be subdued in a strange situation and to display their bad behavior only when they feel at home. The explanation may lie in a stress-induced release of norepinephrine in the brain cells. Thus, *a state of anxiety may produce the same effect as a dose of amphetamine—through exactly the same mechanism*" (emphasis added). With relentless logic, Stewart then discusses the behavior of lobotomized monkeys.

Two points on the physical aspects of drugs demand emphasis. First, John Oates of Vanderbilt University has found that "chronic use of amphetamine in small doses may produce symptoms which very closely resemble paranoid schizophrenia." Second, Stewart discredits the alleged "paradoxical effect" by pointing out that "it has been found that amphetamine has a somewhat similar effect on the performance of normal adults who are assigned a boring or complex task."

Would it then be unduly provocative and aggressively argumentative to phrase the question: "Does a long-term dosage of amphetamine and/or Ritalin induce stress in the bored child, producing a perfect student, whose anxiety-ridden behavior may be paranoid schizophrenic and resemble that of a lobotomized monkey?"

It was to speak to a considerably less loaded version of that question that Gallagher invited the provocative educator John Holt. Holt's contempt for orthodox teaching is well known; he compares today's schools to maximum security prisons. Gallagher had phrased his concern, "I fear there is a great temptation to diagnose the bored but bright child as hyperactive, prescribe drugs, and thus deny him full learning during his most creative years," and he introduced Holt's testimony as putting the discussion in the most important context, that of the child.

Holt's response did nothing to lower the issue's hyperbolic content:

> We take lively, curious, energetic children, eager to make contact with the world and to learn about it, stick them in barren classrooms with teachers who on the whole neither like nor respect nor understand nor trust them, restrict their freedom of speech and movement to a degree that would be judged excessive and inhuman even in a maximum security prison, and that their teachers themselves could not and would not tolerate. Then, when the children resist this brutalizing and stupefying treatment and retreat from it in anger, bewilderment and terror, we say that they are sick with "complex and little-understood" disorders, and proceed to dose them with powerful drugs that are indeed complex and of whose long-run effects we know little or nothing, so that they may be more ready to do the asinine things the schools ask them to do.

Unfortunately, there are those of us who have either forgotten our own grammar school experiences or who think that only an in-depth, scholarly, jargonized study can yield an accurate description of reality. As a result, Holt's testimony needs reinforcement. This was made distressingly clear to me when, during the weeks prior to the hearing, I would describe our witness list and state: "John Holt, a former grammar school teacher." Invariably, the reply would be, "Yes, but what are his credentials?"

Among the abundance of supportive evidence of Holt's findings is that contained in Charles Silberman's recently published *The Crisis in the Classroom*. This study, commissioned by the prestigious Carnegie Corporation, found today's schoolrooms to be "grim" and "joyless." Could we not then wonder if the predicted "zoom" in hyperkinetic diagnosis and its concomitant drug therapy will not be used against precious childhood joy? Has Hutschnecker become institutionalized within the medical-educational complex? Have we put the Dachaus in the pill and then put the pill in the kid?

Dr. Rada Dyson-Hudson of Johns Hopkins University begins a letter to Gallagher: "As an anthropologist with a background in genetics and biology who is also the parent of a hyperactive son," and goes on to describe how her family moved to a rural setting to avoid being mangled by urban society. Based on her own personal observations, she says, "Where there are important, tiring or responsible physical jobs to do, a hyperactive child is a joy to have around." But a hyperactive child is no joy in overcrowded city classrooms or to the modern housewife.

Dyson-Hudson's professional judgment is also fascinating. She suggests that the prevalence of MBD in the population could mean that it is an inherited trait, has a selective advantage and, therefore, should not be regarded as pathological. She says that the selective advantage must be quite large, in order to counterbalance the higher mortality rate in hyperactive children. This is confirmed in dozens of letters to Gallagher that describe the MBD child as a mass of bandages and stitches, and Mark Stewart finds that many of the children he has studied have been victims of accidental poisoning.

On the other side, a recent New Jersey report states that in 80 children studied, four times as many children who show learning disabilities are adopted than those not adopted. But Dyson-Hudson's point demands further extensive research for two reasons.

First, pediatricians, psychiatrists and educators, particularly school administrators, contend that parents of hyperactive children are excitable, have a history of alcoholism and instability and fail to provide the child with a warm and loving upbringing. (This point is directly denied by hundreds of letters disclosing a real agony in parents who must finally go to drugs as a last resort.) With that sort of finding buttressing the experts' faith in themselves, it is easy automatically to write off the complaints of a child's parents and to coerce them into acquiescing to or embracing drug therapy.

Second, it is fair to speculate that hyperactivity may well be a considerable advantage for children, especially for ghetto kids. The latter truly have no childhood; they are instantly forced to match wits with hustlers, gang leaders, police and antipolice violence and an entire milieu where the prize of physically growing up goes to the toughest and the shrewdest. Theodore Johnson, a black chemist from Omaha, testified to the problems of coming of age in the ghetto and listed causative agents that could produce MBD-like behavior. In the school, he mentioned racist attitudes among teachers and administrators, inferior and outdated textbooks, irrelevant curriculum and inadequate facilities; and for the child, he found malnutrition, broken rest patterns, unstable home environment and physical fatigue.

On a larger social plane, it is possible to speculate that the use of drugs to make children sit perfectly still and reproduce inputs may once have had some functional purpose. Schools formerly trained the vast majority of students to become effective cogs in giant factories, and they were designed so that assembly line learning would result in assembly line production during working years. Yet, it is now obvious that service-oriented businesses are rapidly replacing manufacturing as the major source of employment. It is not unreasonable to suggest that children no longer need to be preconditioned for the rigid regimentation involved in earning a livelihood; an inquiring mind in an inquiring body is now marketable.

There would be far less need for many additional McLuhanesque probes into MBD drug medication if we could rely on the testimony of the Department of Health, Education, and Welfare before the Gallagher Privacy Subcommittee. If that testimony could stand up under informed scrutiny and if it reflected a conscientious effort to understand and to disclose all the facts, this article would also be unnecessary.

When the federal government sends officials to the Congress to defend a program of such impact, one has a right to expect that rigorous research and rigid control have gone into the decision. In my judgment, both were lacking, and several examples will illustrate my conviction that this massive technological incursion into the sanctuary of the human spirit operated on intelligence just as faulty as that surrounding last winter's Laotian sanctuary incursion.

First, with $3 million from NIMH alone, and with at least 300,000 children and 30 years' experience in the program, it could be expected that hundreds of studies could be cited to show the long-term effect on the children who have been given drugs. Yet, only in 1970 had funds been granted for this essential study, and the man selected to follow up on 67 children was Dr. C. Keith Conners. The HEW witnesses bristled when Gallagher offered the comment that Conners was engaged in evaluating "his own thing," but it is a fact that, prior to the grant for evaluation of these specific children, Conners had been given $442,794 in grants beginning in 1967 to test the effectiveness of drugs on children. Those studies were cited by HEW witnesses as confirming the validity of the treatment.

Wanted: Scientific Dedication

So, as we zoom up to and beyond six million grammar school children on drugs, we are offered a study of 67 cases that was begun in 1970, is now only in its preliminary data-gathering phase and is being carried out by a man whose professional career has been spent proving how effective the therapy is. One can scarcely imagine the cries of rage that would greet any mayor or governor proposing to evaluate road construction in this manner, but one can only assume that scientific research rises above such petty considerations as conflict of interest. In fairness to the selection of Connors, Ronald Lipman, Ph.D. (chief, Clinical Studies Section, National Institute of Mental Health), pointed out at the hearings: "I think one of the reasons why there have been so few followup studies is that they are so very difficult to do. They involve going back into medical records that are very difficult to come by. They involve tracking down people after a period of 20 years. This is very difficult logistically. *It requires a certain kind of scientific dedication that you just don't find too many people have*" (emphasis added).

Other testimony confirmed Lipman's pessimistic view of his colleagues. Dr. Dorothy Dobbs, director of the Food and Drug Administration's Division of Neuropharmacological Drug Products, and HEW's chief witness, Dr. Thomas C. Points, deputy assistant secretary for health and scientific affairs, both testified that they had conducted "cursory" investigations of the administration of these drugs in Omaha and that nothing was wrong. Later in the hearing it was disclosed that Dr. Byron Oberst, the program's primary proponent in Omaha, was unaware that the Food and Drug Administration (FDA) had listed two of the drugs he was using as "not recommended for use in children under 12." Dr. John Peters, director of the Little Rock Child Study Center, was found to be equally in the dark about FDA guidelines on one of the drugs he dispensed. (It must be mentioned that FDA has no authority to insist that drugs not be used; it has a formal mechanism that permits just about anything to be administered under a doctor's prescription.)

Two points are crucial, however: 1) the HEW witness did not volunteer the information that the department had communicated with Oberst pointing out his oversight; and 2) leading practitioners of drug therapy were unaware of FDA's recommendations.

Moreover, while the HEW witnesses cited some 40 studies conferring validity on the use of drugs to mask hyperactive behavior, they did not refer to Crinella's Office of Education study referred to earlier—"one of our most fashionable forms of consensual ignorance" is a line certainly worth repeating—nor did they mention HEW's own studies by John Oates and Mark Stewart. But perhaps most compellingly, we heard nothing of the June 1970 statement of the American Academy of Pediatrics Committee on Drugs. In light of the supposedly wide support within the medical community for the efficacy of drugs, the academy's words are particularly significant:

> An accurate assessment of the effectiveness of the chemotherapeutic approach poses enumerable difficulties. These stem from factors such as 1) the lack of uniform terminology, 2) marked variability in methodology for evaluation, 3) the absence of standardized requirements for precise diagnosis and classification of the symptomatology constituting learning impediments, and 4) the paucity of long-term, properly controlled studies. As a result, a valid evaluation of response and objective comparison of the effectiveness of drugs administered in an attempt to mitigate or lessen learning impediments becomes impossible.

Finally, the HEW testimony dismissed any possible connection between children relying on drugs during grammar school and the incredible problem of drug abuse in high schools and in the rest of society. The hearing ran for approximately eight hours, and Gallagher hammered away all day long on this most obvious "paradoxical effect," but it was only during the questioning of Sally Williams, chief of the School Nurse Division of the National Education Association, that a glimmer appeared. She had strongly supported the use of behavior modification drugs (controlled, naturally enough, by the school nurse), but, almost as an afterthought, she disclosed that ten students at her school were now on Ritalin at their own discretion. Her exact testimony is most revealing: "They were taken off the medication and they still came back to the 'springs inside,' the inability to control their behavior. So the doctor has put it on a PRN, which means when necessary, so because they are senior high school students they come up to the health office and come to me and say, 'I think I need my Ritalin now.' "

Apparently, the administration shared some of these doubts, because two short weeks after the hearing, the director of the Office of Child Development at HEW announced his intention to form a "blue ribbon" panel to consider the problem. Dr. Edward F. Zigler's statement of 12 October is very different from the tone of the HEW testimony of 29 September: he said the panel would "inform educators that perhaps it is as much a problem of the kind of schoolroom children have to adjust to rather than what is wrong" with the nervous systems of the children. On 10 March 1971 the panel issued its report, and Gallagher commended it for approximately one-half of his remarks in the *Congressional Record* of that day. He singled out two sentences:

> It is important to recognize the child whose inattention and restlessness may be caused by hunger, poor teaching, overcrowded classrooms, or lack of understanding by teachers and parents . . . . Variations in different socio-economic and ethnic groups must be considered in order to arrive at better definitions of behavior properly regarded as pathological.

In light of the evidence we gathered that drug company salesmen were huckstering their products' wonder-working capabilities at PTA meetings and at professional educational society gatherings, Gallagher also praised this stern warning: "These medicines should be promoted ethically and *only* through medical channels" (emphasis in original).

Unfortunately, the second half of Gallagher's statement was not reflected in media reports. He was sharply critical of the panel's failure to do any independent investigation; they had only produced a compendium, in layman's terms, of existing studies. Moreover, while the report reiterated many of the criticisms surfaced by the Privacy Subcommittee, the report made no comment on the desirability of having a mechanism within the federal establishment to encourage sensible caution at the local level. Gallagher said that "the suspicion still exists that these programs will be used to modify the behavior of black children to have them conform to white society's norms," and that "as admirable as the recommendations in the report are, they will be nothing but high sounding platitudes unless supervision of local schools can assure that they are given the attention I think they deserve." He called for the Office of Child Development to become the mandated overseer of the increasing nationwide use of behavioral modification drugs.

Assumption of this responsibility became absolutely essential when the Privacy Subcommittee was abolished by its parent Committee on Government Operations on 31 March 1971. Along with a special panel under Congressman Benjamin Rosenthal (D-New York) that had a remarkably effective record of protecting the consumer, the new committee chairman, Chet Holifield (D-California), decreed, as was his right with subcommittees without direct jurisdiction over specific federal agencies, that these issue-oriented studies were outside the committee's ambit. (Holifield has been either chairman or vice-chairman of the Joint Committee on Atomic Energy since its inception. At the risk of being labeled hyperactive myself, it is disquieting that the man who now says there is no valid reason for concern over privacy or consumer matters in the House has consistently stated that there are no dangers from nuclear power plants.)

It would be possible to continue to discuss privacy generally and behavior modification therapy specifically at a length only slightly less than that of the collected works of Dickens, but a brief reference to the National Education Association (NEA) is essential. It has become one of the most effective lobbies in the legislative and executive ambits in Washington, and its proposals often quickly turn into public policy. For that reason, it is important to find out just what it has in mind for future generations of American children. A particularly relevant example comes from the *NEA Journal* of January 1969 in an article entitled "Forecast for the 1970's." Two professors of education at Indiana University point to a radically altered school environment, but one of their statements says it all: "Biochemical and psychological mediation of learning is likely to increase. New drama will play on the educational stage as drugs are introduced experimentally to improve in the learner such qualities as personality, concentration, and memory. The application of biochemical research findings, heretofore centered on infra-human subjects, such as fish . . . . "

Fish? Fish! Gallagher has long been concerned with the privacy-invading aspects of credit bureaus, electronic surveillance, the computer and psychological testing, and he has said that the Age of Aquarius will become the Age of Aquariums, in which all our lives are lived in a fish bowl. His assumption, up until the investigation of drugging grammar school children, was that there would still be ordinary water in those aquariums; now the concern must be that human rights will be drowned in an exotic brew of biochemical manipulators, stirred and watched by an untouchable medical-educational complex.

The implications and ramifications to our future were well expressed in June 1970 by America's most highly placed social critic. Social scientists would do well to take action on the words of the former president of the Baltimore County Parent-Teacher Association, Spiro T. Agnew: "We as a country have hardly noticed this remarkable phenomenon of legal drug use, but it is new, it is increasing, and the individual and social costs have yet to be calculated."

6

Seymour Martin Lipset

Education and Equality: Israel and the United States Compared

Both the United States and Israel are nations of immigrants attracted by the dream of a better life. Although obviously quite different in many ways, both nations have a number of things in common. Their immigrants are of multi-national origin with European groups dominant. Each society has a predominant political ideology as a cornerstone of its foundation. Each is characterized by an emphasis in formal values on egalitarian beliefs. The United States has Americanism, which in its key document, the Declaration of Independence, proclaimed that "all men are created equal." Israel's Zionist ideology has been predominantly labor-oriented, and it remains the only democratic nation in the world in which diverse socialist parties have a persistent majority.

Some may question using the same term equalitarianism to characterize the values of Americanism and Zionist-Socialism. Clearly these societies vary enormously in their internal social structure, economy and political systems. Yet, some similarity in values can be maintained. An American socialist, Leon Samson, in a book written in 1930s which sought to explain "why no socialism in the U.S." argued that the basic factor weakening the socialist appeal is that the values of socialism and Americanism, property relations apart, are very similar. To demonstrate the point, he quoted copiously, comparing the writings of Marx, Engels, Lenin and Stalin, with those of leading American figures as to the nature of the "good society." Instead of citing such obvious defenders of the egalitarian ideal as Jefferson, Jackson, Lincoln and Franklin D. Roosevelt, he took his representative American citations from John D. Rockefeller, Andrew Mellon, Calvin Coolidge, and Herbert Hoover. And as he indicated, their conceptions of desirable goals in human relations, namely equality of opportunity, regardless of social origins, and equal treatment, regardless of social role, are highly similar to those advanced by the leading Marxists.

Similar ideological forces have been at work in Israel. Most of the Israelis, particularly the earliest group of settlers and consequently the dominant minority of East European origin, support socialist parties. It is hard to say what "socialism" means to these Israelis. It is a fact, however, that all socialists of whatever stripe tend to favor some emphasis on equality of reward and opportunity.

To move from the dream to hard reality, an examination of the history and current social structure of the United States and Israel points up ways in which the emphasis on egalitarianism in the founding political doctrines of each has determined much in its institutional practices and patterns of behavior, and the repeated efforts of each to "equalize" hierarchies imposed seemingly by social necessity.

Equality Through Education

Much of the social history of the United States may be read in terms of an attempt to elaborate on the egalitarian promise of the Declaration of Independence. Before other countries, the United States expanded its suffrage to cover all white males (slavery was its great exception and horror, and continued racism its Achilles's heel). It led other nations in providing education to its inhabitants. The Census of 1840 indicated over 90 percent of whites were literate (undoubtedly an exaggeration). But then and later, this country expended more public funds for education than other societies. A much larger percentage of the appropriate age population attended secondary schools and institutions of higher education from the nineteenth century down to the present than elsewhere. In other words, education has been more equally distributed in the United States than in other countries for a century and a half. Further, a myriad of foreign observers, such as Tocqueville, Martineau and Bryce in the nineteenth century, have commented on the emphasis in social relations on symbolic equality. They noted, in effect, that no man need doff his cap to another, that the symbols of rank, present in Europe, were absent in America. Populism and anti-elitism have characterized its political style.

Most noteworthy of all in the American conception of equality has been the stress on equality, not of rank, status, income or wealth, but of opportunity. The American ideal has predominantly been one of open social mobility, everyone starting at the same point in a race for success.

The vigor of this doctrine in early America may be seen in its most extreme form in the program of the Workingmen's parties formed in various eastern seaboard cities in the 1820s and 1830s. These parties, which secured as much as 20 percent of the urban vote, were particularly concerned with education. In a profound document written in 1829, the New York party anticipated the conclusions of a much later report by James Coleman by asserting that access to equal education in day schools was far from sufficient to provide equal opportunity in the race for success. For, they said, a few hours in school cannot counter the highly unequal effects of varying cultural and material environments supplied by families of unequal wealth and culture. They therefore proposed that all children regardless of class background or parental wishes, be educated from six years of age on in boarding schools, to assure that all had the same environment 24 hours a day. Clearly, this American political party made the most radical proposal ever advanced—to nationalize not property but children. Obviously this policy was not popular and never came close to carrying, but the fact that a party which was a contender for public office and which did elect representatives to various legislative bodies could even make such a proposal is indicative of the strength of egalitarianism a half century following American independence.

It is noteworthy that this party, which incidentally gave Karl Marx the idea that the working class could and should organize politically on its own behalf, did not call for equality of wealth or income. This was never the meaning of equality in Americanism. The Workingmen of 1830 approved of inequality as long as it was the result of success in a competitive race for the top. Close to a century later, a highly successful American multimillionaire, Andrew Carnegie, advocated a confiscatory inheritance tax, in which all wealth returned to the state on death. Carnegie also believed that new ways should be found to equalize the race for success.

Although the Workingmen's parties did not secure boarding schools, the idea that all should begin with an equal education helped strengthen the more successful efforts of those who, like Horace Mann, urged the creation of publicly supported "common" schools in the 1840s. By common schools was meant what are now called "intergrated" schools, that is, schools attended by children from diverse social backgrounds, natives and immigrants, rich and poor. The proponents assumed that such schools were necessary to create a common culture, to absorb those from varying backgrounds, to make possible more equality of opportunity, as well as to create the kind of citizenry who could participate in a one man, one vote democracy.

The spread of the common school idea, it should be noted, included a practice which would have far-reaching consequences. These schools, designed in part to Americanize the immigrant and to civilize the lower classes, deliberately set their educational sights at the levels of the culturally deprived. In a sense they consciously lowered standards or rather educational aspirations from the levels upper-middle-class children could attain so as to make it possible for those of "deprived background" to catch up. It was assumed that all would eventually reach higher levels of attainment, of knowledge, in the upper grades and ultimately in college and university. This pattern has continued in U. S. education, so that world-wide comparisons show that American youth study less than their equivalents in upper-level European gymnasia or lycées. As Max Weber noted in 1918, "The American boy learns unspeakably less than the German boy." By age 20, however, the Americans have more than caught up. And a much greater percentage of them than those of any European country have secured higher education. By going slowly through elementary school and high school, the U.S. system has permitted many more to enter and graduate an institution of higher education.

It would be misleading to credit the growth of education and other institutional practices fostering social mobility, solely or primarily on forces stemming from an egalitarian political ideology. The ideology itself, the educational growth, and equalitarian social relations were fostered as well by the fact that so much of America was a rapidly expanding "new society," a frontier culture, in which all families were first settlers, or their immediate descendants. More important, perhaps, may have been the impact of Protestantism. The United States was and remains the only country in which the majority of the citizens adhere to Protestant sects, mainly Baptists and Methodists, rather than to denominations which had been state churches in Europe, such as the Catholic, Lutheran, Anglican and Greek Orthodox. The latter were hierarchically organized, and linked to monarchy and aristocracy; thus part of the alliance between Throne and Altar also served to mediate between man and God.

The Protestant sects, on the other hand, insisted that man deal directly with God, follow his conscience rather than obey the church or state, and that to be qualified to do so, he must be literate, a student of the Bible.

The Protestant denominations, therefore, supported the spread of public education, the growth of universities. They started many themselves. The Protestant Ethic, of course, also contributed directly to mobility and economic growth by its emphasis on hard work. It also favored a political orientation which had the state helping the individual to help himself, i.e., through education, but not through collectivist welfare measures. The commitment of the Protestant sects to education, of course, had its roots in the same Biblical injunctions which many Jews had obeyed through much of their history.

The identification of Jews with education and intellectual endeavors is proverbial. The Jews were probably the first people with almost total literacy among males. This stemmed from the religious obligation of every man to be literate and to study the Bible, that is, Torah. The highest prestige within ghetto communities in the Middle Ages and later in Eastern Europe was given to religious scholars. Although women could not secure such recognition on their own, well-to-do Jewish businessmen would seek to buy prestige by marrying their daughters to scholars.

The emphasis on religious education among European Jews was gradually secularized after the Enlightenment. Jewish youth poured into secular schools. In Czarist Russia, where they faced enormous handicaps and discriminatory restrictive quotas, they still were able to form a much larger proportion of students in gymnasia and universities than they were in the population. In the period prior to World War I, Jews contributed so enormously to the European world of science and scholarship that Thorstein Veblen felt disposed to write an article in 1919 seeking to explain the reasons for "The Scientific Preeminence of the Jews in Europe." And as millions of East European Jews migrated to America they strengthened the Protestant-initiated commitment to education.

The emphases on egalitarianism and education in Americanism and the socialism of labor Zionism did not, however, produce similar educational concerns in the United States and Israel. Americanism, as noted, focused on individual opportunity by attempting to equalize the means for upward mobility. In Israel, as in Europe, it is significant that the socialist parties and labor movements placed greater emphasis on collectivist measures to lift up the economic level of the bottom, than on opening the door to a race for the top. That is, social democracy spent its money disproportionately on social welfare, old age pensions, state medicine, unemployment benefits, public housing, etc. The United States, conversely, has devoted more of its resources on education as the road to success. (These differences, of course, while still existent, have narrowed considerably. The United States is increasingly a welfare state. Social-Democratic Europe—Sweden, Germany, Britain—has in recent decades been consciously modifying the educatonal systems in the U.S. direction, stressing the comprehensive, common or integrated school, to replace the old elite-mass school divisions in which only a small privileged group attended gymnasia, lycées, or grammar schools.)

In spite of its emphasis on equality of opportunity the United States has never really approached the ideal, even in the spread of formal education itself. Two great nineteenth-century radical thinkers, Karl Marx and Henry George, the single-tax theorist, independently pointed out that publicly supported higher education in the United States involved taking money from the poor to subsidize the education of the well-to-do, that it was a negative "transfer payment" so to speak. Henry George put the thesis in colorful terms when he said in the 1890s that the University of California is a place to which the poor send the children of the rich. Recent analyses by economists indicate George is still right. In spite of the enormous spread of state higher education in California—over 50 percent of the college age population are in school in that state—the families of those who attend the University of California have a higher income than those who go to the state colleges or junior colleges, who in turn are more affluent than the families whose children do not go on to higher education.

Attendance at higher education which has now reached close to 50 percent of the cohort nationally still varies greatly with family income. Thus in 1967, 87 percent of those youths whose families earned $15,000 or more attended college, and only 20 percent from families with less than $3,000 a year income attended college. Yet this 20 percent figure for the very poor is higher than the total figure for many European countries.

Academic aptitude or intellectual ability though highly correlated with family socioeconomic class, of course, also operates independently as a predictor of propensity to secure higher education. Thus only a quarter of those in the lowest aptitude quartile among the upper income quartile attend college, as compared with about 90 percent of those in the highest quartile aptitude group. But most significant of all, in illustrating the way in which low income handicaps youth is the fact that less than half (48 percent) of those in the highest aptitude segment, those who clearly are extremely able academically, but whose families fall in the lowest quarter of the population income-wise, attend college.

Yet, in spite of the pessimistic conclusions in the Coleman Report and Jencks study, *Inequality*, concerning the efficacy of education as a road to social mobility, other data suggest considerable progress has been made. Thus in 1973, the U.S. Census Bureau reported one of the most significant statistics in American history. For the first time, the percent of black

Americans of college age entering an institution of higher education is identical with the proportion of comparably aged white youth. This is the first major piece of evidence that the United States is finally really beginning to right the ancient wrongs of slavery and racism. Clearly, of course, the education received by many blacks is far from equal, for this indicator of educational equality conceals the fact that a very large proportion of black students are attending the more inferior segments of higher education: junior colleges, black colleges in the South, the less prestigious state colleges, etc. Yet the statistic is very important, for college attendance has a major credentialing function. To obtain a job in the better paid sector of the American economy, one has to go to some sort of college.

Some indication of the implications of the downward spread of higher education may be seen in the data bearing on the social class origins of the American business elite, the top executives of the major American corporations. Mabel Newcomer, an historian, has studied such backgrounds, for the top three executives of the largest American businesses in 1900, 1950, and 1964. She found that in 1900 close to half of them (45 percent) came from "wealthy" families and 10 percent from "poor" ones. As of 1964, however, the proportion from wealthy parents had dropped to 10 percent (it was 25 percent in 1950), while those from economically poor backgrounds had risen to 26 percent from 15 percent in 1950. Two developments account for these striking changes. First is the shift from family capitalism to corporate ownership, which sharply reduced the importance of direct inheritance of wealth as a determinant of business executive status. Flowing from this change is the fact that the corporate elite is increasingly drawn from the ranks of those who first enter business as junior executives directly from college. This shift means that the second factor, the spread of college education downward, permits many from relatively poor families to enter the corporate bureaucratic hierarchy if they go to college. This development shows up in Newcomer's data on the college background of the business elite. At the turn of the century, graduates of Ivy League colleges (Harvard, Yale and Princeton), predominated. In the 1964 group, the largest supplier of business leaders came from state institutions, particularly those in the Midwest, e.g., Illinois and Michigan. Similar changes in class background have occurred in other high status occupations which require college background.

It should be obvious, however, that the diffusion of college education and even the broadening of the social class background of those who hold privileged positions, does not demonstrate a leveling of income, wealth or power in America or elsewhere. Jencks has properly emphasized that in spite of the growth of higher education, the distribution of wealth has not narrowed in the United States in recent decades. The evidence does suggest that wealth distribution is today much more egalitarian than in pre-Civil War days, and that there was a narrowing in the period of the Depression and New Deal. But the sharply stratified distribution which sees the lowest quartile holding about 5 percent of the wealth and the highest tenth having well over a third still continues. Raymond Boudon, the French sociologist, drawing on data from western Europe and North America, has in fact shown that increases in education have the effect of widening the salary gap from top to bottom.

Sharp inequality continues to characterize American society as it does all other complex social systems. Well-to-do parents in America are able to provide their offspring with a more academically stimulating environment, real assistance in the form of better schools and teachers, the motivation to attain success, and various forms of direct help in the ways of contacts and financial aid to get started well in the race for success. Those who control large financial resources may convert these into various forms of power in affecting key decisions in the society, as in a different way, may those at the summit of intellectually-important and opinion-molding institutions. Race, ethnic and class background may be less of a handicap in the race for success than earlier, but the inequality between those who succeed and those who do not has not been reduced.

The stress on equality of opportunity, the presence of those who have visibly moved up, the sheer magnitude of the good life possible for those who have succeeded, may be related to another area in which the United States is a leader, particularly among developed countries — that is, in diverse forms of deviant behavior, particularly crime, drug use, etc. It has been argued by many sociologists following the lead of Robert Merton, that the very pressure on everyone to succeed, and the evidence that it is possible for many, makes the experience of not succeeding, frequently defined in the American context as personal failure, a more painful one for Americans than it is for those living in societies which do not place as manifest an emphasis on competitive personal success. That is, in countries which retain elements of a more rigid status system and legitimate inheritance of position and also have leftist parties which stress the extent to which the economic system blocks opportunity for the lowly, failure to be successful is not as strongly perceived as personal failure.

The logic of this analysis suggests that a larger proportion of Americans than others, will, if unable to succeed legitimately (i.e., through school or hard work), feel pressed to do so illegitimately, through various forms of criminal behavior. In America what counts is whether you have won the game, not how you have played it. Thus, Robert Merton and others suggest that Americans faced with the prospect of failure, of losing, will violate the rules more than will those in societies which still take their cues from the aristocratic stress on proper behavior. The latter phenomenon, of course, the stress on playing the game well, is the code of the upper classes, whose ancestors won the game some time back, and who have institutionalized a code of morality which reduces the possibility that others will push them out of their privileged position.

Flowing also from the assumption that failure in a highly competitive system is highly painful, is "anomic behavior," withdrawal from the effort to succeed by engaging in forms of ruleless hedonistic activities frowned on by the conventional work-a-day world. This takes the form of alcoholism, and more recently of drugs, as well as other forms of deviant behavior. Traditionally, such behavior was found more typically among the "failures," the very poor, the lumpenproletariat, the oppressed ethnic-racial minorities. The spread of such behavior within segments of the elite and their offspring in recent years, combined with the overt espousal of anti-competitive ideologies in political and personal life-styles (the counterculture, communes, hippies, etc.), suggest that the pain, the psychic anxiety, involved in the competitive system may be becoming too much even for many who are seemingly privileged. It may also be a sort of inverted consequence, and thus a "tribute" to the fact that the spread of higher education has increased the competition, and the concomitant spread of anxiety up the class ladder, than when the numerical ratio of those competing for elite status was much smaller. After all, when few went to university, the privileges of rank associated with university graduation were much more assured than now.

Tocqueville, an early observer of the United States' ideological emphasis on egalitarianism, was a political conservative who believed that aristocracy and social stratification were necessary for the preservation of liberty. Yet he felt that once the idea of equality entered the world it was politically unbeatable. Tocqueville said this in part because he believed there were more deprived people than affluent ones, and that the deprived majority would back movements which promised equality, to take from the rich and give to the poor, and would thus overwhelm the more privileged. More recently, however, John Kenneth Galbraith, in *The Affluent Society*, argued that in addition to the growth of a well-paid middle class, characteristic of an industrial society, there exists a proportionate decline of the poverty-level population to include primarily the socially invisible (the elderly, the mentally less-endowed, widows and orphans). Thus, the affluent society could ignore its politically impotent underprivileged.

Events of the last decade argue more for Tocqueville's anticipation than for Galbraith's even though, as Galbraith notes, Tocqueville's poor are no longer a majority in many countries, as in the United States. The idea of equality continues to secure many adherents, particularly within the ranks of the affluent themselves. And when impoverished minorities, led or assisted by radical offspring of the powerful, begin to press their claim on the body politic, the latter give way, in part because they too are committed in principle to the idea of equality of opportunity.

Gunnar Myrdal, in his classic work, *An American Dilemma*, published in 1944, noted that most white Americans professed a belief in equality and that this fact could be a tremendous potential political asset for black Americans. He urged the black community to demonstrate harder in order to dramatize the reality of discrimination for whites who sought to repress their awareness of the fact. He predicted white Americans would yield to black pressures, that they would be morally incapable of resisting, and of suppressing an aroused Negro population.

The history of the past few decades, from A. Philip Randolph's March on Washington Movement, occurring while Myrdal was writing, to Martin Luther King's movement and the ghetto riots of the late 1960s, testifies to the validity of Myrdal's anticipations. The gain in black enrollment in higher education referred to earlier did not occur simply as a consequence of structural changes. Colleges and universities, white dominated legislatures, changed policies and laws to open doors of education and economic opportunity which had been closed. Other minority claims associated with black demands, from Chicanos, Indians, women, and others, are also being responded to.

The renewed contemporary fight for more equality, legitimated by the historic commitment to the ideal, it should be noted, is still waged in terms of the old American emphasis on equality of opportunity, the demand of the Workingmen's party that none be handicapped by reason of social origin in the race for success. Almost none of the battles, however, are concerned directly with equality as such. That is, blacks and women are demanding their appropriate share of corporation presidencies, university professorships, government positions, etc. They are not, however, arguing that the prerequisites associated with these statuses be lowered or eliminated.

But as some of the battles for equality of access are in the process of attainment, voices are beginning to be heard (of which Jencks is currently the best known) for equality of result, for reducing the gap between the top and the bottom. Equality which in America once meant equality of opportunity for white males only, but which has now been expanded to include blacks, women, Indians and Chicanos, may, once these struggles are over, change to include something of the old Communist goal, to each according to his needs, not according to his socially recognized achievements. This emphasis on equality of result has, as we shall see, been more characteristic of Israel than of other countries almost from the start of modern Zionist settlement.

Equality Through Social Reward

Israel, like the United States in the nineteenth and early twentieth century, has faced the task of making equality real to a mass of relatively uneducated and unskilled immigrants, the Sephardic and Oriental Jews from North Africa and the Middle East. It may, of course, seem unfair to compare what has happened within Israel in 25 years to American developments which occurred over a century or more. In addition, while the United States absorbed many millions of immigrants, at no time did the proportion of foreign-born in this country even approach the ratio of Israel's Oriental immigrants to its equivalent of WASP natives, the European Ashkenazim. Yet some analytic comparisons can be made.

In establishing a social system, Israel, more so than the United States, may be described as a nation whose very identity is ideological. As its leading sociologist, Shmuel Eisenstadt has stressed, "the egalitarian ideology of the pioneers . . . placed an unmistakable imprint upon the Jewish community . . . there was from the start a powerful tendency towards egalitarianism in social rewards, . . . attempts were made especially by the Histadrut [the powerful Federation of Labor] to narrow the pay differentials between types of jobs and to reduce manifest distinctions in social status . . . ."

As noted earlier, the pre-1948, largely European immigrants to Palestine brought with them a high level of educational attainment and a tradition of belief in the value of education. In 1948, the average education of the adult population may have been the highest in the world. Among European-born adult male immigrants over 25 years of age, 22 percent had some higher education, only one-third had not gone beyond elementary school. The comparable U.S. figures as reported in the 1950 Census are 14 percent with some college or more, and 46 percent with eight grades or less of schooling. And not unnaturally, as Chaim Adler has noted, the pre-state community created "an open, uniform and demanding educational system."

> It was open, in view of the socialist ethos of the founding fathers of the community; it was uniform so as to facilitate the welding of a new nation out of the many newcomers who were gathered in from different parts of the world; it was demanding as an expression of the community's dedication to its European heritage and of its commitment to found a new, modern and progressive social order.

These two emphases, egalitarianism and educational excellence have, though necessarily much modified in content, continued to inform Israeli policy. Thus, Israel has maintained one of the most narrowly spread wage and income structures in the world. The graduated taxation system there would be regarded as confiscatory by middle and upper classes in most other societies. Import duties and taxation are extremely high on luxury items such as automobiles, foreign travel, and the like. Privately purchased housing costs a great deal; publicly built apartments for low income families are much cheaper. Medicine is largely socialized. Welfare benefits are high. As any one who has visited Israel knows, the life of its educated and professional classes is difficult compared to that of equivalent strata in America or Europe. In 1971, "a family of four with 36,000 Israeli pounds per year, the average income in the top decile (roughly $7,800) . . . paid 45 percent of total income in taxes."

The lowest 30 percent of wage earners had about 15 percent added to their total income through transfer payments (government services), while "the upper 16 percent suffered a decrease from 33 to 26 percent of total income." There has been a considerable increase in the income and standard of living of those coming from Asia and Africa in the past decade. According to Schlomo Avineri, the Israeli political scientist, "The average income per standard equivalent adult among families of Asian-African origins" rose from 63 percent of the overall average for Jewish families in 1963-64 to 70 percent in 1970. The differences between those of Oriental background and other Israelis are less striking than these figures indicate, since the "average age of Asian-African family heads was 39.2 in 1971, compared to 49.4 for European-American family heads. The ten years separating the two groups of family heads are the prime years of life in which incomes can be expected to rise significantly." The changes over a decade with respect to ownership of consumer durables are even more impressive than the reduction in income differentials. For example, 92 percent of the Oriental Jews had refrigerators in 1970 compared to 17 percent in 1960." Currently, there is very little difference in possession of such items between the Oriental and European communities. Housing conditions for Orientals also improved remarkably. Among those who immigrated since 1948, the proportion "living in a density of three or more persons per room declined during the same period from 49 percent to 17 percent." Much of these changes are a result of deliberate government policies. It can truthfully be said that in no other democratic country are the egalitarian emphases of socialism as real as in Israel. (In stating this, of course, I am not suggesting Israel is socialist. Clearly much of its economy is capitalist, and considerable private and corporate wealth exists and is, in fact, increasing with the growth of the economy.)

The decline in occupational income and standard of living differentials among the two main Jewish ethnic groups has been paralleled by a steady increase in the rate of intermarriage between them. It is growing by about one percent per year, so that by 1969, "17.5 percent of all Jewish marriages in Israel were intermarriages in the sense that one of the partners came from European background whereas the other came from Asian-African background."

Yet, although the Israeli standard of living and income distribution is spread more equitably, as compared to other countries, the Israeli educational system does not fit an egalitarian model. Rather the original European settlers established a classic pre-World War I school structure. The Israeli high schools copied the model of the German gymnasia, not the American common schools. From the perspective of the average American or poor Israeli youth, the high school system is impossible. An Israeli student in an academic high school has to take something like 14 subjects. Every year he studies chemistry, physics, biology, math, English, Arabic or French, history, Jewish culture, etc. He goes to school six days a week, and has four to five hours of homework every day. In this kind of system no child from an underprivileged background, where he does not have the whole apparatus of the family to support him, can possibly do well, unless he is by some some miracle super-motivated.

Israeli social scientists have documented the implications of the school system in abundant statistical detail. Thus Chaim Adler points out that as of 1969-70, only "6 out of 100 seventeen-year-olds in the population who are of Oriental parentage are fully certified academic high school graduates" as contrasted to 35 out of 100 among those of Occidental parentage.

Many Israelis, Ashkenazim and others — in the government, in the universities, in the Education Ministry — are aware of this. They are consciously concerned with the problem, and are making important changes. But the problem lies in large part with those committed to the old system, the parents and the teachers. To suggest lowering the educational level of the Israeli high school by creating common schools threatens the status of an Israeli high school teacher, who is like the *professeur* at a French lycée. Lowering the intellectual content challenges his status, identity and job. It is understandable that he and his union resist.

The parents who themselves are well educated, or moderately well educated, also object to changes which appear to give their children a much worse education than earlier generations received. The middle-class parents oppose lowering the level of the school — and they constitute a tremendous bloc. The larger Jewish ethos is also involved. It assumes that Jews should have the best education possible, that the great contribution of the Jews is as intellectuals, as scientisits, as educated people. To propose that Israel should lower its educational level rather than raise it is the worst possible thing that may be suggested. Thus the very commitment of European Jewry to education serves to strengthen resistance to proposals which may upgrade the educational aspirations and attainments of Oriental Jews.

Suggesting that Israel (and other Social Democratic states) differs from the United States in emphasizing income and standard of living, rather than educational, equality is not meant to indicate that Israel has not shown a strong interest in upgrading the educational attainments of the less privileged. Where the efforts mainly require more financial resources, changes have been dramatic. The "culturally deprived" are given an extended school life and day. The large majority of children aged three to five years are in nurseries. About a third of the two and three-year-olds are in day creches. Kindergarten for five-year-olds is compulsory. Extensive programs of remedial instruction are provided for those in grades two to five. There are a variety of enrichment programs going up through grade eight.

Yet even on the elementary school level, these policies do not result in a large proportion of those from Oriental backgrounds achieving the standard deemed necessary to permit them to enter the highly demanding academic high schools. In 1966, for example, three-quarters of the students of Western background passed the *Sekur*, the test determining secondary school placement, while two-thirds of those of Oriental families failed it.

In an effort to improve such results, the Education Act was amended to provide for a 6-3-3 year school system, i.e., 6 year elementary, 3 year middle, and 3 year senior high schools, to replace the 8 and 4 system. The assumption is that the new 3 year "middle school" or junior high would provide for a more ethnic and class integrated school (drawing on wider geographical areas) and better trained teachers. Many, including the teachers' unions, opposed the Reform, some arguing disadvantaged students would do worse if integrated with high achievers from wealthier families, that age 12 is already too late to change intellectual abilities, and, therefore, that the new funds should be provided at earlier ages. Still the program is in effect for a growing part of the system. It is too early to tell how much improvement it will make in the proportion of the disadvantaged who go on. The new system includes tracking. By the eighth grade, vocational education is introduced. By the ninth, most studies are separated into tracks leading to academic or vocational high schools, or a terminal ninth grade.

Thus, even the policy of the Reform anticipates that only a minority of high school age Israelis (largely from privileged backgrounds) will go on to academic high schools, that a considerable majority (predominantly from poorer families) will either drop out after middle school, or continue in a vocational high school.

This comparison of the American and Israeli approaches to equality points up the extent to which the

United States has focused on increasing educational opportunity, while until very recently ignoring any collectivity responsibility to upgrade the standard of living of the poor, e.g., by eliminating bad housing, providing public medical care, etc. Israel, like other social democratic states, has followed the alternative policy of spreading non-educational community resources more than academic ones, thus keeping those elite leadership roles which require education largely in the hands of its WASPs, those of Western origin.

Still both types of societies appear to be converging. In the United States, there has been a gradual commitment towards guaranteeing group rights to equality of status, as distinct from the focus on equality of opportunity. This may be seen in its most controversial and questionable form in the efforts to establish quotas, according to racial, ethnic and biological criteria, as a way of measuring institutional concern for equality. But it also is evident in the growth of the welfare state, although the United States is obviously still far away from providing an adequate minimum in the way of housing, medical care and income for the underprivileged. In Israel, in spite of the considerable limitations of opportunity to get on to the academic high school and university ladder of opportunity, there have been some remarkable achievements in education in a quarter of a century. Illiteracy has vanished among Jews. About four-fifths of native-born Israelis, over 14 years of age, have at least some high school, and 20 percent have had some higher education. Although less than 10 percent of youth of Oriental origin graduate from academic high schools, almost half of them are in some form of post-elementary education, over 30 percent in academic high school, a tri-fold jump as compared to 1956.

Since Oriental Jews have increased their income and occupational status considerably, while sharply reducing their birthrate, the evidence would suggest that they will also move towards educational equality. The process is much slower than is desirable. It can and should be speeded up by more political pressures by the Oriental population. They have the votes, though not the leadership or organizational know-how, to press the political elite to further bend the educational system in their direction. Conversely, however, with greater national wealth, education, and the inevitable decline of Zionist collectivity values of responsibility for deprived and persecuted Jews, pressures should grow from the educated elite to widen the income spread. Such pressures are already reflected in strikes for higher income by professors, physicians and media people. Shlomo Avineri pointed out some years ago that the proletarian classless ideals of Labor Zionism, while still official doctrine, were disintegrating under the experience of "an unprecedented boom," in which people begin to grumble "because the man next door is making an even greater packet." As a result, "Studying and making as much money as possible are becoming more and more the general ethos of society." Social scientists are already publishing articles on "Middle and Upper Class Delinquency in Israel," in which they note in terms derivative from Merton's analysis of the comparable United States phenomena the diffusion within Israel of the orientations of Veblen's "ideal pecuniary man," which produces the "urgent necessity to satisfy desires, drives and greeds [which] might be quenched by lawful means but if these are not available the resort to illegal means (deliquency) becomes an almost natural course."

Thus, we may anticipate that over time the structure and values of Israeli society and of U.S. society will be more in tandem with each other. At the present moment, however, Israel's situation is complicated further by the problems of continuing immigration and of the growing Arab proletariat, the two of which are related. As a Zionist state, Israel seeks to bring in Jews from all over the world, which today means Jews from relatively affluent, well educated communities: the United States, Western Europe, South America, and above all, the Soviet Union. The need to encourage immigration involves, in fact, a commitment to further inequality. These potential new immigrants are largely advantaged people who, in most cases, are accustomed to standards of living that are higher than those of most Israelis. Except for the Georgians, the bulk of Russian Jewish immigrants are well educated, and in Russia occupied relatively good positions, as did almost all of the Jews who come from the United States and Latin America. Clearly, to encourage such immigration it is necessary to say to those interested: "We cannot give you the standard of living you're accustomed to, but we can give you a decent apartment, economic opportunity, a good chance for your children to go to college," and so on. That is, Israel must commit itself to placing the new immigrants close to the top of the social hierarchy.

In most countries which in the past have admitted large numbers of immigrants, the bulk of the newcomers almost invariably entered at the bottom. This certainly was the American experience. (It is currently being repeated in much of northern Europe.) Unskilled people, relatively poorly educated people came in from Ireland, Italy, Russia and other places. The census shows this very clearly. The first generation came in and took the lowly jobs. The second generation, as reported in the census from 1880 on, had higher jobs; the third generation as a group was equal to or even a little better off than the native born of native parents. (There were, of course, great variations in success rates among the varying ethnic immigrant groups.) In effect, each second native-born generation could move up because there always was a recent immigrant wave at the bottom.

Currently, the blacks, the Puerto Ricans and the

Mexican-Americans are playing this role. They have migrated into the lowest level of the urban system. The only way to have massive upward group mobility in one generation is to have new people come in at the bottom. In a sense, Oriental Jews played this role in Israel from 1948 to 1967.

Since 1967, however, the Arabs, particularly those from the occupied territories have entered the Israeli economy as manual workers, often highly paid skilled construction workers, but more typically as unskilled ones, who may like blacks in America become invisible servants, such as the Arab waiting staff in the Faculty Club of the Hebrew University.

With the rapid growth of the Israeli economy between 1967 and 1973, the need to create high level jobs for East European immigrants, and opportunities for Oriental Jews, Israel unwittingly adopted the "solution" of creating a new Switzerland, with West Bank and Gaza Arabs playing the role that one million Italians currently fulfill for the Swiss. This possibility — a Jewish bourgeoisie and an Arab proletariat — was once the nightmare of the Labor Zionists. It means recreating the situation of the Jews in the affluent Diaspora.

The beginning of such a system could be seen in Israel at five o'clock every day before the Yom Kippur War. The Arab workers would line up at the bus stops to go back home to the West Bank. There are tens of thousands of Arab workers. These Arabs truly have had all the economic advantages that the Israelis boast about, as workers employed by Jews. They are the best-paid Arab workers in the Middle East.

There is a real danger, however, that Israel may continue to slip into the Swiss situation: a labor reserve from outside the country which does the dirty jobs. This, of course, will permit poor Jews, the Sephardim and others, to move up rapidly. In the long run, however, it is a terrible prospect for Israel as a nation. It would mean the failure of the aspirations of Zionism. It is very tempting for the Israelis to accept Arab labor; even to boast about it, since it is true that since 1967 they have raised the standard of living of the Gaza and the West Bank Arabs. But it is also true that, like the Swiss, they have acquired a proletariat without political rights.

It is noteworthy that Israeli universalism and egalitarianism have thus far fostered little interest in the situation of the Israeli Arabs. Almost none of the academic research and policy discussions about the problems of education, or social mobility, ever deal with the Arab citizens of the country. Except for the not unimportant Histadruth efforts to gain equal pay for them, and their inclusion in various welfare benefits, they, like American blacks before World War II, do not concern the dominant majority ethnic group. Articles about the Israeli situation which break down attainments and statuses by ethnic background usually are generally headed "The Israeli_______System," but have no column for the over 400,000 Israeli Arabs who comprise 14 percent of the population of the state. As of 1971, the average Gross Annual Income of all Israelis was £12,800, of those of Western Jewish origin 14,400, of Oriental background, 10,700 and of non-Jews 8,600. The average Israeli family head had 9.9 years of education, among Western-born Jews it was 10.9, among Orientals the figure was 8.1, and among non-Jews, it was but 6.4 years. Israelis may correctly point to the considerable But in the 1969-1970 school year, there was one teacher for every 17 Jewish students. The figure for Arabs was one for ever 38 attending school.

The depressed situation of the Palestinian Arabs, the limited participation of Israeli Arabs in the cultural, economic and political activities of the state, and the military activities of the Arab states and terrorism by the guerrillas, combined to sustain negative stereotypes of Arabs among most Jewish Israelis. Negative group stereotypes, even though grossly exaggerated, are generally rooted in some sort of reality, some characteristic of the group. For example, groups which are poor, who live in slums, generally do have high crime rates, as the blacks do in the United States, or as some of the North African Jewish groups and urban Arabs do in Israel. As a result, the average person in the society, who is relatively unsophisticated, judges or generalizes about these groups from his surface impression. He says, "These people are dirty, violent, poor; they are not as educated or hard-working as we are. There must be something wrong with them." That kind of reaction to the facts of social and economic inferiority occurs everywhere in the world. It is almost inevitable. Once it occurs, it becomes part of the mechanism which perpetuates inequality, because the feeling that you are superior, or that there is something wrong with the other group, makes you less sympathetic, less inclined to do something about the inequality.

Opinion polls taken before the Yom Kippur War indicated clearly that the majority of the Jews regarded the Arabs as an inferior people. As in other multi-ethnic societies, the long continuation, within one nation, of different peoples living with sharply different levels of culture, education, and skill, produces or sustains the phenomenon described as institutionalized racism in the United States. In effect, the varying components of the social system serve to prevent the depressed group from gaining access to the good things, while they give the dominant one an ideological defense for their birthright superiority. The Sephardim will improve their situation, but Israel, if it ignores its Arab population and relies on a large "external proletariat" could become a racist state.

Concern for equality in Israel remains buttressed by the nation's fundamental values, much as in the United States. Myrdal's anticipations concerning the situation of black Americans discussed earlier may, therefore, also be highly applicable to the future of Arabs in Israel. Israeli Jews, like most American whites, believe they believe in equality for all, regardless of ethnic or religious background. As noted, most of the "privileged" Ashkenazim are socialists, and the bulk of the Orientals have accepted this political culture, insofar as they have one. Self-identified socialists are more likely to feel guilty about ethnic inequality than conservatives. Most conservatives believe in the social value or necessity of inequality and hierarchy and, therefore, have less tendency to feel guilty about being privileged.

This suggests the same operative strategy for the underprivileged in Israel, whether Oriental Jews or Arabs, that Myrdal recommended to American blacks: aggressive protest. Some Oriental Jews are beginning to adopt it with some success.

The Arab situation is much more complicated. Sociologically, it is much more comparable to that of the blacks in the United States than of white immigrants. The position of the various Oriental Jewish groupings is much more comparable to the latter since, as Avineri noted, "despite differences, the various communities in Israel regard themselves as belonging in fact, and not only in principle, to a single nation, and the consciousness of being Jewish is stronger than the much more abstract . . . consciousness of being, say, American." But in any case, more than other aspects of Israeli life, the condition of the Arabs is not likely to take on a "normal" form until a real peace is attained. As long as Israeli Arabs, or foreign Arab workers are linked to the outside enemy, it is too much to expect the emergence of significant support among Jewish Israelis for the plight of Arabs.

Yet if we can think realistically that peace with the Arab world must come, we can also anticipate an Israeli future in which Israeli intellectuals, youth, and others respond to the need to support an Arab demand for equality, much as the American scions of affluent Jewish families of East European socialist background formed the main white support for black civil rights groups and struggles. The same sentiments which have repeatedly been activated among American Jewry, who, more intensely than other white Americans, hold to a combination of American and East European egalitarian values, exist in Israel.

As Israel hopefully moves towards a future which includes affluence and national security in a peaceful world, it may experience many of the social patterns that developed in the most advanced industrial society including higher rates of deviance and a series of political struggles for a fully integrated multi-ethnic society on the model of the racially linked conflicts here. Jewish Israeli socialist parents and teachers may find themselves challenged as hypocrites by their activist offspring who demand that they fulfill the universalistic values of socialism. But these values have an even higher basis of authority than *Das Kapital* or the Declaration of Independence, for in Leviticus, chapter 19, verse 34, we may read:

"A stranger who resides with you shall be to you as one of your citizens. You shall love him as yourself, for you were strangers in the land of Egypt; I am the Lord, your God."

SUGGESTED READINGS

Israel: Social Structure and Change by Michael Curtis and Mordecai Chertoff (New Brunswick, N.J.: Transaction Books, 1973).

Israeli Society by S. N. Eisenstadt (New York: Basic Books, 1967).

Inequality by Christopher Jencks et al. (New York: Basic Books, 1973).

Revolution and Counterrevolution, rev. ed., by S. M. Lipset (New York: Doubleday-Anchor Books, 1970.

Section VIII

Jobs

While all of us are linked to the larger society through our families, and (typically) younger people are linked to it through the educational institution, many adults are tied to society through their jobs. The world of work is an extremely complex one and, like other large institutional structures, both reflects and shapes the larger society. In Berg's "Rich Man's Qualifications for Poor Man's Jobs," the issue is joined about the qualifications employers demand for skilled jobs. The real question, Berg insists, does not involve an increase in skilled jobs but, rather, whether academic credentials are really important for doing a job—or just for getting it. Faith in education as *the* cure for unemployment reflects individualism as a philosophy rather than the real needs of the job market. Berg suggests that the American property system limits government to promoting employment through growth. Most of the growth, moreover, is in middle-level jobs for which both the well- and the not-so-well-educated must compete. We do not know whether people with better education do better work in these jobs. Citing case study material, Berg argues that education does not explain effectiveness; in fact, on "piecework" jobs the more highly educated tended to have a higher rate of turnover, to produce less and to be less satisfied. His solution is the suggestion that emphasis be shifted to demand rather than supply of labor.

Tussing, in "The Dual Welfare System," presses us to look at the whole economic sector in a different way. His main point is that there are two welfare systems in America. One of them, for the poor, is stigmatized and illegitimate, and is called the welfare system; the other, for jobholders and "taxpayers," is a legitimate (in the social sense) system that involves tax loopholes and shelters and social security. Both, Tussing says, are costly, but the legitimate welfare system makes a much larger demand and is excessively regressive. He goes on to suggest that there are five major differences between the two systems: the amounts of money involved; the camouflage, or lack of it, that makes the programs appear to be something else; the level of government involved in administrating the program—federal, state or local; the varying incentive and distributional side effects of the programs; and the degree of intervention into personal and family life.

An important part of working life for many Americans is the labor union. Berger, in "Organized Labor and Imperial Policy," examines the conservative foreign policy of the AFL-CIO and suggests that unions (representing only about one-quarter of the American labor force, but with disproportionate power because of organizational strength) have tied their fortunes to American corporate capitalism and, therefore, tend toward the Right in foreign policy matters. He elaborates the complex interplay of union elites and the rank and file through the use of poll data on worker attitudes toward foreign policy.

1 *Ivar Berg*

Rich Man's Qualifications for Poor Man's Jobs

It is now a well-known fact that America offers more and more jobs to skilled workers while the increase in unskilled jobs has slowed down. Newspaper articles regularly remind us that we have a shortage of computer programmers, and, at the same time, too many unskilled laborers. The conventional solution is to correct the shortcomings of the labor force by educating more of the unemployed. Apart from its practical difficulties, this solution begs the important question: Are academic credentials important for *doing* the job—or just for *getting* it?

My studies of manpower use indicate that although in recent years requirements for many jobs have been upgraded because of technological and other changes, in many cases education requirements have been raised arbitrarily. In short, *many employers demand too much education for the jobs they offer.*

Education has become the most popular solution to America's social and economic ills. Our faith in education as *the* cure for unemployment, partly reflects our inclination as a society to diagnose problems in individualistic terms. Both current and classical economic theories merely reinforce these attitudes; both assume that the labor supply can be significantly changed by investments in education and health. Meanwhile private employers, on the other side of the law of supply and demand, are held to be merely reacting to the imperatives that generate the need for better educated manpower.

Certainly the government cannot force private employers to hire people who have limited educations. Throughout our history and supported by our economic theory, we have limited the government's power to deal with private employers. According to law and the sentiments that support it, the rights of property owners and the protection of their property are essential functions of government, and cannot or should not be tampered with. In received economic doctrine, business stands apart as an independent variable. As such, business activity controls the demand for labor, and the best way the government has to reduce unemployment is by stimulating business growth.

Some of the methods the government uses to do this are direct subsidies, depreciation allowances, zoning regulations, fair-trade laws, tax holidays, and credit guarantees. In return for these benefits, governments at all levels ultimately expect more jobs will be generated and more people employed. But when the market for labor does not work out according to theory, when employer demand does not increase to match the number of job seekers, attention shifts to the supply of labor. The educational, emotional, social, and even moral shortcomings of those who stand outside the boundaries of the social system have to be eliminated, we are told—and education seems to be the best way of doing it.

Unfortunately, economists and public planners usually assume that the education that employers require for the jobs they offer is altogether beneficial to the firm. Higher education, it is thought, means better performance on the job. A close look at the data, however, shows that here reality does not usually correspond with theory.

In recent years, the number of higher-level jobs has not increased as much as personnel directors lead us to believe. The big increase, rather, has been in middle-level jobs—for high-school graduates and college dropouts. This becomes clear when the percentages of jobs requiring the three different levels of education are compared with the percentages of the labor force that roughly match these categories. The comparison of census data with the U.S. Employment Service's descriptions of 4,000 different jobs also shows that (1) high-education jobs have expanded somewhat faster for men than for women; (2) those jobs in the middle have expanded faster for women than for men; and (3) that highly educated people are employed in jobs that require *less* education than these people actually have.

The fact is that our highly educated people are competing with lesser educated people for the jobs in the middle. In Monroe County, N.Y. (which includes Buffalo), the National Industrial Conference Board has graphically demonstrated this fact. Educational requirements for most jobs, the board has reported, vary with the academic calendar: Thus, requirements rise as the end of the school year approaches and new graduates flood the market. Employers whose job openings fall in the middle category believe that by employing people with higher-than-necessary educations they are benefiting from the increasing educational achievements of the work force. Yet the data suggest that there is a "shortage" of high-school graduates and of people with post high school educations short of college degrees while there is a "surplus" of college graduates, especially females.

The economic and sociological theories that pour out of university computers have given more and more support to the idea that we, as a society, have more options in dealing with the supply side of employment —with the characteristics of the work force—than with demand.

These studies try to relate education to higher salaries; they assume that the income a person earns is a valid measure of his job performance. The salaries of better-educated people, however, may not be closely related to the work they do. Female college graduates are often employed as secretaries; many teachers and social workers earn less than plumbers and others who belong to effective unions. What these rate-of-return studies lack is productivity data isolated according to job and the specific person performing the job.

In any event, it is circular reasoning to relate wage and salary data to educational achievements. Education is often, after all, the most important criterion for a person's getting a job in the first place! The argument that salaries may be used to measure the value of education and to measure the "value added" to the firm by employees of different educational backgrounds, may simply confirm what it sets out to prove. In jobs for which educational requirements have not been thoughtfully studied, the argument is not an argument at all, but a self-fulfilling prophecy.

Despite the many attempts to relate a person's achievements to the wages he receives, researchers usually find that the traits, aptitudes, and educational achievements of workers vary as greatly *within* job categories as they do *between* them. That is, people in job A differ as much from one another as they differ from people in job B. Only a small percentage of the labor force—those in the highest and those in the lowest job levels—are exceptions. And once workers become members of the labor force, personal virtues at even the lower job levels do not account for wage differences—intelligent, well-educated, low-level workers don't necessarily earn more than others at the bottom of the ladder. Marcia Freedman's study of employment patterns for Columbia's Conservation of Human Resources project, indicates that, although many rungs of the organizational ladder are linked to differences in pay, these rungs are not closely related to differences in the employees' skills and training.

Educational requirements continue to go up, yet most employers have made no effort to find out whether people with better educations make better workers than people with inferior educations. Using data collected from private firms, the military, the federal civil service, and public-educational systems, and some collected from scratch, I have concentrated on this one basic question.

Business managers, supported by government leaders and academics interested in employment problems, have well-developed ideas about the value of a worker's educational achievement. They assert that with each increment of education—especially those associated with a certificate, diploma, or degree—the worker's attitude is better, his trainability is greater, his capacity for adaptation is more developed, and his prospects for promotions are rosier. At the same time, those workers with more modest educations, and especially those who drop out of school, are held to be less intelligent, less adaptable, less self-disciplined, less personable, and less articulate.

The findings in my studies do not support these assertions.

A comparison of 4,000 insurance agents in a major company in the Greater New York area showed that an employee's productivity—measured by the dollar value of the policies he sold—did not vary in any systematic way with his years of formal education. In other words, those salesmen with less education brought as much money into the company as their better educated peers. When an employee's experience was taken into account, it was clear that those with *less* education and *more* experience sold the most policies. Thus, even an employer whose success in business depends on the social and psychological intangibles of a customer-client relationship may not benefit from having highly educated employees. Other factors such as the influence of colleagues and family obligations were more significant in explaining the productivity of agents.

In another insurance agency, the job performances of 200 young female clerks were gauged from the number of merit-salary increases they had received. Researchers discovered that there were *no* differences in the performance records of these women that could easily be attributed to differences in their educational backgrounds. Once again, focusing on the educational achievements of job applicants actually diverted attention from characteristics that are really relevant to job performance.

At a major weekly news magazine, the variation in educational achievement among over 100 employees was greater than among the insurance clerks. The magazine hired female college graduates, as well as high-school graduates, for clerical-secretarial positions. While the employers argued that the girls needed their college degrees to qualify for future editorial jobs, most editorial positions were *not* filled by former secretaries, whether college graduates or not, but by college graduates who directly entered into those positions. And although the personnel director was skeptical of supervisors' evaluations of the secretaries, the supervisors determined the salary increases, and as many selective merit-pay increases were awarded to the lesser-educated secretaries as to the better-educated secretaries.

Executives of a larger well-known chemical company in New York told me that the best technicians in their research laboratory were those with the highest educational achievement. Therefore, in screening job applicants, they gave greater weight to a person's educational background than to his other characteristics. Yet, statistical analysis of relevant data revealed that the rate of turnover in the firm was positively associated with the employees' educational achievement. And a close look at the "reasons for leaving" given by the departing technicians showed that they intended to continue their educations. Furthermore, lesser-educated technicians earned higher performance evaluations than did their better-educated peers. Understandably, the employer was shocked by these findings.

Over Educated Are Less Productive

The New York State Department of Labor's 1964 survey of employers suggests that technicians often possess educational achievements far beyond what employers themselves think is ideal for effective performance. Thousands of companies reported their minimal educational requirements to the Labor Department, along with their ideal requirements and the actual educators of the technicians they employed. In many industries and in respect to most types of technicians, the workers were better educated than they were required to be; in 10 out of 16 technical categories they were even better educated than their employers dared hope, exceeding the "ideal" requirements set down by the employers.

Upper- and middle-level employees are not the only ones who are overqualified for their jobs. Nor is the phenomenon only to be observed in metropolitan New York. In a study of eight Mississippi trouser plants, researchers found that the more education an employee had, the less productive she was. Several hundred female operators were paid by "piece work" and their wages therefore were a valid test of workers' productivity. Furthermore this study showed that educational achievement was positively associated with turnover: The better-educated employee was more likely to quit her job.

Education's negative relationship to jobs can be measured not only by the productivity and turnover of personnel, but also by worker satisfaction. It may be argued that dissatisfaction among workers leads to a desirable measure of labor mobility, but the funds a company spends to improve employee morale and make managerial personnel more sensitive to the needs of their subordinates strongly suggest that employers are aware of the harm caused by worker dissatisfaction. Roper Associates once took a representative sample of 3,000 blue-collar workers in 16 industries in all parts of the United States. Among workers in lower-skilled jobs, dissatisfaction was found to increase as their educational achievements increased.

These studies of private firms suggest that many better-educated workers are assigned to jobs requiring low skills and that among the results are high turnover rates, low productivity, and worker dissatisfaction. Nonetheless, the disadvantages of "overeducation" are best illustrated by employment practices of public-school systems.

Educated Teachers Opt Out

Many school districts, to encourage their teachers to be highly educated, base teachers' salaries upon the number of credits they earn toward higher degrees. However, data from the National Opinion Research Center and the National Science Foundation's 1962 study of 4,000 teachers show that, like employees elsewhere, teachers become restless as their educational achievements rise. Elementary and secondary school teachers who have master's degrees are less likely to stay in their jobs than teachers with bachelor's degrees. And in a similar study done by Columbia Teachers College, it was evident that teachers with master's degrees were likely to have held jobs in more than one school system.

Thus, for school systems to tie pay increases to extra credits seems to be self-defeating. Teachers who earn extra credits apparently feel that their educational achievements reach a point beyond which they are overtrained for their jobs, and they then want to get administrative jobs or leave education for better paying jobs in industry. The school districts are, in a sense, encouraging teachers not to teach. This practice impedes the upgrading of teacher qualifications in another way. Thanks to the extra-credit system, schools of education have a steady supply of students and therefore are under little pressure to furnish better and more relevant courses.

For the most part, though, employers in the public sector do not suffer from problems of unrealistic educational requirements. For a variety of reasons, they do not enjoy favored positions in the labor market and consequently have not been able to raise educational requirements nearly so fast as the private employer has. But for this reason alone, the experiences of government agencies are significant. How well do their employees with low-education backgrounds perform their jobs?

The pressure on the armed forces to make do with "what they get" has forced them to study their experiences with personnel. Their investigations clearly show that a person's educational achievement is not a good clue to his performance. Indeed, general tests developed for technical, military classifications and aptitude tests designed to screen individual candidates for training programs have turned out to be far better indicators of a person's performance.

In a 1948 study of Air Force personnel, high-school graduates were compared with nongraduates in their performance on the Army Classification Tests and on 13 tests that later became part of the Airman Classification Battery. The military's conclusion: "High-school graduates were not uniformly and markedly superior to non-graduates. . . . High-school graduation, unless supplemented by other screening measures such as tests or the careful review of the actual high-school record, does not insure that a basic trainee will be of high potential usefulness to the Air Force."

In 1963, the Air Force studied 4,458 graduates of eight technical courses. Comparing their performances in such courses as Reciprocating Engine Mechanic, Weather Observer, Accounting, and Finance Specialist with the education they received before entering the service, the Air Force found that a high-school diploma only modestly predicted the grades the airmen got in the Air Force courses. In other Air Force studies, aptitude tests were consistently found to correlate well with a person's proficiency and performance, while educational achievement rarely accounted for more than 4 percent of the variations.

These Air Force data do not conclude that education is unimportant, or that formal learning experiences are irrelevant. Rather, it points out the folly of confusing a man's driver's license with his driving ability. Just as different communities have different safety standards, so schools and school systems employ different kinds of teachers and practices. It should surprise no one that a person's credentials, by themselves, predict his performance so poorly.

Army and Navy studies confirm the Air Force findings. When 415 electronic technicians' scores on 17 concrete tasks were analyzed in conjunction with their age, pay grades, and education, education was found to be negatively associated with performance. When the Navy updated this study, the outcome was the same. For high performance in repairing complicated electronic testing equipment, experience proved more significant than formal education.

Perhaps the military's most impressive data came from its experiments with "salvage" programs, in which illiterates and men who earn low scores on military classification tests are given remedial training. According to research reports, these efforts have been uniformly successful—as many graduates of these programs develop into useful servicemen as the average, normal members of groups with which they have been regularly compared.

Naval Manpower Salvage

In a 1955 study done for the Navy, educational achievements were not found to be related to the performance of 1,370 recruits who attended "recruit preparatory training" courses. Neither were educational achievements related to the grades the recruits received from their company commanders and their instructors, nor to their success or failure in completing recruit training. In some instances, the low-scoring candidates with modest educational backgrounds performed at higher levels than better-educated men with high General Classification Test scores. The military recently expanded its "salvage" program with Project 100,000, and preliminary results tend to confirm the fact that training on the job is more important than educational credentials.

Military findings also parallel civilian studies of turnover rates. Reenlistment in the Navy is nearly twice as high among those men who have completed fewer than 12 years of school. But reenlistment in the military, of course, is related to the fact that the civilian economy does not particularly favor ex-servicemen who have modest educational achievements.

Wartime employment trends make the same point. During World War II, when demand for labor was high, both public and private employers adapted their recruiting and training to the labor supply. Productivity soared while a wide range of people mastered skills almost entirely without regard to their personal characteristics or previous circumstances. Labor's rapid adjustment on the job was considered surprising; after the war, it was also considered to be expensive. Labor costs, it was argued, had gone up during the war, and unit productivity figures were cited as evidence. These figures, however, may have been misleading. Since the majority of wartime laborers were employed in industries with "cost-plus" contracts—where the government agreed to reimburse the contractor for all costs, plus a certain percentage of profit—such arrangements may have reduced the employer's incentives to control costs. The important lesson from the war period seems to be that people quickly adjust to work requirements once they are on the job.

A 5 percent sample of 180,000 men in the federal civil service shows that while the number of promotions a person gets is associated with his years of education, the link is far from complete. Education has a greater bearing on a person's rank at *entry* into the civil service than on his prospects for a promotion. Except for grades 11-15, in accounting for the promotion rates of civil servants, length of service and age are far more significant than education. A closer look at one government agency will perhaps clarify these points.

Few organizations in the United States have had to adapt to major technological changes as much as the Federal Aviation Agency has. Responsible among other things for the direction and control of all flights in the United States, it operates the control-tower facilities at all public airports. With the advent of jet-powered flights, the F.A.A. had to handle very quickly the horrendous technical problems posed by faster aircraft and more flights. Since no civilian employer requires the services needed by the F.A.A. in this area, the agency must train its own technicians and control-tower people. The agency inventively confronted the challenge by hiring and training many new people and promoting those trained personnel it already had. Working with the background data on 507 men—all the air-traffic controllers who had attained grade 14 or above—it would seem that, at this high level, education would surely prove its worth.

On the Job Training for Tower Controllers

Yet in fact these men had received very little formal education, and almost no technical managerial training except for the rigorous on-the-job training given by the F.A.A. itself. Of the 507 men in the sample, 211, or 42 percent, had no education or training beyond high school. An additional 48, or 10 percent, were high-school graduates who had had executive-training courses. Thus, more than half of the men had had no academic training beyond high school. There were, however, no patterns in the differences among the men in grades 13 or 15 with respect to education. That is, education and training were *not* related to the higher grade.

The F.A.A.'s amazing safety record and the honors and awards given to the tower controllers are good indicators of the men's performance. The F.A.A.'s Executive Selection and Inventory System records 21 different kinds of honors or awards. Only one-third of the men have never received any award at all. Half of the 77 percent who have been honored have been honored more than once. And a relatively high percentage of those with no education beyond high school received four or more awards; those with a B.A. degree were least likely to receive these many honors. Other breakdowns of the data confirm that education is not a factor in the daily performance of one of the truly demanding decision-making jobs in America.

The findings reported in these pages raise serious questions about the usefulness of raising educational requirements for jobs. They suggest that the use of formal education as a sovereign screening device for jobs adequately performed by people of lower educational achievements may result in serious costs—high turnover, employee dissatisfactions, and poorer performance. Programs calculated to improve employees' educations probably aim at the wrong targets, while programs calculated to reward better-educated people are likely to miss their targets. It would be more useful to aim at employers' policies and practices that block organizational mobility and seal off entry jobs.

There Are More Job Openings in the Middle

Given the facts that there are more job openings in the middle, and that many people are overqualified for the jobs they do have, policies aimed at upgrading the educational achievements of the low-income population seem at best naïve. It would make better sense to upgrade people in the middle to higher jobs and upgrade those in lower-level jobs to middle positions, providing each group with an education appropriate to their age, needs, and ambitions. The competition for lower-level jobs would then be reduced, and large numbers of drop-outs could move into them. (Only after young people, accustomed to a good income, develop middle-class aspirations are they apparently interested in pursuing the balance of their educations.) Current attempts to upgrade the labor supply also seem questionable in light of what psychologists and sociologists have to say. Changing people's attitudes, self-images, and achievements is either enormously time-consuming—sometimes requiring half a generation—or it is impossible. At any rate, it is always risky.

If the much-maligned attitudes of low-income Americans were changed without establishing a full-employment economy, we might simply be adding fuel to the smoldering hatreds of the more ambitious, more frustrated groups in our urban ghettos. And if we wish to do something about the supposed shortcomings in the low-income Negro families, it will clearly require changes in those welfare arrangements that now contribute to family dissolution. The point is that rather than concentrate on the supply of labor, we must reconsider our reluctance to alter the *demand* for labor. We must have more realistic employment requirements.

Unfortunately, attempts to change people through education have been supported by liberal-intellectuals who place great value upon education and look appreciatively upon the economic benefits accruing to better-educated Americans. Indeed, one of the few elements of consensus in present-day American politics may well be the reduction of the gap between the conservative and liberal estimate of the worth of education.

Obviously, the myths perpetuated about society's need for highly-educated citizens work to the disadvantage of less-educated people, particularly nonwhites who are handicapped whatever the state of the economy. Information obtained by economist Dale Hiestand of Columbia does not increase one's confidence that educational programs designed to help disadvantaged people over 14 years old will prove dramatically beneficial. Hiestand's studies show that even though the best-educated nonwhites tend to have more job mobility, they are more likely to enter occupations that are *vacated* by whites than to compete with whites for *new* jobs. Since the competition for middle-education jobs is already very intense, it will be difficult to leapfrog Negroes into jobs not yet vacated by whites, or into new jobs that whites are likely to monopolize.

Now, nothing in the foregoing analysis should be construed as suggesting that education is a waste of time. Many jobs, as was stated at the outset, have changed, and the need for education undoubtedly grows quite aside from the monetary benefits individuals derive from their educations. But I think it is fundamentally subversive of education and of democratic values not to see that, in relation to jobs, education has its limits.

As the burden of evidence in this article suggests, the crucial employment issue is not the "quality of the work force." It is the overall level of employment and the demand for labor in a less than full-employment economy.

SUGGESTED READINGS

In Pursuit of Equity: Who Serves When Not All Serve? National Advisory Commission on Selective Service (Washington: U.S. Government Printing Office, 1967).

The Draft: A Handbook of Facts and Alternatives edited by Sol Tax (Chicago: The University of Chicago Press, 1967).

Photos by Euan Duff
Text by David Marsden

Workless

This essay was excerpted from *Workless* (Pelican Books) by Euan Duff and David Marsden.

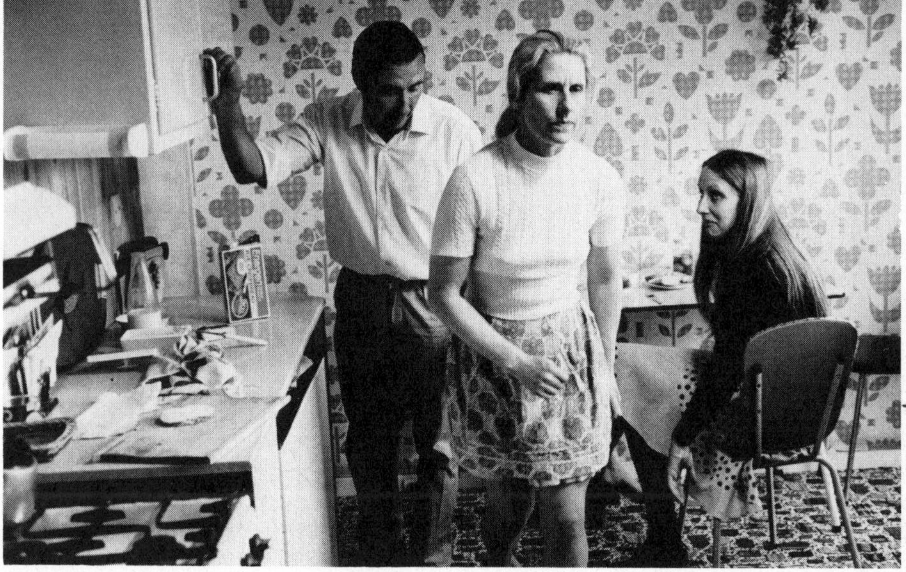

It is by now increasingly recognized that workers may be thrown out of work by industrial forces beyond their control, and that the unemployed are in some sense paying the price of the economic progress of the rest of the community. The unemployed are not mere statistics: they are people, workers without work, whatever the national unemployment figures.

In arguments about unemployment there seems an oversimplification in the idea that either the provision or the performance of much of the available work can be seen idealistically in terms of the fulfilment of a social duty either by industry or the worker. A neglected perspective is how limiting work can be; how dirty, dangerous, monotonous, boring or lonely. This makes it a very interesting question why many men work at all. And indeed it has been suggested that to fill many jobs our educational and occupational systems are calculated to limit talent and to persuade individuals how little they are capable of doing. Certainly the large numbers of men who remain in work for wages below subsistence levels would lend support for the existence of such pressures in society, or to the presence of a work ethic which impels men to work for little intrinsic reward.

Questions about workers' motivations and their control over, and responsibility for, their work careers and unemployment are large ones which may be approached from a number of different perspectives and to which no simple final answers are possible. Indeed there are already large numbers of detailed studies of workers' motivations and the sources of their satisfaction with their work. Nevertheless, perhaps because of their low, "forgotten" status in society, apart from some pioneering studies of redundancies the workless have seldom been questioned about what is the meaning and importance of work to them. Through lack of evidence the notions of work as a social contract and the social costs of unemployment to the individual have been discounted. There was complacency about the adequacy of the material living standards of the workless, and evidence of social costs, such as Orwell's writing about the demoralization of the 1930s, could too easily be dismissed as no longer relevant in the 1970s.

Men who are workless spend their days in very different ways. Some continue with activities very like the work they have lost; others do a housewife's job, looking after the children while their wives work; others use the time to fulfil their individual creativity, perhaps in making pictures or writing; and still others satisfy their idealism by carrying out unpaid community work. A few do nothing. At first glance a number of families seem to have enough money to manage on, and relationships appear cosy; but there are also couples who fight like cat and dog, quarrelling openly over money. Workless men may lead isolated and lonely lives, or alternatively they may spend much of their time in the company of friends who are also unemployed. Some search cheerfully and hopefully for work; others chafe bitterly and angrily at the constraints of unemployment; others work illegally at small jobs which seem to act as a kind of safety valve for their energies and the various pressures which they experience. There are a few who seem to welcome the chance to remain out of work. But there are also those who despair.

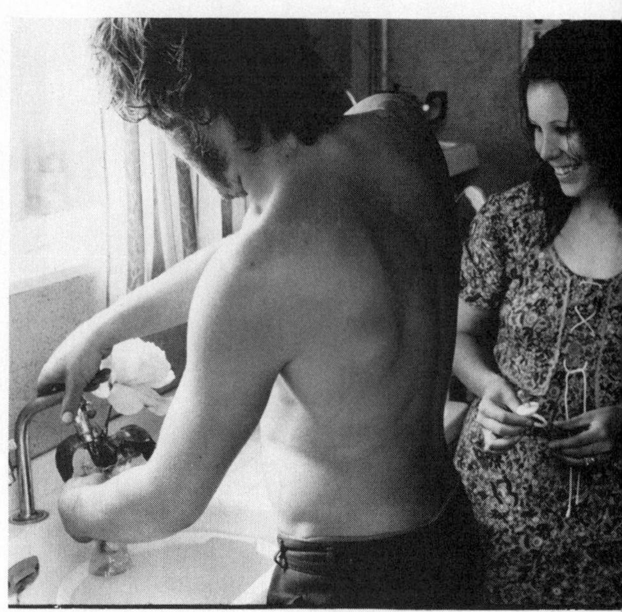

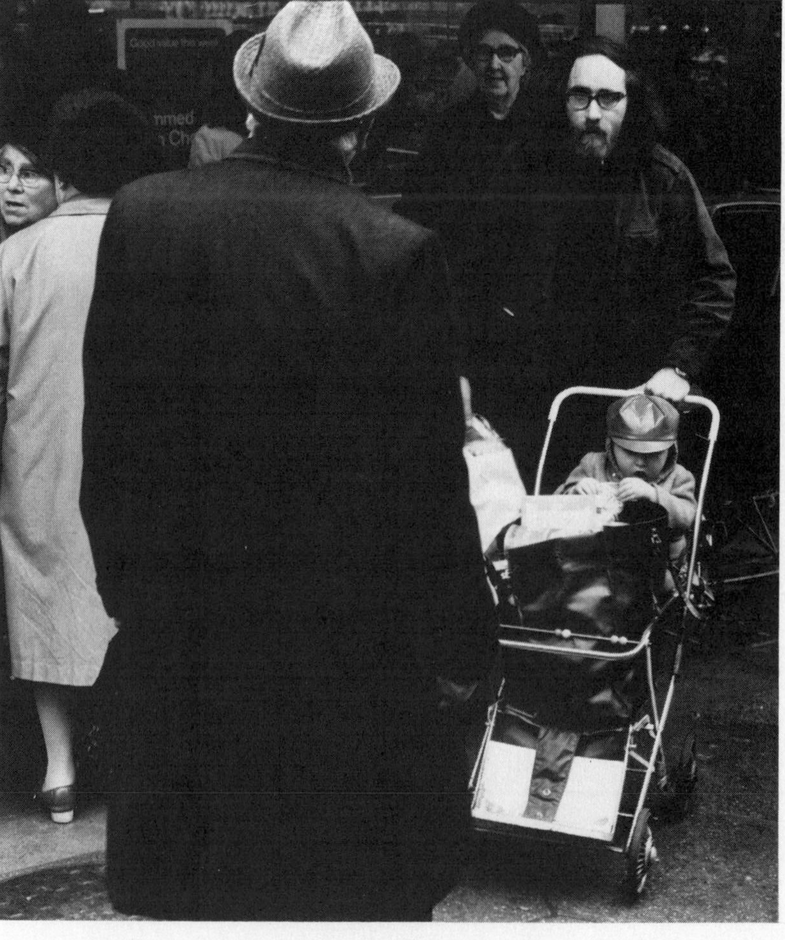

2 The Dual Welfare System

A. Dale Tussing

Two welfare systems exist simultaneously in this country. One is well known. It is explicit, poorly funded, stigmatized and stigmatizing, and is directed at the poor. The other, practically unknown, is implicit, literally invisible, is nonstigmatized and nonstigmatizing, and provides vast but unacknowledged benefits to the non-poor—whether working class, middle class or well to do.

Despite the attention given to programs for the poor, they are dwarfed by the programs for the non-poor. As Gordon Tullock has observed, "Almost all standard discussions of redistribution imply that it is normally from the rich to the poor. Some such redistribution does indeed go on, but it is a trivial phenomenon compared to the redistribution within the middle class. I find the concentration of discussion of redistribution upon the very minor phenomenon of redistribution from the wealthy to the poor and the general ignoring of the major phenomenon—redistribution back and forth within the middle class. . . remarkable."

The legitimacy of one's income and, especially, one's position in the overall distribution of income, are central preoccupations in America. No welfare programs are inherently legitimate in the United States, where the dominant ideology of individualism still appears to reject the welfare state in principle (while applying it in practice—a conflict of some significance). In the view of many people, job-holders are members of and contributors to society; non-job-holders are not. Job-holding legitimates one's political role, as well. In local, state and national politics, more is heard today about "taxpayers" than about "citizens."

Other socially legitimate sources of income exist, but their legitimacy traces directly or indirectly to someone's job. For instance, one can *save* out of one's earnings to provide for one's own retirement, either with a bank or some formal pension scheme. Similarly, one can provide through savings or insurance for an income while sick, or for one's family when one is "no longer there." Virtually all private provisions of this sort are automatically legitimate.

When a recently urbanized and industrialized America found that it could no longer rely on the old, traditional, nongovernmental forms of income protection and maintenance (the extended family, the community and systems of obligation) and had to create a governmental welfare apparatus, a major problem was that American ideology opposed such welfare devices in principle. If both the need for welfare programs *and* the ideology were to be satisfied, either the ideology would have to change, or the *form* and *name* of welfare programs would have to be carefully designed to make them seem to fit the ideology. In particular, they would have to have (or seem to have) a productivity basis.

Two systems were created. Clair Wilcox has labeled the explicit transfer parts of them "social insurance" and "public charity." "Social insurance," the heart of the welfare system for the non-poor, has been constructed to be legitimate, to protect the integrity and dignity of the people involved. To a large extent, this legitimacy is provided by some form of camouflage—by protective nomenclature such as "parity," "compensation" and even "social insurance"; by the paraphernalia of private programs, such as Social Security account numbers; and by burying welfare programs in tax laws.

"Public charity," or the welfare system for the poor, has been constructed to be illegitimate. Thus it too leaves the ideology intact. The illegitimacy of poor people's welfare is multifold. There is, first, the illegitimacy of dependency—living off the incomes of others. Second, there is the separate illegitimacy of apparent idleness, and the usual association with sin. And third, there is the inherent illegitimacy of government spending, financed by taxation. Most welfare programs for non-poor people either do not take the form of government spending (tax relief to some increases others' taxes, but most people do not consider a loophole comparable with an expenditure item), or use earmarked payroll taxes and segregated trust funds, and are thought of, and officially treated as, generically different from spending out of the general revenues of government.

Three examples illustrate the importance of the *form* of a program, and the association of form (rather than content) with legitimacy.

In 1968, Wilbur Cohen, then Secretary of Health, Education and Welfare, advocated a program of "income insurance," as preferable to a guaranteed income, negative income taxes and similar schemes, to cover unemployment as well as more chronic poverty. Cohen pointed to the greater acceptance of Social Security and other programs financed by payroll taxes and with separate trust funds. He argued that the poverty gap could be closed in America—that there were no "economic" reasons that we couldn't afford to redistribute income to eliminate poverty altogether—that the only barriers were "psychological."

In New York State, union members on strike have

been eligible to draw public assistance checks. In one upstate city, a prominent labor leader, an outspoken foreign-policy hawk and vehement critic of public assistance recipients, found his membership receiving benefits, and was asked for a justification, both in light of his general antipathy for public assistance, and in light of the argument that public assistance was created to help the poor survive, not to underwrite strikes. His response was that his union members had for years been taxpaying members of the community, and were now only drawing on a fraction of what they had paid in. By contrast, he argued, regular welfare recipients were *less* entitled to public assistance, since they had not (he said) been taxpayers. He was in effect converting the program into a contributory one—for his members, but not for the poor. In both cases, changed perceptions converted a welfare program to a contributory basis, and thereby made it legitimate.

The third example concerns the Brannan Plan, which provides for farm products to be sold for whatever prices they bring in the market while farmers' incomes are supplemented by government checks. Farmers opposed this plan, despite its general superiority to the price-support programs (no storage costs, lower food prices) because a subsidy through the market was less explicit and therefore more legitimate than a direct cash transfer. Opponents used words like "socialism" to describe the Brannan Plan. More revealing still, some said they "didn't need charity." Only when farm surpluses turned into shortages in 1973 was a Brannan Plan-type program seen by farmers as preferable.

Social Security—a Closer Look

Legitimacy of welfare programs for the non-poor is provided by some form of camouflage, and acceptability requires changing the form, not the content, of welfare programs. The classic case of a legitimate welfare program is Old-Age and Survivors and Disability Insurance under Social Security. Social Security has existed for more than 35 years, and has covered millions of beneficiaries. And yet it is almost uniformly misunderstood. Its protective camouflage consists in part of widespread mythology.

The details of the Old-Age and Survivors and Disability Programs are as follows: effective 1974 (but subject to change), there is an employee tax of 5.85 percent on the first $12,000 of payroll income, and an identical tax paid by the employer. Economists believe that the employer share is passed on to the employee, in the form of a lower wage rate, so that it is fair to say that there is a tax of 11.70 percent on the first $12,000 of payroll income. There is a rough relationship between the amount a worker pays in, and the amount to which he is entitled, but only a rough one. Each person is given an account number, and a record is kept of his tax contributions. Each year's benefits (approximately $40 billion annually in the early 1970s) are paid from that year's tax contributions. In addition, there has typically been a small surplus, so that over the years a balance has built up in the Old-Age and Survivors and Disability Insurance trust funds of about $45 billion (as of 1972).

Many people conclude from these details that the Old-Age and Survivors and Disability Insurance system is not a welfare program at all, but is merely a compulsory pension or compulsory saving scheme. As recently as June 1971, NBC newsman David Brinkley, commenting on a news item which stated that Social Security was the largest program of government payments to persons, said, "Social Security is not a government payment to individuals. It is just the government giving the people's own savings back to them."

A second, somewhat more subtle myth, often appears in the conservative press—that Social Security is inefficient, and that individuals could do better by saving on their own through banks and other investments than through a government program. The argument runs as follows: if a man were to "tax" himself at current Social Security payroll tax rates (employer and employee shares combined) and to deposit the proceeds in a savings account, and at age 65 were to stop paying and start drawing a "pension," he would do better (on the average—age of death is, of course, unknown) than under present Social Security benefits.

The argument contains a serious conceptual error: it misunderstands the nature of Social Security by comparing present benefit levels and present tax rates. Yet no one will spend a lifetime paying present tax rates, and then retire and receive present benefit levels. The fact is that tax rates have been rising throughout the existence of Social Security, and that benefit levels have been rising even faster. The fact is also that Social Security payments are, on the average, well over four times the amount paid in by each taxpayer (counting employer and employee shares, and interest) rather than slightly less than he could earn from a bank on the same payments.

How is it possible for a trust-funded program to pay out over four times as much to each beneficiary as he paid during his working life? Three things make this possible: a rising population and work force, which means that more people will always be currently paying taxes than will be receiving benefits; a rising aggregate income level; and rising tax rates. Could a private pension program do the same—relying on growth in the number of clients, and paying out more to each retired person than what he has paid in, together with earned interest? Obviously not. Only a government unit can be completely confident of its ability to continue growing, as only a government has the power to tax.

Social Security is not, then, essentially a scheme by which individuals pay into a fund, from which they later withdraw. Instead, it is a scheme by which those who are now employed are taxed to pay benefits to those who are now unemployed. It is a transfer at this time rather than across time. It is a welfare program, not a savings program.

The resemblence between Social Security and private, funded pension programs is illusory in other ways, too. In a funded pension program, the more you pay in, other things being equal, the more you get. The later in life you enter the program, other things being equal, the less you get. And your eligibility is not typically affected by your eligibility for other pension benefits. None of this is necessarily true with Social Security. As Professor Milton Friedman has written,

> . . . the relationship between individual contributions (that is, payroll taxes) and benefits is extremely tenuous. Millions of people who pay taxes will never receive any benefits attributable to those taxes because they will not have paid for enough quarters to qualify, or because they receive payments in their capacity as spouse. Persons who pay vastly different sums over their working lives may receive identically the same benefits. Two men or two women who pay precisely the same taxes at the same time may end up receiving different benefits because one is married and the other is single.

Because private pension programs are a form of individual saving, in which beneficiaries receive what they have paid in, together with interest, but less administration costs, private pension programs *do* save for their members, and in fact, acquire massive amounts of stocks and bonds. Over the years, Old-Age and Survivors and Disability Insurance members have paid in more in payroll taxes than have been paid out to beneficiaries, and by 1972 the Social Security Trust Funds had acquired $45 billion in U.S. government securities. Since both own billions in assets, ownership of Treasury securities makes Social Security resemble a funded pension program in still another way. But that ownership actually reflects another *dis*similarity.

These trust funds' ownership of over $45 billion worth of U.S. government securities in 1972 meant that one agency of the federal government (the U.S. Treasury) owed money to another agency (the Social Security Trust Funds). (The other dozen trust funds—most of which, like Railroad Retirement, Medicare and Unemployment Compensation, are linked to welfare programs along the lines of Social Security—owned an additional $40 billion in U.S. government securities.) Since almost every year, receipts exceed payments, the assets of these trust funds continue to grow, though they are far lower than would be necessary to place the system on the same actuarial footing as a private insurance company.

To the extent that Social Security taxes exceed benefit payments, and the excess is "lent" to the U.S. Treasury, Social Security taxes are actually being used to finance expenditures on defense, interior, agriculture, foreign affairs and the rest of the budget. The "lending" is merely a bookkeeping entry. The earmarking of these taxes turns out to be less than perfect—present about $2 billion a year. The point is not that Social Security taxpayers are being bilked, their money being siphoned off into the Treasury. They receive over four times, on the average, what they have paid in—hardly a bilking. The point is, instead, that the Social Security system is not a segregated, quasi-private, compulsory insurance scheme, but rather a government welfare program, fully integrated in fact if not in form with the other functions of the government.

This fact makes it all the more important that Old-Age and Survivors and Disability Insurance payroll taxes are America's most regressive major tax—exempting interest, profit, rent, capital gains, and all payroll income over $12,000, and with no allowance for number of dependents. Moreover, the higher one's income, the larger the ratio of the benefits received to the taxes paid. Friedman has called Social Security "the poor man's welfare payment to the middle class."

Differences Between the Systems

There are five major differences between the welfare programs for the non-poor, and those for the poor. They are: the amounts of money involved; the camouflage, or lack of it, in making the programs appear to be something else; the level of government—federal, state and local—involved in administering the program; varying incentive and distributional side-effects of the programs; and the degree of intervention into personal and family life.

Levels of Support

Both in the aggregate and on a per-person basis, the welfare system for the non-poor provides more liberally than that for the poor. Side-by-side comparisons are hazardous, because coverage from program to program varies according to circumstances (for example, age, number of children and so forth) because the specifications of welfare for the poor and non-poor are different, because there are state-to-state differences in a number of programs, and because some recipients have dual coverage. Nonetheless, the following comparisons are revealing. In March 1973, the average unemployment compensation recipient received $256.76 per month; the average family receiving General Assistance (including, among others, families of those unemployed persons who are ineligible for unemployment compensation) received $114.15. The average retired worker received $164.30 from Old-Age Assistance under Social Security, while the average recipient of Old-Age Assistance under public assistance received $78.65. On the whole, the excess of non-poor over poor welfare programs seems to be in the 20 to 30 percent range for most programs, though some items go up to 100 percent or more.

There are interesting differences even within public assistance. The amount per person averaged as follows in March 1973: Aid to the Blind—$110.10; Aid to the Permanently and Totally Disabled—$106.55; Old-Age Assistance—$78.65; General Assistance—$68.81; and Aid to Families with Dependent Children—$54.20. (As of 1974, benefits for aged, blind and disabled are the same.)

Far more dramatic differences than these exist. In Mississippi the average monthly Aid to Families with Dependent Children payment per recipient was only $14.39. In that same state, a corporate farm, Eastland, Inc., owned by the family of a U.S. senator, received over $250,000 annually in various farm subsidies.

Our welfare systems do not distribute benefits on the basis of need. Rather, they distribute benefits on the basis of legitimacy. Poor people are viewed as less legitimate than non-poor people, and among the poor, those who are disabled, blind and old are seen as more legitimate than those in the General Assistance or Aid to Families with Dependent Children categories—both heavily dominated by minority group members, including ghetto mothers and their children, and even including small numbers of unemployed men.

Implied here is a social judgment that—rhetoric to the contrary notwithstanding—America's poor are poor because they *should* be poor. This judgment takes the following form. Most non-poor Americans would probably be willing to agree that poor people are poor because of circumstances rather than lack of merit, except that to do so would also imply that they themselves were comfortable, affluent or rich because of circumstances rather than because of merit. Poor people are not necessarily thought to be inferior. Rather, non-poor people are thought to be superior. The success/failure, deserving/undeserving distinctions lead us to create categories of assistance which on the surface appear to be functional, but which on deeper examination prove to be moral and ideological rationalizations. Poverty reflects inadequate performance; and high levels of welfare support for the poor would be tantamount to rewarding sin.

Concealment of the Welfare Nature of the Program

By and large, welfare programs for the poor are obvious, open and clearly labeled, and those for the non-poor are either concealed (in tax laws, for instance) and ill understood, or are clothed in protective language and procedures (such as "parity," "social security" and "unemployment insurance," for instance, or both ("tax relief," for instance).

Whether a person is poor or not can often be determined by the names of his welfare programs. If his programs are called "relief," "welfare," "assistance," "charity" or the like, he is surely poor; but if they are called "parity," "insurance," "compensation" or "compulsory saving," he is surely a member of the large majority of non-poor persons who do not even think of themselves as receiving welfare payments.

The degree of concealment in turn influences the level of support, in a number of ways. First, welfare programs for the poor, being more noticed, are more in the public eye. Concealed and camouflaged programs are more likely to escape the wrath of taxpayers' groups. The deductibility of interest on home mortgages and of property taxes, known as "tax expenditure" items, cost the federal government $2.4 billion and $2.7 billion, respectively, in 1971. These tax deductions for home owners serve as a massive "rent supplement" for homebuyers. Either, if acknowledged as such, would be the largest single housing program in the federal government. Together they are more than quadruple the size of all programs combined for housing poor people—including public housing, rent supplements, assistance in purchase of homes and all others. Yet they are all but unknown, except as computations on one's income tax return. According to U.S. Treasury figures, 85 percent of the benefits from these provisions go to taxpayers with over $10,000 of adjusted gross income, while less than .01 percent go to those with adjusted gross incomes of $3,000 or less.

In the eyes of many Americans, the openness of poor people's welfare reinforces the sense that the poor are undeserving. Poor people are viewed as idle and dependent (characteristics often attributed to even the most hard-working and independent); and the publicity given to public assistance and to public assistance recipients is likely to (and often is calculated to) reinforce this impression.

This difference in concealment permits taxpayers to demand and legislators to provide differential levels of support without being conscious of discriminating. Those who have convinced themselves that they are wholly independent and self-reliant, in spite of vast camouflaged welfare programs, will not feel they have provided less generously for poor people. In their opinion, they have provided only for poor people.

The degradation and humiliation involved in some poor people's programs, and the sense of failure in life which is instilled in those who accept poor people's welfare, makes poor people strive mightily to "stay off welfare." This is undoubtedly a major reason that the majority of those legally eligible for public assistance do not receive it at all. The number who decline to claim special tax deductions and other tax preferences in order to preserve their dignity is by contrast surely quite small.

The techniques used for concealment of welfare programs for the non-poor often provide for automatic increases in amount as the years go by. This is especially true of "tax expenditures," which require no annual appropriations, but only that the same tax structure remain intact with higher and higher levels of income.

Level of Government

The third difference between welfare for the poor and

welfare for the non-poor concerns the level of government involved. Welfare programs for the non-poor tend to be federally financed and federally administered, with decisions on eligibility and on levels of support made nationally, with but two exceptions (unemployment compensation and workmen's compensation), and those exceptions involve federal-state partnerships. Programs for the poor, on the other hand, while they may be partially or almost totally supported by federal funds, are characteristically administered as local programs, primarily by county welfare departments (or as state programs in those states where welfare departments are state operated). Even the War on Poverty efforts of the Office of Economic Opportunity and such related programs as Model Cities are tied to local government and local politics.

There is one important and revealing exception to this statement. In 1969, President Nixon proposed a major revamping of the public assistance system, including federal administration and a federally determined minimum payment level, for all four federally aided groups—families with dependent children, the aged, the blind and the disabled.

For nearly four years the Congress labored, and in 1972 it completed its work. The major changes were all rejected, and a bill was passed which made few departures. The most significant of these was the federalization, effective 1974, of a combined program, called Supplementary Security Income, replacing three federally aided state and local programs: Old-Age Assistance, Aid to the Blind and Aid to the Permanently and Totally Disabled. Benefit levels in the new Supplementary Security Income program are, however, lower than those of a number of states in the antecedent Old-Age Assistance, Aid to the Blind and Aid to the Permanently and Totally Disabled programs. Since states are permitted to supplement the federal payments (making the federal benefit the floor or minimum payment), and since a number of states are expected to do so in order not to reduce payments, even the 1972 legislation does not fully federalize assistance to these groups. Benefit levels still depend on state decisions, and state taxes are still involved.

The public assistance system is now left with three levels of federalization: the new, semi-federalized Supplementary Security Income program, for the most "deserving" poor—the aged, blind and disabled; the federally aided program, Aid to Families with Dependent Children, with eligibility and support-level decisions made by the states, and with state and local administration—viewed by many people as the "ghetto mother" program; finally, there is no federal contribution at all for General Assistance, which covers the least socially legitimate of all dependent poor, unemployed single and childless married persons, and unemployed fathers. It is clear that the degree of federalization, like level of support, depends on legitimacy or worthiness. All three of these degrees of federalization are in contrast to the complete federal control, administration and financing of such regular, mainstream welfare programs as Old-Age and Survivors and Disability Insurance under Social Security.

With these partial exceptions, the rule consistently applies: programs for the non-poor are federal; programs for the poor are state and/or local. This fact increases the exposure of poor people's welfare (not only because these programs are subject to local decisions, closer to home and easier to see, but because poor people's welfare legislation will be debated and acted upon on at least two and probably three levels of government, when the Congress, the state legislature, and the local council or board of supervisors passes on public assistance, housing, food and other programs). Poor people's welfare is limited, simply because it is tied to inelastic local and state revenue sources, such as the property tax, while the regular welfare system can provide vast benefits, since it is tied to the overproductive federal tax system.

Local and state administration of poor people's welfare means control over the size of the population of the poor in given areas. Just as many cities, counties and states compete with one another to attract and keep industry and high-income population, so also do they (with less fanfare, of course) compete to discourage or drive away low-income population. Before Department of Agriculture reforms prompted by the Poor People's March and Resurrection City, hundreds of counties, primarily in the South, refused to participate in surplus food distribution, and a few openly stated their motive: to drive away once-needed farm workers, tenant farmers and sharecroppers, made unnecessary when technology affected agriculture. Competition to get rid of poor people is not limited to the South. A city councilman in a northern city, commenting on the council's recent negative vote on a public housing issue, was quoted as saying that the majority would be delighted to build more public housing for the city's poor, except that construction of public housing would merely attract more poor people to the community. Suburbs have steadfastly refused (with, since 1971, Supreme Court approval) to provide public housing. And, despite the fact that residence requirements for public assistance were declared unconstitutional in 1969, states continue to adopt them and enforce them.

This direction of thought has some apparent logic. In most cases, poor people's welfare programs will require state and/or local tax money; and even where they don't, taxes paid by poor people will not cover the costs of their public education, police, fire and other services. However one feels about the morality of trying to drive away people for purely economic gain, no amount of local competition to get rid of them will reduce the national total of poor people; it just affects their geographic distribution. In fact, there is good reason to believe that these policies increase the amount of poverty. Since they reduce the mobility of poor people, such people are unlikely to be able to leave unpromising regions to move to growing and prosperous ones. At the same time, low levels of services and support to poor people trap them into poverty's vicious circle.

Incentive and Distributional Side-Effects

Poor people's welfare programs discourage poor people from becoming self-supporting, from being thrifty and from maintaining a regular family life. The regular welfare system frequently provides nothing to those with the greatest need, and then provides increasing benefits as need declines. The best-known disincentives to the poor are in the public assistance program, particularly in Aid to Families with Dependent Children. The manner in which most recipients are covered provides that every dollar they earn reduces their assistance check by a dollar. If a family is entitled to $150 per month, and the family earns nothing, it will get a check for $150; if it earns $50, it will get a check for $100; and so forth. This means that, in effect, there is a "tax" of 100 percent on earned income. Since businessmen with marginal tax rates of far less complain of the disincentive effects of taxation, it should hardly be surprising that the motivation of someone with a tax rate of 100 percent should be affected adversely.

In some poor people's welfare programs, the effective marginal tax rate may even exceed 100 percent. This is true wherever a food-stamp, public housing, medical care or other program has a fixed eligibility threshold—an income level above which families or individuals become ineligible to participate in the program. A family may find that any further increases in its income will force it to leave public housing, and pay a rent increase which exceeds the pay increase; force it off food stamps, increasing the grocery budget by more than the pay increase; and force it out of other programs as well.

The Work Incentive program for certain Aid to Families with Dependent Children parents reduces the effective tax rate from 100 percent to 66.67 percent. President Nixon's proposed welfare reforms would have reduced the rate to 50 percent. These lower rates still remain high enough to discourage effort. While recent research indicates that this kind of disincentive is less potent than was once thought, it nonetheless constitutes an added burden on the poor, a "sandbagging" of those who need no such handicaps.

There are other kinds of disincentives in poor people's welfare. The best known is the incentive to break up the family. In a majority of states, Aid to Families with Dependent Children, the largest public assistance program, is available only where there are no employable, unemployed adults in the household. In practice, this has meant that virtually all such families are headed by husbandless mothers. Chronically unemployed husbands often must desert their families in order for the families to become eligible for assistance.

Mainly because of their concealment, many mainstream welfare programs provide in ways which are inversely related to need. The most glaring examples are found in welfare programs buried in the tax laws. The general proposition is: the dollar value to the taxpayer of any item which reduces his taxable income, whether it is a deductible expense, a dependents' exemption or an exclusion (nontaxable income item), is equal to the size of that item multiplied by the marginal tax rate applicable to that taxpayer. A $100 deduction for someone in the 25 percent marginal tax bracket is "worth" $25.00. With a progressive income tax, the dollar value of any given deduction, exemption or exclusion rises as income rises.

The simplest example of the inverse relation to need is the extra dependents' exemption allowed those over 65. The extra $750 exemption is worth nothing to the person whose taxable income is so low that he pays no taxes; it is worth $105 (14 percent of $750) to a person in the 14 percent bracket, a person with up to $1,000 taxable income; and it is worth $325 to a person in the highest, 70 percent bracket, for families with over $200,000 in taxable income. The added exemption is worth the least to those with the most need, and the most to those with the least need.

Even though the amount of this extra dependents' exemption is the same for all people, its value to the taxpayer rises as income rises. This effect is aggravated whenever the amount of the deduction or exclusion itself rises with income.

The "income-splitting" provision (husband-wife joint tax returns) also provides benefits which increase with income. The effect of the joint return provision is to double the size of each tax bracket. The 14 percent rate applies to 0-$500 for single persons and 0-$1,000 for married couples filing jointly. The 15 percent bracket is $501-$1,000 for single persons, and $1,001-$2,000 on the joint return, and so on. The greatest benefit comes at the highest end of the income scale, because the brackets are much wider (for example, $100,000-$200,000). People with high incomes are, in effect, paid thousands of dollars to be married (which helps explain why many rich persons are well known for having wife after wife, or husband after husband—they formalize their affairs, for tax reasons). As incomes decline, so do the tax advantages of being married. And when the family is so poor as to qualify for public assistance, they instead are paid to break up!

There are ways to design income tax provisions, using credits instead of exemptions, and using such devices as disappearing deductions, to avoid making their benefits inverse to need. The regressive effects that are found in U.S. law are not inherent in progressive taxes. The regressive effects are a by-product of the concealment of these implicit welfare programs. Can anyone believe that the American people would permit Congress to establish an explicit old-age pension which paid nothing to those with zero income or only Social Security or public assistance income, paid $105 to a person with $1,000 in income, and $525 to someone with over $200,000 a year? The same question might be asked of farm programs, which also pay inversely to the size of the farm operation, and hence presumably inversely to need.

Intervention into Personal and Family Life

A final distinction between the regular or non-poor welfare system and that for poor people is the degree of intervention into personal and family life. Programs for the non-poor make little or no intrusion into sensitive family decisions; programs for the poor exact, as the price of assistance, an element of control and a surrender of autonomy.

Control over the family's budget is control over important family decisions. Whenever someone can tell you what to buy, he is really telling you how to live. The poor people's welfare system does so in two ways: by providing goods instead of money (public housing, medical care, uplifting symphony concerts for ghetto kids and so forth), and by controlling the use of money transfers (through vouchers, such as food stamps, or through close administrative supervision, as in Aid to Families with Dependent Children).

Another way that poor people's welfare weakens autonomy is that people change behavior and family characteristics to become or stay eligible. Can anyone doubt that one reason that there are so many husbandless mothers who head poor families is that the government has for years paid husbandless mothers? Can anyone doubt that some poor people have children because most states do not provide assistance for childless single or married people, no matter how impoverished? President Nixon's family assistance reform proposals would correct the first but not the second of these. It would reduce assistance by a crucial $500 a year for mothers who did not work, unless they had pre-school-age children. Who can doubt that some mothers, faced with the choice between required employment out of the home, and having another baby in order to continue to have pre-school children, will choose the latter? Such choices are not coldly calculated. Rather, the government subtly influences such decisions by determining the environment and reward system in which decisions are made. In precisely the manner described by former Selective Service Director Lewis Hershey, in his famous "channelling" memorandum, just as college students were led to think that becoming engineers or clergymen was their own decision, so poor people are led to think that having children or breaking up a home is theirs.

A third invasion of personal privacy is that various bureaucrats in the poor people's welfare system actually monitor the behavior of their "clients." Public assistance caseworkers, public housing tenant-relations officers and social workers in a variety of agencies view their role as anything from mere advisor and family friend through parent- or husband-surrogate to warden. Mothers have had assistance checks held up because they were seen in bars. Families have been evicted from housing because of delinquent children. Families have been denied surplus food because they owned a television set.

By contrast, the use of Social Security or Unemployment Compensation checks is never monitored. Though families get a dependent's exemption in the income tax for each minor child, no one checks to make sure the family spends at least as much as the exemption on the child. Home buyers who have drunken orgies will not have their F.H.A. loan insurance revoked, Farmers may spend their farm surplus money as they please.

This double standard makes liars and cheaters out of the stronger poor people, and psychologically dependent grown-up children of the weaker ones. Neither characteristic is conducive to personal development. Moneylessness is only one side of chronic poverty, and the larger and more difficult problem is powerlessness. While some poor people's welfare programs attack this powerlessness, a great many of them aggravate it. An important consequence of stunting independence and reinforcing dependence is to keep many poor people poor.

The differences between poor people's and regular welfare programs are systematic and significant. They mean minimal survival for poor people, and reasonable comfort for non-poor; they mean degradation for poor people, and dignity for non-poor; and most important, they imply continued poverty and dependence for many poor, and continued security and apparent self-reliance for the non-poor.

America's dual welfare system is unique in the world, at least in degree. In other developed countries, while there is persistent debate between the advocates of "universal" and of "selective" social welfare programs, the former win out far more frequently than they do in the United States, where virtually every welfare, health, housing and employment program is designed specifically either for the poor or the non-poor.

We have noted the harmful effects of this dual approach. Separate programs for the poor are typically inferior; they involve demoralizing stigmata; and they tend to be built on assumptions which attribute poverty to defects in the poor. Their structures tend, whether accidentally or not, to inhibit economic and personal development among the poor.

Worse than all of these is the fact that the segregation of social welfare programs has separated, or seemed to separate, the interests of the poor from the interests of the rest of society. This separation helps account for a mutual hostility between the poor and lower-income non-poor, notably the working class, which has been enormously destructive to the interests of both. It is hard to believe that much progress can be made against poverty in America as long as this separation and hostility persist.

SUGGESTED READINGS

Background Papers of the President's Commission on Income Maintenance Programs (Washington: Government Printing Office).

"Social Security: Unfair to Those Who Pay It: Unfair to Those Who Receive It" by Carolyn Shaw Bell in *Challenge*, July–August, 1973.

"The Poor Man's Welfare Payment to the Middle Class" by Milton Friedman in *The Washington Monthly*, May 1972.

The State of Welfare by Gilbert Y. Steiner (Washington: The Brookings Institution, 1971).

"Uncle Sam's Welfare Program for the Rich," by Phillip M. Stern in *New York Times Magazine*, April 16, 1972.

"The Charity of the Uncharitable" by Gordon Tullock in *Western Economic Journal*, January 1971.

3 *Henry W. Berger*

Organized Labor and Imperial Policy

For some time now, liberal and radical critics of the AFL-CIO have condemned labor's foreign policy. The federation's rigid anti-communism, its interference in labor affairs abroad, its support of conservative and authoritarian foreign governments (as in Brazil and Vietnam), the assistance which it received in the past from the CIA, the unsavory alliance which it is claimed to have formed with the United States government and American business firms (particularly in underdeveloped nations), its quarrel with the International Labor Organization (ILO), its withdrawal from the International Confederation of Free Trade Unions (ICFTU) and its unyielding approval of America's intervention in Vietnam are specific actions which the critics say demonstrate the conservative and even reactionary character of the AFL-CIO foreign policy.

The reaction of the Executive Council of the AFL-CIO to President Nixon's China policy illustrates this continuing posture. The chief decision-making body of the 13.5 million-member labor federation in a vote of 24 to four advised the president to reexamine his position. The head of the AFL-CIO, George Meany, characteristically went further and suggested the dangers involved in Nixon's planned visit to China could result in another Munich. He reminded the president that during the 1930s the League of Nations "abandoned its principles and sacrificed Ethiopia and gave support to the fascist Mussolini and his friend Hitler."

How did it come about that the strongest and largest labor organization in America has followed a consistently conservative foreign policy? Who makes that policy, how representative of the rank and file are the views and actions of the leadership, and how effective is labor in achieving its aims overseas? Finally, to what extent does the foreign policy which labor spokesmen articulate contradict the interests and needs of the American working class?

The centrality of foreign policy to American society today is obvious. In virtually every significant respect domestic and foreign concerns are closely related—as the current economic crisis illustrates. American workers are very much affected by and involved in those concerns as they touch their personal lives.

At the outset, it is important to establish a proper perspective. Unions, both affiliated and non-affiliated with the AFL-CIO, represent about a fourth of the total work force in this country. At no time have more than about a third of the workers outside agriculture been organized and for much of our history those enrolled in unions totaled less than 10 percent. The bulk of union membership consists of manual workers engaged in manufacturing, mining, construction and transportation. Large numbers of blacks, other racial minorities and women have, however, remained outside the ranks of organized labor.

Even so, like most groups in America, it is not sheer numbers alone which determine power or influence. More important are the quality of organization, the location of the particular organizations within the structure of the society and the ability of such groups to maximize pressure at crucial times and in critical places. The building trades, the teamsters, the unions of the mass production and mining industries, railroad labor and those unions engaged in defense production have been the powerhouses of American labor. And service employees and government workers are gaining a strong voice. These organizations influence decision making in the United States. Since most of these unions are affiliated with the AFL-CIO, it has been that organization's leaders who have commanded the attention of those who formulate and direct American foreign policy, and it is those union leaders who have been identified with labor's activities abroad.

Any effort to examine the nature of labor's foreign policy must take account of these factors. Unfortunately, most of what is published is either largely descriptive in nature or of the exposé type, emphasizing cloak-and-dagger operations of such celebrated personalities as Jay Lovestone, presently director of the AFL-CIO's Department for International Affairs. The "who, what, when and where" are important. But much of that information, especially for the post-World War II period is either classified, destroyed or was never committed to paper in the first place. And it is not enough to say that personalities have always played a dominant role and leave it at that. That kind of assessment tells us little about why American labor leaders hold the particular views they do or what historical influences have shaped labor's international perspective.

Some critics argue that workers in general are not concerned with foreign affairs; they are concerned with more immediate matters such as bargaining grievances. In the absence of interest from the rank and file, the leadership has devised and executed foreign policy. But this is nothing more than an adroit attempt to explain away the elitist character of decision making in the AFL-CIO. These same critics argue that those who make labor's foreign policy do so largely in accordance with the wishes of most unionists, and that these unionists would approve the attitudes and actions of the leadership if they were asked their views. But there is significant evidence to the contrary.

Studies of worker attitudes do indicate differing opinions. The Gallup polls from 1966 to 1969, for instance, indicate a generally growing opposition to the war in Vietnam among manual workers (see Table 1).

TABLE 1
In view of the developments since we entered the fighting in Vietnam, do you think the U.S. made a mistake sending troops to fight in Vietnam?

Manual Workers:		Yes, Mistake	No	No Opinion
1966	March	22%	63%	15%
	May	35	49	16
	September	36	47	17
	November	30	52	18
1967	May	36	49	15
	July	39	49	12
	October	44	47	9
1968	February	42	46	12
	March	45	46	9
	April	43	45	12
	August	50	37	13
	October	49	40	11
1969	February	49	43	8
	October	56	34	10

But the usefulness of this data is limited. There is no distinction made between union and non-union workers. Most important, there is no breakdown of the category of manual laborers into skilled, unskilled, service workers and day laborers. The Roper surveys, however, do provide such data (see Table 2).

TABLE 2
Do you think it was a mistake for the United States to get involved in Vietnam?

	Yes	No	No Opinion
March 1966			
Skilled Workers	16.6%	71.0%	12.2%
Unskilled Workers	26.7	59.3	13.8
Service Workers	21.5	57.3	21.0
Laborers	30.8	50.2	18.8
February 1967			
Skilled Workers	32.2	57.9	9.7
Unskilled Workers	36.3	54.1	9.4
Service Workers	38.5	45.9	15.5
Laborers	45.3	45.3	9.2
April 1968			
Skilled Workers	41.8	48.3	9.8
Unskilled Workers	44.5	41.9	13.5
Service Workers	39.2	47.6	13.0
Laborers	57.1	38.0	4.7

The Roper figures show that skilled workers have supported American involvement in the war far more than other groups of workers; but among all workers anti-war sentiment grew at a rate not reflected by the succession of pro-war statements issued by the AFL-CIO during the same period. A Harris poll taken in 1968 provided different data concerning views on Vietnam among union members only but without any breakdown by trades (see Table 3). The results show that two-thirds of the AFL-CIO members asked either favored a more aggressive policy in Vietnam or supported the present involvement.

TABLE 3
Which statement about Vietnam do you agree with most?
(Harris Poll, April 16, 1968)

	Total queried	Union members	AFL-CIO	Teamsters
I disagree with our present policy. We are not going far enough. We should go further, such as carrying the war more into North Vietnam.	21%	23%	27%	31%
I agree with what we are doing but we should increase our military effort.	38	41	37	44
I agree with what we are doing, but we should do more to bring about negotiations, such as stop bombing North Vietnam.	17	21	15	15
I disagree with our present policy. We should pull out our troops now.	15	10	13	11
Not sure.	9	6	8	—

On the other hand, when public opinion pollsters asked in 1968 and 1969 if defense spending should be increased, decreased or remain the same, workers supported a decrease in such expenditures in significant percentages (see Table 4). However, no breakdown between the union and non-union members was provided.

TABLE 4
December 1968

Should defense spending be:

	Decreased	Increased	Stay the Same	No Opinion
Skilled workers	51.3%	19.8%	22.9%	5.8%
Unskilled workers	47.3	26.8	18.0	7.8
Service workers	57.1	20.2	20.2	2.3
Laborers	43.7	22.9	25.0	8.3

July 1969

Is government spending for defense:

	Too little	Too much	Just right	No opinion
Skilled workers	8.9%	39.9%	35.6%	13.3%
Unskilled workers	7.5	39.0	37.5	14.0
Service workers	3.7	50.6	34.1	11.3
Laborers	7.8	36.8	44.7	10.5

These polls, of course, do not cover all foreign policy issues or even all aspects of the questions which were asked. The time period is limited and the information does not provide explanations for the answers workers give to such questions. Nor do they tell us why differences exist between various categories of workers. But they suggest very strongly that the question of rank-and-file thinking on foreign policy matters is much more complicated than is usually depicted by the defenders and detractors of official AFL-CIO policy on the subject.

We do know that the building trades are the power base of George Meany's position in the AFL-CIO, and they have been the strongest supporters of anti-communism and the Vietnam War for a variety of mixed reasons. We also know that 10 percent of the entire labor force owes its pay check to defense spending and that nearly all that group is unionized. Thus workers employed in those industries are dependent upon defense expenditures for their livelihood. The impact of the defense economy upon working-class values should be investigated more thoroughly, but I think it is safe to say that this relationship is important in explaining a good deal of the cold war mentality of AFL-CIO leadership.

But the conservative, hard-line views of labor's leaders existed even before the Vietnam War or before the postwar defense establishment of the present magnitude was created. The development can only be understood in the context of domestic American labor affairs, in the fact that the AFL emerged as an interest-group trade union association (rather than a class-conscious labor organization), that the craft unionists sought to win recognition and power in their struggles with the corporations by adopting conservative union beliefs and objectives, and that AFL president Samuel Gompers and others considered foreign labor ideologies and movements different from their own a threat to their successes. Because the IWW and the Socialists constituted or seemed to pose a challenge to Gomper's version of trade unionism during precisely those years when the AFL achieved success and power (1890-1913), the AFL leaders had to demonstrate that their brand of unionism would prevail. That involved, among other things, the acceptance of corporate capitalism and opposition to radicals. But the trade union leaders of the AFL were not co-opted, tricked or lured into their allegiance to capitalism. They knew what they were doing and always sought first of all to protect the interests of their organizations. They increasingly linked such interests to those of corporate capitalism. Foreign policy was and has remained a splendid example of this development.

The period of general prosperity after 1897 was an era of rapid trade union expansion. At the same time government and business leaders sought commercial expansion abroad which they concluded was necessary and desirable for the future vitality of the American economy. Some went further, advocating the export of ideas and institutions—and the annexation of territory; between 1898-1899 Hawaii, the Philippines and other areas became colonies of the United States.

Union Capitalism

Some labor organizations (the typographical union, the iron molders and the railroad brotherhoods for example) supported annexation, believing new jobs would open up. But Gompers and most of the AFL were opposed. Annexation could mean competition from goods produced by cheap labor in those areas and unrestricted immigration of orientals, flooding the United States labor markets and threatening union members' jobs. This outlook reflected the earliest positions taken by unions on foreign policy questions. Most important, these positions were clearly related to the domestic repercussions of foreign affairs. At the same time, early contacts with European unionists were aimed at gaining support for the AFL position.

But the AFL did not oppose American economic or political expansion or the extension of the AFL's brand of unionism overseas. The labor leaders came to share the ideas which largely dominated American foreign policy after 1897 and did so because of their acceptance of corporation capitalism and their belief that the vital interests of the unions would be served in the process. There were, of course, disagreements over particular policies (tariff questions and the recent China issue readily come to mind), tactics (American policy toward Cuba from 1959 to the present) and matters involving union rivalries as in the case of the AFL and the CIO before the two federations merged. Conflicts about principles and broad goals were and have been exceptional, and most American labor leaders have accepted and supported the extension of American economic and political interests throughout the globe.

American Supremacy

For example, the unions advocated the construction of the Panama Canal, to be built by American capital and American labor. Tying it to the domestic economic interests of American workers, Gompers declared in 1903 that the canal must be "the result of American enterprise, American genius and American labor." Similarly, the AFL championed Cuban independence before the war in 1898. While a commitment to freedom was involved, the AFL also emphasized that only after independence could Cuban workers be organized, stopping the flow of cheap labor and cheap non-union goods to the United States.

The annexation question produced a crisis for labor unions. There was no quarrel with Americans who wanted to expand American interests abroad, in particular to conquer the markets of the world. But there was sharp disagreement about whether it was necessary to obtain colonies and the AFL opposed such action. Gompers joined the Anti-Imperialist League, campaigned vigorously against annexation, but still extolled the virtues of expansion. He maintained that the latter was possible and desirable without all the burdens and dangers of old-style colonialism. "The nation which dominates the markets of the world will surely control its destinies," the AFL leader proclaimed. Arguing for a fair deal for workers at home as the most important means of increasing production and consumption, Gompers then advocated American supremacy in economic competition abroad:

> To make of the United States a vast workshop is our manifest destiny, and our duty, and thus side by side with other nations, in industrial and commercial rivalry, we are basing the conditions of the workers upon the highest intelligence and the most exalted standard of life. No obstacle can be placed in our way to the attainment of the highest pinnacle of national glory and human progress.

When annexation did occur, the AFL moved quickly to obtain legislation to protect labor's interests at home and also to organize unions in the newly acquired regions. Gompers equated the extension of AFL unionism to the territories with the spread of "the gospel of Americanism." Efforts were made to create AFL locals, to secure higher wages, shorter hours, better working conditions and the right to strike—goals which were not always easy to implement or always achieved. Also involved was opposition to indigenous labor organizations and radical ideologies in conflict with AFL policies.

This pattern of activities in Puerto Rico, Cuba and to a lesser extent in the Philippines was repeated in Mexico after revolution began in that country in 1910. Cooperation was also sought from government and business to secure AFL aims. This was not always forthcoming, but World War I created the conditions for a reciprocal relationship in which AFL adherence to American foreign policy was formally instituted and solidified. The Bolshevik revolution of 1917, which AFL leaders strongly opposed, fortified the alliance. Indeed, the bitterness of AFL leaders against communism and the Soviet Union meant that the AFL increasingly became part of the more conservative wing of the foreign policy consensus. The theoretically international character of the Soviet revolution was viewed as potentially dangerous to workers to whom the Bolsheviks had made their appeal, and there was concern that the Soviet success in Russia would erode the international position of the AFL.

In the meantime, AFL leaders hoped that American economic expansion into the world would provide greater opportunities for AFL-style trade unionism to flourish in other countries. The power and prestige of the AFL would then be increased and trade union standards would remove the threat of cheap labor competition from abroad. American business did not always cooperate in this regard, of course, but after World War II many corporate leaders came to see the advantages of this arrangement. Anti-communism emerged as the common denominator by which labor and bussiness could cooperate overseas.

Foreign Intervention Supported

That the United States government has sought labor's cooperation in foreign policy, especially during wartime, is clear enough. That the unions have, by and large, supported not only the objectives but also the assumptions of official American policy abroad is also true. Anti-communism has provided the basis for AFL-CIO endorsement of American intervention everywhere, including military invasions of the Dominican Republic and Vietnam, to combat real and alleged communist threats. Union self-interest and militant foreign policy were thus joined.

At various times, some opposition to prevailing policies did exist among union members and leaders. But the policies and the assumptions underlying them were not altered in any important way. Not even the CIO after 1946 had much of a different outlook. It also had anti-communist agents in the foreign field beginning at least in 1946. There were more similarities than differences between AFL and CIO foreign policy, and one of the prerequisites for the merger was agreement on foreign policy. This was possible after the CIO purged the left unions from its ranks and broke from the Communist-controlled World Federation of Trade Unions (WFTU) in 1949. The most protracted dispute involved in the unification negotiations between the AFL and CIO in 1955 concerned which group would exercise dominant influence over the administration of foreign affairs in the new federation—but there was no argument about fundamentals.

Similarly, it may be that the Walter Reuther/United Auto Worker (UAW) break with the AFL-CIO involved more than questions of decision-making, personalities and style, but the UAW statements on foreign policy issues after the schism contained very little that was new. The opposition to the war in Vietnam did not produce a revision of basic assumptions about foreign relations.

Sometimes, as has been mentioned, there have been differences with government officials. AFL-CIO opposition to friendlier relations with Communist China is not only the result of a long established anti-communist frame of mind and a general ideological obsession. There is concern too about the possible effects of Chinese imports into the United States and about the removal of the requirement that half of what America exports to communist nations be carried in United States vessels. Meany and the others made all this clear when Nixon lifted trade restrictions in June of 1971.

All this suggests that the sources of labor's foreign policy are historical in character, relate to domestic concerns and attitudes and are the product of indigenous factors. American labor's support of United States foreign policy has not been just for logrolling purposes. Its views have frequently originated quite independently of government initiatives and have been in accord with self-interests and ideological convictions rooted in historical experience and inexorably linked to American corporation capitalism to which American unions, for the most part, have tied their fortunes. The rigid and sometimes excessive character of labor's international outlook since World War II is undeniably due in some measure to the personalities involved in making labor's foreign policy and to a habitual frame of mind. But it is also derived, I think, from the intense allegiance of labor unionists to the American success ethic, to the historical struggle which organized labor had to make to secure legitimacy in this country, to the extraordinary hostility to radicalism in our society (to which the AFL has contributed) and to the high premium which has been placed on Lockean values in America.

Has labor's foreign policy met the needs of the workers in this country? In a narrow sense and on a limited basis, perhaps. But in the long run and in terms of actual worker economic and psychological security, I think the answer is no. American economic expansion abroad has provoked war, with its price of physical casualties, higher taxes, inflation and discriminatory economic and political controls and dislocations; it has created gigantic multinational corporations which compete with American labor rather than foreign enterprises; it has stimulated a vast armaments industry in which employment has become an unreliable dependency of war.

Bankruptcy of Cold War Politics

Above all, the independence and integrity of the labor movement have been sacrificed to the Cold War and its excesses. The AFL-CIO has participated extensively in Cold War politics throughout the world—with results that are uncertain at best. Leftist unions are very strong in France, Italy, Japan and elsewhere despite AFL-CIO efforts to dislodge them. The American labor federation has withdrawn from the ICFTU and is regarded with widespread distrust nearly everywhere. B. J. Widick states flatly that the AFL-CIO "has less influence overseas today than at any time since World War II." All this even though 25 percent of the federation's budget is allocated for international affairs and that since 1945 there has developed a considerable union bureaucracy devoted to international activities. The end result is the most ridiculous of all conditions: an interventionist AFL-CIO isolated from most of world labor and a divided, insecure working class at home.

The answer is not simply to change young leaders for old or to democratize the decision-making and administrative processes of labor's foreign policy. All that is desirable, of course, and the increasing numbers of young and minority-group persons entering the working force have given hope to some that the values which these new members of the working class hold will produce alternative policies. But it is important, I think, to realize that it is the whole set of assumptions about the world and American society which must eventually change. This need not involve total withdrawal from the world or conversion of American labor into a branch of the Communist International. Neither is desirable nor likely. It does mean a reordering of priorities at home, an end to anti-radical crusades around the globe, a willingness to set limits on American power, and a conversion from narrow-interest-group politics to a politics which is dedicated to the interests of the whole community. American labor unions possess the power base from which they can undertake these efforts. It remains to be seen whether or not the workers will use this power.

Section IX

Agencies

Our concern in this part of the text/reader has been with linking institutions. The larger environing society (that is, those in the larger society who have the social power to do so) sets up institutional structures that process people. In "Professionalization and Power in a Community Hospital," the Nanrys present a case study of one such processing institution, a big-city hospital. Their discussion of the conflict of the goals of various interest groups tied into the hospital as an institution illuminates the process whereby an institution becomes a battleground for various definitions of the situation. In spite of good will and good intentions, the community hospital becomes a place where social power is manifested in the struggle for limited resources. The processing mechanisms that they discuss may be generalizable to other institutions that have the task of delivering needed services. It is a microcosm of the larger American social order. The Colburns, in "Integrity House: The Addict as a Total Intsitution," suggest that "the Integrity House approach to rehabilitation is an apolitical myth-oriented method reinforcing the pseudopsychological notion that addiction is exclusively the problem of the addict." After discussing the use of identity stripping and degradation ceremonies in Integrity House, two techniques common to many socializing institutions, they suggest that the real aim of this therapeutic community is to use pseudopsychology in order to exercise social control and to subvert class and political consciousness among ex-drug users. The whole enterprise, they argue, ends up as an apolitical "ad hoc religious community."

One of the definitions Webster gives for an agency is "an establishment for executing business in behalf of others, as at a distance . . ." Hightower advances the thesis that the land grant college complex (a sacred cow of American mythology) has worked to the advantage and profit of large corporations involved in agriculture, and not to that of customers, in "Hard Tomatoes, Hard Times: Failure of the Land Grant College Complex." "Agribusiness," the mechanization of agriculture at public expense, has helped crush the subsistence farm and the family farm way of life. Agricultural research in these institutions, Hightower tells us, in oriented primarily toward agribusiness, with little public accountability or control. The land grant college complex is a closed community serving commercial interests at the expense of people.

1 *Charles Nanry & Jacqueline Nanry*

Professionalization and Poverty in a Community Hospital

"Central" Hospital is a 780-bed institution that was founded in the late nineteenth century under the control of the local city administration. Long a focus of controversy in the city where it is located, this hospital became a state medical college in 1968. Before 1968 hospital jobs were viewed as plums in the spoils system of the city's politics, and the hospital was a haven for political appointees. In fact, the administrative head of the hospital at the time of the state medical college takeover was a local photographer who was active in city politics. Hospital employees were regularly given election day off in order to solicit votes for the local political machine.

The city served by Central Hospital has a population of more than 300,000. In recent years there have been several serious racial conflicts, which burgeoned into a major insurrection in the late sixties. Area residents, angered by an urban renewal project which cleared vast tracts of land surrounding the hospital for medical school construction, fired at the hospital building during the disturbance. Most of the city's residents are black and Puerto Rican, although large white ethnic neighborhoods lie within and adjoining the city. The community is badly polarized along racial lines.

Traditionally, the Central Hospital staff saw as its primary function the treatment of the acutely ill. Under the auspices of the medical college the hospital now has an additional mission of teaching and research. In order to meet these goals the hospital staff attempts to control its patient population to provide appropriate teaching and research cases for the medical students, as well as providing mandated acute-care services.

People in the community, in contrast, view the hospital as a place to take both major and minor medical problems and general problems in living. In their view the hospital is a general service institution that ought to expand its services and broaden available health care. Slum residents who often cannot afford rudimentary health care and family physicians, use the hospital in order to get medication and treatment for relatively minor maladies. Parents who feel the need to get away from their children for a night on the town may use the hospital as a babysitting service, saying, "My baby has diarrhea, please admit him to the hospital." Occasionally, children are simply left in clinic waiting rooms for the weekend. Parents and grandparents are committed to the hospital when the burden of their care is too much to bear.

The conversion of the hospital to a medical school represented a critical sharpening of the divergent lay and professional definitions of the institution's goals. Most of the statements issued by the hospital at that time (and since) have stressed the need for upgrading skills within its own organization. These statements clearly reflect the assumption made by the hospital and medical school staffs that upgrading staff skills and professionalizing areas such as social service would significantly improve the services rendered to the community. Appeals for state, federal and local funds were and still are made on that basis.

In our judgment, without either a change in the hospital's size (i.e., number of beds), the addition of supplementary services in the community or a shift in the allocation of resources (for example, more community control over hospital beds), substantial change is unlikely for those who depend on the hospital. A hospital is limited by institutionalized patterns of use. Some marginal flexibility may be introduced by increasing the number of beds within it. Other small gains may be made by shortening the length of stay per patient, since patient care involves some temporal flexibility. For the most part, however, once a physical plant is designed and built, its ecology, coupled with community concepts of hospital use, limit its expansion. If the supply of hospital beds remains fairly constant, demand for those beds, no matter how pressing, will not change things substantially. The major thrust of the hospital's public relations campaign following the medical college takeover has been that things would be much better because of professional upgrading of the hospital's personnel.

It is often assumed that professionalization in institutional settings leads to better service for clients. Our research experience has led us to believe that that assumption ought to be reevaluated. If professionalization involves the notion of an ideal client, then those who do have problems which differ from those of the ideal client may not be served well. Professional social workers oriented toward psychoanalytic casework or medical practitioners interested in narrowly defined specialties may reveal a trained incapacity for dealing with the real, if often mundane, problems of poor people. Large sums of state and federal monies channeled into the hospital during the period of our study went to hire more professionals, particularly more black professionals, and into upgrading the medical school facilities. On the whole, this infusion of resources meant very little to the average patient.

At issue here is a triangular conflict of goals for the hospital as an organization. The community wants and needs broad-gauged health-care facilities, including care for the chronically ill. The hospital administration wants and needs to limit the definition of the hospital to an acute-care facility. Medical college staff wants and needs a training facility that provides teaching cases. Because of the magnitude of the health problems in the city served, the hospital is always in grave danger of being overwhelmed by the needs of sick people who have few other resources at their command. A social law of large numbers is at work here: the number of persons needing help approaches infinity, while the hospital, as an organization, attempts to rationalize its limits and satisfy internal demands, especially the professional pursuit of special limited and clearly defined problems. There is some danger of deflating the value of each person seeking services since the fact that a large number of people are taken care of does not mean that the institution reaps a larger profit. Service institutions such as hospitals do not work within the same parameters as commercial institutions.

We gathered data for the report during January and February 1967 and January and February 1969. The method of collection included participant observation, review of patient emergency-room records and an examination of charts of patients discharged on one medical and two surgical floors. We have presented our case-study material in narrative form. Employing a technique widely used in industrial sociology, we will discuss the "processing" of patients as a problem of inputs and outputs. What follows, then, is a description of how inputs into the hospital are discouraged and outputs encouraged.

Inputs

The manifestly ill patient brought to the emergency room by ambulance is examined, given urgent services and admitted directly to surgery or to a hospital ward. Medical and paramedical staff respond to such an admission with a humane, professional and patient-centered attitude. The definition of the situation as a crisis is shared by members of the emergency-room staff, and has been generated, at least in part, by external forces, such as ambulance sirens and flashing lights, stretchers wheeled in frantically, patients' shortness of breath or bleeding and so forth. A brochure published by the hospital aptly describes the crisis atmosphere involved in such an admission:

> The white night supervisor taking from the arms of a black grandmother a small boy hemorrhaging from the nose and wrapped in a dirty blanket—the supervisor acutally running with her precious bundle to the pediatric treatment room where swift emergency procedures stem the bleeding.
>
> The sight of blood everywhere—routine are the stab wounds, the slashed throat, the ripped belly.

The emergency room of a big city hospital represents a negotiated order where all of the action-packed stereotypes of the medical team snatching life from the jaws of death approach reality. When the pressure for emergency treatment approaches the overload point, however, certain steps have become institutionalized to defuse the situation. David Sudnow has brilliantly pointed out some of the defusing mechanisms used to forestall overloading. He points out how ambulance drivers label some cases as "possible DOAs." Cues such as special siren signals and voice tone tell the emergency-room staff to take their time in treating an incoming case. Sudnow also points out how the "social value" of a patient affects the kind of effort that will be made to save him. Older patients and morally stigmatized patients, such as alcoholics, drug addicts, prostitutes, attempted suicides and vagrants, get less extraordinary care than do young children and middle-class patients. Sudnow's insights have been substantiated in our research and extend beyond medical care to hospital entry itself, especially for those persons who walk in seeking help.

Ambulatory persons seeking admission through the emergency room are routinely given a number on arrival and directed to a small, crowded waiting room. One by one they are called into the admissions office, where they must laboriously answer questions relating to their personal, medical and financial history.

A guard is stationed by the entrance to this office. His primary function is to deter any potential patient from entering out of turn and to keep relatives and/or friends from accompanying patients beyond this room into the hospital. This separation has important consequences, since it contributes to the total mystification of the patient and restricts admission eligibility status to the discretion of the physician in charge.

The indigent person seeking admission is removed from the support of family and friends as well as the advocacy of a private physician during a health crisis. (Private physicians are retained, in part, to guard their patients' best interests in the medical maze; poor people often cannot afford an advocate doctor.) The poor patient is wheeled into a technically sophisticated environment where medicine-man language is spoken and where he is questioned, poked, X-rayed and probed by a host of white-coated specialists. Unless he is a very sophisticated consumer of medical services he is going to be mystified by the whole emergency-room ritual. Therefore, his admission rests wholly with the examining physician. Failure to submit meekly to this ritual through an outburst of anger or a demand for "rights" may result in the denial of admission.

Theoretically, the decision for admission is based on the urgency of the medical problem. In practice, however, there must be some discretionary process to insure that beds are allocated according to the hospital's predetermined criteria. Among the many arbitrary reasons for a doctor's refusal to admit a patient are service quotas (medical service team A has enough patients) and prognosis (doctors do not like to admit terminally ill patients who will linger and then die or people who appear to be eventual placement problems such as elderly stroke patients or malnourished alcoholics). The overloaded hospital admissions process must discriminate between those who will and those who will not get in. Here again, "social value" criteria are used. Sudnow's proscriptions about avoiding the dead or dying label applies also the the admissible or nonadmissible label:

> Within a limited temporal perspective at least, but one which is not necessarily to be regarded as trivial, the likelihood of "dying" and even of being "dead" can be said to be partially a function of one's place in the social structure, and not simply in the sense that the wealthier get better care, or at least not in the usual sense of that fact. If one anticipates having a critical heart attack, he had best keep himself well-dressed and his breath clean if there is a likelihood he will be brought into County [hospital] as a "possible."

In the hospital we studied, contracting a rare disease might increase one's chances for admission. Failing that, the best way to insure admission is to come on a day when the quota for the necessary service has not yet been filled.

Patients judged ineligible for admission are given clinic slips and/or prescriptions and told to go home and rest. Persons who repeatedly make "inappropriate" attempts to be admitted are received less enthusiastically and are gradually denied even superficial treatment or examination. One particular category of nonadmissible patients is most troublesome to the admitting department and receives special attention: the barely ambulatory person.

The barely ambulatory person who is refused admission is referred to the social service department for placement. If the social worker responding to the referral is unable to locate family to come for the patient, or if rooming- or boarding-home placements seem inappropriate, the worker approaches the physician on behalf of the patient's admission. The success of this advocacy depends on the physician's appraisal of the worker's ward service. In 1967 the social work staff did not have professional credentials, and therefore was not "specialized." The social worker called to the emergency room also shared responsibility for hospital wards where he or she was involved in many needed but not necessarily professional social work functions. For example, the worker directed discharge planning, but also secured prosthetic appliances; he coordinated consultations with other hospitals, but also arranged transportation and acted as a referral agent for other community medical and paramedical services.

In general, the 1967 definition of the role of social worker was that of an organizational jack of all trades. Many departmental members were employed at the hospital as a result of political patronage. Some even held other full-time jobs. For a time the social service office even served as a boutique where one member of the department sold allegedly stolen clothing and fancy contraceptives. In spite of the abuses, however, the social worker was free to adopt an advocate-entrepreneur role in the hospital and to exchange favors with the medical staff in order to get services for patients. And patients did get social services even though some of the social service staff members were primarily interested in quick processing in order to get on with outside activities.

If the individual social worker's competence as an organizational "utility infielder" was recognized by the admitting physician, he was more likely to reclassify the patient as admissible for the social worker's services. In a sense, the social workers had what Amitai Etzioni has called the "power of lower participants."

Throughout the period of the study, proper use of hospital beds for the acutely ill remained the central admission issue. However, because of the addition of medical education as a hospital goal, selectivity of potential patients has become more important. Patients who are interesting may be admitted, even though others who are more critically ill have been denied admission. Quota systems related to types of diagnoses are more closely considered; the question becomes: How many CVAs or ulcerated legs do we have? Many more patients are classified as nonadmissible.

Although outpatient clinic facilities have been enlarged and modernized, the number of nonambulatory persons denied hospital admission has also increased dramatically. This is another result of more stringent admission standards. It is important to note again that the number of hospital beds has not increased, nor have medical services in the community been expanded to any large degree.

Nonadmissible and nonambulatory patients are routinely labeled "social problem" on their admission sheet, and are referred to the social service department. Two interesting developments occurred which dramatically differentiated the transaction between the social worker and the physician in 1969 from that in 1967.

The social service department has been professionalized. Since 1968, there has been an almost complete turnover of staff. The new workers have MSW credentials. The department has divested itself of many of the old tasks which are now labeled clerical or nonprofessional. Furthermore, the new staff laments the fact that they are presently unable to devote all of their time to in-depth casework rather than "merely" to referral services. The social-work staff is now more specialized, and one worker is assigned exclusively to the emergency room.

The visibility of increasingly larger numbers of persons labeled nonambulatory and nonadmissible has distressed the new professional emergency-room manager. His ability is judged on the criterion of rapid processing of patients. His aim is perfectly clear: "The amazing thing is the rapid movement of patients. No more do you see stretchers lining the walls of the corridors while patients await treatment."

To bring about this state of affairs in the emergency room and resolve the crowding problem a holding room has been created. This room is in the hospital but not of it. Patients there have not been admitted and are kept in it until their status is resolved. This anteroom to the hospital is designated for "patient observation." It functions as a limbo where persons wait for the social worker to come to decide their fate. Unfortunately, the social workers have lost their exchange power; physicians in the hospital typically value psychological and psychoanalytic insight much less than resourcefulness. Therefore, the holding room becomes a market where bargaining and barkering takes place over the patients' bodies.

> Social Worker (pointing to the first of six patients on stretchers): Dr. Smith, I can try to place Mr. X if you will admit Mr. B.
> Medical Doctor: Another ulcer (referring to Mr. B) is the last patient that I want to admit.
> S.W.: What about Mrs. R, no one is going to take her . . . she's too much trouble and care.
> M.D.: O.K. If you get Mr. X and Mr. B out of here I'll check with Dr. L. . . . Maybe he'll take her on Medicine, but you had better be able to place her this week!

One category of patients that is particularly troublesome to the hospital staff is the chronic, indigent alcoholic. These men, and there are a large number of them in the city served by the hospital, are beset by a variety of illnesses that stem from gross neglect, malnutrition, infections of various kinds, cirrhosis of the liver, exposure to the elements and so forth. Many of them are on an informal "blacklist" which excludes them even from the various soup kitchens in the area (run mostly by religious organizations). Since they tend to spend any money received (welfare or otherwise) on alcohol, they cannot even afford the cheap flophouses in the downtown area of the city.

But our concern here is with the treatment of alcoholics at the hospital. These unfortunates suffer from what we choose to call the "Johnny comes marching home syndrome." They show up at the hospital needing food and shelter and are referred to social service for help. There are no facilities in the area that will care for them, and they are ineligible for hospital service. They are turned back out on the street. (Care is provided for the acutely ill, not for chronics.) Sooner or later acute illness follows, and then care is provided. The most common acute illness suffered by these men is frostbite. The diagnosis: amputation. The result of treatment: eventually the patient with this kind of career dies of attrition, his body gradually cut away.

Everything seems to work against the victim of the "Johnny syndrome." He does not fit the definition of the proper client until it is too late. Even good medical practice conspires to do him in, a piece at a time. Frostbite is very painful. Along with regular surgery the frostbite victim is often given a sympathectomy; that is, nerves are cut to reduce sensation and therefore pain. When "Johnny" is put back out on the street—which he will be since no one will take him—if it is winter, or when winter comes, he will be frostbitten again. When he is he will not feel it until it is further advanced than before because of the sympathectomy. The cycle is repeated again and again until "Johnny" is gone.

It should be noted that the hospital has added an alcohol treatment unit with a fairly large staff of professionals. But this and other efforts are aimed at motivated alcoholics and employ an anti-alcohol posture. Less glamorous but more useful aid might be provided by a no-questions-asked soup kitchen and flophouse. Admittedly, the person suffering from the "Johnny syndrome" represents an extreme example of the nonadmissible individual. But his plight is not unique in the community. Legions of others suffer from the same type of neglect. There is no room.

Outputs

Emptying hospital beds is just as critical a problem as selectivity in admissions for an acute care or teaching hospital. Understandably, the timing and spacing of discharges is subject to a variety of curative factors within the limits of medical diagnosis and technology. Several other variables, however, influence discharge decisions, and these are coupled with a host of coercive measures to remove patients.

Patients routinely leave Central Hospital after receiving a medical discharge from their physician, together with a clinic appointment for follow-up. Difficult patients, that is, those who do not adapt well to the hospitalized patient role (they challenge orders, make discomforting inquiries or just ask too many questions), are released as early as is medically and/or legally possible. Likewise, the terminally ill patient is encouraged to return home or to allow himself to be placed elsewhere if he threatens to die during a physician's service on a ward (discharges involve less paperwork than death) or badgers the hospital staff by frequently talking about the imminence of his death. In addition, there is a tendency to discharge patients before the rotation of doctors in order to avoid the time-consuming task of writing transfer-of-patient medical summaries that are expected for each patient being transferred to another doctor.

There are two other common routes of exodus for patients: death and release against medical advice. A patient who is not satisfied with medical or auxiliary services may sign himself out of Central Hospital against the advice of his doctor. Difficult patients are often subtly invited to take this measure by medical and paramedical staff. Once the patient makes his intention known, however, the staff rallies together ritualistically to warn the delinquent patient of the potential medical hazards of such a decision; to express their individual sincerity in helping him to health; and to advise him that they will no longer be legally responsible after he signs the patient release form. With the exception of interesting teaching cases and the infrequent patient perceived as having political or charismatic clout, little meaningful effort is expended to keep an "ungrateful patient." In spite of the concerned medical team ritual, staff persons safe from any professional or legal ramifications (aides, ward clerks and others) are not discouraged from supporting the patient's decision to sign himself out. "Mr. R, you're just a mean old man who don't belong here."

There are, however, as in the case of admissions, a group of patients who for physical or psychological reasons are not agreeable to the doctor's expectations about discharge scheduling. Hospital personnel employ four techniques to remove a reluctant patient: social service placement; transfer to another service; psychiatric commitment; and isolation as punishment.

Social Service Placement

Most discharge problems are referred to the ward social worker who tries to convince the patient that he is indeed ready to be discharged and then locates available space for the patient with his family, in boarding or rooming houses, nursing homes or other suitable places. In a large urban hospital, serving an economically deprived population, "discharge planning" is more of a fiction than a real service to the patient because of the dearth of placement facilities. As a consequence, the actual task of physically moving a patient from his hospital bed to a boarding or nursing home bed is carried out perfunctorily, with or without the patient's complete understanding of or consent to the placement. The critical issue becomes one of space and availability, although there is verbal acknowledgement of the importance of an "appropriate placement"; that is, virtually everyone would agree that a 27-year-old amputee should not be tucked away in a chronic-care nursing home, yet that happened. The elderly patient who has trouble signing his name to the transfer papers is arbitrarily sent to the first opening in a nursing home despite his protests. Central Hospital will supply a squiggly "X" and verification. Other patients are deceived into signing by being told that they are signing discharge papers or are signing papers to release them to the "discharge center" which they must visit before going home.

Transfer to Another Service

Another common practice in response to patients who are seen as discharge problems is transfer to another service. This procedure became far more common after the addition of the medical school, because it served two goals at the same time: it supported the discharging physician's patient-turnover scheduling; and it supplied less populated specialty services such as plastic surgery with teaching cases who had already undergone the necessary routine hospital tests and examinations, such as X-rays and various lab and blood work. The staff on plastic surgery was particularily anxious for patients upon whom they might perform cosmetic surgery. It was often the case, moreover, that they would recruit or accept transfers of discharge problem cases, as would the staffs of other services in Central Hospital. We should note, though, that most services were less motivated to receive than to give; physicians would often try to transfer discharge problems for additional hospital services (hemorrhoidectomy, ligation of varicose veins and so forth), but these patients were usually not enthusiastically welcomed by the receiving physician unless he was fulfilling an exchange bargain with another service or needed to demonstrate hemorrhoidectomies to a group of medical students. Let us illustrate with an actual case from our field notes.

> A social worker was called to the female surgical floor in order to begin discharge plans for a 40-year-old postoperative appendectomy patient. The patient way lying in bed staring at the ceiling and singing to herself. She appeared to be joyfully disoriented. Dr. P, one of the plastic surgeons, walked into the ward during the social worker's visit. When he became aware of the general surgeon's discharge plan for this patient. he cancelled the discharge immediately. As he explained to the social worker, plastic surgery was desperate for good teaching cases this month, and the patient in question was an ideal candidate for nipple reconstruction.

Psychiatric Commitment

Patients who become placement problems because of a prolonged dearth of beds in a placement facility or because of absolute refusal to accept placement plans (assuming these persons are alert and able to resist "railroading" into a placement) are referred to the hospital psychiatrist. The psychiatrist, in turn, routinely commits them to a mental institution on the basis of "impaired judgment." The reasoning behind such a decision is somewhat circular: if a patient is temporarily or permanently nonambulatory, and he has no family to whom he may be discharged, nursing-home placement is necessary. If this same patient refuses placement or insists that he be returned to an "inadequate home situation" rather than be placed, his judgment is impaired. If his judgment is impaired, commitment is necessary. A neat syllogism! In addition to numerous cases in our field notes concerning nonambulatory patietns who wanted to return to a life of living alone, we have the following case:

> An elderly woman was admitted to the hospital by ambulance after falling in her apartment building. Mrs. S consented to several X-rays and tests at the time of admission, but soon afterward requested that she be transferred back home. Mrs. S refused medical service and could not be influenced to stay by a medical student, chaplain or social worker. The problem peculiar to this situation was that Mrs. S, although mentally alert and intact, could not walk. The hospital would not take the responsibility of transporting her back to her apartment.
>
> Mrs. S lived alone and without family or close friends in the area. Since in the judgment of the hospital staff Mrs. S could not manage alone in her apartment the psychiatrist was called in to "dispose of" Mrs. S; that is, vacate her bed. He administered the routine battery of commitment questions: Where are you? What is today's date? Who is the President? Mrs. S answered each question correctly, she even could tell the examiner the names of the last four presidents. As she was counting backwards by 7s the psychiatrist drew up the commitment papers. Later, when questioned about his action, he agreed that there were no obvious bases for psychiatric commitment, but in order to vacate her bed he had cooperated by sending her off. "After all," he said, "shall we not say that this patient is merely wrapping herself in the cloak of sanity?"

Mrs. S. went off to a psychiatric institution under protest and very much alone. But others who are not alone and are a problem to friends and/or family may get the compliance of the psychiatric staff in commitment proceedings. For example, we have in our files the case of a little boy sent off because he played hookey. His mother thought that commitment "would do him some good." Many persons do not understand the full implications of psychiatric commitment for themselves and for their loved ones and the problems that the mental illness label can lead to, as well as the difficulty involved in getting out of mental institutions.

Isolation as Punishment

Two less obvious, but nevertheless frequent responses to patients who have long-range discharge or placement problems (some terminally or chronically ill patients fall into this category) are physical punishment and/or isolation. These patients are either removed to a place where they are physically cut off from contact with others on the ward and/or given less and less support for their patient status role. Doctors stop making daily rounds to their bedsides; nurses spend little time with them; medications and meals are given to them last.

> A 49-year-old terminally ill postlaryngectomy patient was slowly abandoned and isolated on the ward as it became apparent that he would be hospitalized indefinitely. Physicians' visits became infrequent. No progress notes were entered into his chart for months, and nurses scurried past his door, avoiding eye contact and paying little attention to his gestures to them. The nurses' aides soon became his only link with the rest of the hospital. His life dragged on for several months and then he died.

This man was regarded as a hopeless case, and the additional disability involving loss of voice meant extra time and effort would have to be made in order for him to communicate. The staff made the decision that he was not worth the effort. Although this case was extreme it was not atypical.

We have here an ethnography of current hospital practices in one community setting. But, more than that, some serious questions have been raised in two areas. First, there is the question of conflicting goals. Much political corruption was cleaned up by the state medical school takeover, but in our estimation the effect on the poor persons who have long depended on this institution for all forms of health care has been minimal. The goals of medical education meant that scarce resources were divided even more thinly as interesting teaching and research cases were sought out and emphasized. Additional resources brought to the hospital tended to be poured into the second area of concern, professionalization.

Professionalization may not lead to salvation. A common theme of professionalism is the automony of the profession. Many students, doctors and other professionals (such as the social service staff) spoke often about the joys of private practice and the kind of clients that they preferred. (Some medical students referred to the hospital as "the zoo.") As we see it, most people in the community want to get into the hospital for a variety of services and to be able to stay there until their lot is improved. The hospital staff wants efficiency in controlling the flow of patients in terms of its own internal needs. Both congeries of partisans have legitimate claims on the available resources. But legitimate claims (and illegitimate ones as well) may not be reconcilable under the conditions described above. Conventional wisdom about the necessity of professional upgrading and the clarification and rationalization of organizational goals may not bring those goals and interests into a hierarchy that serves the common good.

Two consequences of the medical college takeover have profoundly affected the stratification system of the hospital. The first is the addition of more American doctors to the medical staff. The second is the addition of more black administrators and other professionals to the paramedical staff.

While the hospital was under the aegis of the city, many foreign doctors were on the medical staff. The state medical school has replaced many of these doctors with their own faculty members and with medical students. One myth that ought to be dispelled is that foreign doctors are less medically competent than American doctors. The problem with foreign doctors centered around language and cultural difference between them and their patients. Since medical diagnosis depends heavily on verbal communication, the dysfunctional consequences of the language barrier are easy to understand. Many doctors from other cultures, especially in the Third World, ascribe to a different value system about the parameters of medical treatment. In their homelands it may be considered frivolous for physicians to deal with social problems and minor maladies. In absolute terms, the conditions in the city served by the hospital we studied can hardly be compared to conditions in Calcutta. The character of medical staff, then, has changed, and there can be little doubt that the quality of medical care has improved. But from the point of view of the local community, the amount and kinds of medical services is a paramount issue.

Decentralization of health-care facilities and the development of satellite centers (especially for chronic care and other services unwanted by the medical college) may meet some of the needs of poor people. The danger here is that a two-class system of health-care delivery may be institutionalized as the teaching hospital gains more prestige and narrows its focus to highly specialized medicine while the satellite centers find themselves flooded out by the legions of the sick poor. The community will hardly be better off with the political pressure points moved but not relieved.

The blacks who have been added to the paramedical staff have been placed in a double bind. As blacks, many of these persons realize that they hold their present jobs because of community pressure following in the wake of extraordinary racial tension. They represent the hospital's black constituency. As professionals, they have an obligation to be professional, to apply some set of universal criteria to their work. One criterion of administration is to protect the ogranization within its own definition. For many blacks their hospital job represents upward mobility and a chance to assume power, to become the new professional elite. For some it represents an opportunity to cut short the process of adequate professional training.

While some of the new administrators and other medical paraprofessionals have succeeded in their quest to improve the lot of poor people whom the hospital serves, many have not. We have discovered three categories for those who have failed under the new regime: the ineffectual militants, the retreatists and the ritualists.

Ritualists and retreatists follow the patterns of response to organizational demands of just "doing their job." For whatever motives—mobility or lack of social concern—their behavior devolves into routinely stamping forms and staring out of windows or "going downtown" on working days. Immunity from the wrath of bureaucracy and/or the community is sometimes claimed and even achieved on the basis of their self-professed negritude.

Ineffectual militants adopt the rhetoric of revolution and justify their excesses in terms of "ripping off" the system by not taking care of business. This posture is often just an ideological defense for retreatism or withdrawal from effective strategies of social change. Wearing Afro hairdos and clutching copies of ***Soul on Ice*** under their arms, those who follow this pattern of response expend vast amounts of energy spouting the Crow Jim black racism of the new true believers. When confronted with the suggestion that they offer a paradigm for a better medical system for their brothers and sisters they answer with high-flown and often empty slogans. Meanwhile, people are sick and dying.

The category of black paraprofessionals who are really taking care of business are those who came into the hospital out of the community and worked themselves up through the ranks out of a genuine compassion for and grasp of the real needs of the poor people whom they wish to serve. These extradorinary paraprofessionals tend to continue their education (often at night) and offer themselves as advocates for people whose problems arise not from some textbook case but from real problems of living in an oppressive and racist social situation. They adapt and adjust their strategies to the problem at hand and are loath to use sick poor people for any other purpose than to make things better for the sick poor.

2 *Deborah Colburn & Kenneth Colburn*

Integrity House: The Addict as a Total Institution

Integrity House is a nonprofit, tax-exempt corporation founded in May 1968 by its present executive director, David H. Kerr. It is part of a larger drug rehabilitation program in Newark, supervised, funded (through a five-year, $2.2 million grant from the National Institute of Mental Health) and evaluated by the Division of Drug Abuse at the Newark College of Medicine and Dentistry.

Statistics show that only a small percentage of ex-addicts are ever fully rehabilitated at Integrity House.

The Integrity House approach to rehabilitation is an apolitical, myth-oriented method reinforcing the pseudopsychological notion that addiction is exclusively the problem of the addict. Blame is placed solely on the addict; neither social ills nor any other factors share the responsibility for drug abuse. That all addicts are "emotionally immature" and must be forced to undergo rehabilitation are sacred, universal and unfounded assumptions of the Integrity House method.

"We feel that drug use is only a symptom of an underlying character disorder," maintains Kerr, a former parole officer. If the addict were not suffering from a character disorder, "Why . . . would he be on drugs?" Long hair, voluptuous breasts, passivity and political consciousness are treated as symptoms of this character disorder. Haircuts, men's clothing for women and other image-breaking changes are used to redefine, punish or arbitrarily impose "injustices" on inmates.

The pre-interview of a prospective inmate begins the image-breaking process, first by stripping away any sense of identity the applicant may have, and second, by providing him with a new identity as a "sick" person. The staff stresses that the applicant will be required to demonstrate his need for help: if he is admitted to the program, the relationship will be that of the server and the served. The successful applicant must begin to demonstrate his willingness to believe that he not only has a problem but that he *is* the problem at the very first interview. He must begin to think of himself as an "emotional infant," the definition given him by Integrity, whether or not such a description has any empirical truth.

Punishment Techniques

Every applicant submits to this degradation ceremony if he wishes to enter the program. Once an applicant is accepted, the staff's first task is to erase any outward manifestations of his sense of personal identity. Men are often given crew-cuts; if the staff feels that hair is "too important" to the new resident, they may shave his head entirely. A woman's hair might be trimmed, or if the staff feels that her breasts are too obvious, she is forced to wear baggy clothing or even men's apparel.

Such things are done as punishment, but also arbitrarily or, as the staff likes to say, to "teach the resident that injustice exists in the world and that he must learn to deal with it." Integrity's staff feels that inmates should accept injustice without complaint or even feeling that any injustice has been committed. As for those persons who think that an alternative response to injustice is to try to change it—such persons are only demonstrating to the staff that they are still sick with a "character disorder" and are yet "emotionally immature."

The staff's favorite tactic is the "haircut," which is used for various reasons: to punish either passivity or infractions of the rules, or to teach injustice.

"Haircuts," formally defined as verbal reprimands, are extremely effective punishments and social controls. A staff member calls in several inmates for help in administering one; since no one is told in advance who is to get the "haircut," much less what it is for, an inmate reports to the director's office without knowing whether he will be on the giving or receiving end. The staff might even have one of the inmates lead the procedure. In one case, the staff felt that a resident had not carried out his job with proper responsibility. The night-shift expeditor had been ordered by a staff member to wake another inmate for a scheduled trip to the hospital. The expeditor did wake his charge, but somehow the inmate thought he was to go to the hospital on his own, which he did. The staff blamed this misunderstanding on the expeditor, and a "haircut" was ordered for him.

Learning about Injustice

The expeditor was brought to the director's office, the others having already been gathered inside. The expeditor did not know what he was accused of, nor would he have the opportunity to defend himself:

Leader: [Screaming out] "Is that mother-fuck X outside the door?"

X: [Obediently answering] "Yes, Sir!"

Leader: [Still yelling] "Open the fucking door and get your ass in here!"

X comes in, standing at attention, military style.

Leader: "You motherfucking idiot, what the hell's wrong with you?"

A, B and C: [Simultaneously] "You goddam asshole!" "You so damn stupid and fucking ugly, hey what's the matter with you?" "You fat and silly motherfucker!"

Leader: "How the hell come you woke A without telling him to wait for an escort? You dirty fuck!"

A: "Yeah, how come you're so stupid? You want me to shoot dope again, don't you? How come you're such a fucking dope?"

Everyone in the room was there to contribute in some manner to the verbal reprimand. It was "positive behavior" for the inmates to yell whatever came to their mind, although none of them knew what lay behind the degradation they were administering. The major purpose for this group assault was to make all punishment look like it was coming from the community, and to make it difficult for the individual to resist or defend himself.

As it turned out, the night-shift man was innocent, for the day-shift expeditor had misinformed the inmate. Later questioned about how he felt for being blamed and punished for something he had not done, the night-shift expeditor obediently replied, "It teaches me about injustice."

The problem of drug addiction touches many fields of inquiry: there are medical, legal, psychological and sociopolitical perspectives. Differing perspectives will produce different sets of questions and answers. Whatever the merits and validity of these other approaches, they all tend to pass over our primary interest: the sociopolitical considerations of class and conflict. The psychological model deals with drug addiction as a personal problem, but is not necessarily insensitive to sociopolitical questions; on the contrary, at times the psychologist does recognize that certain kinds of persons result from certain environments. We separate psychology proper (with its potential for sociopolitical insight) from what we refer to as *pseudopsychology*: *pseudo*, because it identifies all problems as individual problems, and acts accordingly—on the individual. Pseudopsychology is an ideology that places all responsibility for any state of affairs solely on the individual and dictates that he not only must change himself but also that he is the only one who requires changing. The result is that the social status quo goes unquestioned.

Integrity's methods and presumptions about drug addiction all run counter to the view of deviance as a social phenomenon. Irving Louis Horowitz and Martin Liebowitz note: "Deviance is a conflict between at least two parties: superordinates who make and enforce rules, and subordinates whose behavior violates those rules." To see deviance as a conflict between two parties, the ruler and the ruled, is to see deviance not as a property of any individual, but as a property imputed to the ruled by the ruler. Deviance is fundamentally of a social nature, and both ruler and ruled share responsibility for their interaction. At any given time, then, deviance is the result of a conflict between the ruler and the ruled seen through the looking-glass of official reality. Deviance is treated apolitically when the official view of reality does not permit identifying the true causes of a social inequity.

While the banner of psychology is waved by Integrity, not one bona fide psychologist was involved in the Integrity program during our research period. Ex-drug users, themselves "graduates" of other treatment programs, formed the core of treatment personnel and were hired as staff; the closest to a psychologist was Kerr, with his A.B. in psychology, but his practical work experience was as a parole officer.

Reaching Phase II

Integrity has taken an active role in the public relations area of propagating the official myth of the apolitical, pseudopsychological account of drug deviance. According to the first *Newsletter*: "It is our intention to publish monthly and send [this publication] free of charge to all those interested in the work done at Integrity House (judiciary, legislators, probation departments, residents' families and supporters)." A group of Integrity staff members and inmates are readily available for speaking engagements for any social or civic organizations who request speakers. At these occasions it is typical for one of the inmates to tell the audience what a terrible person he was before he came to Integrity, how irresponsible he was, and the rest of the self-blaming tale.

Integrity is distinguished not only for being the largest residential drug rehabilitation program in the state of New Jersey, but also for the originality it claims for the second phase of its therapeutic program, the "re-entry phase." The resident theoretically advances to the second step after completing the first, or "pre-re-entry" phase, which is the now-popular, strictly supervised 24-hour "therapeutic community." The second phase differs from the first and from programs such as Synanon in that the resident holds an outside job while living at the institution. Most of the ex-addicts are in the first phase of the program.

In the three years of its existence, while Integrity has grown from 14 to 160 residents, and from one to two houses, no more than 38 percent of the total residents have been in phase II of the program at any one time; in 1971, of 160 total residents, only 30 (18 percent) were in phase II. The high dropout rate accounts for those ex-addicts who never reach phase II: in February 1970 there was at least a 33 to 50 percent dropout rate of new residents within the first two or three weeks of their stay; and in April 1971, the public relations staff was reporting a dropout rate of 40 to 50 percent during the first three weeks of an ex-addict's stay.

A COMPARISON OF THE NUMBER OF RESIDENTS AT INTEGRITY IN PHASE I AND PHASE II FROM 1969-71

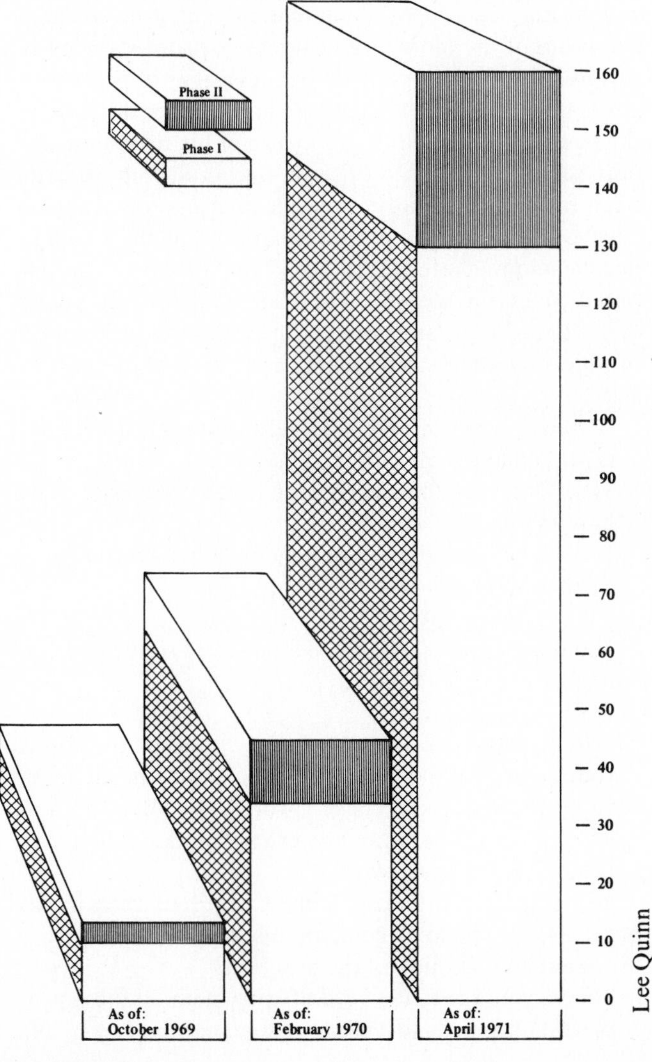

The April 1971 *Newsletter* reported that 30 residents were "in the community on outside jobs," but *11 of these jobs were actually on the staff at Integrity*! At the same time, the total number of residents in the program had increased to 160.

An applicant's decision to go to Integrity House is often a forced choice between "rehabilitative therapy" or a correctional or penal institution. Kerr writes:

> How can an individual labeled an "emotional infant" by many, possess the maturity to have true motivation? A motivated person has a fair degree of emotional growth by definition. The confusion is that the majority of heroin addicts would like to stop using drugs but don't want to at the present. The courts, probation and parole *can play a very important role in forcing the active drug abuser* to do "what he would like" but what he doesn't want to do; that is stop using drugs. . . . What seems to work is the *imposition of heavy court pressure on an addict at the beginning of treatment.* The reason for this is that *the "raw" addict, for the most part, only understands fear of jail as an immediate alternative to rehabilitation.* "If I leave here I'll go to jail. I'll stay here to beat my sentence." *This is the best motivation that anyone can expect from a person with this degree of emotional immaturity. . . .*

Since Kerr is in the business of remodeling the way a person thinks about himself and his world, and since such remodeling obviously meets with resistance and conflict, his job can be made a good deal easier when those who are to be remolded have little real choice in the matter.

Integrity can exist only in a situation where prisons also exist, for Integrity is a viable choice only when jail is the only alternative. Almost half of those who are admitted might choose to return to jail; one wonders if anyone would remain at Integrity without the threat of jail, and for reasons other than "emotional immaturity."

Applicants, accustomed to the more custodial concept of "doing your own time," or "playing it cool," are unprepared for the reception given them at Integrity. The staff often has the problem of a resident being too passive to elicit much of anything that can be used as "signs" of psychological problems; in this case, the passivity itself becomes the object and "symptom" of "sickness," in true pseudopsychological fashion.

"Haircuts," night probes and other tactics are used to provoke the inmate who, once angry, is over his "passivity" and will raise his new-found "feelings" in the weekly encounter group for the entire community. The staff members then have "data" from which they can work on the inmate. Even though they have elicited this data artificially, they never consider their role in generating the conflict but always focus back on the inmate. This is largely possible because of the structure of the encounter group itself: often, more than one staff member is present and any inmate can say anything he desires about the inmate who is the center of attention. In this manner, any encounter session has the appearance of pitting the entire community against the individual; those who "contribute in this positive manner" are in reality contributing to their own release and advancement and privilege.

Encounter sessions are held twice a week. At these times residents are supposed to confront and be confronted with the "real" reasons for their behavior, as defined to them by the staff. During the sessions inmates can demonstrate to staff that they are "learning" the causes of their "irresponsibility." (That one is irresponsible is never open to question.) This was, as one resident put it, the "name of the game." One either plays it (and this was consciously verbalized by some) and gets the rewards of eventual release and privilege, or one leaves.

The privilege system is connected with the work system, and both build credit toward release. Advancement in the work system is advancement toward release. At the bottom of the list are the members of crews, which change bi-weekly. There are several crews: acquisition, service, kitchen, maintenance, etc. First advancement is to the head of a crew; over heads of crews are the expeditors; and from here one enters the second phase of the program.

The evaluation performed by staff on inmates is crucial. The following is taken from an evaluation sheet used to make weekly evaluations.

How does the resident approach and perform his work?

Shows (too much, proper amount of, too little) initiative
Work output is (low, average, high)
Organization of task is (good, average, poor)

How does the resident react toward his work?

Seems alert, interested, and enthusiastic
Appears indifferent
Displays a negative attitude
Daydreams; gives impression he would rather be doing something else
Indicates little or no interest in areas not related to his specific job
Shows evidence he is exploring total job situation

How does the resident accept suggestions and criticisms?

Resents being shown his mistakes
Makes effort to improve
Has no visible reaction
Welcomes criticism, but shows little or no improvement
Actively seeks suggestions for improvement

How does the resident fit into your organization?

Feels at home and natural in setting
Seems somewhat reserved, shy or passive
Is unduly aggressive and presumptuous
Demands too much attention
Makes little effort to get along with others
Works tactfully and cooperatively with others

Attendance: Regular
Irregular
Dress: Appropriate
Inappropriate
Punctuality: Regular
Irregular
Grooming: Neat
Careless

How does this industrial-sounding form square with Integrity's "psychological" treatment of ex-addicts? Integrity's main concern is to employ ex-addicts, but the form shows clearly that emphasis on the individual which is so antithetical to a socially aware psychology.

Yelling and Screaming

An Integrity House inmate's first conflict with the new system involves the contention that drug use is a symptom of an ***unobserved*** character disorder or, more simply, that drug use equals sickness. It is important to stress "unobserved" because the inmate uses this hole in the equation as the basis and means of his resistance. He may refuse to believe in this rule's general truth, or in its truth for him personally (empirical matters for a genuine psychology; merely a programmatic principle for pseudopsychology), refusing to "see" or "observe" the imputed illness in himself. The staff continuously points this "illness" out, and the inmate evades this imputation of illness by attributing such a description to the staff itself:

A new female inmate was eating breakfast as I sat down to have some coffee.
Her "image" had recently been redone; she wore short hair and baggy clothes.
I asked her how she was getting on in her new home.
"Don't ask me."
"Why, what's wrong?"
[Looking across the table to a seasoned resident] "Is it negative to talk about why?"
"No."
"Well, they've taken away my clothes, you know, wanting me to think they're wrong. And I'm supposed to be wrong, too, because I wore them. But I'm not. They're the ones who are crazy, thinking that ***any*** [kind of] clothes are wrong!"

The words of a female inmate who had been in the program just one week confirm this sentiment.

"What do you think of the program?"
"Well, you know, it's kind of scary with all these people running around yelling and screaming—just like

they were crazy."

"Have you found it difficult getting on?"

"It's difficult for some—the pressure just gets too great."

"What do you mean?"

"Well, at the workathon four or five left."

"Why was that?"

"Well you've got to clean the house for 12 to 14 hours straight, everyone [i.e., the staff] on your back, telling you you've got to learn to take that sort of thing. But it's not too bad if you just remember that cleaning a house that's already clean is kinda crazy—if they want to be crazy, OK."

A recent arrival from Skillman (another drug addiction treatment center) talked about his first impressions of Integrity House:

"How do you like the place so far?"

"I've been in other places like this—most concepts [i.e., programs] are the same."

"How was your initiation yesterday?"

"I was shown to my bed and read a long list of rules. I don't see how they expect you to remember them all. Maybe they don't. This way you're bound to mess up, and when you do, they let you know it's because you're the kind of person who messes up. But you know it's not true—they would be just the same if it was done to them."

Those inmates who decide not to believe in the pseudopsychological definition of themselves as mentally ill have two available options: first, an inmate may leave the program altogether (as already noted, nearly half choose this alternative), or second, he may decide to leave the program in a special way, that is, by trying to evade its definition of him.

The second option presents many difficulties. The therapeutic activity makes it more and more difficult to avoid one's "sickness." The staff constantly refers to incidents from an inmate's life history as evidence of his disorder, and all segments of the community pressure him to accept this "evidence" and to confess his past misdeeds to others. The inmate must engage in self-degradation yet remain distant enough to keep his conception of self as one who is sane. It is difficult to dodge activity in any therapeutic community and, hence, difficult to dodge an identity at Integrity. We believe that the high dropout rate reflects the intensity of the redefining of the self as being "sick." The only effective way to avoid conflict is to talk as little as possible since the staff uses all behavior to indicate one's character disorder. Even silence is interpreted as an indication of passivity, and ultimately, one's "disorder." Integrity's task is to get the inmate to participate sooner or later, through creating "feelings." The following illustrates the response of a black female inmate who had been in the program three months:

X's approach to conflict was a passive one; she avoided participating in anything as much as she could. The staff was eventually able to provoke her into anger, which she displayed at an encounter meeting. Y, a female staff member, had forced X, among other things, to wear men's clothing.

X: [to Y] "You are a no-good motherfucking sonofabitch. . . ."

Y: [smiling] "OK, OK you little bitch; now you're mad, aren't you? How come? Got feelings to act out, don't you? OK, now what's wrong with you? Tell us all.

X: [strangely calm, all anger subsided] "I feel rejected—inadequate about myself."

Y: "I know—we all know that. Now let it all out."

X: "Oh—my hair's too short, I'm not tall enough, I'm black, I'd maybe like bigger breasts—longer fingernails."

Y: "You have to learn to live with yourself as you are. . . ."

X decided to leave the program three weeks later. She said that since that night at the encounter she couldn't go on any longer at the place. She couldn't understand what she was doing there, since she didn't think she was "crazy." The staff reported to the community that X left the program because she was discovered to be on drugs; however, the authors were able to look at her file and found no indication of this on record, but only that X had requested permission to leave the program and was released. The authors were unable to determine the reason for this discrepancy, or the number of similar disparities.

Psychology becomes ideology as it serves as a means of control and subversion of class and political consciousness among ex-drug users. How does or how could one know about an ex-addict's personality "disorder" independent of the fact that he uses or has used drugs? And who asserts this definition? Troy Duster says:

> *If one has observed that addicts are psychologically inadequate . . . under what conditions might the observer be forced to conclude that this observation was wrong?* In other words, what would the observer have to see in order to conclude that addicts are not psychologically inadequate? Once this question is posed realistically to those who hold this position, it is likely that the one piece of evidence they require is that the addict give up narcotics usage. . . . The simple fact that he is "using" is regarded as sufficient evidence of inadequacy. The reasoning is circular, tautological, or simply "true" by definition. . . . Once such a definition is made, it can never be proven wrong.

The fact that such a definition cannot be refuted violates the major canon of scientific inquiry: proof and disproof. Those who assert this definition become important; a definition which conveniently can be used to rationalize certain practices under the banner of psychology and science is obtained by fiat. Such a definition becomes a political license to treat ex-addicts in a particular manner.

In pseudopsychology questions of social structure and social class, the recognition of drug deviance as a political issue, or other policy alternatives which question the wisdom of making drugs illegal or legally unavailable (which, after all, accounts for the addict's criminality) become impossible because unnecessary. In this view, there simply *are* no sociological questions.

C. Wright Mills made a distinction between private "troubles" and public "issues": where a few persons become addicted to drugs, it could make sense to look at those individuals and their personal history for clues to account for their addiction. However, considering that since 1968 the population of addicts has doubled to an estimated 300,000, questions of the intersection of life history and social structure must be asked. The greatest danger of a pseudopsychology is that it will continue to ask the same tired question, and give the same old answer: drug addiction is a problem because of the drug addict. Such a view overlooks the interesting fact that, during our research period, the vast majority of inmates at Integrity were from either a lower- or working-class background; most were high school or elementary school dropouts; and a few could not read and/or write. Lack of money forced many into criminal careers to finance their habit. Would the so-called "cost to society" of the addict exist in the economic sense if the addict were able to obtain his supply from legitimate sources, rather than from the underworld? A vicious circle exists here which could be partially eliminated by a long and serious look at the genesis of drug addiction and crime.

The pseudopsychological point of view does not stand up to either historical or comparative data. Thousands of Americans and Englishmen used opium and heroin legally in the early decades of this century, and the question of emotional immaturity was never raised. The middle and upper classes bought more than the lower and working classes and, in proportion to population, addiction was eight times that of 1970. The English today do not treat addiction as a moral problem; rather they make it possible for the addict to obtain drugs legally.

Drug addiction is a way of life for an individual in certain social conditions, and what Integrity seeks in practice, although unmentioned in theory, is to provide an alternative community. Such a community, which Integrity recognizes to be essential, does not exist for the individual in the real world of society, the ghetto of slums and poverty and drunken fathers and broken homes. But since belief is the prime prerequisite of Integrity's community, it should be sociologically classified as a *religious* community. Once this is clear, it becomes possible to ask whether a secular society such as ours either should or must legislate the living of a religious life for certain of its members.

If the key lies in a community, a theory which Integrity acknowledges only implicitly, then this alternative must be questioned and thought about more thoroughly and openly, and from other than a religious conception.

The main social science issue is whether making such an ad hoc community—separated and segregated from society-at-large—is likely to solve the problem. Such a community would be stigmatized, and as Duster has argued, the drug problem in the United States stems largely from the moral interpretation given to drug users. Can drug users be rehabilitated independent of a change in their moral evaluation by society? "If we speak in terms of the typical case, *any rehabilitation program of social deviants is doomed to failure in its own terms by its own criteria* ["rehabilitation"] *so long as the larger society treats rehabilitation as a passage between two moral categories*." Integrity House and programs like it throughout America engaged in the search for money and grants, contribute to and have a vested interest in maintaining that moral and sociopolitical order.

The ideological thrust of the pseudopsychological account of deviance should be seen in terms of its rising popularity among government personnel who will be charged with formulating future drug treatment programs. Consider the words of Dr. Roger Egeberg, the President's advisor for public health:

> I'm not saying that you shouldn't keep working at cutting off your opium sources .... If heroin were cut off from the thousands of addicts in the United States, most of them would get hooked on something else. *We've got to start focusing on the addict* rather than the agent who addicts him. ... I think more and more we will be focusing on the individual while continuing the law-enforcement aspects.

The same focus on individual rather than societal responsibility extends to forthcoming legislation. Nelson Rockefeller, the governor of New York, has requested a new law which calls for life terms in prison for those who commit crimes while under the influence of drugs.

And so the end is once again a beginning.

SUGGESTED READINGS

The Legislation of Morality by Troy Duster (New York: Free Press, 1970).

"Methadone Maintenance as Law and Order" by Florence Heyman in *Society*, June 1972.

Drugs and the Public by Norman E. Zinberg and John A. Robertson (New York: Simon & Schuster, 1972).

3 *Jim Hightower*

Hard Tomatoes, Hard Times

Corporate agriculture's preoccupation with scientific and business efficiency has produced a radical restructuring of rural America that has been carried into urban America. There has been more than a green revolution out there—in the last 30 years there literally has been a social and economic upheaval in the American countryside. It is a protracted, violent revolution, and it continues today.

The land grant college complex has been the scientific and intellectual father of that revolution. This public complex has put its tax dollars, its facilities, its manpower, its energies and its thoughts almost solely into efforts that have worked to the advantage and profit of large corporations involved in agriculture.

The consumer is hailed as the greatest beneficiary of the land grant college effort, but in fact consumer interests are considered secondarily if at all, and in many cases, the complex works directly against the consumer. Rural people, including the vast majority of farmers, farm workers, small town businessmen and residents, and the rural poor, either are ignored or directly abused by the land grant effort. Each year about a million of these people pour out of rural America into the cities. They are the waste products of an agricultural revolution designed within the land grant complex. Today's urban crisis is a consequence of failure in rural America. The land grant complex cannot shoulder all the blame for that failure, but no single institution—private or public—has played a more crucial role.

The complex has been eager to work with farm machinery manufacturers and well-capitalized farming operations to mechanize all agricultural labor, but it has accepted no responsibility for the farm laborer who is put out of work by the machine. It has worked hand-in-hand with seed companies to develop high-yield seed strains, but it has not noticed that rural America is yielding up practically all of its young people. It has been available day and night to help non-farming corporations develop schemes of vertical integration, while offering independent family farmers little more comfort than "adapt or die." It has devoted hours to the creation of adequate water systems for fruit and vegetable processors and canners, but 30,000 rural communities still have no central water systems. It has tampered with the gene structure of tomatoes, strawberries, asparagus and other foods to prepare them for the steel grasp of mechanical harvesters, but it has sat still while the American food supply has been laced with carcinogenic substances.

The land grant college complex is made up of three interrelated units, all of which are attached to the land grant college campuses. The first unit is comprised of the Colleges of Agriculture, created in 1862 by the Morrill Act. The State Agricultural Experiment Stations are the second unit. They were created in 1887 by the Hatch Act for the purpose of conducting agricultural and rural research in cooperation with the Colleges of Agriculture. The Extension Service, created in 1914 by the Smith-Lever Act completes the picture. It was designed to bring the fruits of research to all rural people.

Reaching into all 50 states, the complex is huge, intricate and expensive. It is estimated that the total complex spends three-quarters of a billion tax dollars appropriated each year from federal, state and county governments. The public's total investment in this complex, including assets, comes to several billion dollars in any given year, paying for everything from test tubes to experimental farms, from chalk to carpeting in the dean's office. But this public investment is being misspent. The land grant complex has wandered a long way from its origins, abandoning its historic mission to serve rural people and American consumers.

The Agribusiness Accountability Project, a public-interest research and advocacy organization based in Washington, D.C., created the Task Force on the Land Grant Complex to look into this issue. In addition to research done in Washington and by correspondence, studies were conducted on the campuses of the University of California, Cornell University, University of Florida, Iowa State University, University of Maryland, Michigan State University, North Carolina State University, Purdue University and Texas A & M University.

It is practically impossible to talk with anyone in the land grant college complex or to read anything about the complex without confronting the staggering achievements wrought by agricultural research. There is no doubt that American agriculture is enormously productive and that agriculture's surge in productivity is largely the result of mechanical, chemical, genetical and managerial research conducted through the land grant college complex. But the question is whether the achievements outweigh the failures, whether benefits are overwhelmed by costs. Ask a family farmer or any rural American about the costs. There is a crisis in the countryside. While the agribusiness conglomerates continue to grow because of agricultural research, the independent farmer is pushed out of the way or, worst of all, just forgotten. Tragically, the land grant complex, the public's primary investment of intellectual and scientific resources in rural America, has not only failed to respond—it has contributed to the problems. There is an obvious failure. You don't even need the readily available statistics to see that rural America is crumbling. And not just the family farm, but every aspect of life is crumbling—entire communities, schools, churches, business and a way of life. For example:

□ 47.1 percent of the farm families in this country have annual incomes below $3,000.

□ More than half of the farms in the country have sales of less than $5,000 a year; together, this majority of farmers accounted for only 7.8 percent of farm sales.

□ Since 1940, more than 3 million farms have folded, and farms continue to fold at a rate of 2,000 a week.

□ The number of black farm operators fell from 272,541 in 1959 to 98,000 in 1970.

□ For the first time since the nation was settled coast to coast, the farm population has fallen below 10 million.

□ During the 1960s, the proportion of farm people over 55 years of age rose by a third, while the proportion of those under 14 years of age declined by half.

□ Hired farm workers in 1970 averaged an income of $1,083 if they did farm work only, while those who also did some non-farm work averaged an income of $2,461.

□ 14 million rural Americans exist below a poverty income, with millions more clinging just on the edge of poverty.

□ Independent, small-town businesses are closing at a rate of more than 16,000 a year.

□ 132 rural counties have no doctor.

□ 30,000 rural communities are without central water systems; 30,000 are without sewer systems.

□ 2.5 million substandard houses—60 percent of the bad housing in America—are occupied by rural families.

□ 64 percent of all rural counties lost population during the sixties.

□ Since 1940, 30 million people have left their rural homes for urban areas, and this migration continues at a rate of 800,000 a year.

□ More than 73 percent of the American people live now on less than 2 percent of the land.

Despite the obvious need, the land grant complex has not provided the answers. For example, in the fiscal year 1969, a total of nearly 6,000 scientific man-years (smy) were spent doing research on all projects at all state-agricultural experiment stations. Based on USDA's research classifications, only 289 of those scientific man-years were expended specifically on "people-oriented" research. That is an allocation to rural people of less than 5 percent of the total research effort at the state agricultural experiment stations. And the experiment stations were doing less of this type of research in 1969 than they were in 1966.

The focus of agricultural research is warped by the land grant community's fascination with technology, integrated food processes and the like. Strict economic efficiency is the goal. The distorted research priorities are striking:

□ 1,129 scientific man-years on improving the biological efficiency of crops, and only 18 smy on improving rural income.

□ 842 smy on control of insects, diseases and weeds in crops, and 95 smy to insure food products free from toxic residues from agricultural sources.

□ 200 smy on ornamentals, turf and trees for natural beauty, and a sad seven smy on rural housing.

□ 88 smy on improving management systems for livestock and poultry production, and 45 smy for improving rural institutions.

□ 68 smy on marketing firm and system efficiency, and 17 smy on causes and remedies of poverty among rural people.

A close analysis of these research projects reveals even less of a commitment to the needs of people in rural America than appears on the surface. In rural housing, the major share of research has been directed not to those who live in them but to those who profit from the construction and maintenance of houses—architects, builders, lumber companies and service industries.

Other people-oriented projects tend to be irrelevant studies of characteristics, seemingly stemming more from curiosity than a desire to change conditions. At Cornell, for example, a study found that "employed homemakers have less time for housekeeping tasks than non-employed homemakers." Other projects are just about as "useful."

□ Mississippi State University researchers discovered "that families in poverty are not of a single, homogeneous type."

□ The University of Nebraska is at work on a study of "factors affecting age at marriage."

□ A cooperative Regional Research study unveiled two findings of such significance that Dr. Roy Lovvorn included them in CSRS' 1970 presentation to Congress: "the rural population is dichotomous in racial composition" and "pre-retirement family incomes have a direct bearing upon economic expectations for retirement."

□ Back at Mississippi State, researchers concluded that "the better educated young individuals are able to recognize and take advantage of economic opportunities attainable through migration."

□ University of Nebraska researchers surveyed football coaches in the state and got 60 percent agreement "that introduction of a federally sponsored school breakfast program would benefit the nutritional health of teenage athletes."

For the most part, then, even this small amount of people-oriented research done by the land grant complex, is nothing more than useless poking into the behavior and life styles of rural people.

Mechanization Research

The agribusiness corporations envision rural America as a factory that will produce food, fiber and profits on a corporate assembly line extending from the fields through the supermarket checkout counters. It is through mechanization research that the land grant colleges are coming closest to this agribusiness ideal.

Mechanization has been a key element in the cycle of bigness: enough capital can buy machinery, which can handle more acreage, which will produce greater volume, which can mean more profits, which will buy more machinery. Mechanization has not been pressed by the land grant complex as an alternative, but as an imperative.

Once again, those who most need the help of the land grant complex are its primary victims. If mechanization research has been a boon to agribusiness interests, it has been a bane to millions of rural Americans. The cost has been staggering.

Farm workers were the first to get the axe. Again and again the message is hammered home—machines either exist or are on the way to replace farm labor. There were 4.3 million hired farm workers in 1950. Twenty years later, that number has fallen to 2.5 million. As a group, those laborers averaged $1,083 for doing farm work in 1970, making them among the very poorest of America's employed poor. The great majority of these workers were hired by the largest farms, which are the same farms moving as swiftly as possible to mechanize their operations.

Farm workers have not been compensated for jobs lost to mechanization research. They were not consulted when that research was designed, and their needs were not a part of the research package that resulted. They simply were left to fend on their own—no retraining, no effort to find new jobs for them, no research to help them adjust to the changes that came out of the land grant colleges. Corporate agribusiness received machines with the tax-payer's help, but the workers who are replaced are not even entitled to unemployment compensation.

Independent, family farmers are also hard hit. Designed to the specifications of the largest-scale producers, mechanization has not been much of a blessing to those who are lacking capital, acreage or management capabilities. Small- and medium-scale farmers, making annual sales under $20,000, (which includes 87 percent of all farmers in the United States), simply are not able to make much use of $25,000 harvesting equipment. Even the great majority of large-scale farmers, with sales ranging up to $100,000 a year, have not been well served by the mechanization research of land grant colleges.

The rapidly increasing cost of farming, in combination with perennially low farm prices, is driving farmers off the land. Tractor prices range from about $7,000 for a small one to $36,000 for huge crawler tractors. A tractor is useless without plows, rakes, harrows and other essential attachments. These cost extra, and dearly. Harvesting equipment is tremendously expensive—for example, a cotton picker costs $26,000 to $30,000 and a tomato harvester runs $23,000. More sophisticated pieces, with electronic sensors and other gadgets developed by land grant scientists, simply are out of the question for all but the very well heeled. Operator of his own 600-acre Nebraska farm, Elmer Zeis told a newspaper interviewer about these costs:

> You can't get a piece of small equipment for under $1,000. The combine I bought this fall cost $20,000; I pay all that and use it one month out of the year. Then I have to trade a piece or two each year just to keep current.

Zeis estimated that he had $50,000 tied up in machinery and another $25,000 in storage buildings and bins.

Like the farm worker, the average farmer is not invited into the land grant laboratories to design research. If he were, the research package would include machines useful on smaller acreages, it would include assistance to develop cooperative ownership systems, it would include efforts to develop low-cost and simpler machinery, it would include a heavy emphasis on new credit schemes, and it would include special extension to spread knowledge about the purchase, operation and maintenance of machinery. These efforts do not exist, or exist only in a token way. Mechanization research has left the great majority of farmers to "get big" on their own, or to get out of farming altogether.

Who then benefits from mechanization research? The largest-scale growers, the farm machinery and chemical input companies and the processors are the primary beneficiaries. Big business interests are called upon by land grant staffs to participate directly in the planning, research and development stages of mechanization projects. The interests of agribusiness literally are designed into the product. No one else is consulted.

Obviously, farm machinery and chemical companies are direct beneficiaries of this research, since they can expect to market products that are developed. Machinery companies such as John Deere, International Harvester, Massey-Ferguson, Allis-Chalmers and J. I. Case almost continually engage in cooperative research efforts at land grant colleges. These corporations contribute money and some of their own research personnel to help land grant scientists develop machinery; in return, they are able to incorporate technological advances in their own products.

In some cases they actually receive exclusive license to manufacture and sell the product of tax-paid research.

But mechanization means more than machinery for planting, thinning, weeding and harvesting. It also means improving on nature's design—breeding new food varieties that are better adapted to mechanical harvesting. Having built machines, the land grant research teams found it necessary to build a tomato that is hard enough to survive the grip of mechanical "fingers"; necessary to redesign the grape so that all the fruit has the good sense to ripen at the same time; and necessary to restructure the apple tree so that it grows shorter, leaving the apples less distance to fall to the mechanical catcher.

Mechanization of fruits and vegetables has been focused first on crops used by the processing industries. Brand name processors—such as Del Monte, Heinz, Hunt, Stokely Van-Camp, Campbell's and Green Giant—are direct beneficiaries of mechanization research. Many of these corporations have been directly involved in the development of mechanization projects.

The University of Florida, for example, recently has developed a new fresh market tomato (the MH-1) for machine harvesting. In describing the characteristics that make this tomato so desirable for machine harvest, the university pointed to "the thick walls, firm flesh, and freedom from cracks." It may be a little tough for the consumer, but agricultural research can't please everyone. The MH-1, which will eliminate the jobs of thousands of Florida farm workers who now handpick tomatoes for the fresh market, is designed to be harvested green and to be "ripened" in storage by application of ethylene gas. Michigan State University, in a proud report on "tailor-made" vegetables, notes that their scientists are at work on broccoli, cauliflower, cucumbers, snapbeans, lima beans, carrots and asparagus. And the processors have benefitted because mechanization has been able to lower the costs of production.

If produce cannot be redesigned by manipulating genes, land grant scientists reach into their chemical cabinet. Louisiana State University has experimented with the chemical "Ethrel" to cause hot peppers to ripen at the same time for "onceover" mechanical harvesting; scientists at Michigan State University are using chemicals to reduce the cherry's resistance to the tug of the mechanical picker; and a combination of ferric ammonia citrate and erythorbic acid is being used at Texas A&M to loosen fruit before machine harvesting. This benefits both the chemical input firms on one end and the processors on the other.

Large-scale farming operations, many of them major corporate farms, are also directly in line to receive the rewards of mechanization research. In the first place, it is these farms that hire the overwhelming percentage of farm labor, thus having an economic incentive to mechanize. Secondly, these are the massive farms, spreading over thousands of acres, a scale of operation which warrants an investment in machinery. Thirdly, these are heavily-capitalized producers, including processing corporations, vertically integrated input and output industries and conglomerate enterprises. Such farming ventures are financially able and managerially inclined to mechanize the food system—that 1 percent of American farms with annual sales of $100,000 or more.

These are the "farmers" who are welcome in the land grant research labs. They bring grants and equipment to those labs, but, more importantly, they also bring a shared vision of assembly-line food production. In turn, they get research to implement that vision. These huge growers are more than clients of the land grant system—they are colleagues.

Genetically redesigned, mechanically planted, thinned and weeded, chemically readied and mechanically harvested and sorted, food products move out of the field and into the processing and marketing stages—untouched by human hands.

The agricultural colleges also are engaged in "selling" the consumer on products he neither wants or needs, and they are using tax money for food research and development that should be privately financed. There are many projects that analyze consumer behavior. Typically these involve consumer surveys to determine what influences the shopper's decision-making. If this research is useful to anyone, it is food marketers and advertisers—and reports on this research make clear that those firms are the primary recipients of the results.

The result of this research is not better food but "better looking" food. These public laboratories have researched and developed food cosmetics in an effort to confirm the consumer's preconceptions about food appearances. Chickens have been fed the plant compound Xanthophyll to give their skin "a pleasing yellow tinge," and several projects have been undertaken to develop spray-on coatings to enhance the appearance of apples, peaches, citrus and tomatoes. Other cosmetic research projects are underway at land grant colleges:

□ Iowa State University is conducting packaging studies which indicate that color stays bright longer when bacon is vacuum-packed or sealed in a package containing carbon dioxide in place of air, thus contributing to "more consumer appeal."

□ Scientists at South Carolina's agricultural experiment station have shown that red flourescent light treatment can increase the red color in green, machine-packed tomatoes and can cause their texture and taste to be "similar to vine-ripened tomatoes."

□ Kansas State University Extension Service, noting that apples sell on the basis of appearance rather than nutrition, urged growers to have a beautiful product. To make the produce more appealing, mirrors and lights in supermarket produce cases were cited as effective selling techniques.

Convenience to the processor often outweighs concern

for the consumer, both as a motive for and as an end result of such research. For example, University of Wisconsin researchers have developed a process of making mozarella cheese in five-and-a-half minutes compared to the usual time of four hours. The flavor of the final product is reported to be "mild, but satisfactory for the normal uses." While this is relatively harmless, there is evidence that some aspects of food engineering at land grant colleges are directly counter to the interests of the consumer. For instance, when ethylene gas is used to ripen tomatoes, in addition to inferior taste, color and firmness, the amounts of vitamin A and vitamin C are known to decrease.

Even more insidious, there is strong evidence the DES, a growth hormone fed to cattle to make them grow faster, causes cancer in man. Yet DES has added some $2.9 million to the treasury of Iowa State University, where the use of the drug was discovered, developed, patented and promoted—all with tax dollars. Eli Lilly and Company, which was exclusively licensed by Iowa State to manufacture and sell the drug, has enjoyed profits on some $60 million in DES sales to date.

More and more, chemicals are playing a role in the processing phase. Ohio State University reports that "chemical peeling of tomatoes with wetting agents and caustic soda reduces labor by 75 percent and increases product recovery." One wonders if the consumer will recover. Lovers of catfish might be distressed to know that this tasty meat now is being skinned chemically for commercial packaging.

At the same time, some of the research products are deceptively harmless—to the point of absurdity. At Cornell a critical issue has been how hard to squeeze a grapefruit in the supermarket:

> Should you squeeze a product firmly or softly to determine its freshness, such as is commonly done with bread and some fruits? By using a universal testing machine, scientists have determined that a gentle squeeze, or more scientifically, a small deformation force, is much more precise in comparing textural differences than a firm squeeze or large deformation force.

Among other mind-boggling land grant college projects, Auburn and Penn State have used tax dollars to study "heat-retaining properties" of Astroturf; the University of Wisconsin has turned to camping for a research challenge; and Purdue has spent years and untold tax dollars on athletic turfs for football fields and golf courses. Except for agribusiness, land grant college research has been no bargain. Hard tomatoes and hard times is too much to pay.

The Extension Service (ES) is the outreach arm of the land grant college complex. Its mandate is to go among the people of rural America to help them "identify and solve their farm, home and community problems through use of research findings of the Department of Agriculture and the State Land Grant Colleges." As with the rest of the complex, the ES has hardly lived up to its mandate.

The focus of ES is primarily on "clients" who need it least, ignoring the obvious needs of the vast majority of rural Americans. The service devotes more than half of its total work to just one-quarter of the farmers in this country—those with sales of more than $10,000 annually. That leaves 2.4 million farmers—75 percent of the total according to ES figures—without the attention that their need and numbers warrant. Included are hundreds of thousands of marginal farmers, with "net incomes insufficient for levels of living acceptable even for rural areas."

Three hundred thirty-one million dollars were available to the Extension Service in 1971. Like the other parts of the land grant complex, Extension has been preoccupied with efficiency and production—a focus that has contributed much to the largest producers. And while the rural poor get little attention from ES professionals, they receive band-aid assistance from highly-visible but marginally helpful programs like nutrition aids.

The poor get even less attention than appears on the surface. 4-H—that social club for youth—received $72 million in 1971 and accounted for the largest allocation of extension agents' time—over one-third of the total. And with this time and money 4-H helps the rural poor by conducting litter clean-up days and awarding ribbons to everybody.

In 1955, a Special Needs Section was added to Extension legislation, setting aside a sum of money to assist disadvantaged areas. But Extension has failed to make use of it. Policy-making within ES fails to involve most rural people, and USDA has failed utterly to exercise its power to redirect the priorities and programs of the state extension services.

Who does the ES serve? Like their research and teaching colleagues in the land grant complex, extension agents walk hand in hand with agribusiness. To an alarming degree, extension agents are little more than salesmen. A recent article in *Farm Technology,* the magazine for county agents, offers this insight into corporate ties to Extension:

> We are impressed with the fact that much time is spent working closely with industry agrifieldmen and other company representatives. Nearly all states reported that this type of cooperation is increasing.
>
> A good example of this can be found in Arizona where weed specialists "hit the road" with the chemical company representatives and are involved in cooperative field tests and demonstrations.

Moreover, the Extension Service's historical and current affiliation with the American Farm Bureau Federation, the nation's largest, most powerful and affluent farm organization, casts a deep shadow over its claim that it can ever be part of the solution of the problems of rural America.

The civil rights record of ES comes close to being the worst in government. In three states suits have been brought against the Extension Service for overt and flagrant discrimination in hiring and service. Median income figures from 1970 show that white farm families averaged $7,016 per year, while black farm families averaged $3,037. Yet of all the rural poor, blacks can expect the least assistance from ES.

This is not the only case of institutional racism within the land grant complex. When the Morrill Act created land grant colleges in 1862, most of America's black population was in slavery. After the Civil War, blacks were barred from admission both by custom and by law. In 1890 a second Morrill Act was passed to obtain more operating money for the colleges. This act also included a "separate but equal" provision authorizing the establishment of colleges for blacks. Seventeen southern and border states took advantage of this provision. But these black colleges have been less than full partners in the land grant complex. Resource allocations have been blatantly discriminatory. In 1971, of the $76,800,000 in United States Department of Agriculture funds allocated to those 16 states with both white and black land grant colleges, 99.5 percent went to the white colleges, leaving only 0.5 percent for the black colleges. Less than one percent of the research money distributed by the Cooperative State Research Service in 1971 went to black land grant colleges. This disparity is not by accident, but by law.

Making Research Policy

Land grant policy is the product of a closed community. The administrators, academics and scientists, along with USDA officials and corporate executives, have locked themselves into an inbred and even incestuous complex, and they are incapable of thinking beyond their self-interest and traditional concepts of agricultural research.

The short range research policy of the land grant system is the product of the annual budgeting process and the substance of that research budget is determined by the Agricultural Research Policy Advisory Committee (ARP-AC), which reports directly to the Secretary of Agriculture. Its members are the agricultural research establishment taken from USDA and the land grant community.

The National Association of State Universities and Land Grant Colleges is the home of the land grant establishment. Their particular corner in the Association is the Division of Agriculture, composed of all deans of agriculture, all heads of state experiment stations and all deans of extension. With eight members on the 24-man ARPAC board, NASULGC's Agricultural Division plays a major role in the determination of research priorities and budgets. The division also represents the land grant college complex before Congress on budget matters.

The top rung on the advisory ladder is USDA's National Agricultural Research Advisory Committee. This 11-member structure currently includes representatives from the Del Monte Corporation, the Crown Zellerbach Corporation, AGWAY, Peavey Company Flour Mills, the industry-sponsored Nutrition Foundation and the American Farm Bureau Federation.

Most national advisory structures are dominated by land grant scientists and officials, but whenever an "outsider" is selected, chances are overwhelming that the person will come from industry. A series of national task forces, formed from 1965-1969 to prepare a national program of agricultural research, were classic examples of this pattern. Out of 32 task forces, 17 listed advisory committees containing non-USDA, non-land grant people. All but one of the outside slots on those 17 committees were filled with representatives of industry, including General Foods on the rice committee, U.S. Sugar on sugar, Quaker Oats on wheat, Pioneer Corn on corn, Liggitt & Myers on tobacco, Procter & Gamble on soybeans and Ralston Purina on dairy. Only on the "soil and land use" task force was there an adviser representing an interest other than industrial, but even there, the National Wildlife Federation was carefully balanced by an adviser from International Minerals and Chemical Corporation.

Agribusiness Links to Land Grant Campuses

The giant agribusiness corporations and the land grant complex are linked in an extensive interlocking web. Corporate executives sit on boards of trustees, purchase research from experiment stations and colleges, hire land grant academics as private consultants, advise and are advised by land grant officials: they go to Washington to help a college or an experiment station get more public money for its work, publish and distribute the writings of academics, provide scholarships and other educational support, invite land grant participation in their industrial conferences and sponsor foundations that extend both grants and recognition to the land grant community.

Money is the catalyst for this tight web of relationships. It is not that a huge sum of money is given—industry gave only $12 million directly to state agricultural experiment stations for research in 1969. Rather it is that enough money is given to influence research done with public funds.

Corporate money goes to meet corporate needs and whims, and these needs and whims largely determine the research program of land grant colleges. A small grant for specific research is just good business. The grant is tax deductible either as an education contribution or, if the research is directly related to the work of the corporation, as a necessary business expense. Not only is the product wrapped and delivered to the corporation, but with it comes the college's stamp of legitimacy and maybe even an endorsement by the scientist who conducted the research. If it is a new product, the corporation can expect to be licensed, perhaps exclusively, as the producer and marketer. Everything considered, it amounts to a hefty return on a meager investment.

There is a long list of satisfied, corporate customers. Prime contributors are chemical, drug and oil corporations. Again and again the same names appear—American Cyanamid, Chevron, Dow Chemical, Esso, Eli Lilly, Geigy, FMC-Niagra, IMC Corporation, Shell, Stauffer, Union Carbide and The Upjohn Company are just a few of the giants that gave research grants to each of three colleges checked (University of Florida, North Carolina State University and Purdue University). Chemical, drug and oil companies invested $227,158 in research at Florida's Institute of Food and Agricultural Science, for example, accounting for 54 percent of research sponsored there by private industry in 1970.

Land Grant Research Foundations

At least 23 land grant colleges have established foundations to handle grants and contracts coming into their institutions for research. These quasi-public foundations are curious mechanisms, handling large sums of money from a wide array of private and public donors, but under practically no burden of public disclosure.

A funding source can give money to a private research foundation, which then funnels the money to a public university to conduct research. By this shell game, industry-financed research can be undertaken without obligation to make public the terms of the agreement. The foundation need not report to anyone the names of corporations that are making research grants, the amounts of those grants, the purpose of those grants or the terms under which the grants are made.

These foundations also handle patents for the colleges. When a corporation invests in research through a foundation, it is done normally with the understanding that the corporation will have first shot at a license on any patented process or product resulting from the research. On research patents that do not result from corporate grants, the procedure for licensing is just as cozy. At Purdue University, for example, a list is drawn of "responsible" companies that might have an interest in the process or product developed, and the companies are approached one by one until there is a taker.

Because of these complex and tangled funding procedures it is often difficult to discover exactly what the land grant complex is doing. For example, most agricultural experiment stations offer an annual report in compliance with the Hatch Act disclosure provisions, but these reports are less than enlightening. Some do not list all research projects, but merely list highlights. Most do not include money figures with the individual projects, and very few reveal the source of the money. Instead they contain only a very general financial breakdown, listing state, federal and "other" funds received and expended. Few offer any breakdown of industry contributions, naming the industry, the contribution and the project funded; and none of the reports contain any element of project continuity to show the total tax investment over the years in a particular investigation.

Data are not supplied uniformly, are not collected in a central location and either are not reported or reported in a form that cannot be easily obtained or understood. Even more significant is the fact that many fundamental questions go unasked and fundamental facts go unreported.

The land grant college complex has been able to get by with a minimum of public disclosure—and with a minimum of public accountability. Millions of tax dollars annually are being spent by an agricultural complex that effectively operates in the dark. The farmer, the consumer, the rural poor and others with a direct interest in the work of the land grant complex can get no adequate picture of its work.

Congress is no help; it does not take the time to probe the system, to understand it in detail and to direct its work in the public interest. It is here that the public might expect some serious questions of research focus—and some assertion of public rather than private interests. But it just does not happen. Congress has relinquished its responsibility and authority to single-minded officials at USDA and within the land grant community. Like spokesmen of the military-industrial complex, these officials and their allies come to the Capitol at appropriations time to assure a docile Congress that its investment in agricultural hardware is buying "progress" and that rural pacification is proceeding nicely.

There is nothing inevitable about the growth of agribusiness in rural America. While this country enjoys an abundance of relatively cheap food, it is not more food, not cheaper food and certainly not better food than that which can be produced by a system of family agriculture. And more than food rolls off the agribusiness assembly line—including rural refugees, boarded-up businesses, deserted churches, abandoned towns, broiling urban ghettoes and dozens of other tragic social and cultural costs.

The solution to the problems of rural America is not a return to the hand plow. Rather, land grant colleges researchers must get out of the comfortable chairs of corporate board rooms and get back to serving the independent producer and the common man of rural America. It means returning to the historic mission of taking the technological revolution to all who need it, rather than smugly assuming that they will be unable to keep pace. Instead of adopting the morally bankrupt posture that millions of people must "inevitably" be squeezed out of agriculture and out of rural America, land grant colleges must turn their thoughts, energies and resources to the task of keeping people on the farm, in the small towns and out of cities. It means turning from the erroneous assumption that big is good, that what serves Ralston Purina serves rural America. It means research for the consumer rather than for the processor. In short, it means putting the research focus on people first—not as a trickle-down afterthought.

It is the objective of the Task Force on the Land Grant College Complex to provoke a public response that will help realign that complex with the public interest. In a recent speech concerned with reordering agricultural research priorities, Dr. Ned Bayley, Director of Science and Education for the USDA said that, "the first giant steps are open discussion and full recognition of the need." The Task Force report has recognized the need and is prompting an open discussion. The time for action is at hand.

SUGGESTED READINGS

Dollar Harvest by Samuel R. Berger (Lexington, Mass.: D. C. Heath, 1971).

Eat This Book: How the Department of Agriculture Serves Corporations Instead of Farmers by Martha M. Hamilton (Washington: Agribusiness Accountability Project, 1972).

Factories in the Field by Carey McWilliams (New York: Barnes & Noble, 1967).

Sowing the Wind: A Report for Ralph Nader's Center for Study of Responsive Law on Food Safety and the Chemical Harvest by Harrison Wellford (New York: Grossman Publishers, 1972).

Section X

Movements

In a way, institutions are frozen answers to burning questions. But answers (adequate or inadequate, humane or inhumane) are arrived at, not generated in a vacuum. Movements are collective institutional answers in process. Some will go on to be fully institutionalized; others will prove to be abortive solutions, at best serving the interests of a few.

In "Black Liberation and Women's Lib," La Rue presents us with an insightful comparison of two current social movements in American society. She suggests that the initial commonalities of the black liberation and women's liberation movements are based primarily on rhetoric. She sees the two movements as looking the same to the casual observer but as not having the same basis. Arguing that blacks are oppressed while women are *repressed*, she poses the idea that, in fact, sexism abets racism. Finding both racism and sexism very American, La Rue develops the idea that the solution of the double bind of these two evils is through role integration and a break away from the American sexual paradigm that traps blacks and whites into stereotypical thinking about alternative futures.

For more than a century, various workers' movements have been a vital part of the history of Western societies. Glaberman hypothesizes that unionism in the United States may be reaching its limits in "Unions vs. Workers in the Seventies: The Rise of Militancy in the Auto Industry." Labor relations, Glaberman asserts, are made up of company and union representatives, not workers. The union structure, through full-time stewards and payroll checkoffs, has reduced direct worker pressure, yielding one-party government in the big American unions. With a new and changing American working class, the real struggle, he says, will occur outside the unions.

Blacks, women and workers make up widely recognized movements in American society. There are, however, many other movements that provide insight into collective behavior precisely because of their outer nature. The cryonics movement is one example. Bryant and Snizek, in "The Iceman Cometh: The Cryonics Movement and Frozen Immortality," provide us with a case study of the rise and fall of a movement that attempts to answer one of mankind's most pressing problem: death itself. Cryonics became a full-scale movement in the late 1960's amid considerable publicity. It offered a technological solution to the problem of death. Employing the motto "Never Say Die," cryonics offered a self-reliant, secular and technological religion to its members. It became a means of living out Woody Allen's fantasy in the movie "Sleeper." But popular interest and membership has shrunk in the face of costly procedures, and boredom has followed the first flush of excitement in being part of a scientific vanguard. The authors suggest that this movement has gone from a vanguard to a cult to a lunatic fringe grouping. They also point out, however, that belonging to a movement provides many other functions for members besides the obvious, announced goals of the movement itself—fellowship, camaraderie, a "quasi-community." These characteristics are part of many, if not all, social movements.

In "Audiences, Art and Power," Berger expands on the theme of how styles may be transplanted from a movement (the vaguely defined "youth movement" in this case, with its attendant "culture") to another sphere. Berger argues that the "rock concert style" has been brought into the college classroom. The result is a reduction of social distance between professor and student, just as the rock concert encourages a reduction in social distance between performer and audience. Under this new definition of the situation, audiences (and, by extension, classrooms of students) become constituencies. The performer (professor) becomes a "leader." Professor Berger avers that this is the result of accepting "epistimological democracy," i.e., the notion that there are an infinity of ways of arriving at provisional truths.

1 *Linda J. M. La Rue*

Black Liberation and Women's Lib

There is always a market for a movement. For Women's Liberation, the market will see to it that, in great quantity and unceasing redundancy, the message of "liberation" gets pushed in a way that women want to hear it, see it and believe it. The market will appeal to their early consciousness with daring historical heroines, myths of great women in crisis, valid and half-baked truths about women's separatism and a new society, deeds or self-defense against exploitation and words and words, pasted, paraded and published so often that they reel, as tired old truths will, pounding the walls of that early consciousness until there is a rip or tear and the beginning of "sobering." And well it should be; it is necessary—it is also familiar.

It was barely 20 historical minutes ago that blacks first celebrated their new consciousness with the palm wine of self-appreciation and the pursuit of liberation. We, too, sang of our fine dark heroes, sported our elaborate dashikis, passed both half-baked and valid tales of our virtues among ourselves and made corporations like Johnson and Company not uncomfortably rich from their sale of "Afro-sheen." And well it was; it was necessary—but it was both unfamiliar and painful.

This essay will speak to the sobering moments in both movements as a new crisis imperceptibly creeps up on an entity who is both black and woman. To date little synthesis has been proposed between the problems of the liberation of women and of blacks. Indeed, it seems that just when Eldridge Cleaver's tribute, "To All Black Women From All Black Men," had at least anesthetized the psychic degradation of mutual disdain and distrust existing between black men and black women, there emerged a new movement to reincense black women against black men and re-open the old wounds with salty agitation. Women's Liberation has and will affect black liberation. The question is how.

At this time, there is little need to enumerate what will eventually come to be cliches of women's "oppression" thoughout the ages. As for accentuation and denunciation of past injustices, let us allow the women in the first stages of consciousness to write that commentary. They will be much more diligent in researching "oppression's" sordid details. It suffices to say, as Gordon Allport pointed out, "For some people . . . women are viewed as a wholly different species from men, usually an inferior species. Such primary and secondary sex differences as exist, are greatly exaggerated and are inflated into imaginary distinctions that justify discrimination."

What is Bad About it?

Let us first discuss what the movement literature calls the "common oppression" of blacks and women. This is a tasty abstraction designed purposely or inadvertently to give validity and seriousness to the women's movement through an appeal to universality of plight. Every movement worth its revolutionary salt makes these headliner generalities about common oppression with others. However, let it be stated unequivocally that the American white woman has had a better opportunity to live a free and fulfilling life, both mentally and physically, than any other group in the United States, excluding her white husband. Thus, any attempt to analogize black oppression with the plight of the American white woman has all the validity of comparing the neck of a hanging man with the rope-burned hands of an amateur mountain climber.

"Common oppression" is fine for rhetoric, but it does not reflect the actual distance between the oppression of the black man and woman who are unemployed and the "oppression" of the American white woman who is "sick and tired" of *Playboy* fold-outs, of Christian Dior lowering hemlines or adding ruffles or of Miss Clairol telling her that blondes have more fun. What does the black woman on welfare who has difficulty feeding her children have in common with the discontent of the suburban mother who has the luxury to protest washing the dishes on which her family's full meal was consumed?

The surge of "common oppression" rhetoric and propaganda may lure the unsuspecting into an intellectual alliance with the goals of Women's Liberation, but this is not a wise alliance. The problem is not that women do not need to be liberated from the shackles of their present unfulfillment, but rather that the depth, the extent, the intensity, the importance, indeed the suffering and depravity of the real oppression blacks have experienced can only be minimized in an alliance with women who have heretofore suffered little more than boredom, gentle repression and dishpan hands

This disproportion of urgency and need can be seen in a hundred examples. It is a fact that when white women received their voting rights most blacks—male and female—were systematically disenfranchised and had been that way since after Reconstruction. And even in 1970, when women's right of franchise is rarely questioned, it is still less than common for blacks to vote in some areas of the South. Or take the tastelessly joined plight of oppressed middle-class and poor women in the matter of abortion. Actual circumstances boil down to this: middle-class women decide when it is convenient to have children, while poor women decide the prudence of bringing into a world of already scarce resources another mouth to feed. Neither their motives nor their projects are the same. But current literature leads one to lump the decisions of these two women under one generalization, when in fact the difference between the plights of these two women is as clear as the difference between being hungry and out of work, compared with skipping lunch and taking the day off.

Recently, Women's Lib advocates demanded that a local women's magazine be "manned" by a woman editor. Other segments of the women's movement have carried on similar campaigns in industry and business. But if white women have heretofore remained silent while white men maintained the better positions and monopolized the opportunities by excluding blacks, can we really expect that white women, when put in direct competition for employment, will be any more open-minded than their male counterparts when it comes to the hiring of black males and females in the same positions for which they are competing? American history is not very reassuring that white females will be any less tempted than their husbands to take advantage of the fact that they are white in an economy that favors whites.

In short, one can argue that Women's Liberation has not only attached itself to the black movement but has done so with only marginal concern for black women and black liberation and functional concern for the rights of white women. It is entirely possible that Women's Liberation has developed a sudden attachment to the black liberation movement as a ploy to share the attention that it has taken blacks 400 years to generate. Max Weber speaks of this parasitic relationship:

> If the participants expect the admission of others will lead to an improvement of their situation, an improvement in degree, in kind, in the security or the value of the satisfaction, their interest will be in keeping the relationship open . . .
>
> The principal motives for closure of a relationship are, a) the maintenance of quality, which is often combined with the interest in prestige and the consequent opportunities to enjoy honour, and even profit, b) orientation to the scarcity of advantages in their bearing on consumption needs, and c) orientation to the scarcity of opportunities for acquisition.

The industrial demands of two world wars temporarily offset the racial limitations to mobility and allowed blacks to enter industry as an important labor force. Similarly, women have benefited from an expanded science and industrialization. With their biological limitations successfully brought under control by the pill and offset by automation, an impressively large and available labor force of women was created.

The black labor force, however, was never fully employed and has always represented a substantial percentage of the unemployed in the American economy. Presently, it may now be driven into greater unemployment as white women converge at every level on an already dwindling job market.

Ideally, Women's Liberation was considered a promising beginning of the "oppressed rising everywhere" in the typically Marxian fashion to which many blacks seem drawn. Instead, the specter of racism and inadequate education, job discrimination and even greater unequal opportunity will become more than ever before a function of neither maleness nor femaleness, but blackness.

Moreover, though most radical white Women's Lib advocates fail to realize the possibility, their liberation, if and when it comes, may spell a strengthening of other status quo values from which they also seek liberation. As more and more women participate in the decision-making process through the movement, the few radical women in the "struggle" will be outnumbered by the more traditional middle-class women. This means that the traditional women will be in a position to take advantage of new opportunities that radical Women's Liberation has struggled to win. Voting studies now reflect that the traditional woman, middle class and above, tends to vote the same way as her husband. Blacks have dealt with these husbands in the effort to secure jobs, housing and education; they know the unlikelihood of either blacks or radicals gaining significantly from the open mobility of less tolerant women whose viewpoints differ little from that of their husbands.

My concern at this historical moment is to prevent any unintelligent alliance of black people with white women in this new liberation movement. Rhetoric and anathema hurled at the right industrial complex, idealism that speaks of a final humanism and denunciations of the system that makes competition a fact of life do not mean that Women's Liberation has as its goal anyone else's liberation except its own.

It is time that definitions be made clear. Blacks are oppressed—and that means unreasonably burdened, unjustly, severely, rigorously, cruelly and harshly fettered by white authority. White women are only *suppressed*—and that means checked, restrained, excluded from conscious and overt activity. And there is a difference.

What is Good About It?

The dangers of an unintelligent alliance with Women's Liberation will bring some to conclude that female suppression is the only way to protect against a new economic threat. For others, a broader answer is required, which will enable Women's Liberation to be seen in perspective.

If we are candid with ourselves, we must accept the fact that, despite our beloved rhetoric of Pan-Africanism, our vision of Third World liberation and perhaps our dreams of a world state of multiracial humanism, most blacks still want the proverbial "piece of the cake." American values are difficult to discard, for, contrary to what the more militant "brothers" would have us believe, Americanism does not end with the adoption of Afro hairstyles on pregnant women covered in long African robes. Indeed, the fact that the independent black capitalism advocated in Richard Nixon's campaign speeches appeared to so many blacks as the way out of the ghetto into the light lends truth with a vengeance to the maxim that perhaps blacks are nothing more than black Anglo-Saxons.

More to the point, for this essay, is the striking coincidence of the rebirth of liberation struggles in the sixties with a whole platform of "women's place" advocates who immediately relegated black women to home and babies. I would argue that this is almost as ugly an expression of black Anglo-Saxonism as is an embrace of Nixon's concept of "black capitalism."

The study of many developing areas reflects at least an attempt to allow freedom of education and opportunity to women. Yet black Americans have not adopted the developing areas' new role paradigm, but rather the Puritan-American status of "home and babies" advocated by the capitalist Muslims. This reflects either ingrained Americanism or the lack of the simplest imagination.

Still, to say that black women must be freed before the black movement can attain full revolutionary consciousness is meaningless because of its malleability. It makes much more sense to say that black women must be freed from the unsatisfactory male-female role relationship, which we adopted from whites as the paradigm of the good family, because it indicates the incompatibility of white role models with the goal of black liberation. If there is anything to be learned from the current Women's Liberation, it is that roles are not ascribed and inherent, but adopted and interchangeable in every respect—except pregnancy, breast feeding and the system generally employed to bring the two former into existence.

Role integration, which will be proffered as the goal and the strength of the black family, is substantially different from the role "usurpation" of men by women, or vice versa. It points to what I see as an essential process of incorporation as equals, a permanent equality of merit, responsibility and respect. The fact that the roles of man and woman are deemed in American society to be natural and divine leads to false ego attachments to these roles. During slavery and following Reconstruction, black men felt inferior for a great number of reasons, among them that they were unable to work in positions comparable to the ones to which black women were assigned. With these female positions often went fringe benefits of extra food, clothes and perhaps elementary reading and writing skills. Black women were in turn jealous of white women and often felt inadequate and inferior because there was constantly paraded in front of them the white woman of luxury who had no need to work and who could, as Sojourner Truth pointed out, "be helped into carriages, and lifted over ditches, and . . . have the best place everywhere."

Yet, despite (or, rather, because of) this history, black people have an obligation, as do white women, to recognize that the designation of "mother-head" or "father-head" does not imply inferiority of one and the superiority of the other. They are merely arbitrary role distinctions that vary from culture to culture and circumstance to circumstance.

Thus to quip, as it has been popularly done, that the only place in the black movement for black women is prone is actually supporting a white role ideal; and it is a compliment to neither men nor women to advocate such sexual capitalism or sexual colonialism.

It seems incongruous that the black movement has sanctioned the revolutionary involvement of women in the Algerian independence movement, even though the circumstances modified and often alternated the common role models. At the same time, however, blacks have been duped into hating even their own slave grandmothers, who in not so admirable, yet equally frightening and demanding circumstances also modified and alternated the common role models of the black family.

Can it not be said that in slavery black women assumed an increasingly important place in the survival action, and that this informed their personalities and their sense of responsibility? And after being outraged, violated and tortured, could the black woman be expected to put herself back into her former state of mind and relive her behavior of an even more distant past?

The crux of this argument is essentially that blacks, since slavery and through their entire existence in America, have also been living in revolutionary circumstances and under revolutionary pressures. Simply because the black liberation struggle has taken 400 years to come to fruition does not mean that it is not every bit as dangerous or psychologically exhausting as the Algerian struggle. Any revolution calls upon the best in both its men and women. This is why Daniel Patrick Moynihan's statement that "matriarchy" is a root cause of black problems is as unfounded as it is inane.

Competition

How unfortunate that blacks and whites have allowed the most trying and bitter experience in the history of black people to be interpreted as the beginning of an "unashamed plot" to usurp the very manhood of black men! But the myth of a plot was perpetuated, and thus what brought the alternation of roles in Algeria was distorted and systematically employed to separate black men and women in America.

Black women take kindness for weakness. Leave them

the least little opening and they will put you on the cross . . . it would be like trying to pamper a cobra. [Eldridge Cleaver]

Unless we realize how thoroughly the American value of male superiority and female inferiority has permeated our relationships with each other, we can never appreciate the role it plays in perpetuating racism, and in keeping black people divided.

Most, but not all, American relationships are based on some type of "exclusive competition of the superior, and the exclusive competition of the inferior." This means essentially that the poor, the uneducated, the deprived and the minorities compete among themselves for the same scarce resources and inferior opportunities. At the same time, the privileged, middle-class, educated and select white minorities compete with each other for rather plentiful resources and superior opportunities for prestige and power. Competition between the two large groups is rare due to the fact that elements who qualify are almost invariably absorbed to some extent (note the black middle class) by the group to which they seek entry. It will be understood that in this situation there is only one equal relationship between man and woman—black and white—in America, and this equality is based on the ability to force one's way into qualifying for the same resources.

Instead of attempting to modify this competitive definition within the black movement, many black males have affirmed it as a way of maintaining the closure of male monopolization of scarce benefits and making the "dominion of males" impenetrable to black females. This is, of course, very much the American way of exploitation.

The order of logic which makes it possible to pronounce, as did Robert Staples, that "black women cannot be free *qua* women until all blacks attain their liberation" assumes that black women will be able to separate their femaleness from their blackness—and thus will be able to be free as blacks, if not free as women; or that male freedom ought to come first; or finally that the freedom of black women and men and the freedom of black people as a whole are not one and the same.

Only with the concept of role integration can we hope to rise above the petty demarcations of human freedom that America is noted for, and that are unfortunately inherent in Staples' remark. Role integration involves the realization of two things. The first of these is that ego attachments to particular activities or traits must be abolished as a method of determining malehood and femalehood. Instead, ego attachments must be distributed to a wider variety of tasks and traits in order to weaken the power of one activity in determining self-worth. And the second is the realization that the flexibility of a people in effecting role alternation and role integration has been a historically proven asset to the survival of any people—witness Israel, China and Algeria.

The unwitting adoption and the knowing perpetuation by black people of the American sexual paradigm reflect three interrelated situations: a) black people's growing sense of security and well-being, and their failure to recognize the extent of black problems; b) black people's overidentification with the dominant group, even though the survival of blacks in America is not assured; and c) black people's belief in the myth of "matriarchy" and their subsequent rejection of role integration as unnatural and unnecessary.

While the rhetoric of black power and the advocates of cultural nationalism laud black people for their ability to struggle under oppressive odds, they simultaneously seek to strip away or incapacitate the phenomenon of role integration—the very means by which blacks were able to survive. They seek to replace it with an intractable role separation that would completely sap the strength of the black movement because it would inhibit the mobilization of both women and men. It was this ability to mobilize black men and women that guaranteed survival during slavery.

A Warmed-Over Throne

The strength of role integration is sorely overlooked as blacks throw away the hot comb, the bleach cream, the lye—yet insist on maintaining the worst of American values by placing the strength of black women in the traction of the white female status. I should think that black men would want a better status for their sister black women—indeed, that black women would want a better status for themselves—than a warmed-over throne of women's inferiority, which some white women have so recently abandoned. If white radical thought has called upon the strength of all women to take a position of responsibility and power, can blacks afford to relegate black women to "home and babies"?

The cry of black women's liberation is a cry against chaining a very much-needed labor force and agitating force to a role that belongs to impotent, apolitical white women. Blacks speak lovingly of the vanguard and the importance of women in the struggle yet fail to recognize that women have been assigned a new place, based on white-ascribed characteristics of women rather than on their actual potential. The black movement needs its women in a position of struggle, not prone. The struggle that blacks face is not taking place between knives and forks, at the washboard or in the diaper pail. It is taking place on the labor market, at the polls, in government, in the protection of black communities, in local neighborhood power struggles, in housing and in education. Can blacks afford to be so unobservant of current events as to send their women to fight a nonexistent battle in a dishpan?

Even now, the black adoption of white evaluations of women has begun to show its effects on black women in distinctive ways. The black liberation movement has created a politicized, unliberated copy of white womanhood. Black women who participated in the struggle have failed to recognize, for the most part, the unique contradiction between their professed renunciation of capitalist competition and their acceptance of sexual colonialism. The failure of the black movement to resolve or even deal with this dilemma has perpetuated the following attitudes in politicized black women in America:

- The belief in the myth of the matriarchy. The black woman has been made to feel ashamed of her strength, and so to redeem herself she has adopted from whites the belief that superiority and dominance of the male are the most "natural" and "normal" relationship. She consequently believes that black women ought to be suppressed in order to attain that "natural balance."

- Because the white woman's role has been held up as an example to all black women, many black women feel inadequate and so ardently compete in "femininity" with white females for black male's attention. They further compete with black females in an attempt to be the "blackest and most feminine," thereby superior to their fellow black sisters in appealing to politicized black men. They compete also with the apolitical black female in an attempt to keep black males from "regressing" back to females whom they feel had more "practice" in the traditional role of white women than they have had.

- Finally, the black woman emphasizes the traditional role of women, such as housekeeping, children, supportive roles and self-maintenance, but she politicizes these roles by calling them the role of black women. She then adopts the attitude that her job and her life is to have more children who can be used in the vanguard of the black struggle.

Black women, as the song "Black Pearl" relates, have been put up where they belong—but by American standards. The birth of Women's Liberation is an opportunity for the black movement to come back to its senses. The black woman is demanding a new set of female definitions and a recognition of herself as a citizen, companion and comrade, not a matriarchal villain or a stepstool baby maker. Role integration advocates the complementary recognition of man and woman, not the competitive recognition of same.

The recent unabated controversy over the use of birth control in the black community is of grave importance here. Black people, even the "most liberated of mind," are still infused with the ascribed inferiority of females and the natural superiority of males. These same values foster the idea of "good blood" in children. If, indeed, there can be any black liberation, it must start with the recognition of contradictions such as that involving black children.

It gives a great many black males pride to speak, as Robert Staples does, of the "role of the black woman in the black liberation struggle [as] an important one [which] cannot be forgotten. From her womb have come the revolutionary warriors of our time."

Conceiving of Bastards

How many potential "revolutionary warriors" stand abandoned in orphanages while blacks rhetoricize disdain for birth control as a "trick of the Man" to half the growth of black population? Why are there not more revolutionary couples adopting black children? Could it be that the concept of bastard, which is equivalent to inferiority in our society, reflects black Anglo-Saxonism? Do blacks—like whites—discriminate against black babies because they do not represent "our own personal" image? Or do blacks, like the most racist of whites, require that a child be of their own blood before they can love that child or feed it? Does the vanguard, of which Dr. Staples so reverently speaks, recognize the existence of the term "bastard"?

Would it not be more revolutionary for blacks to advocate a five-year moratorium on black births until every black baby in the American orphanage was adopted by one or more black parents? Then blacks would really have a valid reason for continuing to give birth. Children would mean more than simply a role for black women to play, or fuel for the legendary vanguard. Indeed, blacks would be able to tap the potential of the existing children and could sensibly add more potential to the black struggle for liberation. To do this would be to do something no other modern civilization has ever done, and blacks would be allowing every black child to have a home and not just a plot in some understaffed children's penal farm.

What makes a healthy black baby in an orphanage different from "our own flesh and blood"? Except for the value of inferiority-superiority, and the concept of "bastard" that accompanies it, there is nothing "wrong" with an orphaned child save what white society has taught us to perceive.

If we confine our reading to the literature of the Women's Liberation movement, it appears that women are just one more group in the march of the rising oppressed masses. If we see it as it is, however, Women's Liberation is a clear threat to an already dwindling job market. It is a threat to the economic well-being and progress of blacks and other minority groups. The few positions opening up in areas of power will be greeted with a surge of new applicants, which means that some women (I expect them to be generally white) will be hired in an effort to be "fair to all oppressed groups" or to be "an equal opportunity employer." Women's Liberation will probably end up having used the black movement as a stepping-stone to opportunities in a highly competitive economy. Women's Liberation represents another mouth to feed in a very stingy economy. In short, it will probably mean less for groups that are really oppressed, since distribution does not care who has been in the line the longest (and it is the squeaky hinge that gets the oil).

At the same time, however, we must see Women's Liberation as a light in which blacks can rediscover their deeply ingrained American values. Had the crisis of Women's Liberation not emerged, we would never really have recognized the myth of matriarchy or the new assignment of black women to roles that radical white women are already vacating. Through Women's Liberation we can see how deeply indoctrinated many blacks are by the concept of inferiority. This is true to the extent that when speaking of their wives and children they have employed American values of their worth and American definitions of their meaning.

Most importantly, we can conclude that black women's liberation and black men's liberation is what we mean when we speak of the liberation of black people. The one cannot be mentioned without implying the other. Many suspect that Women's Liberation will enhance the distrust and dissension existing between black men and black women. I maintain that the true liberation of black people depends on their rejection of the inferiority of women, the rejection of competition as the only viable relationship between men and their reaffirmation of respect for man's general human potential in whatever form—man, child or woman—it is conceived. If both men and women are liberated, then competition between the sexes no longer exists, and sexual exploitation becomes a remnant of social immaturity.

SUGGESTED READINGS

The Authoritarian Personality by T. Atorno et al. (New York: Harper & Row, 1950).

"A Cross-cultural Survey of Some Sex Differences in Socialization" by H. Barry, M. K. Bacon and I. L. Child in the *Journal of Abnormal and Social Psychology*, *55*, 1957, pp. 327–332.

The Black Woman edited by T. Cade (New York: Signet, 1970).

Black Skin, White Mask by Frantz Fanon, translated by Charles Lam Markham (New York: Grove Press, 1967).

"Women as a Minority Group" by Helen Hacker in *Social Forces*, April 1951. See in connection with the appendix to Gunnar Myrdal's *The American Dilemma.*

Sex and Temperament in Three Primitive Societies by Margaret Mead (New York: William Morrow, 1935). Also see the review by R. Thurnwald in *American Anthropologist*, *38*, 1936, pp. 558–561.

2 *Martin Glaberman*

Unions vs. Workers in the Seventies

On the morning of July 16, 1970 the *Detroit Free Press* featured on its front page a large five-column picture of General Motors Vice President Earl Bramblett and UAW President Leonard Woodcock shaking hands as they opened negotiations for a new contract. The headline beneath the picture read: "Negotiations Begin; Auto Talk Key: Living Costs."

The banner headline that morning, overshadowing the ritual start of negotiations, was: "Ousted Worker Kills Three in Chrysler Plant Shooting; 2 Foremen, Bystander Are Slain." A black worker at Chrysler's Elden Avenue Axle Plant, suspended for insubordination, had killed two foremen (one black, one white) and a Polish setup man.

The timing of the events was coincidental—but it is the kind of coincidence that lends a special insight. What is at issue—not only in the auto negotiations but in most relations involving American workers, unions and management—is not living costs but living. Involved is not just dollars and cents, important as always to workers, but an entire way of life.

Take a close look at the union's demands. The UAW left out only one thing: the demand to turn the plants over to the workers. Apart from the usual wage increases and financial improvements, some of the issues raised by the UAW bargaining teams included: pensions after 30 years instead of after a specific age; restoration of the escalator cost-of-living clause to its original form; ending time clocks and putting production workers on salary; inverting seniority so that older workers could take the time off at nearly full pay in the event of layoffs; the problem of pollution, both in the plants and in the community; changing production to deal with boredom on the assembly line. Many of these issues were raised purely for propaganda effect with little intent to bargain seriously over them. But taken as a whole, they provide an interesting picture that reflects, if only in a distorted way, the extent of the worker's concern for the nature of his workplace.

Public Show of Militancy

This technique in bargaining was developed by Walter Reuther and is being continued by Woodcock. It gives the public appearance of great militancy but it means something very different. While the leadership of the union goes through the motions of accepting all the workers' demands and pressing them on the companies, the tactic of publicly demanding almost everything that could be thought of at the beginning of negotiations is intended to get the workers off their backs and keep them quiet when the serious negotiating begins in secret sessions. It leaves the union leadership free to work out any settlement it thinks reasonable and to establish its own priorities in the negotiations.

The range of union demands in the auto negotiations also reflects something else. It is a sign that unionism in the United States is reaching its limit. Not because they will win so little, but because they will win so much and it will prove to be so little. It will not make the life of the black worker at the Eldon Avenue plant of Chrysler or the white worker at the GM Chevrolet plant in Flint one bit more tolerable.

That is one of the reasons that the union leadership has such a hard time with the new generation of young workers in the plants. They tell the workers about the great victories of the union in the past and what it was like in open shop days. They tell the truth—those were genuine victories. But they have become transformed into their opposite by virture of becoming incorporated into contracts and the whole process of what is called labor relations. (Labor relations, it should be noted, has nothing to do with workers; it has to do with relations between company representatives and union representatives.)

The *Detroit Free Press* published the following report in August 1970:

> Some 46 percent of General Motors' hourly workers are below age 35. They have never known a depres-

sion, they have had more schooling than the man who lived through the last one, and they aren't impressed by the old Spartan idea that hard, repetitive work is a virtue.

They are less responsive to authority than even the men who seized the Flint GM plants in the historic 1936-1937 sit-down strikes.

That is precisely the background against which discontent is surfacing throughout the industry today, discontent that has reached its most advanced stage in the auto industry.

At the time of the dispute at the Chevrolet Vega plant in Lordstown, Ohio, production on the assembly line had been rationalized to the point where a job took 35 seconds. There are two categories of time that are difficult to visualize from outside the factory. One is 35 seconds. You cannot light a cigarette or get a drink of water in 35 seconds without a car going by on the assembly line. The other category is the rest of your life. This is where the worker expects to be for all of his working life—accumulating seniority. How can one express the tensions that are inherent in such a situation—doing a job that takes 35 seconds for the rest of your life?

The formation of the CIO in the 1930s settled once and for all the idea that owners or managers or stockholders had the right to run their plants any way they saw fit. Sit-downs, strikes, wildcats, direct on-the-job action, sabotage and violence established the power of workers in the plants. The tactics used and the extent of that power varied from plant to plant and from industry to industry.

Sabotage and violence have long been a part of the auto industry. There were reports of the murder or disappearance of foremen at the Ford Rouge plants in the days before the union; the recent murder of two foremen at a Chrysler plant is not an especially new development. Other forms of sabotage are less severe but nonetheless effective. On some assembly lines where the links are exposed, an occasional rest period or slow down is achieved by the simple (and virtually undetectable) tactic of putting the handle of a long open-end wrench into the chain to shear the pin and stop the line. Sometimes the light bulb that signals the line breakdown is unscrewed or broken so that an extra few minutes are gained before the stoppage is discovered.

Not uncommon is the sabotage of the product. Sometimes this increases the amount of the repair work coming off the lines. Sometimes this saddles a customer with a built-in rattle in a high-priced car because some worker welded a wrench or some bolts into a closed compartment.

The nature of violence and sabotage as a tool of American workers provides an insight into the problems caused by the extensive technological changes of the past 20 years. Although generally called automation, something else is involved: the first and basic reason for technological change is the struggle against workers' power by the employers. Technological advance is designed, directly or indirectly, to eliminate workers or to make them more subservient to the machine. And most changes made in plants are made solely to increase production rather than out of any concern for the workers.

For example, Chrysler stamping operations are now centered in the Sterling Township Stamping Plant, about 15 miles outside Detroit. The plant now does operations that were formerly done at the Dodge, Plymouth and Chrysler plants. Separating 4,000 or so workers from most of their fellows seriously reduced the power and effectiveness of the workers. The shutting down of old plants means that formal and informal organizations are broken up or abandoned. And it takes time for new relations and new organizations to be worked out. Workers at Sterling have indicated that it took approximately four years for the plant to be transformed from just an accidental combination of workers to a relatively well organized and disciplined force.

In the early days of the union the power of the workers could be wielded more openly and more directly. Workers negotiated directly with the lower levels of management and were able to settle things right on the shop floor. How easily they were able to do this depended, of course, on their relative strength and the nature of the technology involved among other things. As an example, the workers in the heat-treat department at the Buick plant in Flint had an especially strong position. One time, shortly after the union was established, they felt themselves strongly aggrieved. But the early contracts did not rigidly define the grievance procedure. So instead of locating the violated clause and leaving their fate to a bureaucracy, they simply sent the steward to see the general foreman. Since their interest in this discussion was very great, they accompanied the steward and stood around outside the foreman's office while the discussion was going on. The time they picked for this meeting was just after they had loaded a heat into the furnace. The heat was scheduled to emerge from the other end of the furnace 20 minutes later. If the heat was not pulled at that time the damage to both the steel being treated and to the furnace itself would have been irreparable.

In the early stages of the discussion the foreman was adamant. He would not accede to the demands—"and you'd better get those guys back to work." As the minutes sped by, the foreman became less and less adamant until, finally, with a couple of minutes left to go, he capitulated. The steward then signalled the workers standing outside and the heat was pulled.

That might be an extreme situation but it was not an unusual one. Workers are very aware of how their jobs fit into the total process of production. To change the scale and to change the time: almost 30 years later, during a wildcat at the Sterling Stamping Plant of the Chrysler Corporation in 1969, the workers made clear their awareness of how their plant fit into the scheduling of Chrysler plants in Detroit, Windsor, Ontario, St. Louis and elsewhere. They knew when and in what order the Sterling strike would shut down other Chrysler plants. The knowledge of the workers' importance in the overall framework is both an instrument in the day-to-day struggle and the essential basis for a new society.

Unions vs. Workers

The instinctive assertion of their own power on the shop floor that workers managed in the thirties was extended in the forties when war production requirements and the labor shortage forced the government and the corporations to make concessions to workers' control. But that was also the period during which the separation of workers from the union structure began. The last major organizing success marks the turn to bureaucracy.

When Ford fell to the union in 1941, both the check-off and full time for union committeemen were incorporated into the contract. But the apparent victories only created more problems. Workers wanted full time for union representatives to get them out from under company pressures and discrimination. Getting elected steward often got you the worst job in a department and stuck away in a corner where you couldn't see what was happening. But full time for stewards did more than relieve union representatives from company pressure — it ended up by relieving representatives from workers' pressure. The steward is less available than he was before, and you have to have your foreman go looking for him should you happen to need him.

The check-off produced a similar situation. Designed to keep the company from pressuring weaker workers to stay out of the union even though they were sharing in its benefits, the check-off ended up reducing worker pressure on the union officials. No longer does the steward have to listen to workers' complaints each month as he goes around collecting the dues. Once a month the dues are delivered in one huge check from the company to the union and the worker never sees his dues payment.

One-Party Governments

American entry into World War II finished what the Ford contract had begun. The top layers of the union leadership were incorporated into the government boards and agencies that managed and controlled war production. In return certain concessions were made in terms of union organization. Union recognition was often arranged from above without the participation of the workers in strike or other action. At this point in time the lower levels of the union leadership were still pretty close to the workers and very often local union officials participated in and supported the numerous wildcat strikes that took place.

This process of bureaucratization was completed with Walter Reuther's victory and his substitution of the "one-party state" in control of the union for the democratic kind of factionalism that had been the norm in the UAW before. And with the Reuther administration the union moved to participate directly in the management and discipline of workers in production. All through the fifties, with intensive automation and decentralization going on in the auto industry, the union collaborated in crushing the numerous wildcat strikes, in getting rid of the most militant workers, in establishing labor peace in the industry.

In the other industrial unions the pace of bureaucratization was much more advanced. In steel, for example, Phil Murray kept a tight and undemocratic hold on the Steel Workers Organizing Committee until after the basic contracts had been negotiated with United States Steel. It was only then that the Organizing Committee appointed from the top was replaced by an autonomous union which could vote on its own officers or contracts. Any worker can illustrate the bureaucratic history of his own union.

The grievance procedure became virtually worthless to the workers. In 1955 at the termination of a contract presumably designed to provide a grievance procedure, there were in some GM plants as many as 10,000 unresolved grievances. The situation has not improved since then. GM complains that the number of grievances in its plants has grown from 106,000 in 1960 to 256,000 in 1969 or 60 for each 100 workers.

What are these specific local grievances? They involve production standards: the speed of a line, the rate on a machine, the number of workers assigned to a given job, the allowable variations in jobs on a given line. They involve health and safety standards: unsafe machines, cluttered or oily floors, rates of production which prevent the taking of reasonable precautions, the absence or misuse of hoists or cranes, protection from flames or furnaces, protection from sharp, unfinished metal, protection from welding or other dangerous chemicals or fumes, the right to shut an unsafe job down until the condition is changed.

They involve the quality of life in the plant: the authoritarian company rules which treat workers like a combination of prison inmate and kindergarten child, the right to move about the plant, the right to relieve yourself physically without having to get the foreman's permission or the presence of a relief man, the right to reasonable breaks in the work, the right to a reasonable level of heat in the winter or reasonable ventilation in the summer. And on and on.

The grievances that crowd the dockets of General Motors and of other companies cover the total range of life in the factory. The fact that they are called grievances helps to conceal what they really are—a reflection of the total dissatisfaction of the workers in the way production is run and of the desire of the workers to impose their own will in the factory. The UAW and the Ford Motor Company recently have been discussing the problem of boredom on the assembly line. The only reason they are discussing it at all—it is by no means a new development—is because more and more workers are refusing to accept factory discipline as a law of nature. And it is not boredom but power which is at stake.

The same worker who for eight hours a day attaches belts to a motor and can't wait to get out of the plant will spend his weekends tinkering with his car and consider it rewarding work. The difference is in who controls the work.

It might be worth noting a couple of things. All workers are exploited to one degree or another. But office workers on the whole do not have to walk past armed guards going to and from work and have a certain amount of freedom in scheduling their work on the job. The coffee break is not a blue-collar institution. It is clear that historically bosses never thought that workers would work without the severest external discipline and control. And they still don't.

In addition, no matter what all the theoreticians of capitalism may say, workers are treated very differently from anyone else. The Industrial Division of American Standard has a plant in Dearborn, Michigan which manufactures industrial air conditioning. The company places ads in trade journals urging employers to air condition their facilities. The office section of the facility is air conditioned. The plant is not. The only thing that makes this situation unusual is that the company manufactures the equipment. But even that isn't enough to get them to provide for blue-collar workers what office workers, engineers, managers and professionals now take as a matter of course.

In 1958 a major depression in the auto industry marked a new stage. Packard, Hudson, Murray Body and other auto companies went down the drain. Employment began to drop considerably and led to the development of new theories about the impending disappearance of the industrial working class and the elimination of the black American from gainful employment. The actual developments were quite different.

The reorganization, technological change and decentralization that characterized the fifties and culminated in the depression gave way to a new expansion which brought significant numbers of blacks and young workers into the industry. These are workers, as the *Detroit Free Press* noted, who couldn't care less about what the union won in 1937. They are not more backward (as the UAW bureaucrats like to pretend) but more advanced. They are attuned to the need to change the nature of work, to the need of human beings to find satisfaction in what they do.

It is this new and changing working class that was the basis for the new level of wildcat strikes, for a doubled rate of absenteeism, for an increased amount of violence in plants where guns are often openly carried. It is a new working class that no conceivable contract settlement can control or immobilize.

Both unions and industry are aware of their problem to some degree. The union wants management to contribute to a Training and Education Fund that the union will use to educate and develop a new corps of porkchoppers. "The UAW believes," says the *Free Press*, "that a better-trained corps of union stewards would be better equipped to cope with these issues and with gut plant problems like narcotics, alchoholism, loan-sharking, weapon-packing, pilfering and gambling. 'A bunch of armed guards isn't the only answer,' said one committeeman."

After 33 years of unionism, they have suddenly discovered that armed guards are not the answer. To put it plainly, they have suddenly discovered that armed guards are not enough.

The slowdown of automation in the sixties (a consequence of the shortage of capital) has led to a relative stabilization. That is, workers in new installations and in old ones that have been reorganized have now had a few years to work out new forms of organization. The complaints against the young workers who make up a crucial force in the factories indicate that the wildcats of the past may be replaced, or at least supplemented, by something new.

The tightly knit structures of the big industrial unions leave no room for maneuvering. There is no reasonable way in which young workers can use the union constitution to overturn and overhaul the union structure. The constitution is against them; the money and jobs available to union bureaucrats are against them. And if these fail, the forces of law and order of city, state and federal governments are against them. If that were not enough, the young workers in the factories today are expressing the instinctive knowledge that even if they gained control of the unions and reformed them completely, they would still end up with unions—organizations which owe their existence to capitalist relations of productions.

The impossibility of transforming the unions has been argued by a number of obervers. Clark Kerr has noted, without disapproval, that "unions and corporations alike are, with very few exceptions, one-party governments." That is the phrase usually reserved for Stalinist or fascist totalitarian governments. But it is not overdrawn. Paul Jacobs has documented this in the case of the unions:

> A study of 70 international union constitutions, the formal instruments that rule a membership of almost 16,000,000 workers, shows among other things that in most of these 70 unions power is generally concentrated in the hands of the international presidents, with few restraints placed upon them, that discipline may be enforced against union members with little regard for due process, and that opposition to the incumbent administration is almost impossible.

And all of this is what young workers are revolting against.

That means that the course of future developments in the factories of America has to be sought outside the unions. Caucuses and factions will still be built and, here and there, will have temporary and minor successes. But the explosions that are still to come are likely to have the appearance of new revolutionary forms, organizations which are not simply organs of struggle but organs of control of production. They are a sign of the future.

SUGGESTED READINGS

False Promises by Stanley Aronowitz (New York: McGraw-Hill, 1974).

Alienation and Freedom by Robert Blauner (Chicago: University of Chicago Press, 1964).

Autocracy and Insurgency in Organized Labor, edited by Burton H. Hall (New Brunswick: *Trans*action, Inc. 1972).

The Company and the Union by William Serrin (New York: Alfred A. Knopf, 1973).

Counter-Planning on the Shop Floor by Bill Watson (Radical America, 1972).

3 *Clifton D. Bryant & William E. Snizek*

The Iceman Cometh

Death—unexplained and inexplicable—has always preoccupied mankind. An enormous amount of intellectual energy has gone toward developing value systems which permit man to cope with his fears of dying and the dead. Rapid technological advance, proliferation of scientific discovery and expansion of knowledge have dispelled many traditional fears of spirits and ghosts. At the same time these forces have also eroded the effectiveness of systems of religious thought in neutralizing the prospect of death. Recent successful efforts to prolong, manipulate and moderate life render even more distasteful the prospect of total annihilation of self. In light of all these factors, man has sought alternate intellectual, even technological mechanisms for handling his anxieties concerning dying and death.

Cryobiology

In 1947, Robert C.W. Ettinger, an ex-GI who was convalescing in a Michigan hospital from a wound sustained in World War II, read of the work of Jean Rostand in successful freezing and thawing of frog sperm. Fired by the implications of the experiments for humans, Ettinger saw the possibility of freezing the dead to preserve them until the day when medical help or widespread immortality might be forthcoming. As he recalled in a later interview in *Cryonics Reports*, 1966, "It struck me then that, even if suspended animation or LTA (low temperature anabiosis) techniques were not fully perfected, one could freeze the newly dead, accepting whatever degree of freezing damage was unavoidable, and still have a non-zero chance of eventual revival."

Ettinger sent a one-page summary of his hypothesis to several hundred people randomly selected from *Who's Who*. When only a few persons responded, he realized the necessity of a more detailed and convincing exposition and presented some of the validating scientific evidence in a manuscript entitled *The Prospect of Immortality*. Ettinger privately published it in 1962, and in 1964 it was published by Doubleday. (It has subsequently appeared in a paperback edition.) The book had some limited, favorable but largely guarded, response from the scientific and medical communities. Ettinger's proposal for frozen immortality attracted considerable attention in the popular press. In time he wrote articles for such periodicals as *Esquire*, and his book appeared in serialized form in several newspapers. It was also translated and published in a number of foreign countries. He was a guest on numerous radio and television shows and for a time became something of a prophetic personage, albeit celebrity, throughout the country. His proposal attracted a considerable following of visionaries, who wished to be in the frosty vanguard. For members of the emerging movement, Ettinger was to be their prophet, and *The Prospect of Immortality*, their holy writ. The true believers awaited their marching orders.

The Cryonics Movement

Shortly after the publication of Ettinger's book, persons in various parts of the country began to meet, compare notes and take action on "cryonic internment." A Life Extension Society was formed. In 1965 a Cryonics Society was organized in New York by several persons interested in both "cryogenic internment" and the logistical problems of such a procedure. The name *cryonics* (referring to the activities surrounding human cold storage) was coined by a vice president of the group. Appropriate legal documents and mechanisms for setting up life insurance trust funds for financing frozen "suspension" were developed. In 1966, a dozen interested persons met in Robert Ettinger's home in Oak Park, Michigan, and two weeks later organized themselves as the Cryonics Society of Michigan. Another group in Los Angeles was organized as the Cryonics Society of California. One individual in Arizona began to manufacture "capsules" for the storage of frozen "patients," as well as to build a facility to house them. He also acquired a license to freeze and store bodies. A national conference of the Life Extension Society was held in 1966 in Washington, D.C. The New York society began to publish a periodical devoted to the cryonics enterprise, the *Cryonics Reports*. (Basically a newsletter, it contained interviews with notables such as Ettinger, a chronological log of signal events in the movement and accounts of recent suspensions.) Within a few years, it assumed a slicker format and a more esoteric title, *Immortality*, and circulation grew to several hundred. By the time of Expo 70 the theme of frozen suspension was considered to have sufficient public interest to justify an elaborate Immortality Pavilion exhibit at the Montreal International Exposition. Among other components of the exhibit were an architect's model of a giant storage facility for frozen bodies—a wheel-like structure called a "cryosanctorum," and coffin-like "resting pockets" in the wall of an auditorium from which Expo visitors could view a short film depicting the freezing process. The faithful were enraged at what they perceived as a banal and misleading effort at publicizing cryonics and attacked the exhibit as lacking seriousness of purpose in the Winter 1971 edition of *Immortality*.

Cryonic Suspension

The aim of cryonic (cryogenic) internment is simple. The recently dead individual is subjected to a series of cooling procedures which will prevent the physical deterioration of the body. Stored at a supercool temperature, the person in cryonic suspension will theoretically "keep" indefinitely. Ultimately medical science may evolve to the point where the cause of the individual's death could have been prevented and even death itself can be reversed. At that time, the frozen corpse could be thawed, death reversed, the cause of the terminal condition cured and the "patient" returned to a normal active life. A corollary hope is that of reversing the effects of the aging process. The important thing is to halt the cellular deterioration of the deceased body as soon as possible after death. (Ideally, freezing an individual before death would make him the perfect candidate for cryonic suspension.)

The freezing of a human body for indefinite preservation is a multistage process. First, after the "patient" has been declared clinically dead, the blood is drained and the body cooled to about 10° C. The arteries and lungs are then perfused with a glycerol fluid to help retard cellular damage due to the expansion of ice crystals following freezing. Once this protective fluid has been injected into the vascular system, the "patient" is wrapped in aluminum foil to protect against accumulated frost due to condensation, and stored in a dry ice container similar to a coffin at a temperature of -79° C. From the temporary dry ice box, the "patient" is later transferred to a permanent cryonics suspension capsule, resembling a large hot water heater, and stored in liquid nitrogen at -196° C (-320° F). At this temperature molecular movement, for all intents and purposes, ceases, thereby arresting further cellular deterioration.

The initial cost of encapsulation is approximately $10,000. This amount covers the cost of chemicals, capsule, preparation and handling of the body, and one year's storage. Continued storage and replacement of liquid nitrogen costs about $1,200 per year. No fixed monetary amount has yet been projected for the restoration to "life and health" of the body, should medical science progress sufficiently to enable such an undertaking.

Apart from the technical and financial aspects involved in the freezing process, there is a legal element as well. Individuals who desire encapsulation are encouraged to personally contract to have their bodies frozen upon death, rather than leaving the necessary arrangements to a relative or close friend. All too often, when such a contract has not been made formally, those individuals entrusted with carrying out the deceased's wishes have reneged. Individuals are encouraged to sign a notarized "cryonic suspension agreement" between themselves and a Cryonic Suspension Society, and to take out an insurance policy for at least $20,000 naming the society as beneficiary.

The Suspended

The cryonic Columbus of the present ice age was James H. Bedford, a 73-year-old retired professor of psychology who died of cancer and was frozen on January 12, 1967, in Los Angeles, according to his wishes. He was shipped to Phoenix, Arizona, to be placed in one of the first "cryocapsules." Because of excessive nitrogen boil-off, he was transferred to a new capsule and was ultimately returned to California for final storage. Several years later, when little had been heard of him, cryonic enthusiasts around the country became alarmed lest he had been secretly thawed. To resolve the matter, a special squadron of the Cryonics Youth Association was dispatched on a fact-finding expedition. Happily, they were able to report that Bedford was "frozen and well in Southern California." Bedford's cryonic internment was of sufficient historical note that a book, *We Froze the First Man*, was written about the event by Robert F. Nelson, a participant in the enterprise.

Within a short time, other members of the Cryonics Society died, and the movement snowballed. Steven Jay Mandell, a 24-year-old aeronautical engineering student at New York University, was an avid science-fiction fan. Having seen, in one of his science-fiction magazines, an ad placed by the Cryonics Society of New York, Steven fell in with the ranks of believers. He joined the society, gave the necessary instructions and set up a Cryonics Society trust fund to pay for his eventual freezing. Seven months later he was dead of cancer and, with the help of five members of the Cryonics Society, funeral directors prepared him for cryonic suspension. Mandell, who had been fearful of brain damage in thawing, had taken the precaution of preparing an audio-tape, to be frozen with him, of the experiences of his life which he wished to retain when revived.

Other "patients" included Helen Kline, who "passed through clinical death" in 1968 in a California Hospital and was cryonically suspended and placed in temporary storage in the face of some opposition by relatives. Unfortunately the problem of finances delayed the prospect of permanent storage.

In 1967, Marie Sweet, an early member of the Life Extension Society and ardent booster of the movement, died in California. Although she had prudently taken out a $3,000 life insurance policy to provide for her own cryonic suspension, the amount was inadequate to purchase a cryocapsule, and as a makeshift arrangement she was wrapped in tin foil and packed in dry ice (which must be replenished weekly) in a casket. As with Helen Kline, an appeal was also made for funds for Marie Sweet.

There were numerous abortive attempts at placing "patients" in cryonic suspension. When, for example, New Yorker Andrew D. Mihak died of a heart attack in 1968, his wife decided on the spur of the moment that she wished to have her husband frozen. After many complications, members of the New York Cryonics Society helped the funeral director get Mihak through the initial stages of cryonic suspension. After two days, however, grim reality had to be faced. Mrs. Mihak was essentially impecunious, and the other relatives were reluctant to assume financial responsibility for the body. Mihak was thawed, and inasmuch as he was a World War II veteran, was given a military funeral in the Long Island National Cemetery.

Fifteen or 16 individuals are reported to have been cryonically suspended. Experts have, however, indicated that some of these individuals have since been thawed. In addition to whole bodies, one couple sent a tissue specimen of their drowned son to be frozen and stored, on the slight chance that ultimately science might be able to reconstruct or regenerate the individual, in the same manner as is now possible with some plants such as a carrot. The "patients" in permanent storage are widely scattered—some in a facility in Long Island, some in a facility in Southern California and others throughout the country.

There does not seem to be a real common denominator in terms of the frozen vanguard. It is a population of both sexes, various ages, of differing economic circumstances, and dissimilar occupational, educational and social characteristics. According to N. L. Ross, in an article in the August 13, 1972, Washington *Post*, Ettinger himself has asked: "Who were these frozen corpses in life? Their one common bond . . . was their love of life. Otherwise they ranged in age from 8 to 74, were of all three major religious faiths and many occupations, and died of a variety of causes: heart attack, cancer, kidney disease, adrenal failure and even suicide." Those who made their own decision, however, did apparently seem to have one thing in common—they all preferred the frozen postponement of their destiny to the absolute finality of the grave.

Candidates for Freezing

Active members of the cryonics society who have themselves contracted to be frozen upon death or who have had some member of their immediate family frozen, share, above all else, a deep-seated concern regarding their eventual demise. Such individuals stress the fact that they have spent considerable time reflecting upon their own death. When questioned concerning the nature of these reflections, Saul Kent, secretary of the New York Cryonics Society, explained, "When you die you have the very nauseous feeling, I suppose, that everyone else in the world is alive and that you're the only one dying, you feel the whole world is deserting you . . . . And beyond this there's the fear of disappearing, of ***not being***, which is a very profound fear."

Activists in the movement firmly believe that their lives are worthwhile or highly meaningful. The cryonics movement represents a vehicle for perpetuating man's existence. So strong is this desire that for many the movement may represent a substitute religion. Unwilling to accept the promises of organized religions regarding a spiritual afterlife, cryonics members opt for a type of materialistic, active mastery over their own destinies. An unusually high proportion of cryonics members have bomb shelters, and fly their own planes—giving another indication of an unwillingness to place their lives in someone else's hands.

According to intensive interviews and content analysis of cryonics publications, the large majority of cryonics advocates are atheists with above average education and lower-middle to middle socioeconomic status. Many are devotees of science fiction.

Our technology-oriented society places a high value on innovation and novelty. Western societies have tended to deify science. Our superb research labs and splendorous science buildings on university campuses are our temples of science, the white smocked practitioners, the priesthood, and our gigantic research budgets, the offerings of supplicants. Science presumably also has an aura of adventure. For the layman, to be an intimate participant in a scientific undertaking of possible historical import is a truly exhilarating experience.

Many persons have been drawn into the cryonics movement because of the chance to be at the pioneering forefront of new discovery. Steven Mandell, the science-fiction fan, stands as an example. His mother described his scientific appetite in an interview in the March 1969 issue of *Cryonics Reports:*

> If my son, Steven, would be one of the lucky ones who could be brought back and made physically well 200 years from now, I think he'd have a ball. He'd love to learn anything that was new and futuristic. He was the kind of kid who would have liked to have been in the first rocket to the moon and he'd have a ball. I hope that it will be a good and better world. We don't know, of course. But I think he'd love it.

One wall of a Long Island cryonic storage facility is decorated with a floor-to-ceiling mural of the moon and outer space. This particular mural has been frequently used as a backdrop when photographing a patient being placed in a cryocapsule.

On yet another level, the cryonics movement offers a strong element of fellowship, camaraderie and ingroupness which is attractive and fulfilling to the membership. It represents, in effect, a community of intellectual adventure and shared participation in the novel and the unknown. The president of the New York Cryonics Society described this phenomenon to L. R. Chevalier. "As soon as you get into this movement, it changes you," he said. "It's 'us,' and the rest of you are 'the others.' "

The discussion meetings, the fund-raising banquets and dances, the conventions and perhaps most of all the group effort often required to implement the cryonic suspension decision of a recently dead convert has thrown the members together in an enterprise of shared endeavor and adventure. The movement even proved to be a fertile setting for romance and marriage. On Saturday, May 18, 1968, Karl Werner, vice president of the Cryonics Society of New York, and Glenda Allen, treasurer, were married by a minister from the Founding Church of Scientology. There is undoubtedly some appeal in being involved in a fellowship of the "enlightened." Some of the leaders and spokesmen for the movement have become national "celebrities" as a result of their widespread publicity in popular periodicals and their numerous appearances on radio and television shows. The fame from being involved may well be more personally rewarding than the ultimate realization of the long-term objective of the movement.

Icy Salvation

A manifest long-term goal of cryonics members is physical immortality; yet even this lofty ideal is tempered with stark realism. Both officers and rank-and-file members of the movement who were interviewed made it clear that at this stage of technological development the chances of revival are admittedly quite minimal, yet a chance, however slim, does exist. As one cryonics spokesman told Chevalier, "If there's a chance that I can come back to life, I'm going to take that chance . . . after all, it's really the only crap game in town. If you're cremated or embalmed and buried to rot in the ground, you're through. If you're frozen, you have a chance."

The prospect of death also arouses anxieties concerning the physical deterioration of the body. The cryonics movement has apparently attracted a large number of individuals who can not face the thought of decomposing after death. In all interviews conducted, references were continually made to the repulsiveness of decaying, rotting or decomposing after death. Gillian Cummings, for example, told N. L. Ross of her sense of elation upon seeing her father encapsulated, in seeing him as she had remembered him, and of her reassurance in knowing that the worms weren't getting him. The frozen "patient" retains a lifelike appearance. One cryonics society official said, in referring to a suspended body and the accumulation of frost on his face, "The frost is due to condensation . . . . When you wipe him off, he looks as good as he did the day he died."

Relatives of suspended loved ones apparently find comfort in this aspect of cryonic suspension. The son of Mildred Harry, who paid a substantial amount to have his mother frozen, says he is "very satisfied with the arrangements and happy every time he sees his mother's freckles beneath her make-up; she also wears purple robes and jewelry."

Cryonic suspension permits a redefinition of death itself as survivors conceptualize the deceased person as simply "frozen but not gone." Steven Mandell's mother, for example, has stated:

> When Steven was placed in the capsule, I was present and I didn't find it hard. There's nothing cemetery-like about it, or death-like. It's scientific. It's like having a patient people are working on, or trying to help. I feel very strongly that freezing a person is almost like doing a medical experiment on them. There's certainly nothing to lose—they're dead. Science has a great future and certainly, if there's any chance at all for Steven or for somebody else because of Steven, we haven't lost anything. Steven certainly hasn't.

Russ Le Croix Van Norden, the husband of Marie Phelps Sweet, speaks of his wife as "an arrested entity whom I hope to recover, although I don't know when," according to H. Junker in an article in *The Nation*, (April 1968). Ann Deblasio's husband maintains a perpetual Christmas tree in the storage facility where his wife's capsule is kept and for a time visited her capsule daily. Gillian Cummings had difficulty initially adjusting to her father's death. After she saw the lifelike appearance of her father in the capsule, she even began to spend some nights at the storage facility in order to be close to him. The motto of the cryonics group is "Never Say Die."

The Melting of a Social Movement

The muezzin cry of Robert C.W. Ettinger was heard, but few heeded the call. In the years since his book first appeared, less than a dozen and a half have actually made the icy trip to "storage." The total membership of the New York Cryonics Society, once numbering in the hundreds, is now down to a few dozen and no formal meeting of the group has been held since 1971. Other state groups have experienced a similar decline in membership and participation. Subscriptions to *Immortality* dropped to the point where publication has ceased. Cryonic suspension storage facilities such as the one on Long Island are still in operation, but with minimal occupancy. In a few instances, storage facilities had no individuals in cryonic suspension, permanent or otherwise. Some of the firms that had hoped to ride the tidal wave (or glacier) of consumer demand are now defunct. Popular interest has dwindled and the scientific community displays something less than enthusiastic optimism concerning the viable prospects of cryonic suspension and ultimate revival.

To what elements can the melting of this social movement be attributed? First, perhaps, there is the very factor that first attracted many—the excitement of being in the vanguard of scientific discovery. Exhilaration, unfortunately, gives way to tedium and ennui in the face of frustration, failure or lack of progress. The faithful expressed an awareness that scientific breakthroughs in reviving frozen corpses might be long in coming, but their span of patience was presumably shorter than they realized. When there were no dramatic scientific developments, many simply lost interest.

Money appears to have been a significant factor in the decline of the movement. The public membership response even at the peak of its appeal was never sufficient to finance the formal aspects of the movement adequately. The aspiring cryonics business ventures apparently did not succeed for the same reason. Cryonic internment and subsequent storage and maintenance is expensive. Ultimately, of course, volume might have brought the price down, but for many individuals an approximate initial outlay of $10,000 and a subsequent $600 to $1,200 per year maintenance fee simply brought their icy aspirations down to a warmer reality. As previously mentioned, in at least one instance a wife had her husband temporarily suspended in dry ice only to discover that she did not have the financial resources for permanent suspension. Others who, like Marie Sweet, went so far as to take out insurance policies against such an exigency were denied permanent suspension after death inasmuch as their estates could not afford capsules. Still others had economic problems once suspended. James H. Bedford, the first man frozen, left an estate of $100,000 to the California Cryonics Society to insure his perpetual maintenance. At the time of his suspension, Bedford's son, Norman, gave evidence of complying fully with his father's wishes. More recently, however, he has gone to court in an attempt to break his father's will. The owner of a California storage facility claims he was never paid for four people whom he froze. Of those in suspension who were later defrosted at the wish of relatives, at least two were buried and one was preserved, but in a less financially burdensome formaldehyde solution. The insurance company refused to pay on Steven Mandell's policy, and even with a donation from his mother, the officials of the New York Cryonics Society were still placed in the position of initially subsidizing his suspension. In the case of Steven Mandell and Ann Deblasio, it became necessary to stage a fund-raising dinner-dance to add to the depleted coffers of the "Ann Deblasio-Steven Mandell Memorial Foundation."

The beneficial aspects of novelty finally wore off, and the estranging experience of the bizarre set in. The popular press became less charitable, and ridicule and derision became more common. "Patients" were acidly referred to as "corpsicles" by some wags. The followers were labeled by critics as a "cult," an offensive term to some cryonics enthusiasts. Rather than being billed as the scientific vanguard, some cryonics spokesmen were instead being presented more as the lunatic fringe. The common bond of exhilaration and pioneering commitment to the novel began to erode and the participants were increasingly forced to close ranks until finally only a small hard core of the faithful (many of whom had a financial stake in cryonics) remained. Although at one time a panel of distinguished scientists and physicians was listed in cryonics publications as the "Scientific Advisory Council," by 1972 the ***Journal of the American Medical Association*** was editorializing against the "propriety of physicians letting their names be used in cryonics literature."

In their enthusiasm to sell the cause, followers may well have oversold it. Some have publicly boasted of their intention to become "immortal supermen"; other spokesmen have suggested future "super armies that never wear out, thanks to a continued supply of rejuvenated men." Such remarks are hardly calculated to convey the image of rational reform. The cryonics movement, like any other attempt at scientific and social innovation, inevitably attracts its share of eccentrics, and writers who covered some of the early conferences and meetings of cryonics groups reported "odd mixtures of people," and specifically mentioned "vegetarians." Funeral directors, clergymen, physicians and public officials, never enthusiastic as a whole about cryonics, are presumably more rigid in their posture of opposition than in the early days, when innovation and prospect outweighed practical disadvantages.

Cryonic suspension techniques may one day be perfected. Given the cultural orientation of the American public, it is not surprising that a number of individuals became sufficiently enamored of postponing the inevitability of death that they would consent to being frozen and stored, or collaborate with such a procedure for their friends and family. Cryonic suspension for a time met various unfulfilled needs for many individuals. But given the seeming slowness of scientific implementation of the cryonics hypothesis, the exigencies of cost and effort, and the erosion of popular support, the movement was doomed to inertia. For the near future, the prospect of frozen immortality seems to have melted.

SUGGESTED READINGS

The Prospect of Immortality by Robert C. W. Ettinger (New York: Macfadden Bartell, 1964).

We Froze the First Man by Robert Nelson (New York: Dell, 1968).

"Sociological Symposium," Fall 1968 (special issue on the sociology of death).

4 Bennett M. Berger

Audiences, Art and Power

These kids can't stand professionalism because it makes them feel inferior. The spectacle of someone exercising a hard-earned skill doesn't always inspire them with admiration. Yet these same kids are instinctive egalitarians, brought up to believe that they're just as good as the next fellow. So the logical resolution of the conflict is to adopt as hero the Schlemiel, the Ugly Duckling, the Super-goof—all those types that distinguish themselves in ways that are not threatening or hard to match with personal identification.

From a review by Albert Goldman
in *Life* of some soon-to-be forgotten
heroine of pop culture.

I want to begin with examples—in the hope that by describing the occasions which stimulated my thinking, that thinking will seem more plausible. Several years ago I went to a performance of *Marat/Sade*, given in the round. It was my first experience of "new" theater. The actors came down the aisles from the rear, already "in role." The play began and ran its course, a major part of which includes the several inmates of the lunatic asylum behaving in a randomly insane manner: slouching around the stage, mumbling inaudibly, scratching, looking blearily at the audience and making aggressive, insane gestures—sort of doing their thing, one might say. When the performance I attended was over, the audience apparently did not know it; there was no culturally familiar ending; the action just ran down, sputtered like a dying engine and then stopped. The audience, therefore, did not get (or missed) its signal to applaud; we sat there restless, anxious, looking for a cue to what was to happen next. Finally, one of the actors, in a manner continuous with his insane role, began to clap his hands very slowly, demonstratively, as one might teach a child, all the while gazing at the audience with what seemed, alternatively, patronization and contempt, in an apparent attempt to give it its cue. Gradually there was a sprinkling of applause, never, however, getting to the magnitude that would have been due even a poor performance. Then the actors went off the stage as they had come, the inmates muttering what seemed like insults and making angry faces at the audience. To this day I do not know whether this was all part of the play or whether it was a contemptuous response by the troupe of actors to a particularly inept matinee audience.

Then, during the exciting and murderous spring of 1968 I went to a performance by Dick Gregory on my campus. He filled an enormous auditorium to overflow, and his voice was piped outside to hundreds more standing in the patios surrounding the auditorium. I mention the size of the crowd only because in the middle of his performance, it suddenly occurred to me ("I flashed," as contemporary parlance has it) that were he to reappear two weeks later with exactly the same show, he would fill the auditorium again—which suggested to me that the audience did not come to hear his jokes and line of patter (which they would have already heard). Which, in turn, raised for me the question of what it is he does, what the genre is, and why the people turn out for it in the numbers they do. Was it a comedy routine? Yes, it was that. A lecture? Yes, it was that. A political rally? Yes, it was that too. A happening? Cèrtainly. A rap? Perhaps that is the best term for Gregory's genre. But in spite of the questions about genre (and with new or ambiguous genres, response is always problematic because there are no established criteria of evaluation to guide and govern response), it seemed clear to me that the audience was not there (nor would they come again) to critically appreciate his wit, his wisdom or his inventiveness, for it seemed to me that they laughed and cheered equally for his good jokes and his bad ones and for his ironies when they were sharp-edged and when they were dull.

Then, about a year and a half ago I went to a joint concert given by a local symphony orchestra and a rock group called It's a Beautiful Day. I went because I knew a member of the symphony who told me that the two groups had been rehearsing some unusual musical experiments which I might find interesting. (But I did not anticipate the differences in the norms that govern audience behavior with symphony orchestras and rock groups, nor consider the question of which norms might prevail.) When I got to the hall, about ten minutes before the scheduled start of the concert, I saw immediately that the audience seemed to be more than half teenagers (the concert had been heavily promoted in the area's high schools and was given the night before a school holiday) and that there were lots of police standing around the lobby. Inside the hall, there was a mass of movement: paper airplanes (made from programs) flying through the air, tangles of legs swinging over the balcony rails, people shouting to friends on the opposite side of the hall, random couples necking thither and yon, knots of kids visiting each other's seats in animated conversation—a very high level of background noise. Ten minutes after curtain time the audience began to clap, whistle and in other ways demand that the music begin. Finally, the rock group came out from the wings to thunderous applause, whistles, rebel yells and shrieks of "White Bird!" "White Bird!"—the group's then current hit record. The group did four of five songs (none of them "White Bird"), the applause at the end of each only moderately audible over the general noise level, which never did die down. The paper airplanes continued to fly, people continued to move through the hall, visiting, talking with friends, moving up close to the stage to sit in the aisles, with further occasional demands for "White Bird" audible through the hubbub. Finally, It's a Beautiful Day went off (they had been playing on a platform at stage front); the curtain was raised, and there was the symphony orchestra ready in their chairs. Cheers, whistles, rebel yells, more paper airplanes soaring across the heads of the audience, clunks of coke cans dropped on the floor, and at one point an enormous crash of something toward the back of the hall—perhaps a whole row of attached folding chairs toppling over backward. Then the conductor strides out from the wings, dressed not in white tie and tails, but in bell bottom pants and an aqua see-through blouse with balloon sleeves and ruffles down the front. Deafening cheers, hoots, whistles, yells, more paper airplanes, more clunks of coke cans. The conductor smiles sweetly, slightly embarrassed but not entirely displeased; the audience is not hostile, just noisy. He bows with elaborate formality (more hoots, cheers, whistles, airplanes), turns to the orchestra, baton in hand, raises his arms to ready the players, then after 20 seconds or so slowly drops them as he realizes that the noise level has not lowered at all. He turns his head, gives the audience a baleful, gently reproving look, turns again to the orchestra and raises his arms with apparent confidence that the audience had got the message. Only it hadn't. Or if it had it didn't care. Finally, someone in the audience shrieks "Shut up, will you!" and a sizable SHHH! rumbles through. The conductor turns to the audience and says, "Well, I'm glad somebody got the idea." And a third time he turns to the orchestra and raises his arms. But still the noise level did not lower much. Apparently giving in to the inevitable, the conductor gives the orchestra the signal, and the first few notes of the Beethoven Fifth Symphony are heard. That's as far as they got. At the dum dum dum DUM, the audience broke into an ecstatic roar. It was the equivalent of "White Bird." They knew that dum dum dum DUM; it was somebody's hit record, and they were duly responsive. And so it went through the concert. The noise never did die, the airplanes never did stop flying. The orchestra, I suppose, gradually realized that the audience's behavior was not evidence of unruliness or disrespect; there were just different rules, different modes of expressing delight or respect.

All That Ritual Jazz

I went also last year to a performance given by Nina Simone, which was sponsored by the Black Student Union at my campus. Now, I remember Nina Simone when she was merely a first class jazz singer, sitting at her piano in small night clubs, improvising beautifully in her throaty, staccato voice. At the University of California in Davis ten years later, she was a Queen of Black Culture. Backed by a group of dashiki-clad musicians, she strode about the stage exuding black pride, interspersing her songs ("Black is the Color of My True Love's Hair" became African) with invocations of the names of black heroes and heroines. I remember being slightly disappointed with her singing, but I remember too that I responded immediately to my own disappointment by recognizing the irrelevance of my own response. The evening was less a jazz recital than a celebration of Black Culture, hence my unconscious use of traditional standards of jazz criticism seemed absurd. She was less a jazz performer than a historical figure, less a singer than a ritual celebrant. As such, she was, of course, superb. Regal, imperious in her bearing, gifted (like Billie Holiday and Frank Sinatra or Paul Robeson and Artur Rubenstein) with that magnetism which, because we do not understand it well and cannot describe it thoroughly, we call "charisma," she got standing ovations for virtually every song she did from an audience whose pride in her very presence was palpable.

Shortly after the Nina Simone concert I went to see a couple of old movies from the mid-fifties (*East of Eden* and *The Caine Mutiny*) shown in the auditorium of an art school and sponsored by the school's film society. The audience was mostly hip types, probably art students from the school. I arrived a little late, but already the announced admission fee was no longer being collected at the door. The air was full of marijuana smoke and the sound of babies nursing contentedly at mothers' breasts. The audience was very noisy, relating to the movies in a quasi-camp style. They booed villains, cheered heroes, and at one point where an unsympathetic character said something particularly ugly and cruel to the young hero of one film, somebody in the audience shouted, "You dirty son of a bitch!" and hurled a beer can (it was not empty) at the screen.

I have not seen any live performances of The Living Theater, but I did read several versions of the events that took place a couple of years ago at a New York forum on problems of contemporary theater, which apparently turned into something not unlike a performance of The Living Theater itself. Some said it was in fact exactly that. The speakers were interrupted several times by obscenities from the audience. There were several violent arguments going at once, much microphone grabbing, and some personal assaults among members of the audience, while others were demanding their money back. And in the middle of the near riot, Judith Malina (co-director of The Living Theater) was heard remarking ecstatically that spontaneous chaos is better than theater, better than art.

Something analogous to at least some of the things I have been describing is happening in the classrooms of American universities and colleges. This was first brought home to me when I began to notice that my classes seemed much more lively, much more "successful" when I came to class relatively unprepared and lectured off the top of my head (rapped) than when I came armed with lecture notes, text, manuscript and other "material" which I conscientiously felt it important that the students know. This produced some conflict in me because I like to rap as well as the next man (and think I have some talent for it), and I found very gratifying the plainly visible interest of the students, the feedback, the admiring faces, their readiness to relate to me as a minor Guru. At the same time, though, my puritan sense of responsibility made me feel furtive and frivolous about my gratification. I wasn't being paid to give them the top of my head, but its depths; I felt responsible to "cover the material," to fulfill the implicit contract between the student and myself to follow the course outline, discuss the reading, stay within the confines of the catalogue description of the course. I felt obliged, in short, to follow the plan, the discipline of the course, rather than to engage in spontaneous interaction, Encounter-style, of intellectual and emotional confrontation, whose "interestingness" I had no doubt of, but of whose lasting academic value I was skeptical because the students seemed less interested in learning or knowing what I consciously had to teach them than they were in knowing me.

I had also heard of (though not myself personally experienced) lecture classes disrupted by shouts of (for example) "bull shit!" from students. And in conjuring up the profound shock and devastation of some traditional snowy-haired professor confronted by this kind of barbarism (with which he would probably have a trained incapacity to cope), I tried to imagine what I might do faced with such an utter and absolute assault on the authority of rational discourse in a university class. My heroic fantasy goes like this: some aggressive student shouts "bull shit!" at some innocuous fact that I mention. A hush falls over the class as they wait with barely repressed delight for my response to this assault on my adequacy. Aware of the character of the crisis, I pause, letting the silence grow in intensity. Then, very deliberately, I raise myself up to my full five feet six and one-half inches, lean forward, rest the heels of my hands on the edges of the lectern and shout with full volume (and just a hint of absurdity), "It is not bull shit," then pause again and say, "Are you going to say it is so bull shit?" then I'll shout still louder, "It is not bull shit. Where do we go from there?" Then as I watch the student's face collapse and shatter in five pieces, I turn gentle and fatherly and say "If all you mean is that you disagree with me, perhaps we can talk about it."

My guess is, however, that my imaginary antagonist may in fact have wanted something quite a bit more than merely to disagree with me. Something is indeed happening here, Mr. Jones, in theaters and in schools, and although perhaps no one fully understands what it is (except for hopeful references to "the revolution"), I think I know a little about what's happening and can describe some of it sociologically.

What's happening? First of all, the blurring of lines, the shortening of distances, the transcendence of barriers, symbolic and actual, between performers and audiences. How? By use (in theater) of things like arena stages, mixed media, continual feedback and audience participation; in school by use of seminar rather than lecture-type arrangements, group research and learning projects, encounter techniques, retreats and experimental living-learning arrangements. For evidence that these represent changes (or differences) with respect to the relation between performers and audiences, one should recall Howard Becker's old study of dance band musicians and the emphasis they put on erecting any symbolic line (a row of chairs would do) that could serve as a barrier between themselves and the dancers. Similarly, the more traditional professors resist vigorously most of the recent curricular innovations which tend to break down the formalities between students and professors.

The transcendence of barriers tends to transform the performer/actor/teacher from a persona into a person, from an enactor of a segmented, specific role into a living figure whom the audience wants to know or vicariously know as a human being rather than as a performing role. Every sociological theory that distinguishes between a primary and a secondary relationship (and they all do) testifies to the consequential character of the distinction; it is a very important transformation. In this process, audiences too are transformed—into constituencies.

As an audience is transformed into a constituency, its orientation toward the performer changes from one that is at least formally critical and/or appreciative of his talent/skill/knowledge (which he and his peers are better able to appraise than audiences) to one that is committed to him as a symbolic personage or figure whose value resides less in his command of that substantive talent/skill/knowledge than in his ability to intuit and reflect the shifting moods and needs and demands of his audience-become-constituency. Whereas an audience is interested in learning what the teacher has to teach or in the illumination of individual experience that the artist/performer has to offer to members of an audience, a constituency is interested in having its collective feelings stirred by the invocation of appropriate symbols, and its group identity expressed and validated through an affirmation of those symbols (or a desecration of negative symbols) by the figure/personage/performer who wields them.

These transformations present great temptations to the performer because they promise to lift the burden of alienation from his frail shoulders. The proverbial alienation of the modern artist/intellectual in the West is an alienation between himself and audiences who do not understand him or are indifferent or are otherwise incompetent to respond meaningfully to his work. One thinks again of Becker's musicians for whom the barrier of chairs symbolized their contempt for the audience. The audience was square; the musicians were hip, and the barrier reminded both parties of their alienation. But Becker's musicians suffered from a double alienation, for they were alienated not only from their audience but from their work as well, because they were playing mickey mouse dance music instead of their jazz art.

These two alienations are quite separable, although they may occur together also. The patronized poet of the eighteenth century who wrote love poems to order for his patron was literally alienated from his work but not from his audience. The modern poet may be starving in a garret (or eating organic vegetables in a communal house) and alienated from society but he is not alienated from his work. Lawrence Welk and Mick Jagger (an unlikely duo) have in common their identification both with their work and their audience. Becker's musicians had neither.

There are analogous patterns in the academic world. The metaphor of the ivory tower suggests the scholar's alienation from (or insulation against) audiences; the cry for relevance in teaching and research calls for a restoration of connection between teacher and student, researcher and researched. Like the artist's garret (that not-so-ivory-tower), however, the scholar's study may be the scene of the performer's very heavy identification with his work (although by no means necessarily), whereas even the most relevant kinds of academic work do not guarantee the scholar's identification with it.

An audience provides an end to alienation for a constituency can offer waves of love to a performer in exchange for his affirmation of them. The performer symbolically expresses or represents the hopes, desires or aspirations of the audience; the audience becomes the performer's constituency—his people. Such symbolic identification requires not one-way performers and spectators, givers and receivers, but two-way communication, dialogue, response, audience participation. The performer must look continually to his constituency for feedback reassuring him that he is invoking the right symbols—or not. The audience, rather than slowly mulling or absorbing the performance and responding only later at an appropriate, institutionalized moment, tends to prefer immediate responses (a "right on!" or a "bull shit!") so that the performer, knowing where they are at, may know where he is at. For example, at a hastily organized forum at my campus not long ago to discuss a volatile local issue, red, white, blue and green cards were distributed to all present with instructions to hold up one or another of them to indicate whether one wanted whoever happened to be speaking to stop, to go on or to indicate other degrees of approval or disapproval of what the speaker was saying. So, isolated experience between audience member and performer is replaced by an emphasis on "getting it together," on collective experience, on unity between performer and audience-as-constituency. The occasion, the encounter between performer and audience is transformed from one of segmental exchange into a celebration of ritual solidarity.

I said that the transformation of audiences into constituencies was a great temptation to the performer, and the quasi-religious connotations of that word require some explanation. I call it a temptation because it is, of course, difficult to resist the honor and the sense of power inherent in the invitation to become an integrative symbolic leader, the eliciter of affirmative feelings, good vibes, pride in membership in a constituency. But whether the temptation is resisted depends not only on the character of the invitation—or the demands—made by the constituency but also upon the particular kind of art/skill/talent/knowledge of the performer and his own relationship to the traditions of his own discipline.

Some art is directly people's art (today, most prominently rock, blues, folk art, ethnic art, youth art) and is therefore directly dependent upon its ability to express its audiences's feelings as distinguished from more traditional or classical forms whose original audiences or constituencies no longer exist in the sense that they did when the form was created. When these feelings take on an ideological character (the desire to have them publicly rendered, thus historical, thus traditional, thus legitimate), an audience becomes a constituency and a performer a leader. There is no performer-audience alienation here. But the problems of alienation from work may still be present, particularly when the performer's art/skill/talent/knowledge has a long tradition, a developed esthetic and a strong body of colleague-professionals who administer the standards of performance internally generated among the professional group. The art of the performer in this context is the analogue of scholarly rigor or objectivity in the academic context. Both pay heed to standards of performance internally generated by a group of colleague-professionals rather than to the audience-as-constituency. This overstates this case a bit, particularly where, as in the case of highly specialized or technical work—science, "difficult" poetry, nonrepresentational art, avant-garde music, the group of colleague-professionals may be near identical with the audience.) But academic work, too, can become people's art or people's science to the extent that the work is done in behalf of or in advocacy of the interests of the group that the work directly bears upon. And this is more likely to occur among scholars whose intellectual interests transcend the fields (or "ologies") in which they were trained than among those whose interests are central to their disciplines. My major point, then, is that technical or professional standards internally generated and administered by a group of colleagues can serve as a point of conflict or alienation between the performer-as-leader and the audience-as-constituency, and that that conflict is likely to be most severe and tension-ridden at the point where the performer must choose between playing to his peers or to the audience whose interests as a constituency have overridden its interests as an audience.

What I have been talking about is closely related to the contemporary issue of community control. Community control is a phrase that has developed mostly in the school context, but notice it is directly applicable to theater. Community controllers of schools usually come into conflict with professional educators on the grounds that professional biases run counter to or are irrelevant to community needs. In its more revolutionary version, the professional's very certification as a professional may be regarded as evidence of his incompetence. In the theater, community control means, as it does everywhere, "power to the people"—in this case to audience-as-constituencies who, like community controllers of schools, seek to wrest power over the professional performer from the group of colleague-experts.

This situation threatens the performer with alienation from work as the price of solidarity with his constituency. I think of what happened to Mort Sahl's work: when he lost his constituency he ceased to be funny, although he continued to behave as if he were a funny man, succeeding usually only in being pathetic. Or remember some of the problems of Soviet artists and intellectuals caught between what the people (or their spokesmen) demand and what their colleagues (at least some) respect. But the "new culture," if it has not exactly solved the alienation problem, has devised some interesting ways of coping with it—perhaps even transcending it, and I want to conclude by mentioning just two of these ways.

First, with respect to alienation from work: when standards of performance in traditional genres have become vulgarized, attenuated or irrelevant, audiences participate with performers in the creation of new genres in which standards of competence or quality are, as it were, up for grabs because there are no preexisting criteria of performance, esthetic or cognitive, which are widely shared. In the recent flowering of urban folk forms, for example, the fact that the performer participates in the creation of the genre helps him with respect to the problem of alienation from work. From the point of view of the audience, the fact that performance does not apparently require great skill, knowledge or training promotes easy solidarity because the audience's vicarious identification with the performer is abetted by their knowledge—or feeling—that "they can do it too." And they often can: musicians tell me that an average journeyman rock group is generally not much less skilled than superstar groups, and my bet is that every campus has at least one undergraduate who can sing almost as well as the voice on the latest smash hit record. Similarly, many current experimental programs in higher education involve joint participation by students and staff not only in the creation of the new curriculum but in the discovery of ways (and sometimes these are unprecedented) of appraising the success or failure of the whole enterprise. Indeed, sometimes the solidarities so engendered create as many problems as the alienation's to which they were a response.

Second, with respect to alienation from audiences: the new genres are often able to recapture lost or drifting audiences by making the audience the subject of the performer's art. Whether the subject be youth, hippies, students, black or other ethnic cultures, and the topic love and other sorrows or Viet Nam, poverty and other injustices, what relevance turns out to mean is that what one learns is oneself. Like a bridge over troubled waters, narcissism is the end of alienation.

All of this has a great deal to do with the cultural revolution, which is the latest great thrust of the principle of egalitarianism into the last remaining bastions of elitism. And its most interesting weapon is one called mind-blowing, for whether they know it or not (and at least some of them clearly do), cultural revolutionaries are practicing ethnomethodologists; break the unstated rules on which civil discourse (hence privilege) is based, and society falls apart. The point is to empty the mind of habitual perceptual categories, of the realities these categories define and the rules they imply. When the process is complete we will have been prepared for the ultimate democracy—metaphysical and epistemological democracy, in which all realities will be equal—although some will probably continue to be more equal than others.

Section XI

Deviants

Herculean efforts are put forth in every society to promote regularity in the behavior of members. A large part of the resources of any society are expended in order to ensure that the socialization process works and that individuals are "tied into" its institutions and culture. Under most circumstances, for most people, most of the time, these efforts pay off for those who benefit from having what is "normal" defined in a certain way. But we know that things do not work this way all the time. Some behave "abnormally" or hold attitudes that are "abnormal." Now, how does this come to pass? Both conforming and deviant behavior are results of the same basic processes. Some become deviant because they are labeled so. Still others personify the aphorism that "if you have the name you may as well have the game" and develop a deviant life-style because the normals expect them to. Others become deviant in a myriad number of ways. (Deviance, in fact, may be fathered by innovation and mothered by creativity. The history of science, art and the humanities is replete with examples of this kind of "deviance," from Michaelangelo to Einstein to Coltrane.) The point is that, as sociologists, it behooves us to think of "deviance" as problem solving outside the model ways of problem solving for any collectivity.

The notion of skid row evokes images in our minds of "bums," "drifters" and Salvation Army soup kitchens. Vander Kooi, in "The Main Stem: Skid Row Revisited," corrects that stereotype to an image of a dying piece of Americana where work, entertainment, lodging, food and other needs of transients are provided. Reputable transients—railroaders, seamen and others—as well as the less reputable types have long been the inhabitants of American skid rows. All together, the denizens of skid row have constituted a "casual labor force" that seems to be less needed now. Skid rows, moreover, constitute, as Vander Kooi tells us, a delicate and complicated social structure that is being ruthlessly exterminated by such forces as urban renewal and "upgrading." His practical solution to the "problem" of skid rows is a humane one: If they must go, we must provide some place that is reasonably congenial for the inhabitants—for example, halfway houses.

Unlike Vander Kooi's portrayal of skid row, a dying subculture in America, Carter's "Reform School Families" gives us a picture of the formation of a subculture, one that thrives in the single-sex communities that are young women's reform schools. We are given a fascinating glimpse into a world in which informal social organization and formal social structural arrangements of a "total institution" are compromised. In the reformatory, make-believe families are created (a distortion of the socialized need for family life, but needed nevertheless) and homosexual courting goes on, as well as adolescent peer group culture. Many of the same activities go on inside this small world that would go on outside of it, but through a glass darkly—distortions of traditional boy-girl relationships that are more symbolic and emotional than truly sexual. In discussing the number language that the girls create, Carter informs us that this coded language has two major functions: secrecy and the creation of emotional distance. The ambivalence of these activities (including ritual marriage ceremonies and family "traditions") provides necessary social control and protection but allows easier role alternation than such relationships would "on the outside." This functional role alternation is neatly illustrated in the rather easy movement of some of the girls between polar "butch" and "femme" role behaviors.

"Massage Parlors: The Sensuality Business," by Velarde and Warlick, demonstrates the difficult path taken by those stigmatized as deviants. In discussing the massage parlor business, the authors show how owners are careful to keep themselves "in the clear," while the masseuses are in constant danger of arrest, harassment or both from the police and local "moral entrepreneurs." The low pay the masseuses receive for their "legitimate" activities often puts pressure on them to go into prostitution. They go to great lengths to protect themselves from the prostitute image. The authors grant us an interesting look into the marginal subculture of the massage parlors, and real food for thought is generated by comparing their activities with those of other subcultures.

Pittman's "The Male House of Prostitution" and Heyl's "The Female House of Prostitution: The Madam as Entrepreneur" provide an opportunity to compare two institutions that, on the surface, might be thought to be similar, yet, upon closer examination, prove to be quite different. Pittman's emphasis is on what he labels the "ephemerality of the male hustler's life." He suggests that the job of being a "call boy" is demanding both physically and psychologically and typically leads to a short career, the disreputability of which is justified through financial distress. Countering the myth that prostitutes do not get emotionally involved with clients, Pittman suggests that male prostitutes often do. He further elaborates the process whereby a "call boy identity" emerges.

Heyl, on the other hand, approaches the study of the activities of a madam in much the same way that a researcher might study any other small service business. As a case history, her article is fascinating insofar as it probes the delicate relationship between the madam, the pimp and the "turnouts," i.e., trainee prostitutes. Heyl suggests that the key to understanding this high-risk, modest-profit enterprise is to understand the delicate system of exchanges that leads the role players into a sense of who they are and what it is that they are contributing to the larger order.

In "Stripper Morality," Salutin raises a question about the very meaning of sexuality. She suggests that in our culture it tends to be shrouded in romanticism, with an aura of sacredness and privacy. Burlesque is sex for the sake of sex, part of the "sex market." As such, it constitutes a threat to conventional morality. Generally despised by many elements of the larger society, the stripper shields her "persona" by developing a rationale for what she does by calling it "show business." Conventional sexual imagination is mirrored and mocked in the stripper's act. Strippers, Salutin tells us, try to upgrade their occupation and keep their front and backstage behaviors separate (the defensive technique of role compartmentalization). With a high rate of lesbianism, often denied by the strippers themselves, and general contempt for the audience, strippers create their own subculture. This subculture has its own system of values and rationales, most of which involve condemnation of the hypocrisy of conventional people, especially police. Strippers also defend themselves as teachers and sex experts, and hold what Salutin calls a "corporeal ideology." Their biggest problem is aging, and prostitution is almost inevitable for them. They are nearly always broke and live from day to day. "Stripper Morality" is an excellent example of the convergence of self and other definitions to create a deviant life-style.

The final reading in Part Three is Goldman's "Prostitution and Virtue in Nevada." It is an extraordinary piece of social history. The story revolves around the tension between married (respectable) women and prostitutes in Virginia City, Nevada, from 1860 to 1875. The notions of good and bad women, Goldman says, were class related, and the various campaigns against prostitution are characterized by her as female class wars. As a result of Victorianism, a dichotomy of women was created; higher-class women could protect themselves from view, while other women could not. In the early period of her study, "shady" women were able to win respect and admiration from the community (read males) for their charity and recreational works. Average respectable women coopted the leadership in these areas from the famous prostitutes. Conventional women degraded prostitutes in order to enhance their own status in the eyes of men.

1 *Ronald Vander Kooi*

The Main Stem: Skid Row Revisited

When downtown slums are razed to make room for clean, modern business areas and parking lots, a small group of men mourn, for one particular kind of poverty area—skid row—has provided them with a comfortable, even productive life-style. And now that skid rows are being urban-renewed out of existence, long-time residents are losing their community, their homes, their job possibilities, their place in society. Their life-style is being obliterated along with their "cage hotels."

Despite its reputation, skid row did not develop in order to accommodate social misfits, such as alcoholics and the habitually unemployed. Rather it formed as a "main stem," as the working men called it, with a number of necessary services concentrated on one street—a home and marketplace for unattached nonpermanent laborers. Skid row is still an important labor distribution center for many seasonal, "casual" and usually undesirable jobs. But it is no longer vital enough to withstand the economic and political forces which demand that it be demolished. By the 1980s skid rows may no longer exist.

Even though the term "skid row" lends itself to connotations of down-sliding personalities and life-styles, and most skid rowers seem to accept this definition of personal failure (referring to their peers and themselves as a "bunch of bums"), the phrase originated in a legitimate economic phenomenon.

According to all available sources, the name "skid row" evolved from the phrase "skid road" (an appellation still used to describe such areas in the Northwest, where the term originated). Originally used to describe various methods employed by loggers in getting timber over muddy paths to water and the saw mills, a skid road might be logs laid across muddy paths to expedite dragging timbers out of the woods or it might be water thrown down on the road in freezing weather to allow easy skidding. In Seattle, "skid road" refers to Yessler Way, a downtown street which drops sharply down to Puget Sound and was actually greased to speed logs into the water.

After loggers had spent months in the woods, they arrived in Seattle and Spokane, Washington, Portland, Oregon, Muskegon and Saginaw, Michigan, Bangor and Portland, Maine and lesser lumber ports. They picked up their pay and, quite naturally, stayed to celebrate at conveniently located saloons, gambling places, houses of prostitution and various kinds of male lodging houses. Many loggers blew all their pay in the cities and after a few days or weeks returned to work. But some stayed on, unable or unwilling to work or unneeded during off-seasons or other periods of unemployment. They became "bums," a term which, opposed to "hobo" and "tramp," denoted those who stayed in one place and did a lot of drinking and little work.

Robbers and Boomers

Nineteenth-century development of both the lumber and railroad industries contributed greatly to the growth of skid row and for several decades remained closely attached to it. While lumbering provides a clear case of an enterprise which encouraged skid row formations, partially through off-season layoffs, and while it contributed the "skid row" label to such areas, railroading did much more to foster the development of skid rows across the nation.

From 1860 to 1890 the railroads went through their great period of expansion. In 1850 there were just 9,021 miles of track; in 1860 there were 30,626. This increased to 93,267 in 1890 and though the pace began to slow, an all-time high of 254,000 miles of track had been built by 1916. Since the steel wheels of locomotives cannot pull loads up hills of much more than two feet rise per 100 feet, extensive grading was done with mule teams, wagons, plows and especially by men with shovels. Track-laying, done by machine today, was done manually, as were many other railroad jobs. Thus, the railroads, like a few other industries, demanded a large, ready, mobile and single male labor force. Unattached European immigrants, rootless Americans and Chinese answered the call.

Like the loggers, railroad builders needed rest and recreation facilities, and looked to the developing cities to fill their needs. Since railroad towns had grown explosively and haphazardly, inner-city slums and poverty areas, labeled "rotten row" or "rum row," were often located near downtown. Railroaders ate, slept and brawled in these sections. Although permanent, "respectable" residents continually demanded that such areas be controlled, they were countermanded by the substantial economic rewards which underwrote payoffs to influential politicians.

The end of the Civil War and the accelerated development of the nation through railroad building provided further impetus for development of skid row areas. Especially in border and southern states, the war left large numbers of rootless men, many of whom took to the road as marauders, train robbers and more numerous transient laborers. Tens of thousands became "boomers," men who worked for dozens of railroads, generally building and maintaining track, until they wanted to move on or their job ended. Like their pre-war predecessors, "boomers" found lodging and recreation in downtown slum areas. By 1900 such "hobohemias" had many saloons and barrel houses (places where men paid in advance, got drunk and were put to bed on floors and wooden shelves). In most if not all American skid rows prostitution was readily available. Adjoining red light districts, such as Chicago's "Levee District," were, until broken up, ecologically as distinct as skid rows.

Providing not only work and entertainment, but also the lodging, food and other needs of transient workers, skid rows have swollen in the depressions of 1885, 1958 and 1929 and at the end of each major war until World War II. Men came to cities during economic upheaval and after wars to seek work, and they have continuously come from poverty areas, adhering to the American injunction that a man should have some "get up and go."

Skid rows are often found adjoining or near railroad stations, for areas close to the terminals served as employment centers where men were hired and dispatched. Surveying the 33 largest American cities and many smaller ones, we have often entered cities on passenger trains and have nearly always found skid row areas just outside the stations. Someone has said that skid rows are always found between a town's railroad station and its city hall. Neighborhoods of outlying freight yards in major cities did not develop skid row areas since they could not provide living and recreational facilities which downtown had.

Rocking Chair Pay

As skid row served as a place to recruit railroad workers, it also served as an off-season home for them. They received "rocking chair," a railroad practice of spreading some pay over unemployed seasons. Some still receive that pay as part-time railroaders and even today many older skid rowers are covered under the Railroad Retirement Act rather than by Social Security.

When cities developed as seaports, their skid rows were affected. Major cities on both American coasts and others on lakes and major rivers offered casual labor on the docks and ships. New York's Bowery, for example, is close to the East River and the docks where many skid rowers once worked. Loading and unloading ships offered heavy and often dangerous day labor until the occupation came under the domination of the Longshoremen's Union. Seamen, many of them foreigners, looked forward, at least as much as loggers, to their shore time in various port cities. Large numbers of seamen still live in American skid rows and many of them are stranded there, being too old or having "lost their papers" (for getting into fights or otherwise offending ship regulations). Loss of papers is a rather widespread predicament among men living in the small, distinct skid row of San Pedro, a major world port, 35 miles south of downtown Los Angeles. Mass-murderer Richard Speck was a part-time seaman who suffered a variety of disruptive and traumatizing personal experiences which left him homeless and unattached, spending much of his time in Chicago skid rows and ending in an Illinois prison.

Hobo Jungles

In addition to railroading, lumbering and seafaring, agriculture also needed the labor of the unattached men of skid row. Prior to mechanization many kinds of farming required migrant workers, especially during harvest seasons, even for single-family-owned farms. Advertising brochures called for hundreds or thousands of men to arrive at a certain time and place, and great numbers responded to the call. They rode freight trains to the job and, if lucky enough to be hired, worked long hours to get done in a few days or weeks. They ate in rough facilities "with the boys" (as did railroaders, lumberjacks and seamen), slept in the fields and, when the work was done, left the area at the urging of the local police who used laws that were neglected during the work season. Agriculture still provides a large number of jobs for skid rowers, as private and state labor agency records show in Chicago, Seattle, Los Angeles and many other American cities, especially in the Far West. Many skid row residents quit fruit and vegetable picking soon after beginning because of the back-breaking labor, horrible housing conditions and very low piece-work wages. They share the plight of all homeless and ethnic migrant workers.

California, with its warm weather and great fruitful valleys, provides ample agricultural work for skid rowers. Many hoboes ride the California freight trains, and inhabit hobo jungles or camps. When the job is done, they retreat, with police encouragement, to the skid rows of Los Angeles, Stockton, Sacramento and other cities.

Skid rows developed in response to industry's requirements for a mobile, at best semi-skilled labor class. Although such needs have decreased, the casual labor market still provides a great variety of generally rough and unskilled jobs in or near the city with daily pay. For a certain breed of men, this type of job and pay arrangement is more desirable than any other. All skid rows have labor agencies, commonly known as "slave markets," and have informal hiring on the street as well. Chicago, with its major skid rows and large number of homeless men (perhaps 12,000), has at least 100 private labor agencies and a state day labor office with branches. Men living in skid row flophouses are wakened to go to work or to seek work every half hour from 4 AM on. Laziness hardly seems to be the theme; the "early bird" catches the city's worst jobs! If one is lucky enough to get a job within an hour or two, he spends another hour or so getting to the workplace. He may get back around 5 PM, cash his pay voucher in a cooperating tavern (where he feels obliged to spend some money), eat and go to bed early, anticipating a similar tomorrow.

Contemporary skid rows continue to provide a "main stem" for unattached men; their concentration of male-oriented facilities includes a variety of housing ranging from decent quarters to "flops," and at least a few taverns (better called saloons with their heavily male clientele, heavy early 1900 furnishings, cheap drinks and generally unsanitary, sometimes filthy, conditions). They also include one or more rescue missions. In this country over 500 skid-row-based missions are affiliated with the International Union of Gospel Missions and many others are independent of it. The majority of labor agencies are also located in skid rows, the exceptions being those which specialize in hiring women or professional workers. Used clothing stores and pawn shops are nearly always found in skid rows, selling and trading work clothes and seasonal changes of coats, and buying items back when the owner needs a little money for lodging, transportation, drink or something else. ("Reliefers" are worn-out shoes which are provided so that a man will have something on his feet after he trades good shoes for money.)

For those men who cook their own meals, grocery stores provide sandwich ingredients, fruits, canned goods, milk and other needs. Most skid row residents choose to eat in "greasy spoons," with such exotic fare as pig's feet, wilting cabbage and other overripe vegetables. Dirty facilities and unchecked employees often increase chances for contracting tuberculosis and other diseases. Nevertheless, some skid row residents contend that greasy spoons were superior to "fried food joints," the only restaurants available in neighborhoods where skid rowers have relocated after their homes have been razed in urban renewal efforts.

Skid rows often house such specialized facilities as barber colleges and blood banks. The colleges provide free shaves and haircuts (and a large helping of disrespect) in exchange for the opportunity to practice on heads. Blood banks provide one of the chief sources for transfusions in American hospitals and they do so under unhealthy circumstances in exchange for a few dollars. (For a thorough description of this practice, see "The Gift of Blood" by Richard M. Titmuss in *trans*action, January 1971.)

While early skid rows provided a good deal of prostitution, gambling, fighting and more active sports, such activities have now declined. Prostitution and even burlesque have long since found more favorable locations. As skid rows have aged, residents have even lost interest in activities like pool playing and the men have turned to TV and passive drinking to pass their time. Many sit for long hours in hotel lobbies, some seemingly in a trance. A large number still enjoy simply watching the street, observing passersby, fights or police action, street work or construction. Many residents like to walk through skid row, greeting acquaintances by name or nickname, and they go into the more prosperous parts of downtown to shop, enjoy parks and public buildings, rummage through trashcans and see the sights.

Bum Wagon

In addition to the physical facilities which make the "main stem" distinct, less tangible services and social factors also characterize skid row. City police departments do an inordinate amount of work there, picking up drunks and others who may be unsightly or unsafe on the streets. Larger cities use the "bum wagon," a van which facilitates the arrest and jailing of dozens of skid rowers per police shift. The men are herded overnight into the "drunk tank," a facility which is both cheap to operate and inhumane. After spending the night on cement slabs, the men are led into the "skid row court" where each is usually tried in less than a minute and then, according to his condition and available jail space, released back to skid row or given a sentence ranging from a few days to three months. Rather than a punishment, the drunk tank is a police-provided service which often saves men from frostbite, heart attacks, jackrolling and death on the street. Even though this service is inferior and the facilities rough, relocated skid row residents will find no substitute protective lodging. The bum wagon can operate efficiently only when its clientele is gathered in a small area. Men in trouble in distant alleys, garages and abandoned buildings will not be found.

The business and professional men who run skid row hotels, bars, missions and other facilities all provide essential social services. While some operators exploit men for financial or personal reasons, most of them are in some way helpful. They protect the older and more dependent men, providing loans (though often with exorbitant interest, up to 50 percent for any duration from a day to a year), holding their money, giving advice, taking them to the hospital and helping in many other ways. Many operators have worked with main stem inhabitants for decades.

Jack-Rollers and Flea-Bags

Mission workers, who are paid very little and are generally considered to be at the low end of the religious occupational status ladder, are particularly devoted to the residents of skid rows. Even though many workers are dogmatic and insist on some kind of lip-service to salvation, they are nearly always available, unlike government workers, who limit themselves to 9 AM to 5 PM weekday office hours.

The social character of skid row, with its easy acceptance, friendship and sharing of money for lodging and drink, makes it a desirable place for those who have no home affiliations. Typical of skid rows is group-centered street activity, such as a cluster of men sharing wine, a group of Indians joking together, a few jack-rollers consorting or a couple of old cronies commiserating on "how bad skid row has gotten." Since skid row is so very social, with only the most pathological of men drinking alone in their rooms or seeking isolation, demolition of skid row means that gathering places are razed and cronies separated. Even though most complaints are voiced about the loss of a bar or hotel, it is clear that skid row residents also suffer from loneliness as old friends disperse to other parts of the city or even to other towns. The isolation of displaced skid rowers is like that of other older people who have lost their anchorage when they are removed, for whatever reason, from their own communities.

The men of skid row can be characterized as middle-aged to elderly since their average age is about 53, and at least 30 percent are over 60 years old. Average residence on the main stem is seven to ten years. Those who are older experience all of the problems of the elderly with even more exaggerated sickness and disease, and they live in accommodations which make the nation's currently scandal-ridden nursing homes look luxurious. Studies indicate that the average age of skid rowers has continued to rise in past decades. Few men are under 35, and the police often try to discourage those who are younger than 30 from staying.

Skid row is primarily a white man's institution. Once heavily populated by European immigrants, today it is primarily a community of whites, including Irish and other immigrants, men from Appalachia and other poverty areas and, increasingly, those from urban backgrounds. Negroes have entered in greater numbers, partially because their own communities have developed the same capability to exile "undesirables" as the white middle class. Welfare regulations have led many black men to spend their days in skid rows where they can drink unmolested and pick up day labor to supplement their incomes. Latin Americans have never been very prominent in skid rows, but Indians have been quite visible. Because Indians cluster in active groups on the street, they are always noticed. But, in 1970 we found only 255 Indians in Chicago's downtown skid rows, less than 2 percent of the skid row population and probably even a lower proportion of all the Indians in Chicago.

Concentrated skid row areas are at least 95 percent male. Traditionally, women are less challenged to leave home to make their own way in the world, and if they behave like skid rowers they are more likely to be institutionalized in jails or mental hospitals. The few women who visit skid rows are discouraged, and those who stay around are assumed to be "flea-bags," the lowest class of prostitute.

Most Americans think of all skid rowers as "drunken bums who won't work." This stereotype has been proven false, and studies have exposed a continuum of drinking practices including about an equal number of teetotalers and derelicts (the former are not usually noticed; the latter are easily recognized as they fall down or sleep on the sidewalks and appear regularly in the drunk court). Between these extremes are the more typical light drinkers, heavy drinkers and bingers.

Working habits are at least as varied as drinking habits. There are teetotalers in the area of work too, but most nonparticipants are too old or handicapped (physically or psychologically) to be employed. Many Americans feel that the unemployed find continual work avoidance a pure pleasure. This seems more a projection of the beholder's regard for his work than of the unemployed for, at least in skid row, men use an inordinate amount of time in their daily search for labor. While skid row residents spend a good deal of time drinking and getting the price of a drink (possibly as a retreat from the problems of life on skid row), they take up at least as much time seeking work and actually working.

Skid row residents find hundreds of types of jobs, ranging from common labor to piano moving (the latter a specialty of certain strong, careful workers). With luck, some jobs run a few days or longer, and some men are offered permanent positions. (Usually such men lose confidence, are found unsuitable or are the first victims of layoffs.) Seasonal jobs in the fields and canning factories, with low pay and poor living conditions, still take men out of town for weeks at a time; but railroads and seafaring employ a relatively small number. The majority of jobs are the most undesirable daily-pay labor: washing dishes, delivering handbills, shoveling dirt and snow, and cleaning up warehouses and trade shows, usually for $1.65 an hour or less.

Studies in New York and other cities show a gradual but steady decline in skid row populations over recent decades. The population loss has meant a drop in the profitability of skid row businesses, but the loss of profits cannot fully explain the vast demolition that has struck skid row in recent years.

While few were watching, a number of our large and smaller skid rows have disappeared, often leaving only small remnants. A decade ago, Detroit's Michigan Avenue was razed and, for the most part, remains unoccupied today. Minneapolis' Gateway Project, whose greater part is parking space, replaced skid row. In St. Louis, the Great Arch project displaced some of skid row. In Chicago in 1970, a multi-million dollar business syndicate bought three core blocks of demolished West Madison skid row, and prior to that, in what was labelled as "The Miracle of West Madison," another motel of a nationwide chain replaced half a skid row block.

American skid rows are being replaced by large projects such as cultural centers, hotel and transportation concentrations. Until financing and other arrangements are completed, and this may take decades, the space is usually used for parking. Replacing the men and buildings with more downtown space for America's cultural centerpiece, the automobile, is considered a wonderful achievement.

Not only is skid row to be eliminated, as many city newspapers have bragged, but money is to be made. The economics of skid row are such that more can be made operating parking lots. In the affluent post-war era, the skid row population has dropped, but more important, there are many more profitable ways to invest money and efforts, even in decaying downtown areas (and theoretically in resisting decay) than in skid row businesses. The buildings are very old, and any rigorous enforcement of building and health codes means that the owners would have to spend excessive amounts to come up to code. No wonder many skid row businessmen have branched out into apartment buildings and other non-skid row businesses.

Skid row businesses have slowly diminished in number. In 1966 I examined the most concentrated block of Chicago's West Madison skid row (which Nels Anderson diagramed in *The Hobo*), and found that non-skid row uses, such as wholesale houses and parking lots had replaced several of the bars, missions and other facilities. In Chicago's other skid rows, private enterprises, such as a business school and parking lots on South State Street and motels, gas stations and parking lots on North Clark, have replaced core skid row businesses.

But there has been great resistance to this privately promoted transition. Larger skid rows are hardly good locations for the businessman who wants to cater to middle-class clients, since most Americans see skid row as a dangerous or at least repugnant place to visit. In cities where notable business ventures have been tried, for example in developing variations of the "Old Town" theme to bring people into the old section of town for "old time" entertainment, the merchants have been at war with skid row and "the bums." In Denver's Larimer Street, New York's Bowery, San Francisco's Tenderloin, Chicago's North Clark and Houston's Old Market Square, efforts have been made to bring back the gay nineties or roaring twenties without the men.

There has been a long-term hesitance to invade the skid row area. Only the federal Urban Renewal Program (a supposedly humane tool), with the power to condemn whole areas as substandard, provided big businesses with a way to break into skid row cheaply and with the confidence that all or most of the territory would soon be rid of "bums." In Chicago a corporation was formed, including some national motel chain owners and the director of the Chicago Housing Association, Charles Swibel. Swibel happens to own several skid row hotels, and is to be paid an estimated four million dollars by the corporation for "advising." With a bidding process that Chicago newspapers found hasty and completely arbitrary, the Department of Urban Renewal Board decided that this corporation's plan for the area was more acceptable than that of three others. Within seven years this group will be given almost seven square blocks of skid row immediately adjoining the Loop at a rock-bottom price of about $30 per square foot. Four large skid row hotels and some smaller ones have already been torn down, and the space is being rented to parking companies.

But where does this leave the men and skid row? While the newspapers in Chicago proclaimed "Skid Row to Go," many have asked, "Go where?" The common assumption is that skid row will simply relocate elsewhere. But if one is to hold to the classical definition of skid row as an ecological "main stem," or to distinguish skid row at all from other slums, then it becomes obvious that a skid row cannot relocate in any cohesive way. For the most part former residents look for their own housing because urban renewal relocation programs are too cumbersome to serve more than a small minority. Men go to areas where they hear other men are going. Businessmen and missionaries have a hard time finding suitable new facilities since they need places where the men will be provided with all their daily needs, not just that which any particular business provides. In some cases labor agents have managed to move up to 20 or more of their regular men, providing lodging, food and liquor, but this kind of relocation has been extremely difficult.

Business-lodging areas are no longer available for new skid rows in most cities. Business-slum areas may house new skid row facilities but other inhabitants and businesses do not automatically flee. So there is no room for the rapid development of a main stem nor is there sufficient economic demand to develop a new complete skid row. Skid row is not relocated; it is demolished, never to appear in any concentrated "main stem" again. The men and the businesses, to the extent that each survives, are dispersed into what have been called "gray sections" of the city, the "world of furnished rooms."

Cage Hotels

Several hundred Chicago men have already been removed from their hotels in the wake of urban renewal, and the great majority have moved into other skid row hotels, which are now more crowded, unsafe and unhealthy than they have been for 30 years. The shake-up within the existing skid row results in more racial conflict, as white men are pushed into Negro areas, as well as individual hardships of readjustment.

A few dozen older men have been placed in senior citizen housing, and they have generally done well, even though they have had to adjust to women and middle-class life-styles, including planned activities and their own kitchens along with perhaps ten times as much space as they had in skid row "cage" hotels. Paradoxically, the new lodgings offer much less paternal care than the old.

Relocation workers have not been able to find adequate space for most men. Many have left the skid row area for other sections of Chicago. The most common expectation was that they would invade Uptown, the northside area that is well known as a southern white ghetto. This expectation, along with the actual presence of many southern white married men who spend much of their time in the labor agencies and bars, has resulted in the initiation of skid-row-type police work; recently a section of Uptown was voted "dry."

Uptown, with its thousands of desperately poor Appalachian and other whites, Puerto Ricans, Indians and increasing numbers of blacks, is a chronic problem area. Its militant youthful political organizations are in conflict with Mayor Richard J. Daley's power structure. Uptown is perhaps the prototype of a community which is already beset with so many problems that it can neither afford nor resist the incursion of large numbers of homeless men. It is so powerless that it was chosen by city and state officials to serve as home for a large number of "halfway houses" for mental patients (read "hotels too run down to maintain a middle-class clientele"). In moving to Uptown, skid rowers and mental patients may gain a few advantages, especially as compared to being institutionalized, but the community and its families experience further hardships and despair.

Skid rowers, too, experience serious disadvantages in Uptown. There are probably more than 1,000 unattached, irregularly employed men in the area, but only one regular cage hotel. Nearly all of the men are forced to live in more expensive hotels and apartment hotels where they are overcrowded and where maintenance is nearly nonexistent. The men compete in a labor market with younger, family men who need the jobs even more. They are very likely to be jack-rolled or abused by young men who live in the area. And one of the central institutions of skid row, the rescue mission, does not exist in Uptown! There is no ready relief for the man who has spent his money or been jack-rolled, who needs a bed, clothing, food or bus fare to a job. Though there are two major business streets that are central to Uptown, urban renewal, with a plan to build a regional college, is entering and there will never be a "main stem." Thus the dispersal, even into a more or less white slum like Uptown, is a costly human event.

Much more serious and common is the increasing confrontation of skid rowers, who hold very explicit racial prejudices, and the worst black slums which usually border skid rows today. The widely held belief that Negroes "are ruining skid row," may be humorous in its absurdity to those who think skid row has always been a ruin or who understand the long tradition of problems, including jack-rolling, which skid row has experienced without blacks. But it represents the perspective of many older skid rowers on the rather natural racial conflict between an older, undefended white male lower-class community and a younger, distressed and angry male Negro population.

When skid rowers are dislocated a few may improve their life-style but at least as many decline to a lower standard of life and die sooner! While some find better housing, more regular jobs and perhaps more satisfactory companionship, most do not. At their advanced age, they are sent into urban sections where they are strangers. Even when they get better housing and, with the help of government or skid row workers, improved old age or other assistance, their initial enthusiasm is often replaced by an uneasy, vague loneliness. They miss skid row, their old companions and even some of the things about which they always complained. And often they try to return.

Institutionalization has frequently been offered as a solution for homeless skid row residents. A good proportion of county jail populations has always been skid rowers arrested on drunkenness, loitering and other petty charges. Jails have wintered men, sometimes at their own request, and the men have been summered on work farms. Various kinds of mental hospital programs have in recent decades housed skid rowers, often in alcoholic wards and programs. (But labeling alcoholism as a disease carries a stigma and, in effect, the punishment of an indefinite sentence in the hospital rather than a prescribed number of days in jail.)

Today, many traditional skid row operations are becoming more institutional. The Salvation Army has erected extensive new residential and work buildings. Here men "on the program" work, eat, play and sleep under relatively strict, businesslike regulations. Other missions have also turned to longer-term "rehabilitation programs" with greatly expanded facilities and some professional medical and social services in preference to the old "soap, soup, salvation" rescue mission emphasis. These extensive programs and facilities almost always lead to more rules and regimentation, and they can easily lead to extensive dependence and a loss of freedom.

These large extensive rehabilitation institutions can be compared with those in Europe, where the important social unit in the world of homeless men is the hostel (rather than the skid row), run by the government, the Salvation Army or other nonprofit groups. European hostels are not nearly as regulated as American rehabilitation centers. Hostels usually have from 200 to 500 beds and do not usually have extensive rehabilitative programs. Given their size and good maintenance, they offer a decent and continuous way of life for men who might otherwise be in the gutter.

Americans often place as much faith in psychiatric and other rehabilitation programs as they once devoted to "salvation" in traditional rescue missions, but programs are usually not realistic for men too run down or too old to be regularly employed, or those with no family to rejoin or non-skid row social ties to reestablish. Until planners give more attention to relocating and reestablishing the displaced bum, and to follow-up, rehabilitation seems a dream—a rationalization for wasteful programs in skid row. Rather than permitting simple institutionalization to become the common answer to the problem of skid rowers, it should be assumed that the freedom of the street is more humane and reasonable.

In 1966 when the Department of Urban Renewal in Chicago began to develop its current West Madison urban renewal project, we were asked to survey the 2,300 men listed on the hotel rosters one October night in order to provide some recommendations. The respondents displayed the usual range of skid row demographic characteristics and the same range of work and other activities and problems, and they requested assistance regarding drinking, employment and other problems. They overwhelmingly said that they would be interested in a local, concentrated set of facilities where they could relocate.

Our major recommendation was that a "halfway community," including all the major facilities of skid row in a radically upgraded and carefully supervised manner, be provided. It was and is our contention that upgrading, rather than some amorphous rehabilitation, is the sociologically sound amelioration that skid row needs. If a large number of men are most comfortable in a specialized male community in the downtown area, working on a daily-pay basis, taking their recreation mostly in bars and public places, and "getting by" in their insecure world with rescue missions to fall back on, they should have this choice and not be forced into any other community. Prohibition cannot reasonably be forced on them, if not on other Americans.

This halfway community would provide a choice of new or rehabilitated housing run by at least a few landlords with skid row experience. The variety of rescue missions and other businesses should not be replaced by a monolithic government agency with a singular bureaucratic approach. Municipal shelters operated during the Depression were a bureaucratic, inadequately staffed failure. Government subsidies in construction and/or rent would be needed. The area would include bars, restaurants and the facilities of missions, labor offices and a large "drop-in" center, improving on the existing and very successful Chicago Municipal Reading Room. Other agencies and businesses would be welcome, but all would be carefully regulated so that the existing filthy, dangerous, illegal and exploitative operations on skid row would not reappear. For the first time, the codes and laws of Chicago would not be subject to the double standard of enforcement that has distinguished skid row from other parts of the city.

This community plan has been widely discussed in Chicago and among those interested in urban planning in this country, but little or no action has been taken. One landlord is fairly close to getting HUD assistance to build a 40-unit building whose large living units and rents will be out of line for nearly all skid rowers.

Strong, widespread resistance to the idea has offered a good study in the politics of skid row and of human concern—everyone is for rehabilitation, but not in his own neighborhood. The alderman of the ward said that he had "had skid row in his area long enough and it was somebody else's turn." The businessmen of the area held demanding meetings with urban renewal officials insisting that new skid row facilities would drive them from the city. The new corporation insisted that any skid row facilities near them would be in bad faith and might slow down their construction. If all these worried forces were not enough to stop the project, it still took money, particularly from the Federal Department of Housing and Urban Development, and thus many delayed negotiations between Chicago and Washington. With the Vietnam war, the much more militantly vehement demands from other residents of slum neighborhoods and a change in Washington administrations in the middle of the effort, things have come to a standstill. The talk went on even while the men were being dispersed. And it will take tremendous, even radical, changes in government policies at the local and national levels to recognize the wisdom of working on skid row human problems, as opposed to land use problems, as a cohesive whole, that is, offering the men a choice of a "halfway community" where, in upgrading themselves, some would begin to recognize better opportunities and realistic rehabilitation for themselves.

Skid row as a concentration of facilities serving great numbers of unattached American males is disappearing. The men are moving into what fringes of skid row remain, and to some extent they go to the cities where classical skid rows still exist—New York, Chicago, Denver,

Seattle, Portland and Los Angeles. But their time is marked. Like Chicago, Los Angeles has been considering the demolition of its large 5,000 man Fifth Street skid row in order to provide parking for the eastern downtown banking and shopping area. New York's Bowery is being encroached on from the north by the Peter Cooper renewal project. Denver's Larimer skid row slowly gives way to Larimer Square, a tourist "Old Town" area, and to more parking lots. And similar inroads have been made in the other large skid rows.

Skid row as an institution has existed for 100 years and will soon be gone. Like another so-called "natural area," the "red light district," it has outlived its economic and political usefulness. Forces are combining to effectively end its existence—the same kinds of forces that recognized that prostitution could be as profitable and less embarrassing if dispersed and run via call-girl rings and other routines. The valuable downtown land can be more profitably used by big business, and City Hall can boast of the project where Skid Row once stood and forget the embarrassment of skid row news stories (including those about skid rowers being jailed so that a president or other dignitary could ride through the street without being exposed to the Other America).

Thousands of men will surely die prematurely as a result of the careless dislocation urban renewal and downtown development have foisted upon them. The millions of new men who would have been recruited to skid row will not have it available. The emergence of hippies, runaway youths, unadjusted veterans, and a range of coal miners and other unemployables will produce new homeless impoverished populations whose housing and social organization will be just as problematic. But well over 100,000 skid rowers, and perhaps five times that many, today face an immediate crisis in their new homelessness caused by the destruction of skid rows and their dislocation by urban renewal.

SUGGESTED READINGS

Skid Rows in American Cities by Donald Bogue (Chicago: University of Chicago, 1963).

You Owe Yourself a Drunk by James Spradley (Boston: Little, Brown, 1970).

Stations of the Lost: The Treatment of the Skid Row Alcoholic by Jacqueline Wiseman (Englewood Cliffs, N.J.: Prentice-Hall, 1970).

by Nathan Farb

Street Life

A strange and unique group of men lives in lower Manhatten — on street corners and truck-loading platforms. I live only a half a block from such men and while at times I pity their poverty and vulnerability, I have grown to respect and admire them for their fortitude and resiliency. They drink — how else could a person survive the winter nights with the wind blowing from the river a block away — but they are not drunks.

Charles — the one with the bottle in hand — has lived at the corner of Washington and Vestry streets for the last eight years. In the winter he keeps a fire going on the corner 24 hours a day. I can hear him breaking up the wooden pallets for firewood in the middle of cold nights. Food, when available, comes from the garbage of a fancy steak and lobster restaurant. Clothing is picked from local garbage cans. Once I saw a man wearing a shirt I had thrown out the night before; I felt shocked and guilty. At times, Charles's house of wooden crates and an old office chair grows complex and extends 8 or 10 feet into the street. When this happens, the garbage men plough it away and Charles must start rebuilding again.

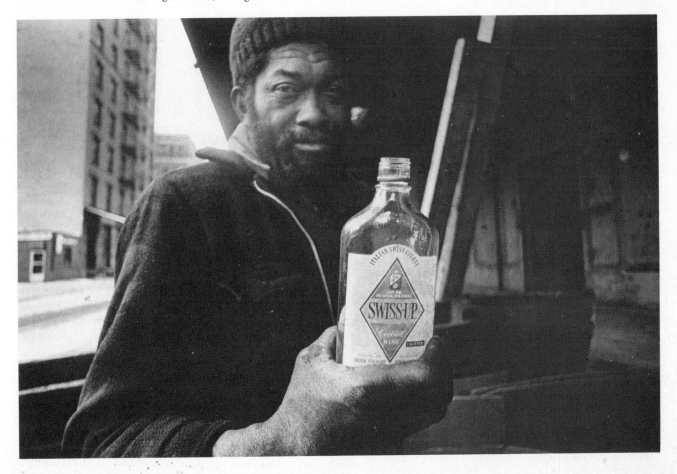

As with all poor people, winter is the worst time of year for the street men. The cold wind blanches their black hands. They look drawn and hungry. Sometimes, when I walk my dog late on an especially cold winter night, I fear that the men will die and I have done nothing more than guiltily given them a quarter or dollar occasionally.

At times the community grows. Often as many as four or five other men stay on the corner with Charles for a few days or even several weeks. Once Charles's cousin came from South Carolina and stayed for a week. Some men inhabit the streets for a month or two, disappear for six months or a year and return to the corner again. Occasionally, the corner becomes too crowded. After the inevitable drunken fight, some of the men will leave.

When I first moved to the neighborhood eight years ago, I thought all of the men were transient. However, some had lived on the streets for years. Clarence, the man with the cast on his foot, has lived in empty trucks and on the corners for 35 years. One afternoon Clarence told me his story. He had been living on the loading platforms, in trucks since 1935. He must have sensed my disbelief because he immediately dragged me off to one of the neighboring warehouses and introduced me to a trucker in his early forties. "Yes," the trucker said, "I knew Clarence when I was a child and my father had this trucking outfit. When I would come down here as a small boy, Clarence would hang around and do odd jobs for my dad." It's true. Clarence has lived in this neighborhood for as long as I can remember."

The neighborhood is changing now. The small truckers and warehousemen are moving out to Jersey. Artists and others are converting many of the old buildings into living quarters. I wonder if the men on the streets will be able to survive this change. Will the new people in the neighborhood view the old street dwellers as nuisances, or perhaps feel uncomfortable with other humans who lead such a bare existence? Sometimes I too wish that these men would disappear so that I would no longer have to face them and their miserable circumstances. Yet the street corners are as much their home as my loft is to me. If they are forced off the streets, my humanity and that of my neighbors would be diminished.

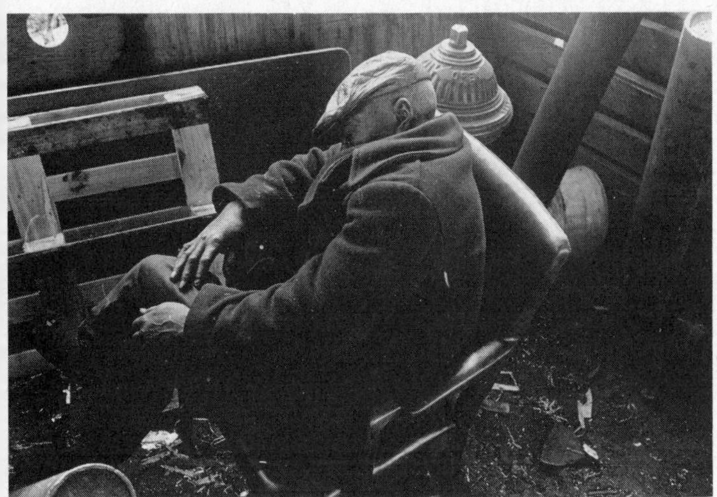

DO not
Park

2 *Barbara Carter*

Reform School Families

Inmate culture in a girls' reform school is best understood as a complex of meanings through which the girls maintain continuity between their lives inside and outside of the institution; and as social forms established to mitigate and manage the pains of confinement and problems of intimate group living. The informal world of reform school girls is one of make-believe families, homosexual courting relations and adolescent peer group culture. It is the world of the adolescent girl on the outside, imported into the institution and appropriately modified to fit the formally structured world of the institution.

Love and Romance: Going with Girls

Adolescent concern with boy-girl love relationships is no less intense for girls in the institution than it is for adolescents in the world outside of the institution. But for these girls, many of whom have gotten into trouble because of their associations with boys, there are no boys around with whom to explore courtship, romance and love. To fill the painful void created by the total absence of boys, the girls turn inward to each other and create their own world of love relationships.

"Going with girls" is a relationship which attempts to capture the characteristics and qualities of the traditional adolescent boy-girl relationship. Girls in the institution go with girls for much the same socio-emotional reasons that boys and girls in the society at large go with each other: they seek recognition, companionship and emotional involvement.

Courtship in the reform school allows a girl to acknowledge a romantic and symbolically heterosexual attachment to another girl. While in part a state of mind and a world of fantasy, this acknowledgement is objectively concretized, like its outside counterpart, by pleas for and declarations of love, flirting and jealousy; by the exchange of letters and verbal messages; and generally, by seeking out a present or prospective courting partner in a variety of informal settings. These courting relationships, like boy-girl relationships in the external world, provide the substance for everyday social conversations.

Smiles, stares, glances, pushes, pats and name-calling take on important and exaggerated meaning for the conversational and romance lives of the training school girls. Physical contact per se is a relatively minor component of the courting relationships and is most often manifested in hand-holding, touching and, to a lesser extent, by kissing. For most girls more extensive physical contact appears to be both undesirable and/or unattainable. The vast majority of the courting relationships are emotional and symbolically sexual rather than physical.

Generally, informal group pressure encourages but does not demand that one go with girls. The decision to do so is entirely voluntary. The threat of force, or its actual use, is neither a socially accepted nor practiced way of inducing girls to participate in the courtship system.

Despite the absence of overt coercion and in the presence of formal restrictions against it, somewhere around 70 percent of the girls participate in the courtship system. This estimate is based on my own counting and familiarity with the declarations and activities of the girls. Girls participating in courting activities estimate that close to 90 percent of all girls go with girls. The specific estimates of the noncourting girls cluster around 50 percent. The few staff estimates elicited tended to be considerably lower and most often characterized as "not many." It is clear that estimates about the extent of participation in the courting system are influenced by one's relationship to that system.

Courtship Roles

"Butch" and "femme" are the two pivotal roles in the courtship system. Auxiliary roles are the "stone butch," the "half-ass butch," the "jive butch" and the "stone femme."

The butch is that position in the courtship system assigned to the girl who assumes the masculine role in the courting relationship. An important part of being a "good butch" is learning to look the part. In a setting where real sex differences are nonexistent, nuances of dress, hair style, carriage and posture take on great social significance.

In summary, then, to be a butch simply means to "act the part of a boy." However, a butch may still show interest in some traditionally feminine activities like knitting, crocheting and sewing. Also she may, like the other girls, decorate her room with dolls, stuffed animals and bric-a-brac. The butch is permitted to play a role without assuming an identity which implies a "real" or permanent commitment. She is permitted to maintain an image of herself as female. It is this permissiveness which gives rise to the distinction between the butch and the stone butch. The butch plays a role while the stone butch purports to have accepted an identity.

A girl may be a butch for the duration of her stay in the institution, or she may be a butch one day and a femme the next—a butch in one relationship and a femme in a concurrent relationship. Most of the terms used by girls in describing roles in the courtship system are terms taken from black culture. That this is so reflects the dominance of the soul orientation in reform school life. For example, the label "half-ass butch" is applied to the girl who calls herself a butch but generally fails to play the part. The black societal counterpart is "half-ass nigger."

The term "jive butch" is most frequently used to describe the butch who courts many girls at once without being "serious" about any. Its equivalent on the outside is the playboy. To call a butch jive is at once to offer a compliment and a criticism; to be jive means that one is popular; but to openly exploit that popularity is bad. The black societal counterpart is "jive nigger."

The female counterpart of the butch is the femme. Within the reform school culture the femme affects in an exaggerated fashion behavioral patterns culturally associated with femininity. Most girls perceive this as just acting "natural." A femme is expected to take pride in her personal appearance and to wear jewelry, make-up and lipstick to make her attractive to butches. The femme is expected to be submissive or, as the girls say, "to do what the butch tell her." She is expected to "obey" her butch.

At any given moment in the courting system femmes probably outnumber butches by at least two to one. This uneven distribution, of course, contributes to the internal dynamics of "going with girls" by further allowing butches—as scarce commodities—to assume a role of dominance by defining the terms of the courting relationship. The ***single*** most important factor determining this distribution is race. Within the context of the institution, race becomes a highly visible constant for imagined sex differentiation. Blacks, grossly disproportionate to

Love Is Here and Now You're Gone, I'm Your Puppet, Hello Stranger, Respect, Ain't No Mountain High Enough, Reach Out

Time — To pen you
Place — My lonely room
Thought — Of you
Reason — I love you
Desire — To be with you
Hope — We meet on the outs
Wish — You were here now!
Want — You and your loving
Need — You and your loving
Care — For you
Hurt — By love
Love — You
Hate — I hate —— (I hope she drops dead)
Happy — Not now
Sad — Yes
Mood — Confused
Songs — I Do Love You, Stand by Me, Since I Lost My Baby

Say Love,

Time plus pleasure permits me to write you these few sweet lines. Hon I hope I did not upset you but I just had to tell you. And if I did not tell you when I did decide to tell you which I probably would you would have either been angry or hurt because I didn't tell you before. Paula I do love you and I mean it but hon I don't know how to prove it to you but believe me I'll do anything to prove it to you. Hon, I want you to go to board and go home why should you suffer because of me oh sure you'll say you're not suffering but I'll know and deep down you will too. And if you go home and behave I'll probably be able to see you in June or even on my Xmas weekend and remember one thing even if we don't meet on the outs or for that matter ever see each other again remember there will always be someone else that you will love and be happier with than me.

You may not think that now but when you do meet that someone you'll look back and say Pony really knew what she was talking about and then after a while you'll forget me and then it will be hard for you to think that we were more than friends but I hope that doesn't happen to us but if it does, well that's life and boy life sure is hard. Isn't it?

Well I got to go see you tomorrow sometime I hope

1 4 3
6 3 7
Little Miss Supreme

P.S. But promise me never again as long as you live to touch that Dope! and I mean it hear?

Well good night and 1 4 3
6 3 7

This love note is typical of those which the girls regularly write to each other. 1 4 3 means "I love you" and 6 3 7 means "always and forever."

their numbers in the institution, become butches, and whites, equally disproportionately, become femmes. The most common and desirable arrangement is a relationship consisting of a black butch and a white femme.

Whether black girls become butches because they have been socialized to be more aggressive than white girls, or are more aggressive because they have become butches, is unclear. I am inclined to believe that the two are mutually reinforcing: the black girls are in fact "tougher" than the white girls but their toughness is made acceptable and manageable to white girls by having the blacks become the symbolic masculine figures in a social context which is microcosmic of a society that assigns toughness and power to males and not females.

A second argument is that the purpose of creating symbolic males in an all-female population is to permit the vast majority of girls to continue to maintain their pre-institution identities as "feminine people." One might then argue that due to past and present position in society, black girls are more willing to temporarily give up their female roles for certain high-status rewards.

The Dynamics of Courtship

Courting relationships in the reform school, like teenage courtships on the outside, are highly charged emotionally and often short-lived. Girls frequently estimate that during the course of nine to 12 months in the institution, the typical girl may go with anywhere from five to ten girls, with five or six girls being the most common estimate given.

Despite, and maybe because of the relatively short duration of most courtships, going with girls is one of the most alive, emotionally intense and conversationally consuming experiences of the girls. These relationships are the source of considerable anxiety for many girls. Girls talk about, dress for, "show-off" for and look forward to seeing each other, even momentarily and at a distance. Girls are excited and joyous when things go well and sometimes angry or sad when things go badly.

Daily courtship relations revolve around the exchange of written and verbal messages; the sharing of "goodies" and the exchange of small gifts; the arranging and engaging in momentary and public rendezvous; hand-holding, smiles, glances, kisses, petty jealousies and continually recapturing these moments in conversations with friends.

The single most prominent feature of going with girls is the regular exchange of "pen notes." These illegal written communications are saved, hidden and treasured by the girls who receive them. The themes of loneliness, frustration and a need for love are common to most of the letters.

A code for various phrases is used. Presented below are some of the most common phrases.

1 4 3	I love you
2 1 6	As a sister
2 2 6	As my mother
2 2 3	As my man
2 4 3	Go fuck off
2 2 4	Go to hell
2 2 5	As my woman *or* It is quits
2 1 8	As a daughter
1 3 3	I dig you
3 2 4	Pen me back *or* Pay me back
6 3 7	Always and forever
2 6 8	We belong together
2 1 7	As a brother
4 4 6	True love always
4 2 3	Kiss my ass
4 2 4	Take me back

The codes reflect the sense of a need for secrecy, but also seem to create some emotional distance. For example, in face-to-face encounters girls are far more likely to say, "1 4 3" than "I love you."

A common pattern observable at recreational activities is the informal sorting of femmes and butches into separate groupings. These groupings are often seen as some combination of the sorting of symbolic males and females to discuss their respective partners and activities and as an informal grouping of blacks (butches) and whites (femmes). In first discussing this phenomenon with the observer, one femme vividly recalled how she had been told to leave an informal grouping of butches, some of whom were her close friends, because the conversation was to be about things which she, as a femme, should not hear. With respect to the second basis for groupings (race), the observer notes that a considerable portion of conversation content for butches centers around the recounting of pre-institution experiences, events and places known to the blacks coming from common urban area ghettos.

The dynamics of the courtship system can be elaborated further by describing the everyday language of courtship. Girls talk about "digging" girls, and this is their way of saying that one girl is attracted to another and would like to enter into or continue a courting relationship. Talk about who is "digging" whom is very common. A girl may communicate this particular attraction for another girl by penning a note or more informally by a variety of nonverbal gestures such as stares, smiles, winks, pushing or hitting. Presented below is one girl's description of how the observer could identify when one girl is "digging" another. "If that name keeps popping up. They keep bringing it up and you get suspicious. That's what Lee did with Helen. We were talking about cars and she said, 'Don't Helen look cute today.' " To accuse a partner of "digging" another girl is to charge her with unfaithfulness. Such accusations of jealousy are common and lively features of the courtship drama. These accusations, often true, lead to many break-ups. While butches and femmes probably make an equal number of accusations, butches are more likely to take the initiative in ending relationships. This is so because femmes are more numerous than butches and consequently, it is easier for butches to find new partners than for femmes to do so. Then too, femmes are less likely to end relationships when partners are suspected of being unfaithful because there is a general consensus that butches, like males, are to some extent "jive." That is, butches, like men, are expected to be playboys.

Girls also talk about "rapping." Girls "rap" to each other, but especially butches to femmes. Rapping is variously described as, "You make a girl think you like her," "You talk bull," or "Play up to her." "Rapping" is the act of artistically persuading one to believe the impossible or improbable. Historically, it is similar to the art of making the master believe that he is loved by his slave.

"Slobbing" is the local and graphic vernacular for "French" kissing. Though frequently described as a "natural" feature of courting relationships, this activity seems to occur as frequently, if not more so, between non-courting partners as it does between courting partners. "Slobbing" is perceived as one of the "big" things that girls can engage in. It certainly carries a greater penalty from the school's administration than writing pen notes. Physical contact for most courting partners seldom goes beyond "slobbing." Most girls say that this limitation is imposed by the girls themselves, but a small number do see it as an expedient reflecting the absence of opportunities for more extensive contacts. The actual amount of "slobbing" occurring in the institution is open to debate. Some girls estimate that it is a frequent activity and say that about three-quarters of courting partners slob each other; others place the figure higher and some estimate that it is an activity in which as few as one-third of the courting girls are engaged.

While the dominant relationship in the romance complex is the courting relationship, marriage relationships are also acknowledged. Except for the name, and a ceremony which accompanies it, it is usually impossible to distinguish between courting and marriage. Girls, however, say that marriage relationships, like those relationships in the external world, imply a degree of permanence, stability, faithfulness and commitment not necessarily implied by a courting relationship.

Most courting girls do not get "married." "Marriage" relationships last no longer than the more common courting relationships, and girls may get married one day and divorced several days later. Many girls involved in courting simply refuse to get married on the grounds that it, unlike courting, is "too unrealistic."

One girls summed up the meaning of marriage by saying, "It means that they like each other a whole lot more than kids just going together. They have to stay together or get a divorce. The girl takes the last name of the butch."

Marriages, like most other activities, take place during recreational periods in the presence of other girls. Like marriages on the outside, they are performed by preachers. Any butch may become a preacher simply by performing a marriage. (There are few female preachers in the outside world and none in the institution.) The marriage ceremony varies both with the style of the preacher, the setting, the risk of discovery, and the amount of time available for performing the ceremony. It may be as simple or as embellished as the preacher desires, but always consists of the lines "Do you (*pen name*) take (*pen name*) to be your lawfully wedded butch/femme." Each marriage must be witnessed by at least two people, but more are usually present, often standing as camouflage or lookouts.

Divorces most often seem to occur because partners lose interest in each other, though it is reported that some girls simply get divorced before they leave the institution, maybe to denote a real end to a symbolic existence. Below is a brief description of how one girl described her divorce and the circumstances surrounding it.

> She quit me for no reason at all. I wasn't going with anybody. At first I thought she was jealous or something, but she wasn't. She just said that she wanted to go with Thelma. [Have you had other break-ups like this?] No we haven't. We quit each other before but usually we were back together in five minutes. . . . Yet we got a divorce. A preacher divorced us. [Did you have to stand together?] No. It was a one-way divorce. I didn't want to get it. She told me that she wanted a divorce and I said no. I thought she would just forget all about it but she didn't. Then the girl who divorced us told me that we were divorced. [What did you do when told about the divorce?] I turned in her dirtiest pen note. She lost her weekend and everything. But I don't care. I'm glad. She hurt me.

New girls learn the language and etiquette of courting by talking with, listening to and observing their peers as they act out the daily courtship drama. These girls learn that it is a voluntary activity which "gives you something to do" and which "helps to pass the time." But, too, they learn of the verbal ambivalence of even those girls who participate in the system: that going with girls is "fun" and "exciting" but also "wrong," "crazy," "sick" and "stupid"—and that one can get in trouble for it. They learn that the staff officially and usually informally disapproves of it and that one can really get in trouble for a "dirty pen note" if it is discovered. They learn that some matrons who are otherwise accepting get really upset when they hear girls talking about going with girls and that a few staff members also see it as a "game" and will laugh or smile when they overhear girls talking about it. Mostly they learn that it's best to try to keep going with girls a secret.

Most girls stop going with girls when they leave the institution, for they know that "it's only something you do up here," and "once you leave you forget all about this place." After all, almost everybody prefers life on the outs to life inside, and boys to girls.

Having a Family

In recreating life on the outside, the girls do not stop at boy-girl relations. Just as they miss having boyfriends, they long for their mothers, fathers, sisters and brothers. The following is a typical letter written by one of the girls to her family at home.

Dear Ma and Dad
I hope this letter finds you in the best of health.
Ma and Dad I lonely and blue and I need you very much. more than I did before. because I know How much you & the kids mean to me now. I never knew how much yous mean tell now. So I am asking for yours and Dad forgives. Please! take me back I need you and I need your love.
I know you say she only fooling around so she can come home. but am not I mean every word I am saying to you. Ma please take me in your arms and love me like you do the other kids. Please! Rock me and hold me in your arms Ma. Someone said to me (You can have a lot of fathers but you can only have one mother. Cause she the one who brought you in this world. I believe that if only you would let me love you and you love me. Ma please understand what I am trying to say. Well thats all for now. Please forgive me.
I already forgave you and ready to try again.

Love & Kisses & Hugs
Dena

Dena writes from the heart and paints a plea for love, acceptance and affection. Her letter, unfortunately, is typical of many I read during my fieldwork at the Girls' Reform School.

Dena, like many girls at the school, is estranged from her family and feels an intense loneliness for them. Families, both loved and hated, are everyday topics of conversation for the girls, their visits anticipated and letters anxiously awaited.

Girls in the institution talk about and long for their families. Yet there is little that one can do about families on the outside except write to them, wait for their visits, hope for an infrequent weekend, send apologies, and ask for forgiveness and acceptance. Perhaps this is the reason that girls create their own make-believe familial relationships within the institution.

Girls use kin terminology to describe a variety of close relationships between them and other girls in the institution and speak of having "sisters," "brothers," "mothers," "fathers" and "daughters." Kin relationships generally lack the tone of emotional excitement so characteristic of the courting relationships, and the vast majority of girls acknowledge not just one but several make-believe relatives on the grounds. This commonly ranges from a low of two or three relatives to a high of 14 or 15. Girls most typically have about four to seven family relations. Having family relations distinguishes courting from non-courting friends and thus reduces feelings of jealousy, suspicion and distrust among courting partners involved in multiple relationships.

I have found it convenient to divide kin relationships into two broad categories: macro- and microfamily groupings. Girls speak of the macrogroupings as "grounds families," meaning that these families are institution-wide. The most popular of these large groupings at the time of my research were the Robinsons and the LaMonts. Girls simply identified themselves as belonging to one of the "grounds families" and often took the family name as their pen note surnames. Belonging to a large family grouping seemed to convey some positive status on girls. The major function of these groupings presently seems to be to provide a sense of social rather than emotional integration.

When asked about the history of the two dominant macrofamilies the responses ranged from "don't know" to constructions of a recent past. Many times I was told that the Robinson family, the larger of the two families, was started up in the fall of 1966 by two girls who were "married" to each other. Others reported that the Robinson and LaMont surnames have been used by the girls for many years. Thus the girls have attempted to create a past and legitimate the families and interrelationships.

One becomes a member of a family grouping simply by being asked or so identified by someone who is already a member. Getting out of a family is as simple as getting into it. A girl simply declares that she no longer wants to be in that family.

From the perspective of the girls the large grounds family groupings are seemingly less important on the level of day-to-day interaction than are the smaller, comparatively more closely knit nuclear and sibling groups into which the girls also organize themselves.

A sizable number of girls are mothers or daughters, and an even larger number of girls acknowledge sister or brother relationships. (Interestingly, there are no "sons." A girl assuming a butch role in a courting relationship will usually become a brother to another girl or even a daughter. In most cases it seems that a girl identifying herself as a butch will not have a parent unless she has alternated between the roles of butch and femme.) It is not uncommon that a girl will be a mother or father in one relationship, a sister or brother in another, and a daughter in still another.

In general, girls who acknowledge kin relations regularly write pen notes to each other, send verbal messages, share with each other and exchange small gifts. These girls seek out each other and talk together at recreational activities, hold hands, exchange affectionate hugs and kisses, and often move in the same circle of friends. In terms of observable content, these relationships are practically indistinguishable from courting relationships. Importantly, however, these relationships lack the talked-about glamour and excitement of the courting relations. Of course in the outside world adolescent girls take families for granted and talk, instead, about boyfriends.

A sister or brother, most commonly a sister, is frequently the first kin relation to be acknowledged by a girl on the grounds and this tie is frequently established within a week or two of a girl's arrival at the institution. Some girls establish these ties within a few days after their arrival but others do not choose or are not chosen until much later. One girl, for example, reported that she was at the institution for five months before she acknowledged a kin relation. At the time of our conversation she acknowledged five sisters, several brothers, an aunt and uncle (both unusual since the term "aunt" is usually reserved for matrons) and a host of "good friends" described as "not worthy" of being called sisters and brothers. Another girl, however, reported that on her first day at the institution she received six pen notes with several of them containing requests for a sister relationship. At present this girl is in the Robinson grounds family and acknowledges a mother, two daughters, four sisters and two brothers.

Mother-daughter relations are less common than sibling associations, and the girls seemed at a loss to describe the parent-child relationship. In explaining why she had chosen a particular girl as her daughter, one girl said it was, "because I like her. She's little. I don't know, I like little people. If they're smaller than me they can be my daughter." Mothers are nearly always older than their daughters. Girls typically describe those who become mothers as "more mature girls."

Mothers give advice, provide a sense of security and help meet material needs. Parents assume some responsibility for socializing their children into the informal culture of the institution. When asked to describe the relationships which commonly exist between parent and child on the grounds, the girls almost always say that the parent tells the child what to do, how to behave and how to avoid trouble. One in fact frequently hears parents, as well as girlfriends and relatives, telling the girls to "be good" or "You'd better make A-Party" (for girls who have adhered to all school rules for the week) or to obey the matrons.

Family members on the grounds, like the idealized concept of families on the outside, "like" and "care" for each other. The girls themselves see the parental role as being one which provides the child with a sense of emotional security, social direction and physical protection. The parent fulfills the desire to nurture; the child has her need to be nurtured fulfilled. These are intensely personal needs which cannot be fulfilled by the formal structure of an institution.

The child-parent relationships are effective channels for socializing recruits into life on the grounds: it is an informal but powerful channel of social control. The girls want to protect their social system and to maintain a comfortable social order where staff discipline is minimal. To the extent that parents (and other kin and friend relations) express concern about the behavior of their children by telling them to "be good" or "make A-Party" and children obey these commands, the child-parent unit becomes an important informal source of support for the formal structure's emphasis on discipline and order. To the extent that the entire enterprise is successful, parents become informal social control agents of the formal institutional structure.

Families—parents, daughters, sisters and brothers—are important to adolescents both inside and outside the institution. For these adolescent girls on the inside, plagued by real family conflicts and often social and emotional estrangement and certainly physical separation, make-believe families function to fill a void not otherwise filled by the institution. There is some interaction between girls and matrons characteristic of child-parent interaction, and though girls may develop special attachments for certain matrons, these attachments clearly do not erase the need for make-believe families. In the final analysis, say the girls, even most of the "nice" matrons are people who just *work* at the institution. Furthermore, not even the matrons themselves feel equipped to provide the 25 girls in their cottages with the "love and affection" they are perceived as needing.

These reform school girls have attempted, consciously and subconsciously, to affect their restricted environment, finding ways to compensate not only for their incarceration but also for deprivation in their lives outside of the institution. Make-believe boyfriends, girlfriends and families provide, at least temporarily, the romantic, sibling and parental relationships that these girls crave.

SUGGESTED READINGS

Society of Women by Rose Geallonbardo (New York: John Wiley, 1966).

"Child Convicts" by Paul Lerman in *Trans*action, July–August 1971.

Women's Prison: Sex and Social Structures by David Ward and Gene Kassebaum (Chicago: Aldine Press, 1965).

3 *Albert J. Velarde & Mark Warlick*

Massage Parlors

The nationwide massage parlor business is booming. Into a world formerly populated by physical therapists and affluent health enthusiasts have come the prostitute, the pimp and a bevy of innocent young girls looking for any kind of employment. The personality of a masseuse, her working conditions, society's reaction to her occupation, and her problems with owners, customers and the police were the targets of our investigation.

We concentrated our study on a suburban West Coast community that is supporting one parlor for every 5,000 people. We interviewed 15 masseuses, four owners, several customers and the husbands of two masseuses. Our subjects were drawn from nine different parlors within the community.

The Masseuse

Why does a young woman choose to enter an occupation that carries the stigma of prostitution? In this particular town, the massage boom hit over two years ago. Word got around slowly at first—friends told friends of friends—then snowballed as the ads in underground newspapers became more blatant. More parlors opened to meet the increasing demand of curious customers. The high rate of unemployment for young, unskilled women in this community has been the major factor in obtaining a work force for massage parlors. "Why did I get into it? Very simple! I needed a job and no other work was available at the time."

Did these girls know what they were getting into? Were they aware of the prostitute image? To answer this question a time element must be considered. For a full year after the boom began, the straight press was virtually ignorant of any illicit activities taking place in the parlors. Many established newspapers (not to mention the underground and campus papers) carried very respectable advertisements for masseuses: "Masseuses needed—part time or full time—training included. An equal opportunity employer." To all outward appearances and to the public, this smacked more of physical therapy than prostitution. Girls who answered these early ads were almost unanimous in expressing naiveté toward the finer points of their new occupation.

Advertisements drew hundreds of women to apply for the few available jobs in the profession. We asked one owner, "How did the job applicants react when you told them about locals (massaging the penis)?" "The first 15 or 20 girls I interviewed I was too ashamed to talk to them about it, I just couldn't do it. I was completely amazed at the girls. I figured maybe one out of 20 would do it (give a local). Well, like 99 out of 100 would! Not all of them would go beyond that, but almost any girl that came in would give a local without even batting an eye!"

Most owners simply said nothing about locals and left informing the new masseuse of her duties to the customer. We found that a sizeable percentage of women quit at this point. One masseuse told us, "I lasted three days at my first place, leaving there at night just totally mind-blown. I couldn't even think about giving a man a local because to me it was a personal sexual involvement which I just couldn't do for money. Here I was, a trained masseuse and these guys were coming in, laying 20 bucks on the table, and expecting me to jump up there."

Most masseuses would give the first local. "If you think about it, you probably won't do it. It's the same with nude modeling or working in topless bars. If you just do it, it's not so bad. You don't have time to feel guilty."

Training to be a masseuse is as varied as the parlors and bosses themselves. An owner may have the prospective employee read a book on massage, then have her perform a massage on him. Others do just the opposite—training girls by giving *them* a massage or by having them witness someone else receiving a massage. Other owners rely on schools to train their employees. One student complained that "the book was really shitty. All kinds of physical detail and nothing at all about the aesthetic side of massage." Others hold a different view: "I learned so much! I got to meet other girls in my profession and learned everything from the names of muscles to the whole nervous system. They even taught us how to operate a fire extinguisher."

Some owners use the training to check out more than a girl's ability to massage. "Jack puts the make on every girl he hires. It's kind of aggravating 'cause he's a real pimp-type, very smooth and slimy. But it's not true that you have to ball him to get hired. He just checks you out real good to see how loose you are. Sure, he gets his kicks out of it but it's more for his own protection. Anybody he hires is in a position to get him in a lot of trouble."

Other owners are more demanding. "I couldn't stand pumping gas anymore so I applied for a job as a masseuse. I had read horrible stories of what went on in there, but I was curious. The sign said I would be a trained masseuse and that interested me also." What kind of training was involved? "Just reading the book he gave me. He also asked me to give him a massage to see if I could do it right. . . .What an ugly, fat ass he had. I massaged him and he told me to jerk him off in the end. I knew that I would be doing this, so I jerked him off until he came all over my hands. There were some paper towels near the table and I wiped my hands off. It wasn't so bad!"

Working Conditions

The first obstacle a prospective masseuse encounters is the law. The local ordinances require eight steps for a masseuse to become licensed: (1) She must present a note from her future employer of his intention to hire her. (2) She must appear at city hall and pay the $15.00 application fee and fill out a two-page questionnaire on her job, legal and personal background. (3) She must proceed to the police department to be fingerprinted and photographed. (4) The police will question her and warn her not to engage in prostitution. (5) She must produce a birth certificate for identification. Driver's licenses are not acceptable. (6) She must then see a doctor for a medical check-up (specifically, a VD check-up). (7) She must show proof of enrollment in a certified massage school. (8) She must take 70 hours of schooling which are to be concluded within 90 days. Schooling averages $250.00 for 70 hours.

These ordinances assure proper training, but authorities generally treat the masseuse as a legalized prostitute. "They made me feel like a whore while trying to get licensed. The medical check doesn't do any good. They don't care if I have infectious sores on my hands or TB. They simply want to assure that I won't give VD to my customers. Now what does that imply?"

Most full-time masseuses work eight to 12 hours per day, five to six days per week. The hours are long and tedious when the masseuse is busy; boring, when she's not. Many masseuses work 12 hours per day or more without overtime pay. They are usually paid on a commission basis that averages 40 percent (between $3.00 and $5.00) per massage. Very few get paid for sitting around waiting for a customer to come in.

One parlor gives $1.25 per hour plus commission. We found one higher class parlor paying its girls $2.50 an hour or $5.00 a massage, whichever was greater on a weekly basis.

Few businesses can maintain themselves financially without a regular clientele. As one masseuse put it, "If you're giving straight massages you might as well be on welfare." "You couldn't make it in this business without giving locals." Low pay forces the girls to cater to customers' wishes in hopes of getting a tip. If the customer is satisfied, he may become a regular, which makes the masseuse's rate of pay less sporadic. When a masseuse moves to another parlor, she may advertise in an underground paper so her regular customers will know where to find her. "Looking for Katie from N.Y.? I've moved to El Gato. Come see me soon."

The Massage Parlor

The physical layout of a massage parlor varies according to the type of customer and the amount of capital invested. Parlors range from dives to very plush operations. An owner who wishes to attract working-class customers looking for sex and thrills need make only a small investment. Homes in unincorporated areas and low-rent, downtown storefronts have been converted into blue-collar massage parlors with the addition of partitions, curtains, a couch, a chair, massage tables and linen. Advertising is a necessity. Ads need only show a semi-nude girl with the caption "Your complete satisfaction on request."

A few higher class parlors cater to wealthier businessmen and financially influential people, yet offer much the same services. These parlors advertise subtly, preferring to attract a select clientele. Customers are provided such comforts as plush carpets, soft couches, clean linen, piped-in music and soft lighting. All of this may demand a few thousand dollars extra, but as one manager said, "You wouldn't want to pay for a massage in a filthy place, would you?" Almost all parlors feature saunas and showers; the latter is required by law. Some even have their own laundry room for a constant supply of fresh linen.

Occupational Precautions

Masseuses must have a basic knowledge of solicitation laws. Women who engage in sexual acts must be certain that the customer does the soliciting. A mere hint for a tip could be distorted to infer solicitation. The question, "Is there anything else you'd like me to massage?" is far more suggestive than, "Is there anything you'd like massaged again?" Little word games such as these become crucial in a courtroom.

Since few owners stay on the premises during business hours, the masseuses must sniff out undercover policemen. Some are incredibly adept, cataloging a large variety of data before continuing with anything illegal. General appearance, mannerisms, tone of voice, type of language, overconfidence or excessive nervousness—all are studied carefully. The masseuse may direct conversation in an attempt to discover any contradictions.

If a customer says he is a student, yet doesn't know when finals are, calls the school by the wrong name and doesn't know any teachers in his department, he is obviously a liar and possibly an undercover policeman. One masseuse told us, "This dude came in and everything was cool until he told me he was in the real estate business. I asked him to help me with a problem involving the sale of an inherited home with depreciation value conflicts. He stuttered and stammered on that one. Shit, he didn't even know what a tax write-off was! We both laughed about it and he was pretty embarrassed. Needless to say he didn't get anything extra from me, tip or no tip!"

The one-to-one nature of the masseuse-customer relationship adds to the legal difficulties of both parties. One masseuse told me, "It doesn't matter what goes on in that room. When they're assigned to bust you they're gonna bust you. Those cops will get up on the witness stand and lie through their teeth. It's your word against his and who do you think a jury is going to believe—the cop or the masseuse?" Some parlors have gone as far as installing tape recorders to protect them against undercover policemen in court. Even when who solicited whom is clear, a jury is likely to frown on a masseuse who performed a lewd act.

Handling phone calls is an art in itself. As a rule, one girl in a parlor will handle most of the calls. Crank calls are common, be they from genuine perverts, women trying to antagonize the masseuses or policemen involved in harrassment. Some girls have an incredible memory for phone voices: "There's this one cop who calls now and then. Once he asked if he could bite my panties. He said he'd give me $50.00 if I'd wear them for a week after that. He gets real pissed when we say something like, 'Aw Fred, cut it out. Why don't you come on in and we'll talk about it.'"

Another caller asked, "How much does straight sex cost?" The masseuse replied, "Tenderness, sincerity, loving care and another person." This caller wanted and expected either a straight dollars and cents answer or a flat rejection. Instead, he received an answer that forced him to think. Such answers arouse curiosity, which is the main commodity that a customer brings with him into a parlor. One masseuse even turned several gutter-level, obscene phone callers into regular customers.

Locals

Of all the legal questions involved in the massage profession, one stands out above them all: Is it legal for a man to enter a place of business, pay a fee, and eventually have his penis massaged in such a manner as to result in an ejaculation? On one side of this controversy are the enforcers of the law who are arresting girls right and left for soliciting to commit a lewd act. On the other side, of course, are the owners, masseuses and customers. Lewd or not, locals are popular. We asked one masseuse, "What percentage of customers ask for locals?" She replied, "I kept track of that once. While working at this one parlor I did over 500 massages and only four guys *didn't* ask for a local."

Owners use a variety of methods to isolate themselves from the illegal activities in their parlors. Most owners never mention anything against the law to their employees. Some have even gone as far as filing the business in someone else's name. They still collect the profits while their dupe receives all the pressure.

One owner was asked if massages in his parlor included locals. "It was always up to the girl's discretion." We asked if masseuses ever told him about it. "I didn't want to know about it! I knew about it in the beginning and that just got me into trouble. I might as well have been running a whorehouse with all the problems I had."

As might be expected, a brothel has a higher profit ratio than a semi-straight massage parlor. A parlor owner generally wants his girls to accomodate customers to the greatest degree possible. Owners protect themselves in two ways. First, if the owner knows that the employee is a prostitute, he will tell her openly not to ball the customers, while knowing all along that she will. He can always say that he knew nothing of what was going on. Second, the owner may give his total consent to the illicit activities. At the same time he will demand that the masseuse sign a contract asserting that she will *not* engage in anything sexually illegal. With this paper signed, as one owner said, "The girls are free to fuck like a bunny! It's very difficult for the cops to convict an owner on that. Almost impossible."

Personality

Masseuses come from nearly all walks of life and all types of economic and social backgrounds. We met women who were from 14 to 64 years old, with the majority being in their 20s. There are women in the profession with fifth grade educations as well as several graduate students from nearby universities. There is simply no quality or characteristic which typifies the average masseuse.

Most find the work boring and react accordingly. Most customers, regardless of age, background or personality, are interested basically in receiving sexual pleasure. Some want to talk about personal problems.

Susan N. said, "It gets boring after awhile. The minute someone comes in, you know what that sexist, male chauvinist wants and you know that you'll get hassled for not giving him *everything* he wants. It gets to be a drag real quick. Now, when someone comes in who isn't after sex, he's unusual and your curiosity perks up. He's new and refreshing and you want to talk to him. And he talks back, not about what he can get out of you, but what's in your mind. Imagine! Someone, especially a customer, who's interested in you as a person, not as a body with a pair of tits and a cunt. We meet so many men that are sex-hungry that mental relationships become latent, stuffed away in a closet until someone comes around and asks what's on your mind."

How do masseuses handle grabby customers? One woman who believed that a relaxed, sensual atmosphere should be maintained at all costs, said she merely treated such a man like a baby: "I take his hands, fold them across his chest and say: 'Now, now! Let's be a good little boy. We don't want to ruin everything by being grabby now, do we?' That usually makes him laugh and get embarrassed, and I never have any trouble with him after that." What if he persists? "I'd probably act insulted and leave the room. I'd never do him any physical harm."

Another masseuse handles things differently. "It's all a personality thing. I was having a bad day once and this dude really capped it off. He paid $30.00 for a half and half (consisting of a regular massage followed by the customer massaging the masseuse) and didn't even wait for his turn to massage me when he reached for my snatch. I grabbed his hand and bent his finger back 'til it really hurt. I said, 'Goodbye, this massage is over,' and left the room." We asked, "Didn't your actions ruin the atmosphere of the massage?" "As far as I'm concerned *he* ruined the massage. I'm up to here with these people who think they can get away with anything just because they paid their money."

While most masseuses can readily justify their own actions, we found many have a low opinion of other masseuses, particularly those in other parlors. They are quick to label another masseuse "a whore" but reluctant to turn the same scrutiny on themselves.

One masseuse told us: "I couldn't figure out what was going on at the first place I worked. I was twice as pretty and built better than the other girls but they were getting all the customers. I found out later that most of them were turning tricks. Hey man! Those whores even have rooms rented by the month at the motel across the street!"

Many masseuses share society's contemptuous view of the massage game. They accept society's tendency to label as undesirable any incomprehensible area of behavior. While masseuses understand and accept their own behavior, they lack objectivity to pass judgment on their peers. This negative feeling towards other masseuses eventually becomes a self-judgment.

Women who remain in the profession go to great lengths to protect themselves from the prostitute image. We asked two masseuses about this. "How do you reply to inquiries about your occupation?" Sue L.: "I say I work in an office." Linda P.: "I usually tell them, but I get a lot of hassle. I find some guys will avoid me, where others think I'm really loose and will lay them that night if they take me out. Some think I'm a nymphomaniac. Then if I don't go to bed with them, they accuse me of being a lesbian." Sue L.: "Either way they want to look down on you. I'm searching for a house to live in now. If I was to tell the owner about my occupation, it would be all over." Linda P.: "Either that or he'd want to screw you for the rent!"

We found the rate of lesbianism among masseuses to be low if not non-existent. Though many express contempt for men (as customers) we found very few bisexuals by admission or accusation from other employees. Most masseuses in these parlors are married, or have boyfriends, and do not demonstrate any desire to massage women or engage in sexual activities with them. There were no male homosexual massage parlors in our area of observation.

Owners

The principal factor in determining massage parlor working conditions is the boss. There is a distinct difference between owners who rely on the parlor for their sole support and owners to whom it is just another business venture. Because a massage parlor is primarily a small business—one can be opened for as little as $2,000—most owners fall into the former category. This results in a high level of exploitation and the general opinion among masseuses that an owner is little better than a pimp. As one masseuse told us, "It basically takes a pimp mentality to be an owner. They usually don't like to work and enjoy making money off other people's labor." Personality conflicts occur often between employer and employee. Several bosses have made deductions from paychecks (for arrest insurance, vacation pay, savings) while having no intention of ever returning it or using it for its set purpose. Masseuses have been fired for everything from rejecting a boss's sexual advances to changing the station on the parlor radio. One boss lives with two of his masseuses. As might be expected, they do his housework, laundry and cooking. Once a boss bails a masseuse out of jail, their relationship often changes. Some bosses use this to pressure a girl to do topless or nude massages. Others demand longer hours or personal sexual favors. One boss was accused of addicting his employees to amphetamines in order to exert control. A masseuse's husband said that the pills separated him from his wife.

> It was some sort of speed that made her horny. She got it from her boss/boyfriend who likes to make sure that his chicks have lots of energy. He started giving the stuff to her a little bit at a time to make her work those long hours. After awhile she demanded more, and got it. That's why she started making so much money and couldn't stand to be fucked by me when she got home. The speed wore off and all she could do was doze off until he would give her some more at work the next day. A year later when I last saw her,

she had his kid and was still fucked up on those pills; it was her whole life, those pills and the job.

There are many other tales of conflict between masseuses and bosses. This relationship is the main reason that many masseuses become transients in their own profession. The turnover of employees is large in nearly every parlor and the search for a better boss is widespread.

That search, it must be noted, is not always in vain. We have found several owners who carry on honest, trusting relationships with their employees. One owner keeps out of the bookkeeping entirely, believing explicitly that the masseuses are telling him the truth about the volume of business. Another takes his girls who can't massage (for legal or medical reasons) and puts them to work in his office until they can massage again. The only thing that these types of owners have in common is the fact that, for them, the massage business is a sideline. They receive the main portion of their income from another source and they can afford to be honest, trusting and non-exploitative.

Getting Started

One massage parlor existed in this community from 1960 to 1970. In 1970 the second parlor opened. Two more opened in the first 6 months of 1971. Masseuses in the fourth parlor gave locals more freely than employees of the other parlors. Soon the fourth parlor began to attract hordes of customers. Among the pre-boom customers were men with capital who recognized a profitable business when they saw one. Three of these men opened parlors of their own within the following year.

One of the early owners explains how he got started.

> A friend of mine, kind of a wilder sort, had been going to ________'s place for years when one day she whipped him off. It was one of the greatest experiences of his life and he got all excited about opening a parlor. He was in it to play around and I was always looking for an easy buck, so he talked me into it.
>
> There were only three other places in town and we were the first to have young, attractive masseuses. We brought in some really great stuff. Our parlor was running the others out of business by sheer quality! Our only real competitor opened the following month. They started right in with blow jobs and fucking the customers and that's when the other owners started screaming bloody murder.

From the end of 1971 to the present a new parlor has opened every two months. The peak has now been reached, and many owners are feeling the pinch of a glutted market.

Owners do not have nearly as many problems getting licensed as a masseuse. The prospective owner has but four requirements to meet. (1) He must pay a $50.00 fee to cover the cost of investigating his background. (2) He must not have been convicted of a sexual offense. (3) He must get a business license. (4) He must be fingerprinted and photographed by the police department.

The police department and city hall have 30 days to accept or reject the application. Instances of an applicant being rejected are rare. Most businessmen have their affairs in order before they apply.

The owner usually hires a manager to keep the place open on a regular basis, watch the girls, and act as a bouncer when necessary. A business will often fail when the girls alone are responsible for keeping regular business hours. Katherine L. said, "I was supposed to open the place up at 10:00 but I'd hardly ever get there before 11:30. If I didn't get a customer or a phone call in an hour or two, I'd split. What's the sense in staying open if there's no business?"

The manager is often a silent partner or unemployed friend of the owner. Since most owners depend on their parlor for their bread and butter, they often watch the manager as diligently as the manager is supposed to watch the masseuses.

Recruitment

Attractive, intelligent and personable girls are in great demand as employees. Even with an overcrowded market, a new parlor can still succeed if the quality of the girls hired is high. Thus, recruiting strategies and techniques have become increasingly important.

□ A straight newspaper ad can bring in dozens of applicants. This method requires a great deal of screening, but can be productive if the owner knows what he is looking for.

□ An excellent way to find masseuses is to have a good employee solicit her friends and acquaintances for the job. This eliminates a sizeable amount of guesswork and research on prospective employees. Having friends work together adds to the relaxed environment of a parlor.

□ Scouting has been a successful method. Each parlor has at least one masseuse with considerably more charisma than the others. Many owners will send a friend to a parlor to seek out this employee. If she proves to be a capable masseuse, and is dissatisfied with her present job situation, she may accept a better offer from another parlor.

□ A recommendation from a customer or especially an ex-owner has been known to bear fruit. Many masseuses leave the profession because of long hours, low pay or personality conflicts with an owner. An informed owner may make a better offer to attract a disgruntled masseuse back into the business.

Owners' Problems

The owner of a massage parlor must also deal with his landlord. Some wealthy owners get around the landlord problem by buying the building that houses their parlor. Others are not so fortunate and find that a paranoid landlord can cramp their style. We asked an ex-owner about the person who recently purchased his parlor. Would he be a successful owner?

> I think he'll get buried! I sat down with this guy for three hours and told him every hassle, every detail about the business as I knew it and all he could do was stare at Mary's big tits. He's obviously not in it for the money, so he won't make much. Oh, he could draw $100, maybe $200 a week, but it'll be very difficult for him to make a pile of money without really opening up. If he does that, the landlord will boot him out of the building. He doesn't want a whorehouse operating there.

In several cases the police have attempted to stop the transfer of ownership. They can legally reject an application only if their investigation reveals contradiction in the applicant's background. The head of the local vice squad tried to block one transfer by slowing down the bureaucratic processes. The present owner eventually had to go to his superiors and threaten a law suit against the city. The processes were suddenly speeded up and the transfer approved!

Business pressures have forced owners to go to great lengths in order to protect themselves. One owner likes to go into a parlor where he is a silent partner and test the masseuses. He plays the role of undercover cop in an attempt to discover how far his unknowing employees will go. Another owner has a mirror on the end of a stick to check on his masseuses. The massage rooms are separated by eight-foot partitions and watching a masseuse in action is easy with his little gadget. Other owners, especially those with respected positions in the community, endeavor to make friends in the police department. As one masseuse told us, "________ always knew when a bust was coming 'cause he was in with all those people. He would either leave town or just cool it for a couple of weeks." After a parlor is busted, even if the owner was not directly involved, he may be asked to make an appearance at the police station. Upon arriving there, days or even weeks after the bust, he may suddenly find himself under arrest. A long list of charges may be thrown at him which, more often than not, are drastically reduced after an extended period of court dates, public embarrassment and harassment.

As a precaution, most parlors maintain a brief file on their customers. This serves to inform a masseuse of the preferences of regular customers as well as the identities of undercover policemen. Most of these files are kept on a first name basis only. One highly respected parlor went further, however. Barbara C. said, "Before a customer could get even a local, he had to submit three things: a valid I.D., a business card, which was stapled to his card in the file, and a current credit card. In the future, then, we could just check his card before the massage and we would know how far we could go with him." Another parlor has a steady clientele of a dozen influential people who have agreed to testify that they were never solicited at that parlor.

The higher class owners have themselves pretty well covered. This has forced the small-time owners to organize a Massage Parlor Association. Roughly half of the parlor owners in town are dues-paying members of this organization. While its original purpose was to fight city ordinances while they were in the process of being legislated, a police crackdown around this time forced the association to divert its funds from public relations (offense) to legal fees (defense). This severely weakened the affiliation and caused much internal feuding. Half of the members ran reasonably legitimate parlors while the other half operated parlors of the whorehouse variety. Illegitimate parlors were busted first and the legitimate owners resented pumping money into the legal defense of prostitutes. The association showed early signs of being a significant force on the local massage scene. At this point, however, the burden of defending the few has rendered it virtually powerless.

One owner presented his view of the situation:

> It's weird. The laws are supposedly there to prevent prostitution, yet they actually encourage it. An owner is better off in the long run to open a whorehouse and make a big pile of money in a hurry. That way he can afford good lawyers and hire girls who don't care about morals charges. Chances are you're gonna get busted regardless of what goes on in your place. If society and the law treat a masseuse as a whore, she's likely to become one. Treat a legitimate parlor as a whorehouse and it's likely to become one. It sounds paradoxical, but that's the way it is.

Customers

In our research we were able to determine that there is no such thing as a typical masseuse. Customers, on the other hand, fit several general categories. Most of our conclusions concerning customers are necessarily based primarily on what the masseuses told us about them and upon our impressions of customers as they entered the parlors we frequented. The largest group consists of white men over the age of 35. (In over six months of hanging around the parlors and talking to masseuses, we heard of only two black customers.) As a rule they are white-collar businessmen. Curiosity and boredom with a daily routine are the two outstanding characteristics of the average customer. Many are simply starving for attention, and this need may be the chief reason for the success of the parlors. Where else can a person enter a business establishment, pay a fee, and for the next hour have an attractive girl pay attention to him and cater to his pleasure?

The second largest category of customers is composed

of transients who have little to call their own. Sandy R. said, "We get a lot of transients through here. We get a lot of traveling salesmen, but more often it's a guy who just moved to the area and doesn't know anybody. He'll come in maybe once a week for three or four months, then less frequently as he begins to meet people and make some friends. Most of them drop in now and then to say hi. A lot of them admit that we kept them from going crazy while they were going through their changes."

The word "changes" refers to much more than a shift in geographical location. A sizeable number of men will frequent a parlor when their personal lives are taking turns that they cannot comprehend. Cheryl T. told us, "Lately we've been getting a lot of young married guys. They've been married for, oh, two to five years and can't understand why their sex lives have gone stale. I try to rap to them about communication, you know, get 'em to tune into their old ladies. All they need, as far as I can see, is some confidence and a desire to work things out." Another side of this category consists of men whose wives have already left them. "I've had three customers who came home from work to find a 'Dear John' letter in a half-empty house. They all thought things were fine up until then. I couldn't believe they could be so out of touch with reality. I mean, if a guy's wife finally up and split physically, she'd probably left mentally a long time ago."

The final group of customers includes those men who, by current social standards, are physically or mentally unattractive. Men with deformities are frequent visitors to the parlors. These men may be too ashamed and withdrawn to approach females in everyday situations and find relief in being able to pay money for the attention they receive. A considerably larger group is composed of sexual deviants. Approximately half of the parlors employ one or two masseuses to service these men. What they receive comes under the general heading of a dominant massage. A dominant costs at least twice as much as a normal massage and large tips are commonplace.

What does a dominant massage consist of? Paula B. explained, "Well, since they pay more, it's usually whatever they want. Basically they want to be treated like a piece of shit. I had one guy who had me do nothing but cuss at him for a half hour. Man, I threw out every obscenity I could think of and he tipped me well for it. It really wore me out." Another masseuse related this story: "This guy about 45 came with five pairs of high-heeled shoes. He had me put on each pair during the course of the massage. To cap it off he had me tie his hands with a bra he brought in, pull down the nylon panties he was wearing, and spank him with one of the spiked heels." Another masseuse had a customer with an invalid wife who, he said, treated him like a dog. "He wanted to play the role for real. He brought in his own leash, had me put it on him and lead him around the room. I kicked him a few times and told him what a bad dog he was. He really got off on that."

Surprisingly, many customers come into a parlor just to talk. They are content with taking off their clothes and relating pieces of their private lives to a masseuse. "A lot of guys are just getting over the hangup of being nude and alone with a girl. We get things said to us that a customer would never dream of saying to someone he knows. Some things they say are just plain gross, but, more often we get dudes who rap about their personal relationships. homosexual tendencies or their sexual hangups. I guess they figure they're never gonna see us again if that's the way they want it." Discretion is a valuable commodity to all customers.

It's hard to go shoplifting in a massage parlor, yet some men still manage to make off with a free thrill now and then. One owner told us,

> Sure, we have our share of rip-offs. One guy ripped us off for five massages in a two-week period. The girls would usually collect after the massage in hopes of getting a tip. Well, this dude slipped out the front door twice and the back door twice. We were laying for him the fifth time, but he somehow managed to crawl out the bathroom window. Another guy came in and asked if he could take the girls' measurements. This one girl, who's a bit naive, said sure. So he breaks out his tape measure and measures her, copping a free feel here and there. He then asked for some kleenex and disappeared behind the bamboo curtain. The girl wondered where he went when she heard the thumping noise from behind the curtain. She looked and there he was, jacking off right in the parlor!

Incidents of exhibitionism are not foreign to masseuses. They occasionally become the objects of voyeurs exposing themselves. Janet H. said, "I remember this one guy, though he wasn't a customer. He came up to the parlor window, looked in and saw me behind the desk talking on the telephone. Right in the middle of downtown, he whipped out his cock and started jacking off; rubbing it against the window and all. It wasn't long before he came and shot sperm all over the window. I happened to be talking to the police at the time and told them to come get this weirdo, but he was finished and gone before I knew it."

Rates for massages vary according to the parlor, clientele and volume of business. We found prices from a $4.00 "special" to the popular "half and half" for $30.00. Customers are often fooled by the money factor. Is the sauna counted as part of the hour long massage? Masseuses have been known to stick undesirable customers in the sauna for longer than usual in order to avoid giving him his money's worth. Seven dollars looks very economical in an advertisement, but is that for an hour or a half hour? Some parlors are notorious for skimping on the massage and getting down to what the customer really came for.

We found that one parlor employed a "blow-job (fellatio) specialist." It was said that there wasn't a single guy she couldn't get to come in less than three minutes flat. Volume was so high at this parlor, that on busy evenings she might perform the oral sex act up to 20 times. It was her sole function there. She absorbed the responsibility for anything illegal and the owner only had to cover for one girl.

Typical rates for the average parlor are $10 to $15 for an hour's massage. A masseuse at one of the looser parlors explained their policy: "It's $15 for an hour long massage including a local. An extra $5 will get my top off and $5 more takes my bottom off. For $10 more he can bathe with me for a half hour. (This is a rare practice.) Anything after that is negotiable between me and the customer. I have to soak him for $35 before negotiating a blow-job or a lay." It is nearly impossible for an owner, a landlord, a policeman or a researcher to determine which parlors are engaged in illegal activities and which are not. A whorehouse today may be a health spa tomorrow, according to a number of variables. Financially though, if a parlor is a front for a house of prostitution, oral sex will cost between $30 or $40 and complete sexual intercourse between $40 and $60.

Law Enforcement

The law governing prostitution and solicitation in this community reads as follows:

> It shall be unlawful for any person to keep or carry on or become an inmate of, or a visitor to, or to in any way contribute to the support of any house of ill fame or prostitution, or to induce, or attempt to induce by any solicitation, prostitution to be carried on in any house, room or place or to solicit by word, act, gesture, sign or otherwise, any person for the purpose of prostitution.

Compared to the type of crime that proliferates in a large metropolitan county, the massage business—prostitution or no prostitution—is in reality a miniscule problem. Control of the businesses rests more with the legislative branch than the sheriff's department. Several parlors in the area were recently closed because laws were enacted that the parlor owners couldn't possibly comply with. One such law states that the owner of a massage parlor must be a licensed masseur. Few, if any, owners—be they enterprising businessmen or pimps—qualify as masseurs. The owners can scream and file suits against the county, but, during the period of litigation, the padlocks of the sheriff's department remain securely on the parlor doors.

As far as we could discover, the massage business in the nearest major city is under the control of an organized crime syndicate. The authorities in this city do not seem to be too concerned about the proliferation of parlors. Because their ownership is centralized, competition and sensationalism in advertising are virtually nonexistent. New competitors are forced to run wide-open parlors which are dealt with swiftly and decisively by the syndicate. Rumors of payoffs proliferate to no one's surprise or concern.

This makes the smaller suburban areas ripe for the massage business. These cities do not possess the capital to fund a well-staffed vice squad. Investigation, arrests and court proceedings have proved to be a heavy financial burden. The most recent raids in this community saw five masseuses arrested on charges of solicitation to commit a lewd act. One manager estimated that this raid will ultimately cost the city $30,000. This is a high price to pay for putting five masseuses out of business for a day or two despite favorable publicity for the police.

Sisterhood Really Is Powerful

We have painted a rather dismal picture of the life of a masseuse. Her hours are long, the pay low, the employer is pressured and he, in turn, pressures her. She is constantly confronted with the fact that, in society's eyes, she is a deviant.

Is there any hope for a better life? The answer is yes. We found one unique parlor within the community. The masseuses were directly involved in virtually every area of setting up their working environment. The girls work seven hours per shift and the pay is comparatively high at $2.50 per hour. The owner of this parlor is well off financially. We have determined, however, that this fact plays a minor role in the total make up of the parlor.

There are many reasons for the parlor's overall success. The people involved took great care in preparing their establishment. The owner thoroughly investigated the other parlors in the community. The types of women in the work force, the physical layout of the parlor, the types of customers catered to and, most important, the amount of capital invested and returned, all were considered before the first girl was even approached for employment. Most of the girls eventually hired came from another parlor in town. They had banded together in a "sisterhood" as an intellectual reaction to the oppressive situation in that parlor. They shared two basic ideals. One was a sincere desire to understand the psychological nature of their profession. The second was an important realization: that the owner needs the masseuses much more than they need him.

What is a sisterhood of masseuses? How did it form? How did it (or could it) affect the life and working conditions of a masseuse?

> When I started being a masseuse I knew what the hussling game was. When I started working at The Palace all of the girls there were just finding out where they were at. They were either at the stage of being used or not knowing what they were doing. I met Sherry and could really relate to her and then I started

relating to the other chicks. When you work at a bar, you have to handle about 30 to 50 men at a time, there are just masses of people out there. When you work at a massage parlor it's like one to one with the guys and the group was the girls. So I started being able to relate to the girls and it was really good for my head. Sherry was writing a paper for one of her classes in college which really caused us to start thinking about different psychologies we applied in that room and what we had going for us. When we started really wording it, verbalizing it, and thinking about it, we started rapping to the other chicks about it. I was into reading Tarot cards real heavy then, so I brought that into work with me and that became another way to teach people to reflect on themselves, and look inside themselves. More and more the whole place started becoming like a trip. Look around you and see what your environment's really like and what's motivating you to do things and what kind of control you have.

The best part about it was that it didn't get canabalistic like most group therapy gigs do. Because we had a common cause we had a common ground where the "other" was the customer. You had your own private life so you didn't have to confront your personal life with the other people out there, you know, society. And when you can pit the girls against that, they start taking what they have learned in their experiences with the customers and start applying it into their own personal life. You avoid the direct confrontation that a group therapy has, where you are attacking your own personal life constantly. That's what made it good. It was like getting a group sanity together which really got us closer and closer, and the girls got to know each other better and we spent a lot of time with each other. Which is something I never did on any other job I had been in. I had always totally dissociated myself from the people I worked with. I never wanted them to know what my personal home life was like because people would usually use it as a weapon. Everytime a new girl got hired we had to bring her into the sisterhood. That's where we ran into trouble with the boss because all of a sudden his neat plan of keeping everyone alienated wasn't working anymore. He couldn't quite figure out why it wasn't!

We asked the masseuse another question: "The final break with The Palace was actually over vacation pay, right?"

Yeah, but that was after we already had decided to quit. It simply came to that we had a sisterhood going and a guy had offered us a job—what are we staying here for? The vacation pay was owed to us and that was a crisis that initiated it. Now we're going to test our strength, we're going to stand up to him and see if our sisterhood really works, and it did! It was a test of strength and we met him on his ground and we won. All the girls who heard about it had that as an example. You don't have to let him push you around. . .if you get organized. The enemy isn't the other girls or the customers. The enemy is whoever is trying to make you feel ashamed or guilty. . .because it's really *good* to be a sensual person; that gives people pleasure. But you can't turn that against yourself if you have these secret guilts and secret doubts and that's where the strength of the sisterhood is. Most of the girls I've seen working in other massage parlors aren't proud of their work and that's because they accept the way other people look at it. . .instead of seeing it as a calling. Rather than seeing a massage parlor as a kind of sanctuary that can bring about change, they look at it the way the customers look at it when *they* come in there, and it drags them down. That's where they keep all the girls working for them, in all the bars, all the massage parlors and anything that has to do with men-women relationships. Instead of the girls looking at themselves as people who offer solace, and that's being a good thing in society, they see themselves as being degraded.

Although one masseuse told us that working in a massage parlor absolutely kills your sex drive, the members of the sisterhood disagreed. "She's talking about her own bitter experience." We noted that the sensual level of the parlor was very high. It's obvious that the masseuses were not getting burned out by their work.

That's because we don't have a boss that sucks our energies. The girl you talked to is how a lot of girls can end up because when she goes in the room, she goes in there alone. . . .When I go in there, I'm not alone; all my sisters are with me. Anything he says to me he says to all of us. Several of my customers had come in very upset that their wives were starting to express Women's Lib ideas. I try to make them see why their wives were unhappy and why I was unhappy when I led that kind of life. You aren't supposed to relate to people intelligently, to be independent, or to be able to take care of yourself, and he's got all the sexual liberties. So if you want to do anything you have to sneak off and lie about it and feel like a criminal. More and more guys come with some remark like, "Well, are you married?" and I'll say "Yes," and that will really stun them. "Why, your husband will let you work here?" "Let you," that phrase, "allows you!" I happen to know that my husband is proud of what I'm doing. More people should make other people feel better and my husband feels that way about it too. What I do here is no threat to him.... The young guys who are in their early twenties have been asking us for advice and they go home and take what they learn from us back to their wives. It surprises me that more and more young guys come in now than a year ago, maybe because we have a nice place.

We responded strongly to this liberated masseuse. "Your place *is* nice. The atmosphere is very warm and friendly. Walk into another parlor in town—and we've been to most of them—and they make you feel like a chauvinist pervert of some kind." There is one basic reason that this liberated parlor is a success. The masseuses are simply not mind hungry. They have thought about what they're doing. They're on top of all the games. Here are the principles of Women's Liberation in a place where they are totally unexpected. These women have met the male chauvinist on his home ground, making the massage parlor a creative environment—a place for self-realization—rather than sexual exploitation.

4 *David J. Pittman*

The Male House of Prostitution

Drift, impermanence, ephemerality—such is life for the male hustler. The homosexual market (like many others) craves two things most of all, novelty and youth. Necessarily, then, the hustler drifts from city to city, from 42d Street in New York to Saint Louis' Forest Park, seeking his fortune (he may say) but also running from scenes and people to which he is no longer new, trying to catch the impossible dream of eternal youth and undying virility. Failing that, and he must fail of course, there is, as we shall see, the dream of something much more ordinary—love, shelter, home.

But a house, as Polly Adler observed some time ago, is not a home, and this is as true of male houses of prostitution as it is of more familiar sorts of brothels. The house I am going to describe here, which caters exclusively to homo- or bisexual tastes, is really a composite of several known to me in a large metropolitan center in the United States. I will be no more specific in identification than this, for obvious reasons.

The Male House of Prostitution

The house stands in a residential area of single-family dwellings, duplexes and apartment houses. From the outside, one would imagine it to be occupied by the same sort of middle-income people who live in the neighborhood. The inside, needless to say, offers a different prospect. The doorway opens onto a reception room exquisitely decorated with occasional chairs, an overstuffed couch, brightly painted walls and wall-to-wall carpeting. Off the reception room is the business office of the house, containing a desk, chair and two telephones; this is where Jay works. Whether out of irony or deference to a possibly older tradition I do not know, but Jay is known as the madam. Officially, Jay runs a modeling agency.

The rest of the house contains four bedrooms, a kitchen, two bathrooms with showers and a sitting room for the models when they are not involved with the customers. There is a color television set in the sitting room, as well as a stereo set and a bar. The madam supplies the models with drinks free of charge, but he keeps the liquor cabinet locked. Of the four bedrooms, one can be said to be fairly typical. It is furnished with a queen-sized bed, flanked on each side by a nightstand table each of which contains a towel and a tube of K-Y lubricating jelly. The room is lavishly furnished with zebra skins on the floor, linen curtains and a quilted bedspread. Illumination is provided by lights recessed behind the bed and/or candles. Two straight-back chairs (for the model's and customer's clothes) complete the room's accoutrements.

The Business Enterprise

Jay is an active homosexual himself, but he manages his business with the same goals as a legitimate enterprise. He wants to make a profit and to have satisfied customers who will return to use his personnel's services. His typical question to a departing customer is, "Did everything go all right?" If the model goes on a call to a customer at a downtown hotel or a private residence, Jay will often telephone the customer later and ask the same question.

The madam prides himself on the fact that his business is no fly-by-night operation, and that his customers are completely protected against being cheated, robbed, assaulted or blackmailed in the sexual encounter; furthermore, he protects his clients, many of whom are socially prominent, against their homosexuality becoming public knowledge.

As he would in another business, Jay also advertises, discreetly. In the underground press and periodicals that cater to homosexuals Jay will occasionally run an ad announcing that he has models for hire and giving a telephone number. Jay always interviews a caller over the phone to discover his motives; if he has any doubts, he schedules an appointment to interview the man personally. Most customers, however, are referred by other individuals.

Jay's staff is composed of a core group of approximately 15 full-time models and a fringe group of 20 models who supplement their income by doing modeling in their off-hours. The ages of the models range from 18 to 26, although there are exceptions. One of the most successful models in the city, for example, is in his mid-thirties, but given the primacy of youth as a value in the homosexual subculture, he is a rarity. In his ads, Jay usually bills his models as being from one to three years younger than they are, but seldom does a model pass more than three birthdays while in Jay's employ. The demands on them are heavy, physically and psychologically. As one former core model stated: "You were never free from the job. Jay would wake me up at 2 A.M. to go on a call, or if business was active, I might have four or five calls in one day."

Recruitment of Models

A new model can be recruited either through the recommendation of a current employee or through the advertisements Jay runs calling for "young, well-built and good-looking" men who are needed to pose for photographers. Or Jay might meet a potential recruit at parties or other social gatherings. One model who was recruited in this 4, I met Jay at a party. I indicated that I was having a hard time financially and was looking for a new job. Jay asked me if I would like to go to work for him, and I asked him what he did. He stated bluntly, "I run a male house of prostitution. If you are interested, why don't you drop by." He gave me his address and telephone number, and several days later I dropped by.

The indication of interest by a young male is only the first step in the recruitment process. Jay must then determine his suitability through an interview that follows a fairly standard format. If Jay has never met the young man personally, he will try to make him feel at ease by stating, "Call me Jay, I'm the madam of the house." The interview begins with Jay's asking the model his name, his level of education, his last employment and whether he is homosexual. This, or at least bisexuality, is mandatory. If, for example, the potential recruit claims to be heterosexual but wishes to earn some money by indulging in homosexual encounters, he is denied employment. The young man is then queried whether he has any qualms about whom he goes to bed with. To have certain qualms is perfectly acceptable; Jay doesn't disqualify someone for not desiring to go to bed with a member of another race, a sadist or a masochist. Jay next establishes whether the applicant is "versatile" or "aggressive," trade terms as well as code words in the homosexual subculture. Versatile means one will indulge in both active and passive acts of fellatio and anal intercourse. Aggressive refers to the model who will take only the active role in anal intercourse but will engage in active and passive fellatio. Jay prefers that his models be versatile, but he does accept on occasion those who are only aggressive if they are extremely attractive. Furthermore, Jay asks the young man whether he has any qualms about his nude photographs appearing in magazines or movies, under an assumed name of course. He also establishes whether the applicant has any sadistic or masochistic tendencies. This is important to Jay as he will not turn away a customer desiring such services, and he has special models to accommodate them.

Further questions elicit whether the candidate has ever been arrested on a morals charge. It is Jay's strict policy never to employ a model who has ever been officially labeled "queer" by police officials; the risk is too dangerous for him. The young man is then asked whether he has had venereal disease or hepatitis in the last five years. If he has been cured of these disorders, he is employable, but a physical checkup in any case is required before he begins work.

The Physical Examination Interview

If, after an hour of questioning, the prospective model has satisfied Jay with respect to his personality and mental stability, the candidate is then asked to go to one of the bedrooms. There the young man is asked to remove all his clothes and to have an erection. If the latter proves impossible, Jay calls in another model and asks him to go down on the applicant. If this does not cause an erection, the candidate is dismissed on the theory that if he could not perform at this point, in all probability he would be unlikely to be able to perform with the customers.

The prospective model is next photographed with a color Polaroid camera in the nude, with his penis both in the flaccid and erect states. Jay then measures the model's erect penis from the dorsal side and makes a note on its thickness. The photographs and measurements go into a book that the customer can view in selecting his model. Other vital statistics are included such as height, weight, eye color, age, body build and so forth. Jay does not have sexual intercourse with the prospective model, which stands in contrast to what has been reported in some accounts of female houses of prostitution. The model-to-be is also warned not to have sexual encounters with other models, as this causes conflicts and interpersonal attachments to develop among the business staff. The applicant then is told that once he is dressed (he may take a shower if he desires), he should return to the business office. One model in commenting on this aspect of the interview stated: "I was very nervous throughout the whole thing, but I kept thinking how good the money was." When the applicant returns to the business office, Jay informs him whether he is acceptable for employment.

Acceptance for Employment

Since one of the primary motivations for engaging in prostitution is for material gain, Jay then explains in explicit detail the monetary arrangements. Jay makes all appointments for the models with the customers. Business calls fall into three categories: in-calls, out-calls and overnight calls. An in-call occurs in the house itself, for which the charge is $20 an hour, of which the model retains $14 and Jay takes $6. On out-calls the fee ranges from $25 to $35 per hour, with the model retaining $19 to $25; the customer is required to pay the model's taxicab fare to and from the hotel or place of meeting. An overnight call can take place at the customer's place of choosing for a period of seven or eight hours. The fee ranges from $100 to $150, with the model retaining $70 to $110 and the remainder going to Jay. Thus, the fee split is approximately 70 percent for the model and 30 percent for the madam of the house. The model is allowed to keep all tips, which range from nothing to as high as $50, with the most usual tip being from $5 to $10. Although he is not required to tell the madam of his tips, he is encouraged to do so.

Finally, Jay discusses the question of the new model's assuming a new name. A model rarely chooses to use his legal name but takes a new one, as is frequently the case in the entertainment industry. He is billed under his new name, always a first name, in keeping with the mores of the homosexual subculture.

Socialization of the Model

In a classic article, the sociologist Kingsley Davis stated that prostitution was characterized by emotional indifference to the customer, by barter and by promiscuity. Basically, these are the same values that Jay attempts to instill in the new models. They are told not to become emotionally involved with their customers or to see them outside the business context; they are forbidden to give customers their real names, addresses or telephone numbers. Breaking these rules is grounds for dismissal. The barter aspect is simple enough: on in-calls the customer either pays the model or the madam after the sexual liaison; on out-calls the model collects the fee in cash, unless he has been instructed by the madam to accept a check. Finally, a prostitute is by definition promiscuous; he is expected to accept all calls assigned to him unless he can provide an acceptable explanation for refusing.

Preparing for a Call

The model is given general instructions about preparing for a call. Since the accent is on "young, well-built and attractive" males, the models are expected to maintain an excellent physical appearance. Their hair is to be always well groomed and trimmed within acceptable lengths. Facial preparations are used to remove the telltale signs of lines in the face, especially during periods of heavy sexual activity. Models generally trim their pubic hair, and almost all models remove buttocks hair with a cream preparation.

Both versatile and aggressive models prepare for a specific call in almost identical ways. The model showers, using a deodorant and body powder; the versatile model will also douche his rectum. Clothing worn by the model depends upon the occasion, a dinner engagement with the customer before the liaison calling for one kind of attire, a request for a "butch" or masculine model calling for another, usually a formfitting shirt with tight trousers.

The First Calls

Since all the models are practicing homosexuals or bisexuals, homosexual experience is scarcely unfamiliar to them. For a number of the models, however, the first call is their initial experience in receiving money for their sexual favors, in being a prostitute. Previous encounters may have brought them gifts of clothing, weekend trips or no-expense vacations, or loans of money, but there had been no explicit understanding that the benefactor had to be satisfied in every way. In other words, the previous experiences, generally with men older than the models, carried with them expectations of reciprocity but no feeling of prostitution.

Many young men enter the house intending to stay only for a short period of time until they are financially on their feet. For example, one model stated:

> When I first started I told myself I would do it for only one week—until I had all my bills paid off and a few dollars saved. However, the money was so good, and the life was exciting and thrilling to begin with, so I continued. But after a few months it became boring and tiresome.

This initial experience of good money and thrills is an entirely predictable outcome, inherent in a career of male prostitution. New faces are always in demand by Jay's customers; and since the models have been carefully screened to obtain young, well-built, attractive and versatile males, they receive more calls during the first two weeks at the house than do the older models. This means, of course, more money than the man is accustomed to, as well as high status as the new star of the house. The latter should not be underestimated; as one informant put it:

> All my customers treated me good. No one was ever cruel or mean to me. Of course, occasionally some trick did not tip me, but this was the exception, not the rule. And I had a number of them who always asked for me when I was working for Jay.

Another young man made a similar point:

> At first I thought it was so wonderful to have love made to me by so many wealthy and socially elite men. I will never forget my first experience with a trick. We met in the reception room where Jay introduced me to Bill. We then went to the bedroom and took off our clothes and got into bed. I was very nervous. We began to talk, and he told me he was married with a wife and two children. He said that he did not realize that he had strong gay tendencies until after his marriage and now that he was in his early forties that he wanted both his family and also to have homosexual relations. He was very nice—an airline pilot I think. He then asked me what I liked to do in bed, and I told him. I asked him what he liked, and he said he liked to be screwed, so I did it to him. We talked for the rest of the hour, and he gave me a $10 tip.

In this particular case, the model's initial experience was a financially and psychologically rewarding one. At first the number of calls the models receive is heavy—as many as seven within a 24-hour period of time. However, unless he is exceptional, he is considered one of the regular members of the business staff after approximately two weeks. The term "exceptional" is given to those models who are outstandingly good-looking, well hung, versatile and have a pleasing personality. His physical assets are the subject of much talk in the homosexual community, and Jay's customers seek the exceptional model's services frequently until his newness, too, finally wears off. After the model becomes an established member of the business staff he will receive an average of three calls a day, although some models may have only one call per day.

Part of the model's socialization to his role involves learning to satisfy the customer. Jay strongly inculcates his models with the necessity of this. The model is to remember that for one hour he exists to gratify the customer's desires. Part of this means being pleasant, talking with the trick but never asking questions about his personal and business affairs, unless such information is volunteered. Conversely, the model is not to discuss his own personal life with the customer except in the most general terms.

According to my informants, the typical customers are financially affluent white professional or businessmen in their forties or early fifties; a sizable proportion of these men are married, with various models estimating the number as being between one-third to one-half of their customers. (This is in basic agreement with Laud Humphreys' findings that a majority of the known participants in homosexual encounters in public places are married.) Their relatively advanced age makes it difficult for them to compete for youth in the free market of the homosexual subculture, but their financial status makes it possible for them to purchase the youth and physical attractiveness so strongly desired in the homosexual (as in the heterosexual) world. Most of the customers are what would be termed in the homosexual argot as "size queens," that is, they are fixated on the size of the penis—the larger, the better. The men constantly comment on the size of the call boy's organ. If there is fetishism here, it is rather analogous to the American heterosexual male's alleged fetishism for large breasts. In any case, one call boy, with frankness, stated: "My big peter was the reason I was chosen so frequently—I want to be liked for myself, not my body." It seems clear, too, that the customers are men whose social and political position as well as marital status require them to keep their deviance a secret. Jay is the key figure here, and he apparently merited the trust his customers place in him.

Progression in the Career of a Model

As previously noted, the typical model does not begin his work with the expectation that he will become committed to the role of a call boy. The career is begun with the rationalization that it will be for only a few days or weeks until pressing financial problems are resolved. In the initial interview Jay, the madam, always explains to the young man the difference between a whore and a prostitute. According to him, a whore is "one who gives his sexual favors without being rewarded financially," whereas a prostitute is "one who receives money for his sexual favors." Jay, although avoiding the label prostitute for his business staff, does try to make the model understand what his role will be. Although in moments of anger the models will refer to each other as "whore," "slut" or "prostitute," Jay and the models refer to their role as that of a call boy—never prostitute. This self-identification, according to one informant, came "about the third week on the job. It was easy money, and I did not desire to trick on the side. I was having more than enough sex at work. I always had nice clothes and money in my pockets." In other words, he is a businessman like anyone else in the society, above all emotionally uninvolved with his customers.

Sexual Encounters

Whatever the psychological gratification obtained by either call boy or client in the conversations that occur during the hour, the primary purpose of the male prostitute is to provide sexual gratification to the customer. Sexual encounters fall into a typical pattern. This can be best described in the words of the call boys themselves. Bill, in recounting an episode stated:

> The customer picked me from the book of photos that Jay has of the boys. Jay got me from our room [the models' sitting room] and took me to the reception room where he introduced me to Jack. Jack was about 35 years of age with blond hair and was good-looking. We went into one of the bedrooms, and he asked me to undress. He admired my body, especially my cock, and stated that I was really well hung. He then undressed, and we got in the bed and embraced. He asked me if I liked to have sex with the lights on or off. I said I preferred sex in the dark, so he turned off the lights. We talked for a while; he told me he was from Texas and had heard about our house from some of his friends, so he decided to visit it.
>
> He then told me how good-looking I was and that we wanted us to perform "69," which we did. I told him to tell me when he was going to come as I don't like for tricks to come in my mouth. It makes me sick. He said he would, and he did. I did not come myself.
>
> We conversed after this about Texas, and he told me about his wife and his son. He said he never tricked with a male unless he was out of town on a business trip. He was very nice to me. He then asked me what I liked to do. I told him I liked to fuck, and he said he liked to be fucked, so I got the K-Y out of the drawer and fucked him. He said he enjoyed it. We talked awhile, and he said that he would like to see me again when he was in town again. I said all right—just call the house.
>
> We then got up and took a shower together. He then dressed, and he gave me a $10 tip—Oh, I guess I had him about once a month over the next five months.

The major thing to note about this episode is that the call boy follows the interactional leads of the customer on both sexual and conversational activities. This liaison also illustrates the statement of most informants that most customers prefer to have fellatio performed on them and to be the passive partner in anal intercourse.

The frequent performance of fellatio on customers raises the question for the call boy of what to do with the fluid at ejaculation. Some require the customers to inform them before they ejaculate. One call boy stated:

> I had this trick who did not tell me he was coming. He came in my mouth. It made me so sick that I had to

jump out of bed, grab the towel and vomit in it. I was sick for hours after that. I just can't stand that.

Some call boys, however, accept the swallowing of the seman as part of the job even though they may not enjoy the taste or the sensation. And there are some who do enjoy it.

Anal Intercourse

Generally speaking, certain physical attributes of the model determine whether he is to be the active or passive partner in anal intercourse. Customers prefer to be the passive partner when the model is of the butch type, with a larger than average penis. Customers who want the active role in anal intercourse seek models who are more slender, with smooth bodies and an average-sized penis. It should be emphasized that there are exceptions to these generalizations, but on the whole they hold up.

One of the call boys, Ben, related the following experience concerning anal intercourse:

> There was this young guy of about 30 years old who came to the house one night. Much to my surprise he was a guy who I had known from the bar. He was always trying to get me to go home with him, but I always refused. I'm sure he did not know I was a model. Well, he picked me from Jay's photo book, and Jay introduced us as usual. Once we were in the bedroom he said to me, "It's funny that we meet this way finally—in bed." The first thing he did was to blow me, and I came in his mouth, as he wanted it that way. Then after some talk about his always wanting to have sex with me and how much of a crush he had on me from seeing me in the bars, he said, "I'm going to fuck you." I said, "All right, but be careful (as he was well built). Don't ram me as I am built small." To be honest, I enjoyed it—especially the sensation of his coming inside me. He said he would be coming back to the house frequently.
>
> In a few days he returned and told me how much he liked me. He asked me what I liked to do. I said I liked to fuck, but he refused to let me do it as he was almost a virgin—he had been screwed only once or twice before. Well, we did "69" that night. He said he would return soon.
>
> About a week later, he returned. I was attracted to him, and he said he really liked me. I told him that I wanted to screw him. At first he hesitated and said I was too large, that it would hurt him. In the end he consented if I would be careful. I told him the easiest way would be for him to lean over the bed and that I would use Vaseline as it does not dry as fast as K-Y. Well, I took it easy and was very careful not to hurt him, and it took me about ten minutes to get it in, as he was so tight. He did not really enjoy it, but he did it for me.

One hears in this story a contradiction of Davis' observation that the prostitute shows emotional indifference. And, in fact, this customer desired the call boy to become his lover, but Jay, sensing that the model might reciprocate these feelings, saw to it that Ben was never available to this customer again.

It should be noted that some customers are so oriented to anal intercourse that after the model has performed the active role the customer will request that the model use a dildo on him for the rest of the hour. One model quoted a married man who was a regular customer of his as stating: "I like to get fucked and suck a cock. These are two things my wife cannot do for me." Call boys, however, generally view this type of customer as a "weirdo."

Masturbation and Voyeurism

Less frequent than fellatio and anal intercourse are sexual activities that involve masturbation by the model and/or customer. Customers for this sort of service are often "watch queens," men who receive gratification from watching the sexual activities of others. They may ask the model to walk around the room nude, and he may or may not masturbate. Or the client may request the model to lie in bed with him while he watches him masturbate, or, a variation on this, the model may sit on the customer's chest and masturbate. Or, while the two lie in bed together, the customer masturbates the model and may or may not expect the model to masturbate him.

Less frequently a customer will request to watch the sexual activities of two models as they perform fellatio and/or anal intercourse. Some models think of voyeurism of this classic type as incomprehensibly odd. As one model stated: "He is paying for something he does not participate in."

Violations of House Regulations

One of the cardinal rules of the madam is that the models are not to have sex with each other, the reason being that the models, all young, physically healthy and attractive, might become emotionally involved with each other, which would lead either to their becoming lovers (with the possibility of leaving his employment) or to friction with other models. Given the transitory nature of many homosexual liaisons, Jay is probably more concerned with the bitterness that might develop between two models at the end of the affair. In his mind, emotional attachments among his staff could only lead to business problems, and that would reduce his profit.

As with all group norms, the rule of no sex between models is violated. As one model stated: "What else could you expect to happen when you had so many virile, young homosexuals together? Sex was bound to occur." The madam is realistic about this and does not dismiss a model for an occasional indiscretion with another model unless they become too emotionally involved.

The major prohibition, which the madam states time after time to the models, also concerns emotional involvement, this time with the customers. However, Jay desires to have satisfied customers who return frequently, and some of them are bound to ask for the same model for each sexual encounter. As long as the model and the customer satisfy the madam that no personal attachments are developing, he approves of such an arrangement. If, however, he discovers an emotional relationship, Jay no longer allows the pair to be together. He would rather risk losing the customer than the model. If they met socially outside the house, he would dismiss the model.

Models and customers, nevertheless, do become emotionally attached to one another, given the context of single, wealthy middle-aged men and striving, attractive young males. The natural history of one such attachment is told by the model Joe:

> Aaron selected me from Jay's book of photographs. We hit it off from the first time. In the next month he asked for me seven times. On his eighth visit he asked me to have dinner with him, but I refused. He kept begging me to go out with him and said that he was very attracted to me. On his next visit he again invited me to dinner, and I accepted his invitation to meet him at a gay bar and then go out to dinner. At that time I was living at the house, and I telephoned the madam to tell him that I was not going to work that night as I was tired and was going to spend the night with a friend. Aaron and I met for dinner, and he invited me to stay overnight at his apartment. I accepted, and we went to his home where we had sexual relations, but he did not give me any money. I was so happy after that night; I felt that at long last I had found someone to love me. We made arrangements to keep meeting outside my business hours.
>
> Several times in the next week the madam intercepted telephone calls to me from Aaron, as I was living in the house. About two weeks after Aaron and I had been meeting outside the house the madam called me to the office. Bluntly Jay asked me, "What in the hell is going on between you and Aaron? He is always telephoning you, and he hasn't been to the house in the last few weeks. What's the score?"
>
> I replied that I thought I loved Aaron and wanted him for a lover. The madam was furious with me and shouted, "No! No! I will not permit it. It's bad for business. I told you when you first started working here not to become emotionally involved with the customers. You must break it off at once." I replied that I was moving out of the house and going to live with Aaron—that nothing he said would change my mind.
>
> At this point Jay had calmed down somewhat. He said, "I'm against it, and it won't work out. Go ahead if that's what you want. You're a good model, and I'll hate to see you leave. But you'll still work with me, won't you?"
>
> Although I really wanted to stop being a model, I replied that I would, but I was still going to move to Aaron's apartment. I discussed the matter with Aaron. I told him I didn't want to work anymore for Jay. Well, I should have known better when Aaron told me that it would be good for me to continue working at the house until I found another job. I guess I was so attached to Aaron at that time that I would have agreed to anything.
>
> Almost immediately I began to have problems with Aaron. He expected me to work and at the same time to have sex every night before I went to work. Then the newness of the affair began to wear off after a few weeks. I was tired all the time—physically and mentally. I began to drink more heavily and became very depressed. That only made my situation worse. I also began to take more and more "bennies" [amphetamines] to keep me going. But I could not keep up with my work at the house; I could not perform for the customers.
>
> Around a month after I originally left the house to live with Aaron, the madam called me to the office and read the riot act to me. He said that my performance with the customers was poor—that either I leave Aaron or he would fire me. He also said that if I left Aaron I could go visit my parents in another state for a two-weeks' vacation and return to work if I pulled myself together. I told him I would leave Aaron as I was already regretting ever getting involved with him. He was tricking on the side, and he also drank heavily, which did not help my drinking problem.
>
> Aaron did not seem to care about my leaving him, and I went home to visit. I returned to Jay's house a few weeks later, but it was not the same. I just did not have it in me to be a model anymore.

Joe's recollections are presented here in detail to establish the point that the prostitute does, at times, become very emotionally involved with his clients. It is perhaps doubtful whether such relationships as developed between Joe and Aaron have much of a chance of developing into long-term relationships. But it is difficult for many models not to see a solution to their life situations in the permanent attachment that a customer may provide them. If one recalls the strong motives of material gain that led the models into their present jobs, it is understandable that they should prefer being "kept" by a wealthy client to the life of a call boy.

Disenchantment with Modeling

As I said at the outset, a call boy's career is a short one; it generally comes to an end in the mid- or late twenties. We do not have systematic longitudinal data on a significant number of models, but we can discuss some of the reasons why a model might call it quits. Above all, there is disenchantment with the profession, added to this the physical and psychological decline of the model.

Many models, after the initial excitement, become fed up with their lives. They begin to perceive their occupation as being dead-end, a journey to nowhere. As one former model poignantly stated:

> The job was making me depressed. I was young and wanted to go out and have some fun. If I did, it would take me away from the job, and I would lose money. I could not start a romance—who would want a call boy as a lover. I was lonely all the time. I wanted someone to love me for myself, not just my body.

Hustlers and call boys are stigmatized in the homosexual subculture, despite the fact that the group itself is stigmatized by the larger society, and despite the fact that a significant number of homosexuals are almost as promiscuous as the hustler or call boy. Behaviorally there is little difference between the homosexual's "one-night-stands" and the call boys's activities. The former, however, justify their behavior on the grounds that it does not involve the exchange of money.

Beyond this, the model is always fighting a battle to keep the appearance of youth and good looks, and against odds made impossible by irregular hours and periods of heavy sexual activity. He becomes physically tired and turns to stimulant drugs to keep him vibrant and awake. Or in moments of depression about his work and stigmatized position he drinks heavily and becomes intoxicated. Whether through drugs or alcohol, his sexual performance with the customers is inevitably affected—he becomes irritable, tired, unable to have an erection. His face begins to show the effects of such a life style—"bags" under the eyes that no amount of make-up can hide, bloodshot eyes or weight loss, etc. His physical desirability decreases, and slowly he loses customers until he arrives at the inevitable day when the madam fires him.

Psychologically, the strain of many short, intensive encounters with his customers threatens his mental stability. He constantly searches for either a lover to provide him with emotional security, such as the case of Aaron and Joe, or a "sugar daddy," a successful business or professional man, sometimes married, who will support him and provide him with an apartment.

5

Barbara Sherman Heyl

The Female House of Prostitution

Most material on the operation of houses of prostitution deals with the highly urbanized setting. This article, however, is based on interview data from Ann, who owns and runs a small "joint" in Prairie City, population approximately 127,000. Prairie City has a colorful history dating back to its early days as a riverboat landing community. Although many nearby communities remained small and rural, Prairie City industrialized and grew during the late nineteenth century. Before World War I it boasted numerous small manufacturing firms and processing plants. In 1913, in the midst of a nationwide reform movement to halt "white slavery," a State Senate investigating committee came to Prairie City and heard testimony that there were over 20 houses of prostitution operating at that time in the city. The committee felt there was a relationship between the very low wages women were paid in the industrial firms and retail establishments ($3-$10 per week) and the large number of houses of prostitution, where women could earn $25-$75 per week. The effects of the pre-World War I legislation on prostitution are unclear in the case of Prairie City, as in most other parts of the country, but during World War II there was organized prostitution supported by nearby military bases. The 1950s brought another serious attempt to clean up the community, but although prostitution has declined consistently over the years in Prairie City its long-established reputation as an open city hangs on. The largest community in a 200-mile radius, it draws clients from the smaller, neighboring towns, as well as from its own industrialized metropolitan area, to several small houses and a number of hotels and bars supporting prostitution.

The Business

Ann's was not an endeavor long in the planning; instead, it grew out of her previous employment and a chance opportunity. Ann, who is 38, turned out in a midwestern city 23 years ago. She came to Prairie City in 1961 after having worked in several states out of houses and as a call girl ("I've never been a street girl or a bar girl"); in Prairie City she began working in a joint under a madam ("landlady"). She was a successful hustler in the house, with a growing clientele of her own. As it happened, a competitive house in the district had been closed down by the police, and the realtor was attempting to sell the building. Ann began thinking of buying the building and opening a place of her own. She contacted the realtor, who offered her a contract to rent with an option to buy. The arrangement involved little initial capital, and Ann decided to go ahead. During the two weeks of deliberation, however, Ann had been telling her tricks of her potential plans. When her landlady learned of her intentions, she was furious and fired Ann. So Ann proceeded to open the new place as soon as she could; her tricks followed her and spread the word. ("Tricks have a grapevine you wouldn't believe!") In her new establishment she had three women working for her, many customers, but she was arrested 13 times in her first year of operation. As a result of these arrests, she eventually served one year in the state penitentiary for "owning and operating" a house of prostitution.

At the end of her prison term Ann was undecided about staying in the prostitution business, but the friend who picked her up on her release was then a madam in Prairie City. Very soon Ann was working for Sal. Not long thereafter, however, Sal was in the hospital for a considerable stay. With Sal's bills running up and the business running down, she prevailed on Ann to manage the house for her. Ann did. Six months later Sal died. When Sal's mortgagee repossessed the house, Ann had to relocate.

Ann did not find her new building. "One of the fellows [pimps] found it—empty. The first time I saw it, I thought it looked terrible. But it was in an ideal location–a commercial district, where I'd have only one or two neighbors." Thus, although Ann had not initially chosen the site, she recognized the assets of the building's location with respect to her working-class clientele—in an older business district, not far from several major manufacturing industries. She contracted to buy the place. Having invested $1,000 of her own to paint the building, to pay the first and last months' rent and to start the utilities, she was ready to open for business.

The Customers

Ann's place of business is an ordinary, very simply furnished apartment. It includes a living room, two and one-half bedrooms, a kitchen, and "a room out in front that I fixed for myself so I could get away someplace." The living room contains a large color TV set, which is watched alternately by the waiting women or the waiting clients. The entrance to the apartment is hidden in a narrow passageway between two buildings; one would never venture there without prior knowledge of the establishment. The joint opens in late afternoon as the businesses around her close and stays open through to the early morning hours Ann employs a housekeeper who helps supervise when Ann is away and cooks the evening meals for Ann and her staff.

Many of Ann's current customers are clients she has known for a long time. A good number of them have followed her from her working-girl days to her present location. Ann describes them as working middle class, listing their occupations as farmers, truck drivers and workers in Prairie City's large machinery plants. Some college men visit the joint; she has very few wealthy customers, and a number of clients come in regularly from neighboring towns.

The Police

Ann maintains that Prairie City is not a pay-off town. (She has mused that at times she wishes it were!) In fact, she could be arrested at any time and, as noted above, her first joint was busted 13 times. When asked why she suffered so many arrests during one year and many fewer during other years, she cites two main reasons: (1) heavy arrests can reflect particular political decisions either in the community or within the police department to get tough on prostitution and (2) her year of 13 arrests reflected a negligence on her part in screening persons she admitted to the joint as customers. After her state prison sentence, Ann decided to let in only customers she knew personally; any new customers would have to be accompanied into the house by a regular client. Ann states:

> I get new customers from old customers. Now remember that most of these customers are ex-customers of mine personally when I was working, and I have known them for 10, 15, 20 years; and when an old customer like that brings a friend, then I'll let that stranger in with the girl because that guy knows that if he brings the cops down, he's going downtown too—so he's not going to take any chances.

Since this rigid admittance policy went into effect, Ann's joint has not been busted. But she pays a price; the size of her group of clients is not expanding.

To be sure, Ann is known to the police; she, in turn, knows members of the force, particularly vice squad members, due to her previous arrents.

> When the police come and take you to jail time after time, you can't help but develop a mutual respect; they are doing their job and doing it consistently well. But they see that *you* are doing your job and doing it well. They can see I run a clean place—no drugs, no thefts, no trouble, no minors in here—either girls or customers; the girls' weekly medical check-up forms are always in plain sight.

She adds: "The only way I know of to pay off in this town is through respect." Police relationships with professional law-breakers can become businesslike; the term does not imply bribery but rather describes relationships founded on a mutual trust that the other will behave as expected, i.e., professionally.

Ann may be allowed to continue her business because at present there are few houses open in Prairie City and because she runs a small, stable business. Communities tend to tolerate a limited number of known deviants as long as their behavior is predictable and does not menace others. Prairie City's history of prostitution suggests that for this community a small house or two is tolerable. In addition, Ann's joint is not a rapidly growing enterprise. Most small businesses need to grow to survive. Yet Ann has, by her admittance policy, deliberately restricted her ability to increase her pool of clients, that is, to expand her market. This decision, however, may be a key to survival since it inhibits arrests and insures that her joint will remain a small—therefore tolerable— illegal business in the community.

The "Girls"

In addition to the important business decisions with regard to location and policy for admittance, Ann made a significant decision concerning the staffing of her house. She decided her "girls" would all be turnouts, young women who had never worked as prostitutes before. This decision developed, as did the others, out of Ann's previous work experiences. In Sal's joint there were always a few turnouts, but before Ann came, "there was no one turning them out," that is, no one was teaching them how to be professional hustlers. The new prostitutes just "went to work." Since they were neophytes, they were in a vulnerable position with respect to clients and the professional prostitutes in the house. Ann frequently took these women under her wing. ("I found I had a knack for teaching, and there was a definite need for it!") Ann's first house had been staffed wholly by professionals, and she remembered the distance that existed between her, as madam, and the pros. ("I didn't know who they were, where they came from, or how they felt about anything.")

Ann's decision to staff her house exclusively with turnouts was similar to the businessman's decision on the choice of line. Ann opted for a closer relationship with her staff and more control over the services being provided. Her decision had a number of important repercussions for the operation of the business.

1. The turnouts are always young (19-24). The clients approve of this.
2. Ann seldom has more than two or three women working for her at any one time. (She asserts that supervising and teaching more than one or two at a time is difficult. This limits client choice at any one time.
3. The prices at Ann's house are low; $10 is the basic rate. Ann insists she cannot charge the same as a house staffed with professional prostitutes because her girls are not professional yet; they are inexperienced. Another reason that she has not raised her prices is

that she can more likely keep her old clientele, upon which she is dependent.

4. Ann has a high turnover rate among those working for her. Since the turnouts come to Ann's house for training, they leave any time they (or their pimps) feel they are ready—after one week or after several months. This situation poses staffing problems for Ann, who recently instituted a new rule enabling her to hold back one-half of the girl's first week's earnings until her third week at the house. Since the first week's take is usually quite high (word gets around that "Ann has a new girl working"), this provides an incentive to the turnout to stay at least three weeks. The longest anyone has stayed is six months. The average stay is two to three months. Ann feels that usually the women would like to remain at her joint, but the pimps want to get their ladies trained and move them on to call girl work or a joint for professionals, which bring in more money. Ann's customers like the high turnover rate; novelty is valued highly by clients. But the high turnover race makes Ann more dependent on her sources for acquiring new prostitutes—a small group of pimps and their acquaintances.

5. Ann asserts, however, that she conceived of running a house for turnouts as a "gimmick" to help keep her joint staffed. She claims that pimps frequently have difficulty placing their inexperienced ladies. "Most professional houses don't like to take girls who've never hustled before." Moreover, since a prostitute cannot make much money in Prairie City, Ann can tell the pimp that, even if his lady is not a high earner in Ann's house, she will learn how to be a professional hustler. Ann emphasizes, then, the professional training she gives the turnouts in order to manage the pimps as suppliers of staff for her business.

The Pimps

Ann will seldom accept a woman without a pimp. The turnout with a pimp, due to her commitment to him, is more likely to stay in the business; and from the standpoint of the teacher, Ann says she would much prefer to train someone who is going to use the knowledge and experience over someone who will quit as soon as she finds out that the prostitute's life is not an easy one.

The difference in attitudes toward pimps may well be explained by how integrated into the prostitution subculture the madam is. "High-class" madams would not do business with pimps. Ann in contrast runs a low-budget house and is dependent on pimps to obtain staff for her house.

Ann accepts women with pimps because she has little choice. Her house is a small one, located in a mid-sized, relatively isolated city. She is operating an illegal business as part of a sexually stratified subculture in which the men (the pimps) have the more powerful position. Ann states this clearly: "The men lay down the rules in the rackets. The men are the leaders: they absolutely control the rackets." One of the rules the men laid down—obviously to their financial advantage—is that prostitutes and pimps go together. If Ann consistently took "outlaws" (those without pimps), she could not expect much help from the pimps to supply her with her staff. In that case she would have to rely on other landladies or women who have worked for her in the past to find turnouts for her. It would be a very difficult situation. There is, according to Ann, very little solidarity in the rackets in Prairie City. At present the few madams are in competition with one another and would almost rather find some way to put each other out of business than to help each other. In order to staff her business, then, Ann must work with pimps and convince them that she offers a valuable service: turning a straight girl into a "working" girl.

Ann accepts turnouts from a group of some six pimps—three in Prairie City and three in other communities—and their acquaintances. One of the main pimps recently became a partner in her business. When a pimp has a woman who wants to start in the business he calls Ann, says he has "a package" and asks if she is interested. He must give as a reference another pimp whom Ann knows and leave his own phone number. If she has an opening, Ann calls the reference, verifies the information, calls the first pimp back, and they make arrangements for him to bring the woman to Ann's house. When they arrive, they discuss the rules and financial arrangements. Ann says: "I prefer to deal with the men; they know what's happening and usually know the rules and money matters—like holding half of the first week's take until three weeks, etc." As soon as he leaves, she spends several hours with the woman (Ann prefers that they not arrive during working hours) and begins the turning-out process.

Taking the name of the interested pimp allows Ann to check on the recent state of his relationship with other pimps she works with. Since acquiring a partner, Ann frequently checks with him before dealing with a new pimp. "I won't accept a girl from someone my partner doesn't want to deal with, and I won't deal with anyone tied to a Big Organization." Ann indicates that the rackets in Prairie City are very disorganized. As a result it is easy to get busted in this community "[because] the people in the rackets here don't stick together." But one advantage to the disorganization is that there is no big organization to compete with. Moreover, that there is some cooperation among pimps in Prairie City is attested to by the fact that there is little prostitution in neighboring communities. The reason: "They [the pimps] don't want it." It appears that Prairie City pimps have effectively cornered the market on prostitution in their area by concentrating it in one location.

The Partner

Until Ann acquired a full partner, she ran the business with no man in the background. When asked how she survived in the male-dominated rackets, she claims that it was at least partly due to her independent behavior.

> The pimps really just don't know what to make of me. There aren't many women in the rackets as independent as I am. They know I'm really handy with a gun, and, actually, the pimps think I'm crazy. So I just let them think that, and they leave me alone.

Ann's partner is a white pimp (in Prairie City most are black) for whom she has turned out more than 20 women over a five-year period. During that time they developed a strong respect for each other as business persons.

> He's one of the best in the business. I would rather turn out one of his old ladies than anybody else's. He really makes them toe the line. It's easy with his help to turn them into real professionals. That is one reason why I respect him; he is a great businessman. We have a complete mutual trust about money, and that's important.

After four years of bringing turnouts to Ann's joint, he acquired a 25-percent interest in the business. In return, he safeguarded the business' cash and guaranteed that Ann would always have one woman working. Ten months later (immediately following a period of illness for Ann), he became a 50-percent partner, sharing bills as well as profits. As partner, he "handles the hiring and firing of the girls, does some scolding when that's necessary, and when it comes time to pay, he counts the money and gives it to the pimps. But I keep all the books."

The Budget

The following are the approximate monthly totals in income and expenditures for Ann's business:

MONTHLY BUDGET

Income:	Approximately 15 tricks per night (@ $10), six nights per week	$4000
	To the "girls" and their pimps	-2000
	Approximate income from clients, per month	$2000
	Usually two "girls" each pay $5 a day for board, six days a week	240
	Approximate net income for the business: Ann and Partner, per month	$2240
Expenses:	Rent and utilities	$ 270
	Housekeeper:	
	to supervise the house	200
	to cook ($200 for services, $280, estimated food costs)	480
	Other	400
	Total regular expenses, per month	$1350
	Approximate net profit for the business: Ann and Partner, per month	$890

Thus, after splitting the earnings with her partner, Ann may make $450 per month *before* any expenses other than those listed above. Other expenses are hairdresser and florist costs (she has fresh flowers in the house regularly); doctor's fees (she has no medical insurance and was recently in the hospital for a moderate stay—$2,000); and lawyer's fees ($2,000 over the last few months). Her partner helps with lawyer's fees, bond, etc., because it is considered part of the business, but contributes nothing to her personal expenses (such as the medical fees). The prostitutes pay for their own medical examination costs. Ann does not own a car and does not drive; her partner frequently provides necessary transportation. Her wardrobe expenses are modest now, "nothing compared to my days as a call girl." Ann sells no liquor in the joint.

The above figures indicate a narrow profit margin for Ann's joint. It may be that in the sensitive area of financial figures Ann has quoted the income conservatively. On the other hand, there is some evidence that the profits from houses of prostitution are not as high as widely believed. In any case, madams indicate that their businesses yield low profits.

Ann pays approximately $200 monthly rent for a small apartment in dilapidated condition in an undesirable part of town. Only the most disadvantaged members of straight society would pay such rent, which would fetch a two- or three-bedroom home in a residential area of Prairie City. Ann's contract with her landlord assures him a clear profit. He has no improvement obligations whatever; when the furnace needs replacing or the roof fixing, she must pay for it. Ann confirms that the doctor, attorney and virtually every legitimate business contact gets a share of her profits. "They see me coming and raise their fees." A madam's rental and housekeeping costs, in addition to any protection costs she might be paying, must be met every month, whereas her income reflects the seasonal variations in client expenditures (e.g., low in December and January) and is dependent on the prostitutes who come and go. Moreover, her long-term profits can be rapidly diminished by illness or legal prosecution. Owning and operating a house is a high-risk enterprise.

The Madam Role

In order to run her business Ann must keep her customers. To keep her customers, she needs prostitutes; to have a staff of prostitutes, she needs pimps, especially her partner, who has been (and is now obligated to be) her main supplier of "working girls." This triangular set of relationships—clients, prostitutes and pimps—has been described in many discussions of prostitution. The money flows from trick to prostitute to pimp and then back to the tricks via the pimps' purchases of expensive cars, clothes, TVs, jewelry, etc. Ego gratification flows in both directions, in one form or another, for all involved. The madam, it is suggested here, should be thought of as operating in the center of the triangle: she is dependent on all three groups for her business success (and therefore must provide each with something); she both gives and receives ego gratification from all three; and she is to some extent pimping off all three—she gets money from the clients, service from the girls and supplies from the pimps. The successful madam keeps the triangle in balance: if she keeps enough of the people happy enough of the time, she will make a profit.

Keeping her customers happy seems to be the simpler part of the business for Ann. Like a manager of a service business, she must meet a fixed set of customer needs: to have in stock what he wants, to keep regular and convenient hours, to be in a convenient location, to keep prices down and to give him attention when he wants it. Thus, she must have attractive, friendly, healthy women working, and she must have time to chat with the trick who comes in more for company than for sex. It is easier to keep customers satisfied when there are few misunderstandings on the essentials of the transaction. For this reason, Ann much prefers her old clientele—who are "housebroken"—to new customers who do not know what to expect or the rules of the house. Of course, Ann has been dealing successfully with tricks for a long time, so this part of the business poses relatively few problems for her. But she is dependent on her clients for her source of income; thus, she must keep them in mind when she plans any changes in the business.

The pimps and their ladies are Ann's suppliers in the business, and the mutual demands and expectations are much more complicated with them than with the tricks. Ann's pool of tricks is a remarkably stable group, whereas her staff of prostitutes changes every few months. As noted, this high turnover rate forces Ann to be heavily dependent of the pimps to supply her with new staff and no doubt reduces her profits. When asked why she does not run a house staffed with professional hustlers rather than turnouts—so that she could be more independent, charge the tricks more money and cut down on her constant staffing problems—Ann replies: "I've asked myself that. It's because I am needed. The turnout needs someone to teach her, to help her." Ann values highly being able to play the teacher role to each new set of turnouts.

Ann feels strongly that her teaching is the critical factor affecting her success as a madam: her ability to meet the demands of the clients, girls and pimps.

> If I'm good at my teaching, the girl will be a success with the tricks (the clients are happy). When that's the case, she'll be making money, and *that* makes her and her old man happy. *How* the girl gives service determines completely how much money she makes; and I'm here to teach her to give professional service.

Ann prides herself on her strict standards of professionalism. Cleanliness, self-pride, social skills and fair hustling techniques are emphasized and carefully taught along with some of the old customs of prostitution, such as, no kissing of clients, taking the money "up front" (before the action) and thorough checking of the client for venereal disease. Ann states that the turnouts are frequently appreciative toward her. "They find that I am teaching them how to make money, to dress tastefully, to converse and be poised with men, to be knowledgeable about good hygiene, to have good working habits (like punctuality) which will help them whether they stay in the rackets or not, and to have self-respect." Ann gains from any positive attitudes the women may have toward her during the training, for she needs their cooperation to run her business.

More critical than how the women feel about what they are learning at Ann's is how the pimps evaluate Ann's training of their "old ladies." For if they are displeased with what Ann is teaching, they will not bring their turnouts to her. Ultimately, then, it is the pimp Ann must satisfy. As far as the pimp is concerned, Ann's responsibility is to turn the straight girl into a professional hustler but, just as important, Ann must teach her how to behave toward him. It is very clear in the rackets what the pimp-prostitute behavioral relationship should be: the men are dominant. Ann teaches each woman the racket's four rules governing her behavior toward her "old man"; (1) no talking back; (2) no lying; (3) no holding back (money); and (4) no chippying (dating anyone else). "The pimps hold me responsible for their old ladies' behavior, even after they leave here. If a girl breaks one of the four rules and I know about it, I tell her old man. If I don't, then it's like her behavior is my fault, because I didn't teach her right." Pimps will sometimes bring their ladies back for a "refresher course," "Pimps will come to me and say, 'She's doing this and doing that. Can you tell her how she's supposed to talk to me!' " Since the pimp's status among his peers depends partly on how well he controls his women, he may hope (or expect) Ann will put the woman's behavior back in line with his demands. Keeping good relations with the pimps depends as much on Ann's ability to train the women to make money as on assuring the men that she's teaching the rules.

When confronted with the discrepancy between perpetuating (through her teaching) the male dominance in the rackets and her own position of relative independence, Ann replies that it poses no problem for her:

> The girl needs him [the pimp] now. When she matures and gets a job on her own, it'll be different. But since she does need him now, she should be helped to know how to keep him.

Ann notes that not all the women she turns out are in love with their pimps, though she adds that, "Personally, I can't imagine people giving the money they've earned to someone they don't love." Some prostitutes maintain a business arrangement with the pimp. Ann summarizes their feelings: "He got me the job and takes care of me; I give him the money." The women Ann turns out have chosen to be with a pimp before coming to her; and Ann notes that "when the girl is ready to leave him, she will." Thus Ann's view of her work with turnouts is that as long as the woman is going to enter the rackets, she might as well learn the rules of the game so that she can play it well and make some money while she is in it.

Ann's recent decision to take a partner into her business (after almost ten years of working without a pimp) reflects the persistent pressure of a culture—both in and out of the rackets—that says the woman needs a man and that he should be dominant in the relationship. Ann explains: "Why did I take on a pimp for a partner after ten years of being alone? After being alone for ten years, why not?! Actually, I entered into the partnership for one main reason: to get some of the responsibility for the business off my shoulders." She claims she had wanted him to share the business with her for a long time, but she had to wait for *him* to make the proposition. During her recent hospitalization he apparently recognized his involvement in the business and decided to formalize it by sharing expenses with Ann and splitting the profits. Finding competent help with a business is the mark of a good entrepreneur. Ann knows that, within the rackets, a lone woman indeed has limitations; and she has with the partnership decision succeeded in marshalling support for her enterprise.

Ann insists that her relationship with her partner is primarily a business one, though it is somewhat complicated by her personal commitment to him and growing emotional involvement with him. Though he has supported Ann's business venture for several years, he has made no personal commitment to her. Ann feels that one explanation for that is her well-established position in the rackets: if they linked up personally, he would become known in the rackets as "Ann's old man" rather than her being known as his "old lady," becasue he is younger and much newer to the business and to Prairie City than Ann.

Ann rationalizes the present state of their relationship another way:

> I can't really ever be his old lady because I doubt that I could not talk back. We bicker and squabble, and I sass him all the time. And that's the number one rule, remember? You can't talk back to your old man. So we have to have a special relationship because of my independence and my knowledge of the business. I know so much more about it than he does. And we *do* have that special relationship.

Ann sees their relationship as an unusual one in the rackets because it is characterized by an approximate balance of power. In answer to the question on what ways her partner is more powerful than she, Ann replies: "(1) he's bigger than I am and (2) the way I feel about him gives him power." Regarding her sources of power with respect to him, she answers, "If I were out of the picture, there's be no business! He can't turn girls out, work the door or take money. Without me there's no business—it's that simple and he knows it." The man's power is that he is a man in a culture that says the man is necessary and important. To balance that power—to be on an equal footing with the pimp—the madam must have her business enterprise.

Because her business is a source of power (it yields more profit than a single prostitute), Ann will be in a stronger position with respect to her partner than will any of his old ladies. Consequently, she can, and does, assume a "main lady" role in her partner's "family," even though she has no personal commitment from him and is not a part of his personal life. She lives in her apartment (where the joint is), while he and his two ladies live elsewhere.

Ann insists that she is not treated as a main lady, which sometimes has a number one favorite status associated with it, but she definitely functions as one. The main lady helps turn out her man's new ladies, helps him control his "family," and generally supports him in any way she can, in hopes "he will stick by her when the other women have gone." Ann clearly exemplifies this attitude in the following statement:

> My main responsibility is to my partner. I run the joint for his benefit and mine. Everything I do is geared to help him—either with the joint or with turning out his old ladies and keeping them happy. And that helps me.

Ann's own personal profits have probably decreased since accepting a partner, but she may have gained in certain other respects that could assure the survival of the business. She has strengthened a tie with someone who will supply her with her staff and who may stand by her in the future. Also, she is free from harrassment from other pimps who either resent her functioning as an independent woman in the rackets or who would like a part of the business themselves. Finally, Ann is assured that as long as the joint is doing well, her man will be around. For money and love, the world's most powerful incentives, Ann is working hard at being a successful entrepreneur.

SUGGESTED READINGS

"Apprenticeships in Prostitution" by James H. Bryan in *Deviance: The Interactionist Perspective*, 2nd ed., edited by E. Rubington and M. S. Weinberg (New York: Macmillan, 1973) pp. 268–277.

Ladies of the Night by Susan Hall (New York: Oridant Press, 1973).

Black Players: The Secret World of Black Pimps by Christina Milner and Richard Milner (Boston: Little, Brown, 1972).

Hustling: Prostitution in Our Wide-Open Society by Gail Sheehy (New York: Delacorte Press, 1973).

6 *Marilyn Salutin*

Stripper Morality

The corner of Dundas and Spadina, at the center of downtown Toronto's garment district, is one of the dirtiest areas of town, a conglomeration of hot, smoky dress and pants factories, wholesale outlets, delicatessens, bargain houses, bookie joints, noise, dust, cigarette stands and outdoor food markets run by Portuguese, Chinese, Italian and Jewish shop owners. Showroom models and working women walk past cheap rooming houses and beer parlors. Tempers are apt to explode easily here. In summertime, soft music flows out of the upper-story apartments on top of the stores.

Dundas and Spadina is just the sort of area where one might expect to find a burlesque show. Conventional standards of middle-class public morality aren't always in play here. And, of course, the spectacle of nude women simulating intercourse and orgasm onstage does not precisely conform to conventional mores either. Thus, there is a nice social symbiosis here between street and theater. On the street the casual passerby is not expected to adhere to any particular standard of dress or behavior, as would be the case, for example, in the highly stratified social landscape of the financial district. On the contrary, Dundas and Spadina is a salad of social identities and personality types. Here the individual can lose himself, so to speak, in the street. He can slip into the burlesque during the afternoon without being given a second glance by other passersby. His presence in the theater will go unnoticed, and for $2.25 he can sit there, if he so desires, from 1:30 in the afternoon until late in the evening.

The theater itself is called the Victory, and it stands across from Switzer's, the most famous delicatessen in Toronto, where the strippers traditionally grab their evening meal before they go onstage and frontstage. For the passersby, the Victory's big neon lights and bold posters promise sexual delights. Huge blowups of famous strippers such as Sexotica, Sintana, Busty Haze and SintoLation — posed in the traditional floor positions or bumping and grinding with larger-than-life red lips and lunging torsos — entice the audience while it is still on the street. For the linear minded there are captions: "One Hot Woman," "Sexual Delights Never Before Experienced," "Bare-Breasted Beauties" and "We Go All the Way — No Strings Attached." It is the big sex thrill in a world where, as Norman Mailer says, sex is sin and sin is paradise. Sin is also good for business at the Victory.

From the bright marquee to the little old man taking tickets and promising you that you haven't missed too much if you come late, the Victory might appear a haunting relic of the days of Broadway and working-class vaudeville. Inside, the stage is flanked by two statuesque cardboard strippers who stand like pillars setting off an altar. Perhaps they are guarding the sacred ritual of the burlesque from contamination or invasion by outsiders, or perhaps they are the fading afterimages of the time when Gypsy Rose Lee might have come down the aisle to wow the audience with her bumps and grinds.

No Lilies and Roses

But this is not the scene for Gypsy Rose Lee or even for Lili St. Cyr. It is the scene for some would-be Gypsy Rose Lee who doesn't have what it takes, or for some Gypsy Rose Lee who made it several years ago and has had it or for some Gypsy Rose Lee who just never made it at all.

Because this is not Las Vegas with its gorgeous show girls, nor New York and Paris with their Lidos and Copas — it is Toronto, and it is the Victory at Dundas and Spadina, and I call it "poor man's burlesque." Still, poor man's burlesque is probably better than no burlesque at all, and it certainly is for the thousands of men in Canada and the Midwest who go to hundreds of other Victorys in search of a kind of "satisfaction."

At any rate, the Victory is a fag end of the day gone by, of which some still say "when men were men," because the Victory is run-down and old, with sleazy seats and cigarette-smoking, hunched-up, shabbily dressed men waiting, it seems, for equally jaded strippers to come out and turn them on with their make-believe sexuality, learned perhaps in Libby Jones' book on *How to Striptease*.

Burlesque in Toronto today means the nude dramatization of the sex act, including the orgasm. As such, it is, of course, considered an affront to the public definition of sexual morality. It is considered obscene.

In our society the spoken or unspoken reference point of all discussions of sexual morality is the animal. Sexually man is not supposed to be an animal — he is expected to attach social meanings and purposes to the sex act. Sex is associated with marriage and procreation, the preservation of the family system and is, in essence, useful for the maintenance of the ritual ordering of our way of life. Sex is usually exchanged by women for the financial security and honorable social status of marriage. Sex is also shrouded in romantic mystique. An aura of sacredness and privacy is associated with it, as is emotion and affection between the two love partners. Now, obviously, burlesque destroys all that. It is an exhibition of sheer animalistic physical sex for the sake of sex. This is offensive. It is offensive to lovers because they want to feel secure with each other, with the feeling that they are wanted and needed. It is offensive to women because women like to feel that they are usually more admired by men (and by other women) if they do not appear too eager to engage in sex. Many women, as Fred Davis has noted, feign contempt, or really feel contempt for sex, unless the submission of their bodies to their husbands brings them some material rewards. Strippers demand nothing like this from their public. They demand to be accepted as erotic people, sexual experts who can meet the needs of all men, who can excite all men no matter who they are, where they are from or where they are at. The public nudity, the portrayal of orgasm and masturbation, the open and public enjoyment of eroticism is something most people have been trained to condemn, or even to fear. It represents a devaluation of their sex values and a threat to what Herbert Marcuse has called the repressive nature of Western civilization's sexual order.

Strippers are viewed as "bad," then, because they strip away all social decorum with their clothes. They taunt the public with their own mores by teasing them and turning them on. The privacy of the sex act disappears as does its personal quality, that is, the physical touching of one another and the sharing of affection. In burlesque theater and in the strip bars, open to the public for the price of admission, the sex act is made a packaged commercial deal, one of a variety of sex deals offered in a large sex market aimed at exploiting the contingencies in our society that make it hard for some people to get the sex they think they want.

One of the most important aspects of burlesque is that sex is made impersonal. It has to be impersonal because it has to be available to large numbers of people at the same time, and it has to offer anonymity to the participants, to the audiences and performers. It has to be impersonal because, as a salable, exchangeable commodity, it confers some semblance of normalcy and stability to the occasion. And it has to be impersonal because, when the participants don't know one another and yet understand each other's needs, the deviant act becomes much easier to perform, more acceptable; it becomes something that can be engaged in and then forgotten as soon as it is over.

Burlesque is also made more acceptable by going under the guise of "entertainment" and "show business." But its function as a sex outlet is there for all to see who will see. Says one stripper in this respect, "I am really a professional cockteaser." She would not say this to a stranger, however, and most of the performers stick (at least in public) to the show business definition of burlesque. Audiences don't; they are more likely to see burlesque for what it is and to treat it as such. This is because the performers have more at stake in trying to protect their identities and pass themselves off as normal. For they are considered to be the initiators of the deviant act and are therefore regarded with more social contempt. The audience is merely the witness.

Moreover, audiences have more protection from social condemnation in that they are fully clothed whereas the strippers are naked. They can make all kinds of excuses to rationalize their attendance. Even if they masturbate in their seats, which some do, members of the audience aren't nude and can't be accused of public exhibitionism, which, of course, the strippers are accused of all the time. Until very recently, indeed, the accusation was often legal: strippers were subject to arrest if they showed their pubic hair or "flashed." Now they "show everything" with "no strings attached," but the tolerance of the law has scarcely improved their esteem in the eyes of the public. (For audiences the rules are clearly defined: they aren't to undress or go onstage with the strippers; if they do, they can be arrested.)

Ned Polsky would call burlesque hard-core pornography done to music and designed to stimulate masturbation in the audience. It does this, as well as act as an occasion for public voyeurism. In keeping with these functions, strippers learn and professionalize special techniques and skills. They adopt gimmicks such as wearing a particular costume or do something unusual such as eating fire while they strip. They learn how to move their bodies so that the act becomes a kind of sexual extravaganza, and because of that available to everyone there. Just to make sure, strippers often ask the audience if they can see what they are doing and point to whatever part of their body they want to "feature" for that moment.

The girls, needless to say, show no inhibitions or shyness or modesty about the body or about sex generally. But at the same time, they show no affection or emotional response towards the audience either. Instead, there is either a blank look, a wink or contempt expressed on the face of the stripper. If strippers choose a face that is shy, it is because they want their "floor work" (crouching or lying on the floor and simulating intercourse) and "dirty work" ("flashing" and spreading their legs) to remind the audience of demure girls. They feel this is more erotic; it is supposed to be like seeing the girl next door up there stripping.

Burlesque serves a market mainly composed of men from all walks of life. To the strippers they become indistinguishable from one another. They are seen as a collectivity representing all men. Yet they play to lonely men, frustrated men, happy men and unhappy men. They play to men who go there a lot and to men who may go once a year or once a month. They are businessmen, traveling salesmen, high school and university students, office clerks, professionals, immigrants, truck drivers and transients. They are married and unmarried, and sometimes men and women go together.

There are five shows daily at the Victory every day of the week, and almost every performance is filled. Men pour in during the day, some on lunch breaks, some on out-of-town business, and some just come in off the street. Groups of students bring their sandwiches and drinks and eat their lunch while they watch the show. They laugh and heckle the stripper and reach out for her as she comes down the ramp. They never take their eyes off her whether they are laughing at her or with her. Businessmen, well dressed, hurry in and sit either alone or with one or two others. After the show, they rush out and go back to work. Others, such as transients and immigrants, stop and stare at the photographs of strippers in the lobby on their way out. They walk slowly and stand outside for long periods of time, go away and come back for a later show or for the show the next day.

Strippers note the full houses, the cheering and jeering and excitement in the audience. It tells them that no matter what the public says about them, they are needed. This is gratifying to them. Equally so, perhaps, is the knowledge, if they have it, that burlesque today is a take-off and put-down of most people's sexual fantasies, a burlesque in the true sense, in which the conventional sexual imagination is mirrored and mocked in the act.

Strippers: Frontstage and Backstage

Like all stigmatized people, strippers, offstage, try to

negotiate a more favorable self-image. Briefly, they do this in two ways. First of all, they try to upgrade their occupation in a redefinition of stripping that says it is socially useful, constructive, good and generally all right to do. Secondly, strippers conceal backstage information about their own personal lives that would label them as sexual deviants if known publicly. Their public face is designed to demonstrate that they are sexually normal and therefore moral, and that they are really entertainers, that stripping and sex shows in general are true forms of entertainment that require an artistic talent and openness and honesty about sexual matters. When strippers claim to be "exotics" or "dancers," they are giving the job a face-lifting. But they are not denying the fact that they are strippers, merely describing what they do and who they are in a more flattering way, in a way to save themselves embarrassment, shame and degradation. Still, replacing the negative definition of stripping with a positive one does replace the negative definition of themselves with a more positive one. It says they are engaged in a moral enterprise and therefore must be regarded as moral people.

Strippers' self-concepts are integrally tied up with what they do onstage. Their definition of stripping as good, legitimate entertainment is based largely on the fact that they never saw themselves as anything but strippers, that is, they never were or intended to become real singers, dancers or Broadway stars. They admire famous strippers like Oneida Mann, Babette and Amber Haze. Offstage, they talk about them—about their acts and the problems they have in their personal lives. Strippers feel complimented and flattered if one tells them they were good onstage and especially if you tell them they remind you of a famous stripper. For example, one girl remarked: "When they see me and say it looks like her [Oneida Mann] I know I'm doing good." They are proud if you refer to them in a flattering way about being part of a good show doing good work, meaning highly sexy, erotic work. Their vested interest is in the job as it stands, and it is this they are trying to protect in their various encounters with members of the public.

Strippers are realistic in their interpretation of their job and admit they are "with it" or "in it," or at least are "trying to make the most of it." Because strippers never envisioned themselves as show business stars in the normal sense of the word, they naturally do not fall back on lost dreams in the ways, for example, that their fellow troupers, the comics, do. Whatever lost dreams strippers have in their private worlds aren't tied up with ambitions in show business but with ambitions in life as normal women. This is why their stress is on the morality of sex shows in the sense that they are justified in doing them because they are "socially useful."

In short, strippers take the stance of a deviant minority forming and adhering to subcultural values of its own. This means, among other things, that they attempt to normalize or neutralize their roles by downgrading the public, condemning them for being hypocrites, ignorant and dishonest. Strippers blame many of their problems on the repressive nature of the public sexual order, especially as represented by the police. In the strip bars, for example, strippers resent the police coming in and busting hookers. They are afraid they, too, will be arrested, even if they are just stripping, or that the cops will find dope of one kind or another on them. One stripper declared: "I hate these guys . . . . I can smell them whenever they're near, and I hate them . . . . Why don't they just go away and leave us alone. They could never understand the problems of people." How can the public condemn what it has created a need for and which it supports not just privately in ideology but openly with money (admission fees)? Skid rowers and prostitutes also blame the public for their problems in an attempt to normalize their role. Said one stripper: "We just want to be left alone without any hassles with the public. We aren't trying to make them be like us, just understand us and let us go our way . . . leave us alone."

The public face of strippers should be seen as a cooling-out trick. It is a difficult stance to take because it involves the denial of social attitudes that form the basis of real social facts. For example, strippers must negate or deny that sex for the sake of sex is bad or immoral behavior in public. They must also negate the public typification that all strippers are whores. Strippers, consequently, must be seen as very complex personalities, not simply the middle-class stereotypes of them. What they do in their relations with others is difficult; they are constantly engaged in conscious manipulation of behavior, in concealing and revealing what they deem to be situationally proper and what they believe will bring them the most respect. They are always involved in what Erving Goffman calls strategic interaction—putting their best foot forward.

To illustrate how complicated these self-cooling-out or "passing" devices are, think of what strippers, in dealing with outsiders, have to conceal about themselves: their often ambivalent sexual activities, the kinds of men they become emotionally involved with and the exact nature of their heterosexual relationships, why they went into stripping in the first place, what other work they do that is directly related to stripping, what they might be getting out of stripping in addition to money.

Strippers can never reveal, offstage or on, if they want to keep their self-esteem, that they aren't normal women-very sexy and desirable women to be sure, but normal nonetheless. Any kind of contrary information can be a threat to their posited conception of who they really are. Little things, such as saying who they live with and what their husband does for a living, become obstacles in interaction with others who aren't part of their subculture, either because they fully support their husband or lover by stripping and prostitution or because they are living with a girl in a lesbian relationship. Their habits, and their pasts, have to be concealed from strangers because they might incriminate them. Strippers often invent elaborate tales about why they began stripping as an excuse for their participation in the show. One girl said she is using stripping as a means to get to Hollywood where she wants to become a movie star in the style of Jayne Mansfield. The idea is that they are doing it temporarily as a means to an end. Another girl said she was "tricked into it" and really thought she was going to be a "go-go girl to back up the Feature [an out-of-town star]." Others claim to be doing it just "temporarily" until they earn enough money to go into business. One girl said she wants to buy a flower shop in Chicago where she was born. She also says she wants to raise a family with her husband and that she is only killing time and making lots of money until that day. In reality, the girl is a lesbian who is constantly searching for a female lover in every city she visits, claiming: "I'm just not satisfied with my husband . . . . I need a girl, one who is nice . . . . anyone can satisfy you sexually, but I need somebody I can talk to and have a deep emotional relationship with, just like most women want from men." All this came out after a long talk in which, for the first hour or so, she tried to create the impression that, "like every other girl," she loved her husband and desired no other kind of sexual or emotional relationship. Another girl claimed she was stripping only until she saved enough money to go into the rooming house business. She asserted that her husband loved her to strip "because he knows he can really have me when all those other guys want me but can't get me."

Strippers place a high value on money and believe it should be made in the easiest way possible—their way. But they don't hold on to it for very long. One reason is that they usually are totally supporting the man they live with. Some are also supporting children. They feel a sense of power handing over money to their man because they enjoy his financial dependency, but at the same time they are being exploited because the man usually spends most of the money on himself. One night I listened for hours as a stripper and her husband argued over how he had spent her paycheck. He claimed he had bought a radio and some liquor. The girl was upset because she told me she was broke and that she couldn't control the way he spent the money. She wanted to buy a new costume but wouldn't be able to now, and she also owed her agent some money but couldn't pay him. Her husband tried to joke about it to cool her off. He asked her what she would do without him. She laughed and smiled and explained that they were both bad with money, that they couldn't save a dime, owed money all over town and lived from day to day never knowing what tomorrow would bring. She also told me she spends some of her money on pills she takes to "keep her going" and that the main reason she dislikes being so broke all the time is that it prevents them from taking off whenever they like (traveling) and that money is a constant source of argument between them.

And so they say that stripping is fun and that they are sexy "artistic" performers who are better than most women because they are more honest and direct about sex. They also take the following lines, in general—that they are happily married and look forward to the day when they can quit and "settle down with a family," or that the kind of men they go with admire them because they are sexy and actually prefer them to other women. That they are financially or emotionally exploited in their personal relationships with men, or that men go with them for any reasons other than their being sexually desirable, these facts are hidden. Like most other people, they also try to create the impression in public that their living arrangements are normal. They are apt to say, for example, that they are married rather than that they are "living common-law," which is usually the truth. Such are the pressures of conventional morality on these women.

Strippers don't end up stripping because they have skidded downwards in their careers as have the burlesque comics. They chose stripping as an occupation, and their decision was based upon what they knew of the world. The experiences they have had in the world formulate themselves into a common-sense rationality of how best to put their bodies to use, how best to live their lives. In their own view, they haven't fallen in status. After all, one alternative would have been full-time prostitution, which has neither the social status nor the economic payoff (the prostitutes they know only get $5.00 to $10.00 a trick in Toronto).

To strippers, stripping is a good thing, and they do it as naturally as stenographers type. It earns them a minimum of $165 a week and offers what they call an "easy life." They can sleep late each day, watch soap operas on television, get dressed, go to the theater, get into their costumes, sit around backstage until it is time to work, work, repeat the same process four or five times a day and pick up their pay at the end of the week. If they work steadily, they earn a fair amount of money.

What strippers don't mention, initially, is that stripping also facilitates lesbian relationships. This is backstage information, the kind that would label them as "unnatural." Backstage, however, they joke around a lot about sex and show a playful affection for each other by touching each others' bodies. One stripper explained that the constant exposure and manipulation of the body and the body contact backstage are often the beginning of lesbian experiences for strippers. They maintain it is very easy for a stripper to become a lesbian because it is "all around." If you add to this a contemptuous feeling for the public, especially the "johns" and "marks" in the audience, lesbianism, as an occupational contingency, is quite understandable. Contempt for men is expressed in terms like this: "All they need is a cute ass and a pair of tits wiggling." Strippers themselves say that more than 75 percent of their colleagues are lesbians and that often their first experiences came as a direct result of stripping-which is not to deny that some lesbian strippers are also married to men and continue to have sex with them. One stripper explained this situation like this: "It's quite simple, you see . . . . I'll go out and meet a girl and go home with her—that's all—and he'll do whatever he likes . . . . he knows I'll come back again . . . . he doesn't mind if I pick up a girl . . . . he knows what I am . . . . he sometimes picks up women . . . . but we have a companionship, a kind of love." Nevertheless, it is common for strippers to be bisexual or lesbian, but not straight.

Another occupational contingency of stripping is prostitution. And yet, strippers very carefully, in public, differentiate themselves from full-time prostitutes, whom they perceive to be of a lower social status. They stress the fact that they strip and don't hook for a living, whereas prostitutes just hook. If they do hook, they make sure one understands that it is "just once in a while" and for a very good reason, like "eating and putting a roof over my head."

Once You Start . . .

Nevertheless, and for all that they take pains to deny it, prostitution is almost an inevitable consequence of stripping. One woman remarked, for example: "My girl friend just hooks because she is afraid to do what I do in public, and if I was afraid to strip, I'd be doing it all the time too [hooking]." In my sample, most of the strippers hooked part time to supplement their income. They also performed at stags. They often get their customers in strip bars. Having a career in commercial sex makes prostitution easy to do, even if one doesn't really want to do it. For one thing, the general public regards all strippers as prostitutes anyway, and for another, strippers are always being propositioned. One stripper recalled: "It's so easy to start hooking for some guy . . . . You think, well, I really could use the extra money . . . . but once you start, you never stop. And most them never even save any of this money." Nevertheless, strippers much resent being labeled a prostitute. One woman said: "I hate clubs, especially small ones in northern Ontario. They'll treat you like a prostitute whether you are one or not just because most of them have been who were here before you . . . . When you finish the show, you never know what drunk is going to be waiting for you at the top of the stairs."

The strippers in my sample are poorly educated. The average level of education of the 20 strippers in this sample was grade seven or eight. They have no office skills or any other kind of talent suitable for an urban labor market. They cannot sing, dance or act nor could they ever. They do not have bodies suitable for modeling; they are too large, in all dimensions. (Amber Haze, a current favorite, measures 52 inches around the bust.) Nearly all said they left home at an early age—by the time they were 14 or 15 years old. They learned early that they had to support themselves. Most had what they described as unhappy home lives, either because they didn't get along with their parents or because they had too much work to do at home or because their sexual experiences upset their parents. For example, one girl said she had to leave home because she was a lesbian and her mother wanted to have her committed to a mental hospital because of it.

Most developed early, that is, their bodies matured early. Sexuality (their own and others') came early, too, often in a violent form such as being beaten or raped; and for as long as they can remember, their bodies were objects of talk, staring and sexual passes. They were used to being cheered and jeered as they walked down the street. They were used to being whistled at and pawed over. Yet even as they were often humiliated by the nature of some of their sexual experiences, most strippers, by the time they reached their late teens, had come to the conclusion that the body, because it attracts men, can bring in money. This knowledge, plus the desire for attention, plus the exhibitionist tendencies they acknowledge, led them to stripping. One girl claimed, for example: "I like it because to me it seems glamorous, and I like attention. I'm an exhibitionist really." They were also encouraged by people they knew—other girls who were doing it and boy friends who urged them to do it.

Strippers like stripping because it makes them feel important, especially when the audience claps and cheers. They feel exhilarated. They also like the money. By the time they are "in the life" they have developed an exploitative attitude to men and people in general. They become harder and tougher in their attitudes to men, money and sex. However, they do not feel badly about this, merely smart, one-up on the world. Said one girl, "If I don't exploit them, they'll do it to me." Stripping becomes easy to do with this kind of attitude.

Being paid to display their bodies in public means they are beating the world at its own game. It is no more immoral in their eyes than getting a man to marry them in exchange for intercourse. Indeed, in their own eyes or at least in the face they turn to the public, they are no different from other women with regard to sex, just more blunt, honest, open and direct. Other women are hypocrites; they may not strip for money, but they ask a price just the same. It's usually marriage, but it could be just a dinner. Strippers also claim all women are exhibitionists. Said one stripper, "All women are in spirit exhibitionists and prostitutes." Said another, "All women are exhibitionists . . . . haven't you ever seen a woman wearing an extra-tight sweater?"

Both onstage and off, strippers like to be referred to as erotic, sexy people, professional sex experts, skilled in ways others aren't. They pride themselves on their knowledge of eroticism, and unlike the average woman, they aren't ashamed of their sexual knowledge and expertise. In fact, strippers often say that one of their special roles is to teach people about sex, for most people, especially women and most men in their audiences, don't know anything about it. For example, they say college students come to the Victory to learn about sex in a sort of initiation ritual. One stripper told me: "They're still wet behind the ears and embarrassed. We have to show them a few things."

The line they take is that society needs strippers in the same way it needs teachers or doctors. Without sex shows, men would be lonely and frustrated and lacking a sex outlet. Thus, their work is actually as good and helpful and socially constructive as any other kind of work, and because the work is useful, they are moral. This, of course, is a "passing" device and a cooling-out trick. Another line is their claim that strip shows are really good entertainment, as are all sex shows from live stag exhibitions to stag movies. One stripper performs at stags with her husband. He encourages it, and they both maintain it is good entertainment as well as a good way to make money.

The line that "anybody will do anything for a buck anyway" is perhaps their principal legitimizing tactic. They feel generally that any dealings they have with members of the public should be of a contractual nature—and that they should be paid for whatever they do. One girl said, "I'm being stared at anyway, so why not be paid for it?" Said another, "I don't care what they say or do to me as long as they pay." They should be paid, then, for just being around, for being sexy. They should be paid also for showing people the "truth" when they strip, which is doing everybody a favor. The "truth" here means the truth about sex—actually, the truth about life.

Who Profits

At the same time, however, strippers also maintain that they really aren't being so terribly exploitative, especially if one remembers that "all men are sexually frustrated and in need of their services," as one of them put it. They claim that if they didn't exploit the public's need for a sex outlet, that is, making a profit on it, men would be making a profit on them—that is, they, as women, would be taken advantage of by men. They would be touched, screwed and not paid.

Strippers, offstage, also argue that stripping is just a job like any other and that what they do is done in a routinized way (this despite their open acknowledgement that they are exhibitionists). One stripper told me:

> I don't think anything about stripping . . . . I don't stand nude . . . . I always wear a G-string even though it looks like I don't. I do my act as a routine, automatically . . . . sometimes I don't even see the audience . . . . I can black them out . . . . lots of girls do that . . . . we just do our act and do it again the next night . . . . but other girls get orgasms right on the stage . . . . they get a charge out of turning the guys on right there in the club or in the theater . . . . I saw a guy finish once right in this girl's face, and she thought it was cute.

Needless to say, if a stripper does get a sexual thrill out of performing, she wouldn't say so in public; it would make her seem unnatural, and that would be to contradict all the legitimizing lines she may have developed. By the same token, strippers never admit that their boy friends are often pimps or addicts who would push them onto the street if they didn't strip.

Backstage, however, these facts do emerge. They also reveal that they are constantly broke, their money being spent mainly on liquor, debts, drugs, traveling expenses, costumes, props as well as the usual rent and food. Other backstage information would include the fact that in certain centers, strippers are controlled by the Mafia, and they must turn tricks in the bars in order to keep their jobs. Strippers complain about insults from drunk customers, unwanted propositions, depression due to fights with theater owners, club managers and other strippers, being lied to, cheated and stolen from. Bosses are divided into categories of "nice guys" and "bad guys" according to how they treat them. By the same token, audiences are divided into "nice squares" and "bad squares" according to how they react to their performances—as one girl put it, "according to how hypocritical they are about their need for us." Loneliness is also a constant problem, whether traveling the circuit including New York, Chicago, Montreal, Toronto, Los Angeles and San Francisco or traveling from one small town in Ontario to another (Peterborough, Timmins, Sudbury). One girl claims she "carries her husband with her everywhere she goes" just to avoid this loneliness. Sometimes they make friends when they visit a town, but they become depressed because they know the chances of ever seeing the person again are slim. So they talk of writing letters to one another and express the hope they will meet again sometime.

But it is what happens to old strippers, or, more precisely, what the aging process does to them, that is perhaps their worst problem. They fear getting old, and if they are getting old, they will work desperately to create the illusion that their bodies are firm and still sexy. Growing old is an incontrovertible denial of a future in terms of the lines they adhere to, and even the youngest stripper is aware of this. What happens to older strippers is that they can't get by anymore with the "sex is fun and I am very sexy" line, and as a result, they have to "spread themselves" more and act as the butt of the MC's dirty jokes. In fact, they become the joke itself, the source of all the dirty humor. They are no longer very persuasive sexually, but they are still usable, and perhaps this is the biggest difference between them and the younger women. Their usability is what keeps them working, not their desirability, and this is a difficult thing to rationalize to anybody, especially themselves.

Often older strippers become alcoholics and do what they do drunk. Younger strippers know about this, too, but they don't seem to have any way of stopping it from happening to them. They have no plans for the future. They live from day to day and plan only far enough ahead for tomorrow.

As suggested earlier, life to a stripper is a game of one-upmanship where everyone has the potential to be had. To be a winner, one must be on top of the situation at all times, whether onstage or off. If one lets one's defenses down, she becomes vulnerable to attack and shame.

When audiences clap for them at the end of performances at the Victory, strippers really feel they have put one over. They are being paid and applauded, but they have given nothing of themselves in return. Even their nudity is neutralized by becoming just a part of the job. Winning at the end of a performance lets them see themselves as successful not only as strippers but in life itself.

Strippers expect one another to adhere to the same line in normal interaction with the public. They attempt to reinforce their definition of the situation within the ranks of their own group. They need solidarity in order for the definition of their situation to have any kind of social reality. For this reason, strippers rarely downgrade each other in the presence of strangers. Only if a stripper disobeys norms does she come under public attack. A stripper who "flashes" too easily, who doesn't demand a higher price for doing it, is immensely disliked by the others and is not considered to be a "good stripper," meaning a loyal member of the group. They also avoid and dislike strippers who act superior, who are snobs. One stripper commented about another: "She'll just have to learn she's no better than we are."

Newcomers are initiated into the business by being handed down practical advice. They are taught how to handle verbal insults while they perform. They are taught what to say if they spot a man masturbating and they don't dig it too much: "Put it away and save it for later" and "Do up your pants; I'm being paid, and you're not" are common methods of turning the guy off. Other tricks they learn are how to handle police by lying to them or "being nice to them when they're around"; the same holds true for any outsider. These protective tricks are taken for granted and are part of their normal daily behavior. It is normal to offer the following kind of advice to one another or a novice: "Think with your head, not with your pants . . . . keep a cool head, or you'll get sucked under and never get out. They'll own you." Only most of them are in it for life regardless.

Sexual standards aren't generally imposed on one another. A person's sexual status is regarded as a private matter, nobody's concern but that particular individual's. As one girl put it: "Each to his own . . . . they leave me alone, so I leave them alone . . . . they know it if you're really straight, so they leave you alone usually . . . . that's the way it is." Another girl said: "I only initiate a girl if she approaches me first, and most of them like it after, especially after doing a show." However, there are, of course, exceptions. For example, some straight strippers resent playing the same bill as a well-known lesbian and will try to get out of the job or else ask for a separate dressing room. Also, some lesbians disobey the norm and try to initiate an affair with a novice.

When strippers do make friends, they put themselves out for them because friends aren't easy to find in this world. If they hit if off, they will try to get each other jobs, teach each other routines, loan props and costumes, sometimes loan money for drinks, socialize in bars after work, go to parties together, protect each other from the police and other outsiders, visit each other at home, introduce each other to their men and go out in mixed groups. But perhaps most important, they will sit and listen to each other's problems with sympathy, because after all, one girl's troubles are those of every other.

Strippers don't downgrade comics but accept them as part of the show, though not too important a part. They joke around with them after work and go out for drinks with them. They also treat them as confidants, telling them all their troubles, hopes and dreams.

With respect to the master of ceremonies, strippers like to have him on their side, especially if they are having a fight with another girl. But the MC can also be the cause of friction. If he shows more attention to one stripper than another, the rejected one will feel jealous and malicious. For example, in one of the strip bars in Toronto, the MC always gave a more elaborate introduction to one stripper than to the other. He also joked more with her offstage. His favorite was black, the other white. One evening, the white stripper whispered across the table: "He always spends more time with her than me . . . . I don't know. I guess he just prefers niggers . . . . Oh, I guess that isn't nice, is it? Well, it's the truth anyway, isn't it?" She then began to laugh about her whispered confession of jealousy.

In essence, their everyday world is one of what to do next, after the show, before the next show, what to drink, where to drink it, when to go home, writing to one another, when they might see each other again—about the "old days of burlesque," how good they are onstage, about "14-year-old boys" (college students) who are still wet behind the ears, about owing the agent, a "bum," a fin, about an old friend accused by the police of this or that, in one case murder—and teasing each other about picking up other men or women and about who will pay for the drinks this time.

A stripper's persona can be thought of as a sexual extravaganza—a way of being and living in the world as a sexual creature, larger than life. It is for this reason they often appear onstage and off as caricatures of female sexuality. Perhaps the silicone injections most of them have had done to their breasts best illustrate this point. Their breasts are made so large that whether they want to be "in play" offstage or not, it would be difficult to disguise the nature of their work. This might be an additional reason for playing up, offstage, the artfulness of stripping until it takes on a socially significant meaning. However, the attention they pay to the body, to their costumes, facial expressions, makeup and so forth is all a part of a ritual they go through every day to help make the performance more of a show. It also makes it more unreal and impersonal. It is a kind of sexual circus.

This almost parodic quality in the face they turn to the world perhaps explains why only one woman in my sample tried to deny what she did, and she said she was really a model. It also explains why they don't distance themselves from the occupation itself but rather try to redefine it so that it suits their bodies, so to speak. By endowing their overblown bodies with a useful social function, a sex extravaganza, they are saying they are moral bodies inhabited by moral people. Their "passing" technique, then, involves a new definition of sexual morality rather than an attempt to live up to the existing one.

All the skills they learn as strippers can be seen, in a sense, as working up to this new definition of sexual morality and sexual worth. It is the only stance they can take, which is why it is so strictly enforced among members of their own group.

Corporeal Ideology

What I am saying is that as their work is expressed in their bodies, so, too, is their ideology. The body becomes an object that every member of the audience is supposed to identify with and use in his own way. If it stimulates masturbation, that is perhaps not in keeping with the official norms governing the occasion, but it is still in line with the expressed function the strippers declare as being theirs.

Because strippers manifest a certain sameness in their self-presentations, they become almost indistinguishable from one another in the same ways that members of the audience become indistinguishable from one another to the strippers.

Their coping device, then, is to make the body moral in the same way they make the show and themselves moral, all being part of the same phenomenon and sharing in stigma. At the same time, it is to state that, other than having this extravagant body and sexual presence, they are normal, that is, no different than any other woman. To state this, as I discussed, is to conceal any kind of information about themselves that would give the lie to their self-presentation. Strippers are constantly playing this kind of show in a conscious way; it illustrates the complicated nature of destigmatizing processes and the complexities of those who have to work out a suitable identity.

7 *Marion Goldman*

Prostitution and Virtue in Nevada

Some of the most direct, vicious and persistent attacks by one class of American women against another occurred in the guise of crusades aimed at punishment and abolition of prostitution. Respectable women's antagonism against shady ladies was particularly visible in late nineteenth-century frontier boom towns, where prostitutes often outnumbered married women. Prostitutes were the first female settlers in many such towns, and the arrival of upright women produced many tensions and overt conflicts, some of which led to passage of laws limiting and regulating prostitution.

Between 1860 and 1875, Virginia City, Nevada, the great Comstock boom town, grew from a crude shanty town of 2,500 to a relatively sophisticated city of 25,000, making it imperative that a system of social control develop in a short time. The whole pattern of legal development from informal social control, to semi-formal vigilante rule, to formal law making and enforcement occurred in less than a decade, reflecting the arrival of powerful new social groups bringing new definitions of deviance. Rapid changes in Virginia City's demographic composition and economic organization affected the community's ethos and its labeling of behavior. The arrival of relatively large numbers of upright matrons brought the iron Victorian distinctions between good and bad women into focus, where they previously had been blurred because of the absence of females other than prostitutes.

As Virginia City developed a differentiated status structure and imported culture from established cities, the hard-working, tenacious frontier woman faded as a social ideal, to be replaced by the delicate, passive lady. Ladies seldom labored outside the home, and women who did often had their moral standards both questioned and assaulted. Thus the classifications of women as either good or bad were strongly (though not entirely) class related.

In this sense, the Virginia City campaigns against prostitution were female class wars, and laws resulting from them affected working men's prostitutes who lived in cribs and wretched houses rather than the mistresses of rich or middle-class men. The presence of this large, visible group of poor women thought to be irrevocably tainted served as both impetus and weapon for the upper- and middle-class woman's fight to sustain her own precarious social and economic position at the expense of her less fortunate sisters.

Information on prostitution in early Virginia City is somewhat sketchy—few prostitutes left the letters or diaries commonly providing information about respectable women of the era. Instead, painted women's lives must be pieced together, from various sources such as histories of the period, personal documents, city council minutes and even coroner's reports. A random sample of 30 *Virginia City Territorial Enterprises* published between 1860 and 1875 proved helpful in this respect, as did census records listing sporting women in categories such as housekeepers, courtesans, hurdy girls, prostitutes, and prostitutes of the lowest order.

In order to understand the roots of this conflict between matrons and prostitutes, it is essential to understand Victorian definitions of female sexuality which constrained in different ways the lives of all women of the period.

The rigid moral code attributed to nineteenth-century men and women originated in the middle class, and even within that class there was probably a good deal of discreet deviance. Despite the fact that Victorians left numerous records of lip service to strict morality, popular scandals of the age and large private collections of erotica discovered after their owners' deaths conflict with public moral ideals and suggest that both men and women privately loosened constricting sexual codes.

While there was a good deal of deviance from norms of appropriate female sexual behavior, there was also of course widespread adherence to those rules. Norms forbidding respectable women to have sexual relations outside marriage and even discouraging sexual enjoyment within marriage severely limited their freedom. But at the same time those norms offered women a sense of certainty. They provided clear definitions of femininity and offered many women a definite sense of who and what they were. Distinctions between good and bad women were rooted in conceptions of "natural" man/woman, and while those clear sex roles tended to benefit males far more than females, they did at least offer women an explicit set of standards.

Good women were thought to be nature's highest creation, totally devoid of sensuality or passion. They fulfilled maternal functions in the home and sometimes in the community through charity work. Insisting that good women functioned as men's consciences and represented the higher things in life, Victorian men could sin so long as they guarded the purity of their female consciences.

Bad women were defined solely in terms of their sexuality. Once a woman had intercourse with a man to whom she wasn't married and was discovered by many other community members or bore evidence nine months later, she was permanently labeled as bad. She often accepted that label and sometimes saw prostitution as the only course open to her. Many immigrant women were deliberately seduced so that they could be placed in bawdy houses.

Generally men were not held culpable in relationships with bad women. Popular doctrine held that the strength of male drives coupled with the intensity of a fallen woman's sexual attractiveness triggered situations in which men could not be held responsible for their actions. Women were saddled with the burden of guilt for initially allowing themselves to be deflowered and later acting as seducers themselves.

The whole Victorian celebration of womanhood and glorification of legitimate maternity served to justify upper- and middle-class women's isolation from work. Good women were considered too delicate to engage in the sordid world of commerce, and those women not cut off from productive labor were denied the deferential treatment and respect men accorded their more fortunate sisters. Middle-class, single women working as school teachers and social reformers were regarded as well-meaning cranks at best, but most women working in factories, mills and other peoples' homes were considered half-persons.

Only through relationships with men could Victorian women be socially and financially secure—sometimes as spinster daughters, but usually as wives. During that era marriage was the sole respectable vocation for women, and they competed fiercely to find suitable partners. Once married, most women were willing to pay high emotional costs in order to hold their husbands. These costs commonly included tolerance of frequent affairs with women of easy virtue. Labeling such women "bad" allowed matrons to dismiss the influence and importance of such individual women, or attack them as a class, while it afforded their husbands opportunities for dalliance with a minimum of guilt.

Social Class and Sexual Virtue

Since the concept of good and bad women was strongly class related, it was less difficult for the rich than the poor to avoid being labeled bad and to sustain the illusion, if not the reality, of fidelity or chastity. The many working-class and poor women who conformed to strict sexual norms were often forced to make enormous efforts to maintain their virtue.

Women factory workers were often expected to dispense their favors to foremen and supervisors, and female domestics were frequently hounded by the master of the house and/or encouraged to conduct sexual initiation rites with the master's sons. Refusal brought about dismissal, and sometimes strong-willed working women were finally forced into prostitution in order to support themselves.

Close quarters in tenement districts and shanty towns were conducive to both sexual intimacy and widespread knowledge about its occurrences. It was usually the public knowledge of such experiences, rather than sexual intimacies themselves, which led to ruined reputations and ruined lives. Rumors about working and poor women's reputations seldom remained among members of their own class, but spread upward through gossip which employers often used as grounds for dismissing domestics.

Poor women were vulnerable to censure not only because of the visibility of their sexual activities, but also because of the potential consequences of their affairs. Abortionists practiced in most American cities during the late nineteenth century, sometimes advertising openly in newspapers. But only relatively well-to-do women could afford medical abortions or visit distant friends or relatives until after their babies were born. Others went to quacks or availed themselves of dangerous, ineffective potions promising relief from pregnancy.

Without economic security and social status it was almost impossible to engage in extramarital sexual relations with the amount of style and caution necessary to avoid disgrace. Lower-class women were suspected of sexual misbehavior by others simply because of their living conditions and their contact with strange men in the course of their work. At some point in their lives, most women venturing outside their homes to earn a living found their sexual standards open to question, if not threat.

Early Prostitution in Virginia City

Prostitutes were the first women to appear in numbers in the Comstock camps, many traveling across the Sierras from San Francisco. Most of them accepted the popular social definitions of their sullied souls and were determined to maximize the financial advantages of degradation. Mark Twain described frontier prostitutes:

> They are virtuous according to their lights, but I guess that their lights are a little dim.

While some painted women were American born, a large number were natives of Europe, Central and South America and China. Many originally secured passage to San Francisco by allowing their ship captains to sell them to the highest bidder once they reached port. Chinese were sold for life, but most others served as indentured prostitutes or one man's concubine for a specified period. However, the high frequency of syphillis often turned comparatively short term agreements into life commitments—many prostitutes died before fulfilling their contracts.

A widespread American myth describes prostitution as a popular mode of social mobility. Women came West, made their fortunes and journeyed back to their homes or to other frontier towns where they had no pasts. It was supposedly possible for them to cross the line between respectability and notoriety, turn a tidy profit and cross back again to respectable comfort.

A few red light ladies did manage to hide their questionable activities and marry well or assume respected positions in new communities. But the majority ended their careers in poverty and shame. Along with exposure to syphillis and gonorrhea, painted women were ravaged by gin, laudanum, opium and other drugs; they were physically abused by customers and financially exploited by madams and other auxilliary personnel associated with prostitution. Frontier prostitutes often died from overdoses of drugs or committed suicide.

Despite these fairly well known dangers of the skin trade and the stigma attached to it, most American-born shady women came to the Comstock of their own volition, and only a relatively small number of women were tricked into prostitution by the domestic agencies offering free passage West. The first prostitutes coming from California were soon joined by others traveling overland from other mining camps in the West, and from Chicago, New Orleans and other cities. It is difficult to discover whether they were accompanied by cadets (pimps), since there is no record of campaigns for legislation against such men and the sampled newspapers did not mention them. Still it is probable that some were present in Virginia City since they were quite active in San Francisco during that era.

From the first prostitutes' arrival, the social organization of prostitution in Virginia City was racist. A very small number of blacks were employed as prostitutes' maids, but there is no record of black women being permitted to join the line. Also, no native American Indian women were allowed to work in the red light district, although they were easily available in an encampment outside town. Chinese prostitutes were rigidly segregated in the "celestial quarter" (Chinatown), although they frequently entertained white customers.

Until the mid-1870s, when plush parlor houses were built, most prostitutes in Virginia City plied their trade in small whitewashed cabins set below the town's main thoroughfare. Women who lived and worked there maintained strict social boundaries among themselves. European- and American-born women looked down on Chicanas and Latinas, charging higher prices and occupying better locations. Within this upper-status group, women were ranked according to their youth (few of the early prostitutes were less than 25 years old) and attractiveness. As a group, the western Europeans were novelties and tended to attract wealthier customers than Americans.

Despite prostitutes' traditional degradation, miners were as hungry for female companionship as they were for pure sexuality, and they accorded bawdy women measures of attention and deference usually reserved for ladies. Since they were almost the only women in town, prostitutes assumed integral roles in community life, nursing the sick, doing charity work and organizing much desired general recreations such as picnics, parades and dances. Of course not all prostitutes participated in these activities, and those who did usually belonged to the high-status ethnic groups.

The legendary harlot heroines of the Old West derived much of their fame from good deeds of this type. While working for charity and group leisure, prostitutes performed broadly "maternal" functions for the whole community rather than their own nuclear families. They were among the few whole women of the Victorian era, fusing the bad women's sexuality with the good women's kindness and sacrifice.

Shady women gained community (male) gratitude and recognition for their charity and recreational works, rather than for their sordid occupation. This community recognition was one factor motivating respectable women to work for laws regulating prostitution and effectively limiting prostitutes' involvement in civic life.

Respectable Women as Moral Reformers

As ore strikes proliferated and the town grew, mine owners, engineers, attorneys and merchants moved in with their wives and children. Some miners' families also came, although most working men could not afford more than one passage. A few upright single women arrived to work as school mistresses and as seamstresses, but most of these women had neither the time nor interest to participate in anti-prostitution campaigns. This group was extremely small and many women workers traded marginal respectability for the more tangible rewards of the sporting life.

The campaigns to regulate prostitution that corresponded with the arrival of upper- and middle-class women generated a minimal amount of legislation. Their influence on laws relating to prostitution in Storey County occurred on three levels: 1) overt, organized moral crusading, 2) sporadic group action and 3) individual conformity to norms emphasizing divisions between good and bad women.

During the seventies a few women on the Comstock stood out as conspicuous reformers crusading for all types of moral legislation, including laws against prostitution. However, most respectable Virginia City women acted against prostitution within the confines of acceptable female behavior, meeting informally at each others' homes and acting spontaneously against prostitutes' encroachment into their own social territory.

There are many records of respectable women banding together to take away foundlings from prostitutes' care, to drive bawdy houses away from residential areas, to publicly reject "tainted" contributions to charity (although often these contributions were later accepted if donated anonymously) and to limit in other ways prostitutes' role in community life.

Respectable women on the Comstock made their most dramatic gesture of contempt after the brutal murder of a famous, well-loved local courtesan, Julia Bulette. While miners and workingmen clamoured to lynch her assassin, the town's good women visited the prisoner, bringing fruit, flowers and various homemade delicacies.

An elaborate code of manners emphasized the enormous social distance between prostitutes and upright women. A respectable woman seen in or near the restricted district even in broad daylight courted disgrace, while any prostitutes walking in residential areas would be totally snubbed. When matrons encountered shady ladies in the shopping district, they were expected to treat the bad women as if they didn't exist.

Reasons for Anti-Prostitution Crusades

Virginia City women's crusades against prostitution were rooted in a number of social motives, many of which reflected indirect rebellion against constricting feminine roles. Although respectable women had been taught to suffer in silence when their husbands relieved their base instincts with disreputable females, they often felt pangs of jealousy. This bitterness was usually directed at the prostitutes who led their men astray rather than at the men. For example, when Mrs. Adolph Sutro found her bonanza king husband in compromising circumstances in a bedroom of the International Hotel, she promptly broke a bottle of champagne over his unfortunate female companion's head, but did nothing to him.

Despite the ideology dismissing good women's capacity for sexual enjoyment, many such women must have been hurt by their husbands' preference for prostitutes. The fact that a woman was unable to satisfy her man implied that she was incomplete. Even though her sexual limitations may have indicated her refinement, they also indicated that she was not considered a whole person by a husband who turned to other women for basic forms of female companionship.

Prostitutes presented more tangible threats in the form of venereal diseases, which they transmitted to husbands who passed them on to their wives. Syphillis and gonorrhea were major public health menaces in frontier towns. While no preliminary research on Virginia City revealed community anti-prostitution campaigns organized around fear of disease, it is probable that such fear figured in private discussions and intimate motives for such crusades. During the same period in New York City, feminists outspokenly protested against prostitution on grounds that it endangered their own and their unborn children's health.

Some women, particularly those in marginal financial circumstances, feared their own temptation into prostitution. Upright women of all classes were apprehensive about the example prostitutes might set for their children. They imagined that their sons would be drawn into dissipation in their early teens and their daughters, yearning for flashy finery displayed by shady ladies, might set out to earn money in a similar manner.

In 1876 and 1877 moral crusaders closed the Barbary Coast, a small red light district generally considered more lewd and depraved than the larger area on D Street. The campaign centered around the Fourth Ward School's opening and parents' apprehension that the Barbary Coast's proximity to a place of learning might endanger their children's morals. These anxieties evidently still influence Nevada state law, which currently permits prostitution so long as it is not practiced within 400 yards of a school or church.

Somewhat surprisingly, religion does not appear to have been a major social factor in anti-prostitution campaigns. Clergymen were not central figures in such campaigns, and there is no record that women used established church groups as bases for their moral crusades. Religious justification was probably so much assumed by matrons that they used other, more practical rationales for their moral stance.

Prostitutes' community activities particularly vexed respectable women. Volunteer work was one of the few avenues of civic participation open to nineteenth-century women. Through performance of good deeds they could gain recognition for their own achievements, rather than for those of their fathers or husbands. Charitable activities were within the sphere of respectable women's duties yet allowed them partial escape from confining marital roles. At the same time, volunteer work served as a means for women to affirm their own and their families' status and importance in the community.

If prostitutes had been permitted to continue charitable work, such activities would not have remained a route to recognition for respectable women. The high mindedness and personal goodness associated with charity work could easily have been questioned if socially ostracized women routinely performed such deeds. Moreover, if prostitutes and good women went about these duties side by side the good women would be socially tainted by the bad women's influence. Thus, the town's matrons had to choose between forcing prostitutes out of volunteer work or abandoning one of the few routes of recognition open to them.

In gaining control of charity and philanthropy, the upright women both maintained their social distance from shady ladies and sustained their social dominance. As they cared for the sick during frequent mine disasters, took charge of orphans and organized general recreation, they appropriated a good deal of power, making decisions affecting the lives of almost everyone in the community. Upper- and middle-class women's appropriation of these activities affirmed the ascendency of their social classes and values.

Results of Comstock Anti-Prostitution Campaigns

Respectable women pushed prostitutes out of community life through informal pressures. These pressures were supplemented by city ordinances against prostitution which functioned to formally stigmatize prostitutes and limit their access to respectable districts. Ordinances were modified every few years in the early period of community growth. However, by the mid-seventies they had been formulated to cover a broad range of offenses and were not substantially changed after 1878.

One of these ordinances prohibited women from working in dance halls or saloons, either as waitresses or as attendants of patrons (B-girls). An 1878 ordinance held both waitresses and patrons culpable but by 1888 employers and patrons were not subject to punishment. Ordinances were also passed confining houses of ill fame to the restricted district and prohibiting their inmates or individual women plying the trade from using loud talk, fancy dress or other means to attract the passerby. Although there was little systematic enforcement of these laws, they served to keep painted women in their appropriate, subordinate places and affirmed anti-prostitution norms and values.

Despite relatively frequent attempts to regulate and restrict prostitution in Virginia City, there were few campaigns to abolish it. The absence of strong movements to abolish prostitution can be traced to three related sources: 1) popular theories about male sexuality, 2) men outnumbering women in Virginia City by at least two to one and 3) anti-prostitution groups' limited power and legitimacy.

Victorians subscribed to a bucket theory of male emotions, believing that men were filled with monstrous, seething sexual urges which if left unsatisfied would eventually overflow. Unless prostitutes were available single men would seduce or attack good women, consort with other men or, worst of all, satisfy their urges through masturbation. Prostitution was considered the least offensive sexual outlet outside marriage and was defined as a single man's only acceptable alternative to celibacy. Painted women also exerted a stabilizing influence on the labor pool, providing workers with rewards for labor, and acting as an incentive for men to continue in the mines so they could afford their sexual services. If the red light ladies had vanished, the working men might have followed them.

Even without numerous rationalizations for its endurance, prostitution in Virginia City could not have been legislated out of existence. The upper and middle classes were neither large enough nor prestigious enough to abolish prostitution. Although the arrival of these classes marked the beginnings of a differentiated status structure in Virginia City, social boundaries were still fairly fluid and the upper and middle classes lacked authority to force their values on the lower classes. If they had formally outlawed prostitution, their legislation would have been ignored by the majority of townsmen and prostitutes, and the ascendent classes might have lost what prestige and power they did have.

The minimal legal restrictions on prostitution and painted women's informal exclusion from civic life could not have been achieved without general belief in the popular dichotomy between worthy and debased women. It was in the interests of affluent men and women to subscribe to this ideology, but it was also generally accepted by prostitutes themselves and the miners who patronized them. There is a legend that in the first days of the Comstock boom miners payed more in gold to gaze at a respectable woman than they did to sleep with a red light lady.

During the boom years, influential men's support was essential for passage of anti-prostitution ordinances. Some men wanted to clean up the mining towns in order to emulate more sophisticated eastern cities. Others advocated legislation against certain kinds of prostitution, such as brothels and cribs, because it would increase patronage at their own gaming tables and dance halls. Still others were married to women dedicated to regulating prostitution or associated with those women's husbands.

Painted women in Virginia City, like their counterparts elsewhere, had little ammunition to fight moral reformers. Some shady women maintained liaisons with important men who could be cajoled into publicly standing against vice regulation. But prostitutes were essentially powerless. Their degradation was a central feature of the era's moral code. None had the legitimacy to speak in her own behalf, and few had enough money to pay attorneys or newspaper writers to speak for them.

Virginia City's early anti-prostitution laws resemble those passed throughout the nation up to the present time. Male clients were not condemned while prostitutes were penalized. Moreover, laws regulating prostitution were directed against the humblest prostitutes who worked on the streets, in cribs and in low dance halls, serving miners and working men. The law did not attack wealthy men's "housekeepers" or shady women residing in plush hotels and catering to the bourgeoisie. Although today's legislation is more comprehensive, it is primarily enforced against streetwalkers—the lowest status prostitutes.

The single, most striking characteristic of the process of legislation of female morality in Virginia City was that both prostitutes and reputable women assumed their respective roles in the conflict because of the same economic and ideological forces. Reputable women gained their socioeconomic status and security from their husbands' positions. Prostitutes, too, were entirely dependent upon men for their livelihoods and professional standing. Both groups had been forced into these positions of dependency because the occupational structure and its supporting ideology offered no possibility for women to earn a comfortable living and community esteem at the same time.

While respectable women succeeded in crowding prostitutes out of civic life and separating them from the community, the painted woman's confinement in the restricted district was nothing more than a distorted image of the respectable woman's insulation in her family parlor. Both groups of women suffered from being classified as either good or bad; both groups were dependent upon men not only in a financial sense, but for their respective identities. This sexual ideology not only contributed to both the spread of prostitution and the growth of forces opposing it, but served to isolate all women from full and meaningful participation in the social world.

PART FOUR

Macro-sociology

In the previous two parts of this text/reader, we have considered the micro and middle levels of social life. In Part Four, our focus shifts to the macro-level. In other words, we have moved from interaction itself, to the linkages of interaction into the larger social structure, to our present concern: patterned public behavior. It should be clear that these levels are analytic; that is, each level links up with and penetrates the other. The institutional level of society is interaction writ large, and more or less stabilized. At the same time, institutions themselves play a significant role in shaping patterns of interaction.

Each of the readings in this part illustrates in one way or another how sociology represents the intersection of biography and history. Some institutional arrangements make life easier for us all by providing a script for the round of daily activities. Others, however, lock people into patterns of interaction that supply pain, suffering and even death. Institutions themselves have traditionally been at the very heart of the sociological enterprise and its major *raison d'être* as a discipline.

To examine society at the macroscopic level is an implicit, even explicit, admission that individuals are shaped by forces beyond primary groups or observed reference groups. It is to understand that agencies of an impersonal sort may indeed be as forceful in shaping individual lives as friendships and families. When the Department of Defense orders a military draft of young people, it directly effects those people in every intimate form of life. Hence, the macro level is nothing short of the interpenetration of individuals and institutions: an interplay as fateful as any between people.

Section XII

Law and Justice

A legal system in any society represents codified conventions of the moral order. Lawyer–sociologist Blumberg, in "Law, Order and the Working Class," explores the real meaning of the hapless phrase "law and order." Blumberg suggests that true law and order, based on justice and equality, is gravely subverted by the institutional arrangements that now exist in American society. The key role in defining what law and order will come to really mean (it is, after all, a highly abstract notion) will be played by the "middle mass"—those trapped between the welfare poor and the educated professionals and white-collar technicians. The middle mass represents an American problem, the "in-betweens": Historically, other "classes" in America have been oppressed and exploited by a more privileged group from above and threatened by emerging groups from below. The frustrations of the American middle mass will lead to action, and the legal institution will be a focus of that action. "Law and order" has become an ideology used by the wealthy to make a weapon of the middle mass against the poor. It represents a diversion from real problems in the United States. Its application is unequal: The well-to-do receive the *substance* of law and order, others the *form*, says Blumberg. He goes on to discuss in detail how crime and punishment in America are tied to our stratification system. (For example, one-third of all arrests in the United States are for some variation of the prosaic charge of drunkenness.) His wide-ranging discussion of the criminal justice system reviews particulars from the way the Juvenile Court operates to the use of psychiatric testimony during trials. The entire article is an excellent example of the fruitful wedding of legal and sociological insights.

The execution of justice does not happen in a vacuum. Nagel and Weitzman, in "Double Standard of American Justice," explore the application of legal sanctions and protections to the largest "minority" group in our society: women. The authors have discovered that there are two patterns that occur in the treatment of minorities. The first is widely recognized and involves the discrimination visited upon the disadvantaged. The second, paternalism, represents the systematic violation of civil rights and safeguards. Juveniles have long suffered from this second type of treatment. The authors document the notion that in some circumstances women are treated as "childlike." Black women, as one might suspect, suffer from both types of discrimination. This article is an excellent example of the technique of controlling (that is, looking within a particular category in order to see the effects of two additional variables without the contamination of the third, or categorical, variable) in order to articulate the relationships among sex, race and type of crime.

Another kind of methodology is represented in Heussenstamm's "Bumper Stickers and the Cops." The author developed an interesting natural social science experiment in order to discover whether or not the display of lurid Black Panther bumper stickers on automobiles would stimulate the police to issue more traffic tickets during a period of hostility between the police and the Panthers. Heussenstamm found a dramatic increase in the number of tickets issued to people with such stickers affixed to their cars. While controlling for as many factors as possible, the author points out how many more variables would have to be controlled in order to demonstrate fully the relationship. Although it is useful to employ all of the statistical knowledge available about sampling design and variable control, this article demonstrates how a hypothesis may arise and be partially supported in less than perfect methodological circumstances. It is an excellent example of "science as doing one's damnedest."

Miller's "Our Mylai of 1900: Americans in the Philippine Insurrection" is a bone-chilling reminder that not to know history is to condemn ourselves to reliving its errors. He draws a historical parallel between the actions of American civilians and servicemen in the Philippine war at the turn of the century and the recent Vietnam war. Through the use of historical data, Miller is able to document the idea that Vietnam, and American reactions to it, were not new but, rather, part of a continuing pattern.

1 *Abraham S. Blumberg*

Law, Order and the Working Class

The relationship of the current themes of "law and order" and "crime in the streets" to the growing resentments and belligerence of the middle mass of Americans—that group found somewhere between the welfare poor and the educated professional—will tend to dominate the politics and social life of the United States in the decade ahead. As the struggle unfolds there will undoubtedly be shifts in alliances, new targets, new slogans to match new grievances and new violence and disorder. What is certain is that the legal system, the enforcement apparatus, and the courts as political instruments will be at the center of the social upheavals that are bound to occur. Rather than the traditionally passive role ascribed to them by Marx and Mills, the middle mass is going to perform a critical function in determining the directions we are likely to travel in shaping our legal institutions, in either preserving or destroying the remnants of democracy in America.

The middle mass is likely to attribute the deteriorating quality of life, disappointments and frustrations in regard to life chances as a breakdown in law and order traceable to the deviant or minority group which threatens to limit opportunity. Implicit in the concept of law and order is the promise that it will provide the machinery for orderly change in the allocation of rewards, opportunity structures and access to the means of life in our social system —in a word, justice.

Yet what is at once vexing and embarrassing about the pledges that are embodied in the law and order concept is that they are simultaneously unredeemed, if not denied outright, by our society's institutional arrangements for their effectuation. The law and order ideology conceals the real problems of the middle mass by concentrating on a technological order which protects the moneyed and powerful and overrides the injustices which generate the anger and desperation that produce violence, criminality, marginality and illness. Our criminal process is primarily oriented to bureaucratic goals of efficiency and production rather than humanistic goals of remedy and assistance. Our law enforcement, public welfare and court systems have become the very agencies which blunt the possibility of orderly change and the more equitable distribution of life chances while claiming to protect the guaranteed rights of citizens.

Excerpted from the introduction to the second edition of *Law and Order: The Scales of Justice*, published by Transaction Books.

It is the police and their supporters in the legislatures and the mass media who have perpetuated the myth that the United States Supreme Court has promoted a crime wave through its rulings. But a close examination of our history reveals that we have always been in the midst of a "crime wave," long before the Supreme Court ever ruled on the very issues that the law and order ideology insists have caused crime. For example, the Mapp decision excluding illegally obtained evidence did not come until 1961, after a long history of abuses at the local level by police authorities who searched people, their homes and personal effects almost at will, and generally maltreated them in the process. The requirement that indigent defendants in felony cases be provided with counsel did not come until 1963 in the Gideon case. The Miranda ruling in 1966 aroused the special fury of police buffs and the supporters of the law and order ideology. Yet the purpose of the Miranda ruling was to equalize rights, to require that regardless of a person's intelligence, social class, race or legal sophistication that he be advised that what he said may be used against him, that he had a right to remain silent and a right to a lawyer. What was good enough for the professional and organized criminal was certainly good enough for the ordinary person.

Miranda and the other decisions simply spelled out rights declared in our Constitution over 180 years ago, a delivery on the pledges that were contained in the Bill of Rights. It is well to remember that prior to these decisions it was not uncommon for police and enforcement officials to kick doors down, to search in a fishing expedition fashion, to apply the rubber hose to one's back or genitals or use a well-placed blow to the side of the head with a phone book to encourage people to confess. Indeed, the Supreme Court sought to establish a sense of order and decency to an area which had become a quagmire of police lawlessness in the various states.

The irony of the attacks on the Supreme Court over Miranda is that research returns indicate that it has not hampered the police at all. It is estimated that only about 20 percent of all crime is ever reported and that only approximately 25 percent of this total is cleared by an arrest being made. But confessions have never been an important element in this rather low overall clearance rate, which has generally depended on independent evidence and the testimony of witnesses. In spite of Miranda, people continue to confess even after warnings have been given and the endless crush of cases in our courts and overcrowding of our prisons continue. Some lawyers and judges had hoped that one of the by-products of the court's rulings would be an overhauling of the American police system, and an upgrading of the personnel and administrative procedures affecting the almost 500,000 police and the over 40,000 departments. But the limited reforms have not been without some ominous developments of police politicization which are potentially destructive to the democratic process.

The law and order mystique of the American middle mass possesses a rather fascinating internal inconsistency. At the international level, for example, the United States government was the prime mover of a resolution which was unanimously adopted by the United Nations General Assembly on December 11, 1946 establishing the proposition that genocide is a crime under international law. Although it has been ratified by 75 nations, we have not done so for fear of the questions that might be raised in connection with out internal racial strife. At the national level, the law and order ideology conveniently ignores the kind of lawlessness inherent in the numerous ploys and strategies which have been designed to blunt the impact of the 1954 Supreme Court decision in ***Brown*** vs. ***The Board of Education***. Similarly, the most vehement middle mass law and order adherents heap calumny on the Supreme Court while opposing any gun control legislation as a step toward crime prevention.

The counterparts of the middle mass crusaders who oppose gun control are to be found in the various enforcement and domestic intelligence agencies such as the Bureau of Narcotics and Dangerous Drugs and the FBI. Federal and local narcotics enforcement agents in their cruel harassment of drug users and physicians have deliberately chosen to ignore the legal doctrine established in *Lindner* vs. *United States* (1925), which would treat addiction as a disease, and the addict as a sick person for whom the medical profession could legally prescribe and treat in the course of private practice.

Illicit wiretapping and bugging are commonplace activities of late, and the FBI has been employed on more than one occasion as a not too subtle vehicle to stifle criticism (as in the case of the investigation of Daniel Schorr who had been critical of the federal administration). But far more ominous is the development of a proliferating network of domestic surveillance agencies and related activities involving the creation of files and dossiers on almost any person or group that may seize their fancy.

Although our bail laws are in effect an insidious form of preventive detention, there are well organized efforts at the federal and local level to formalize these procedures which are ostensibly designed only for dangerous offenders who are likely to commit crimes while on bail or parole. The crucial feature of the preventive detention proposals is the difficulty of predicting who will commit a crime which threatens life. The most serious constitutional shortcoming of the concept of preventive detention is that it seriously compromises any notion of a presumption of innocence.

The role of the middle mass in directing the law and order crusade is best demonstrated by the stop-and-frisk decision of the Supreme Court. In response to pressures generated by the drug traffic and violent street crime, state legislatures, noting that police were not observing the standard of "probable cause," passed the stop-and-frisk legislation. This legislation wrote into law the much lower standard of "reasonable suspicion" as a basis for police stopping and interrogating persons in the street and frisking them for a possible weapon when the officer reasonably believes that he is in danger. Thus, the police were given statutory comfort and support for actions already being performed under the guise of probable cause. It is noteworthy, however, that the President's Commission on Law Enforcement and Administration of Justice (popularly known as the Crime Commission) indicated in its report that the stop-and-frisk power is employed by the police primarily against the inhabitants of our urban slums, against racial minorities and the underprivileged. Police will make field interrogations of persons simply because their clothing, hair, gait or other mannerisms square with preconceived police notions of "suspicious characteristics"—characteristics that, for the most part, don't fit the middle mass mold. Quite often these suspicious persons are Puerto Ricans, blacks, Mexicans or Indians. The police practice of illegal arrests on suspicion or for investigation rather than probable cause was fairly widespread prior to the passage of stop-and-frisk legislation, especially in neighborhoods inhabited by the poor and racial minorities. Most of these arrests (about 300,000 per year) are made as part of an "aggressive patrol" tactic to demonstrate police "rep" and "muscle," as well as a fishing expedition. Most of these arrests are terminated without any formal charges being brought.

In June, 1968 the United States Supreme Court after considerable agonizing upheld the stop-and-frisk practices of the police. The lone dissent of Justice Douglass is of interest: "To give the police greater power than a magistrate is to take a long step down the totalitarian path....If the individual is no longer to be sovereign, if the police can pick him up whenever they do not like the cut of his gib, if they can seize and search him in their discretion, we enter a new regime."

The grave danger incurred by the extreme sensitivity of officeholders and office seekers to the middle mass concern with crime in the streets is that there will be increasing pressure by the law and order ideologues to neutralize the Bill of Rights, which in effect establishes a "friendly fascism." Despite the rather elaborate instruments of control now available to the law and order crusade—an 80 to 90 percent conviction rate, electronic eavesdropping and other more elaborate technologies, stop and frisk, a bail system which amounts to preventive detention, maximum security prisons and mental hospitals which are filled to capacity, the middle mass remains sold on the notion that more of the same is the answer to the "crime problem." The middle mass has bought the illusion of a crime-free society without confronting the underlying issues of poverty, race, housing, education, health and employment. And they are almost ready to accept some version of a blue-coated garrison state to achieve it.

Photos by Stanley Bratman

Text by Anne Stevens

Cook County Jail

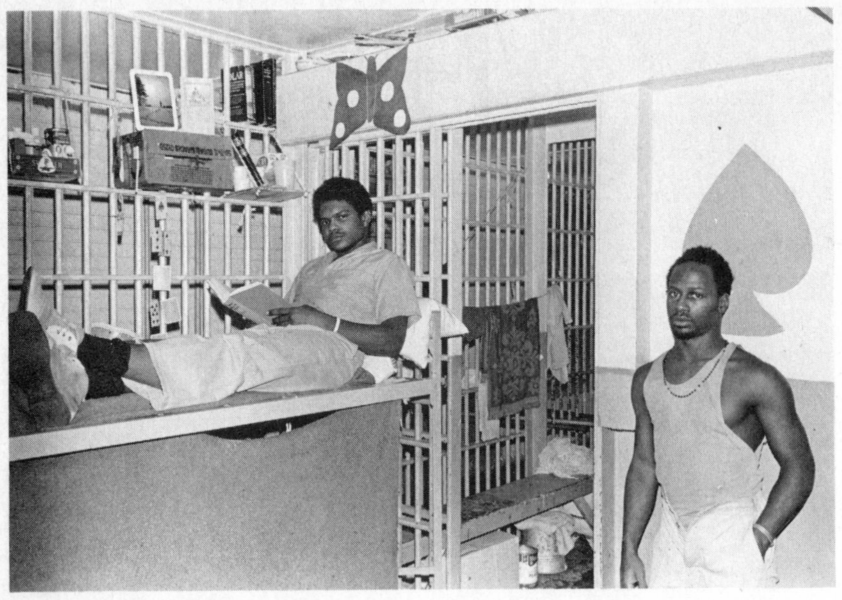

Cook County Jail is isolated—unconnected to the daily life of most Chicagoans by both location and purpose. It is dreary, fortress-like and foreboding from the outside. Windows are hidden high in dirty limestone walls. Parapets—hiding gun towers—loom over the adjacent street. The only accessible public entrance is through a courtyard between the jail and the Criminal Courts Building next door. More parapets for guns hang over the courtyard. The doors are heavy steel with tiny windows high off the ground.

People in the jail are usually those who cannot make bond and are being held to guarantee appearance in the court. There are some serving minor sentences, usually less than a year. Most of them are black, unemployed males, aged from 18 to 25. But there are also always some older, white, middle-class men, serving 30 days to 6 months sentences for reckless driving or failure to provide child-support. Women, a growing minority in the jail, form a more cohesive group than the men.

Prisoners live on tiers—groups of cells that are handled as administrative and social units. There is some rudimentary screening, but beyond separating sick from well and men from women, the social makeup of the tiers is fairly arbitrary. The six-by-ten cells contain a sink, a urinal, a cot and a small metal cabinet for clothes. Each tier has a dayroom

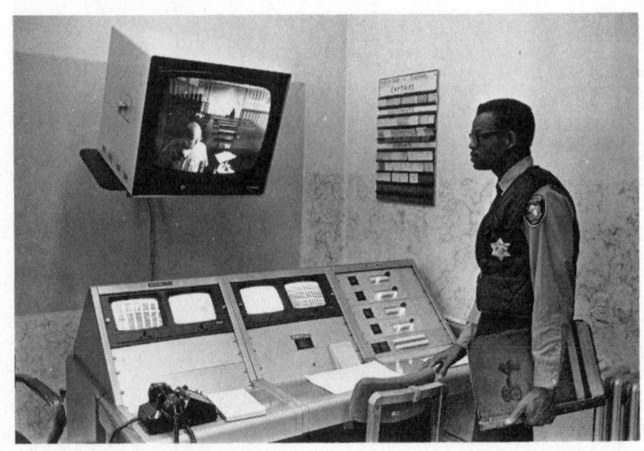

with tables, chairs and a television. Inmates are allowed to accumulate some possessions in their cells. For most, the first thing to be acquired is a radio so they can hear something of the outside.

The chief occupation is waiting. Waiting for hearings, waiting for trial, waiting to leave. Life revolves around the television, the radios and things to read. Clusters form and reform; people rap to each other. But the conversation is about the criminal courts or the streets, the outside or how to get outside. Rarely does anyone talk about self or feelings or ideals or ideas. Social barriers from the outside are preserved. Only through concentrated effort do dissimilar people get to know each other. There is a kernel of self held apart from all the others; each person reflects the isolation of the jail building. Each is separate, not dependent. Each gives only the surface of self to occupying time. The rest is given to hope, to plans of what to do when out, to schemes of how to get out.

The pattern of days is always the same. There is a time for the lights to go on in the morning and there is a time for the lights to go out in the evening. There is a time to be in the dayroom and there is a time to eat each meal. On some days there is mail; on some days there may be visitors. Some days there are showers and some days there is inspection of the cells. The only important days are the ones spent in court, for they are the days

on which there is real contact with outside, a real chance of getting back on the streets.

There are the usual misnamed "rehabilitative" programs; vocational and academic programs are offered through the Pace Program, staffed by clergy and ex-offenders, and the special visual arts programs run by the social workers. But all are underfunded and understaffed and only a minority of the people in the jail benefit. Most people in the jail are too busy with private plans and hopes. Besides, as many of those who've been inside will tell you, these programs are all based on the idea that there is something wrong with the people they are designed to serve.

Political scandals periodically rock the jail. The most recent large-scale scandal a few years ago revolved around the special treatment afforded to some illustrious prisoners being held for the federal courts. Sam Giancana, the Conspiracy Seven and other federal prisoners were being held on a special tier which allowed more visitors, less regimented treatment, better food. The ensuing investigations revealed that the administrative structure of the jail was dependent on a few convicted prisoners called "barn bosses." Privileges were bought and sold on the tiers with cigarettes, drugs, sexual favors. Uncooperative prisoners were "lost" on court days regularly. Barn bosses even had the ability to send prisoners to isolation for rules infractions.

Though most prisoners were and are black, most guards—in a city that is over 20 percent black—were white, as was the warden and virtually all of the administrative personnel. There was a general shakeup of the jail staff. The warden was replaced by a hard-nosed, career corrections officer who also happened to be black. Federal prisoners were integrated with the rest of the jail population. Overt racist actions were administratively outlawed. But the jail, more often than not remains overcrowded. Cells built for one often contain two. Showers, mail, visitors and any access to the outside are still considered privileges. And the jail, grey and flat, is there—dominant—still based on a contradiction in our legal tradition. Though supposedly innocent until proven guilty, those unable to post bond are held in a punitive setting and treated as guilty until proven innocent.

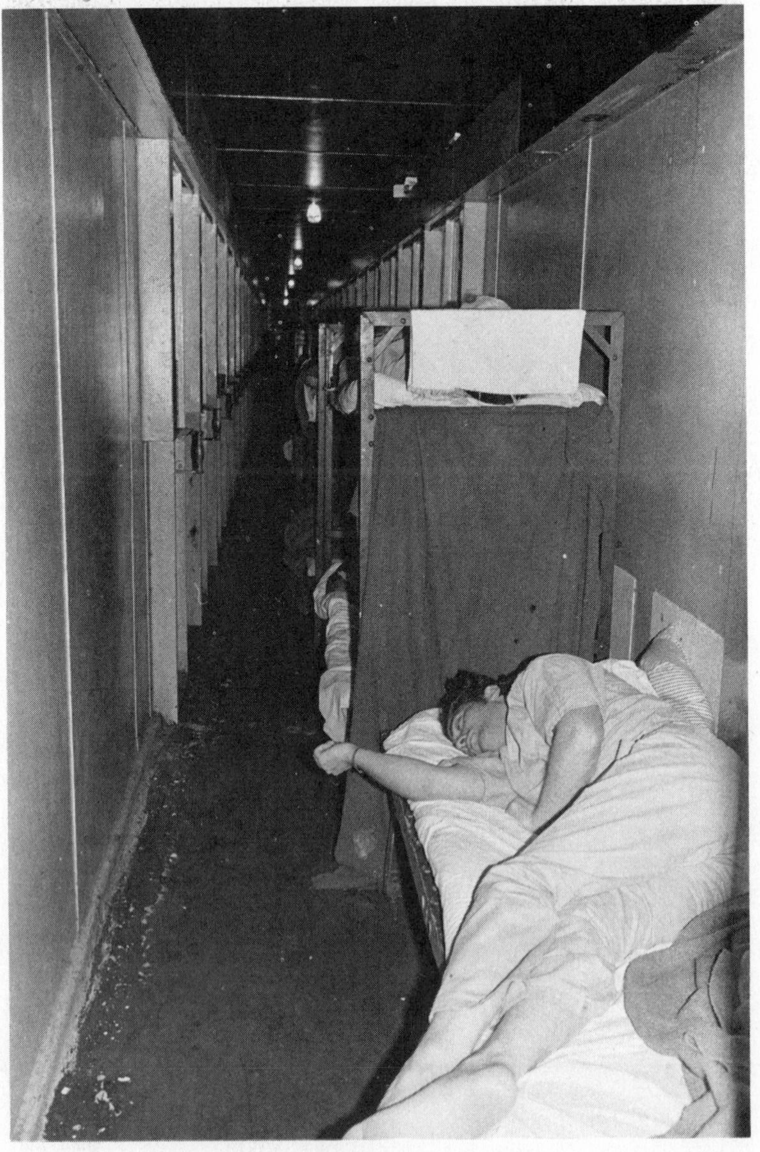

2

Stuart Nagel & Lenore J. Weitzman

Double Standard of American Justice

Are women treated equally in American courts? Or does sexism tip the scales of American justice against women when they are defendants and litigants before the bar? In the literature dealing with women's rights, researchers have found that "in several states, higher penalties are imposed on a woman who commits the same crime." However, this conclusion is based on those few state statutes and appellate test cases which describe the law on the books rather than law in action. Our research will focus instead on the law in action. We will ask if, in practice, women are sentenced to more time in prison than men for the same crimes. Are women favored or disfavored in criminal, personal injury and divorce proceedings? How does the presence of women jurors and judges affect the relative treatment of male and female litigants?

Analogies are frequently drawn between the treatment of women and blacks in many areas (e.g., employment) of American society. Is this similarity applicable to the courtroom? A comparison of black-white and male-female sentencing practices is examined for comparative insights.

Women as Criminal Defendants

In 1962, Lee Silverstein of the American Bar Foundation (ABF) compiled data on 11,258 criminal cases, using 194 counties located in all 50 states as his sample. While the main focus of his study was on procedures for providing attorneys to indigent defendants, Silverstein also gathered information on the race, sex and age of the defendants and the treatment they received at all stages of the criminal justice process—from preliminary hearing through sentencing.

Two basic patterns of discrimination emerge. The first—the disadvantaged pattern—involves unfavorable treatment of defendants who are poor, black or have only elementary education. These defendants in socially inferior positions receive unfavorable treatment at virtually all stages of the criminal justice process, including 1) receiving a preliminary hearing, 2) being released on bail, 3) having a hired attorney rather than assigned counsel or no attorney, 4) being subjected to relatively shorter pretrial detainment while in jail if not released on bail, 5) receiving a jury trial, 6) being dismissed or being acquitted, 7) receiving probation or a suspended sentence if convicted and 8) receiving a relatively short sentence if jailed.

The second discriminatory syndrome—the paternalistic pattern—particularly applies to juvenile offenders and involves unfavorable treatment only in the area of safeguards for the innocent, such as having an attorney or a jury trial. It involves favorable treatment, however, in being kept out of jail pending trial, in not being convicted and in not being sentenced to jail if convicted.

Both the disadvantaged and paternalistic patterns of discrimination against women are apparent to some degree in the ABF findings. However, when female criminal defendants are compared with their male counterparts, the resulting treatment pattern most readily fits the paternalistic mold. Paternalistic discrimination against and for women, as in the case of juveniles, is found in both grand larceny cases and in felonious assault cases, although women are somewhat more likely to be jailed when they commit assault. Due perhaps to the fact that assault is considered a more masculine type of crime than larceny, women's and men's jail sentences correspond more closely in these cases.

To the extent that male and female larceny and assault cases are comparable, the data suggest that the difference in treatment may be explained by a judicial attitude which assumes women (and juveniles) to be weaker, and therefore more likely to be harmed by pretrial and postconviction jailing.

Although blacks and indigents are particularly discriminated against when it comes to being released on bail, in the larceny and assault cases studied, the opposite holds true for women (Table 1). Of the 63 female larceny defendants, 76 percent were released on bail, while of the 771 male larceny defendants, only 50 percent were released on bail—a 26 percent difference. This practice works to avoid keeping juveniles and women in jail pending trial or after conviction. The same pretrial jail-avoidance phenomenon is evident in the assault cases, where there is a 19 percent difference.

Likewise, the data show that women receive more lenient treatment if they are convicted in grand larceny cases; 64 percent of the women received a suspended sentence or probation, as compared to only 43 percent of the men. A related although weaker difference is also apparent in the felonious assault cases studied.

Of those defendants who actually received jail sentences, there are too few (20 or less) women in the sample who were jailed pending trial or imprisoned after conviction to

Table 1
How the Treatment of Females Differs From Males As Defendants in Criminal Cases

	NUMBER OF DEFENDANTS *Percentage Receiving Treatment*			
	Females	*%*	*Males*	*%*
GRAND LARCENY CASES				
A. BEING JAILED				
1. Released on bail	63	76	771	50
2. Had less than 2 months delay of those awaiting trial in jail	10	60	231	67
3. Case dismissed or acquitted	71	24	841	13
4. Received suspended sentence or probation of those convicted	47	64	656	43
5. Received less than one year imprisonment of those imprisoned	9	33	241	45
B. FORMAL SAFEGUARDS				
6. Received preliminary hearing	42	57	606	55
7. Had or given a lawyer	61	90	781	87
8. Received a jury trial of those tried	18	47	283	31
FELONIOUS ASSAULT CASES				
A. BEING JAILED				
1. Released on bail	43	77	615	58
2. Had less than 2 months delay of those awaiting trial in jail	6	17	152	49
3. Case dismissed or acquitted	45	36	638	23
4. Received suspended sentence or probation of those convicted	25	44	415	36
5. Received less than one year imprisonment of those imprisoned	9	89	172	57
B. FORMAL SAFEGUARDS				
6. Received preliminary hearing	31	74	451	73
7. Had or given a lawyer	42	88	620	89
8. Received a jury trial of those tried	24	19	262	45

make a meaningful comparison possible on length of imprisonment. Possibly as a means of avoiding imprisonment and the stigma of a criminal record, fewer women are convicted than their male counterparts. The study shows that 24 percent of the women were acquitted or had their larceny cases dismissed, as compared to only 13 percent of the men. A similar difference is present in the assault cases cited.

Convicted defendants given indeterminate sentences were not included when computing the number imprisoned because these sentences lack the necessary precision for comparison. Of the 363 women sentenced in the total sample, 27 percent received indeterminate sentences, while 35 percent of the 5,898 men's sentences were indeterminate. Although these sentences are usually associated with such crimes as murder and arson (which men are more likely to commit), men usually receive a slightly higher percentage of indeterminate sentences than do women for the same type of crime. Such sentences generally have higher maximums than fixed terms and may result in longer prison stays.

When it comes to formal safeguards for the innocent, judicial treatment is mixed. When women defendants are compared with men defendants in either larceny cases or assault cases with respect to having a lawyer, no discriminatory pattern emerges. Likewise, no discrimination is evident with regard to receiving a preliminary hearing, although this is probably not as important a safeguard for the innocent as are having counsel or receiving a jury trial. (Of these three safeguards, only preliminary hearings have not been made a due process right for adults by the Supreme Court.)

However, women—in conformity with the paternalism hypothesis—are more likely to receive informal treatment with regard to not receiving a jury trial, at least in the assault cases, where the percentage difference between men and women is 26. This disparity is contrary to the best interests of women, because juries are generally less likely to convict than are judges. To be convicted by a jury normally requires the unanimous agreement of 12 persons, a task harder for the prosecutor to achieve than that of convincing a single judge. The University of Chicago Jury Project research indicates that while both juries and judges tend to favor women in their criminal verdicts, juries do so to a greater extent.

Although the numbers are small, a comparison of women by race indicates that white women are less likely to be jailed before or after conviction than are black women, and they are also less likely to have a lawyer to represent them. This is because they are less apt than blacks to be so poor that they are appointed counsel by the court. And while black women (unlike black men) receive more favorable treatment than do white men with regard to being jailed before or after conviction—in this case, sexual paternalism and racial discrimination are mixed—there is no consistent pattern whereby black women receive or do not receive a jury trial. Therefore, white women seem to fit the paternalistic mold more neatly.

The ABF data, then, indicate that women are substantially less likely to be held in jail before or after trial, but are more likely to lack a jury trial. While all the differences discussed were sufficiently significant that they could not readily be attributed to chance, some of them might be attributable to the fact that women commit grand larcenies and felonious assaults on a less grand scale than men do, and that therefore they have less at stake to merit a jury trial and less guilt to merit a severe sentence.

It is interesting to note that male juveniles and female adults are treated about equally. Although the male juveniles are less likely to have an attorney, a jury trial or a preliminary hearing, the female adults are more likely to be kept out of jail before and after conviction.

In addition to assuming that women are weaker and more open to harm from jailing, judges may also give shorter sentences to women than to men convicted of similar crimes because they think this weaker nature also makes women less dangerous to society, more easily deterred from repeating their crime and more speedily rehabilitated. Custodial care, deterrence from further crime and rehabilitation being the official goals of imprisonment in any case, women are thus already assumed to be in a position of conforming to them. Women and especially juveniles are also less likely to be hardened criminals—in the sense that they are somewhat less likely to have prior criminal records.

Likewise, judges might feel that both juveniles and women should be treated in a more fatherly, less legalistic way, and that jury trials and defense counsel interfere with this paternalistic informality.

The few statutes which provide different sentences for women and men for the same type of crime generally provide more indeterminate sentences for women, just as juvenile statutes provide more indeterminate sentences for juveniles. The legislators who pass these laws probably believe that women and juveniles are more accessible to rehabilitation than are adult males, and that indeterminate sentences contingent on progress made in prison will facilitate rehabilitation. (However, we know that indeterminate sentences usually result in a longer period of incarceration.) Testing this explanation would require determining the legislators' attitudes, although the judges who apply criminal statutes allowing for discretion are probably more instrumental to the increase or decrease of sexual discrimination than are the legislators who write them into law.

Women as Personal Injury Plaintiffs

In personal injury cases, where the defendant is usually an insurance company rather than an individual man or woman, the difference in the sex of the plaintiffs who have suffered personal injuries may be an important variable. How do sex differences affect treatment received?

There are separate stages at which discrimination can occur in personal injury cases—the first being whether or not the injured party files a complaint.

In Alfred Conard's 1964 study of the economics of personal injury cases in the state of Michigan, he compiled data on the background characteristics of automobile accident victims who subsequently became personal injury claimants. His key sex data (Table 2) show that of the seriously injured male accident victims, 38 percent filed suit, whereas of the seriously injured female accident victims, only 30 percent filed suit. This difference might be due to a higher rate of precomplaint settlements for women or to less severe injuries sustained by them. An even more telling explanation might be that women are encouraged to be less aggressive in asserting their legal rights in personal injury cases.

Once the suit is filed, the next stage is establishing the defendant's liability to pay something to the injured plaintiff. The 1970 Department of Transportation study of personal injury claims (which used nationwide data) shows that there is virtually no difference between men and women in the likelihood of their winning claims (see Table 2). It is interesting to note that there is a lower victory rate in cases which go to a jury decision as compared to cases heard by a judge or settled without coming to trial—possibly because the nontrial cases more clearly favor the plaintiff—but there is no differentiation related to whether the plaintiffs are men or women.

Sexist on Sex

A discriminatory pattern begins to appear if one leaves out minors and compares only adult male plaintiffs with adult female plaintiffs, since adult males win 76 percent of their jury trials and adult females only 69 percent of theirs. Sexual discrimination seems less prevalent in the comparison between boy and girl minors (especially preteenage minors) because the tendency is to class them simply as "children." The data reveal, however, that adults, whether male or female, have a better chance of winning their cases than children of either sex, probably because children frequently contribute through negligence to their own injuries, and juries tend to identify more closely with adult defendants than with child plaintiffs.

Once liability has been established, the next stage involves determining the amount of money to be awarded. Again there is little difference in the average amount awarded to male and female plaintiffs when adults and minors are grouped together, although a small percentage difference may involve a substantial number of dollars. However, the pattern of amounts awarded is again more favorable to men when only adults are compared: men received 6 percent above the average personal injury award for similar cases of injury with similar compensation for medical expenses and lost wages, while women averaged 2 percent below this figure.

The more interesting male-female comparisons relate to specific kinds of personal injuries. For instance, when husbands sue for loss of consortium (affection and sex) caused by their wives' injuries they collect more than when wives sue for loss of consortium caused by their husbands' injuries. This is so even though when women sue for their own injuries, they tend to collect less than men do. Our data also shows that there are more than 11 times as many suits by husbands for the loss of their wives' services as by wives for the loss of their husbands' services—another odd phenomenon. Does this represent the fact that more wives than husbands suffer personal injuries, or is it rather a reflection of outmoded legal tradition? It would seem to be the latter, for in fact, these 28 suits in which the wife is plaintiff represent a sizeable increase over the three such cases shown in the 1964 Jury Verdict Research Report, and in some states the law still permits only husbands—and not

Table 2
How the Treatment of Females Differs from Males As Victims and Plaintiffs in Personal Injury Cases

	Female Plaintiffs	*Male Plaintiffs*
I. SUIT FILED		
1. Suit filed by seriously injured victim	30%	38%
II. LIABILITY ESTABLISHED		
2. Claim was paid in bodily injury cases	80%	77%
3. Victory in jury trial cases (to plaintiffs of all ages)	61%	62%
4. Victory in jury trial cases (to adult plaintiffs)	69%	76%
III. AVERAGE AMOUNT AWARDED		
5. Award in jury trial cases (to plaintiffs of all ages)	-2% below average	+1% above average
6. Award in jury trial cases (to adult plaintiffs)	-2% below average	+6% above average
7. Award for loss of victim's services (to spouse plaintiffs)	$5,585	$6,524
8. Award for victim's death (to spouse plaintiffs where victim employed age 21-29)	$67,524	$39,820
9. Award for urinogenital injuries	$11,835	$31,966

wives—to sue for loss of a spouse's services—a holdover from the time when wives were considered part of their husbands' property—and one's property cannot sue for damages to the owner of the property. It may also have been felt unseemly for a woman to sue for the loss of the sexual services of her husband.

The generally larger amounts awarded to male plaintiffs for their personal injuries may be in part explained by the greater earning power of males, which may be temporarily or permanently reduced by the injury. This greater earning power may reflect employment and educational discrimination against women over which personal injury juries have no control. In cases where the injury results in death, male victims are clearly valued more highly than women in terms of monetary awards; because of this, women seem to be favored as plaintiffs. However, it must be remembered that where a wife-plaintiff is seeking to collect for a killed husband rather than a husband-plaintiff for a killed wife, one is mixing favoritism as to the victim's sex with discrimination as to the plaintiff's sex.

Differences in the amounts awarded to male and female plaintiffs for injuries not generally related to an individual's work capacity cannot be readily explained in terms of differential earning power. Urinogenital injuries fall into this category, and the inequality pattern here is greater than with any other type of bodily injury. In the sample studied, the average male plaintiff who wins a urinogenital injury case collects $31,966, while the average female plaintiff collects only $11,385. This represents an absolute difference of $20,131 or 170 percent. Monetary awards for injury to male genitalia run almost three times as high as those for injury to female genitalia—a direct indication of an apparently sexist value system in American courts.

Some of the difference may be accounted for by the fact that urinogenital damage was usually more severe and more likely to be permanent among the male plaintiffs. Because the child-bearing capacity of women is especially valued in American society, a more useful comparison would be between women who lose their capacity to bear children with men who lose their potency.

An overall view of the findings seems to reveal a pattern in which adult women are less likely than men to file suit, to establish liability and to receive a relatively high award, especially for certain types of injury. In this regard, the pattern of discrimination against women resembles that of black plaintiffs rather than juveniles. The victory rate for black plaintiffs was 57 percent as compared to a general rate of 61 percent and a rate of 46 percent for children under 12. Damage awards to black plaintiffs averaged 15 percent lower than the general level of awards. If children collect anything in court, they tend to get either very small or very large awards. This uneven distribution gives them an average award close to that of the general population. In personal injury cases, children, blacks and women, in that order, do worse on liability than adults, whites and men. Given this order of discrimination on a victory-rate continuum, women plaintiffs are thus closer to blacks than to children in the treatment they receive. On a damages-awarded continuum, however, women are closer to children than to blacks, with blacks farthest behind.

The basic issue in personal injury cases is whether the plaintiff succeeds in collecting money for damages. Since women are usually less favored in economic matters in our society, a similar pattern of negative discrimination should be evident in personal injury cases. This has, on examination, turned out to be correct. The paternalism hypothesis, which made some sense in relation to the treatment of women as criminal defendants, cannot be applied in the same terms to personal injury plaintiffs, because they are not in jeopardy of being placed in jail or stigmatized with criminal records. It could, however, be defined here as favoritism toward the weak in imposing negative sanctions, but disfavoritism in awarding or enforcing monetary awards. If it is so defined, we can legitimately say that the discrimination women experience fits both the disadvantaged and the paternalistic patterns. Its causes are probably: the traditional subordination of women in the family, employment and educational discrimination, the rationing of scarce monetary resources, even, in some cases, a Freudian castration fear and other sexual anxieties, as indicated by the huge discrepancy in awards for loss of urinogenital functions. As contemporary pressures for societal and legal change steadily erode these causal factors, differential victory rates and damages awarded should become more nearly equal.

Women as Divorce Litigants

The predominant impression among the general public is that divorce cases are a manifestation of female domination or even exploitation of men, because normally only women litigants seek and obtain alimony or child support. Despite this prevailing opinion, the facts about women as divorce litigants could well be said to show actual male domination and even exploitation.

In a sample of divorce cases in 22 states taken in 1963, wives were plaintiffs in 72 percent of the cases. Yet, even where women are the formal plaintiffs, existing data indicate this is often really a nominal status, and in reality it is the husband who has taken the de facto rather than the de jure initiative in dissolving the marriage. William Goode, on the basis of extensive interviews with a sample of 425 divorced women in 1956, concluded that "the husband more frequently than the wife is the first to desire a divorce, and it is the husband more often than the wife who adopts (whether consciously or not) a line of behavior which forces the other spouse to suggest a divorce as the appropriate solution."

Among the poor, desertion by the husband is a frequent substitute for divorce and is a major cause of eligibility for welfare aid. In the year 1967, 76 percent of the 1.3 million Aid to Dependent Children families in the United States had fathers absent from the home. Once again the man appears to be the active partner in the dissolution of the family.

The fact that wives seem to have better formal grounds for divorce and thus become the plaintiff-complainants may possibly show greater provocation on the part of husbands. An alternative explanation is that both husband and wife recognize that the wife has a better chance of winning the case. In divorce cases where decrees were granted, the wife as plaintiff lost only about 2 percent of the time, whereas the husband as plaintiff lost about 10 percent of the time.

Although women have become more independent as a result of increased employment opportunities, they are still more economically dependent upon their husbands than their husbands are on them and would therefore tend to resist divorce were it not for their husbands' provocation, which may take the form of cruelty, nonsupport, desertion or some other ground.

In descriptions of the divorce trial process, there are many references to the often degrading paternalistic procedures to which women litigants are subjected. Begging for alimony may be particularly degrading, even if alimony is considered 1) income accrued as a result of inadequately compensated wifehood and motherhood and 2) payment for obtaining educational rehabilitation and training. Seeking child support may also be a frustrating ordeal, even if the judge recognizes the concept as covering both some of the considerable work the mother must do in caring for her children and some of the many out-of-pocket expenses involved in raising the children which the husband has fathered. Although it might at first glance appear to be a victory when the wife obtains custody of and responsibility for the children, which she does in about 95 percent of cases, husbands in fact admitted that about 85 percent of the time they agreed with the custody decrees.

A double standard of morality may also prevail in custody disputes, condemning extramarital activities by wives but tolerating them on the part of husbands. In some states, the double standard actually allows husbands to obtain a divorce on sexual grounds which are not allowed to wives—as, for example, a common provision that allows husbands to divorce wives who were pregnant at the time of the marriage, whereas there is no comparable legislation allowing wives to divorce husbands who have made other women pregnant at the time of the marriage.

The real test of possible discrimination in the judicial process comes not at the stage of initiation or filing suit, nor even at the stage of judgment, but rather at the stage of that judgment's enforcement. To a lesser extent, this reasoning also applies to criminal and personal injury cases, but a far higher percentage of the results of such cases are determined at the prejudgment stage. In addition, there seems to be no data available on the collection of personal injury damages by sex—as distinct from the awarding of damages—nor on the paroling of convicts by sex. We do however have some data on the monetary judgments awarded to women divorce litigants.

Table 3 illustrates the probability of a divorced woman being able to collect any child-support money. It is based on data gathered by Kenneth Eckhardt from a sample of fathers who were ordered to pay child support in divorce decrees in a metropolitan county in Wisconsin in 1955. Within one year after the divorce decree, only 38 percent of the fathers were fully complying with the support order. Twenty percent had only partially complied, and in some cases partial compliance constituted only one payment. Forty-two percent of the fathers had made no payment at all. By the tenth year, the number of open cases had dropped from 163 to 149 because of the death of the father, termination of his parental rights or the maturity of the children. By that year, only 13 percent of the fathers were fully complying and 79 percent were in total noncompliance.

If noncompliance with child-support orders is so great, we can reasonably expect it to be even greater with alimony orders, although alimony orders are in fact relatively infrequent. In a 1956 analysis of 12,000 Chicago divorce cases, the wife requested post-divorce alimony in only 7 percent of the cases. In 1922, the last year the United States Census Bureau kept alimony data, their figures showed alimony decreed in only 15 percent of a nationwide sample, although women were considerably less independent at that time.

Of 172,000 minor children involved in divorces in Chicago in the period 1949-50, one third were awarded no child support at all. It should also be noted that the original child-support orders given by a court probably do not meet the full support needs of the children. Some of the orders may also be further judicially reduced when the husband remarries or when his financial status otherwise worsens. Thus, if only a minority of husbands are paying anything at all, and those husbands are paying only a substantially less than full support order, this means in practice that most of the actual child support is being carried by the mother or by the state.

In spite of potential sanctions such as contempt of court, civil action and criminal prosecution and despite the considerable incentive to the state to avoid unnecessary welfare payments, legal action is seldom initiated against the nonpaying father. This is especially the case as the children grow older and probably require even more support money. Yet Table 3 shows that only 19 percent of the 101 nonpaying fathers at the end of the first year had legal action taken against them, and in the tenth year only 1 percent of the 128 nonpaying fathers were faced with legal action. Indeed, monetary divorce awards may well be the least complied with and the least enforced of criminal or civil court orders.

The explanation for the lack of enforcement is not that the fathers are unable to comply. Support orders take into account the father's ability to pay. In fact, working-class fathers, though less financially well off, are more likely to

Table 3
The Possibility of a Divorced Woman Collecting Any Child Support Money

Years since court order	*Number of open cases*	*Compliance* Full	Partial	No	*Nonpaying Fathers**
One	163	38%	20%	42%	19%
Two	163	28	20	52	32
Three	161	26	14	60	21
Four	161	22	11	67	18
Five	160	19	14	67	9
Six	158	17	12	71	6
Seven	157	17	12	71	4
Eight	155	17	8	75	2
Nine	155	17	8	75	0
Ten	149	13	8	79	1

*Nonpaying fathers against whom legal action was taken.

Based on data from Kenneth Eckhardt, "Deviance, Visibility, and Legal Action: The Duty to Support," 15 *Social Problems* 470, 473-74 (1968).

be prosecuted than are middle-class fathers, because their ex-wives are more likely to be on welfare, and they themselves are more likely to have criminal records. The explanation for general nonenforcement of support orders probably lies in the pro-male bias of the prosecutors, judges and legislators who could more effectively enforce the law if they cared to. Some of the nonenforcement may also be due to the greater complexity of nonsupport cases (especially where there is a question of interstate enforcement) and to the less current nature of nonsupport decrees, as compared to the crush of other cases.

A realistic remedy for the nonenforcement of child-support orders may lie not in the more vigorous prosecution of errant males—although in some flagrant cases this might be merited—but in the imposition of some system of social insurance to cover the situation and preserve the dignity of those concerned. The concept of survivorship under Social Security could be expanded to include children of a deserting or divorced father, as well as of a deceased father. Other social alternatives include child allowances, the negative income tax or an expanded Family Assistance Plan. A national program of wholesome, well-run daycare centers and a government stimulation of possible employment opportunities would also enable those women who wish to work to support themselves and their children to do so, rather than have to ask for child support or welfare.

The Effect of the Sex of the Jury

The amount and direction of inequality between treatment of male and female litigants may be affected by whether the judge is a man or a woman and the predominance of male or female jurors. While there is a significant lack of female judges and a corresponding lack of data comparing them with male judges in their treatment of male and female litigants, it may be possible to extrapolate some findings about male and female jurors to male and female judges. (The concern here is with the effect of the sex ratio of judicial decision-makers on discrimination against women as litigants. Studies that deal with the effect on sentences or awards in general are not directly relevant. However, such studies do show that housewives are less punitive in burglary and possibly in other theft cases too, but more punitive in father-daughter incest and possibly other male-female sex crimes.)

There are five meaningful hypotheses which one can formulate about the effect of the jurors' own sex on their treatment of male and female defendants in criminal and personal injury cases. (Since jury trials are a rare occurrence in divorce cases, they will not be considered here.) One hypothesis might be called the attraction-of-opposites hypothesis, predicting that men will favor women and women men. "If you are representing a personable young man," advises John Appleman in his *Successful Jury Trials* (1952), "try to seat kindly old ladies in the jury box. If you are presenting an attractive young woman, have as many male jurors, old or young, as possible."

Second is the chivalry hypothesis, which predicts that men will favor women and women will also favor women, because women need special treatment. A third, the brainwashing hypothesis, says men and women both favor men because they have both been indoctrinated to believe men are more valuable. Fourth is the equality hypothesis, which says men favor neither sex, and women favor neither sex. This is the implicit or explicit hypothesis in those court cases which have held that it is not a denial of equal protection for a state to systematically decrease the chances of women serving on juries. Fifth is the likes-attract-likes hypothesis, which says men favor men and women favor women.

With regard to criminal cases, the most relevant data appear in a study by Arnold Rose and Arthur Prell. In 1953, they asked a sample of students taking courses in introductory sociology and social psychology at the University of Minnesota what sentences they would hand down if they were serving as judges or jurors in a variety of hypothetical fact situations. One situation involved a male convicted of a certain crime. Another, placed elsewhere on the list of situations, involved a female convicted of the same crime. The male respondents tended to give the male defendant a lower sentence than the female defendant, whereas the female respondents tended to give the female defendant a lower sentence than the male defendant. In other words, men tended to favor males and women tended to favor females. To the extent that this finding can be extrapolated to real juries or real judges, it confirms the likes-attract-likes hypothesis.

There is data available from the Jury Verdict Research Corporation on the way actual juries have treated females as distinct from males in personal injury cases, taking into consideration the sex of the jury. The study answers two questions: "If I know the sex of the plaintiff, what can I predict with regard to victory and damages before male-dominated and female-dominated juries?" and, "If I know the dominant sex of the jury, what can I predict with regard to victory and damages for male and female plaintiffs?"

Both parts of the study show that controlling for the sex of the jury makes no significant differences with regard to establishing liability. Both parts, however, show that controlling for the sex of the jury does make a substantial difference with regard to the average amount awarded. For instance, male-dominated juries gave awards to male plaintiffs that were 12 percent above the average to be expected for the type of injury, medical expenses and lost wages, whereas male-dominated juries gave female plaintiffs awards 17 percent below the average expected. Female-dominated juries reversed the direction of favoritism between female and male plaintiffs, further reinforcing the data that the likes-attract-likes hypothesis is the valid one, at least for average amounts awarded.

Discrimination, or at least inequality, between men and women seems to be greater in the amount of damages awarded than in the establishment of liability. This may be attributed to the fact that extremely large awards, those over $100,000 for instance, tend to be rendered for work accidents that result in crippling injuries—and relatively few women are injured in such circumstances. But some of the liability-damages difference may be because the differential earning power rationale only applies to assessing damages, not to establishing liability, and male jurors may place more emphasis on that rationale.

Much of the difference may also be attributed to the greater subjectivity involved in determining the extent of damages, which allows prejudice to enter more readily than in the more legalistic decision involved in establishing liability. Likewise the greater inequality present at the bail and sentencing stages in criminal cases, as compared to the pretrial procedural safeguards, may also be partly attributable to the relatively greater subjectivity and lesser legalistic restraint involved in the setting of bail and sentencing.

Because the disparities in the treatment of male and female litigants can be affected by the sex of the decision-makers, this should be further reason for society to seek out more women judges and jurors, in addition to the reasoning that emphasizes more democratic representation. To obtain more women judges, we must encourage more women to become law students and lawyers who will in due course be eligible to become judges. As for jurors, a majority of states by law still allow women to be more easily excused or exempted from jury service than men, and women are therefore probably underrepresented on the juries of those states.

Although women are more easily exempted from jury service in most states, local administrators and judges play a crucial role in applying jury selection laws. A Pennsylvania study showed an imbalance toward male jurors in Lancaster County, an imbalance toward female jurors in Philadelphia County and approximate equality in Allegheny County—all under the same state law.

From this general review, we can conclude that women as litigants do not receive the same treatment as men. In criminal cases women are much less likely to be jailed before or after conviction and are more likely to lack a jury trial than are men charged with the same crime. In personal injury cases, adult women are less likely to win than are adult men, and they collect awards that are substantially smaller, especially for certain types of injuries and especially before male-dominated juries. In divorce cases, where there is always a woman on one side and a man on the other, the woman seems to win on the basis of a simple analysis of divorce decrees; but these decrees become meaningless when we look at the collection records.

These findings seem consistent with how women are treated in American society in general. There is a kind of paternalistic protectiveness, at least toward white women, which assumes that they need sheltering from such manly experiences as being jailed or being treated in an overly formal fashion in family law or criminal cases. At the same time, when it comes to allocating scarce valuable resources, such as personal injury monetary awards or money for child support, women are more likely to be slighted.

More equal treatment might be achieved by increasing the public awareness of the disparities in the treatment of male and female litigants and by increasing the representation of women as jury and judicial decision-makers. Needed, however, are more specifically focused changes within the legal system, which will in turn improve the legal process for men and women alike.

For example, the remedy for the disparities in the jailing of women lies not in lessening the frequency of their release on bond, or increasing their postconviction term of imprisonment, but in providing pretrial release for all persons—regardless of sex—mainly on the basis of the likelihood that they will in fact appear for trial. Likewise, society needs to provide postconviction sentencing for everyone, regardless of sex, again, mainly on the basis of whether that person is likely to be rehabilitated or deterred from future crime by a period of imprisonment.

Along related lines, the remedy for disparities in personal injury awards and child-support collections probably does not lie in lowering the damages awarded to males or in prosecuting wayward nonpaying fathers more vigorously. Instead, society should perhaps seek collective action, such as no-fault insurance and an expanded Social Security program.

Neither these measures nor any others, however, will be sufficient in themselves. Nothing will succesfully eliminate the discrimination that exists against women litigants—save the complete eradication of discrimination against all women in our society.

SUGGESTED READINGS

Sexist Justice by Karen DeCrow (New York: Random House, 1974).

Sex Roles in Law and Society by Leo Kanowitz (Albuquerque: University of New Mexico Press, 1973).

"Women as Litigants" by Stuart Nagel and Lenore Weitzman in *Hasting's Law Journal*, *23*, pp. 171–198, Winter 1971, Symposium on Women's Rights.

3 *F. K. Heussenstamm*

Bumper Stickers and the Cops

A series of violent, bloody encounters between police and Black Panther Party members punctuated the early summer days of 1969. Soon after, a group of black students I teach at California State College, Los Angeles, who were members of the Panther Party, began to complain of continuous harassment by law enforcement officers. Among their many grievances, they complained about receiving so many traffic citations that some were in danger of losing their driving privileges. During one lengthy discussion, we realized that all of them drove automobiles with Panther Party signs glued to their bumpers. This is a report of a study that I undertook to assess the seriousness of their charges and to determine whether we were hearing the voice of paranoia or reality.

Recruitment advertising for subjects to participate in the research elicited 45 possible subjects from the student body. Careful screening thinned the ranks to 15—five black, five white, and five of Mexican descent. Each group included three males and two females. Although the college enrolls more than 20,000 students (largest minority group numbers on the west coast), it provides no residential facilities; all participants, of necessity then, traveled to campus daily on freeways or surface streets. The average round trip was roughly ten miles, but some drove as far as 18 miles. Eleven of the 15 had part-time jobs which involved driving to and from work after class as well.

All participants in the study had exemplary driving records, attested to by a sworn statement that each driver had received no "moving" traffic violations in the preceding twelve months. In addition, each promised to continue to drive in accordance with all in-force Department of Motor Vehicles regulations. Each student signed another statement, to the effect that he would do nothing to "attract the attention" of either police, sheriff's deputies or highway patrolmen—all of whom survey traffic in Los Angeles county. The participants declared that their cars, which ranged from a "flower child" hippie van to standard American makes of all types, had no defective equipment. Lights, horns, brakes and tires were duly inspected and pronounced satisfactory.

The appearance of the drivers was varied. There were three blacks with processed hair and two with exaggerated naturals, two white-shirt-and-necktie, straight caucasians and a shoulder-length-maned hippie, and two mustache-and sideburn-sporting Mexican-Americans. All wore typical campus dress, with the exception of the resident hippie and the militant blacks, who sometimes wore dashikis.

A fund of $500 was obtained from a private source to pay fines for any citations received by the driving pool and students were briefed on the purposes of the study. After a review of lawful operation of motor vehicles, all agreed on the seriousness of receiving excessive moving traffic violations. In California, four citations within a twelve-month period precipitates automatic examination of driving records, with a year of probation likely, or, depending on the seriousness of the offenses, suspension of the driver's license for varying lengths of time. Probation or suspension is usually accompanied by commensurate increases in insurance premiums. Thus, the students knew they were accepting considerable personal jeopardy as a condition of involvement in the study.

Bumper stickers in lurid day-glo orange and black, depicting a menacing panther with large BLACK PANTHER lettering were attached to the rear bumper of each subject car and the study began. The first student received a ticket for making an "incorrect lane change" on the freeway less than two hours after heading home in the rush hour traffic. Five more tickets were received by others on the second day for "following too closely," "failing to yield the right of way," "driving too slowly in the high-speed lane of the freeway," "failure to make a proper signal before turning right at an intersection," and "failure to observe proper safety of pedestrians using a crosswalk." On day three, students were cited for "excessive speed," "making unsafe lane changes" and "driving erratically." And so it went every day.

One student was forced to drop out of the study by day four, because he had already received three citations. Three others reached what we had agreed was the maximum limit—three citations—within the first week. Altogether, the participants received 33 citations in 17 days, and the violations fund was exhausted.

Drivers reported that their encounters with the intercepting officers ranged from affable and "standard polite" to surly, accompanied by search of the vehicle. Five cars were thoroughly gone over and their drivers were shaken down. One white girl, a striking blonde and a member of a leading campus sorority, was questioned at length about her reasons for supporting the "criminal activity" of the Black Panther Party. This was the only time that an actual reference to the bumper stickers was made during any of the ticketings. Students, by prior agreement, made no effort to dissuade officers from giving citations, once the vehicle had been halted.

Pledges to Drive Safely

Students received citations equally, regardless of race or sex or ethnicity or personal appearance. Being in jeopardy made them "nervous" and "edgy" and they reported being very uncomfortable whenever they were in their automobiles. After the first few days, black students stopped saying "I told you so," and showed a sober, demoralized air of futility. Continuous pledges to safe driving were made daily, and all expressed increasing incredulity as the totals mounted. They paid their fines in person immediately after receiving a citation. One student received his second ticket on the way to pay his fine for the first one.

No student requested a court appearance to protest a citation, regardless of the circumstances surrounding a ticketing incident. When the investigator announced the end of the study on the eighteenth day, the remaining drivers expressed relief, and went straight to their cars to remove the stickers.

Some citations were undoubtedly deserved. How many, we cannot be sure. A tightly designed replication of this study would involve control of make and year of cars through the use of standard rented vehicles of low-intensity color. A driving pool of individuals who represented an equal number of both extreme-left and straight-looking appearance with matched age-range could be developed. Drivers could be assigned at random to pre-selected, alternate routes of a set length. Both left-wing and right-wing bumper stickers could also be attached at random after drivers were seated in their assigned vehicles and the doors sealed. In this way, no subject would know in advance whether he was driving around with "Black Panther Party" or "America Love It Or Leave It" on his auto. This would permit us to check actual driving behavior in a more reliable way. We might also wish to include a tape recorder in each car to preserve the dialogue at citation incidents.

No More Stickers

It is possible, of course, that the subject's bias influenced his driving, making it less circumspect than usual. But it is statistically unlikely that this number of previously "safe" drivers could amass such a collection of tickets without assuming real bias by police against drivers with Black Panther bumper stickers.

The reactions of the traffic officers might have been influenced, and we hypothesize that they were, by the recent deaths of police in collision with Black Panther Party members. But whatever the provocation, unwarranted traffic citations are a clear violation of the civil rights of citizens, and cannot be tolerated. Unattended, the legitimate grievances of the black community against individuals who represent agencies of the dominant society contribute to the climate of hostility between the races at all levels, and predispose victims to acts of violent retaliation.

As a footnote to this study, I should mention that Black Panther bumper stickers are not seen in Los Angeles these days, although the party has considerable local strength. Apparently members discovered for themselves the danger of blatantly announcing their politics on their bumpers, and have long since removed the "incriminating" evidence.

SUGGESTED READINGS

Justice Denied: The Black Man in White America by Peter Collier and William M. Chace (New York: Harcourt Brace Jovanovich, 1970).

Report from Black America by Peter Goldman (New York: Simon & Schuster, 1970).

Another View: To Be Black in America by Gerald Messner (New York: Harcourt Brace Jovanovich, 1970).

4 *Stuart C. Miller*

Our Mylai of 1900

"Kill everyone over ten."

General Jacob H. Smith

Few Americans are aware that 70 years ago this country fought a long and bloody war of counterinsurgency, one that was remarkably similar to our struggle today in Vietnam. Even to the well educated, this lesson seems to have been lost. Only recently, Harvard professor Lawrence Kohlberg stated that 100 years ago, or even as recently as World War II, "nobody would have raised an issue such as the Song My massacre." In fact, such an issue was raised in 1902; and what began as the court martial of a major, ended up with a general standing trial and the army's chief of staff being forced into early retirement—precisely for permitting a policy of terror against another people.

Rarely do historical events resemble each other as closely as the involvements of the United States in the Philippines in 1899 and Vietnam in 1964. The murky origins of the fighting; the quick adoption of unsuccessful Spanish techniques for suppressing the Filipinos; an unrealistically optimistic, handsome, martial-looking commander whose ineptness was rewarded with accolades from Washington; a peace movement with "teach-ins" at universities and a more activist radical faction; rumors and finally evidence of American atrocities; complaints of rainy seasons, hidden jungle entrenchments and clandestine enemy soldiers who blended with the peasants after ambushing and booby-trapping American soldiers; talk of getting our native allies to assume the burden of fighting; and, finally, a scandal involving one officer and seven top sergeants, who pocketed commissary funds—all of this should make the war in the Philippines between 1899 and 1903 sound uncannily familiar to the American of 1970. Indeed, to follow the Philippine Insurrection in old newspapers and magazines is like sitting through a shabby drama for the second time.

We are becoming accustomed to the idea that the Tonkin Gulf incident of 1964 was possibly provoked by the U.S. Navy whose destroyers were gathering electronic intelligence while their South Vietnamese allies were bombarding two islands a few miles off the coast of North Vietnam. Even so, the alleged enemy torpedo attacks "appear doubtful" in the words of the skipper of the *S.S. Maddox*. He stressed that "no actual visual sightings" had confirmed them, and they could have been invented by "overeager sonarmen" and "freak weather effects." It now seems probable that the incident that led to full-scale American intervention in Vietnam was either deliberately contrived by our military brass, who were eager to bail out their faltering allies in Saigon, or it was the product of military bumbling.

The fighting that broke out on February 4, 1899, between Filipino nationalists under the command of General Emilio Aguinaldo and American troops occupying Manila was also to the advantage of the military brass. Back in Washington anti-imperialist sentiment in the Senate was threatening to block the two-thirds vote necessary to ratify the Treaty of Paris which, apart from ending the Spanish-American War, also provided for U.S. annexation of the Philippines. The vote was scheduled for February 6 and, by presenting the Senate with a full-scale war, the military was able to stampede some undecided senators. That it was the Americans who started the action in the islands is also indicated by other circumstantial evidence that Aguinaldo was not prepared to be attacked, much less to launch one of his own. Three of his key lieutenants were away from their posts when the fighting began, and his personal secretary was visiting in Manila where he was easily captured by the Americans.

Once fighting erupted in the Philippines, General E. S. Otis assured the nation that he would speedily put down the rebellion within a few weeks, an optimistic prediction he reiterated throughout the next 12 months. General Otis reports were filled with inflated statistics of enemy casualties and claims of spectacular American victories. Typically, they provoked headlines such as "Climax at Hand in Philippines," although a few less reverent editors wondered aloud why each optimistic report was invariably accompanied by a demand for more troops. By the end of his first year, Otis had 70,000 troops under his command (a 350 percent increase over the initial 20,000 which he had once insisted was "more than adequate"); and he was demanding an additional 30,000 to complete the job.

Less awed by the military brass than their counterparts of today, American editors at the beginning of this century openly began to question Otis's competence. Some called for an investigation of the army, and others ran headlines accusing the War Department of manufacturing statistics to conceal the actual cost of holding the Philippines. Such doubts sent Otis back to Washington to reassure Congress that, with a little more effort, victory was at hand. He was hailed as a conquering hero in the nation's capital; and all doubts were washed away in a sea of toasts and patriotic testimony. Once Otis was relieved, at his own request, it was rumored that he was slated to be the new secretary of war; but there was no cabinet shift to make room for him; and, unlike General Westmoreland, he was a "volunteer" and ineligible to become chief of staff.

Back home, Otis exchanged his sword for a pen and began to attack the anti-imperialists for encouraging the Filipinos to continue fighting after they had been obviously beaten. He also blamed the failure to end the war on his political superiors who imposed impossible limitations on his activity; nowhere was there even a suggestion of any personal responsibility. Perhaps the most striking similarity in the analogy between the Philippines and Vietnam affairs lies in the tortured logic and the humorless, turgid, self-righteous prose in which these two generals, Otis and now Westmoreland, rationalize the successes of their enemies.

Stop the War

The anti-imperialist movement, like the abolitionists a half-century earlier, was nurtured in Boston where Edward Atkinson published a magazine, *The Anti-Imperialist,* to protest the war. Atkinson featured articles entitled "The National Crime" and "Criminal Aggression: By Whom Committed?" and a July 4 issue in 1899 depicted an American flag at half-mast on the cover with the legend, "in memory and in honor of the brave soldiers of the United States whose lives have been sacrificed in the effort to subjugate the people of the Philippine Islands and to deprive them of their liberty." The postmaster general acted quickly to confiscate any copies destined for addresses out of the country and in San Francisco the post office seized a copy destined for Admiral George Dewey in Manila.

In the Senate the attack on the war was led almost single-handedly at first by the distinguished and respected Republican senator from Massachusetts, George Frisbee Hoar. Like Fulbright many decades later, Hoar was in the awkward position of fighting his own party then in office. Like Fulbright too, he was not only morally indignant over the tactics being employed in the Philippines, but very practically concerned over the domestic political effects of such imperialist ventures for the United States.

Senator Hoar was joined by a good many other respected Americans, from the industrialist Andrew Carnegie to Henry Wade Rogers, president of Northwestern University. College campuses at Ann Arbor, Chicago, and Cambridge sponsored mass antiwar rallies, addressed by leading professors. "Alas, what a fall is here, my countrymen. Within the circuit of a single year to have declined from the moral leadership of mankind into the common brigandage of the robber nations of the world," Michigan professor Charles A. Towne told an assembly of colleagues, students and townsmen in Ann Arbor. At similar gatherings, Charles Elliot Norton of Harvard denounced the war; and at the University of Chicago Lawrence Laughlin evoked cries of treason when he described the Stars and Stripes as "an emblem of tyranny and butchery in the Philippines." Pro-administration newspapers, such as the *New York Times,* decried the evolution of the universities into political instruments over the Philippine affair.

In the Vietnamese conflict, Mill Valley in California's Marin County was the first local government to pass an antiwar resolution. That honor went to New York City in 1899, although a patriotic plea, asking why "Lawton's [a popular general killed early in the war] slayers" should be "upheld by representatives of New York," caused the council quickly to rescind the resolution. Attempts to get other local governments to pass antiwar resolutions were unsuccessful. Petitions to end the war were as ubiquitous 70 years ago as they are today. Senator Hoar presented one to Teddy Roosevelt shortly after he assumed the presidency; it called for an immediate end to "a contest professedly waged in the interest of humanity" but which was being "degraded into an inhuman war of extermination." This petition accused American soldiers of murdering Filipino women and children; burning down native villages; using torture to extract confessions and information from prisoners, suspects and local officials; and employing "savage allies to settle old scores under the aegis of the United States." Needless to say, Teddy was as receptive to such petitions as Nixon was when he inherited the war in Vietnam last year.

There were also some antiwar radicals who were not content with rallies, speeches and petitions to get American soldiers out of the Philippines. One group in Meadville, Pennsylvania, actually attacked Americans enlisting in the army to fight the Filipinos. "Meadville seems to be afflicted by the presence of Aguinaldinos even more reckless in act and statement than those of Boston," exclaimed the *New York Times.* Other activists smuggled antiwar literature into army camps; and nine American soldiers deserted to the side of Aguinaldo, proclaiming him to be the George Washington of the Philippines.

Enemies Without and Within

Today one can quickly recognize the rationalizations offered by the McKinley administration and its apologists to defend the policy in the Philippines, for they differ only in specifics from the justification for American intervention in Vietnam. We were fighting in the Philippines, they insisted, to protect the Filipino people externally from imperialistic Germans lurking by; and, internally, from Aguinaldo himself, who was attempting to enslave his countrymen. A *New York Times* editorial in 1899 explained that McKinley was "the liberator" baffling Aguinaldo, "the enslaver, the criminal aggressor, the designing tyrant." The editor denounced "the heartless indifference of the anti-imperialists to the cruel fate in store for the non-combatant natives if we fail to crush Aguinaldo." Every Atkinson pamphlet, Hoar speech, and peace rally "forges a link in the chains which Aguinaldo is trying to foster upon the wrists of his unfortunate countrymen," the editorial asserted.

To make this argument more viable, proadministration editors ran sensational stories describing "the massacre and rapine" that "marked the course of Aguinaldo." Thus, "the dearest illusion of Senator Hoar" has been "shattered by the beastly behavior of the *insurrectos* against their own countrymen," the *New York Times* commented. Ironically, the administration had to reverse itself quickly once Aguinaldo was captured early in 1901 and thereupon urged his compatriots to surrender and swear allegiance to the United States. Overnight, the "bloodthirsty tyrant" became an "honest, sincere . . . natural leader of men with considerable shrewdness and ability . . . highly respected by all." General Funston, who captured Aguinaldo, added, however, that while the Filipino commander was "a man of humane instincts," he was not always able to control his followers.

Another key rationalization for those who supported American policy in the Philippines was that only the peace movement in the United States kept the insurrection going by encouraging the Filipinos to think that the Americans would pull out of the islands short of victory. "I know from observation, confirmed by captured prisoners, that the continuance of fighting is chiefly due to reports that are sent out from America," General Lawton told a correspondent in 1899. Back home, this contention was repeated over and over, and one magazine carried a picture of Aguinaldo on a flap pasted on the cover, under which was the caption, "What is behind Aguinaldo, that *Fiend Who Has Slain American Soldiers?*" By raising the flap, the reader found a picture of William Jennings Bryan, the presidential candidate running on an anti-imperialist platform. In his chronicle of the period, *Our Times,* Mark Sullivan commented that "the spirit of America became sour" as a result of the debate over the Philippines; we taste that sourness again today.

Rumors of American atrocities were part of the peace propaganda very early in the war; but by 1900 letters from soldiers to relatives back home, describing the use of dum dum bullets, torture, retaliatory shooting of prisoners and the creation of concentration camps for civilians, began to reach the desks of local editors. One soldier bragged in a letter that Americans were shooting Filipino men, women and children "like rabbits." A Lieutenant Hall reported that General Funston had all prisoners shot as a matter of course, and described how one was dispatched on his knees still begging for his life. This disclosure dampened the administration's plans to give Funston a hero's welcome back to the United States after capturing Aguinaldo.

Another soldier freely confessed that he had used the "water cure" on 106 Filipinos, all but 26 of whom died in the process. This was the favorite method of torture. The victim was placed on his back and forced to swallow huge amounts of water, often salted. Periodically, a soldier jumped on his distended stomach; and the process was started over again. When the victim did confess, he was usually shot and his village burned. "It is now the custom to avenge the death of an American soldier by burning to the ground all the houses and killing right and left natives who are only suspects," the *New York World* explained to its readers.

The army responded to these charges by first denying them and forcing those letter writers who were still in service to retract their statements. Private Baker, for example, publicly confessed that his statement that "we shoot people like rabbits was not so of course; and I thought they [his family] would understand it was intended as a joke." The soldier who confessed to killing scores of Filipinos with the water cure retracted his confession, claiming that it was motivated by boredom and designed to thrill a maiden aunt back in the states. "Another yarn which has failed to stand the test of time," gloated the *New York Times* in accepting the army's "proof" that such atrocities only existed in the imagination of the anti-imperialist, or, as the editor liked to call him, "the anti-everything." But not all editors were so easily convinced, and the *Springfield Republican* accused the *Times* of "suffering morally from a case of blind staggers on the Philippine question."

Not content with a simple denial, the army in the next breath usually attributed any atrocities that did occur to our Macabebe allies. The latter were scorned by most Filipinos for having served in the Spanish army before allying themselves with the Americans, just as our allies in Vietnam today once served the French. Representative John Gaines of Tennessee denounced the Macabebes on the floor of Congress as "the scum of the islands, traitors to their cause, thieves by nature and by tradition, who are hated by the Filipinos."

Lies and Euphemisms

After vigorously denying the atrocities, then attributing them to our allies, the army went on to invent euphemisms to cover these practices. The concentration camps didn't exist; but in any case they should be called "camps of instruction and sanitation" designed "to protect the natives from guerrilla bands," one official explained, apparently oblivious to the contradiction. While insisting that no "white man" ever used "the so-called water cure," General Funston went on to explain that the water cure was "by no means so severe an ordeal as would be indicated." It was merely "an unpleasant experience" for the victim. But the prize for the best euphemism produced in this war must go to President McKinley who called the process of subduing the Filipinos one of "benign assimilation."

Foreign correspondents in the Philippines began to corroborate the reports of American atrocities in spite of the crude attempts to manage the news made by General Otis and his successor, General Arthur MacArthur. A report in the *New York Journal* described how two *presidentes,* or mayors, were beaten to death by Americans with rattan rods in an unsuccessful attempt to force from them confessions of collusion with the guerrillas. Even the *New York Times* published an account of Captain Rowan's response to the assassination of a corporal in his company. Rowan not only had the assassin executed but burned his village down, and a neighboring village as well. This report was buried in the lower right-hand corner of page 6 and what the *Times* left out was that the corporal had raped the girl friend of the assassin and the second village burned was the home of the girl raped by the murdered corporal.

A front page in the *Philadelphia Ledger* carried the eye-witness account of a large-scale retaliatory killing of civilians by Americans:

> American troops have been relentless, have killed to exterminate men, women, and children, prisoners and captives, active insurgents and suspected people, from lads of 10 and up . . . have taken prisoner people who held up their hands and peacefully surrendered; and an hour later, without an atom of evidence to show that they were even insurrectos, stood them on a bridge and shot them down one by one to drop into the water below and float down as examples to those who find their bullet-riddled corpses.

Not that the correspondent was critical of such tactics. On the contrary, he attempted to justify them. "It is not civilized warfare," he conceded; "but we are not dealing with a civilized people. The only thing they know and fear is force, violence, and brutality; and we give it to them."

Savages

Essentially, this was the army's last line of defense in the face of increased reports of American atrocities. After denial was no longer feasible, the military simply insisted that the tactics of the Filipinos made unorthodox methods of warfare a necessity; and, furthermore, the classification of the insurrectos as "bandits" and "criminals" legalized such methods in the eyes of the generals. "Men who participate in hostilities without being part of a regular organized force, and without sharing continuously in its operations but who do so with intermittent returns to their homes and vocations, divest themselves of the character of soldiers and, if captured, are not entitled to the privileges of war," MacArthur proclaimed in 1900. In a lengthy order "to all station commanders," a year later, General J. F. Bell carefully spelled out MacArthur's proclamation. Prefaced with the usual disclaimer that the United States had "exercised an extraordinary forbearance and patiently adhered to a magnanimous and benevolent policy toward the inhabitants," Bell accused the Filipinos of carrying out "a reign of terror" in direct violation of "the well-known laws and usages of war," as "announced in General Orders #100, Adjutant General's Office, 1863 (signed by Lincoln)." In the manner of a lawyer's brief, Bell's orders cited all the infractions and the corresponding code they violated. The Filipinos falsely swore allegiance to the United States "solely for the purpose of improving their opportunities and facilities for deceiving American officials and treacherously aiding and assisting the insurrection in violation of Section 26." It apparently never occurred to Bell that the Filipinos would not consider their lack of "special markings" and resemblance to "the ordinary peasant" a violation of any code of warfare, and certainly not Section 63 of Lincoln's orders.

What is interesting is that the charges MacArthur and Bell made against the Filipino insurrectos are almost identical to those made against the Viet Cong today. Bell accused them of constructing what today are called "booby traps." They "improvised and secreted in the vicinity of roads and trails rudely constructed infernal machines propelling poisoned arrows or darts" when triggered by an unwary American soldier. They also camouflaged pits lined with bamboo spears. These are, of course, the age-old tactics of guerrillas. Facing a superior force but enjoying popular support, the insurrectos, like the Viet Cong today, blended into peasant surroundings and resorted to ambushes, assassinations, booby traps and sabotage.

But Bell's orders would never be committed to writing by today's publicity-conscious generals. Bell ordered his commanders to "avail themselves of retaliation," to select prisoners by lot and shoot one of them for every American soldier killed. "The innocent must suffer with the guilty for the sake of speedily ending the war," his orders concluded.

Bell was an old Indian fighter, as were many of the senior army officers in the Philippines. He had never suffered any rebuke for employing such tactics against "savages" in the old Southwest. He enjoyed comparing the Filipinos to Sioux, Comanches and Apaches. "I have been in Indian campaigns where it took 100 soldiers to capture each Indian; but the problem here is more difficult on account of the inbred treachery of the people . . . and the impossibility of recognizing the actively bad from the only passively so." In endorsing Bell's orders, General Chaffee, another veteran Indian fighter, commented that "personal contact with the people and knowledge of their methods and sentiments made it [unorthodox tactics] necessary." Chaffee also warned a correspondent: "If you should hear of a few Filipinos more or less being put out of the way, don't grow too sentimental over it."

To justify further their illegal tactics, the army released a great many horror stories of atrocities committed against American prisoners. One even accused the Filipinos of injecting American prisoners with leprosy and releasing them to spread the disease among the troops. "Only a few incidents like the beheading of a captured American soldier will justify putting into effect the administration's long contemplated plan for treating the rebels not as belligerents, but as brigands; and for punishing their acts of slaughter not as war but as murder," an editorial in the *New York Times* reasoned.

Clearly, this enemy was not human and, ultimately, the key justification for using uncivilized tactics was a racist one. General S. B. Young expressed this directly when he told a group in Pittsburgh commemorating the birth of Ulysses S. Grant: "The keynote of the insurrection among the Filipinos past, present, and future is not tyranny, for we are not tyrants. It is race. This, then, gentlemen, is the whole thing in a nutshell. If you ask me the quickest and easiest way to bring peace and good order to the Filipino, I can only say that, like the chameleon, we must put him on such a background that he can change his color!" General Young was loudly applauded by the group which included several senators, congressmen and governors, along with a bevy of retired generals. An editorial "On Filipino Character" in the *New York Times* explained that they were "veritable children" with all "the weaknesses and the vices of the resourceless and unmoral human infant." Whitelaw Reid warned that the Filipinos could never attain the intelligence, morality, self-restraint and self-governing abilities "developed in the Anglo Saxon bone and fibre through all the centuries since Runnymede." General A. G. Greenwood suggested that after the war the United States could solve its racial problems by colonizing the Philippines with American blacks to mix with the "Filipino niggers." In the ranks, the soldier summed up these attitudes by referring to the Filipinos as "goo goos," who were no more human than were Indians, Negroes or Chinese.

Officers on Trial

By the end of 1901, it was impossible for the Senate to ignore the reports of American atrocities. A committee on Philippine affairs under the chairmanship of Senator Henry Cabot Lodge, a staunch supporter of the administration's imperialist policy, undertook an investigation. In spite of Lodge's partisan position, the testimony of witnesses called before the committee proved to be much more damaging to the administration than had been anticipated. In attempting to defend American tactics in the Philippines, a former army surgeon (Henry Howland) freely admitted to having personally administered the water cure to prisoners and suspects, as well as having witnessed prisoners being shot in retaliation. But he insisted that the "treacherous nature" of Filipinos necessitated such modes of warfare. "After so many betrayals, the men decide that the only chance of pacification lies in a wholesale cataclysm—an inundation of human blood that will purge the islands of treachery," he explained.

Another witness, ex-soldier Charles Riley, repeated charges that he had made earlier in a Northampton, Massachusetts, newspaper—the first to receive sensational treatment in the nation's press. The committee was unable to shake his testimony, and the military was unable to impugn his character as they had done to other witnesses. But most disturbing to the war department was Riley's citing a staff officer (Captain Edwin Glenn) as having personally administered the water cure on several occasions. The administration's defense that these were isolated instances and not part of policy was beginning to crumble.

To demonstrate that American crimes in the Philippines did not go unpunished, Secretary of War Elihu Root released a memorandum listing 44 trials of Americans in the islands. But this document also backfired when the press examined it more closely and discovered that one officer found guilty of assaulting and murdering prisoners had been given a reprimand and fined $300. The case of Lt. Preston Brown became a cause celebre in the press. For murdering a Filipino, he had been dismissed from the service and sentenced to five years in prison; but the reviewing authority commuted the sentence to forfeiture of half of his pay for nine months and a loss of 35 places on the promotion list.

The yellow press that had once sensationalized Spanish atrocities in Cuba now began to raise a hue and cry over similar American tactics in the Philippines. "The hideous acts of barbarities were committed under our flag by men wearing the uniform of the United States and commanded by American officers," the *New York World* complained while the *Philadelphia North American* ran headlines on "American Atrocities in the Philippines." Overnight the charge of the anti-imperialists appeared to be vindicated. The *Boston Evening Transcript* described "a great transfer" in the "sentiments of both parties in Congress" and in editors generally. Even the *New York Times* began to express some doubts over the conduct of American troops in the islands, "Reports of cruelty, torture, and inhuman procedures in the Philippines have come to their [Americans'] ears. They have been shocked . . . when so much is known, the rest cannot remain concealed."

News that Marines on the island of Samar had summarily executed nine native bearers reached the ears of Secretary of War Root at this juncture; it appeared to be a perfect opportunity for the administration to demonstrate its ability to punish such malfeasance severely. The press, too, began to call for the head of the brigade commander, Major Littleton Waller. "Don't let the Butcher of Samar" escape, demanded a headline in the *North American*. In short, Waller was the scapegoat, and the public eagerly awaited his trial to assuage its feeling of guilt over the Philippine question.

Search and Destroy

Waller had landed on Samar with a brigade of marines only five months earlier. This was a few months after Company C of the U.S. Ninth Infantry had been massacred in their quarters in the town of Balangiga on that island. Waller was temporarily under the command of the army's Brigadier General Jacob Smith, an old cavalryman and veteran Indian fighter known as "Hell-Roaring Jake" because his loud voice was out of proportion to his slight stature. Smith made it clear to Waller that he wanted revenge on Samar as well as pacification. He told the Major, "I want no prisoners. I wish you to kill and burn; the more you kill and burn, the more you will please me. I want all persons killed who are capable of bearing arms." Waller was no stranger to carnage. He had participated in a brutal attack on Arab cavalry at Alexandria in 1882 and had fought the Chinese Boxers only the year before. But even he was taken aback at Smith's orders and asked what "limit of age to respect." "Ten" was Smith's reply. Later Waller told his officers that they were to fight in a "civilized manner," and not make war on women and children. But, given the nature of guerrilla warfare, the racist view of the "goo goos," and the anger over the fate of Company C, who had served with Waller's men in China, it was perhaps inevitable that conventional restraints in warfare would be lost on Samar during the last few months of 1901.

The slain commander of Company C, Captain Connell, had been something of a humanitarian by army standards. To establish good relations with the natives of Balangiga, he had forbidden the use of the term "goo goo," any dealings with the women, or the bearing of arms in the town, except when officially posted as sentries. Such measures earned him the epithet "nigger lover" from his own executive officer. Waller made it clear that he was not going to repeat Connell's fatal errors. His initial orders to his officers read, "It must be impressed upon the men that the natives are treacherous, brave, and savage. No trust, no confidence can be placed in them." His concluding statement set the tone for the kind of warfare that was to follow, "We have also to avenge our late comrades in North China—the murdered men of the Ninth U.S. Infantry."

To set up what would today be called "a free fire zone," Waller ordered all natives in the interior to move to the coast; and two days later began to burn systematically every village in the interior, destroy food and hemp ready for market, kill any work animals found and sink all native boats discovered. If American uniforms or personal artifacts were discovered in any of these villages, Waller's men assumed they had belonged to Company C and simply shot down every remaining inhabitant—man, woman and child. Evidently Waller thought such behavior within the scope of "civilized warfare."

Waller also reacted harshly to the slightest infraction of his orders to the natives. When the presidente of a nearby barrio visited the brigade's headquarters at Basey without seeking Waller's permission, he was thrown in jail and his entire barrio burned to the ground. The natives retaliated by cutting the telephone cable to army headquarters elsewhere on the island, and Waller sent out repair parties with orders to shoot any natives seen in the vicinity of the line.

Waller was hardly secretive about all this. On the contrary, he made detailed reports to General Smith of every village burned, every native and carabao killed. Smith was delighted and wired back encouragement. "The interior of Samar must be made a howling wilderness," he ordered, which was to earn for the general the new nickname of "Howling Jake" in the press once Waller's court-martial began.

After a brilliant victory over the heavily fortified headquarters of the insurrectionists on Samar, Waller insisted on leading a platoon of marines on a vain, pointless and fatally miscalculated march across the island. Facing heavy rains and swollen rivers in the jungle with an inadequate food supply, only an advance party of Waller and a handful of marines made it across. The remainder turned back when they failed to receive word from Waller, losing ten men who died from exhaustion, exposure and hunger. The native bearers grew less cooperative with this group, foraging and constructing shelters of leaves for themselves and ignoring the marines. When a lieutenant threatened them with a gun, the bearers knocked him down and wounded him with a bolo. Yet, these bearers voluntarily returned to marine headquarters with a rescue party sent out by the army, only to be immediately executed. As before, Waller dutifully reported the executions to Smith; but the political climate in Washington had changed, and such behavior was no longer countenanced. At Secretary Root's insistence, General Chaffee ordered Waller court-martialed.

Represented by the same Captain Glenn who had been cited in the Senate hearings for using the water cure on prisoners, Waller freely admitted the executions, but insisted that he was following Smith's orders. While this defense won Waller an acquittal, it left the War Department with no choice but to order that Smith be court-martialed. The court found the general guilty and ordered him admonished, although Root in his review recognized extenuating circumstances in "the condition of warfare with cruel and barbarous savages." Teddy Roosevelt, too, cited "the cruelty, treachery, and total disregard of the rules and customs of civilized warfare" on the part of Filipinos to justify Smith's behavior. Nevertheless, Roosevelt astutely ordered the general to be retired from active service immediately to avoid any more unfavorable publicity.

Glenn was next to stand trial, and he fared poorly with Waller's defense. He cited the orders of Generals Bell and Chaffee to justify his use of the water cure. One telegraphed directive from Chaffee submitted in Glenn's defense read, "The Division Commander directs that no matter what measures may have to be adopted, information as to the whereabouts of the force [*insurrectos*] must be obtained." Nevertheless, Glenn was found guilty and reprimanded.

It would almost seem that Americans had had their surfeit of horror stories about the Philippine campaign by the middle of 1902. At least they seemed eager to sweep the dirt under the rug and forget it. Hence, Glenn's trial produced few sensational headlines, nothing comparable to the "Butcher Waller Testifies to Dastardly Crimes" which appeared in the *Philadelphia North American* during the earlier trial. *The Evening Journal* in New York was roundly criticized by other newspapers for publishing a cartoon depicting American soldiers shooting women and children in the Philippines. The *New York Times* called this "a new low in yellow journalism." *Harper's* ran an article on the humanitarian aspects of the water cure and the killing of Filipino hostages; in the long run, it shortened the war and saved lives. "A choice of cruelties is the best that has been offered in the Philippines. It is not so certain that we at home can afford to shudder at the 'Water cure' unless we disown the whole job . . . the army has obeyed orders. It was sent to subdue the Filipinos. Having the devil to fight, it has sometimes used fire." The *Times* thanked *Harper's* for publishing "a particularly sane view of the situation in the Philippines."

The revelation during Glenn's trial that orders for such tactics had been endorsed all the way up the chain of command to Washington failed to provoke cries for the heads of Bell, Chaffee or their superiors. Teddy Roosevelt quietly retired the chief of staff, General Miles, but in his Memorial Day address of 1902 the president was able to say that the U.S. Army in the Philippines was "fighting for the triumph of civilization over forces which stand for the black chaos of savagery and barbarism."

Although the insurrection was officially declared over on July 4, 1902, fighting continued for another year. In 1903, the death of a Filipino priest being given the water cure by a Captain Ryan did evoke a few headlines; but the captain was acquitted by a court-martial, and the army made it clear that such tactics were necessary in order to terminate a war that was officially over. Captain Glenn was swiftly promoted to major and went on to serve many more years, attaining the rank of brigadier general. Waller served until 1920, retiring as a major general; but the notoriety of his trial clearly cost him the post of commandant of the Marine Corps.

The analogy between the two counterinsurgencies fought by Americans in the Philippines and in Vietnam six decades later is not yet complete. It will remain to be seen if Lieutenant Calley will utilize a defense similar to that of Major Waller and open up another Pandora's box for the army. Already, there are signs that higher authorities may be implicated before the trial is over. Meanwhile, Americans should realize that Vietnam is not a unique phenomenon in our history but rather the rerun of a tragic tale witnessed by our grandfathers.

SUGGESTED READINGS

Twelve Against Empire: The Anti-Imperialist 1898–1900 by Robert L. Beisner (New York: McGraw-Hill, 1968).

American Occupation of the Philippines, 1898–1912 by James Blount (New York: Putnam, 1912, reprinted by Calaya Books, Quezon City, Philippines, 1968).

American Imperialism and the Philippine War, edited by Henry Graff (Boston: Little, Brown, 1969).

The Ordeal of Samar by Joseph L. Schott (Indianapolis: Bobbs-Merrill, 1964).

Anti-Imperialism in the United States: The Great Debate 1898–1920 by E. Berkeley Tompkins (Philadelphia: University of Pennsylvania Press, 1970).

Little Brown Brother by Leon Wolff (Garden City, N.Y.: Doubleday, 1961).

Section XIII

Minorities and Masses

Currently, there is considerable debate about whether America is a "melting pot," a nation headed toward assimilation, or a "salad of nationalities," a nation made up of unmeltable ethnics. In "Black Crusaders: The Rise and Fall of Political Gangs," Helmreich discusses the natural history of a militant black organization dedicated to the goals of black self-help and militancy. Although the Crusaders did accomplish some of their goals, they ultimately failed, Helmreich suggests, for four reasons: (1) the continuing opposition of the local power structure and harassment by the police, (2) a negative media image, (3) failure to gain consensus in the black community on the goals of the organization before antagonizing the power structure, and (4) a general spirit of apathy and lack of unity within the community. The generalizability of these four elements to other militant interest groups warrants further investigation.

While Helmreich has documented a recent case history of unassimilability, Hill, in "Anti-Oriental Agitation and the Rise of Working-Class Racism," uses broad historical materials to address the larger question of assimilation. His fundamental research question is: Who can be an American? His conclusion is that the historical answer to this question revolves around the deep-seated Anglo-Saxon normative structure in the United States.

Hill's material is drawn from labor history and the Chinese experience in America after 1850. Chinese workingmen were brought to this country around 1850 to work as cheap labor in the urban factories and on the western railroads. The jobs they had were, for the most part, highly undesirable and resulted in a caste labor system. Hill argues that organized labor's response to Oriental workers was racist as soon as they were perceived as a threat to white workers. The Chinese were blamed for the depression of 1873 (although there were relatively few Chinese, especially in the East), and an anti-Chinese stance became a vehicle for political party demagoguery and craft union leaders' tirades (although the craft unions had the least to fear from unskilled laborers). Hill discusses the historical origins of the union label and the rise of a labor aristocracy in America, as well as suggesting that labor's treatment of the Chinese provides a classic example of scapegoating. He further documents how this process was extended to Japanese workers and finds the roots of anti-black labor orientations in the institutionalized racism produced.

Lyman, in "Japanese-American Generation Gap," provides us with a view of ethnicity from the inside. He suggests that the stereotype of the Japanese as mysterious and inscrutable, as well as highly achievement oriented, is part of the same character. Lyman's discussion of Japanese-Americans suggests an interesting variation on the theme of three-generational differences. His point of focus is the nisei (second-generation) and their adoption and adaptation of the *samurai* ethic of stoicism and antiindividualism to America. The contrast with isei (first-generation) and sansei (third-generation) norms emphasizes the geogenerational emphasis (of time and person) in the Japanese-American language and culture.

The American Indian represents a nation within a nation in America. After pointing out how demographic characteristics (for example, very high rates of infant mortality, high unemployment, etc.) suggest that Indians are clearly separate and unequal in America, Westermeyer, in "Indian Powerlessness in Minnesota," documents the failure of major institutions to aid Indians. His data clearly show that Indians are systematically excluded from the institutions that shape their lives. Whites tend to be in high-status positions and Indians (especially males) in menial jobs in medical and welfare agencies. Westermeyer argues that there is a danger of "pseudoequality" in ignoring the special problems of minorities like the Indian.

1 *William B. Helmreich*

Black Crusaders: The Rise and Fall of Political Gangs

The Black Crusaders, an organization of militant young ghetto dwellers, were determined to influence and improve both their own political and economic situation and that of the residents of their community. During their brief lifespan—August 1968 to January 1969—they were cool, stone-faced, menacing figures clad in black uniforms. Potential liberators of blacks in the inner city they, like the Black Panthers, were a threat and an enigma to whites. How did their organization work? What were the members like as people? What caused the rapid demise of the organization?

Central City is a midwestern metropolis with a population of over one million. Not too far from the central business district of the city 35 blocks of slum made up the ghetto from which the Crusaders emerged. Unemployment in the area was high (about 40 percent for blacks between 16 and 24), and young men lounging about on street corners, passing time in conversation, were part of the daily scene. Based on a breakdown of police district crime rates, crime in the area was almost twice the already high city average. Even the police were reluctant to enter some of the more dangerous parts of the neighborhood. Relations between the police and the local residents were generally characterized by fear, mistrust and hostility.

The Beginning

In early August of 1968 the Crusaders opened an office on a busy street in the heart of the ghetto. Headquarters consisted of one large room furnished with a desk, two telephones and some folding chairs. The walls were adorned with posters and leaflets relating to different aspects of the Crusaders' programs. Around the corner from the office was a gas station, and behind it was a windowless wall that formed part of a three-story brick building. Painted on the wall were pictures of various leaders and heroes of the black nationalist movement.

Crusader leaders began an intensive campaign to recruit youths who lived in the immediate area. As part of these efforts, leaflets urging people to join the organization were distributed throughout the area. Five thousand copies of ***The Black Crusader*** were printed and given to local residents. Posters, buttons and various other items were also sold in order to raise money for the group. Stokely Carmichael came to Central City and spoke under the sponsorship of the Black Crusaders.

Members

The average Crusader was about 17 years old and came from a lower-class background. He was likely to be a member of a large family. His father was probably away from home often (because he had two jobs, because he had deserted his family or for other reasons familiar in the ghetto). Many of the Crusaders were still in school and, for most, membership in the organization represented their first involvement in an activist cause on behalf of black people.

According to both the police and the leaders of the organization, most of the Crusaders had criminal records of one sort or another. Although it was not possible to obtain the Crusaders' police files, evidence from other sources indicates that very few had ever been convicted of anything more serious than a misdemeanor.

Leaders

The leaders of the Crusaders differed from the members in several respects. To begin with, they were older, ranging in age from 18 to 28. Almost all had some previous experience working in civil rights movements. They also appeared to be more articulate than most of the members, a fact which probably influenced their designation as leaders of the group.

James Reese was prime minister of the Black Crusaders. Twenty-three years old, with a college degree, he regarded his formal education as a distinct advantage in being accepted by the Central City community. After being a Student Nonviolent Coordinating Committee (SNCC) organizer in the early sixties, Reese came to Central City where he received public attention for leading demonstrations against several radio stations.

By virtue of his abilities, his charismatic qualities and his position in the organization, Reese exerted a considerable amount of influence on the Crusaders. Although most of the internal decision-making power was vested in a central committee of seven Crusader leaders, Reese was usually responsible for announcing these decisions to the community at large.

George Watts, 28 years old, a general in the Black Crusaders, had come to Central City 12 years earlier from a small town in the Deep South where he and his eight brothers and sisters had picked cotton for $1.50 a day.

Until he joined the Crusaders Watts' life had been marked by limited opportunities in education and employment. The disappointments and frustrations he encountered in Central City may have been even harder to bear in light of his expectations. The Crusader organization appealed to him because one of its goals was the improvement of the economic, political and social conditions of black people in Central City.

Although *Fred Miles* grew up in Central City, his life history was similar to that of George Watts, especially in terms of his schooling, family life and employment patterns. Miles, a 26 year old with a reputation in Central City as a black activist, frequently represented the Crusaders at various rallies and meetings. An intelligent, articulate man, Miles seemed frustrated by his lack of opportunity to channel his capabilities in a constructive direction. After leaving school at 18, he worked at menial jobs for several years. Some time during this period he became friendly with local black leaders and community organizers who appear to have played a significant role in shaping some of his attitudes toward society. Perhaps the greatest source of Miles's anger and resentment was the police, whom he seemed to regard as the major immediate enemy of black ghetto residents.

> Many times I was stopped on the street by racist police who would get out of their car and tell me to lean against the car with my hands flat and spread my legs as they pulled everything from my pockets. I turned around and attempted to ask what I had done and got a good strike against my face. This happened a number of times. Many times I would be taken down to the station and. . .they would refuse to bring me back. I would maybe have to walk a mile.

Nina Parker, 23 years old, was president of the Sister Organization of the Crusaders. Bright and highly verbal, she had completed a year of college and had previously been involved in a black culture group made up of black women. Although she was not a separatist, Parker believed that blacks had to develop without the help of whites in order to "get themselves together." Her experiences prior to joining the Crusaders do not reflect the same degree of hardship and deprivation of the other leaders, yet she was well aware of the conditions which existed in the ghettoes.

Few of the Crusaders (three at the most) came from a middle-class background, even though Central City had a large black middle-class community. There was a good deal of antagonism between those who were poor and lived in the ghetto and those who had "made it." In the sense that the backgrounds of both the leaders and the members were lower-class, it would be accurate to define the Crusaders as a grass-roots organization.

First Projects

One of the Crusaders' first projects was helping the Brothers of Unity (a culturally oriented black militant organization) paint the Wall of Respect. The wall was located near the Crusaders' headquarters and consisted of a collection of paintings of national black leaders like Martin Luther King, Jr., Malcolm X and Elijah Muhammed. Shortly after the project was begun, the police arrested several Crusaders at the wall and charged them with disturbing the peace and disorderly conduct. In discussing this incident, George Watts asserted,

> The biggest problem in forming the Crusaders was police harassment. We was . . . the brothers at that time, the artists, was modeling the Wall. We would meet up there every evening and there was about 50 of us on the lot. It was a public gas station. All of a sudden we looked up and here come all these policemen about 25 or 30 squad cars . . . and we was thrown in jail. The next morning we were sentenced for 30 days although we only stayed for a day and a half. While we were in there we talked to a lot of the brothers in the jail and we began to put the pieces together. We began to see that we were going to have to do something to move against the injustices.

Another problem that faced the Crusaders at the onset was finances. The monied segments of the black community in Central City were generally apathetic and in some instances even hostile and resentful of the Black Crusaders and their efforts. Some leaders saw the Crusaders as a threat to the power and influence of their own organizations and looked on them as outsiders trying to get a "piece of the action." Others felt that the activities of the group were counterproductive and not in the interest of the black community as a whole. Despite such attitudes, the Crusaders were able, within a three-week period, to pay the rent for their office, get the lights turned on and have a telephone put in.

Organizational Structure

The Black Crusaders organization was paramilitary. The standard uniform consisted of a black beret, black jacket, black shirt and pants, and black combat boots. (Members were not required to wear the uniform, but most chose to.) The leaders were almost always referred to by the membership as general, captain, sergeant, etc. Participation in drills, marches and military training was required. Whenever leaders spoke publicly members were assigned to stand guard. They were required to stand at attention and to maintain absolute silence.

The leadership revealed three basic reasons for the military structure. Self-defense was the obvious primary reason, and developing discipline among the members was almost as important. According to George Watts, "The only way we felt we could get discipline within ourselves was to go through military training, and every group that's ever been formed to move against injustice had to go through the same thing." A third reason for the organization's military orientation was to promote a feeling of solidarity among the Crusaders. According to Nina Parker, "Wearing the uniform, marching and drilling gave people a feeling of belonging to something."

At the top of the Crusaders' formal hierarchy was the prime minister; immediately under him were three generals, followed by one major, two captains, two lieutenants, three sergeants and one corporal, who were all elected by the rank-and-file membership. Several national leaders were eventually named to posts, largely as a result of nominal coalitions formed by the Crusaders with other groups.

The membership of the Crusaders was divided into four groups. The Black Crusaders, males over 16 years of age, comprised the regular membership; the Junior Crusaders were males 16 and under; the Sister Organization was made up of females over 16; and the Junior Sisters were females 16 and under.

Questions of policy and matters of major importance to the entire organization were generally decided by the central committee, which consisted of the seven top officers in the organization. Meetings of the central committee, which took place at least twice a week, were closed to other members and outsiders.

The Sister Organization of the Black Crusaders was primarily a community service group and was separate from the main organization. Although it maintained liaison with the male leaders of the Crusaders and was under their control in terms of decision-making, meetings were held separately—usually in private homes, rather than at the office (where the general meetings were held). The Sister Organization's officers were a president, a vice-president, a secretary and a treasurer.

The Junior Crusaders and the Junior Sisters sometimes met separately from the older members but were also present at the general meetings of the organization. They helped out wherever and whenever possible.

Fund Raising

The Crusaders had seven ways of raising money.

□ Members of the Central Committee requested payment for their frequent speaking engagements. If funds were unavailable, they would ask for contributions and pass the hat at the conclusion of the presentation. In addition, buttons and posters featuring pictures of the leaders were also sold for prices ranging from a quarter to a dollar. The Crusaders made at least 30 such appearances during the time I was actively involved with the organization.

□ The Crusaders held five or six parties which were open to the public. Admission was charged. Refreshments, prepared by the Sister Organization, were sold for a nominal fee. In addition to providing relaxation and entertainment, these functions also emphasized black culture and developed black pride and awareness through presentations of African music and dances, black poetry and so on.

□ On several occasions, the Crusaders invited national figures, such as Stokely Carmichael and Adam Clayton Powell, to Central City to speak. Sometimes tickets were sold; at other times individuals were asked to donate whatever they could when they arrived to hear the speaker.

□ Although the leaders of the Crusaders told me that sympathetic groups in the community had donated unspecified sums, only one group, a liberal labor union local, was officially on record as having done so.

□ The only national organization reported to have given financial support to the Crusaders was SNCC, with whom the Crusaders eventually formed a nominal coalition. However, this source of aid was never confirmed. In view of SNCC's own financial status at the time, it seems unlikely that they could have made a very substantial contribution.

□ The Crusaders' office was located in the center of the business district that served the black community. From time to time the Crusaders approached the merchants, mainly whites, for donations—for bail to "spring" a member from jail, for funds for a benefit performance or other causes. When the Crusaders first formed, representatives went to a meeting of the Merchants' Association and offered to protect the merchants' stores at night from burglars. (The offer was turned down by the merchants, who asserted that they were already "protected.") In addition, merchants were asked to place advertisements in the Crusaders' newspaper. With one or two exceptions, merchants turned down these requests.

□ Each Crusader was required to pay weekly membership dues of $2.00. I could not determine if these dues were collected on a regular basis.

It is not possible to state accurately how much money the Crusaders received from each of the sources cited, largely because they did not seem to keep financial records. Financial problems were, however, a major cause for the eventual breakup of the organization.

Rules and Regulations

Being black was the only formal membership requirement. The regulations of the organization fell into two broad categories. First were rulings which applied to personal conduct, concerning, for example, drinking, stealing and using drugs. The second category of rules and regulations pertained largely to the paramilitary nature of the Crusader organization. All male Crusaders (including the Junior Crusaders) had to attend self-defense classes and participate in drills and marches, which were held several times a week.

Members were also required to attend the general meetings of the organization, which were held at least twice a week, usually on Tuesday and Friday. Meetings gave the members an opportunity to increase their knowledge of black history and culture; to review local developments of importance to the organization and, if necessary, to make decisions concerning them; to deal with internal problems such as discipline and sharing responsibilities. Fred Miles's comments concerning the third aspect give an idea of how formal sanctions were applied to those who broke the rules of the organization:

> Any member violating any rules was dealt with accordingly. Many times he would be suspended; many times special privileges would be taken away from him such as socializing and reading black history with the group. If he had done something very serious his name would be stricken from the organization completely.

The organization probably had about 200 active members at its peak.

Crusader Politics

The Crusaders viewed the economic and political structure as diametrically opposed to the interests of the black masses. The leaders saw themselves not only as part of an oppressed race but also as members of an oppressed class that was economically exploited by a ruling elite. They also felt that poor whites were manipulated by the power structure.

There was a difference of opinion about the usefulness of violence as an approach to solving black problems. Ray Davis's assertion that the Crusaders would do "anything that's necessary" to attain their objectives, coupled with his acknowledgement that the "system" had succeeded elsewhere in quelling opposition to its policies, illustrates the difficulties the Crusaders faced in translating their rhetoric into reality.

An Economic Base for Blacks

The dominant theme of the Crusaders' ideological critique of capitalism was that a small group of people in this country controls much of the wealth and uses it to advance their own interests. One of the Crusaders' primary objectives was to establish an economic base for black people.

This objective was both a belief *and* a goal. The Crusaders were expressing a general view that land equaled power. In a more limited sense, they were referring to the importance of owning property in the ghetto so that black people could control their destiny and their lives.

A Black Guard

The Crusaders' attitude toward the police was that of many black ghetto residents—fear and hostility. The Crusaders saw themselves as protectors of ghetto residents from the police. One of their stated objectives was to establish a black guard which would protect the black community from racist cops. The Crusaders often spoke bitterly of the lack of respect shown black people by the local police. Regardless of how well Crusaders may have known that the police were often simply carrying out orders from higher authorities, it was, nevertheless, the police who questioned, arrested and, at times, even insulted and brutalized them. The police often represented an immediate threat to ghetto residents' physical safety. The Crusaders' sometimes violent response to the police must be considered within its emotional and situational context rather than simply as ideological inconsistency.

Many of the Crusaders, particularly the younger members, found it difficult to see themselves as combating an insidious yet unseen enemy such as "the system" or "the power structure." By focusing on the police, the Crusaders made the "enemy" not only easily identifiable but also relevant to many of the members' personal experiences.

Despite the members' feelings concerning the need for black pride and unity, and even though some of their programs dealt with different aspects of black culture, the Crusaders were by no means a culturally oriented organization. Don Neal, a captain in the Crusader organization, once said, "Whoever heard of starting a revolution with writing poetry? You can write poetry *after* the revolution's over but you can't make one *with it*."

Attitudes Toward Whites

Crusaders expressed ambivalent attitudes toward whites. Although they were pessimistic about ending racism, they regarded certain segments of white society, particularly college students, favorably. Discussing the 1968 Democratic convention in Chicago, Reese said:

> The blacks who were sitting in their living rooms looking at the TV set realized for the first time that there are many young whites who are radical enough to be involved in that type of brutality. Therefore, they recognized that many of them were sincere and this brought a closer relationship.

Not all the members shared this positive attitude toward students or young whites in general. One youth about 18 years old asked me, "Don't many of the students at the university criticize you for associating so much with the Black Crusaders?" "No," I replied, "quite a few of them are with you all the way." He appeared very surprised by my response but said nothing. Some of the members seemed to regard their occasional trips to universities as forays into enemy territory. This attitude is not surprising in light of the limited contact that many of the younger members had had with sympathetic whites. Their attitudes probably were shaped by their encounters with the whites who worked in the ghetto as merchants, policemen and landlords.

Another Crusader goal was to convince black people to look on whites as individuals, not simply as members of a race that oppressed blacks. Although it would have been much simpler for the Crusader leaders to look on all whites as enemies, their professed ideology prevented them from doing so. Their political stance forced them to define all those who were not within the power structure, the "system," as members of an oppressed class; this category, of course, included many whites. Yet the "system" they attacked was composed almost exclusively of whites.

Making this distinction clear to the members, since many lacked the political sophistication of the leaders, was therefore very difficult. Moreover, the leaders' actions in confrontations with the police often contradicted their own analysis of the "system." How could they ideologically justify to the members their opposition to the police, when they had already identified the police as part of an oppressed class? Given the oppressive nature of some of the things the police did, how could they justify not taking a stand against them?

Elections were held about three months after the Crusaders formed. By that time, members had already been involved in a series of confrontations with local law enforcement authorities which were threatening to destroy the organization. Out of necessity the Crusaders became interested in working for candidates who approved of their organization. The group became involved, to varying degrees, in a total of seven different campaigns—for governor, state attorney general, mayor, U.S. representative, state representative and state senator. The local political power structure regarded this activity as threatening, yet the Crusaders were, with one exception, ineffective in determining the results of the elections in which they took active part. There are several reasons for this lack of influence. The Crusaders' brief span of existence meant that they had insufficient time to develop a powerful political base. Even the black residents of Central City were unimpressed with the group, partly because the media had generally portrayed them in a negative light. Their support may not have been considered an asset by the various candidates, especially those who were running for election in districts where whites formed a large part of the constituency. Another factor was the large amount of time the Crusaders had to spend on police-related matters, time which had to be spent away from political activities. A final reason for the Crusaders' inability to influence elections was the fact that the entrenched political structure adopted an antagonistic position toward them.

From the time the Black Crusaders first opened their office they were under constant police surveillance. Adam Clayton Powell came to speak in Central City on August 17, 1968, at the invitation of a group of black businessmen. During his stay in Central City, Powell took a walk through the ghetto area—accompanied by six Crusaders armed with rifles and shotguns (these were legal if not concealed, according to state law). Powell's aides, concerned over the tenseness of the situation, cut short the tour and whisked him away from the scene. Shortly after Powell left, the police, who were present in force, arrested two Crusaders as they were transferring their weapons from one car to another, charging both with carrying a concealed weapon and one with possession of a sawed-off shotgun.

The Crusaders' actions were not merely an attempt to incite the police by openly displaying weapons. There is little doubt that the Crusaders were well aware that they would be observed and remembered by the police. The Crusaders were really attempting to assert their identity and demonstrate their courage to the enemy.

In order to raise bail money for the two Crusaders arrested in the Powell incident, the organization sponsored an appearance by Stokely Carmichael. Carmichael arrived in Central City on August 29, and spoke to an audience of about 1,000. The rally was guarded by the Crusaders who frisked everyone entering the hall and stood guard through Carmichael's speech. After the rally, police arrested four Crusaders and charged them with carrying concealed weapons—two pistols found in the car the members were riding in. According to eyewitnesses, the arrest incident involved at least six marked patrol cars, four unmarked cars, three canine vehicles and a command car.

Following the arrests at the Carmichael rally, the Crusaders announced that another rally, featuring SNCC chairman Phil Hutchins, would be held on September 7, to raise money to get the members out of jail.

Early in the evening of September 4 police stopped the Crusaders' car for having no light illuminating its license plate. Five Crusaders, including Reese and Watts, were arrested and four were charged with peace disturbance after police claimed that the Crusaders had tried to incite a crowd of about 150 persons who had gathered at the scene. A television reported at the scene later stated to me that the Crusaders had not tried to "stir up" the crowd, which, according to him, numbered only ten persons. A police report also claimed that diagrams pertaining to the construction of explosive devices had been found in Reese's right boot.

Shortly after Watts and the others were taken to the police station, a crowd gathered outside and demanded their release. Later that evening shots were fired through the window of the police station and through the window of a police lieutenant's home, and a firebomb (which failed to explode) was tossed into the office of Ray Wilson, a black member of the civilian Police Board of Central City. (Wilson had told the Crusaders earlier that the best thing they could do for Central City would be to disband.) Police theorized that the Crusaders were responsible for these acts, although the accusation was never substantiated. Ray Wilson later told me: "I think that saying the Crusaders bombed my office makes good copy. There's no evidence."

In the early hours of the morning, the Crusaders' office was broken into and virtually destroyed. In addition, the organization's car was set afire and demolished. Witnesses at the scene, including a fireman who had been called to put out the fire, later swore in court that they had seen about seven or eight people, at least one of whom they recognized as a plainclothes police officer, breaking into the office and destroying the furniture inside. The police claimed that when they entered, the Crusaders' office had already been wrecked. Even though the Crusaders' headquarters was totally destroyed, the police were able to display, in undamaged condition, a flag, a crossbow, bullets, papers and other materials they had seized from the office.

On September 7, Phil Hutchins, the new national chairman of SNCC, spoke at a rally in a rented auditorium sponsored by the Black Crusaders. As Hutchins, Reese and Johnny Wilson (a leader of the antiwar movement within SNCC) drove away from the rally, they were arrested by the police and charged with unlawful assembly. The following morning a city court judge found them all guilty and fined Hutchins and Wilson $500, the maximum penalty.

By this time, liberal segments of the community had begun to react. In an editorial, the *Central City Times* accused the police of deliberate harassment of black militants, condemning their actions as a violation of the First Amendment. The American Civil Liberties Union filed suit, asking that the court enjoin the police from unlawfully arresting black militants in Central City. Local student, church and civic groups began to hold meetings to protest the Crusaders' treatment at the hands of the police.

On September 12, black ministers, the head of the Community Welfare Council and the mayor met privately to discuss the Crusaders. Less than 24 hours later, Reese and Fred Miles were stopped by the police for faulty brake lights. They were arrested and taken to the district police station where they were severely beaten by police officers. Police said that they had reacted in self-defense after Reese and Miles attacked them while in the station. However, the city hospital lends considerable support to Reese's claim that he and Miles were beaten while attempting to protect themselves. The doctor issued the following statement to the press on the incident:

> Reese had received numerous stitches in his scalp and had lost a considerable amount of blood. If he had hurt his hands when hitting someone the metacarpal bones would have been folded up. These bones were cracked across as if, as the patient said, he was struck by nightsticks while trying to protect his head.

Five days later the police board met to discuss the incident. Based on a reading of the police report, it suspended one policeman for 30 days, another for ten days, and issued letters of reprimand to four other officers. The board, which had previously regarded the Crusaders unfavorably, stated in its decision that it felt that excessive force had been used. By this time the entire community was in an uproar. A petition signed by 700 police officers demanded that the members of the police board resign, and leaders of several unions announced their support of the police. The governor of the state, who had appointed the members of the board, called a press conference in which he denounced the board's decision to suspend the officers and said he would order a public investigation of the matter (which was never implemented). On the other side of the issue, the liberal *Central City Times* accused the governor of being a meddler. Various civic groups held protest rallies in which they called for an end to police harassment and brutality.

On September 15, more than 2,000 persons attended a rally in Central City, sponsored by a wide range of community, labor and civic organizations. Never before and never afterward did the Crusaders attract such a large crowd or enjoy such widespread support within the community. Police harassment had become a rallying point for liberals and ghetto residents.

October was relatively quiet for the Crusaders. There were no real confrontations between the police and the members of the organization, who were still under almost constant surveillance. It appeared that the events of the past month had brought about an uneasy truce between the two groups.

The Crusaders busied themselves throughout this period with various activities, including contacting other organizations and groups in Central City and elsewhere in an attempt to raise bail money. In addition they made plans to invite speakers for local benefits. Finally, they began preparing for the November elections.

The decrease in police harassment may well have been caused by adverse public action. It is also possible that the police felt that the Crusaders would die out more quickly if there were no publicity concerning their actions, particularly since the organization's financial problems were mounting steadily.

On December 4, 1968, according to a police report, about 40 or 50 Crusaders marched through the district police station, dressed in full uniform, to protest police harassment of the organization. The police did nothing and arrested no one. Ray Davis said that the purpose of the march was "to show them that we are not afriad, that we are ready to get what's due. And besides about an hour before that, one of the leading sisters in the organization had been arrested for some charge: peace disturbance,"

After this incident, the Crusaders became inactive, and often when I visited the office no one was there.

On January 29, 1969, Reese was charged with possession of marijuana. Although Reese claimed that the marijuana had been planted in his car by the police in an attempt to frame him, the prime minister announced his resignation from the Crusaders two days later. Although Ray Davis and Fred Miles were named as the new leaders, the organization, for all practical purposes, ceased to exist.

Accomplishments

The Crusaders felt that their anti-drug program was one of their most significant accomplishments. Leaders occasionally would lecture members on the hazards of drug abuse. The Crusaders were quite active in draft counseling. In addition to forming loose coalitions with various antiwar groups in the city, the Crusaders gave out leaflets in the ghetto urging blacks not to join the army. Generally speaking, the reasons they gave for opposing the draft centered on propositions that the war was unjust and that there were more important problems to be solved in the black community.

Another Crusader activity was raising the general level of consciousness of the older residents in the ghetto, talking to domestics, the elderly and hospital patients. The Sister Organization was active in community service programs, such as collecting old clothing donated by people in the neighborhood and giving it to the poor, and visiting patients in the hospital. The news media in Central City rarely if ever mentioned these activities in its coverage of the Crusaders. The Crusaders seemed to be accorded more space whenever they had confrontations with the police and less when they announced benefits or rallies, community programs and so on.

Bringing speakers to the city was a significant accomplishment of the organization. Speakers fulfilled several functions; most important, perhaps, was demonstrating to young blacks that many of the problems that faced black ghetto residents in Central City (police brutality, the need for unity, lack of control over their own institutions) were shared by millions of black people throughout the country.

Despite serious attempts to accomplish their goals, the Crusaders organization broke up after only five months of existence. Primary causes for this failure were: (1) the continuing opposition of the city's power structure to the organization, particularly as manifested by the actions of the police; (2) the role of the media in projecting a negative image of the organization; (3) the Crusaders' failure to teach the black community about the organization's goals and objective ***before*** making public their active opposition to the city power structure; (4) general apathy and a lack of unity even among sympathetic elements in the community.

The Crusaders' accomplishments were not too significant in relation to the effort and problems involved in the attempt. Yet the experience of the Crusaders may be valuable for similar groups with similar goals. The history of the Crusaders is a model of the problems and pressures encountered by black self-help groups in many American cities.

SUGGESTED READINGS

The Black Panthers Speak, edited by P. Foner (Philadelphia: Lippincott, 1971).

The Blackstone Rangers by R. T. Sale (New York: Random House, 1971).

Seize the Time: The Story of the Black Panther Party and Huey Newton by B. Seale (New York: Random House, 1970).

Jazz in New Orleans

by Jack V. Buerkle

This essay was excerpted from *Bourbon Street Black* (Oxford University Press) by Jack V. Buerkle and Danny Barker.

Though some say jazz now exhibits a kind of hardness in its people, there is a place where it shouts a warm and vibrant simplicity: New Orleans, where it all began. Driven by the spirits of Bienville and Vaudreuil, by the memory of Congo Square, the burial societies and the voodoo drums, here a 100-year-old subcommunity of black musicians and their families lives on. Just a fleeting 75 years ago Charles "Buddy" Bolden's cornet blasted out of the bottom lands proclaiming a new element in the world's music. This rough, daytime barber-nighttime musician was probably unaware of his role as harbinger of America's unique contribution to the arts — a new music form — *jazz*. To understand why Buddy had not intellectualized what he came to do with his horn is simple. The salmagundi of humanity that peopled New Orleans since 1718 had set the tempo for a kind of perpetual hedonic binge, with style, a style that resulted in the gradual merging, in their music, of elements from Africa, Europe and the Caribbean. As the twentieth century emerged, the music surfaced as a distinct improvisational form owing debts to the blues, gospel songs, ragtime, minstrelsy and European instrumental techniques.

Booze, the "chicks" and mental illness soon dampened the hot fire of Buddy Bolden. Others, though, had quickly adopted this new music born in the hip-swinging brass street bands and later nurtured in the whorehouses and clubs in Storyville. Men like Joe "King" Oliver, Freddie Keppard, Sidney Bechet, Jelly Roll Morton, Kid Ory and Louis Armstrong would spread its distinctiveness throughout much of the Western world. Now they are all dead, but Bourbon Street Black continues.

Come to New Orleans virtually any day and you will see the progeny of the creators of jazz continuing to add that distinctive flair to the emotional tone of the city. Music is still a very serious business to the people of Bourbon Street Black. With only a passing glance you can see the studied pride each takes in entertaining those who have come to listen. Unlike jazz players with a more contemporary approach, they draw much of their own satisfaction with their craft in pleasing others.

The
FAIRVIEW
BAPTIS

2 *Herbert Hill*

Anti-Oriental Agitation and the Rise of Working-Class Racism

From the beginning of the new nation on the North American continent until our own time, each generation has been confronted by the question of who can be an American. The assumption that white Anglo-Saxons are the real "Americans" has permeated virtually the entire society. Conformity to Anglo-Saxon physical appearance, religion, language, traditions and culture was long assumed to be the decisive factor in determining who could and who could not be considered an American.

From the colonial period through the early history of the United States, the white settlers developed policies that resulted in genocide, sequestration and slavery for the non-white populations. The Indians who survived the white man's slaughter were confined to limited territories or reservations. Most blacks were held in a condition of slavery that legally declared them to be subhuman property; and blacks who were not slaves were denied basic rights and could not achieve equal citizenship with the white population. But whatever difficulties successive waves of non-Anglo-Saxon white immigrants might face, they could eventually become naturalized and gain the rights of citizenship.

The Chinese immigration beginning in 1848 and the subsequent conflict between the forces of inclusion and exclusion are a prime example of the effect of racism on the "Americanization" process. For the first time a non-white population had arrived in this country for whose fate there was no precedent within the policies of the established system. The Chinese were not pressed into slavery nor sequestered on reservations. Because of new manpower needs that required a free but controlled and mobile work force, a different model for dealing with non-white labor had to be constructed—a model that encompassed a racial labor caste system together with rigid segregation for a non-slave but racially dintinct people. The Chinese were from the moment of their arrival a conflict population: though not slaves they were limited to certain categories of employment, denied basic rights, not considered as potential Americans and not allowed to become citizens. The Chinese were to be available for a very high degree of exploitation but were to be kept separate and apart from the rest of society. In part, this model of labor exploitation was derived from the earlier experience with a racially distinct slave labor force; in turn it provided a model that significantly influenced the treatment of blacks who were to be emancipated more than a decade later.

When the Chinese began to arrive in large numbers after 1850, the labor needs of the burgeoning urban factories and the vast railroad construction projects in the western part of the country could no longer be met by the existing white labor force. A slave system—which required a large capital outlay, ownership and resale and continuity of work over a long period—was not suited to these new conditions. The Chinese, easily exploitable as cheap labor by virtue of their endurance, skills and availability, were an excellent solution. They had an additional advantage for their white employers: since, unlike slaves, they were not property and since, unlike the white work force, they could not become citizens, no one had to take responsibility for them when their usefulness came to an end.

Still, the solution was only partial. The white workingman—faced with a racially separate work force that could be manipulated to the white worker's competitive disadvantage—had to come to terms with the cross-currents of both class and racial conflict on a vast scale. The choice made by labor organizations—their vigorous participation and leadership in the anti-Oriental agitation and their use of racial distinction to keep categories of workers outside their organizations—was an important factor in setting a pattern for the establishment of a racial labor caste system which was to develop into a major characteristic of the American labor movement. The relationship of racism to labor unionism, expressed in exclusionary and other discriminatory practices against Orientals and blacks, must be understood as part of a continuing historical process, rather than as one of direct causal effect.

For white labor these issues were not theoretical abstractions. They involved fundamental matters of work and social status. As successive generations of white immigrants effectively used labor unions to acculterate and become Americans, they acted through the same labor organizations to exclude non-whites from certain occupations and from society. Thus, organized labor has played an important role in the inclusion-exclusion process of Americanization.

Organized labor's role in the anti-Oriental agitation illustrates the process by which racism was institutionalized. From 1850 to 1875 the main thrust of the anti-Oriental movement was confined to California, Oregon and the state of Washington where the Chinese were sought out by entrepreneurs who saw great advantages in their industriousness and their capacity to work together in teams. They were simultaneously regarded as a threat by white workers who found it more and more difficult to compete against them. The Chinese settled overwhelmingly in the mining districts; they nearly always worked the abandoned or least desirable mines, making these mining operations profitable. As early as 1852 white miners in several areas forced Chinese workers out of mining operations and called for the prohibition of Chinese immigration. That year white miners in Marysville, California adopted a resolution denying mining claims to Chinese. Other communities passed laws excluding Chinese from mining and forced Chinese workers to leave mining camps. Not infrequently the expulsion of Chinese miners was accompanied by violence, as at Coal Creek Mine in King County, Washington, where the living quarters of Chinese were burned to the ground.

The Chinese, under pressure from white miners and special tax assessments against them levied by the state, began to leave the mining districts. Most of those forced to leave went to the cities, mainly San Francisco, Sacramento and Los Angeles. They later went to Wyoming, Oregon, Idaho and other states where the problem took on new and more ominous dimensions.

Chinese labor was also later used extensively in railroad construction. Historian Walton Bean writes:

> The first experiment, with a crew of 50 Chinese in 1865, was so phenomenally successful that agents were soon recruiting them by the thousands, first in California and then in South China. At the peak of construction work, the Central Pacific would employ more than 10,000 Chinese laborers.... Labor unions in San Francisco protested, but as the railroad advanced into the mountains and construction continued throughout the year, white workers lost all interest in jobs that required the performance of hard and dangerous labor under the conditions of winter in the Sierras.

Meanwhile, the state of California continued to punish the Chinese, preventing them from becoming citizens (even as they were accused of disdaining the privilege), excluding their children from public schools and attempting repeatedly to restrict their immigration (though white foreigners were encouraged to enter). Various anti-Chinese legislative measures, including special taxation, were eventually ruled illegal by the California courts. So long as the issue was confined to California, the racist attacks against the Chinese could simply be regarded as a response to regional conditions. But once the Chinese issue transcended the borders of California, its regional peculiarity could no longer be argued.

The enlargement of the obsession with the problem of Chinese labor corresponded roughly with the integration of the western mining economy into the national economic structure. Prior to the completion of the transcontinental railroad, influential eastern leaders, particularly politicians, businessmen and newspaper editors, had looked rather indulgently on the use of Chinese laborers in western mining and manufacturing. But during 1869 and 1870 this attitude shifted dramatically. The "problem" was spreading across the nation to the consciousness of the East. Henry George sounded the alarm against multitudes of cheap "coolie" labor in the New York *Tribune* on May 1, 1869. Southern planters at a meeting in Nashville in 1869 called for coolie labor to replace recently emancipated blacks (the call went unheeded), and 75 Chinese boot and shoe workers were introduced into the shoe factory of Calvin Sampson in North Adams, Massachusetts for the purpose of breaking a labor strike in 1870.

Because it involved the actual introduction of Chinese workers into eastern industry, the North Adams incident especially seemed to labor unions to be the opening trickle in a tidal wave of coolie labor that would overwhelm the East. Labor unions were then able to argue that the Chinese threatened the entire union movement and that only a national policy of exclusion could save the nation from destruction and contamination. At the moment when the Chinese were brought into North Adams the American economy was on the threshold of a protracted decline. With the depression of 1873, widespread unemployment provided a docile and readily available surplus work force. In essence, the depression destroyed organized labor's hope that without Chinese workers the labor supply would be small enough to allow trade unions to maintain control over wage scales in certain occupations. Both labor leaders and rank-and-file workers assumed a priori that the Chinese posed a definite economic threat to their interests, and that this cheap coolie labor was largely responsible for the depressed conditions of the American economy after 1873.

This "fact" soon became an unquestioned belief of the labor movement during the last part of the nineteenth century. For example, the Colorado Bureau of Labor Statistics' first report in 1887 solicited the general opinions and attitudes of Colorado workers in an effort to present rank-and-file views of "what labor wants." A white miner in Lake County, Colorado responded to the Bureau of Labor Statistics' questionnaire: "Laws should be passed compelling equal pay to each sex for equal work; making all manual labor no more than eight hours a day so workers can share in the gains and honors of advancing civilization; prohibiting any more Chinese coming to this country on account of physiological, labor, sanitary and other considerations, as the country would be happier without Chinamen and trusts." Note the automatic equation of Chinese labor and trusts, as if these were the twin (and equally dangerous) menaces that American labor had to combat. What makes this equation especially significant is the fact that there was not a single Chinese person living in Lake County, Colorado, either five years before or five years after the miner made that statement.

It should also be noted that since the Chinese numbered only 368 outside the West in 1870, even the most insistent labor politician could not factually argue that the depressed conditions of white workers were the result of competition from Chinese labor in that early period. Another problem with the apologies for labor's racism on economic grounds is that such a view ignores the ideological content of the anti-Chinese efforts within the labor movement. Selig Perlman, one of the writers at the forefront of that view, blatantly reveals the confusion of class interests with racial consciousness. Summing up what was obviously labor's own conception of its role in securing adoption of the Chinese Exclusion Act of 1882, Perlman writes that "the anti-Chinese agitation in California, culminating as it did in the Exclusion Law passed in 1882, was doubtless the most important single factor in the history of American labor, for without it the entire country might have been overrun by Mongolian labor, and the labor movement might have become a conflict of races instead of classes." These words, let it be emphasized, are quoted not because they are true but because they reflect the view held by organized labor and many of its academic apologists, even at the present time.

Three major factors after 1873 kept the Chinese question alive as a national issue: local western demagoguery, the fact that organized labor took up the anti-Chinese litany after 1870, and, in the wake of this, the recognition by both major national political parties that an anti-Chinese stand could win votes. The Democratic party, attempting to revive itself after the Civil War, used an anti-Chinese position to appeal to working men. The Democrats demonstrated an amazing resurgence in California and elsewhere on a labor platform that featured, above all else, attacks on Chinese labor and immigration. Soon the Republican party perceived the possibilities of the anti-Oriental agitation for its own purposes. The compromise of 1876 in effect dismissed the Negro as a factor in national politics and forced the Republicans to look elsewhere for political support. By then, the Republicans had come to understand that working men were important in building a successful national coalition and that the anti-Chinese position was winning politics.

Prior to 1876 and after 1882, the leadership of the anti-Chinese movement was held by the leaders of the craft unions—precisely those unions that had the least to fear in terms of economic competition with the Chinese. For the leaders of these unions the anti-Chinese movement became a means by which they could manipulate the political and organizational energy of the entire labor force, skilled and unskilled, thereby using the Chinese issue as a device to prevent an active challenge to their leadership and to their control of unionized occupations by unemployed and unskilled workers. This is not to say that at times hysterical xenophobia against the Chinese on the part of labor leaders was merely a convenient device. They were also vehemently asserting Caucasian superiority as an ideology. In 1906 Samuel Gompers went so far as to say that "Maintenance of the nation depended upon maintenance of racial purity," and that it was contrary to the national interest to permit the arrival of "cheap labor that could not be Americanized and could not be taught to render the same intelligent efficient service as was supplied by American workers." The equation of racism and Americanism was reaffirmed.

Given the great effort generated in the ranks of labor, passage of the Exclusion Act of 1882 could be regarded as only a partial victory. It of course barred all Chinese workers from entering the United States in the future, but it did not address itself to the 100,000-plus Chinese who were already here. As labor finally understood the act, it was not adequate, it was not a full solution, and labor had a mixed reaction to the passage of the law. Therefore, the anti-Chinese position was kept alive after 1882 by labor leadership. For example, Terrance Powderly of the Knights of Labor called for the total elimination of all Chinese in the United States at the end of 1882, even while he celebrated the passage of the Exclusion Act as a labor victory.

This new stage of anti-Chinese agitation corresponded to a period of national economic decline. The difference between 1876 and 1882 was not that the Chinese had flooded out of the West into eastern industry as had been feared in 1870 (there were still only 3,663 Chinese living outside the western states in 1880), but rather that the national political system in the seventies had given credence to labor's extreme anti-Chinese stance. The onset of the industrial depression in 1882 served as an excuse for labor to renew and extend its anti-Chinese campaign. The effects of the 1882-86 depression were borne largely by workers and consumers in terms of declining wage rates and high unemployment. As the ranks of the unemployed grew there was increasing pressure on labor leaders and politicians to give some direction to the discontent of both organized and unorganized workers. Anti-coolieism was their response. Anti-coolieism meant good politics in 1882 as it had in 1876, not only for the labor politicians but also for the trade union leaders who used the issue to divert pressure on them to make more meaningful or effective challenges to the political and economic order.

The politics of anti-coolieism was translated into direct action in the form of violence against Chinese along the Pacific Coast and in some areas of the mountain states during 1885 and 1886. The pattern of these attacks conformed to a standard pathology. In 1885 the nationwide depression reached its most severe stage. As this point was reached in a given locale, white workingmen, usually under the combined leadership of union officials and local politicians, often formed anti-Chinese organizations and sounded the call for the physical removal of the Chinese and their belongings from the area. The expulsion of Chinese usually followed one of three patterns. Often it took place very rapidly and spontaneously. Sometimes it followed a period of agitation which saw a rather intensive involvement of white workers in the local politics of anti-coolieism. Finally, agitation to expel Chinese would lead to savage violence, as in Rock Springs, Wyoming where some 30 Chinese were killed by white miners in 1885. Similar violence occurred in Eureka, California and in Tacoma and Seattle, Washington where entire Chinese populations were driven out by force in 1886.

Pogroms and organized actions against the Chinese were hardly new. There had been periodic outbreaks of violence against the Chinese in California, while they were blamed for everything from drought in San Francisco to the full-scale depression that struck California in 1877. The depression of 1877 in California is worth noting because it gave rise to the Workingman's Party of California—which combined a platform of idealism and compassion toward poor white workers with an extreme racism toward non-white workers. It was founded by one of the most interesting demagogues in American history, Denis Kearney. Kearney was a self-educated Irish drayman who had spent his early years as a poor lad in County Cork. Seizing his opportunity, he rose overnight from obscurity to national fame. He became so notorious that Lord Bryce, writing in the early 1880s, devoted an entire chapter of his great study of America to "Kearneyism in California."

The governing assumption of the Workingman's Party of California was that the rich and the Chinese were engaged in a tacit conspiracy to oppress white workers, small farmers, mechanics and struggling businessmen. The party's platform proposed a number of far-reaching economic reforms, including a system of progressive taxation, an extensive welfare state program "for the poor and unfortunate, the weak, the helpless and especially the young," the election of humble men to office and the destruction of "land monopoly." On the Chinese question, the platform was violently racist. "We propose to rid the country of cheap Chinese labor as soon as possible and by all means in our power, because it tends still more to degrade labor and aggrandize capital." They would "mark as public enemies" employers who refused to discharge their Chinese help. Throughout the winter of 1877, workingmen's clubs proliferated in the poorer neighborhoods of San Francisco. Having found their scapegoat, Germans, French, Scandinavians and Italians, socialists and anti-socialists alike, all overcame their differences in their haste to join the new party.

Economic improvement sounded the death knell of the Workingmen's Party and eventually forced Kearney's retirement. Historically, radical or labor parties arise in the United States during periods of high unemployment; economic despair drives the workers to seek new political solutions. In prosperous times these parties disappear or merge with the two major parties. The Workingmen's Party of California suffered this fate. By mid-1880, it was finished in all but name, and Kearney's influence was gone.

During this period the California state legislature and various cities subjected the Chinese to extreme legal persecution. As early as 1870 the state legislature categorically outlawed the employment of Chinese in certain public works projects. Two years later it mounted a full-scale attack on them by prohibiting Chinese from owning real estate or securing business licenses.

Meanwhile San Francisco was imposing its own restrictions. For example, a license fee of $8.00 a year was demanded of one-horse laundry wagons. But those laundrymen who collected and delivered by foot (the Chinese) had to pay $60.00. The case of the vegetable peddlers was similar. The Chinese, who carried their vegetables in baskets, were required to pay five times as much—$40.00 a year compared to $8.00—as those who used wagons. San Francisco also passed a Cubic Air Ordinance, which prohibited any tenant or factory worker from occupying a room that provided less than 500 cubic feet of air for him. So many Chinese were arrested that the jails were violating the law. Especially galling to the Chinese was the so-called Queue Ordinance, which stipulated that criminals must have their hair cropped. For the Chinese this meant loss of their pigtails—a form of sacrilege. Eventually all these ordinances were declared unconstitutional, but they caused much hardship during the years they were enforced.

And, as usual, whites often took matters into their own hands. No one knows how often the police looked away while the Chinese were violently attacked in the streets. It can be assumed that crimes against them were commonplace and almost always went unpunished. Generally, Chinese did not register formal complaints as they were legally prevented from testifying against whites. The most serious instance of organized violence against them took place in Los Angeles where a mob shot and hanged 20 Chinese, pillaged homes and stores and tortured Orientals.

With the return of prosperity and the decline of "Kearneyism," anti-Chinese agitation among the white workers of California entered a new phase. The cause was now taken up primarily by trade unions, representing the craftsmen and mechanics—the labor aristocracy. In April 1880, delegates from 40 labor unions met in San Francisco and established a so-called League of Deliverance (from the Chinese menace). The man most responsible for organizing the League—he was elected chairman—was one Frank Roney. Roney had been the leader of the anti-Kearney faction of the Workingmen's Party before becoming a socialist and a member of the violently racist San Francisco Seamen's Protective Union. Over the years he had assiduously built up support within the union movement to oust the Chinese from their jobs and, of course, keep them out of the country. His efforts had resulted in the formation of the League of Deliverance, which, within months after its founding, had 13 branches throughout the state and over 4,000 members. Persuading the public to boycott Chinese-made goods was the main tactic employed by the League, and it was a smashing success. Merchants refrained from buying commodities made by Chinese labor and many factories dismissed Chinese workers. How were the Chinese workers supposed to live? Leaders of the white labor organizations had no interest in such matters.

The League of Deliverance dissolved in 1882, its mission accomplished. In that year Congress enacted the Chinese Exclusion Law. The League's highly successful tactic of boycotting Chinese-made goods had actually been introduced earlier by white unionized cigarmakers.

From the start, the white cigarmakers marched in the forefront of the assault on the Chinese. It was the white cigarmakers, too, who discovered a most ingenious method of punishing their Chinese competitors. In 1874 they adopted a white label to indicate that they, the white union men, had produced the cigars. Accompanying the label was a certificate granted to those proprietors who sold only their cigars. The certificate contained the following message:

> Protect Home Industry. To All Whom It May Concern: This is to certify that the holder of this certificate has pledged himself to the Trades Union Mutual Alliance, neither to buy nor sell CHINESE MADE CIGARS, either wholesale or retail, and that he further pledges himself to assist in the fostering of Home Industry by the patronage of PACIFIC COAST LABEL CIGARS of which the above is a facsimile.

The facsimile of the label showed a dragon on one side, the union mark on the other, and the words, "White Labor, White Labor." The practice of issuing labels quickly caught on. In 1875 the St. Louis cigarmakers followed suit with a bright red one. Finally, in their general convention three years later, the Cigar Makers' International Union decided on a blue one. Thus, the great tradition of the union label began as a racist stratagem.

In California the proponents of the union label came not only from the ranks of organized labor but from small cigar producers, such as the White Cigar Makers' Association. By the mid-1880s the industry was becoming rapidly rationalized, meaning that the larger concerns, using a more refined division of labor, could manufacture cigars at a cheaper price than the smaller ones. Usually it was the larger concerns that employed Chinese who learned their trade quickly and well. The label thus "became a means of product differentiation by which small producers could cling to a toe-hold in the market." But the process of rationalization had gone so far that by 1885 almost seven-eighths of the cigarmakers of San Francisco were Chinese. The manufacturers hired them against prevailing public opinion because they had to meet the competition from the East or perish.

Precisely at this point the Cigar Makers' International Union (CMIU) entered the picture. Under the leadership of erstwhile Socialists like Adolph Strasser and Samuel Gompers the CMIU concentrated on securing higher wages and better working conditions for its skilled members, leaving the unskilled and disadvantaged to fend for themselves. In this way an aristocracy of labor emerged, enjoying increasing benefits while the rest of the work force, having no leverage in the open labor market, stagnated.

In 1884 the CMIU established Local 224 in San Francisco to drive Orientals out of the trade and give the unemployed white cigarmakers of the East (themselves casualties of rationalization) the jobs then held by the Chinese. The astonishing fact was that the whites were content to work at the same rate of pay—a complete reversal of roles. Now it was the whites who were entering into competition with the Chinese.

The Cigar Makers' International Union attacked the companies that employed the Chinese, and of course the Chinese themselves. The large manufacturers were the only major obstacle in the way of the union. The union's tactic was to persuade one large concern to hire just a few white workers. This occurred when the firm of Koeniger, Falk and Mayer took on a handful of whites. Soon the handful had turned into nearly half of the 160 man work force. The Chinese employees of Koeniger, Falk and Mayer knew that their days were numbered, and, with nothing to lose, organized a strike in protest against their displacement. The white community of San Francisco was shocked by this unprecedented show of audacity.

Other Chinese cigarmakers, employed elsewhere, stayed at their jobs. But the CMIU took advantage of the threat, now raised for the first time, of massive, industry-wide resistance by the Chinese. The Chinese were always regarded as servile and congenitally incapable of standing up for the rights of labor. Now the white cigarmakers union was claiming that its men were more compliant and trustworthy than the refractory Chinese. Once again the whites unhesitatingly reversed roles when it suited them to do so.

In any case, the job walkout by the Chinese prompted the entire labor movement in San Francisco to take up the cause of the beleaguered white workers. The Knights of Labor and other organizations led a boycott of all brands of cigars except that of Koeniger, Falk and Mayer. The campaign was successful. By the end of November 1885 the large producers had agreed to the demands of the union. Jake Wolf, president of the San Francisco Cigar Makers' Union, extracted a promise from them that all of the Chinese would be removed from the industry the moment white workers replaced them. The target date was January 1, 1886. The target date was not met, but the Chinese were in time eliminated completely from the industry. A process of racial occupational eviction had begun that would soon be used by organized labor against black workers in many occupations.

Meanwhile organized labor in general responded to the controversy in the cigar trade by mounting a new attack on the Chinese. On November 30, 1885 delegates from 64 Pacific Coast organizations gathered at an extraordinary congress to frame a program against the Chinese "menace." Represented were trade unions, radical and conservatives alike, the Knights of Labor, the Anarcho-Communists of the International Working People's Association, and the Socialist Labor Party. "It was," said the chairman of the congress, "a queer combination of heterogenous elements." But on one thing they could all agree: that the Chinese must go. The question was how and when.

It did not take the congress long to take up the question. One of the representatives of the Sailors' Union offered a resolution to expel the Chinese from San Francisco within 60 days. But the conservatives, consisting mainly of Knights of Labor delegates, thought labor should not lay down ultimatums which it could not enforce except by insurrectionary violence. Opposing the resolution too were the more principled members of the Socialist movement.

The advocates of immediate expulsion came from the left. Generally, those of the extreme left were the more intense in their desire to take up arms against the Chinese. One member of the International Working People's Association, a sailor named Alfred Fuhrman, maintained that the Chinese should be thrown out of the city at once. "By force," he asserted, "is the only way to remove the coolie and 20 days is enough to do it in." Under this kind of pressure, the congress passed the resolution by a vote of 60 to 47. Most of the representatives of the Knights of Labor then left the hall; they refused to be part of an organization openly advocating force and violence.

The other trade unions in the congress were perhaps as adverse as the Knights to force and violence, and they had no intention of honoring the resolution. But they wanted the Knights to leave the congress, and so used the militant radicals for their own ends. After the Knights left, the trade unions demanded that the resolution be reconsidered on the floor. Reference to an exact time period for the expulsion of the Chinese was deleted. In its final form the resolution merely expressed the sense of the congress that the Chinese should leave San Francisco and the Pacific Coast. The congress did, however, establish a trade union council for San Francisco (later the Federated Trades Council, then the San Francisco Labor Council) that over the next decades remained in the forward ranks of the crusade against the Oriental races in America.

The American Federation of Labor's predecessor and parent organization, the Federation of Organized Trades and Labor Unions, at its first convention in 1881, condemned the Chinese cigarmakers of California and recommended that only union label cigars be bought. But the leaders of the Federation (after 1886 the AFL) were not content merely to sanction, perhaps cynically, the movement against the Chinese. Instead, they became the most articulate champions of the anti-Oriental cause in America. No man was more persistent in providing leadership and support than Samuel Gompers, the president of the AFL (except for one year) from its inception to his death in 1924. He was himself an immigrant Jew who had early in his life embraced socialist ideals of brotherhood and the solidarity of the toiling class. But he later repudiated these ideas and became the major spokesman for concepts of racial and national superiority within organized labor.

What he really thought of Oriental workers—leaving aside his professions of "profound respect" for them in the autobiography he wrote in the last years of his life—is best revealed in a tract that he and another official of the AFL, Herman Gutstadt, co-authored at the turn of the century. Its title, *Some Reasons For Chinese Exclusion: Meat vs. Rice, American Manhood Against Asiatic Coolieism—Which Shall Survive?* will give an accurate enough idea of its content. First published in 1902, the pamphlet was written at the behest of the Chinese Exclusion Convention of 1901. Its purpose was to persuade Congress to renew the Exclusion Law, due to expire the following year. Gompers states that "...the racial differences between American whites and Asiatics would never be overcome. The superior whites had to exclude the inferior Asiatics by law, or if necessary, by force of arms." The Chinese were congenitally immoral: "The Yellow Man found it natural to lie, cheat and murder and 99 out of every 100 Chinese are gamblers."

Gompers draws all the arguments that the anti-Chinese forces had been advancing since the 1850s. Only now they are decked out in new dress, for this is the period when the West trembled at the yellow peril and imagined that the dread Mongol hordes were about to march again. The Chinese conspire to overcome class differences, thereby placing white labor at a serious disadvantage. He stresses a familiar theme—the tendency of the Chinese to relentlessly degrade labor and create a new servile element in society.

Modeling himself on a Victorian dime novelist, Gompers conjures up a terrible picture of how the Chinese entice little white boys and girls into becoming "opium fiends." Condemned to spend their days in the back of laundry rooms, these tiny lost souls yield up their virgin bodies to their maniacal yellow captors. "What other crimes were committed in those dark fetid places," Gompers writes, "when these little innocent victims of the Chinamen's wiles were under the influence of the drug, are almost too horrible to imagine.... There are hundreds, aye, thousands, of our American girls and boys who have acquired this deathly habit and are doomed, hopelessly doomed, beyond a shadow of redemption."

Meat vs. Rice was reissued by the Asiatic Exclusion League in 1908, six years after it had been first published. Yet the Chinese question was long since closed, the third and final exclusion law having been enacted in 1902. Gompers and the labor federation arranged for its reissue because the "Mongolian menace" had suddenly reemerged. This time the enemy were the Japanese, several thousand of whom were immigrating to the United States every year. Accordingly, all that Gompers had said about the Chinese was applied with equal force to the Japanese. Having learned much from its experience in the attack upon the Chinese, organized labor once again assumed leadership of the campaign and did not rest until the Japanese too had been driven out of competing occupations and denied entry into the United States.

Before 1890 only a handful of Japanese had emigrated to the United States, less than 150 in all. Japan was closed to the world until 1853, when Admiral Perry's fleet opened Japan to the western world. Between 1886 and 1890, 3,000 Japanese came to America. During the next ten years the number rose to 27,000; and during the next eight to 127,000. In the period of the greatest immigration—1902 to 1908—the yearly total fluctuated between 11,000 and 30,000. At the beginning the *issei* (or first generation Japanese) faced little discrimination. Issei dressed and otherwise bore themselves like Westerners and were unfailingly "polite, courteous, smiling" as one newspaper put it. Most of them served as railroad men, as domestics, in some places as miners, lumbermen or fishermen, or they became storeowners catering to their own people. They quietly lived in their own communities, notably around San Francisco, Sacramento and the upper San Joaquin Valley. Later, the bulk of them moved to southern California.

Until 1905 attacks against the issei were sporadic and brief. As early as 1888 the San Francisco Trades Council called attention to a "recently developed phase of the Mongolian issue." Four years later, Denis Kearney came out of retirement to alert the public to "another breed of Asiatic slaves" who were filling the gap "made vacant by the Chinese." "We are paying out our money," he cried, so that "fully developed men who know no morals but vice (may) sit beside our... daughters to debauch (and) demoralize them. The Japs Must Go!" But Kearney's day was over. The public paid no heed to his ranting; nothing was heard of him again.

In 1900 a rather serious upsurge of anti-Japanese sentiment took place in San Francisco. It was instigated by the local labor unions and their friends, among them the mayor of San Francisco. He spoke a language which must have sounded familiar to many of his listeners. "The Chinese and Japanese are not bona fide citizens. They are not the stuff of which American citizens can be made." Later that same year the AFL took official notice of the Japanese and included them in demanding the total exclusion of "cheap coolie labor." And in 1901 the Chinese Exclusion Convention, which consisted largely of delegates from organized labor (800 out of 1,000) was told that it had better become aware of "the Japs," for they were "more intelligent and civilized... than the Chinamen."

By mid-1905 the labor unions of California had joined forces to establish the Asiatic Exclusion League. Four prominent San Francisco labor union executives were primarily responsible for launching the League's career; all four, it should be mentioned, were themselves immigrants (as were Kearney and Gompers). They were Patrick H. McCarthy (from Ireland), chief of the San Francisco Building Trades Council; his assistant, Olaf Tveitmoe (from Sweden), later to be convicted of participating in a plot to bomb the Los Angeles *Times;* Walter MacArthur (from Scotland) and Andrew Furuseth (from Norway), both representing the Sailors' Union.

Historians and biographers have duly acknowledged Furuseth's achievements. By the sheer force of his personality, he persuaded Congress to improve working conditions on American merchant ships. But beneath the aura that encircles his life and work lies the specter of racism. Improving the lot of seamen was less important to him than excluding "the Oriental" from American ships. The power of the white races, he claimed, rested on its mastery of the seas. That control over the world which the white race—or a segment of it—had maintained unimpaired for 3,000 years now stood in jeopardy because "Oriental" seamen were replacing the whites. It followed that the law Furuseth wanted passed should include a provision forcing Asian seamen off the ships. Such a provision was indeed incorporated into the LaFollette Seamen's Act.

Such thinking was typical of the Asiatic Exclusion League. Its purpose was not only to stop all further Japanese immigration to America; it was also to deny or circumscribe their right to a livelihood. Usually the exclusionists depended on sweeping demagogic verbal attacks on the issei. The League, for example, declared in its statement of principles: 1) that the Japanese (like the Chinese) were unassimilable 2) that "foreigners so cocky, with such distinct racial, social and religious prejudices" would only cause "friction" 3) that Americans could not compete "with a people having a low standard of civilization, living and wage" 4) that American women must not be allowed to intermarry with "Asiatics" 5) that they must not be allowed to become citizens and 6) that if "the Jap" is not excluded how can the Chinese continue to be kept out?

During this period the AFL refused charters to agricultural worker's unions whose membership consisted mainly of Mexican and Japanese farm laborers in the sugar beet fields of California. There were Japanese trade unions in the early 1900s, but whenever they turned to their white "brethren" for help, they found none other than Samuel Gompers and the AFL in their path. In 1902-1903, the Japanese workers and contractors (middlemen who supplied labor and maintained discipline) of the Oxnard, California beet fields organized a strike after the owners, acting in concert, decided to eliminate the contractors and recruit the men themselves. The strike proved successful. More important, it resulted in the creation of the Sugar Beet and Farm Laborer's Union of Oxnard, its members consisting of Mexican as well as Japanese field hands. The Union promptly did what other unions were doing at the time—it applied to the American Federation of Labor for a charter.

In reply, Samuel Gompers wrote, "Your union must guarantee that it will under no circumstances accept membership of any Chinese or Japanese." In short, Gompers was asking the union to disband as the condition for securing a charter. J. H. Larraras, secretary of the Oxnard union, denounced Gompers' racism and inhumanity. He pointed out that "our Japanese here were the first to recognize the importance of cooperating and uniting in demanding a fair wage scale."

But Gompers refused to grant the charter. His blatant repudiation of earlier working class principles was excessive even for a number of unions within the Federation. The Los Angeles Labor Council resolved, in a show of solidarity with the Sugar Beet and Farm Laborers' Union, "that time has come to organize Japanese workers in fields into the Federation." And these sentiments were shared by the Chicago-based *American Labor Union Journal*. It wrote, in June 1903, that so long as non-whites were barred from membership in the AFL, just so long would it be impossible "to organize the wage workers of California for the protection of their interests."

As before with the Chinese, Gompers led the attacks upon the Japanese within organized labor. What Gompers thought of the prospect of organizing the Japanese can be gauged by his remarks at the 1904 convention of the American Federation of Labor. "The American God," he solemnly stated before his audience of delegates representing more than a million workers, "was not the God of the Japanese." The convention went on to give his anti-Japanese position its seal of approval by passing a resolution specifying that the "Japanese were as difficult to assimilate into the American culture as were the Chinese."

At the turn of the century, the American Federation of Labor was committed to a policy of racial superiority and national glorification and many of its affiliates engaged in a variety of overt discriminatory practices against Negroes and Orientals. This development, together with the refusal to organize the unskilled and mass-production workers, further alienated non-whites from organized labor. The discriminatory pattern was now firmly established and would continue for many decades.

Throughout the early months of 1906 tension continued to build in San Francisco as the Japanese were subject to one harassment after another. It was commonplace for them to be assaulted and beaten by gangs of hoodlums. Between May and November 290 cases of assault were reported; none of the white assailants was captured, but seven Japanese were arrested for defending themselves.

While Japanese individuals feared to walk the streets, Japanese restaurants were terrorized by a boycott organized by the labor-dominated Asiatic Exclusion League. In June 1906 the League's executive board concluded that too many "wage earners, laborers and mechanics" were eating in Japanese restaurants and ordered union members to cease eating in them or face penalties. The ban went into full effect four months later. Picket lines were formed around the restaurants and matchbooks were distributed with the label, "White men and women patronize your own race." The organizers frequently punctuated their racial admonitions by smashing windows and beating up owners. Again no arrests were made. The boycott illustrated the racism of the white trade unionists. Significantly, the Japanese restaurant workers applied for admission to the San Francisco Cooks' and Waiters' Union—the prime movers of the boycott—but were resoundingly turned down. The boycott also revealed the corruption to which racism naturally lent itself. When the Japanese consented to pay over $350 for "protection" the boycott was lifted. The union leaders had made a modest killing.

In 1920 the California State Federation of Labor helped form the Japanese Exclusion League of California; the other contributing charter organizations were the Native Sons of the Golden West, the American Legion, the California Federation of Women's Clubs, the California State Grange, the Farm Bureau and the Loyal Order of Moose. The old League had been led by San Francisco labor; this one was dominated by middle-class and small-town elements. It was the farmers, the small businessmen and other "respectable" citizens of California who were principally responsible for pressuring the legislature to enact a second Alien Land Law in 1920. More important, they were largely responsible for getting Congress—in the face of vigorous protests from the Japanese government—to pass an immigration law that barred all but a handful of Japanese (or members of any other non-white race) from entering the United States. The chapter was thus closed. The Japanese had officially joined the Chinese as a people declared unworthy of becoming American.

White working-class racism did not suddenly emerge full-blown. It gestated over a long period of time, advancing from stage to stage, incorporating the "Chinese question," the "Japanese question" and the "Negro question." Their success in excluding what they called "Mongolians" from the labor force suggested to the leadership of the American Labor movement how they could deal with the black worker. In each instance the objective was the same: to drive the workers of the offending "non-Caucasian" race from the job market, either (as in the case of the Chinese and the Japanese) by keeping them out of the country or (as in the case of blacks, Mexican-Americans and other "tainted" groups) by limiting them to low-paying, unskilled, non-mobile jobs outside of the mainstream of the American labor force.

It may be objected that the racial views of Gompers, Furuseth and other labor leaders should not be singled out for special notice or criticism, for as some have argued they merely reflected the zeitgeist. But the fallacy of the zeitgeist argument is that it receives its justification in retrospect from those labor historians who either eliminated or diminished the choices that confronted the major figures in the period under investigation. The zeitgeist did not command American labor organizations to embrace a policy of racism, and it certainly did not command the AFL, which spoke for the overwhelming majority of organized workers from the 1890s on, to be even more militantly racist than Americans in general.

The responsibility for what the AFL and its affiliated unions did lay with the AFL itself—it could have taken an alternative course at the time. It could have practiced what its leaders occasionally preached, namely, that all workers were equal, that no person should be treated as a commodity, that capital was the common enemy of all workers. Instead, the American Federation of Labor acted on the assumption that non-Caucasians were inferior, that they deserved to be used as commodities, that differences of race, not class or wealth, defined the important issues between men.

The ground rules that organized labor created made conflict between the races inevitable. Organized labor chose the path it walked in the years following the Civil War. In fact, it created its own zeitgeist. How different American Life might have been if organized labor had not repeatedly acted against the interests of non-Caucasian workers, both Oriental and black, who could have joined in a racially unified struggle for the equal rights of all working people.

SUGGESTED READINGS

Bitter Strength: A History of the Chinese in the United States, 1850–1870 by Gunther Barth (Cambridge: Harvard University Press, 1964).

The Asian in the West by Stanford M. Lyman (Reno: Western Studies Center, University of Nevada, 1970).

The Anti-Chinese Movement in California by Elmer C. Sandmeyer (Urbana: University of Illinois Press, 1939).

The Indispensable Enemy: Labor and the Anti-Chinese Movement by Alexander Saxton (Berkeley: University of California Press, 1971).

3 *Stanford M. Lyman*

Japanese-American Generation Gap

When the first Japanese embassy arrived in the United States in 1860, the *Daily Alta Californian* reported with mingled approval and astonishment that:

> Every beholder was struck with the self-possessed demeanor of the Japanese. Though the scenes which now met their gaze must have been of the most intense interest for novelty, they seemed to consider this display as due the august position they held under their Emperor, and not one of them, by sign or word, evinced either surprise or admiration.

Thus, with their first major debarkation in the New World, the Japanese appeared to Americans to lack emotional expression. Indeed, San Francisco's perceptive journalist went on to observe: "This stoicism, however, is a distinguishing feature with the Japanese. It is part of their creed never to appear astonished at anything, and it must be a rare sight indeed which betrays in them any expression of wonder." In the 85 years between Japan's first embassy and the end of the Second World War, this "distinguishing feature" of the Japanese became the cardinal element of the anti-Japanese stereotype. Characterized by journalists, politicians, novelists, and film-makers as a dangerous, hostile people, the Japanese were also pictured as mysterious and inscrutable.

When the Second World War broke out, Japanese-Americans in the United States were automatically presumed to be loyal to Japan, and incarcerated for the duration of hostilities—a violation of their fundamental civil rights justified in the minds of many ordinary Americans by the perfidious character they imputed to all Japanese.

The Japanese stereotype was so widespread that it affected the judgments of some sociologists about the possibilities of Japanese assimilation. In 1913 sociologist Robert E. Park predicted their permanent consignment to minority status, and although he later reversed this prediction, his observations on Japanese emphasized their uncommunicative features, stolid faces and apparently blank character. "The American who is flattered at first by the politeness of his Japanese servant will later on, perhaps, cite as a reproach against the race the fact that 'we can never tell what a Japanese is thinking about.' "

Others were quick to recognize the remarkable record of achievement by Japanese-Americans. As early as 1909 Chester Rowell pointed to their refusal to accept unprofitable contracts, their commercial advancement beyond the confines of the ghetto and to their geniality and politeness. More recently, Rose Hum Lee vividly contrasted Chinese-Americans with their Japanese counterparts, noting that the *nisei* (American-born Japanese) "exhibit greater degrees of integration into American society than has been the case with the Chinese whose settlement is twice as long." Others have declared that the record of the Japanese in America is an achievement perhaps rarely equaled in the history of human migration. Careful statistical measures indicate that present-day Japanese in America have outstripped all other "colored" groups in America in occupational achievement and education.

Interestingly, analyses of Japanese-American achievement lay stress on those very same character traits which once made up the notorious stereotype. During World War II personnel managers and fellow workers in California and Chicago admired the nisei working in their factories as an alternative to detention. "What has happened here," wrote William Caudill and George de Vos, "is that the peers, teachers, employers and fellow workers of the nisei have projected their own values onto the neat, well-dressed and efficient nisei in whom they saw mirrored many of their own ideals." What were these ideals? They included patience, cleanliness, courtesy and minding one's own business—the same ideals that could be distorted into the negative characteristics of unwarranted aloofness.

Time-Person Perspectives

Both time and person are perceived in terms of geographic and generational distance from Japan. Japanese-Americans are the only immigrant group in America who specify by a linguistic term and characterize with a unique personality each generation of descendants from the original immigrants. They do not merely distinguish native-born from foreign-born but rather count geogenerationally forward or backward with each new generational grouping. Each generation removed from Japan is assumed to have its own characteristics, qualities which are derived at the outset from its spatio-temporal position, and are thus not subject to voluntary adoption or obviation.

Immigrants from Japan are called *issei*, literally "first generation," a term referring to all those who were born and nurtured in Japan and who later migrated to the United States. The children of at least one issei parent are called nisei, literally "second generation," a term that encompasses all those born in the United States of immigrant parentage. The grandchildren of issei are called *sansei*, literally "third generation," and include all those born of nisei parentage. The great-grandchildren of issei are called *yonsei*, literally "fourth generation," and include all those born of sansei parentage. The great-great grandchildren of issei are called *gosei* and include all those born of yonsei parentage. In addition, those who were born in the United States of issei parentage, were educated in Japan, and then returned to the United States are called *kibei*, literally "returned to America," and their children are considered sansei.

The Japanese in America lay great emphasis on contemporaries. This does not mean that they have no sense of predecessors (those who lived in the past), successors (those who will live in the future), and consociates (those contemporaries with close personal relationships). Rather their ideas about these categories are vague and diffuse, or in the case of consociates, deemphasized and deprecated.

The basic conception of the nisei phenomenon depends ultimately on the objective existence of their own generational group. The Japanese community in general and the nisei group in particular provide a nisei with emotional security and a haven from the turbulence and unpredictable elements of the outer world. But the nisei group is threatened by both centripetal and centrifugal forces, by individual withdrawal and acculturative transcendence. Should individuals withdraw into dyadic relationships or small cliques or transcend the generational group by moving out into the world of their non-Japanese contemporaries, both the objective and subjective senses of nisei identity would lose their compelling force and the group's collective identity would be dissolved.

Thus, the nisei must worry on two fronts about the risks of intimate association. On the one hand the very close contacts inherent in the segregated yet secure Japanese community allow for intimate association below the level of the generational group; on the other hand the breakdown of prejudice and discrimination threatens to seduce the nisei individual away from the confines of his racial group. It follows that, for the nisei, social and interpersonal relations are governed by a permanent interest in maintaining an appropriate social distance, so that individuals do not escape into integration or withdraw themselves from group solidarity.

For the nisei to preserve the objective identity of their own generational group, interpersonal relations must be kept formal. The Japanese language itself is one of social forms, indicative politeness and status identifiers. It is also one of indirection, removing the subject (speaker) in a sentence from direct relation to the predicate, and utilizing stylistic circumlocutions so that the intended object of the particular speech is reached by a circular rather than linear route. The result is that individuals are held at arm's length; potential consociates remain simply contemporaries—quasi-strangers and quasi-friends.

The issei were able to transmit the basic ideas of this culture to their offspring; however, not all of its conventions remain viable. Although the bow, whose rigid rules the Japanese imposed upon themselves while exempting all foreigners, did not survive the generational passage except in vestigial form of the quick jerk of the head offered by nisei to elders, issei and visitors from Japan, other forms, especially verbal ones, could be translated into English. Japanese-Americans are likely to pay careful attention to titles, to employ the terms of genteel propriety, to avoid obscenity and to use the passive voice. Further, they attempt to employ tonal control, euphemisms, and circumlocutive forms in speaking English. Europeans who speak English and most native-born Americans employ tonal change for emphasis and object indication. The nisei strive for flatness of tone and equality of metre, which make it hard for the uninitiated to distinguish between important and insignificant items in any verbal encounter. For the nisei this style of speaking provides a continuous demonstration to self and comprehending others of the proper state of emotional equanimity; for the "foreigner" it induces wonder about what is really being said and in some instances suspicion of ulterior motives.

Nisei employ euphemisms whenever the more direct form might indicate a state of emotional involvement or evoke an undesirable emotional response and especially when the precise term could be insulting or otherwise provocative. Where no English euphemism is available a Japanese term may be employed. For example, nisei understand that race is a touchy subject in America so they substitute more neutral terms derived from Japanese—and this despite the fact that nisei tend not to speak Japanese to their peers. The term "Caucasian" is sometimes used, but one is more likely to hear *hakujin*, which means, literally, "white man," and occasionally one might overhear the pejorative *keto*, literally, a "hairy person" but freely translated as "barbarian." For "Negro," the nisei, who combine a culturally derived, mild antipathy to blackness of skin with an unevenly experienced and ambivalent form of the American Negrophobia, use the denotatively pejorative *kuron-bo*, literally, "black boy," usually in a neutral and unpejorative sense, at least on the conscious level. For "Chinese," another people toward whom nisei are ambivalent, the mildly pejorative Hawaiian term, *pake*, is quite commonly used.

Indirect speech is also affected by the use of go-betweens to mediate delicate matters. An intermediary may be employed to inform one friend that another wishes to borrow money from him and to sound out the former on his willingness to lend it. This saves the would-be borrower from a direct face-losing refusal should his friend decide not to lend the money, and the borrowee escapes the mutually embarrassing situation that would arise if he had to refuse to oblige his friend. An intermediary is also employed, occasionally, to warn someone that he will receive a social invitation or to inform him that a "surprise party" is planned for him.

One difficulty in using indirect speech is that it is the listener's duty to ascertain the context of what he hears and to glean from it and from his knowledge of the speaker and the context just what the important point is. Violations of this tacit ritual speech relationship occur fairly often, sometimes among nisei themselves, but more often in encounters with outsiders. If a non-nisei, frustrated by the apparent pointlessness of a conversation, asks a specific, pointed question, the nisei is troubled. He may refuse to answer, change the subject or more subtly redirect the conversation back to its concentric form. To maintain the appropriate ritual and calm state of speaker and audience, important items are buried beneath an avalanche of trivia, and in the most perfected of conversations, they are never brought to the surface at all, but are silently apprehended by the listener.

This emphasis on composure lends itself to unstated but widely held norms of conversational propriety appropriate to different social occasions. Because it is at informal parties, dinners and tête-à-têtes that one's speech partners and oneself are vulnerable to conversion from contemporaries to consociates, it is precisely such occasions that require careful monitoring. Nisei "rules" for social gatherings include 1) an emphasis on "democratic participation" in speech, that is, no one should speak too long or too much and everyone should have an opportunity to speak, 2) circulation—small clusters of people conversing are permissible but these should regularly decompose and reform with new elements, while lengthy dyadic conversations at a gathering of ten or 20 people are actively discouraged, 3) unimportance—the content of conversations should be restricted to trivial matters. The most fruitful items for conversation, consequently, are sports, stocks and bonds, and technical subjects.

Nisei emotional management is also seen in their emphasis on form over function. Nisei golfers and bowlers who are performing poorly, or who believe they will do so, may justify their bad scores by pointing out that they are working on their stance, body form, follow-through. Because it is widely accepted that form and content are analytically separable but related aspects of a variety of activities, the claim to be emphasizing the former irrespective of the latter is perfectly acceptable, and prevents any attribution of the poor scores to the inner or actual state of the performer. Nisei behavior at pornographic movies shows a similar use of the emphasis of form to mask emotional discomfiture. For example, a nisei may comment on the physical anatomy, aesthetic quality or gymnastic innovation of the nude bodies copulating on the movie screen, thus neutralizing stimulation.

Another response is to tease a member of the group about his excessive interest in the films, alleged similarities or dissimilarities between his behavior and that depicted on the screen, or his remarkable quietness in the presence of an obviously stimulating event.

To communicate their perfect control of body, mind and feelings, nisei strive to set their faces at the expressionless level. Some nisei are so disturbed at the possibility of facial disclosure that they avoid facing others for any length of time or employ newspapers and magazines as a means of reducing eye contact during a conversation. The fact that they share a common concern over face management facilitates a mutual avoidance of staring.

Dissimulation is a regular feature of nisei life. Its most elementary form is the self-imposed limitation on disclosure. Nisei tend not to volunteer any more information about themselves than they have to. Thus, a nisei will sometimes not tell about an important event or will casually dismiss it with a denial or only a partial admission, suggesting by style and tone that it was not important at all. Direct questions are usually answered with vague or mildly meretricious replies. Still another element of dissimulation is concealment of feelings, opinions or activities, especially in the presence of employers, colleagues and guests. Colleagues and superiors of middle-management nisei have sometimes been astonished at their silence during conferences or executive meetings. But the nisei do not feel the need to justify these omissions, "white lies," or evasions; rather the burden would appear to be on the listener to demonstrate why such tact and tactics should not be employed.

Nisei avoid persons and situations likely to evoke embarrassment, personal disorganization or loss of self-control. When a nisei takes on a new line of endeavor, especially one that requires learning a new skill or taking a risk, he does so in secret or with people he does not know well. After the skill has been mastered or the risk evaluated as worthwhile, he will casually tell close associates that he might be about to undertake the line of action in question. Fellow nisei will understand that all preparations, rehearsals and calculations have already been made and if they later see a performance of the new skill, they remain silently aware that it is in fact an exhibition of an already perfected ability.

When a nisei recognizes a close associate's excessive *amae* (dependence) toward him, he may become upset by this fact, retreat even further behind a formal facade of etiquette and attempt to establish greater social distance. Or he might clandestinely request that a third party tactfully urge the friend to be less demanding. An alternative is to gently but firmly tease the offending party until he realizes that he has overstepped the bounds of propriety. Still another tactic is to make sure that all contacts with the offending party will take place with other friends present, so that his excessive affection will be diffused among the whole body of friends rather than centered on just one person.

Building Nisei Character

The fundamental source of nisei character is to be found in the samurai ethic. *Chambara* (samurai) stories always emphasize the stoic character of the solitary and often tragic warrior, who though beset by personal or clan enemies, political misfortunes and natural disasters, nevertheless retains inner psychic strength and emotional equanimity. These heroes, familiar to non-Japanese-Americans by the poignant screen portrayals of such actors as Toshiro Mifune and Tatsuya Nakadai, serve the nisei as ideal character models and reminders of the appropriate presentation of self.

The patterns of hierarchical society were predominant in the early life of the issei, who grew up in a time of great technological and political but little ethical or interpersonal change in Japan. The modernization of the country was achieved not by overturning the old cultural order but by adapting Western industrial, educational and military forms to its framework. The educational system fostered the study of classics and, later, the more technical subjects; it also and more importantly directed its major attention to the development of virtue, humble modesty before superiors, self-control and etiquette. Consequently, though few of the issei were of samurai rank they bore the cultural marks which had been part of the Japanese tradition for at least two centuries.

In addition to the samurai ethic, elements of the rural farmer's outlook helped forge the orientation with which the issei reared their children. The *ie* system, by which Japanese farmers represented both the contemporary physical house and the permanent family household, operated through the notion of preservation and continuity to forestall the development of individualism. In Japan's rural villages the *honke-bunke* (stem-branch family system) allowed nuclear families to split off from one another in a partial sense, so that nothing like the extended Chinese clan system developed, but atomization below the *ie*, or household, level was strongly discouraged. The *ie* was far more important than the individuals who comprised it, and village people would speak of the *iegara* or *kakaku*, that is, the reputation or standing of a family, rather than the *hitogara* or *jinkaku*, the personality or social standing of individual members.

In America the issei men, often married by proxy to women whom they had only seen in pictures and who were sometimes quite a bit younger than they were, applied traditional principles of child rearing to the nisei offspring. In certain respects, perhaps because the issei fathers lacked the outlet of Japan's bath houses and geisha, child rearing was harsher than in Japan; the nisei offspring in turn lacked the presence of an indulgent grandmother to counterbalance the severity of parental authority. Physical punishments were rarely used, although in one known instance an Okinawan nisei reported that his father purposely cut his ears when giving him a haircut. When the boy screamed in pain, his father would slap him across the face with the stern admonition: "You don't scream. Japanese boys do not scream." However, physical punishment is unusual in issei-nisei families. Much more likely is the use of ridicule and teasing, a common theme being to tease a recalcitrant, noisy, emotionally upset or otherwise obstreperous boy about behaving like a little girl.

Emphasis was placed on individual superiority, achievement and education as criteria for both individual and group maturity. Nisei children would not be invited to discuss family matters at the dinner table until age and achievement had demonstrated their worth. Children and adolescents would be admonished with the statement *nisei wa mada tsumaranai*, that is, they were told that the nisei generation was still worthless. Until manhood had been demonstrated the nisei were treated as immature but developing children.

Central to this demonstration of maturity was self-control. Emotional management, even in childhood, was always worthy of exhibition and constantly tested. A line of family authority extended downward from the issei father through the mother to the first-born, second-born, third-born and so on, while a line of obligation extended upward from the youngest to the eldest. This authority system was not infrequently tested by an elder brother harshly rebuking a younger, sometimes for no apparent reason. Younger brothers learned that if they could take these rebukes with outward calm they would ultimately be rewarded with a recognition of maturity. First-born sons received similar treatment from their fathers, and daughters sometimes found that they had to live up to both the precepts of manhood maturity and of womanliness.

Among the nisei, peer-group teasing and ridicule function to monitor behavior. Cuts, digs, put-downs and embarrassing stories are the stuff of verbal life in the clubs, cliques and gangs of nisei teenagers. The didactic purpose of this teasing is widely accepted and regular "victims" have on occasion reported to me their heartfelt gratitude for it.

Two rules appear to govern nisei teasing. First, the relative status position of any particular nisei may render him either ineligible or preferable for teasing. There is a tendency, for instance, for nisei whose parents hail from peasant and poor prefectures not to tease those whose parents are from urban and socioeconomically better-off areas; for nisei from rural parts of California to be somewhat awed by those from San Francisco or Los Angeles; and for clique leaders to be less eligible for cuts than ordinary members.

Second, nisei ridicule and joking must steer a careful course between the Scylla of ineffectiveness and the

Charybdis of associative break-up. If jokes and cuts are too mild, too obscure or always mitigated by apologies and explanations, then the straying party is not brought to heel. If, on the other hand, the jokes are too pointed, if they cut to the very heart of a person and leave him no room for maneuver or retreat, then he may withdraw from the group in shame or anger and be lost, perhaps permanently, to its benefits and protections.

To indicate that a teasing person has gone too far, a nisei "target" may warn his persecutor by directing a telling remark at a third party within earshot. Once I was watching two youthful nisei friends of mine escalate their reciprocal cuts when the offended party turned to me and said, "Man, he's a chilly dude, isn't he?" The other recognized the rebuke for what it was and began to de-escalate his humorous assaults. And so the appropriate relationship—not too close, not too distant—was maintained.

The nisei ideal character is not unfamiliar. It was once thought to be peculiar to aristocrats, Orientals and urbanites, but today's industrial societies seem to require of everyone that they be blasé, sophisticated and, in more recent times, cool. For the nisei this means, ideally, combining courage, that is, willingness to proceed on an anticipated dangerous course of action without any manifestation of fearfulness; gameness, that is, sticking to a line of action and expending energy on it despite setbacks, injury, fatigue and even impending failure; and integrity, that is, the resistance to temptations that would reduce the actor's moral stance. The greatest emphasis is on composure, which includes all its ramifications of physical and mental poise, calmness in the face of disruptions and embarrassing situations, presence of mind and the avoidance of "blocking" under pressure, emotional control during sudden changes of situation and stage confidence during performances before audiences.

In everyday discussions with nisei, any non-nisei listener would be impressed by their pointed perceptions and shrewd observations of others. These observations are made about absent third parties and are never uttered in the presence of the person under discussion. Many people would be surprised at how keenly quite ordinary nisei have paid attention to the minute details of interpersonal situations, placed brackets around particular sets of events, and interpreted words and gestures in light of the general theory of nisei character.

Parlor psychoanalysis is quite common. One nisei may speak of another in terms of the latter's essential inability to mask his "inferiority complex," "fear of failure" or "feelings of inadequacy." These perceptions may in fact be projections. Nisei tend to function as one another's mirrors, showing up the defects in each other's character. This is possible because the wall which the nisei have built to prevent others from seeing their own emotions is really only a set of personal blinders that keep the individual from introspection. In attempting to separate personal feeling from particular action the nisei have alienated their emotional from their behaving selves. Thus they see their fellow men from an angle not shared by those with less self-detachment.

Witty repartee is a well developed and highly prized art among the nisei, but precisely because skill at it is differentially distributed, no nisei feels quite comfortable about it. They often have trouble deciding whether a joke is didactic or destructive. Beyond adolescence, nisei occasionally confess discomfiture about being permanently locked into a system of competitive relations with their fellows. Social visits are occasions for the reciprocal giving of humorous remarks calling attention to invidious distinctions. Birth, sex and growth of children, richness and style of furniture, occupational advancement, skill at leisure-time activities and many other everyday things may become grist for the wit's mill.

Nisei encounters with friends and colleagues tend to be episodic rather than developmental, as is normal in non-nisei interactions. Among nisei, there is a limit in expressing feelings which may not be deepened without loss of inner equanimity or outer poise. Hence, nisei tend to treat each encounter almost as if the participants were meeting for the first time. To Americans, who usually assume that each new social encounter will begin at the emotional level or feeling-state reached at the end of the last meeting, the apparent coldness of response may be puzzling.

It does sometimes occur that ceremony and etiquette collapse and nisei find themselves locked in the mutually embarrassing relationship of consociates. This most often happens when one party in an encounter is unable to sustain appropriate emotional equipoise and ceremony collapses. The others present will try to restore the proper social distance—either by studied non-observation of the other's embarrassment or by a warm but unmistakably triumphant grin signalling simultaneously a victory in the ever played game of social testing and the social reinstatement of the losing player.

The Crisis of the Future

The Japanese geogenerational conception of time and person evokes the recognition that each generation with its attendant character structure will eventually decline and pass away. The issei generation is by no means gone, but its influence has been declining since 1942, when the enforced incarceration propelled the nisei into positions of prison camp and community leadership. At the present moment the nisei group is beginning to sense its own decline and eventual disappearance as the sansei generation comes to maturity and establishes its independent existence and special group identity in America.

The census of 1960 reported that 82 percent of all Japanese in 13 western states were born in the United

States, its territories or possessions. The manner of taking the census prohibits any further breakdown of these figures into their respective geogenerational groupings; but we can arrive at a crude approximation by looking at age distribution. Out of 159,545 persons of Japanese descent living in California the 1960 census recorded 68,015 between the ages of zero and 24. Most of these are the children, grandchildren or occasionally great-grandchildren of nisei. So the nisei can clearly see the end of their generational existence in the not too distant future.

The inevitability of this end has provoked a mild crisis in the *Lebenswelt* of the nisei. They are coming to realize with a mixture of anxiety, discomfort and disillusion, but primarily with a sense of fatalistic resignation, that the way of life they are used to, the presentation of self they have always taken for granted, the arts of self-preservation and impression management they have so assiduously cultivated and so highly prized, will soon no longer be regular features of everyday existence among the Japanese in America, and what they have accomplished by living this way will no longer be accomplished this way or perhaps at all. The sansei, and for that matter, the other successor generations, will be different from the nisei in certain fundamental respects.

Nisei have always seemed to recognize the sociocultural and psychic differences between themselves and the sansei. Some of these are based on clearly distinguishable generational experiences. Few sansei are old enough to have experienced the terrible effects of imprisonment during World War II; many come from homes in which there is no noticeable cultural division between America and Japan and very often have received support for their educational pursuits from parents who have been materially successful. Finally, very few of the sansei have borne the oppressive burden of racial discrimination or have felt the demoralizing agony of anti-Japanese prejudice with the same intensity as the nisei. In all these respects the nisei recognize that sansei are the beneficiaries of their own and their parents' struggles and acknowledge that if the sansei do behave differently it is only right and proper that they do so.

But there is one aspect of sansei behavior that worries and disappoints the nisei: their lack of appropriate nisei character. Some nisei see this characterological loss as a product of increased urbanization and Americanization; others emphasize the loss of Japanese culture in the third generation. Whatever the explanation, many nisei perceive a definite and irremediable loss of character in their successor generation. To illustrate this point, note that nisei often use the term sansei to indicate at one and the same time the existence and the cause of social impropriety. Thus in the face of an individual's continued social errors in my presence, a nisei explained to me, "What can you expect? He's a sansei."

Ironically, nisei child rearing and parental practices contribute to the creation of the very character that disappoints them, just as their own issei parents helped to lay the groundwork for nisei character. Despite the general respect and personal deference the nisei render their parents, they recall the isolation, the harshness, and the language and communication difficulties that marred their own childhoods, and many of them determined to raise their children differently. As a result nisei parents rarely emphasize the ethics of samurai stoicism, endurance and discipline, preferring to follow the white middle-class ethos of love, equality and companionship.

From the point of view of most nisei, the results have been disappointing. Sansei, they complain, lack the drive and initiative which once was a hallmark of the Japanese; they have no interest in Japanese culture, especially its characterological elements; they are more prone to delinquency and have less respect for authority than the nisei; they are "provincial" and bound to the "provincialisms" of Los Angeles, which has probably the single largest aggregate of sansei. They also deplore the lack of psychological self-sufficiency and independent capacity for decision making among sansei.

A nisei scoutmaster told me how his scout troop, mostly sansei, became homesick and upset when away for a week's camping trip, and how their projected wiener roast would have been ruined if he had not stepped in and directed the planning for food purchases. He attributed these "failings" to their sansei background, but admitted that his own intervention in the scouts' plans was a distinct departure from what his own parents would have done in a similar situation during his childhood. Issei parents would probably have let their children fail in such an endeavor in order to help them cultivate responsibility and initiative. But to many nisei such a seemingly unfeeling response to their own children is anathema.

Sansei indicate an ambivalence and a mild anxiety over their own situation. They do exhibit a desire to recover selected and specific elements of the culture of old Japan, but find that their own Americanization has limited the possibility of very effective recovery. If juvenile delinquency among them is on the rise (in fact the evidence is inconclusive) they attribute it in small part to parental misunderstandings and in larger part to the effects of the great social change taking place in America. They find their parents old-fashioned, often unprepared to understand their hang-ups and unwilling to offer sufficient love and understanding. At times they seem about to claim the right to dissolve their own geogenerational identity and that of their successor generations in order to achieve deeper intimate associations below the level of the generational group and interracial intimacies that transcend it. Yet they also wonder how and in what manner they can or should retain their Japanese identity.

As for the nisei, they have not merely survived the hatred and oppression of America's racism, but they have triumphed over it. In nearly every objective measure they outstrip their minority competitors, and in education they have surpassed the white majority. They have turned almost every adversity into a challenge and met each with courage and cool judgment. In all this their own subcultural character has been an invaluable aid and an ever-present source of pride. Inevitably, their own generation and this character are both coming to an end; they cannot turn back the generational clock, but only wonder what psychic supports will provide mental sustenance for the generations to come. In one sense the nisei are the last of the Japanese-Americans; the sansei are American-Japanese.

4 *Joseph J. Westermeyer*

Indian Powerlessness in Minnesota

Social institutions practice gross discrimination against Indian people in Minnesota—and they do so in the name of equality. Besides ignoring the real social needs of Indians, they often attempt to undermine Indian mores and values. Those institutions having the greatest contact with Indian people—the courts, police, welfare agencies and others—are the least adept at problem-solving and rehabilitation in the majority society. And institutions with a record of successful problem-solving have very little to do with Indians.

The incidence of infant mortality, child abuse, foster home placement, state guardianship of children, arrest (especially alcohol related arrest), imprisonment (especially property offenses), unemployment and accidental and homicidal death is many times higher for Indians than for the general population of Minnesota. Conversely, neonatal death, psychiatric hospitalization for both children and adults and suicide occur less often among Minnesota Indians. These rates are related to the degree of success or failure achieved by social institutions in solving Indian problems.

This relationship between Indian people and social institutions was the subject of a two-year investigation conducted between 1969 and 1971. Field activities concentrated on the three largest Indian reservations in Minnesota, larger towns near these reservations and the Twin Cities area. Church groups, private social agencies, federal bureaus, state departments, city police and city administration, county welfare and county sheriffs, teachers and attorneys, clinics and hospitals were consulted. Time spent with various officials and institutions ranged from a few hours, to several consecutive days, to repeated contacts throughout the study. Observations were made on the behavior of institutional workers toward Indian clients, patients, prisoners, students and parishioners.

Authority positions within the schools, clinics, social agencies, religious organizations and businesses serving Indian communities have been occupied almost exclusively by non-Indian people. The structure of these organizations has tacitly implied that Indian people are incapable of assuming responsibility for their education, health services, social welfare, religious needs and so forth. Where social institutions have included Indian people, they include them on the lowest levels.

Indian education in Minnesota demonstrated an important example of this structure and mode of thought. Minnesota society was attempting to teach majority-oriented material under the direction of majority educators to Indian children, despite the prevalent distrust of white people and disdain for middle-class values. The drop-out rate exceeded that of any other group in Minnesota. Indian students prematurely left their educational experience ill-prepared for life in either the majority society or in Indian society.

One of the factors affecting this educational experience was lack of local autonomy and control. While not an official tabulation, Table 1 shows positions held in several reservation schools in September 1969, as noted by observation and informant reporting. This sample showed the aggregation of white people in status positions and Indian people at menial tasks.

Table 1 — SCHOOL POSITIONS ON THREE INDIAN RESERVATIONS IN MINNESOTA, 1969

Position	Indian	White
Principal	1	4
Teacher	3	47
Secretaries	4	1
Bus drivers	6	0
Maintenance men	7	0

Based on observation and informant reporting (requests to the Minnesota State Department of Education for a racial categorization of employees have remained unanswered).

Indian school advisory boards have recently come into vogue both on the reservation and in urban centers. However, these boards can only advise. Unlike real boards of education, they are unable to set policy and cannot hire or discharge school employees. Thus Indian parents had, in effect, no authority over their children's education. Such administrative organization assumed that professional education was all important, while local autonomy and leadership capability had little value. Were Indian leaders to determine goals and priorities, then professional and technical people (Indian and non-Indian) could implement them with an assurance that either success or failure would reflect on Indian leadership. But in the present context, the outcomes depend on an evermigratory series of non-Indian bureaucrats.

Another untoward finding was the tendency of Indian females to have more education than males. In the 1960 Minnesota census, the median school years completed among those 14 years of age and older was 8.6 years for Indian males and 9.0 years for females. In a 1969 survey of Indian students age 16 years and over, the number of females exceeded males. This suggested a subtle bias was operating to keep Indian males in a socioeconomic position not only inferior to non-Indian males but often inferior to Indian women as well.

High Unemployment, Low Income

As a whole, Indian people had the highest rate of unemployment and the lowest income of any racial group in Minnesota. Mean incomes averaged about one-third of income levels for the state. But it should also be noted that Indian men not only had less education than Indian women, but also more unemployment and generally lower status jobs. The male unemployment rate on reservations averaged 42 percent in 1969. In addition, these data demonstrated the trend for women's employment rates to equal and even slightly surpass those of men (58.2 percent for females, 58.0 percent for males in this survey).

Minnesota business and industry, while often glorifying "the Indian" in advertisements, have given Indian people short shrift when it comes to hiring them. Mostly Indians have worked at seasonal jobs which no one else wants—cutting pulpwood, ricing, guiding, road work and fishing.

One community psychiatrist practicing near a reservation gave a straightforward explanation of these figures, declaring that "discrimination is rampant in this town." While my own experiences in his area supported such a viewpoint, a number of fairly liberal men—mostly local businessmen and professionals—attested that such was not the case. They disavowed any malice toward Indians and considered them in no way different from other people. When they were asked the question: "But what if your son or daughter wanted to marry an Indian?" without exception a score of them admitted they would be strongly opposed (one volunteered that it would be worse if his daughter married an Indian than if his son did).

Medical services have had a major impact on Indian health in those areas where effective preventive measures are available. For example, these measures have reduced tuberculosis and other communicable diseases, as well as neonatal mortality (where prenatal care reduces infant death in the month following birth). Post-neonatal infant mortality, diarrhea and pneumonia deaths continue at an inordinately high rate, however. Deaths strongly influenced by individual behavior have increased over the last few decades: accidents, homicide, suicide, cirrhosis of the liver. Longevity is slowly increasing, but it is still two-and-a-half decades behind the general population. While mortality measures general health in a crude fashion, mortality statistics did suggest that medical care services (as distinct from preventive services) have had doubtful impact on Indian health problems.

As in the field of education, medical services also imputed to Indian people an inability to provide for themselves. Table 2 classifies Indian Health Service personnel on Chippewa reservations in Minnesota by race, sex and position. There were no Indian physicians, dentists or pharmacists. Chippewa women occupied higher status positions (nurses, medical secretaries) than did Chippewa men (janitor, maintenance work). Also, non-Chippewa Indian women tended to work at higher status jobs. Non-Indian men occupied the highest paid, most prestigious positions.

Indian people rarely used the Community Mental Health Clinic system in northern Minnesota. Staff people in those areas had a remarkably similar tale to tell. Most of their Indian referrals came from courts and social agencies; in these instances, the patient and family ordinarily gave less than willing cooperation. To the Indian citizen, the C.M.H.C. system served primarily as a way station for incorrigible psychotics and suicidal patients on their way to state psychiatric hospitals. Occasionally a patient with epilepsy or brain disease arrived for consultation. Notable by their absence were reactive or crisis difficulties, family problems, mental illness in early phases and alcoholism.

Nut Doctors

Psychiatric facilities in the Twin Cities area encountered Indian people in much the same fashion as in the northern mental health clinics. Indians did not utilize psychiatry as a first-call resource to find remedies for problems, but rather as a last resort on which to dump intolerable difficulties. As a result Indian informants perceived psychiatrists as "nut doctors" or some variant thereof. In turn, psychiatric health workers commonly described Indian patients and their families in psychiatric jargon using terms with negative connotations.

Except for occasional provision of hand-me-down clothes and secondhand refrigerators, the missionary, too, has not served significantly as a social resource among Indian people. Few Indians have attained status in church circles. Despite large numbers of nominal devotees, Catholics could not claim a single Indian priest in Minnesota; there was only one ordained Episcopal priest. A few Indian lay ministers could be found,

Table 2 — INDIAN HEALTH SERVICE POSITIONS ON CHIPPEWA RESERVATIONS IN MINNESOTA - July 1, 1970

Position	Chippewa		Other Indian		Non-Indian	
	Male	Female	Male	Female	Male	Female
Physician	none	none	none	none	6	none
Dentist	none	none	none	none	4	none
Pharmacist	none	none	none	none	4	none
Nursing	none	17	none	2	none	7
Administration	3	4	none	1	1	none
Lab, X-ray	1	1	none	none	1	2
Dental Assistant	none	4	none	1	none	none
Clerical	4	6	none	none	none	4
Environmental Health	3	none	none	none	none	none
Dietary	5	8	none	none	none	none
Maintenance	14	2	none	none	1	1

Data obtained from Indian Health Service at Bemidji and supplemented by medical officers of I.H.S. as well as personal observation.

but—like the priest—they were men well over 50 years of age.

Recently a fundamentalist evangelical sect has been gaining in popularity as Indian men have assumed ministerial roles. Of course the Native American Church (a pan-Indian religion in which peyote is used) has a long history in Minnesota. The traditional spirit religion still plays a role in the lives of some.

In both the rural counties and in the Twin Cities, police personnel possessed a wider experience with Indian people than did most other institutional workers. Complaints of police brutality suggested that the total police-Indian experience was solely a detrimental one. But such a simplistic viewpoint failed to appreciate the complexity of police-Indian relationships.

Police often played a paternal "rescuer" role to Indian people, especially when the latter were drinking. Inebriated Indians were removed from railroad tracks or highways where they had fallen asleep, rescued from snowbanks and inoperable cars in cold weather, taken off the streets when they posed a danger to themselves and traffic. As one might expect, regular "clients" dutifully acted the child's part. They even came to some jails while sober to seek a free meal or a night's lodgings when out of money. In repetitive scenarios demonstrating this police-Indian entente, officers of the law were seen cajoling their drunken, pseudo-belligerent charges into custody. The opposite reportedly occurred as well, especially in larger towns and cities—drunken Indians have been deprived of their bankrolls and obstreperous offenders have been beaten. Some officers appeared to have no patience with behavior they condemned morally and could not understand.

A private Indian organization in the Twin Cities developed an innovative cooperative program with police officials to subvert both these paternal and enemy roles played by peace officers. During the evenings, especially during warm weather, an Indian Patrol walked the streets around the Indian neighborhood. Originally started to watch the police (that is, to play the "adversary" game), it gradually developed service functions such as taking intoxicated persons home or injured persons to the hospital. Eventually police officers turned minor offenders over to the Patrol, and Patrol members assisted police in managing difficult situations.

Welfare departments ranked second only to the police in number of contacts with Indian people in trouble or distress. As with the police, their performance varied with the individuals concerned, the specific department and prevailing policy. Despite considerable range, however, certain generalizations could be made.

Lack of mutual trust and understanding marked the white social worker-Indian client relationship. Workers accused the clients of uncooperative attitudes, sloth and attempting to manipulate the worker. Clients accused workers of prejudice, excessive curiosity and superior attitudes.

Why should it be thus? Certainly differing value systems and communication skills accounted for part of it. But it went beyond that. Social workers wielded great power over Indian lives in Minnesota. Workers were restrained by laws and agency rules, yet there was much room to maneuver depending upon the elements of the case as they saw it. At one time or another the finances of virtually all Indians rested upon personal decisions made by social workers.

An even more potent cudgel was the worker's capability to take children away from Indian parents, a power which—as indicated by the large numbers of Indian foster children—was employed frequently. Many Indian parents, considered reasonably responsible by their ethnic peers, did not hesitate to leave young children in the care of an eight- or ten-year-old child while they went shopping, working, partying or visiting. Appearance of a social worker on the scene has resulted in abandonment charges. Also, an Indian child in ordinary trouble at a good home or momentarily angry at his parents may opt to take off for the home of a friend or relative to spend a night or two until things settle down at home (a legitimate option for children in Indian families). Should the child choose a white social worker as "friend," he may be headed for a foster home.

Most Indian children were placed in white foster homes (of over 700 foster homes noted to be caring for Indian children in Minnesota during 1969, only two had an Indian parent). This fact was especially bothersome in that the rate of foster placement and state guardianship for Indian children ran 20 to 80 times that for majority children in all counties studied. An explanation for this may be found, not in humanistic philosophy, but in economics. Especially in rural communities the excessively large number of Indian children in foster care bolstered the local community, since federal funds rather than local funds paid for the foster home care and the welfare supervision. Again, this was an instance where the administration of Indian funds by state and county officials worked to the detriment of Indian people and the benefit of the nearby non-Indian community.

When the children were taken away by a social agency, the Indian couple split up immediately or soon afterwards (no exceptions to this were encountered by the author or reported by informants). Rather than working for family integration, the average worker simply took the children. And by the decision to do so, the social worker destroyed the family as a functioning unit.

Kinship ties were not totally broken for most foster children, however. Such children maintained kin ties with their defunct families as they went from one foster home to another. When they reached maturity, most of them rejoined Indian society, but without skills enabling them to live productively. That is, they were not adept at hunting or fishing or wild rice harvesting—skills useful on the reservation—nor had they obtained the skills or education necessary for a job in town. Appended to this were the psychosocial disabilities associated with the foster child syndrome (inability to trust, insecurity, free floating anxiety, difficulty in maintaining satisfying family living).

Another problem was the maze of rules and regulations governing county residence, tribal affiliation, responsible government unit (whether city, county, state or federal) and so on. Each level of government averred that another level held responsibility for Indian people.

Private social agencies varied widely in their services for Indian people. However, most social agencies serving Indians could be characterized as having non-Indian men in the highest positions, Indian women along with non-Indian people in intermediate jobs, and Indian men in the lowest positions. To compound matters further, Indians occupying intermediate levels often came from other tribes outside of Minnesota (sometimes from traditional enemies of local tribes).

In small towns near reservations, private social organizations were exclusively white-dominated and white-oriented in their services. Around Minneapolis a few agencies, such as the Community Information and Referral Service, assisted a sizeable proportion of Indian people. However, even in Minneapolis the services were relatively sparse when compared to the great needs. For example, the Directory of Community Services in Minneapolis included the following number of private agencies for various categories: unwed mothers, 8; Catholics, 6; Jewish, 4; Indian,2.

Indian Agencies

Those few agencies under Indian control deserve special mention. While these were few in number, their achievements were notable—especially in view of the long tradition of agency failures under non-Indian leadership. For example, a white attorney with a reservation Legal Aid agency controlled by Indians related that his clients trust him and present their problems openly:

> They need legal help badly. All reservations are crying for it. But the Legal Aid programs have been attacked by whites in reservation areas, including ours, and the Indians feel that if this is true we must be all right. They align themselves with us.

Statistical information concerning the relationships between Indians and social institutions and the resultant generalizations were, of course, important in understanding the treatment of Indians in Minnesota. Equally important were the attitudes of the people who made up these institutions. Interviews with institutional personnel abounded with surprises. Just as interactions with Indian citizen committees fractured old stereotypes of Indian incompetence, so too did these interviews disrupt many preconceived notions. Patience and frankness could be encountered in a sheriff's office, nihilism in a principal's office, rigidity in a community mental health clinic. Sufficient range of interview experiences was garnered to demonstrate that every social institution harbored entire spectrums, from nihilism to activism, from extreme flexibility to extreme rigidity. No one institutional form had cornered the market on backwardness or on enlightenment.

Many institutional leaders maintained a know-nothing attitude about Indian life, and how their institution might interrelate with and contribute to Indian life. Pressed to comment on the role of his school in the community, a white principal of a reservation school said:

> We'll tell you anything or give you any information about the school. We're the experts here. But we don't know anything about conditions outside of the school. We keep to ourselves.

Such an attitude implies that the educational function

operates independently of the community whose children attend the school. In the face of such a stance (honestly and directly spoken by the principal), the high drop-out rate at his school came as no surprise.

Pseudo-egalitarianism was rife within the social institutions of Minnesota. According to official doctrine all citizens were treated equally, but in fact Indians were treated unequally by expecting all people to have the same Judeo-Christian Euroamerican system of values and behavior. Since all people in Minnesota were *not* the same in regard to their cultural mores and social problems, gross inequality in services resulted from treating everybody as though they were "the same." In effect, the true needs of Indian people were blatantly ignored or poorly handled. The argument could not be illustrated better than it was by a community psychiatrist who, when asked about statistics on Indians in his case load, spoke heatedly:

> All of the people in these counties pay for this (sic) data. If it can't benefit them, it won't be released. There aren't Indians and non-Indians in these communities. They're all citizens. They all benefit from the services here.

According to this man's staff, the Indian community did not use the services offered at the clinic. The single "preventive psychiatry program" for Indian people in this community consisted of stringently enforced school attendance, an action taken independently of the Indian community and enforced by the local sheriff's office.

A further social harm resulted from this pseudo-equal policy—the forcing of foreign social values on a minority people. In order to benefit from social institutions as constituted, Indian people were expected to behave in ways which are odious to them. This amounted to de facto attempts at ethnicide.

"Save the Indians"

Many young social and health workers openly admitted an initial messianic motivation to "save the Indians" when they began their work with Indian people. They wished to help the noble savage, fallen from grace, back to his rightful place of honor. But fatalism soon replaced their altruistic ardor. One young physician with the Indian Health Service acknowledged:

> The hard core alcoholics are irritating to the point you'd want to shoot them. They're mean and vicious when they're drunk. The police come and drop them in your lap. The medical set-up here is perfect, but you can't call this a hospital . . . . These (alcoholic) patients chew up the most time and money. Generally they die anyway. You might say our worst problems have been resolved by death.

Indians were observed to respond to such treatment by social institutions with three types of behavior: 1) open noncooperation, 2) covert passive-aggressive harassment and 3) deception. Personnel from social institutions complained that one or all of these dispositions characterized Indian-institution relationships. In my own experience with hospitalized Indian patients, each of these was indeed encountered frequently and in combination.

It should be noted that almost all such cases of noncooperative, passive-aggressive ploys and manipulation occurred in a context of majority-dominated institutions. Within Indian-dominated organizations, such unproductive mechanisms (while not altogether absent) were significantly less prominent. In the absence of such maneuvers within the ordinary Chippewa or Sioux family in Minnesota, one could not avoid the implication that these Indian people have learned or have been trained to behave this way as a result of contact with various institutions.

Institutional Mismatch

Those social institutions with which Indian people have the most direct contact emphasized neither rehabilitation of their clients nor removal of clients from the cycle of need for continued services. Courts, jails and prisons protected society. State mental institutions served to hide deviant behavior. Missionary religions wanted faithful converts. Acute medical services operated in crises, with little care for health maintenance. Educational systems were trying to acculturate Indian children into the majority society. Welfare and federal agencies served the legislative programs which created them and which annually infused fiscal sustenance; and they did this in a way which primarily benefitted non-Indian people.

Social resources with problem solving or rehabilitation emphasis had little or no contact with Indian people in Minnesota. These included business, industry, unions and co-ops; community clinics and general hospitals; trade schools, colleges and universities; city and county government; private social agencies and attorneys; self-run parish groups. They are smaller, more responsive to individual and family needs, more goal-oriented than procedure-oriented and more prone to repeated performance evaluation from within and without. These social forms tend to foster autonomy. Faced with a problem, they lend themselves to a period of mutual cooperation after which the individual or family fades as an identified "problem" and resumes status as an ordinary citizen.

Cooperative efforts between social institutions and Indian communities have been peculiarly absent. Where such cooperation does occur to some degree, problems are solved. Where non-Indian authority dominates, problems persist—problems which can only be resolved by surrendering responsibility for Indian lives to the Indian community.

Section XIV

Religions and Belief

A major institution that affects the lives of many is religion. In this section facets of belief are discussed for the three major religious groups in America: Protestants, Catholics and Jews. To set the stage for that discussion, however, we present Rokeach's "Paradoxes of Religious Belief." This article explores the fundamental paradox of organized religion, namely, that most religious groups have a basic tenet that says believers should love everyone, yet, at the same time, encourage communicants to believe that their own faith is the only true one. Everyone is equal, but only some will be saved. Rokeach argues that religion brings both good (golden rules) and evil (exclusivity). His review of the empirical evidence leads him to conclude: "The empirical results show that religious people are on the average less humanitarian, more bigoted, more anxious; also that the greater the religious differences, the greater the likelihood of conflict in marriage."

In "Is There An American Protestantism?" Glock and Stark raise the issue of unity of belief in America. Their review of relevant research in this area leads them to conclude that there are substantial differences within Protestantism and that, in fact, there are more differences among Protestant groupings than between Protestants and Catholics. The motif of religious paradox, as articulated by Rokeach, is strongly suggested by Glock and Stark. Their conclusion is that there are four or five major theological groups in the United States and that these cut across the traditional Protestant-Catholic dichotomy.

Vallier's "Challenge to Catholicism in Latin America" provides us with an important sociohistorical perspective on the role of the Church in Latin America. The article opens with a consideration of the traditional importance of the religious elite in Latin America and the role of the Roman Catholic Church there. He suggests that the formal Church has always been at odds with folk religion, that the Church has developed major organizational weaknesses, that it has been under secular control and that it has evidenced moral confusion. The Church's achievement of influence and social control did not depend on its capacities as a Christian religious system but, rather, drew its importance from alliances with secular powers and multiple involvements in education, social welfare and administration. This power has severely eroded, Vallier says, in the twentieth century—the rise of Protestantism and "the Left" have broken the monopoly the Church traditionally enjoyed in many areas. With the "new" Latin America integrated at the national level, the Church finds itself in deep trouble because it lacks such integration. Pressure from within (in the Latin American context) and external pressure stemming from overall Church reform has led to the development of at least four types of elite postures within the Church: those of the traditionalists, the pluralists, the papists and the pastors.

"Jewish Radicalism in Transition" by Dreier and Porter, explores the flight of "New Left" Jews into mystical and messianic religions. They consider the history of Jewish radicalism and return to a theme sounded in other articles in Part Four: generational differences. Youthful radicalism among Jews, the authors argue, is represented by a rebellion against the softer liberalism of their parents. Outflanked by the Black Power and Women's Lib groups, many young Jewish radicals have retreated. Dreier and Porter suggest that sociopolitical concerns for Jews revolve around four things: the fate of the state of Israel, Soviet Jewry, the Jewish establishment and Jewish culture. The struggle of Jewish identity revolves around a search for commonality in these areas. The authors also suggest that, from a historical perspective, we are witnessing the abandonment of politics by younger Jews. The 1950's was a time when politics were unnecessary; in the 1960's politics were hopeful, and in the 1970's they are futile. A turning inward is the result.

1 *Milton Rokeach*

Paradoxes of Religious Belief

All organized western religious groups teach their adherents, and those they try to convert, contradictory sets of beliefs. On the one hand, they teach mutual love and respect, the golden rule, the love of justice and mercy, and to regard all men as equal in the eyes of God. On the other hand, they teach (implicitly if not openly) that only *certain* people can be saved—those who believe as they do; that only *certain* people are chosen people; that there is only one real truth—theirs.

Throughout history man, inspired by religious motives, has indeed espoused noble and humanitarian ideals and often behaved accordingly. But he has also committed some of the most horrible crimes and wars in the holy name of religion—the massacre of St. Bartholomew, the Crusades, the Inquisition, the pogroms, and the burnings of witches and heretics.

This is the fundamental paradox of religious belief. It is not confined to history. In milder but even more personal forms it exists in our daily lives.

In 1949 Clifford Kirkpatrick, professor of sociology at Indiana University, published some findings on the relationship between religious sentiments and humanitarian attitudes. Professor Kirkpatrick investigated the oft-heard contention that religious feeling fosters humanitarianism; and, conversely, that those without religious training should therefore be less humanitarian. His conclusions were surprising—at least to the followers of organized religion. In group after group—Catholic, Jewish, and the Protestant denominations—he found little correlation at all; but what there was was negative. That is, the devout tended to be *slightly less* humanitarian and had more punitive attitudes toward criminals, delinquents, prostitutes, homosexuals, and those who might seem in need of psychological counseling or psychiatric treatment.

In my own research I have found that, on the average, those who identify themselves as belonging to a religious organization express more intolerance toward racial and ethnic groups (other than their own) than do non-believers—or even Communists. These results have been found at Michigan State University, at several New York colleges, and in England (where the Communist results were obtained). Gordon Allport in his book, *The Nature of Prejudice,* describes many of the studies that have come up with similar findings. In a recent paper he read at the Crane Theological School of Tufts University, he said:

> On the average, church goers and professedly religious people have considerably more prejudice than do non-church goers and non-believers.

Actually, this conclusion is not quite accurate. While non-believers are in fact generally less prejudiced than believers toward racial and ethnic groups, it does not follow that they are more tolerant in every respect. Non-believers often betray a bigotry and intellectual arrogance of another kind—intolerance toward those who disagree with them. Allport's conclusion is valid if by "prejudice" we only mean ethnic and religious prejudice.

Organized religion also contends that the religious have greater "peace of mind" and mental balance. We have found in our research at Michigan State University—described in my book, *The Open and Closed Mind*—that people with formal religious affiliation are more anxious. Believers, compared with non-believers, complain more often of working under great tension, sleeping fitfully, and similar symptoms. On a test designed to measure manifest anxiety, believers generally scored higher than non-believers.

If religious affiliation and anxiety go together, is there also a relation between religion and serious mental disturbance? What is the relative frequency of believers and non-believers in mental hospitals, compared to the outside? Are the forms and courses of their illnesses different? I recently discussed this with the clinical director of a large mental hospital. He believes without question that religious sentiments prevail in a majority of his patients; further, that religious delusions play a major part in the illnesses of about a third of them.

It is pretty hard to conclude from such observations anything definite about the role religion plays in mental health. This is an area that needs much research, not only within our own culture but also cross-culturally. I am thinking especially of the Soviet Union. What is the relative frequency of mental disease in the Soviet Union as compared with western countries? To what extent could such differences be attributable to differences in religious sentiments? What is the proportion of believers and non-believers in Soviet mental hospitals? Many questions could be asked.

In a study in Lansing, Michigan, we found that when you ask a group of Catholics to rank the major Christian denominations in order of their similarity to Catholicism, you generally get the following order: Catholic first, then Episcopalian, Lutheran, Presbyterian, Methodist, and finally

Baptist. Ask a group of Baptists to rank the same denominations for similarity, and you get exactly the reverse order: Baptist, Methodist, Presbyterian, Lutheran, Episcopalian, and finally Catholic. When we look at the listings of similarities they seem to make up a kind of color wheel, with each one of the six major Christian groups judging all other positions from its own standpoint along the continuum. But actually it turns out that all these continua are basically variations of the same theme, with Catholics at one end and Baptists at the other.

Apparently people build up mental maps of which religions are similar to their own, and these mental maps have an important influence on everyday behavior. If a Catholic decides to leave his church and join another, the probability is greatest that he will join the Episcopalian church—next the Lutheran church—and so on down the line. Conversely, a defecting Baptist will more probably join the Methodist church, after that the Presbyterian church, and so on. The other denominations follow the same pattern.

The probability of inter-faith marriage increases with the similarity between denominations. When a Catholic marries someone outside his faith, it is more likely to be an Episcopalian, next most likely a Lutheran, and so on.

What of the relation between marital conflicts and inter-faith marriages? In general we find that the greater the dissimilarity, the greater likelihood of conflict both before and after marriage.

We determined this by restricting our analysis to couples of whom at least one partner was always Methodist. We interviewed seven or eight all Methodist couples; then another group in which Methodists had married Presbyterians; then Methodists and Lutherans; and on around. We not only questioned them about their marital conflicts, but also about their pre-marital conflicts. How long did they "go steady"? (The assumption is that the longer you go steady beyond a certain point, the more likely the conflict.) Did parents object to the marriage? Had they themselves had doubts about it beforehand? Had they ever broken off their engagement? For marital conflict, we asked questions about how often they quarreled, whether they had ever separated (if so, how many times), and whether they had ever contemplated divorce. From the answers we constructed an index of pre-marital and post-marital conflict.

These findings raise an issue of interest to us all. From the standpoint of mental health, it can be argued that inter-faith marriages are undesirable. From the standpoint of democracy, is it desirable to have a society in which everyone marries only within his own sect or denomination? This is a complicated matter and cannot be pursued here. But these findings do suggest that somehow the average person has gotten the idea that religious differences—even minor denominational distinctions within the Christian fold —*do* make a difference; so much difference in fact that inter-faith marriages must result in mental unhappiness.

To pull together the various findings: I have mentioned that empirical results show that religious people are on the average less humanitarian, more bigoted, more anxious; also that the greater the religious differences, the greater the likelihood of conflict in marriage. Does a common thread run through these diverse results? What lessons can we learn from them?

It seems to me that these results cannot be accounted for by assuming, as the anti-religionists do, that religion is an unqualified force for evil; nor by assuming, as the pro-religionists do, that religion is a force only for good. Instead, as indicated at the beginning, I believe that these results become more understandable if we assume that there exist simultaneously, within the organized religions of the West, psychologically conflicting moral forces for good *and* evil—teaching brotherhood with the right hand and bigotry with left, facilitating mental health in some and mental conflict, anxiety, and psychosis in others. I realize that this seems an extreme interpretation; but the research bears it out.

Gordon Allport makes a similar point:

> Brotherhood and bigotry are intertwined in all religion. Plenty of pious persons are saturated with racial, ethnic, and other prejudice. But at the same time many of the most ardent advocates of racial justice are religiously motivated.

We are taught to make definite distinctions between "we" and "they," between believer and non-believer; and sometimes we are urged to act on the basis of these distinctions, for instance in marriage. The category of man that comes to mind when we hear the word "infidel" or "heretic" is essentially a religious one. It is part of our religious heritage. But it is pretty difficult psychologically to love infidels and heretics to the same extent that we love believers. The psychological strain must be very great; and a major result must be guilt and anxiety.

This kind of dichotomy is not confined to religion. Gunnar Myrdal, in *The American Dilemma,* described the conflict between American ideals of democracy and practice of discrimination against minority groups, and the guilt, anxiety, and disorder it spawned. We are familiar in international affairs with the enormous psychological discrepancy between the humanitarian ideals of a classless society advocated by the Marxists and the anti-humanitarian methods employed by them for its achievement. No wonder there have been so many defections from the Communist cause in America and Europe! When the strain between one set of beliefs and another set of beliefs—or between belief and practice—becomes too great, one natural response is to turn away from the whole system.

I suspect that such contradictions lead often to defection from religion also. Most of the time, however, the result is psychological conflict, anxiety, and chronic discomfort arising from feelings of guilt. The contradictions in religious teachings are more subtle than those in politics and would, for the most part, be denied consciously. A conflict between ideological content and ideological structure—between *what* is taught and *how* it is taught—must be very subtle. A particular religious institution not only must disseminate a particular religious ideology; it must also perpetuate itself and defend against outside attack. It is this dual purpose of religious institutions, I hypothesize, which leads to the contradiction between the *what* and the *how*. It leads to the paradox of a church disseminating truly religious values to the extent possible, while unwittingly communicating anti-religious values to the extent necessary.

RESOLVING CONTRADICTIONS

Gordon Allport, writing on the relation between religion and bigotry, has suggested two types of religious orientation. He calls them the *extrinsic* and the *intrinsic*. The extrinsic outlook on religion is utilitarian, self-centered, opportunistic, and other-directed. The intrinsic, in contrast, includes basic trust, a compassionate understanding of others so that "dogma is tempered with humility" and, with increasing maturity, "is no longer limited to single segments of self interest." Allport does not imply that everyone is purely either intrinsic or extrinsic; rather, all range somewhere along the continuum from one pole to the other.

The extent to which a particular person has an intrinsic or extrinsic outlook depends largely on the way he is able to resolve the contradictory teachings of his religious group. This in turn depends on the particular quality of his experiences with others, especially with parents in early childhood. A person is more apt to be extrinsically-oriented if his early experiences included threat, anxiety, and punishment or if religion was used punitively, as a club to discipline and control him.

Good empirical evidence exists which supports Allport's distinctions. W. Cody Wilson has succeeded in isolating and measuring the extrinsic religious sentiment and in showing that it is closely related to anti-Semitism. Also, one of my collaborators, Dr. G. Gratton Kemp, has isolated two kinds of religiously-minded students, all enrolled in one denominational college. One group was open-minded and tolerant. The other group was closed-minded and highly prejudiced. Dr. Kemp studied their value orientations over a six-year period. He found that while they expressed similar values when in college, they diverged sharply six years later. Both groups ranked their religious values highest but then parted abruptly. The open-minded group put social values next and theoretical values third. The closed-minded group also ranked religious values highest, but political values were second in importance for them and economic values third. It is obvious that the total cluster of values is quite different between the open-minded and the closed-minded groups. These findings clearly suggest that religious people do indeed differ strongly in their orientations toward life to the extent that their religious outlook is, as Allport claims, extrinsic or intrinsic.

AN ANTI-HUMANITARIAN VICTORY?

All the preceding leads to the following tentative conclusions: the fact that religious people are more likely to express anti-humanitarian attitudes, bigotry, and anxiety and the fact that religious similarity and dissimilarity play an important role in marital conflict may both be interpreted as the end result of the emergence of the extrinsic rather than the intrinsic orientation toward religion. They also suggest that, in most people, the extrinsic orientation predominates. This greater prominence of extrinsic attitudes in turn seems to arise out of the contradictory beliefs transmitted through organized religion: humanitarian on one side, anti-humanitarian on the other. One constructive suggestion that might be advanced is that ministers, rabbis, and priests should better understand the differences between the *what* and the *how* of belief, and the fact that contradictions between the *what* and the *how* can lead to excessive anxiety, pervasive guilt, and psychic conflict and, therefore, to all sorts of defensive behavior capable of alleviating guilt and conflict. Representatives of organized religion should consequently become more sophisticated about the unwitting contradictions introduced into religious teachings, and try to eliminate them—as the Catholics are doing now with belief in Jewish guilt for the crucifixion.

Parents are really the middlemen between the forces of organized religion and the child. What factors in rearing, in parental attitudes, in discipline techniques, in the quality of reward and punishment are likely to lead to what Allport has called the intrinsic orientation toward religion? What factors lead to the extrinsic? The data suggest that the more the parent encourages the formation and development of extrinsic attitudes toward religion, the more he hinders the growth of the child into a mature and healthy human being. The more he strengthens the intrinsic religious orientation, the more he helps his child grow healthy, mature, tolerant, and happy.

The conflict between the ideal and what seems to be the practical is widespread. But the current readjustment in racial relations, in which clergymen have taken so large a part, for all its upset and pain indicates that these dichotomies are neither eternal nor inevitable. Nor is the extrinsic orientation necessarily the "practical" one. Research and practice in race relations, criminology, and child-rearing have consistently shown that the non-punitive and accepting approach brings better results.

Change is underway, in the church and in the home, and brings with it, hopefully, greater emphasis on resolving the paradox between the what and the how of religious belief.

2 *Charles Y. Glock & Rodney Stark*

Is There an American Protestantism?

"Do you, personally, believe in God?" To this recurrent question on Gallup polls, 97 percent of Americans answer "Yes." Supported by such findings, commentators on contemporary American life are unanimous in asserting that all but an insignificant fraction of Americans believe in God.

Another prevalent judgment about religious life in this country is that all Americans are coming to believe pretty much in the same things. The primary feature of American religion today seems to be no longer its diversity—based on the existence of several hundred Christian bodies—but its unity of outlook. Furthermore, the recent series of denominational mergers has fostered rising hopes for a general ecumenicalism.

Will Herberg in his now famous book, *Protestant-Catholic-Jew,* speaks of the "common religion" of America; the differences between Protestant denominations he considers to be organizational and ethnic rather than theological, and far outweighed by the consensus of beliefs. Robert Lee, in the *Social Sources of Church Unity,* suggests that a "common core Protestantism" exists because our urban, mobile, national society has broken down old parochial religious boundaries.

The major arguments have shifted away from whether this convergence in American religion has taken place, to the question of whether it is a blessing or a curse. Some churchmen contend that the homogenization of belief portends a loss of religious concern and authenticity; some social scientists condemn it as another symptom of the moral corrosion of mass society and the "O.K. world" of suburban complacency. On the other hand churchmen and social scientists hail the sloughing off of old divisions as symbolic of a new era of brotherhood, in which all can unite in a common quest to ennoble the human spirit.

We believe this debate is much too premature. We mean to raise a much more basic question: Have such changes really taken place? Is there really a "common core" belief in American Protestantism? Do the 97 percent of Americans who believe in God believe in the *same* God?

Our extensive survey shows that there are still a great many basic differences of belief among Protestant denominations in America.

The notion that American religion has undergone doctrinal agreement rests on two main premises:

■ That the old disputes (such as adult versus infant baptism) have lost their force and relevance; that nobody much believes in, or cares about, the idiosyncracies that once rent Christendom.

■ That the demise of these historic differences leaves Americans in general agreement, sharing in the essential core of Christian (and Judaic) teachings. That is, Americans now are in consensus on such bedrocks of faith as the existence of an all-powerful, personal God, the moral authority of the Ten Commandments, and the New Testament promise of salvation.

But systematic evidence supporting these premises has been extremely scanty. Important and sweeping assertions about American religion need more careful examination, and firmer evidence. So we shall draw upon empirical data from our study of Christian church members to see to what extent American religion really is homogeneous.

SUPERNATURALISM

As noted at the outset, American adults report a virtually unanimous belief in God. But what do they believe *about* God? And to what *degree* do they believe?

Table I demonstrates definitely that Americans are anything *but* unanimous in their beliefs about God; and that the distinctions are not only sharp between individuals, but between denominations as well.

Only 41 percent of the Congregationalists indicated unquestioning faith in a personal God. (Table 1.) This rises to 60 percent of the Methodists, 63 percent of the Episcopalians, about 75 percent among the center denominations, and is virtually unanimous among Southern Baptists and members of the fundamentalist sects. Overall, 71 percent of the Protestants endorsed the orthodox position, as compared with 81 percent of the Roman Catholics.

The second line shows that most of those who rejected unquestioning faith did not hold a different image of God, but were uncertain in their belief. They conceived of a personal divinity, but had doubts about his existence. Denominational differences here too are marked: 34 percent of the Congregationalists doubted; but only 1 percent of the Southern Baptists.

The fourth question is especially interesting, for it indicates a different conception of God, rather than mere doubt.

1 Belief in God — "Which of the following statements comes closest to what you believe about God?"	Congregationalists	Methodists	Episcopalians	Disciples of Christ	Presbyterians	American Lutherans	American Baptists	Missouri Lutherans	Southern Baptists	Sects	Total Protestants	Catholics
"I know God really exists and I have no doubts about it."	41%	60%	63%	76%	75%	73%	78%	81%	99%	96%	71%	81%
"While I have doubts, I feel that I do believe in God."	34	22	19	20	16	19	18	17	1	2	17	13
"I find myself believing in God some of the time, but not at other times."	4	4	2	0	1	2	0	0	0	0	2	1
"I don't believe in a personal God, but I do believe in a higher power of some kind."	16	11	12	0	7	6	2	1	0	1	7	3
"I don't know whether there is a God and I don't believe there is any way to find out."	2	2	2	0	1	*	0	1	0	0	1	1
"I don't believe in God."	1	*	*	0	0	0	0	0	0	0	*	0
No answer	2	*	1	4	*	*	2	0	0	1	1	1
Number of respondents	(151)	(415)	(416)	(50)	(495)	(208)	(141)	(116)	(79)	(255)	(2326)	(545)

Note: Asterisk denotes less than ½ of 1 per cent.
Some columns fail to sum to 100% due to rounding error.
The number of respondents shown for each denomination in this table is the same for all other tables.
American Lutherans include The Lutheran Church in America and the American Lutheran Church.
Sects include The Assemblies of God, The Church of God, The Church of Christ, The Church of the Nazarene, The Foursquare Gospel Church and one independent Tabernacle.

Again, contrasts are striking: 16 percent of the Congregationalists, 11 percent of the Methodists, 12 percent of the Episcopalians—and *none* of the Southern Baptists—substituted some kind of "higher power" for a personal God.

Two percent of the Congregationalists, Episcopalians, and Methodists were agnostics, and 1 percent of the Congregationalists said they did not believe in God at all.

If the first four lines are added, then 98 percent of both Protestants and Catholics may be said to believe to some extent in some kind of God. Superficially, this supports the Gallup figures. But the Gallup poll implication of uniformity and piety are entirely misleading.

Gallup studies also report that American Christians are virtually unanimous in believing Jesus Christ to be the Divine Son of God. But this faith too needs to be qualified.

Table 2 shows important contrasts in belief in the divinity of Jesus. Denominational differences are virtually identical to those in the belief in God. Only 40 percent of Congregationalist had *no doubts* that "Jesus is the Divine Son of God." This rose abruptly to 99 percent of Southern Baptists. The total Protestant figure is 69 percent versus 86 percent for Catholics.

Examining some of the other orthodox beliefs about Christ (Table 3) brought differences into even sharper focus. Only 57 percent of all Protestants believed it "completely true" that "Jesus was born of a virgin," compared to 81 percent of Catholics. But the differences between the purportedly "common core Protestants" was much more startling: only 21 percent of Congregationalists believed it, rising to a peak of 99 percent of Southern Baptists.

The Southern Baptists remain rockbound in their faith in Jesus for all questions. Was it "completely true" that "Jesus walked on water"? Here the firm believers in this miracle fell to a small minority of the large liberal denominations, and counted only half of all Protestants. Even the Catholics fell to 71 percent. But the Southern Baptists held at 99 percent.

THE SECOND COMING

Like the existence of God, the Saviorhood of Christ causes mixed reactions among American Christians. On the promise of the second coming of Christ ("Do you believe Jesus will actually return to the earth some day?") the differences between the Protestant denominations was far greater than that between Protestants as a whole and Catholics. A sizable majority of Congregationalists felt that Jesus would "definitely" or "probably" not return, compared to only 2 percent of Southern Baptists. Only 13 percent of Congregationalists and 21 percent of Methodists thought he would "definitely" return—compared to 75 percent of Missouri Synod Lutherans and 92 percent of the unshakeable Southern Baptists. Less than half of Protestants as a whole, as well as Catholics, thought the second coming "definite," and less than 60 percent thought it probable. Protestants can no longer sing, "Christ crucified, risen, coming again," with one voice, since less than half of total American Christendom really believes it true.

Table 4 deals with two basic religious beliefs about deity.

2 Belief in the Divinity of Jesus

"Which of the following statements comes closest to what you believe about Jesus?"

	Congregationalists	Methodists	Episcopalians	Disciples of Christ	Presbyterians	American Lutherans	American Baptists	Missouri Lutherans	Southern Baptists	Sects	Total Protestants	Catholics
"Jesus is the Divine Son of God and I have no doubts about it."	40%	54%	59%	74%	72%	74%	76%	93%	99%	97%	69%	86%
"While I have some doubts, I feel basically that Jesus is Divine."	28	22	25	14	19	18	16	5	0	2	17	8
"I feel that Jesus was a great man and very holy, but I don't feel Him to be the Son of God any more than all of us are children of God."	19	14	8	6	5	5	4	0	0	*	7	3
"I think Jesus was only a man, although an extraordinary one."	9	6	5	2	2	3	2	1	1	*	4	1
"Frankly, I'm not entirely sure there was such a person as Jesus."	1	1	1	0	1	*	0	0	0	0	1	0
Other and no answer	3	3	2	4	1	0	2	1	0	1	2	2

3 Additional Beliefs About Jesus

	Congregationalists	Methodists	Episcopalians	Disciples of Christ	Presbyterians	American Lutherans	American Baptists	Missouri Lutherans	Southern Baptists	Sects	Total Protestants	Catholics
"Jesus was born of a virgin."												
Completely true	21	34	39	62	57	66	69	92	99	96	57	81
"Jesus walked on water."												
Completely true	19	26	30	62	51	58	62	83	99	94	50	71
"Do you believe Jesus will actually return to the earth some day?"												
Definitely	13	21	24	36	43	54	57	75	94	89	44	47
Probably	8	12	13	10	11	12	11	8	4	2	10	10
Possibly	28	25	29	26	23	18	17	6	0	1	20	16
Probably not	23	22	17	12	12	6	6	4	1	2	13	11
Definitely not	25	17	11	6	8	7	5	1	1	3	10	12
No answer	3	3	6	10	3	3	4	6	0	3	4	4

4 Life Beyond Death and Belief in the Devil

	Congregationalists	Methodists	Episcopalians	Disciples of Christ	Presbyterians	American Lutherans	American Baptists	Missouri Lutherans	Southern Baptists	Sects	Total Protestants	Catholics
"There is a life beyond death."												
Completely true	36%	49%	53%	64%	69%	70%	72%	84%	97%	94%	65%	75%
Probably true	40	35	31	32	21	23	19	10	3	4	24	16
Probably not or definitely not true	21	13	13	0	7	5	7	4	0	2	9	5
"The Devil actually exists."												
Completely true	6	13	17	18	31	49	49	77	92	90	38	66
Probably true	13	15	16	34	17	20	17	9	5	5	15	14
Probably not or definitely not true	78	66	60	38	48	26	29	10	1	5	43	14

5 Sin

	Congregationalists	Methodists	Episcopalians	Disciples of Christ	Presbyterians	American Lutherans	American Baptists	Missouri Lutherans	Southern Baptists	Sects	Total Protestants	Catholics
"Man can not help doing evil."												
Completely true	21	22	30	24	35	52	36	63	62	37	34	22
Probably true	36	36	34	36	35	30	28	20	14	15	31	29
Probably not or definitely not true	39	38	31	38	25	15	27	13	22	42	30	43
"A child is born into the world already guilty of sin."												
Completely true	2	7	18	6	21	49	23	86	43	47	26	68
Probably true	2	4	7	2	7	12	9	4	3	3	6	10
Probably not or definitely not true	94	87	71	90	68	37	65	9	55	46	65	19

Congregationalists Methodists Episcopalians Disciples of Christ Presbyterians American Lutherans American Baptists Missouri Lutherans Southern Baptists Sects Total Protestants Catholics

■ "There is a life beyond death." On this central tenet of Christianity only 36 percent of Congregationalists thought the statement "completely true," along with 49 percent of Methodists, and compared to 97 percent of Southern Baptists.

■ The controversial statement "The Devil actually exists" brought on a much wider spread of Protestant opinion. Only 6 percent of Congregationalists and 13 percent of Methodists consider Satan's existence certain, against 92 percent of Southern Baptists. Overall, 38 percent of Protestants and 66 percent of Roman Catholics were certain.

CONCEPTS OF SIN

Unlike the supernatural, sin is related directly to the nature of man. Acceptance of man as sinful by nature increases in the usual pattern (Table 5), from the more liberal denominations on the left to the more conservative ones on the right; however, compared to differing beliefs in the supernatural, the spread is generally more even.

But on the acceptance of "original sin" ("A child is born into the world already guilty of sin"), there are some abrupt departures from the spectrum: those denominations with a liturgical or "high church" tradition are readily distinguishable by their willingness to accept this belief. Original sin cannot be absolved by personal efforts, but only through the church, especially those churches which emphasize ritual. Thus, the ritualistic Episcopalian church stands out sharply from the liberal group, and the American Lutherans from the other center groups. The strongly ritualistic Catholic church contrasts greatly with the Protestants in general, 68 percent to 26 percent.

It is clear that a general relationship exists between belief in original sin and theological conservatism, so that Lutherans are much more likely to hold this view than Episcopalians; yet the marks of the formal doctrine show up all across the table. Thus, on the left of the table the traces of old doctrinal differences on original sin may still be detected, while on the right these differences retain much of their old force.

SALVATION

What of the central concern and promise of all Christianity: salvation?

FAITH. Christians have long battled over the question of whether faith *and* works were necessary to be saved; but there has been no argument that faith at least was absolutely required. The central tenet of this required faith is belief in Jesus Christ as the divine son of God who died to redeem men from their sins. Some Christian traditions hold that more is necessary ("Faith without works is dead"); but all agree that there is no salvation outside of Christ.

However, we have seen that members of American denominations do not all believe Jesus divine. Therefore, it is not surprising to find them also disagreeing over whether belief in Christ is absolutely necessary for salvation.

In the liberal groups, only a minority consider faith in Christ "absolutely necessary." (Table 6) Among the conservative and fundamentalist groups, however, there is almost complete consensus about the necessity of faith in Christ for salvation. Overall, 65 percent of Protestants and 51 per cent of Roman Catholics gave this answer.

It seems likely that among all Protestant groups, persons who accept the promise of eternal salvation beyond the grave are also likely to feel that this eternal reward is contingent upon belief in Christ as savior.

All denominational groups are less likely to feel that one must hold "the Bible to be God's truth" in order to be saved. Overall, the pattern follows the now familiar increases from left to right, with one notable exception. The Southern Baptists had been most unanimous in their assertion of traditional Christian positions, yet they are not importantly different from the center on the importance of Bible literalism. This probably reflects the great emphasis they put on Christ as the primary source by which one attains grace.

WORKS. Having become accustomed to increases from left to right in proportions of those holding faith necessary for salvation, it comes as a surprise to see these trends reverse in Table 7.

Table 7 deals with the necessity of *works.* Those denominations weakest on the necessity of faith for salvation are the strongest on the necessity of "doing good for others." In fact, the proportions of people on the left who think doing good for others is required for salvation is higher than those of the same groups who think faith in Christ absolutely necessary. More people in the liberal churches believed in the absolute necessity of doing good than believed in life after death. On the other hand, the conservative groups do not give "good deeds" any special importance in the scheme for salvation.

We suggest that these responses on "doing good" by those who essentially reject the traditional notion of salvation represent their desire to ratify the ethical components of their religious outlook. Indeed, ethics are likely *the* central component of their religious beliefs.

Turning to the matter of tithing, it is clear that Christians in general are not inclined to connect this with salvation. Only 14 percent of the Protestants and 10 percent of the Roman Catholics thought tithing absolutely necessary.

To sum up: marked contrasts do exist among Christian denominations in their conceptions of what is required for salvation.

BARRIERS TO SALVATION

IMPROPER FAITH. If faith in Christ is essential for salvation, what acts and beliefs are an absolute barrier to it? Looking at the data in Table 8, those denominations strongest on requiring faith in Jesus for salvation are also strongest on rejecting salvation for non-Christians. How-

	Congregationalists	Methodists	Epsicopalians	Disciples of Christ	Presbyterians	American Lutherans	American Baptists	Missouri Lutherans	Southern Baptists	Sects	Total Protestants	Catholics
6 Requirements for Salvation: Faith												
"Belief in Jesus Christ as Saviour." Absolutely necessary	38	45	47	78	66	77	78	97	97	96	65	51
"Holding the Bible to be God's truth." Absolutely necessary	23	39	32	58	52	64	58	80	61	89	52	38
7 Requirements for Salvation: Works												
"Doing good for others" Absolutely necessary	58%	57%	54%	64%	48%	47%	45%	38%	29%	61%	52%	57%
"Loving thy neighbor" Absolutely necessary	59	57	60	76	55	51	52	51	41	74	58	65
"Tithing" Absolutely necessary	6	7	9	12	10	13	16	7	18	48	14	10
8 Barriers to Salvation: Improper Faith												
"Being completely ignorant of Jesus as might be the case for people living in other countries." Definitely prevent salvation	3	7	3	8	11	15	17	36	41	32	14	4
Possibly prevent salvation	13	23	16	38	24	29	31	28	39	46	25	24
"Being of the Jewish religion." Definitely prevent salvation	1	3	3	8	7	16	7	31	25	23	10	1
Possibly prevent salvation	6	9	10	18	12	16	25	23	28	33	15	11
"Being of the Hindu religion." Definitely prevent salvation	1	5	4	10	14	20	14	40	32	37	15	2
Possibly prevent salvation	12	11	12	28	15	22	25	16	27	31	17	13
9 Barriers to Salvation: Improper Acts												
"Drinking liquor." Definitely prevent salvation	2	4	2	0	2	2	9	1	15	35	8	2
"Practicing artificial birth control." Definitely prevent salvation	0	0	2	2	1	3	1	2	5	4	2	23
"Discriminating against other races." Definitely prevent salvation	27	25	27	34	22	20	17	22	16	29	25	24
"Being anti-Semitic." Definitely prevent salvation	23	23	26	30	20	15	13	22	10	26	21	20

ever, in all denominations there were many who held faith in Christ to be absolutely necessary who were also unwilling to deny that persons *outside* the Christian faith could be saved. For example, only 14 percent of the Protestants and 4 percent of the Catholics said that "being completely ignorant of Jesus, as might be the case for people living in other countries," would definitely prevent salvation. Among Protestants, the proportion varied from a mere handful of Congregationalists, Methodists, Episcopalians and Disciples of Christ to 36 percent of the Missouri Lutherans, and 41 percent of the Southern Baptists. However, an additional and sizable group of Christians were somewhat inclined to accept this view. Twenty-five percent of the Protestants and 24 percent of the Roman Catholics thought ignorance in Jesus would "possibly prevent" salvation.

Jews, of course, are not "completely ignorant" of Jesus. Can they be saved? Relatively few thought it impossible for a Jew to be saved: only 10 percent of all Protestants and 1 percent of Catholics. Again, however, there were great contrasts among Protestant groups. One percent of the Congregationalists and 3 percent of the Methodists and Episcopalians took this position, while 31 percent of the Missouri Lutherans and 25 percent of the Southern Baptists saw no hope for Jews. A sizable group thought it "possible" that a Jew could not be saved, and taken together, more than half of the members of the more fundamentalist groups at least doubted the possibility of a Jew's salvation.

In summary, a substantial minority of American Christians consider persons in non-Christian religions as beyond the hope of salvation.

IMPROPER ACTS. American Christians no longer regard drinking as a certain road to damnation (Table 9). Only 8 percent of Protestants and 2 percent of Catholics thought it was. Only among the Baptists and the followers of fundamentalist sects did more than a handful attach temperance to their scheme of salvation.

Virtually no Protestants (only 2 percent) thought the practice of artificial birth control would prevent salvation, but perhaps even more interesting and surprising, *less than a quarter of the Catholics held this view.* Whether or not Catholics approve of birth control, more than three-quarters of them are unwilling to agree it carries the supreme penalty of damnation.

The last two items in Table 9, dealing with racial discrimination, seem especially interesting, and repeat the pattern of evaluation of good works. On virtually all other "barriers to salvation," the conservative and fundamentalist bodies have been most likely to see them as absolutely necessary. However, on questions of racial discrimination and anti-Semitism, the Southern Baptists are the *least* likely of all religious groups to see them as relevant to salvation. Thus, while 27 percent of the Southern Baptists thought cursing would definitely prevent salvation, only 10 percent of them viewed anti-Semites as disqualified from entrance into God's Kingdom, and only 16 percent saw racial discrimination as a definite barrier. On the other hand, while only 13 percent of the Congregationalists thought that taking the name of the Lord in vain would definitely prevent salvation, 27 percent thought that racial discrimination and 23 percent that anti-Semitism would be barriers. Perhaps an even more suggestive contrast appears when we consider that about half of the members of all denominations thought it necessary to "love thy neighbor."

To sum up the findings on salvation: Christian denominations in America differ greatly in their beliefs about what a man must do to be saved. While most denominations give primary importance to faith, the liberal Protestant groups are inclined to favor good works. Protestants in a ritualistic tradition and Roman Catholics place greater emphasis on the sacraments and other ritual acts than do those from low-church traditions.

UNITY AND REALITY

To return to the questions posed at the beginning of this article: Is religion in modern America accurately characterized as unified? Do such concepts as "common core Protestantism," and "common American religion" bear any important resemblance to reality?

We suggest that they do not. Differences in the religious outlooks of members of the various denominations are both vast and profound. On the basis of our data it seems obvious that American religion has indeed undergone extensive changes in recent decades, but it seems equally obvious that these changes have been greatly misperceived and misinterpreted.

Has American religion become increasingly secular? As noted, many commentators claim that the mystical and supernatural elements of traditional Christianity have been replaced by a demythologized (ethical rather than theological) religion.

In light of the data, important changes of this kind have indeed occurred to *some* American denominations. We have no comparable data on the past; but compelling historic grounds exist for assuming that the typical Episcopalian or Congregationalist in the mid-19th century firmly believed such tenets as the Virgin Birth and the Biblical miracles. If true, obviously secularization has indeed taken place in these religious bodies, for only a minority of them adhere to these beliefs today. On the other hand, among the Southern Baptists and the various sects, commitment to traditional Christian theology has been virtually impervious to change. The fact that these more evangelical and traditionalist denominations have been growing at a faster rate than the mainline denominations suggests that two simultaneous and divergent trends have been taking place:

- Many people have been staying with or turning to "old-time" Christianity.
- Others have been, to some extent, changing their theological outlook away from the supernatural and miraculous toward a more naturalistic view.

These opposed trends seem to hold significant implications for the future.

THE NEW DENOMINATIONALISM

Historically, the schisms in Christianity were largely marked by subtle doctrinal distinctions, and disagreements on proper ritual or organization. All observers generally agree that these issues have lost much of their relevance and divisive potential in contemporary America. Our data confirm these judgments.

But the data also suggest that new and generally unnoticed splits have appeared in Christianity that may well hold greater potential for division than the old disputes.

Earlier disagreements were bitter; nevertheless they took place among men who usually shared belief in such basic components of Christian theology as the existence of a personal and sentient God, the Saviorhood of Christ, and the promise of life-everlasting.

But today, our data indicate, the fissures which map what might well be called the "New Denominationalism" fragment the very core of the Christian perspective. The new cleavages are not over such matters as how to properly worship God—but whether or not there is a God it makes any sense to worship; not whether the bread and wine of communion become the actual body and blood of Christ through trans-substantiation, but whether Jesus was divine at all, or merely a man. These disagreements, it must be emphasized, are not only between Christians and secular society, but exist *within* the formal boundaries of the Christian churches themselves.

How, therefore, can we account for all the hope and talk about general ecumenicalism? For those groups close together to begin with, such a possibility may well exist. At least there seem no overwhelming theological barriers to merger. But how are we to interpret exploratory talks between Roman Catholics and Episcopalians, or between Methodists and Baptists? Do the participants in the ecumenical dream simply misperceive one another's theological position, or do they consider such matters unimportant? Perhaps both of these factors are operating; but there are also signs that church leaders are becoming more aware of the doctrinal chasms that separate them.

Apparently most general ecumenical rhetoric comes from the most secularized mainline denominations. Probably the theological changes in these bodies have been accompanied by a lessening of concern for theology itself. Therefore, they may not view theological barriers as especially significant. But it is not true that the conservative groups are similarly unconcerned about doctrine. A good illustration comes from the relations between the National Council of Churches and fundamentalist bodies. Fundamentalists continually and bitterly denounce the National Council; yet it retains its composure and continues to encourage these hostile groups to become members.

Note that those bodies least amenable to the idea of ecumenicity are those which have the greatest consensus in religious belief. Among Southern Baptists and the various sects, for example, from 90 to 99 percent take similar positions on major articles of faith.

In bodies most concerned about ecumenicity, however, such as the Congregationalists and Episcopalians, members tend to be spread across a wide range of views on theology. Looking at these apparent conflicts on doctrine, the question rises: How do the liberal bodies manage to remain united? Examination of the data suggests several reasons:

- Persons in the more liberal bodies place considerably less importance on religion and on their own church participation than do members of the more conservative bodies.
- Persons in the liberal bodies who do hold traditional beliefs have many friends in the congregation, while persons with more secularized outlooks report that most of their friends are outsiders.
- The sermons preached in these denominations tend to be topical and ethical rather than doctrinal, while confessions and other rituals retain traditional form and content.

Thus it seems possible that the orthodox minority could remain unaware that the majority do not share their beliefs because the people they know in the congregation, their friends, do share these beliefs. Meanwhile, the majority, not being linked into the congregation by friendship bonds, may remain largely unaware of the fundamentalist segment of the congregation.

These factors may largely prevent potential conflicts from coming into the open. There are recent signs, however—such as the rise of theologically conservative lay groups within the more liberal denominations and the current growth of "tongues speaking" groups—that strains are developing even in these bodies because of theological differences.

One further fact ought to be mentioned. The liberal bodies that have most transformed their doctrines generate the least participation and concern among their members. By a strikingly wide margin, proportionately fewer attend worship services, join church organizations, pray privately, or believe in the importance of religion in their daily lives. Even within these more secularized denominations, those members who retain an orthodox theological outlook are consistently the more active in the life of the church. Probably, therefore, if a denomination is going to adopt new theological forms, it may have to find new organizational and ritual forms as well, or run the risk of becoming less significant in the lives of men. Mission societies, the Ladies Aid, and other traditional church activities may be inappropriate and even distasteful to those who bring an ethical rather than a theological concern to the church, and who are perhaps more interested in social betterment than world-wide conversion. Such persons may also be more attracted to sermons raising moral questions about social problems than in messages of peace of mind in Christ. In any event, the churches are presently failing to obtain much participation from members with the most modernist religious views.

THE PROTESTANT SPECTRUM

At least four and probably five generic theological camps can be clearly identified among the American denominations. The first, the *Liberals,* comprises the Congregationalists, Methodists, and Episcopalians, and is characterized by having a majority of members who reject firm belief in central tenets of Christian orthodoxy. It is likely that the changes that have gone on in these bodies, since they are among the highest status and most visible Protestant groups, have largely produced the impressions that Protestantism in general has shifted toward a secular and modernized world-view.

The second group, the *Moderates,* is composed of the Disciples of Christ and the Presbyterians. This group is less secularized than the Liberals, but more so than the *Conservatives,* who are made up of the American Lutheran group and the American Baptists. The *Fundamentalists* include the Missouri Synod Lutherans, the Southern Baptists, and the host of small sects.

Because of historic differences with Protestantism, the Roman Catholics are perhaps properly left to form a fifth distinct group by themselves. But on most theological issues, both those presented here and many more, the Roman Catholics consistently resemble the Conservatives. Only on special Protestant-Catholic issues such as Papal infallibility (accepted by 66 percent of the Roman Catholics and only 2 percent of the Protestants) were the Catholics and the Conservatives in any extensive disagreement.

Merging the denominations to form these five major groups is the greatest degree of clustering that is statistically permissible. It seems very unlikely that ecumenical clustering could result in fewer.

Finally, the data seriously challenge the common practice of contrasting Protestants and Roman Catholics. Protestant-Catholic contrasts are often large enough to be notable (and often, too, remarkably small), but they seem inconsequential compared to differences found among the Protestant groups. The overall impression of American Protestantism produced when members of all denominations are treated as a single group (the "Total Protestant" column in the tables) at best bears resemblance to only a few actual Protestant denominations. Indeed, in some instances these "average Protestants" do not closely correspond to *any actual* denomination.

When we speak of "Protestants," therefore, we tend to spin statistical fiction. It seems unjustified to consider Protestantism as a unified religious point of view in the same sense as Roman Catholicism. Not that Roman Catholicism is monolithic either—clearly there are several theological strands interwoven in the Catholic church—but at least it constitutes an actual, organized body. Protestantism, on the other hand, includes many separate groups and the only possible grounds for treating them collectively would be if they shared a common religious vision. This is clearly not the case.

This article is based on a random sample of church members in four metropolitan counties in Northern California. Key questions from the original questionnaire were repeated on a national sample, with results parallel with those presented here. This article, previously published as "The New Denominationalism," in the *Review of Religious Research*, is reprinted with permission of the Religious Research Association.

---

3 *Ivan Vallier*

Challenge to Catholicism in Latin America

Religious elites and professional holy men hold a more distinctive place in history than warriors or kings. As the guardians of spiritual values and moral authority, they may emerge as the centers of ideological ferment in periods of social crisis and transformation. Such is the situation in Latin America today.

Latin American religious elites are composed of the varying complexes of leadership within the Roman Catholic church. This leadership is not confined simply to those occupying the top statuses in the religious system; a person belongs in the religious elite if, as an individual or group member, he is able to exert a decisive influence on the development of the Catholic system or the wider social order. This influence may be tradition-oriented, innovative, or simply neutralizing.

Elitism in Latin America must be viewed within its historical context, within the institutional framework which gives it social meaning. In the case of Latin American Catholicism this framework is the church in relation to its history and thus to its evolving connections with the social structure. It sets the context for developments within the church, and for the developing impact of the church on the social situation. To know what the Roman Catholic church is today in Latin America and what internal and external lines of change it is taking, it is necessary to know what it *was*—where it stood in the traditional social order. Four major patterns of the traditional church emerge.

FORMAL VS. FOLK RELIGION. During the seventeenth century a deep cleavage began to develop between the formal church and the "Catholic" religion. Because of a shortage of clergy, the hierarchy's fusion with the ruling classes, and the missionaries' "in-name-only" conception of Christian conversion, a major part of the religious needs of the masses came to be satisfied through extrasacramental practices, private devotions, worship of patron saints, and participation in festive religious-social activities. This gap between ecclesia and religious needs became institutionalized. Although the church as a formal body was to be found in the cathedrals and chapels, Catholicism became grounded in nonecclesiastical social units—in the family, in brotherhoods, in the community, and in the informal contacts of the everyday world. The priest and his sacramental authority tended to be peripheral to man's quest for salvation.

ORGANIZATIONAL WEAKNESS. The Latin American church, as an administrative and policy-making organization, emerged as a series of isolated ecclesiastical units, each one focused almost exclusively on its immediate situation. The traditional system can be characterized as decentralized, extremely uncoordinated in its regional and diocesan activities, and structurally awkward; lines of communication and authority were weak and confused. Since routine administration and ad hoc problem-solving outweighed planning and programming, the church's activities were not oriented to a set of central and shared religious goals or autonomous, long-range policies. Because the church was hierarchically undeveloped, internally divided, and relatively incapable of using its canonical structure as an effective system of command and action, its elite groups were not able to take a clear and unified position as *religious* leaders.

SECULAR CONTROL. Traditional Catholic elites have been subjected to secular control over most of the past 450 years. The Spanish crown exercised close control over the church in the New World, and as a result the hierarchy had to work through secular elites in order to survive and initiate religious activities of every sort. In this situation the clergy's energies were consumed in short-run political maneuvering and in creating viable coalitions with other power groups. Religious elites were prepared to maximize their position when secular conditions were favorable, to exercise restraint in periods of uncertainty, and to be inconsistent if the situation demanded it.

MORAL CONFUSION. Because they lacked a unified vision of the church's mission and were subjected to inconstant secular domination, Catholic elites failed to create and institutionalize a religious and moral foundation for the growth of a common system of societal values. Their potential capacity to symbolize and require conformity to a higher moral order was never realized. Instead of functioning as creators of a religiously based value system and as impartial leaders in the moral realm, the Catholic elites actually fomented moral confusion. Consequently an enduring association between secular political strength and moral legitimacy was established, and politics became an arena in which a "religious" battle over ends, rather than a competition over who is best qualified to lead, took place. There is little doubt that this early link between secular power and moral authority has helped to create the political turmoil characteristic of contemporary Latin America.

Thus, the church's achievement of influence and social control did not depend on its capacities as a Christian religious system. In the main, the church and its leaders drew their importance from alliances with secular powers and from their multiple involvements in education, social welfare, and administration. The scope of the church's functions was very wide, but each function was dependent on the maintenance of the status quo. For this reason, the church continued to align itself with the conservative factions of Latin American society as a major survival strategy until the beginning of the twentieth century.

During the twentieth century, the traditional church in one Latin American country after another has discovered that its capacity for influence has been severely weakened, not only by the nineteenth century anticlerical legislation, but also by a series of subtle sociological trends: the growth of an urban social class, internal population shifts, the strengthening of technical and scientific centers in secular universities, and the emergence of many competing interest groups. These trends have tended to weaken or obscure traditional lines of influence and sources of status. In addition to these broad patterns of change, specific trends on the local, national, and international levels have rendered traditional Catholicism's position of influence especially tenuous.

Local: New Value Movements

Until the turn of the century Catholicism held a dual monopoly as the official national religion of many Latin American republics and as the universal religious culture. But the rise of secular political movements of the left and of salvation-oriented Protestant sects has broken this monopoly. Both movements offer a new reward system, assume a militant posture against the existing social order, and articulate a cohesive set of anti-Catholic values. By competing with Catholicism at the value level they have forced it to assume the guise of an ideology for conservative groups rather than a major cultural system. In addition, the new movements provide their adherents with a program of social action to be carried out in lay organizations which combine enthusiasm with group responsibility at the grass-roots level. Even the novice layman has a definite status, a meaningful set of responsibilities to be carried out.

The traditional Catholic system is ill equipped to counter such militant sects. For more than four centuries it has made no attempt to utilize the layman as a religious system resource or even to integrate him meaningfully into the system. Since the entire Catholic system was entwined with the institutions of the total society, there was no real *need* to utilize the layman as an instrument of religious influence. Why organize the grass roots to "win the neighbor"? All the neighbors were baptized Catholics, as were the people of the next village, *patrones* and slaves, peasants and military officers. Moreover, the hierarchical divisions within the church and within the laity provided no basis for integration, whereas the Communists and Socialists, as well as the Pentecostal sects, stress horizontal solidarity and communality, both ideologically and structurally. Such slogans as "From each according to his ability; to each according to his needs," and "We are all brothers in Christ: no priests, no servants, no rich, no poor," provide a feeling of solidarity which is closely related to existing kinship and community ties and with which Catholicism cannot compete, even on religious grounds.

National: Institutional Integration

There is a characteristic tendency for a modern, nationally focused society to move and adapt as a total system. As the Latin American countries develop economically and politically, the growth of institutional interdependence brings all specialized functional units together into a more integrated whole such that the *primary* integrative level is found at the level of the total society. National, rather than regional or local, events and institutions dominate the rhythm of social life. This means that special interests, including influence-oriented religious groups, require clear-cut national strategies and forceful national organizations if they are to make an impact on society. An ambitious religious system must fulfill several organizational tasks: Religious impact must be developed to cope with the total society's trends, rhythms, and problems; religious action must depend on generated, rather than "gathered," loyalty and must be consciously planned and coordinated; and religious programs must have both a long-term goal and a short-range adaptability to specialized local circumstances.

Traditional Catholicism is not integrated at the national level and therefore not prepared to cope with the new rhythm of social life. It is given to localized, ad hoc problem-solving, situational alliances, and a short-run goal perspective. It is thus extremely handicapped in the face of national institutional integration.

International: Pressures from Other Catholics

The Latin American church is under heavy pressure from various hierarchies of international Catholicism to resolve its problems and "put its house in order." Both the Holy See and various national episcopal conferences in France, Belgium, Germany, Canada, and the United States are concerned over the Latin American church, for it not only encompasses more than one-third of the church's total baptized membership, but also appears to be impotent in the face of Communist expansion among the masses. Moreover, the Second Vatican Council dealt quite plainly with issues, policies, and innovations bearing directly on the problems of traditional Latin American Catholicism, and the Latin American church is thus considered a key "test site" for the conciliar reforms and for the future of Catholicism in general.

Under the foregoing pressures to maintain and regain an influential position in a changing society, Catholic leaders in Latin America are desperately seeking new mechanisms to strengthen the church's spiritual life and provide it with new bases of influence in the wider institutional order. Although there are still major internal divisions and much disagreement over goals, certain patterns are emerging with respect to the church's internal organization and to its links with society.

Transforming the Church as a System

Considerable energy and leadership in the Latin American church are being diverted to the task of making the church relevant and effective in the modern situation. The most noticeable change which has occurred is centralization, the establishment of tighter lines of authority and communication within the hierarchies, and the enlargement of the de facto powers of national and continental episcopal councils. The traditional isolation and autonomy of bishops and local clergy has been reduced in favor of coordinated activities and policies oriented toward the church as a whole.

Another theme of elite activity is the creation of a socially relevant Catholic ideology, drawn largely from the social encyclicals and new theologies which have been produced in the church over the last 75 years. Leo XIII's *Rerum Novarum* (1891), Pius XI's *Quadragesimo Anno* (1931), and John XXIII's *Mater et Magistra* (1961) are frequently quoted documents, and the names of Maritain, Congar, Rahner, Teilhard de Chardin, Kung, Suenens, and de Lubac—all Europeans—are frequently heard in the socially progressive sectors of the church. Perhaps the greatest source of ideological support for the agents of change within the church has been the ideas and proposals produced by Vatican II, which have given the liberal sectors of Catholicism so much popular reinforcement that those who earlier hesitated to act are gaining new confidence. In Latin America the Catholic liberals have fashioned a powerful and appealing ideology calling for social justice for the deprived, fundamental institutional reforms, social action in the world as the key means of Christian influence, and a concern for man and the human community.

To realize this ideology and to meet the pressing demands of the modern situation, Catholic leaders are attempting to mobilize a new lay missionary force or lay apostolate. Laymen are organized into priest-led cells or associations, in which they are educated and persuaded to infuse their daily relationships with Christian principles. Thus the usually passive layman is to promote Catholicism in his routine activities as worker, friend, club member, or family member in order to re-Christianize the dormant masses, and regain a prominent place in society for the church.

Forming New Church-Society Linkages

Clusters of elite activity have also differentiated around the political and cultural priorities of the church—that is, its strategy of survival and its role in social change. Four types of elite development can be identified. The first is the traditional base from which the others have differentiated, and three are "new" types.

■ Traditional Catholic elites in Latin America are oriented to the power structure of secular society. Because they feel that the church's interlocking connections with the polity and its manipulation of secular power groups are essential to its survival, these traditional elite members may be called the *politicians.* They look to secular groups for support, protection, and legitimation, and they see the church as a structure of formal, hierarchical positions from which they receive status which is useful in the wider community. They ignore the laity, carry out rituals pro forma, make the sacraments available to those who can pay the fee, and define social evils as implicit in the human situation. Secure in their positions, the traditional elites strongly resist and even satirize the innovations of Vatican II bearing on changes in the liturgy and lay involvement.

■ Of the three new elites, the *papists* (not meant with any opprobrium) stand for a militant, modern Catholicism oriented toward re-Christianizing the world. They reject traditional sources of political involvement in favor of creating a church which relies on its own authority and resources to achieve visibility and influence. These resources are seen as the church structure, social action, and the sacraments. The hierarchy, the clergy, and the laity constitute a missionary elite concerned with expanding the frontiers of Catholic values under the aegis of a hierarchy which extends beyond the local or national level to Rome. Religious action is defined according to traditional Catholic premises on the nature of the church, the validity of its dogmas, and its monopoly of religious charisma.

This militant, apostolic conception of modern Catholicism's relation to society is drawn from developments in the European situation over the past two generations. The most decisive expression of the new mission emerged during the pontificate of Pius XI, and was adopted, with some modifications, during the mid-1930's in areas of the Latin American church, where it was expressed in terms of youth programs, apostolic units, and episcopally directed strategies. Although actual successes have been minimal, often because they provoked latent anticlericalism, the papists remain a major elite cluster in Latin America, especially in Colombia, Argentina, and Mexico.

■ The *pastors* are a small but growing group of bishops and clergy who see their main task as that of building up strong, worship-centered congregations. They seek a formula for effectively welding the priest, the laity, and the sacraments into a single spiritual body. Among the changes the pastors propose are: elaboration of the priest's role from that of isolated ritual leader to include preaching, counseling, and mingling with the laity; involvement of the laity in the liturgy; alteration of parish boundaries to create smaller, more homogeneous congregations; and design of church buildings that reduces the physical distance between priest and worshippers. The vocabulary of the pastors is studded with such terms as cooperation, community, communication, pastoral care, and the meaning of the sacraments—clear indicators of their concern over the quality of religious life.

■ The third new elite group, the *pluralists,* are a rather mixed group whose central premise is that Catholicism in Latin America is but one faith among many others, both secular and religious, and that the church therefore ought to assist in the institutionalization of social justice whereever possible. They are more concerned with grass-roots action than with political alliances, hierarchy and clericalism, or worship and the sacraments; the essential religious task is that of furthering economic development and social integration.

The pluralists pay special attention to the problems of the poor and the exploited, and they are not averse to cooperative undertakings with other faiths in order to benefit the disadvantaged. Their planning is long-range and societal in scope, since they feel that the church must, as a differentiated agency of moral and social influence, play a positive role in the social revolution occurring in Latin America. And they tend to be highly critical of the other elite groups' methods and orientations as inadequate and misguided. They refer to the conforming, clerical Catholic Action elite as "sacristans" or "goon squads." They talk with bitterness about the traditional "politicos" and their maneuverings. The pastors' exclusive concern with the church's inner life is criticized as "escapism," "retreatism," and "withdrawal."

The foregoing elite groups do not exhaust the kinds of religious elite differentiation to be found in contemporary Latin American Catholicism, but they differ along two major analytical dimensions: the sphere from which they feel the church should gain its influence—either from its internal resources (organization and ritual) or from its external involvement with secular groups and events—and the organizing principle which they feel should structure religious-social relationships. These dimensions can be utilized to construct the following typology:

		Structural principle of Catholic activity	
		HIERARCHICAL	COOPERATIVE
Sphere from which church influence is to be drawn	EXTERNAL	Politicians	Pluralists
	INTERNAL	Papists	Pastors

Two patterns are clear with respect to the conditions of the "new" elites' emergence. First, the strength of the politicians in the national hierarchy is directly related to the number of remaining church-state links; where these ties are numerous, the politicians' survival strategies are viable, and they in turn tend to limit the growth of the papists and the pastors. But pluralist counterelites develop as a reaction against the political posture and conservatism of the politicians. Although the papists and the pastors cannot undertake the upgrading or restructuring of church organization and life because the church is neither autonomous nor, at this point, in need of it, the pluralists are able to counter the politicians in the sphere of secular action and thereby flourish.

On the other hand, the papists appear to play a key facilitating role in the development of the other two new elites, pastors and pluralists. With their emphasis on political detachment, improving church organization, involving laymen, and on defining an articulated set of theological conceptions of "mission in society," the papists form a bridge between the traditional politicians and the new pastors and pluralists. Institutional change in Roman Catholicism requires the imprimatur of the hierarchy, and the papists provide for a structural reorganization which makes the granting of this imprimatur to the efforts of the pluralists and pastors much more likely. Once the church has undergone a series of structural and ideological changes, including a "liberalization" of the hierarchy, the pluralist and pastoral strategies become a fully integrated part of a total mission and thus may add strength to the church and aid in the positive development of society.

It may be possible for the pastors and pluralists to form a working alliance if they can manage to utilize the organizational capacities of the papists without having to accept their parallel emphases on authoritarianism, monopolism, and ultramontanism. Unless the two more radical groups recognize the importance of centralized coordination and integration, they run the risk of dispersion and thus defeat. They actually have a long-range advantage in that there are certain well-developed trends in Latin America toward sociological pluralism and increased religious competition, factors which will require the church to forego some of its rigidity and emphasis on ritual and organizational uniformity in favor of the changes proposed by the pastors and pluralists if it is to retain its influence. The institutional dilemma, of course, is how to achieve the advantages of "denominationalism"—internal religious, ritual, and ideological differentiation—without falling into the pattern of fragmentation which characterizes the Protestant tradition.

We hear a great deal in the church today about *aggiornamento* or "bringing the church up to date." From these phrases and the ideas that accompany them, the observer tends to see the whole dynamic of the church's development in terms of the struggle between the "conservatives" and the "liberals." But within the present typological distinctions, it is possible to clarify the crucial distinction between "bringing the church up to date" or "renewal" and "reform" of the Catholic system. Many Catholic leaders and laymen champion Pope John XXIII as the most advanced spokesman of the "liberal" camp. But this is a mistake. His major emphasis was on renewal—on raising the internal effectiveness of the church's structure and adjusting traditional ideas to the modern times. He was not bent on making deep structural changes in the church—such as those taken seriously by the pastors and the pluralists. To renew is not to reform. Consequently, one of the most critical tasks of the new Catholic elites is how to secure basic structural changes that bear decisively on the special religious problems and social issues in Latin America. The "happy days" of John XXIII created a phase of risky optimism that has already suffered some deep shocks.

Sequence of Development

The strength of the four elites varies from country to country. Colombia, Argentina, and Peru are strongholds of the politicians, and, as expected, there are also pluralist religious groups in these countries. The papists are also strong in Argentina and Colombia, as well as in Mexico. Brazil, Venezuela, and Chile, on the other hand, are the main centers of pastor-pluralist developments, and strong pastoral emphases are to be found in certain regions of Bolivia and Guatemala.

The broad comparative picture suggests two generalizations. First, elite developments in Chilean and Brazilian Catholicism appear to be on the threshold of a new phase, having partially broken the political tradition and, in turn, moved through a modified papist period. Thus, in these countries, as in certain Venezuelan and Argentinian dioceses, an institutional basis for effective pastoral and pluralist developments exists to a limited degree. Second, the pastoral and pluralist elites gain in importance as Christian Democratic parties emerge within the national political system. These Catholic-oriented political movements serve to absorb political-type strategies within the church, thus allowing pluralists and pastors to concentrate on religious values and religious action. Moreover, they provide an institutionalized means for the papists to link political action with Catholic values without formally involving the church in politics.

Within the total context of Latin American development, each of the new elites plays a different role in what can be seen as a three-stage sequence. In the first stage, the problem of development is to create frameworks of meaning that legitimate change, especially for status groups with a vested interest in the status quo. A broad ideology which links traditional symbols of authority and meaning to the idea of change and thus fuses the past with the future in the context of familiar cultural elements is required not only to win the support of vested interests but also to motivate and activate those middle class groups which may already be predisposed to change.

The second-stage development problem involves the translation of ideological commitments to change into social arrangements that bring together hitherto uncoordinated scarce resources, that promote cooperation and compromise, and that mobilize the population to undertake common developmental tasks. This is the stage at which many Latin American sequences falter: Key sectors of a society may be committed to change, modernization, and even revolution, but they find it impossible, even when they have political power, to get the system moving—to work committed energies and capacities into a steady, disciplined pattern of growth. The mechanisms of mobilization—pooling resources, delegating authority, and "trusting the system"—are extremely weak and in some instances almost nonexistent.

The third stage of Latin American development is full-fledged modernization, a phase in which the mobilization mechanisms have been institutionalized, and change, both social and ideological, is accepted by all major groups in society. In this third stage old forms of solidarity and integration have been shattered, and people are "on the move" in both physical and social space. The developmental problem is to establish a new level of social integration, both vertical and horizontal, that is congruent with the demands of modernization. Thus a sequence of societal development poses three major imperatives:

—shifting the locus of meaning from tradition to change;
—transforming societal acceptance of the desirability of change into actual mobilization patterns;
—developing new modes of integration to replace traditional bonds and sustain full modernization.

Though these developmental requisites are of a different order from the ones normally considered imperative for modernization—capital, industry, or the universal franchise—they call attention to the deeper social transformations that development requires.

If the foregoing model of Latin American development is accepted, the distinctive contributions of the new religious elites can be identified at each stage. The papists perform at least two critical functions during the first stage of change. First, they link traditional Catholic values with the concept of social change, thereby utilizing papal authority as expressed in the social encyclicals to legitimate the idea of change. Second, they emphasize the principle that the church does not intend to impose its conceptions of the good society on others by political means. Rather it intends to promulgate the Catholic social ideology through a lay apostolate which will link church and society and carry the new values.

The papists' contributions are particularly relevant at the first stage because it is at this point that the church is under heavy attack for its political involvements and resistance to change. By giving Catholic legitimation to social change the papists help to overcome conservative reactions. Moreover, their efforts to strengthen the internal spiritual resources of the church within a traditional hierarchical framework ready the Catholic system for the competitions to be met in a modern pluralistic society.

In their attempts to bring about social justice and to aid other reforming groups, the pluralists assist in the mobilization required for the second stage of development. To be effective, their approach depends upon the incorporation of some of the emphases of the papists: lay responsibility in the world, an ideology linking Catholic values with social change, and the noninvolvement of the church in political affairs. Within this context, the pluralists cooperate with non-Catholic groups in economic, technical, and welfare projects characterized by a maximum of lay responsibility and a minimum of church presence. These cooperative efforts, though decidedly modest in scale, hold an enormous potential for mobilizing disparate groups to undertake the tasks of social development.

With the lack of strong support for interpersonal cooperation, the vulnerability of social consensus when attained, and the absence of functional integration between levels of social structure, the pluralists' efforts to bridge traditional social and functional cleavages under the aegis of an ideology which can draw upon wide consensus of a religious nature are especially valuable for mobilization purposes. They serve not only as actual centers of mobilization efforts but also to demonstrate symbolically that much social good can come out of intergroup cooperation.

The contributions of the pastors to long-range social development are more indirect than those of the papists and pluralists, but they are equally important. When the society has begun to move into the third stage of full modernization, old patterns of identity, association, and integration have been broken and new modes of integration are urgently needed to prevent social and personal disorganization. In their efforts to strengthen the internal spiritual life of the church at the grass-roots level by transforming the parish church into a source of identity and basis of social integration for the individual, the pastors function as creators of small religious and social systems on the local level which answer some of the problems stemming from mobility and social isolation. The local church provides a stable source of social identity, religious expression, and cultural anchorage, as well as mediating between the individual and society. Because the church is omnipresent in an otherwise constantly changing society, these pastoral trends provide for the critical modicum of integration needed at the grass-roots level to overcome individual and communal disorientations which might otherwise erupt in social conflict.

An overall picture of the role of the three new elites can be obtained by linking the model of Latin American development, the levels of the sociocultural system, and the activities required at each point in time. (See below.)

A Missed Link in Colombia

Examples of the actual operation of this model can be seen in Colombia, Argentina, and Chile. Despite its recent land reforms, its coalition government, and its internationally oriented economy, Colombia is generally considered an extremely traditional country. Roman Catholicism is the official religion, and the church controls most of the country's educational system. The clergy walk the streets with a casualness that can only come from a secure position in society. Colombia is not only a clerical country, it is also a country that is not yet fully committed to the necessity for social change. Many power groups not only resist the idea of change but manage to obstruct even minor social reforms.

The most visible new elites in the Colombian church are the pluralists: There is a solid core of pluralists engaged in activities bearing directly on the solution of social problems, but there is also a growing, volatile group of pluralists who want to make a direct frontal attack on changing the social order, through revolution if necessary. This latter group has become highly visible recently, especially through the activities of a recently killed priest who had renounced his priesthood, openly criticized the Cardinal, joined the mountain guerillas, and published a manifesto for social revolution. Like many of the other radical pluralists, he claimed that true Christianity was not possible under Colombia's present social and political conditions.

These radical pluralists appear to be a concrete manifestation of a "missed stage" in the evolution of the church. Because the crucial contribution of the papists has not been made, the new elites are turning directly to secular change without the support of a Catholic social ideology

ROLE OF NEW ELITES—CHRONOLOGICAL DEVELOPMENT

		Legitimating Change	Mobilizing Resources	Reintegrating Society
Levels of the Sociocultural System	Culture	PAPISTS		
	Intergroup		PLURALISTS	
	Person-Group			PASTORS

which legitimates development and modernization. This is a tragic situation for both the church and Colombian society. For the traditional hierarchy to legitimate the more radical pluralist strategies at this time would be too destructive of their own authority; at the same time, the conservative secular groups are not prepared to confront the problems pointed up and attacked by the pluralist priests and laity. If both of these tradition-oriented sectors had been prepared for these developments by contact with a modern Catholic ideology, the pluralists might have won their support in building an effective social action movement. Theoretically, if the more radical pluralists were to retrench and concentrate their energies on the development of such an ideology, the stabilization and reintegration of the church could be accomplished and the context set for the pluralists to move out into direct social action again.

Transition in Argentina

Argentina faces a different set of developmental problems. Urbanization and technology, bursts of vigorous economic growth, and a commitment to change by major societal groups are basic features of the society; much of the groundwork for complete modernization already exists. However, the pattern of development is not steady because there are only weak bases for long-range mobilization. Factionalism, nonproductive competition, and distrust deplete energies and resources. During the Peronist era, skilled workers achieved levels of economic gratification that were unrealistic in the economic long run, and these groups are now unwilling to relinquish their gains for the national good. Intergroup tensions are especially strong in the metropolitan area of Buenos Aires, where both Protestants and Jews constitute sizable minority groups. In short, Argentina's central developmental problem is that of mobilization, drawing the already present commitments to change into a working framework of cooperative effort. The resources are available, but they remain uncombined and unaligned at strategic institutional junctures.

In this period of transition, the Argentinian church is a curious mixture of the traditional and the progressive. The leadership tends to be traditional without being reactionary, perhaps because all hierarchical vacancies must be filled with the approval of the government. Many of the top positions are filled by the sons and grandsons of Italian immigrants, a circumstance which has produced a combination of Italian Catholic orientations and a nationally focused church, ultramontanism mixed with particularism. The social encyclicals are quite influential at the lower levels of the church, and Catholic Action groups are relatively strong, especially among students and some of the middle-class groups. Thus, the church actually stands midway between papist and pluralist elite developments. Catholicism and the idea of change have been fused at numerous points throughout the system, but very little in the way of action-oriented cooperation has been undertaken. Part of the pluralist deficiency is due to divisions within the hierarchy and factionalism among lay groups. There is no doubt but that a greater participation in intergroup and interfaith action projects, such as the pioneering ventures in the Buenos Aires area, by church elites would have a major symbolic effect on breaking other forms of deadlock. The new Catholic elites of the pluralist type thus appear to be the key to reinforcing the society's mobilization process.

Modernization in Chile

The Chilean situation is quite different in that Chile appears to be approaching full modernization. The country has experienced chronic economic problems, exasperating political battles, and an internal migration which has created severe problems of urbanization without full industrialization. Yet political development over the past 50 years has been quite steady, and social welfare programs have been institutionalized on a nationwide basis. A major land reform program is currently in the first stages of implementation, as are recent agreements to nationalize foreign-owned mining operations. In short, Chile seems to be "on the way."

The Chilean church is often and appropriately called "the most progressive Catholic system in Latin America." The key positions in the hierarchy are occupied by liberals, and the church has developed and legitimated a powerful social ideology for a "Christian revolution." In Chilean Catholicism, as in the society at large, the idea of social change is fully institutionalized in a variety of programs: technical training for the *campesinos* (peasants), distribution of church lands to underprivileged groups, and credit and production cooperatives in some of the *callampas* (urban slums). In these pluralist activities, the church has developed strong linkages with private and governmental units, but the church itself is not involved in politics. Catholic loyalties are channeled through the recently victorious Christian-Democratic party for political purposes. In short, the Chilean Catholic elites have shown a rare ability to legitimate social change in terms of symbols that bridge past and present and to develop and support cooperative undertakings for the social good.

However, it would be a mistake to conclude that continued development is assured. There is a distinct possibility that the new elites may become so enamored of their success that they will succumb to the temptation of moving directly into politics, a development which might prove disastrous for both the church and the country. On the other hand, while it has a strong, liberalized hierarchy, the Chilean church does not have deep religious anchorages among the people; the local church is not a central focus of spiritual or social activity, and the Protestant Pentecostal groups have made solid inroads into traditionally Catholic populations. The most positive line of development for the Chilean church would thus be to encourage the pastoral elites in their strategies in order to reinforce Catholic loyalties and build up the local church as a new basis of religious and social solidarity.

The three cases of Colombia, Argentina, and Chile suggest that Catholic developments are not merely correlative with societal developments, but actually play a causal role: Both Colombia and Argentina are being held back by the hesitancy and underdevelopment of the Catholic system, while Chile progresses on the basis of a change-oriented Catholic outlook.

These optimistic appraisals of the developmental potential of the new Catholic elites for Latin America imply three things. First, religious elites may play a role in the process of total societal change, particularly at the strategic levels of symbolizing intergroup solidarity, legitimating institutional reforms, and drawing marginal peoples into values and relationships that form the basis of a modern society. Ever since the enunciation of the Weber thesis, centering on the indirect consequences of religiously based motives for economic development, sociologists have been energetically searching other religions to see if parallels to the Protestant ethic are present. Hinduism, Buddhism, and Islam have all been brought under scrutiny. If evidence for something like the Protestant ethic is not found, the whole topic of religion's relevance to institutional change is dropped. Roman Catholicism, with its sacramentalism, its hierarchical system of authority, and its corporatist conceptions of society is, of course, automatically taken to be the complete antithesis to social change. But the Weber thesis has perhaps blinded us to the important theoretical point that religions may have various positive consequences in spheres of life other than the economic and through mechanisms other than the unconscious strivings of believers to transform the world in order to build the Kingdom of God.

The All-Encompassing Church

In giving a major role to the social effects of the Catholic religious factor, it must be remembered that the importance of Catholicism is not adequately indexed by measures of church attendance or the people's conformity to the church's official moral rules. It derives more from the fact that politics, production, and personal meanings are all indirectly imbued with Catholicism and its redemptive weltanschauung. In the midst of misery, confusion, strife, and disillusionment, Latin Americans seek a convincing plan of redemption and membership in some beautiful crusade.

This Catholic culture and its corresponding Catholic psychology must also be joined by the fact that the church as an organization has some impressive sociological features: It is the only formal organization that spans the four and a half centuries of Spanish-American history and that transcends national boundaries. While there are individual national churches, it still remains true that the Latin American church is an entity in and of itself. It possesses a distinct identity in relation to other sectors of the international Catholic church and has formal solidarity and integration in the form of such structures as the Latin American Bishops' Council, the Latin-American Religious Confederation, and the International Federation of Institutions for Socio-Religious and Social Research. These formal structures are augmented by a multitude of durable informal relationships which have developed around common interests, from temporary alliances, and as a number of confidence structures. Finally, the church is the only organization in any given country which maintains close contact with both the people and the rulers. Not only does its vertical span encompass the whole range of the social scale, but its horizontal, or functional, span takes in a wide range of ritual, educational, and social associations. In short, the church is not only historically comprehensive and internationally continuous, but it is also vertically and functionally organized to encompass or touch most of the aspects of social and societal life.

There is no intention here to build the church up into some sort of complete or unique system; the argument here is that any approach to Latin America must consider Catholicism and that any consideration of Catholicism in Latin America must deal with the church as a social system of major historical and contemporary importance. Catholic elites play central roles in the process of total societal change, particularly in symbolizing intergroup solidarity, legitimating institutional reforms, and drawing marginal groups into the relationships that form the basis of an integrated modern society.

It must be noted that the capacity of the new Catholic elites to assist in development depends on their ability to generate "spiritual" authority in the secular realm without falling into a political strategy; once the religious nature of the elites is compromised by political involvements, they lose the motivating and sanctioning halo of the "spiritual" realm and become as other interest groups.

Latin American development also depends on the continuation of the breach between the new Catholicism and the traditional order. Unless secular reformers are willing to link their forms of production, their political objectives, and their goals of social revolution with progressive Catholic elites' efforts, Latin America will continue to manifest regressive swings, political setbacks, and familiar patterns of disturbance and resistance. One cannot expect new conceptions of authority, attitudes toward performance, and norms of trust and cooperation to pervade the social order unless they are anchored in the new Catholic efforts under way. In effect, this new Catholicism is the point of leverage between Latin America's past and its future, and the new Catholic elites may prove to be the most important "transition" groups in twentieth-century Latin America.

4 *Peter Dreier & Jack Nusan Porter*

Jewish Radicalism in Transition

Bob Dylan is rumored to be studying with a Hassidic rabbi, has visited Israel several times, and given money to the Jewish Defense League. Rennie Davis, who once organized antiwar demonstrations, has become a disciple of the 15-year-old Indian perfect master Guru Maharaj-ji, and now organizes mass rallies in his name. Old SDS leaders from Berkeley to Harvard follow Meher Baba, practice Transcendental Meditation, maintain organic food diets, share personal troubles in encounter groups, and get high on Jesus. What does it all mean? What does it tell us about American youth culture at mid-decade?

Radical politics seems to be theologizing. Both the scale and direction of American youth culture have shifted significantly in the first half of the 1970s. With the disintegration of the New Left and Black Power, a variety of new movements has emerged to fill the void. Former radicals now seek peace, personal fulfillment, and a sense of community through religious (and quasi-religious) teachings and fellowships. The form, as well as the substance, of American youth culture is in transition. Today, among a broad spectrum of youth, there is a turn to the mystical, the millennial, and the messianic.

In a recent interview, theologian Harvey Cox suggested that the New Left in the United States was never as anticlerical as its European counterpart. Religious people, including religious professionals such as Martin Luther King, William Sloan Coffin, and Daniel Berrigan, were welcome participants in New Left events. The New Left in America was suspicious of ideology and emphasized spontaneity rather than rigidity.

It is not surprising that, partly out of the fabric of New Left politics, youth movements have emerged that emphasize the personal over the political. It is not accurate to say that one caused the other, for many (if not most) of today's religious youth are not the same New Leftists of the 1960s; they represent a later generation who were in junior high school during the Kent State massacre of 1970. Likewise, many of the earlier New Leftists have maintained their political commitments to social change as white-collar occupations face the specter of young insurgents.

Secular and religious elements have always been a part of Judaism and ethnic Jewish culture. So perhaps it is not strange that amidst all the raging euphoria and desperate search, a new force emerged at the end of the sixties among young Jews that attempted to fuse radical politics and religious culture—the Jewish liberation movement. And in its tensions between particularism and universalism, privatism and social concern, it reflects much of the mood of the post-New Left era.

In 1961, a year before the beginnings of SDS at Port Huron, David Boroff, in an essay on Jewish youth culture, saw a growing assimilation into American mass society and a parallel end to the radical politics of the previous generation. The second (parents') generation of American Jewry, he wrote, "was characterized by a restless groping for meaning and identity . . . [but] as the doors of American society swing open hospitably to talented Jews, the impulse to castigate and criticize becomes attenuated." Indeed, Boroff lamented that "as Jews increasingly become part of the 'Establishment,' [they] will merely see themselves as apprentices rather than critics."

The participation of young Jews in the New Left was widespread. It was the Jewish Establishment's worst-kept secret. The visibility of Mark Rudd, Abbie Hoffman, Jerry Rubin, among others, underscored the Jews' overrepresentation among the leadership and activists of the student movement.

As the New Left began to wane, and in the aftermath of the Israeli-Arab Six Day War in 1967, an upsurge of Jewish consciousness hit the campuses. A new voice—Jewish liberation—appeared. Young Jews began to make demands for Jewish studies programs, to publish Jewish underground newspapers, to protest on behalf of Soviet Jewry, to defend Israel's right to exist against New Left attacks while criticizing the policies of the Israeli government, and to confront the complex of national and local organizations labeled the Jewish Establishment.

Underlying these public actions was a private turmoil, a concern for identity and roots in an increasingly rootless America—questions of power, on the one hand, and alienation, on the other. Now, more than six years since its beginnings, the Jewish youth movement has taken on a less political, and more religious, complexion.

Roots of Jewish Radicalism

The grandparents of today's young Jews brought with them from Eastern Europe, between 1881 and 1914, a variety of radicalisms. In America they organized two mass movements of Jewish labor and Jewish socialism. In the midst of the formative period of the American labor movement, the Jews found work in the sweatshops of the needle trades in New York's Lower East Side and other urban ghettos. Most often their employers were German Jews of an earlier wave of immigration. At the time, the AFL-led labor movement was extremely nativistic and opposed to organizing the unskilled immigrants. When the unskilled Jews did organize, as Louis Ruchames points out in his historical essay on American Jewish radicalism, in *The Ghetto and Beyond,* they did so as Jews.

In 1907 the United Hebrew Trades comprised 74 affiliated unions and 50,000 members. By 1914 the numbers had soared to 104 and 250,000, respectively. The Jewish unions were the backbone of the Socialist party, which had its own Yiddish-speaking wing. The radical Yiddish press—anarchist, Communist, and Socialist, religious and secular, Zionist and anti-Zionist—was widely read and influential. The radicalism of Yiddish-language playwrights, poets, and novelists dramatized the plight of the Jewish masses. The largest and longest-lasting Yiddish paper, Abraham Cahan's *Jewish Daily Forward*, reached a circulation of over 200,000 in 1916.

In the 1930s Jews were active in the Depression-era radicalism. Nathan Glazer notes that perhaps one-third of the American Communist party membership was Jewish and the number of Jewish fellow travelers was even greater. Hal Draper recalled that support for the 1934 Student Strike for Peace was strongest in the three city colleges with highest Jewish enrollments — C.C.N.Y., Hunter College, and Brooklyn College.

A mixed bag of radical activity is found among the grandparents and the parents of today's Jewish students. Unlike the Jewish New Leftists of the 1960s, they were acutely aware of their Jewishness. Although they were divided over issues of Zionism, religion, and assimilation, they were united on issues of anti-Semitism, discrimination against Jews in college and employment, and encroaching fascism in Europe. They were, for better or worse, part of a Jewish milieu—outsiders looking in.

After World War II, the Hitler-Stalin pact caused the desertion of many Jews from the Communist ranks. Disenchanted with Stalinism, upwardly mobile into the free professions, small business, and welfare state bureaucracies such as teaching and social work, the Old Left dissolved. In time, it would spawn a different breed of radical—the New Left.

The great success of this second generation of Jews meant, for the current generation, a ceiling on social mobility. Most of today's young Jews could transcend the struggle for individual secular success, go beyond their parents' liberalism and materialism, and seek social justice (radicalism) and spiritual identity (religion and communalism).

Changes in the social structure of the Jewish community brought about shifts in the patterns of organized Jewish life. Upward mobility and suburbanization meant a shift from an associational to an affiliational locus. Jewish life became more bureaucratic. Ritual observance declined and only those rituals that did not interfere with middle-class culture were maintained. Thus, in many homes, Hannukah became the Jewish Christmas and anxious parents decorated Hannukah bushes with candy and Stars of David. Despite the decline of ritualism, the synagogue became the central institution in Jewish life and took on the responsibility for educating the young in Jewish heritage and ethnic identity. But though large numbers of synagogues were built, they were mostly empty except on Bar Mitzvahs or the High Holidays. In the 1950s and 1960s, the number of young Jews receiving some Jewish education expanded, but the quality of that education was designed to keep Jews within the fold without being "too Jewish."

This negativism was reinforced by the nouveau riche Jewish popular culture—Miami Beach, the Catskills, and the *Goodbye, Columbus* syndrome. For the Jewish generation raised in the 1950s and 1960s, Judaism and Jewish culture became identified with status-striving and conspicuous consumption. Rabbis became administrators and social directors rather than moral or spiritual leaders. American Jewry had its own end-of-ideology period. No longer were the central questions of East European and immigrant Jewish life—socialism, Zionism, and Judaism—debated. To be a Jew meant to be liberal, to support Israel, and to join a synagogue, observe few rituals, and let the rabbi (when he had the time) worry about theology.

During this period the Jewish Establishment—the network of overlapping philanthropies, defense agencies, social clubs, religious and educational institutions, and community centers—pursued a liberal course. It was in the forefront of exposing the Radical Right—McCarthyism and John Birchers. In its pursuit of civil liberties, the Jewish Establishment found a natural ally among blacks. Despite its liberalism, however, the Jewish Establishments wished to wash out the stain of the Commie Jews stigma. And, to a great degree, they were successful. Charles Stember reports that while in 1938, 32 percent of the American public believed Jews to be more radical than others, by 1962 only 17 percent held this view.

And why not? Jewish radicalism was dormant during the cold war. Jewish students were achievement-oriented, fun-seeking, and silent like everyone else. (There were exceptions of course, such as the Student Peace Union and other organizations reacting against nuclear testing and those seeking Fair Play for Cuba.) Barriers were breaking down—in employment, colleges, and fraternities—and Jews were not interested in constructing barriers—political or ethnic—of their own. Intermarriage was increasing and the Jewish community became concerned; even *Life* had a cover story on the vanishing American Jew.

It is ironic, then, that the genesis of the New Left (the Port Huron Statement of 1962) coincided with the Jew-as-radical stigma at an all-time low. And with the coming of the New Left, the Jewish Establishment saw a new threat to the new and hard-fought respectability of Jews. They saw their own children challenging the very ladders of Jewish success.

It was the New Left—and not the Jewish Establishment—that set the stage for what would become the Jewish liberation movement. The early period of the New Left was predominantly a WASP undertaking. But beginning with the Berkeley Free Speech movement (1964), the Freedom Rides in the South, SDS's community organizing projects in northern ghettos and later in the antiwar movement, the New Left saw a large influx of Jews, centered on the selective elite and urban campuses with high Jewish enrollments. In 1969, a profile of Jewish freshmen by the American Council on Education found that Jews were more likely to express radical attitudes about civil disobedience, the draft, race relations, abortion, and other social issues.

During the late 1960s, as militant activity spread from the elite campuses to the less-select colleges, the percentages of Jews in the New Left decreased, but the number of Jews drawn into the radical whirlpool increased. A series of crises—external repression and internal dissension—stung the New Left in the late 1960s. Many Jewish activists were stung in a particularly unnerving way.

In 1966, Stokely Carmichael shocked the country with a cry for Black Power. Soon there followed the ghetto rebellions. Jews, along with other whites, were no longer welcome in the civil rights movement. In liberal circles as well, Jews and blacks had a falling-out, culminating in the New York City teachers' strike of 1968—the controversy in (predominantly Jewish) Forest Hills, New York, over a low-income housing project in a middle-class neighborhood—and the rise of the Jewish Defense League. The so-called Jewish backlash revealed itself in local elections in New York, Philadelphia, and Los Angeles, and found the Jewish vote divided along lower-middle- and upper-middle-class lines. But in the national elections, Jews remained overwhelmingly Democratic. Less than 20 percent of Jewish voters favored Nixon in 1968 and, despite the disaffection of several prominent Jewish contributors from the Democratic party and an intensive campaign to woo the Jewish vote, Nixon received less than 35 percent of the Jewish vote in 1972. It was social issues such as open admissions and affirmative action that divided the Jewish community, with the large Jewish organizations opposing these measures on meritocratic grounds. But back in the mid-sixties, the tensions were just beginning.

Suddenly, the June 1967 Six Day War erupted. The war, and the events in its immediate aftermath, triggered the heightened awareness of Jewish identity in general and the beginnings of the Jewish liberation movement on campus.

The short-term impact of the war found a tremendous outpouring of money, sympathy, and identity, even among closet (unaffiliated or unidentified) Jews. But while most of the Jewish community returned to business as usual soon after the crisis had subsided, for others this new sense of Jewish identity lingered, though without much direction.

For many young Jews sympathetic to or part of the New Left, these feelings caused a considerable dilemma of identity and allegiance. In some New Left circles, Israel's victory was seen as a barrier to Palestinian liberation. Indeed, Israel became the enemy of the Third World in general. Only two months after the war, the New Politics conference in Chicago passed a resolution, at the urging of the black nationalists, condemning Israel as an "imperialist lackey of the United States." The tensions between blacks and whites surfaced. Many Jews felt betrayed. The meeting, for many, was a turning point: How could a generation reared on assimilationist Judaism, whose parents refused to teach them Yiddish, and who knew little about the political struggles of the Old Left (and the central role of Jews within it) reconcile being Jewish and being radical?

An Answer: Jewish Liberation

The early leaders of the Jewish liberation movement were found among those marginal men and women whose experiences combined a positive Jewish identity with the style of the New Left. Four distinct types arose.

The first were those who had been involved in the two major Socialist Zionist youth movements, Habonim and Hashomer Hatzair, as teenagers. Through these activities they viewed Zionism as the national liberation movement of Jews; secular Marxism was taught at summer camps, and the Jewish Establishment's "Israel, right or wrong" ideology was called into question. Indeed, the first high school SDS chapter grew out of a Habonim chapter in Washington, D.C.

The second was a small group of young Jews who grew up in the fading world of Yiddish secular socialism, who attended Jewish secular schools where the Jewish labor-Socialist movements in Eastern Europe and America were taken seriously, whose parents and teachers read the left-wing *Jewish Currents* magazine and attended the Communist Emma Lazarus clubs (purged by Jewish Establishment organizations during the McCarthy period). Their world was one where Jewishness—not Judaism, for they were secularists and humanists—and radicals did not conflict at all.

Third, a group of young Jews had been exposed to United Synagogue Youth, the yough movement of the Convervative branch of American Judaism. At USY's Hebrew-speaking Camp Ramah, they were oriented toward questions of community and tradition yet they shared the general lifestyle of American middle-class youth. Less political than many other Jewish youth, they were nevertheless influenced by the New Left and the counterculture. It was this group that organized *Response* magazine in 1967 and opened the Havurat

Shalom communal religious seminary the following year.

Finally, there was a group comprised of the graduates of Jewish day schools. In 1945 there were only 69 such schools and only 10,000 students in the U.S. By 1970 there were 378 schools and 75,000 students. These Orthodox academies were first organized by refugees from Nazi Europe. Thus, their children were prototypically marginal, with an immediate link to the Nazi Holocaust and the world of European Jewish life, but also to the world of Paul Goodman, teach-ins, sit-ins, civil rights, Bob Dylan, underground newspapers, and the rest of the youth culture. By the late 1960s, the first crop of day school graduates reached the secular campuses, and the New Left.

In time, others who felt Jewish but lacked definition and direction were attracted to the movement, including the confused liberals, the disaffected Orthodox, and sympathetic New Leftists. The mobilization of a specifically Jewish movement was legitimated by the separatist ideology of the Black Power movement. And those interested in Socialist forms of community could take the kibbutz as a living model. Despite a certain ambivalence toward their Jewishness, they sought a place to feel at home in America and on the Left. As the organized New Left began to disintegrate, the Jewish liberation movement helped to fill the vacuum.

The movement began in the winter of 1968-69 when, independent of each other, three Jewish underground papers emerged: *The Jewish Radical* in Berkeley, *Otherstand* in Montreal, and *The Jewish Liberation Journal* in New York. By the next academic year there were 25 new papers, and by 1972-73 more than 65. They were published in such unlikely places as Albuquerque, New Mexico, and Norman, Oklahoma, and they took names like *Chutzpah* and the *Jewish Urban Guerilla*. The movement that these papers expressed is evident in four central areas of concern: Israel, Soviet Jewry, the Jewish Establishment, and Jewish culture and community.

Israel. The initial interest in Israel was almost a knee-jerk response to the New Left, defending Israel against anti-Zionists through debates, forums, leaflets, and letters-to-the-editor of campus and New Lefts publications. As the first issue of *The Jewish Radical* stated, "one of the reasons that so many of us came together to start this paper was a growing concern with our radical communities' increasingly anti-Israel posture." Indigenous local groups banded together in 1970 into the Radical Zionist Alliance. They agreed that Israel depended too much on military superiority and treated Israeli Arabs as second-class citizens. But, they argued, Israel did have a right to exist and Al Fatah (the Palestinian guerilla movement) was not the Vietcong.

While confronting the New Left on radical grounds, they also took on the Jewish Establishment on Jewish turf. For example, when the president of the Zionist Organization of America, Jacques Torczyner, announced he would support U.S. policy in Vietnam in return for its support for Israel, the *Jewish Liberation Journal* called him "Nixon's hatchet man in the Jewish community" and organized a demonstration at the ZOA office in New York. And when Israel's Foreign Minister Abba Eban presented his country's Medallion of Valor to California Governor Ronald Reagan in September 1971, more than 500 Jewish activists protested, charging in a leaflet that it was "time for the Jewish community to cease linking the Jewish homeland to the names and actions of the men who perpetrate injustice in the United States."

In addition to these political activities, Israel had other appeals for young Jews. Israeli folk dancing, coffee houses, and Hebrew study groups mushroomed. The number of college students applying for Hebrew University's junior-year-abroad program increased from 238 in 1967 to 824 in 1971. The American Zionist Youth Foundation's Volunteers for Israel program drew 1,400 participants in 1968 and 4,200 in 1971. More young Jews decided to move to Israel permanently and several groups of radical Jews banded together in garins—collectives—which they later transplanted to Israel as new kibbutzim. By 1975, however, many of these immigrants—perhaps as many as half—had returned to the United States.

By the time of the Israeli-Arab war in October 1973, the New Left was only a memory and thus no radical defense of Israel was necessary. Campus emergency drives, like those in the larger Jewish community, stressed Israel's immediate survival, not its political legitimacy or Socialist beginnings. No upsurge of identity resulted either. For the current (17- to 22-year-old) generation of Jews on campus, indifference or acceptance, rather than ambivalence, are the modal patterns of Jewish identity. The only political response to the October was was a loose-knit group called *Breira* (Hebrew for alternative), composed of postcollege Jews who saw in the military stalemate a possibility for a just settlement of the Palestinian question. In a Yom Kippur Vigil in September 1974, they demonstrated at the United Nations, the Israel Mission, and the Palestinian Liberation Organization office, calling for a mutual acknowledgment of each other's right of self-determination. Not unexpectedly, their efforts had little impact on the Jewish community. Israel, in 1967 the trigger of the Jewish Liberation movement, was now again a given of Jewish life, no longer the symbol of a conflict of ethnic and political loyalties.

Soviet Jewry. Although the campaign to dramatize the plight of Societ Jews has now become part of the platforms of politicians, its origins go back to 1964 and the founding of the Student Struggle for Soviet Jewry by a handful of young, primarily Orthodox, Jews. After 1967, the issue not only played into the logic of politicians anxious over Soviet-American detente, but also provided (along with Israel) a symbolic link between the American and world Jewish community.

Militant, though hardly radical, the activists in the cause of Soviet Jewry adopted the tactics and rhetoric of the New Left. Activists disrupted performances of visiting Soviet ballet troups, orchestras, and circuses; a Freedom Bus carrying American and Soviet Jewish students traveled to 50 cities and campuses in 1971-72 to dramatize the situation of the cultural and political genocide of Soviet Jews and dissenters; sit-ins at Soviet embassies and large demonstrations at the United Nations were held on symbolic holidays, such as Passover and May Day. The larger Jewish community, too, picked up on the campaign for Soviet Jewry, although emphasizing behind-the-scenes diplomacy and appeals to President Nixon instead of confrontation politics.

Jewish radicals, of course, found it difficult to ally themselves, politically and psychologically, with the militant anti-Communist following—such as the Jewish Defense League—attracted to the cause of Soviet Jewry. Here, too, the tension between ideology and identity was resolved by walking a political tightrope. Differences of social class, political ideology, and ethnic identity divide the Jewish community. The political differences over Soviet Jewry among the Jewish radicals and the more populist posture of the now-defunct Jewish Defense League are complicated further by the disdain both groups have for the Jewish Establishment on Soviet Jewry and most other issues.

The Jewish Establishment. Radical Jews responsed to the bureaucratization of organized Jewish life by demanding the reordering of Jewish priorities and a participatory Judaism; increased participation of and programs for Jewish youth, aged, and poor; more support for Jewish education; and an end to the business oligarchy that overwhelmingly controls the Jewish fund-raising philanthropies. While acknowledging that many of the Jewish professionals within the bureaucracies are well-meaning, they also understand that major decisions are controlled by the fund-raisers whose commitment to and style of Jewish life appears hollow.

Jewish "Uncle Jakes" have sold out to the system, they claim. When local Jewish organizations honored conservative public figures, such as S.I. Hayakawa in San Francisco or Frank Rizzo in Philadelphia, radical Jews demonstrated in protest. And when Jewish organizations rewarded their own members of the American power elite—for example, the Jewish federation of Chicago named philanthropist Henry Crown, principal owner of General Dynamics, its Humanitarian of the Year—Jewish radicals challenged the hypocrisy.

Jewish activists registered a list of demands at the 1969 annual meeting of the Council of Jewish Federations and Welfare Funds in Boston. A young rabbinical student took the microphone to castigate the Jewish leadership for its unwillingness to challenge the Jewish and American status quo—and for alienating its youth. At a sit-in at the Jewish philanthropy office in New York, Jewish activists were arrested and soon labeled the "Federation 45."

Jewish women and homosexuals have protested their status as second-class citizens in Jewish tradition and community life. In February 1973, more than 500 Jewish women—from traditional Orthodox to assimilated feminists—met in New York at the first Jewish women's liberation conference, where they scrutinized sexist stereotypes—the Jewish mother and the Jewish princess—and called for equal participation in Jewish life. Local Jewish rap groups emerged; a feminist paper, ***Off Our Backs,*** published an entire issue on Jewish women, and an anthology entitled ***The Jewish Woman*** went into several editions. More cautious, and even more excluded from organized Jewish life, Jewish homosexuals soon came out of the closet. In Chicago's underground paper the ***Seed,*** a member of the Venceremos Brigade, draft resistance, and gay liberation wrote an article on "Coming Out Jewish." In Los Angeles and New York, gays organized their own synagogues.

The response of the Jewish Establishment to all this has been a mixture of righteous indignation, confusion and ambivalence, and anxious acceptance. Given the indifference of the large majority of young Jews, some see these symbolic confrontations with the Jewish Establishment as a healthy breath of Jewish life. Many assume that these young radicals will be the Jewish leadership of the next generation. Internally, some Jewish organizations have made some changes. For example, in September 1973 the Conservative wing of Judaism voted to admit women to the prayer quorum, the ***minyan***, and the Reform branch has already ordained one woman rabbi and accepted others to its seminary. Locally, Jewish organizations have supported Jewish underground papers. Network, the Jewish movement's umbrella organization, relies almost entirely on contributions from the Jewish Establishment. Indeed, many Jewish professionals recognize that their survival of organized Jewish life may depend on graduates of the Jewish liberation movement.

Jewish Culture and Community. Most young Jewish activists, however, find the Jewish Establishment institutions too inflexible to accommodate their own needs for a satisfying Jewish lifestyle. Instead, paralleling the counterculture, they have organized alternative Jewish institutions of their own—a reflection of a generational and cultural, rather than a political gap. They share the general distaste for Jewish popular culture, *Goodbye, Columbus* and Hadassah brunches, Miami Beach and B'nai Brith bowling leagues. And they seek an alternative to both the transient student culture and the intransigent Jewish Establishment.

In seeking to fuse traditional Jewish symbols with everyday concerns, many have acknowledged their own lack of Jewish understanding. Not unlike the black experience, young Jews knew little about their own personal and historical roots. They demanded Jewish studies. Reluctantly, colleges began to introduce courses in Jewish history and sociology, Middle East politics, Jewish theology and literature, Hebrew and Yiddish language. By 1974, more than 300 colleges offered some kind of Jewish studies, a fivefold increase since 1967.

Paralleling the demand for college-credit courses, young Jews also organized Jewish free universities. Like the New Left counterparts, these institutions offered more flexible and innovative courses—Jewish cooking, Jewish mysticism and radical theology, Zionism and the Third World. During the intensity of the Vietnam War, the Jewish Peace Fellowship established draft-counseling centers for young Jews. Once secure in their Jewish identity, young Jews began to question and scrutinize Jewish tradition itself and to select from Jewish tradition the symbols, rituals, and lessons that seemed to apply to their own lives.

The Jewish Catalog, published in 1973, includes recipes for Matzoh, gefilte fish and chicken soup (the "panacea"), instructions for ceremonial candle-making, music for traditional Jewish melodies and other "how-to-Jew-it" guides. Its first printing of 15,000 sold out before publication and has been used in synagogues and Jewish homes.

In magazines such as ***Respone*** and ***Davka***, through poetry, film, drama, fiction, and essays, Jewish Liberation expresses a search for authentic Jewish Liberation expresses a search for authentic Jewish culture. While most young Jews find Jewish tradition (***halakha***) irrelevant for modern concerns, others have returned to Jewish sources for direction and even talk of building on the old to create a new Jewish theology. In recent months radical (theologically as well as politically) Jews have circulated a *New Halakha Newsletter.* In 1969, Arthur Waskow published a first draft of his "Freedom Seder" in ***Ramparts*** magazine, adding to the traditional Passover ceremony quotes from Martin Buber and Eldridge Cleaver.

Part of this encounter with Jewish tradition includes a return to the mystical elements of religious life. Beyond intellectual dimensions of theology and radical humanism, the new Jewish awareness spills over into the more joyous and intense tradition of Hassidism. Following the 1967 Summer of Love in Haight-Ashbury, folksinging Hassidic Rabbi Shlomo Carlebach established the House of Love and Prayer to remind hippies attracted to the Eastern religions of Judaism's own mystical tradition.

Certainly it is not surprising that an outgrowth of the 1960s was an attempt to translate these feelings of Jewish identity into what Rosabeth Kanter calls intentional community. The first of these, the Havurot Shalom communal seminary in Boston, was organized by disillusioned young rabbinical students and their friends; when no Jewish organization would take the risk, the Danforth Foundation offered a grant to establish a community center. Soon after, a small group of Jewish activists in Washington organized Jews for Urban Justice to confront the local Jewish community about its silence toward the black community and the Vietnam War. Within a short time, however, its members felt that using Jewish symbols to justify their own radicalism was inadequate—indeed, unauthentic—and they soon rented a community center, asked local rabbis for guidance, and developed a program of workship and study called Fabrangen. More than 25 similar communes and communities across the country represent the effort to develop an alternative institutional structure to the prevailing pattern of organized Jewish life, culture, and community.

Community and Beyond. It is the emphasis on small-scale community, ritual, religious experience, and interpersonal relations that, in the mid-1970s, best expresses the mood of Jewish youth and youth culture in general. It echoes and mirrors the attraction of the Guru Maharaj-ji, the Jesus freaks, the interest in nostalgia from the 1930s, 40s, and 50s, the spread of encounter groups, astrology, and the occult, and the stylized indifference and self-conscious decadence of the glitter scene represented by pop stars Alice Cooper, Bette Midler, and David Bowie.

Certainly part of the explanation for this trend is found in the New Left's perception of its own failure. Despite the New Left's impact on the country's attitudes and public opinion toward Vietnam and its accurate portrait of American society, more crucial structural changes in the distribution of power, wealth, and equal justice lagged far behind. Perhaps it is not surprising that while the drug culture of the 1960s emphasized uppers, in the Nixon years the mood turned to downers. The students of 1967 are young adults now, while today's college students came of age during a period of profound pessimism and disillusionment about the possibilities of social change; freshman in 1974 were in high school during the invasion of Cambodia and the killings at Kent and Jackson State in 1970. They are far different from the idealistic and somewhat naive students at Port Huron, attracted by Kennedy's Peace Corps and "part of the way with LBJ" in 1964. Today's students tend to be more cynical, privatized, and careerist. But the shifts in psychology and political style are rooted in larger social forces over which today's youth have, and feel, a little control.

For the generation that came of age in the 1950s, insurgent politics seemed unnecessary, because the cold war and the so-called affluent society provided Americans with a sense (however unwarranted) of security and confidence. For the idealistic generation of the 1960s, oppositional politics seemed hopeful; though liberalism had failed them, a coalition of the poor and the alienated could—the word now seems so outdated—overcome. But for the generation of the 1970s, any politics at all seems futile; the air war over Indochina and U.S. aid continues, after Watergate drains the national energy, President Ford pardons Richard Nixon and leaves the draft resisters and deserters to earn their reentry, and even teachers cannot find jobs.

Like other attempts at intentional community of the past decade, the Jewish communes create their own dilemmas. Personal, religious, and political differences remain, despite the common factor of an ascribed, historical status—their Jewishness. Members move, they graduate, or they find their Jewish identity fading and their non-Jewish selves (as parents, spouses, employees, etc.) more salient. Except for occasional peak moments—a wedding or a Sabbath worship—a sense of community becomes difficult to sustain.

Jewish life today cannot replace the East European shtetl. The Jewish family faces increasing divorce rate. Ethnic neighborhoods in large cities are disintegrating and the ethnic lifestyle—with street life, delicatessens, and local synagogues—has virtually disappeared.

Can one, in fact, create something as organic as community? Certainly it is difficult without segregating oneself physically and psychologically from modern life and concerns. Most young people, though seeking authentic community, are nevertheless unwilling or unable to give up the rewards of modern life. And perhaps, in recognizing the futility of this cultural, political, and psychological dilemma, they disengage from larger public issues. Indeed, during the Nixon administration, they glorified sham and put-on. In the 1960s, Bob Dylan and Joan Baez symbolized the authentic self, the search for commitment. In the 1970s, Alice Cooper and Evel Knievel represent the reverse—the pseudoevent and the inauthentic self. The audience knows it's all a sham and this creates its own mystique. Certainly if anything calls to mind Durkheim's notion of anomie—the loss of any guiding standards—this is it.

The fabric of American society today seems remarkably similar to the conditions which German sociologist Herman Schmalenbach described as giving rise to social movements of "communion"—transient and somewhat desperate attempts to achieve coherence, emotion and closeness to fill a void during periods of social, political and economic breakdown. Schmalenbach was describing the conditions of pre-Nazi Germany, and we can see parallels to the United States today—economic dislocation, the loss of political legitimacy. Many elements of American popular culture including the movies Cabaret, Chinatown and Last Tango in Paris—parallel the bourgeois decadence and social pessimism of the pre-Nazi period. Public opinion polls reveal that the Congress, the Presidency, the media, and the corporate sector have lost credibility. Yet the anger is diffuse and the mood is fatalistic. In the absence of a mass progressive political movement to focus and channel these discontents, youth culture has nowhere to go but to retreat and to escape.

SUGGESTED READINGS

The New Left and the Jews, edited by Mordecai Chertoff (New York: Pitman, 1971).

Socialist-Zionism: Theory and Issues in Contemporary Jewish Nationalism by Allan Gal (Boston: Schenkman, 1973).

The Liberation of the Jew by Albert Memmi (New York: Orion Press, 1969).

Jewish Radicalism: A Selected Anthology by Jack Nusan Porter and Peter Dreier (New York: Grove Press, 1974).

The Jewish Catalog: A Do-It-Yourself Kit edited by Richard Michael Seigel and Sharon Strassfeld (Philadelphia: Jewish Publication Society, 1973).

The New Jews, edited by James Sleeper and Alaq Mintz (New York: Random House, 1971).

"The Jewish Women: An Anthology," special issue of *Response Magazine, 18*, 1973 (Box 1496, Brandeis University, Waltham, Mass. 02154).

Section XV

Transportation and Communication

A bench mark of industrial society is the rapid development of transportation and communication channels. An understanding of transportation and communication and their impact on people's lives is essential for comprehending the modern world. Schiller, in "Madison Avenue Imperialism," discusses the penetration of modern American advertising technology into every corner of the world. Starting from the benign notion that free communication is a good thing, Schiller points out how this notion is used by multinational corporations to control markets by flooding national communication networks at home and abroad with American-style advertising. In other words, national communications systems and their programming are being transformed according to the specifications of international marketeers. Advertising penetrates and dominates by creating a "commercial culture" in each medium. It is the mixture, Schiller says, of economics and electronics. Advertising follows business wherever it goes. He goes on to document the control of U.S. ad agencies and their internationalization. The next logical step, already under way, is to employ public relations techniques to legitimate business and business elites as they assume control of larger and larger sectors of everyone's life here and abroad.

It is hardly a secret that the automobile has become a central part of the American (and industrial) way of life. In "Automobile Addiction: The Abuse of Personal Transport," Huttman examines our automobile addiction and dependency. Pointing out that fully one-tenth of the nongovernmental labor force in the United States in involved in auto production, he also suggests that the car is a major status symbol and very nearly an object of worship to many Americans. We are physically and psychologically auto addicted. Automobiles voraciously consume our environment, including space for living. His suggestions for a public system of car ownership is most thought-provoking and worthy of serious consideration.

Whitt continues the auto addiction theme in "Californians, Cars and Technological Death." We are given a careful case history of one mild piece of antiauto legislation, Proposition 18, in California, and its failure at the hands of the enormous auto–oil–highway lobby. The frightening interlock of special interests and their wealth in the anti-Proposition 18 campaign raises important questions about the way in which public interest may be bought and sold through skillful advertising.

A popular response to the problem of private transportation is often a suggestion to bolster mass transit. In "Public Transportation and Black Unemployment," Goering and Kalachek caution against accepting such notions without careful consideration of the entire culture of transportation and its meaning. You can put in buses, but you still have to get people to ride on them. The article is about the Tempo experiment in St. Louis to bus ghetto residents to employment in the suburbs. The project was an expensive and massive failure. Its failure, the authors tell us, flowed from four myths about the situation in St. Louis. First of all, there was a myth that jobs were not available in the inner city. In fact, blue-collar workers come into the inner cities to work in large numbers. Second, there was a myth that suburban employers often need unskilled workers. Third, there was a myth that unemployed black ghetto residents need transportation to the suburbs. Finally, there was a myth that improved and expanded bus transportation cannot be provided through the existing structure of antipoverty agencies. The Tempo project, the authors conclude, was too "technological" a solution. It failed to take social and cultural variables into account and was inflexible. Mass transport is an important solution to car-choked America, but it will work only when planners come to realize that people live in culturally textured groupings that demand sophisticated institutional answers.

1 *Herbert I. Schiller*

Madison Avenue Imperialism

Many currents feed the international flow of communications. Tourists, governmental agents and officials, student travelers, trade (exports and imports), international games and sports, religious organizations and cultural exchanges are only some of the better recognized contributors to international communications. While each element does not necessarily match the next in volume, force or impact, in theory, at least, there is supposed to be no dominant thrusting single component that overshadows the rest. There is, it is claimed, a diffusion of influence, with culture, entertainment, travel and commerce nicely balancing each other in an international equilibrium that offers advantage to all participants. We hear, therefore, that "Trade is good," "Cultural exchanges create understanding," and "Travel is broadening." All this folk wisdom contributes ultimately to the almost mystical and revered concept of the "free flow of information." The free flow of information, until recently at any rate, has been regarded as the ultimate good for which all sensible nations should strive.

Actually, this view of beneficial and pluralistic international communications is about as realistic as the economists' model of free competition and the self-adjusting market economy. Not surprisingly, both systems are disrupted by the same force. Domestically, the giant corporation, as Galbraith and others have effectively demonstrated, makes a shambles of the notion of a free market of countless uninfluential producers and consumers. Internationally, the multinational corporation, the intercontinental extension of the domestic behemoth, now dominates similarly the global economy and has become the chief organizer and manufacturer of the international flow of communications.

The internationally active corporation is not an altogether new phenomenon but its extensive involvement in overseas communications is relatively recent. Since the end of World War II, both the volume and the character of international economic activity have changed considerably. Perhaps $70 billion of direct private overseas investment is owned and controlled by a few hundred U.S.-based companies, the so-called multinational corporations. The massive build-up of private U.S. investment abroad requires no elaboration here. Though American-controlled raw materials and extractive industries have maintained and even extended their holdings around the world, the largest part of the postwar American investment flow abroad has been into manufacturing and service industries in already developed regions and countries (Western Europe, Canada, Australia). The changing nature of this investment has affected directly and consequentially both the apparatus and content of international communications. A trade publication has commented on this shift of activity of private U.S. investment overseas:

> For the international advertiser and marketeer, (for instance), this means expanded horizons. The shift in investment means a greater concentration by international business in the production of goods and services and a more rapid development of consumer markets. *Hence, a growing emphasis on the advertising and marketing of those goods and services is to be expected.*

U.S. raw materials and heavy goods producer interests overseas in the pre-World War II days availed themselves of some communications talent to provide their local activities with favorable imagery but such expenditures were marginal at best. Today the situation is entirely reversed. Now the mass media, wherever U.S. manufacturing companies operate, have been summoned to promote the global expansion of American consumer goods sales and services.

The international community is being inundated by a stream of commercial messages that derive from the marketing requirements of (mostly) American multinational companies. The structure of national communications systems and the programming they offer are being transformed according to the specifications of international marketeers.

Advertising requires total access to the mass media. It is through the multimillion circulation magazines, the car and kitchen radio and the home screen that the marketing message comes across incessantly and effectively. Advertising cannot tolerate, if it wishes to be successful, mass communications channels that exclude its commercials and its commercially oriented "recreational" programming. It strives untiringly, therefore, to penetrate each available communications outlet that has a sizable audience. Advertising's appetite is insatiable and nothing less than the total domination of every medium is always its objective. Once subordinated, the medium, whatever its original attributes, becomes an instrument of the commercial culture.

Accordingly, one measure of a nation's loss of control of its own mass media, (apart from the obvious loss through foreign ownership), is the degree of penetration of foreign advertising agencies in the mechanics of national marketing. Such a penetration signals also fundamental changes in the country's cultural ecology, as a changed communications structure increasingly transmits and reinforces attitudes that fit nicely with the requirements of the multinational corporate goods producers that are financing the new system.

The emerging pattern reveals a mixture of economics and electronics that is enormously powerful.

Spreading Commerce

Sophisticated communications methodologies—those which have proved themselves the most effective in regimenting and securing the attachment of the domestic population—are being applied internationally at an accelerating tempo. The culture of commerce, or more precisely, of corporate power, is radiating from its American base in a dazzling display of vitality. To sell its goods and products and itself, U.S. business overseas employs the familiar services of advertising, public relations, opinion surveys and market research. And to carry the carefully synthesized messages of these bought services, it enlists or subverts the mass media of the many national states in which it operates.

Take television, for example. A couple of years ago I described the process by which Western European broadcasting was being commercialized. "In Western Europe, the most stable noncommercial broadcasting structures of sovereign states are unable to resist the forces that are arrayed against them." Here is one description (from *Television Age*) of how commercials defy national boundaries, especially in the compact North Atlantic region:

> Of course, the continued expansion of commercial television, despite powerful opposition, is playing a major role in making unity of diversity. Although many important countries, particularly in Europe, still forbid TV advertising, there is a certain "spillover" effect that tends to spread commercials even to those countries that originally were adamant. Only this year did the 11-year-old government-controlled Swiss TV service permit commercials on its three regional networks. The move was in large part prompted by the concern of Swiss manufacturers who knew their customers were viewing Italian and German TV across the border. The same process is expected to unfold in the Netherlands, a large part of which is open to German programming and advertising messages. If Netherland TV goes commercial, then Belgium is expected to follow shortly thereafter. Then France and Scandinavia will be the last big holdouts . . . If French television goes commercial, an executive at J. Walter Thompson remarks, then there truly will be a common market for the TV advertiser.

All of this has come true with a vengeance. In Western Europe today, the only countries that have not "gone commercial" are Sweden and Denmark. Beginning in Britain in 1954 and continuing on through the last 16 years, country after country has accepted some form or another of commercial influence. Around the world, except in the Chinese and Soviet blocs, commercialism in broadcasting is now the dominant mode of organization. In the less developed nations, the dependence on outside capital assistance makes it inevitable that commercial broadcasting be established, and such has been the case.

International Message-Makers

Advertising has become the indispensable adjutant of the business system. Not surprisingly, perhaps, its own organizational structure is not different in many ways from the corporations whose interests it promotes and represents. Ad agencies, like the rest of American enterprise, show the same pattern of consolidation and concentration. In 1968, less than 10 per cent of the firms in the industry received almost three-quarters of the domestic business (billings). International billings are much more heavily concentrated.

The major U.S. ad agencies, much like the manufacturing companies they service, possess resources and obtain revenues that put them far ahead of most of their international competitors. Of the world's ten largest agencies in 1969, only one was not an American firm, and in the top 25 international agencies, 23 were American companies.

The rich domestic consumer market in the United States was the original stimulus for the growth of these word and image factories. It hastened their initial development. Now they are grazing in pastures far from home. The stupendous growth of directly owned American business overseas, has brought with it, of necessity, the marketeers. American factories worth more than $10 billion are manufacturing their products in Western Europe. Another $10 billion worth of U.S. plant is in Canada. Latin America, Africa and the Middle East, though mainly still serving as raw material depots of Western enterprise, have some U.S. manufacturing capacity too. The ad men follow their manufacturing clients wherever the potential markets lead, generally where the capital investment is set down. In 1968 American ad agencies operating outside the United States had billings exceeding $1.5 billion, a large part of which, though by no means all, was accounted for by the advertising programs of U.S. companies overseas. This year U.S. companies advertising expenditures abroad are expected to reach $5 billion.

And the big U.S. agencies get most of the business. J. Walter Thompson; McCann-Erickson; Ted Bates; Young & Rubicam; Ogilvy and Mather; Norman, Craig & Kummel; Leo Burnett Co.; Foote, Cone and Belding; Compton; and Kenyon and Eckhardt are the elite ten American agencies in the world marketing swim.

No part of the globe (except, and perhaps only temporarily, the socialist-organized sector) avoids the penetration of the internationally active American ad agency. In a special international issue of *Printers' Ink* in 1967 titled "Who's Where Around the World," 45 U.S. agencies were listed with hundreds of overseas affiliates. Consider, for example, the far-flung activities of the largest agency in the world, J. Walter Thompson. In 1969, JWT had $740 million in billings of which $292 million, a sizable 39 percent, originated in 28 countries outside the United States. JWT world-wide has 700 accounts and employs 8,000 people in 42 offices, in some instances several in one country. It operates in Argentina, Uruguay, Austria, Australia, Belgium, Brazil, Canada, Ceylon, Chile, France, Denmark, Britain, India, Italy, Switzerland, Spain, Japan, Mexico, Holland, Pakistan, Peru, the Philippines, Puerto Rico, South Africa (with five offices throughout the country and billings of $10,000,000) and Venezuela. JWT is the largest ad agency in seven countries outside the United States.

Who's Where Around the World?

As of 1970, only two of the top 25 U.S. ad agencies still did not have overseas offices. If anything, the expansion of U.S. ad agencies is accelerating and foreign competition is being brought increasingly under the American umbrella. For instance, Leo Burnett Company, fifth-ranked U.S. agency in 1969, announced the acquisition of the two largest ad agency subsidiaries of the London Press Exchange—LPE Ltd., one of England's largest agencies, and LPE International, Ltd., a combination of 19 agencies in Europe, Latin America, Africa and Asia. "It is a natural alliance," said Philip H. Schaff, Jr., chairman of Burnett. "Leo Burnett is strong in the United States and Canada and very weak outside. London Press Exchange is strong outside but very weak here.

The internationalization of the American advertising business is an integral part of the expansion of U.S. industry abroad. It is the latter's voracious marketing requirements that elicit and support the agencies' world-wide activities. The client list of American ad agencies operating internationally is a roster of *Fortune*'s Directory of the largest 500 U.S. nonfinancial corporations, supplemented by a heavy representation of major European companies.

In Canada, for instance, the main revenues of commercia radio-television broadcasting come mostly from the giant U.S. companies operating across the border. In 1969, the top ten broadcasting advertisers were: General Motors of Canada Ltd., Procter and Gamble of Canada Ltd., Canadian Breweries, General Foods Ltd., Imperial Tobacco of Canada, Colgate-Palmolive Ltd., Ford Motor Company of Canada, Lever Bros. Ltd., Government of Canada and Bristol-Myers of Canada.

Ninth-ranked U.S. ad agency Ogilvy and Mather, with one-third of its income earned outside the United States and with 30 offices in 14 countries, notes in its 1969 annual report that it serves 17 clients in three or more countries: Air Canada, American Express, Bristol Myers, General Foods, Gillette, Hertz, ICI, Lever, Mars, Mercedes Benz, Rountree, Schweppes, Shell Chemical, Shell, U.S. Travel Service.

In their 1968 Annual Report, the eighth-ranked U.S. agency, Foote, Cone and Belding includes among its clients abroad Monsanto, BOAC, Gillette, B. F. Goodrich, Clairol, Kimberly-Clark Corporation, International Harvester, GM, Hughes Aircraft, Smith-Kline & French, Mead Johnson, Singer Company, Armour-Dial, Kraft Foods and Zenith Radio Corporation.

The omnipresent advertising message, jarring or insinuatingly effective, now constitutes a major voice in international communications. The mass media are the ideal instruments of transmission, especially television which captures the viewer in his own, allegedly secure, living room. The media, if they were not commercial to begin with as they were in the United States, end up eventually as business auxiliaries. The lure of advertising revenues it too tempting. Furthermore, the business system cannot permit as influential a "sales tool" as radio-television to function noncommercially, free to reject the transmission of its consumer messages.

It is no surprise, therefore, to discover that American advertising agencies have made deep inroads in most of the already-industrialized states. In Great Britain, for example, according to the *Financial Times*, "The situation now is that of the top twenty London advertising agencies, only seven are totally British. All the rest are American owned, or, in a few cases, have strong American links. In the top ten, the U.S. dominance is even greater, with only two of the ten retaining total independence." In West Germany, France, Italy and even Japan, U.S. ad agencies now account for the bulk of nationally-placed advertising, says *Advertising Age.* On the other side of the world there is the same loss of national control of the image-making apparatus. A report from *Advertising and Newspaper News* notes that "Overseas agencies gain whole or partial control of 15 of 24 largest Australian ad agencies and Australians berate themselves for lack of self-faith."

In many of the less developed states, the control of internal communications by foreign (generally U.S.) business interests, is often overwhelming. *Le Monde* reports, for example, that in Peru "more than 80 percent of the advertising carried by Peruvian newspapers, radio and television is channeled through big American advertising firms, such as J. Walter Thomson (sic), McKann Erickson (sic), Grant Advertising and Katts Acciones, Inc." Venezuela is even more monopolized by U.S. agencies and a similar pattern, varying in degree, applies in Rhodesia, Kenya, Nigeria, India, Malaysia, Pakistan, Thailand and many other low-income nations.

Advertising, and the mass media which it eventually traduces are, therefore, the leading agents in the business of culture, and the culture of business. Other services such as public relations, marketing research and opinion surveying, all of which are utilized to make the marketing effort more effective, feed further the stream of international commercial communications.

Public relations, a practice of American business since the early years of the twentieth century, also has become an international phenomenon, following the migration of American capital overseas. Compared with the growth of international advertising, PR is still a rather modest but steadily expanding activity. Whereas advertising commonly aims to sell the corporation's output, PR's goal more specifically is to sell the company itself—as a useful, productive and beneficial entity to the society in which it is located. As American capital floods into a country and wrests control of key industries, this is no mean task. Here is the problem as seen by the executive vice-president of Hill & Knowlton, Inc., the most important American company engaged in international public relations:

> Let us review the situation confronting the American corporation today in Western Europe, [Mr. William A. Durbin suggests:] For a time following World War II, American companies found European countries eager for dollar investment—and the markets seemed almost limitless. In the past decade or so, American business responded with a tremendous increase in direct U.S. investments in Western Europe. In 1965 the total approached $14 billion, compared with $1.7 billion in 1950 [closer to $20 billion in 1969—HS]
>
> In recent years the climate has changed: the 'welcome' sign has been replaced with one reading 'Yankee Go Home.' A recent survey of Opinion Research Corporation disclosed considerable pressures to restrict the growth of U.S. firms in four Common Market countries. Fifty-six percent of the *businessmen* (my italics) in Germany believe their government should discourage U.S. investment. For Italy the figure was 44 percent, France 40 percent, and the Netherlands, 31 percent.
>
> . . . Under these circumstances, American corporations face difficult problems. They cannot merely withdraw—they must work harder than ever—and much of their attention must be given to the public relations aspects of their international operations.

Or put otherwise, it is the task of U.S. corporate-supported public relations to overcome widespread resistance to American penetrations of the national economy wherever they may be occurring.

The manipulation of symbols to achieve this objective is applied skillfully, generally unobtrusively and intensively by the professional image-makers. As noted in one business bulletin, "Worldwide PR is, quite simply, the art of using ideas and information through all available means of communications, to create a favorable climate of opinion for products, services and the corporation itself."

When PR has its way, the flow of communications becomes a stream of unidentifiable (by source) promotional messages for the sponsoring company or complex or even the entire business system itself. Years ago, a U.S. business periodical observed: "As expert communicator, PR plays a unique and quite startling role in the whole flow of communications between the business community and the public. This role is often glossed over, but the simple fact is that much of the current news coverage of business by the American press, radio and television is subsidized by company PR effort . . . one hundred thousand public relations practitioners serve as a tremendous source of communications manpower. Without them, only a handful of newspapers and radio or television stations would have the staff or resources to cover business activities . . . "

Emphasizing the fanciful means that are required to promote modern business, a later study concluded: "The relative significance of public relations cannot be gauged by estimating total expenditures for this work. We have no such estimates, and the figure would probably be small in comparison with advertising proper. The most telling test of the significance would be to determine the portion of the contents of our newspapers [and television and radio programming—HS] that has originated from public-relations offices. This portion is probably quite remarkable."

In this curiously inverted state of affairs, the public is supposed to benefit from the privately-prepared press releases which are fed into the mass media, because the latter would be unable, if left to its own resources, to produce enough of such material. Now the international community is receiving these communications benefits as well. *Business Week*, a decade ago, estimated that "among the top three hundred companies in the country, three out of four have full-fledged PR departments, a broad jump from the one out of fifty reported in 1936. New corporation PR departments are starting at the rate of one hundred a year." The top 300 companies, it may be recalled, are the major exporters of capital and are the main owners of overseas plants and facilities. In a survey undertaken by Opinion Research Corporation in January 1968, the 500 largest industrial corporations listed in the *Fortune* directory were asked to fill out questionnaires about their foreign public relations programs. Only 153 replies were received and of these, 43 reported no overseas PR activities. The Survey therefore represents a self-selected response of 110 major U.S. companies engaged in foreign public relations. The basic findings with respect to these firms were:

> The number of companies engaging in international public relations activities has increased markedly in recent years.
>
> These companies are carrying out public relations programs on every continent and in every major country.
>
> The programs are usually handled by staff members based in the overseas countries.
>
> Only one-third of the respondents use either a public relations firm or advertising agency to implement their overseas public relations programs.
>
> The principal activities are press releases, product publicity, and exhibits and special events." Other activities include community relations, employee relations and government regulations. *Public Relations Quarterly* sums up the study in these words: "Not only are more companies entering the overseas public relations field, they also seem to be more active."

National and local mass media systems are infiltrated by business messages not necessarily identified by their sources of origin. Hill and Knowlton have prepared a guidebook to familiarize less knowledgeable PR-men with the techniques of overseas promotion and concern with the local media has the highest priority.

With the advent of space communications, the opportunity to achieve a world-wide audience for promotional ends has not been ignored. In June, 1969, for example, the space satellite system was used to herald the opening of an iron ore complex in Australia, owned and operated by an American multinational corporation in association with other business companies. "Co-ordinated planning, American techniques and Intelsat make Austalian mine opening a world event," reported the *Public Relations Journal.*

The Opinion-Takers and the Marketing Researchers

Two other media-related services supplement the information-generation business which engages so much of the attention and resources of American companies active in international markets. These are the opinion survey organizations and the market research companies which are also involved in opinion-taking as well as in more detailed market analysis.

Opinion polls are considered generally as part of the contemporary political infrastructure of parliamentary-electoral societies. In fact, by volume and character of the work, market-economic undertakings account for a substantial part of the poll-takers' overall business. The distinction between survey and market research is often extremely thin, and the techniques of uncovering political attitudes and desires may serve to give orientation to economic activities and policies. For example, the Opinion Research Corporation recently announced the establishment of a new company, Market and Opinion Research International, Ltd., (MORI) with headquarters in London. This is a joint venture with NOP Market Research Ltd., London. MORI, the new outfit, is expected to provide facilities for research in North America, the United Kingdom and Europe.

The Gallup Organization, Inc., the most well known United States opinion-surveying company, identifies itself as providing "marketing and attitude research." Gallup-International, which includes its autonomous overseas associates in a loose network of affiliate relationships, "covers 36 countries or regions throughout the world. It undertakes surveys on a world-wide or European scale in the fields of marketing research and of public opinion and behavioral sciences, to be conducted on a contract and client basis."

A. C. Neilsen Co., the major market research company in the United States, engages in surveys as a matter of course and operates in 20 different countries on four continents. It supplies some of its research services to 86 international organizations with parent companies located in eight different countries. Its television audience research services have been established directly in Canada and Japan and through joint ventures in Ireland and West Germany. This rating service which creates frenzy amongst commercial TV broadcasters scrambling to achieve high viewing ratios, is described by Arthur C. Nielsen, founder of the company, in this way:

> . . . (Since) this type of research exerts a significant and favorable effect on the efficiency of one of the most important methods of moving goods from producer to consumer (television)—it is lowering the cost of distribution and creating increased profits for manufacturers and greater values for consumers.

The view of television as essentially a "method of moving goods from producer to consumer" explains, of course, the pathetic condition of television in the United States. The "increased efficiency" that the medium provides for the marketing function can be balanced against the human dysfunction imposed on its audience.

Another firm, International Research Associates, Inc. (INRA) conducts market and opinion research in the United States, Latin America, Europe, Africa and the Middle East, Southeast Asia and the Far East. The company has a network of associated research organizations operating in more than 40 countries and principalities around the world.

The opinion survey—whether conducted under national or foreign auspices, which is, incidentally, no easy matter to ascertain—is ostensibly designed to acquire information, not to create it. In fact, however, it often creates not only information but attitudes that it is supposed only to poll. The problem lies not with faulty sampling or poor interviewing; even the questions can be phrased with complete objectivity. Deficiences in these matters can and do appear, but with increasingly sophisticated polling techniques available, amongst well-established organizations, technical errors are likely to be minimal.

A less acknowledged consequence of opinion surveying, however, is what might be termed its legitimization effect. This means that once political, social or economic questions are put in a fixed perspective and called to the attention of the respondent, a validation of certain ideas or even of a frame of reference may occur. Consumer preference studies, for instance, inquire about choices between one product or another, not whether either or both of the products should have been produced in the first place. Political inquiries ask individuals to choose between candidates thereby validating the electoral process rather than questioning its mechanics.

A Way to View

In short, in most instances, and not necessarily with a deliberate intent to influence, the question-answer format creates for the respondent (and the viewer, listener or reader of the poll's published results) a pattern with which to view reality. This is set according to the structure of the inquiry. The conditions of the response are set by the poll-taker in the way he already views the relationships he wishes to uncover. The respondent is forced into that mold once he accepts the role of participant in the survey.

A case in point as an illustration. A Roper poll, conducted and paid for by the National Association of Broadcasters (the commercial broadcasters), asked its respondents, "Do you agree or disagree that having commercials is a fair price to pay for being able to watch [television]?" Roper reports, no doubt to the great satisfaction of the NAB, that "people agreed, eight to one, with the concept that having commercials is a 'fair price to pay.' " Yet what has been learned from this question and the overwhelming affirmative response it obtained? Alternatives of having television without commercials were not offered to the respondents. A commercial structure of relationships was assumed by the question formulated by Roper, and those answering, by the very fact of responding, had to accept the underlying set of assumptions. In effect, the prevailing institutional pattern of commercial television was sanctioned in the very process of poll-taking.

In this way surveys of opinion too often either create opinion or inhibit opinion-creating by restricting the framework in which genuine alternatives can be expressed or considered.

Gallup-International, financed by whomever will foot the bill, conducts periodic omnibus surveys in

> Argentina (every other month); Australia (every other month); Austria (four times a year); Belgium (each week); Chile (every other month); Great Britain (every week); Greece (every two weeks); India (four times a year); The Netherlands (every week); Norway (every month); Phillippines (once a year); Sweden (every month); Switzerland (four times a year); Union of South Africa (alternate months, when the "European" adult population is sampled); Uruguay (every other month); Vietnam (four times a year); West Germany (every month).

Published findings may be expected to have the effect of solidifying status quo sentiments in a generalized though fundamental sense. Moreover, polls conducted under obscure sponsorship may provide information to those with limited social responsibility, which increases their potential for further manipulation of local populations.

In any event, opinion surveys conducted for American corporations or governmental information agencies, present a twofold threat to the societies in which they are undertaken. The polls are structured commercially and when published as national sentiment cannot fail to aggravate the marketeering influence in the country, by legitimizing still further, existing inclinations to consumerism. Of more moment, perhaps, they probe surreptitiously for national opinions that may determine or increase the scope of U.S. official or private information makers' future policy in that country. Certainly, the information that is derived from American-financed overseas surveys hardly promotes the two-way flow of communication which is the objective of so much UNESCO rhetoric.

It should also be clear that in many advanced, industrial market societies, local market research and polling occur alongside of and sometimes without competition from American supported operations in the same territory. To the extent that they do exist independently, they provide for their domestic sponsors the same methodology of control and manipulation that these activities offer their American counterparts. Though this discussion is concerned primarily with the promotion of American business ideology overseas through advertising, PR, polls and market research, the imposition of a value structure riddled with commercialism is made easier to the extent that it finds societies already prepared and enmeshed in these practices.

Conclusion

The economic power of American corporate capitalism has long been manifest. Its postwar global expansion has made it an international system which affects, and is affected by, national decision-making in scores of countries on all continents. Its economic impact, if not thoroughly documented, at least is generally recognized and includes raw material flows and explorations, balance of payments conflicts, dividend and profit repatriation pressures, migrations of human talent ("the brain drain"), currency and gold speculation, and shifting shares of world markets. Political consequences of the international operations of American companies are also beginning to be appreciated. Instabilities or at least tensions in local political structures are sometimes analysed with respect to inflows of American capital.

Only the cultural-informational sphere has gone almost unacknowledged in the appraisal of America's global influence. Yet today the control of men and of societies requires, before anything else, the manipulation of words and images. Whatever the degree of raw power that can be brought to bear on a people, it is unavailing in the long run (which may not be so very long in arriving) if it cannot make its objectives seem, if not attractive, at least benign to those it seeks to control. The methods and the messages of communications therefore are the most significant and indispensable instruments of modern power wielders. Neglect of communications in any analysis of contemporary international relations overlooks one of the sources of ultimate power in our time. For the attitudinal state of a population helps to determine its political behavior. And beliefs and opinions are remarkably vulnerable to the sort of modern mass communications which the American system of power uses with fantastic dexterity.

Commercially-produced entertainment and recreation are the chief channels that convey internationally the values and life styles of U.S. corporate capitalism, but the information generated directly by the sizable American business community overseas also is imposing and far reaching in its effects. It is difficult to overstate the impact of the promotional and "research" activities of the large corporations on peoples subjected to them. Moreover, since the agent of influence is often unrecognized as such, the more powerful though less measurable it is likely to be.

The great American stream of business-financed and commercially-saturated communications, pouring through the mass media, is aimed at protecting the physical operations of U.S. enterprises abroad as well as in fostering values and attitudes of privatism and consumerism, which are the ultimate supports of the business system. Few are the regions removed from this wave of commercialism. The culture of American business is enveloping everything in its path as it appeals to individualistic instincts while it reinforces its messages with the imagery of technological gadgetry and consumer delights.

It derives strength also from its utilization of two of the currently strongest human desires—the yearning of people everywhere for an end to bloody conflict and warfare and in their place some condition of universality, and the equally powerful popular impulse to freedom. Accordingly, the rhetoric of corporate communications, disseminated one way or another through the mass media, makes much of internationalism and freedom, of the special sort that maximizes private benefits. The identification of human freedom with property ownership and classifying the world-wide activities of business corporations as an inspiring model of internationalism, provide the chief ideological underpinnings of today's business-originated messages. For instance, the advice of Tom Sutton, executive vice-president-International of J. Walter Thompson Company, the world's largest advertising agency, on this subject is forthright: "I believe it is the job of international organizations such as [the] International Advertising Association and the International Chamber of Commerce to preach the gospel of freedom and to see that the best systems of control and restraint—in areas where there may have to be some—are exported for adoption everywhere, and not the worst."

On the internationalist theme, Robert Sarnoff, chairman of the board and president of RCA Co., the electronics supercorporation, invokes the image of a boundary-free world, accessible to everyone but especially to the undertakings of the few hundred multinational corporations. In a call for a "global common market of communications," Sarnoff enthusiastically recommends reducing national responsibility in communications so that it can be considered a "global resource." Such a development he claims "would foster an increasing worldwide flow of information that would bring benefits as tangible as the increasing trade among the countries of Western Europe. The distribution of knowledge by such a system would provide greater stimulus to growth than any conceivable program of economic aid."

"For the public of all countries, it would provide entertainment, cultural and informational programming from abroad as a routine rather than a rarity." And, furthermore, Sarnoff adds: "As data transmission becomes less and less expensive, we will see greater use of computerized controls and even long-distance time-sharing to strengthen the multinational firm as a vehicle for the transfer of technology. The increases in production and productivity, resulting from the global surge of business information, could parallel the economic advances made in the common market over the past 20 years."

All this would apparently occur in the absence of genuine international structures of control and alongside diminished national authority. Beneficiaries in this context could only be the giant, transnational corporations.

Economic output, technological mastery and military power have been the traditional strengths of the American corporate economy. Now, increasing reliance is being placed on communications control. The heavy informational flow produced and supported by American companies overseas makes a powerful contribution to the domestic maintenance and global extension of the business system and its value.

SUGGESTED READINGS

The Image Empire by Erick Barnouw (New York: Oxford University Press, 1970).

2 *John P. Huttman*

Automobile Addiction

A status symbol, an object of fantasy, an important source of employment and an indispensible element in the national income accounts, the automobile has had a profound impact upon the quality and character of urban life in the United States. Even those who assert that the automobile has not been one of the basic causes of urban deterioration concede that, at the very least, the car contributes to the complexity of urban problems. The automobile has a voracious appetite for the consumption of urban land. The car provides people with the means for moving away from rather than resolving urban problems, at the same time facilitating the expansion of suburban sprawl. The shift of population and sources of employment from metropolitan centers to outlying areas has reduced the capacity of cities to support services for their remaining, often needy residents. The automobile has played a crucial role in the decline of pedestrian and public transport patterns in the city and in the deterioration of many traditional city functions.

Auto-Addiction

The public's obeisance to the automobile and the critical dependence on cars for employment and economic growth are instrumental in the ordering of social and economic priorities. One-tenth of the nongovernmental labor force in the United States is directly dependent upon the production, sales and service of automobiles for its employment. When embarking on its economic recovery program to bring the country from recession to prosperity, the government quickly acted to lift the automobile excise tax. Optimistic predictions of increased consumer demand for new vehicles and a related rise in automobile-connected employment issued from official quarters.

The growth of industries dependent upon auto-addiction (such as the petroleum companies) is as important to the economy as the direct impact of the production and sales of cars. Hundreds of other spin-offs are involved in highway construction, and it is likely that the imposing Interstate freeway system—a $60 billion investment—will be appraised as inadequate a few years after its completion. Then its deficiencies will probably be repaired with a multi-billion dollar program of expansion.

Cars wear out or owners crave the status and novelty of having the latest innovation. Buyers avidly queue up to examine and place orders for the newest models rolling off the assembly lines. There is a sense of exhilaration and urgency in all this, although new models are differentiated from old mainly by cosmetic touches. Technological innovations are applied to production models less frequently than the industry would care to admit. The small minority of motorists who disdainfully neglect the maintenance of their cars, sometimes deliberately as a mark of their domination over the car, only accelerate the deterioration of their vehicles. The industry does not care whether motorists consume cars to keep pace with current model changes or to replace inoperative wrecks, so long as their output of new automobiles is steadily absorbed.

A conspicuously growing number of motorists pay homage to and pamper their cars, treating them—perhaps most appropriately—as objects of ornamentation rather than as utilitarian machines. Advertising incessantly reminds the public of the status value of the automobile. In one recent advertisement, a car-maker declared that purchase of its top-of-the-line sedan was a more important decision than buying a house. A Los Angeles mechanic recently observed that many of the people who have him service their cars "go hungry at night so that their automobiles can get the care they deserve." Others have all they can do to keep their vehicles out of the hands of recovery agents. Automobiles are expensive. A recent government study indicates that $1,300 is the average annual cost of a moderately priced and sized vehicle which is owned for ten years and driven about 10,000 miles per year. However, since the actual life of a car appears to average only slightly more than six years, and since many cars exceed the purchase price, size and mileage specifications of the government's study, many motorists make substantially higher annual outlays for the ownership and operation of their cars.

Recent legislation compelling manufacturers to publicly reveal mechanical defects and recall their products for repair has disenchanted some motorists. It hurts a motorist's image when his car's manufacturer acknowledges (albeit reluctantly) that the car may disgorge some vital parts or even disintegrate. But a consumer's revolt seems unlikely since the automobile is physically as well as psychologically addictive.

Many Americans seem to think that the evasive qualities of freedom, individuality and creativity are theirs with the purchase of a new car. It is apparent that the translation process generates frustrations: "image" constantly requires updating as models go out of vogue. Illusions of uniqueness suffer from the obvious duplication resulting from mass production. Image conveyed through the automobile becomes superficial and ephemeral, and the manufacturers of cars find it profitable to stimulate and then accommodate this demand.

The automobile insatiably consumes space and resources in its production and operation. In some of the fastest growing cities in the United States, over half the land area has been paved over for purposes directly relating to automobiles. Even older, more traditional cities typically have about one-fourth of total area devoted to roads, driveways, parking lots, garages, service stations and other auto-serving functions. Government at all levels usually responds with alacrity to demands for road improvement. The demands of consumers and producers of cars appear irresistible.

As land is shifted from income-earning and taxable uses to non-income-earning and nontaxable roads, cities and, in some cases, higher political jurisdictions, must depend on a diminished tax base. Typically, improved road systems enable middle-class families to relocate from central city areas to suburbs. Thus the urban tax base declines and, in some cases, reduces city population to the extremes of poor and wealthy. Developers are quick to spot the profits afforded them by new highway systems and housing, so industry and shopping centers follow the roads. The market mechanism subordinates the planning process, and the result is chaotic suburban sprawl.

The cost of our extensive road system appears rational when highways "pay for themselves" through gasoline sales taxes or through tolls levied against road users. However, while such revenue may pay for road construction and upkeep, it is not calculated to compensate for the loss of the income and tax-earning capacity of the land consumed for roads. Such losses are often unevenly distributed, so that cities losing land to road systems may experience income loss or only slight gain while the surrounding suburban areas may realize substantial benefit.

The operation of cars, through exhaust emission byproducts, space consumed by roads and parking areas, and the production of fuels and of cars themselves, has damaged the environment, and it is difficult to transfer these environmental costs to the operators of motor vehicles.

The automobile dilemma defies piecemeal reform. The benefits of offering discounts to multiple-passenger cars at bridge and roadway toll stations—aside from boosting the sale of mannequins—might include a net increase in the number of car pools. Similarly, increasing tolls during peak traffic periods might encourage some to commute during off hours. If increased substantially, the tolls might have a deterrent effect on some rush-hour commuters and even shift a greater share of the costs of roads to users. But the toll stations are not always located where traffic problems are most critical. In many urban areas, toll stations are rare, even on bridges, and it would be unfeasible to erect and operate toll stations in congested urban districts. The impact of toll station rate differentials by number of passengers and time of travel, in the case of privately owned automobiles, would necessarily be limited in terms of its effect on discouraging driving because a large part of the costs of car operation would remain unaffected. The high public costs incurred by automobile operation in congested areas would remain largely intact.

Despite mounting social and economic costs our physical dependence on cars seems inescapable. For practical purposes, there is no way for people to get from one place to another except by car. The continuing need for cars is reinforced by the fact that people already operate cars extensively and that a comprehensive road network exists. Widely dispersed and low-density residential locations, combined with complex patterns of shopping trips and commutes for employment purposes, dictate complicated and extensive travel routes for many persons. These conditions make it difficult to justify creation of comprehensive public transportation networks in many areas of population concentration and, further, they suggest that even with the operation of a modern, efficient public transport system many people will continue to operate cars.

Reducing Auto-Dependency

The strategist intent upon reducing America's dependency upon the automobile must be content, at least initially, to focus upon the modest, realistic objective of reducing rather than eliminating dependency on cars. In fact, recent measures intended to reduce automobile exhaust pollutants and to make cars safer may already have inadvertantly discouraged new car sales.

The Environmental Protection Agency recently extended established deadlines for the enforcement of more stringent automotive emission standards. However, it is likely that more rigorous standards may be introduced in the future. The introduction and enforcement of anti-pollution standards may do little to lessen the aggregate impact of automotive pollution upon the environment if the reduction in pollution output per vehicle is offset by an increased number of vehicles. But if the anti-pollution standards prove sufficiently onerous, manufacturers may be unable to meet these requirements except at a high cost per vehicle produced, reflected in an increased cost to the consumer. This could result in a smaller demand for new cars.

More rigorous anti-pollution standards might reinforce inequities in our society between different socio-economic groups. However, it is a contradiction to denounce inequities introduced as the result of more stringent environmental preservation criteria while viewing with equanimity disparities in the distribution of necessities, as food and housing, because these result from the market mechanism. The argument for lessening inequality in the case of automobile ownership by neglecting anti-pollution standards appears shallow when the inequities regarding basics as shaped by market forces are treated as sacrosanct. Those intent upon achieving an equitable society might more profitably argue for repair of market deficiencies than for neglect of the environment.

Safer cars, particularly if both consumer and producer insist on maintaining existing size and performance characteristics, are likely to be more expensive, so fewer cars may be demanded. Conceivably, it might be more directly effective to discourage automobile production and use through imposing highway tolls, reducing speed limits, introducing more traffic signals and even narrowing and closing off streets. But these direct measures to discourage cars would be less likely to win the support or even the acquiescence of motorists than would the "more respectable" safety and pollution control standards.

People are unlikely to reduce their dependence upon automobiles significantly, even if the costs of owning and operating cars soar, until a viable alternative becomes available. The likely substitute for the private car is a comprehensive public transport network, particularly the urban rapid-transit system. The capacity of a traffic lane is substantially expanded when busses rather than individual cars are the transportation vehicles, and expanded even more when the traffic lane is the exclusive right-of-way of a rail system of rapid transit.

One obstacle to the success of any existing public transport system is that it must co-exist with personal forms of transport offering much greater flexibility. Flexibility in terms of travel patterns is important because jobs, shopping, residence and other activities requiring significant movement have been shaped over decades by the car. It is no surprise that the automobile best serves the conditions which its manufacturers and users have cultivated. Any shift from the automobile to an alternative form of transportation would probably involve considerable inconvenience which only time could alleviate.

Manipulation of the price structure of public transport might offer prospects of weaning motorists from their cars. At the extreme, making a public transport system free to users during peak periods could entice drivers to it for the journey to and from work. Yet when authorities in Rome experimented with free bus travel during rush hour periods they found, to their dismay, that few Italian motorists were willing to be separated from their cars. The busses quickly filled to capacity with pedestrians while the number of cars in use declined but slightly. Conceivably, if public transport were more comprehensive in its network, equipped with fast, comfortable vehicles operating on frequent schedules and yet still offered free or at attractive prices, a substantial number of motorists would switch from their cars. But it is unlikely that a public transport system, for which the financial burden of operation falls upon taxpayers in general, rather than users specifically, would be capable of sustaining these attractive features. Even if public transport were to be provided free to users at peak periods, it is unlikely that the public would tolerate intensively scheduled free public transport for off-peak hours. Motorists compelled to resort to their cars for non-commuting trips might be tempted to use their vehicles for commuting purposes as well.

The total cost per mile to the user of automobile transport may greatly exceed that for public transport, but to the motorist, the price he pays for the public transport alternative is variable, that is, one which is incurred only when he is actually riding on that vehicle. In the case of the automobile, the motorist incurs both variable costs resulting from the operation of the car and fixed costs resulting from ownership of the car, independent of operation. The fixed costs involved include depreciation and insurance while the variable costs consist of such items as gasoline, oil and most maintenance operations. So long as the motorist owns a vehicle, he encounters fixed costs. Therefore, the car owner would only compare the variable costs of automobile use with the total costs of taking the alternative public transport. If the variable costs alone of automobile operation were equal to or, perhaps, only slightly greater than the public transport costs to the user, the motorist would probably choose to drive his car, with its greater convenience and comfort. Possibly over the long run, when the motorist is confronted with the decision as to whether or not the car is to be replaced with a new one, he may opt to forgo ownership. But so many noneconomic factors are involved in buying a new car that psychological and other needs may override economic rationality. Perhaps the only certain way to shift from automobile to public transport would be to eliminate private ownership of personal transport vehicles.

Automobiles as Public Goods

Under the prevailing scheme of private automobile ownership, the motorist is constrained only by the costs which he personally encounters and remains indifferent to the costs imposed upon society. A motorist may impose slight cost upon society when he operates his car very early in the morning, when the road is nearly free of other traffic. Later in the morning, at the peak of heavy rush hour traffic, the same vehicle may impose a much higher cost on society. Similarly, adding another car to an infrequently travelled road may cause society only slight expense while one more vehicle on a more heavily travelled road may impose a much heavier toll. Because of the range and variety of individual values reflected in automotive operating decisions, it is unlikely that the aggregate of automobiles will be distributed over time and place of operation in a pattern which would minimize public cost.

Schemes that might insure that motorists cover the full social costs of operation of their cars would distribute vehicles in a more beneficial pattern. Toll zones within congested parts of cities could discourage traffic. But it may prove uneconomical to establish stations to enforce tolls in less compact areas and it may not prove economically feasible to regulate the toll rate structure fairly.

One inefficiency of private automobile ownership is that a large share of the total number of cars sit idle much of the time. Typically, many of the idle cars are concentrated in intensively used, land-scarce commercial areas during conventional business hours. Duplicate service facilities for cars are also located in these areas, consuming additional land.

Public ownership of personal transportation vehicles could shift the full social costs of automobile operation to the individual motorist. The transfer of personal transport vehicles from private to public ownership does not necessarily represent a serious infringement upon the process of free market choice. In fact, car ownership prevents motorists from shifting between automobiles and other goods and therefore interferes with the ideal mobility implied in connection with market decision-making forces. Actual ownership of goods—as opposed to availability of use—is not critical to the market process.

Public ownership of personal transport vehicles, to have any chance of success, would have to be a comprehensive system, with rates scaled for time and location and with charges levied for vehicles held idle as well as operated. An experimental collective automobile ownership program conducted in Montpellier, France, reveals the limitations of a more circumscribed scheme. The Montpellier program involved a fleet of about 200 small cars, only a small fraction of the total number of automobiles in operation in the immediate area. Access to the cars in the fleet was provided by membership in an organization, with members holding keys for the common door and ignition locks of the vehicles. Special tokens fed meters which timed the operation of the automobiles. The scheme encountered some difficulties in the efficient allocation of resources. A member could leave a vehicle wherever he chose when he had completed a trip. However, with few cars in the fleet, the problem members undoubtedly experienced in locating cars abandoned by others probably encouraged some to hoard automobiles for future use. Because there was no penalty for hoarding, the existing stock of cars in the fleet was often inefficiently allocated.

The individual motorist involved in the Montpellier program was charged the same rate for operating a fleet vehicle in the city center and in the less intensively travelled surrounding countryside, and during rush hour and slack period traffic, since no distinction was made for time and location of use. The only distinct advantage of the scheme over private automobile ownership is that both fixed and variable costs could be incorporated in the established meter rates—if the time and location factors are neglected—whereas under private ownership only variable costs are involved in the decisions relating to each trip.

A publicly controlled automobile rental agency might assume the form of a universal, monopolistic Hertz or Avis, perhaps operating autonomously under general government guidelines and regulations. The car rental agency would have rates established on the basis of time and location of operation, with meter mechanisms adjusting rates over the time of day and over geographic zones. Clock devices could adjust rates by time, and electronic trip cords on roads could trigger rate changes as cars entered one zone from another. The cars would be checked out of rental stations and, upon completion of use, would be checked in at the same or other rental stations. Magnetic credit cards and computerized recording and metering devices would be required for efficient, economical operations. In the absence of privately owned cars and competing rental agencies, the scale of operation of the public car rental agency would be sufficient to sustain a large number of widely distributed stations. Stations would be geared to accept cars on a "rent it here, leave it there" basis with little or no penalty for doing so.

The rates established for the public car rental agency, in addition to differentiation on the basis of time and location as a reflection of social and economic costs incurred, offer the possibility of adjustment to reduce the total number of automobiles in operation. The public can be encouraged to even out its demand for cars over the day through more attractive rate scales for the hours when demand for cars normally declines. The convenient location of car rental stations along public transport system lines, particularly if coordinated with bonuses for dropping cars off at such stations, would encourage travelers to link public transport into their trips. Over time, the inconvenience of dispersed car rental stations in lightly populated suburban areas could restrict further suburban sprawl. Cars might be rented on a permanent basis by isolated individuals who need constant transportation, but the cost would be established at regular rental rates. The high costs involved in long-duration rentals would encourage more compact living, work and shopping arrangements and thereby reduce dependency on cars.

The proposed public car rental scheme could combine rental facilities with refueling and repair agencies, allowing conservation of valuable land, particularly in urban areas, commonly wasted by duplicate gas stations and other auto-serving facilities. The car rental scheme would allow for standardization of automobiles into far fewer models than the prevailing proliferation, with the strong possibility of economies through eliminating the annual model change ritual. The adverse impact upon the automobile industry of a public car rental scheme could be dampened by engineering effective safety and antipollution features into each vehicle. The increased investment in each automobile would mean that manufacturers would not suffer serious economic reverses as production of new cars declines.

Proposals for introducing a public car rental system probably would generate formidible opposition. Objections might be raised regarding restrictions on the appearance and performance of vehicles. These superficial and socially misplaced values have become deeply entrenched and are unlikely to be lightly dismissed by the public. Objections to a public car rental system might also include the charge that such a system is ideologically alien to the United States. This charge cannot be sustained, since the rental phenomenon is expanding greatly in the American economy while, simultaneously, the urgency for private ownership of automobiles is accelerating in the Soviet Union and other socialist countries. Nonetheless, even though ownership is not essential and may even impede the process of consumer choice, it is sanctioned along with sundry other peculiar practices under the guise of being an integral part of the market system. More substantial objections to the replacement of private automobile ownership with a rental scheme might focus on the prospect that while such a scheme might minimize the environmental damage and resource misallocation involved in private car ownership, it would not entirely eliminate such deficiencies. It must be conceded that these conditions inevitably follow from the existence of cars but, importantly, a car rental scheme does offer prospects for assuming an intermediary role, potentially capable of leading to the eventual elimination of personal transport vehicles.

SUGGESTED READINGS

Dead End, The Automobile in Mass Transportation by Ronald A. Buel (Baltimore: Penguin, 1972).

The Urban Transportation Problem by John R. Meyer, John Kain, and M. Wohl (Cambridge: Harvard University Press, 1965).

Technology and Growth: The Price We Pay by Ezra J. Mishan (New York: Praeger, 1969).

Transportation: Selected Readings edited by Denys Munby (Baltimore: Penguin, 1968).

Towns Against Traffic by Stephen Plowden (London: Deutsch, 1972).

A Self-Financing Road System by G. J. Roth (London: The Institute of Economic Affairs, 1966).

Readings in Urban Transportation, edited by George M. Smerk (Bloomington, Indiana: Indiana University Press, 1968).

Beyond the Automobile: Reshaping the Transportation Environment by Tabor R. Stone (Englewood Cliffs, N.J.: Prentice-Hall, 1971).

3

J. Allen Whitt

Californians, Cars and Technological Death

The freeways, like the vehicles that cruise them, are anything but free. The price in misallocation of resources, in deaths, in pollution and environmental disruption are enormous. These costs are social, borne not by auto manufacturers and motorists alone but by society at large. Since California is popularly held to be two years ahead of the rest of the country in social trends it is already in an advanced state of auto-addiction and is a logical proving ground for would-be social solutions to the auto problem.

Little wonder, then, that supporters of one such plan—a measure to fight auto pollution and improve mass transit—were confident that their proposal would be readily approved by the electorate. If anything, Proposition 18, as the measure was known, was felt by its supporters to be too modest an attempt at reform. It had but two provisions: that an unspecified amount of the revenue from gasoline taxes and license fees would go to control environmental pollution caused by motor vehicles; and that local voters could use up to 25 percent of their county's revenues for improving mass transit systems.

But the environmental groups and urban transit interests which supported Proposition 18 had badly misjudged the strength of the highway lobby; the measure never stood a chance. Proposition 18's author, Senator James Mills, later wrote that he was surprised that the bill got as far as the ballot. In fact, on the day it was due to come to a vote he left the Assembly early, "thinking the bill had died." Perhaps some assemblymen voted for Proposition 18 since they were certain it would fail anyway but felt that a token pro-ecology vote would be politically astute. Whatever the reason, Proposition 18 made it through the legislature and was scheduled to appear, just 11 weeks later, on the November 1970 ballot as a referendum. The life history of Proposition 18—certainly a small-scale attempt to mitigate certain of the social costs of the automobile transport system—can prepare us for the course of future contests between environmentalists and their economic and political enemies.

The Campaign

Proponents of the proposition formed an organization called Californians Against Smog. Aided by a $10,000 contribution from the Tuberculosis and Respiratory Disease Association of California (TARDAC) and with active support from the Sierra Club and other environmental groups, Californians Against Smog began to try to raise money for campaign expenses. Also allied with pro-18 groups was the Citizen's Transportation Committee in Los Angeles, which had succeeded in raising around $400,000 for a rapid transit campaign in 1968. CTC spokesman told Proposition 18 proponents: "You are a real army. Your foot soldiers should get the message to the grassroots. . . . You only need $200,000 this time. Eighteen's a good issue. That's all it'll take."

Meanwhile, opponents of Proposition 18 had established a group called Californians Against the Street and Road Tax Trap. Its purpose was to gather forces for a media blitz.

The contest which followed was replete with rhetoric, denunciations, protest, law suits, charges of prevarication and perfidy, and disillusionment.

Proponents of Proposition 18 argued that building more highways cannot solve traffic problems since new roads are overrun by autos as soon as they open, and that funds produced by the automobile should logically be used to control air pollution—also produced by the automobile. Citing studies which were said to show that "up to 87 percent of the travel on State highways terminates within the county of origin," they maintained that the state road system was basically a local transportation system. It followed that local voters should be able to determine the kind of local system of transport they desire. Earmarking of highway funds leads, they argued, to inflexibility and inequality of funding state projects. Under Proposition 18 benefits would also accrue to rural residents, because they would be able to use their 25 percent of highway revenues for the construction and maintenance of local roads, if they so voted. Federal matching funds for rapid transit would become available, easing the present burden of property taxes to pay for such transit. Proponents also argued that the availability of rapid transit facilities would help reduce traffic congestion on the freeways and would decrease air pollution.

Opponents of Proposition 18 countered that the "freeway master plan, adopted by the Legislature in 1959, is only about 36% developed to freeway standards and the remainder of that system may never be finished if highway gasoline tax money is used to finance rapid transit." Rapid transit, they said, is very expensive and will not be able to compete successfully with automobile transportation. Moreover, "it is unfair and economically unsound to impose a tax burden upon one form of transportation to finance another." The building of highways, they continued, is a very complex and long-range process. "The very nature of this type of program demands a predictable, steady, and assured source of revenue, making a special purpose fund and tax source highly desirable." Noting that highway funds were already available for the support of State Air Resources Board and air pollution research, they said that it was not necessary to amend the Constitution for this purpose. Finally, they argued that by the time rapid transit systems could be built, "much will have been accomplished through engine and fuel modifications in the elimination of automobile air pollution."

Early in the campaign, various organizations and individuals went on record as being for or against Proposition 18. Governor Reagan was at first publicly opposed to the bill "because it would endanger the state highway system." Yet by election time, Reagan was *for* the amendment, saying that it gave the people the right to say how public funds should be spent. Reagan's opponent in the November election, Jesse Unruh, called the governor's stand "hypocritical," noting that oil companies had contributed more than $100,000 to Reagan's campaign, and drawing attention to Standard Oil of California's bad record as a polluter.

Declared opponents of Proposition 18 included the Automobile Club of Southern California, California State Automobile Association, the Teamsters Union, California Trucking Association, California State Chamber of Commerce, County Supervisors Association of California, Atlantic-Richfield Company, E.P. DuPont de Nemours & Company, Ethyl Corporation, Gulf Oil Corporation, Humble Oil & Refining Company, Mobil Oil Corporation, Phillips Petroleum Company, Standard Oil of California, Union Oil Company of California, California Taxpayers' Association, California State Employees Association, California Farm Bureau, California Real Estate Association, and the Property Owners' Tax Association of California.

To run their media campaign, opponents of Proposition 18 hired Milton Kramer, a political consultant from suburban Los Angeles who had waged a successful campaign a few months before against a ballot proposition that would have shifted education costs to the state.

Billboard Propaganda

During the second week in October, Kramer saturated the state with billboards reading "More taxes? No No. 18." The 700 billboards were placed to achieve a "100 percent showing"; that is, every person in the state should theoretically have seen such a billboard at least once before election time (except in those few counties, such as Santa Barbara, that ban billboards). The opponents argued that such slogans were justified since the state highway system was already behind schedule, revenues were inadequate to meet the need for highways, and any diversion of monies from the highway trust fund would have to be compensated for by an increase in taxes.

Proponents of 18 cried out in anguish against the contention that the amendment would raise taxes, pointing out that only a *diversion* of money was involved. As campaign rhetoric became more heated, nearly all of the major newspapers in the state announced support for Proposition 18. In endorsing 18, the *Sacramento Bee* said:

> This modest step is too much for the highway lobby, an aggregation of oil companies, cement firms, automobile clubs, truckers, contractors, and others with vested interests in restricting the use of gasoline tax revenue for highway purposes.

The *Los Angeles Times* called the opposition campaign by "powerful special interests" one of "deliberate confusion and misinformation" designed to deceive the voters.

Yet the media campaign was only one impediment that Proposition 18 supporters had to overcome. As organizations and individuals that proponents had counted on for support let them down, it became increasingly apparent during the month of October that their initial optimism was not justified. Californians Against Smog had counted on the aluminum industries to support Proposition 18 since they stood to profit from mass transit systems (Bay Area Rapid Transit, for example, is expected to use two million pounds of Alcoa aluminum) but they proved to be ambivalent towards the amendment since they also have big interests in highway construction and maintenance and in auto manufacture.

Money sources for the measure virtually dried up. Businessmen united with what one supporter of the proposition called "interlocking corporate good will" and spread the word that 18 was bad for business. Quasi-environmentalist organizations like the Los Angeles County Environmental Quality Control Committee voted not to support 18. The Los Angeles Chamber of Commerce did endorse 18, but weakly and very late in the campaign. The San Francisco Chamber of Commerce went on record against 18, though Mayor Joseph Alioto stated he was appalled at their position on an issue that would bring San Francisco between $72 and $90 million to aid the Municipal Railway "as well as fighting pollution." According to Sierra Club president Phillip Berry, the decision of the Chamber was the direct result of pressure from Standard Oil of California, an accusation which, says Berry, "Interestingly, Standard never denied. . . ."

Proponents of Proposition 18 also saw opposition voiced against their amendment in "unofficial" ways.

The Freeway Support Committee of the State Chamber sponsored a six-page supplement which appeared in the *Los Angeles Times* one week before the election. Although the $14,000 supplement did not mention Proposition 18, thus qualifying for the lower "educational" rate rather than the "political" rate, the supplement eulogized the state highway system in pictures and text, and provided a card for registering reader approval. The chairman of the Freeway Support Committee was also president of the Automobile Club of Southern California.

Not unexpectedly, the auto club was opposed to Proposition 18, as was the California State Automobile Association (both affiliates of the American Automobile Association). It has been estimated that the club spends from $30,000 to $35,000 a year lobbying in Sacramento. The club magazines were another source of "unofficial" opposition to the measure. With a combined membership of approximately two and a half million, the clubs may have significantly influenced the final vote.

Most auto club members are concerned only with the road services that such associations offer, services that are generally of a high order. Member apathy is conducive to oligarchical control. Ralph Nader and other critics have charged that the American Automobile Association is not adequately meeting member needs and has extensive ties with the highway lobby. Local auto clubs are also big business. Many sell tires, batteries and automobile insurance. The California State Automobile Association, for example, reported that it wrote more than $120 million worth of insurance in 1970.

Supporters of Proposition 18 were severely hampered by their lack of campaign money. Endorsements by Sugar Ray Robinson, Carol Burnett and Jack Lemmon were taped, but there was too little money to buy time to broadcast them. Two full-time staff members had to be let go and the campaign ran on the efforts of 2,000 to 4,000 volunteers.

In contrast, opponents of 18 were well financed. Expenditures by both sides for their media campaigns have been estimated as follows:

	Opponents	**Proponents**
Billboards	$123,000	—
Television	60,000	$1,400
Newspaper	17,000	1,456
Radio	15,000	2,401
Total	$215,000	$5,257

The advantage of the opposition is even more overwhelming considering that these are the official expenses; not included is the "unofficial" assistance to the opposition campaign by the California State Chamber of Commerce in its mailings to local government officials, nor the newspaper supplement by the Freeway Support Committee, nor the articles against Proposition 18 which appeared in auto club publications. Moreover, there was an enormous organizational advantage on the side of opponents. As E.E.Schattschneider has observed:

> . . . businessmen collectively constitute the most class-conscious group in American society. As a class they are the most highly organized, more easily mobilized, have more facilities for communication, are more like-minded, and are more accustomed to stand together in defense of their privileges than any other group.

About four months before the campaign started, a state-wide attitudinal survey found that 77 percent of California adults favored "spending some of that state gas money (i.e., that currently spent for highways) for smog or air pollution research." Only 17 percent expressed disapproval. About five months later, just before the billboards of the anti-18 forces were erected, the Field poll discovered that only about one in three voters in the state had heard of Proposition 18. However, when they were given a copy of the measure as it was to appear on the ballot, 64 percent said they would vote yes. Twenty-two percent were opposed. It looked as though 18 would pass. Another Field poll was taken a week before the election, after the measure had been more publicized. Still, only 57 percent had seen or heard about Proposition 18. The ballot statement was read to those who had not heard anything about the measure, and 56 percent of that group were in favor. Twelve percent were opposed. On the other hand, 53 percent of those who were previously aware of the issue said they would vote yes, while 29 percent said they would vote no. Among all voters, potential support for the amendment had declined to 52 percent, a drop of 12 percentage points in approximately one month. Since the main voices for and against the measure had been, up until that time, the major newspapers and the billboards, respectively, it must be assumed that the disingenuous message of the laconic billboards was having the greater influence.

During the last days of the campaign, anti-18 forces waged a weekly saturation campaign on television, newspapers and radio. These advertisements, supporters say, were filled with distortions. The central theme was that Proposition 18 would increase taxes. It was suggested that toll booths would appear on freeways if money were diverted from highways.

This ad campaign was as effective as it was misleading: although 52 percent of those surveyed had approved of Proposition 18 one week before the election, on November 3 the amendment was defeated by a vote of 2.7 million (45.9 percent) to 3.2 million (54.1 percent). Proposition 18 passed in only eight of the 58 counties.

Further indication of the last-minute success of the opposition campaign is revealed by the absentee ballots. By law absentee ballots in the state may be requested between seven and 29 days before the election. That means that such ballots could have been filled out as early as October 5, 1970, well before the media blitz at the end of the campaign. Absentee voting figures are available for 35 of the 58 counties, the rest having been combined with general election totals. The total absentee vote in the 35 counties was *favorable* to the measure: 90,148 (58.7 percent) versus 63,480 (41.3 percent). General election totals for the amendment in those counties were close to the statewide percentage (46.2 percent versus 45.9 percent). Assuming that these 35 counties are a representative sample, a comparison of the absentee vote with the general election vote indicates a highly significant relationship between voting absentee and voting for Proposition 18. While we cannot be certain, of course, that other temporal factors were not at work here, there can be little doubt that the opposition media campaign was decisive in the defeat of Proposition 18.

Contributions

More precise identification of the proponents and opponents of Proposition 18 is contained in the campaign contribution reports filed with the secretary of state. It is not possible to determine just how accurate these reports may be, especially since none of them was verified under penalty of perjury as required by the California Elections Code, but they are at least *minimal* indices of the nature of the forces for and against the amendment.

According to these reports, opponents spent about 15 times as much as proponents ($335,445.69 versus $22,721.81). Total contributions for and against 18 were $348,830.00 and $17,714.20, respectively. It is obvious that money was overwhelmingly on the side of the opposition. Those who contributed $10,000 or more to oppose Proposition 18 were:

1. Standard Oil of California	$75,000
2. Shell Oil Company	50,000
3. Mobil Oil	30,000
4. Automobile Club of Southern California	22,000
5. Gulf Oil	20,000
6. Texaco	20,000
7. Union Oil Company of California	20,000
8. Sully Miller Company	15,000
9. Phillips Oil	15,000
10. Humble Oil and Refining Company	12,000
11. California State Automobile Association	11,000
12. Interinsurance Bureau, Los Angeles	10,000

By contrast, supporters of the amendment received only three contributions of more than $1,000. They were from two companies with mass transit interests, Kaiser Industries ($2,500) and Rohr Corporation ($2,000), and from the Citizens Transportation Committee ($3,345.98). The CTC money represented that group's working capital.

Opposition money came primarily from large contributions, while money for 18 came from small donations: the median contribution for the anti-18 campaign was $500; the median contribution for the pro-18 campaign was $5. More than three-fourths of the opposition money came from oil companies. Other anti-18 interests were (in order of contribution): automobile clubs and their insurance bureaus; highway equipment and construction companies; trucking and taxi companies; labor unions representing highway construction employees; forest products and land companies; tire and rubber companies; and individuals.

The full involvement of oil companies in the campaign had not been immediately apparent. The opposition's contribution report, filed about three weeks after the election, listed four "anonymous" donations totaling $95,000.

Kramer, the opposition's campaign manager, had wanted $600,000 with which to conduct a proper campaign. He complained that he did not have enough money for the final weekend media campaign he had been planning. The events of the last week before the election are described by the *Washington Post:*

> The way Kramer tells it, four unidentified cashiers' checks turned up at the committee's Los Angeles offices while he was away in Sacramento. . .the total—$95,000—was put toward a final weekend media blitz, including $60,000 in television spots. . . .

Secretary of State-elect Edmund G. Brown, Jr., decided to force the issue. He sent a letter to the District Attorney of Sacramento County, demanding that he

> . . .launch an immediate investigation and also inquire of each committee member (Californians Against the Street and Road Tax Trap) concerning his knowledge of these anonymous donations to determine whether there has been a violation of the Elections Code through failure to disclose the donors' true identity.

One week later, Mobil Oil Corporation admitted in a letter to Sullivan that it was one of the anonymous donors, its contribution of $30,000 having been made on October 28, five days before the election. The company said that it gave the money in good faith and never asked for anonymity.

When the next campaign expenditure report was filed near the end of December, the three remaining anonymous donations were listed: Anonymous—Mellon National Bank—cashier's check—$20,000.00; Anonymous–California Bank NA,SF—cashier's check—$25,000.00; Anonymous—California Bank NA,SF—cashier's check—$20,000.00.

Another month passed. On January 26, 1971, Brown filed suit in Los Angeles asking permission to subpoena bank records to determine the identities of the contributors. The next day, Gulf Oil confessed that it had given $20,000 to oppose 18. Brown observed, "A Gulf spokesman says the company never requested anonymity, but I am highly suspicious of the circumstances surrounding this matter."

One day later, Standard Oil of California, a company which had already contributed $30,000, admitted that the two remaining anonymous contributions of $20,000 and $25,000 were its own. Standard's story was much like that of Mobil and Gulf. A spokesman said, "There never was any intention on our part to conceal the contribution. It was the responsibility of the campaign organization to make the report, not us."

After these disclosures, Brown continued with his civil suit. The suit asked a $1,000 penalty from each defendant: Standard, Mobil, Gulf, Kramer, Californians Against the Street and Road Tax Trap, and two of its officers. The Sacramento County district attorney had rejected Brown's demand for an investigation. Moreover, the Sacramento County grand jury indicated little interest in the case. A Los Angeles Superior Court judge ruled that Brown's suit was unconstitutional: the election code laws requiring the disclosure of contributions to defeat or pass ballot measures were discriminatory because such requirements were not placed upon donors to the campaigns of individual candidates. Brown persisted. The State Supreme Court overturned the lower court ruling and authorized a continuation of the suit. On January 30, 1972, Brown announced a settlement with one of the defendants. Gulf Oil Corporation agreed to donate $25,000 to the Air Pollution Research Center at the University of California, Riverside.

Oil's Role

There can be little doubt that oil companies played a major part in the defeat of Proposition 18. Their contributions were apparently coordinated by the Western Oil and Gas Association (WOGA). Harry Morrison, general manager of WOGA, says that some oil companies asked him what their "fair share" of contributions against Proposition 18 would be. He maintains he asked the campaign manager how much the anti-18 campaign would need. Kramer told him between $600,000 and $1.25 million. Morrison says that he then calculated that contributions from oil companies totaling $175,000 (the actual oil contributions amounted to $240,000) would be appropriate, "if they were going to give." The sum was apportioned among the various companies on the basis of their "gallonage" sold in California.

When asked why oil companies such as Sun Oil (headquartered in Philadelphia and having no service stations in California) and Standard of Indiana saw fit to donate money to oppose 18, Morrison responded that the oil industry saw the campaign as a very important one. If diversion of gas taxes could happen in California, it "could happen anywhere." A spokesman for an oil company that requested anonymity agreed with Morrison's interpretation: he called the issue a "bellwether nationally" as far as oil companies were concerned.

Even so, one major oil company doing business in California, Atlantic-Richfield, did not (apparently) contribute money to the opposition campaign. ARCO is not listed on the contribution lists although the company was reported early in the campaign to be opposed to Proposition 18. This was confirmed after the election by a company spokesman. An oil company executive later admitted that "not all companies wanted to go along," fearing a bad press. The *Los Angeles Times* quotes one source in the oil industry as saying:

> Some of us . . . wanted to stay neutral. But [Otto] Miller [chairman of the board of Standard Oil of California] and [Fred] Hartley [head of Union Oil] reminded us persuasively of all the joint ventures in exploration where we worked with their companies.

Interlocks

In addition to the unity of purpose brought about by common interests, the business community had more direct means of coordination. The California State Chamber of Commerce, for example, was a primary agent in the planning and execution of the anti-18 strategy. Interlocking boards of directors constitute a second means of coordination. The connections between the Automobile Club of Southern California and other businesses are more impressive than those links between the California State Automobile Association (CSAA) and business. CSAA is interlocked with the Freeway Support Committee (two mutual directors), United California Bank (one) and Bank of America (one). The Automobile Club of Southern California, on the other hand, shares directors with the Freeway Support Committee (two), United California Bank (two), Bank of America (one), Cyprus Mining (three), North American Rockwell (two), Beckman Instruments (one), Getty Oil (one), Stanford University (one), Pacific Mutual Life Insurance (four), University of Southern California (two), California Institute of Technology (one) and Stanford Research Institute (one). All three California oil companies, Getty, Standard and Union, are linked to the Stanford Research Institute, the California Institute of Technology and Bank of America. Some of the links between corporations bind them together very tightly. For example, one person, Asa V. Call, links together the Automobile Club of Southern California, United California Bank, Cyprus Mining, University of Southern California and Pacific Mutual Life Insurance Company.

It is obvious that such interlocks were not without effect in the Proposition 18 campaign. At a minimum, they facilitated communication and coordination among anti-18 forces. More likely they constituted a significant web of influence among the largest corporations in the state which effectively suppressed potential support for Proposition 18 among business interests.

Power to the Automobile

The automobile transportation system produces enormous private profits and massive social costs. Proposition 18 was a mild attempt to reduce these social costs. Not surprisingly, the highway and automotive interests—

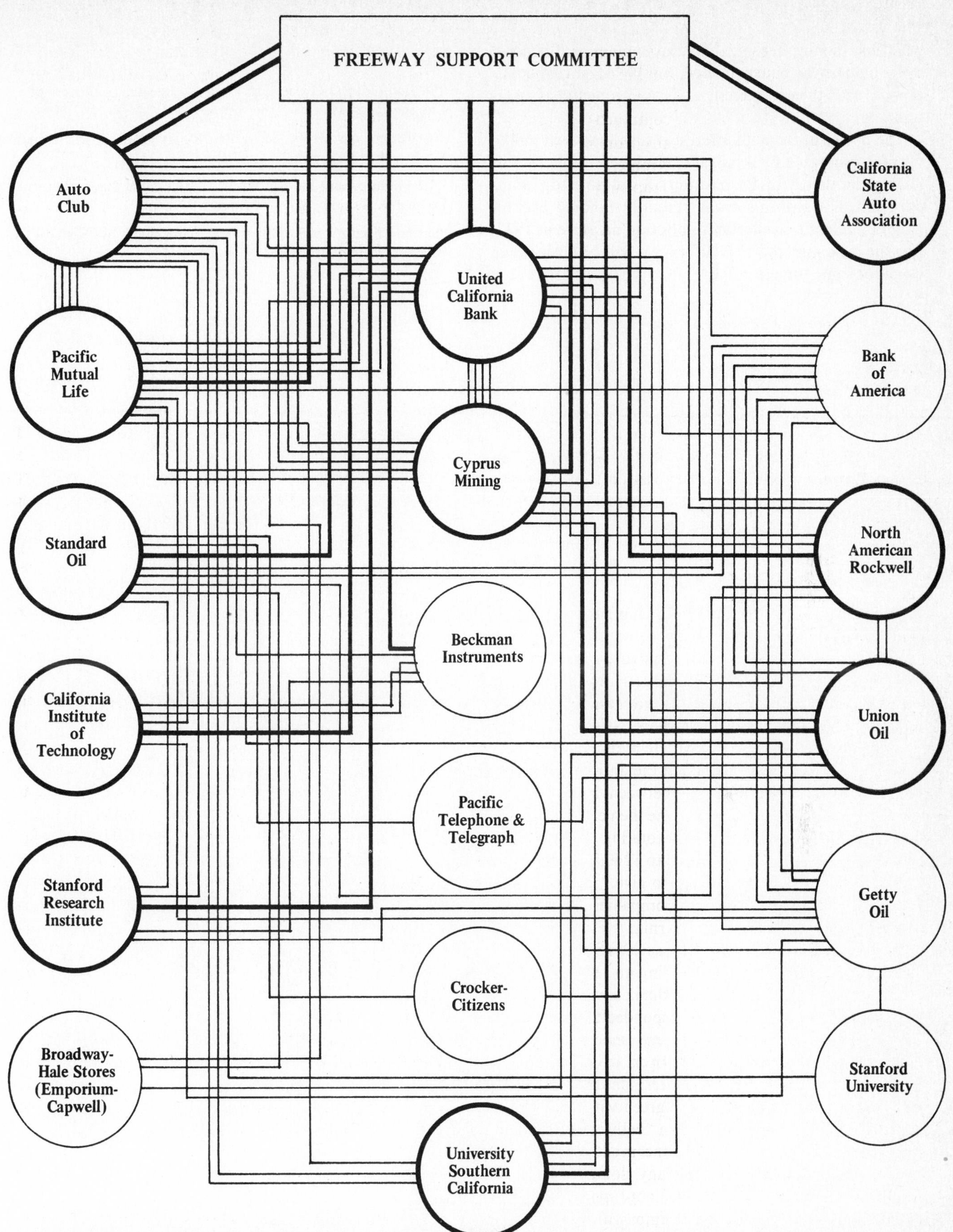

This diagram illustrates directorate interlocks among: the Freeway Support Committee and other California companies; the companies with which the Freeway Support Committee was linked; and several miscellaneous firms, associations and universities. Each line represents one director.

Source: *Poor's Register of Corporations, Directors and Executives* (1970, 1971); *Moody's Industrial Manual* (1970, 1971); *Moody's Banking and Finance Manual* (1971); *Dun & Bradstreet Million Dollar Directory* (1971); corporation files from the office of the California Secretary of State.

with their money, organization and economic influence—overwhelmed the poorly funded, loosely organized coalition of rapid-transit interests and environmental associations.

The power of the auto interest is such that even public outrage generated by a barrage of adverse publicity following the defeat of Proposition 18 did not stop Standard Oil of California from blatantly funding a campaign to defeat a similar anti-pollution measure in 1972. For the auto interests in California it will be business as usual for some time to come.

SUGGESTED READINGS

The Politics of Oil by Robert Engler (Chicago: University of Chicago Press, 1961).

The Pavers and the Paved by Ben Kelley (New York: Donald W. Brown, 1971).

"Air Pollution and Human Health" by Lester B. Lave and Eugene P. Seskin in *Science*, August 1970.

"System Energy and Future Transportation" by Richard A. Rice in *Technology Review*, January 1972.

4 *John M. Goering & Edward M. Kalachek*

Public Transportation and Black Unemployment

Unemployed blacks are trapped in job-scarce urban ghettos, unable to reach suburban plants where many good positions are waiting to be filled. A simple technological improvement—mass-transportation systems to connect the labor resources of the ghetto with the labor demands of industries developing in suburbia—ought to alleviate some pressing racial and economic problems.

These are reasonable-sounding assumptions—so reasonable, in fact, that experiments based on such ideas were funded in about a dozen cities, including Los Angeles, New York, St. Louis and Buffalo. A detailed examination of the metropolitan St. Louis demonstration project, TEMPO NORTHWEST, led to a startling conclusion: ***buying luxury automobiles and giving them free to bus riders would have cost less than the federal treasury expended on TEMPO.***

What kind of misconceptions led to such a fiasco? Why was the initial operation of several large busses making 13 round trips daily from the heart of the St. Louis ghetto to a major industrial complex 20 miles away soon cut back to eight and finally to two round trips a day by the end of the 20-month project?

Four myths combined to insure the program's failure, myths which also underlie other aspects of antipoverty programs.

Myth Number One
☐ *Jobs are not available in the inner city*

Basic to the planning for the mass-transit experiment was the belief that jobs are not and cannot be available in the inner city. The movement of industry to the suburbs apparently has created a condition in which blue-collar and lower skill jobs are increasingly located in the suburbs, while less skilled workers, particularly blacks, continue to live in the inner city. A Department of Transportation official commented in 1968 that "since jobs . . . for the non-driver, especially the poor, are diminishing in the central cities, this means that transportation service to other than central business district destinations must be developed." And a March 20, 1973 *New York Times* headline read, "More Bus Service Urged to Help Poor Get to Jobs."

The 1960 census, however, indicated that in that year only 52 percent of all blue-collar workers lived in the central city, but 59 percent worked there. Forty-nine percent of manufacturing workers lived in the central city, but almost 60 percent worked there. Substantial numbers of the poor lived outside the inner-city ghettoes. Roughly 52 percent of those who resided in metropolitan areas and earned less than $3,000 lived in the central city, while 56 percent of the same group worked there. Thus, the number of blue-collar, industrial, low-skill and low-income jobs located in the central city was greater than the number of blue-collar, industrial, low-skill and low-income workers who lived there. Since then employment has grown more rapidly in the suburbs than in the city, but so has population. Employment still tends to be concentrated in the inner city, while the poor are everywhere. The relocation of industry continues to be matched by the relocation of population. There is little support, then, for the belief in a perverse specialization of jobs and of populations between cities and suburbs.

Myth Number Two
☐ *Suburban employers need unskilled workers*

A major supposition was that unemployed blacks would be hired if they were transported to suburban areas—the jobs were there and waiting. The faultiness of this expectation became immediately apparent in almost every city experimenting with transportation solutions to unemployment. In St. Louis, only 25 percent of the applicants sent to jobs in suburban areas were hired. Suburban employers were not short of labor. In surveying a large number of firms in suburban St. Louis, we found few companies with job vacancies lasting longer than a week. A majority of the firms were unconcerned with public transportation. They assumed the worker would have access to personal transportation. As one employer said, "We would like for workers to have their own personal means of getting here. No other way is reliable. The bus is a ridiculous way to travel." The crucial importance of the automobile is demonstrated by the fact that the firms most distant from the ghetto and from public transportation were most satisfied with their recruiting ability. Employers felt that transportation deficiencies were a "disadvantage for Negroes from the inner city but not for the company."

More generally, because of their favorable recruiting position, most suburban employers were not, through social consciousness or other motivations, concerned about hiring large numbers of inner-city blacks. There was little enthusiasm about actively recruiting black workers, and over half of the personnel managers interviewed saw significant disadvantages in hiring more black workers. Many of these negative respondents distinguished quite clearly between most black workers, whom they regarded as being just as good as white workers, and the applicants sent by the antipoverty agencies, whom they did not regard highly.

A few smaller businesses were actively concerned with developing access to the black labor market. These firms tended to offer relatively low wages (about $2.00 an hour) for production work involving considerable physical drudgery, and frequently had reputations as suburban sweat shops. Plagued by high quit-rates and continuous labor shortage, they gave strong support to the transportation experiments. To a significant extent the experiments were an indirect subsidization of these firms. (In the New York area such firms actually petitioned the government to initiate a mass-transportation program.)

Myth Number Three

☐ *Unemployed black ghetto residents need transportation to the suburbs*

This myth rests on a picture of the unemployed black worker as having been out of a job for a long time, and as likely to remain so in the absence of social intervention. Simple intervention, such as government-supported transportation, would be enough to turn the hard-core unemployed into readily employable individuals. There may be many ghetto residents who fit this description, but in sampling the records of the antipoverty employment agency in St. Louis we were able to discover very few. In interviewing roughly 200 job-seeking blacks living in one of the areas of highest unemployment, we found the average unemployment length (12½ weeks) to be only four weeks longer than the national average. We found only seven individuals who had been unemployed longer than six months. Personal problems rather than inability to find a job appeared responsible for these few extremely long periods.

Many respondents had work histories characterized by an impressive amount of job stability. The average length of a prior job was approximately one year, and 30 percent had lasted three years or longer. There were, of course, a number of workers who changed jobs frequently, but such job instability and resulting unemployment appeared traceable to wages too low to encourage job stability. Inadequate transportation was mentioned by less than 3 percent as a reason for quitting or not taking a job.

With effort and the assistance of friends and relatives, the black job hunter can find employment in the center city. He generally will not be tempted to seek a suburban job which requires a time-consuming and expensive journey to work (the target area for TEMPO was roughly 20 miles from the center of the city, and the round-trip fare was $1.00). There is no reason for commuting to the suburbs unless suburban jobs are appreciably better than city jobs. In surveying a sample of all manufacturing firms in suburban St. Louis we found that pay scales did not increase with distance from the city. Jobs in the suburbs are not synonymous with greater opportunity for advancement or with higher income levels.

It was hardly surprising, then, to find that unemployed blacks were uninterested in travelling for over an hour in a large "poverty" bus. Sixty percent of the blacks we studied lived within five blocks of the new bus route, but in a period of roughly ten months, less than 5 percent of the sample had even used the bus line and only 3 percent were still using it. Two hundred TEMPO bus riders did find jobs, but turnover rates were high, and most jobs were of brief duration. The St. Louis experiment clearly did not activate any latent demand for transportation to the suburbs. The poor, understandably, strongly dislike rides requiring more than one transfer or lasting over half an hour. Distance also introduces a not-so-irrational fear of travelling to alien neighborhoods. The unemployed black may be concerned with the risks involved in travelling to and working in an all-white area. A sense of strangeness often characterizes their image of suburbia. One black resident put it well: "I'm not for going out in the county, cause out in the county people are too different from me, you know, they ain't my bag."

Myth Number Four

☐ *Improved and expanded bus transportation can be provided through the existing structure of antipoverty services*

Since significant numbers of job-hunting black workers were not willing to use the bus on their own initiative, and since few suburban employers were interested in actively recruiting ghetto residents, the bus was unviable as a purely technological solution to black unemployment. An intermediary was needed to develop jobs in the suburbs and to recruit workers in the ghetto. Since TEMPO had funds to publicize its own function but did not have enough money for job development and placement activities, it relied on the existing antipoverty employment agencies. These agencies, however, were unenthused about TEMPO and the type of jobs to which it provided access. Their self-proclaimed function, at least in St. Louis, was to monitor the flow of their clients to select employers, providing specific workers for jobs offering both wages over $2.00 an hour and the possibility of career advancement. These agencies had a well-defined ideology which interpreted the unemployment problem as being as much a function of employer attitudes and sensitivities as of the qualifications of the unemployed worker.

A second difficulty with technological solutions is that they do not recognize the autonomy of neighborhood poverty organizations which seek to control the flow of new resources into and out of their area. There can be little neighborhood control of the planning and routing of a metropolitan area-wide transportation system. The new transportation system was administered and planned by units outside the sphere of community participation. By cutting across and through the boundaries of several neighborhood poverty areas, the new transportation experiment appeared to ignore both the desire for local autonomy and the principle of carefully evaluating who was to be sent to which employer.

Finally, the transportation planners involved in establishing the new mass transportation demonstration projects appear, in both St. Louis and elsewhere, to be primarily concerned with developing balanced, "systems" approaches to transportation in which the entire metropolitan area is laced with a network of economical routes. This system approach has resulted in a reliance on large busses as the most efficient means of mass transit. However, mass transit does not adequately meet the needs of either unemployed blacks or of suburban employers. Since few plants are eager to hire many of the blacks recommended by antipoverty agencies, 50-passenger busses can be used efficiently only if they serve a number of plants. Unfortunately, this is not always feasible. Industrial parks often encompass wide areas. Either a large number of busses must be employed or a cumbersome and time-consuming number of stops instituted if most plants are to be served. Despite the large number of busses originally operated by TEMPO, employer complaints of poor service were frequent. They regarded bus stops five or six blocks or a quarter of a mile from their plant as being unrealistically distant. The ability of a single bus to serve a number of establishments is even more seriously compromised by differences in shift scheduling. A bus well timed for one plant's shift turnover may be premature or late for another plant. Irregular recourse to overtime means that even one plant cannot be adequately served by a bus with a fixed time schedule. Bus service would become far more economically feasible if neighboring plants would cooperate by coordinating shift times. However, most employers have little incentive to institute shift changes. They do not regard busses from the central city as contributing significantly to their recruiting ability. Besides, shift coordination would intensify traffic jams for the majority of employees who own automobiles. In several ways facilitation of bus transit could mean conflict with employees and their unions.

What Should Be Done

The transportation experiments conducted so far have been a dismal disappointment because of the mythical assumptions on which they were based. The criticisms of these assumptions are not, however, intended as criticisms of any one federal or local agency. The Department of Housing and Urban Development, which sponsored the program, has in fact demonstrated a concern with exploratory policies at a time when there was great uncertainty about the magnitude of the unemployment problem and the usefulness of strategies for eliminating the problem. Hopefully, the experiments will contribute to the formulation of a workable transportation program for the poor. The unemployed poor who lack private transportation are at a cruel disadvantage in today's labor market, and there is a distinct role for substantial federal transportation subsidies if realistically planned.

Designers of the St. Louis transportation experiment incorrectly assumed that the unemployment problem had a technological solution. However, the mere existence of the bus elicited very little job-hunting activity and few really attractive job offers. If experiments in transportation are to succeed, other antipoverty agencies must actively develop jobs and match them with unemployed workers. Employment counselors maintained a somewhat critical attitude toward TEMPO, in part reflecting a correct perception that improved transportation did not direct itself to the basic problem of changing the opportunities available to and acceptable to the poor. TEMPO was no substitute for the informal automobile transportation offered by the counselors, a form of transportation which permitted follow-up counseling.

The employment counselors were correct in emphasizing the supportive role of transportation in facilitating job placement and retention. However, this supportive role is unlikely to be achieved so long as transportation funds are allocated to separate transportation agencies. Rather, these funds should be assigned to employment services or to antipoverty agencies which have the responsibility or expertise to find jobs and to provide supportive services for workers with below-average qualifications or interest. Allocating funds in this way will help to ensure that transportation is treated as part of a package for alleviating unemployment and poverty rather than as an end in itself. It would also write an end to the resentments and frustrations created when independent transit units seek to publicize and legitimize their existence by issuing unrealistic promises of better jobs through bussing. In short, planners must recognize the role of the new informal government of local agencies and community action groups operating within poverty areas.

In their use of transportation funds, antipoverty agencies should not be restricted to extending or improving bus lines. Busses cannot economically serve many of the suburban establishments which might hire a few central city residents. They cannot provide unemployed central city residents with the opportunity to range widely over the metropolitan area in their job-hunting endeavors. If central city residents who do not have private transportation are to be given effective access to most suburban jobs, it will be necessary to come to grips with the diffuse location of suburban establishments. Top priority in transportation experimentation should be given to vehicles considerably smaller than 50-seat busses and to schemes for flexible routing. Such vehicles could be used to drive applicants to job interviews, and to transport them to and from work during the initial weeks of employment. If the driver is also the job counselor, transportation services can be closely integrated with job placement and retention services. The stressing of small vehicles would also represent a great humanization of the program. Huge busses with the word TEMPO spelled out on their side in large block letters represent a blatant and unnecessary stigmatization of the poor. After the initial weeks of employment, most workers should be able to afford to rent or buy an automobile or join a carpool. The needs of those not so able might be met if antipoverty agencies subcontracted for the maintenance of a stable of good quality used cars. Jitneys with semifixed routes are a promising alternative to both private cars and large busses. Five- to eight-passenger cars could be licensed to travel along fixed routes between the central city and suburban work centers, but allowed to vary their routes within the work center in order to respond to the shifting locus of job openings.

The failure of TEMPO and other such programs, like that of many other antipoverty efforts, cannot be assigned to any one agency or group. The fault, if one can be identified, is that there is no simple association between technological or transportation reforms and the elimination of unemployment. The conditions of urban poverty are often supported by existing technological and transportation systems and no amount of improvisation on existing public transportation lines will significantly affect the concentrations of unemployment among the black population. In fact, only with careful monitoring will the black worker, rather than low-wage-paying industries, receive the major benefits from transportation experimentation.

SUGGESTED READINGS

"The Mobility of the Poor" by Phillip B. Herr and Aaron Fleisher. Joint Center for Urban Studies, Massachusetts Institute of Technology and Harvard University (unpublished paper).

The Urban Transportation Problem by John R. Meyer, John Kain, and M. Wohl (Cambridge: Harvard University Press, 1966).

Section XVI

Health and Medicine

All of us have marveled at the advances of modern medicine. Yet the very fact that many of the great killer diseases of the past have been conquered means that many of the diseases that are not conquered are of the chronic type and demand continuing care. Strauss, in "Chronic Illness," tells us that 40 percent of all Americans suffer from some form of chronic illness. There is, he further elaborates, a lag between the medical treatment of these diseases and their social treatment. Strauss emphasizes the following issues surrounding the social treatment of chronic illness: coping with crisis—reading the signs of the illness, organizing efforts to deal with the coming crisis and following prescribed regimens of treatment; symptom management, including the risks of interaction and the redesign of the environment and reorganization of time; dealing with the potential isolation that may result from chronic illness; and adjusting to changes in the disease trajectory. These issues all add up to "artful striving"—developing guidelines for "acting normal" under adverse conditions and adjusting to social demands.

Suczek, in "Chronic Medicare," nicely illustrates some of the issues raised by Strauss in the previous article. She documents the high price tag placed on many chronic illnesses, in this case renal failure. Several thousand people every year develop renal failure and need hemodialysis. This results in a two-part trajectory, the first having to do with rescue, the second with maintenance. Rescue costs are often covered by insurance; maintenance is not. Insurance is geared to acute illness, but maintenance plays a major role in determining who will and who will not be saved. Renal failure victims who live have four outstanding characteristics, according to Suczek's research. They are urban (socially and geographically), respectable, affiliated (that is, they have a network of social support), and have a steady employment record. Insurance companies often try to evade responsibility (because of the staggering expense) by banking on ignorance and "loopholing," among other things. Suczek's discussion broadens to consider how most of us treat insurance through "ritual magic" and how many chronic illness problems are dealt with through "ad hoc solutions." She offers some solutions based on her exhaustive analysis of medicare's role in hemodialysis.

In "Apartheid Medicine," Mechanic analyzes how the discriminatory system of medicine in South Africa operates. The entire article is a fine example of how the trained sociological observer can contribute to investigative reporting. Mechanic "sees" things that would be missed by anyone not trained in medical sociology.

1 *Anselm Strauss*

Chronic Illness

Smallpox, diphtheria, polio, measles—conquered through immunization. Tuberculosis, leprosy, plague, yellow fever, malaria—defeated or checked by sanitation, improved living conditions and effective treatment.

In the old days, people who died from diseases contracted them quickly, reached crisis shortly thereafter, and either died or pulled through. Modern medical researchers have changed this dramatic pattern by taming many once-devastating ailments. Improved conditions of living, along with effective medical skills and technology, have altered the nature of illness in scientifically advanced societies. While patients suffering from communicable diseases once filled most hospitals, treatment centers now serve mainly those afflicted with chronic ailments.

Many who would have died soon after contracting a disease now live and endure their affliction. Today most illnesses are chronic diseases—slow-acting, long-term killers that can be treated but not cured. A 1964 survey by the Department of Health, Education and Welfare indicates that about 40 percent of all Americans suffer from one or more chronic diseases; one out of every four so afflicted have lost some days at work because of disabling symptoms.

A large and growing body of medical literature presents detailed discussions of etiology, symptomatology, treatments and regimens. This outpouring of information, however, generally ignores a basic aspect of chronic illness—how to deal with such ailments in terms that are *social*—not simply medical. How can patients and professionals cope with health-related problems of family disruption, marital stress, role destruction and adjustment, stigmatization and even loss of body mobility?

Each chronic condition brings with it multiple problems of living. Among the most pressing are preventing and managing medical crises (that go even to death), managing regimens, controlling symptoms, organizing one's time efficiently, preventing or living with social isolation, adjusting to changes in the disease trajectory, and normalizing interaction and life, despite the disease. To handle those problems, people develop basic strategies which call for an organization of effort (including that of kinsmen, neighbors and health professionals). To establish and maintain this organization requires certain resources (financial, medical, familial and so forth), as well as interactional and social skills in order to make the necessary arrangements.

Medicine and the health professionals are very much included in this scheme but are neither at the scheme's focal point nor even constitute its primary elements. What is primary is simply the question of living: the difference between chronic sufferers and "normal people" merely being that the former must live with their diseases, their symptoms and often with their regimens. Medicine may contribute, but it is secondary to "carrying on."

Coping with Crises

Some chronic diseases carry a constant threat of grave medical crises. Diabetics may fall into insulin coma and die; epileptics can go into convulsions (which of themselves are not lethal) and be killed in a fall or a traffic accident. In order to prevent crises, minimize their effects, get the critically ill person into the hands of a physician or a hospital staff—and if need be actually save him—the person himself and possibly his kinsmen must be organized and prepared to handle all contingencies.

Relevant to the question of crises is how far they can go (to, or short of, death), how fast they appear, the clarity of advance warning signals to laymen or even to health professionals, the probability of recurrence, the predictability of their appearance, the complexity of the saving operations, and the speed and completeness of recovery from them.

The ability to read signs that portend a crisis is the first important step in managing chronic illness. Thus, diabetics or the parents of diabetic children learn how to recognize the signs of oncoming sugar shortage or insulin shock and what to do in case of actual crisis. Likewise, epileptics and sickle cell disease sufferers, if they are fortunate enough to have warning signs before their crises, learn to prepare themselves: if they are in public they get themselves to a place of safety and sit or lie down. Diabetics may carry instructions with them and may also carry those materials, like sugar or candy or insulin, which counteract the crisis; and epileptics may stuff handkerchiefs between their teeth just before convulsions.

When signs aren't properly read, are read too slowly or are interpreted as meaning something else, then people die or come close to dying. This may happen the first time a cardiac patient experiences severe chest pains and doesn't yet know their cause or treatment. (After the first sequence the patient may put his doctor's name close to the telephone for emergency use.) Even physicians may misread signs and so precipitate a crisis—even death. If an unconscious sickle cell anemia sufferer is brought bleeding to a hospital he may die if the natural immediate effort is made to stop his bleeding. Patients who carry instructions with them can sometimes avoid difficulties. Whenever an unconscious individual is brought into the emergency room of the nearest hospital, physicians there understandably may treat him for the wrong disease. Inexperienced patients who are on kidney dialysis machinery may not realize that their machinery is working incorrectly and that their bodies are nearing crisis. The complexity of the human body can cause even experienced persons to misread important signs.

Any breakdown or disruption of the crisis-preventing or crisis-coping organization can be disastrous. Family strain can lead to the abandonment of or lessening control over regimens, and temporary absence of "protective agents" or of "control agents" (such as mothers of diabetic children who are prone to eat too much candy) can also be traumatic. A divorce or separation that leaves an assisting agent (a mother helping her cystic-fibrosis child with absolutely necessary exercises) alone, unrelieved with her task, can gradually or quickly lead to a crisis. (One divorced couple arranged matters so that the father relieved the mother on weekends and some evenings.) Even an agent's illness can lead to the relaxation of regimens or the elimination of activities that might otherwise prevent crisis.

There is also a post-crisis period, in relation to the organization of effort. Some failure of organization right in the hospital can be seen when the staff begins to pull away from a cardiac patient, recently saved from a heart attack, but now judged "less critical" than other patients. Back home, of course, such patients require plenty of family organization to prevent additional attacks. What is not so evident is that the patient and his family may read signs of improvement where few exist, or that contingencies may arise which render faulty the organization for crisis prevention and crisis management. Relevant variables here are the length and rapidity of recovery—since both of these may vary for different disease conditions.

During an extended period of crisis the family may need to make special arrangements about their time (for visiting the hospital, for nursing the patient at home) and their living space (having the bed downstairs rather than upstairs, living near the hospital during the peak of the crisis). They may have to juggle the family's finances or spell each other in nursing the patient during his crisis. Even the patient himself—in trying to get better rather than giving up—may have to contribute to the necessary organization of effort to bring the family through the crisis period.

Unless the physician is absolutely helpless in the face of a given chronic disease, he will suggest or command some kind of regimen. Adhering to regimens, though, is a very complex matter, for regimens can sometimes set problems so difficult that they may present more hardships than the symptoms themselves.

Patients do not adhere to regimens automatically. Those who accept and maintain a regimen must have abiding trust in the physician, evidence that the requirements work without producing distressing or frightening side-effects (or that the side-effects are outweighed by symptom relief or fear of the disease itself), and the guarantee that important daily activities, either of the patient or of people around him, can continue relatively uninterrupted.

In addition to the time it takes and the discomfort it causes, an important property of a given regimen is whether it is visible to other people, and what visibility may mean to the patient. If the regimen means that a stigmatized disease can be suspected or discovered, the person is unlikely to carry it out in public. (Tuberculosis patients sometimes have this problem.) If the visible regimen is no more than slightly embarrassing or is fully explainable, then its visibility is much less likely to prevent its maintenance in public or private.

Another property is also important: if the regimen appears to work for the patient, then that *may* convince him that he should continue with it. But continuance is problematic, not only because the other properties noted above may counteract his best intentions or his good sense, but because once a regimen has brought symptom relief, the patient may forego the routine—no matter what the physician says. This is exactly what happens when tuberculosis patients see their symptoms disappear, and figure that now they can cut out—partially or totally—their uncomfortable regimen.

The very properties of the regimen, then, constitute contributing conditions for adhering, relaxing or even rejecting the prescribed activities. Thus, if the patient simply denies that he has the disease (as with tuberculosis, where many patients experience no symptoms), he may not carry out his regimen. Instructions for a treatment routine may leave him confused or baffled: cardiac patients told to "rest" or "find their own limits" can be frustrated because they don't really know what "sufficient rest" means.

Patients and kinsmen inevitably enter into negotiations with each other, and sometimes with the physician, over relaxing or otherwise changing (substituting one drug for another, one activity for another) the regimen. They are negotiating not only over such matters as the elimination of discomfort and side-effects, but also the possibility of making the management of ordinary life easier or even possible. Physicians, of course, recognize much of this bargaining, but they may not realize just how high the stakes can be for the patient and his family. If a doctor ignores those factors, his patient may go shopping for another physician or, at the least, he may quietly alter his regimen or substitute part of it with something recommended by an amateur—pharmacist, friend or relative.

Symptom Management

The control of symptoms is obviously linked with adherence to effective regimens. Like adherence to regimen, symptom control is not merely a matter of medical management. Most of the time, the patient is far from medical facilities, so he and his family must rely upon their own judgment, wisdom and ingenuity in controlling symptoms—quite aside from faithfully following the prescribed regimens. Some physicians—probably not many—recognize that need for judgment.

Whatever the sophisticated technical references may be, the person who has symptoms will be concerned primarily with whether he hurts, faints, trembles visibly, has had his mobility or his speech impaired, or is evidencing some kind of disfigurement. How much they interfere with his life and social relationships depends on whether they are permanent or temporary, predictable or unpredictable, publicly visible or invisible; also on their degree (as of pain), their meaning to bystanders (as of disfigurement), the nature of the regimen called for to control the symptom; and of course on the kinds of life-style and social relations which the sufferer has been accustomed to.

Even minor, occasional symptoms may lead to some changing of habits, and major symptoms may call for the redesigning or reshaping of important aspects of a patient's life-style. Thus, someone who begins to suffer from minor back pains is likely to learn to avoid certain kinds of chairs and even discover to his dismay that a favorite sitting position is precisely the one he must forego. Major adjustments could include moving to a one story house, buying clothes that cloak disfigurement, getting the boss to assign jobs that require less strength, using crutches or other aides to mobility. In one case a mailman suffering from colitis lived "on a leash," having arranged never to be very far from that necessary toilet. Emphysema patients learn to have "puffing stations" where they can recoup from lack of breath while looking like they have stopped normally.

Ideas for redesigning activities may come from others, too. A community nurse taught an emphysema patient how to rest while doing household chores; a sister taught a patient afflicted with brittle bones (because of a destructive drug) how to get up from the toilet, minus a back brace, without breaking bones in her back. Another woman figured out how her cardiac-arthritic grandfather could continue his beloved walks on his farm, by placing wooden stumps at short distances so that he could rest as he reached each one. Unfortunately, kinsmen and health professionals can function in just the opposite fashion: for instance, a woman with multiple sclerosis had carefully arranged her one-room apartment so that every object she needed was literally within arm's reach; but the public health nurse who visited her regarded the place as in a terrible shambles and proceeded to tidy things up herself.

Perhaps inventiveness, just as much as finances or material resources, is what makes the difference between reaching and not reaching some relatively satisfying redesign of life. The cancer patient with lessened energy who can ingeniously juggle her friends' visits and telephone calls can maintain a relatively unimpaired social life. Arthritic farm women who can get neighbors to bring in groceries can live on their farms during the summer although they must move to town for the winter months. One multiple sclerosis patient who is a student not only has rearranged her apartment but persuaded various people to help her manage despite her increasingly restricted mobility. A veritable army of people have come to her aid: the university architect redesigned certain of the public toilets for her wheelchair and also put in some ramps; the handy men around the university help her up and down stairs, by appointment; they also have rebuilt her cupboards so that she can reach them from her wheelchair; and so on.

Lack of imagination about useful redesigning makes symptom control harder. This lack of imaginative forethought can be seen in many homes for the elderly where stiff-jointed or low-energy people must struggle to rise from sitting positions on low sofas and chairs, or must painstakingly pick their way along highly polished corridors—minus handrails.

The reshaping of activities pertains also to the crucial issue of "interaction." A variety of judicious or clever maneuvers can keep one's symptoms as inobtrusive as possible. Sometimes the tactics are very simple: a college teacher with bronchitis, whose peak load of coughing up sputum is in the morning, arranges his teaching schedule so that he can stay at home, or at least in his office, until after lunchtime. Another person who tends continually to have a runny allergic nose always carries tissue in her hand when in public. Another with a tendency to cough carries cough drops with him—especially important when he attends concerts. An epileptic may have to persuade acquaintances that his epileptic fits are not communicable! Emphysema sufferers learn to sit down or lean against buildings in such a fashion that they are not mistaken for drunks or loiterers.

Agents of various kinds can also be useful—wives who scout out the terrain at a public meeting to find the least obtrusive spot, and then pass on the information to their husbands in wheelchairs or on crutches. Spouses may have prearranged signals to warn each other when a chronic symptom (for example, runny nose) starts appearing. In a more dramatic instance a couple was attending a party when the husband noticed his wife's temporarily slurred speech—a sign of her tiredness and pain from cancer. Since they did not want to have their friends know of her illness, he acted quickly to divert the others' attention and soon afterward manufactured an excuse so that they could leave the party.

When visible symptoms cannot easily be disguised, misleading explanations may be offered—fainting, for instance, is explained away by someone "in the know" as a temporary weakness due to flu or to some other reasonable cause. When a symptom cannot be minimized, then a wife may attempt to prepare others for the distressing sight or sound of her husband's affliction. The sufferer himself may do this, as when a cancer patient who had lost much weight warned friends, over the phone, that when they visited they would find her not looking like herself at all. Each friend who visits is very likely, in turn, to warn other friends what to expect.

Various chronic diseases lead to such disruption that they call for some temporal re-ordering. One all-too-familiar problem is too much time. It may only be temporary, as with persons who are waiting out a post-crisis period, but, for the disabled elderly or victims of multiple sclerosis, it may be a permanent condition. Among the consequences are boredom, decreased social skills, family strains, negative impact on identity and even physical deterioration.

Just as common is not enough time. Not only is time sopped up by regimens and by symptom control, but those who assist the patient may expend many hours on their particular tasks. Not to be totally engulfed, they in turn may need to get assistants (babysitters, housecleaners, cooks) or redistribute the family workload. Occasionally the regimens require so much time, or crises come so frequently (some sickle cell anemia sufferers have been hospitalized up to 100 times), that life simply gets organized around those events; there is not enough time for much of anything else. Even just handling one's symptoms or the consequences of having symptoms may require so much time that life is taken up mainly with handling them. Thus, a very serious dermatological condition forced one woman to spend hour after hour salving her skin; otherwise she would have suffered unbearably. Unfortunately, the people who suffer cannot leave their bodies. Kinsmen and other assisting agents, however, may abandon their charges out of desperation for what the temporal engulfment is doing to their own lives. Abandonment, here, may mean shifting the burdens to a nursing home or other custodial institution, such as a state mental institution.

The term "dying trajectory" means the course of dying as defined by various participants in it. Analogously, one can also think of the course of the chronic disease (downward in most instances). Like the dying trajectory, that course can be conceived as having two properties. First, it takes place over time: it has duration. Specific trajectories can vary greatly in duration. Some start earlier, some end later. Second, a trajectory has shape. It may plunge straight down; it may move slowly but steadily downward; it may vacillate slowly, moving slightly up and down before diving downward radically; it may move slowly down at first, then hit a long plateau, then plunge abruptly even to death. Neither the duration nor shape of a dying trajectory is a purely objective physiological property. Both are perceived properties; their dimensions depend on when the perceiver initially defines someone as diseased and on his expectations of how the disease course will proceed. (We can add further that the dying trajectory consists merely of the last phases of some chronic disease trajectories.) Each type of disease (multiple sclerosis, diabetes and so forth) or subtype (different kinds of arthritis) may have a range of variation in trajectory, but they certainly tend to be patterned in accordance with duration and shape.

It would be much too simplistic to assert that specific trajectories determine what happens to a sense of identity; but certainly they do contribute, and quite possibly in *patterned* ways. Identity responses to a severe heart attack may be varied, but awareness that death can be but a moment away—every day—probably cannot but have a different impact on identity than trajectories expected to result in slow death, or in leaving one a "vegetable" or perfectly alive but a hopeless cripple.

We have alluded to the loss of social contact, even extending to great social isolation, that may be a consequence of chronic disease and its management. This loss is understandable given the accompanying symptoms, crises, regimens and often difficult phasing of trajectories.

It is not difficult to trace some of the impact on social contact of varying symptoms, in accordance with their chief properties. The disfigurement associated with leprosy leads many to stay in leper colonies; they prefer the social ease and normal relationships that are possible there. Diseases which are (or which the sufferer thinks are) stigmatizing are kept as secret as possible. But talking about his illness with friends who may understand can be comforting. Some may find new friends (even spouses) among fellow sufferers, especially through clinic visits or special clubs formed around the illness or disability (such as those formed by kidney failure victims and people who have had ileostomies). Some virtually make careers of doing voluntary work for those clubs or associations. People can also leave circles of friends whom they feel might now be unresponsive, frightened or critical and move to more sympathetic social terrain. An epileptic who has used a warning tactic and has moved to a supportive terrain said:

> I'm lucky, I still have friends. Most people who have epilepsy are put to the side. But I'm lucky that way. I tell them that I have epilepsy and that they shouldn't get scared if I fall out. I go to things at the

church—it's the church people that are my friends. I just tell them and then it is okay. They just laugh about it and don't get upset.

Some people may chose to allow their diseases to advance rather than put up with their regimens. One cardiac patient, for instance, simply refused to give up his weekly evening playing cards with "the boys"—replete with smoking, beer drinking and late hours—despite his understanding that this could lead to further heart attacks. Another cardiac patient avoided coffee breaks at work because everyone smoked then. He stayed away from many social functions for the same reasons. He felt that people probably thought him "unsociable," but he was not able to think of any other way to stop himself from smoking. Perhaps the extreme escape from—not minimization or prevention of—social isolation was exhibited by one woman with kidney disease who chose to go off dialysis (she had no possibility of getting a transplant), opting for a speedy death because she saw an endless time ahead, dependence on others, inability to hold down a job, increasing social isolation and a purposeless life. Her physicians accepted her right to make this choice.

Those who cannot face physically altered friends may avoid or even abandon them. One individual who was losing weight because of cancer remarked bitterly that a colleague of his had ducked down the street, across campus, to avoid meeting him. Spouses who have known great intimacy together can draw apart because of an illness: a cardiac husband may fear having sex or may be afraid of dying but cannot tell his wife for fear of increasing *her* anxiety. The awkwardness that others feel about discussing death and fear of it isolates many chronically ill people from their friends—even from their spouses. During the last phases of a disease trajectory, an unbridgable gap may open up between previously intimate spouses.

Even aside from the question of death fears, friends may draw apart because the patient is physically isolated from the mainstream of life. One stroke patient who temporarily lost the ability to speak described what happened between himself and his friends: "I felt unguarded and my colleagues— who pretty soon found their conversation drying up in the lack of anything from me—felt bored, or at any rate I thought they were. My wife, who was usually present, saved the conversation from dying—she was never at loss for a word." A cardiac patient hospitalized away from his home town at first received numerous cards and telephone calls, but once his friends had reached across the distance they chose to leave him alone, doubtless for a variety of reasons. He and his wife began to feel slightly abandoned. Later, when he had returned to part-time work, he found that his fellow executives left him relatively alone at first, knowing that he was far from recuperated. Despite his conscious knowledge that his colleagues were trying to help, he still felt out of things.

Friends and relatives may withdraw from patients who are making excessive demands or who have undergone personality changes caused by a crisis or the progress of a disease. Abandonment may be the final result. Husbands desert, spouses separate and adult children place their elderly parents in nursing homes. In some kinds of chronic diseases, especially stigmatic (leprosy) or terribly demanding (mental illness), friends and relatives and even physicians advise the spouse or kinsmen quite literally to abandon the sick person: "It's time to put her in the hospital." "Think of the children." "Think of yourself—it makes no sense." "It's better for her, and you are only keeping her at home because of your own guilt." These are just some of the abandonment rationales that are offered, or which the person offers himself. Of course, the sick person, aware of having become virtually an intolerable burden, may offer those rationales also—though not necessarily alleviating his own sense of estrangement.

The chief business of a chronically ill person is not just to stay alive or to keep his symptoms under control, but to live as normally as possible despite his symptoms and his disease. In the case of chronically ill children, parents work very hard at creating some semblance of a normal life for their offspring. "Closed awareness" or secrecy is the ruling principle of family life. No one tells the child he is dying. Parents of children with leukemia, for example, have a very difficult time. For much of the time, the child actually may look quite well and live a normal life—but his parents have to work very hard at *acting* normal unless they can keep the impending death well at the back of their minds. The parents with children with longer life expectancies need not work so hard to maintain a normal atmosphere in their homes, except insofar as the child may rebel against aspects of a restrictive regimen which he feels makes *his* life abnormal. Some of the difficulties which chronic sufferers experience in maintaining normal interaction are reflected in the common complaint that blind and physically handicapped people make—that people assume they cannot walk and work like ordinary mortals, but rush up to help them do what they are quite as capable of doing as anyone else. The non-sick, especially strangers, tend to overemphasize the sick person's visible symptoms, so that they come to dominate the interaction. The sick person fights back by using various tactics to disavow his deviant status: he hides the intrusive symptom—covers it with clothes, puts the trembling hand under the table—or if it can't be hidden, then minimizes its impact by taking attention away from it—like a dying woman who has lost a great deal of weight but who forces visitors to ignore her condition by talking cheerfully and normally about their mutual interests.

Artful Striving

In setting guidelines for "acting normal" there is much room for disagreement between the ill person and those near to him about just how ill he is. The sick person may choose more invalidism than his condition really warrants. After a crisis or a peak period of symptoms, the sick person may find himself rushed by others—including his helping agents—who either misjudge his return to better health—or simply forget how sick he might still be since he does not show more obvious signs of his current condition. All patients who have partial-recovery trajectories necessarily run that hazard. ("Act sicker than you look or they will quickly forget you were so ill" was the advice given to one cardiac patient who was about to return to his executive job.)

The more frequent reverse phenomenon is when the sick person believes his condition is more normal than others believe. His friends and relatives tell him, "Take it easy, don't rush things." His physician warns him that he will harm himself, even kill himself, if he doesn't act in accordance with the facts of his case. But it sometimes happens that the person really has a very accurate notion of just how he feels. One man who had had a kidney transplant found himself having to prove to his fellow workers that he was not handicapped—doing extra work to demonstrate his normality. A slightly different case is the ill person who may know just how ill he is but wishes others to regard him as less ill and allow him to act accordingly. One dying man who was trying to live as normally as possible right down through his last days found himself rejecting those friends, however well intentioned, who regarded him as "dying now" rather than as "living fully to the end."

As the trajectory of the ill person's health continues downward, he may have to come to terms with a lessened degree of normality. We can see this very clearly with those who are slowly dying, when both they and their friends or kinsmen are quite willing to settle for "something less" at each phase of the downward trajectory, thankful at least for small things. It is precisely when the chronically ill cannot settle for lower levels of functioning that they opt out of this life. When their friends and relatives cannot settle for less, or have settled for as much as they can stand, then they too opt out of his life: by separation, divorce or abandonment. Those who are chronically ill from diseases like multiple sclerosis or other severe forms of neurological illness (or mental illness, for that matter) are likely to have to face this kind of abandonment by others. The chronically ill themselves, as well as many of their spouses, kinsmen and friends, are remarkably able to accommodate themselves to increasingly lower levels of normal interaction and style; they can do this either because of immense closeness to each other or because they are grateful even for what little life and relationship remains. They strive manfully—and artfully—to "keep things normal" at whatever level that has come to mean.

We must not forget, either, that symptoms and trajectories may stabilize for long periods of time, or in fact not change for the worst at all: then the persons so afflicted simply come to accept, on a long-term basis, whatever restrictions are placed on their lives. Like Franklin D. Roosevelt, they live perfectly normal (even super-normal!) lives in all respects except for whatever handicaps may derive from their symptoms or their medical regimens. To keep interaction normal, they need only develop the requisite skills to make others ignore or de-emphasize their disabilities.

Helping those afflicted with chronic diseases means far more than simply displaying compassion or having medical competence. Only through knowledge of and sensitivity to the *social* aspects of symptom control, regimen management, crisis prevention, handling dying and death itself, can one develop truly beneficial strategies and tactics for dealing with specific diseases and chronic illness in general.

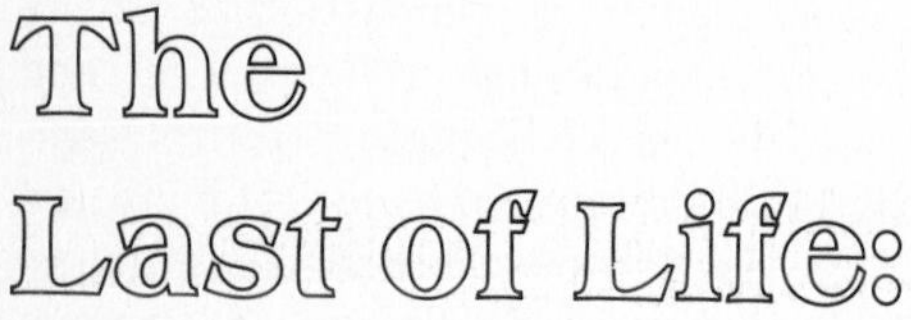

The Last of Life: Dignities and Indignities

by Harvey Stein

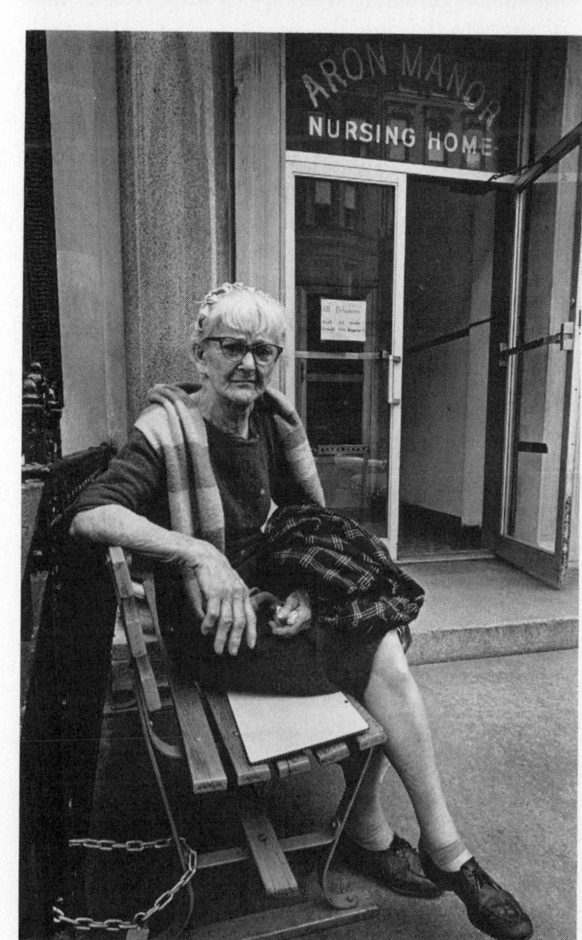

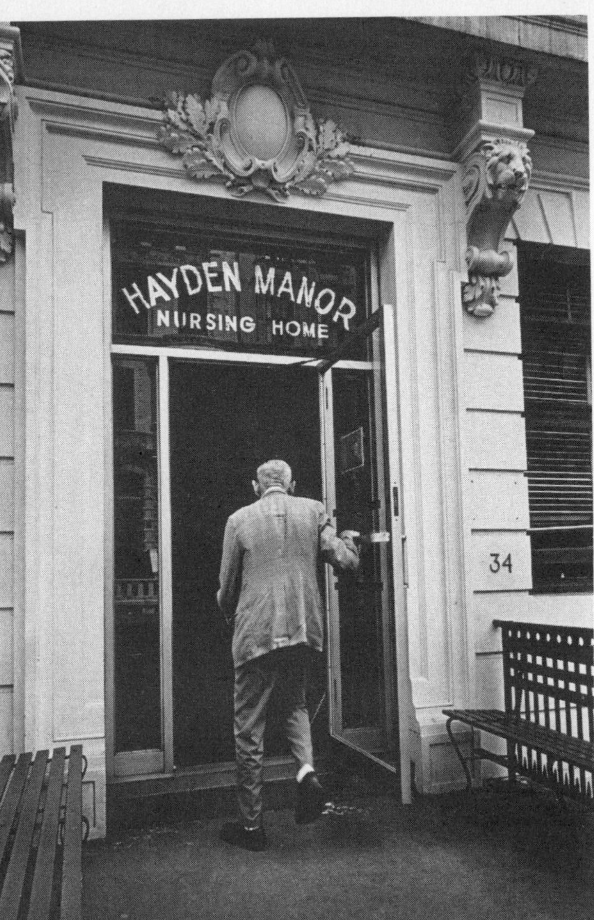
HAYDEN MANOR
NURSING HOME
34

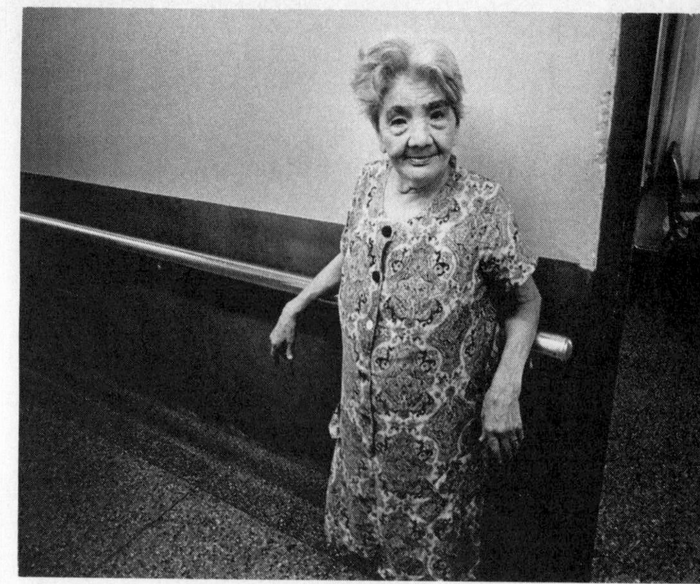

Green
APPLE
PIE
FLOUR
CHERRY PIE

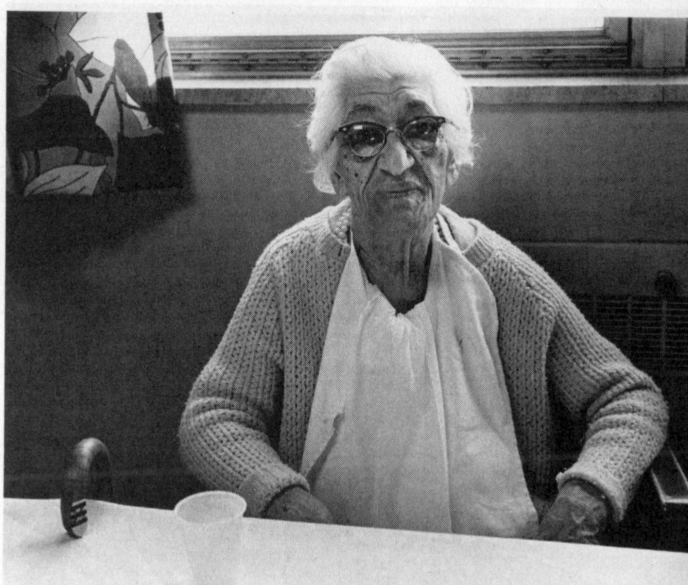

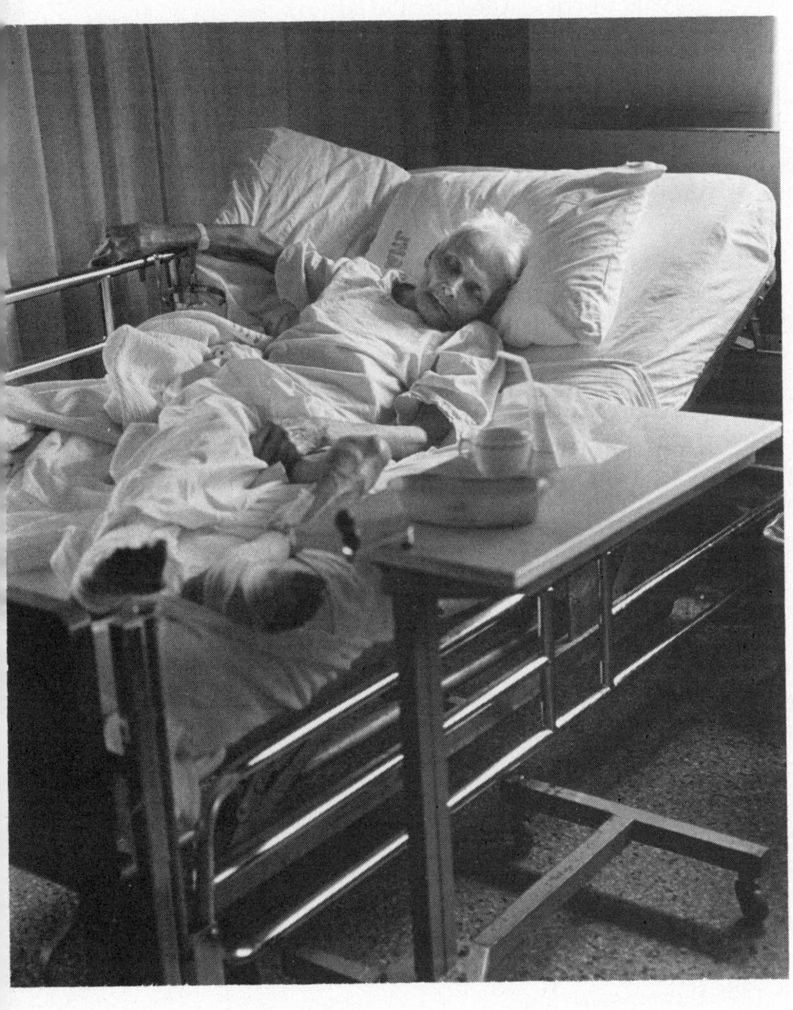

2 *Barbara Suczek*

Chronic Medicare

What is a human life worth? For a people readily moved to personal generosity when catastrophe hits friend or stranger we are strangely reluctant to commit ourselves to the expense of instituting a federally financed health-care policy. One result of this fear of changing the social system is that the life of a victim of a chronic ailment is virtually price-tagged at whatever the cost of treatment is. In the case of renal failure (kidney disease) victims, this figure is at least several thousand dollars a year—the cost of hemodialysis, the process of filtering toxic substances which accumulate in a renal patient's blood. Despite its time-consuming and psychologically demanding nature, dialysis holds out dramatic hope to chronic renal failure victims. But the same society whose technology offers this life-sustaining promise cruelly impedes its fulfillment with random, arbitrary methods of making funds available to those who need treatment.

Regardless of his economic status, the chronic renal failure patient—sick and worried—is forced to chart a perilous physical and financial course. Unfortunately, the physically healthy seem to lack the imagination, the time and the emotional energy to sustain any deep involvement with seemingly interminable medical problems. Bolstered by a proud but largely unexamined assumption that "we," as Americans, are probably doing as well as can be expected in providing for general health care, the chronically sick and those intimately involved with their care are essentially left to cure their own financial ills.

The two major phases of the illness trajectory—the acute, or *rescue* period and the chronic, or prolonged *maintenance* period—are each accompanied by their own special funding problems. Since the latter phase may extend over an entire lifetime, it will almost certainly be accompanied by a sequential depletion of funding sources—each failure initiating a new crisis that propels the patient into a search for new funds.

Without public monies the fund-raising process takes on the ongoing, never-consummated quality of running on a treadmill. A successful kidney transplant may seem the only real hope for escape. Such an escape is not, unfortunately, a panacea. It involves massive problems of its own, such as locating donors, the inevitable risks associated with major surgery and the hovering possibility of organ rejection. Though it is also an expensive procedure, its financial advantage lies in the fact that the costs involved are circumscribed and at least roughly calculable. If it is successful, there is hope for genuine relief at the economic as well as the physical level. If it is unsuccessful, the patient returns to the treadmill.

Originally, at least, the victim of chronic renal failure who has health insurance coverage may be saved from financial worries. Although the costs of the rescue period will probably be higher than those of subsequent phases, the patient may actually experience less financial distress than later in his illness since health insurance generally cushions the initial blow.

Health insurance as it now stands, however, falls far short of meeting the funding needs of dialysis patients. Since health insurance policies are primarily geared to protect the insured against the cost of acute illness, they are rarely adequate for coping with the long-term financial drain associated with chronic illness.

Essentially, health insurance coverage may determine which renal failure victims live and which die. About 80 percent of survivors (those stabilized and on dialysis) carry some sort of major medical coverage at the onset of illness. This figure is higher than the national average. Without recourse to the lifesaving machines or sufficient funds to pay for using the machines, renal failure victims die early in the course of their illness. Many more renal failure victims die than are saved. Of those who die, many could be saved.

Competing for Dialysis

Those who live—even though semi-permanently attached to a dialysis machine—are not randomly selected. As a group they have four outstanding characteristics: urbanity, respectability, affiliation and a record of fairly steady employment.

Urbanity is intended in both its geographical and psychological sense. It takes an urbane, sophisticated know-

Author's note:

On July 1, 1973 new provisions for funding hemodialysis went into effect under Medicare. Such provisions offer some hope for easing the financial burden of many chronic renal failure victims. What the actual effect will be, of course, nobody knows, but professionals with whom I have spoken are cautiously optimistic. At the very least this sort of funding proves that efforts *are* being made in response to lobbying pressure.

Despite the fact that this article was written prior to the new rulings, none of its basic points has been invalidated. The new guidelines simply demonstrate the ongoing struggle over funding which will not, I am convinced, reach any satisfactory resolution until we face the need to socialize medical services for all.

how to locate sources of funds. Further, dialysis units are almost exclusively located in large urban centers so patients must live in or within commuting distance of the city. Even patients on home dialysis must have some means of reaching the city for the six-week training period, for periodic checkups and for medical and mechanical emergencies. There are, moreover, rural areas that are not suited to the installation or operation of dialysis machinery.

Respectability is less an inherent personal trait than a value judgment made by others who must choose among patients competing for limited medical facilities. Persons who are viewed as "unbalanced" or socially irresponsible are obviously less likely to qualify for selection.

Affiliation, that is, whether the patient has recourse to a social network, will also have bearing on alternatives available to him, especially on the choice between center- and home-based dialysis. Home care is possible only if the patient has a responsible person available to help him use the machine. There are, at present, no trained professional assistants.

A steady employment record is necessary because health insurance policies are frequently sponsored by labor groups or business organizations and are, as such, available only to employees in good standing: and because—regardless of sponsorship—some stable base of income is obviously needed in order to meet a schedule of regular payments.

There is little that can be confidently stated with regard to the overall health insurance picture. Not only do various plans differ widely from one another in the kinds and amounts of benefits they offer, but even within the framework of a specific plan there are wide disparities in coverage, varying according to such criteria as the relationship of the patient to the policyholder (in cases where dependents are covered), type of facility used (many policies will cover hospital treatment but will not pay for outpatient or home care—a source of running dispute, incidentally, between an organization of New York kidney disease victims and New York City Blue Cross), length of time the policy has been in effect (the Kaiser health plan stipulates, for example, that the claimant must have been a member of the plan for at least two years prior to qualifying for prepaid dialysis). Nearly all policies carry clauses that specifically limit the liability of the carrier to prestated amounts. The relationship of the patient to the subscriber, the particular and peculiar conjunction of points in personal, occupational and disease careers, the site and type of available treatment all have their bearing on how the terms of a specific policy will be interpreted.

Coding categorical differences is not the major difficulty, although it is true that here—as in any coding operation—there will be cases whose disposition is not readily clear and apparent. Rather, the major source of confusion stems from a seemingly universal effort to evade the issue of financial responsibility.

Health insurance policies are formulated and contracts negotiated in an atmosphere of uncertainty. One side does not know what reasonably to demand; the other does not know what to refuse. The central issue is the extent to which the surety shall be liable for claims that were unforseeable at the time of contract. Little more than a decade ago the alternative of hemodialysis did not exist in the treatment of kidney failure, and its effect, therefore, could not be anticipated in actuarial calculations. There seems no reason to assume that the present procedure and its attendant costs will long endure; the probability is that any day now some new technological breakthrough will render them both obsolete.

One tactic insurance companies might adopt would be to refuse to honor any claim based on future technological developments. But such a policy could be strategically inadvisable since business competitors might be able to exploit that stand to their own advantage.

Liability Loopholing

Corporate tradition dictates that the problem of competition could be resolved by collusion were it not for the spectre of that anathema to insurance companies—socialized medicine. Certainly it would seem imprudent for anyone with a vested interest in private enterprise to pursue a course that might tip the balance of public sentiment in the direction of state-financed medical care.

The fear of making firm, definitive statements that might inadvertently establish precedents leads both sides to a vagueness of position. The result is that there is a wide area for loopholing for both claimant and corporation.

Further adding to the confusion is the fact that the claimant may be simply and overwhelmingly ignorant. It is a rare person who has the slightest idea what his insurance can be expected to cover. There is simply no way for an individual to be able to anticipate all eventualities and their consequences. Who could have guessed a few years ago that even "forever" might be barely adequate as a time stipulation? Yet this is only a slight overstatement of what has become a fact of life for thousands of victims of renal failure.

A policy carrying a $20,000 liability limitation may seem, to the healthy, more than adequate to protect a family from the costs of even major illnesses. However, in the case of one young woman—a wife and mother—who was stricken with kidney failure, $13,000 of such a policy was consumed in less than four months. This amount covered only 80 percent of her overall medical expense. Thus, the family was already more than $2,000 out of pocket, the insurance was 65 percent depleted and there was still a lifetime of expense ahead which, for a woman of 27, might be expected to extend for upwards of 50 years. This young and previously prospering family watched a carefully planned insurance program melt away before their eyes, carrying with it many of their hopes and plans for the future.

The simple truth is that, for many individuals, health insurance seems to function like ritual magic: they trust that the powers-that-be, having been duly placated by the proper observances and offerings, will come to their rescue in time of need.

Ignorance of content is often accompanied by ignorance of procedure. For patients who are unfamiliar with the intricacies of bureaucratic paperwork or for those who are too sick to concern themselves with it, filling out the required forms according to prescribed time schedules may present an almost insurmountable problem. One patient reported:

> I owe about $300 in hospital bills that I'll have to pay for myself. I didn't fill out the state disability form so the insurance doesn't cover it. I'm just out of pocket. I was too sick to deal with that. I didn't know *anything* for two weeks and that was when I was supposed to fill out the form. After I was well I called them about it but I found out it was too late. . . .

Diffidence can also limit the patient's knowledge: "I don't know why it's taking so long. I'd kind of like to know, but. . . well, I don't like to call them . . . . Oh, I hate to go causing people trouble."

It seems clear that there are various reasons that patients may need help with insurance formalities. At present, responsiblity for assisting patients falls to a motley crew of agents whose efforts are not necessarily closely coordinated.

The hospital employs social workers, administrators and other professionals to recover costs that the institution cannot afford to absorb. There are also unofficial assistants—often nurses and doctors whose work brings them into close and frequent contact with individual patients—who, in addition to their regular duties, may find themselves involved in efforts to unsnarl a patient's financial difficulties. There are two basic reasons for this sort of involvement: first, since effective functioning of the treatment process can be seriously impeded by recurring financial problems, frustrated professionalism may demand their solution by whatever or whosever intervention seems most expedient; second, the close association between dialysis patients and the professionals who supervise their care often leads to a sympathetic involvement with the patient's affairs. Dialysis room concern often manifests itself in efforts above and beyond the normal call of professional duties. No one, anywhere, serves primarily to help the patient understand and order his financial affairs strictly in accordance with his own needs and interests.

Rejected Claims

The usual procedure followed by insured patients seems to be that of submitting claims on an *ad hoc* basis until such time as payment is refused. If refusal is based on a technicality, a running dispute with the company may ensue:

> I had trouble with the insurance company, but Dr. A. finally got it settled. They wouldn't pay for the dialysis unless you spent the night in the hospital and the dialysis unit here isn't open at night. It just didn't make sense . . . all through October and November it was under debate: Dr. A., the hospital and the insurance company. Finally I guess Dr. A. convinced them . . . since December the insurance company has started paying . . . but I think the hospital took the loss.

If refusal is based on the fact that the company's liability is spent—that the source of funds is exhausted—a new crisis is precipitated. Rarely does a patient make any advance plans for dealing with the crisis. "I just don't know *what* I'll do when the insurance runs out!" is a typical comment. This is undoubtedly because there are few—terrifyingly few—available options. The patient, helpless and bewildered, simply drifts into crisis, hoping that, when the point is reached, some solution will present itself.

Rescue Efforts

Individuals are occasionally rescued by charitable intervention: organizations and groups may have funds available or may undertake fund-raising drives in a patient's behalf. Appeals through the media sometimes meet with surprisingly generous public response. In such cases, however, novelty is a powerful ally. Every fund drive that depends on a human interest motif to insure its success probably serves, in a degree, to desensitize its audience and may decrease the chance that such drives will be similarly successful in the future. A time of increasing need, therefore, may unfortunately be merging with a period of diminishing returns.

It is also true that fund-raising ventures probably do better when it is possible to define a single, specific objective—some indicator that can be used both as the measure of success and the end of the project. Interest and energy flag in confrontation with the demoralizing drain of unremitting need. The renal failure patient thus has a much better chance of receiving aid in some specific amount—the sum needed to defray the cost of a heroic rescue, for example, or to buy a machine for home use—than he has of tapping charitable or voluntary resources for long-term maintenance.

The prolonged maintenance period is one in which the renal failure patient's condition has stabilized. Although it is impossible to keep the body chemistry in perfect balance—there will always be periodic flurries and alarms and medical supervision must be regularly maintained—the physical condition is basically under control and the situation permits some opportunity for predicting and planning of future needs. Despite this, however, the period is characterized by a series of funding crises. While it is presumably true that in California, for example, since the state offers funds under the provisions of MediCal, no Californian need die for lack of money for treatment, there is so much personal misery and financial distress entailed in accepting state medical aid that recourse to public funds will almost certainly be postponed as long as possible.

How early and to what extent an individual will experience the treadmill effect of the prolonged maintenance period hinges on many contingencies. It makes a critical difference, for example, whether a patient is financially dependent, self-supporting or the breadwinner for a family. The most difficult position is that of the afflicted person who must earn a living.

Renal failure is hardest on the breadwinner for three reasons. First, the time needed for dialysis may cut seriously into working hours. Second, physical debility not only hampers productivity and overall efficiency but also limits the sort of work that can be undertaken. Occupations that involve a considerable outlay of physical energy or require extensive travelling, for example, may have to be abandoned. Third, it may be difficult to find any sort of suitable work since employment policies are frequently associated with insurance regulations that will, almost certainly, reject persons suffering from serious chronic disease.

Early retirement is a frequent solution among those whose age and seniority status permit them that alternative. The person who can retire on a pension and is qualified to receive help from Medicare is in a relatively good financial position, providing there are no extraneous complicating factors. Under other circumstances, however, retirement—by cutting down income and changing insurance status—may be extremely threatening. Consider, for example, the plight of a man who had reached the compulsory retirement age but whose wife—20 years his junior—was on hemodialysis that was being funded through his occupational insurance.

Medical Aid

The Californian who is already on welfare at the time of kidney failure—if he survives the many hazards in the path to rescue—will, theoretically, qualify by definition for medical aid from MediCal. Ironically, such patients are often among those whose treatment is the most expensive to maintain since they lack the stable conditions necessary to qualify them for home care.

In California, the whole issue of state-financed medical help is fraught with bitterness and altercation, and the financing of renal failure—because of its chronic nature and its extraordinarily high cost—is a particularly touchy point.

There are three sources of major dispute: welfare restrictions, governmental responsibility and administrative red tape.

Welfare Restrictions. In order to qualify for funds from MediCal, a patient must divest himself of any personal property or income he may have in excess of that permitted to recipients of state welfare. The MediCal plan is apparently so designed in order to insure that an individual will not freeload at the taxpayers' expense—that he will assume liability and share the cost of his illness. In operation it is like a deductible clause that is based on the patient's income. A single person, for example, with an income of $500 a month may be permitted a maintenance need allowance of $110 a month (the fact that specifications are subject to unpredictable change is another source of ambiguity and worry); all income above that amount must be used for medical expenses before MediCal will intervene. In addition, according to its policy, MediCal will not assist anyone who owns cash or property in excess of a value of $1,200 (personal dwelling excepted) and/or cash value of life insurance over $100 per dependent. Thus, if the patient has been fortunate enough or foresighted enough to be able to provide some security for his family, he is expected to see to the dispersal of that security before he can apply to MediCal for the funds needed to save his life. To lose one's financial foothold is never a happy eventuality, but to do so at a time when the physical realities of illness are making the course of the future extremely uncertain is particularly distressing. Once he has been reduced to the welfare level, there seems little likelihood that a patient can find the means to regain his independence.

To many persons involved in it—patients and professionals alike—the situation seems not only unfortunate but contrary to American principles and goals. Such prescriptions may even be generating a *welfare race* of persons who no longer have any incentive to self-help. That a victim of illness through no perceivable fault of his own should be reduced to such a plight is thoroughly unjust. In the words of one administrator:

> Most people are not millionaires. Most people are middle income—six to ten thousand dollars a year. I, myself, just don't think it's worth all that hassle. Especially when you stop to think that these people never feel very good—well, you get accustomed to feeling half-good . . . . But when you work all your life and you pay taxes all your life and taking care of yourself has always been a source of pride to you, and then you get turned down because *you've got too much!* Well, it's demoralizing.

Governmental Responsibility. California's state legislature is caught in a crossfire of constituent demands: reconciliation of public and private interests is not often reached at a single bound. Simultaneously pressured by demands for increased assistance, lower taxes, less governmental intervention and universal health benefits, the result is, not surprisingly, lacking in clarity and direction. The fight over hemodialysis is a case in point:

> The whole dialysis issue is a big problem in Sacramento—an embarrassment. The legislature didn't re-

ally want to pay for dialysis. But dialysis, after all, came into being here—here and at a sister center in Seattle. There was a sort of local proprietary pride . . . . And then it turned out there wasn't enough insurance to go around, so great pressure was put on the Reagan administration to accept hemodialysis. This was in 1967. Now they regret it. They didn't know what they were getting into. The State Department of Public Health estimates that by 1977 there will be 3,000 people on chronic dialysis in California. The money men say, "My God! Who's going to support their habit?"

While the legislature allegedly regrets its decision, lobbies of patients and/or professionals fight desperately to maintain and increase their financial foothold—frustration and exasperation with the ins and outs of bureaucratic evasion sometimes leading to unexpected political and ideological configurations. Because there seems to be no source of funds other than the federal government that is capable of absorbing the potential burden of technological medicine, physicians and other professionals who, in different circumstances, might have been expected to form a bulwark of resistance to socialized medicine may now—for both humane and career reasons—begin to agitate in its favor.

Administrative Red Tape. The organization and distribution of state health-care funds is apparently so tangled in a web of duplication, evasion and conflicting purpose that the overall result is mass confusion. Presumably the outgrowth of legislative ambivalence, the present situation seems to be characterized by overlapping jurisdiction, conflict of policy, bureaucratic shuffling of responsibility, and a general lack of coordination and accountability. The following is a description given by a representative of a community hospital:

> We've had reforms and we've reformed the reforms . . . . The providers are so entangled in confusion it is virtually impossible to get reimbursed. Blue Cross pays for MediCal. Welfare establishes eligibility. But the criteria of the Department of Health say *everybody* is eligible. These two agencies controvert each other. So they spend now and eligibility may be established six months from now, but the provider doesn't know whether it will be or not . . . . There's a subtle move—not to *refuse*—but to pressure the provider: 45% of the applications "disappear" or are returned for no valid reason and usually too late to resubmit them. Do you know that there are *218* reasons why a thirty-four item form can be returned? And after that there's "Other"! . . . I think they're deliberately stalling . . . . The provider is caught in a bind . . . . Eventually *somebody* has to reimburse *somebody!*

Loopholing is an informal device whereby officially proscribed actions may be unofficially redefined in terms that permit their accomplishment without open infraction of rules. There is considerable evidence to suggest that—even as lack of clear definition in the private insurance transaction sometimes leads to exploitable loopholes—confusion and ambiguity at the state level inadvertently leaves gaps whereby patients may escape some of the more devastating effects of eligibility rulings.

Paper Statements

Because loopholing must, of necessity, be evasive in method as well as in goal, it entails some special problems. In the case of dialysis patients, for instance, the medical staff or a case worker may point out the possibility of making "paper statements" that will indicate intent but may not be binding in actual commission. This is a task of considerable delicacy: such patterns of evasion are usually couched in subtle terms as a protection against the danger of legal and political repercussions.

> . . . the social workers can't say right out what is going on. They have to hope the patients will catch on when they say things like, "Well, in your case I wouldn't worry too much!" Once in a while but not very often, they'll just come right out with it. But this is dangerous.

Some persons take loopholing easily in stride, seeing it in the light of a sensible and innocuous business arrangement—like maneuvering all possible personal advantages from income tax regulations—or as a more-or-less empty ritualistic gesture. Others view it as simple dishonesty and suffer accordingly—either because desperation leads them to comply with evasionary tactics against the dictates of their scruples, in which case they suffer from the demeaning pangs of bad conscience, or because they do not, and bear, in consequence, the effects of financial anguish.

Patients as Prisoners

Loopholing can sometimes be accomplished by making a change in legal status (a device not infrequently employed by the urban poor). One such case was reported by a social worker:

> The husband, who was the patient, was in his fifties but he had a young family from a second marriage . . . . It was a working class family: the mother had a job as a salesgirl and he was a garage attendant. When they applied for MediCal, the welfare guidelines for a family of their size were just impossible—if they kept their combined income they would just be working for the state. It was a total mess! Well, the upshot of the matter was that after he had been on dialysis for a month, the marriage broke up. They got a divorce. It was the only way to save the income . . . . The woman continued to take care of him and was obviously very fond of him.

To be successful, loopholing ususally depends upon an alliance of, for example, patient, case worker and eligibility worker. If participants do not share understandings of need or definitions of loyalty the situation may dissolve into one of personal rancor and agency infighting, with counter-attributions of bureaucratic inhumanity and fiscal irresponsibility being hurled back and forth to the apparent benefit of no one.

The patient, meanwhile, stands helplessly by. He is like a prisoner at the bar waiting for the result of adversary action to decide his fate: in this case, a negative decision will condemn him to the humiliation and distress of ultimate financial wipeout.

At present several treatment alternatives exist for dealing with chronic renal failure. Chief among these are center-based hemodialysis, home-based hemodialysis and kidney transplant. Each has major drawbacks and each offers its own special advantages. The patient is not likely to have much of a say in deciding on a method, first because he usually inherits certain preselected programs and equipment along with the physician and/or institution which circumstances have assigned him; second, because personal limitations—physical, social and economic—dictate what alternative may be practical or even possible in an individual case; and third, because medical paternalism is such that the situation of the patient as it is perceived by persons in decision-making relationships to him will greatly influence what choices are brought to his attention.

For center-based dialysis the patient comes to a central unit two or three times a week for treatment. There are four major advantages to this arrangement: constant supervision by personnel trained and equipped to deal with emergencies; relief for family members from some of the burden of work and anxiety; availability to many persons who lack a suitable home or who do not have a responsible assistant regularly available; usefulness in transient holding cases—patients awaiting a transplant, for example—where investment for home equipment would be impractical.

The chief disadvantages of center-based dialysis are higher cost, transportation problems and loss of independence. The high cost of center-based as compared with home-based dialysis is an interesting problem. In theory, centralization of services and multiple use of equipment suggest an economic efficiency that should produce the opposite effect. In practice, however, high hospital overhead, inefficient administrative practices (few centers, for example, are operated on a 24-hour schedule), a certain degree of professional and institutional profiteering, and competition among providers combine to make centralization more costly. The fact that dialysis centers have no assurance as to time or extent of reimbursement for their services makes it even harder to cut costs.

Home-based dialysis was initially designed as a program to reduce operating costs and to reach patients otherwise inaccessible for treatment—goals it has achieved with some success. Home dialysis does not eliminate the need for the center, which still provides training, medical—and sometimes mechanical—supervision and emergency care. In addition, it is customary for the patient to return to the center at specific intervals—perhaps four times a year—for a period of followup study and medical workup.

The chief drawback to home dialysis is probably the patient's need for a qualified home helper, one who can bear the physical, emotional and temporal burdens and meet high standards of intelligence, character and training. In addition, even well-qualified helpers are not unfailingly reliable: they fall ill themselves; they leave to get married; they simply grow tired of it all and quit. Their places are not readily filled.

Another problem that may beset the home-dialysis candidate is the fact that his insurance may not cover outpatient care. Unless he can convince his insuror that home dialysis is not in that category, the patient may have no choice but to accept center-based treatment, with all the irony of its additional cost.

A machine for home use can be either purchased or rented. Unless the patient has reason for anticipating an early release—by transplant, for example—it is cheaper to buy it. Once he has paid for the machine (an expense of, roughly, \$4,000) and has completed the launching period of physical stabilization and home training (altogether, perhaps, a matter of \$12,000) a patient's home dialysis expenses will probably range from \$2,500 to \$3,000 a year (as compared with estimates of center-based costs that run from \$22,000 to \$30,000 annually).

The funding process for home dialysis follows the pattern for center-based dialysis. There is an initial high cost period that may be cushioned by insurance as the patient is rescued and launched into his home-dialysis career. This is followed by a period of somewhat lower and more predictable cost for prolonged maintenance. Treadmilling problems typically attend this situation of continuing need and diminishing supply.

Kidney transplant, the only alternative to dialysis, is the most dramatic and theoretically the most promising of the solutions now available for chronic renal failure. Although an enormously expensive process, like any major surgery, the cost of transplant in no way compares with the financial burden imposed by a lifetime of dialysis. Furthermore, such expenses are often covered by major medical insurance policies, with the unfortunate exclusion of the financial burden of the donor. These latter can be considerable: the surgical process involved in removing a kidney is more difficult than that required for implanting one. However, there are a number of possibilities for defraying donor expenses, including such resources as personal savings, personal loans and charitable subscription.

Unfortunately, the possibility of rejection is high. Figures based on a one-year success rate suggest, very roughly, a 70 percent success with transplants from live donors and a 50 percent or less chance with cadaver kidneys. Further, the antirejection regimen is itself unpleasant and restrictive. If rejection occurs, the patient is once more caught up on the treadmill—searching for funds and probably for kidney donors as well.

Groups of enterprising patients occasionally organize themselves into kidney clubs, which are usually oriented to consumer activities such as group buying in order to reduce the cost of supplies, pressuring insurance companies for certain policy redefinitions, challenging doctors on details of care, small-scale legislative lobbying and fund-raising for specific purposes. (One such project involved an effort to provide flight money for members in the event that an individual awaiting a transplant is suddenly informed, by computerized matching service, that a suitable kidney is available in a distant city.) The effectiveness of such organizations is seriously hampered by basic lack of group cohesion. Since the membership is composed of persons who are chronically ill, there is a marked dearth of the physical energy and stamina needed to sustain a concerted drive towards large objectives. Additionally, members, by and large, are committed to one another only at the financial level. For many, particularly those who exhibit the most vitality and talent for leadership, there seems to be a tendency to disavow the invalid identity and therefore resist any real involvement with persons who are ill, maintaining their own membership only as long as it seems to provide personal, material advantages. Participation in the group is thus apt to be ambivalent and transitory: members who, by good fortune or good management, find better solutions for their problems, typically withdraw from the club.

There are some who object to the present emphasis on the treatment of chronic renal failure, arguing that research might more profitably be directed towards prevention than toward cure. A spokesperson for the Northern California Kidney Foundation argues, for example, that a program of periodic urinalysis among school children might provide an effective early warning system, predicting potential renal failure at a phase in its trajectory when it may still be reversible.

Such views are, at present, much overshadowed by public and professional interest in the more dramatic possibilities of artificial organs and transplant. In addition, research findings tend to rule out the effectiveness of any single preventative program.

There is a significantly higher incidence of suicidal behavior among chronic renal failure patients than for the population at large or even as compared with victims of other chronic disease. Suicidal behavior refers both to deliberate action taken by the patient to terminate his own life and to his refusal to undergo treatment with an intent to accomplish the same end.

Over the past few years considerable attention has been directed to identifying predisposing psychological factors that may contribute to the self-destructive impulse. Personality variables such as ego strength and self-esteem have been defined and measured as factors controlling the suicidal tendency. It may be that being in bondage to the machine sends those patients with unresolved dependency conflicts into a state of suicidal despair.

The conditioning effect that circumstance and status can exert on the direction of personal decision is demonstrated in the following examples. The first was reported by the administrator of a dialysis center:

> There are lots of cases where patients just haven't showed up. Patients have been referred to private centers, say, where they demand a deposit of $10,000, and they just toss in the towel. One man I know of personally—thirty-seven years of age with three children and $19,000 in the bank—elected to die. He was perfectly frank. He said if he went into treatment he would destroy his family.

Another patient—a 27-year-old father of two young children—faced a different situation and, in accordance with his perception of it, reached a different decision:

> . . . the way I see it, I'm going to be in the hole all my life. I worry about bills. I worry about a change in the laws that will cut off what we're getting now. Most of my worry is money . . . . It's my kids. They're forcing me to stay alive. I keep seeing myself caring for them until they're on their own. I imagine what it will be like for them if I die. They'll hardly have anything. My wife didn't even finish high school and she wouldn't be able to take care of them . . . . They'd hardly get anything to eat, maybe. The thought keeps me going. I want to live . . . .

In neither of these cases did the patient—by demeanor or behavior—manifest lack of self-esteem or neurotic fear of dependency. Opposite decisions were apparently reached according to real differences in external conditions.

The funding process pursued by the renal failure patient dramatically highlights, by the urgency of its precarious balance between financial wipeout and death, a course that is probably typical of that to which desperate persons may, in the end, be always reduced—including crisis-oriented, *ad hoc* decision-making and rule-evading loopholing tactics that undermine personal morale, social values and, possibly, in the end, established social systems.

Future Proposals

A number of proposals for alleviating the distress of chronic renal failure patients have emerged from our study of the problem:

- ☐ That insurance carriers reimburse claimants for outpatient treatment.
- ☐ That unions assign trained persons to act as insurance advisors to their members, on an individual basis.
- ☐ That providers of dialysis treatment work together to relieve expensive duplication and overlap that often

result from competitive efforts.

- ☐ That dialysis centers be operated on a 24-hour basis.
- ☐ That paramedical personnel be trained in hemodialysis techniques in order to assist home-care patients, if not on a regular, at least on an emergency basis.
- ☐ That prepaid transportation service be provided for center-based patients—urban, suburban and interurban.
- ☐ That some relaxation be made in insurance regulations in order to encourage businesses to employ chronically ill individuals who are able and willing to work.
- ☐ That state health insurance policies and their administration be completely reorganized in order to cut red tape, to give health care providers a reasonable basis for predicting the time and extent of reimbursement for services rendered, and to remove health care assistance from the restrictions of welfare eligibility rules.

The implementation of any or all such suggestions would bring some measure of relief to the individual patient. It would not, however, eliminate the basic problem and the crisis-to-crisis course of the funding process. That will happen only when we are ready to take the financial responsibility for our espoused humanitarianism and pay for a federal health care program.

SUGGESTED READINGS

"Suicidal Behavior in Chronic Dialysis Patients" by Harry S. Abram, Gordon L. Moore, and Frederic B. Westervelt, paper delivered to the American Psychiatric Association at San Francisco, May 1970.

"Psychosocial Aspects of Hemodialysis" by George L. Bailey and "Funding for End-Stage Renal Patients" by Margaret B. Wilkins in *Hemodialysis: Principles and Practice*, edited by George L. Bailey (New York: Academic Press, 1973).

"Help Patterns in Severe Illness: The Roles of Kin Network, Non-Family Resources and Institutions" by Sydney H. Croog, Alberta Lipson, and Sol Levine in *Journal of Marriage and the Family*, February 1972.

3 *David Mechanic*

Apartheid Medicine

The Republic of South Africa is a country of great contradictions and striking contrasts. Differences in medical care between blacks and whites reflect existing inequalities. The most advanced transplant teams exist side by side with widespread malnutrition and starvation among blacks. The white infant mortality rate is comparable to that of advanced nations; but if you are born in some black reserves you may have no more than a 50-50 chance of reaching the age of five.

While the total population of South Africa is 21,500,000, the approximately four million whites dominate every aspect of its social and economic life. The remaining population, consisting of approximately fifteen million Africans, two million coloreds (mulattoes), and more than half a million Asians, is by law and by social custom subjected to a variety of indignities and deprivations. While the Asians have the least deprived economic status among the non-whites, and the coloreds hold an intermediate position, the great mass of Africans live under conditions of abject poverty.

Apartheid is the Republic of South Africa's official policy of segregation. It preserves and sustains the economic, political and social domination of the white minority over all other groups. This forced separation leaves the black majority with 14 percent of the land, gives the white full control over the productive capacities of the nation and results in enormous hardship and misery for the non-white population.

The patterns of disease and health care in the country reflect this social and economic organization. For example, in 1970 the number of white infant deaths per 1,000 live births was 21.1. For Asian infants the number was 37.1, and for colored infants it rose to 136.2. Registration of births among Africans is incomplete and infant mortality is not reported, but a 1966 survey found that half of the children in a typical reserve die before reaching age five and doctors practicing among Africans in rural areas report that it is quite typical for African women to have lost half of their children.

In the summer of 1972 I was asked by the University of Witwatersrand in Johannesburg to be a visiting professor and to initiate a teaching program for medical students in the sociology of medicine. I visited South Africa for 25 days, spending approximately half of my time in Johannesburg and surrounding areas and the remainder in visiting medical facilities and physicians in other parts of the country. If there are any biases in my observations, they result from having seen more urban than rural facilities and more prestigious than ordinary hospitals, and from having spent a disproportionate amount of time visiting "model" facilities. For example, I spent more time in the African township of Soweto than in other more impoverished townships and had an official tour of the "most progressive" of the reserves, medically speaking, the Tswana homeland in Hammanskraal. I made some effort to see medical facilities in different townships and reserves in varying parts of the country and visited several mission hospitals in rural areas. I saw white, colored and African units in urban areas that were funded by the same authorities and thus had some opportunity to examine the degree of inequality in the provision of medical services.

Twenty-five days is a very limited exposure, and I am well aware of the difficulties in arriving at a balanced picture in so short a time. Thus I have made special effort to verify my personal observations by consulting available publications on social and medical conditions in South Africa. I have tried to state my observations with care, and I feel confident that they are valid.

The Republic of South Africa, according to the Minister of Health, has one doctor for every 450 whites and one for every 18,000 blacks. There are relatively few non-white doctors in the country, with one colored doctor for every 6,200 colored and one African doctor for every 44,400 Africans. South Africa has four medical schools for whites which exclude Africans but have a very limited number of colored and Asian medical students who are given special permission to attend. In 1971 the one black medical school at the University of Natal had 247 Indians, 172 Africans and 38 coloreds. Blacks have difficulty entering medical school because of deficiencies of prior education, lack of economic resources to support themselves and limited access to medical education.

The legal exclusion of Africans and most other non-whites from white medical schools relegates them to an inferior social and medical status, and those who become doctors receive lower wages by law than comparably trained whites. Moreover, non-white doctors may never be in a position to give orders to whites, thus greatly affecting training opportunities and possibilities of occupational mobility, and they may not use white dining facilities at hospitals nor participate in other social activities.

The high doctor-patient ratio among whites makes white medical practice in South Africa highly competitive, and the white population receives exceedingly responsive care. Doctors are highly accessible, make home calls and night calls, and their services are relatively inexpensive by American standards. The basic organization of services is private and on a fee-for-service basis; ordinarily hospitalization is provided in nursing homes (somewhat akin to proprietary hospitals in the United States). Superspecialist hospital services are available in government-financed hospitals. Such institutions as Groote Schuur in Cape Town have medical capabilities comparable to those found anywhere in the world.

The vast majority of the white population of South Africa is affluent, well fed and well doctored, and suffers from disease patterns comparable to other affluent Western nations. Studies of peripubertal growth among Pretoria children show nutritional status among whites to be comparable or superior to anywhere else in the world, while blacks are clearly disadvantaged. Such problems as schistosomiasis, trachoma and idiopathic endomycardial fibrosis, which are extremely common in the black population, receive relatively little medical attention.

The organization of health care services in African areas varies from that available in urban areas, to rudimentary services in some reserves, to non-existent services or inaccessible services for large parts of the population. In order to understand the differences in organization, it is necessary to consider the differences between the townships and the reserves.

Reserves (frequently referred to as Bantustans and Homelands) are those land areas in which Africans of various tribes in South Africa have pseudo-independence and some citizen rights. Thus, in most of the country they are treated as "guest workers" and have no political rights. The reserves are not economically viable and are an inadequate basis for separate development. The African townships, such as Soweto and Alexandra in Johannesburg, are defined as "legally" inside of white areas, and Africans require a permit to be there. Access to these areas is controlled, maintaining the fiction that the urbanized African's home residence is in one or another of the reserves. Africans living in Soweto are denied citizenship and property rights, and the government at its pleasure evicts populations from areas in which they have lived when it serves the political, economic or social needs of the white population.

Disease and Low Wages

White society in South Africa depends on African labor, and the Africans, in turn, depend on work in urban areas for their subsistence. The social and economic situation for Africans is sufficiently severe in the reserves to encourage large numbers to remain in urban areas without permits despite harassment and a high risk of arrest. Such "illegal residence" is frequently encouraged by whites who desire access to cheap African labor. Conditions in the townships are generally harsh and contribute in major ways to disease and social pathology. Africans coming from the reserves to the townships cannot bring their families with them and this results in long separations and family disruptions.

In one township I observed large numbers of malnourished and neglected young children near a day care center. Personnel at the center—in telling me of their work—indicated that they had sufficient places for all of the children who wished to come. When I inquired about the children playing outside, I was informed that since their parents did not have residence permits the day center was prohibited by the government from taking the children despite available places. These children were just some of the many victims of brutal attempts to enforce apartheid.

Many of the disease problems arise from economic inadequacies. In the summer of 1972 the first national survey of African wages, made by the Productivity and Wages Association, was released. The survey results came from 1,086 companies, mainly in manufacturing and financial and commercial sectors (excluding mining), involving more than 188,000 employees. The return rate among firms surveyed was only 13 percent, and it is likely that those responding paid somewhat higher wages than those who did not participate. Moreover, since the survey was based on what firms paid rather than on what Africans earned, it excluded the large number of unemployed Africans and those who do a variety of casual work and household work at even more exploitative wages.

Chronic Malnutrition

Despite the conservative nature of the survey, it was found that 80 percent of Africans in the private sector earn less than 70 Rand a month (approximately $93 at current exchange rates, which constitutes the poverty line). The Johannesburg Chamber of Commerce has estimated that a family of five in Soweto requires at least a minimum of R82.19 a month to live acceptably. In 1970 the Human Sciences Research Council estimated that the minimum effective income level necessary for a white family of five in Pretoria was R158.90 per month; and if one takes into account the changes in the cost of living, R170 would be a more reasonable figure.

The problem of low wages is compounded by discriminatory wage scales for white, colored and African workers doing the same job, by the exclusion of Africans and coloreds from many jobs reserved for white labor, and by indentured service characteristic of mining and other aspects of the economy. In mining, Africans are paid 50 to 60 cents a shift of eight hours, approximately one-seventeenth of what white miners earn.

The average social pension for an African is about R5.00 a month (approximately $7). He is expected to pay approximately half of that total for housing in the township. The Reverend David Russell, in attempting to make visible the plight of the African, has been trying to survive on R5.00 a month. I quote in some detail from his letter of July 28, 1972 to the *Rand Daily Mail:*

> I wish to emphasize that these conditions of tearing hardship do not only involve the so-called "unproductive units." The situation is just as frustrating and harsh for the few able-bodied men "lucky enough to be working as casual labourers for R20.00 per month. For this they must work a 46-hour week, starting at 7.30 am and finishing at 5.12 pm. Monday to Friday, with only half hour for lunch, and no tea break at all ....For a casual labourer with a wife and only four children there is a mere R3.34 a month per person for living. These wages and working conditions are shocking....The R5.00 per month I have been living on for the last three months leaves me significantly better off than most Dimbaza inhabitants [an African Resettlement Township near King William's Town]. Nevertheless I am feeling the strain. It is like serving a prison sentence—I hold on grimly counting the days. My life revolves around my stomach! Human joy is shrivelling up; my capacity for giving out is shrinking. My friends notice the difference in me.

The common health problems of Africans are those generally found in the impoverished and underdeveloped world. The Africans are in a chronic state of malnutrition, and this contributes to a wide variety of disease problems and consequences. Protein-calorie deficiency disease is extremely common, and there is a considerable amount of pellagra and other nutritional diseases as well. Stunted physical and mental growth, often a consequence of chronic malnutrition, is also extremely common. There is a very high prevalence of gastroenteritis and pneumonia, diseases which are major causes of death among infants. Tuberculosis is rampant and so are its complications. Severe burns resulting from falling into open fires used to keep dwelling units warm are a very common problem among children in winter. Because of poor penetration of immunization and preventive medicine among Africans—particularly in the rural areas—measles, diphtheria, dysentery and many other preventable diseases are quite common.

A Great Tiredness

I was told over and over again that malnutrition was a product of the ignorance of the African, of his unwillingness to follow a healthy diet, of his need for health education. This concerned note became the great rationalization used to explain the human deterioration so evident at every clinic and hospital. It is probably correct that Africans with a limited income could eke out a technically balanced diet if they adhered to a standard of austerity and self-denial that few whites could conform to. It is true that the African can eat what David Russell and other outraged people are attempting to eat as a means of protest; a daily food ration of 306 grams of mealie meal (ground maize), 125 grams mealies, 75 grams of beans, 30 grams skim milk, 15 grams margarine and 7 grams salt. But to argue that the failure to follow this diet is primarily a product of ignorance is to engage in the worst type of sophistry. On October 14, 1972, the *New York Times* reported that the Reverend David Russell was at the point of collapse and planning to end his ordeal. He was quoted as saying, "Trying to live on 5 Rand a month has been long and dreary....I feel a great tiredness deep within me. I just do not know how Africans manage."

It is extremely difficult to obtain adequate figures on the scope of malnutrition in South Africa. At one time kwashiorkor was a notifiable disease, but now notification has been discontinued; thus, the Minister of Health has remarked to Parliament that there is no malnutrition in South Africa. But a survey in Pretoria suggested that half of the Urban African school children studied in the age group 7-11 are adapted to a suboptimal protein intake although the basis of the estimate may not be fully valid. Dr. Neser of the National Nutrition Research Institute has written, on the basis of his survey, that "at least 80 percent of school-going children from Bantu households in Pretoria suffer from malnutrition and under-nutrition." These estimates are both conservatively based, since rural children are obviously more malnourished than those from urban areas, and those most malnourished are less likely to be in school.

Identified malnutrition is only a small proportion of such cases existing in the population. One estimate suggests eight or nine additional potential cases for every one recognized, and an assessment made at the University of Cape Town suggests that for every case of kwashiorkor seen by doctors at clinics, there are 40 undefined cases of malnutrition. Similarly, it is well known that the occurrence of tuberculosis is related to nutrition, and this may serve as a proxy for estimates of malnutrition. As in the United States, tuberculosis is relatively uncommon among the white population of South Africa. In some African areas as much as one-fifth of the population may have tuberculosis.

Soweto, the major African township in Johannesburg, is served by a large provincial hospital, Baragwanath, which occupies the physical facilities of a restored army barracks. It is a teaching institution of the University of Witwatersrand Medical School. The medical and nursing staff is well trained, concerned about the health status of the Africans, and copes admirably with an unending flow of pathology within considerable budgetary constraints. Despite an enormous number of beds (approximately 2,200), the needs are so great that only the very sickest patients are admitted and released sooner than desirable. Particularly impressive is the pediatrics unit which is especially dedicated and is doing extraordinary work despite severe limitations of funds and space.

Unending Flow of Pathology

In the townships, medical responsibility is highly fragmented between curative hospital medicine, preventive and curative clinics and the social services. They are each under different authorities, making it extremely difficult to develop or coordinate a wholistic approach to the problems of the Africans in the townships. The hospital has no authority or funding for preventive work and must deal with an unending flow of pathology with few tools to alter the conditions producing pathology in the community. Physicians often find their efforts futile, having patients return time and time again for the same difficulties that recur on return to noxious community conditions.

The curative clinics in the townships are crowded dispensaries providing limited and superficial care. Waiting periods to see a doctor are long—with patients queuing up early in the morning—and the number of patients processed by each doctor is extremely large. Dental and ophthamological services are virtually non-existent. Despite the fact that I made special efforts to visit pediatric services, day care centers and preventive clinics, I never saw a black child in the Republic of South Africa with eyeglasses, but I assume there must be some.

The preventive clinics are worthy institutions but have inadequate financing and manpower to cope with the existing difficulties in the community. They provide immunizations, pre- and postnatal care, health education and birth control services. Staffed by nurse-midwives and health visitors, they make considerable effort to improve prevention, but the inadequacy of financing and staffing makes community penetration difficult. The government subsidizes the availability of skimmed milk powder which can be obtained at the preventive clinics for young underweight children. More subsidy is approved than utilized, indicating a clear inability to reach much of the population in need.

Birth control programs are probably more enthusiastically implemented than any other by the authorities, and wherever I went, this facet of prevention was emphasized. This is no surprise since the white community fears the growing black population and would like to limit their fertility. Although many black women are amenable to birth control, existing conditions make others in the black community skeptical. The main strength of the blacks in South Africa, they maintain, is in their numbers, and they are reluctant to support efforts to control their population. Similarly, women are frequently skeptical about limiting their fertility when so many of their youngsters die. Children are not only culturally valued, but also provide some security in old age since social services are almost non-existent. It is my impression that birth control, without associated efforts to limit infant mortality in the black community and to improve the social situation of the blacks, will be a futile effort. The authorities have not as yet been willing to confront these issues.

In the reserves medical care is within the jurisdiction of the Office of Bantu Affairs, and it is possible to develop an integrated approach to preventive and curative medicine. I was taken to part of the Tswana homeland near Hammanskraal—by the Secretary of Health and three of his major assistants heading up various aspects of the health department in Pretoria—to see the evolving plan for health services in the homelands which, in their view, was well developed in this specific area. I was told that the population of that particular area was approximately a quarter of a million and that it was fairly widely dispersed with limited access to transportation. All of the hospital services for the population are provided by the mission hospital, having a staff of five physicians.

Mission Hospitals Impressive

The rural African population has depended heavily on the various mission hospitals for the limited medical services available to them. These hospitals are frequently staffed by mission doctors from abroad and vary in their orientations—some mixing religion with medicine as a condition of service, others with a much more secular attitude. The mission hospitals that I visited were staffed by physicians with dedication and concern. Some limit the patients they serve in terms of available space and resources, others never turn away a patient in need, keeping beds in every available place—indoors and on outdoor porches. These hospitals obviously have made and continue to make an important contribution, and without them the health status of the African would be even more dismal.

Mission hospitals sometimes hospitalize young infants with their sick mothers, for their survival is often precarious when the mother goes to the hospital. A common practice in both urban and mission hospitals is to have mothers stay in the hospital with their dehydrated infants, assuming part of their care and having some exposure to health education concerning nutrition and child care. This was one of the few practices I saw in South Africa that we would do well to follow.

Most impressive of the mission hospitals I visited was the Charles Johnson Memorial Hospital in Nqutu, KwaZulu. The hospital has some 338 beds with an average daily case load of approximately 650 people, administers clinics in outlying areas, has its own school for training African nurses and deals impressively with an unending flow of pathology and disease. Understanding the basic plight of the region they serve, the hospital personnel do what they can to assist in preventive and community matters, but the task is immense and resources extremely limited. Although the hospital has made important contributions to the region over the past three decades, it is clear that no hospital or clinic has the means to intervene effectively in the conditions causing disease.

Not far from the Johnson Memorial Hospital there is a settlement of some 500 people uprooted from white farms and forced to resettle elsewhere. Officially their presence in the area is illegal, and sooner or later they will be moved on again. Food is difficult to scrape together and water is scarce. The people dig holes in the dry earth with the hope that they might collect some underground water, and since their presence in the area is "temporary" (they have been there two years already), the authorities will take no measures to provide a decent and safe water source. *The Guardian* of September 23, 1972 reported that when the director of the hospital took the issue up with the authorities and tried to do something to improve the situation, he was told to mind his own business and that he was interfering with the Bantu. It may be a coincidence that at the same time an official telephoned the hospital questioning the permit of its welfare officer to enter the reserve.

The mission hospitals now receive financial support from the government, although they are underfinanced to meet the needs of the regions they serve. The existing plan is to provide primary medical care and preventive services from satellite clinics dispersed throughout the region, but it has not as yet been made operational in most areas. In the Hammanskraal area, where the plan was said to be in practice, I visited satellite clinics staffed by nurse-midwives who provide other than hospital services, and the clinics are visited occasionally by physicians from the hospital; I was told that there was approximately one session every two weeks. These clinics give considerable attention to family planning and immunizations, prenatal care and midwifery, and are the primary site for milk powder distribution. There are no dental or ophthamological services at these clinics, and the basic medical care is rudimentary. Staffing is far too inadequate to reach many people in need in the population. Although these clinics provide sites of care which are of value, the character, scope and quality of service would be totally unacceptable to the white population of South Africa.

Separate and Unequal

In order to get some measure of the extent of inequality of medical care, I visited white, colored and African pediatric units in the same evening—all funded by the same governmental authority. In the African hospital, the wards were extremely crowded with very limited staffing. In one of the infant units we saw two nurses attempting to feed, change and generally cope with 37 very sick children. We then went to the comparable white hospital where we found two nurses caring for five white children who were less ill. The comparable unit for coloreds in the same hospital was somewhere between these two extremes. Generally the physical facilities and amenities followed the same pattern.

I also visited the major hospital serving the colored community in Johannesburg—Coronation Hospital—and the various areas in which these persons live. Although conditions are not quite as harsh as in the African community, they are generally comparable. Housing is inadequate and frequently unavailable, community conditions are poor, and malnutrition and preventable diseases are common. Medical services cannot cope with the magnitude of disease and pathology created by community conditions. From many of the colored areas, transportation is especially difficult to Coronation Hospital, and medical services in the community are rudimentary.

Few medical facilities are available in the African and colored communities after dark; and should problems develop, it is frequently difficult to get to the hospitals serving these areas. In both Johannesburg and Cape Town there are projects carried out by medical and law students which provide some health and legal services to a colored community. These projects are carried out by volunteers and deserve to be commended, but it also should be noted that the type of patchwork service provided by a large number of volunteers—each contributing a little time—does not provide first-rate care, nor is it an ideal educational experience. The clinics tend to be erratic, depending on the academic schedule, and supervision is spotty. The medical schools involved have a responsibility to make such community services part of the overall approach to medical education and to provide the resources and supervision that guarantees a more adequate service. The practice of community medical care should be as much a part of medical education as work in the teaching hospital, and it should be more than a volunteer effort among those students who feel some sense of social responsibility. It must be clear, however, that the medical schools also are a reflection of South African society and are largely meeting the needs of its white elite. The basic problem is much deeper than the social responsibilities of medical education since the health of the African population is determined primarily by social and political policies, and these affect the performance of medical education and all other human services as well.

It is a well-known principle that the assumptions and conditions under which people live have a pervasive effect on their perceptions and behavior regardless of their particular ideologies. Social structures have the capacities to accent the best or worst in people, and under some conditions even well-meaning and idealistic persons come to take for granted behavior they would not condone if they lived in a different social context. In this regard, I often had the impression that people thought they were showing me one thing, but I was seeing quite another.

At one point I visited a landscaped park in Soweto, which is a stopping point for the visitors' bus tour. Sitting on a hill overlooking the township, there is an elegant tearoom pleasantly surrounded by flowers and plants. Since I had noticed no parks or playgrounds or any green areas in Soweto, I asked whether Soweto residents used the park. My escort, somewhat embarrassed by the inquiry, indicated it was off limits; as an afterthought she indicated that this was to protect against vandalism.

Sources for Information on South Africa's Health and Medical Care

Although seeing conditions with one's own eyes adds a dimension to experience and judgment, the facts reported in this paper are almost entirely taken from previously published sources. Much of the reported data comes from *A Survey of Race Relations in South Africa,* published by the South African Institute of Race Relations in Johannesburg. The Institute, an organization promoting racial cooperation and research on existing social conditions, is presently being harassed by a government investigation of its activities. The survey of race relations is published annually but the data reported here are based on the most recent survey published in 1972. Other publications of the Institute of particular value to this paper are: Ellen Hellmann, *Soweto: Johannesburg's African City* (1971) and J.V.O. Reid, *Malnutrition* (1971). Various articles appearing in Johannesburg newspapers, *The Star* and the *Rand Daily Mail*, were also useful in describing conditions in various African areas.

There are few general articles on medical conditions in South Africa. I found the paper by Raymond Hoffenberg ("Inequality in Health Care in South Africa," U. N. Unit on Apartheid, December, 1970) useful. Also very valuable is the book edited by S. L. Kark and G. W. Steuart, *A Practice of Social Medicine* (Edinburgh: E. and S. Livingstone, 1962). For studies on growth and development in various groups, the published work of P. V. Tobias, Professor of Anatomy at the University of Witwatersrand, was particularly relevant.

To grasp the conditions of medical practice among the Africans in rural areas, a vivid and exciting description is provided by Anthony Barker (*The Man Next to Me: An Adventure in African Medical Practice,* New York: Harper, 1959). For a moving pictorial description of social conditions among Africans in South Africa, see Ernest Cole, *House of Bondage* (New York: Random House, 1967). A detailed description of the horrendous conditions based on an extensive personal survey of such areas is provided by Cosmas Desmond, (*The Discarded People,* Baltimore: Penguin Books, 1972). Father Desmond has been banned by the South African government.

David Mechanic

I had similar experiences in my visits to various hospitals. For even among persons of conscience and commitment a certain callousness and disregard of human factors were frequently evident. It was apparent in many little ways. Some doctors who were obviously persons of integrity and compassion would lecture me loudly on the ignorance and superstitiousness of the African as we went from bed to bed. Few thought it necessary to explain to patients, whose treatment was being disrupted by my visit, who I was or why the disruption. When I embarrassedly requested that a patient be asked for permission so that I could take his picture, I was assured over and over again that I could take pictures of anything I wanted and that I did not have to ask anyone.

White Callousness

Disregard for human dignity is found in hospitals the world over and is in no sense unique to South Africa; but in South Africa it would take saintly qualities to be anything but paternalistic and hardened under the social and political conditions that prevail. One falls in with the culture and those with whom one must cooperate in assumptions and behavior. Even in my short stay I could observe the process occurring in myself; by the time I left I was beginning to unconsciously accept conditions that I found shocking when I first confronted them. Human survival depends on steady concessions to the social and cultural milieu. Thus I have come to have the greatest respect for those South Africans in all walks of life who speak out loudly against the brutalities and indignities of the social structure of South Africa; and if they sound paternalistic from time to time, it is not too difficult to understand why. Already Africans are rejecting their more paternalistic white advocates and, indeed, the time may be coming when they reject all whites. This reaction is also clearly understandable, a product of the limited options available.

These economic, social and medical inequalities are already known to informed physicians, government officials and the involved public in South Africa. But existing conditions make it difficult for many concerned persons to speak out without personal risk. Yet, throughout my visit I was impressed by the concern of many South Africans who were struggling to do what little they could within the constraints imposed on them. There were many concerned physicians in the hospitals; but curative medicine, however important, is somewhat of a smoke screen if not complemented by better preventive efforts and improved conditions in the community. Moreover, it is obvious that progress and decency in South Africa must involve more than good will and concern of individuals; it must be embedded in the social structure and social conditions which are the primary determinants of health and illness in society. Social policies that divide men, disrupt communities, separate family members against their wishes and breed distrust and hate cannot create a healthy society.

Some South Africans maintain that theirs is a poor country, and that it is inappropriate to impose the kind of standard I have in my observations. They point to poverty elsewhere in Africa and to the fact that there are other starving Africans. I would be less likely to regard this as a grand rationalization if the country were not so rich in natural resources, if the white population did not dominate so much of the country's resources, and if it did not live in ostentatious affluence in the midst of such great poverty. South Africa has had an enormous rate of economic growth, but it has not shared its growing affluence with its black population. The only relevant comparison is an internal one that takes into account the economic resources and capacities of the country and compares the differences in how the white and black populations live and the impact of social policies on maintaining or closing these differences.

Similarly, I would be more impressed with concerns about the ignorance of the African if education among Africans were encouraged, if they were not legally excluded from white schools and universities, and if they did not have to pay from their meager wages for education that is freely available to whites. The fact is that many of the Africans in the Republic of South Africa are highly urbanized, and their disabilities arise not from ignorance or ineptitude but from systematic exclusion from social and economic opportunities enforced by apartheid policies. South Africa persists in plundering its greatest resource—the capacities, labor and potentialities of its people.

SUGGESTED READINGS

Modernizing Racial Domination: The Dynamics of South African Politics by Herbert Adam (Berkeley: University of California Press, 1971).

The Man Next to Me: An Adventure in African Medical Practice by Anthony Barker (New York: Harper & Row, 1959).

A Short History of South Africa, rev. ed., by Leo Marquard (New York: Praeger, 1968).

The Peoples and Policies of South Africa, 4th ed., by Leo Marquard (London: Oxford University Press, 1969).

Law, Order and Liberty in South Africa by A. S. Mathews (Berkeley: University of California Press, 1972).

Section XVII

Economy and Society

Social life is affected by and, in turn, affects economic life. Horowitz, in "Capitalism, Communism and Multinationalism," provides an analysis of the thaw in the cold war and ties that analysis to the development of the gigantic multinational corporations and the rise of the Third World as a force in international political and economic life. In articulating the interrelationships on which the new world order will depend, he says: "The multinationals help to bridge the gap between revolutionary nationalism and establishment internationalism by acquiescing to the symbolic demands of nationalists and revolutionists, while satisfying the very real economic demands of conservative middle-sector elements in Third World societies." Internationalism, Horowitz argues, is corporate rather than proletarian because of consumer demand and technological triumph. These tendencies, however, may produce a new kind of galvanized worldwide worker movement.

In "Benign Neglect in the United States," Heilbroner raises the question: Why is there so much social neglect in a country as rich as America? In addition, he points out that by all standard measures this neglect is greater than in many other industrialized countries. His suggestion is that it has more to do with national character than just with the consequences of capitalism. Democracy and economic success have yielded institutionalized unconcern and antipathy for government intervention and created by antiwelfare, frontier spirit. The American social conscience, he states, has been anesthetized, and a great fear of a "pinch" on middle-class wealth has fed that spirit. America lacks a socialist movement and programs of reform for the lower classes, as well as working-class interest groups and political parties. Heilbroner sees a new "New Deal" from movement in the areas of racial inequality, from the realization of environmental limitations and the youth movement.

"Post-1984 America" represents Rainwater's vision for the future of America. Using the technique of extrapolating current trends into the future from demographic and socioeconomic data, he sees two key life-style changes. In the economic area, there will be a very large rise in median income, educational attainment and cosmopolitanism. In the cultural area, he sees the elaborating and perfecting of existing class-related life-styles, that is, a growth in pluralism. Rainwater suggests that the role of women will change and that norms governing marriage will also undergo change. Time will become more important as an "inelastic commodity" where there are people financially well off in glutted commodity market. There will be a large growth in service industries. All of this applies, he says, to the middle classes; there will be little improvement for the underclass. Rainwater's article is an example of the sociologist's imagination applied to the venerable art of forecasting.

1 *Irving Louis Horowitz*

Capitalism, Communism and Multinationalism

A well-known party is looking for revolutionary ideas. It may come as a surprise, but the communists are no longer claiming they've invented every good idea under the sun. On the contrary, they're eagerly hoping that Westerners may have invented a few before them. The fact is that the communists—in particular the East Europeans—are building a broad consumer society. They're in a hurry. And they're in the market for advanced technology in a staggering number of fields. The point is this: if you own the patented or proprietary technology that East European countries need, you could work out some highly profitable arrangements. Sell technology to the communists? Can it even be done? The answer is that today it finally can be done. And is being done. In fact, over the past couple of years, major American corporations have been doing it with increasing frequency. Naturally, the technology must be non-strategic. Exactly how do you go about it? You go about it with infinite patience. As you can imagine, selling American technology in Eastern Europe is a highly complex economic, political and technical problem. Obviously, it's absolutely crucial to develop the right contacts and the right communication. That's where we, World Patent Development Corp. come in. For years now, we've maintained close technological contacts with the proper governmental agencies in all East European countries. Because of our unique position, we've been able to locate markets and negotiate licensing agreements for the sale of almost every kind of technology. Conversely, we're also presiding over the transfer of East European technology to the West. In fields ranging from synthetic copolymers to pollution control equipment. From advanced textile equipment to natural cosmetics.

The preceding ad, placed by the World Development Corporation in the *New York Times* (October 1, 1972), is a far cry from Cold War rhetoric; and helps place in perspective the obvious thaw *cum* rapprochement reached between Nixon and Kissinger for the American side and Brezhnev and Kosygin for the Soviet side. For the emergence of the multinational corporation is the paramount economic fact of the present epoch, and helps to explain current trends in the political sociology of world relations.

The struggle for supremacy between capitalism and communism has been the overriding ideological posture of the twentieth century. Now, however, the struggle has been broken by two developments: first, the rise of a Third World in Africa, Asia and Latin America, accompanied by a pluralization of economic forms, political systems and social doctrines; and second, the rise of multinational corporations which are primarily loyal to industrial growth and financial profitability, rather than to any one national regime. Multinationalism has had an extraordinary impact on relations between capitalist and socialist states, taking us beyond a model premised on a showdown struggle between old capitalism and new communism.

The Nature of Multinationalism

Definitions of the term "multinational corporation" vary. Nonetheless, there is general agreement on the following operational guidelines:

- Multinationals are corporations that operate in at least six foreign nations.
- Multinationals are corporations whose foreign subsidiaries account for at least 10 to 20 percent of its total assets, sales or labor force.
- Multinationals have annual sales or income of more than $100 million (which effectively reduces the number of firms we are dealing with to about 200, of

which roughly 75 percent are primarily affiliated with the United States).

- □ Multinationals have an above-average rate of growth and profit margins when measured against exclusively national firms.
- □ Multinationals are found most often in high-technology industries, specifically those that devote a high proportion of their resources to research, advertising and marketing.

Many firms, such as Singer Sewing Machines, National Cash Register, Unilever, General Motors and others, have been conducting overseas business for many years; it is, however, the fusion of these older firms with more basic (high-level-technology-producing) industrial firms, such as Xerox Corporation, International Business Machines, British Petroleum, Phillips of the Netherlands, International Nickel and others that has tipped the balance within them from national to international corporate participation. Since each of these giants of industry reveals annual sales that exceed the individual gross national product of all except several dozen nations, the political and economic power they wield is obviously potent, although highly diffuse.

That which is new about multinationals can be summarized as follows. Firms which in the past maintained classical imperial relations, that is, imported raw materials and exported finished commodity goods at superprofits, have new arrangements, forced partially because the old system was so limited that the masses were barred from participation and reacted accordingly. National liberation and socialist movements of various types and structures simply invalidated the classical mode of colonialism. Now multinational firms share research and development findings and patent rights distribution; manufacture in the economic periphery at lower costs rather than producing the same goods in the cosmopolitan center (which has the additional payoff of quieting nationalist opposition); develop profit-sharing arrangements between local firms and foreign firms, which involve training and tooling. Beyond that, one finds a reverse multinationalism, one based on raw materials rather than on finished goods. Thus, the oil-rich countries of the Arab Middle East form a bargaining collective to do business directly with major oil companies of the West. National governments, such as the Arab oil states, joined by Venezuela, Iran, Nigeria, Indonesia, and other members of OPEC, barter and bargain with private-sector multinationals like the powerful oil corporations of America and Western Europe, thus bypassing governmental agencies of the big powers.

What is new about the multinational is not simply the transcendance of the nation-state boundaries to do business, an old ploy of corporations in wealthy nations but, more profoundly, a reduction in profits through increased payment of high prices for raw materials (like petroleum) and the acceptance of lower prices and hence less profit for finished manufactured goods (such as automobiles). This is the aspect of multinationals which most sharply points to the need for a modification of classical and new forms of Marxism-Leninism alike, since the very essence of politics as a reflection of national and economic exploitation is reversed. What we have now is economics as a managed, manipulated form of political exploitation and domination.

The multinationals help to bridge the gap between revolutionary nationalism and establishment internationalism by acquiescing to the symbolic demands of nationalists and revolutionists, while satisfying the very real economic demands of the conservative middle-sector elements in Third World societies.

The Buying of Western Capitalism by Eastern Socialism

The post-World War II thrust of nationalism prevented any undue optimism about the capacity of socialism to triumph as a world system and as an international ideology. So intense did nationalist sentiments become in Third World areas of Asia, Africa and Latin America that the Soviets, after much hesitation, had to readjust their policy and ideology, and finally recognize a third way, something more than capitalism and less than socialism; a cross between a Keynesian economic mechanism and a Leninist political machinery. But in that act of recognition, the dream of an international proletarian revolution, with or without a Soviet vanguard, gave way to more parochial dreams of peoples' democracy and socialist republics that would no more dare try to transcend nationalist sentiments than would the older capitalist regimes in Western Europe. Between 1945 and 1970, the nationalist thrust profoundly diminished belief in a socialist utopia.

When internationalism finally did make its move, it did so in corporate rather than proletarian guise. The multinational corporation, pointing to an international brotherhood of the bourgeoisie and the bureaucracy, to a transcendant class loyalty beyond the national aspirations of even the United States or other principal capitalist social systems, discredited the socialist utopia no less than had the earlier nationalist phase. The multinationals offered a basket of commodity goods that the socialist states, no less than the Third World states, desire. The relative ease with which such multinationals of the capitalist sector penetrated the societies and economies of the socialist sector stands in marked contrast to the difficulties involved in concluding the most elemental treaty arrangements between East and West at the policy and political level. Doing things in a businesslike way has become as much a touchstone for rational efficiency in the Soviet Union as in the United States. The culture of multinationalism permeated Eastern Europe and the Soviet Union long before the actual economic penetration, with the mass consumer demands of the Soviet public following the Stalinist period. Multinationalism, like nationalism in an earlier era, has stymied the socialist utopia, at the very same time that it has improved the commodity conditions of the socialist nations.

One need only consider the extensive trade agreements reached between the United States and the Soviet Union in September 1972, to gauge the velocity and the extent of multinational penetration. Not only do these trade agreements solve fiscal imbalances by intensifying internal shortages; they also place both major powers in a financial mosaic that can hardly be described in conventional terms of capitalism or socialism. As *U.S. News and World Report* indicated,

> White House adviser Henry Kissinger, negotiating in Moscow between September 11 and 14, achieved substantial progress in trade talks with the Soviet Union. . . . On September 14, the U.S. Department of Agriculture confirmed a private sale of 15 million bushels of American wheat to Communist China, the first to that nation in many years. A few days earlier, the Boeing Company announced sale of 10 of its 707 jetliners to the Red Chinese for 125 million dollars in cash. The chairman of Occidental Petroleum Corporation, Armand Hammer, said in Moscow on September 14 that details of the trade pact his firm had signed in June with the Soviet Union were being arranged. Among other things under consideration, said Mr. Hammer, were sales of chemical fertilizers and construction of a 70-million-dollar U.S. trade center in the Russian capital, complete with a 400-room hotel. . . reports from Moscow indicate that the overall trade agreement now being negotiated could increase business between the two countries to as much as 5 billion dollars a year by 1977. At present, U.S.-Russian trade amounts to about 220 million dollars annually. That figure, however, does not include around a billion dollars in purchases by the Russians of American grain in recent weeks. . . . Agreement also was reported near on a maritime pact that would guarantee to U.S. and Russian merchant ships at least a one-third share each of the cargoes involved in the billion-dollar grain sale to Russia.

The question then becomes: Can the Soviet Union maintain its basic commitment to production development rather than to consumption modernization in the face of foreign business penetration? Obviously, the Russians and to a lesser degree the Chinese think the answer is affirmative. However, the inexorable logic of consumer orientations is toward satisfying utilitarian needs of a social sector able to pay, rather than delaying such gratifications in favor of long-range moral goals of economic equality at home, and certainly rather than fulfilling ambitious political goals of national liberation abroad.

The political potential of multinationals, even those dominated by the United States, are revealed by their use in East European nations like Rumania and Hungary. One finds Pepsi-Cola Corporation, Hertz Rent-a-Car Agencies, Pan American and ITT-supported hotels in the center of Bucharest, and of course the most conspicuous multinationals in such a country, Western-dominated commercial airlines. This serves a double purpose: it permits Rumania to become the Switzerland of the East—the meeting place of Chinese, Russians, Israelis, Arabs and others, and it also weakens the socialist doctrine of development as a unique function of bootstrap industrialization. There can be no doubt that a number of East European regimes (Yugoslavia, Rumania and Poland, in particular) are fully aware of both the risks and possibilities in multinationalism.

Such firms, which do business on a licensing basis in East Europe, open up channels of communication to the West. If the socialist republic's dependence on the Soviet Union is lessened more symbolically than in reality, it nonetheless has the effect of displaying the physical presence of the West in Eastern Europe. It also permits higher numbers of international conferences at which Westerners participate and interact with participants from China and the Soviet Union. In short, the multinational firm provides a much-needed meeting place for the East Socialist bloc; a place where Israelis, Albanians, Russians and Chinese interact freely and to the greater benefit of the open-ended socialist regime. In the East European setting, national sovereignty is strengthened rather than weakened by the existence of the multinational corporations. This is, of course, at considerable variance with the impact of multinationals in a Western European context. For example, the combined power of Dutch multinationals (Royal Dutch Shell, Unilever, KLM Airlines, Phillips) is much stronger than the standard vehicles of political life in the Netherlands. Holland shows how national sovereignty can be weakened rather than strengthened by multinationalism.

Raymond Vernon, in ***Sovereignty at Bay: The Multinational Spread of U.S. Enterprises,*** has indicated his own belief that labels of socialism will do as much to promote as to dissuade multinationals from penetrating the socialist and Third World sphere.

> The fact that many less-developed countries associate themselves with some form of socialism needs no detailed documenting. The number may even have increased somewhat in the course of time. It is not clear, however, just what that espousal means for the role of the multinational enterprise. During recent years, several genuinely socialist countries have been exercising enormous ingenuity to find a way of assigning a role to foreign-owned enterprises in their economies. The Yugoslavs, of course, have moved furthest in this direction; by 1970, foreign-owned enterprises were in a position to negotiate for rights that were the de facto equivalent of those available in such non-socialist states as Mexico or Brazil.

Many other less-developed countries—for example, Pakistan, Tunisia, and Iraq—though committed to socialism of some sort, have nevertheless cultivated a certain deliberate ambiguity over the future position of multinational enterprises in their economies. As India edges her way toward national identification with socialism, it is not at all clear that the country's policies toward foreign investors will grow any more restrictive. Besides, the actual shift of less-developed countries toward state ownership of the means of production has not been irrevocable—witness the cases of Indonesia and Ghana. Neither is it clear that the countries that do not yet see the future in these terms will eventually make the shift. Mexico, with her abiding coalition of local big business, bureaucracy, and a single party of ambiguous ideology, seems as likely a model as Guinea; Yugoslavia, with her bent for improvisation and pragmatism, seems no less likely a model of the future than Cuba.

The idea of a single world market has so deeply permeated Soviet socialism, that the Soviet Union is now in the position of accepting as part of its own economic codebook the rules on any given day of the much-reviled free market economy. The recent "wheat deal" between the superpowers indicates an increasing sophistication price, or 37 cents. This deal, profitable as it was to the Soviets, was equally advantageous for the United States, who without this gas arrangement, would have had to pay 87 cents per thousand cubic feet to Algeria for such gas purchases, or similarly high prices to Middle East nations in the near future. The rise of sophisticated multinational dealings across East-West boundaries clearly services the major powers at the expense of Third World nations.

Huge trading blocs for shares of corporations are now developing. This gradual emergence of a single world market for securities rationalizes relationships between East and West. The increasing concentration of capital in the West permits a movement from multinational corporation to an interrelated fiscal network which readily connects up to the Soviet interrelated fiscal network.

The Selling of Eastern Socialism to Western Capitalism

The fundamental antagonism within the socialist bloc has been the development of an industrial society without a corresponding modernized society. The Soviet Union can mount trips to outer space, but cannot satisfy consumer demands for automobiles; it can launch supersonic jet aircraft; but cannot supply the accoutrements of personal satisfaction to make such travel enjoyable. It can mass-produce military hardware, but cannot individualize stylistic consumer components. In every aspect of socialist society, the duality between industrialism and modernism has emerged as a central factor. In this, the socialist sector is the opposite of the Third World, where modernization is purchased at the cost of development, where production is increased with relatively low technology inputs, and product is exchanged for commodity goods produced in the advanced capitalist sector. Both the Second World (socialist nations) and Third World need and want consumer goods from the First World (capitalist nations). The Third World pays for such consumer goods with agrarian goods, while the Second World wants to pay for such consumer goods with industrial products.

The lessening of tension since the end of the Stalin era in 1952 has taken the form of opening consumption valves in the Soviet Union, consequently maintaining tight political, statist controls. The assumption was that as the valves were opened wider, and as more demands for immediate consumer gratification were met, the stability of the socialist bureaucratic regimes would also increase. So far, this theory has proven correct. Protest in the socialist bloc has been limited to a narrow stratum of intellectuals who have been declared malcontents or madmen in the face of the general satisfaction of consumer demands of ordinary people. Whatever the long-term secular trends may be, and whatever the consequences to socialist legitimacy and class interests, the fact remains that consumer orientations have worked. Multinational penetration must therefore be seen as part of a general commitment of the Soviet leadership to political quietude through economic gratitude.

The most obvious commodity that the Soviets have to sell is not agrarian products, and certainly not consumer goods—both of which are in profoundly short supply within the socialist orbit. However, it does have a high technological sophistication, built up over more than 50 years of emphasis on industrialization at the expense of nearly every other economic goal. To an increasing degree, American companies looking for ways to reduce costs in their own research and development are buying the latest Soviet technology. The trend is most apparent by Soviet "business" in these areas of market management and manipulation. Twenty Soviet buying teams negotiated independently and without any apparent coordination, yet the actual high level of commercial orchestration enabled the Soviet Union both to fulfill an agrarian internal need for wheat, and to buy a low-cost surplus for high-profit resale on the world market. In this way the Soviets have become part of the "paper economy"—for the wheat deal involves the movement of money no less than the transfer of a basic crop.

The Soviets have done as well in the area of natural gas as in wheat negotiations. In 1966, they negotiated with Iran to purchase gas that had previously been flared off in the fields because there was no market for it. In turn, the Iranians received Soviet financing and assistance to construct the necessary pipelines and associated equipment as well as a steel mill. While the Iranians gained a valuable steel plant, the Soviets began negotiating its sale of the Iranian gas to both East and West European nations. These deals culminated in sales equal to the total Iranian gas supply. The Soviet purchase price from Iran for the natural gas was 19 cents per thousand cubic feet, while its sale price was nearly double that in the metallurgy field.

Since consumer goods are purchased largely through Western-dominated multinationals, the character of international banking communism has drawn closer to international banking capitalism, in short to the essence of banking principles, profits from interest on loans secured by equity arrangements. Coming into existence is a banking network that has the capacity to rationalize multinational exchanges. Banking capitalism links up with banking socialism precisely because banks are involved in similar international activities and investment in profitable enterprises. In the absence of direct industry-to-industry contacts, given East-West structural constraints at the manufacturing level, the banking system is the fluid which pumps life into an East-West economic detente. This detente permits arms reduction negotiations to take place in an atmosphere of political entente cordiale.

The Fusion of Capitalism and Socialism as Social Science Ideology

The multinationalist framework has already demonstrated a cultural impact on an East-West accommodation beyond any level reached in the past. Led by the United States and the Soviet Union, scientific academies of a dozen nations have set up a "think tank" to seek solutions to problems created by industrialization and urbanization of societies. Such problems as pollution control, public health and overpopulation are to be studied by an International Institute of Applied Systems Analysis with overseas headquarters in Vienna, Austria. Even the broad composition of this new knowledge industry reflects multinational thinking. Its director will be a professor of managerial economics at Harvard, and its council chairman will be a member of the Soviet Academy of Sciences, Jerman M. Gvishiani, the son-in-law of Premier Aleksei N. Kosygin. In this remarkable display of East-West fusion, representatives from Czechoslovakia, Bulgaria, Poland and East Germany will be joined by representatives of Japan, Canada, Great Britain, West Germany and Italy. The director of the program, Dr. Howard Raiffa, indicated that the accumulated findings of management techniques, particularly as these have evolved in the aerospace industry, would be applied to a wide variety of health and welfare problems in Eastern Europe. This international think tank will be technocratic and non-ideological in nature; in short, the perfect cultural and educational coefficient to the rise of a multinational framework.

The rise of a multinational cultural apparatus has been made possible by the widening exchange of contact between scientists, scholars and performers from East and West alike. Underneath such widening contacts, in reality its presupposition, has been the declining fervor of ideology. Both Marxism and Americanism have yielded to considerations of efficiency and effectiveness and have cooperated in a vigorous effort to provide methodological guidelines that will provide accurate and exchangeable data. The new technology, with its potential for simultaneous translation and rapid publication, has also served to bring East and West together. This coalescence occurs precisely in areas of intellectual activities relatively uncontaminated by inherited ideological sore points. Hence it is that such diverse subjects as futurism, computer technology and machine learning by virtue of their newness permit widening contact points. Of course it is precisely these areas that are most significant from the viewpoint of multinationalist exchanges of goods and services.

The Reemergence of Proletarian Internationalism as a Function of Multinationalism

The strangest, or certainly the least anticipated, consequence of the multinational corporation is the reappearance of militant unionism. The emergence of worker resistance to the multinationalist attempt to seek out the cheapest supply of labor as well as raw materials, wherever they are available, is still in an infant stage, but clearly on the rise. High-paid West German optical workers must compete against low-paid workers from the same industries in Eastern Europe. Auto workers in Western Europe find themselves competing against workers in Latin America producing essentially the same cars. Chemical plants of wholly owned U.S. subsidiaries are put up in Belgium and England, to capitalize on the cheaper wage scales of European chemical workers and to gain greater proximity to retail markets. Even American advertising agencies are protesting the manufacture of commercials in Europe. Such stories can be repeated for every major multinational firm and every nation.

One can well appreciate the rationale offered by the multinationals. They can take advantage of the protectionist system of closed markets in the United States while pursuing an antiprotectionist approach for trading abroad. They can thereby derive the payoffs of having the American workers as a customer at high price, while employing overseas workers at low wages. Investment abroad is also a way to get beyond antitrust laws that apply fully within the United States but scarcely at all in other countries.

This new situation, whatever the merits or demerits of the rationalizing capacity of multinationals, has created a partially revivified working class, that, in contrast to earlier periods, shows greater class solidarity than cross-class national solidarity. Certainly, in the major wars of the twentieth century, the working classes have lined up solidly behind nationalism and patriotism; and in so doing have frustrated just about every prediction made on their behalf by left-wing intellectuals. Now, precisely at the moment when so much left-oriented rhetoric has itself become infused with an anti-working-class bias, we bear witness to the emergence of proletarian militance, this time as a function of self-interest rather than lofty ideology.

The organization of working-class life is still along national lines; but when confronted with middle-class internationalism, as represented by the multinationals, it must either create new trade union mechanisms or revitalize old and existing ones. According to Gus Tyler,

> foreign resentment against U.S. multinationals flares up most dangerously when these corporations do to the workers of other countries what they have been doing to American workers all along: shut down a plant for company reasons. Within two weeks, General Motors closed down a plant with 685 employees in Paris, because of Italian competition, and Remington Rand closed down a plant with 1,000 employees to relocate in Vienna. The French government—then under Charles de Gaulle—decided to get tough with the U.S. multinationals; so GM opened a plant in Belgium instead of France and proceeded to ship the product into France—duty free.

It is intriguing to note how a relatively insular trade union movement such as the British Trades Union Congress has vigorously responded to multinationals as a threat. It has put forth demands for making union recognition a precondition for setting up foreign subsidiaries in the United Kingdom; and likewise to have organizations such as the Organization for Economic Cooperation and Development serve as an agency for funneling and channeling working-class demands on wider multinationals.

While British responses have been legalistic and profferred through government agencies. European workers on the mainland have become more direct and forthright in their dealings, engaging in strike actions and corporate lockouts led by international unions. According to John Gennard,

> The International Federation of Chemical and General Workers' Union has acted as a coordinating body for different unions in various countries in negotiations with St. Gobain, a French-owned glass manufacturing multinational. Some success for international action coordinated through International Trade Secretariats has been achieved; for example: In 1970, strikers at May and Baker, a British subsidiary of Rhone-Poulenc, won a 16 percent pay rise "largely due to large-scale international intervention" at the company's French headquarters and at other May and Baker plants in the Commonwealth. Peugot workers in Founee threatened a 15 minute stoppage in 1968 to back 1,000 workers suspended in an Argentinian subsidiary. After two days, the company agreed to take back nearly all the suspended workers.

This renewed working-class activity has had a stunning effect on East-West trade union relations. It is axiomatic that socialism does not tolerate or permit strikes since, in the doctrine of its founders, socialism is a workers' society, and a strike against the government is a strike against one's own interest. That such reasoning is a palpable hoax has never been denied; and the leaders of Poland, Hungary and other East European states have become quite sensitized to such mass pressure from below. Yet the impact of this reasoning is that strike actions have been rare, and met most often with repressive measures. The concept of working-class international action between laborers in "capitalist" and "socialist" countries has been virtually non-existent. Nevertheless, such is the force of multinationalism, that even these deep political inhibitions are dissolving. We may be entering an era of working-class collaboration across systemic lines, perhaps resembling the coalescence between the bourgeois West and bureaucratic East.

Several important features of this special variant of proletarian internationalism must be distinguished. (1) It cuts across national lines for the first time in the twentieth century. (2) It cuts across systemic lines, being less responsive to Cold War calls for free labor or socialist labor than at any time in the post-World War II period. (3) The vanguard role in this effort is being assumed by the workers in the better paid and better organized sectors of labor; in the specialized craft sector more than the assembly-line industrial sector. (4) While new mechanisms are being created to deal with multinational corporations, the more customary approach is to strengthen the bargaining position of available organizations, such as the International Metal Workers' Federation and the International Federation of Chemical and General Workers Unions.

What we have, then, is an intensification of class competition, but on a scale and magnitude vastly unlike the conventional national constraints. It is still difficult to demonstrate or to predict whether such class struggles can be as readily resolved short of revolution in the industrial areas as the previous epoch was resolved in the national areas. In effect, if Marxism as a triumphal march of socialism throughout the world has thoroughly been discredited, it manages to rise, phoenix-like, out of the bitter ashes of such disrepair. The intensification of class struggles at the international level remains muted by the comparative advantages of multinationalism to countries like Japan and the United States. But if such comparative advantages dissolve over the long pull of time (and this is beginning to happen as less developed nations play catch-up), then the quality of class competition might well intensify.

The Theory of Big Power Convergence and Multinational Realities

Multinationalism has served to refocus attention on the theory of convergence, that set of assumptions which holds that over time, the industrial and urbanizing tendencies of the United States and the Soviet Union will prevail over systemic and ideological differences, and form a convergence, or at least enough of a similitude to prevent major grave international confrontations.

The evidence for the convergence theory has been generally made much stronger by the rise of multinationals. Without entering into an arid debate about whether capitalism and socialism can remain pure and noble if this can take place, the empirics of the situation are clear enough: the United States (whatever its economic system can be called) and the Soviet Union (whatever its system can be called) have shown a remarkable propensity to fuse their interests at the economic level and collapse their differences at a diplomatic level, for the purpose of forming a new big power coalition that dwarfs the dreams of Metternich for a United Europe in the nineteenth century. Indeed, we now have a situation in which the doctrine of national self-interest has been fused into one of regional and even hemispheric areas of domination by the two major world superpowers.

The issue of systemic convergence is certainly not new. The existence of commonalities between the major political and economic powers has long been evident. Geographical size, racial and religious similitudes, even psychological properties of the peoples of the United States and the Soviet Union, all conspire to fuse American and Soviet interests. What has been in dispute is whether such root commonalities would be sufficient to overcome long-standing differences in the economic organization of society, ideological commitments and political systems of domination. This argument remained largely unanswered and unanswerable as long as the mechanism, the lever, for expressing any functional convergence remained absent. The unique contribution of multinationalism to the debate over convergence between the major superpowers is precisely its functional rationality; its place in contemporary history as the Archimedean lever lifting both nations out of the Cold War. Multinationals take precedence over political differences in prosaic but meaningful ways. They serve to rationalize and standardize international economic relationships. They demand perfect interchangeability of parts; a uniform system of weights and measurements; common auditing languages for expression of world trade and commerce; standard codes for aircraft and airports, telephonic and telegraphic communications; and banking rules and regulations that are adhered to by all nations. Convergence takes place not so much by ideological proclamation (although there has even been some of this) but primarily by organizational fiat; that is, by seeming to hold ideological differences constant, while rotating every other factor in international relations.

Multinationalism has played a major role in breaking the Cold War struggle between capitalism and socialism. Indeed, doing so has profoundly lessened the bargaining power of smaller nations vis-à-vis the superpowers. But whatever problems this leaves in its wake, this myth-breaking event at least makes possible a more realistic international political climate.

Pax Americana Plus Pax Sovietica: The Politics of Multinationalism

The politics of multinationalism is not so much an illustration of convergence as it is an example of pragmatic parallelism. Michael Harrington points out that, underlying the Nixon-Kissinger position, there is a shared metaphysical belief that the division of the world is both necessary and desirable.

> Internationally, then, Nixonism has a profoundly conservative, shrewd yet utterly flawed approach. It seeks a Metternichian arrangement among the superpowers, capitalist and communist, according to which change would be relegated to controllable channels. In pursuit of this goal it is, unlike the moralistic policy of Dulles, willing to strengthen the power of its enemies if only they will accept the model of a global equilibrium. Nixonism is rhetorically dedicated to the virtues of the global division of labor but actually committed to utilizing America's state power to socialize the enormous advantage of our corporations on the world market. . . . Capitalist collectivism, in other words, wants to make a deal with bureaucratic collectivism to preserve the status quo.

Edward Weisband and Thomas M. Frank, aside from assigning causal priority to this doctrine to the West, assert nonetheless the similitude of the Brezhnev approach toward peaceful coexistence as big-power sovereignty over smaller areas.

> The Brezhnev doctrine, which continues to govern the policies of the Warsaw Pact governments, to some degree represents a tradeoff or division of the world by the Soviet Union and the United States into spheres of influence or "regional ghettos." Not that our policy-makers in Washington planned it that way: little or no evidence has been adduced to show that the U.S. government ever willfully intended to trade control over Latin America for recognition of absolute Soviet dominance over Eastern Europe. Nor can it be said that any actions we have taken in relation to Latin America are the same as Russia's brutal suppression of Czechoslovakia. . . . What we do wish to assert is that virtually every concept of the Brezhnev doctrine can be traced to an earlier arrogation of identical rights by the United States vis-á-vis Latin America . . . it is important to realize that the search for new norms in the world must begin with a clear understanding that we, as much as the Russians, bear responsibility for conceptualizing the Brezhnev norms . . . In the Soviet view, regional determination and prerogatives take precedence over those of the inter-

national community including the United Nations.

Curiously enough, the connection between international politics and the rise of multinationalism was not clearly articulated, even by the above prescient commentators on international affairs. Lesser analysts seem to prefer to think of the new Nixonism as some sort of magical mystery tour; a transformation of high spiritual beliefs into policy matters. My contention is that the current foreign policy initiatives of Henry Kissinger derive precisely from a new American policy-making realization of changes in corporate relationships as necessitating an end to the Cold War, and establishing a new detente based on economic realities. Throughout 1972 President Nixon clearly articulated such a geopolitical realignment based on economic realities.

As early as January 1972 Nixon articulated the point of view which he sustained on his diplomatic initiatives in Moscow and Peking.

> We must remember that the only time in the history of the world that we had any extended periods of peace is when there has been a balance of power. It is when one nation becomes infinitely more powerful in relation to its potential competitor that the danger of war arises. So I believe in a world in which the United States is powerful. I think it would be a safer world and a better world if we have a strong, healthy United States, Europe, Soviet Union, China, and Japan, each balancing the other, not playing one against the other, an even balance.

The peculiar linkage is China, since it alone has yet to participate fully in the multinational system. Further, it can be said to be by far the poorest of the countries with which power balance has to be sought. But with that admittedly crucial exception, and this can be argued to be a requirement of political tradeoff preventing an undue Soviet impact on the Western world and an undue Japanese presence in the Eastern world, what Nixon has outlined is quite clearly the politics of multinationalism, and not of capitalism triumphant or socialism defeated. The trade and aid agreements between East and West during this period serve to confirm the accuracy of this appraisal. Even China is entering the multinational race with its increased sale of specialized consumer goods to the United States, and its purchase from Boeing Aircraft of an international fleet of advanced jets.

This new Metternichian arrangement among the superpowers is precisely a repudiation of the earlier moral absolutism of anticommunism and anticapitalism. In a sense, and one step beyond an acknowledged end of the Cold War, is the fact that such a geopolitical redistribution also serves to solve a major problem of the multinational corporation, its transcendence of the limits and encumbrances placed by national sovereignty. By an international linkage of the superpowers, the problems of multinational regulation, which loom so large in the established literature can be rationalized, if not entirely resolved, by appeals to commercial rationality rather than to political sovereignty.

The thesis presented by George Kennan that the end of the Cold War came about as a result of a series of victories of the United States over the Soviet empire, is simply untenable. The plain fact is that Soviet foreign policy has remained consistently legalistic whatever its resort to extralegalities and terrorism internally. Beyond that, the Soviet Union has neither dissolved nor shrunk. Current Soviet policy, especially as it effects Eastern Europe, can only be described as extremely aggressive. It is precisely the absence of victory, of a thoroughly stalemated situation, that led the major powers to reconsider their collision course—a course that could threaten both empires at the expense of outsider factions in the Third World, China and even nonaligned nations like India, waiting in the wings to pick up the pieces.

Arms control agreements, direct executive rapprochement, new trade and purchasing agreements, exchanges of research and development technology in basic fields have all been instituted in rapid succession. These have signaled the real termination of the Cold War. Multinationalism, in its very extra-nation capacities, has served to rationalize this new foreign policy posture on both sides. Terms like "have" versus "have-not" states have come to replace and displace an older rhetoric of capitalism versus socialism, not simply as an expression of the uneven international distribution of wealth, but as an indication of the current sponginess of any concept of capitalism or socialism. It is precisely the inability of the Cold War to be resolved through victory that has led to a feeling on the part of the leadership in powerful states that the coalition of the big against the small, of the wealthy against the impoverished, and even of white-led nations against colored-led nations, that can best guarantee the peace of the world, and the tranquilization of potential sources of rival power like China in the East or Germany and France in the West. With one fell swoop the mutual winding down of the Cold War settles the hash of rival powers and determines the subordinate position of the Third World for the duration of the century. The cement for this new shift in fundamental policy is the multinational corporation. An end to ideology? No. An end to capitalist and communist rhetoric? Possibly. An end to the Cold War epoch? Yes.

SUGGESTED READINGS

The World Corporation: Problematics, Apologetics and Critique by Gyorgy Adam (Budapest: Hungarian Scientific Council for World Economy, 1971).

Roots of War by Richard J. Barnet (New York: Atheneum, 1972).

Capital, Inflation and the Multinationals by Charles Levinson (London: George Allen & Unwin, 1971).

Sovereignty at Bay: The Multinational Spread of U.S. Enterprises by Raymond Vernon (New York: Basic Books, 1971).

2 *Robert L. Heilbroner*

Benign Neglect in the United States

The United States is by all conventional measures the wealthiest nation in the world. Why is it not at the same time the most socially advanced? To put the question differently, why is it that a nation that could afford to remove social and economic inequities more easily than any other has been so laggard in doing so?

Note that my question hinges on the *comparative* performance of the United States. I am not concerned with measuring the absolute level of neglect in America, or assessing the trend of that neglect or trying to estimate by how much it could or should be reduced in the future. My problem here is broader and more far-reaching, and perhaps correspondingly more difficult. It is why social neglect in the United States is greater than in other nations with similar institutions, such as Norway, Sweden, Denmark, Switzerland, New Zealand, England or Canada. In the end, of course, the matter that concerns us is the alleviation of neglect in this country—a matter to which I shall turn at the end of this essay—but the primary focus of my inquiry lies in the roots of the problem rather than in the specifics of its remedy.

Let me begin by documenting briefly the premise from which I start. I shall do so in broad brush strokes, partly because the statistical information is lacking to make finer comparisons, and partly because I do not think the basic evidence is apt to be called into question.

I start with habitat itself. It is not a simple matter to make precise comparisons of social neglect with regard to housing and living environment among nations, because accepted standards differ from one country to the next. Swedish housing projects, for example, have fewer rooms per family and less room space per person than similar projects in the United States, while in Japan only 13 percent of all urban and less than 2 percent of all rural dwellings have flush toilets, a condition that in the United States is virtually prima facie evidence of extreme social disrepair. Thus the unwary statistical comparison shopper could easily come to the conclusion that American housing projects are better than Swedish, or that the vast bulk of Japanese live in conditions similar to those of the worst of our slums.

Such considerations make it exceedingly difficult, or even impossible, to arrive at a simple ranking of living habitats that will disclose where the United States belongs on an international spectrum of neglect. Hence I shall content myself with two generalizations based on personal observations at home and abroad. First, I believe that in no large city in the United States do we find a concern for the living habitat comparable to that commonly found in the cities of such nations as the Netherlands, Switzerland or the countries of Scandinavia; and second, I maintain that to match the squalor of the worst of the American habitat one must descend to the middle range of the underdeveloped lands. These are, I repeat, "impressionistic" statements, for which quantitative documentation is lacking, but I do not think they will be challenged on that account.

Let me now turn to a second and somewhat more objective indicator of the comparative performance of the United States with regard to social well-being—the neglect of poverty. Here again, however, a degree of statistical prudence is necessary. The income of a family of four at the "official" threshold of poverty in the United States is roughly $3,500. This is an income approximately equivalent to that of a family in the middle brackets in Norway. Poverty is therefore a matter of relative affluence quite as much as absolute income. Nevertheless, just as the definition of poverty reflects the differing levels of productivity of different countries, so the neglect of poverty also mirrors the differing capabilities of nations to create a surplus that can be transferred to those in need. Thus, a rich nation may define its level of need higher than its poor neighbor, but it should also be in a better position to devote more of its income to the remedy of that need.

Unfortunately, we do not have detailed statistics that allow us to match the specific antipoverty efforts of different nations, as percentages of their national incomes. But as a very rough indicator of the allocation of resources for this purpose we can turn to the percentage of Gross National Product used for income transfers of all kinds. In the 1960s, for the nations of the European Economic Community the average ratio of social security expanditure to GNP was approximately 14 percent; for the Scandinavian trio it was around 12 to 13 percent; for Canada 9.9 percent. In the United States the ratio was 6.5 percent, barely above the level for Portugal.

Furthermore, to this general indicator of comparative performance we can add a second consideration. The existential quality of poverty is profoundly affected by the surrounding conditions in which it is experienced. The difference between "genteel" and "degrading" poverty is not alone one of private income but of public environment. Thus, a factor worsening the relative neglect of poverty in the United States is that it is here concentrated in the noisome slums of our cities or rural backwaters, rather than being alleviated, as in the Scandinavian or better European nations, by clean cities, attractive public parks and a high general level of basic life support.

Another related, and yet distinct, area of social neglect is that of public health. Here we possess the most detailed statistics of international performance, but once again the results are not comforting for the United States.

Just Above Hong Kong

At first blush, one would expect to find the United States as a world leader in the field of health. No nation devotes as large a fraction of its gross output—some 6.5 percent—to health services. None has produced more important advances in drugs or medical techniques or spent more on basic research. Yet the comparative showing of the United States can only be described as disastrous. In 1950 the United States ranked fifth safest in the world in risk of infant mortality. This less-than-best rating could perhaps be explained by the generally admitted inferior health services provided the Negro population, much of which still lived in rural areas in the South. Since then, however, the Negro has moved northward and to the cities, but despite (or because of?) this migration, our infant mortality rate has steadily worsened. By 1955 we had fallen to eighth place; by 1960, to 12th. Today it is estimated that we rank 18th, just above Hong Kong.

It is not only in infant mortality that comparative neglect in matters of health is visible in the United States. Despite our overall expenditure on health services, we ranked only 22nd in male life expectancy in 1965 (down from 13th in 1959) and tenth in female life expectancy (down from seventh in 1959). Our death rates from pneumonia and TB are far from the best. Diseases of malnutrition, including kwashiorkor—long considered a disease specific to underdeveloped areas—have been discovered in the United States.

The causes for this deplorable showing are complex and involve many cultural attributes of Americans, who overeat and oversmoke, as well as reflecting the effects of sheer neglect. But the steady deterioration of our comparative showing does not result from an absolute impairment of American health (with minor exceptions) as much as from the spectacular successes of other nations in applying social effort to the improvement of their national health. Judged against this steady comparative decline, the finding of extreme social neglect in the area of health seems inescapable.

Last, let me direct attention to a somewhat unrelated but surely no less important area of social concern. This is the manner in which we and other advanced nations treat that aberrant fraction of the population that is apprehended for criminality. I put the matter this way since it is well known that the infringement of laws is much more widespread than the prosecution of illegality. Estimates of crimes committed, but unreported, range from twice the number of recorded instances of criminality to much larger than that. Indeed, a recently reported survey of 1,700 adults without criminal records brought out that 99 percent of them had committed offenses for which they could have ended in prison. Furthermore, it is clear that among those who do commit crimes, it is the economically and socially least privileged that bear by far the heaviest incidence of prosecution and punishment. In 1967 the President's Crime Commission reported that 90 percent of American youth had done something for which they could have been committed by a juvenile court. Yet only 5 percent of the children in institutions for juvenile delinquency come from families in "comfortable circumstances."

I have no evidence to indicate that this differential apportionment of punishment is more pronounced in this nation than in others. But I have some distressing statistics with regard to the measures taken by our nation in its treatment of the "criminal" stratum compared with the measures taken by other nations. The total population of Sweden, for example, is about half that of California. Yet her prison population is only one-fifth that of California's, and one-third of that prison population is in small light-security camps enjoying "open" conditions. In the United States, such work-release camps are available only in four states. The caseloads of prison psychologists in Denmark average 20 to 30 per doctor; in the United States the average ratio of psychiatrists or trained therapists per inmate is one to 179, and this ratio is for our federal penal institutions which are far superior to our state institutions. In no Scandinavian (or European) country have prison camps or institutions been reported that can match for brutality the conditions recently discovered at the Arkansas state farm. All this must have some bearing on the fact that 20 to 40 convicted persons out of 100 in Scandinavia go back to jail for some other offense, while an average of 73 out of 100 do so in the United States.

Capitalism and Character

It would not be difficult to add evidence of neglect in other areas of American social life. One thinks, for example, of the niggardliness of American social security payments as a percentage of preretirement earnings compared with those of Sweden, or of the greater American than European indifference with regard to the protection of the consumer in many areas. But I think the basic premise does not require further detailed argument. Instead, let us now turn to the central and critical question with which we began. How can we account for the anomaly that the United States, which among all nations can most easily afford to remedy social neglect, has been so lax in doing so?

We move now from the reasonably solid ground of evidence to the quicksands of explanation. Any effort to unravel the problem of American relative social backwardness must be suppositive and conjectural. But let me begin by stressing an essential aspect of this inquiry. It is that the terms of the problem, as we have posed it, make it impossible simply to declare that the social neglect all too visible in America is nothing but the "natural" result of the class stratification, the hegemony of property interest or the blind play of market forces characteristic of capitalism. Speaking of the failure of American society to provide low-cost housing, two radical critics, Paul Baran and Paul Sweezy, have declared: "Such planning and such action [that is, the provision of low-rent housing] will never be undertaken by a government run by and for the rich, as every capitalist government is and must be." The trouble with such an explanation is that it overlooks the fact that there is no significant difference in income distribution, concentration of private or corporate wealth or play of market forces among the various countries that we have used to establish the laggard social record of the United States. The top 5 percent of income receivers in Denmark received 17.5 percent of national income in 1955; 19 percent in (urban) Norway in 1948; 24 percent in Sweden in 1945; 20 percent in the United States in 1955–59 (before tax). Concentration of corporate assets and sales among all capitalist nations is also roughly similar. Nor does the degree of intervention into the market seem inordinately different as between, say, Switzerland on the one hand and the United States on the other. It may very well be that the institutions and ideologies of capitalism place fundamental inhibitions on the reach of social amelioration in all capitalist nations, but the problem remains as to why the United States has not reached the limits of improvement that have been attained by other nations in which the same basic inhibitions exist.

This initial orientation to our inquiry suggests that the reasons must be sought in the most treacherous of all quicksand regions—those that account for the subtle differences in basic institutions, attitudes or responses that we call "national character." Evidently factors and forces in the American past made American capitalism less attentive, or less responsive, to large areas of social neglect than was the case with her sister societies abroad. What might these elements have been?

We might start by considering what is perhaps the most obvious difference between the United States and the European nations—the matter of size. One hypothesis would then be that the higher level of American neglect could be ascribed to social changes induced by the larger scale of our continent, with its obvious spatial obstacles in the way of creating a tight-knit society with a strongly felt sense of communal responsibility and concern.

The hypothesis is a tempting one and perhaps contains a modicum of explanatory power. Sheer distance undoubtedly works against the growth of community spirit. But the effects of scale cannot possibly bear the whole burden of the problem. Canada, with a better record of legislative social concern than we, has an even larger territory. More to the point, the density of population per square mile, which is perhaps the most important way in which scale becomes translated into human experience, is not markedly different in the United States than in many smaller nations. The United States averages 55 persons per square mile; Sweden averages 44; Norway, 31; New Zealand, 26; Canada, 5. Thus the effects of scale in separating man from man, and presumably thereby reducing the level of shared concerns and mutual responsibilities, should operate in the opposite direction, toward a higher level of concern in the United States than in any of the above countries.

A second intuitive possibility seems more convincing. If size does not provide a convincing answer to the problem of why America lacks a relatively high-ranking program of social repair, the striking diversity of the American scene may serve as a better reason. In the heterogeneity of the American population there would seem to be a prima facie cause for its lack of community feeling.

As with the matter of size, it may be that heterogeneity has its role to play, but—with one special exception to which I will shortly turn—I do not believe it can be made a central causative factor. There is, to begin with, the awkward fact that the most heterogenous of all European nations—Switzerland with its three language groups—is certainly one with a high level of public amenities. Canada is another example of a culturally diverse nation, in which political frictions have not stood in the way of the development of an advanced welfare system. Perhaps even more telling, we cannot easily establish within the United States any strong association between homogeneity of culture and community concern. The high level of social neglect among the white population of the southern states and the inattention paid to the decline of Appalachia by its white kinsmen in more affluent areas of that region are cases in point.

However, if homogeneity, in itself, seems an uncertain source of social concern, there is no doubt that the special case of racial heterogeneity is an all too certain cause of social neglect. The problem of racial animosity is by no means confined to this country and wherever it appears greatly intensifies the problem of neglect: witness the Maori in New Zealand and the Ainu in Japan. But there is no parallel to the corrosive and pervasive role played by race in the problem of social neglect in the United States. It is an obvious fact that the persons who suffer most from the kinds of neglect we have mentioned—residents of the slums, recipients of welfare payments, the medically deprived and the inmates of prisons—are disproportionately Negro. This merging of the racial issue with that of neglect serves as a rationalization for the policies of inaction that have characterized so much of the American response to need. Programs to improve slums are seen by many as programs to "subsidize" Negroes; proposals to improve the conditions of prisons are seen as measures to coddle black criminals, and so on. In such cases, the fear and resentment of the Negro take precedence over the social problem itself. The result, unfortunately, is that society suffers from the results of a failure to correct social evils whose ill effects refuse to obey the rules of segregation.

If the subject of race is discouraging, at least it gives us a clue as to where to search for the causes of the comparative social neglect in the United States. For the important role played by race in the etiology of the problem gives us one clear-cut reason why the institutions of capitalism in America have failed to develop in the same way as in other nations. Moreover, the importance of this special factor in our past suggests that other distinctively "American" facets of our history should also be examined to see if they too bear on the problem.

Whoever searches for such distinctive shaping forces of our past quickly fastens on two: the unique role of democracy and the extraordinary success of the economic system in shaping the American heritage. But if democracy and economic success are familiar touchstones in our history, they are surely disconcerting candidates for the role of social retardants. We are accustomed to pointing to our strong egalitarian sentiments and to the exuberant pace of economic progress when asked why we did so much "better" than Europe in the nineteenth century, not why we are doing so much "worse" in the twentieth century. To consider the possibility that these very elements of our past success may now act as social retardants would seem to require us to reverse the verdict of considered historical judgment.

That is not, however, what I intend. My thought, rather, is to suggest that the traits and institutions that admirably served the needs of one period may not be equally well suited to those of another. Consider, to begin with, the much-admired democratic cast of American political thought. This is usually extolled for the impetus it gave to self-government, the limits it established against tendencies to tyranny and so forth. That judgment remains valid. But the democratic bias of American thought can also be seen in another light, when we consider it as a background factor that has conditioned our attitude to social need. The idea of the self-government of equals, as has often been remarked, has brought with it a deep suspicion of government for any purposes other than to facilitate the intercourse of the (presumably) successful majority. And beyond that it has meant as well a denigration of an important aspect of the more ancient conception of a government of unequals—namely, that one of the justifications of government was the dispensation of charity and social justice to the neediest by those entrusted with state power.

Antiwelfare

I have no wish to romanticize this elitist ideal of government. Indeed, it is probable that the homely realities of American democratic social justice were preferable by far to those of the "benevolence" of the rulers of nineteenth century Europe. Nonetheless there remained within the older "feudal" conception of government a latent legitimization of authority that, once given the changed mandates of the twentieth century, provided the basis for a much stronger and more penetrating attack on social neglect than did the much more restricted democratic concept. In a word, the elitist tradition was ultimately more compatible with the exercise of a compassionate and magnanimous policy than was the democratic.

As always, Alexis de Tocqueville sensed the difference. "The bonds of human affection," he wrote, "with regard to the democratic state, are wider but more relaxed" than those of the aristocratic:

> Aristocracy links everybody, from peasant to king, in one long chain. Democracy breaks the chain and frees each link. As social equality spreads there are more and more people who, though neither rich nor powerful enough to have much hold over others, have gained or kept enough wealth and enough understanding to look after their own needs. Such folk owe no man anything and hardly expect anything from anybody. They form the habit of thinking of themselves in isolation and imagine that their whole destiny is in their own hands. Thus, not only does democracy make men forget their ancestors, it also clouds their view of their descendants, and isolates them from their contemporaries. Each man is forever thrown back on himself alone, and there is danger that he may be shut up in the solitude of his own heart.

What Tocqueville alerts us to is a restriction of the reach of concern in democratic societies—a tendency to cultivate a general solicitude for those who remain within a few standard deviations from the norm of success, but that ignores those who drop beyond the norm into the limbo of failure.

In its general antipathy for government policies that transgressed these narrow boundaries of social concern, the "antiwelfare" animus of American democracy was further abetted by two other attributes of our experience. One of these was the frontier spirit with its encouragement of extreme individualism and self-reliance. The other was the enormous influence of economic growth. What E. H. Kirkland has called "that great human referendum on human conditions, the number of immigrants" provided striking confirmation throughout the late nineteenth and early twentieth centuries of the relative superiority of life chances in America to those elsewhere, including the Scandinavian countries that now appear as paragons of capitalism. This vast encouragement in the field of economic life powerfully reinforced the prevailing political belief that those who failed to reach the general level of average well-being had no one to blame but themselves. Not only among the upper classes, but in the middle and working classes as well, the conviction was gained that social failure was more a matter for scolding than for indignation. Thus the rampage of Social Darwinism in late nineteenth-century America, with its long-abiding legacy of antiwelfare attitudes in the twentieth, cannot be divorced from the myth (and the reality) of the frontier or the facts of economic life itself.

The result was a peculiarly American anesthetizing of the public's social conscience which, coupled with its profound suspicions of government "from above," led toward a mixed indifference and impotence with regard to social neglect. This is not to say that American culture produced a people that was less sensitive to suffering than other peoples; on the contrary, Americans have shown their quick human sympathies more readily than many other nationalities, especially for victims of misfortune in other parts of the world. It is, rather, that the ingredients of the American experience made Americans loath to acknowledge the social causes of neglect and reluctant to use public authority to attend to them.

Middle-Class Attitudes

It is informative in this regard to reflect on how much of the social legislation in America has come about as the result of determined work by the "aristocrats" of the system, against the opposition of the middle classes. Today as well, proposals for the elimination of social grievances receive much more support from the elites of national government than from the county administrators, state legislators or small-town congressmen who continue to express the traditional philosophy of the American past. When it comes to the alleviation of the specific forms of neglect we have discussed in this essay, it is not a pinch on the profits of the great corporations but a pinch on the principles of middle-class Americans that often stands in the way.

To this enthronement of middle-class attitudes must be added one last and exceedingly important supplement. This is the combined efficacy of the American democratic ethos and the American economic élan in preventing the socialist movement from gaining a foothold in the United States. On the one hand, as Leon Samson has pointed out, the political ideology of America, with its stress on equality, came very close to that of socialism, to the detriment of the special appeal of the latter less democratic milieux. On the other hand, the sheer economic advance of the United States greatly lessened the traditional appeal of socialism in terms of its promised economic benefits. As Werner Sombart remarked crudely but tellingly: "On the reefs of roast beef and apple pie, socialist Utopias of all sorts are sent to their doom."

The absence of a socialist movement in turn exerted two effects. First, it removed from American political life the abrasive frictions of a class-oriented politics that proved the undoing of parliamentary government in many nations of Europe. That was sheer gain. Second, however, it also removed the combination of working-class political power and intellectual concern for social reform that provided the moving force behind much of the reform legislation that eventually emerged in the rest of the Western world. If there seems to be one common denominator within the variety of capitalist governments that have developed a high level of response to social neglect, it is the presence within all of them of powerful social democratic parties combining trade union strength and moderate socialist ideology. Per contra, one cause for the relative neglect of social ills in this country seems to be the failure of a comparable alliance to emerge in America.

In focusing attention on the roles played by the democratic and economic elements of American history in giving rise to her present condition of relative social backwardness, I do not wish to overlook consideration of numerous other factors that we have not considered, primary among them the peculiarly tangled and ineffective structure of American political power. The impotence of city government, the rivalry of the states, the power of sabotage inherent in the seniority system in Congress—all these and still other factors surely deserve their places in an examination of the roots of social neglect. Nevertheless, with all the risks inherent in an effort to simplify a multicausal phenomenon, I believe that we can offer a reasonably cogent answer to the question with which we began: why has American capitalism lagged behind other capitalist nations in the repair of its social defects?

The reasons, as I see them, are threefold. First, the remedy of neglect has been stymied because of the identification of need with race and the unwillingness to take measures of which a principal effect would have to be a marked improvement in the condition of the Negro. Second, social reform has been retarded due to the lingering heritage of the democratic conception of limited government and to its lack of the ideal of social magnanimity. Finally, social neglect has persisted because the American credo and the American experience have inhibited the formation of a social-democratic, working-class party dedicated to the improvement of the lower classes.

Is it possible to go beyond diagnosis to prognosis? Can an examination of the roots of American inertia give us some clues as to the chances of remedying the neglect from which the country suffers? From the material we have covered I shall venture a few comments that may seem surprising, for in an age of general pessimism they carry a message of qualified optimism. By this I mean that new social forces capable of bringing about a substantial betterment of the prevailing level of social neglect seem to me to be at hand, but that we cannot yet say whether the potential for change inherent in these forces will be allowed to exert its influence.

A New New Deal?

Few would deny the presence of the first force. It is the belated arrival on the American scene of significant improvement in the relative economic well-being of the Negro community. Median incomes of black families, which averaged 55 percent of white incomes at the beginning of the decade, moved up to 63 percent at the end. Moreover, the preconditions for further increases are present in the existence of legislative measures that, however inadequately, bring some power of remedy against the remaining barriers of discrimination. I do not wish in any way either to exaggerate the progress of the average black family, which is still much too little, or to brush aside as inconsequential the obstacles to social equality that remain, which are immense, but only to state as an indisputable fact that a beginning has been made, and that it seems unlikely that it will come to a halt.

My second cause for qualified optimism is the tardy arrival of another necessary force for the repair of social neglect in America. This is the basis for a possible new New Deal—that is, for a second great massing of public energies for the improvement of social conditions in the United States. Here, the stimulus is provided by the challenge of the ecological crisis which, in the short run, threatens the comfort, decency and convenience of life in America and in the long run imperils its very continuance. There is no doubt that the reckless abuse of the environment must come to an end and that the present mindless extraction of raw materials and heedless disposal of wastes must give way to an orderly administration of the entire economic process from start to finish. In this imperious requirement, imposed on us not by a division within society but by a potentially fatal imbalance between the system as a whole and its adjustment to nature, there lies an issue that may be sufficiently impelling—and yet also homely and personal enough—to bring about the needed public acquiescence in the bold use of government authority for social ends. What the ecological crisis offers is the basis for a new reform movement in America whose potential for improving our habitat, health and general well-being could be very great.

My third cause for qualified optimism lies in the presence of still a last necessary ingredient for social change. This is the discovery in our midst of a social force that may provide a substitute for the social-democratic political conscience that has been missing from the American experience. That substitute is the party of the young.

I am aware that the young are not currently in full favor with other Americans, and I shall have something to say about their shortcomings. But at this juncture, while we are looking for possible counterforces against the traditional American inertia in the face of social neglect, surely we must count the energy and idealism of the youth movement as one of these. Whatever their faults, the vanguard of angry young people has succeeded, where all else has failed, in causing Americans to reexamine the condition of their own house. Do not forget that the movement for civil rights was begun by the young, that the opposition to the war has been led by them, that the "discovery" of the ecological crisis was and is their special concern. It would be foolish to glorify everything that the youth movement has produced in America, but it would be wrong to deny the role that the young have played as the enforcement agents for the nation's conscience.

The presence within contemporary America of the first real signs of racial improvement, of the basis for a new New Deal and of a corps of idealistic and determined youth constitutes new and promising possibilities for the repair of social neglect. Yet I would be remiss if I did not make clear the basis for the qualifications that I must also place against these optimistic possibilities.

The Failure of Success

Let me begin with the risks that must be faced in the rise of black well-being. They derive from the fact that we cannot expect a continued improvement in the social neglect suffered by blacks to follow "automatically" from the workings of a growing economy, or even from a rise in the average income of blacks. On the contrary, the past decade of "average" improvement tells us that the deprivations of black ghetto life, the prison brutalities suffered by blacks, the terrible differentials in conditions of health or the persistent poverty of the black fatherless slum family will not melt away quickly even under the warming sun of a general rise in relative Negro incomes. To repair these resistant areas of social failure will require continued agitation on the part of the black community to bring its neglect incessantly and insistently before the attention of the white community. The prerequisite for improvement, in a word, is a continuation of black militancy, meaning by this demonstrations, confrontations and the like.

The dangers here are twofold. On the one hand, the prospect of a decade or more of continual turmoil and pressure from the black minority hardly promises a peaceful or easy political atmosphere for the nation as a whole. More ominous, there is the risk that black militancy, if pushed beyond the never clearly demarcated line of social tolerance, may result in white countermilitancy, with the possibility of an annulment of black gains, or even of a retrograde movement. If the rise of black power thus opens the way to a long overdue repair of the single greatest source of social neglect in America, it also holds the worrisome prospect of a polarization of race relations that could result in a major social catastrophe, for whites as well as blacks.

Second, the possible basis for a new New Deal, based on the need to work toward an intelligent management of our economy, carries a considerable price. For the achievement of an ecological balance in America will not be won by the imposition of a few antipollution measures. In the long run it will require an unremitting vigilance over and a penetrating regulation of large areas of both production and consumption. In a word, the functional requirements of a new New Deal must include a far-reaching system of national planning.

Is it possible that such a profound change in the structure of the American economy will be easy to achieve? The experience of the first New Deal is hardly reassuring in this regard. Yet the problem this time may not lie at first with the recalcitrance of business management—it is significant that two major corporate leaders, Robert W. Sarnoff of RCA and Thomas J. Watson, Jr., of IBM, have already called for national planning as the necessary first step if we are to exert effective control over the future. The difficulties may lie, instead, with the unwillingness of the great mass of average Americans to give up the easy freedom of an unrestrained economic carnival for the much more self-denying life style necessary for a truly balanced economic equilibrium. And beyond that lies the still more difficult problem of reorienting our whole economic system away from its accustomed goals of growth to new goals of a cautiously watched relationship with nature itself. In the end, the demands placed on the adaptive powers of the system by the requirements of ecology may constitute the life-or-death test of capitalism itself.

Finally, there are the qualifications with regard to the young. These are of two kinds. The first I need not dwell upon. It is the risk that the energies and idealism of the young will focus on petty issues rather than central ones, will be directed to rhetoric rather than remedies, or will culminate in a senseless fury that will only bring upon itself the repressive countermeasures of their elders. The second danger is perhaps even greater, although it is one to which we usually pay less attention. It is simply that the party of the young will vitiate its strength in internecine quarrels, as have so many parties of reform, or will become a party of the few rather than one of the many. The danger, in a word, is that the present energy and idealism of the young will peter out into exhaustion and futility. There are those in the older generation, I know, who would welcome such a disappearance of youthful activism. But where, we must ask ourselves, would we then find an equally effective force of conscience in America?

Offsets to Optimism

All these qualifications come as chastening offsets to the optimism offered by the advent of new forces for social change. The threat of the difficult adjustments, clashes and crises that seem certain to arise from the need for continued black militancy, for expanded government planning, and from uncertain temper, appeal or staying power of youth, which makes it impossible to look forward to a smooth transition from a relatively neglectful America to a relatively concerned one. Indeed, it is entirely possible that the decade ahead will not be one of improvement at all, but only one of growing tensions between the forces for change and those of indifference or inertia, and that the indices of social neglect will show little or no gain. In a word, America ten or 20 years hence may be as ugly, slum-ridden, unconcerned with poverty, unhealthy, negligent in her treatment of criminals—in short, as laggard with regard to her social problems—as she is today.

Before this indeterminate outlook, predictions can only be fatuous. More important, they are beside the point. For what our diagnosis has brought to the fore is a recognition that social neglect in America is but the tip of an iceberg of attitudes and institutions that deter our society, not alone in dealing generously with respect to its least fortunate members, but in dealing effectively with respect to the most pressing issues—racial, ecological, ideological—of our times. In this sense, the remedy of neglect in America comes as a challenge much larger than the immediate problems to which it addresses itself. What is at stake is not only whether the richest nation in the world will finally become the most decent but whether a nation whose very greatness is now in jeopardy can recognize—and thus perhaps begin to remedy—the degree to which its present failures are rooted in its past success.

SUGGESTED READINGS

The First New Nation by Seymour Martin Lipset (New York: Basic Books, 1963).

Toward a Social Report (Washington, D.C.: Department of Health, Education and Welfare, 1969).

by Lewis W. Hine

Work or Starve!

Lewis Hine came from the Midwest. He studied at the University of Chicago and took a Ph.D. in sociology at Columbia University in 1905. A few years earlier he had started using a camera to teach students about nature. By 1908 he had become a reformer, using pictures instead words, and his exposure of the life and work of the poor, children and immigrants was a major weapon in the social welfare movement of his day.

This group of photographs comes from the files of the National Child Labor Committee for whom he worked from 1908-1921. For them he photographed working children — newsboys, miners, mill hands, farm workers and oyster shuckers. He called himself "a social photographer" on his lanterns slides made from these photographs, and his pictures show the terrible conditions of work. They are also individual portraits which is why, perhaps, he is one of the most important American photographers. Hine continued working on various projects until the middle of the 1930s. However, his style and approach had been largely passed by — he died in near poverty in 1940.

These photographs are reproduced by courtesy of the National Committee on the Employment of Youth (the successors to the National Child Labor Committee) and the Witkin Gallery.

Portrait of a worker — Georgia, 1913

Workers in a glass factory — New Jersey, 1911

Piecework, picking nutmeats — New York, 1911

Bundle carrier — New York, 1912

3 *Lee Rainwater*

Post-1984 America

The way of life of Americans changes constantly yet somehow over long periods of time is recognizably the same. Indeed, whether the life style of particular groups of Americans is seen as changing or stable is somewhat a matter of emphasis and purpose. Moreover, when predicting what life styles will be in a decade or so, the issue of change versus stability, of emergence versus repetition, is a complex one. Demographic and economic analysis shows that there will be striking changes in these objective indicators of socioeconomic position. On the other hand, during the past two or three decades—during which there have been similarly striking socioeconomic changes—the life styles of the various social classes have been remarkably stable despite all the technological innovation and socioeconomic progress.

Changes in life style and values in the future are likely to be subtle, or even superficial, in the sense that they represent adaptations to basic core values and patterns of interpersonal relationships to a new social, economic and ecological situation. The stability of life style is maintained in exactly this way—by constant reinterpretation of the meanings and use of particular products and services to make them consistent with the basic themes of various life styles.

The Next 15 Years

We are often misled into thinking about social problems by fastening too much on the present and the immediate past in developing the paradigms by which we seek to understand and control problems. As antidote for that let us look at what seems to be the most likely course of development of the broad segments of the American society over the period of the next 15 years.

The nation is now heavily urban in its pattern of settlement; by the mid-1980s it will be slightly more urban, the proportion of the population in metropolitan areas having increased from 68 percent to 71 percent. But there is another side to this increased urbanization. Because of the transportation revolution brought on by the automobile and the superhighway, within the urban areas the population is less and less densely settled—the population per square mile in urbanized areas will have decreased from 6,580 in 1920 to around 3,800 in 1985. And the proportion of the population living in the suburban areas will have increased from 39 percent to 45 percent. This is what suburbanization is all about; it is a trend that can be expected to continue into the future. This means that more and more land will be subject to the stresses of suburbanized development.

The population will grow, but current indications are that the growth will not be nearly as great as has been previously thought. The rate of population growth seems to be slowing down and some of the most experienced demographers believe that somewhat greater perfection of contraceptive technology will lead to zero population growth without any special need for exhortation. The population of the mid-1980s is likely to include some 240 million Americans—about 35 million more than today.

This growth is not particularly dramatic although it will certainly require a great deal in the way of new facilities. The most dramatic aspect of population change is the change in the age distribution. If the sixties and early seventies have been the generation of youth—of the teenager and early twenties adult—the late 1970s and 1980s will be the era of the young marrieds. The number of men and women between the ages of 24 and 34 will increase by 60 percent; the younger group will increase less than 10 percent. There will be a 37 percent increase in the number of adults between 35 and 45, a small decrease in the number 45 to 54, and a 27 percent increase at the over-65 level. The big demographic impact on the society, then, will be in the years of youthful maturity.

Most indications are that the economy will grow fairly steadily through the 1970s and 1980s. This will result in an increase in the size of the GNP from one to 1.7 trillion dollars. It is expected that the service sector of the economy will grow much more rapidly than the goods sector but the growth in the latter will not be inconsiderable.

In the daily life of members of the society the concomitant impact of this growth is a very large increase in personal income. The median income for families is expected to grow from around $10,000 to over $16,000 (in dollars of 1970 purchasing power).

However, there are no indications to suggest that this income will be distributed more equitably in the future than it is at present. As has been true for the post-World War II period it seems likely that, although each income class will participate in the rising personal income, those at the bottom will not be increasing their share of the pie. That would mean that in the future as today the richest 20 percent of families would still be receiving over 40 percent of all of the personal income, and the poorest 20 percent would still be receiving less than 5 percent of the money income.

Of these various changes, two principal ones seem likely to have the greatest import for life style changes that have taken place over the past decades and that will take place (in all likelihood with increasing intensity) in the next two decades. The first of these is economic and the second cultural.

We are so used to the steady increase in affluence (despite occasional periods of two or three years of relative stagnation) and we adapt so rapidly to each successive level of affluence, that it is often difficult to realize how very large the shifts in personal income are. For example, the median income of families and unrelated individuals is projected to increase by $6700 from 1971 to 1985 (1970 dollars). One way of looking at this increase is to say that over a 17-year period median income will increase as much as it has over the previous 50 years. Thus, although the proportionate increase in income year by year, decade by decade is projected to be about the same over the next few years as it has been over the past half-century, the absolute increase is much larger because of the larger base on which the constant proportionate increase takes place. The result of these increases will be that by the mid-1980s half of the population will enjoy the level of living that characterized only the top 3 percent of the population in 1947 or the top 15 percent of the population in 1970. The very large bundle of goods and services that goes with this very large absolute increase in median income can be expected to have important interactions with the emerging life styles of the 1980s, both affecting and being affected by those styles. The table presents comparative data for 1968 and 1985.

Comparing Actual 1968 with Predicted 1985 Family and Individual Income in the United States.

	Families		Families and Individuals	
Income levels	**1968**	**1985**	**1968**	**1985**
Number (millions)	50.5	66.7	64.3	85.9
Percent	100	100	100	100
Under $3,000	10	4	19	9
$3,000 to $4,999	12	6	14	8
$5,000 to $9,999	38	18	34	19
$10,000 to $14,999	25	23	21	21
$15,000 to $24,999	12	33	10	29
$25,000 and over	3	16	2	15
Aggregate income (billions)	$486	$1,074	$544	$1,277
Percent	100	100	100	100
Under $3,000	2	1	4	1
$3,000 to $4,999	5	1	6	2
$5,000 to $9,999	29	8	30	9
$10,000 to $14,999	31	18	30	17
$15,000 to $24,999	23	37	21	35
$25,000 and over	10	35	9	36
Mean income	$9,600	$16,100	$8,500	$14,900
Median income	$8,600	$14,700	$7,400	$13,500

The median educational attainment of the population is expected to grow to only 12.6 years by 1985, and the proportion who attend college is projected to increase to 31.5 percent, with 18.8 percent completing college.

While these upward shifts in educational attainment are not particularly dramatic, the small increases there, in addition to numerous other forces expanding the knowledgeability of the population (and shifting its values and tastes in a more sophisticated and cosmopolitan direction) will combine to make important changes in the world view of consumers in the 1980s. The continuing urbanization of the population and the impact of modern communications have the effect of exposing the average citizen to a much wider range of information, and a much wider range of perspectives for interpreting that information, than has ever been true in the past. The citizen in the 1980s is therefore likely to be less insulated from national and worldwide trends in taste, style and innovation than has ever been true.

Life styles will increasingly be built out of a rapidly expanding multiplicity of choices—choices made possible by the interaction of affluence and cosmopolitanism. One of the most striking things about American society since World War II (or longer than that) has been the extent to which the lives of most Americans involve what they put together out of the choices available to them rather than to what they are constrained to do by their socioeconomic situation. Much of the conflict and turmoil in the society probably has as much to do with anxiety and uncertainty engendered by continuing massive increases in the range of choices available to people as with more frequently cited factors. Indeed the "oppression" that many of those who "protest" feel (aside from blacks and other minorities) is probably more the oppression of having many choices and not knowing how to choose among them than of being "forced" to do things one does not wish to do.

Out of the current ferment about life styles is very likely to come the institutionalization of a set of pluralistic standards which legitimate a far wider range of ways of living in American society than has previously been the case. From the various liberation movements (black, brown, red, women, gay men, gay women, youth) will probably come a more widespread ethic of pluralism in life styles. (And this will be more than toleration in that it will involve recognition of the legitimacy of different kinds of identities and life styles.)

The ability to pursue a life style more tailored to individual choice (and less constrained by standards as to what a respectable conforming person should be like) is tremendously enhanced by the increases in material affluence and cultural sophistication. Because of higher incomes one can afford to take up and put aside different styles of living without regretting the capital investment that each may take. The security about the future which goes with steady increases in prosperity allows for the deferral of more permanent life style choices to the future; without this kind of security individuals feel they must make the permanent commitments relatively early in life. To the extent that sanctions against what has been nonconforming behavior decline, individuals are paradoxically less likely to be fixed in nonconforming identities and styles once chosen, since the "road back" is not blocked by discrimination or the necessity to repent. And by the same token, the nonconforming life style can be pursued more fully and more vigorously because of less need for secretiveness if a respectable future is desired.

For the most part these shifts in opportunity for choice will not involve dramatic changes in life for the great bulk of Americans because their exercise of choice will tend to be in the direction of elaborating and perfecting the existing class-related life styles. However, given the resources available to them it is likely that their particular version of those life styles will become increasingly distinctive, increasingly tailored to the needs and identities which they bring to their life situation and which evolve out of its year to year development. It is likely that more and more individuals and families will find it possible to elaborate particular arenas in which they can indulge one or another special taste or interest in a major kind of way. As in the past the increasing level of affluence and sophistication will allow the great middle majority of the population to increase their psychological and financial investment in leisure time activities, and there will be a broadening range of the kinds of activities chosen by different families of equal resources for this kind of investment.

At the level above the middle majority, where the absolute dollar amounts of the increase are even greater, one can expect to find, as in the past, even more highly specialized interests and pursuits. The "class mass" will be in the vanguard of the development of new styles—styles which as time goes on will tend to filter down, be reinterpreted and assimilated to the ongoing middle majority styles.

More of the Same

In the post-World War II period the life styles of each of the major social classes have evolved in terms of a logic dictated by the values and needs of families in each class as these interact with the increasing resources and possibilities available. The dominant trends of each class can be expected to continue to be important as families from these classes use the resources that come to them to further accomplish their goals and aspirations.

For the working class the dominant theme has been the solidification of the nuclear family base. Traditionally the working class has been very much enmeshed in kinship, ethnic and peer group ties, and the nuclear family has tended to be relatively "porous" to influences from the outside. Already in the early 1960s the affluence of the post-World War II period had produced a modern working-class family in which husband and wife interacted in a closer and less rigid way, and in which they directed themselves together toward the goal of perfecting a secure, comfortable and pleasant home as the central focus of their lives. Their relationships, particularly the father's, with the children also reflected this sharp focus on the home as opposed to previous external ties. This development was central to the consumer goals of the modern working-class family which were strongly oriented toward investment in the home to perfect it as a secure, comfortable, cozy place. In many ways this modern working-class family seemed to be adopting the styles of the lower-middle class. But that class also was in the process of change.

The lower-middle class has traditionally centered its life style on a necessity to achieve and maintain respectability. (This has been a lesser point of elaboration for the working class. Even as the modern working class developed in ways that made it seem superficially similar to the lower-middle class in day-to-day life, the importance of the striving after respectability was not so apparent.) While respectability certainly continues to be a touchstone for the lower-white-collar way of life, it is increasingly taken for granted and decreasingly an issue of preoccupation for lower-middle-class men and women.

The growing economic affluence and the wider horizons that come from higher education and constant attention to the messages of the mass media have highlighted the striving after wider horizons as perhaps the central theme in the development of a modern lower-middle-class life style. Affluence allows the working-class family to turn in on itself since it no longer has to be so deeply enmeshed in a mutual aid network of community and peers. Affluence allows a lower-middle-class family to reach outward to experience and make use of a wider slice of the world outside the family. This is true both for lower-middle-class individuals who move toward expression of personal interests and for the lower-middle-class family as a whole, which is able to increasingly define as central to family interaction the experiences they have as individuals or together in the outside world. These wider horizons, however, are pursued from a very solid family-oriented base, and with the assumption that the experiences of the wider world will not change the members in any essential way or change their relationships to each other. Therefore the traditional base of family togetherness as a core goal of the lower-middle-class life style is not challenged. Thus lower-middle-class people come to have a wider range of experiences and possessions that have previously been considered characteristic of the upper-middle-class taste and way of life. Here too, however, the reinterpretation of new life style elements and the changes in the social class above them result in a continued distinctiveness about the life style.

In the upper-middle class the push out to the larger world is intensified. The central characteristics of the upper-middle-class orientation towards living have always been self-sufficiency and the pursuit of self-gratification. It is a more egocentric class in that the claims of respectability and of membership in diffusely obligating groups such as kindred are subordinated to personal goals and desires. Increasing resources and knowledgeability intensify the striving after exploration and fuller self-realization. This is particularly apparent among upper-middle-class youth where parental indulgence, current life situation and family resources combine to maximize the possibilities for fullest realization. At the level of older upper-middle-class persons the experimental approach to perfecting life styles is more subdued but is also often pursued with greater resources. Upper-middle-class people are in a position to afford, and are likely to have the knowledge to select, major new additions to their way of life—whether this be a vacation home and the frequent use of it to develop an alternative social world, or the development of a fairly systematic plan of vacation travel that, for example, allows one to see the U.S.A., then Europe, then Asia, with in-between excursions to the Caribbean and Latin America. Because of the extremely large absolute increase in income that will accrue to this group, one can expect a considerable strengthening in the 1980s of this propensity toward elaborate life style innovations. Thus while the median increase in family income projected for 1970 to 1985 is $6700, the median increase for the upper-middle class will more likely be on the order of $17,000 to $20,000. Such a large absolute increase obviously provides a very rich resource for upper-middle-class experimentation with new life styles without the necessity of sacrificing the material base that supports the more traditional life style.

In addition to the unfinished agenda of the social classes discussed above, one can expect life style changes in response to the changing circumstances that future developments will bring. In some cases (as in fertility) these changes represent a reversal of previous trends, in other cases simply an intensification of changes that have been taking place over a longer period of time.

Changes in Family Living

Adults will spend less time in the "full nest" stage of the family life cycle. This will come about through a later age at marriage and birth of the first child, an unchanging age at the birth of the last child and an unchanging or perhaps slightly declining age at which the child ceases to live at home.

As a lasting legacy of youth and Women's Liberation thinking we are likely to find that young people marry somewhat later than they have in the past. There is no evidence of a major revolution in the extent of premarital sexual relations—the Kinsey Institute study of college youth completed in the mid-1960s showed essentially no change over the first Kinsey study in the proportion of women who had had premarital relations. In both cases approximately half the women had had premarital sexual relations. However, there do seem to be important changes in the pattern of sexual relations for that portion of the female population that has premarital sexual relations at all. Sexual relationships are likely to be more frequent and more institutionalized, more open and more accepted within the peer group than was true in the 1930s. Since there is reason to believe that the post-World War II trend toward earlier marriage in the middle class (the lower and working class had always married young) was in large part responsive to an effort on the part of young people to establish their maturity and adult status, the development of alternate modes of being "grown up" should mean less of a rush to marriage. The beginning of legitimation of premarital sexual relations in the context of youth peer group relations (rather than as furtive and hidden activities) should go a long way toward reducing pressure for marriage to establish legitimate adulthood. (For that matter the 18-year-old vote and the consequent courting by politicians may bring somewhat the same result.)

It seems likely that at the level of the class mass (as least the highly urban and more cosmopolitan portion of it) relationships that involve young couples living together will become fairly widespread. Under these circumstances marriage will come when the couple decide to settle down either to have children or to begin seriously to build incrementally a career and its related family base. For large numbers of other young men and women, less institutionalized patterns of heterosexual relationships may serve to allow a sense of adulthood without marriage. We have already seen the development in a few cities, particularly on the West Coast, of a wide range of singles institutions. One can expect this pattern to continue to spread across the country and to become more elaborate as the level of affluence of young adults permits this.

Social and heterosexual relationships of the kind sketched above (involving as a common, though not majority pattern, reasonably regular participation in sexual relationships) depend, of course, on a high possibility of preventing unwanted births. The continued development of more and more effective contraceptive devices (and in the 1980s a once-a-month technique such as the prostaglandins should be well established) means that the technical base for this pattern of social relationships will be available. Legalization of abortion on demand (which should be the case by the 1980s in the states with the great majority of the population) allows for the clearing up of "mistakes" which often currently precipitate marriages (apparently about one-quarter of all brides are pregnant at marriage). While there is ample evidence that the availability of contraception does not have much impact on women's willingness to give up their virginity, the willingness to establish a regular premarital sexual relationship is much more responsive to the possibility of effective and interpersonally simple contraception.

Of course the same contraceptive techniques and the availability of abortion which make possible lower rates of premarital fertility also allow couples to space births and to have exactly the number of children they want. Analysis of surveys already conducted suggests that if couples had only the children they chose to have—that is, if pregnancy was completely voluntary—the average completed fertility of married couples would be on the order of 2.6 children (whereas in fact average completed fertility has been running more on the order of 3.3 children).

We have almost no information as to why there seems to be a shift towards smaller family ideals during the past decade. There is no way of predicting with much assurance what fertility desires will be in the late 1970s and 80s. However, according to fertility survey data, even in a period of fairly high fertility a great deal of the expressed preference for medium and large families may well have been a rationalization of "accidents" and unplanned pregnancies. This makes it seem most reasonable to predict a continued trend toward lower fertility.

The results of these various changes in mating behavior are that women would be likely to complete their fertility in the late twenties as they do now, having (again on the average) started their families somewhat later than they do now. The children would be grown and old enough to leave home while the parents are on the average somewhat younger than they are now. For example, the median case might be one in which the mother marries at 22 or 23 and has 2 children. The last one is born when she is 27 or 28 and, the children leave home for college or a job and "singles" living when the mother is not yet 50. Whereas the typical time period between the marriage and the last child leaving home is now between 25 and 30 years, given these patterns of marriage and fertility the more typical range in the 1980s might be 20 or 25 years. The life style elaborations both prior to marriage—the various "singles" styles—and those after the children leave home would loom larger than is presently the case.

Changing Role of Women

The new feminism seems to contain two strains of thought for women, one of which may very well have a pervasive effect and the other a more limited effect. The first involves a greater self-consciousness on the part of women about their subordinate status within the family and in the larger world, and a drive for more autonomy, self-respect and self-expression.

The second involves a challenge to the still established notion that a woman's place is (really) in the home. The implications of the new feminism are easy to misconstrue because of a peculiarity of the interests of the leaders versus the subjects of the movement. By definition women who seek leadership or elite positions within the Women's Liberation Movement are persons whose major identity goals are bound up with activities in the public world, and often also with career aspirations. Such interests, aspirations and the relevant skills are entailed in the elite roles. Therefore the leaders of the Women's Liberation Movement will probably consistently underplay the importance of equality goals and aspirations that do not relate in one way or another to the larger, more public, world. More specifically, the leaders will tend not to regard as legitimate the homemaker role as a major commitment on the part of women. The mass of the followers, however, will be much concerned with their ability to fulfill the homemaker role in a way that is personally gratifying, in a way that allows for the development of autonomy, self-respect, and a sense of valid identity within the narrower and more private worlds that they themselves construct. Even though they will often find the public level of discussion of feminine equality frustrating because it does not take these aspirations as fully legitimate, they probably will prove remarkably tenacious (as people do generally in such a situation) in pursuing their own interests by reinterpreting a great deal of the public ideology of the movement to support the actual roles that they play in their private worlds.

As quickly becomes apparent in any discussion between men and women on this subject, the liberation of women also involves a very significant change in attitudes on the part of men and in relationships between men and women. The kind of thinking that is apparent in the new feminism (except in its more radical version) clearly assumes the viability of marriage but points in the direction of greater equality between husbands and wives in their functioning. This amounts to a strengthening of trends apparent over the last several decades in the middle-class family towards more sharing of power and duties and a less sharply defined division of labor. It has in the past been a point of considerable ambivalence among middle-class women as to whether they are the servants of their families, the hidden bosses of their families, or persons of equal status whose duties happen to be those of keeping things running smoothly within the home. It is the latter definition which is likely to be strengthened by the new feminism.

As incomes rise, the need for the woman's management of the home, and the complexity of that activity of manager, purchasing agent and doer of tasks also rise. If more and more goods and services are brought into and used within the home the woman's work there becomes more valuable rather than less. Yet women have the problem that the values of the society do not define the wife's work as general manager of the home as productive and worthwhile in the same sense that paid-for labor is regarded as productive and worthwhile. Thus women can define themselves as oppressed and "underpaid" for their valuable work for other members of the family. Many women's first impulse is to get out of the home and to earn self-respect and respect from others by work in the labor market. Such work not only earns a clear-cut status, but the demands in jobs are more specific and less diffuse than are homemakers' tasks. Women sometimes find it easier to feel that they are doing a good job at those more specifically defined tasks than at home where a woman's work is never done—nor is it unambiguously judged. Yet with the rise in affluence and productivity in the commodity sector, the kinds of services that a woman might buy to take care of her home become increasingly expensive so that women will be loath to buy on the outside market much of the labor that will be necessary to maintain the home.

There may well be a class difference in response to the combination of affluence and a continuing emphasis on feminine equality. Very likely at the working- and lower-middle-class level, the two will combine to give women a greater sense of worth and to encourage them toward more autonomous functioning within the homemaker role. At the upper-middle-class level, however, there may be an increasing emphasis on career for purely self-expressive goals. (At all class levels there may be some increase in the proportion of women in the work force—because of the decline in fertility and the fewer years in which a woman has children in the home.) Upper-middle-class women have always included activities outside the home (either in voluntary activities or at jobs) as a central part of their role definition. They will certainly expect, as part of rising affluence, to be able to engage in these self-enhancing and self-validating activities more fully. This will put a strong premium on work organization and homemaking products which facilitate labor and timesaving. While on the one hand the home will be a more elaborate and complex place, on the other hand the woman will want to spend less time there. This will create a great demand for innovations which make homes easier to keep clean and neat, meals quicker to prepare and so forth.

Since families are smaller it is likely that there will be greater opportunities for the development of individual interests and activities on the part of all members of the family. The lesser burden of child care and rearing certainly enhances these possibilities for the mother, and for the father. The children too, because of greater resources available and a lessened tendency to treat the children as "a group," will be more likely to move in individualistic directions. (During the height of the large-family enthusiasm of the 1950s this potentiality was viewed negatively, as encouraging the "selfishness" of both parents and children.)

For the same reasons the family as a group becomes more "portable." The smaller family can more easily leave the home base for travel—both short-run travel as to a weekend cottage, and longer-run vacations. The heavy home-centeredness that was a concomitant of the large-family enthusiasm of the 1950s can be expected to decline as families feel themselves less space-bound.

Modern communications combined with the greater sophistication of the audience have the effect of bringing the world in on the average citizen in more and more forceful terms as the years go on. He reacts to what he sees in various ways—sometimes with fright and intimidation and other times with interest, approval and fascination. Both of these responses can be expected to be at least as characteristic of the 1980s citizen as of today's, assuming that all the world's problems are not solved between now and then. But the need to pull back, to disengage from exposure to the world's events (not just the large scale events seen on the evening news but also those observed and important in one's day-to-day life at work, on the street, in the local community and elsewhere) strengthens people's commitment to home as their castle, as well as encouraging them toward seeking to relax and vacation in other locales which are tranquil, isolated, private. The feeling that the world is too much with us leads to an interest in getting away from it all, getting "back to nature."

There Won't be Enough Time to Spend All the Money

People become busier the more affluent they are. Paradoxically, people whose affluence is increasing tend to make choices which result in their having less free or uncommitted time rather than more. There is considerable evidence to suggest that, with increasing affluence, workers do not choose greater leisure rather than more income; work hours tend either not to decrease at all or to decrease very slightly. None of the predictions made in the early 1950s concerning significantly shorter working hours seem to have held up. Indeed, in the few cases where unions have bargained for a short work week the slack seems to have been taken up for a fair number of the workers by more moonlighting. This makes good economic sense. After all, a man doesn't have to have anything extraordinarily interesting to do with his leisure time if his only choice is earning 50 cents an hour. On the other hand, at ten dollars an hour the leisure time needs to be pretty gratifying to cause him to forego his money.

With increasing affluence people are able to buy more and more goods and services, but then they run into the hard fact that the using of the products and services requires time. And the time available for consumption does not change. One cannot really buy time; all one can do is try to buy more efficient use of time. This fact has profound implications for life styles—many of these implications are discussed within the framework of economic theory by Steffan Linder in *The Harried Leisure Class* (Columbia University Press, 1970).

In general, when there are so many products to use and things to do and gratifications to be derived from both, people will tend to become impatient with routine, purely instrumental activities which seem to consume a great deal of time and effort relative to the gratification they produce. Similarly, people will tend to shift their commitments in the direction of activities that seem to provide more gratification per time unit and away from those which seem time-consuming in relation to the amount of gratification they provide.

The principal effect of this time/affluence dynamic is to make daily life more "commodity and service intensive." That is, people will tend to use more and more products and services in ways that maximize the satisfaction in a given period of time. Linder argues that with rising incomes pure leisure time (that is time in which you do nothing much) tends to decline because the degree of gratification that is available from goods and services, that were previously too expensive, is now greater than the gratification that is available from leisure and from one's own efforts to turn leisure into gratifying activity. Similarly, activities that are less productive of gratification tend to be given up or the time devoted to them sharply curtailed in favor of activities that are more productive and more expensive. The less time goods take per unit of satisfaction provided, the more in demand they will be. The cheapness of the product in terms of time becomes more and more important as the importance of their cheapness in terms of money declines. Individuals tend to give up relatively less productive activities such as reading or taking long walks in familiar territory or leisurely engagement in lovemaking in favor of activities that require less time investment per unit of gratification. The same activities may be pursued in more exotic settings as a way of heightening satisfaction through the use of economic resources—thus the man who would hardly waste his time to view nature in the city park a few blocks away from his home may be ecstatic about the beauties of the Scottish countryside. People are notorious in not being tourists in their own cities because they are "too busy," but they will spend a great deal of money to visit a distant city and end up knowing more about its interesting sights than they do about the ones in their own home town.

These trends, coupled with the trends toward freeing women even more from their household duties, will tend to heighten awareness of the home as a "system" involving shelter, furnishings, production processes and their maintenance, a view in line with at least one economic theory of how households operate (Gary S. Becker, "A Theory of the Allocation of Time," *American Economic Review*, September, 1965). The home will become a more and more capital-intensive place as the cost of both externally supplied labor and household labor increases.

The Consumption of Services Will Grow and Broaden

A large segment of the multiplicity of choices that become available to people as their affluence rises has to do with the wide range of services which they can afford. People are able to buy expensive services which they previously had to forego (like regular medical care) or perform for themselves. As their own time becomes more and more valuable they are more willing to pay others to do things for them, if those others can perform the task more efficiently (often at the cost of possession of special equipment) or in a more satisfying way. This trend toward having others do work previously performed by household members is most dramatically evident in the rapid growth of franchise food operations. In the future one would expect an increase in the proportion of the family food budget used for meals away from home.

A second area in which a large expansion of services is likely has to do with the public sector. If the current national consensus toward disengagement from worldwide empire becomes a more or less permanent feature of the nation's stance towards the larger world, then one can expect an even greater rate of growth in public sector services than has been apparent over the last decade. The basis of support of demand for a broader and more fully developed range of public sector services is provided both by increasing affluence and by the broad exposure of most of the population to "informed opinion" through the mass media. Also, a higher proportion of the population attends college and is exposed there to welfare-oriented teaching which emphasizes public sector services of all kinds.

Future of the Underclass

So much for likely life style developments affecting the fortunate majority of Americans who are above the level of economic marginality. But what of the groups that have occupied so much of the public attention during the decade just finished—the poor and the oppressed minorities?

All of the income projections currently made predict no change in the distribution of income. Thus from 1947 (and very likely for much longer than that) through 1985 there is no present reason to imagine a major change in the distribution of income among families. In 1985, as at present and as in past decades, it is projected that slightly less than 20 percent of families will be living on incomes that are less than half of the median family income.

By 1985 the income that marks the top of the underclass will stand at $8,200 a year, an increase of $3,400—even larger than the absolute increase since 1947. However the constant dollar gap between the underclass income and that of the man in the mainstream also grows—from $2,800 in 1947 to $5,600 in 1971 to $8,400 in 1985.

There are obviously two ways to look at what happens to disadvantaged groups under these economic circumstances. If one focuses on the absolute changes, one can say that they are far better off than today. If one focuses on changes relative to the majority segments of the society, one can say that they are not at all or only slightly better off.

The people we would have called poor on the basis of an examination of their way of life in 1950 we would very likely call poor in 1970 because their way of life is much the same despite the fact that it includes slightly more in the way of material goods. Their affluence has increased somewhat but in absolute amounts the affluence of the bulk of the population has increased even more and they will find themselves further away from the going standard of American life now than they did in 1960. The issue of poverty then and the apparent progress toward eliminating it has concealed all along the issue of inequality and the fact of no progress toward eliminating it.

If membership is the key issue in the human's effort to find a meaningful life and if in affluent industrial societies membership can be achieved only through the command over the goods and services that are required for mainstream participation, then it follows that we will continue to have poor people and oppressed minorities so long as a significant proportion of Americans have incomes far removed from that of the average man. It follows that the underclass will be alive and well in 1985. And all of the pathologies of the city which are generated by the oppression and deprivation which produce the underclass will also still be with us.

Just as there are reasons for predicting no change in the income distribution, there are good reasons for predicting only small changes in the relative incomes of white and black families by 1985. The 1960s saw a significant increase in black family incomes relative to whites—from around 53 percent of white income to around 63 percent of white income. However, there has been no improvement in that figure in the last couple of years—emphasizing again the crucial role of high unemployment rates in black economic oppression. Indeed, an economist, Harold W. Guthrie, has projected the comparative experience of white and nonwhite families from 1947 through 1968 into the future by calculating the number of years required for equality of family income between the two races under various employment conditions. His results suggest that at current unemployment rates equality of income between black and white families would take well over 100 years to achieve.

At the so-called full unemployment rate of 4 percent it would still require 30 years to achieve equality of income. Only with a sustained unemployment rate lower than 3½ percent would black and white incomes be equal by 1985. Given the kinds of swings in unemployment experienced in the 1960s we could perhaps expect black family incomes to increase to between 70 and 75 percent of white family income. At 75 percent of white family income, blacks would be enjoying the standard of living purchased by over $12,000 a year, significantly better than the median family income for whites today. Their incomes would have almost doubled. Yet relative to whites the absolute difference in income would be slightly larger than it is today.

As we have seen, without marked improvements in their economic situation the black underclass will continue to grow in numbers. Because the black migration from the rural South to the major metropolitan areas does not seem to be abating very fast, it is likely that the size of the urban ghettos will continue to grow, in some cities spilling over into the suburbs. In any case the ghettos will remain the locales of concentrated trouble and violence that they are today.

Because the underclass will still be there, and because of the much higher level of affluence, property crime rates will probably continue to increase, and crimes of violence will probably not decrease very much. There may or may not be recurrent periods of urban rioting—but then the riots are really less important to the day-to-day lives of people living in the ghetto than the more random and individual violence to which they are subjected. One can expect larger and larger areas of the city to deteriorate and become abandoned, and one can expect more no-man's-lands to develop in cities, areas where no one wants to go for any legitimate purpose, and which are abandoned to whatever use marginal persons may want to put them. Again, although the financial cost to individuals with whose commercial or residential investments in the areas of deterioration may be great, the net cost of the deterioration of the cities will continue to be fairly small relative to the general level of affluence, and relative to the opportunities that the expanding suburban and exurban rings provide.

Finally, while one can expect to see a very large growth in the "human service" industries—with perhaps a large part of that growth directed toward doing something about the problems of the underclass—it seems likely that these service-oriented programs will continue to prove to be failures. They will provide opportunities for middle-class professionals and hopefully for a few mobile persons from the underclass to earn a good and steady income but will not do much in fact to improve life for the "clients" of these services.

Only if there is a very major shift in the way Americans think about and cope with the problems of poverty, race, urban distress and the like is 1985 likely to appear much better to us in these respects than 1972.

SUGGESTED READINGS

Rich Man, Poor Man by Herman P. Miller (New York: Crowell, 1971).

The Future of Inequality by S. M. Miller and Pamela Roby (New York: Basic Books, 1970).

Section XVIII

Politics and Power

1 *James M. Graham*

Amphetamine Politics on Capitol Hill

The American pharmaceutical industry annually manufactures enough amphetamines to provide a month's supply to every man, woman and child in the country. Eight, perhaps ten, billion pills are lawfully produced, packaged, retailed and consumed each year. Precise figures are unavailable. We must be content with estimates because until 1970, no law required an exact accounting of total amphetamine production.

Amphetamines are the drug of the white American with money to spend. Street use, contrary to the popular myths, accounts for a small percentage of the total consumption. Most of the pills are eaten by housewives, businessmen, students, physicians, truck drivers and athletes. Those who inject large doses of "speed" intravenously are but a tiny fragment of the total. Aside from the needle and the dose, the "speed freak" is distinguishable because his use has been branded as illegal. A doctor's signature supplies the ordinary user with lawful pills.

All regular amphetamine users expose themselves to varying degrees of potential harm. Speed doesn't kill, but high sustained dosages can and do result in serious mental and physical injury, depending on how the drug is taken. The weight-conscious housewife, misled by the opinion-makers into believing that amphetamines can control weight, eventually may rely on the drug to alter her mood in order to face her monotonous tasks. Too frequently an amphetamine prescription amounts to a synthetic substitute for attention to emotional and institutional problems.

Despite their differences, all amphetamine users, whether on the street or in the kitchen, share one important thing in common—the initial source of supply. For both, it is largely the American pharmaceutical industry. That industry has skillfully managed to convert a chemical, with meager medical justification and considerable potential for harm, into multihundred-million-dollar profits in less than 40 years. High profits, reaped from such vulnerable products, require extensive, sustained political efforts for their continued existence. The lawmakers who have declared that possession of marijuana is a serious crime have simultaneously defended and protected the profits of the amphetamine pill-makers. The Comprehensive Drug Abuse Prevention and Control Act of 1970 in its final form constitutes a victory for that alliance over compelling, contrary evidence on the issue of amphetamines. The victory could not have been secured without the firm support of the Nixon Administration. The end result is a national policy which declares an all-out war on drugs which are *not* a source of corporate income. Meanwhile, under the protection of the law, billions of amphetamines are overproduced without medical justification.

Hearings in the Senate

The Senate was the first house to hold hearings on the administration's bill to curb drug abuse, The Controlled Dangerous Substances Act (S-3246). Beginning on September 15, 1969 and consuming most of that month, the hearings before Senator Thomas Dodd's Subcommittee to Investigate Juvenile Delinquency of the Committee on the Judiciary would finally conclude on October 20, 1969.

The first witness was John Mitchell, attorney general of the United States, who recalled President Nixon's ten-point program to combat drug abuse announced on July 14, 1969. Although that program advocated tighter controls on imports and exports of dangerous drugs and promised new efforts to encourage foreign governments to crack down on production of illicit drugs, there was not a single reference to the control of domestic manufacture of dangerous drugs. The president's bill when it first reached the Senate placed the entire "amphetamine family" in Schedule III, where they were exempt from any quotas and had the benefit of lesser penalties and controls. Hoffman-LaRoche, Inc. had already been at work; their depressants, Librium and Valium, were completely exempt from any control whatsoever.

In his opening statement, Attorney General Mitchell set the tone of administrative policy related to amphetamines. Certainly, these drugs were "subject to increasing abuse"; however, they have "widespread medical uses" and therefore are appropriately classed under the administration guidelines in Schedule III. Tight-mouthed John Ingersoll, director of the Bureau of Narcotics and Dangerous Drugs (BNDD), reaffirmed the policy, even though a Bureau study over the last year (which showed that 92 percent of the amphetamines and barbiturates in the illicit market were legitimately manufactured) led him to conclude that drug companies have "lax security and recordkeeping."

Senator Dodd was no novice at dealing with the pharmaceutical interests. In 1965 he had steered a drug abuse bill through the Senate with the drug industry fighting every step of the way. Early in the hearings he recalled that the industry "vigorously opposed the passage of (the 1965) act. I know very well because I lived with it, and they gave me fits and they gave all of us fits in trying to get it through."

The medical position on amphetamine use was first presented by the National Institute of Mental Health's Dr.

Sidney Cohen, a widely recognized authority on drug use and abuse. He advised the subcommittee that 50 percent of the lawfully manufactured pep pills were diverted at some point to illicit channels. Some of the pills, though, were the result of unlawful manufacture as evidenced by the fact that 33 clandestine laboratories had been seized in the last 18 months.

Dr. Cohen recognized three categories of amphetamine abuse, all of which deserved the attention of the government. First was their "infrequent ingestion" by students, businessmen, truck drivers and athletes. Second were those people who swallowed 50-75 milligrams daily without medical supervision. Finally, there were the speed freaks who injected the drug intravenously over long periods of time. Physical addiction truly occurs, said Dr. Cohen, when there is prolonged use in high doses. Such use, he continued, may result in malnutrition, prolonged psychotic states, heart irregularities, convulsions, hepatitis and with an even chance of sustained brain damage.

As the hearings progressed, the first two classes of abusers described by Dr. Cohen would receive less and less attention, while the third category—the speed freaks—would receive increasing emphasis. The amphetamine industry was not at all unhappy with this emphasis. In fact, they would encourage it.

Ingersoll had already said that BNDD statistics indicated that only 8 percent of illicit speed was illegally manufactured. Thomas Lynch, attorney general of California, testified that his agents had in 1967 successfully negotiated a deal for one-half million amphetamine tablets with a "Tijuana café man." Actual delivery was taken from a California warehouse. All of the tablets seized originated with a Chicago company which had not bothered to question the authenticity of the retailer or the pharmacy. Prior to the 1965 hearings, the Food and Drug Administration completed a ten-year study involving 1,658 criminal cases for the illegal sale of amphetamines and barbiturates. Seventy-eight percent of all convictions involved pharmacists, and of these convictions 60 percent were for illicit traffic in amphetamines.

The pharmacists were not the source of illicit diversion, according to the National Association of Retail Druggists (NARD) and the National Association of Chain Drug Stores. Indeed, NARD had conducted an extensive educational program combating drug abuse for years, and, as proof of it, introduced its booklet, "Never Abuse—Respect Drugs," into the record. Annual inventories were acceptable for Schedule I and II drugs, NARD continued, but were unwarranted for the remaining two schedules which coincidently included most of their wares—unwarranted because diversion resulted from forged prescriptions, theft and placebo (false) inventories.

The amphetamine wholesalers were not questioned in any detail about diversion. Brief statements by the National Wholesale Druggists Association and McKesson Robbins Drug Co. opposed separate inventories for dangerous drugs because they were currently comingled with other drugs. Finally, the massive volume of the drugs involved—primarily in Schedule III—was just too great for records to be filed with the attorney general.

Dodging the Diversion Issue

The representative of the prescription drug developers was also not pressed on the question of illicit diversion. Instead, the Pharmaceutical Manufacturers' Association requested clarifications on the definitional sections, argued for formal administrative hearings on control decisions and on any action revoking or suspending registration, and endorsed a complete exemption for over-the-counter nonnarcotic drugs.

With some misgivings, Carter-Wallace Inc. endorsed the administration bill providing, of course, the Senate would accept the president's recommendation that meprobamate not be subjected to any control pending a decision of the Fourth Circuit as to whether the drug had a dangerously depressant effect on the central nervous system. On a similar special mission, Hoffman-LaRoche Inc. sent two of its vice-presidents to urge the committee to agree with the president's recommendation that their "minor tranquilizers" (Librium and Valium) remain uncontrolled. Senator Dodd was convinced that both required inclusion in one of the schedules. The Senator referred to a BNDD investigation which had shown that from January 1968 to February 1969, three drug stores were on the average over 30,000 dosage units short. In addition, five inspected New York City pharmacies had unexplained shortages ranging from 12 to 50 percent of their total stock in Librium and Valium. Not only were the drugs being diverted, but Bureau of Narcotics information revealed that Librium and Valium, alone or in combination with other drugs, were involved in 36 suicides and 750 attempted suicides.

The drug company representatives persisted in dodging or contradicting Dodd's inquiries. Angry and impatient, Senator Dodd squarely asked the vice-presidents, "Why do you worry about putting this drug under control?" The response was as evasive as the question was direct: There are hearings pending in HEW, and Congress should await the outcome when the two drugs might be placed in Schedule III. (The hearings had begun in 1966; no final administrative decision had been reached and Hoffman-LaRoche had yet to exercise its right to judicial review.)

In the middle of the hearings, BNDD Director Ingersoll returned to the subcommittee to discuss issues raised chiefly by drug industry spokesmen. He provided the industry with several comforting administrative interpretations. The fact that he did not even mention amphetamines is indicative of the low level of controversy that the hearings had aroused on the issue. Ingersoll did frankly admit that his staff had met informally with industry representatives in the interim. Of course, this had been true from the very beginning.

The president of the American Pharmaceutical Association, the professional society for pharmacists, confirmed this fact: His staff participated in "several" Justice Department conferences when the bill was being drafted. (Subsequent testimony in the House would reveal that industry participation was extensive and widespread.) All the same, the inventory, registration and inspection (primarily "no-knock") provisions were still "unreasonable, unnecessary and costly administrative burden(s)" which would result in an even greater "paper work explosion."

For the most part, however, the administration bill had industry support. It was acceptable for the simple reason that, to an unknown degree, the "administration bill" was a "drug company bill" and was doubtless the final product of considerable compromise. Illustrative of that give-and-take process is the comparative absence of industry opposition to the transfer of drug-classification decision and research for HEW to Justice. The industry had already swallowed this and other provisions in exchange for the many things the bill could have but did not cover. Moreover, the subsequent windy opposition of the pill-makers allowed the administration to boast of a bill the companies objected to.

When the bill was reported out of the Committee on the Judiciary, the amphetamine family, some 6,000 strong, remained in Schedule III. Senator Dodd apparently had done some strong convincing because Librium, Valium and meprobamate were now controlled in Schedule III. A commission on marijuana and a declining penalty structure (based on what schedule the drug is in and whether or not the offense concerned trafficking or possession) were added.

Debate in the Senate—Round I

The Senate began consideration of the bill on January 23, 1970. This time around, the amphetamine issue would inspire neither debate or amendment. The energies of the Senate liberals were consumed instead by unsuccessful attempts to alter the declared law enforcement nature of the administration bill.

Senator Dodd's opening remarks, however, were squarely directed at the prescription pill industry. Dodd declared that the present federal laws had failed to control the illicit diversion of lawfully manufactured dangerous drugs. The senator also recognized the ways in which all Americans had become increasingly involved in drug use and that the people's fascination with pills was by no means an "accidental development": "Multihundred million dollar advertising budgets, frequently the most costly ingredient in the price of a pill, have, pill by pill, led, coaxed and seduced post-World War II generations into the 'freaked-out' drug culture. . . . Detail men employed by drug companies propagandize harried and harassed doctors into pushing their special brand of palliative. Free samples in the doctor's office are as common nowadays as inflated fees." In the version adopted by the Senate, Valium, Librium and meprobamate joined the amphetamines in Schedule III.

Hearings in the House

On February 3, 1970, within a week of the Senate's passage of S-3246, the House began its hearings. The testimony would continue for a month. Although the Senate would prove in the end to be less vulnerable to the drug lobby, the issue of amphetamines—their danger and medical justification—would be aired primarily in the hearings of the Subcommittee on Public Health of the Committee on Interstate and Foreign Commerce. The administration bill (HR 13743), introduced by the chairman of the parent committee, made no mention of Librium or Valium and classified amphetamines in Schedule III.

As in the Senate, the attorney general was scheduled to be the first witness, but instead John Ingersoll of the BNDD was the administration's representative. On the question of amphetamine diversion, Ingersoll gave the administration's response: "Registration is. . . the most effective and least cumbersome way" to prevent the unlawful traffic. This coupled with biennial inventories of all stocks of controlled dangerous drugs and the attorney general's authority to suspend, revoke or deny registration would go a long way in solving the problem. In addition, the administration was proposing stronger controls on imports and exports. For Schedules I and II, but not III or IV, a permit from the attorney general would be required for exportation. Quotas for Schedules I and II, but not III or IV, would "maximize" government control. For Schedules III and IV, no approval is required, but a supplier must send an advance notice on triple invoice to the attorney general in order to export drugs such as amphetamines. A prescription could be filled only five times in a six-month period and thereafter a new prescription would be required, whereas previously such prescriptions could be refilled as long as a pharmacist would honor them.

The deputy chief counsel for the BNDD, Michael R. Sonnenreich, was asked on what basis the attorney general would decide to control a particular drug. Sonnenreich replied that the bill provides one of two ways: Either the attorney general "finds *actual street abuse* or an interested party (such as HEW) feels that a drug should be controlled." (Speed-freaks out on the street are the trigger, according to Sonnenreich; lawful abuse is not an apparent criterion.)

The registration fee schedule would be reasonable ($10.00—physician or pharmacist; $25.00—wholesalers; $50.00—manufacturers). However, the administration did not want a formal administrative hearing on questions of registration and classification, and a less formal rule-making procedure was provided for in the bill.

Returning to the matter of diversion, Sonnenreich disclosed that from July 1, 1968 to June 30, 1969 the BNDD had conducted full-scale compliance investigations of 908 "establishments." Of this total, 329 (or about 36 percent) required further action, which included surrender of order forms (162), admonition letters (38), seizures (36) and hearings (31). In addition to these full-scale investigations, the Bureau made 930 "visits." (It later came to light that when the BNDD had information that a large supply of drugs was unlawfully being sold, the Bureau's policy was to warn those involved and "90 percent of them do take care of this matter.") Furthermore, 574 robberies involving dangerous drugs had been reported to the Bureau.

Eight billion amphetamine tablets are produced annually, according to Dr. Stanley Yolles, director of the National Institute of Mental Health, and although the worst abuse is by intravenous injection, an NIMH study found that 21 percent of all college students had taken amphetamines with the family medicine cabinet acting as the primary source—not surprising in light of the estimate that 1.1 billion prescriptions were issued in 1967 at a consumer cost of $3.9 billion. Of this total, 178 million prescriptions for amphetamines were filled at a retail cost of $692 million. No one knew the statistics better than the drug industry.

Representing the prescription-writers, the American Medical Association also recognized that amphetamines were among those drugs "used daily in practically every physician's armamentarium." This casual admission of massive lawful distribution was immediately followed by a flat denial that physicians were the source of "any significant diversion."

The next witness was Donald Fletcher, manager of distribution protection, Smith Kline & French Laboratories, one of the leading producers of amphetamines. Fletcher, who was formerly with the Texas state police, said his company favored "comprehensive controls" to fight diversion and stressed the company's "educational effort." Smith Kline & French favored federal registration and tighter controls over exports (by licensing the exporter, *not* the shipment). However, no change in present record-keeping requirements on distribution, production or inventory should be made, and full hearings on the decisions by the attorney general should be guaranteed.

The committee did not ask the leading producer of amphetamines a single question about illicit diversion. Upon conclusion of the testimony, Subcommittee Chairman John Jarman of Oklahoma commented, "Certainly, Smith Kline & French is to be commended for the constructive and vigorous and hard-hitting role that you have played in the fight against drug abuse."

Dr. William Apple, executive director of the American Pharmaceutical Association (APhA), was the subject of lengthy questioning and his responses were largely typical. Like the entire industry, the APhA was engaged in a massive public education program. Apple opposed the inventory provisions, warning that the cost would be ultimately passed to the consumer. He was worried about the attorney general's power to revoke registrations ("without advance notice") because it could result in cutting off necessary drugs to patients.

Apple admitted organizational involvement "in the draft stage of the bill" but all the same, the APhA had a "very good and constructive working relationship" with HEW. Apple argued that if the functions are transferred to Justice, "We have a whole new ball game in terms of people. While some of the experienced people were transferred from HEW to Justice, there are many new people, and they are law-enforcement oriented. We are health-care oriented." Surely the entire industry shared this sentiment, but few opposed the transfer as strongly as did the APhA.

Apple reasoned that since the pharmacists were not the source of diversion, why should they be "penalized by costly overburdensome administrative requirements." The source of the drugs, Apple said, were either clandestine laboratories or burglaries. The 1965 Act, which required only those "records maintained in the ordinary course of business" be kept, was sufficient. Anyway, diversion at the pharmacy level was the responsibility of the pharmacists—a responsibility which the APhA takes "seriously and (is) going to do a better job (with) in the future."

Congress should instead ban the 60 mail-order houses which are not presently included in the bill. (One subcommittee member said this was a "loophole big enough to drive a truck through.") The corner druggist simply was not involved in "large-scale diversionary efforts."

The Pharmaceutical Manufacturers' Association (PMA) was questioned a bit more carefully in the House than in the Senate. PMA talked at length about its "long and honorable history" in fighting drug abuse. Its representative echoed the concern of the membership over the lack of formal hearings and requested that a representative of the manufacturing interests be appointed to the Scientific Advisory Committee. Significantly, the PMA declined to take a position on the issue of transfer from HEW to Justice. The PMA endorsed the administration bill. PMA Vice-President Brennan was asked whether the federal government should initiate a campaign, similar to the one against cigarettes, "to warn people that perhaps they should be careful not to use drugs excessively." Brennan's response to this cautious suggestion is worth quoting in full:

> I think this is probably not warranted because it would have the additional effect of giving concern to people over very useful commodities. . . . There is a very useful side to any medicant and to give people pause as to whether or not they should take that medication, particularly those we are talking about which are only given by prescription, I think the negative effect would outweigh any sociological benefit on keeping people from using drugs.

"Limited Medical Use"

There was universal agreement that amphetamines are medically justified for the treatment of two very rare diseases, hyperkinesis and narcolepsy. Dr. John D. Griffith of the Vanderbilt University School of Medicine testified that amphetamine production should be limited to the needs created by those conditions: "A few thousand tablets (of amphetamines) would supply the whole medical needs of the country. In fact, it would be possible for the government to make and distribute the tablets at very little cost. This way there would be no outside commercial interests involved." Like a previous suggestion that Congress impose a one cent per tablet tax on drugs subject to abuse, no action was taken on the proposal.

The very next day, Dr. John Jennings, acting director of the Food and Drug Administration (FDA), testified that amphetamines had a "limited medical use" and their usefulness in control of obesity was of "doubtful value." Dr. Dorothy Dobbs, director of the Marketed Drug Division of the FDA further stated that there was now no warning on the prescriptions to patients, but that the FDA was proposing that amphetamines be labeled indicating among other things that a user subjects himself to "extreme psychological dependence" and the possibility of "extreme personality changes. . . (and) the most severe manifestation of amphetamine intoxication is a psychosis." Dr. Dobbs thought that psychological dependence even under a physician's prescription was "quite possible."

Congressman Claude Pepper of Florida, who from this point on would be the recognized leader of the anti-amphetamine forces, testified concerning a series of hearings which his Select Committee on Crime had held in the fall of 1969 on the question of stimulant use.

Pepper's committee had surveyed medical deans and health organizations on the medical use of amphetamines. Of 53 responses, only one suggested that the drug was useful "for *early* stages of a diet program." (Dr. Sidney Cohen of NIMH estimated that 99 percent of the total legal prescriptions for amphetamines were ostensibly for dietary control.) Pepper's investigation also confirmed a high degree of laxness by the drug companies. A special agent for the BNDD testified that by impersonating a physician, he was able to get large quantities of amphetamines from two mail-order houses in New York. One company, upon receiving an order for 25,000 units, asked for further verification of medical practice. Two days after the agent declined to reply, the units arrived. Before Pepper's committee, Dr. Cohen of NIMH testified that amphetamines were a factor in trucking accidents due to their hallucinatory effects.

Dr. John D. Griffith from Vanderbilt Medical School, in his carefully documented statement on the toxicity of amphetamines, concluded "amphetamine addiction is more widespread, more incapacitating, more dangerous and socially disrupting than narcotic addiction." Considering that 8 percent of all prescriptions are for amphetamines and that the drug companies make only one-tenth of one cent a tablet, Dr. Griffith was not surprised that there was so little scrutiny by manufacturers. Only a large output would produce a large profit.

Treatment for stimulant abuse was no easier than for heroin addiction and was limited to mild tranquilization, total abstinence and psychiatric therapy. But, heroin has not been the subject of years of positive public "education" programs nor has it been widely prescribed by physicians or lawfully produced. A health specialist from the University of Utah pointed out that the industry's propaganda had made amphetamines: "One of the major ironies of the whole field of drug abuse. We continue to insist that they are good drugs when used under medical supervision, but their greatest use turns out to be frivolous, illegal and highly destructive to the user. People who are working in the field of drug abuse are finding it most difficult to control the problem, partly because they have the reputation of being legal and good drugs."

The thrust of Pepper's presentation was not obvious from the questioning that followed, because the subcommittee discussions skirted the issue. Pepper's impact could be felt in the subsequent testimony of the executive director of the National Association of Boards of Pharmacy. The NABP objected to the use of the word "dangerous" in the bill's title because it "does little to enhance the legal acts of the physician and pharmacist in diagnosing and dispensing this type of medication." (The Controlled Dangerous Substances Act would later become the Comprehensive Drug Abuse Prevention and Control Act of 1970.)

As in the Senate hearings, Ingersoll of the BNDD returned for a second appearance and, this time, he was the last witness. Ingersoll stated that he wished "to place. . . in their proper perspective" some "of the apparent controversies" which arose in the course of testimony. A substantial controversy had arisen over amphetamines, but there was not a single word on that subject in Ingersoll's prepared statement. Later, he did admit that there was an "overproduction" of amphetamines and estimated that 75 percent to 90 percent of the amphetamines found in illicit traffic came from the American drug companies.

Several drug companies chose to append written statements rather than testifying.

Abbott Laboratories stated that it "basically" supported the administration bills and argued that because fat people had higher mortality rates than others, amphetamines were important to the public welfare, ignoring the charge that amphetamines were not useful in controlling weight. Abbott then argued that because their products were in a sustained-release tablet, they were "of little interest to abusers," suggesting that "meth" tablets per se cannot be abused and ignoring the fact that they can be easily diluted.

Eli Lilly & Co. also endorsed "many of the concepts" in the president's proposals. They as well had "participated in a number of conferences sponsored by the (BNDD) and. . . joined in both formal and informal discussions with the Bureau personnel regarding" the bill. Hoffman-LaRoche had surely watched, with alarm, the Senate's inclusion of Librium and Valium in Schedule III. They were now willing to accept all the controls applying to Schedule III drugs, including the requirements of record-keeping, inventory, prescription limits and registration as long as their "minor tranquilizers" were not grouped with amphetamines. Perhaps, the company suggested, a separate schedule between III and IV was the answer. The crucial point was that they did not want the negative association with speed and they quoted a physician to clarify this: "If in the minds of my patients a drug which I prescribe for them has been listed or branded by the government in the same category as 'goofballs' and 'pep pills' it would interfere with my ability to prescribe. . . and could create a mental obstacle to their. . . taking the drug at all."

When the bill was reported out of committee to the House, the amphetamine family was in Schedule III, and Hoffman-LaRoche's "minor tranquilizers" remained free from control.

Debate in the House—Round I

On September 23, 1970, the House moved into Committee of the Whole for opening speeches on the administration bill now known as HR 18583. The following day, the anti-amphetamine forces led by Congressman Pepper carried their arguments onto the floor of the House by way of an amendment transfering the amphetamine family from Schedule III into Schedule II. If successful, amphetamines would be subject to stricter import and export controls, higher penalties for illegal sale and possession and the possibility that the attorney general could impose quotas on production and distribution. (In Schedule III, amphetamines were exempt from quotas entirely.) Also, if placed in Schedule II, the prescriptions could be filled only once. Pepper was convinced from previous experience that until quotas were established by law the drug industry would not voluntarily restrict production.

Now the lines were clearly drawn. The House hearings had provided considerable testimony to the effect that massive amphetamine production coupled with illegal diversion posed a major threat to the public health. No congressman would argue that this was not the case. The House would instead divide between those who faithfully served the administration and the drug industry and those who argued that Congress must act or no action could be expected. The industry representatives dodged the merits of the opposition's arguments, contending that a floor amendment was inappropriate for such "far reaching" decisions.

"Legislating on the floor. . . concerning very technical and scientific matters," said subcommittee member Tim Lee Carter of Kentucky, "can cause a great deal of trouble. It can open a Pandora's Box" and the amendment which affected 6,100 drugs "would be disastrous to many companies throughout the land."

Paul G. Rogers of Florida (another subcommittee member) stated that the bill's provisions were based on expert scientific and law enforcement advice, and that the "whole process of manufacture and distribution had been tightened up." Robert McClory of Illinois, though not a member of the subcommittee, revealed the source of his opposition to the amendment:

> Frankly. . . there are large pharmaceutical manufacturing interests centered in my congressional district. . . . I am proud to say that the well-known firms of Abbott Laboratories and Baxter Laboratories have large plants in my (district). It is my expectation that C.D. Searl & Co. may soon establish a large part of its organization (there). Last Saturday, the American Hospital Supply Co. dedicated its new building complex in Lake County. . . where its principal research and related operations will be conducted.

Control of drug abuse, continued McClory, should not be accomplished at the cost of imposing "undue burdens or (by taking) punitive or economically unfair steps adversely affecting the highly successful and extremely valuable pharmaceutical industries which contribute so much to the health and welfare of mankind."

Not everyone was as honest as McClory. A parent committee member, William L. Springer of Illinois, thought the dispute was basically between Pepper's special committee on crime and the subcommittee on health and medicine chaired by John Jarman of Oklahoma. Thus phrased, the latter was simply more credible than the former. "There is no problem here of economics having to do with any drug industry."

But economics had everything to do with the issue according to Representative Jerome R. Waldie of California: "(T)he only opposition to this amendment that has come across my desk has come from the manufacturers of amphetamines." He reasoned that since the House was always ready to combat crime in the streets, a "crime that involved a corporation and its profits" logically merits equal attention. Waldie concluded that the administration's decision "to favor the profits (of the industry) over the children is a cruel decision, the consequences of which will be suffered by thousands of our young people." Pepper and his supporters had compiled and introduced considerable evidence on scientific and medical opinions on the use and abuse of amphetamines. It was now fully apparent that the evidence would be ignored because of purely economic and political considerations. In the closing minutes of debate, Congressman Robert Giaimo of Connecticut, who sat on neither committee, recognized the real issue: "Why should we allow the legitimate drug manufacturers to indirectly supply the (sic) organized crime and pushers by producing more drugs than are necessary? When profits are made while people suffer, what difference does it make where the profits go?"

Pepper's amendment was then defeated by a voice vote. The bill passed by a vote of 341 to 6. The amphetamine industry had won in the House. In two days of debate, Librium and Valium went unmentioned and remained uncontrolled.

Debate in the Senate—Round II

Two weeks after the House passed HR 18583, the Senate began consideration of the House bill. (The Senate bill, passed eight months before, continued to languish in a House committee.) On October 7, 1970, Senator Thomas Eagleton of Missouri moved to amend HR 18583 to place amphetamines in Schedule II. Although he reiterated the arguments used by Pepper in the House, Eagleton stated that his interest in the amendment was not solely motivated by the abuse by speed freaks. If the amendment carried, it would "also cut back on abuse by the weight-conscious housewife, the weary long-haul truck driver and the young student trying to study all night for his exams."

The industry strategy from the beginning was to center congressional outrage on the small minority of persons who injected large doses of diluted amphetamines into their veins. By encouraging this emphasis, the drug companies had to face questioning about illicit diversion to the "speed community," but they were able to successfully avoid any rigorous scrutiny of the much larger problem of lawful abuse. The effort had its success. Senator Thomas J. McIntyre of New Hampshire, while noting the general abuse of the drugs, stated that the real abuse resulted from large doses either being swallowed, snorted or injected.

Senator Roman Hruska of Nebraska was not suprisingly the administration and industry spokesman. He echoed the arguments that had been used successfully in the House: The amendment seeks to transfer between 4,000 and 6,000 products of the amphetamine family; "some of them are very dangerous" but the bill provides a mechanism for administrative reclassification; administration and "HEW experts" support the present classification and oppose the amendment; and, finally, the Senate should defer to the executive where a complete study is promised.

It would take three to five years to move a drug into Schedule II by administrative action, responded Eagleton. Meanwhile amphetamines would continue to be "sold with reckless abandon to the public detriment." Rather than placing the burden on the government, Eagleton argued that amphetamines should be classed in Schedule II and those who "are making money out of the misery of many individuals" should carry the burden to downgrade the classification.

Following Eagleton's statement, an unexpected endorsement came from the man who had steered two drug control bills through the Senate in five years. Senator Dodd stated that Eagleton had made "a good case for the amendment." Senator John Pastore was sufficiently astonished to ask Dodd pointedly whether he favored the amendment. Dodd unequivocally affirmed his support. Dodd's endorsement was clearly a turning point in the Senate debate. Hruska's plea that the Senate should defer to the "superior knowledge" of the attorney general, HEW and BNDD was met with Dodd's response that, if amphetamines were found not to be harmful, the attorney general could easily move them back into Schedule III. In Schedule II, Dodd continued, "only the big powerful manufacturers of these pills may find a reduction in their profits. The people will not be harmed." With that, the debate was over and the amendment carried by a vote of 40 in favor, 16 against and 44 not voting.

Dodd may have been roused by the House's failure, without debate, to subject Librium and Valium to controls which he had supported from the beginning. Prior to Eagleton's amendment, Dodd had moved to place these depressants in Schedule IV. In that dispute, Dodd knew that economics was the source of the opposition: "It is clearly evident... that (the industry) objections to the inclusion of Librium and Valium are not so much based on sound medical practice as they are on the slippery surface of unethical profits." Hoffman-LaRoche annually reaped 40 million dollars in profits—"a tidy sum which (they have) done a great deal to protect." Senator Dodd went on to say that Hoffman-LaRoche reportedly paid a Washington law firm three times the annual budget of the Senate subcommittee staff to assure that their drugs would remain uncontrolled. "No wonder," exclaimed Dodd, "that the Senate first, and then the House, was overrun by Hoffman-LaRoche lobbyists," despite convincing evidence that they were connected with suicides and attempted suicides and were diverted in large amounts into illicit channels.

By voice vote Hoffman-LaRoche's "minor tranquilizers" were brought within the control provisions of Schedule IV. Even Senator Hruska stated that he did not oppose this amendment, and that it was "very appropriate" that it be adopted so that a "discussion of it and decision upon it (be) made in the conference."

The fate of the minor tranquilizers and the amphetamine family would now be decided by the conferees of the two houses.

In Conference

The conferees from the Senate were fairly equally divided on the issue of amphetamine classification. Of the eleven Senate managers, at least six were in favor of the transfer to Schedule II. The remaining five supported the administration position. Although Eagleton was not appointed, Dodd and Harold Hughes would represent his position. Hruska and Strom Thurmond, both of whom had spoken against the amendment, would act as administration spokesmen.

On October 8, 1970, before the House appointed its conferees, Pepper rose to remind his colleagues that the Senate had reclassified amphetamines. Although he stated that he favored an instruction to the conferees to support the amendment, he inexplicably declined to so move. Instead, Pepper asked the conferees "to view this matter as sympathetically as they think the facts and the evidence they have before them will permit." Congressman Rogers, an outspoken opponent of the Pepper amendment, promised "sympathetic understanding" for the position of the minority.

Indeed, the minority would have to be content with that and little else. All seven House managers were members of the parent committee, and four were members of the originating subcommittee. Of the seven, only one would match support with "sympathetic understanding." The other six were not only against Schedule II classification, but they had led the opposition to it in floor debate: Jarman, Rogers, Carter, Staggers and Nelsen. Congressman Springer, who had declared in debate that economics had nothing to do with this issue, completed the House representation. Not a single member of Pepper's Select Committee on Crime was appointed as a conferee. On the question of reclassification, the pharmaceutical industry would be well represented.

Hoffman-LaRoche, as well, was undoubtedly comforted by the presence of the four House subcommittee conferees: The subcommittee had never made any attempt to include Valium and Librium in the bill. On that question, it is fair to say that the Senate managers were divided. The administration continued to support no controls for these depressants.

At dispute were six substantive Senate amendments to the House bill: Three concerned amphetamines, Librium and Valium; one required an annual report to Congress on advisory councils; the fifth lessened the penalty for persons who gratuitously distributed a small amount of marijuana; and the sixth, introduced by Senator Hughes, altered the thrust of the bill and placed greater emphasis on drug education, research, rehabilitation and training. To support these new programs, the Senate had appropriated $26 million more than the House.

The House, officially, opposed all of the Senate amendments.

From the final compromises, it is apparent that the Senate liberals expended much of their energy on behalf of the Hughes amendment. Although the Senate's proposed educational effort was largely gutted in favor of the original House version, an additional 25 million dollars was appropriated. The bill would also now require the inclusion in state public health plans of "comprehensive programs" to combat drug abuse and the scope of grants for addicts and drug-dependent persons was increased. The House then accepted the amendments on annual reports and the possession charge for gratuitous marijuana distributors.

The administration and industry representative gave but an inch on the amphetamine amendment: Only the liquid injectible methamphetamines, speed, would be transferred to Schedule II. All the pills would remain in Schedule III. In the end, amphetamine abuse was restricted to the mainlining speed freak. The conference report reiterated the notion that further administrative action on amphetamines by the attorney general would be initiated. Finally, Librium and Valium would not be included in the bill. The report noted that "final administrative action" (begun in 1966) was expected "in a matter of weeks." Congress was contented to await the outcome of those proceedings.

Adoption of the Conference Report

Pepper and his supporters were on their feet when the

agreement on amphetamines was reported to the House on October 14, 1970. Conferee Springer, faithful to the industry's tactical line, declared that the compromise is a good one because it "singles out the worst of these substances, which are the liquid, injectible methamphetamines and puts them in Schedule II." If amphetamine injection warranted such attention, why, asked Congressman Charles Wiggins, were the easily diluted amphetamine and methamphetamine pills left in Schedule III? Springer responded that there had been "much discussion," yes and "some argument" over that issue, but the conferees felt it was best to leave the rest of the amphetamine family to administrative action.

Few could have been fooled by the conference agreement. The managers claimed to have taken the most dangerous and abused member of the family and subjected it to more rigorous controls. In fact, as the minority pointed out, the compromise affected the least abused amphetamine: Lawfully manufactured "liquid meth" was sold strictly to hospitals, not in the streets, and there was no evidence of any illicit diversion. More importantly, from the perspective of the drug manufacturers, only five of the 6,000 member amphetamine family fell into this category. Indeed, liquid meth was but an insignificant part of the total methamphetamine, not to mention amphetamine, production. Pepper characterized the new provision as "virtually meaningless." It was an easy pill for the industry to swallow. The Senate accepted the report on the same day as the House.

Only Eagleton, the sponsor of the successful Senate reclassification amendment, would address the amphetamine issue. To him, the new amendment "accomplish(ed) next to nothing." The reason for the timid, limpid compromise was also obvious to Eagleton: "When the chips were down, the power of the drug companies was simply more compelling" than any appeal to the public welfare.

A week before, when Dodd had successfully classified Librium and Valium in the bill, he had remarked (in reference to the House's inaction): "Hoffman-LaRoche, at least for the moment, have reason to celebrate a singular triumph, the triumph of money over conscience. It is a triumph. . . which I hope will be shortlived."

The Bill Becomes Law

Richard Nixon appropriately chose the Bureau of Narcotics and Dangerous Drugs offices for the signing of the bill on November 2, 1970. Flanked by Mitchell and Ingersoll, the president had before him substantially the same measure that had been introduced 15 months earlier. Nixon declared that America faced a major crisis of drug abuse, reaching even into the junior high schools, which constituted a "major cause of street crime." To combat this alarming rise, the president now had 300 new agents. Also, the federal government's jurisdiction was expanded: "The jurisdiction of the attorney general will go far beyond, for example, heroin. It will cover the new types of drugs, the barbiturates and amphetamines that have become so common *and are even more dangerous because of their use*" (author emphasis).

The president recognized amphetamines were "even more dangerous" than heroin, although he carefully attached the qualifier that this was a result "of their use." The implication is clear: The president viewed only the large dosage user of amphetamines as an abuser. The fact that his full statement refers only to abuse by "young people" (and not physicians, truck drivers, housewives or businessmen) affirms the implication. The president's remarks contained no mention of the pharmaceutical industry, nor did they refer to any future review of amphetamine classification. After a final reference to the destruction that drug abuse was causing, the president signed the bill into law.

2 *Walter Dean Burnham*

Crisis of American Political Legitimacy

The American political system was organized and achieved its concrete behavioral reality under social, economic and international conditions which have ceased to exist in our time. The whole system is based upon several primordial elements, elements which may well be sine qua non for its survival in recognizable form. The first of these was a belief, revolutionary in its time and for many decades thereafter, in the inherent equality and dignity of the individual. Associated with this was a political machinery developed by the founders which explicitly denied that sovereign power existed anywhere within it in domestic affairs, while concentrating such sovereignty in the president so far as the country's relations with foreign powers were concerned. This denial of internal sovereignty is of course enshrined in two key elements of the Constitution: the separation of powers at the center and the centrifugal force of federalism.

Thirdly, the whole enterprise was based upon the development and maintenance of a very broad consensus within society on fundamentals involving the place of organized religion in the political system and the place of private initiative and the private sector generally in the political economy. Without such a consensus the cumbersome machinery would have collapsed; but that is another way of saying that sovereign power in the state develops historically in response to fundamental conflicts among sharply discrete social groups over control of society through politics. It represents the victory of one coalition of such groups over another and the positive use of state power to consolidate the control of the new group over the social system—for example, the bourgeoisie over pre-modern feudal and clerical elements.

In the American case, we find one spectacular example of this in the Civil War. And it is precisely here for a short season that we find the collapse of the Constitution and the development of sovereign power to an astonishing degree. The episode was temporary, though leaving some permanent residues, but it is also exceptionally instructive. Otherwise, however, the social consensus survived, changing in emphasis and shape as the society was transformed by industrialization. This consensus was essentially the ideology of liberal capitalism, coupled after the 1870s by an increasingly explicit racism which justified the reduction of the southern black to a limbo halfway between the slavery of old and genuine citizenship.

When we find ourselves in a political crisis, it is extraordinary to see how often older theorists of American politics—particularly those steeped in a juristic-institutional tradition—can illuminate the problem. An individualist, liberal-capitalist theory and practice of politics assumes by definition that the state, and above that the public, has no collective business to transact apart from the most marginal welfare and police-keeping functions. In turn this presupposes a socioeconomic system which is not dominated by collectivist concentrations of power. It also presupposes, far more than we have realized until recently, that American involvement with the outside world is episodic rather than permanent: a lack of external empire and the power structures which go with imperial world involvement.

In 1941 the late E.S. Corwin made precisely this point and coupled it with a warning for the future of American politics—and of constitutional liberty in this country, as that term had hitherto been understood. He identified two changes in the contexts of American politics which had arisen since 1929 and whose implications profoundly disturbed him. The first, of course, was the emergence of a permanent federal presence in the private sector necessitated by the collapse of free-market capitalism in the Great Depression. The second was the permanent mobilization of the United States in world politics—in a context of acute military threat.

Naturally, Corwin approached these issues from a juristic perspective which many today would describe as conservative if not reactionary. The same is even more true of the warnings which Herbert Hoover continually issued in the 1930s about the dangers of the kind of corporatist syndicalism which the New Deal was bringing into being. Yet in our own day such warnings may well be taken more and more seriously. While we cannot review all of these issues, we can give some indication of their relevance to the current crisis of political legitimacy which grips the United States.

We have argued that the American political system was set up according to a certain conception of liberty which denied the normal existence of sovereign governmental power in domestic affairs. This implied the lack of need for permanent public regulation of or intervention into the private sector. Yet during industrialization this sector had elaborated one of the great collectivist organizations of all time—the business corporation; and the corporation became and remains the dominant form of social organization in the United States. It was not long after the turn of this century that the leaders of corporate capitalism discovered the uses of public authority to achieve some rationalization of their competitive activities and to avoid some of the more ruinous implications of truly free competition.

But the Great Depression which began in 1929 revealed that such marginal public-sector efforts were not enough even to protect the basic interests of entrepreneurs and management, not to mention those of the rest of society. So permanent public-sector involvement came with the New Deal but it came without any basic change in the political system. That system remained, as before, the kind of essentially non-sovereign collection of middle-class economic and political feudalities which it had been since the end of Reconstruction.

The interaction between this archaic political system and an overwhelming demand, which it could not resist without courting social and political revolution, produced the hybrid phenomenon known as "interest-group liberalism." This in turn promptly received an ideological support base from political scientists and others who celebrated the virtures of pluralism and veto groups in the political process and of incremental change in policy outputs. Yet there were two significant problems in this rewriting of Locke, this recasting of atomistic individualism from the level of the individual to the level of the group. The first was that such a huge proportion of the American people were not actually included in the new groupist system. They belonged to no groups with political leverage, and—if not subject to outright disfranchisement and political persecution, as were the southern blacks—were excluded from the most elemental mode of participation, that is, voting.

Throughout the New Deal and down to the present time, these excluded people formed not less than two-fifths of the total adult population—concentrated, of course, at the bottom of the socioeconomic system. As the late E.E. Schattschneider pithily observed, "The flaw in the pluralist heaven is that the heavenly choir sings with a markedly upper-class accent." It is virtually impossible to overstate the importance of this steep class bias in our politics for the workings of interest-group liberalism since the New Deal.

The second major problem in interest-group liberalism was accurately pinpointed by Herbert Hoover, of all people. Such liberalism amounts to a kind of unresponsive syndicalism which can work oppression on individual human beings in several different ways. Such syndicalism rests upon the creation of very large-scale or "peak" organizations and ultimately upon power transactions between the top leadership of these organizations and the top leadership of Congress, executive agencies and independent regulatory commissions. Needless to say, the interests of the ordinary individual can and very often do get lost in this process at all levels—in the private-sector organizations themselves, in the interface transactions between peak groups and government, in the shaping of public policy and in the ordinary transactions between individual citizens and bureaucracies. This, of course, applies to individuals who are fortunate enough to be covered by the umbrellas provided by the corporation, the labor union or other group active in the pressure system. How much more forcefully does it apply to the very large fraction of the population which is outside these groups.

"Power speaks to power;" if there is any part of the "old politics" which has generated more passionate opposition among Americans than any other, it is this. Such opposition is crystallized implicitly or explicitly around the belief that there is a common public interest which trancends group negotiations; that this interest is somehow grossly violated by the power game played by peak associations and top-level government people and that legislation is or of right ought to be the product of more than the temporary balance of power among these organized groups.

Pluralists either ignore or categorically deny the existence of such a public interest at home, though they find it easy enough to discover an American national interest abroad. But this rejection of the notion of a public interest reveals the true extent to which pluralism is bourgeois ideology—a logic of justification for an established order of things. The trouble with this line of argument is that it enshrines naked power relationships among group and political elites while arguing that these processes are beneficial because of social harmony. It is laissez-faire ideology writ large. But it is vulnerable when and to the extent that individuals come to disbelieve in this harmony; and in fact, the long-term workings of this syndicalism destroy, almost dialectically, public belief in the justness of political solutions and the legitimacy of government itself. At the "end of liberalism," as Theodore Lowi has precisely argued, is a felt lack of justice, of simple human equity in the political system.

It is no wonder that academic pluralism has been so hostile to the notion of a public interest. The existence of a public interest presupposes that there is collective business to transact at home. It necessarily presupposes a fundamental opposition to the theory and practice of corporate syndicalism. To the extent that such collective business is perceived to exist, a first and very long step has been taken toward the creation of a government which is responsible not merely to the leadership of private power concentrations but to the people of the United States. The struggle to create such a government is a basic ingredient in today's political turmoil. It will go on for the foreseeable future. Only such a government is likely in the long run to generate the moral authority necessary to function effectively without resort to armed force.

Corwin was also apprehensive about the political implications of permanent mobilization of the United States in international politics. In his farewell address in 1961, President Eisenhower voiced a very similar concern when he warned against the acquisition of influence, sought or unsought, by the military-industrial complex. It is a pity that all of his successors have been so patently insensitive to this warning.

The reason for this worry is inherent in the American constitutional structure. It cannot be said often enough that the American political system is extremely archaic by comparative standards and that in foreign and military affairs it presupposes that the president will act very much like a seventeenth-century patriot king. Not only does sweepingly sovereign power exist so far as foreign and military affairs are concerned; in practice the power has been concentrated even beyond the Constitution's very broad grant in a very narrow executive elite.

Since World War II a well-known combination of factors—contextual (military threat from the Communist world), ideological (reflexive anti-communism) and economic (the possibility of large Keynesian public-sector expenditures without competition with private enterprise)—have contributed to the development of a colossal military and defense-related organizational structure. This structure ramifies throughout the political system. Four-fifths of all congressional districts now have defense installations or plants which are of more or less significance to the local economy. Perhaps one way to capture graphically the change which has occurred since Corwin wrote is to present the per capita expenditures on defense, space and military-assistance programs. In current dollars, these amounted to \$4.19 per capita in 1935, \$89.18 in 1950, \$245.97 in 1960 and \$387.75 in 1970. Even taking inflation into account, the burden of empire for the average American has grown enormously in the past generation.

The political implications of this immense proliferation in military activity and expenditure have been fundamental. In the first place, a vast new syndicalist complex has come into existence since the New Deal era. It is based squarely upon the top management of the leading industrial corporations, the political foreign-policy establishment around the president and in leading universities, the top Pentagon elite and the armed services and appropriations committees of Congress. It has been actively supported by another major element in the New Deal syndicalist coalition, the top leadership of organized labor—not only on grounds of international anti-communist ideology, but above all because where defense is, there are jobs also. Any effort to organize a domestic political movement calling for reallocation of our scarce resources and budget priorities must recognize the pervasiveness of this complex and the multitude of very large material and ideological interests which are permanently mobilized around it.

Granted the realities of international power configurations since World War II, it would be unrealistic to argue that defense and related burdens on American resources can be done away with or that they are not needed. But even if we cannot dismantle the military-industrial-academic complex if we would, the future of American domestic politics depends in a very real sense upon whether this immense set of power concentrations can be tamed and made politically accountable. This complex represents at its highest point of development the syndicalist interest-group liberalism which has dominated American politics. Perhaps the supreme example of the coercions which play upon the little man who is subject to power he cannot begin to control is the drafting of young men to fight in a war which was initiated entirely by the president and his narrow elite of military, civilian and academic advisers.

It is not possible to devote much time here to the Vietnam War. It has vastly accelerated the domestic political crisis in the United States and may even come to be viewed in retrospect as the most durably influential such experience since the Civil War itself. The decision to make war in Vietnam captures the essence of Corwin's worries about the operation of this political system under conditions of permanent imperial involvement in the outside world. It was an executive decision. It was made by a president who had campaigned a few months earlier on a pledge not to do so. The president so acted with the advice and consent not of the Senate but of a rarified elite of advisers who were accountable to no one but themselves and the chief executive. But it was also a decision which ordinary people had to pay for—in the case of 50,000 young men, with their lives. Naturally, the latter point, not less than the barbarously inhumane methods by which this war was and is being carried on, contributed immensely to the volcanic alienation of college youth and others in the late 1960s. But these considerations, however important, should not deflect our view from the core of the issue which the war has raised. This issue, baldly put, involves the ascendancy of a narrow executive-military elite in our politics and the absence of any organized institutional means for restraining the exercise of that power.

Lurking just beneath the once calm surface of American politics is a fundamental constitutional crisis, the gravest indeed since the Civil War a century ago. On the domestic scene the syndicalist politics of groups has produced in dialectical contradiction waves of antagonistic mobilizations and countermobilizations. The final product of the old politics of interest-group liberalism is the wavelike spread of acute relative deprivation feelings among more and more people. This is so not only because such a system "lacks justice" in Lowi's abstract sense, but because concretely it tends to operate only in response to organized pressures and protests. Action and reaction lead to ever wider senses of frustration and alienation; power groups proliferate at all levels; and the system jams in its practical operation while its very legitimacy suffers cumulative erosion. On the international front we find ourselves half-republic, half-empire; and one may doubt that this house divided can indefinitely survive divided any more successfully than did the house of which Lincoln spoke a century ago.

A number of revolutions have been unfolding during the past generation and pushing us toward and beyond the present political crisis. We have discussed the two most basic—the post-1929 revolution in political economy and the imperium revolution. But there have been others.

1) The demographic revolution. This involves the social and political effects of an enormous exchange of population since 1945: the urbanization of American blacks (and other groups such as Puerto Ricans and Chicanos) and the massive middle-class white flight from central cities to suburbs.

2) The civil-rights revolution and the political mobilization of the black and the poor, a revolution which, by destablilizing race relations and destroying the repressive compromise of 1877, has also effectively destroyed the old New Deal political coalition.

3) The combined education and media revolutions, themselves the product of increased economic affluence in American society. The education revolution has in a sense created the conditions, at least, for the emergence of a college-based class for itself among young people with common concerns and political values. But the media revolution may prove at least as important. In a very curious way, it has permitted people who are physically separated but have common interests and problems to find one another. Moreover, it has drastically reduced the costs of political information and—even more subversively, from an official point of view—has permitted ordinary people to judge for themselves the falsity of official pronouncements about such basic events as the Vietnam War. The two revolutions together are producing a very large group of Americans who are well educated, who are politically committed and who are independent actors in the political arena.

4) Closely associated with both preceding revolutions—and the industrial affluence which underlies both—is a very far-reaching cultural revolution. One need not accept all of Charles Reich's pieties or naivetes in *The Greening of America* to realize that, among growing numbers of people—young and not so young—the traditional bonds and moral imperatives of such elemental social groupings as organized religion and the family, not to mention those of the old puritan work ethic, are rapidly dissolving. A worldwide crisis of authority is going on: as J. H. Plumb has pointed out, basic social institutions which in one form or another go back to the Neolithic era have suddenly become visibly fragile if not evanescent.

One primary feature of this cultural revolution is that—with all its bizarre and even repellent manifestations—an active search is going on for a new meaning in the lives of individuals. When old social myths and mazeways collapse, when they lose their coercive moral authority, predictably strange things happen to people in society. Group struggles and personal anxieties increase drastically. Some people move into politics with the kind of "Puritan saint" commitment of which Michael Walzer has written. Cults flourish, along with chiliastic and millenarian movements; "the end of the world" in one form or another seems remarkably close at hand to many. Ultimately, the quest is for revitalization: for some new set of social myths and routines which, because people come to believe in them, have the power to reintegrate this social chaos in some new and acceptable order.

Unhappily such conditions are not the stuff of which political pluralism or incremental bargaining in the policy process are made. They appear in fact to be essential ingredients of every truly revolutionary situation; and that is because, consciously or not, increasing numbers of people are searching for a reconstruction of themselves through a reconstruction of the social order itself. What they seek they will find, though not necessarily in the form that any individual might either foresee or desire a priori. At the same time, what makes revolutions what they are is the fact that this drive for revitalization, for political and social reconstruction, always encounters increasingly desperate resistance not only from established elites but from very broad masses of the population. Revolutions are virtually never matters of unanimous consent: the very revitalization which becomes psychically necessary to the person who supports the revolution becomes psychically intolerable to the person who cannot imagine his survival without his traditional beliefs.

If all the foregoing has some relationship to today's reality, several propositions can be made about the near future of American politics:

The overall thrust of our revolutions, especially the last, is to rediscover the worth and dignity of the individual, be his social estate never so low. It is also to attack the fundamental legitimacy of political decisions based upon syndicalist bargains among elites and of the political processes by which such decisions are made.

The political thrust of these revolutions is aimed squarely against the coercive power of Big Organization, whether nominally public or nominally private. One very difficult question is the extent to which such attacks can proceed before they compromise or destroy the capacity of these organizations to perform their functions. In any case, the political organization of prisoners in jails, the emergence of storefront lawyers and many other signs of the times have come into being to give the little man the elemental leverage on his life that interest-group liberalism has denied him.

To the extent that the contemporary crisis in American politics is founded in a far-reaching if uneven collapse in traditionally held values, it can be resolved only through revitalizations of some sort. Whatever this revitalization turns out to be at the end, one thing is certain: it will not be liberal, for Lowi is quite right in claiming that liberalism has really come to an end.

Because of this, it seems increasingly certain that American political processes and structures will undergo profound transformation before the end of this century. It is possible that this change, when it occurs, will be revolutionary (or counter-revolutionary); it will in any case be sweeping in practical operation, even though the forms of the Constitution itself may not change very much. In view of the tremendous durability of this archaic political system, such a prediction seems rash, to say the least. But it is based upon certain basic propositions: first, that the system cannot operate without consensus on social fundamentals; second, that such consensus is now very rapidly disappearing; and third, that political involvement with both the value and operational problems of American society will of necessity create permanent sovereign political power resources in its national government. To the extent that the existing operation of American politics is based upon the denial of such sovereign power, it can hardly survive such a transition in recognizable form.

There is no reason to suppose with Charles Reich that the cultural revolution must succeed or that revitalization centered around its rediscovery of the individual's human, social and political needs must prevail. Indeed, it is very unlikely to prevail without political organizations which collectively concentrate the power of individuals and which will therefore articulate new needs in an organizationally familiar way. Every revolution has its counter-revolution, and counter-revolutions sometimes succeed.

The genius of American politics, as its past history abundantly demonstrates, has lain in the capacity of the system as a whole to undergo renewal and revitalization through critical realignments in the electorate and in the policy structure. Thus far the revolutionary thrust of the present-day changes we have discussed has been contained remarkably well through the existing instrumentalities of politics. But a trade-off is required sooner or later: at some point the old must yield at least partially to the new or resort to force, to breaking the system in the name of its preservation, and the preservation of the ascendancy of the old. If one thinks as a whole about all of the revolutions we have discussed, the most striking thing about them is that they point in increasingly polar-opposite directions. The older revolutions in political economy and world politics taken together point to a state with an explicitly clearly defined ruling class based upon an oligarchy of sydicalist elites and one whose leaders deal with revolutions abroad and discontent at home in an increasingly militarized, technocratic way.

The newer revolutions in media, education and culture have served to mobilize groups whose former passivity and non-participation have been essential preconditions for the smooth operation of the syndicalist welfare-warfare state. The Vietnam War somehow crystallizes for the newer America what has gone wrong with our national life under its bipartisan ruling class. It spells out for this newer America how far the syndicalist leadership of the old order has been prepared to drift away from the humane premises of the Republic in their pursuit of ideology, interest and, it may be, Empire. It is the dialectical polarization which our revolutions have generated, taken together in the same period of time, which has fueled the present crisis and which has eroded the legitimacy of the existing political order.

Now few sensible people seriously think that all the ills or dysfunctions of a social order undergoing such massive doses of change can be resolved by politics. But few would doubt either that politics is somehow integrally related to redefining the terms of conflict and compromise among major social forces. It seems to me that we have about reached the point in our national life where a clear breakthrough of the newer forces in American politics cannot be longer deferred without catastrophic intermediate-run consequences for the prospects of political freedom in the United States. Realignments have been the price which American politics pays for timely change which does not foreclose future options and which does not short-circuit the system into authoritarianism. A realignment is obviously due if not overdue: and this is clearly what the political struggles of 1968 and 1972 have been all about. If the old America, working through its entrenched syndicalist groups, can effectively choke off this peaceful revolutionary upsurge, I would regard the future of the Republic as very dim indeed.

Political forces such as those which are now on the move represent objective conflicts in society; these conflicts are long-term; and very broadly, they can be settled only by peaceful if rapid change, by violent revolution or by authoritarian reaction with clearly fascist overtones. The first alternative presupposes that the rot of syndicalism at home and of imperialism abroad has not gone so far that democratic revitalization has become excluded as a practical option. It presupposes that we have not yet crossed the point of no return on the march to the construction of the *Imperium Americanum*. This may seem to some an heroic assumption, but all the returns are not quite in yet. The second alternative is virtually certain to fail as such: but the danger is very real that newer America may be driven by desperation to violent collisions with the established political order if they cannot gain access to it peacefully. Such collisions would serve, in all probability, to speed up the processes involved in the third solution, one which carries out the implications of syndicalism and militarized foreign policy to their logical extreme. To the extent that manifest destiny dominates the political-economy and foreign-policy revolutions of our time—as an orthodox Marxist, for example, might well argue—it must candidly be said that this third option would clearly be the most likely one.

But this is to foreclose a future which has not yet occurred, in the name of a social and political determinism which cannot rest upon an adequate scientific basis. The precise point is that struggle is going on. This struggle is over peaceful penetration of democratic elements into an elite-controlled political system. But in a larger, perhaps almost mystical sense, the struggle is for the American soul. On its outcome, in my view, literally hangs the future of human freedom in United States.

SUGGESTED READINGS

Hopes and Fears of the American People by Albert H. Cantril and Charles W. Roll, Jr. (New York: Universe Books, 1971).

Why Men Rebel by Ted Robert Gurr (Princeton: Princeton University Press, 1970).

The End of Liberalism by Theodore J. Lowi (New York: Norton, 1969).

Pentagon Capitalism by Seymour Melman (New York: McGraw-Hill, 1970).

3 *William J. Crotty*

Presidential Assassinations

American exposure to assassination represents a recent occurrence, or so most would like to believe. On November 22, 1963 President John F. Kennedy was murdered while on a political trip to Dallas. People were shocked. The world's mightiest government momentarily staggered. An investigation was initiated into the events surrounding the act with the intention of fixing responsibility for the murder.

The Warren Commission Report, as it became known, was a comprehensive although not flawless examination of the assassination. The report's conclusions, despite a continuing controversy, were generally accepted by the American people. Within five years of John Kennedy's assassination, his brother Robert was murdered while seeking the Democratic nomination for the presidency. Robert Kennedy's assassination followed almost two months to the day the killing of the Reverend Martin Luther King, black civil rights leader and the adaptor of Gandhian principles of non-violence to the turbulent racial crises of the 1960s. Between the deaths of the two Kennedys and Dr. King, at least two other political leaders representing polar extremes of political philosophy, Medgar Evers, the NAACP leader in Mississippi dedicated to achieving peaceful electoral participation of blacks, and Lincoln Rockwell, a fascist and outspoken head of the revived American-German Party, were assassinated.

The continuing assassinations in concert with a decade of seemingly endless violence brought serious concern to Americans. While assassinations, it turns out, are not unknown in the United States, these acts were new to the consciousness of the vast majority of living Americans.

The immediate outcry was one of confusion. Was America a sick society? Was some sinister long-range plot wreaking its vengeance? Was the United States headed toward a new era of open political warfare and potential police-state repression? Was the delicate fabric of American social and moral behavior collapsing?

Assassinations of political consequence can be defined as the murder of an individual, whether of public prominence or not, in an effort to achieve political gain. The classic conception of the assassination act is as a tactic in struggles for political power. Julius Caesar was assassinated by a group of friends and senators who feared the evil consequences of his great power; the legendary Rasputin was assassinated by Prince Felix Yusupov and a coconspirator who resented his evil influence over the Czar; two premiers of Japan, Hanaguchi and Inuiki, plus a number of cabinet officials were assassinated by political opponents in pre-World War II Japan. Each of these assassinations and the vast majority that stud the pages of history had explicitly political motives behind them.

This definition of assassination must be modified to have meaning within the American context. The statement assumes an element of rationality in the planning of the murder as it relates to the achievement of specified political objectives. Any assassin will deliberate on how to assault his victim—the time, the place, the weapon to be used, the nature of the encounter and so on. The concept of rationality is not intended to convey the idea of the preplanning of the details of the act. Rather, it means that the execution of the victim has a tangible relationship to a policy goal the conspirators wish to achieve. In other words it is motivated by political concerns. The chief factor isolating assassinations in the United States from those in other countries hinges on this distinction.

Lonely Figures

It can be argued with some limited support that the assassinations of prominent American political leaders, or at least of presidents, are best understood as individual acts that result from the pathological drives of the killer. All of the presidential assassins have been lonely figures, mentally unstable and through these murders have acted out inner fantasies. Such explanations may be partially acceptable for explaining simple acts; they are of little value for understanding the persistence of the murders over time or their broader implications. Why should an individual choose a public personage as his target if he is irrationally responding to internal needs? Why after seemingly peaceful interludes do assassinations reoccur? Why are assassinations more frequent in one nation than another? An approach that focuses on the peculiarities of a given assassination or number of assassinations cannot begin to address such questions. Assassinations are social acts with broad political consequences. They cannot be treated as isolated phenomena and thus not subject to systematic, comparative analysis or interpretation. Rather, they are acts that reflect a variety of cultural forces and social conditions, culminating in bizarre outlets for personal behavior.

A classification of assassinations can serve to explain patterns of assassination in the United States compared to other nations. Assassinations can be divided into five categories.

☐ *Anomic assassination* is the murder of a political figure for essentially private reasons. The justification for the act is couched in broadly political terms, but the relationship between the act and the advancement of the political objectives specified is impossible to draw on any rational basis. The connecting link then is assumed to be the fantasies of the assassin. This type of act is the most familiar to those concerned with presidential assassinations.

☐ *Elite substitution* is the murder of a political leader in order to replace him or those he represents in power with an opposing group at essentially the same level. The palace guard assassination of a dictator or the power struggle among groups for governmental leadership would result in this type of assassination. The continuing blood struggle between the Karageorgevich and Oberenovich dynasties in Serbia is a case in point. Transfer of power through elite assassination became almost a matter of court routine in nineteenth-century Turkey.

□ *Tyrannicide* is one of the oldest forms of assassination and the one with the greatest philosophical justification—the murder of a despot in order to replace him with one more amenable to the people and needs of a nation. That assassination developed beyond the simple act to the preoccupation with tyrannicide and regicide in particular can be traced to the latter half of the nineteenth century. The struggles in Russia against the czar developed the systematic and tactical use of assassination as a broad-scale political weapon. The intention was to punish the government or its minions for specified acts, to decentralize and weaken it and eventually to incapacitate it. This in turn developed into a fourth type of assassination.

□ *Terroristic assassination* can be employed on a mass basis to demonstrate a government's incapacity to deal with insurgents, to neutralize a populace's allegiance to a government, to enlist their support in a revolutionary movement or, more ambitiously, to allow a minority to suppress and subjugate a population. Examples of mass terror in history are many. The era associated with the French Revolution, the Inquisition, the Russian purges of the 1930s, the Mau Mau rebellion in Kenya during the 1950s, the Nazi persecutions, the American South following the Civil War and the terror used by the Viet Cong in the rural provinces of South Vietnam are examples of the systematic use of assassinations by an organized group within a population to achieve political goals.

The terror can be random, choosing targets for no reason indigenous to the victim. The intention is to erode any faith in the government and intimidate the population. In this, the terrorists are willing to deliberately murder innocents to achieve their broader objectives.

A case study in random mass terrorism was the Algerian nationalists' fight against the French. Reportedly in the first three years of the terrorism (November 1954 to November 1957) the Algerian rebels assassinated 8,429 civilians of whom only 1,126 were Europeans. The rest were brother Moslems. Curiously, the OAS (the Secret Army Organization of French Algerians) resorted to mass terror when it became apparent that the De Gaulle government was willing to accede to an independent Algeria. During the latter part of 1961 and early 1962, the OAS was credited with responsibility for 500 deaths in Algeria.

Terroristic assassinations directed toward specified categories of civilians or officials represents a more limited and systematic attempt to achieve the same ends as mass terror assassinations. The Viet Cong focused on village leaders, allegedly killing or kidnapping over 2,400 in the period 1957-1959, with an additional 7,982 civil officials assassinated and 40,282 abducted in the period 1961-1965. Macedonian, Armenian and Bulgarian terror directed against their Turkish rulers at the turn of the century are other examples of more discrete, highly specific assassination strategies.

□ *Propaganda by deed* is a type of assassination employed to direct attention to a broader problem (for example, the subjugation of a people) with the hopes of bringing some alleviation. The assassinations during the 1950s by the Algerian nationalists were of this nature, although the volume of political murders would have to place them in the category of mass terror. The French colonial OAS organization in the early 1960s attempted to assassinate military figures and journalists in Paris to direct the attention of the French people to their difficulties. The assassination of Czar Alexander II was in part for propaganda purposes, as was the assassination attempt directed against President Truman and the explanation given for Senator Robert Kennedy's assassination. In Truman's case the Puerto Rican nationalists hoped to publicize their cause, independence for Puerto Rico, through their attack on the president. Sirhan Sirhan, the Jordanian immigrant who murdered Robert Kennedy, wanted to emphasize the plight of the Arab nations and the supposed favoritism shown Israel by Kennedy.

A comparison of the level of assassinations in the United States with other nations reveals a disquieting fact: the United States has a disturbingly high level of political assassinations. By virtually any measure, this country ranks near the top of any list of political assassinations. For the fifty-year period 1918-1968, information on assassinations and attempted assassinations reveals that the United States ranked thirtieth of the 89 nations studied. In another study of the frequency of assassinations for a more recent time period—the two decades immediately following the Second World War—the United States ranked fifth among the 84 nations analyzed.

Ivo Feierabend and his associates, in their comparative study of assassinations cross-nationally during this latter period, uncovered a number of interesting relationships. They demonstrated, for example, an association between a high incidence of political assassination and social disruption and political instability in a nation. Assassinations were also related to less developed nations and those in transitory economic situations, cases to which both France and the United States proved to be curious exceptions. There was a strong relationship between assassinations and politically violent acts more generally; in fact, the incidence of specified types of politically violent occurrences represented one of the most consistent predictors of assassination. The link with violence—both violent acts directed against other nations and internally violent events of political significance—was clearcut.

Carl Leiden and associates, in reviewing assassinations for the entire 50-year period, argue much the same relationship between political stress in a nation (as manifested in politically violent events) and a high level of assassinations. In noting that four periods accounted for 70 percent of the assassinations that took place over the entire five decades, they point out that each was a time of unusual political turbulence. The years 1919-1923 represented the immediate post-World War I period; 1932-1934 encompassed the heart of the Great Depression; 1946-1951 witnessed the readjustment after World War II; and 1963-1966 highlighted the midpoint of a decade noted for its political unrest.

Many commonalities appear in the assassination attempts directed against American presidents or presidential candidates. A convenient way of examining those factors is to arbitrarily divide the assassination acts into similarities common to the intended victims and those associated with the assailants.

The Targets

One explanation for the assassinations that has enjoyed some vogue develops the assumption that certain types of politicians attract would-be assassins. The argument really breaks into two subthemes, one stressing a psychological interpretation of a politican's approach to life and the other dealing with the nature of political demands and the officeholder's reaction to these.

Some contend that certain personalities entertain an implicit death wish. These individuals are attracted to high-risk occupations. While politics does not compare to auto racing, it does represent a precarious calling and does prove attractive to adventuresome types. High-risk politicians are characterized by a willingness to extend themselves—actually overextend themselves—in seeking to advance their careers. They are willing to expose themselves to dangerous situations, possibly even subconsciously seek out such encounters, assumedly to satisfy internal psychological drives.

Robert Kennedy purportedly represents a prime example of this thesis. The senator's death wish, or at least his willingness to open himself to personal hurt, evidenced itself in private life in such treacherous pastimes as mountain climbing, navigating waterways such as the Amazon, and shooting dangerous rapids. He was known for his love of other physically taxing sports. In public life, the same drive surfaced in his pushing to the limits of physical stamina in the incessant campaigns, the tumultuous motorcades and the large and engulfing crowds regularly featured on the candidate's itinerary. This strain of argument contends that an individual places himself in situations that if not inviting attack permit the conditions that make it a possibility. Similar contentions were heard after John Kennedy's death. In retrospect, Theodore Roosevelt would fit this mold rather nicely also. After being shot by John Schrank when leaving a Milwaukee hotel to make a campaign speech, he insisted on making his speech although carrying the bullet in his chest and bleeding profusely.

The validity of such arguments cannot be easily assessed. They depend for verification upon an in-depth analysis by experts of the psychological mechanisms that motivate individual personalities. But it is unlikely that explanations of this nature can serve to develop a general understanding of political behavior as it relates to violent personal attacks. Whether such an explanation applies to the Kennedys is a moot point. McKinley, Garfield, Franklin Roosevelt and Truman do not appear to fit the theory.

At best, it is an explanation sufficient for understanding individual cases one by one. It serves to divert attention from broader and more important themes that focus on an interlocking network of circumstantial and situational factors that at least offer hope of remedy.

A second type of argument emphasizes the image and intentions of the victim rather than his psychological drives. This school of thought claims that the presidents most prone to physical attack are those who challenge the status quo. The movers, the doers in office and those seeking election who associate themselves with change invite controversy and become targets for the frustrations of those inclined toward political murder.

Robert Kennedy as a leader of the New Politics and champion of the Negro, Mexican-American and the young appears to have been such an individual. John Kennedy may have seemed an innovator to his contemporaries. Franklin Roosevelt certainly introduced basic changes into American society. On the other extreme, Herbert Hoover and Dwight Eisenhower appeared to be complacent, less innovative presidents, and they were not attacked.

The argument claims a superficial credibility, but it does not hold up under examination. John Kennedy, while a personally glamorous figure, was not a particularly rash or disruptive president by present assessments. It appears that his reputed assassin, Lee Harvey Oswald, previously attempted to kill retired General Edwin Walker, a hero of the far Right. It is difficult to ascertain the link between Oswald's two targets, unless it lies within the killer rather than his victims. Indeed, Robert Kennedy was a product of the Old Politics more than the new, as was his brother. A more reasonable target, if this line of reasoning is extended to its logical end, was Eugene McCarthy. Senator McCarthy successfully mobilized and personified throughout his own 1968 presidential nomination campaign the politically charged elements of dissent within the United States. Further, Robert Kennedy's assassin, Sirhan, offered a different explanation for his attack. Senator Kennedy's support of Israel, a minor point in his prenomination campaign, was Sirhan's stimulus to attack. Beyond this, the love-hate relationship (as perceived by the murderer) with the politician offers another explanation of Sirhan's behavior, but again one that deals with the psychological workings of the assassin and is difficult to relate to his victim.

Franklin D. Roosevelt was an unquestioned mover, a prime molder of the domestic economic system of modern America. His achievements were profound, far outlasting his stewardship. Certainly he is the most powerful example to be offered in support of this line of contention.

Yet Giuseppe Zangara attacked Roosevelt after his election and prior to his inauguration, well in advance of any indications of the impact the president-elect would have on the country. The Democratic party platform Roosevelt had run on in the 1932 election was a conservative document and Roosevelt's campaign oratory was not designed to alarm anyone.

Zangara was concerned with the office, not the man. He believed it to be a symbol of oppression and disregard for the problems that beset the ordinary citizen. Zangara justified his action as striking a blow on behalf of the poor men of the world against capitalism. That Roosevelt, given his place in history and the contemporary groups that opposed him, should symbolize the rejection of the common man is anomalous.

Zangara was an Italian immigrant. Before leaving Italy, by his own admission, he desired to assassinate King Victor Emmanuel III for the same reasons he later employed to justify his attack on Roosevelt. He also intended to assassinate Presidents Coolidge and Hoover, hardly symbols of change, but he never had the opportunity. The factor that distinguished Franklin Roosevelt as a target for assassination from either Hoover or Coolidge, or for that matter the king of Italy, was not his personality, his politics, or his potential impact on national politics, but the opportunity that he accidentally gave Zangara. Roosevelt happened to appear in Miami for a speech while Zangara was living there. While not a chief of state at the time, he was the president-elect, which was good enough for his assailant.

Zangara made the point unmistakably clear at his own trial. When asked if he would have attacked President Hoover he replied, "I see Mr. Hoover first I kill him first. Make no difference. President just the same bunch—all same. No make no difference who get that job. Run by big money. Makes no difference who he is."

It is difficult to envision Presidents Garfield or McKinley as significant threats to the status quo. The classification of Presidents Jackson and Truman and, at the time, presidential candidate Theodore Roosevelt, would depend on one's interpretation of their role in and contribution to the political development of the United States. Lincoln certainly must be regarded as a president who had a fundamental impact on his society. Overall, however, the evidence for this particular line of reasoning is not persuasive. The argument has an intrinsic popular appeal, but it is not substantiated by what is known concerning the assassinations.

The Assassins

Discernible patterns do emerge when the focus shifts from the victims to their assailants. First, and of greatest importance, only two of the nine attempts on the lives of presidents or presidential candidates can be considered the work of a conspiracy (see Table 1). And of these two, the Booth plot against President Lincoln was a pickup conspiracy involving friends and acquaintances of his, and the attempt on President Truman was little more. The attack against Lincoln was not known or supported by the southern Confederacy, which it was intended to help, and only conjectural evidence can be cited to implicate Lincoln's Secretary of War, Edwin M. Stanton, directly or indirectly in a coup d'etat.

The attempt by Oscar Collazo and Griselio Torresola to storm Blair House, the temporary residence of the president, and attack Harry Truman was a conspiracy, but a poorly conceived and ineptly executed one. The potential assassins were members of a Puerto Rican liberationist group centered in New York. They traveled to Washington with the intention of murdering the president as a symbolic propaganda act designed to draw attention to Puerto Rico's plight. The scheme was born of blind fanaticism. Truman had done more than any of his predecessors in recognizing the island's difficulties and in attempting to stabilize its political and economic conditions. Nonetheless, he was the intended victim by virtue of the office he held. What tangible public benefit could be expected to accrue from the attack is difficult to conceive. The attempt was not designed to gain control of the government, quite obviously, or to give an opposition leader or party political advantage, classic objectives in traditional assassination conspiracies.

The conspirators themselves had only the most freewheeling of plans for gaining access to the president and engaged in the sketchiest of preparatory planning. The effort resulted in a wild gun battle leading to the deaths of Torresola, one Secret Service agent, and the wounding of two other agents and Collazo and the eventual imprisonment of the latter for life.

People find it difficult to understand how one lone, demented gunman can bring down the most powerful leader on earth. A pressing necessity exists to explain the murder in broader and more acceptable terms. Rather than a quirk happening, the act is reconstructed as part of a well-conceived plan with important ramifications. People want to believe that Oswald was a Communist agent, a representative of a right-wing hate group, or the tool of the CIA. Facets of his confused background could be interpreted to lend support to each of these possibilities. Richard Lawrence was accused of being the gunman of a Whig conspiracy designed to intimidate President Andrew Jackson. John Wilkes Booth and his accomplices were considered agents of the South. Charles Giteau supposedly represented the Republican party faction—the Stalwarts—that opposed Garfield. President McKinley's assassin, Leon Czolgosz, reportedly executed the wishes of the anarchists, a group that paid dearly for this asseumption. And Zangara was said to be carrying out the orders of mobsters—one rumor had it that his intended target was Mayor Anton Cermak of Chicago whom he did in fact kill and not President-elect Franklin Roosevelt.

An element of psychological reassurance resides in attempts to attribute assassinations to conspiracies. However, these speculations are fed by more than the individual's desire to relieve his mental anguish. The nature of the American presidency has grown in the mythology of the times far out of proportion to the presumed abilities of one man to fill it. The president assumes the attributes of a god, a king, a political leader without equal, the super-American in every respect. In contrast, the British divorce the traditional and symbolic roles (in the person of the king or queen) from the seat of actual political power, and they also discourage interpretations of the prime minister as the sole mover of events. While the American presidency has been humanized through media incredibly intrusive into every aspect of the occupant's life, paradoxically the president at the same time assumes almost superhuman dimensions.

The protective paraphernalia that surrounds the president reinforces an image of invincibility. All are familiar with the much publicized Secret Service and their role in providing for the safety of the president and his family. Television constantly exposes even the casual viewer to the

Table 1 – Presidential Assassinations and Assaults

Assailant	*Target*	*Date of Attack*	*Outcome*	*Activity of Victim at Time of Attack*	*Age*	*Assailant's Occupation*	*Weapon*	*Place of Birth*
ASSASSINATIONS:								
John Wilkes Booth	President **Abraham Lincoln**	4/14/1865	Lincoln's Death 4/15/1865	Attending "Our American Cousin" at Ford's Theatre, Washington, D.C.	26	Actor	Pistol	U.S. (1st generation born in U.S.)
Charles Julius Giteau	President **John Garfield**	7/2/1881	Garfield's Death 9/19/1881	Waiting to board train for vacation trip, Washington, D.C.	38	Lawyer, Lecturer, Evangelist	Pistol	U.S.
Leon F. Czolgosz	President **William McKinley**	9/6/1901	McKinley's Death 9/14/1901	Standing in receiving line, Pan-American Exposition, Buffalo, N.Y.	28	Mill Worker	Pistol	U.S. (1st generation born in U.S.)
Lee Harvey Oswald	President **John F. Kennedy**	11/22/1963	Kennedy's Death 11/22/1963	Motorcade through Dallas, Texas	24	Worker in Book Depository	Rifle	U.S.
Sirhan Sirhan	Senator **Robert F. Kennedy** Candidate for Democratic Presidential Nomination	6/5/1968	Kennedy's Death 6/5/1968	Returning from talk claiming victory in Calif. Democratic Primary, Los Angeles, Calif.	24	Stable boy, Clerk	Pistol	Jordan
ASSAULTS:								
Richard Lawrence	President **Andrew Jackson**	1/30/1835	Pistols misfired, Jackson unhurt	Leading funeral procession for deceased Congressman, Washington, D.C.	36	House Painter	Pistols	England
John Schrank	Presidential Candidate **Theodore Roosevelt**	10/14/1912	Roosevelt wounded, but survived	Leaving hotel to make campaign speech, Milwaukee, Wisc.	36	Bartender, Landlord	Pistol	Bavaria
Giuseppe Zangara	President-Elect **Franklin D. Roosevelt**	2/15/1933	Missed Roosevelt, killed Mayor Anton Cermak of Chicago standing near FDR	Speaking at political rally, Miami, Florida	32	Construction Worker	Pistol	Italy
Oscar Collazo and **Griselio Torresola**	President **Harry F. Truman**	10/31/1950	President unhurt; 1 Secret Service Agent killed, 2 wounded; Torresola killed; Collazo wounded	Assailants stormed Blair House, temporary residence of President, Washington, D.C.	36 25	Metal Polisher None	Pistols	Puerto Rico Puerto Rico

presidential guardians in their supposedly unobtrusive execution of their duties. The president's car with its various gimmicks, including the famed (and as it later turns out) non-bulletproof bubble-top is well publicized, an object of curiosity every time he appears in a motorcade. Certainly with such an office, such a man and such protection, one sick gunman, it is thought, could not be the true explanation for assassination—a devilishly clever group of conspirators must have designed a plan to penetrate the impenetrable defenses around the president's life.

As with most erroneous beliefs that large numbers of people persist in subscribing to, there must be some credibility attached to them, some reason for believing. The ineptitude surrounding the immediate events following President Kennedy's assassination and the history of occurrences since then lend support to a wide range of conspiratorial theories. The events developing out of the assassination were poorly handled. Without straining, a variety of questions can be put forward for which no satisfactory answers exist. Why didn't a Secret Service man drive the route immediately preceding the presidential motorcade seeking trouble spots? Why didn't anyone of the spectators who saw Oswald with a rifle in the window awaiting the presidential party mention it to the police officers standing with them? Why did the president's car slow down after the first shot rather than speeding away? Why wasn't the hospital alerted to receive the mortally wounded president? Why weren't contingency plans immediately available for implementation? Why wasn't the Texas School Book Depository sealed off, if not immediately, then as soon as the police had an indication the shot had come from there? Why wasn't a record kept of Oswald's interrogation (in which the Secret Service, the FBI, the Texas Rangers, the county prosecutor's office and the Dallas police all participated)? Why wasn't Oswald allowed legal counsel? Why wasn't Oswald given over to the Dallas sheriff's office immediately after he was remanded to their custody in the hearing before the judge? Why were both of Oswald's preliminary hearings, one for Officer Tippett and the second for John Kennedy, held in camera? How could a civilian known to the police kill Oswald while he remained in police custody?

The later reluctance of the government to make available the full autopsy reports and the delicacy with which some witnesses were treated by the Warren Commission and others never requested to appear reveal a laudable but misplaced sympathy with the sensibilities of the individuals involved. A chief intention of the Warren Commission was to restore a sense of legitimacy and trust to the government. This concern also had to influence their deliberations. Placing the burden of the investigation into the assassination on the FBI, an agency facing judgment as to its own responsibilities in the sequence of events leading to the murder, invites distrust. The price paid for all this was high, a series of reflections made on the credibility of the official explanation put forward. Since such reports are always suspect, those who frame them should extend themselves to insure skeptics no basis for argument that can be avoided. The procedures employed and the evidence collected should be characterized by the greatest objectivity. The one intention should be to develop and make public the most comprehensive, accurate and impartial report of the events as they occurred. Anything less is totally unacceptable.

Within such a vortex of influences—the psychological need for reassurance, the overpublicized and personalized nature of the office, the invincible security arrangements and the official bungling in handling the murder and its ramifications—the desire to believe in a conspiracy appears not so unwarranted a response.

The assassins enjoyed several other things in common besides being non-conspirators. Most were fringe members of society. Virtually all were mentally unstable. Few had succeeded in any walk of life. Oswald, Sirhan and Torresola worked irregularly at odd jobs; Czolgosz, a factory worker, quit his job three years prior to McKinley's assassination and did not work regularly after that. Giteau was an itinerant lawyer and lecturer of no great renown; Schrank, a bartender and tenement landlord, spent the bulk of his time reading, scribbling notes and wandering around Manhattan in the years preceding his attack on Theodore Roosevelt. John Wilkes Booth was a noted actor, although not of the calibre of his father or brothers, but one with declining opportunities to work and in jeopardy of losing his career altogether due to a throat ailment. Zangara was a bricklayer and contractor although holding no job for any length of time in the two years preceding his attack on FDR; Lawrence, a house painter, worked infrequently in the two years leading up to his attempted murder of Jackson. Collazo, the exception, held a variety of jobs but was employed steadily preceding his trip to Washington from New York City to make a strike for Puerto Rican independence.

Collazo was an exception in other respects. While each of the others had difficulty in establishing and maintaining mature emotional relationships, he had a wife and a settled family life. Collazo was proficient at his job and respected in his community—a type of recognition that eluded each of the others except Booth. Collazo's fanaticism, and again the parallel to Booth is appropriate, placed a cause above life. Excepting Collazo, each of the others gave demonstrable evidence of emotional instability in the years immediately prior to their assassination attempts.

Richard Lawrence, the would-be assassin of President Jackson, appears to have been totally irrational. He had threatened assassination before. He saw himself as a king, believed the United States was subtly persecuting him as he believed it had his father before him and that the country owed him large amounts of money.

Czolgosz felt McKinley "was the enemy of the good people—the good working people" and reported feeling no sorrow for his crime. Schrank coupled Theodore Roosevelt's try for a third term (actually Roosevelt served the major part of McKinley's second term after his death and was elected to only one full term on his own) with an apparition of McKinley's ghost in a bizarre explanation. According to Schrank, "God . . . called me to be his instrument." Apparently the deceased McKinley did also, appearing before him in a dream and declaring, "This is my murderer [pointing at an image of Roosevelt], avenge my death." And finally, Schrank argued that "every third termer [must] be regarded as a traitor to the American cause . . . it is the right and duty of every citizen to forcibly remove a third termer."

Zangara wanted to strike a blow on behalf of the working man and to ease a pain in his abdomen, caused he felt by the capitalists, and for which no physical explanation could be found in his autopsy. In his words, "I have trouble with my stomach and that way, I make my idea to kill the president [President-elect Franklin Roosevelt] —kill any president, any king." Booth wished to gain immortality, to be remembered as the man who toppled the colossus. Vaguely, he intended his plan to aid the South also.

Two strains run through the Warren Commission assessment of Oswald's motive. One is that Oswald needed to overcome feelings of impotency, to assume the heroic proportions he fantasized for himself. The second is that he, as did Booth, craved historical notoriety.

One thing is clear: the assassins struck at the office, not the man. They had no personal relationships with their victims, no animosity directed against them as individuals and frequently even no knowledge of their personalities or policies when in office. Zangara typified the majority when he stated it made no difference to him whether he assassinated Coolidge or Hoover rather than Roosevelt, or for that matter, the king of Italy.

Most of the assailants felt they acted under divine inspiration. And although post facto diagnosis has its risks, most would have to be classified as patently unbalanced.

Public Revenge

The response of most Americans and the courts to the presidential assailants depended on whether their attempts on the lives of the presidents succeeded or not. If they failed in their attacks they were dealt with humanely. Collazo, Schrank, Lawrence and Zangara (in his first trial which took place prior to Cermak's death) were institutionalized for life.

If the assassins succeeded, however, vengeance became the dominant public mood. Neither the courts specifically nor the legal safeguards provided by society as a whole have stood up well under the attack. Neither Oswald nor Booth came to trial. Both were killed. Oswald died within 48 hours of John Kennedy. Booth succumbed in a fiery barn within 12 days of Lincoln's death, killed either by his own hand or the bullet of a Union soldier. Four of Booth's co-conspirators were tried and hung, at least one on questionable evidence. Four others were imprisoned on the Florida Keys, one dying from disease before and one shortly after all were pardoned by Andrew Johnson in 1869. The lot included the boy who held Booth's horse outside of Ford's Theatre.

Zangara's second trial took place three days after Cermak's death. Within 24 hours he was judged guilty and 33 days after his attack he was electrocuted. Czolgosz was tried four days after McKinley's death. His trial lasted eight-and-one-half hours over a two-day period. The jury took 34 minutes to deliver the verdict and Czolgosz was electrocuted 40 days after McKinley's death. Sulfuric acid was poured into the coffin, apparently a custom of the time. Giteau's trial for the assassination of Garfield turned into a circus that lasted almost three months, although the results ultimately were the same.

Richard Lawrence's trial for his unsuccessful attack on President Jackson's life in 1835 represents a noteworthy gauge against which to assess the others because of the manner in which the law was applied to the case. In his introductory remarks the prosecutor, who was Francis Scott Key, drew attention to a British precedent as a basis for dismissing the prevailing criteria for determining legal responsibility for the crime, which was an individual's capacity to judge right from wrong. The prosecutor argued that a defendant who acted on the basis of a delusion should be judged insane and treated accordingly. The defense's responsibility was to prove the defendant suffered delusions that led to the attack against Jackson and this they did with ease. Lawrence pled insanity, was imprisoned for life and died in a mental institution.

None of the three sets of defense lawyers in the Giteau, Czolgosz or Zangara cases argued the precedent established in the Lawrence trial. Czolgosz had no legal representatives until two days before his trial, and then they put forward no defense witnesses on his behalf. The most eminent medical authorities concluded that Czolgosz was "unqualifiedly" sane, and the court assumed this was the case unless proven otherwise. The contention was not challenged. A thorough reanalysis of his life begun a year after his death by two highly competent psychiatrists, however, came to quite dissimilar conclusions.

In Zangara's case, a board of two court-appointed psychiatrists examined him but made no determination as to sanity. No psychiatric witnesses were called to testify on his behalf and his sanity was assumed, although one of the psychiatrists who examined him declared to author Robert Donovan 20 years later that "medically, he was not sane."

Giteau did plead insanity. He had a determined if unspectacular set of lawyers, testimony by experts was presented to the effect that he was insane, and his outbursts and consistently unpredictable behavior during the trial should have been sufficient to convince disbelievers of his illness. The court persisted in crediting him with being sane, partly because Giteau wanted to be judged mentally incapable and threatened God's personal intervention on the court if any other verdict was delivered. The public demanded blood in payment for President Garfield's assassination. The court convicted Giteau, an appeal to the Supreme Court was rejected, President Arthur refused clemency and, to the satisfaction of a large crowd of onlookers, Giteau was hung.

The office of presidency has been the target of assassins because of its power and visibility as the kingpin of American government. A depersonalization of the office and its incumbent would be helpful as would an emphasis on the complex responsibilities of competing centers of governmental power—the Congress, the state capitals and the mayors' offices.

Violence in America

A number of studies and presidential commissions have dealt with violence in American society with particular focus on some of its more unpleasant aspects—urban riots, crime, assassinations and death and disorders on college campuses. Main themes in all the reports are the need for greater tolerance and understanding, less rhetoric, more equitable distribution of the society's resources and truly representative governing bodies. The commissions have helped society to reexamine its past and they have done commendable jobs of explanation. But the net practical results measured in legislative gain and changed governmental procedures emanating from the work of the Warren, Kerner, Eisenhower and Scranton Commissions have been few. The public and its representatives content themselves with broad discussions of the problems involved and accept the recommendations of the commissions with grave reservations.

The public attitude toward political assassination is fatalistic. In 1963 the American people were deeply shocked by the assassination of President Kennedy and expected nothing of like nature to happen again. Five years later they were resigned to believing that assassination represents a necessary risk of political life.

In the nationwide poll on political violence conducted by Louis Harris and Associates, 51 percent of the respondents agreed with the statement that "if people go into politics they more or less have to accept the fact that they might get killed." Fifty-five percent agreed that "a lot more people in government and politics will probably be assassinated in the next few years."

Most discouraging of all has been the cautious response of public officials. Minor pieces of legislation are passed—such as weak gun control laws and increased Secret Service protection for presidential candidates. Commissions are appointed to study outbreaks of violence in order to defuse tense situations. But as long as no more serious solutions for dealing with the roots of the problem are offered, the results are predictable. A sober assessment of present conditions portends ominous future events.

SUGGESTED READINGS

Assassinations and the Political Order, edited by William Crotty (New York: Harper & Row, 1972).

The Politics of Assassination by M. Havens, C. Leiden, and K. Schmitt (Englewood Cliffs, N.J.: Prentice-Hall, 1970).

Assassination and Political Violence by J. Kirkham, S. Levy, and W. Crotty (New York: Praeger, 1970).

Political Violence by H. L. Nieburg (New York: St. Martin's Press, 1969).

PART FIVE

Social Science and Public Policy: Sociology as a Public Statement

The role of social science links up with the policy effort, first, to satisfy the bureaucratic needs of managing a postindustrial economy—and that means managing the competing needs of an entrenched bureaucracy as well as a powerful industrial working class. Beyond that, perhaps equally powerful, are intermediate classes of a nondescript variety: everything from secretaries to schoolteachers. Social science also relates to the second part of our paradigm concerning postindustrial capitalism—namely, satisfying the needs of people who themselves are largely without voice, even though they may sometimes have a vote. In that special sense, the role of social science involves advocacy as well as analysis, that is, giving voice or representation to that difficult to grasp phenomenon called "the people" and also giving expression to an even more ubiquitous concept called the "general interest" over and against special interests represented by the class and race system within American society.

Any examination of how the social sciences impart policy guidelines in the United States and the ways in which the policy-making apparatus supports and underwrites social science activity is an extremely complex exercise. The magnitude of the undertaking invites skepticism at the least and scorn at the most. Cries and whispers will be evoked concerning the autonomy of the social sciences, followed by declarations that policy has no more dependency on social science research than do apples on oranges. Beyond that is the lurking suspicion that American social science may employ a different rhetoric, but scarcely exhibits a noticeable or notable superiority, to social sciences elsewhere in the world. Given these and other Herculean objections to this sort of study, it is perhaps necessary to set forth plainly and frankly the scope and limits of this ambitious, yet exploratory, effort.

Alternating between case study materials and empirically grounded theory, this section of *Sociological Realities II* attempts to set forth the intriguing relationships between the community of social scientists and the still-larger cluster of policy makers in the United States. This is a large-scale task. Throughout, the emphasis is on the institutional setting of policy research rather than the headier realm of ideology. This is necessary by virtue of the simple fact that, in the great majority of cases, policy research is sponsored research. What is involved is an exchange system of buyers and sellers of presumably scarce or difficult to generate information. To begin elsewhere, with a general system of ideas, for example, would exaggerate the role of an intelligentsia and, therefore, only becloud and falsify the actual context in which policy-oriented research takes place in the United States.

So much emphasis has been placed on the role of the federal government as patron and donor in social policy research that there has been a shortsighted tendency to ignore how social scientists participate in community, local, city and state policy making. Indeed, a considerable amount of successful, if unheralded, work goes on at these subnational levels. One finds here a high degree of isomorphism between social science and policy implementation. As a result, this section considers in detail how each social science discipline, through its own inner history, responds to the policy-making demands of the present. The level of sophistication and stage of professionalization heavily influence the exact impact of a particular social science upon policy making. Our analysis is selective, that is, based on case study material, attempting to show how each discipline provides unique mechanisms to deal with particular policy issues.

A final theme that characterizes this section is the examination of interactional frameworks and paradigms governing the relationship between social scientists and administrators and perpetrators of public policy. This section focuses on the sorts of problems that social science researchers throughout the world can expect to encounter when they involve themselves with the policy process. Beyond that, we present a number of modest recommendations that should enable researchers to avoid the pitfalls encountered in the United States. We do not, however, suggest that social scientists should discard the effort to use scientific knowledge to solve practical human problems.

One can detect in most policy writings within sociology the resurfacing in modern guise of the old fact–value dualism, with the assumption that, somehow, information provided and decisions made are discrete entities. It is no exaggeration to say that a considerable amount of current thinking in the United States is predicated on this central assumption. Laswell's idea of a "science of policy making" has largely given way to a de facto operational view that the social scientist is concerned primarily with facts while the policy makers are concerned with implementation. While a considerable amount of analysis is based on the assumption that the research performed is utterly distinct from the applications devised, a growing body of social science opinion operates on an entirely different set of premises: what might be referred to as the monist in contrast to the dualist framework.

Edel, in "Scientists, Partisans and Social Conscience," raises the key issue in the consideration of social science and public policy, namely, the issue of responsibility. Science itself is, we know by now, not "value free." In fact, it arises in historically and socially bound contexts. Edel discusses the history of the growth of science in the larger context of the growth of social conscience. Yet, as sociologists from Emile Durkheim onward have pointed out, this growth of social conscience includes a paradox: the growth of individual decision as well. Proposing a breakdown of the individual–social dichotomy (another lesson from the discipline of sociology itself)—the author discusses the external and internal factors that have changed the very nature of science in our times. He emphasizes the internal factors. Among them are a shift in the view of human interference in the course of events, the growth of the scope of the scientific enterprise, the development of what may be called an "ecological mode of thought" and an apparent change in the relation of practice to theory in the scientific enterprise. Edel discusses the impact of all of these things on science and presents us with a sophisticated discussion of the responsibilities of scientists themselves.

In "Social Science for Social Policy," Gans addresses the origins and nature of policy research and offers a model for social policy design and research. He argues that academic social science is, in large measure, unsuitable because it is not aimed at intervention. To illustrate this point he discusses the norms of the sociological enterprise. Sociology, Gans says, is detached, holds a norm of impersonal universalism, has high levels of generality, is characterized by conceptual abstractness and is wrapped up in the "metaphysics" of academia, i.e., creates a political naiveté among its practitioners.

Schorr is harsher with both academics and policy makers than Gans. In "Public Policy and Private Interest," he suggests that social policy often follows a random pattern in its development. Systematic evidence and experience, he argues, are not used; instead, the "Protestant ethic" and a circular process of defining problems in terms of political answers operates. This flows, Schorr tells us, from the pragmatic nature of government. Social scientists in government must steer a course between the Charybdis of reductionism and the Scylla of elaborationism. Schorr also warns against the narrow self-interest of empire-creating social scientists who are tempted to give their clients what they want, betraying their disciplines in the process.

The two articles by Horowitz constitute a set. In the first, "Social Science Yogis and Military Commissars," he presents an analysis of the contents and implications of a confidential report on how social science research can benefit the Defense Department. The report was written by eminent social scientists. He then presents some constructive proposals based on another report in which the integrity of true research is maintained.

"The Pentagon Papers and Social Science" is a case study of the social scientist's role in world affairs. It provides a useful review of how Vietnam happened and how "war gaming" instead of political sophistication became the basis for American policy. This process, Horowitz argues, resulted in a one-sided policy that "mandarinized" the social scientists involved; that is, the social scientists became part of the system rather than analysts of it. Those involved with policy were essentially cut off from the informed public and fell into a posture of "crackpot realism." The crux of the issue involves full disclosure versus confidentiality and secrecy. It is a control issue. The dimensions of autonomy versus involvement and secrecy versus publicity becomes the twin axis on which the tragic game is played. The Pentagon Papers also grant us oblique evidence on the nature of the ruling elite in America and some evidence on how former President Nixon became a victim of "presidentialism."

The best argument for the widest possible implementation of social scientists in the legislative, executive and judicial branches of government at national and subnational levels is the brake on idiosyncratic decision making that often results from too narrow a consideration of evidence and contexts. The worst argument for such social science talents being more widely used is to avoid or bypass the democratic processes, a situation in which the role of expertise comes to displace the will of the people on major issues. Between these two poles the tightrope must be walked. Again, there are no magic formulas: Populism can degenerate into jingoism, just as assuredly as social science can issue into elitism. But given a context in which decision making becomes increasingly sensitive and complex, and the technological demands are for immediacy of decisions no less than accuracy of forecasting, there can be no question that the tilt is toward the wide deployment of social science. For at this time there is widespread utilization of economists as the one group that is held to be reliable and worthwhile in a policy context. And yet, more and more, the problems are at the qualitative rather than quantitative levels—problems of how good, no less than how much. Under such circumstances, definitions of what constitutes the good, of how the aims of the society can be meshed and blended to the constraints of the economy, indicate the need for much wider use of psychologists, sociologists, anthropologists and political scientists. Indeeed, the very proliferation of the social sciences at policy levels will itself provide a democratizing effect on governments and agencies that at present confine themselves to economists and engineers.

There is such a heavy emphasis on the training of policy-oriented sociologists on behalf of local communities or national agencies that we sometimes forget the essential role of criticism performed by sociology. In this context, what we would urge is the widest possible training of sociologists for policy-making roles in counterestablishment institutions no less than established institutions. The role of social science in setting policy may more readily take place in connection with the advice and support of industrial unions, ethnic minorities and special-interest groups such as women, the aged or the youth. Social science could even be utilized to formulate the political platforms of out-of-power and out-of-favor parties. In short, in considering the role of social science as a policy-making device, we have always to emphasize not simply the subnational levels at which such relationships between science and policy can be maintained but also the ideological content of such sociological services. The failure to admit this possibility in the past has led to an undue and unfair assumption that sociology was intrinsically a conservative agency working on behalf of the established system. In point of fact, only the widest possible utilization of social science in counterestablishment institutions can break down these powerfully rooted prejudices, which are equally dangerous both to social scientists and to the policy sector (which, after all, needs the best available information—not the loudest or noisiest forms of patriotism).

One exceedingly important consequence of the high participation of sociologists in public policy is that the very doing of social science becomes directly pegged to public policy definitions of needs and goals. That is to say, if the problems of ecology and environment become central, then the fundings open up in this area. This "mandarin effect" signifies several dangerous possibilities: first, that no research will get done outside of policy-stated needs, since no funding will be in the offing; second, that the social science research will be of a crude, empiricist variety, veering sharply away from any sort of speculation that might tend to damp the enthusiasm of project sponsorship for future research; and third, that social science will set its priorities in strictly fiscal terms and, hence, fail to challenge prevailing orthodoxies. In some measure, the very tension that must exist between social science and public policy needs is a safeguard against such a premature atrophy. However, for this "creative tension" to remain intact, sources of funding independent of projects themselves are required. And it is precisely the unwillingness of donors and sponsors to provide for "free-floating" funds that jeopardizes autonomy in social science.

Sociology operates best on public policy when there is a preexisting, broad-based consensus; it operates worst under conditions of public dissension. Hence, the areas of greatest success are in areas of denied equity: equal rights for black enlisted men, equal educational opportunities for children from minority backgrounds and equal rights for women. Within this national arena, in which a perceived sense of injustice exists, the impact of social science is quite large. When consensus is lacking, such as in the American overseas involvement in Southeast Asia, then the efforts of social sciences are subject to extreme criticism from without and serious shortcomings at the analytical level from within, i.e., misevaluations of Viet Cong capacities, mistakes over Cuban support for Castro, etc. When social science services the powerful groups, it is perceived as a reactionary instrument and a fallacious one; when it services the poor and the oppressed, social science is viewed as a legitimate exploratory device. There seems to be an inverse relationship in the perception of social science: as a good thing when operating on shared national aspirations and issues, and as a bad thing when operating on a divided set of international aspirations.

All research, like all thinking, is done by real people, individuals. However "collective" the nature of an enterprise, individual talent and even genius cannot be slighted or ignored. Whether the genius of a Machiavelli, a Hobbes or a Marx can ever be replaced by a team research effort is a moot point. Suffice it to say that the work of individuals like Morgenthau or Arendt still represents a profound input into the policy process. Sometimes this input is affirmative, as in the work of the "war gamers" of the sixties like Herman Kahn; sometimes it is in the negative, cautionary spirit, illustrating what cannot be done, as in the work of David Reisman. What we mean to say is that support for individuals, and failing that, respect for the same individuals, is an essential element in any sound federal approach to the relationship between social science and public policy. It is easy to develop the sort of conceit and arrogance that stems from money, influence and power in high places. The best corrective and antiseptic for such sins of the powerful is the research of the lonely individual, the critical voice raising doubts and even obstacles to what may appear as self-evident propositions. The European approach, with its built-in respect for the intellectual tradition over and against the scientific tradition, is perhaps better able to withstand the arrogance of social science power than the American approach, with its pragmatic predilections.

The growth of sociology for policy purposes will require a large-scale shift in the understanding of what science, no less than social science, is all about. Models of science that frankly take into account the role of advocacy procedures, the place of social forecasting and the need for large-scale as well as small-scale planning mechanisms must begin to augment the traditional empirical and historical forms of description. The present divisions between "pure" and "applied" science only serve to prolong the myth of dualism, the idea that "facts" and "values" or "professionalism" and "occupationalism" are in different realms. The need for cross-fertilization has never been greater, and the rise of policy-making roles for the sciences only points out further this need to maintain a balance between scientific theory and scientifically based actions. The political content of sociology is simply the potentials of the truth about the world to be implemented over and against the claims of blood ties, impulse, collective will, national rights, etc. And, thus, it is the rational core of sociology that gives it its special qualities and uses for policy agencies.

1 *Abraham Edel*

Scientists, Partisans and Social Conscience

Nearly every group in our society—from businessmen to policemen to teachers—finds no difficulty in talking about social responsibilities. Why has there been confusion about it in the case of the scientific enterprise? At least one reason, apart from historical and sociological considerations, has been the conception of science—the strange mixture of the timorous and the lordly stance—which attempted to give a single answer in terms of a particular conception of the lone scientist as intrinsically a truth-seeker. This is both narrow and wide—narrow because it ignores the understanding of the scientific enterprise in terms of its changing historical relations, and wide because the very pursuit of truth itself, if faced as a path in the contemporary world, carries its practitioner much farther than he may think on empirical and historical grounds.

In a time of crisis the problem of the responsibilities of scientists as scientists should constantly recur. What is surprising is that it should keep coming back in the same old terms and with the same old dichotomies, and—in spite of twentieth-century philosophy having been characterized as an Age of Analysis—without a clearer analysis of the questions themselves and their presuppositions. It is as if we started with some fixed definition of the scientist, whether the layman's image of a father-figure in white coat or the philosopher's fallibilistic doubter, and set it against an equally fixed concept of a social conscience embodying the usual hard-line division between individual and social responsibility. And it is as if we simply held up and compared the two pictures and reported that there was or was not a path between the two conceptions.

There is something very wrong with this procedure and its results. Science is a historically changing enterprise and its responsibilities flow not only from its perennial features but from its place in a given time and level of social development. A sense of social responsibility does not take its character from the perennial features of the human conscience alone, but from the whole sociocultural complex in its historical development. Hence any picture of the relations of the two rests on assumed pictures of the whole of the human world in its operations in our age. Once we realize this we can see how complex is the scope of our problem.

I shall therefore discuss at the outset the changing character of the scientific enterprise, go on to the changing character of social conscience, and finally draw conclusions about the contemporary social responsibilities of science.

The Scientific Enterprise

The material and sociological changes in the scientific enterprise are familiar enough. There are more scientists now alive and at work than the past total in all human history. Science is also more systematically organized. It has large resources. Basic research is now encouraged and subsidized. Sociologically, science is not a self-determining field. In spite of the occasional dreams of technocracy or the occasional entry of a scientist into the directory of ruling classes, science is the servant, not the Platonic guardian. It has many masters and many strings by which it is pulled, even in the freer atmosphere of the better university where its practitioners can soothe themselves with a truth-for-truth's-sake ideology. We know that some scientists have shifted from physics to theoretical biology, despairing of any physical research outside the grasp of a war machine. By contrast, the relation of the scientific enterprise to business and the search for profits seemed almost benign, till sociology produced the concept of the "military-industrial complex." But at this point I want to explore the internal changes in the scientific enterprise—both in the theory of knowledge and in the practical attitudes of men—that the progress of science has brought about; it is these changes that determine the responsibility of scientists in the contemporary world. I want to distinguish four such changes:

- ☐ A shift in the view of human interference in the course of events.
- ☐ The growing scope of the scientific enterprise.
- ☐ The development of what may be called an "ecological mode of thought."
- ☐ An apparent change in the relation of practice to theory in the scientific enterprise.

1) *The model of human interference.* Men have always wanted to extend their control of the world and themselves, but the ideal of science has not always been associated with that of control. In ancient Greek philosophy the ideal of science was the intellectual grasp of the eternal; the purer the science, therefore, the less the extent of human control. The idea of knowledge as power had a slow growth. We can see this clearly in the human attitudes to crisis. First there is a kind of weather-model; you wait till the crisis blows over, if you are lucky. Economic crises were treated in this way till quite recently. Then there is

the intervention-model: you intervene only to remove obstacles, so that nature can take its course. This was the medical model under the older teleological approach that nature works for the best. With the Cartesian view of the body as a machine, the idea of interfering to control came to the fore; now some see the body as a mechanism with replaceable, even improvable parts.

In the social field, resistance to intervention is old. We may recall Aristotle's story, in his *Politics*, of the society in which a person who moved a change in the laws had a halter put around his neck, and if his motion lost, he was hanged on the spot. The adulation of tradition has an almost parallel character—to try consciously to remake, to plan the whole, is to exhibit the height of folly. The contemporary attitude is one of the control-model permeating all fields. It reflects not only the vast expansion of science, but also the desperate state of many of our problems, in which a weather-model would mean the acceptance of disasters. Of course even the attitude to the weather is changing: the next generation may think such a name for a resignation-model rather queer and inaccurate.

2) *The growing scope of the scientific enterprise.* It was barely yesterday that arguments were still popular about the inherent limitations of science. First a sharp line was drawn between the physical and the human-social, and the latter declared out of bounds. Then parts of psychology and the social were surrendered, but the cultural and the historical were ideographic, empathetic, value-ridden. We need not track down all the barriers that were thrust aside. Of course, the conception of science changed in the process; it ceased being the universalistic, mechanical-quantitative in the nineteenth-century sense; probability and statistics made their sweep into the human field; generalized and refined mathematical conceptions of order upset the sharp distinction of quantity and quality; and so on. The outcome is that the whole domain of knowledge lies open to the attempts of science. To attempt is not to succeed, but *a priori* and metaphysical limitations seem to be a thing of the past. The domain of ignorance is and will be indefinitely vast. But from a practical point of view it can no longer be used as an *a priori* veto on attempts at knowledge and control. In more stable days, it could be said that no experimental ventures should be made in human life which involved a plunge into the unknown, because disasters might result. Now the same argument often can be urged against *not* making experimental ventures; for the consequences of continuing in the old ways in a rapidly changing world may be quite as unknowable and quite as disastrous. This argument does not justify recklessness in experiment; we are learning how reckless we have been. But it underlines the recklessness of conservatism too. In short, the emphasis falls on responsible attempts at control. The burden of responsibility falls with increasing weight on the scientific enterprise.

3) *The ecological mode of thought.* Part of the recklessness has come not from ignorance but from neglect of knowledge in other fields. There is arising a changed mode of thought which we may call "ecological" because it is so sharply illustrated in ecological studies. We have become very sensitive to the way in which attempts at control in one direction have upset the balance of nature in others, as in the case of insecticides and the disposal of industrial wastes. So we now demand that the application of knowledge be carried out in terms of the whole range of relevant knowledge available. In a column in the *New York Times* James Reston quotes Prime Minister Clement Attlee's remark that, when he concurred in President Harry Truman's decision to drop the atomic bomb on Hiroshima, they knew nothing about the genetic effects of fallout, though in fact, as Reston points out, H.J. Muller had won the Nobel Prize in 1927 for his evidence of the genetic effects of radiation.

Another aspect in the shift in outlook is a demand that one-sided evaluation should not dominate policy; for example, when offshore oil drilling springs a leak, the oil industry may worry about the seepage of salt water into oil, and the seashore population about dispersing the oil lest it cover the beaches. But the chemical used to disperse the oil may have a more deleterious effect on marine life than the oil itself.

On the theoretical side, an ecological mode of thought involves a systems approach, in which there is not only a meeting of different sciences in relation to a particular problem, but there may be a recasting of formulations in the hitherto isolated disciplines. This approach may in part constitute a critique of isolated abstract formulation of knowledge itself in an unduly narrowed domain—the fallacy, for example, of the presidential candidate in the late 1920s who argued that the American economy was in fine shape but something happened abroad and it spread to cause the Great Depression. He failed to realize that the description of an economy in the modern world should be as part of a world-system.

It is probably space research which best dramatizes the need for a full picture which combines the work of many sciences. Applied to the whole of human life, we begin to think of the planet itself as a spaceship, a relatively closed system in which the cyclical processes maintaining a balance have to be known and reckoned with if disaster is to be avoided.

4) *The relation of practice to theory in the scientific enterprise.* Practical questions are playing a greater role in scientific work today. Experiment itself requires more extended use and organization of resources. In part it is because developed sciences experiment over a broader field. Nuclear tests involve a wide geographic area; medical experiments may require a large population of subjects; economic and political experiments have to take place in the on-going life of a society. In part it is because the very tools of testing and observation become large and complex technological achievements, whether it be the telescopes of astronomy or the standardization of tests in psychology and the use of computers in behavioral science generally. In part it is because the field of practical application may itself be furnishing a test in experience which adds weight for or against a theoretical position. For example, the collapse of a bridge brings to a test the strength of the materials, the appearance of side-effects tests the safety of a drug, the day-by-day sessions of the psychoanalyst constitute some kind of check on the theory of therapy, and so on. And in part it is because the subject matter of experiment, especially in social science, may itself be the practical issue

of human well-being, so that the experiment is one of how to diminish crime or use of drugs or to achieve fewer family breakups. In fact this is so widespread that some theoretical attempts have been made to redefine the social sciences by human objectives, for instance, economics as the science of securing high productivity and wide distribution without depressions.

In much of this, where the scientific study is of human beings, the integration of practical application and experiment becomes so close that they seem almost two different ways of saying the same thing. Thus in medicine the line grows thin between the experimental effect of a drug and its medical efficacy. In recent governmental hearings on the contraceptive pill, one outcome was a recommendation that every doctor regard every use of it by a patient as an experiment. One could draw an interesting parallel from the history of thought between the integration of the empirical element in science and the symptoms of integration of the practical element now taking place. In its early history, the model of science was wholly mathematical-conceptual and experience had merely an outside suggestive role. In time, not only did the areas that were "merely empirical" achieve respectability as fit subjects for science, but science itself became thought of as "empirical science." Practical application too has been traditionally conceived as having merely an illustrative or facilitating role. But its closer relations seem to bring it near to occupying the place of an insider in the scientific enterprise. The integration of practical application within the complex of theory and experience may mean that the concept of the scientific enterprise is itself being refashioned.

If these four tendencies constitute a trend in our understanding of the scientific enterprise, there will as a consequence be serious inroads on the traditional view that the scientist as individual or the scientist as citizen may have social responsibilities, but not as scientist. How is such a view of science possible when the scientific enterprise has come to take a control-stance, to range over the whole of human life, to adopt an ecological mode of thought, and to bring practical application within the scope of its work? Does not such an emerging view of the scientific enterprise itself demand a social conscience?

It is possible to invoke the metaphysical dogma of the sharp separation of value and fact as an *a priori* barrier to this demand. But it must not be assumed that science is equivalent to fact in such a dichotomy; science may very well involve some facts and some values, no matter how strongly the dogma be held to. If the scientific enterprise is allowed an internal value of the pursuit of truth, it becomes an empirical matter how far into the value domain this carries the scientist. For he is committed to defending the pursuit of truth as scientist, not merely as citizen or individual. And if the picture of the world should happen to be that only a particular political policy will preserve the pursuit of truth, and all others will subvert it, he may find himself as scientist committed to political action. Of course, there is the possibility of drawing back.

It might be said that while the scientific enterprise, as a human affair, involves values, science as an ideal type of activity does not. But this argument is, I suspect, a desperate move. It will end up by holding that the aim of science is not the discovery of truth, but only the discovery of theoretical systems to fit accumulated data—that the aim is only to show which theoretical formulations are assigned with what degrees of probability on the basis of what evidence. This can, I think, be worked out to a refined extent. But the result will bear little resemblance to what we think of as the scientific enterprise; it is rather a particular redefinition of science. And it would be question-begging to argue that it is justified because it would preserve the value-free character of science.

Social Conscience

The social conscience of a society can be described as a pattern of assumed and felt responsibility for others, a concern for the well-being of people and for the solution of dominant social problems. Every society has some such pattern. Individuals may differ in the extent and intensity in which they exhibit responsibility. But the scope of social conscience, its mode of expression, the kinds of topics on which it is directed, are historically variable and can be seen as sociocultural formations. The only way to understand the present character of our social conscience is to see it as the outcome of a historical development of the last few centuries.

By the seventeenth century, a new pattern of conscience was in the making. We need not enter into the background of the emerging economic order in which an acquisitive individualism became dominant nor the religious break with the older authoritarian church as a result of which the lone individual directly faced his God. Soon the individual was no longer enmeshed in the guilt of original sin with its weight of obligations. He became increasingly an atomic will, exercising his choice and recognizing no obligation that did not issue from his will. This *moral voluntarism* or, in interpersonal and social relations, *moral contractualism*, became enshrined as an individualistic pattern of obligations and responsibilities. It is clearly marked in political, legal and moral theory. In politics the very state was conceived as contractual in origin: atomic individuals entered with an initial capital of natural rights, and took on burdens only by consent, for the effective maintenance and expression of their rights. In law, the field of contract increasingly took over human relations that had been the subject of institutional regulation; in Maine's familiar phrase, the movement of progressive societies was from status to contract. In the theory of tort and crime, men went far toward shedding fault and responsibility for anything that could not be traced by direct connection to their intentional acts or by indirect connection to their negligence.

It is perhaps the abstract regions of ethical theory that show most starkly the character of the shift. The older pattern of duties imposed on men by God's will and applied by derivation from natural law, without consulting individual will or consent, gives way to a primary dichotomy between self and other. In the "other" are telescoped all the intermediate kinds of ties—family, kin, small group, as well as society at large. Moral philosophers in the eighteenth century, faced with Hobbes' stern egoism, attempted to justify benevolence, that is, to persuade the individual to stretch out his hand toward others, his non-self. They seemed to think, as Hobbes himself had done, that a sober rationality would take a man beyond himself, even if only to protect himself, that a greater wisdom would find an identity of interest with others, that beneficence would be a good investment yielding appropriate return, or that private profit pursued would redound to public well-being through greater productivity.

These roundabout routes for mustering a social conscience are familiar enough. Nor were they questions of abstract theory alone. For their anxious character reflected the breakdown in traditional ways of handling widespread poverty, suffering and social displacement. The career of parish relief and poor laws in England, supplemented by Dickens' novels and the bitter history of trade-union organizational struggles, is evidence enough. When the twentieth-century outburst of industrial progress faced men with the familiar dislocation—industrial accidents, unemployment, poverty, social insecurity—the intellectual equipment for social responsibility was utterly inadequate, and justification for what was socially unavoidable and socially desirable had to be fashioned almost afresh.

I need not recapitulate the familiar story of the growth of social responsibility and the struggles in this century, both theoretical and practical, that were waged to secure workmen's compensation, unemployment insurance, social security, welfare support, medical care, extension of educational opportunity, and so on. It is a somber paradox that human treatment was often argued for *not* because of any sense of the fellowship of man, but because the worker was seen as a factor in production, whose depreciation should be borne by those who gain from using it, just as they had to stand the losses in the wear and tear of machinery. But of course this presupposed that men, unlike worn-out machines, could not simply be thrown on the scrap-heap or would not endure being so thrown. Nowadays even the scrap-heap has become a problem of social responsibility and the debate goes on whether pollution is to be faced as a social problem met through the tax fund or through throwing the burden as "external costs" on the enterprises that produce the pollution as a normal part of their operation. But perhaps the best example of how far we have moved in developing a pattern of social responsibility is the current consideration of a guaranteed minimum annual income.

The growth of a social conscience in all these ways does not, however, spell the end of the individualistic tradition in morality. Strangely enough, it is becoming more not less powerful and taking over provinces hitherto marked as social. Perhaps the most extreme form of individualist reconstruction is seen in the rise of individual responsibility *against* authority and the state, as contrasted with the older social conception of patriotism, obedience and loyalty. A number of diverse forces have fed this growth of individual judgment. One is no doubt the weakening of patriotism as a dominant binding relation, in the development of the wider loyalties of an increasingly unified humanity. A great share of causal responsibility goes to the discrediting of the mystique of the state in the evidence of Hitlerism and its deeds; this is best seen in the outcome of the Nuremberg trials in which even disobedience to military commands is enjoined where basically immoral action is commanded. I think that a third factor in elevating individual judgment lies in the lessons of experience with intellectual repression—for example, such impositions of ideological dogmatism in the Soviet Union as the notorious Lysenko affair and its domination of genetics, or our own experience of the drive for conformity in the so-called McCarthy period of the 1950s.

In the 1960s a fourth factor was added to our experience—the civil rights movement, in which legality was on the side of discrimination, and, later, the opposition to the Vietnam War. The growth of civil disobedience as a technique of social change has thus been rapid, and the movement to give greater legal scope to conscience is a serious one; for example, to allow conscientious opposition to a particular war, not merely to war itself, as a ground for draft-exemption.

The ambivalent attitude to individual judgment in contemporary society reflects, I believe, two conflicting forces. On the one hand, the growth of corporate enterprise and large-scale organization presses for conformity. On the other, the complexity of technological and social organization and the weight of problems and the rapidity of change in all fields of life demand a high degree of inventiveness, individual initiative in thought, a constant stream of new ideas. And so we have almost the paradox of nonconformity becoming a conformist demand. The weight of individual decision and the lack of social guidance for decision in many areas of life are greater than ever before.

On the theoretical side, too, the individualistic form of morality has been growing rather than receding. And yet, though individual decision and responsibility are the central focus of theoretical developments, this is no longer the old individualism of the atomic self, cut off by initial stipulation from society as its opposite. Dewey's individualism proposes the rich development of the person as a social goal for education and morals and social institutions. And Sartre's intensely individual focus has him assume responsibility for all that is immoral around him. A man cannot, says Sartre, shift off responsibility for a war that he had no part in making, for he could always be asked what he has done to stop it. The depth of social responsibility for the individual conscience in the moral philosophies of today is central, no longer peripheral or a good business transaction.

What is happening is a long overdue breakdown of the individual-social dichotomy. Both the growth of our knowledge of man and the development of our complex, interrelated modern life make this dichotomy less significant for understanding what kind of self a man develops and what his obligations and responsibilities are. It is not yet clear what kind of categories will emerge as central in ethics and human understanding. That of the active or creative, as against the fixed, currently looms large, but this too may reflect the intensity of change. Yet it does contain the permanent lesson that man's self-knowledge is an active point of self-reconstruction rather than a learning of what is already fixed by nature. This lesson was already clear in the nineteenth century. In historical terms it is found in the Marxian conception of freedom as the growth of human awareness of the laws of the world and man, which enables man to make greater progress in the attainment of his human values. In individualistic subjective terms it is clearly stated by Kierkegaard when in his *Either/Or* he contrasts the Socratic moral maxim of "know thyself" with his own maxim of "choose thyself."

Morality is self-making and society-making and there is no cut between the two. The growth of social conscience in the contemporary world represents a profound transformation in the life of men, breaking into their consciousness, reshaping thought and sentiment, and creating the opportunity for a freer reconstruction. Whatever historical and social sources, it has a growing firmness which imparts to it the voice of judgment. It is with this conscience and its demands that the scientist must reckon as he attempts to shape—whether to expand or limit—the responsibilities of his profession.

The Scientific Enterprise and Social Conscience

Let us now ask what role the scientist should take in relation to the social conscience, what specific pattern of responsibilities he should assume. On the one hand, the scope of scientific knowledge suggests the greater share in the social conscience; on the other, the high standards of evidence and the disinterested character of scientific inquiry suggest distinguishing sharply between the scientist and the citizen and assigning responsibility to a man as citizen or as individual, not as scientist.

There are two ways to deal with this line of argument. One is basically revolutionary in the sphere of thought, for it upsets the categories and dichotomies in terms of which the question is framed. Thus it may be said that the role-playing which distinguishes the man as scientist, as citizen, as individual, is becoming an increasingly meaningless game, that it will go the way of the older distinctions between the economic man and the moral man, or the self as individual and the self as social. There are particular moral problems of conflict in different relationships, but no general partitioning of the person and his responsibility; man and human life are becoming too integrated for that, and even in the past such distinctions were never more than relative isolation of systems and practices in a basically unified human life. The second path is less drastic: it is the argument that even if one wishes to preserve the distinctions between the various roles, the decision about what social responsibilities fall within which role is itself a scientific or empirical one, contextual rather than general. I want to pursue the second path here, though I think in the long run the first is the more profound. Yet to be more than a general insight it will have to work out its detailed modes of assigning responsibilities.

Suppose then that the scientist argues against taking a policy stand on social matters because as scientist he is aware of the vast amount of justifying evidence needed in authoritative judgment; one has fewer cognitive responsibilities if he judges social matters as a citizen or as an individual, since it permits more subjective judgment. The difficulty is, however, that on many questions the scientist knows the central evidence only as a scientist—the genetic effects of nuclear fallout as a biologist, the inflationary effects of the Vietnam War as an economist, the psychological effects of ghetto life as a social psychologist, and so on. As a private citizen he might have had quite aberrant notions. Of course, part of the evidence may come from other scientific fields than his own. And part may indeed be just his belief as a layman. If these scruples stand in the way of expressing a scientific social judgment, the scientific thing to do is not to plead subjectivity and individual bias, but to be more precise about the extent of his evidence and specify its credentials. Thus, a particular social stand by biologists might be advanced with the addendum: 70 percent as biologist, 10 percent as relying on economists, 12 percent as general intellectual (all intellectuals presumably having a more sharpened sense of evidence or relevance), 5 percent as citizen (in terms of accepted social obligations), and 3 percent as individual subjective conviction.

Think of the generally educative effect of such pronouncements. If a classification were developed for social judgments, think of the height of sophistication if the public could respond to a flaming headline—"Political Scientists Issue 4D Condemnation of Federal Pollution Policy; Ecologists Concur with 2A Resolution."

Sometimes I have the impression that the scientists' plea for exemption from social judgment as scientists is a normative judgment parallel to an occupation's plea for automatic draft exemption on the grounds of its social importance. Scientists are too busy for political activism or incipient rebellion. Yet here again, the answer is unfortunately not open to antecedent determination. Whether or how much rebellion is involved is an empirical matter and depends on the state of the country and the character of the issues. In Nazi Germany, to make a biological assertion about the lack of evidence for Aryan superiority was probably equivalent to revolt. And in the Oppenheimer case, as we recall, it was a scientific hesitation about the feasibility of the hydrogen bomb that played some part, as well as moral consideration of the consequences of pushing on with its development.

But a large part of social action that can fall into the province of scientists is scarcely of this dramatic kind. Many social questions are not a matter of introducing new and revolutionary categories, but of shifting mutually acceptable categories. Thus if ecologists want a nationally directed water policy or economists and sociologists want a governmental housing industry, they need not be voting on socialism versus capitalism. The categories exist within our society: for example, our army is a collective institution, but we do not advertise for a war to be waged by the lowest private bidder. Nor was the recent suggestion in New York, that subway rides should be free, an anarchistic-collectivist aspiration: it was simply saying that subways should be the same kind of municipal service as garbage collection.

Certainly these are social-science issues in large part. I am reminded of the clarity with which, if I recall a newspaper account correctly, Milton Friedman, when he was testifying for the negative income tax, cut through the remark of a senator to the effect that at least people who got public money in this way should forfeit their right to vote; he replied that if putting one's hand in the public trough warranted loss of the vote, businessmen would be the first to lose it.

A number of different types of social responsibility for the scientific enterprise may be distinguished. Some would fall on individual scientists, some would more effectively be carried out by scientists in associated groups. There are, first, obligations that arise in the professional and public milieu with respect to the scientific work itself. For example, Bentley Glass, in his *Science and Ethical Values*, lists such obligations as: to publish one's methods and results in such a way that another may confirm and extend the results; to see that one's work is properly abstracted and indexed; to write critical reviews in the field; to communicate to the general public the new revelations of science; to transmit the knowledge to the succeeding generation. Such obligations follow from the state of the field as well as the general objectives of the enterprise; thus proper indexing rises to importance because of the stream of contributions in the contemporary world, so that the dangers of work being lost are very real in some fields. Again, the obligation to ensure communication to the general public reflects the tremendous importance of a wide base of public understanding if the lessons of science are to play a part in the advance of culture and social life; this obligation is distorted if scientists think of it only as a way of ensuring financial support for science. It is not implied of course that every scientist has to be busy on all these fronts. Some of the obligations can be carried out in an organized professional or even institutional way, for example, the rise of scientific journalism as a profession itself, rather than as an additional burden to a scientist who may not be gifted in this respect. While there is no scientific obligation to be polemical about conflicting theories and approaches, the obligation to do critical reviews seems to suggest not only the wider purview of the field but participation in the sharpening of theoretical approaches.

There are, in the second place, direct social responsibilities to others who are involved in the work or come within its ambit. Familiar examples of such responsibilities are those of medical researchers to subjects; psychological experiments which involve lying to or misleading the subjects (the extreme case of the Milgram electric shock tests, in which the subject is told to increase an alleged electric shock in order to see when the subject will revolt and draw the line as he watches the faked tortured response); relations of anthropologists to informants in native villages whose ordinary relations may be quite upset after the researcher's departure; questions of invasion of privacy of informants in modes of research and modes of publication; participant observation as a technique and its effects.

Responsibilities of Science

There is further the general responsibility of maintaining the conditions under which science can be continued. This may become a matter of direct political participation when general freedom of inquiry is threatened. Other issues may have a comparable status. For example, the imposition of secrecy on research projects where they are connected with military or political applications has been much opposed by scientists as a hindrance to the free flow of scientific communication. The imposition of political qualifications on scientists as a condition of engaging in research is often seen as disruptive of the community of science and its professional criteria. There is no advance way of knowing what kinds of conditions may turn out to interfere with scientific work and progress, but when scientists individually or in organized fashion oppose these conditions, it is as a scientific responsibility or an exercise of a scientific social conscience.

Moving gradually into the context of scientific work, it would seem to be a scientist's responsibility to know or be aware of the various social relations of his scientific work—how it is supported and financed, what practical purposes motivate the support and the work, what applications are likely to be made of it, who will benefit and who will be affected in what way. So far I speak merely of the obligations not to remain in the dark on these matters. But knowledge about one's scientific work and its context would seem to carry some responsibility for decision—whether to abandon the research under these conditions, to do it but make public or agitate against its intended applications, to work out alternative ways of carrying it on. With the development of such large-scale problems in our scientific culture, paradigms may well be established in the ethical code of the profession. For example, research in biological warfare might well have been banned by scientists even before its recent partial rejection by national edict. Many fuzzy borderlines still remain to be dealt with. It is not inconceivable that a union of engineers should include, in its bargaining with a given corporation, provision of nonpolluting processes of waste disposal, just as a teachers' union may include in its bargaining the provision of school breakfasts or lunches for children—in part because of the help this gives to the educational process, in part because of the general obligation for the welfare of those affected.

Where there are crucial problems affecting the whole life of the society, it may well be a responsibility of all intellectual, scientific and cultural leadership in the community to ask itself what it can do to help face the problems. Thus, in our contemporary world one could pinpoint the problems of war, discrimination in its various forms, overpopulation, pollution of the environment and exhaustion of natural resources as the four great threats to mankind. Hence there would be no question about the scope of social conscience in general with respect to them and about the obligation of scientists to ask themselves what their fields could do to ameliorate the situation. In fact, the obligation of scientists here is directly greater because of the part science has played in generating the situation, even where its action was directly beneficial as, for example, in increasing life expectancy by reducing infant mortality. Two excellent examples of the exercise of this obligation of science to crucial problems and threats are the reaction of anthropologists in the 1930s to Nazi racism and the agitation by atomic scientists in the 1940s and 1950s for controls of nuclear power against war uses. The geneticists nowadays are much worried about the impending breakthrough in their field and the questions of control over human biological development it may raise.

Let me conclude with a few reflections on the modes of action a sense of social responsibility among scientists may call for. Again there is no simple answer. We may distinguish individual action, informal group action, and action in structured associational groups. Individual action may take the form of public criticism, withdrawal from a field of work, or engagement in some form of political action. Informal group action has tended to be ad hoc; it is a familiar feature of our society to see advertisements of scientists speaking on the question of the Vietnam War or on overpopulation or occasionally even on some particular flagrant injustice.

Organized group action is less developed. We may distinguish briefly three types. One is the exercise of negative fighting functions, parallel to strikes by unions for specific demands; this has not been employed very much by organized scientists but is quite conceivable in the present state of things. The second is the exercise of what we may call a ferment-function, to generate all sorts of new ideas and plans and intensify consciousness of the problems and possible solutions. The third is what we may think of as institution-making, which has been more common than we may think. Thus the development of insurance as an idea was a mathematical discovery which underlies vast social transformation in modern societies, though not directly applied by scientists themselves. Group medicine was an invention of medical practitioners. The development of clinics for psychotherapy and the growth of schools for mentally ill children arose from the work of professionals and readily passed into government programs. Recent attempts to organize the poor to take part in a concerted pursuit of their own welfare also had professional origins.

There is nothing implausible in current suggestions that organized scientists market their own discoveries for public welfare, for example, in drugs or even in certain industries. We may compare the fostering of housing and banks by certain unions, or even the suggestion that Harold Ickes made after World War II that what the government had built up for industry during war production should be turned over to a corporation with all veterans as shareholders, instead of being sold at a cheap price to industrial corporations.

Of course such suggestions run up against the realities of basic power. But the amount of free play in our society would be tested by social experiments along these lines. My point is simply that there are avenues for the legitimate exercise of the social conscience of scientists, far beyond the mere expression of a collective voice where there is one. There could very well be sections of the scientific societies on institution-making and on international scientific cooperation, for example, on implementing the abolition of biological warfare. It may not even be too early to think about the possibilities of international citizenship for scientists.

SUGGESTED READINGS

The Social Functions of Science by J. P. Bernal (New York: Macmillan, 1939).

Science and Ethical Values by Bentley Glass (Chapel Hill: University of North Carolina Press, 1965).

The New Sociology by Irving Louis Horowitz (New York: Oxford University Press, 1964).

The Sociological Imagination by C. Wright Mills (New York: Oxford University Press, 1959).

2 *Herbert J. Gans*

Social Science for Social Policy

In recent years, planners, systems analysts, policy specialists and others at work on the formulation or design of public policy have begun to develop a niche for themselves in government, particularly in Washington and in the larger American cities. At the same time, social scientists have become interested again in policy research, partly to train the policy designers but also to conduct studies that support, broaden and criticize government policies. Much of this research has itself originated or taken place in government agencies, but it is now also emerging in the universities, so much so that institutes of policy studies may soon complement or even replace institutes of urban studies on the campus.

Intellectually speaking, policy research is still in its infancy, deriving its theory and concepts largely from the existing academic social sciences. However, since policy researchers are concerned with changing society rather than understanding it, they must have—and create—a policy-oriented social science, independent of but related to and not estranged from the academic disciplines.

I want here to describe some of the characteristics of a policy-oriented social science. My analysis begins by considering the nature of social policy and policy design, and then suggests some conceptual and theoretical requirements of a policy-oriented social science through a discussion of the shortcomings of academic social science for policy research. A final section lists these requirements in summary form. The analysis of both types of social science will draw largely on my own discipline of sociology.

The Nature of Social Policy and Policy Design

By social policy, I mean any proposal for deliberate activity to affect the workings of society or any of its parts. Properly speaking, the prefix social is superfluous, because all policies that affect more than one person are social. However, the prefix is often used to distinquish some types of policy from others, for example, economic or environmental policy. I shall use the term social policy in its broadest meaning, to include economic, environmental and other policies, because they too are intrinsically social. Some semantic confusion might be alleviated by the term societal policy, except that it connotes deliberate activities to affect the society in toto, and I could use the term public policy, since most policy is designed for and by public agencies, except that I do not wish to exclude consideration of "private policy," designed by and for non-public agencies.

As I understand it, social policy differs from planning or social planning only in scale; a plan is nothing more than a set of interrelated social policies. Similarly, social policy differs from politics largely in degree; politicians also engage in deliberate activities to affect society. They tend, however, to choose activities which can be implemented through the political institutions, whereas the designers of social policy are less limited in their choice of activities or institutions. (Of course, policy design cannot take place without attention to political considerations, and policy implementation must normally take place with the help of politicians.)

The distinctive quality of social policy is its aim for what might be called programmatic rationality; it seeks to achieve substantive goals through instrumental action programs that can be proven, logically or empirically, to achieve these goals. Political activity, on the other hand, must by its very nature emphasize the politically rational, which places greater priority on political goals such as keeping the party in office than on substantive ones, and is as likely to stress expressive programs as instrumental ones. For example, politicians may well resort to symbolic appeals for "law and order" when faced with a public demand for crime reduction, even if these appeals do not achieve the substantive goal. The designer of social policy, however, will be concerned first and foremost with programs that actually lead to a reduction in crime. (Even so, he will also and inevitably pursue his own political goals, and work to expand his own agency's budget.)

A Model for Social Policy Design

Inherent in these observations is a model of social policy design, which not only describes the components of the social policy process but also spells out the kinds of social science data needed by the policy designer. As I conceive it, social policy design has three major components: goals, programs and consequences, and the policy-designer works toward the achievement of a (social) goal by the development of programs that can reasonably be predicted to achieve that goal, accompanied by an optimal set of consequences. By programs, I mean simply the specific activities required for goal-achievement; by consequences, the by-products, effects or externalities of a given program. Consequences may also be understood as the benefits and costs of a program for the various sectors of society affected by it, and an optimal set of consequences is that array of maximal benefits and minimal costs which will be most effective in achieving the goal. (Obviously, there can be no single optimum here, for not only do different programs have different benefits and costs, but alternative programs which may achieve a given goal differ widely as to which sectors of society obtain benefits and which must endure costs. Indeed, the major value question the policy designer must answer is, as Harold Lasswell put it over a generation ago, who gets what.)

The determination of consequences is a vital part of social policy design, for all programs have costs and benefits, and these must be determined or at least estimated before the final draft of the policy design so that the program can be revised to eliminate costs which would prevent it from being carried out, or which would be less desirable than the goal being sought. For example, a program which is so costly that funds for it cannot be obtained obviously needs revision; similarly, a delinquency prevention program that helps to make delinquents into heroin users should be revised, for the individual and social costs of delinquency are undoubtedly less than the costs of drug addiction.

The policy designer is typically most active in three stages of the policy design process: goal-operationalizing, determining goal-program relationships and dealing with program-consequences relationships. Although he may play a role in deciding what goal is to be achieved in the first place, in most instances his employer or sponsor, whether a public agency or a ghetto protest group, will make the final decision about the goal for which policy is to be designed. The designer's role, then, is to operationalize that goal, reformulating it so that he can design programs which will achieve it, estimate their consequences, and undertake the program revision to make sure that the array of consequences is optimal. In this process, he must pay particular attention to assuring that the program and its consequences are beneficial to the intended clients.

The Role of the Policy Researcher

So far, I have limited the discussion to policy design, as carried out by policy designers (and, of course, implementers). The policy researcher's role in this process is to provide conceptual and theoretical inputs, the necessary empirical data, the empirical "guesstimates" when data are unavailable, and a critical analysis of the policy design when it is completed.

In the model I have presented, the policy researcher participates in the same three stages of the process as the designer. At the goal-operationalizing stage, the researcher may have to do some intensive interviewing in the sponsoring agency, for sponsors are often vague about the goals they seek, and when the sponsor is an agency, there is likely to be disagreement about goals as well. Without knowing how different parts of an agency feel, the policy designer may find that he has designed a program that will not engender the participation or allegiance of the total agency, for example, the lower bureaucracy of a public agency, or the less active members of a ghetto protest group. And if the goal requires participation or allegiance from clients outside the sponsoring agency, information will be required on how they feel about the goal. For example, if a sponsor seeks to improve the quality of housing among poor people, he ought to know what kind of housing these clients want and will accept: whether they will live in public housing or would prefer rent subsidies to help them compete in the private housing market. If more than one goal is being sought by the various participants in the policy design, as is often the case, the researcher can also help the designer in determining which goals are most important, if all cannot be incorporated into a single policy design.

The policy researcher must also make the designer aware of latent goals, particularly institutional maintenance or growth, for sponsoring agencies rarely pursue a policy which does not at least maintain its present level of resources or power.

The major need for policy research is, however, in the other two stages of the policy design process. First, the policy-designer needs information about which programs will achieve his goal, and wherever possible, empirical evidence to this effect. Ideally, the policy researcher should be able to provide what I have elsewhere called a policy-catalog, that is, a list of programs relevant to all possible conceivable goals from crime reduction to economic equality that have been proven, by empirical research, to achieve these goals. Since both goals and programs are nearly infinite, putting together such a catalog would require an immense amount of action research, social experimentation and evaluation studies. The policy catalog would allow a policy researcher to supply a policy designer with generalized programmatic statements, based on as many cases and studies as possible, which the designer can then apply to the specific situation or community in which he is working. In this application, he may require some bridging research to move from the generalized statement to a specific program.

When the goal in question is the elimination of a social problem the policy researcher must provide findings on the major causes, those explaining most of the variance, and on the immediate causes, for the most rational programs are those that eliminate the major causes, while the most easily implemented programs are usually those that get at immediate causes.

Moreover, policy research ought to provide the policy designer with a model, as empirically based as possible, of all the components and stages of the social-political process by which a social problem is eliminated or a goal achieved. This model should include all of the *activities* involved in the process, the *agents* (institutional and other) whose normal social role is to bring these activities into being or who can be recruited to do so, and the *levers* (incentives and sanctions) needed to activate these agents. Needless to say, activities, agents and levers must all be spelled out in highly specific terms, the ideal being a step-by-step model of the process by which a present state is transformed into an end state.

Finally, the policy researcher must provide information, or at least estimates, of the consequences of a given program, from first order to nth order effects, preferably in terms of benefits and costs of all participants, direct and indirect, in both the program and its implementation. (By indirect participants, I mean especially the bystanders of a process, who may not be directly involved but who always play a role in the political climate that can spell success or failure to a program.) Ideally, the previously described policy catalog should also provide information on the various consequences of each program, and here the research task is even more massive, for effects research is difficult to do, at best, and many of the important consequences of any program cannot be isolated empirically. Thus policy designers may have to be satisfied with informed guesses on the part of policy researchers.

The major types of research needed are about financial and political consequences. The policy designer must have data to help him determine the money costs of a program, but he must also have some estimate of indirect costs paid by various participants, as well as financial benefits that might accrue to others. Data are also needed to estimate political consequences for direct and indirect participants, that is, for whom will a given program result in increases or decreases of political power. Political must be defined broadly, however, for data are also needed on the status consequences of a policy, for any program which results in a loss of status to some indirect participants in the process will inevitably result in political opposition to the policy.

In addition, the policy researcher needs to trace all other possible consequences of a program. Ideally, he should know how the beneficiaries and all other participants will be affected by it, that is, to what extent their own behavior and important attitudes may change as a result, if only to assure the political survival of his policy. He must also have such data to make sure that programs do not cause unintended harm to intended clients or other participants in the social process being generated. For example, the policy researcher must know that a birth control program will not wreak havoc with other aspects of the conjugal relationship among the intended beneficiaries; that the cooling of interethnic or interracial conflicts among teenage gangs in a mixed neighborhood does not just transfer such conflicts to the adults; or that a racial integration program on the job or in the community does not result in a white exodus. Such data are needed, as noted before, to revise programs so that optimal consequences result, or to encourage the design of additional programs to deal with unintended but harmful consequences.

Needless to say, most of the policy research I have suggested here will never be done, and in most policy design situations, a policy researcher can draw only on his understanding of society, the social process, and the effects of deliberate intervention in the process to offer help to the designer. But even this modest role cannot be carried out properly until we begin to develop policy-oriented social science.

The Unsuitabilities of Academic Social Science

One way of thinking about the characteristics and requirements of policy-oriented social science is to look at the unsuitabilities of academic social science for policy research. That such unsuitabilities exist is obvious; academic social science seeks to understand society, not to intervene in it, resulting in many organizational, theoretical and methodological features that cannot be applied to policy research. This is not a criticism of academic social science, for understanding society is a prerequisite to intervening as well as a useful task per se, and besides, policy-oriented social science needs its academic peer.

It is of course impossible to generalize about as large and variegated a phenomenon as academic social science, but it is possible to identify some prevailing theoretical and conceptual features that make it unsuitable for policy purposes. These are: its detachment, "impersonal universalism," high levels of generality and abstractness, and last but not least, its metaphysical perspectives. Moreover, as noted earlier, I will limit my analysis to one social science, sociology.

Detachment. Academic sociology, like most academic social science, views itself as detached from society. For example, academic sociologists rarely make studies to affect the workings of society; instead, they are more likely to study the people who do so. By detachment, I do not refer here to the illusory attempt at objective or value-free research, but rather to a general perspective: that of the outside observer who is examining a society in which he is not involved, at least as researcher.

The detached perspective is not helpful in policy-oriented research, for it generates theories and concepts more suitable for the bystander to the social process than the participant. Although participants must sometimes take the bystander role to be able to evaluate their participation, the policy researcher must provide dynamic theories of the social process to the policy designer so that he can find footholds from which to intervene. Parsonian theory may be useful in understanding how society as such is put together, but it does not, despite its concern with "action," supply concepts that help the policy-designer initiate action. Even Mills' study of the power elite, though hardly detached in terms of values, does not enable a policy designer to come up with policies to obtain more power for his sponsor.

Impersonal Universalism. One of the correlates of detachment is "impersonal universalism," by which I mean the concern with identifying the broad impersonal causal forces that underlie events. Academic sociology developed in reaction to older personalistic theories of human behavior, for example the Great Man theory, and sought to show that individuals cannot be understood apart from society. This mode of explanation was and still is highly useful in discouraging the overly facile application of moral opprobrium to socially caused actions, and it is useful for policy design in that it tends to focus on major causes, but policy designers also need a less universal and less impersonal approach. For example. although there can be no doubt that urbanization and industrialization are responsible for many structural changes in the family, policy designers in the area of family policy cannot do anything significant about these broad forces and require analyses that deal with more manageable causes.

Policy designers also need less impersonal theories for they must, after all, design policies to be implemented among persons. The policy designer works in a sociopolitical context in which moral judgments are made, praise and blame are dealt out, and hypotheses about the motivations of actors are all important. Consequently, he must be able to understand how impersonal causes are translated into—and affect—moral judgments and motives. Similarly, while it is useful for the policy designer to know that all human beings play a multiplicity of roles and that conflicts between roles can lead to social and individual strain, he must design policies for people as combinations of roles and must know how to judge the consequences of a policy for a person who is at once a worker, homeowner, landlord, father and deacon of his church.

High Levels of Generality. The universalism of academic sociology also produces levels of generality that are often too high for the needs of policy. Although many of the social problems with which the policy designer deals may well be the results of urbanization, he must have research which tells him what specific aspects of urbanization are at play and how they affect people. Urbanization can mean many things: for example, the actual move from country to city, living at higher density than in the country, having more heterogeneous neighbors, holding an industrial rather than a rural job, participating in a more complex division of labor, or encountering the life-styles and forms of social participation that are typically found in the city. A social problem resulting from rural in-migration will have to be treated quite differently than one resulting from living at high density, and what is the policy designer to do when confronted with a group which, though it holds industrial jobs and lives in tenements in a heterogeneous neighborhood still practices the peasant life-style it brought from Europe?

Similarly, the policy designer is absolutely lost when confronted with a concept like social change, for it lumps into one term all the various activities in which he is involved. Like the Eskimo who requires more than 20 different words for snow, the policy designer must have very specific concepts of social change, which spell out for individuals, groups and institutions who or what is changing from what original position to what subsequent one, in which aspects of a person's life or group's activities, and with what consequences for the rest of his life or their activities.

Conceptual Abstractness. The high levels of generality at which much of academic social science operates also breeds conceptual abstractness which results in concepts that cannot be applied to the real-life situations in which the policy designer works. Such concepts as social structure, culture and institution are helpful in the academician's task of generalizing about human behavior, but the policy designer can only work with specific human organizations that play roles in the policy he is designing. He cannot deal with political institutions; he must deal with city hall, political parties and citizen groups. He will often be helped by information about what such groups have in common as political institutions, and what roles they play in the structure of power, but his policy must eventually involve individual organizations, and he must know exactly where the power lies in a specific situation if he is to be able to act.

Perhaps one of the most important concepts in modern sociology is class, but this concept is also of little use to the policy designer. Since classes do not exist in America as concrete entities, he cannot design policy to act on them directly; he must have data which is analyzed in terms of the specific and concrete variables that he can affect. In effect, he must break down the concept into its major components: income, occupation, education, power and prestige; for he can only design policies that affect people's earnings, jobs, schooling, political position and status. Likewise, the policy designer finds little of relevance in the descriptions of the class structure and the class cultures that sociologists develop; he can do something about poverty and poor schools but not about lower-class culture, and the sociologist's careful qualification that class cultures and life styles overlap cannot help a policy designer who must know how a specific group of people will react to a policy. He wants to know what this reaction is, not whether it is lower class or working class. He needs to know how different types of poor people will feel about the choice between a poorly paying or dirty, dead-end job and being on welfare; whether these feelings are part of a larger lower- or working-class set of norms is only of parenthetical interest. Moreover, his interest in whether people can be classified as lower or working class is limited to the consequences of the hierarchical fact that working-class people are higher in the sociopolitical pecking order than lower-class people, and may express discontent if the distinctions between the strata are altered by an antipoverty program.

Another aspect of the policy designer's conceptual needs may be illustrated by the term "slum." Aside from the fact that it is a value-laden term with some questionable empirical assumptions, it is, like class, a concept that lumps many components into one often useless whole. The policy designer's problem is that until American housing policy makes some provision for low-cost housing or rent subsidies at a scale that would allow him to propose tearing down anything that is or might be a slum, he must allocate limited resources in the most beneficial manner. Thus, he must know, not whether and how an area is a slum, but the various physical and social components of the area in question and what impact they have on their residents. This will enable him to determine which of these components are harmful and not harmful, and which are more and less harmful, so that, given limited resources, he can design a policy that will get rid of the most harmful components first.

I do not want to suggest that abstract academic concepts are irrelevant to policy; often, they are crucial but not sufficiently developed for the policy designer's purposes. A good example is the sociologist's emphasis on the distinction between manifest and latent phenomena and formal and informal groups. A great deal of highly useful research has shown the impact of latent functions and informal group patterns on the goals, structure and activities of formal organizations, and the policy designer could not work effectively without knowing about the latent and informal arrangements in group life. By and large, however, he can deal only with formal groups and their manifest activities, and he must know therefore how to develop policies which affect their informal and latent components.

The final and perhaps most important drawback of conceptual abstractness is the inaccessability of the relevant data. Until there is a plethora of policy-oriented and academic research, the policy designer will have to work with the data that are available, and these are usually limited to basic and not very subtle types, for example, census statistics. Thus, the highly developed conceptual virtuosity of the academic sociologist who has studied a lower-class community or a delinquent subculture is of little relevance to the policy designer who may know no more about a poor neighborhood than is available in census tract statistics or a health and welfare council analysis, or about delinquents than he can dredge up from police records or case worker reports. This is not the fault of academic sociology, of course, but the policy designer needs to know what he can make of the data he has.

The Metaphysics of Academic Sociology. Last but hardly least, the metaphysical assumptions of much academic sociology also make it unsuitable for policy research and design. I am not concerned here with its often conservative political bias or with the fact that all kinds of political values and implications usually enter into manifestly value-free research in the selection of topics, hypotheses and concepts. These issues have received much discussion of late, and besides, policy design is not wedded to a particular political outlook. Although most social scientists currently interested in what they call policy research tend to be left-liberals, other social scientists doing a form of policy research they call systems analysis are more frequently conservative, if not in intention at least in their work. Moreover, policy design can also be reactionary, radical or anarchist. It is even possible for policy designers or researchers to be politically neutral, acting as technicians who develop programs and consequences for goals determined by others. In this case, they are neutral only in intent, for they are actually adopting the political values of those who determine the goals. As Amitai Etzioni points out, "some policy research serves those in power, some—those in opposition, but it is never neutral."

Whether the goals are conservative, liberal or radical, all policy designers and researchers must accept one political value, the desirability of intervention, and in so doing, they depart from the paths of academic research. Policy design and research must be concerned with *what can be* or should be, whereas academic researchers see their task as studying *what is*, or if they are predictive, what will be. This is only another way of saying that policy research must be normative, but this in turn demands a different perspective. For one thing, the policy researcher must have a thorough understanding of what is, but only for allowing him to see how the present can be changed and at what points he can help the policy designer intervene. He must develop conceptual bridges to enable the designer to make the transition from what is to what can be, from the present to some desired future.

Academic sociology's emphasis on what is also results in what might be called a perspective of adaptation; it is mainly interested in studying how people adapt to the situations they face, and whether they are satisfied or dissatisfied with these situations, but it is not much interested in considering how people would adapt to different circumstances, or what circumstances they want. To put it another way, academic sociology has largely studied behavior, and attitudes about that behavior (how people feel about what is), it has not often studied aspiration, or what people feel they should be. Ironically, despite the great influence of Talcott Parsons on American sociology, most of his colleagues have ignored one of his central themes, that individuals and groups are goal-seeking, striving to achieve their aspirations. The policy researcher must of course place great emphasis on aspirations, for here is one major bridging concept between what is and can be.

Academic sociology is also especially sensitive to obstacles to change, not because researchers are conservative, but because of its emphasis on what is. Of course, the policy designer must be aware of such obstacles, but he must also have research on the readiness for change, a subject about which academic sociology has been relatively silent, except in some recent studies of black militancy. Similarly, studies of cultural factors in behavior have often defined culture as a conservative influence, partly because it has been assumed that culture is naturally persistent and hard to change. As a result, there has been little research on the "intensity" with which cultural norms are held and except in ethnic acculturation studies, on how culture changes when opportunities improve. For example, there have been many studies of the culture of poverty or lower-class culture among the poor, but none that I know of which investigated changes in culture when poor people obtained higher incomes, or what happened to behavior when people escaped from poverty. These are the kinds of studies policy designers must have; they need to know what forms of situational change bring about cultural change and vice versa, and they require measures of the intensity or nonintensity and persistence or nonpersistence of all of the components of culture, social structure and personality. Instead of academic sociology's passive stance, the policy researcher must take an active one toward the subject of his study.

Another unsuitable metaphysical stance of academic sociology is the systemic bias, that is, concern with the social system rather than with its parts that prevails among more traditional sociologists. For example, most functionalists study the functions and dysfunctions of social phenomena for the society as a whole, paying less attention to the functions and dysfunctions these phenomena have for individuals and groups within the society. Similarly, traditional students of deviance and social control concern themselves with the effect of deviant behavior on society, without asking who defines deviance and society or for whose benefit social control is instituted.

Likewise, when sociologists say that society defines certain activities as criminal or that it encourages deviant behavior to reinforce conformity to its norms, they reify society as a social unit that acts for its members. This reification is based on the ideas of Emile Durkheim, who developed the concept of society from his studies of small independent tribes living in a clearly bounded territory with a distinctive social structure and often without a formal government, but such an approach is not applicable to large interdependent nations.

This is clear when one looks at American society and asks not what it is but what it actually does as a society, for an identifiable unit that acts as a society does not exist. Of course, the State, that is, government, sometimes acts as a body, occasionally on the basis of considerable consensus, but more often by shoehorning a set of political minorities into a temporary majority so that a decision can be reached by majority vote. However, that decision is made by the State, not by society, and when sociologists use the term society, they really mean the State—although even it is rarely a homogeneous monolith, but rather an array of agencies which do not always act in concert. Thus it is not American society which deprives the heroin addict of easy access to his fix, and not even the State, but certain governmental agencies, who may argue and feel that they are supported by the majority of the population, but actually only speak in the name of the State and those citizens who favor taking a hard line toward the addict. This becomes evident when one looks at governmental decisions for which consensus is clearly lacking, for example, the search for victory in Vietnam or the prohibition of marijuana. In these instances, agencies of the State are pursuing actions favored by only part of the nation, and no one would suggest that these actions are approved by society.

The systemic bias encourages findings that identify the activities and interests of dominant social groups with society as a whole, and tends to underestimate the amount of dissensus and conflict. Aside from its implicit or explicit political position, however, this bias produces data that are of little help to the policy designer. Unless he is working for the federal government or for city hall and is asked to design policies that enhance control over their territories, he needs research based on a more pluralistic perspective. Most of the time, the policies he is concerned with are intended for selected clients, and the consequences of almost any program will result in benefits for some groups and costs for others. He must therefore know more about specific populations, interest groups and institutions than about society.

A final drawback of academic sociology for the policy designer is its relative inattention to theories and concepts of power. Because of the emphasis on what is and the systemic bias, sociologists in the past have not dealt sufficiently with the role that power plays—in maintaining what is, in holding the social system together, and in the life of nonpolitical institutions generally. For example, family studies have only rarely dealt with the use of power by its various members against each other—or against other families.

The policy designer who usually works in a political institution is constantly aware of the role of power in any social group, and because he is concerned with implementing as well as designing policy, he needs research on the nature and use of power, for example, by groups who would oppose a specific program. He must also know how power can be used to implement policies—and when the power of sanctions or of incentives is called for. He particularly needs data on the extent to which the use of governmental power is effective in overcoming cultural obstacles to change. Often, cultural norms, for example, in support of racial or sexual discrimination, are weaker than they seem and can be overcome by the exercise of governmental power.

Some Positive Functions of Academic Social Science. I have dwelt at length on the ways in which academic social science is unsuitable for policy design and research, but its positive role in policy must also be acknowledged, if more briefly. Indeed, policy research could not exist without academic research.

From what little is known so far of the sociology of policy design, it is clear that both policy designer and researcher frequently become so involved in the bureaucratic and political contexts in which they operate that their own perspective extends only as far as their side of the political game. Also, both are forced to pay so much attention to minor details that they lose sight of the larger picture. And when the political battles are over and their policy is implemented, both can becoame so enchanted with their victory that they fail to see the faults of their policy. The war on poverty is a good example, for many thoughtful researchers and policy designers became wedded to the policies they were able to get passed by Congress and soon forgot how little relevance these policies had for eliminating poverty. Moreover, because of the bureaucratic and political contexts in which they work, policy designers and researchers often find it difficult to be innovative, to scrap bad policies or to come up with ideas for new ones.

Ideally, these faults would be best dealt with if policy researchers could look at their problems with the detachment, universalism, generality and abstractness of the academic, for they would then be able to see their policies from both sides of the political fence, evaluate them coolly for their ability to achieve the intended goal, and look for innovation when it is needed. Since it is unlikely that most policy researchers can be both policy-oriented and academic in their perspective at the same time, they need to rely on academic researchers to function as outside evaluators and critics, although these academics should obviously have a general interest in policy as well as theory.

But policy research needs its academic counterpart in at least three other ways. First, one cannot design policy for intervening in society without first understanding society, and generally speaking, the better the academic research, the better the resulting policy research and design. This is particularly true at present, when policy research is an infant industry which must build on what academics have produced before, but I suspect it will always be true, for most policy research will, by definition, be specific and concrete, and must therefore look elsewhere for more general and abstract theories and generalizations.

Second, one of the major contributions of academic research, at least potentially, is its serendipity; its ability to spawn fresh ideas, unexpected findings and productive new tangents. To put it more simply, academic research will probably always be more innovative than policy research, and as such may also be a major source of innovation in policy research. This is especially true because almost all academic studies have some implications for policy, even if they are unintended, and usually unrecognized by the academic researcher. A good policy researcher should be able to spot these implications—or the leads to implications—in even the most abstract academic study.

Third, academic research is and probably always will be the methodological model for policy research, since policy researchers are typically forced to come up with quick answers and can therefore do only quick or "dirty" research. It is quite possible that they will make some significant methodological innovations for policy research, but it is also true that when it comes to rigor, reliability, validity and the like, academic researchers will provide the technical models and will themselves be the role models for their colleagues in policy research. Moreover, once the policy researcher has made the value commitments inherent in policy research, he must follow the same norms of rigor and objectivity in data collection that appear in the academic sphere.

Some Conceptual and Theoretical Requirements For A Policy-Oriented Social Science

Academic research may often be unsuitable for policy purposes, but clearly, policy research cannot develop without it. If policy research ever becomes a viable institutional activity, and policy-oriented social science disciplines are able to become equal in size and competence to academic disciplines, policy researchers working in government and other action agencies will satisfy many of the academic needs I have described here from academically inclined and located policy-oriented social scientists. Until this state of affairs is reached, however, they will continue to place heavy reliance on existing academic social science.

My analysis of the unsuitability of academic social science for policy has already indicated or implied most of the major requirements of a policy-oriented social science, so that it is possible to list these here in brief and summary form.

First, the purpose of policy-oriented social science is to provide the policy designer (as well as the policy implementer) with "general" and "specific" research. The former would deal with such general issues as the nature of social policy, the role of the policy designer in its various institutional contexts, the relationship between policy and the ongoing social-political process, the nature and problems of intervention in that process. General research would presumably be the distinctive task of academic policy-oriented social scientists. Specific research, done both in the academy and in action agencies, would provide detailed data on specific substantive policy fields, such as health, housing, family life and so forth, cataloguing for each issue the programs which would achieve specific goals and the resulting consequences.

Second, specific research must be based on highly specified theories and concepts which can, wherever possible, analyze the concrete groups, organizations and institutions with which the policy designer must deal.

Moreover, such theories and concepts must lend themselves to maximal operationalization, so that the findings which result from them can be easily applied to the policy process.

Third, a fundamental necessity of policy-oriented social science is a model of the social-political process that is tailored to the needs of the policy designer. Such a model must have the following features:

- □ It must view the social-political process as composed of goal-seeking groups and individuals, and must therefore provide concepts about the nature of goal-formation; the relationship between goals and behavior on the one hand, and goals and underlying values on the other.
- □ It must analyze the socio-political process in terms of the specific activities (rather than abstract behavior patterns) by which goal-seeking groups and individuals proceed, and the incentives and restraints that impinge on them and their activities.
- □ It must attempt to explain the process in terms of specific causes, particularly major and immediate ones, for the policy designer seeks to encourage or overcome these causes in the programs he proposes.
- □ It must be a normative and future-oriented theory of action, which analyzes both what is and what can be, developing concepts that allow the policy designer to develop programs that bridge the present and the desired future. In each case, the theory must spell out the obstacles to change, the agencies and norms behind these obstacles, the strength or intensity of these obstacles, and the kinds of rewards or sanctions by which they could be overcome. (The theory must also specify what cannot be, identifying those elements of the sociopolitical process which cannot be changed by policy design and political action.)
- □ One of the central concepts in the theory of the social process must be power, for the policy designer must understand how power functions in both political and nonpolitical institutions, and what kinds of power can be exerted to implement programs.

Fourth, policy-oriented social science must of course be concerned with values; it cannot delude itself that it is value free, for it must provide the policy designer with the means to achieve values stated as goals. However, the data-gathering process must follow scrupulously the dictates of rigor and objectivity prevailing in academic social science; otherwise, it is possible that the policy researcher will supply the policy designer with findings that underestimate the difficulties and the obstacles to implementing programs.

Fifth, policy-oriented research must also be particularly concerned with the values of all those participating in or affected by a specific policy, not only to discourage the policy designer from imposing his own or his sponsor's values on the beneficiaries of the policy, but also to make sure that the designed policy bears some relevance to the aspirations of those affected by it. This is not to say that policy design must honor all exisitng values, for policies which provide benefits to some will also create costs to others. The policy researcher must therefore collect data not only on what values are held by people affected by a specific policy, but also how intensely these are held, and what incentives or sanctions would change them if necessary.

Finally, one of the prime values underlying policy-oriented social science and its research methods must be democracy. The policy researcher, like the policy designer, must be responsive to the values and aspirations of the people for whom they are designing policy, but their relationships with people involved in both research and policy design phases must also eschew the elitism sometimes found in academic social science which treats the researched as "subjects." People who want to participate in the research itself must be allowed to do so whenever possible, and policy research and design must be predicated on the notion of planning with, not planning for people.

3 *Alvin L. Schorr*

Public Policy and Private Interest

It was said of Samuel Johnson that he was a pessimistic man, but cheerfulness kept breaking through. This distinction should be set forth explicitly. I am a reformer by temperament, and by training disposed to believe that scientific method can show the way. This combination produces a powerful optimism that may flicker but does not die. Still, I have spent ten years observing the development of national welfare policy at close hand and must acknowledge that social science had rather little to do with it. So the optimism in this essay will be temperamental and the pessimism a reflection upon by experience—which is limited, after all. When optimism and pessimism are mixed in the open air, the result is anger; a little of that may be discerned too.

Theory of Randomness

My point of departure in this essay is a theory of randomness concerning the movement of social policy. This means that the nation does not move from trial and error to new trials, from experience to correcting errors, or from systematic evidence to programs based on that evidence. It means also that, although needs produce solutions, the correspondence is very far from point to point, and some needs are never noticed. I use randomness here in this narrow but, I dare say, rational sense. Of course, social policy does not develop randomly from a political point of view, but responds to the desires of the electorate as these are expressed through the political process. In effect, this is to say that, so far as welfare policy is concerned, the electorate has not been attentive to systematic evidence or even to experience. Although governments are permitted considerable flexibility within the broad issues to which electorates pay attention, they have not used this latitude to be more systematic than the electorate.

Several illustrations of the point come to mind. In welfare policy, we have for at least 15 years been behaving as if dependency were a curable handicap. Therefore, we enact programs of social services for fatherless children and their mothers, and vocational rehabilitation for unemployed men and women. Congressmen vote for these programs, in part, because they believe that they promise a reduction in the cost of public assistance. None of these programs has produced such a result and so, from time to time, officials discover that few people receiving public assistance are curable of the need for it. One such Eureka speech was delivered by then Secretary Abraham Ribicoff and another by then White House Special Assistant Joseph Califano. Each was greeted with public surprise. Yet the in some ways excellent new welfare proposals of President Richard Nixon have been wrapped in the same promise. In three or four years, no doubt, some high government official will make a speech like those of Ribicoff and Califano, which will again be greeted with surprise.

Another illustration of the point is the community action program. Probably, its central function was to act as a collaboration of social services that would bring down barriers to opportunity. If that was the intent when it was enacted, it went against the evidence that was beginning to accumulate. The so-called juvenile delinquency projects of the early 1960s were intended specifically as tests of the effectiveness of such programs in opening opportunity. The evidence was only beginning to come in when the poverty program began, and it was cloudy, but one would have had to read the findings at that point as negative.

The history of the search for comprehensive urban planning offers a final illustration. For 20 years, we have moved from urban renewal, through comprehensive redevelopment, workable programs, community renewal plans and into model cities, not troubling to alter the slogans with each new name. We have acted each time as if the earlier conception was partial and, by directing attention to the need for comprehensiveness, we were entering a new era. Comprehension has been in shorter supply than comprehensiveness. It is dangerous to oversimplify—some changes were introduced with the new programs—but comprehensiveness was not new. And nothing was done about the central reason that comprehensiveness never took hold, namely, that the planners lacked responsibility for or control over events.

(Presumably, it is not necessary to say that I support the provision of social services, and think community action and comprehensive planning good things. I simply object to justifying them on grounds we know or ought to know are unsound, or to distorting *other* programs by stuffing these good ideas down their bellies.)

Obviously, we do from time to time develop good new programs and reshape old programs in ways that evidence would suggest is sound. Community action was fine because it moved poor people toward participation—a good in itself—and because in some small way it redistributes social services. The Elementary and Secondary Education Act of 1965 has produced marginal improvements in the education of rural children and, perhaps, slowed the deterioration of central city schools; and it has fed quite a lot of children who would have gone hungry. Nixon's welfare proposals will, if enacted in the shape he offered them, raise levels of assistance in four or five states and considerably broadened eligibility in most states.

If one reflects on these or other progressive moves, however, it is evident how little they have to do with their ostensible objective or with social science. The three programs listed probably owe their genesis more to the desperate financial plight of cities and states than to any other single factor. The poverty program and the Education Act came in a time and manner dictated by more powerful developments than the need for them: the guilt of a decade of dividing affluence among the affluent (a guilt which has now, apparently, dissipated); the death of John Kennedy and the inauguration of Lyndon Johnson, with all the passion and ambition that were aroused; and the turning in frustration of the still powerful civil rights movement to goals it *could* achieve. A strong force behind the poverty program and the president's welfare proposals is middle- and working-class hatred of bureaucracy (entirely akin to the anger that leads our young people to protest). But since the real objective is war against bureaucracy, it is not necessary to test or discard ideas that are dear to us—that eating is a sign of merit, for example. And when these programs fail to wipe out poverty or hunger—because we set the programs firmly on the road to failure—it adds fuel to our anger at the bureaucrats who balked us once more, as it seems.

The point being illustrated may be clear: We get forward movement in social policy out of the resonance of developments that are quite unrelated to social science and may be unrelated to reason. Because such forward movement must satisfy its sources before anything else, the actual design of programs shows little fundamental influence of social science. Along with that, as has already been said, on some matters we get no movement at all.

If social policy moves randomly, one constructive question is why. Ideas about this will be discussed under two headings—first, public values and definitions and then, limitations in the practice of social science.

Greed

It must be self-evident that public values determine the direction of social policy. It would be difficult to argue that it should be otherwise. It is hardly novel to observe that the Protestant ethic is at the root of the problem in welfare policy. If failure and dependency are signs of God's displeasure, truly those who suffer from it need treatment more than money—and evidence to the contrary is frivolous. Quite possibly, we deal with a similar value problem in educational policy. We are generally conscious of and troubled by the fact that we do not know very much about how to improve the quality of education. But we seem to be untroubled by the fact that generally rising levels of education do not greatly affect poverty in the United States. A grade school education was once a pretty good thing. A high school education sufficed not so long ago. Very soon, a college degree will be required to assure a moderate level of income. With education as with income, apparently, the absolute level achieved matters less than one's position relative to the average.

The point has been made by an international comparison: The average duration of education in Great Britain is no more than the educational level our poor people achieve. The fact that our poor people would be quite adequately educated in Britain—a country widely regarded as industrial—does them no good here. In short, it is the distributional pattern in education that affects one's ability to compete for a job. Yet, with our stubborn faith in self-improvement, we provide Head Start and special funds for high schools in the ghettoes and ignore the fact that we are improving the education of the rest of the population at least as quickly. (We are running to stand still and, to be sure, few would argue that we should do less.)

One is tempted to shrug fatalistically, leaving the work ethic and Calvinist theology in undisputed possession of the field. However, when values are asserted again and again despite experience that should qualify them or where they are irrelevant, one must look for their roots. One comes to see the underlying values at play as more primitive and not so sweetly overlaid with religion. The values being asserted are greed for money and status and the right of the powerful to the spoils. Most people in the country appear to be unwilling to give up having more than someone else or feeling better than someone else, whatever peace or sense of community might be produced. (In everyday speech, this is expressed as: "Who helped us when we came!" and "I worked hard all my life and now they're giving it away!") Those are the values we are dealing with. They have made us great and powerful—I say that without irony—but we are paying a terrible price for them.

Circular Definitions

Closely (even circularly) related to public values is the public definition of issues. One understands in general that the way a problem is defined may determine the conclusions about it. For example, the fiscal problem of federal, state and local governments is in large part a result of the growing welfare burden, according to widespread public definition. Yet the figures demonstrate that in recent years welfare costs (including social security) have grown less rapidly than health costs or education costs, considered either as federal expenditures or as state and local expenditures. Indeed, federal expenditures on health have tripled and education quadrupled while welfare was growing by only half. State and local expenditures have also increased faster in health and education than in welfare. An instinctive reaction, upon absorbing these figures, is to observe that the increases in health and education costs are not relevant; they are increases on a smaller base and, more important, the public is willing to bear them. Welfare increases are scandalous mainly because they are quite unwanted. That is the point, of course. Welfare costs are defined as the fiscal problem *because* welfare is disliked. So the definition of welfare as the cause of the fiscal problem is circular. Yet it fuels public resentment of the program.

Similarly, it is intriguing to observe which facts and research findings gain currency and which do not. For example, the steady, sharp increase in public assistance rates in New York City began leveling off in the fall of 1969. It was a gratifying development; the mayor and other prominent officials took pains to speak about it in public. But the newspapers did not pick it up until it had been said quite a number of times in their presence. Again, most sociologists are aware how little research supports the view that interfaith marriage is inordinately risky. But article after article on the subject has appeared that failed to make this point, although at least some of the authors understood it. The boldest statement that is permitted—and when it came, the writer regarded it as a breakthrough—is that interfaith marriages can be successful, *if the partners are especially mature.* These examples are not cited to look for a devil in the newspapers, or to say once again that Madison Avenue can shape our minds. Rather, the newspapers are in the public grip quite as much as the other way around. If the public has seized upon rising welfare rates or the breakdown of religious barriers to account for its troubles, it is not news to cite findings to the contrary. The newspaper that insists will be thought dull and preachy.

Pragmatism

Apart from public definition, public values also find support or at least protection from challenge in the pragmatic nature of government. Pragmatism is not used here to mean that the government relies on no assumptions or generalizations at all. At the other extreme, one does not expect government to seek a complete set of generalizations accounting for all the behavior in some field. But even short of this, government is not hospitable to the development of plausible new generalizations, derived from social science, on which policy may or would be based. This probably is not true of economic theory, which seems to be well, if only recently, established.

It may help to illustrate the point. I have written elsewhere of the almost clinical depression, as it seemed to me, with which high government officials responded to the Detroit riots of 1967. Detroit deflated the assumption on which the government was then operating, namely, that if competent men worked desperately to create visible programs for the disadvantaged, people would respond with satisfaction or at least patience. When that innocent formulation was swept away, the administration was left with nothing to put in its place. Officials might well have found themselves depressed. It would appear that the succeeding administration did not try to develop a theory, but rather shifted attention to other problems or client groups.

A few programs may seem to rest on theories—the juvenile delinquency program, the poverty program, Model Cities. On closer examination, it appears that some of the people involved in the formulation of these programs had theories, but one person's theory differed from another's. The programs that were put together compromised these differing views, and accommodated the views of others who had no theories at all but would describe themselves as pragmatists. When the programs were launched, administrators selected for application the theories or non-theory that they found congenial. That accounts, in some measure, for the difficulty in securing agreement about the theory of the poverty program. When an administration turns over, of course, there is a certain loss of interest in demonstrating the validity of a theory of the prior administration. And so the Model Cities program, which may have held a theory, was quickly converted from experimentation into a simple conduit of federal funds to cities.

In any event, the juvenile delinquency, poverty and Model Cities program were exceptional in even dealing with theory. The bulk of federal programming in these fields—welfare, education, youth and alienation, mental health—involves very little theory at all. Why should that be so? Theories or, at any rate, theorists are resistant to compromise in an arena where compromise is an everyday necessity. Theories are natural targets for hostile Congressmen or special interest groups. For example, Secretary Robert F. Finch began his introduction of the Family Assistance Act of 1969 to the House Ways and Means Committee with the following language: "We sought, in designing the Family Assistance Plan, to identify and deal directly with the most pressing problems facing public welfare today. While it is a far-reaching and fundamental reform of public welfare, the Family Assistance Plan is a practical and pragmatic program . . . . This problem solving approach, rather than a theoretical approach . . . ." and so on. It is a particularly interesting statement because the Family Assistance Plan was, in fact, based on a theory about the significance of work in public assistance and how it may best be maintained. But the Secretary solicited the support of Congress by opposing his pragmatism and theirs to theory.

Theories themselves can also be tools of one interest group or another, limiting the inclination of officials to deal with them academically. For example, any reasonable theory about the social impact of the distribution of income in the United States might make it difficult to justify the 1969 tax cut. At the same time, the dubious theory that inflation hurts poor people more than anyone else helped to justify a policy that created unemployment. To continue with reasons that the government may be hostile to theory, as has already been implied, the fact that the time perspective of each administration is three years or less is inimical to the testing of theories which, in these complicated days, requires a little time. A final reason for abjuring theory may be a governmental tendency to rely on incremental developments. Increments have the advantage of accommodating old interests even while attempting to develop new patterns. Yet, some theories simply cannot be tested by increments. That is the heart of the argument about the Coleman report, for example, that children who do not demonstrably respond to *somewhat* better classroom situations would respond to *much* better classroom situations. Or, as another example, it can be argued that we will not get desegregation with any program less powerful in the 1970s than FHA was in the 1950s. No demonstration effort or small program can tell us what would happen in such a case, that is, if we arranged matters so that private enterprise profits on a large scale from desegregation.

To sum up so far: Social science has rather little relation to policy development because policies are determined by values that are often unrecognized. These values, in turn, determine the very definition of the issues, and so we get fed back to us the solution to the issues that our values demand. Then our resolutely pragmatic approach to government makes it hard from one decade to the next to know what theories, and therefore what programs, are serving us well or poorly. To be sure, pragmatism is said to keep the body politic at peace (is someone asking, "What peace?") and to help to contain a temperamentally violent people in a highly stable government. One must place considerable value on stable government. The point is merely that, despite considerable testimony to the contrary, in certain areas we have a relatively inflexible set of values. This set of values is embedded in a system that protects it from searching examination. That does not contribute to rational or social scientific policy development, which is to say that policy develops at random.

We now turn to the way social scientists operate in and in relation to government. Included in what follows are clinicians such as social workers and psychiatrists who, while working on policy development, seek guidance in systematic research. I will consider intellectual difficulties first and then self-interest.

Intellectual Problems

A worrisome intellectual problem is that social scientists take a narrow view of problems that require a broader view. That is, they approach problems by way of a single discipline. It is barely necessary to repeat what has been said so often, but it is perhaps useful to illustrate how this limitation affects policy development. For example, "culture of poverty" explanations of the behavior of poor people draw vitality from two sources that are peripheral to the evidence. One source of vitality that should bring no surprise is that this set of ideas defines the problem in a way that supports current values. The other source of vitality is that social scientists are expert in description of attitudes and status situations. They are largely inexpert on such matters as nutrition and in understanding what makes social patterns change over time. So "culture of poverty" reflects the expertise of the researchers more than it explains the situation or prospects of poor people. Yet this notion is the major support for social service and educational strategies in dealing with poverty.

Economists, more than others, often offer a warning that they are about to take too narrow a view of a problem. Having come to a conclusion about some economic aspect of a question, they mutter *ceteris paribus* before making their policy recommendation. "All things being equal" ought to be treated as a proclamation of ignorance, but is more often a ritual defense against considerations that one understands not to be very important at all. An illustration of the hazards when an economist moves narrowly from his discipline occurred in the deliberations of a United Nations group concerned with social defense. They were interested in the cost-effectiveness of various approaches to crime and delinquency—that is, dollar for dollar, is prevention more effective than jails, and so forth? At one point, they found themselves discussing the most cost-effective approach to preventing juvenile delinquency in Vietnam. The war, as it did not lend itself to cost analysis in quite the same terms, was never mentioned, nor was its relationship to juvenile delinquency.

Another intellectual problem in the applicability of social sciences is the value that is placed on elaboration. Our universities may be directly responsible for this. Students are taught to abandon unlearned common sense and, with it, simplicity. Somehow the necessary search for rigor in thinking is converted into overvaluing the complex and technical. Therefore, simple matters may be overlooked. For example, the significance to social behavior of nutrition and shelter were all but ignored in post-World War II research. When one seeks a policy recommendation from people so disposed, the result is either a retreat to the need for more research or a hopelessly involved recommendation. This is not to plead for reductionism but only to name the parallel error of elaborationism. People who have been trained in this manner teach or do highly technical work; they tend not to address themselves to policy development anyway. However, the pattern of thinking influences those who do set out to deal with policy matters.

A third intellectual problem lies in the relevance to policy of the research that is done. On one hand, many of the issues that trouble sociologists and psychologists have very little consequence in the social policy world. The fact is too well known to require elaboration. On the other hand, a good deal of research is dominated by the government's needs and definitions. It is not necessary to argue that actual slanting of findings occurs very often. But the choice of research subject and the terms in which it is pursued quite often determine the outcome. As an example, it is not an accident that the negative income tax is the only substantial departure in income maintenance that has been experimented with. Staff at the Office of Economic Opportunity, the Department of Health, Education and Welfare and the President's Commission on Income Maintenance Programs decided before President Nixon assumed office that that was the program the country should have. And so an administration that came into office encouraging experimentation in various forms of income maintenance was, in less than a year, instructed by the president himself to support only income maintenance projects that had been approved in the White House. That may not be unusual behavior in a government. But how does one account for the fact that, with interest in the subject high, not a single university developed a study that broke through the government's definition or predilection?

Another intellectual issue troubles those social scientists who get directly involved with high government officials on a policy issue. They are likely to be offered friendly advice on how to shape their recommendations for maximum political effect. They may be told that a recommendation is sound, but needs to be clothed in different rhetoric. Or they may be told how large a step or what sort of strategy is likely to be effective at the moment. It is a difficult problem. One does not want to be intransigent or ingenuous nor, however, to abandon solid professional or technical ground. I offer you only my own observation. Social scientists err much more often in accommodating themselves to political advice than in intransigence.

From social scientists who are barely concerned with social policy—the elaborationists—the discussion has moved to those who are so concerned that they have to decide how purely to deal with their discipline. It is necessary to make a final point about the intellectual problem of those social scientists who try to affect social policy most broadly. Social scientists and professional organizations carrying such a role find that evidence that leads directly to policy recommendations is comparatively rare. Rather, these spokesmen are usually bringing to bear the basic values of their discipline—humanism, rationality, a therapeutic rather than a penal approach. Either that, or more explicitly, they are arguing the merits of the disciplines they know—the economist urging econometrics, the sociologist urging the importance of institutions, the social worker promoting group work and casework. The public is not really faced with social science but with contending values and interests. Decisions are not made on evidence but on who happens to have acceptance, power or the most persuasive line. The intellectual problem for these social scientists is that research and analysis are not being conducted in a manner that is useful to them. They argue from their values or intuitions, or desist.

Self-Interest

We have been cataloguing intellectual difficulties in bringing social science to bear upon social policy, and perhaps it is already obvious how closely involved with these difficulties is the self-interest of social scientists. If social scientists are trained in elaborationism, it is because their professors are most secure with that. It is the surest route to academic success for faculty and students as well. The National Academy of Sciences and Social Science Research Council put the point as follows: "Many academic scientists value the prestige that their contributions to basic research and theory give them in the eyes of their peers more than whatever rewards might be obtained from clients who would find their work useful. It . . . leads not only to scientific knowledge, but also to respect and status tendered by those whose judgments they value most." If universities waste no time on research that the government will not fund anyway, more students will be taught and provided stipends and more status and resources accrued to the department. If social workers promote social services and social scientists promote research, higher salaries and richer perquisites will be available all around. An example of the exception that proves the rule was the testimony of the National Committee for the Day Care of Children concerning the 1967 amendments to the Social Security Act. The association testified against those amendments because they would be damaging to children and their families, even though day care programs in particular were to be greatly expanded. There are not so many examples of that sort; not all the testimony on the 1967 amendments was so disinterested.

More insidious than the narrow self-interest of each discipline and more difficult to explain without being misunderstood, is the coalition of self-interests that gather around social research. Daniel Bell has made the argument that the intellectual class is now maneuvering for political power, a development that facilitates and is in turn supported by building up financially secure bases of operation for intellectuals. Noam Chomsky makes a finer charge, that experts or "scholar-technicians" are maneuvering to take power from "free-floating intellectuals" who tend to be more attentive to values than techniques. The two observations are not incompatible, and one may think them both right. The scholar arguing the merits of research asserts a class interest quite as much as the miner arguing the merits of coal. Certainly, excessive claims have been made for research. The point is beginning to be acknowledged retrospectively, but nothing prevents social scientists from asking that funds for research be written into each new piece of legislation. There are matters we know how to study and others we do not. There are studies for which personnel is available and others for which it is not. Some research ought to be initiated by government and other research not. How is it that social scientists all together support—by silence, if not affirmatively—requests for funds for social research of any sort?

I do not, more than anyone else, want to seem impolite. One can bring to mind very fine work by social scientists, and some examples of courage and self-sacrifice. Yet it is necessary to examine the possibility that they do not represent the generality. It appears that the nation is now structured on professions and occupations as the medieval world was structured on guilds. There is no yielding of self-interest on any side, not among social scientists and not among the professions. If they believe their own dire prophecies—those social scientists who make dire prophecies—should they not on occasion find recommendations to make to Congress and the country that are counter to their self-interest?

Conclusion

The simplest conclusion is a summary that will itself seem simple: Public policy is dominated by public values—naturally. These values are comparatively inflexible, and are protected from critical examination by social forces and the tendencies of government. That is convenient, as it permits greed to operate unimpeded and even unnamed. Social science is a mirror image of the larger situation, despite the fact that its traditions demand that it be quite different. Social science, too, has impediments to substantial critical examination of major policy issues, and tends—so the record shows—to pursue its own self-interest. Therefore, in relationship to reason or social science, one would expect social policy to move at random—as indeed it appears to do.

That is how it seems to me; do I see any hope? The intellectual tradition of social scientists provides grounds for hope. Ideologies tend to carry on even when they are not practiced, and young social scientists continue to be taught integrity and scientific rigor. When they mix those ideas with the ones they are developing for themselves—rejection of materialism and self-interest and a demand for relevance, we may see a different social science with different effects.

As for the older social scientists, perhaps we may rely on their sense of irony. We have already noted the cost-effectiveness approach to juvenile delinquency in Vietnam. I have in mind also a federal program that provides food for pregnant and nursing mothers if their doctors will prescribe it. Jonathan Swift could have thought of nothing finer. We might run all of public assistance on the basis of physicians' prescriptions. One day such black humor will be too much for social scientists, and they will take on social policy in earnest.

4 *Irving Louis Horowitz*

Social Science Yogis and Military Commissars

"The bonds between the government and the universities are . . . an arrangement of convenience, providing the government with politically usable knowledge and the university with badly needed funds." The speaker of these words, Senator J. William Fulbright, went on to warn that such alliances may endanger the universities, may bring about "the surrender of independence, the neglect of teaching, and the distortion of scholarship." Many other distinguished Americans are worried by the growing number of alliances between the military and the university.

The Setting

Instead of the expected disclaimers and denials from university officials, however, in recent months these men—from both the administrative and academic sides—have rushed to take up any slack in doing secret research on campus, asking that the number of projects they are already handling be increased. Arwin A. Dougal, assistant director of the Pentagon's office for research and engineering, has indicated that while some major universities are gravely concerned about academic research for military ends, most universities realize how important "classified research" is to the national security. Indeed, Dougal has said that many professors involved in secret research actually try to retain their security clearances when their projects are completed. Rather than disengaging themselves, they, like many university leaders, are eager to participate to an even greater extent.

Symptomatic of the ever-tightening bond between the military and the social scientist is a "confidential," 53-page document entitled *Report of the Panel on Defense Social and Behavioral Sciences.* It was the offspring of a summer 1967 meeting, in Williamstown, Mass., of members of the Defense Science Board of the National Academy of Sciences. This board is the highest-ranking science advisory group of the Defense Department. The meeting's purpose: to discuss which social-science research could be of most use to the Department of Defense (DoD).

The Report of the Panel on Defense Social and Behavioral Sciences throws a good deal of light on current relations between the national government and the social sciences. Unlike Project Camelot, the abortive academic-military project to investigate counterinsurgency potentials in the Third World, this Report was not inspired by government contractual requests. It is the work of leading social scientists who have been closely connected with federal research. Unlike *Report from Iron Mountain,* this Report can hardly be described as a humanistic hoax. The authors are known, the purpose of the Report explicit, and the consequences clearly appreciated by all concerned. What we have in this Report is a collective statement by eminent social scientists, a statement that can easily be read as the ominous conversion of social science into a service industry of the Pentagon.

Most of the scholars who prepared this Report have one striking similarity—they have powerful and simultaneous academic and government linkages. They move casually and easily from university to federal affiliation—and back again to the university.

The panel's chairman, S. Rains Wallace, the exception, is president of the American Institutes of Research, a nonprofit organization that does research under contract for government agencies, including the DoD.

Gene M. Lyons, who is executive secretary of the Advisory Committee on Government Programs in the Behavioral Sciences of the National Research Council (affiliated with the National Academy of Sciences), is also a professor at Dartmouth College. (He maintains, however, that he attended only one day of the meeting, and as an observer only.)

Peter Dorner, functioning through the Executive Office of the President on the Council of Economic Advisers, is also a professor of economics at the Land

Tenure Center of the University of Wisconsin.

Eugene Webb, listed as a professor at Stanford University, is now serving a term as a member of the Institute for Defense Analysis, specifically, its science and technology division.

Other panel members—Harold Guetzkow of Northwestern University; Michael Pearce of the RAND Corporation; anthropologist A. Kimball Romney of Harvard University; and Roger Russell, formerly of Indiana University and now Vice-Chancellor for Academic Affairs at the University of California (Irvine)—also shift back and forth between the polity and the academy. It is plain, then, that these men have penetrated the political world more deeply than members of past project-dominated research activities.

In addition to this similarity, nearly all of these social scientists have had overseas experience, and are intimately connected with federal use of social science for foreign-area research. Yet, as in the case of Camelot, this common experience does not seem to produce any strong ideological unanimity. The men range from relatively conservative political theorists to avowed pacifists. This underscores the fact that patriotism and professional purpose tend to supersede the political viewpoints or credos these men may adhere to.

The Report

The Report closely follows the memorandum that John S. Foster Jr., director of Defense Research and Engineering of the Department of Defense, issued to the chairman of the panel. Foster's marching orders to the panel members requested that they consider basically four topics: "high-payoff" areas in research and development—"areas of social and behavioral science research in which it would be reasonable to expect great payoffs over the next three to ten years"; research to solve manpower problems; Project THEMIS, a DoD project for upgrading the scientific and engineering capabilities of various academic institutions so they can do better research for the Defense Department; and, finally, broad-ranging government-university relationships.

Before commenting on the Report, let me provide a summary of its findings and recommendations.

To begin with, the Report urges increased effort and funding for research on manpower, in all its aspects; for research on organization studies; for research on decision-making; for increasing the understanding of problems in foreign areas; and for research on man and his physical environment.

- Under "Manpower," we read, among other things:

  "In order to make full use of the opportunities provided by Project 100,000 [to make soldiers out of rehabilitated juvenile delinquents] both for the military and for the national economy, we recommend that fully adequate funds be invested to cover all aspects of the military and subsequent civilian experience of the individuals involved."

- Under "Organization Studies":

  "Research on style of leadership and improved methods of training for leadership should be revitalized."

- Under "Decision-Making":

  "Techniques for the improvement of items which might assist in forecasting alliances, neutralities, hostile activities, etc., and for use in tactical decision-making need to be expanded, applied, and tested in the real world."

- Under "Understanding of Operational Problems in Foreign Areas":

  "Despite the difficulties attendant upon research in foreign areas, it must be explicitly recognized that the missions of the DoD cannot be successfully performed in the absence of information on (a) socio-cultural patterns in various areas including beliefs, values, motivations, etc.; (b) the social organization of troops, including political, religious, and economic; (c) the effect of change and innovation upon socio-cultural patterns and socio-cultural organization of groups; (d) study and evaluation of action programs initiated by U.S. or foreign agencies in under-developed countries.

  "Solid, precise, comparative, and current empirical data developed in a programmatic rather than diffuse and opportunistic fashion are urgently needed for many areas of the world. This goal should be pursued by: (a) multidisciplinary research teams; (b) series of field studies in relevant countries; (c) strong representation of quantitative and analytic skills; (d) a broad empirical data base."

- Under "Man and His Physical Environment":

  "Continuing and additional research are needed on the effect of special physical and psychological environments upon performance and on possibilities for the enhancement of performance through a better understanding of man's sensory and motor output mechanisms, the development of artificial systems which will aid performance, and the search for drugs or foods which may enhance it."

- Under "Methodology":

  "We recommend increased emphasis upon research in behavioral-science methodology. While this is basic to all of the areas listed above, it needs to be recognized as worthy of investment in its own right. The systematic observation of the many quasi-experimental situations which occur in everyday military activities must be made possible if we are to learn from experience. We recommend that a capability be established in one or more suitable in-house laboratories to address the question of how the logistical problems of such observation can be solved."

Why the DoD is No. 1

The Department of Defense (DoD) is the most sought-after and frequently-found sponsor of social-science research. And the DoD is sought and found by the social scientists, not, as is often imagined, the other way around. Customarily, military men provide only grudging acceptance of any need for behavioral research.

There are four distinct reasons why the DoD is sponsoring more and more social-science research.

■ First, money. In fiscal 1968, Congressional appropriations for research and development amount to the monumental sum of $14,971.4 million. Of this, an incredible $13,243.0 million, or about 85 percent, is distributed among three agencies whose primary concern is the military system: the Atomic Energy Commission, the National Aeronautics and Space Administration, and the DoD. The figure for the DoD alone is $6680.0 million. This means that a single federal agency commands nearly two-fifths of the government research dollar. So it is easy to see why so much effort and energy is expended by social scientists trying to capture some of the monies the DoD can experiment with. As bees flock to honey, men flock to money—particularly in an era when costly data-processing and data-gathering strain the conventional sources of financing.

■ Second, the protection that research has when done for the DoD. I am referring to the blanket and indiscriminate way in which Congressional appropriations are made for both basic and applied research. Policy-linked social scientists operate under an umbrella of the secrecy established by the DoD's research agencies. Reasons of security ward off harassment by Congressional committees. Attacks over supposed misallocation of funds and resources—undergone by the National Institutes of Health at the hands of the committee headed by Rep. L.H. Fountain of North Carolina—are spared those academics with Defense Department funding.

This dispensation is strikingly illustrated by the fact that DoD allocations for research and development are not itemized the way allocations are for Health, Education, and Welfare. This auditing cover allows for even more experimenting in DoD spending than its already swollen funds might indicate. Such a *carte blanche* situation probably places far less of a strain on social scientists than would be the case if they worked for other agencies. In the world of research, power provides the illusion of freedom.

■ Third, the relatively blank-check Congressional approach to DoD funds, and the security umbrella of the auditing system, provide social scientists with unlimited resources. DoD allocations are not broken down into sub-agencies, nor are any of their specialized activities or services checked—unlike the usual scrutiny directed at other agencies.

That this fact has not gone entirely unnoticed is shown by the Congressional demand that as of 1968 the DoD be called to account on an appropriation budget.

■ Fourth, the DoD's connection with the "national security" —which protects the DoD and those who work for it—offers great temptations to social researchers interested in the "big news." For it enables the DoD not only to outspend such agencies as the National Science Foundation in university-based activities, but to penetrate areas of non-Defense research that are central only to the social-science researcher. Programs to support juvenile-delinquency research (Project 100,000) and others to upgrade academic institutions (Project THEMIS) are sponsored by the DoD rather than by the Office of Economic Opportunity, and not simply because of their disproportionate fundings. Just as important is the legitimation the DoD can provide for policy-oriented researchers in sensitive areas.

These are the main reasons why many social-science researchers are now enlisting the support of the DoD in their activities—despite the negative publicity surrounding Project Camelot and other such fallen angels. I.L.H.

■ On government-university relations:

"There is disagreement concerning the involvement of first-rate academic groups in behavioral science research relevant to long-term DoD needs. The task statement implies that DoD has not been successful in enlisting the interest and service of an eminent group of behavioral scientists in most of the areas relevant to it. This panel does not concur. We therefore recommend that the [National Academy of Sciences] Panel on Behavioral and Social Sciences be asked to address this problem and to determine whether, in fact, an acceptable proportion of first-rate academic workers are involved in DoD behavioral-science research."

"More high-quality scientists could probably be interested in DoD problems if DoD would more frequently state its research needs in terms which are meaningful to the investigator rather than to the military. . . . Publicity concerning the distinguished behavioral scientists who have long-term commitments to the DoD should be disseminated as a way of reassuring younger scientists and improving our research image."

The Panelists

Why did these distinguished social scientists accept the assignment from the DoD? Most of them seemed particularly intrigued by the chance to address important issues. They view the work done by the DoD in such areas as racially segregated housing, or the rehabilitation of juvenile delinquents through military participation, as fascinating illustrations of how social science can settle social issues. It is curious how this thirst for the application of social science led the panelists to ignore the *prima facie* fact that the DoD is in the defense business, and that therefore it inevitably tends to assign high priority to military potential and effectiveness. Further, the question of what is important is continually linked to matters of relevance to the DoD. In this way, the question of professional autonomy is transformed into one of patriotic responsibility.

In general, the idealism of social scientists participating in DoD-sponsored research stems from their profound belief in the rectifiability of federal shortcomings, as well as in the perfectibility of society through the use of social science. Despite the obviousness of the point, what these social scientists forget is that the federal government as well as its agencies is limited by historical and geopolitical circumstances. It is committed to managing cumbersome, overgrown committees and data-gathering agencies. It is committed to a status quo merely for the sake of rational functioning. It can only tinker with innovating ideas. Thus federal agencies will limit investigation simply to what is immediately useful not out of choice, but from necessity.

The social scientist often imagines he is a policy formulator, an innovating designer. Because of the cumbersome operations of government, he will be frustrated in realizing this self-image and be reduced to one more instrumental agent. His designing mentality, his strain toward perfecting, will appear unrealistic in the light of what he can do. He gets caught up in theoryless applications to immediacy, surrenders the value of confronting men with an image of what *can be*, and simply accepts what others declare *must be*. Thus, what the social scientist knows comes down to what the Defense Department under present circumstances can use.

Although the initiative for this Report came from the social scientists, the DoD provided the structure and direction of its content. To a remarkable degree, the study group accepted DoD premises.

For example, the two major assumptions that influenced its thinking are stated baldly. First, since the DoD's job now embraces new responsibilities, its proper role becomes as much to wage "peacefare" as warfare. Peacefare is spelled out as pacification of total populations, as well as a role in the ideological battle between East and West. Toward such ends, it is maintained, social science can play a vital part.

Nowhere in the document is the possibility considered that the DoD ought not to be in many of these activities—that perhaps the division of labor has placed too great an emphasis upon this one agency of government at the expense of all others. Nor is it anywhere made clear that similar types of educational and antipoverty programs the DoD is engaged in are already under way in other branches of government—that DoD activities might be duplicating and needlessly multiplying the efforts of the Department of Health, Education and Welfare or the National Science Foundation.

The second explicit assumption the group makes is that hardware alone will not win modern wars; manpower is needed, too. Here the panelists see social science as providing data on the dynamics of cultural change and a framework for the needs and attitudes of other people.

But here, too, there is a remarkable absence of any consideration of the sort of "manpower" deployed in foreign environments; or of the differing responses of overseas peoples to such manpower. The foreign role of the U.S. Defense Department is simply taken as a given, a datum to be exploited for the display of social science information. In this sense, U.S. difficulties with foreign military activities can be interpreted as a mere misunderstanding of the nature of a problem. Expertise and objectivity can then be called upon where a policy design is lacking or failing. Thus even the DoD can mask policy shortcomings behind the fact of a previously inadequate supply of data. In this way, the credibility gap gets converted into a mechanical informational gap. Which is exactly what is done in the Report. All efforts, in other words, are bent to maximizing social science participation rather than to minimizing international conflict.

Still a third assumption of the panel participants—one that is not acknowledged—is that their professional autonomy will not be seriously jeopardized by the very fact of their dependence upon the DoD. Indeed, many scholars seem to have abandoned their primary research interests for the secondary ones that can be funded. And the main responsibility for this shift lies not with the DoD but with the social-science professions and the scholarly community at large.

As one panel member ironically noted, in response to my questionnaire, the position of the DoD is an unhappy reflection of university demands that individual scholars and university presidents pay for expanding university overhead and enlarge graduate programs—rather than any insistence by federal agencies that the nature of social science be transformed. Another panel member indicated that, whatever dishonor may exist in the present relationships between social science and the DoD, the main charge would have to be leveled at the professoriat, rather than at the funding agencies. And while this assignment of priorities in terms of who is responsible for the present era of ill will and mistrust can be easily overdone, and lead to a form of higher apologetics in which there is mutual accusation by the social scientists and government policy-makers, it does seem clear that the simplistic idea that the evil government corrupts the good social scientist is not only an exaggeration but, more often, a deliberate misrepresentation.

The Findings

Reexamining the specific findings of first section of the Report, "High Payoff Research in Development Areas," leaves no doubt that the panelists mean by "high payoff" those potential rewards to be netted by the DoD, rather than advantages to be gained by social scientists. This is made explicit in the section on "Manpower," in which the main issues are contended to concern problems of improving the performance of soldiers equipped with high-level technology. It is in this connection that the panelists heartily approve of Project 100,000. Although (with the exception of two panelists) there is a special cloudiness as to the nature of Project 100,000, the panelists have no doubt that the employment of delinquents in this fashion makes the best use of marginal manpower for a "tremendous payoff" for the future efficiency of the defense establishment.

A number of the Report's recommendations amount to little more than the repetition of basic organizational shibboleths. But even at this level, special problems seem to arise. There is confusion in the minds of the panelists, or at least throughout the Report that they prepared, about what constitutes internal DoD functions as opposed to those belonging to general military functions. The phrase "military establishment" functions as an umbrella disguising this ambiguity. Not only is the relationship between a civilian-led DoD and a "military establishment" unresolved, but beyond that the panelists appear willing to discount the organizational intermingling of the DoD with other governmental agencies—such as the Census Bureau, the Department of Labor, and the Department of Health, Education, and Welfare.

This leads to a tacit acceptance of DoD organizational colonialism. Not only is the DoD urged to be on the lookout for other agencies' collecting similar data and doing similar sorts of analyses, but also an explicit request that the DoD exert a special effort to use the work of outside agencies is included. On behalf of "cooperation," there exists the risk of invasion of privacy, and other dangers encountered when any single department functions as a total system incorporating the findings of other sub-units.

The Report contends that those parts of the armed services responsible for developing basic knowledge about decision-making have done their work well. It is interesting that no examples are given. Moreover, the military and civilian personnel who provide support for decision-making within the military establishment are said to have a rare opportunity to contribute to this steadily-improving use of sound decision-making models for areas like material procurement for front-line battle medical services. Nothing is said about the nature of the conflict to be resolved, or the values employed in such decisions.

While several members of the panel, in response to the questionnaire of mine, indicated that they held this Report to be an indirect resolution of problems raised by Project Camelot, the formulations used in this Report are similar to those used in the Camelot study concerning overseas research.

The Report states: "Comparative organizational work should not be done only within civilian groups such as large-scale building and construction consortia and worldwide airlines systems, but also within foreign military establishments." In Project Camelot, the same desire for military information was paramount. Curiously, no attention is given to whether, in fact, this is a high-payoff research area; or if it is, how this work is to be done without threatening the sovereignty of other nations. In other words, although the Report superficially is dedicated to the principle of maximum use of social science, this principle is not brought into play at the critical point. The ambiguities and doubts raised by previous DoD incursions into the area of foreign social research remain intact and are in no way even partially resolved.

The panelists are dedicated to the principle of high-payoff research, but appear to be disquietingly convinced that this is equivalent to whatever the members of the panel themselves are doing, or whatever their professional specialties are. Thus a high-payoff research area becomes the study of isolation upon individual and group behavior; or the area of simulation of field experiences that the military may encounter; or the study of behavior under conditions of ionizing radiation. It is not incidental that in each instance the panelists themselves have been largely engaged in such kinds of work. One is left with the distinct impression that a larger number of panelists would have yielded only a larger number of "high-payoff" areas, rather than an integrated framework of needs. This leads to a general suspicion that the Report is much more self-serving than a simple review of its propositions indicates.

The references to methodology again raise the specter of Camelot, since it is evident that no general methodology is demonstrated in the Report itself and no genuine innovations are formulated for future methodological directions. There is no discussion of the kind of methodology likely to yield meaningful prediction. Instead, the DoD is simply notified of the correctness of its own biases. We are told that "predictive indicators of a conflict or revolutionary overthrow are examples of the type of data which can gain from control applications." No illustrations of the success of such predictors is given. The purpose turns out to be not so much prediction as control of revolutionary outbreaks. This, then, constitutes the core methodological message of the Report.

Project THEMIS

As for Project THEMIS, designed to upgrade scientific and engineering performances at colleges and universities for the benefit of the Defense Department, the project titles at the institutions already selected do not furnish enough information to assess the actual nature of the research. A proposal of more than $1.1 million for research into "chemical compounds containing highly electro-negative elements" was turned down by the dean of faculties at Portland State College. Said he: "I know what the proposal was talking about. It could very easily be interpreted as a proposal involving biological warfare. The proposal could be construed as committing the university to biological warfare."

Among the universities now contracted for Project THEMIS work is the University of Utah, with the project title "Chemistry of Combustion." Newspaper accounts during the summer of 1967 indicated clearly that this project was aimed at improving missile fuels. Additional illustrations could be given, but the point is clear: Project THEMIS is what it claims to be, a program to involve universities in research useful to the Defense Department.

The panelists assure us that "DoD has been singularly successful at enlisting the interest and services of an eminent group of behavioral scientists in most of the areas relevant to it." They go on to say that, indeed, "the management of behavioral science research in the military department should be complimented for long-term success in building the image of DoD as a good and challenging environment in which to do both basic and applied research." No names are cited to indicate that there are eminent clusters of behavioral scientists working in the DoD. Nor is there an indication whether "the eminent men" connected with DoD are in fact remotely connected as part-time consultants (like the panelists themselves) or intimately connected with basic work for the government. And even though Foster's letter indicates that there is a problem of recruitment and government-university relations, the panel simply dismisses this as insignificant. Yet members go on to note that the DoD image is perhaps more tarnished than they would like to think; that, for example, the Civil Service Commission discriminates against the behavioral scientist with respect to appointments, and that it is hard to persuade behavioral scientists that the DoD provides a supportive environment for them. Despite the censure of the Civil Service Commission, it is claimed that the DoD has not been as attractive and as successful in social-science recruitment as we were earlier led to believe.

More damaging, perhaps, is the allegation of the panelists that quality control of research at universities is not in any way superior to that exercised within other research sources, such as the DoD. They tend to see "quality control" as something unrelated to university autonomy and its implications for objectivity. Lest there be any ambiguity on this point, they go on to indicate in an extraordinary series of unsupported allegations that the difficulty is not one of social-science autonomy versus the political requirements of any agency of government, but rather one of bad public relations—which is in turn mostly blamed on "Representatives of Civilian Professional Organizations" who lack a clear picture of DoD requirements and yet testify before Congressional committees, which in turn are backed up by social and behavioral scientists who regard such DoD activities as a threat to academic freedom and scientific integrity, and who "are usually ignorant of the work actually being performed under DoD's aegis."

The specific committee hearings referred to are nowhere indicated. Certainly, the various hearings on such proposed measures as a national social science foundation, or on social accounting, do exhibit the highest amount of professional integrity and concern. It might be that DoD intellectuals are concerned precisely over the non-policy research features of such proposed legislation.

Finally, the panelists offer a gentle slap on the wrist to defense research managers who allegedly lack the time to address themselves to these kinds of problems. In short and in sum, the Report ignores questions having to do with social science autonomy as if these were products of misperceptions to be resolved by good will and better public relations between the DoD and the Academy. That such conclusions should be reached by a set of panelists, half of whom are highly placed in academic life, indicates the degree to which closing the gap between the academy and the polity has paradoxically broken down the political capabilities of social science by weakening its autonomous basis.

The panelists have enough firmness of mind to make two unsolicited comments. But the nature of the comments reveals the flabbiness that results from the tendency of social scientists to conceive of their sciences as service activities rather than as scientific activities. They urge, first, that more work be done in the area of potential high-payoff fields of investigation that might have been overlooked in their own Report, given the short time they had available in preparing it. They further urge the establishment of a continuous group with time to examine other areas in greater depth and to discuss them more deliberately, so that high-payoff areas can be teased out and presented for cost considerations. In other words, the unsolicited comments suggest mechanisms for improving these kinds of recommendations and making them permanent. They do not consider whether the nature of social science requirements might be unfit for the bureaucratic specifications of Foster's originating letter.

Advise and Dissent

In some ways, the very tension between social scientists and policy-makers provided each group with a reality test against which basic ideas could be formulated about policy issues. But the very demand for a coalescence of the two, whether in the name of "significant" research or as a straight patriotic obligation, has the effect of corrupting social science and impoverishing policy options.

The question that the Report raises with terrible forcefulness is not so much about the relationship between pure and applied research, but about what the character of application is to be. Applied research is clearly here to stay and is probably the most forceful, singular novel element in American social science in contrast to its European background. What is at stake, however, is a highly refined concept of application that removes theoretical considerations of the character and balance of social forces and private interests from the purview of application. The design of the future replaces the analysis of the present in our "new utopian" world.

The panelists simply do not entertain the possibility that the social world is a behavioral "field" in which decisions have to be made between political goals no less than means. Reports cannot "depoliticalize" social action to such an extent that consequences do not follow and implicit choices are not favored. Innovation without a political goal simply assumes that operations leading to a change from one state to another are a value. The Report does not raise, much less favor, significant political changes in the operations of the DoD; and its innovative efforts are circumscribed to improving rather than to changing. However, efficiency is a limited use of applicability because it assumes rather than tests the adequacy of the social system.

The era of good feelings between the federal government and social science, which characterized the period between the outbreak of World War II and extended through the assassination of President John F. Kennedy, no longer exists. In its place seems to be the era of tight money. The future of "nonprofit" research corporations tied to the DoD is being severely impeded from both sides. Universities such as Pennsylvania, the University of California, and Princeton have taken a hard look at academic involvement in classified research for the Pentagon. Princeton, with its huge stake in international-relations programming, is even considering cancelling its sponsorship of a key research arm, the Institute for Defense Analysis. On the other side, many of the "hard" engineering types have continued to press their doubts as to the usefulness of software research. And this barrage of criticism finds welcome support among high military officers who would just as soon cancel social science projects as carry out their implications.

With respect to the panelists, it must be said that a number of them have indicated their own doubts about the Report. One of the participants has correctly pointed out that the Report has not yet been accepted by the DoD, nor have the findings or the recommendations been endorsed by the National Academy of Sciences. Another member claimed that his main reason for accepting the invitation to serve on the panel was to argue against the Defense Department's involving universities in operations such as Project Camelot. He went on to point out that his mission was unsuccessful, since he obviously did not influence the other panelists.

A third panelist points out that the Camelot type of issue was not, to his recollection at least, a criterion in any discussion of the topics. Yet he strongly disclaims his own participation as well as membership in the National Academy of Science Advisory Committee on Government Programs in the Behavioral Sciences. He also indicates that his panel had nothing but an administrative connection with the National Academy of Sciences, and he, too, seems to indicate that he had an ancillary advisory role rather than an integrated preparatory role.

Trying to gauge the accuracy with which the final Report represented a true consensus of the panelists proved most difficult. While most panelists, with hedging qualifications, agreed that the Report reflected an accurate appraisal of their own views, the question of the actual writeup of the document brought forth a far from consistent response. One panelist claims that "all members contributed to the basic draft of the Report. Each assumed responsibility for composing a section, all of which were then reviewed by the panel as a whole." Another panelist declared his participation only "as an observer," and that he was not involved in any final writeup. Yet a third panelist disclaimed any connection with preparing the Report.

A final, and still different, version was stated as follows: "The report was written by members of the committee and the overall editing and bringing-together responsibility was undertaken by Rains Wallace. One or two members of the committee were assigned to specific topics and drafts were prepared at Williamstown. These went to Wallace, who organized them, did some editing, and sent them back to us. Each person responded and the final version was then prepared by Wallace." In other words, the actual authorship of a document that was released "in confidence" over the names of some of America's most distinguished social scientists is either the work of all and the responsibility of none, or perhaps—as is more likely the case—the work of one or two people and the responsibility of all.

F.A.R. *vs* DoD

The issuance, even in semi-private form, of this Report reveals the existence of a wide gap between the thinking of the two chief departments involved in sensitive research and in research in foreign areas—namely, the Department of Defense and the Department of State. Indeed, the issuance of this Report is likely to exacerbate the feelings of high officials in the State Department that the Defense Department position represents an encroachment.

The memorandum issued in December 1967 by the Department of State's Foreign Area Research Coordination group (F.A.R.), in which it set forth foreign-area research guidelines, represents a direct rebuke or, at the very least, a serious challenge to the orientation that the Report of the Defense Science Board represents. It is a high point in federal recognition that real problems do exist.

The F.A.R. Report is broken into two different sections with seven propositions in each section. First, under Guidelines for Research Contract Relations Between Government and Universities, are the following:

(1) The government has the responsibility for avoiding actions that would call into question the integrity of American academic institutions as centers of independent teaching and research.

(2) Government research support should always be acknowledged by sponsor, university, and researcher.

(3) Government-supported contract research should, in process and results, ideally be unclassified, but given the practical needs of the nation in the modern world, some portion may be subject to classification. In this case the balance between making work public or classified should lean whenever possible toward making it public.

(4) Agencies should encourage open publication of contract research results.

(5) Government agencies that contract with university researchers should consider designing their projects so as to advance knowledge as well as to meet the immediate policy or action needs.

(6) Government agencies have the obligation of informing the potential researcher of the needs that the research should help meet, and of any special conditions associated with the research contract, and generally of the agency's expectations concerning the research and the researcher.

(7) The government should continue to seek research of the highest possible quality in its contract program.

A second set of seven recommendations is listed under Guidelines for the Conduct of Foreign Area Research Under Government Contract, and these too bear very directly on the panel Report and do so most critically and tellingly.

(1) The government should take special steps to ensure that the parties with which it contracts have the highest qualifications for carrying out research overseas.

(2) The government should work to avert or minimize adverse foreign reactions to its contract research programs conducted overseas.

(3) When a project involves research abroad, it is particularly important that both the supporting agency and the researcher openly acknowledge the auspices and financing of research projects.

(4) The government should under certain circumstances ascertain that the research is acceptable to the host government before proceeding on the research.

(5) The government should encourage cooperation with foreign scholars in its contract research program.

(6) Government agencies should continue to coordinate their foreign-area research programs to eliminate duplication and overloading of any one geographical area.

(7) Government agencies should cooperate with academic associations on problems of foreign-area research.

This set of recommendations (with allowances made for the circumstances of their issuance) unquestionably represents the most enlightened position yet taken by a federal agency on the question of the relationship between social science and practical politics. These sets of recommendations not only stand as ethical criteria for the federal government's relationship to social scientists, but—even more decisively—represent a rebuke to precisely the sort of militarization of social science implicit in the panel Report. The reassertion by a major federal policy-making agency of the worth to the government of social science autonomy represented the first significant recognition by a federal agency that Project Camelot was the consequence, not the cause, of the present strains in social science-federal bureaucracy relationships.

5 *Irving Louis Horowitz*

The Pentagon Papers and Social Science

Today, no major political event, particularly one so directly linked to the forging of American foreign policy as the publication of the Pentagon Papers by the *New York Times* and the *Washington Post* can be fully described without accounting for the role of the social scientist. In this case, the economists clearly performed a major role. From the straightforward hawkish prescriptions offered in 1961 by Walt W. Rostow to the dovishly motivated release of secret documents on the conduct of the war in 1971 by Daniel Ellsberg, the contributions of social scientists were central. As a consequence, it is fitting, nay imperative, that the import of these monumental events be made plain for those of us involved in the production and dissemination of social science information and insight.

The publication of the Pentagon Papers is of central importance to the social science community in at least two respects: social scientists participated in the development of a posture and position toward the Vietnam involvement; and at a more abstract level, the publication of these papers provides lessons about political participation and policy-making for the social sciences.

We live in an age in which the social sciences perform a special and unique role in the lives of men and in the fates of government, whatever be the status of social science theory. And because the questions of laymen are no longer "is social science scientific," but "what kinds of recommendations are offered in the name of social science," it is important that social scientists inquire as to any special meaning of the Pentagon Papers and documents, over and above the general and broad-ranging discussions that take place in the mass media. Thus, my effort here is not to be construed as a general discussion of issues, but rather a specific discussion of results.

I. Findings

The Pentagon's project director for a *History of United States Decision-Making Process on Vietnam Policy* (now simply known as *The Pentagon Papers*), economist Leslie H. Gelb now of Brookings, remarked: "Writing history, especially where it blends into current events, especially where the current event is Vietnam, is a treacherous exercise." Former Secretary of Defense Robert S. McNamara authorized this treacherous exercise of a treacherous conflict in 1967. In initiation and execution this was to be "encyclopedic and objective." The actual compilation runs to 2.5 million words and 47 volumes of narrative and documents. And from what has thus far been made public, it is evident that this project was prepared with the same bloodless, bureaucratic approach that characterizes so much federally inspired. social science and history. The Pentagon Papers attempt no original hypothesis, provide no insights into the behavior of the "other side," make scant effort to select important from trivial factors in the escalation process; they present no real continuity with past American foreign policy and in general eschew any sort of systematic survey research or interviewing of the participants and proponents. Yet, with all these shortcomings, these materials offer a fascinating and unique account of how peace-keeping agencies became transformed into policy-making agencies. That this record was prepared by 36 political scientists, economists, systems analysts, inside dopesters and outside social science research agencies provides an additional fascination: how the government has learned to entrust its official records to mandarin types, who in exchange for the cloak of anonymity are willing to prepare an official record of events. An alarming oddity is that, in part at least, the chronicle was prepared by analysts who were formerly participants.

For those who have neither the time nor the patience to examine every document thus far released, it might be worthwhile to simply summarize what they contain. In so doing, it becomes clear that the Vietnam War was neither a Democratic nor a Republican war, but a war conducted by the political elite, often without regard to basic technical advice and considerations, and for reasons that had far less to do with curbing communism than with the failure of the other arms of government in their responsibility to curb executive egotism. The publication of these papers has chronicled this country's overseas involvement with a precision never before available to the American public. Indeed, we now know more about decision-making in Vietnam than about the processes by which we became involved in the Korean War. For instance, we have learned that:

1. The United States ignored eight direct appeals for aid from Ho Chi Minh in the first half-year following World War II. Underlying the American refusal to deal with the Vietnamese leader was the growth of the cold war and the opposition to assisting a communist leadership.

2. The Truman administration by 1949 had already accepted the "domino principle," after the National Security Council was told early in 1950 that the neighboring

countries of Thailand and Burma could be expected to fall under communist control if Vietnam were controlled by a communist dominated regime.

3. The Eisenhower administration, particularly under the leadership of Secretary of State John Foster Dulles, refused to accept the Geneva accords ending the French-Indochina war on the grounds that it permitted this country "only a limited influence" in the affairs of the fledgling South Vietnam. Indeed, the Joint Chiefs of Staff opted in favor of displacing France as the key influence rather than assisting the termination of hostilities.

4. The final years of the Eisenhower administration were characterized by a decision to commit a relatively small number of United States military personnel to maintain the Diem regime in Saigon and to prevent a détente between Hanoi and Saigon.

5. The Kennedy administration transformed the limited risk gamble into an unlimited commitment. Although the troop levels were indeed still quite limited, the Kennedy administration moved special forces units into Vietnam, Laos and Cambodia—thus broadening the conflict to the area as a whole.

6. The Kennedy administration knew about and approved of plans for the military coup d'état that overthrew President Diem. The United States gave its support to an army group commited to military dictatorship and no compromise with the Hanoi regime.

7. The Johnson administration extended the unlimited commitment to the military regime of Saigon. Under this administration between 1965 and 1968, troop levels surpassed 500,000 and United States participation was to include the management of the conflict and the training of the ARVN.

8. After the Tet offensive began in January 1968, Johnson, under strong prodding from the military Chiefs of Staff, and from his field commanders, moved toward full scale mobilization, including the call-up of reserves. By the termination of the Johnson administration, the United States had been placed on a full-scale war footing.

Among the most important facts revealed by the Papers is that the United States first opposed a settlement based on the Geneva accords, signed by all belligerents; that the United States had escalated the conflict far in advance of the Gulf of Tonkin incident and had used congressional approval for legitimating commitments already undertaken rather than as a response to new communist provocations; and finally that in the face of internal opposition from the same Department of Defense that at first had sanctioned the war, the executive decided to disregard its own policy advisers and plunge ahead in a war already lost.

II. Decisions

Impressive in this enumeration of policy decisions is the clinical way decisions were made. The substitution of war game thinking for any real political thinking, the total submission of the Department of State to the Department of Defense in the making of foreign policy, and the utter collapse of any faith in compromise, consensus or cooperation between nations, and the ludicrous pursuit of victory (or at least non-defeat) in Vietnam, all are so forcefully illustrated in these Pentagon Papers, that the vigor with which their release was opposed by the Attorney General's office and the executive branch of government generally, can well be appreciated.

Ten years ago in writing *The War Game* I had occasion to say in a chapter concerning "American Politics and Military Risks" that "a major difficulty with the thinking of the new civilian militarists is that they study war while ignoring politics." The recent disclosure of the Pentagon Papers bears out that contention with a vengeance; a kind of hot house scientology emerges, in which the ends of foreign policy are neatly separated from the instruments of immediate destruction. That a certain shock and cynicism have emerged as a result of the revelations in these papers is more attributable to the loss of a war than to the novelty of the revelations. The cast of characters that have dragged us through the mire of a bloody conflict in Southeast Asia, from Walt W. Rostow to Henry A. Kissinger, remain to haunt us and taunt us. They move in and out of administrations with an ease that belies political party differences and underscores the existence of not merely a set of "experts," but rather a well defined ruling class dedicated to manufacturing and manipulating political formulas.

The great volume of materials thus far revealed is characterized by few obvious themes: but one of the more evident is the utter separation of the purposes of devastation from comprehension of the effects of such devastation. A kind of Howard Johnson sanitized vision of conflict emerges that reveals a gulf between the policy-makers and battlefield soldiers that is even wider and longer than the distance between Saigon and Washington. If the concept of war gaming is shocking in retrospect, this is probably due more to its utter and contemptible failure to provide battlefield victories than to any real development in social and behavioral science beyond the shibboleths of decision theory and game theory.

III. "Scientists"

A number of researchers as well as analysts of the Pentagon Papers were themselves social scientists. There were political scientists of considerable distinction, such as Morton Halperin and Melvin Gurtov; economists of great renown, such as Walt W. Rostow and Daniel Ellsberg; and systems analysts, such as Alain Enthoven. And then there was an assorted group of people, often trained in law, such as Roger Fisher and Carl Kaysen, weaving in and out of the Papers, providing both point and counterpoint. There are the thoroughly hawkish views of Walt Rostow; and the cautionary perspective of Alain Enthoven; and the more liberal recommendations of people like Roger Fisher. But it is clear that social scientists descend in importance as they move from hawk to dove. Walt Rostow is a central figure, and people like Carl Kaysen and Roger Fisher are at most peripheral consultants—who in fact, seem to have been more often conservatized and impressed by the pressurized Washington atmosphere than to have had an impact on the liberalization or softening of the Vietnam posture.

The social scientific contingency in the Pentagon, whom I christened the "new civilian militarists" a decade ago, were by no means uniform in their reactions to the quagmire in Vietnam. Political scientists like Morton H.

Halperin and economists like Alain C. Enthoven did provide cautionary responses, if not outright criticisms of the repeated and incessant requests for troop build-ups. The Tet offensive, which made incontrovertible the vulnerability of the American posture, called forth demands for higher troop levels on the part of Generals William C. Westmoreland and Maxwell Taylor. Enthoven, in particular, opposed this emphatically and courageously:

> Our strategy of attrition has not worked. Adding 206,000 more U.S. men to a force of 525,000, gaining only 27 additional maneuver battalions and 270 tactical fighters at an added cost to the U.S. of $10 billion per year raises the question of who is making it costly for whom. . . . We know that despite a massive influx of 500,000 U.S. troops, 1.2 million tons of bombs a year, 200,000 enemy killed in action in three years, 20,000 U.S. killed in action in three years, 200,000 U.S. wounded in action, etc., our control of the countryside and the defense of the urban areas is now essentially at pre-August 1965 levels. We have achieved stalemate at a high commitment. A new strategy must be sought.

Interestingly, in the same month, March 1968, when Enthoven prepared this critical and obviously sane report, he wrote a curious paper on "Thomism and the Concept of Just and Unjust Warfare," which, in retrospect, seemed to be Enthoven's way of letting people like myself know that he was a dissenting voice despite his earlier commitment to war game ideology and whiz-kid strategy.

As a result of these memoranda, Assistant Defense Secretary Paul Warnke argued against increased bombing and for a bombing pause. He and Assistant Secretary of Defense for, Public Affairs, Phil G. Goulding, were then simply directed to write a draft that "would deal only with the troop issue;" hence forcing them to abandon the internal fight against an "expansion of the air war." And as it finally went to the White House, the report was bleached of any criticism. The mandarin role of the social scientists was reaffirmed: President Johnson's commitments went unchallenged. The final memo advocated deployment of 22,000 more troops, reserved judgment on the deployments of the remaining 185,000 troops and approved a 262,000 troop reserve build-up; it urged no new peace initiatives and simply declared that a division of opinion existed on the bombing policy, making it appear that the division in opinion was only tactical in nature. As the Pentagon Papers declared:

> Faced with a fork in the road of our Vietnam policy, the working group failed to seize the opportunity to change directions. Indeed, they seemed to recommend that we continue rather haltingly down the same road, meanwhile, consulting the map more frequently and in greater detail to insure that we were still on the right road.

One strange aspect of this war game strategy is how little the moves and motives of the so-called "other side" were ever taken into account. There is no real appreciation of the distinction between North Vietnam and the National Liberation Front of South Vietnam. There is not the slightest account taken of the actual decisions made by General Giap or Chairman Ho. The Tet offensive seems to have taken our grand strategists by as much surprise as the political elites whom they were planning for. While they were beginning to recognize the actual balance of military forces, Wilfred Burchett had already declared, in 1967 to be exact, that the consequences of the war were no longer in doubt—United States involvement could not forestall a victory of the communist factions North and South. Thus, not only do the Pentagon Papers reveal the usual ignorance of the customs, languages and habits of the people being so brutally treated, but also the unanticipated arrogance of assuming throughout that logistics would conquer all. Even the doves like George W. Ball never doubted for a moment that an influx of a certain number of United States troops would in fact swing the tide of battle the way that General Westmoreland said it would. The argument was rather over tactics: is such a heavy investment worth the end results? In fact, not one inner circle "wise man" raised the issue that the size of the troop commitment might be basically irrelevant to the negative (from an American viewpoint) outcome of the Southeast Asian operations. One no longer expects good history or decent ethnography from those who advise the rulers, but when this is compounded with a heavy dose of impoverished war gaming and strategic thinking in the void, then the question of "science for whom" might well be converted into the question of "what science and by whom."

All of this points up a tragic flaw in policy-making by social science experts. Their failure to generate or to reflect a larger constituency outside of themselves made them continually vulnerable to assaults from the military and from the more conservative sectors of the Pentagon. This vulnerability was so great that throughout the Pentagon Papers, one senses that the hawk position is always and uniformly outspoken and direct, while the dove position is always and uniformly ubiquitous and indirect. The basis of democratic politics has always been the mass participation of an informed electorate. Yet it was precisely this informed public, where a consensus against the war had been building, that was cut off from the policy-planners and recommenders. Consequently they were left in pristine isolation to pit their logic against the crackpot realism of their military adversaries within the bowels of government.

IV. Disclosures

Certain serious problems arose precisely because of the secrecy tag: for example, former Vice President Hubert Humphrey and Secretary of State Dean Rusk have both denied having any knowledge whatsoever of these papers. Dean Rusk went so far as to say that the research methodology was handled poorly: "I'm rather curious about why the analysts who put this study together did not interview us, particularly when they were attributing attitudes and motives to us." (*New York Times,* Saturday, July 3, 1971.) Perhaps more telling is Dean Rusk's suggestion that the Pentagon Papers have the characteristics of an anonymous letter. Along with Dean Rusk, I too believe that the names of the roughly 40 scholars connected with the production of these papers should be published. To do otherwise would not only prevent the people involved from checking the veracity of the stories attributed to them, but more important, would keep the social science community from gaining a clearer insight into the multiple roles of scholars, researchers, professors and government analysts and policy-makers. The nature of science requires that the human authorities behind these multi-volumes be identified, as in the precedent established by the identification of the authors of the various bombing surveys done after World War II and the Korean War.

One serendipitous consequence of the Pentagon Papers has been to provide a more meaningful perspective toward the proposed "Code of Ethics" being advanced by so many social science professional associations. They all deal with the sanctity of the "subject's rights." All sorts of words guarding privacy are used: "rights of privacy and dignity," "protection of subjects from personal harm," "preservation of confidentiality of research data." The American Sociological Association proposals for example are typical:

> Confidential information provided by a research subject must be treated as such by the sociologist. Even though research information is not a privileged communication under the law, the sociologist must, as far as possible, protect subjects and informants. Any promises made to such persons must be honored. . . . If an informant or other subject should wish, however, he can formally release the promise of confidentiality.

While the purpose of this code of ethics is sincerely geared to the protection of individuals under study, if taken literally, a man like Daniel Ellsberg would be subject to penalty, if not outright expulsion, on the grounds that he was never allowed by the individuals concerned to make his information public. What so many professional societies forget is that the right to full disclosure is also a principle, just as significant as the right of the private subject to confidentiality, and far more germane to the tasks of a social scientific learned society. The truly difficult ethical question comes not with the idea of maintaining confidentiality, but with determining what would be confidential, and when such confidentiality should be violated in terms of a higher principle. All social science codes of ethics presume an ethical standpoint which limits scientific endeavor, but when it is expedient to ignore or forget this ethical code, as in the case of the Pentagon Papers, the profession embarrassingly chooses to exhibit such a memory lapse. The publication of the Pentagon Papers should once again point the way to the highest obligation of social science organizations: to the truth, plain and simple, rather than the preservation of confidentiality, high and mighty. And unless this lesson is fully drawn, a dichotomous arrangement will be made between making public the documents of public servants whose policies they disapprove of and keeping private the documentation on deviants whom supposedly the social scientists are concerned with protecting. This is not an ethical approach but an opportunistic approach. It rests on political and professional expediency. The need therefore is to reassert the requisites of science for full disclosure, and the ethics of full disclosure as the only possible ethics for any group of professional scientists. If the release of the Pentagon Papers had done nothing else, it has reaffirmed the highest principle of all science: full disclosure, full review of the data, full responsibility for what is done, by those who do the research.

V. Secrets

Another area that deeply concerns the social scientist and that is highlighted in the Pentagon Papers is the government's established norms of secrecy. While most officials in government have a series of work norms with which to guide their behavior, few forms of anticipatory socialization have applied to social scientists who advise government agencies. The professionalization of social scientists has normally been directed toward publicity rather than secrecy. This fosters sharp differences in opinion and attitudes between the polity and the academy, since the reward system for career advancement is so clearly polarized.

The question of secrecy is intimately connected with matters of policy, because the standing assumption of policy-makers (particularly in the field of foreign affairs) is not to reveal themselves entirely. No government in the game of international politics feels that its policies can be candidly revealed for full public review; therefore, operational research done in connection with policy considerations is customarily bound by the canons of government privacy. But while scientists have a fetish for publicizing their information as a mechanism for professional advancement no less than as a definition of their essential role in the society, the political branches of society have as their fetish the protection of private documents and privileged information. Therefore, the polity places a premium not only on acquiring vital information, but on maintaining silence about such information precisely to the degree that the data might be of high decisional value. This leads to differing premiums between analysts and policy-makers and to tensions between them.

Social scientists complain that the norm of secrecy oftentimes involves yielding their own essential work premises. A critical factor reinforcing an unwilling acceptance of the norm of secrecy by social scientists is the allocation of most government research funds for military or semi-military purposes. Senate testimony has shown that 70 percent of federal funds targeted for the social sciences involve such restrictions.

The real wonder turns out to be not the existence of the secrecy norm but the relative availability of large chunks of information. Indeed, the classification of materials is so inept that documents (such as the Pax America research) designated as confidential or secret by one agency may often be made available as a public service by another agency. There are also occasions when documents placed in a classified category by sponsoring government agencies can be gotten without charge from the private research institute doing the work.

But the main point is that the norm of secrecy makes it extremely difficult to separate science from patriotism and hence makes it that much more difficult to question the research design itself. Social scientists often express the nagging doubt that accepting the first stage—the right of the government to maintain secrecy—often carries with it acquiescence in a later stage—the necessity for silence on the part of social researchers who may disagree with the political uses of their efforts.

Steinfels quote goes here

The demand for government secrecy has a telling impact on the methodology of the social sciences. Presumably social scientists are employed because they, as a group, represent objectivity and honesty. Social scientists like to envision themselves as a wall of truth off which policy-makers may bounce their premises. They also like to think that they provide information which cannot be derived from sheer public opinion. Thus, to some degree social scientists consider that they are hired or utilized by government agencies because they will say things that may be unpopular but nonetheless significant. However, since secrecy exists, the premises upon which most social scientists seek to work are strained by the very agencies which contract out their need to know.

The terms of research and conditions of work tend to demand an initial compromise with social science methodology. The social scientist is placed in a cognitive bind. He is conditioned not to reveal maximum information lest he become victimized by the federal agencies that employ his services. Yet he is employed precisely because of his presumed thoroughness, impartiality and candor. The social scientist who survives in government service becomes circumspect or learns to play the game. His value to social science becomes seriously jeopardized. On the other hand, once he raises these considerations, his usefulness to the policy-making sector is likewise jeopardized.

Social scientists believe that openness is more than meeting formal requirements of scientific canons; it is also a matter of making information universally available. The norm of secrecy leads to selective presentation of data. The social scientist is impeded by the policy-maker because of contrasting notions about the significance of data and the general need for replication elsewhere and by others. The policy-maker who demands differential access to findings considers this a normal return for the initial expenditure of risk capital. Since this utilitarian concept of data is alien to the scientific standpoint, the schism between the social scientist and the policy-maker becomes pronounced precisely at the level of openness of information and accessibility to the work achieved. The social scientist's general attitude is that sponsorship of research does not entitle any one sector to benefit unduly from the findings—that sponsorship by federal agencies ought not place greater limitations on the use of work done than sponsorship by either private agencies or universities.

VI. Loyalties

A major area that deeply concerns social scientists is that of dual allegiance. The Pentagon Papers have such specific requirements and goal-oriented tasks that they intrude upon the autonomy of the social scientist by forcing upon him choices between dual allegiances. The researcher is compelled to choose between participating fully in the world of the federal bureaucracy or remaining in more familiar academic confines. He does not want the former to create isolation in the latter. Thus, he often criticizes the federal bureaucracy's unwillingness to recognize his basic needs: 1) the need to teach and retain full academic identity; 2) the need to publicize information; and above all 3) the need to place scientific responsibility above the call of patriotic obligation—when they may happen to clash. In short, he does not want to be plagued by dual or competing allegiances.

The norm of secrecy exacerbates this problem. Although many of the social scientists who become involved with federal research are intrigued by the opportunity to address important issues, they are confronted by some bureaucracies which oftentimes do not share their passion for resolving social problems. For example, federal obligations commit the bureaucracy to assign high priority to items having military potential and effectiveness and low priorities to many supposedly idealistic and far-fetched themes in which social scientists are interested.

Those social scientists, either as employees or as consultants connected with the government, are hamstrung by federal agencies which are in turn limited by political circumstances beyond their control. A federal bureaucracy must manage cumbersome, overgrown committees and data gathering agencies. Federal agencies often protect a status quo merely for the sake of rational functioning. They must conceive of academicians in their midst as a standard bureaucratic type entitled to rise to certain federal ranks. Federal agencies limit innovating concepts to what is immediately useful, not out of choice and certainly not out of resentment of the social sciences but from what is deemed as impersonal necessity. This has the effect of reducing the social scientist's role in the government to that of ally or advocate rather than innovator or designer. Social scientists begin to feel that their enthusiasm for rapid change is unrealistic, considering how little can be done by the government bureaucracy. And they come to resent involvement in theoryless application to immediacy foisted on them by the "new utopians," surrendering in the process the value of confronting men with the wide range of choices of what might be done. The schism, then, between autonomy and involvement is as thorough as that between secrecy and publicity, for it cuts to the quick well-intentioned pretensions at human engineering.

The problem of competing allegiances is not made simpler by the fact that many high ranking federal bureaucrats have strong nationalistic and conservative political ideologies. This contrasts markedly with the social scientist, who comes to Washington not only with a belief in the primacy of science over patriotism but also with a definition of patriotism that is more open-ended and consciously liberal than that of most appointed officials. Hence, he often perceives the conflict to extend beyond research design and social applicability into one of the incompatible ideologies held respectively by the social scientist and entrenched Washington bureaucrats. He comes to resent the proprietary attitude of the bureaucrat toward "his" government processes. The social scientist is likely to consider his social science biases a necessary buffer against the federal bureaucracy.

VII. Elitists

The publication of the Pentagon Papers sheds new light on political pluralist and power concentrationist hypotheses. When push finally did turn to shove, President Nixon and the government officials behaved as members of a ruling class and not as leaders of their political party. President Nixon might easily have chosen to let the Democratic party take the burn and bear the brunt of the assaults for the betrayal of a public trust. Indeed the Nixon administration might have chosen to join the chorus of those arguing that the Democratic party is indeed the war party, as revealed in these documents; whereas the Republican party emerges as the party of restraint—if not exactly principle. Here was a stunning opportunity for Mr. Nixon to make political capital at a no risk basis: by simply drawing attention to the fact that the war was constantly escalated by President Truman, who refused to bargain in good faith with Ho Chi Minh despite repeated requests, by President Kennedy, who moved far beyond anything President Eisenhower had in mind for the area, by making the fatal committment not just to land troops but to adopt a domino theory of winning the war, by President Johnson, whose role can well be considered as nefarious: coming before the American people as a peace candidate when he had already made the fatal series of committments to continuing escalation and warfare. That the president chose not to do so illustrates the sense of class solidarity that the political elites in this country manifest; a sense of collective betrayal of the priesthood, rather than a sense of obligation to score political points and gain political trophies. And that too should be a lesson in terms of the actual power within the political structure of a small ruling elite. Surely this must be considered a fascinating episode in its own right: the reasons are complex, but surely among them must rank the belief that Mr. Nixon behaved as a member of the ruling elite, an elite that had transcendent obligations far beyond the call of party, and that was the call of class.

One fact made clear by the Pentagon Papers is the extent to which presidentialism has become the ideology and the style in American political life. The infrequency of any reference to the judicial situation with respect to the war in Southeast Asia and the virtual absence of any reference to congressional sentiments are startling confirmations of an utter change in the American political style. If any proof was needed of the emerging imbalance between the executive and other branches of government, these papers should put such doubt to rest. The theory of checks and balances works only when there are, in fact, groups such as senators or stubborn judges who believe in the responsibility of the judiciary and legislative branches to do just that, namely, establish check and balance. In the absence of such vigor, the war in Southeast Asia became very much a series of executive actions. And this itself should give pause to the advocates of consensus theory in political science.

The failure of the Vietnam episode has resulted in a reconsideration of presidentialism as the specific contemporary variant of power elite theory. The renewed vigor of Congress, the willingness, albeit cautionary willingness, of the Supreme Court to rule on fundamental points of constitutional law, are indicative of the resurgence of pluralism. In this sense, the darkest hour of liberalism as a political style has witnessed a liberal regrouping around the theme of mass politics. Even the domestic notions of community organization and states rights are indicative of the limits of presidentialism—so that Mr. Nixon, at one and the same time, is reluctantly presiding over the swan song of presidentialism in foreign affairs, while celebrating its demise in domestic affairs. The collapse of the Vietnam War and the trends toward neo-isolationism are in fact simply the reappearance of political pluralism in a context where to go further in the concentration of political power in the presidency would in all likelihood mean the upsurge of fascism, American style. If the concept of a power elite was reconfirmed in the Pentagon Papers, so too, strangely, was the concept of political pluralism in the public response to them. The countervailing influence of the Supreme Court was clearly manifested in the ringing affirmation of the First Amendment, in the denial of the concept of prior restraint and prior punitive actions, and in the very rapidity of the decision itself. This action by the judiciary, coupled with a show of muscle on the part of the Senate and House concerning the conduct of the war, military appropriations, boondoggles and special privileges for a select handful of aircraft industries in their own way served to underscore the continued importance of the open society and the pluralistic basis of power. Even executives, such as Hubert H. Humphrey, have declared in favor of full disclosure and reiterated the principles guiding the publication of the Pentagon Papers.

Power elites operate behind a cloak of anonymity. When that cloak is lifted, an obvious impairment in the operational efficiency of elites occurs. What has happened with the release of the Pentagon Papers is precisely this collapse of anonymity, no less than secrecy. As a result, the formal apparatus of government can assert its prerogatives. This does not mean that the executive branch of government will be unable to recover from this blow at its prestige, or that it will no longer attempt to play its trump card: decision-making by executive fiat. It does mean, however, that the optimal conditions under which power elites operate have been seriously hampered. The degree of this impairment and the length of time it will obtain depend exclusively on the politics of awareness and participation, no less than the continuing pressures for lowering the secrecy levels in high level international decision-making.

Probably the most compelling set of reasons given for President Nixon's bitter opposition to the release of the Pentagon Papers is that provided by Melvin Gurtov, one of the authors of the secret Pentagon study and an outstanding political scientist specializing in Asian affairs. He speaks of three deceits in current American Vietnamese policy: "The first and most basic deceit is the Administration's contention that we're winding down and getting out of the war." In fact, Vietnamization is a "domestic political ploy that really involves the substitution of air power for ground power." The second deceit is that "we're truly interested in seeing the prisoners of war released." Gurtov notes that "as far as this administration is concerned the prisoners of war are a political device, a device for rationalizing escalation, by saying these are acts that are necessary to show our concern for the prisoners." The third deceit "is that under the Nixon Doctrine the United States is not interested in making new committments in Asia." In fact, the administration used the Cambodia coup "as an opportunity for creating for itself a new commitment in Southeast Asia, namely the survival of a non-Communist regime in Pnompenh." This outspoken position indicates that the defense of the power elite of the past by President Nixon might just as well be construed as a self-defense of the power elite in the present.

VIII. Conspiracies

The Pentagon Papers provide much new light on theories

of power elite and power diffusion and also provide an equal measure of information on conspiracy theory. And while it is still true that conspiracy *theory* is bad theory, it is false to assert that no conspiracies exist or are not perpetrated by the government. It might indeed be the case that all governments, insofar as they are formal organizations, have secrets; and we call these secrets, conspiracies. From this point of view, the interesting question is how so few leaks resulted from an effort of such magnitude and involving so many people as setting policy in the Vietnam War. Rather than be surprised that these papers reached the public domain four to six years after the fact, one should wonder how the government was able to maintain silence on matters of such far-ranging and far-reaching consequence.

Cyrus Eaton, American industrialist and confidant of many communist leaders, indicates that the Vietnamese almost instantaneously were made aware of United States policy decisions. But I seriously doubt that they actually had copies of these materials. Rather, like the American public itself, they were informed about the decisions but not the cogitations and agitations that went into the final decision. Perhaps this is the way all governments operate; nonetheless, it is fascinating—at least this once—to be privy to the process and not simply the outcome, and to see the foibles of powerful men and not just the fables manufactured for these men after the fact.

These papers tend to underwrite the common-sensical point of view that governments are not to be trusted, and to undermine the more sophisticated interpretation that governments are dedicated to the task of maintaining democracy at home and peace abroad. As bitter as it may seem, common sense cynicism has more to recommend it than the sophisticated, well elaborated viewpoints which take literally the formal structure of government and so readily tend to dismiss the informal response to power and pressure from men at the top. The constant wavering of Lyndon B. Johnson, his bellicose defiance of all evidence and information that the bombings were not having the intended effect, followed by shock that his lieutenants like Robert McNamara changed their position at midstream (which almost constituted a betrayal in the eyes of the president) were in turn followed by a more relaxed posture and a final decision not to seek the presidency. All of this forms a human drama that makes the political process at once fascinating and frightful; fascinating because we can see the psychology of politics in action, and frightful because the presumed rationality is by no means uniformly present.

The publication of the Pentagon Papers, while a considerable victory for the rights of a free press and of special significance to all scientists who still uphold the principle of full disclosure as the norm of all political as well as scientific endeavor, is not yet a total victory for a democratic society—that can only happen when the concept of secrecy is itself probed and penetrated, and when the concept of undeclared warfare is finally and fully repudiated by the public and its representatives. The behavior of the government in its effort to suppress publication of the Pentagon Papers cannot simply be viewed as idiosyncratic, but rather as part of the structure of the American political processes in which the expert displaces the politician, and the politicians themselves become so beholden to the class of experts for information, that they dare not turn for guidance to the people they serve. For years, critics of the Vietnam War have been silenced and intimidated by the policy-makers' insistence that when all the facts were known the hawk position would be vindicated and the dove position would be violated. Many of the facts are now revealed—and the bankruptcy of the advocates of continued escalation is plain for all to see. Hopefully, this will strengthen the prospects for peace, and firm up those who, as an automatic reflex, assume the correctness of the government's position on all things military. It is to be hoped that the principle of democracy, of every person counting as one, once more becomes the source of fundamental decision-making and political discourse.

SUGGESTED READINGS

The basic text is *The Pentagon Papers: The Secret History of the Vietnam War*, as published by the *New York Times*. Based on investigative reporting by Neil Sheehan. Written by Neil Sheehan, Hedrick Smith, E. W. Kenworthy, and Fox Butterfield. Articles and documents edited by Gerald Gold, Allan M. Siegal, and Samuel Abt. (New York: Bantam Books, 1971).

Notes on Authors

BACK, KURT W. ("The Way of Love and Trusts"), is professor of sociology and psychiatry at Duke University. Author of many books and articles including *Slums, Projects and People: Social Psychological Problems of Relocation in Puerto Rico*, his most recent book, written with Alan C. Kerckhoff, is *The June Bug: A Study of Hysterical Contagion.*

BECKER, HOWARD S. ("Consciousness, Power and Drug Effects"), senior editor of *Society*, is the author of *Outsiders: Studies in the Sociology of Deviance.* A professor at Northwestern University and a fellow at the Center for Advanced Study in the Behavioral Sciences, Stanford, he has written extensively on deviance and social control.

BERG, IVAR ("Rich Man's Qualifications for Poor Man's Jobs"), is professor of sociology and associate dean of faculties at the Columbia University Graduate School of Business. His books include *Education Credentials for Jobs in a Democratic Society and Sociology and the Business Establishment*, with David Rogers.

BERGER, BENNETT M. ("Audiences, Art and Power"), is professor of sociology at the University of California, La Jolla. He is the author of *Working Class Suburb: A Study of Auto Workers in Suburbia* and *Looking for America: Essays on Youth, Suburbia and Other American Obsessions.*

BERGER, HENRY ("Organized Labor and Imperial Policy"), is associate professor of history at Washington University where he teaches American labor history and U.S. foreign relations. Author of several articles in these two fields, he is currently at work on a book-length treatment of labor's role in American foreign affairs.

BLUMBERG, ABRAHAM S. ("Law and Order: The Counterfeit Crusade"), is professor of sociology and law and associate dean of faculty at John Jay College of Criminal Justice of the City University of New York. He has written extensively on criminal law and his most recent book is *Current Perspectives on Criminal Behavior.*

BOWLES, SAMUEL ("Getting Nowhere: Programmed Class Stagnation"), associate professor of economics at Harvard University, has been active in the Union for a Radical Political Economics. He is currently writing a book with Herbert Gintis on schooling and class structure.

BRADFORD, C. H. ("Creating a World for Research"), assistant professor of education in the Graduate Institute of Education at Washington University, is a research associate at the university's computer center. His interests are in pychometrics and the application of computers in education research.

BROWNING, HARLEY L. ("Timing of Our Lives"), is associate professor of sociology at the University of Texas at Austin and director of the Population Research Center. His major research interests are the modernization process, particularly urbanization and internal migration in Latin America, and explorations in social demography.

BRYANT, CLIFTON D. ("The Cryonics Movement"), is professor and head of the department of sociology at Virginia Polytechnic Institute and State University. His books include *Social Problems Today, The Social Dimensions of Work* and *Deviancy and the Family and Deviant Behavior: Occupational and Organizational Bases.*

BURNHAM, WALTER DEAN ("Crisis of American Political Legitimacy"), is professor of political science at MIT. He has written extensively on American politics and his primary research interest is American voting behavior and electoral politics. His latest book is *Critical Elections and the Mainsprings of American Politics.* At present he is at work developing a general theory of American political dynamics.

CARTER, BARBARA L. ("Reform School Families"), is associate professor of sociology and associate provost at Federal City College, Washington, D.C. Her current activities include extensive research on the experiences of adult and adolescent females in prison. Her most recent publication is *On the Grounds: Informal Culture in a Girls' Reform School.*

CHRISTIE, NILS ("The Scandinavian Hangover"), is professor of criminology and director of the Institute of Criminology and Criminal Law in Oslo, Norway. He is currently visiting the School of Criminology, University of California, Berkeley.

COLBURN, DEBORAH ("Integrity House"), a recent graduate of Livingston College, Rutgers University, attends York University as a graduate student of sociology.

COLBURN, KENNETH, JR. ("Integrity House"), is a doctoral candidate in sociology at York University in Canada.

CRESSEY, DONALD R. ("The Respectable Criminal"), dean of the College of Letters and Science and professor of sociology at the University of California at Santa Barbara, is author of *Other People's Money* and co-author of books on criminology and prisons. Dr. Cressey's research is in social organization, particularly law enforcement.

CROTTY, WILLIAM J. ("Presidential Assassinations"), is professor of political science at Northwestern University. Coauthor of two books on assassination, he was co-director of the Task Force on Assassination and Political Violence of the National Commission of the Causes and Prevention of Violence.

DENZIN, NORMAN K. ("Children and Their Caretakers"), is professor of sociology at the University of Illinois, Urbana. He is the author of *The Research Act* and editor of *The Values of Social Science* and *Children and Their Caretakers.*

DEVEREUX, EDWARD C. ("Practical Problems and the Uses of Sociology"), is professor of child development and family relations at Cornell University. He has published papers in the fields of sociological theory, the sociology of deviant behavior and research methodology, and is the author of numerous articles on participation in community life.

DREIER, PETER ("Jewish Radicalism in Transition"), teaches sociology at DePaul University. He is a Ph.D. candidate in sociology at the University of Chicago, writing a dissertation on the social organization of the press. He co-edited *Jewish Radicalism* (with Jack Nusan Porter) and has written articles for the *Encyclopedia of Sociology.*

EASTO, PATRICK C. ("Carnivals, Road Shows and Freaks"), assistant professor of sociology at Eastern Michigan University, was born and raised in a carnival family and traveled the circuit with them from northern Indiana to Florida every carnival season. His father was a girl show talker; his mother, a star stripper. He himself worked as a carnie from age 8 to 17 at all kinds of jobs from ticket seller to concession operator.

EDEL, ABRAHAM ("Scientists, Partisans and Social Conscience"), is distinguished professor emeritus of philosophy, City University of New York, and research professor of philosophy, University of Pennsylvania. He is the author of several works on ethics and science, including *Ethical Judgment: The Use of Science in Ethics, Science and the Structure of Ethics* and *Method in Ethical Theory.*

ETZIONI, AMITAI ("Social Analysis and Social Action"), is professor of sociology at Columbia University and director of the Center for Policy Research. He is the author of *The Active Society: A Theory of Societal and Political Processes* and *Comparative Analysis of Complex Organizations.*

GANS, HERBERT J. ("Social Science for Social Policy"), is professor of sociology at Columbia University and senior research associate, Center for Policy Research. Among his books are *The Urban Villagers, The Levittowners* and *People and Plans.* He is currently completing a study and book on how the national news media cover American society.

GLABERMAN, MARTIN ("Unions vs. Workers in the Seventies"), is professor of sociology at Wayne State University. He spent 20 years in the labor movement as a production worker and union activist and was editor of two independent labor journals. He has written extensively on the labor movement and Marxism.

GLOCK, CHARLES Y. ("Is There an American Protestantism?"), is professor of sociology and director of the Research Program in Religion and Society, Survey Research Center, at the University of California, Berkeley. He has also been president of the American Association for Public Opinion Research and the Society for the Scientific Study of Religion. He is senior author of *Adolescent Prejudice*, editor of *Religion in Socological Perspective* and co-editor of *Beyond the Classics?*

GMELCH, GEORGE ("Baseball Magic"), is assistant professor of anthropology at McGill University. He played three years in the Detroit Tiger organization (minor leagues) and two seasons in a professional league in Quebec, Canada. His recent major research interest is the adaptation of Irish tinkers and other European itinerants to settled life.

GOERING, JOHN M. ("Public Transportation and Black Unemployment"), is associate professor of sociology at the Graduate Center of the City University of New York and director of a research and technical assistance project in East Harlem. He is presently conducting a study of the role of interorganizational linkages in community housing and health organizations.

HEILBRONER, ROBERT L. ("Benign Neglect in the United States"), is the chairman of the department of economics, graduate faculty at the New School of Social Research. He is author of numerous books, the latest of which is *Between Capitalism and Socialism.*

HELMREICH, WILLIAM B. ("Black Crusaders: The Rise and Fall of Political Gangs"), is assistant professor of sociology and Jewish studies at City College, City Universtiy of New York. He is the author of *The Black Crusaders*, from which this chapter was excerpted.

HENRY, WILLIAM E. ("Actors' Search for Self"), is professor of psychology and human development at the University of Chicago. He has conducted similar studies of business executives and mental-health professionals. The author of many books and articles, he is currently interested in personality development during the adult years.

HEUSSENSTAMM, F. K. ("Bumper Stickers and the Cops"), is associate professor of sociology at California State College, Los Angeles. Her research interests focus on black, white and brown adolescent militancy.

HEYL, BARBARA SHERMAN ("The Female House of Prostitution"), is currently a doctoral candidate in sociology at the University of Illinois. She taught two years at Illinois State University and has published "The Harvard 'Pareto Circle'" in the *Journal of the History of the Behavioral Sciences.* Her article is a revised version of one that appeared in *Sociological Symposium.*

HIGHTOWER, JIM ("Hard Tomatoes, Hard Times"), is director of the Agribusiness Accountability Project, a watchdog research agency concerned with the influence of big government and big business on rural America. A freelance writer on politics and rural affairs, he was formerly legislative assistant to Senator Ralph Yarborough.

HILL, HERBERT ("Anti-Oriental Agitation and the Rise of Working-Class Racism"), is author of *Black Labor and the American Legal System* and other books. He has taught at the University of Wisconsin, Princeton University and elsewhere in the United States and abroad. Mr. Hill is the national labor director of the NAACP.

HOCHSCHILD, ARLIE ("Communal Life-styles for the Old"), is assistant professor of sociology at the University of California, Berkeley. Winner of the 1968 A.S.U.C. Teaching Award, she has written extensively on aging and on women's roles and is the author of *The Unexpected Community.*

HOROWITZ, IRVING LOUIS ("Sociological Snoopers and Military Commissars," "Capitalism, Communism and Multinationalism," "The Pentagon Papers and Social Science" and "Social Science Yogis"), is co-editor of *Sociological Realities II*, professor of sociology and political science at Rutgers University, director of *Studies in Comparative International Development* and editor in chief of *Society* magazine. He is the author of numerous books, including *The Rise and Fall of Project Camelot* and *The New Sociology.*

HOWARD, JOHN R. ("The Making of a Black Muslim"), is chairman of the department of political science at the State University of New York, Purchase. His research interests include the relationship between community structure and the participation of the poor in the war on poverty and institutional resistance to innovation in the public schools.

HUTTMAN, JOHN ("Automobile Addition"), is associate professor of economics at San Francisco State University. His major areas of research, in addition to urban transportation, include housing, new towns and environmental problems. His articles have appeared in several publications, including *The Annals of Regional Science, Growth and Change*, the *Journal of Regional Development* and *Environment.*

KALACHEK, EDWARD ("Public Transportation and Black Unemployment"), is chairman of the department of economics at Washington University. A former consultant to the Presidential Commission on Income Maintenance, he served as director of the Washington University Transportation and Employment Project. He has written numerous articles on the labor market.

KELMAN, HERBERT C. ("Deception in Social Research"), is Richard Clarke Cabot professor of social ethics at Harvard University. He is past president of the Society for the Psychological Study of Social Issues.

KIESLER, CHARLES A. ("Conformity and Commitment"), associate professor of psychology at Yale, is chairman of the interdisciplinary honors major in culture and behavior. His research interests are in experimental social psychology, attitude change, and interpersonal influence and group effects on the individual. He has published books on *Conformity* (1969) and on *Attitude Change* (1969) with other authors.

LARUE, LINDA J. M. ("Black Liberation and Women's Lib"), a native of Indiana, is pursuing a Ph.D. in government at Cornell University. She and her husband are currently working on a joint project in exploring crosscurrents of different social-political movements.

LIPSET, SEYMOUR MARTIN ("Education and Equality"), is George D. Markham professor of government and sociology, vice-president (social sciences) of the American Academy of Arts and Sciences and chairman of the section on the social and economic sciences of the AAAS. He is the author of numerous books, and most recently, he edited *Failure of a Dream: Socialism in America* with John Laslett.

LYMAN, STANFORD M. ("Japanese-American Generation Gap"), is professor and chairman, Department of Sociology, Graduate Faculty of Political and Social Science, New School for Social Research. Among his books are *The Black American in Sociological Thought: A Failure of Perspective and Chinese Americans.*

MACK, RAYMOND W. ("Science as a Frame of Reference" and "Intellectual Strategy"), is professor of sociology and vice-president and dean of faculties at Northwestern University. His recent publications include *Prejudice and Race Relations, Transforming America: Patterns of Social Change,* and *The Changing South.*

MAHIGAL, E. LOUIS ("How Card Hustlers Make the Game"), is executive director of the Legal Advocacy Project at the University of Minnesota Law School. Prior to his college education he was a professional gambler.

MECHANIC, DAVID ("Apartheid Medicine"), is professor of sociology and director of the Center for Medical Sociology and Health Services Research at the University of Wisconsin. He is the author of *Students Under Stress: A Study in the Social Psychology of Adaptation, Public Expectations and Health Care, Mental Health and Social Policy* and *Medical Sociology: A Selective View.*

MEIER, DOROTHY L. ("Creating a World for Research"), is assistant professor of sociology at Washington University and has conducted investigations with Inter-Nation Simulation for four years, both at Northwestern University and at Washington University. Her areas of study are research methods and political sociology.

MERTON, ROBERT K. ("Practical Problems and the Uses of Sociology"), is university professor of social science at Columbia University. His books include *Social Theory* and *Social Structure, Science, Technology and Society in Seventeenth Century England, Mass Persuasion* and *The Sociology of Science.*

MILLER, STUART C. ("Our Mylai of 1900"), is professor of social science at San Francisco State University. He is the author of *The Unwelcome Immigrant: The American Image of the Chinese* and is currently completing a book on the American conquest of the Philippines.

MORRIS, MARIAN GENNARIA ("Psychological Miscarriage"), has graduate degrees in both nursing and social work and was research associate at Hahnemann Medical College and Hospital in Philadelphia. At the Children's Hospital of Los Angeles, Department of Psychiatry, she has done work on abusive parents.

MOSKOS, CHARLES C., JR. ("Why Men Fight" and "Third World Research"), is professor and chairman of the department of sociology, Northwestern University. He is the author of *The American Enlisted Man* and *Peace Soldiers: The Sociology of a United Nations Military Force.*

MOTZ, ANNABELLE B. ("Family as a Company of Players"), is professor of sociology at The American University. She is the author of many articles that reflect her research interest in social psychology, social organization and family living.

NAGEL, STUART S. ("Double Standard of American Justice"), is professor of political science at the University of Illinois and a member of the Illinois Bar. He has authored numerous articles and books dealing with the judicial process and related matters, including *Improving the Legal Process: Effects of Alternative,* in which a longer version of this chapter appears.

NANRY, CHARLES ("Professionalism and Poverty in a Community Hospital"), co-editor of *Sociological Realities II,* is associate professor of sociology at Rutgers University College. He has edited *American Music: From Storyville to Woodstock* and is co-editor of the *Journal of Jazz Studies.*

NANRY, JACQUELINE ("Professionalism and Poverty in a Community Hospital"), holds an MSW from Rutgers University. A medical social worker for over five years, she is currently a psychotherapist at the Middlesex County Crisis Intervention Center.

OLEXA, CAROL ("Programmed for Social Class"), teaches sociology at Evergreen State College. Her interests include the reaction of the school to students' nonconforming behavior and the effect of the school experience on students' self-concepts. With Walter Schafer she is co-author of *Tracking and Opportunity: The Locking Out Process and Beyond.*

PALSON, CHARLES ("Swinging in Wedlock"), is a doctoral candidate in anthropology at the University of Chicago. He is national president of the Student Evaluation Project (STEP), which publishes student evaluations of graduate departments of anthropology.

PALSON, REBECCA ("Swinging in Wedlock"), has studied anthropology and art. Co-author with her husband of several articles on the culture of sex and the structure of swingers' relationships, she is working with him on a book, *Friends and Lovers: A Study in the Use and Meaning of Sex.*

PITTMAN, DAVID J. ("The Male House of Prostitution"), is director and professor of sociology at the Social Science Institute of Washington University. He has published widely in the areas of alcoholism, drug addiction and criminology and is co-author of *Revolving Door: A Study of the Chronic Police Case Inebriate.*

POLK, KENNETH ("Programmed for Social Class"), is professor of sociology at the University of Oregon. Widely consulted by local, state and national agencies on juvenile delinquency, he is principal investigator of a 13-year basic research grant studying rural delinquency. With Walter Schafer he is co-author of *Schools and Delinquency*.

PORTER, JACK NUSAN ("Jewish Radicalism in Transition"), teaches sociology at Pine Manor Junior College. Previously active in Zionist youth movements, he co-edited *Jewish Radicalism* with Peter Dreier and has written numerous articles and reviews for Jewish and sociological journals. Currently he is writing a book on the sociology of film.

RAINWATER, LEE ("The Sociologist as Naturalist" and "Post-1984 America"), is professor in the department of sociology and the John F. Kennedy school of government at Harvard University. Among his many publications are *Behind Ghetto Walls* and *Family Design*. Research for this article was supported by grant No. 1-PO-MH-15567 from the National Institute of Mental Health.

ROKEACH, MILTON ("Paradoxes of Religious Belief"), is professor of sociology and psychology at Washington State University. The author of approximately 80 articles in psychological, sociological and popular journals, his books include *The Open and Closed Mind*, *The Three Christs of Ypsilanti* and *The Nature of Human Values*. His research interests are long-term attitude, value and behavioral change; race prejudice; belief systems and personality; and cultural, social and personal determinants of values and value change.

ROSSI, PETER ("Evaluating Social Programs"), is professor of sociology at the University of Massachusetts and director of the Social and Demographic Research Institute. His books include *The Education of Catholic Americans* (with A. M. Greeley) and *The New Media and Education* (with B. Biddle). This article was taken from a paper delivered at the 1966 American Statistical Association meetings.

SALUTIN, MARILYN ("Stripper Morality"), is on the staff of the John P. Robarts Research Library, Centre of Criminology, University of Toronto. This article is based on her M.A. thesis. She has written about strippers and comedians.

SCHAFER, WALTER E. ("Programmed for Social Class"), is director of research and special programs at the School of Community Service and Public Affairs at the University of Oregon and an associate professor of sociology. He is author of numerous articles and co-author with Carol Olexa of the book *Tracking and Opportunity: The Locking Out Process and Beyond* (Chandler, 1971).

SCHILLER, HERBERT I. ("Madison Avenue Imperialism"), is professor of communication at the University of California, San Diego. He is author of *Mass Communications and American Empire* and *The Mind Managers*.

SCHORR, ALVIN L. ("Public Policy and Private Interest"), is general director of the Community Service Society, a non-profit, nonsectarian social agency devoted to the improvement of family and community life in New York. He is the author of *Poor Kids: A Report on Children in Poverty* and *Explorations in Social Policy*.

SCOTT, JOHN FINLEY ("Sororities and the Husband Game"), is associate professor of sociology at the University of California, Davis. His publications deal with kinship in complex societies and the role of norms in sociological theory. This article is based on his paper "The American College Sorority: Its Role in Class and Ethnic Endogomy" published in the *American Sociological Review*.

SILBERBERG, MARGARET C. ("Reading Rituals"), is psychological consultant to several programs, including one providing services to American Indians and one to deaf children, and lecturer in the Continuing Education Program at Sister Kenny Institute. She has done research on reading readiness and reading abilities and directed the development of a bookless program in eleventh-grade humanities. She is also author with Norman E. Silberberg of *Who Speaks for the Child?*

SILBERBERG, NORMAN E. ("Reading Rituals"), is vice-president for research and education at Sister Kenny Institute in Minneapolis. He has been a school psychologist and has conducted research in the areas of remedial reading, reading readiness and bookless programs. He is co-author with Margaret C. Silberberg of *Who Speaks for the Child?*

SIMS, JOHN ("Actors' Search for a Self"), is professor of psychology and human development at George Williams College, Downers Grove, Illinois. He is co-author of *The Fifth Profession: Becoming a Psychotherapist* and is currently engaged in research projects including a study identifying the ideologies of college youth.

SKEDGELL, ROBERT A. ("How Computers Pick an Election Winner"), has been with CBS radio and television since 1939 as writer, news editor, reporter, producer and administrator. He served as assistant general manager of CBS News for radio until 1964 when he joined the CBS News election unit and was named director of Vote Profile Analysis.

SNIZEK, WILLIAM E. ("The Cryonics Movement"), is assistant professor of sociology at Virginia Polytechnic Institute and State University. His areas of interest include metasociology and the sociology of occupations and professions. He has published in the *American Sociological Review* and numerous other sociological journals and is currently director of a study on game wardens funded by the U.S. Department of Agriculture.

STARK, RODNEY ("Is There an American Protestantism?"), is professor of sociology at the University of Washington, Seattle. He collaborated with Charles Y. Glock on *By Their Fruits: Christian Belief and Anti-Semitism*.

STEINMETZ, SUZANNE K. ("The Family as Cradle of Violence"), is completing her doctorate at Case-Western Reserve University and is a member of the faculty at the University of Delaware. She is currently conducting crosscultural studies of family violence. With Murray A. Straus she co-edited *Violence in the Family* (published by Dodd, Mead and Co., Inc.).

STEVENS, EVELYN P. ("Machismo and Marianismo"), is associate professor of political science at Loyola University of Chicago. She served as public information director for the governor of Puerto Rico and has written extensively on Latin American politics and on woman's role in Latin America.

STONE, GREGORY P. ("How Card Hustlers Make the Game"), is professor of sociology at the University of Minnesota and founder and co-chairman of the Society for the Study of Symbolic Interaction. He has a long-time interest in play, sport and nonverbal communication, contributing many articles in these areas. He edited *Games, Sport and Power* and co-edited *Social Psychology Through Symbolic Interaction*.

STRAUS, MURRAY A. ("The Family as Cradle of Violence"), is professor of sociology at the University of New Hampshire.

The author of over 60 articles on research methods, he is co-editor with Suzanne K. Steinmetz of *Violence in the Family* (published by Dodd, Mead and Co., Inc.), from which this article was excerpted.

STRAUSS, ANSELM ("Chronic Illness"), is professor of sociology at the University of California in San Francisco. A former member of the *Trans*action (now *Society*) editorial board, he has written over 20 books on social psychology and medicine and is currently the principal investigator in a federal study on nursing care and management of pain. This article was printed by permission of the Russell Sage Foundation

STURGES, GERALD D. ("1000 + 1000 = 5000: Estimating Crowd Size"), was legislative assistant to David R. Obey, Democratic congressman from Wisconsin. A reporter for the *Oakland Tribune* with the city of Berkeley and the University of California campus and board of regents as his beat, he was subsequently an American Political Science Association congressional fellow.

SUCZEK, BARBARA ("Chronic Medicare"), is a doctoral candidate in sociology at the University of California in San Francisco. Her major areas of interest include the social experience of aging, self-concept in women and deviant behavior. The renal failure study was made under a grant to Anselm Strauss by the Russell Sage Foundation.

TRUZZI, MARCELLO ("Carnivals, Road Shows and Freaks"), is associate professor of sociology at New College in Sarasota, Florida. Author of *Caldron Cookery* and editor of the *Subterranean Sociology Newsletter*, his primary research interest at present centers around occult movements in the United States. He comes from a well-known circus family and is working on a long-term study of the American circus.

TUSSING, A. DALE ("The Dual Welfare System"), is professor of economics at Syracuse University. His writings on the economics of the public sector, education, welfare and poverty have been widely published. This article is excerpted from *Poverty in a Dual Economy* (permission granted by St. Martin's Press, Inc.).

VALLIER, IVAN ("Challenge to Catholicism in Latin America"), is professor of sociology at Crown College, University of California, Santa Cruz. This article is adapted from *Elites in Latin America* edited by Seymour M. Lipset and Aldo Solari (reprinted by permission of Oxford University Press).

VANDER KOOI, RONALD ("The Main Stem: Skid Row Revisited"), is associate professor of sociology at Calvin College in Grand Rapids, Michigan. He has done research on the growing popularity of country music in urban America and on the relationship between Christian missions and urbanizing American Indians, in addition to his on-going study of America's skid rows.

VELARDE, ALBERT ("Massage Parlors: The Sensuality Business"), is doing graduate work at Northwestern University. He plans to earn a Ph.D. in sociology.

VON HOFFMAN, NICHOLAS ("Sociological Snoopers and Journalist Moralizers"), is a columnist for *The Washington Post*. He is also the author of *Mississippi Notebook*, *Multiversity*, *We are the People Our Parents Warned Us Against*, *Left at the Post* and *Fireside Watergate*.

WARLICK, MARK ("Massage Parlors, The Sensuality Business"), recently received a B.A. degree in philosophy from California State University at Hayward. His plans include further research, travel and graduate school.

WEBBER, MELVIN M. ("The Politics of (Social) Information"), is professor of city planning and director of the Institute of Urban and Regional Development at the University of California, Berkeley. This article is an excerpt from a paper in the *Journal of the American Institute of Planners*.

WEISS, MELFORD S. ("Rebirth in the Airborne"), is associate professor of anthropology at California State University, Sacramento. He is the author of *Valley City: A Chinese Community in America*. His current research endeavors center upon the life-styles of contemporary "swinging singles."

WEITZMAN, LENORE J. ("Double Standard of American Justice"), is assistant professor of sociology at the University of California, Davis, and also on the faculty of the law school where she teaches a course on the legal status of women. This article was written while she was a Russell Sage fellow at the Yale Law School. Her research interests include socialization, missing persons and identity change and the sociology of law.

WESTERMEYER, JOSEPH J. ("Indian Powerlessness in Minnesota"), is assistant professor of psychiatry at the University of Minnesota. An expert on alcoholism, drug addiction and the crosscultural provision of health services, he spent two years leading a public health unit in Laos and is currently a consultant to Laotian methadone programs and to a halfway house for Indian alcoholics in St. Paul.

WHITT, J. ALLEN ("Californians, Cars and Technological Death"), is a Ph.D. candidate in sociology at the University of California, Santa Barbara. He is preparing his dissertation on the politics of mass transportation systems.

WITTER, CHARLES ("Drugging and Schooling"), was staff director for Congressman Cornelius E. Gallagher's Special Subcommittee on Invasion of Privacy until March 31, 1971, and is now staff consultant to the House Committee on Foreign Affairs. He is working on a book on privacy with the working title *Big Brother is a Mother*.

Name Index

Subject Index

75 76 77 9 8 7 6 5 4 3 2 1